Rick Steves®

EASTERN EUROPE

Rick Steves & Cameron Hewitt

CONTENTS

Eastern Europe

100 kilometers
100 miles

FINLAND ☆Helsinki

Uppsala

Stockholm☆

ESTONIA
☆Tallinn

SWEDEN

Visby

LATVIA
☆Riga

RUSSIA

Moscow☆

Kalmar
Växjö
Öland

LITHUANIA
Vilnius☆

Minsk☆

Malmö

RUSSIA

Baltic Sea

Dnieper River

Gdańsk Malbork

BELARUS

Poznań

Toruń

Warsaw☆

G E R M A N Y

P O L A N D

Kiev☆

☆Berlin

Oder River

Vistula R.

Dresden

Elbe R.

Lviv

U K R A I N E

Auschwitz

Kraków

☆Prague

TATRA MTNS.

CZECH REPUBLIC

Levoča

MOLDOVA

Český
Krumlov

Brno

SLOVAKIA

Chișinău☆ Odessa

Danube R.

Melk

Bratislava

Eger

Iași

BUCOVINA

Vienna☆

MARAMUREȘ

Salzburg

Győr

☆Budapest

Cluj-Napoca

Hallstatt

HUNGARY

Sighișoara

AUSTRIA

Pécs

Szeged

R O M A N I A

Bled

SLOVENIA

Novi
Sad

TRANSYLVANIA Brașov

Ljubljana☆

☆Zagreb

Timișoara

Venice

CROATIA

Constanța

ISTRIA

Plitvice
Lakes

**BOS.-
HERZ.**

Bucharest☆

Varna

Rovinj

Pula

Belgrade☆

Danube R.

Veliko
Tarnovo

Black
Sea

Ravenna

SAN
MARINO

Ancona

Split

Sarajevo☆

SERBIA

BULGARIA

USCANY

DALMATIAN
COAST

Mostar

Podgorica

Priština

☆Sofia

Plovdiv

Istanbul

Assisi

UMBRIA

Adriatic Sea

Dubrovnik

Kotor

MONT.

KOSOVO

Rila

ivita

Rome☆

Tiranë☆

☆Skopje

MACEDONIA

T U R K E Y

ITALY

Bari

ALBANIA

Thessaloniki

VATICAN
CITY

Naples

Pompeii

Brindisi

Meteora

Sorrento

AMALFI
COAST

Paestum

Corfu

GREECE

Tyrrhenian
Sea

Aegean Sea

Ephesus

Delphi

Athens☆

Sámos

Palermo

Cefalù

Ionian
Sea

Olympia

Nafplio

Mykonos

Bodrum

Sicily

Taormina

PELOPONNESE

Paros Naxos

Agrigento

Kardamyli

Santorini

MALTA

Gorge of
Samaria

Crete

Poland

LEGEND

A-4	Freeway/Autobahn
	Major Roads
	Major Rail Line
✈	Airport
■	Ruin, Museum, Other Point of Interest

100 Kilometers
100 Miles

Prague

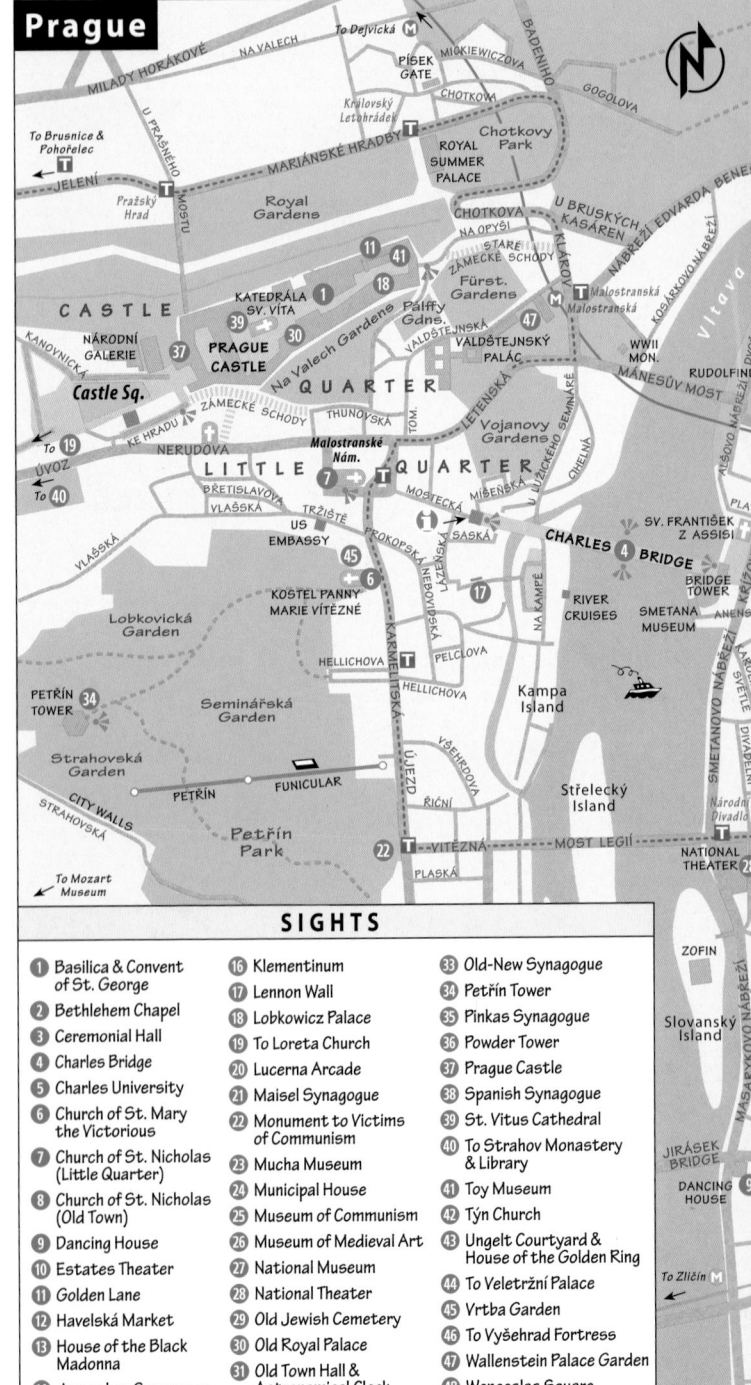

SIGHTS

1. Basilica & Convent of St. George
2. Bethlehem Chapel
3. Ceremonial Hall
4. Charles Bridge
5. Charles University
6. Church of St. Mary the Victorious
7. Church of St. Nicholas (Little Quarter)
8. Church of St. Nicholas (Old Town)
9. Dancing House
10. Estates Theater
11. Golden Lane
12. Havelská Market
13. House of the Black Madonna
14. Jerusalem Synagogue
15. Klaus Synagogue
16. Klementinum
17. Lennon Wall
18. Lobkowicz Palace
19. To Loreta Church
20. Lucerna Arcade
21. Maisel Synagogue
22. Monument to Victims of Communism
23. Mucha Museum
24. Municipal House
25. Museum of Communism
26. Museum of Medieval Art
27. National Museum
28. National Theater
29. Old Jewish Cemetery
30. Old Royal Palace
31. Old Town Hall & Astronomical Clock
32. Old Town Square
33. Old-New Synagogue
34. Petřín Tower
35. Pinkas Synagogue
36. Powder Tower
37. Prague Castle
38. Spanish Synagogue
39. St. Vitus Cathedral
40. To Strahov Monastery & Library
41. Toy Museum
42. Týn Church
43. Ungelt Courtyard & House of the Golden Ring
44. To Veletržní Palace
45. Vrtba Garden
46. To Vyšehrad Fortress
47. Wallenstein Palace Garden
48. Wenceslas Square

LEGEND

- Pedestrian-Friendly Area
- **T** Tram #22 Stop
- **M M** Major Metro Stops
- Landmark or Point of Interest
- Tourist Information Offices
- Viewpoint

400 Meters

400 Yards

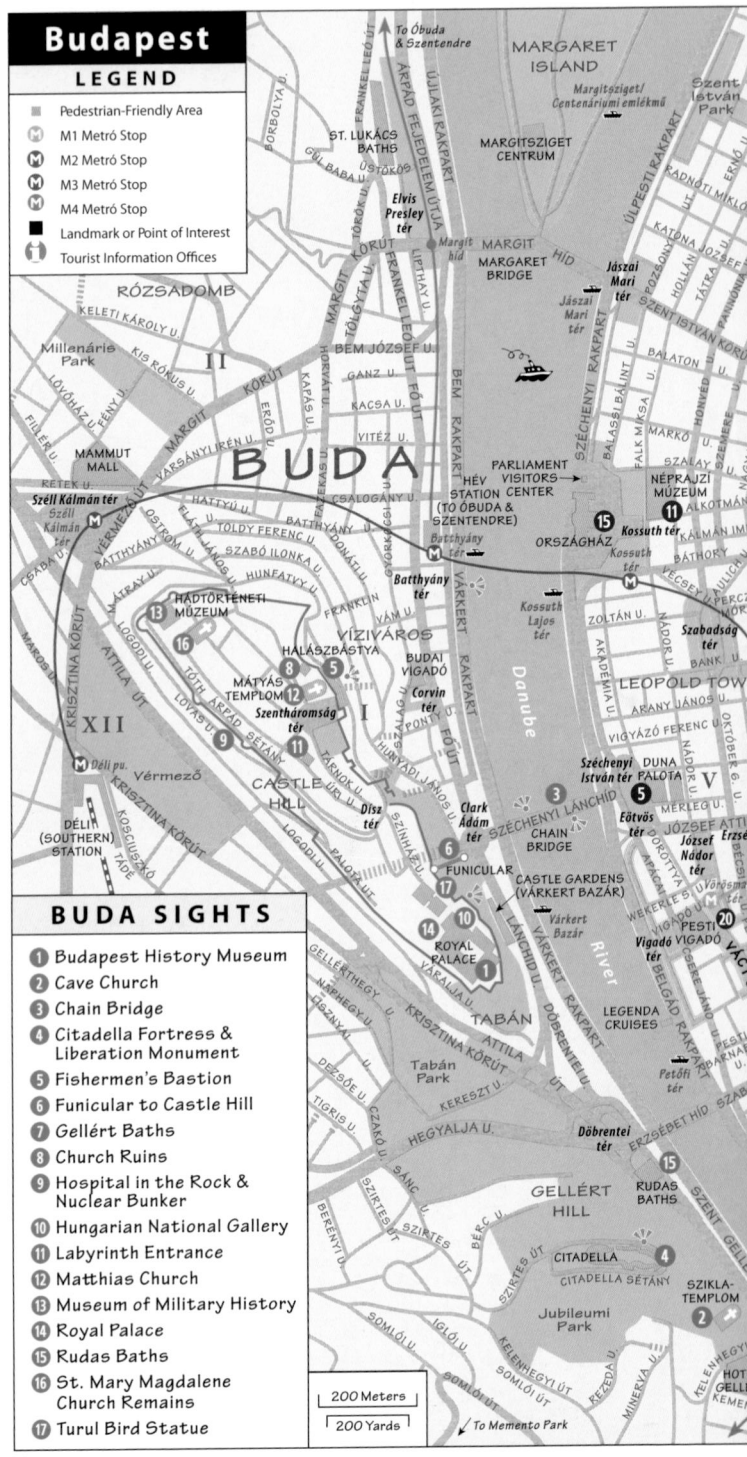

Budapest

LEGEND

- ▪ Pedestrian-Friendly Area
- Ⓜ M1 Metró Stop
- Ⓜ M2 Metró Stop
- Ⓜ M3 Metró Stop
- Ⓜ M4 Metró Stop
- ■ Landmark or Point of Interest
- ⛉ Tourist Information Offices

BUDA SIGHTS

1 Budapest History Museum
2 Cave Church
3 Chain Bridge
4 Citadella Fortress & Liberation Monument
5 Fishermen's Bastion
6 Funicular to Castle Hill
7 Gellért Baths
8 Church Ruins
9 Hospital in the Rock & Nuclear Bunker
10 Hungarian National Gallery
11 Labyrinth Entrance
12 Matthias Church
13 Museum of Military History
14 Royal Palace
15 Rudas Baths
16 St. Mary Magdalene Church Remains
17 Turul Bird Statue

200 Meters
200 Yards

PEST SIGHTS

1. Franz Liszt Museum
2. Franz Liszt Square
3. Great Market Hall
4. Great Synagogue & Jewish Museum
5. Gresham Palace
6. Heroes' Square & Millennium Monument
7. To Holocaust Memorial Center & Applied Arts Mus.
8. House of Terror
9. Hungarian Nat'l Museum
10. Műcsarnok (Hall of Art)
11. Museum of Ethnography
12. New York Café
13. Opera House
14. Orthodox Synagogue
15. Parliament
16. St. István's Basilica
17. Synagogue at Rumbach Street
18. Széchenyi Baths
19. Vajdahunyad Castle
20. Vörösmarty Square

SIGHTS

1. Academy of Fine Arts
2. Albertina Museum
3. Am Hof Square
4. Augustinian Church & State Hall
5. To Belvedere Palace & Mus. of Military History
6. Butterfly House
7. Börse (Stock Exchange)
8. City Hall
9. Dorotheum Auction House
10. To Freud Museum
11. Haus der Musik
12. Hofburg Imperial Apartments
13. Hofburg New Palace Museums
14. Hofburg Treasury & Boys' Choir Chapel
15. Jewish Museum Dorotheergasse
16. Jewish Museum Judenplatz
17. Kaisergruft (Crypt)
18. To Karlskirche
19. To Kunst Haus Wien & Hundertwasserhaus
20. Kunsthistorisches Museum
21. Mozarthaus Vienna Museum
22. Museum of Applied Art (MAK)
23. MuseumsQuartier
24. Naschmarkt
25. Natural History Museum
26. Opera
27. Plague Column
28. To Prater Park
29. To Schönbrunn Palace & Imperial Furniture Collection
30. Secession Building
31. Spanish Riding School
32. St. Michael's Church Crypt
33. St. Peter's Church
34. St. Stephen's Cathedral
35. Wien Museum Karlsplatz
36. Wien Ticket Kiosk

LEGEND

- Pedestrian-Friendly Area
- **U** U-1 U-Bahn Stop
- **U** U-2 U-Bahn Stop
- **U** U-3 U-Bahn Stop
- **U** U-4 U-Bahn Stop
- **T** Tram Stop along Ringstrasse
- Landmark or Point of Interest
- Tourist Information Offices

500 Meters

500 Yards

Rick Steves

EASTERN
EUROPE

Top Destinations of Eastern Europe

GDAŃSK AND THE TRI-CITY

POMERANIA

WARSAW

POLAND

AUSCHWITZ-BIRKENAU

KRAKÓW

PRAGUE

NEAR PRAGUE

ČESKÝ KRUMLOV

CZECH REPUBLIC

SLOVAKIA

VIENNA

BRATISLAVA

EGER

BUDAPEST

AUSTRIA

HUNGARY

ROMANIA

JULIAN ALPS

LAKE BLED

SLO-VENIA

LJUBLJANA

CROATIA

BOSNIA-HERZEGOVINA

TO BULGARIA

MONTE-NEGRO

200 Kilometers

200 Miles

INTRODUCTION

Until 1989, Eastern Europe was a foreboding place—a dark and gloomy corner of the "Evil Empire." But the dismal grays and preachy reds of communism live on only in history books, museums, and kitschy theme restaurants. Today's Eastern Europe is a traveler's delight, with friendly locals, lively squares, breathtaking sights, fascinating history, reasonable prices, and a sense of pioneer excitement.

Wander among Prague's dreamy, fairy-tale spires, bask in the energy of Kraków's Main Market Square, and soak with chess players in a Budapest bath. Ponder Europe's most moving Holocaust memorial at Auschwitz. Enjoy nature as you glide across Lake Bled to a church-topped island in the shadow of the Julian Alps. Taste a proud Hungarian vintner's wine and say, *"Egészségedre!"* (or stick with "Cheers!").

This book covers Eastern Europe's top big-city, small-town, and back-to-nature destinations—from the Hungarian metropolis of Budapest to the quaint Czech village of Český Krumlov to the pristine Julian Alps of Slovenia. It then gives you all the specifics and opinions necessary to wring the maximum value out of your limited time and money. If you're planning for a month or less in this region, this book is all you need.

Experiencing Europe's culture, people, and natural wonders economically and hassle-free has been my goal for several decades of traveling, tour guiding, and writing. With this book, I pass on to you all the lessons I've learned.

I've been selective, including only the top destinations and sights. For example, Poland has dozens of medieval castles—but Malbork is a cut above the rest. The best is, of course, only my opinion. But after spending much of my life exploring and researching Europe, I've developed a sixth sense for what travelers

Map Legend

Viewpoint	Airport	Tunnel	
Entrance	Taxi Stand	Pedestrian Zone	
Tourist Info	Tram Stop	Railway	
Restroom	Metro Stop	Ferry/Boat Route	
Castle	Bus Stop	Tram	
Church	Parking	Mtn. Pass	
Synagogue	Park	Walk/Tour Route	
Statue/Point of Interest	Cruise Ship Terminal	Trail	
		Funicular	

Use this legend to help you navigate the maps in this book.

enjoy. Just thinking about the places featured in this book makes me want to polka.

ABOUT THIS BOOK

Rick Steves Eastern Europe is a personal tour guide in your pocket. Better yet, it's actually two tour guides in your pocket: The co-author of this book is Cameron Hewitt. Cameron writes and edits guidebooks for my travel company, Rick Steves' Europe. Inspired by his Polish roots and by the enduring charm of the Eastern European people, Cameron has spent the last decade closely tracking the exciting changes in this part of the world. Together, Cameron and I keep this book up to date and accurate (though for simplicity we've shed our respective egos to become "I" in this book).

Eastern Europe is a sprawling region; a comprehensive guidebook would span many volumes. To keep things simple and focused, this book covers the best of Eastern Europe in three sections.

The **core countries** of the Czech Republic, Poland, Hungary, and Slovenia—where most travelers focus their time—receive full coverage.

I've also included full coverage for two important **gateway cities**: Vienna, Austria, and Bratislava, Slovakia. While there's not room in this book to cover other destinations in those countries, you're likely to pass through these capitals on your way between the major core destinations.

The **"More Eastern Europe"** section, near the back of the book, is a roundup of other countries in this area that may serve as logical add-ons. These include Croatia, Bosnia-Herzegovina, Montenegro, Bulgaria, and Romania. (Some of these are covered in greater depth in separate guidebooks—such as *Rick Steves Croatia & Slovenia*.)

Key to This Book

Updates
This book is updated regularly—but things change. For the latest, visit www.ricksteves.com/update.

Abbreviations and Times
I use the following symbols and abbreviations in this book:

Sights are rated:

▲▲▲	Don't miss
▲▲	Try hard to see
▲	Worthwhile if you can make it
No rating	Worth knowing about

Tourist information offices are abbreviated as **TI**, and bathrooms are **WC**s. Accommodations are categorized with a **Sleep Code** (described on page 1073); eateries are classified with a **Restaurant Price Code** (page 1080). To indicate discounts for my readers, I include **RS%** in the listings.

Like Europe, this book uses the **24-hour clock.** It's the same through 12:00 noon, then keeps going: 13:00, 14:00, and so on. For anything over 12, subtract 12 and add p.m. (14:00 is 2:00 p.m.).

When giving **opening times,** I include both peak season and off-season hours if they differ. So, if a museum is listed as "May-Oct daily 9:00-16:00," it should be open from 9:00 a.m. until 4:00 p.m. from the first day of May until the last day of October (but expect exceptions).

A Ω symbol indicates that a free, downloadable self-guided Rick Steves audio tour is available.

For **transit** or **tour departures,** I first list the frequency, then the duration. So, a train connection listed as "2/hour, 1.5 hours" departs twice each hour, and the journey lasts an hour and a half.

For places with full coverage, each destination is organized as a minivacation on its own, filled with exciting sights, strollable neighborhoods, affordable places to stay, and memorable places to eat. In the core-country chapters, you'll find these sections:

Planning Your Time suggests a schedule for how to best use your limited time.

Orientation has specifics on public transportation, helpful hints, local tour options, easy-to-read maps, and tourist information.

Sights describes the top attractions and includes their cost and hours. Major sights have self-guided tours.

Self-Guided Walks take you through interesting neighborhoods, pointing out sights and fun stops.

Sleeping describes my favorite hotels, from good-value deals to cushy splurges.

INTRODUCTION

Eating serves up a range of options, from inexpensive eateries to fancy restaurants.

Connections outlines your options for traveling to destinations by train, bus, and boat. For car-friendly regions, I've included route tips for drivers, with recommended roadside attractions along the way.

Country Introductions give you an overview of each country's culture, customs, money, history, current events, cuisine, language, and other useful practicalities.

The **Practicalities** chapter near the end of this book is a traveler's tool kit, with my best advice about money, sightseeing, sleeping, eating, staying connected, and transportation (trains, buses, boats, car rentals, driving, and flights).

The **appendix** has the nuts and bolts: useful phone numbers and websites, a festival list, recommended books and films, a climate chart, a handy packing checklist, and a guide to pronouncing Eastern European place names.

Throughout this book, you'll find money- and time-saving tips for sightseeing, transportation, and more. Some businesses—especially hotels and walking tour companies—offer special discounts to my readers, indicated in their listings.

Browse through this book, choose your favorite destinations, and link them up. Then have a great trip! Traveling like a temporary local, you'll get the absolute most of every mile, minute, and dollar. I'm happy that you'll be meeting some of my favorite Europeans as you visit places I know and love.

Planning

This section will help you get started on planning your trip—with advice on trip costs, when to go, and what you should know before you take off.

TRAVEL SMART

Your trip to Europe is like a complex play—it's easier to follow and fully appreciate on a second viewing. While no one does the same trip twice to gain that advantage, reading this book before your trip accomplishes much the same thing.

Design an itinerary that enables you to visit sights at the best possible times. Note festivals, holidays, specifics on sights, and days when sights are closed (all covered in this book). For example, most museums throughout Eastern Europe close on Mondays. Hotels in resort towns (such as those in the Julian Alps) are most crowded on Fridays and Saturdays, whereas weekdays are tight in convention cities (for instance, Budapest and Warsaw). Expect seasonal closures. To connect the dots smoothly, read the tips in Practicalities

"Eastern Europe" vs. "Central Europe"

"Eastern Europe" means different things to different people. To most Americans, it includes any place that was once behind the Iron Curtain—from Berlin to Moscow. But people who actually live in many of these countries proudly consider themselves "*Central* Europeans." In fact, some even get a bit offended by the "Eastern" label. (To them, "Eastern Europe" means Russia and its immediate satellites.) While I'm careful to describe this area as "Central Europe" when I'm actually traveling there, if I used that term back home, many Americans might wonder if I meant Switzerland or Italy.

And so, while I have deep respect for the people of this region, I'm calling this book "Eastern Europe" so as to best serve its target audience—North Americans. These travelers readily identify the countries I cover here—**Czech Republic, Poland, Hungary, Slovenia,** and highlights of **Austria** and **Slovakia**—as "Eastern Europe." For those venturing beyond that core zone, this book also includes tips to help you get started in a few more countries that Americans also tend to label this way: **Croatia, Bosnia-Herzegovina, Montenegro, Bulgaria,** and **Romania.**

Taken together, this list represents a striking cultural diversity that scatters across a huge swath of Europe. But, while each country certainly has its own strong identity, they share a common legacy. All of them (except Austria) fell under communist control during the last half of the 20th century. And perhaps even more importantly, for centuries leading up to World War I, they were all part of the Austrian Habsburg Empire. Before the Habsburgs, the kings and emperors of these countries also frequently governed their neighbors. And all of these countries (except Hungary and Romania) are populated by people of Slavic heritage, who share common ancestors and speak closely related Slavic languages.

I hope that natives, sticklers, and historians will understand the liberties I've taken with the title of this book. After all, would you buy a book called *Rick Steves Former Habsburg Empire*?

on taking trains and buses or renting a car and driving. Designing a smart trip is a fun, doable, and worthwhile challenge.

Make your itinerary a mix of intense and relaxed stretches. To maximize rootedness, minimize one-night stands. It's worth taking a long drive after dinner (or a train/bus ride with a dinner picnic) to get settled in a town for two nights. Every trip—and every traveler—needs slack time (laundry, picnics, people-watching, and so on). Pace yourself. Assume you will return.

Reread this book as you travel, and visit local tourist information offices (abbreviated as TI in this book). Upon arrival in a

Please Tear Up This Book!

There's no point in hauling around a big chapter on Vienna for a day in Prague. That's why I hope you'll rip this book apart. Before your trip, attack this book with a utility knife to create an army of pocket-sized miniguidebooks—one for each area you visit.

I love the ritual of trimming down the size of guidebooks I'll be using: Fold the pages back until you break the spine, neatly slice apart the sections you want with a box cutter or utility knife, then pull them out with the gummy edge intact. If you want, finish each one off with some clear, heavy-duty packing tape to smooth and reinforce the spine, and/or use a heavy-duty stapler along the edge to prevent the first and last pages from coming loose.

To make things even easier, I offer a line of laminated covers with slide-on binders. Every evening, you can make a ritual of swapping out today's pages for tomorrow's. (For more on these binders, see www.ricksteves.com.)

While you may be tempted to keep this book intact as a souvenir of your travels, you'll appreciate even more the footloose freedom of traveling light.

new town, lay the groundwork for a smooth departure; confirm the train, bus, boat, or road you'll take when you leave.

Even with the best-planned itinerary, you'll need to be flexible. Update your plans as you travel. Get online or call ahead to learn the latest on sights (special events, tour schedules, and so on), book tickets and tours, make reservations, reconfirm hotels, and research transportation connections.

Enjoy the friendliness of the local people. Connect with the culture. Set up your own quest for the best bit of communist kitsch, mug of Czech beer, bowl of borscht, or scenic seafront perch. Slow down and be open to unexpected experiences. Ask questions—most locals are eager to point you in their idea of the right direction. Keep a notepad in your pocket for confirming prices, noting directions, and organizing your thoughts. Wear your money belt, learn the currency, and figure out how to estimate prices in dollars. Those who expect to travel smart, do.

TRIP COSTS

The countries in this book—more than two decades removed from communism—are no longer Europe's bargain basement. Although the global recession hit their economies along with everyone else's, the cost of living in most of Eastern Europe is approaching what it is in the West. But it can still be a good value to travel here. Things that natives buy—such as food and transportation—remain fairly inexpensive. Hotels can be pricey, but if you use my listings to find the best accommodations deals, a trip to these countries can be substantially cheaper than visiting, say, Italy, Germany, or France.

Five components make up your trip costs: airfare to Europe, transportation in Europe, room and board, sightseeing and entertainment, and shopping and miscellany. The prices I've listed below are more or less average for all of the destinations in this book. Prices are generally lower in Poland and higher in Slovenia and Vienna; the Czech Republic and Hungary are in between. Of course, big cities (such as Prague and Budapest) are much more expensive than smaller towns (like Český Krumlov and Eger).

Airfare to Europe: A basic round-trip flight from the US to Prague can cost, on average, about $1,000-2,000 total, depending on where you fly from and when (cheaper in winter). Consider saving time and money in Europe by flying into one city and out of another; for instance, flying into Prague and out of Vienna is almost certainly cheaper than the added expense (and wasted time) of an overland return trip to Prague. Overall, Kayak.com is the best place to start searching for flights on a combination of mainstream and budget carriers.

Transportation in Europe: For a three-week whirlwind trip of my recommended destinations by public transportation, allow $300 per person. If you plan to rent a car, allow $230 per week, not including tolls, gas, and supplemental insurance. Car rentals are cheapest if arranged from the US. Rail passes normally must be purchased outside Europe but aren't necessarily your best option— you may save money simply by buying tickets as you go. Don't hesitate to consider flying—a short flight can be cheaper than the train (check www.skyscanner.com for intra-European flights). For more on public transportation and car rental, see "Transportation" in Practicalities.

Room and Board: You can thrive in Eastern Europe on $100 a day per person for room and board. This allows $15 for lunch, $25 for dinner, and $60 for lodging (based on two people splitting the cost of a comfortable $120 double room that includes breakfast). Students and tightwads can enjoy Eastern Europe for as little as $50 a day ($30 per hostel bed, $20 for groceries and snacks).

Sightseeing and Entertainment: Sightseeing is cheap here. Figure $3-6 per major sight (with some more expensive sights at around $10), and $10-25 for splurge experiences (e.g., going to concerts, taking a lake cruise, or soaking in a Budapest bath). You can hire your own private guide for four hours for about $100-150—a

Not Your Father's Eastern Europe

Americans sometimes approach Eastern Europe expecting grouchy service, crumbling communist infrastructure, and grimy, depressing landscapes. But those who visit are pleasantly surprised at the area's beauty and diversity, as well as how safe and easy it is.

Travel in Eastern Europe today is nearly as smooth as travel in the West. Most natives speak excellent English, and many pride themselves on impressing their guests. Service standards can sometimes be a bit lower than in other parts of Europe, but on the other hand, locals are generally less jaded and more excited to meet you than their counterparts in many big-name Western European destinations. Any rough edges add to the charm and carbonate the experience.

The East-West stuff still fascinates us, but to people here, the Soviet regime is old news, Cold War espionage is the stuff of movies, and oppressive monuments to Stalin are a distant memory (and those under age 25 have no firsthand memories of communism at all). More than 25 years after the fall of the Iron Curtain, Eastern Europeans (or, as they prefer to be called, Central Europeans) think about communism only when tourists bring it up. Freedom is a more than a generation old, and—for better or for worse—McDonald's, MTV, and mobile phones are every bit as entrenched here as anywhere else in Europe. All of the countries in this book (except Bosnia and Montenegro) belong to the European Union, and everyone seems to be looking forward to more progress in the future.

great value when divided among two or more people. An overall average of $20 a day works for most people. Don't skimp here. After all, this category is the driving force behind your trip—you came to sightsee, enjoy, and experience Eastern Europe.

Shopping and Miscellany: Figure $2 per postcard, coffee, beer, and ice-cream cone. Shopping can vary in cost from nearly nothing to a small fortune. Good budget travelers find that this category has little to do with assembling a trip full of lifelong memories.

SIGHTSEEING PRIORITIES

So much to see, so little time. How to choose? Depending on the length of your trip, assuming you are focusing on the core countries, and taking geographic proximity into account, here are my recommended priorities.

3 days:	Prague
5 days, add:	Budapest
7 days, add:	Český Krumlov, slow down
10 days, add:	Kraków, Auschwitz

14 days, add:	Ljubljana, Lake Bled
16 days, add:	Vienna
18 days, add:	Julian Alps, Bratislava
20 days, add:	Eger, slow down
25 days, add:	Gdańsk, Warsaw, Toruń (or save these for a Poland-focused trip)

This includes nearly everything on the map on page 13. If you don't have time to see it all, prioritize according to your interests. The "Eastern Europe a Glance" sidebar can help you decide where to go (page 10). The three-week itinerary (see sidebar) includes all of the stops in the first 20 days.

With more time—or for a different focus to your trip—consider some of the neighboring countries. See the "More Eastern Europe" section near the end of this book for ideas on how to splice in Croatia, Bosnia-Herzegovina, Montenegro, Bulgaria, and Romania.

WHEN TO GO

The "tourist season" runs roughly from May through September. Summer has its advantages: the best weather, very long days (light until after 21:00), and the busiest schedule of tourist fun.

In spring and fall—May, June, September, and early October—travelers enjoy fewer crowds and milder weather. This is my favorite time to travel here. Cities are great at this time of year, but some small towns get quieter and quieter the further off-season you get, and are downright deserted and disappointing in early May and late October.

Winter travelers find concert season in full swing, with absolutely no tourist crowds (except in always-packed Prague), but some accommodations and sights are either closed or run on a limited schedule. Confirm your sightseeing plans locally, especially when traveling off-season. The weather can be cold and dreary, and night will draw the shades on your sightseeing before dinnertime. (For more information, see the climate chart in the appendix.)

KNOW BEFORE YOU GO

Check this list of things to arrange while you're still at home.

You need a **passport**—but no visa or shots—to travel in the countries covered in this book. You may be denied entry into certain European countries if your passport is due to expire within six months of your ticketed date of return. Get it renewed if you'll be cutting it close. It can take up to six weeks to get or renew a passport (for more on passports and requirements for Eastern European countries, see www.travel.state.gov). Pack a photocopy of your passport in your luggage in case the original is lost or stolen.

Book rooms well in advance if you'll be traveling during **peak**

Eastern Europe at a Glance

This covers only the core destinations of Eastern Europe. For some add-on options, see page 974.

Czech Republic

▲▲▲**Prague** Romantic Czech capital with a remarkably well-preserved Old Town, sprawling hilltop castle, informative Jewish Quarter, and rollicking pubs.

▲**Near Prague** Kutná Hora's offbeat bone church and grand cathedral, Terezín's Nazi concentration camp memorial, and Franz Ferdinand's residence at Konopiště Castle.

▲▲**Český Krumlov** Picturesque town hugging a river bend under a castle.

Poland

▲▲▲**Kraków** Poland's cultural, intellectual, and historical capital, with a huge but cozy main square, easy-to-enjoy Old Town, thought-provoking Jewish quarter, and important castle.

▲▲▲**Auschwitz-Birkenau** The largest and most notorious Nazi concentration camp, now a compelling museum and memorial.

▲▲**Warsaw** Poland's modern capital, with an appealing urban tempo, a reconstructed Old Town, and good museums.

▲▲**Gdańsk and the Tri-City** Historic Hanseatic trading city, with a cancan of marvelous facades and the shipyard where the Solidarity trade union challenged the communists in 1980.

▲**Pomerania** The Teutonic Knights' gigantic, Gothic Malbork Castle and the red-brick, gingerbread-scented city of Toruń.

Hungary

▲▲▲**Budapest** Grand Danube-spanning cityscape peppered with opulent late-19th-century buildings, excellent restaurants, layers of epic history, and uniquely exhilarating thermal baths.

▲▲**Eger** Strollable town with a gaggle of gorgeous Baroque buildings and locally produced wines.

Slovenia

▲▲**Ljubljana** Slovenia's vibrant, relaxing capital, with fine architecture and an inviting riverside promenade and market.

▲▲▲**Lake Bled** Photogenic lake resort huddled in mountain foothills, with a church-topped island and cliff-hanging castle.

▲▲The Julian Alps Cut-glass peaks easily conquered by a twisty mountain road over the Vršič Pass, ending in the tranquil Soča River Valley, with the fine WWI museum in Kobarid.

Gateway Cities
▲▲▲Vienna, Austria Glorious onetime Habsburg capital boasting stately palaces and world-class museums, convivial wine gardens, a rich musical heritage, and a genteel elegance that has long outlived the emperor's reign.

▲▲Bratislava, Slovakia The Slovak capital, with a rejuvenated Old Town and lots of new construction.

Eastern Europe: Best Three-Week Trip by Public Transportation

Day	Plan	Sleep in
1	Fly into Kraków	Kraków
2	Kraków	Kraków
3	Side-trip to Auschwitz	Kraków
4	Travel to Prague (cheap flight, long train ride, or private driver)	Prague
5	Prague	Prague
6	Prague	Prague
7	Prague (side-trip to Kutná Hora)	Prague
8	Train to Český Krumlov (tour Konopiště Castle en route)	Český Krumlov
9	Český Krumlov	Český Krumlov
10	Shuttle bus to Vienna	Vienna
11	Vienna	Vienna
12	Vienna	Vienna
13	Train to Budapest (stop in Bratislava en route)	Budapest
14	Budapest	Budapest
15	Budapest	Budapest
16	Budapest (side-trip to Eger)	Budapest
17	Train to Ljubljana (direct, leaves Budapest at 8:30)	Ljubljana
18	Ljubljana	Ljubljana
19	Rent a car to explore Lake Bled	Lake Bled
20	Lake Bled and Julian Alps	Lake Bled
21	Fly home from Ljubljana Airport	

This is an urban-focused itinerary—spending most nights in big cities (except for Český Krumlov and Lake Bled), and side-tripping to smaller towns. This itinerary assumes you're using public transportation (partly to spare you some very long drives, and partly to avoid costly international drop-off fees for rental cars). Get creative. From Kraków to Prague, you could take a nine-hour night train or a complicated daytime connection—or you could look for a cheap flight. Better yet, splurge on a private driver based in Kraków (see page 247) or Prague (page 154) to take you there (5-hour drive), and fit in a stop at Auschwitz en route—

season (July and August in resort towns, September and October in convention cities), or over any major holidays or festivals (see list on page 1110).

Call your **debit- and credit-card companies** to let them know the countries you'll be visiting, to ask about fees, and to request your PIN if you don't already know it. See page 1063 for details.

figure about $400-500 for a carload. Train connections between Český Krumlov and Vienna require multiple changes, but various shuttle services do the trip affordably in under four hours. Also, it's very smart to strategically rent a car for a few days in places where it's warranted—for example, to explore the countryside between Prague and Český Krumlov, or between Ljubljana and Lake Bled; as long as you're dropping off the car in the same country, there's usually no (or minimal) extra charges.

Two-Week Variation: If you're tight on time, skip Slovenia and cut out some of the side-trips (Kutná Hora, Eger) to squeeze this plan into two weeks.

Do your homework if you're considering **travel insurance.** Compare the cost of the insurance to the cost of your potential loss. Also, check whether your existing insurance (health, homeowners, or renters) covers you and your possessions overseas. For more tips, see www.ricksteves.com/insurance

If you're taking an **overnight train** and need a couchette or

🎧 **Rick Steves Audio Europe** 🎧

My free **Rick Steves Audio Europe app** is a great tool for enjoying Europe. This app makes it easy to download my audio tours of top attractions, plus hours of travel interviews, all organized into destination-specific playlists.

My self-guided **audio tours** of major sights and neighborhoods across Europe are free, user-friendly, fun, and informative. In this book, these audio tours include my Prague City Walk, Vienna City Walk, St. Stephen's Cathedral, and Ringstrasse Tram Tour. Walks and sights covered by my audio tours are marked with this symbol: 🎧. These audio tours are hard to beat: Nobody will stand you up, your eyes are free to appreciate the sights, you can take the tour exactly when you like, and the price is right.

The Rick Steves Audio Europe app also offers a far-reaching library of insightful **travel interviews** from my public radio show with experts from around the globe—including many of the places in this book.

This app and all of its content are entirely free. (And new content is added about twice a year.) You can download Rick Steves Audio Europe via Apple's App Store, Google Play, or the Amazon Appstore. For more information, see www.ricksteves.com/audioeurope.

---

sleeper—and you must leave on a certain day—consider booking it in advance through a US agent (such as www.ricksteves.com/rail), even though it may cost more than buying it in Europe. If you're planning on **renting a car,** bring your driver's license and an International Driving Permit (see page 1092). Confirm pickup hours; many car-rental offices close Saturday afternoon and all day Sunday. Many countries require drivers to buy a toll sticker for driving on expressways; for details per country, see page 1098.

If you plan to visit the **Auschwitz-Birkenau Concentration Camp Memorial,** you're required to reserve ahead on their website (see page 352). You'll want to do this as far ahead as you can set a date.

If you'd like to **tour the Hungarian Parliament in Budapest,** consider reserving online a few days ahead to ensure your choice of entrance time (see page 570).

If you plan on visiting **Schönbrunn Palace in Vienna** during the summer or on a weekend, make a reservation in advance (see page 903).

If you plan to hire a **local guide,** reserve ahead by email. Popular guides can get booked up.

If you're bringing a **mobile device,** consider signing up for an

> ## How Was Your Trip?
>
> Were your travels fun, smooth, and meaningful? You can share tips, concerns, and discoveries at www.ricksteves.com/feedback. To check out readers' hotel and restaurant reviews—or leave one yourself—visit my travel forum at www.ricksteves.com/travel-forum. I value your feedback. Thanks in advance—it helps a lot.

international plan for cheaper calls, texts, and data (see page 1084). Download any apps you might want to use on the road, such as translators, maps, transit schedules, and **Rick Steves Audio Europe** (see sidebar).

Updates to This Book: Check www.ricksteves.com/update.

Traveling as a Temporary Local

We travel all the way to Europe to enjoy differences—to become temporary locals. You'll experience frustrations. Certain truths that we find "God-given" or "self-evident," such as cold beer, ice in drinks, bottomless cups of coffee, "the customer is king," and bigger being better, are suddenly not so true. One of the benefits of travel is the eye-opening realization that there are logical, civil, and even better alternatives. A willingness to go local ensures that you'll enjoy a full dose of European hospitality. And with an eagerness to go local, you'll have even more fun.

Fortunately for you, hospitality is a local forte. The friendliness of the Eastern Europeans seems to have only been enhanced during the communist era: Tangible resources were in short supply, so an open door and a genial conversation were all that people had to offer. For many Eastern Europeans, the chance to chat with an American is still a delightful novelty. Even so, some people—hardened by decades of being spied on by neighbors and standing in long lines to buy food for their family—seem brusque at first. In my experience, all it takes is a smile and a little effort to befriend these residents of the former "Evil Empire."

Europeans generally like Americans. But if there is a negative aspect to the image of Americans, it's that we are loud, wasteful, ethnocentric, too informal (which can seem disrespectful), and a bit naive.

INTRODUCTION

While Europeans look bemusedly at some of our Yankee excesses—and worriedly at others—they nearly always afford us individual travelers all the warmth we deserve.

Judging from all the happy feedback I receive from travelers who have used this book, it's safe to assume you'll enjoy a great, affordable vacation—with the finesse of an independent, experienced traveler.

Thanks, and happy travels!

Rick Steves

Back Door Travel Philosophy

From *Rick Steves Europe Through the Back Door*

Travel is intensified living—maximum thrills per minute and one of the last great sources of legal adventure. Travel is freedom. It's recess, and we need it.

Experiencing the real Europe requires catching it by surprise and going casual..."through the Back Door."

Affording travel is a matter of priorities. (Make do with the old car.) You can eat and sleep—simply, safely, and enjoyably—anywhere in Europe for $100 a day plus transportation costs. In many ways, spending more money only builds a thicker wall between you and what you traveled so far to see. Europe is a cultural carnival, and time after time, you'll find that its best acts are free and the best seats are the cheap ones.

A tight budget forces you to travel close to the ground, meeting and communicating with the people. Never sacrifice sleep, nutrition, safety, or cleanliness to save money. Simply enjoy the local-style alternatives to expensive hotels and restaurants.

Connecting with people carbonates your experience. Extroverts have more fun. If your trip is low on magic moments, kick yourself and make things happen. If you don't enjoy a place, maybe you don't know enough about it. Seek the truth. Recognize tourist traps. Give a culture the benefit of your open mind. See things as different, but not better or worse. Any culture has plenty to share. When an opportunity presents itself, make it a habit to say "yes."

Of course, travel, like the world, is a series of hills and valleys. Be fanatically positive and militantly optimistic. If something's not to your liking, change your liking.

Travel can make you a happier American, as well as a citizen of the world. Our Earth is home to seven billion equally precious people. It's humbling to travel and find that other people don't have the "American Dream"—they have their own dreams. Europeans like us, but with all due respect, they wouldn't trade passports.

Thoughtful travel engages us with the world. It reminds us what is truly important. By broadening perspectives, travel teaches new ways to measure quality of life.

Globetrotting destroys ethnocentricity, helping us understand and appreciate other cultures. Rather than fear the diversity on this planet, celebrate it. Among your most prized souvenirs will be the strands of different cultures you choose to knit into your own character. The world is a cultural yarn shop, and Back Door travelers are weaving the ultimate tapestry. Join in!

THE CZECH REPUBLIC

Česká Republika

CZECH REPUBLIC

Česká Republika

The Czech Republic is geographically small. On a quick visit, you can enjoy a fine introduction while still packing in plenty of surprises. The country has a little of everything for the traveler. Quaint villages? Check. Beautiful landscapes? Check. World-class art? Czech, Czech, and Czech.

While the Czechs have long occupied the lands of the present-day Czech Republic, for most of their history they were treated as second-class citizens, under the thumb of foreign rulers (generally from Germany or Austria). That the Czech nation exists as an independent state today is practically a Cinderella story. So let's get to know the underdog Czechs.

In Czech towns and villages, you'll find a simple joy of life—a holdover from the days of the Renaissance. The deep spirituality of the Baroque era still shapes the national character. The magic of Prague, the beauty of Český Krumlov, and the lyrical quality of the countryside relieve the heaviness caused by the turmoil that passed through here. Get beyond Prague and explore the country's medieval towns. These rugged woods and hilltop castles will make you feel as if you're walking through the garden of your childhood dreams.

Given their imaginative, sometimes fanciful culture, it's no surprise that the Czechs have produced some famously clever writers—from Franz Kafka (who wrote about a man waking up as a giant cockroach) to Karel Čapek (who wrote about artificially created beings he dubbed "roboti" or robots). The unique entertainment form of Black Light Theater—a combination of illusion, pantomime, puppetry, and modern dance—exemplifies Czech creativity (see page 124). And beloved Czech characters—such as the smiling Good Soldier Švejk, who befuddles his Austro-Hungarian army officers by cleverly playing dumb, and the ubiquitous little cartoon mole called Krtek—will quickly become familiar, as you'll see them all over the streets of Prague. (For more on Czech lit, see page 1113.)

Czechs refuse to dumb things down; if you want to visit one of the pretty countryside castles, they'll only let you do it on a thoughtfully guided tour—as if to guarantee that every visitor will come away with a complete appreciation for the place. Education and intellect are important, and academics are honored in Czech society. At the end of communism, the nation elected a poet, playwright, and philosopher, Václav Havel, to serve two terms as president.

Beyond his intellect, voters no doubt also appreciated Havel's independent thinking and bold actions (he had been imprisoned by communist authorities for his activities promoting human rights). Perhaps because they've seen their national affairs bungled by centuries of foreign overlords, many Czechs have a healthy suspicion of authority, and an admiration for those willing to flout it. Other Czechs with a rebellious spirit are national hero Jan Hus (who refused to recant his condemnation of Church corruption, and was burned at the stake), contemporary artist David Černý (whose outrageous stunts are always a lightning rod for controversy), and, of course, the man voted by a wide margin to be the greatest Czech of all time, Jára Cimrman. A fictional character originally created in the 1960s by a pair of radio satirists, Cimrman has taken on a life of his own—and today is something of a nationwide practical joke. (For more on Cimrman, see the sidebar later in this chapter.)

The Czechs' well-studied, sometimes subversive, often world-weary outlook can be perceived by outsiders as cynicism. Czechs have a sharp, dry, often sarcastic sense of humor, and a keen sense of irony. They don't suffer fools lightly...and watching a united nations of clueless tourists trample their capital city for the past generation hasn't done wonders for their patience. Cut the Czechs some slack, and show them respect: Be one of the very few visitors who bothers to learn a few pleasantries—hello, please, thank you— in their language. (See "Czech Language," later.) You'll notice the difference in how you're treated.

Czech Republic Almanac

Official Name: As of 2016, the country's new official short name is Czechia. It's better known as the Česká Republika, born on January 1, 1993, along with Slovakia, when the nation of Czechoslovakia—formed after World War I and dominated by the USSR after World War II—split into two countries.

Population: 10.6 million people. About 64 percent are ethnic Czechs, who speak Czech, and another 5 percent are Moravian. Unlike some of their neighbors (including the very Catholic Poles and Slovaks), Czechs are inclined to be agnostic: One in 10 is Roman Catholic, but the majority (54 percent) list their religion as unaffiliated, and another 35 percent list none.

Latitude and Longitude: 50°N and 15°E (similar latitude to Vancouver, British Columbia).

Area: 31,000 square miles (similar to South Carolina or Maine).

Geography: The Czech Republic comprises three regions (called "lands" here)—Bohemia (Čechy), Moravia (Morava), and a small slice of Silesia (Slezsko). The climate is generally cool and partly cloudy.

Biggest Cities: Prague (the capital, 1.3 million), Brno (378,000), Ostrava (300,000), and Plzeň (167,000).

Economy: The gross domestic product equals about $332 billion (similar to Minnesota). The GDP per capita is approximately $31,600 (compared to $51,490 for the average American). Major moneymakers for the country include machine parts, cars and trucks (VW subsidiary Škoda is a highly respected automaker),

Of the Czech Republic's three main regions—Bohemia, Moravia, and small Silesia—the best-known is Bohemia. It has nothing to do with beatnik bohemians, but with the Celtic tribe of Bohemia that inhabited the land before the coming of the Slavs. A longtime home of the Czechs, Bohemia, with Prague as its capital, is circled by a naturally fortifying ring of mountains and cut down the middle by the Vltava River. The winegrowing region of Moravia (to the east) is more Slavic and colorful, and more about the land.

Tourists often conjure up images of Bohemia when they think of the Czech Republic. But the country consists of more than rollicking beer halls and gently rolling landscapes. It's also about dreamy wine cellars and fertile Moravian plains, with the rugged Carpathian Mountains on the horizon. Politically and geologically, Bohemia and Moravia are two distinct regions. The soils and climates in which the hops and wine grapes grow are very different... and so are the two regions' mentalities. The boisterousness of the and beer (the leading brand is Pilsner Urquell). Industrial production declined during the economic slowdown, but not beer consumption, which dropped only minimally (the vast majority of Czech beer is consumed domestically). More than a third of trade is with next-door-neighbor Germany; as a result, Germany's economic health one year generally predicts the Czech Republic's fortunes the next.

Currency: 25 Czech crowns (*koruna*, Kč) = about $1.

Government: From 1948 to 1989, Czechoslovakia was a communist state under Soviet control. Today, the Czech Republic is a member of the European Union (since 2004) and a vibrant democracy, with about a 60 percent turnout for elections. Its parliament is made up of 200 representatives elected every four years and 81 senators elected for six years. The president is selected every five years. No single political party dominates; the current leadership is a coalition of Social Democrats (left), Christian Democrats (center), and an unpredictable one-man populist party. Ailing President Miloš Zeman, elected in 2013 in the first-ever popular presidential vote, is viewed as increasingly out of touch with the public and bent on steering the country's foreign policy toward Russia and China.

Flag: The Czech flag is red (bottom), white (top), and blue (a triangle along the hoist side).

The Average Czech: The average Czech has 1.4 kids (slowly rising after the sharp decline that followed the end of communism), will live 78 years, and has one television in the house.

Czech polka contrasts with the melancholy of the Moravian ballad; the political viewpoint of the Prague power broker is at odds with the spirituality of the Moravian bard.

Only a tiny bit of Silesia—around the town of Opava—is part of the Czech Republic today; the rest of the region is in Poland and Germany. (The Habsburgs lost traditionally Czech Silesia to Prussia in the 1740s, and 200 years later, Germany in turn ceded most of it to Poland.) People in Silesia speak a wide variety of dialects that mix Czech, German, and Polish. Perhaps due to their diverse genes and cultural heritage, women from Silesia are famous for being intelligent and beautiful.

Ninety percent of the tourists who visit the Czech Republic see only Prague. But if you venture outside the capital, you'll enjoy traditional towns and villages, great prices, a friendly and gentle countryside dotted by nettles and wild poppies, and almost no international tourists. Since the time of the Habsburgs, fruit trees have lined the country roads for everyone to share. Take your pick.

HELPFUL HINTS

Telephone: In Prague, dial 112 for medical or other emergencies and 158 for police. To summon an ambulance, call 155. For more details on dialing, see page 1086.

Tolls: If you're driving on highways in the Czech Republic, you're required to buy a toll sticker *(dálniční známka)* at the border, a post office, or a gas station (310 Kč/10 days, 440 Kč/1 month). Your rental car may already come with the necessary sticker—ask.

Rail Passes: The Czech Republic is covered by a Czech Republic pass, a Central Europe Triangle Pass (Vienna-Budapest-Prague or Vienna-Salzburg-Prague), a four-country European East pass, the Global Pass, and the Select Pass. If your train travel will be limited to a handful of rides and/or short distances (for example, within the Czech Republic), you're probably better off without a pass—Czech tickets are cheap to buy as you go. But if you're combining Prague with international destinations, a rail pass could save you money.

For more detailed advice on figuring out the smartest rail pass options for your train trip, visit the Trains & Rail Passes section of my website at www.ricksteves.com/rail.

CZECH HISTORY

The Czechs have always been at a crossroads of Europe—between the Slavic and Germanic worlds, between Catholicism and Protestantism, and between Cold War East and West. As if having foreseen all of this, the mythical founder of Prague—the beautiful princess Libuše—named her city "Praha" (meaning "threshold" in Czech). Despite these strong external influences, the Czechs have retained their distinct culture...and a dark, ironic sense of humor to keep them laughing through it all.

Charles IV and the Middle Ages (500s-1300s)

The pagan, Slavic tribes that arrived in this part of Europe in the sixth century A.D. were first united by the Prague-based Přemysl dynasty. The main figure of this era was Duke Václav I (A.D. 907-935)—later immortalized in a Christmas carol as "Good King Wenceslas"—who converted the Czechs to Christianity and founded a cathedral at Prague Castle, on a bluff overlooking the Vltava River.

In 1004, Bohemia was incorporated into the Holy Roman Empire (an alliance of mostly German-speaking kingdoms and dukedoms). Within 200 years—thanks to its strategic location and privileged status within the empire—Prague had become one of Europe's largest and most highly cultured cities.

The 14th century was Prague's Golden Age, when Holy Roman Emperor Charles IV (1316-1378) ruled. Born to a Luxembourger nobleman and a Czech princess, Charles IV was an ambitious man on the cusp of the Renaissance. He lived and studied in several European lands, spoke five languages, and counted Petrarch as a friend—but always felt a deep connection to his mother's Czech roots. Selecting Prague as his seat of power, Charles imported French architects to make the city a grand capital, founded the first university north of the Alps, and invigorated the Czech national spirit. (He popularized the legend of Wenceslas to give his people a near-mythical, King Arthur-type cultural standard-bearer.) Much of Prague's history and architecture—including the famous Charles Bridge, Charles University, St. Vitus Cathedral, and Karlštejn Castle—can be traced to this dynamic man's rule. Under Charles IV, the Czech people gained esteem among Europeans. Charles was born under a lucky star: During his time the dominance of divinely sanctioned monarchs peaked. A generation later, after a religious and social upheaval, his son faced much stronger opposition when trying to implement Charles-like absolute power.

Jan Hus and Religious Wars (1300s-1600s)

Jan Hus (c. 1369-1415) was a local preacher and professor who got in trouble with the Vatican a hundred years before Martin Luther. Like Luther, Hus preached in the people's language rather than in Latin. To add insult to injury, he complained about Church corruption. Tried for heresy and burned in 1415, Hus became both a religious and a national hero. While each age has defined Hus to its liking, the way he challenged authority while staying true to his beliefs has long inspired and rallied the Czech people. (For more on Hus, see page 60.)

Inspired by Hus' reformist ideas, the Czechs rebelled against both the Roman Catholic Church and German political control. This burst of independent thought led to a period of religious wars. Protestant Czech patriots—like the rough-and-rugged war hero Jan Žižka (often depicted in patriotic art with his trademark eye patch)—fought to maintain Czech autonomy. But ultimately, these rebels were overwhelmed by their Catholic opponents. The result of these wars was the loss of autonomy to Vienna.

Ruled by the Habsburgs of Austria, Prague stagnated—except during the rule of King Rudolf II (1552-1612), a Holy Roman Emperor. With Rudolf living in Prague, the city again emerged as a cultural and intellectual center. Astronomers Johannes Kepler and Tycho Brahe flourished, as did other scientists, and much of the inspiration for Prague's great art can be attributed to the king's patronage.

Not long after this period, Prague entered one of its darker spells. The Thirty Years' War (1618-1648) began in Prague when Czech Protestant nobles, wanting religious and political autonomy, tossed two Catholic Habsburg officials out the window of the castle. (This was one of Prague's many defenestrations—a uniquely Czech solution to political discord, in which offending politicians were literally thrown out the window.) The Czech Estates Uprising lasted two years, ending in a crushing defeat in the Battle of White Mountain (1620), which marked the end of Czech freedom. Twenty-seven leaders of the uprising were executed (today commemorated by crosses on Prague's Old Town Square), most of the old Czech nobility was dispossessed, and Protestants had to convert to Catholicism or leave the country.

Often called "the first world war" because it engulfed so many nations, the Thirty Years' War was particularly tough on Prague. During this period, its population dropped from 60,000 to 25,000. The result of this war was 300 years of Habsburg rule from afar, as Prague became a German-speaking backwater of Vienna. While the Austrian rule contributed to economic prosperity—and was fairly liberal compared to its Russian and Prussian neighbors— Czechs still tend to despise the Habsburgs. They see them as a pompous royal family that invented the concept of the modern zoo (at Vienna's Schönbrunn Palace) and then tried to impose it on the people of their empire (before deciding it was better to turn them into cannon fodder).

Czech National Revival (1800s-1918)

The end of Prague as a German city came gradually. During the centuries that the Czech language and culture were suppressed, "Prag" and other cities were populated mainly by German-speaking urbanites, while "backwards" peasants kept the old Czech ways alive in the countryside. But as the Industrial Revolution attracted Czech farmers and peasants to the cities, the demographics of the Czech population centers began to shift. Between 1800 and 1900—though it remained part of the Habsburg Empire—Prague went from being an essentially German town to a predominantly Czech one.

As in the rest of Europe, the 19th century was a time of great nationalism, when the age of divine kings and ruling families came to a fitful end. The Czech spirit was first stirred by the work of historian František Palacký, who dug deep into the Czech archives to forge a national narrative. During this time, Czechs were inspired by the completion of Prague's St. Vitus Cathedral, the symphonies of Antonín Dvořák, and the operas of Bedřich Smetana, which were performed in the new National Theater.

Alfons Mucha, a prodigiously talented Czech artist who made a name for himself in the high society of turn-of-the-century Paris, embodied this wave of nationalism. When he could have lived out his days in the lap of luxury in Paris or New York City, Mucha chose instead to return to his homeland and spend decades painting a magnum opus celebrating the historic journey of the Czechs and all Slavs—the *Slav Epic*.

After the Habsburgs' Austro-Hungarian Empire suffered defeat in World War I, their vast holdings broke apart and became independent countries. Among these was a union of Bohemia, Moravia, and Slovakia, the brainchild of a clever politician named Tomáš Garrigue Masaryk (see sidebar on page 108). The new nation, Czechoslovakia, was proclaimed in 1918, with Prague as its capital.

Troubles of the 20th Century (1918-1989)

Independence lasted only 20 years. In the notorious Munich Agreement of September 1938—much to the dismay of the Czechs and Slovaks—Great Britain and France peacefully ceded to Hitler the so-called Sudetenland (a fringe around the edge of Bohemia, populated mainly by people of German descent; see sidebar on page 192). It wasn't long before Hitler seized the rest of Czechoslovakia...and the Holocaust began. Under the ruthless Nazi governor Reinhard Heydrich, tens of thousands of Jews were sent first to the concentration camp at Terezín, and later to Auschwitz and other death camps. After Heydrich was assassinated by a pair of Czech paratroopers, the campaign of genocide grew even worse. Out of the 55,000 Jews living in Prague before the war, more than 80 percent perished during the Holocaust; throughout Czechoslovakia, an estimated 260,000 Jews were murdered.

For centuries, Prague's cultural makeup had consisted of a rich mix of Czech, German, and Jewish people—historically, they were almost evenly divided. With the Jewish population decimated, part of that delicate tapestry was gone forever. And after World War II ended, more than 2 million people of Germanic descent who lived in Czechoslovakia were pushed into Germany. Their forced resettlement—which led to the deaths of untold numbers of Germans (what some today might call "ethnic cleansing")—was demanded by the public and carried out by Czechoslovak President Edvard Beneš, who had ruled from exile in London throughout the war. Today's Czech Republic is largely homogenous—about 95 percent Czechs.

Although Prague escaped the bombs of World War II, it went directly from the Nazi frying pan into the communist fire. A local

Jára Cimrman: The Greatest Czech?

"I am such a complete atheist that I am afraid God will punish me." Such is the pithy wisdom of Jára Cimrman, the man overwhelmingly voted the "Greatest Czech of All Time" in a 2005 national poll. Who is Jára Cimrman? A philosopher? An explorer? An inventor? He is all these things, yes, and much more.

Born in the mid-19th century, Cimrman studied in Vienna before journeying the world. He traversed the Atlantic in a steamboat he designed himself, taught drama to peasants in Peru, and drifted across the Arctic Sea on an iceberg. He invented the lightbulb, but Edison beat him to the patent office by five minutes. It was he who suggested to the Americans the idea for a Panama Canal, though, as usual, he was never credited. Indeed, Cimrman surreptitiously advised many of the world's greats: Eiffel on his tower, Einstein on his theories of relativity, Chekhov on his plays. ("You can't just have *two* sisters," Cimrman told the playwright. "How about three?") Long before the world knew of Sartre or Camus, Cimrman was writing tracts such as *The Essence of the Existence*, which would become the foundation for his philosophy of "Cimrmanism," also known as "nonexistentialism." (Its central premise: "Existence cannot not exist.")

Despite Jára Cimrman's genius, the "Greatest Czech" poll's sponsors had a single objection to his candidacy: He's not real, but the brainchild of Czech humorists Zdeněk Svěrák and Jiří Šebánek, who brought this patriotic Renaissance Man to life in 1967 in a satirical radio play.

How should we interpret the fact that the Czechs chose a fictional character as their greatest countryman over any of their flesh-and-blood national heroes—say, Charles IV (the 14th-century Holy Roman Emperor who established Prague as the cultural and intellectual capital of Europe), or Martina Navrátilová (someone who plays a sport with bright green balls)?

I like to think that the vote for Cimrman says something about the country's enthusiasm for blowing raspberries in the face of authority. From the times of the Czech kings, who used crafty diplomacy to keep the German menace at bay, to the days of Jan Hus and his criticism of the Catholic Church, to the flashes of anticommunist revolt that at last sparked the Velvet Revolution in 1989—the Czechs have maintained a healthy disrespect for those who would tell them how to live their lives. Their vote for a fictional personage, says Cimrman's co-creator Svěrák, shows two things about the Czech nation: "That it is skeptical about those who are major figures and those who are supposedly the 'Greatest.' And that the only certainty that has saved the nation many times throughout history is its humor."

uprising freed the city from the Nazis on May 8, 1945, but the Soviets "liberated" them on May 9.

The period of 1945 to 1948 is a perfect case study of how, in trying times, a country can lose its freedom through its own folly. The popular perception that Czechoslovakia simply fell into the Soviet sphere of influence is only partly true. While the Soviets had special interest in controlling Czechoslovakia (particularly because of its uranium deposits), Czechoslovakia was represented by an internationally recognized exile government during the war. This government was allowed to come back and rule until the 1946 election. And up until 1948, Czechoslovakia was still a sovereign state (although under pressure), whose elected leaders were responsible for shaping its eventual orientation.

The first mistake was that the government in exile (despite Churchill's warnings) signed a binding cooperation pact with the Soviet Union in 1943. Then the communists won the most seats in the 1946 election—garnering over 40 percent of the vote in the Czech lands (they came in only second in Slovakia). In 1947 the parliament voted against the Marshall Plan. When the country's leaders and electorate realized the communists weren't playing according to any rule book, it was too late. By 1948 the communists controlled all the powerful ministries and suppressed student-led protests calling for democracy. For over 40 years they would not hold a free election.

The early communist era (1948-1968) was a mixture of misguided zeal, Stalinist repressions, and attempts to wed socialism with democracy. The "Prague Spring" period of reform—initiated by a young generation of progressive communists in 1968, led by the charismatic Slovak politician Alexander Dubček—came to an abrupt halt under the treads of Warsaw Pact tanks (for details, see page 82). Dubček was exiled (and made a backwoods forest ranger), and the years of "normalization" following the unsuccessful revolt were particularly disheartening. A wave of protests spread through the country in 1969, as furious young Czechs and Slovaks lit themselves on fire to decry communist oppression. But the status quo would hold strong for another 20 years.

In the late 1980s, the communists began constructing Prague's huge Žižkov TV tower (now the city's tallest structure)—not only to broadcast Czech TV transmissions, but also to jam Western signals. The Metro, built at about the same time, was intended for mass transit, but was also designed to be a giant fallout shelter for protection against capitalist bombs.

Every small town had its own set of loudspeakers for broadcasting propaganda. (You'll still see these if you look closely as you pass through the countryside.) Locals remember growing up with these mouthpieces of government boasting of successes ("This year, despite many efforts of sabotage on the part of certain individuals in service of imperialist goals, we have surpassed the planned output of steel by 195 percent"); calling people to action ("There will be no school tomorrow as all will join the farmers in the fields for an abundant harvest"); or quelling disturbances ("Some citizens may have heard about alien forces in our society taking advantage of this week's anniversary to spread unrest. This is to reassure you that the situation is firmly under control and nothing is happening in Olomouc or in Prague. Nevertheless, for their own safety, we suggest all citizens stay home").

Eventually the Soviet empire crumbled, beginning with reforms in Hungary in the summer of 1989 and culminating in the fall of the Berlin Wall that October. A few weeks later, Czechoslovakia regained its freedom in the student- and artist-powered 1989 "Velvet Revolution," so-called because there were no casualties...or even broken windows (see page 87). Václav Havel, a poet, playwright, and philosopher who had been imprisoned by the communist regime, became Czechoslovakia's first postcommunist president.

"It's Not You, It's Me": The Peaceful Breakup (1989-1993)

In the postcommunist age of new possibility, the two peoples of Czechoslovakia began to wonder if, in fact, they belonged together.

Ever since they joined with the Czechs in 1918, the Slovaks felt overshadowed by Prague (unmistakably the political, economic, and cultural center of the country). Slovakia, which in the preceding 50 years had been stripped even of the right to run schools in its own language, stood no chance of independence on its own after World War I. And over the years, the Czechs resented the financial burden of carrying their poorer neighbors to the east. In this new world of flux and freedom, longstanding trends and tensions came to a head. You could argue that Austro-Hungary's multiethnic successor states—such as Czechoslovakia and Yugoslavia—were miniature copies of the mother country. Once the idea of a multiethnic state represented by that mother fell apart, it was only a matter of time until the children would dissolve into national states as well.

The dissolution of Czechoslovakia began over a hyphen, as the Slovaks wanted to rename the country Czecho-Slovakia. Ideally, this symbolic move would come with a redistribution of powers: two capitals and two UN reps, but one national bank and a single currency. This idea was rejected, and in June 1992, the Slovak nationalist candidate Vladimír Mečiar fared surprisingly well in the elections—suggesting that the Slovaks were serious about secession. The politicians plowed ahead, getting serious about the split in September 1992. The transition took only three months from start to finish.

The split became official on January 1, 1993, and each country ended up with its own capital, currency, and head of state. For most, the breakup dissolved tensions, and a decade and a half later, Czechs and Slovaks still feel closer to each other than to any other nationality.

The Czech Republic Today (1990s to Present)

In recent times, the Czech Republic has had three significant turning points. In March 1999, it joined NATO. Then on May 1, 2004, the country joined the European Union. Three and a half years later, it entered the Schengen Agreement, effectively erasing its borders for the purposes of work and travel.

After 14 years in office, a term-limited Václav Havel stepped down in 2003. He died in 2011. While he's fondly remembered by Czechs as a great thinker, writer, and fearless leader of the opposition movement during the communist days, many consider him to have been less successful as a president.

The next president, Václav Klaus, had been the pragmatic author of the economic reforms in the 1990s. Klaus' surprising win in the 2003 election symbolized a change from revolutionary times, when philosophers became kings, to modern humdrum politics, when offices are gained by bargaining with the opposition (Communist Party votes in the Parliament were the decisive factor in Klaus' election).

Behind-the-scenes deals in Parliament allowed Klaus to be re-elected, drawing public outrage and eventually a change in the country's constitution, which allowed for the first election of a president directly by the people (rather than by Parliament) in January 2013.

The winner of this historic presidential election was Miloš Zeman, the other political heavyweight of the 1990s. President Zeman, a tobacco, pork, and Becherovka-powered man of the people, has since suffered ill health, and critics say he's become so confused that he can no longer tell East from West. He's been criticized for courting Russian President Vladimir Putin, and during the 2016 visit of Chinese President Xi Jinping, Zeman took a page from Prague circa-1980, ordering a police assault on peaceful protesters.

But the president is largely a symbolic head. The main power broker, the prime minister, is chosen in parliamentary elections. In 2017, the country faces a choice: settle for its imperfect traditional parties, or empower a recently emerged antiestablishment candidate—food industry mogul and former secret police collaborator Andrej Babiš, head of the Action of Dissatisfied Citizens party.

Wary Czechs debate whether the out-of-control Zeman or the cunning finance minister Babiš—who seems to be a cross between Vladimir Putin and former Italian Prime Minister Silvio Berlusconi—is more dangerous for the country overall.

But every country has its political wrangling and corruption scandals. What really matters to Czechs is sports. Like most Europeans, Czechs are obsessed with soccer. The Czech national team routinely finishes impressively in international tournaments. Domestically, the two oldest and most successful soccer clubs are the bitter Prague rivals, AC Sparta and AC Slavia. But Czechs are an even more impressive world power when it comes to hockey; the national team has won several world championships and Olympic medals. Currently, more than two dozen Czech players take the ice in America's NHL; think of Jaromír Jágr, one of the NHL's all-time leading scorers, and Dominik "The Dominator" Hašek, a top goaltender.

Overall, the recent trajectory of Czech history is trending positive. Both in the capital and in rural villages, the country feels more affluent than ever before, all while celebrating its inherent Czech-ness. And Prague is, quite justifiably, one of the most popular tourist destinations in Europe.

CZECH FOOD

The Czechs have one of Europe's most stick-to-your-ribs cuisines. Heavy on meat, potatoes, and cabbage, it's hearty and tasty—designed to keep peasants fueled through a day of hard work. Some people could eat this stuff forever, while others seek a frequent break in the form of ethnic restaurants (bigger towns such as Prague, Český Krumlov, and Kutná Hora have several options).

A Czech restaurant is a social place where people come to relax. Tables are not private. You can ask to join someone, and you will most likely make some new friends. After a sip of beer, ask for the *jídelní lístek* (menu).

Soups: *Polévka* (soup) is the most essential part of a meal. The saying goes: "The soup fills you up, the dish plugs it up." Some of the thick soups for a cold day are *zelná* or *zelňačka* (cabbage), *čočková* (lentil), *fazolová* (bean), and *dršťková* (tripe—delicious if fresh, chewy as gum if not). The lighter soups are *hovězí* or *slepičí vývar s nudlemi* (beef or chicken broth with noodles), *pórková* (leek), and *květáková* (cauliflower).

Bread: *Pečivo* (bread) is either delivered with the soup, or you need to ask for it; it's always charged separately depending on how many *rohlíky* (rolls) or slices of *chleba* (yeast bread) you eat.

Main Dishes: These can either be *hotová jídla* (quick, ready-to-serve standard dishes, in some places available only during

Czech Dumplings

Czech dumplings *(knedlíky)* resemble steamed white bread. They come in plain or potato *(bramborové)* varieties; are meant to be drowned in gravy (dumplings never accompany sauceless dishes); and are eaten with a knife and fork.

Sweet dumplings, listed in the dessert section on a menu, are a tempting option in summer, when they are loaded with fresh strawberries, blueberries, apricots, or plums, and garnished with custard and melted butter. Beware, though, that many restaurants cheat by filling the sticky dough with a smattering of jam or fruit preserve; before ordering, ask the waiter for details, or discreetly inspect that plate at your neighbor's table. Dumplings with frozen fruit lose some of the flavor, but are still worth trying.

lunch hours, generally 11:00-14:30) or the more specialized *jídla na objednávku* or *minutky* (plates prepared when you order).

The word *pečené* (roasted) shows up frequently on menus, whether it's *vepřová pečeně* (pork roast), *pečené kuře* (roasted chicken), or *pečená kachna* (roasted duck). Other popular meat dishes are *smažený řízek* (fried pork fillet, like Wiener schnitzel), *guláš* (a thick, meaty stew), and *svíčková na smetaně* (beef tenderloin in cream sauce). If you're spending the night out with friends, have a beer and feast on the huge *vepřové koleno* (pork knuckle), usually served with mustard *(hořčicí)*, horseradish sauce *(křenem)*, and yeast bread *(chleba)*.

In this landlocked country, fish options are typically limited to *kapr* (carp) and *pstruh* (trout), prepared in a variety of ways and served with potatoes or fries—although recently, Czech perch and Norwegian salmon have cropped up on many local menus.

Vegetarians can go for the delicious *smažený sýr s bramborem* (fried cheese with potatoes) or default to *čočka s vejci* (lentils with fried egg).

Starches and Garnishes: *Hotová jídla* come with set garnishes, but if ordering à la carte *(jídla na objednávku)*, you'll typically need to order your garnishes separately (otherwise you'll get only the main dish). In either case, the most common sides are *knedlíky* (bread dumplings, described in the sidebar), *zelím* (cabbage), and *bramborem* (potatoes).

Salad: *Šopský salát*, like a Greek village salad, is usually the best salad option (a mix of tomatoes, cucumbers, peppers, onion, and feta cheese with vinegar and olive oil). The waiter will bring it with the main dish, unless you specify that you want it before.

Dessert: For *moučník* (dessert), there are *palačinka* (crêpes served with fruit or jam), *lívance* (small pancakes with jam and

Czech Beer

Czechs are among the world's most enthusiastic beer *(pivo)* drinkers—adults drink an average of 80 gallons a year. The pub is a place to have fun, complain, discuss art and politics, talk hockey, and chat with locals and visitors alike. Whether you're in a *restaurace* (restaurant), *hostinec* (pub), or *hospoda* (bar), a beer will land on your table upon the slightest hint to the waiter, and a new pint will automatically appear when the old glass is almost empty (until you tell the waiter to stop). Order beer from the tap (*točené* means "draft," *sudové pivo* means "keg beer"). A *pivo* is large (0.5 liter—17 oz); a *malé pivo* is small (0.3 liter—10 oz).

The Czechs perfected a Bavarian's invention—Pilsner-style lager—in nearby Plzeň and the result, Pilsner Urquell, is on tap in many local pubs. But the Czechs produce plenty of other good beers; most of the famous brands, including Krušovice, Gambrinus, Staropramen, and Kozel, are owned internationally. Budvar, from the town of Budějovice ("Budweis" in German), is the last state-owned (and as locals like to point out, mismanaged) brewery. For years, the Czech and the American breweries disputed the "Budweiser" brand name. The solution: Czech Budweiser is sold under its own name in Europe, China, and Africa, while in America it is marketed as Czechvar.

The big degree symbol on beer bottles doesn't indicate alco-

curd), *zmrzlinový pohár* (ice-cream sundae), or fruit-filled dumplings. Many restaurants will offer different sorts of *koláče* (pastries) and *štrůdl* (apple strudel), but it's much better to get these directly from a bakery. A *větrník* is a super-decadent, glazed cream puff.

All over Prague's Old Town, you'll find kiosks selling a treat called *trdlo* or *trdelník*. This is a long ribbon of dough wrapped around a stick, slowly cooked on a rotisserie, then rolled in cinnamon sugar or other toppings. While these aren't "traditional Czech" (they were imported quite recently from Hungary), they do offer a fresh, sweet treat. Try to get one that's still warm, rather than one wrapped in plastic—it makes a big difference.

Beverages: No Czech meal is complete without a cup of strong *turecká káva* (Turkish coffee—finely ground coffee that only partly dissolves, leaving hol content. Instead, it is a measurement used by brewers to track the density of certain ingredients. As a rough guide, 10 degrees is about 3.5 percent alcohol, 12 degrees is about 4.2 percent alcohol, and 11 and 15 degrees are dark beers. The most popular Czech beers are about as potent as German beers and only slightly stronger than typical American brews.

Each establishment has only one brand of beer on tap; to try

a particular kind, look for its sign outside. A typical pub serves only one brand each of 10-degree, 12-degree, and dark beer. Czechs don't mix beer with anything, and they don't hop from pub to pub (in one night, it is said, you must stay loyal to one woman and to one beer). *Na zdraví* means "to your health" in Czech.

While the trend for much of the last 20 years has been for the biggest beer corporations to buy up or edge out the smaller companies, Czechs have been moving beyond "eurotaste" beers to creative microbrews. Now, more and more restaurants are making their own beer or serving beer only from independent breweries.

On the other hand, alcoholism is cited as the chief cause of homelessness in the country, leading many to question the ethics of a culture in which beer costs less than bottled water.

"mud" on the bottom, highly caffeinated and drunk without milk). Although espressos and instant coffees have made headway in the past few years, some Czechs regard them as a threat to tradition.

Czech mineral waters *(minerálka)* have a high mineral content. They're naturally carbonated because they come from the springs in the many Czech spas (Mattoni, the most common brand, is from Carlsbad). If you want still water, ask for *voda bez bublinek* (water without bubbles). Tap water is generally not served. Water comes bottled and generally costs more than beer.

Bohemia is beer country, with Europe's best and cheapest brew (see the sidebar). Moravians prefer wine and *slivovice* (SLEE-voh-veet-seh)—a plum brandy so highly valued that it's the de facto currency of the Carpathian Mountains (often used to barter with farmers and other mountain folk). *Medovina* ("honey wine") is mead.

In bars and restaurants, you can go wild with

memorable liqueurs, most of which cost about a dollar a shot. Experiment. *Fernet,* a bitter drink made from many herbs, is the leading Czech aperitif. Absinthe, made from wormwood and herbs, is a watered-down version of the hallucinogenic drink that's illegal in much of Europe. It's famous as the muse of many artists (including Henri de Toulouse-Lautrec in Paris more than a century ago). *Becherovka,* made of 13 herbs and 38 percent alcohol, was used to settle upset aristocratic tummies and as an aphrodisiac. This velvety drink remains popular today. *Becherovka* and tonic mixed together is nicknamed *beton* ("concrete"). If you drink three, you'll find out why.

CZECH LANGUAGE

Czech is a Slavic language closely related to its Polish and Slovak neighbors. These days, English is widely spoken, and you'll find the language barrier minimal. Among older people, German is a common second language.

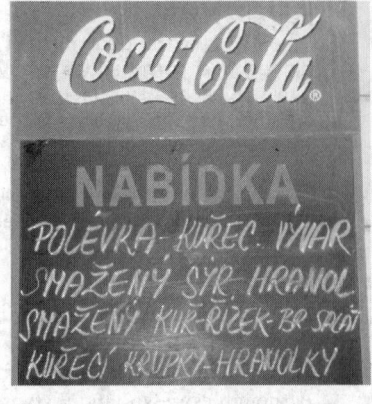

Czech pronunciation can be tricky. The language has a dizzying array of diacritical marks (little doo-hickeys over some letters that affect pronunciation). Most notably, some letters can be topped with a *háček* (*č, š, ž, ň, ě*). Here are some clues for Czech pronunciation:

j sounds like "y" as in "yarn"
c sounds like "ts" as in "cats"
č sounds like "ch" as in "chicken"
š sounds like "sh" as in "shrimp"
ž sounds like "zh" as in "leisure"
ň sounds like "ny" as in "canyon"
ě sounds like "yeh" as in "yet"
ď sounds like the "dj" sound in "ledge"

Prague is flooded with tourists, most of whom don't bother to learn a single word of the local language. To ingratiate yourself to your hosts—not to mention be a sensitive traveler—take some time to learn the Czech essentials. You'll find Czech survival phrases and pronunciation tips on the following pages.

When navigating town, these words might be helpful: *město* (MYEHS-toh, town), *náměstí* (nah-myehs-tee, square), *ulica* (OO-leet-sah, street), *nábřeži* (NAH-bzheh-zhee, embankment road), and *most* (mohst, bridge).

Czech Survival Phrases

The emphasis in Czech words usually falls on the first syllable—though don't overdo it, as this stress is subtle. A vowel with an accent (á, é, í, ú, ý) is held longer. The combination ch sounds like the guttural "kh" sound in the Scottish word "loch." The uniquely Czech ř (as in Dvořák) sounds like a cross between a rolled "r" and "zh"; in the phonetics, it's "zh." Here are a few English words that all Czechs know: super, OK, pardon, stop, menu, problem, and no problem.

English	Czech	Pronunciation
Hello. (formal)	Dobrý den.	**doh**-bree dehn
Hi. / Bye. (informal)	Ahoj.	**ah**-hoy
Do you speak English?	Mluvíte anglicky?	**mloo**-vee-teh **ahn**-glits-kee
Yes. / No.	Ano. / Ne.	**ah**-noh / neh
I don't understand.	Nerozumím.	neh-roh-zoo-meem
Please. / You're welcome. / Can I help you?	Prosím.	**proh**-seem
Thank you.	Děkuji.	**dyeh**-kwee
Excuse me. / I'm sorry.	Promiňte.	**proh**-meen-teh
Good.	Dobře.	**dohb**-zheh
Goodbye.	Nashledanou.	**nah**-skleh-dah-noh
one / two / three	jeden / dva / tři	**yay**-dehn / dvah / tzhee
four / five / six	čtyři / pět / šest	**chtee**-zhee / pyeht / shehst
seven / eight	sedm / osm	**seh**-dum / **oh**-sum
nine / ten	devět / deset	**dehv**-yeht / **deh**-seht
hundred / thousand	sto / tisíc	stoh / **tee**-seets
How much?	Kolik?	**koh**-leek
local currency	koruna (Kč)	koh-**roo**-nah
Write it?	Napište to?	**nah**-pish-teh toh
Is it free?	Je to zadarmo?	yeh toh **zah**-dar-moh
Is it included?	Je to v ceně?	yeh tohf **tsay**-nyeh
Where can I find / buy...?	Kde mohu najít / koupit...?	guh-**deh moh**-hoo **nah**-yeet / **koh**-pit
I'd like... (said by a man)	Rád bych...	rahd bikh
I'd like... (said by a woman)	Ráda bych...	**rah**-dah bikh
We'd like...	Rádi bychom...	**rah**-dyee **bee**-khohm
...a room.	...pokoj.	**poh**-koy
...a ticket to ___. (destination)	...jízdenka do ___.	**yeez**-dehn-kah doh ___
Is it possible?	Je to možné?	yeh toh **mohzh**-neh
Where is...?	Kde je...?	guh-**deh** yeh
...the train station	...nádraží	**nah**-drah-zhee
...the bus station	...autobusové nádraží	**ow**-toh-boo-soh-veh **nah**-drah-zhee
...the tourist information office	...turistická informační kancelář	**too**-rih-stit-skah **een**-for-mahch-nee **kahn**-tseh-lahzh
...the toilet	...vécé	**veht**-seh
men / women	muži / ženy	**moo**-zhee / **zheh**-nee
left / right / straight	vlevo / vpravo / rovně	**vleh**-voh / **fprah**-voh / **rohv**-nyeh
At what time...?	V kolik...?	**fkoh**-leek
...does this open / close	...otevírají / zavírají	**oh**-teh-vee-rah-yee / **zah**-vee-rah-yee
Just a moment, please.	Moment, prosím.	**moh**-mehnt **proh**-seem
now / soon / later	teď / brzy / později	tedge / **bir**-zih / **pohz**-dyeh-yee
today / tomorrow	dnes / zítra	duh-**nehs** / **zee**-trah

In a Czech Restaurant

English	Czech	Pronunciation
I'd like to reserve... (said by a man)	Rád bych zarezervoval...	rahd bikh **zah**-reh-zehr-voh-vahl
I'd like to reserve... (said by a woman)	Ráda bych zarezervovala...	**rah**-dah bikh **zah**-reh-zehr-voh-vah-lah
...a table for one / two.	...stůl pro jednoho / dva.	stool proh **yehd**-noh-hoh / dvah
Non-smoking.	Nekuřácký.	**neh**-kuhzh-aht-skee
Is this table free?	Je tento stůl volný?	yeh **tehn**-toh stool **vohl**-nee
Can I help you?	Mohu vám pomoci?	**moh**-hoo vahm poh-**moht**-see
The menu (in English), please.	Jídelní lístek (v angličtině), prosím.	**yee**-dehl-nee **lee**-stehk (**fahn**-gleech-tee-nyeh) **proh**-seem
Service is / isn't included.	Spropitné je / není zahrnuto.	**sproh**-pit-neh yeh / **neh**-nee **zah**-har-noo-toh
"to go"	s sebou	**seh**-boh
with / and / or	s / a / nebo	suh / ah / **neh**-boh
ready-to-eat meal	hotová jídla	**hoh**-toh-vah **yeed**-lah
meal on request	minutky	**mih**-noot-kee
appetizers	předkrm	**pzhehd**-krim
bread	chléb	khlehb
cheese	sýr	seer
sandwich	sendvič	**sehnd**-vich
soup / salad	polévka / salát	poh-**lehv**-kah / **sah**-laht
meat	maso	**mah**-soh
poultry	drůbež	**droo**-behzh
fish	ryby	**rih**-bih
fruit / vegetables	ovoce / zelenina	**oh**-voht-seh / **zeh**-leh-nyee-nah
dessert	dezert	**deh**-zehrt
(tap) water	voda (z kohoutku)	**voh**-dah (**skoh**-hoht-koo)
mineral water	minerální voda	**mih**-neh-rahl-nyee **voh**-dah
carbonated / not carbonated (spoken)	s bublinkami / bez bublinek	**sboob**-leen-kah-mee / behz **boo**-blee-nehk
carbonated / not carbonated (printed)	perlivá / neperlivá	**pehr**-lee-vah / **neh**-pehr-lee-vah
milk	mléko	**mleh**-koh
(orange) juice	(pomerančový) džus	(**poh**-mehr-ahn-choh-vee) "juice"
coffee / tea	káva / čaj	**kah**-vah / chai
wine	víno	**vee**-noh
red / white	červené / bílé	**chehr**-veh-neh / **bee**-leh
sweet / dry	sladké / suché	**slahd**-keh / **soo**-kheh
glass / bottle	sklenka / lahev	**sklehn**-kah / **lah**-hehv
beer	pivo	**pee**-voh
light / dark	světlé / tmavé	**svyeht**-leh / **tmah**-veh
Cheers!	Na zdraví!	nah zdrah-**vee**
Enjoy your meal.	Dobrou chuť.	**doh**-broh khoot
More. / Another.	Více. / Další.	**veet**-seh / **dahl**-shee
The same.	To samé.	toh **sah**-meh
The bill.	Účet.	**oo**-cheht
I'll pay.	Zaplatím.	**zah**-plah-teem
tip	spropitné	**sproh**-pit-neh
Delicious!	Výborné!	**vee**-bohr-neh

PRAGUE

Few cities can match Prague's over-the-top romance, evocative Old World charm...and tourist crowds. Prague is equal parts historic and fun. No other place in Europe has become popular so quickly. And for good reason: Prague—the only Central European capital to escape the large-scale bombing of the last century's wars—is one of Europe's best-preserved cities. It's filled with sumptuous Art Nouveau facades, offers tons of cheap Mozart and Vivaldi concerts, and brews some of the best beer in Europe.

Prague is a photographer's delight. You'll wind through walkable neighborhoods, past statues of bishops and pastel facades adorned with gables, balconies, lanterns, and a zillion little architectural details. Prague itself seems a work of art. Besides its medieval and Baroque look, it's a world of willowy Art Nouveau paintings and architecture. You'll also see rich remnants of its strong Jewish heritage and stark reminders of the communist era. And you'll meet an entrepreneurial mix of locals and expats, each with a brilliant scheme of how to make money in the tourist trade.

Escape the crowds into the back lanes and pretend you're strolling through the 18th century. Duck into pubs to enjoy the hearty food and good pilsner beer, and tour museums packed with fine art. Delve into one of Europe's top stops.

PLANNING YOUR TIME

A few days in Prague is plenty of time to get a solid feel for the city and enjoy some side-trips. If you're in a rush, you'll need a minimum of two full days (with three nights, or two nights and a night train) for a good introduction to the city. Keep in mind that

Jewish Quarter sights close on Saturday and Jewish holidays. Some museums, mainly in the Old Town, are closed on Monday.

Prague in Two or More Days

Here's my plan for fully experiencing Prague in two days. With more time, I've offered more suggestions. Split your nights between beer halls, live music, or Black Light Theater.

Day 1

9:00	Take my Prague Old Town Walk to get oriented to the city's core. Along the way, enter some of the sights (including the Municipal House) and climb at least one of the old towers—at the Old Town Hall, or at either end of the Charles Bridge—to enjoy the view.
13:00	Have lunch either in the Old Town or Little Quarter. Explore the Little Quarter (Kampa Island, Lennon Wall, Little Quarter Square).
15:00	Explore the Jewish Quarter.

Day 2

8:00	Get an early start from your hotel, and zip up to Prague Castle on the tram. Be at St. Vitus Cathedral when it opens at 9:00, then visit the rest of the castle sights.
11:00	As you leave the castle, tour the Lobkowicz Palace.
12:00	Have lunch in the Little Quarter, below the castle.
13:00	Visit Wenceslas Square, and tour the Mucha Museum or the Municipal House (if you didn't visit it already) to enjoy some Art Nouveau.
16:30	Squeeze in one more museum—perhaps the Museum of Medieval Art or the Museum of Communism.

Note: If you'd rather sleep in today, flip this plan—visit Wenceslas Square, the Mucha Museum, or Municipal House; then tram up to the castle in the early afternoon (by about 14:00), as the crowds disperse.

Day 3 and Beyond

With more time, fit in additional museums that interest you. If you have at least four days, Prague has a variety of worthwhile day trips at its doorstep. I'd prioritize Kutná Hora (delightful small town with gorgeous cathedral and famous bone church), the Terezín Memorial (Holocaust history), and/or Konopiště Castle (with a lived-in Habsburg interior). Český Krumlov is another wonderful destination, but it's a bit far for a day trip—it's much better as an overnight.

Prague Overview

HOLEŠOVICE

VELETRŽNÍ PALACE

← To Airport

CASTLE QUARTER (Hradčany)

PRAGUE CASTLE

River

OLD TOWN (Staré Město)

ŽIŽKOV →

ROYAL WAY

Little Quarter Square

CHARLES BRIDGE

JEWISH QUARTER

POWDER TOWER

LITTLE QUARTER (Malá Strana)

Old Town Square

ROYAL WAY

MAIN TRAIN STATION

Petřín Hill

Wenceslas Square

NEW TOWN (Nové Město)

Not to Scale

Vltava

VINOHRADY

SMÍCHOV

VYŠEHRAD

VYŠEHRAD FORTRESS

PRAGUE

Orientation to Prague

PRAGUE BY NEIGHBORHOOD

Residents call their town "Praha" (PRAH-hah). It's big, with about 1.3 million people (swelling to 2 million in the metropolitan area). But during a quick visit, you'll focus on its relatively compact old center.

The Vltava River divides the city in two. East of the river are the Old Town and New Town, the main train station, and most of the recommended hotels. To the west of the river is Prague Castle, and below that, the sleepy Little Quarter. Connecting the two halves are several bridges, including the landmark Charles Bridge.

Think of Prague as a collection of neighborhoods. In fact, until about 1800, Prague actually was four distinct towns with four town squares, all separated by fortified walls. Each town had a unique character, drawn from the personality of its first settlers. Today, much of Prague's charm survives in the distinct spirit of these towns.

Old Town (Staré Město): Nestled in the bend of the river, this is the historic core, where most tourists spend their time. It's pedestrian-friendly, with small winding streets, old buildings, shops, and beer halls and cafés. In the center sits the charming Old Town

PRAGUE

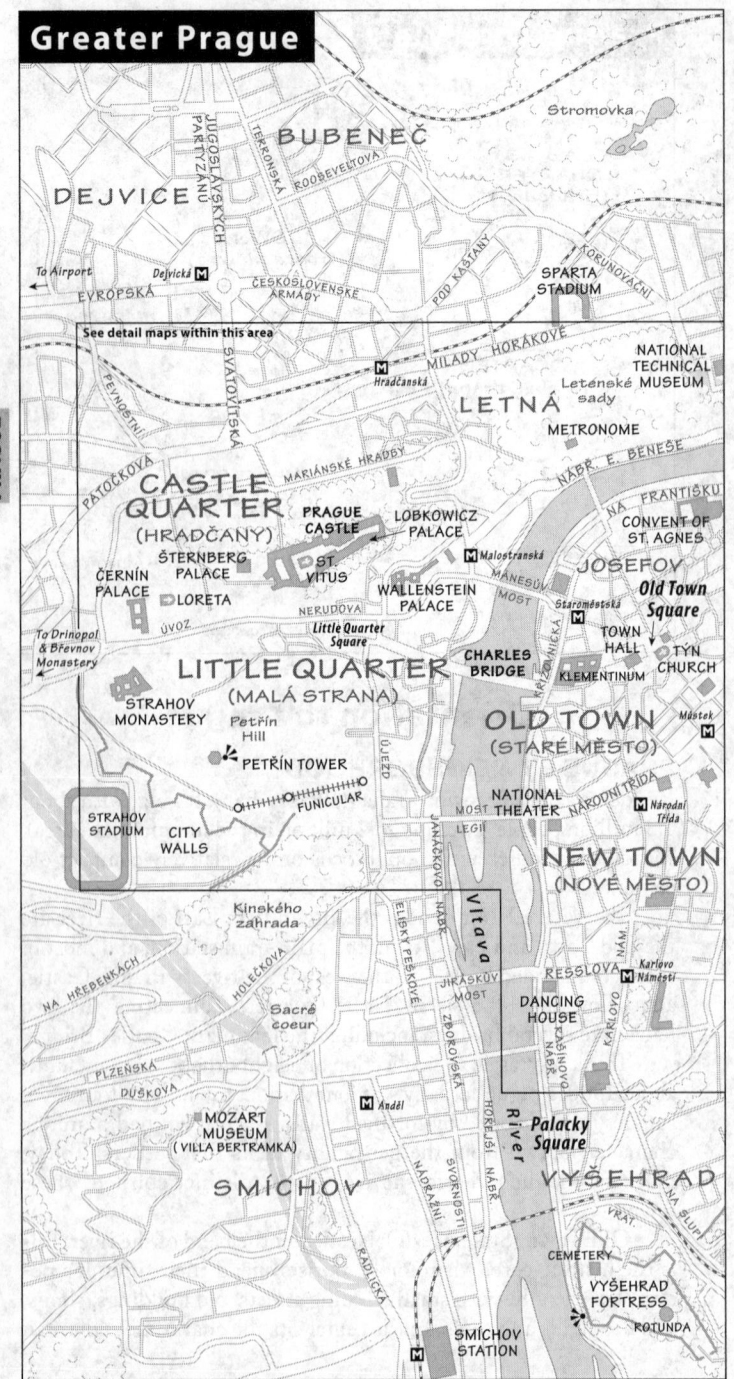

Greater Prague

Stromovka

BUBENEČ

DEJVICE

To Airport   Dejvická Ⓜ   ČESKOSLOVENSKÉ ARMÁDY

EVROPSKÁ

SPARTA STADIUM

See detail maps within this area

MILADY HORÁKOVÉ   Hradčanská Ⓜ

LETNÁ   Letenské sady

NATIONAL TECHNICAL MUSEUM

METRONOME

NÁBŘ. E. BENEŠE

CASTLE QUARTER (HRADČANY)

MARIÁNSKÉ HRADBY

PRAGUE CASTLE

LOBKOWICZ PALACE

NA FRANTIŠKU

CONVENT OF ST. AGNES

ČERNÍN PALACE   ŠTERNBERG PALACE   ST. VITUS

Malostranská Ⓜ   MÁNESŮV MOST

JOSEFOV

Old Town Square

LORETA

WALLENSTEIN PALACE

NERUDOVA   Little Quarter Square

Staroměstská Ⓜ

TOWN HALL

TÝN CHURCH

To Drinopol & Břevnov Monastery

ÚVOZ

CHARLES BRIDGE   KLEMENTINUM

LITTLE QUARTER (MALÁ STRANA)

OLD TOWN (STARÉ MĚSTO)

Můstek Ⓜ

STRAHOV MONASTERY   Petřín Hill

PETŘÍN TOWER

ÚJEZD

NATIONAL THEATER   NÁRODNÍ TŘÍDA

Národní Třída Ⓜ

STRAHOV STADIUM   CITY WALLS

FUNICULAR

MOST LEGIÍ

NEW TOWN (NOVÉ MĚSTO)

JANÁČKOVO NÁBŘ.

Kinského zahrada

Vltava

ELIŠKY PEŠKOVÉ NÁBŘ.

JIRÁSKŮV MOST

RESSLOVA   Karlovo Náměstí Ⓜ

KARLOVO NÁM.

NA HŘEBENKÁCH

HOLEČKOVA

Sacré coeur

ZBOROVSKÁ

DANCING HOUSE

RAŠÍNOVO NÁBŘ.

PLZEŇSKÁ

DUŠKOVA

Anděl Ⓜ

HOŘEJŠÍ NÁBŘ.

SVORNOSTI

MOZART MUSEUM (VILLA BERTRAMKA)

River

Palacky Square

VYŠEHRAD

SMÍCHOV

NÁDRAŽNÍ

RADLICKÁ

VRAT

CEMETERY

NA SLUPI

VYŠEHRAD FORTRESS

SMÍCHOV STATION   Ⓜ

ROTUNDA

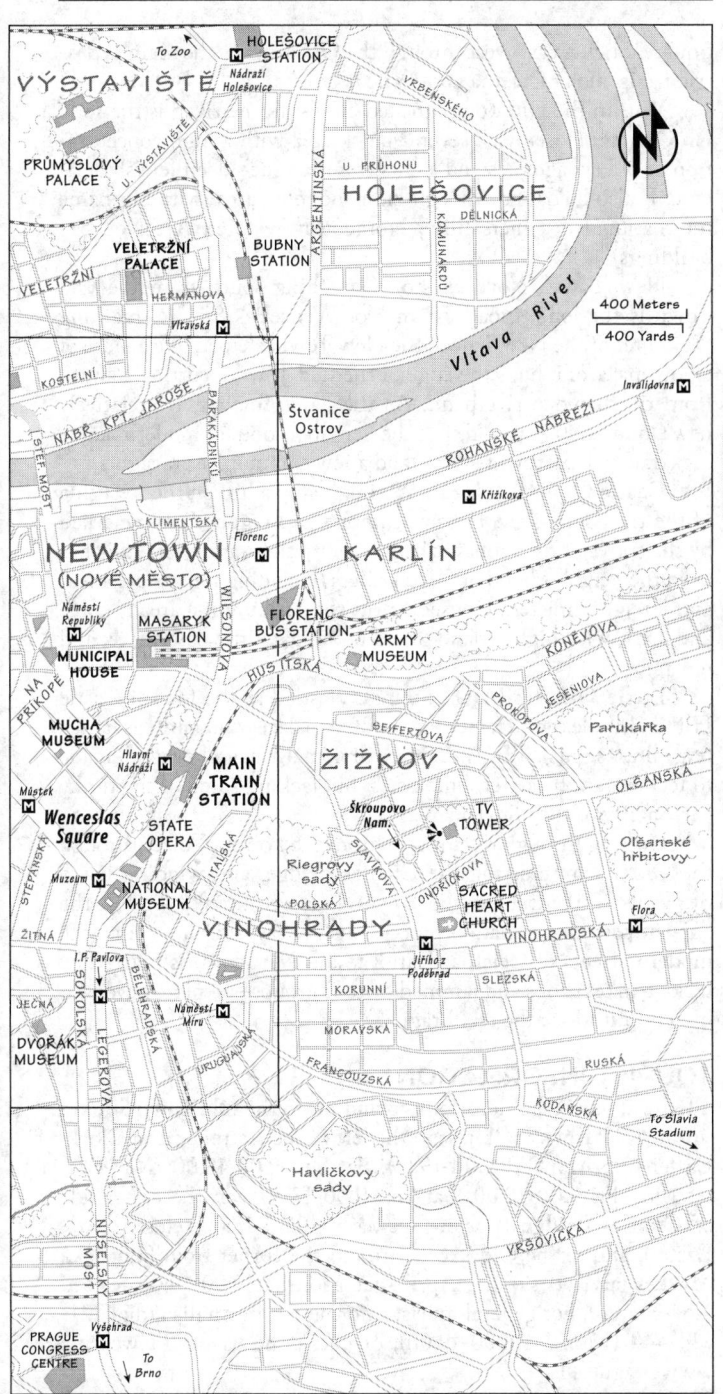

Square. Slicing east-west through the Old Town is the main pedestrian axis, along Celetná and Karlova streets.

Within the Old Town, tucked closest to the river, is the **Jewish Quarter** (Josefov), a several-block area with a high concentration of old synagogues and sights from Prague's deep Jewish heritage. It also holds the city's glitziest shopping area (with big-name international designers filling gorgeously restored Art Nouveau buildings).

New Town (Nové Město): Stretching south from the Old Town is the long, broad expanse of Wenceslas Square, marking the center of the New Town. The New Town, shaped like a piece of elbow macaroni, hugs the edge of the Old Town—cutting a swath from riverbank to riverbank. As the name implies, it's relatively new ("only" 600 years old). It's the neighborhood for modern buildings, fancy department stores, and a few communist-era sights.

Castle Quarter (Hradčany): High atop a hill on the west side of the river stands the massive complex of Prague Castle, marked by the spires of St. Vitus Cathedral. For a thousand years, this has been the neighborhood of Czech rulers (including today's president and foreign minister). Consequently, the surrounding area is noble and leafy, with high art and grand buildings, little commerce, and few pubs.

Little Quarter (Malá Strana): Nestled at the foot of Castle Hill is this pleasant former town of fine palaces and gardens (and a few minor sights). This is Prague's diplomatic neighborhood, made to feel elegant by stately embassies, but lacking some of the funky personality of the Old Town.

Cutting through the towns—from the Powder Tower through the Old Town, crossing the Charles Bridge, and winding up to St. Vitus Cathedral—is the **Royal Way** (Královská Cesta), the ancient path of coronation processions. Today, this city spine (the modern streets of Celetná, Karlova, and Nerudova) is marred by tacky trinket shops and jammed by tour groups—explore beyond it if you want to see the real Prague.

TOURIST INFORMATION

TIs are at several key locations, including on the **Old Town Square** (in the Old Town Hall, just to the left of the Astronomical Clock; Easter-Oct Mon-Fri 9:00-19:00, Sat-Sun 9:00-18:00; Nov-Easter Mon-Fri 9:00-18:00, Sat-Sun 9:00-17:00); on the castle side of **Charles Bridge** (Easter-Oct daily 10:00-18:00, closed Nov-Easter); and in the Old Town, around the corner from **Havelská Market** (at Rytířská 31, April-Oct Mon-Sat 9:00-19:00, closed Nov-March). For general tourist information in English, dial 221-714-444 (Mon-Fri 8:00-19:00), or check the useful TI website: www.prague.eu.

The TIs offer maps, a helpful transit guide, and information on guided walks and bus tours. They can book local guides, concerts, and occasionally hotel rooms.

Monthly event guides—all of them packed with ads—include the *Prague Guide* (29 Kč), *Prague This Month* (free), and *Heart of Europe* (free, summer only).

Prague Card: This pricey sightseeing pass covers public transit (including the airport bus); admission or discounts to a number of sights (including a few biggies—such as Prague Castle and Jewish Quarter sights); a free bus tour and river cruise; and discounts to other attractions, including some concerts and guided tours. For most travelers, it's not worth the steep cost (e.g., €48/2 days); check what's included and do the math before you buy (pick up a brochure at the TI, or use the calculator feature at www.praguecard.com).

ARRIVAL IN PRAGUE
Prague has multiple train stations, but most visitors arrive at the main train station (Hlavní Nádraží), on the eastern edge of downtown—a 20-minute walk, short taxi ride, or bus ride to the Old Town Square and many of my recommended hotels. Prague's Václav Havel Airport—12 miles from downtown—is easily connected to the city center by public bus, airport bus, minibus shuttle, and taxis. For details on all of these options, see page 148.

HELPFUL HINTS
Exchange Rate: 25 Kč = about $1

Country Calling Code: 420 (see page 1086 for dialing instructions)

Rip-Offs: There's no particular risk of violent crime in Prague, but—as in any heavily touristed city—naive tourists can get taken by con artists. Most scams fall into the category of being charged a two-scoop price for one scoop of ice cream, having extra items appear on your restaurant bill, or not getting the correct change. Jaded salesclerks in the tourist zone know that the 25-to-1 exchange rate mystifies American visitors, and may try to take advantage of your carelessness. Any time you pay for something, make a careful mental note of how much it costs, how much you're handing over, and how much you expect back. Count your change. Beware the "slow count," where clerks give back part of your change, then pause...hoping you'll think they're done and walk away. Wait until you get all the money you're due. Plainclothes policemen "looking for counterfeit money" are con artists—ask to see their badges and they'll shrink away.

Pickpockets: They're abundant in Prague. They can be little children or adults dressed as professionals—sometimes even as tourists with jackets draped over their arms to disguise busy fingers. Thieves work crowded and touristy places in teams—for example, they might create a commotion at the door to a Metro or tram car. Keep your wits about you, assume any big distraction is a smokescreen for theft, and wear a money belt. All of this can sound intimidating, but Prague is safe. Simply stay alert.

Medical Help: A 24-hour **pharmacy** is at Palackého 5 (a block from Wenceslas Square, tel. 224-946-982). For above-standard assistance in English (including dental care), consider the top-quality **Hospital Na Homolce** (less than 1,000 Kč for an appointment, daily 8:00-16:00, call 252-922-146, for after-hours emergencies call 257-211-111; bus #167 from Anděl Metro station, Roentgenova 2, Praha 5). The **Canadian Medical Care Center** is a small, private clinic with an English-speaking Czech staff at Veleslavínská 1 in Praha 6 (appointment—3,000 Kč, house call—4,500 Kč, halfway between the city and the airport, tel. 235-360-133, after-hours emergency tel. 724-300-301).

Sightseeing Tips: The Museum of Medieval Art is closed on Mondays, and Jewish Quarter sights are closed on Saturdays. St. Vitus Cathedral at Prague Castle is closed Sunday morning for Mass.

Bookstores: Shakespeare and Sons is a friendly English-language bookstore with a wide selection of translations from Czech, the latest publications, and a reading space downstairs overlooking a river channel (daily 11:00-19:00, one block from Charles Bridge on Little Quarter side at U Lužického Semináře 10, tel. 257-531-894, www.shakes.cz). In the heart of the Jewish Quarter, the **Franz Kafka Society** has a fine little bookstore with a thoughtfully curated shelf of Czech lit in English translation—from Kafka to Švejk to tales of the Little Mole (daily 10:00-18:00, Široká 14, tel. 224-227-452).

Maps: A good map of Prague is essential. For ease of navigation, look for one with trams and Metro lines marked, and tiny sketches of the sights (30-70 Kč; sold at kiosks, exchange windows, and tobacco stands). The *Kartografie Praha* city map, which shows all the tram lines and major landmarks, also includes a castle diagram and a street index. It comes in two versions: 1:15,000 covers the city center (good enough for most visitors), and 1:25,000 includes the whole city (worthwhile if you're sleeping in the suburbs).

Also consider getting a mapping app for your smartphone, which uses GPS to pinpoint your location. To avoid data-roaming charges, look for an offline map that can be

Prague's Best Views

Enjoy the "Golden City of a Hundred Spires" during the early evening, when the light is warm and the colors are rich. Good viewpoints include the following:

- The garden terrace in front of **Strahov Monastery,** above the castle (see page 114);
- The many balconies and spires at **Prague Castle;**
- **Villa Richter** restaurants, overlooking the city from just below the castle past the Golden Lane;
- The top of either tower on **Charles Bridge;**
- The **Old Town Square clock tower** (with a handy elevator);
- **Hotel u Prince**'s rooftop dining terrace overlooking the Old Town Square (also with an elevator);
- The steps of the **National Museum** overlooking Wenceslas Square; and
- The top of the **Žižkov TV tower,** offering spaceship views of the city, in the Žižkov/Vinohrady neighborhood east of the city center (150 Kč for elevator to observatory at 300 feet, free access to Oblaca restaurant at 200-foot-level for customers).

PRAGUE

downloaded in its entirety, such as those offered by **City Maps 2Go** (searchable offline).

Laundry: A **full-service laundry** near most of the recommended hotels is at Karolíny Světlé 11 (200 Kč/8-pound load, wash and dry in 3 hours, Mon-Fri 7:30-19:00, closed Sat-Sun, 200 yards from Charles Bridge on Old Town side, mobile 721-030-446); another laundry is at Rybná 27 (290 Kč/8-pound load, same-day pickup, Mon-Fri 7:00 or 8:00-18:00, closed Sat-Sun, tel. 224-812-641). **Prague Andy's Laundromat** offers both self- and full-service (self-service-160 Kč/load, full service-300 Kč/load—weekdays only, free Internet access, daily 8:00-20:00, near Náměstí Míru Metro stop at Korunní 14, Praha 2, mobile 723-112-693, www.praguelaundromat.cz).

Bike Rental: Prague has improved its network of bike paths, making bicycles a feasible option for exploring the center of the town and beyond (see http://mapa.prahounakole.cz for a map). Two bike-rental shops are located near the Old Town Square: **Praha Bike** (daily 9:00-22:00, Dlouhá 24, mobile 732-388-880, www.prahabike.cz) and **City Bike** (daily 9:00-19:00, Králodvorská 5, mobile 776-180-284, www.citybike-prague.com). They rent bikes for about 300 Kč for two hours or 500 Kč a day (1,500-Kč deposit), and also organize guided bike tours. Another shop offers **electric bikes** (590 Kč/half-day, 890 Kč/day, April-Oct daily 9:00-19:00, tours available, just above American Embassy in Little Quarter at Vlašská 15, mobile 604-474-546, www.ilikeebike.com).

Car Rental: You won't want or need to drive within compact Prague, but a car can be handy for exploring the countryside. All the biggies have offices in Prague (check each company's website, or ask at the TI).

Travel Service and Tours: Magic Praha is a tiny travel service run by Lída Jánská. A Jill-of-all-trades, she can help with accommodations and transfers throughout the Czech Republic, as well as private tours and side-trips to historic towns (mobile 604-207-225, www.magicpraha.cz, magicpraha@magicpraha.cz).

GETTING AROUND PRAGUE

You can walk nearly everywhere. Brown street signs (in Czech, but with helpful little icons) direct you to tourist landmarks. For a sense of scale, the walk from the Old Town Square to the Charles Bridge takes less than 10 minutes (depending on crowds).

Still, it's worth figuring out the public transportation system, which helps you reach farther-flung sights such as Prague Castle. The Metro is slick, the trams fun, and the taxis quick and easy. Prague's tram system is especially wonderful—trams rumble by frequently and take you just about anywhere. Be bold and you'll swing through Prague like Tarzan. For details, pick up a transit guide at the TI. City maps show the Metro, tram, and bus lines.

By Metro, Tram, and Bus

Excellent, affordable public transit is perhaps the best legacy of the communist era (locals ride all month for 300 Kč).

Tickets: The Metro, trams, and buses all use the same tickets:

- 30-minute **short-trip ticket** *(krátkodobá)*, which allows as many transfers as you can make in a half hour—24 Kč
- 90-minute **standard ticket** *(základní)*—32 Kč
- **24-hour pass** *(jízdenka na 24 hodin)*—110 Kč
- **3-day pass** *(jízdenka na 3 dny)*—310 Kč

Buy tickets from your hotel, at Metro stops, newsstand kiosks, or from machines. To avoid wasting time looking for a ticket-seller when your tram is approaching, stock up on tickets before you set out. Since Prague is a great walking town, most find that individual tickets work better than a pass.

Be sure to validate your ticket as you board the tram or bus, or as you enter the Metro station, by sticking it in the machine, which stamps a time on it—watch locals and imitate. Inspectors routinely ambush ticketless riders (including tourists) and fine them 700 Kč on the spot.

Schedules and Frequency: Trams run every 5-10 minutes in the daytime (a schedule is posted at each stop). The Metro closes at midnight, but nighttime tram routes (identified with white numbers on blue backgrounds at tram stops) run all night at 30-minute intervals. You can find more information and a complete route planner in English at www.dpp.cz.

Trams: Navigate by signs that list the end stations. At the platform, a sign lists all the stops for each tram in order. Remember that trams going one direction leave from one platform, while the other direction might leave from a different platform nearby— maybe across the street or a half-block away. When the tram arrives, open the doors by pressing the green button. Once aboard, validate your ticket in the machine.

As you go, follow along carefully so you'll be ready when your stop comes up. Newer trams have electronic signs that show either the next stop *(příští),* or a list of upcoming stops. Also, listen to the recorded announcements for the name of the stop you're currently at, followed by the name of the stop that's coming up next. (Confused tourists, thinking they've heard their stop, are notorious for rushing off the tram one stop too soon.) The surest way to know whether it's your stop is to check the platform for a sign that shows the name of the stop.

Tram #22 is practically made for sightseeing, connecting the New Town with the Castle Quarter (find the line marked on the Prague Metro map). The tram uses some of the same stops as the Metro (making it easy to get to—or travel on from—the tram route). Of the many

PRAGUE

Prague Public Transportation

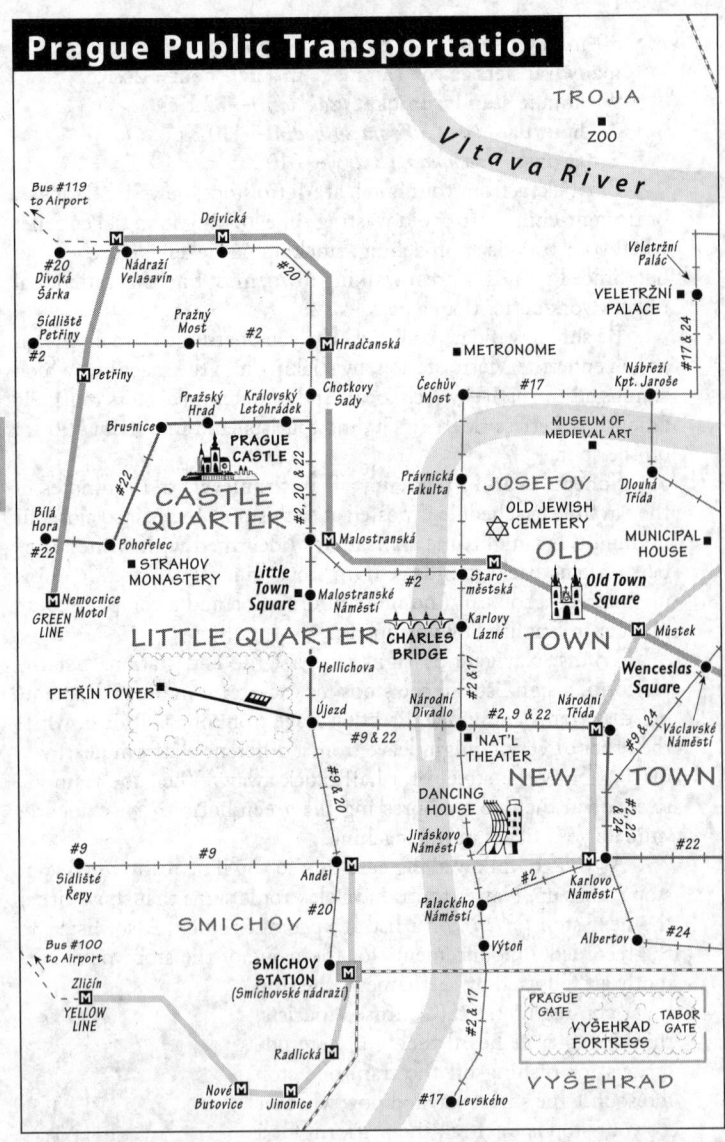

stops this tram makes, the most convenient are two in the New Town (Národní Třída, between the bottom of Wenceslas Square and the river; and Národní Divadlo, at the National Theater), two in the Little Quarter (Malostranské Náměstí, on the Little Quarter Square; and Malostranská Metro stop, near the riverbank), and three above Prague Castle (Královský Letohrádek, Pražský Hrad, and Pohořelec; for details, see page 99).

Metro: The three-line Metro system is handy and simple, but doesn't always get you right to the tourist sights (landmarks such as the Old Town Square and Prague Castle are several blocks from the nearest Metro stops). Although it seems that all Metro doors lead to the neighborhood of Výstup, that's simply the Czech word for "exit."

By Taxi

I find Prague to be a great taxi town and use them routinely. That said, the city has more than its share of dishonest cabbies, so here are a few tips to avoid being overcharged.

Legitimate local rates are cheap: Drop charge starts at 40 Kč; per-kilometer charge is around 30 Kč; and waiting time per minute is about 6 Kč. These rates are clearly marked on the door, so be sure the cabbie honors them. Also insist that cabbies turn on the meter, and that it's set at the right tariff, or "sazba" (usually but not always tariff #1). Unlike in many cities, there's no extra charge for calling a cab—the meter starts only after you get in. Tip by rounding up; locals never tip more than 5 percent.

Have a ballpark idea of what your ride will cost. Figure about 150-200 Kč for a ride between landmarks within the city center (for example, from the main train station to the Old Town Square, or from the Charles Bridge to the castle). Even the longest ride in the center should cost under 300 Kč.

To improve your odds of getting a fair metered rate, call for a cab (or ask someone at your hotel or restaurant to call for you), rather than hailing one on the street. **AAA Taxi** (tel. 222-333-222) and **City Taxi** (tel. 257-257-257) are the most likely to have English-speaking staff and honest cabbies. Avoid cabs waiting at tourist attractions and train stations, who are far more likely to be crooked—waiting to prey on unwary tourists.

And what if the cabbie surprises you at the end with an astronomical fare? If you think you're being overcharged, challenge it. Point to the rates on the door. Get your hotel receptionist to back you up. Pull out your phone and threaten to call the police. (Because of new legislation to curb dishonest cabbies, the police will stand up for you.) Or simply pay what you think the ride should cost and walk away.

Tours in Prague

WALKING TOURS

A staggering number of small companies offer walking tours of the Old Town, the castle, and more (for the latest, pick up fliers at the TI). Since guiding is a routine side-job for university students, you'll generally get hardworking young guides at good prices. While I'd rather go with my own local guide (described later), public walking tours are cheaper (4 hours for about 450 Kč), cover themes you might not otherwise consider, connect you with other English-speaking travelers, and allow for spontaneity. The quality depends on the guide rather than the company. Your best bet is

Prague Pronunciations

English	Czech
Main train station	Hlavní Nádraží (*HLAV-nee NAH-drah-zhee*)
Old Town	Staré Město (*STAR-eh MYEHS-toh*)
Old Town Square	Staroměstské Náměstí (*STAR-oh-myehst-skeh NAH-myehs-tee*)
New Town	Nové Město (*NOH-vay MYEHS-toh*)
Little Quarter	Malá Strana (*MAH-lah STRAH-nah*)
Jewish Quarter	Josefov (*YOO-zehf-fohf*)
Castle Quarter	Hradčany (*HRAD-chah-nee*)
Charles Bridge	Karlův Most (*KAR-loov most*)
Wenceslas Square	Václavské Náměstí (*vaht-SLAHF-skeh NAH-myehs-tee*)
Vltava River	Vltava (*VUL-tah-vah*)

to show up at the Astronomical Clock a couple of minutes before 8:00, 10:00, or 11:00, then chat with a few of the umbrella-holding guides there. Choose the one you click with. Guides also have fliers advertising additional walks.

"Free" Tours: As is the case all over Europe, "free" walking tours are not really free; you're expected to tip your guide (with paper bills rather than coins) when finished. While these tours are fine for the backpacker and hostel crowd (for whom they're designed), the guides are usually expat students (generally from the US or Australia) who memorize a script and give an entertaining performance as you walk through the Old Town, with little respect for serious history. When it comes to guided tours, nothing is free (except for my ∩ Prague City Walk audio tour; see page 14).

LOCAL GUIDES

In Prague, hiring a guide is particularly smart (and a ▲▲ experience). Guides meet you wherever you like and tailor the tour to your interests. Visit their websites in advance for details on various walks, airport transfers, countryside excursions, and other services offered, and then make arrangements by email. Because prices are usually per hour (not per person), small groups can hire an inexpensive guide for several days.

Small Companies

Personal Prague Guide Service's Šárka Kačabová uses her teaching background to help you understand Czech culture, and has a team of personable and knowledgeable guides (600 Kč/hour for 2-3 people, 800 Kč/hour for 4-8 people, fifth hour free, mobile 777-225-205, www.personalpragueguide.com, sarka@me.com).

Prague at a Glance

Rather than a checklist of museums, Prague is a fine place to wander around and just take in the fun atmosphere.

In the Old Town

▲▲▲The Old Town Square Magical main square of Old World Prague, with dozens of colorful facades, the dramatic Jan Hus Memorial, looming Týn Church, and fanciful Astronomical Clock. **Hours:** Týn Church generally open to sightseers Tue-Sat 10:00-13:00 & 15:00-17:00, Sun 10:30-12:00, closed Mon; clock strikes on the hour daily 9:00-21:00, until 20:00 in winter; clock tower open Tue-Sun 9:00-21:00, Mon 11:00-21:00. See page 61.

▲▲▲Charles Bridge Atmospheric, statue-lined bridge that connects the Old Town to the Little Quarter and Prague Castle. **Hours:** Always open and crossable. See page 72.

▲▲▲Jewish Quarter Finest collection of Jewish sights in Europe, featuring various synagogues and an evocative cemetery. **Hours:** The quarter can be visited any time; museum sights open April-Oct Sun-Fri 9:00-18:00, Nov-March until 16:30, closed Sat and on Jewish holidays; Old-New Synagogue open Sun-Thu 9:30-18:00, off-season until 17:00, Fri closes one hour before sunset, closed Sat and Jewish holidays. See page 74.

▲▲Museum of Medieval Art Best Gothic art in the country, at the former Convent of St. Agnes. **Hours:** Tue-Sun 10:00-18:00, closed Mon, may close sporadically due to budget cuts. See page 81.

▲Havelská Market Colorful open-air market that sells crafts and produce. **Hours:** Daily 9:00-18:00. See page 69.

In the New Town

▲▲Wenceslas Square Lively boulevard at the heart of modern Prague. **Hours:** Always open. See page 81.

▲▲Mucha Museum Easy-to-appreciate collection of Art

Nouveau works by Czech artist Alfons Mucha. **Hours:** Daily 10:00-18:00. See page 88.

▲▲**Municipal House** Pure Art Nouveau architecture, including Prague's largest concert hall and several eateries. **Hours:** Daily 10:00-18:00. See page 89.

▲**Museum of Communism** The rise and fall of the regime, from start to Velvet finish. **Hours:** Daily 9:00-21:00. See page 89.

▲**National Memorial to the Heroes of the Heydrich Terror** Tribute to members of the resistance, who assassinated a notorious Nazi architect of the Holocaust. **Hours:** Tue-Sun 9:00-17:00, closed Mon. See page 92.

PRAGUE

In the Little Quarter
▲**Petřín Hill** Little Quarter hill with public art, a funicular, and a replica of the Eiffel Tower. **Hours:** Funicular—daily 8:00-22:00; tower—daily 10:00-22:00, shorter hours off-season. See page 98.

In the Castle Quarter
▲▲▲**St. Vitus Cathedral** The Czech Republic's most important church, featuring a climbable tower and a striking stained-glass window by Art Nouveau artist Alfons Mucha. **Hours:** Daily 9:00-17:00, Nov-March until 16:00, closed Sunday mornings year-round for Mass. See page 106.

▲▲**Prague Castle** Traditional seat of Czech rulers, with St. Vitus Cathedral (see above), Old Royal Palace, Basilica of St. George, shop-lined Golden Lane, and lots of crowds. **Hours:** Castle sights—daily 9:00-17:00, Nov-March until 16:00; castle grounds—daily 5:00-24:00. See page 102.

▲▲**Lobkowicz Palace** Delightful private art collection of a Czech noble family. **Hours:** Daily 10:00-18:00. See page 113.

▲**Strahov Monastery and Library** Baroque center of learning, with ornate reading rooms and old-fashioned science exhibits. **Hours:** Daily 9:00-11:45 & 13:00-17:00. See page 114.

PragueWalker is run by Katka Svobodová, a hardworking historian-guide who knows her stuff and manages a team of enthusiastic and friendly guides (600 Kč/hour for individuals, families, and small groups; mobile 603-181-300, www.praguewalker.com, katerina@praguewalker.com).

Individual Guides

These generally young guides (which is good, because they learned their trade post-communism) typically charge about 2,000-2,500 Kč for a half-day tour.

Jana Hronková has a natural style—a welcome change from the more strict professionalism of some of the busier guides—and a penchant for the Jewish Quarter (mobile 732-185-180, www.experience-prague.info, janahronkova@hotmail.com). **Zuzana Tlášková** speaks English as well as Hebrew (mobile 774-131-335, tlaskovaz@seznam.cz). **Martin Bělohradský,** formerly an organic chemistry professor, is particularly enthusiastic about fine arts and architecture (mobile 723-414-565, martinb5666@gmail.com). **Jana Krátká** enjoys sharing Prague's tumultuous 20th-century history with visitors (mobile 776-571-538, janapragueguide@gmail.com). Friendly **Petra Vondroušová** designs tours to fit your interests (mobile 602-319-420, www.compactprague.com, petra.vondrous@seznam.cz).

To combine a highlights tour with exploration outside the main circuit, contact this book's co-author, **Honza Vihan** (mobile 603-418-148, honzavihan@hotmail.com). **Kamil and Pavlína** run a family business specializing in tours of Prague and beyond. They also provide sightseeing and transport as far as Vienna and Berlin (mobile 605-701-861, www.prague-extra.com, info@prague-extra.com). **Running Tours Prague** are guided by Radim Prahl, a local with an appetite for ultra-marathons; he'll run you past monuments, through parks, and down back alleys at your own pace (1,500 Kč for two people; mobile 777-288-862, www.runningtoursprague.com).

JEWISH QUARTER TOURS

Jewish guides meet small groups twice daily in season for three-hour tours (of varying quality) in English of the Jewish Quarter. **Wittmann Tours** charges an 880-Kč fee that includes entry to the Old-New Synagogue and the six other major Jewish Quarter sights (which cost 480 Kč total), so the tour actually costs only 400 Kč (May-Oct Sun-Fri at 10:30 and 14:00, Nov-Dec and mid-March-April Sun-Fri at 10:30 only, no tours Sat and Jan-mid-March, minimum 3 people). Tours meet in the little park (just beyond the café), directly in front of Hotel InterContinental at the end of Pařížská street. They also offer guided side-trip minibus tours to Terezín

Memorial (tel. 603-168-427 or 603-426-564, www.wittmann-tours.com). In addition, several of the **private local guides** recommended earlier do good tours of the Jewish Quarter.

TOURS OUTSIDE OF PRAGUE

To get beyond the sights listed in most guidebooks, or for a deeply personal look at the usual destinations, call **Tom and Marie Zahn.** Tom is American, Marie is Czech, and together they organize and lead family-friendly day excursions (in Prague and throughout the country). Their tours are creative and affordable, and they teach travelers how to find off-the-beaten-track destinations on their own. Their specialty is Personal Ancestral Tours & History (P.A.T.H.)—with sufficient notice, they can help Czech descendants find their ancestral homes, perhaps even a long-lost relative. Tom and Marie can also help with other parts of your Eastern European travel by linking you with associates in other countries, especially Germany, Hungary, Poland, Romania, Slovakia, and Ukraine (US tel. 360-450-5959, Czech tel. 257-940-113, www.pathways.cz for tours, www.pathfinders.cz for genealogy research, info@pathfinders.cz).

Reverend Jan Dus, an enthusiastic pastor who lived in the US for several years, now serves a small congregation about 100 miles east of Prague. Jan can design itineraries, and likes to help travelers connect with locals in little towns, particularly in northeastern Bohemia and Moravia. He also has an outstanding track record in providing genealogical services (toll-free US tel. 800-807-1562, www.revjan.com, rev.jan.services@gmail.com).

TOUR PACKAGES FOR STUDENTS

Andy Steves (Rick's son) runs **Weekend Student Adventures** (WSA Europe), offering 3-day and 10-day budget travel packages across Europe including accommodations, skip-the-line sightseeing, and unique local experiences. Locally guided and DIY unguided options are available for student and budget travelers in 12 of Europe's most popular cities, including Prague (guided trips from €199, see www.wsaeurope.com for details).

Prague Old Town Walk

Nestled in the bend of the river is Prague's compact, pedestrian-friendly Old Town. A boomtown since the 10th century, the Old Town has long been the busy commercial quarter, filled with merchants, guilds, and supporters of the Church reformer Jan Hus (who wanted a Czech-style Catholicism). Today it's Prague's tourism ground zero, jammed with tasteful landmarks and tacky amusements alike.

Old Town Walk

(map of the Old Town with numbered walk stops, showing the Vltava River, Charles Bridge, Old Town Square, Castle Quarter, Jewish Quarter, Little Quarter, Kampa Island, and labeled streets and landmarks including Rudolfinum, Museum of Decorative Arts, St. Nicholas, Old Town Hall, Klementinum, St. Francis of Assisi, Bridge Tower, Smetana Museum, Bethlehem Chapel, St. Bartholomew, St. Martin, National Theater, Nová Scéna, Tesco Dep't Store)

This walk, which takes two to three hours, starts in the heart of the neighborhood—the **Old Town Square** (rated ▲▲▲)—then dips into the New Town before winding back into the Old Town and ending at the Charles Bridge.

🎧 My Prague City Walk audio tour covers sights in both the Old Town and New Town.

• *Begin with the square's centerpiece, the...*

❶ Memorial to Jan Hus

This monument is an enduring icon of the long struggle for Czech freedom. In the center, Jan Hus—the religious reformer who has

become a symbol of Czech nationalism—stands tall. Hus, born in 1369, was a Prague priest who stood up to both the Catholic Church and the Austrian Habsburg oppressors. His defiant stance—as depicted so powerfully in this monument—galvanized the

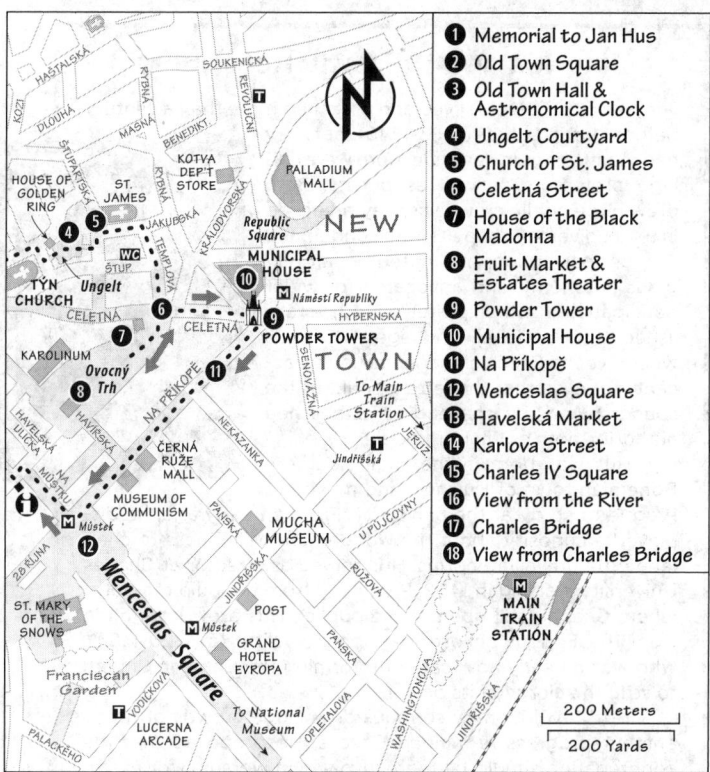

1. Memorial to Jan Hus
2. Old Town Square
3. Old Town Hall & Astronomical Clock
4. Ungelt Courtyard
5. Church of St. James
6. Celetná Street
7. House of the Black Madonna
8. Fruit Market & Estates Theater
9. Powder Tower
10. Municipal House
11. Na Příkopě
12. Wenceslas Square
13. Havelská Market
14. Karlova Street
15. Charles IV Square
16. View from the River
17. Charles Bridge
18. View from Charles Bridge

Czech people, who rallied to fight not just for their religious beliefs but for independence from foreign control.

But Hus was about a century ahead of his time. He was arrested, charged with heresy, excommunicated, and, in 1415, burned at the stake. His followers picked up the torch and fought on for two decades in the Hussite Wars, which killed tens of thousands and left Bohemia a virtual wasteland.

Surrounding Hus's statue are the Hussite followers who battled the Habsburgs. One patriot holds a cup, or chalice. This symbolizes one of the changes the Hussites were fighting for: the right of everyone (not just priests) to drink the wine at Communion. Look into the survivors' faces—it was a bitter fight. In 1620, their rebellious cause was brutally crushed by the Catholic Habsburgs at the pivotal Battle of White Mountain fought outside Prague—effectively ending Czech independence for three centuries.

Each subsequent age has interpreted Hus to its liking: For Protestants, Hus was the founder of the first Protestant church (though he was actually an ardent Catholic); for revolutionaries, this critic of the Church's power was a proponent of social equality; for nationalists, this Czech preacher was the defender of the lan-

Jan Hus and the Early Reformers

Jan Hus (c. 1369-1415) lived and preached more than a century before Martin Luther (1483-1546), but they had many things in common. Both were college professors as well as priests. Both drew huge public crowds as they preached in their university chapels. Both condemned Church corruption, promoted local religious autonomy, and advocated for wider paticipation in worship rituals. Both established their national languages. (It's Hus who gave the Czech alphabet its unique accent marks so that the letters could fit the sounds.) And, by challenging established authority, both got in big trouble.

Hus was born in the small southern Bohemian town of Husinec, and moved to Prague to study at the university. From an early age, he displayed a curiosity about the world and a willingness to challenge the prevailing norms. Hus served as a rector at Charles University starting in 1402. Preaching from the pulpit in Bethlehem Chapel (still open to the public), Hus drew inspiration from the English philosopher John Wycliffe (c. 1320-1384), who was an early advocate of reforming the Catholic Church to strip the clergy of its power.

Hus' revolutionary sermons drew huge crowds of reverent but progressive-minded Czechs. He proposed that the congregation should be more involved in worship (for example, be allowed to drink the wine at Communion) and have better access to the word of God through services and scriptures written in the people's language, not in Latin. Even after he was excommunicated in 1410, Hus continued preaching.

In 1414, the Roman Catholic Church convened the Council of Constance to grapple with the controversies of the day. First they posthumously excommunicated Wycliffe, proclaiming him a heretic and exhuming his corpse to symbolically burn at the stake. Then they called Hus to Constance, where on July 6, 1415, they declared him a heretic. After refusing to recant his beliefs and praying that God would forgive his enemies, Hus was tied to a stake and burned alive. But by this time, Hus' challenging ideas had been embraced by many Czechs, and sparked the bloodiest civil war in the country's history.

This early Catholic precursor to the Counter-Reformation kept things under control for generations. But in the 16th century, a German monk named Martin Luther found a more progressive climate for these same revolutionary ideas. Thanks to the new printing press, invented by Gutenberg, Luther was able to spread his message cheaply and effectively. While Hus loosened Rome's grip on Christianity, Luther orchestrated the Reformation that finally broke it. Today, both are honored as national heroes as well as religious reformers.

guage; and for communists, Hus was the first ideologue to preach the gospel of socialism. But regardless of who was in power, Hus' importance to the Czech people has never wavered.

• *Stepping away from the Hus Memorial, stand in the center of the Old Town Square, and take a 360-degree...*

❷ Old Town Square Orientation Spin-Tour

Whirl clockwise to get a look at Prague's diverse architectural styles: Gothic, Renaissance, Baroque, Rococo, and Art Nouveau. Remember, Prague was largely spared the devastating aerial bombardments of World War II that leveled so many European cities (like Berlin, Warsaw, and Budapest). Few places can match the Old Town Square for Old World charm.

Start with the green domes of the Baroque **Church of St. Nicholas.** Originally Catholic, now Hussite, this church is a popular venue for concerts. The Jewish Quarter is a few blocks behind the church, down the uniquely tree-lined "Paris Street" (Pařížská)—which also has the best lineup of Art Nouveau houses in Prague, and arguably in all of Europe.

Spin to the right. Behind the Hus Memorial is a fine yellow building that introduces us to Prague's wonderful world of Art Nouveau: pastel colors, fanciful stonework, wrought-iron balconies, colorful murals—and what are those statues on top doing? Prague's architecture is a wonderland of ornamental details.

Continue spinning a few doors to the right to the large, red-and-tan Rococo **Kinský Palace,** which displays the National Gallery's Asian arts collection (and has a handy WC in the courtyard).

Farther to the right is the towering, Gothic **Týn Church** (pronounced "teen"), with its fanciful twin spires. It's been the Old Town's leading church in every era. In medieval times, it was Catholic. When the Hussites took power (c. 1420-1620), they made it the headquarters of their faith. After the Hussite defeat, the Habsburgs returned it to Catholicism. The symbolism tells the story: Between the church's two towers, find a golden medallion of the Virgin Mary. Beneath that is a niche—now empty. But in Hussite times, a golden chalice stood there, symbolizing their cause. When the Catholics triumphed, they melted down the chalice and made it into this golden image of Mary.

If you want to go inside, make your way through the cluster of buildings in front of it, entering at #14 (under the arcade that faces the square; 30-Kč requested donation, generally open to sightseers Tue-Sat 10:00-13:00 & 15:00-17:00, Sun 10:30-12:00, closed Mon). The structure is full of light, with soaring Gothic arches. The ornamentation reflects the church's troubled history: medieval Catholic; Hussite iconoclasm (stripped of decoration); and post-Hussite Habsburg (Baroque exuberance).

The row of pastel houses in front of Týn Church has a mixture of Gothic, Renaissance, and Baroque facades. If you like live music, check out the convenient **Via Musica box office** near the church's front door to find out all your options (see page 124); we'll pass it later on this walk.

Spinning right, to the south side of the square, take in more **glorious facades,** each a different color with a different gable on top—step gables, triangular, bell-shaped. The tan house at #16 has a steepled bay window and a mural of St. Wenceslas on horseback, and Albert Einstein once lectured at the light-orange house at #18.

Finally, you reach the pointed 250-foot-tall spire marking the 14th-century **Old Town Hall.** The tower is Neo-Gothic. In the 19th century, a building was constructed on the square's west side that once stretched from the Old Town to the Church of St. Nicholas. Then, in the last days of World War II, German tanks knocked it down...to the joy of many Prague citizens who considered it an ugly 19th-century stain on the medieval square.

Approach the Old Town Hall. At the base of the tower, near

the corner of the tree-filled park, find **27 white crosses** inlaid in the pavement. These mark the spot where 27 Protestant nobles, merchants, and intellectuals were beheaded in 1621 after the Battle of White Mountain—still one of the grimmest chapters in the country's history.

• *Around the left side of the tower are two big, fancy, old clock faces, being admired by many, many tourists.*

❸ Old Town Hall and Astronomical Clock

The Old Town Hall, with its distinctive trapezoidal tower, was built in the 1350s, during Prague's Golden Age. Check out the ornately carved Gothic entrance door to the left of the clock; a bit farther to the left is another door, leading to the TI, a pay WC, and the ticket desk for the clock tower elevator and Old Town Hall tours (see "Sights Inside the Old Town Hall," later in this walk).

For now, turn your attention to that famous **Astronomical Clock.** See if you can figure out how it works. Of the two giant

dials on the tower, the top one tells the time on two rings: The outer one, with Roman numerals, is similar to present-day clocks, while the inner one, numbered 1 through 24 in a strange but readable Bohemian script, rotates to reset each day at sunset. Within the dial is yet another revolving disc, where today's zodiac sign is marked.

If all this seems complex to us, it must have been a marvel in the early 1400s, when the clock was installed. Remember that back then, everything revolved around the Earth (the fixed middle background—with Prague marking the center, of course). The clock was heavily damaged during World War II, and much of what you see today is a reconstruction.

The second dial, below the clock, was added in the 19th century. It shows the signs of the zodiac, scenes from the seasons of a rural peasant's life, and a ring of saints' names. There's one for each day of the year, and a marker on top indicates today's special saint. In the center is a castle, symbolizing Prague.

Four statues flank the upper clock. These politically incorrect symbols evoke a 15th-century outlook: The figure staring into a mirror stands for vanity, a Jewish moneylender holding a bag of coins is greed, and (on the right side) a Turk with a mandolin symbolizes hedonism. All these worldly goals are vain in the face of Death, whose hourglass reminds us that our time is unavoidably running out.

The clock strikes the top of the hour and puts on a little glockenspiel show daily from 9:00 to 21:00 (until 20:00 in winter). As the hour approaches, keep your eye on Death. First, Death tips his hourglass and pulls the cord, ringing the bell, while the moneylender jingles his purse. Then the windows open and the 12 apostles shuffle past, acknowledging the gang of onlookers. Finally the rooster at the very top crows and the hour is rung. The hour is often wrong because of Daylight Saving Time (completely senseless to 15th-century clockmakers). I find an alternative view just as interesting: As the cock crows, face the crowd and snap a photo of the mass of gaping tourists.

Sights Inside the Old Town Hall: Go through the door to the left of the Astronomical Clock, where the ticket desk shares a space with the TI. From here, continuing deeper into the building, you'll find pay WCs and a bank of elevators.

Ride the elevator to floor 3 to buy your ticket to ascend the **town hall's tower** (via another elevator—if it's busy, you may have to wait a few minutes), with ▲▲ views over Prague's prettiest square (110 Kč, Tue-Sun 9:00-21:00, Mon 11:00-21:00; after 19:00 the entry is through the door immediately to the left of the clock rather than through the TI).

On floor 1, you can take a 45-minute **tour of the Old Town Hall,** which includes a Gothic chapel and a close-up look at the inner guts of the Astronomical Clock, plus its statues of the 12 apostles (100 Kč, or 160-Kč combo-ticket with tower, about 3 tours/day in English—see the schedule at the ticket desk).

• *Let's leave the Old Town Square. Our next stop is directly behind the Týn Church: Cross through the square and head down the street along the left side of the church (Týnská) for about 100 yards, passing the convenient **Via Musica box office.** A bit farther along, on the left, you'll pass the **House of the Golden Ring,** worth considering if you're curious about 20th-century Czech art.*

Continue straight through a sturdy gate, into a courtyard called...

❹ Ungelt

This pleasant, cobbled, quiet courtyard of upscale restaurants and shops is one of the Old Town's oldest places. During the Bohemian Golden Age (c. 1200-1400), it was a multicultural hub of international trade. Prague—located at the geographical center of Europe—attracted Germans selling furs, Italians selling fine art, Frenchmen selling cloth, and Arabs selling spices. They converged on this courtyard, where they could store their goods and pay their customs (which is what *Ungelt* means, in German). In return, the king granted them protection, housing, and a stable for their horses. By day, they'd sell their wares on the Old Town Square. At night, they'd return here to drink and exchange news from their native lands. Notice that, to protect the goods, there are only two entrances to the complex. After centuries of disuse, the Ungelt has been marvelously restored—a great place for dinner, and a reminder that Prague has been a cosmopolitan center for most of its history.

• *Exit the Ungelt at the far end. Just to your left, across the street, is the...*

❺ Church of St. James (Kostel Sv. Jakuba)

Perhaps the most beautiful church interior in the Old Town, the Church of St. James has been the home of the Minorite Order

almost as long as merchants have occupied Ungelt. A medieval city was a complex phenomenon: Commerce, prostitution, and a life of contemplation existed side by side. (I guess it's not that much different from today.) Step inside (free, Tue-Sun 9:30-12:00 & 14:00-16:00, closed Mon); or, if it's locked, peek through the glass door. Artistically, St. James is a stunning example of how simple medieval spaces could be rebuilt into sumptuous feasts of Baroque decoration. The original interior was destroyed by fire in 1689; what's here now is an early 18th-century remodel. The blue light in the altar highlights one of Prague's most venerated treasures—the bejeweled Madonna Pietatis. Above the pietà, as if held aloft by hummingbird-like angels, is a painting of the martyrdom of St. James.

• *Exiting the church, do a U-turn to the left (heading up Jakubska street, along the side of the church, past some rough-looking bars). After one block, turn right on Templova street. Head two blocks down the street (passing a nice view of the Týn Church's rear end, and some deluxe toilets) and go through the arcaded passageway, where you emerge onto...*

❻ Celetná Street

Since the 10th century, this street has been a corridor in the busy commercial quarter—filled with merchants and guilds. These days, it's still pretty commercial, and very touristy.

• *To your right is a striking, angular building called the...*

❼ House of the Black Madonna (Dům u Černé Matky Boží)

Back around the turn of the 20th century, Prague was a center of avant-garde art second only to Paris. Art Nouveau blossomed here (as we'll soon see), as did Cubism. The Cubist exterior is a marvel of rectangular windows and cornices—stand back and see how masterfully it makes its statement while mixing with its neighbors...then get up close and study the details. The interior houses a Cubist café (the recommended Grand Café Orient, one flight up the parabolic spiral staircase)—complete with cube-shaped chairs and square-shaped rolls. The Kubista gallery on the ground floor shows more examples of this unique style.

• *The long, skinny square that begins just to the left of the House of the Black Madonna is the...*

❽ Fruit Market (Ovocný Trh) and the Estates Theater

This long, narrow square with a bulge in the middle is typical of medieval Central European market towns. Market stalls would pop up along the busy main drag right in the center of town—making it easy to see how a town can swell as it grows. While no fruit vendors still sell their wares here, this square has retained its traditional name.

The green-and-white building squatting in the middle of the square—right at the bulge—is the **Estates Theater** (Stavovské Divadlo). Built by a nobleman in the 1780s, this Classicist building was the prime opera venue in Prague at a time when an Austrian prodigy was changing the course of music. Wolfgang Amadeus Mozart premiered *Don Giovanni* in this building (with a bronze statue of Il Commendatore duly flanking the main entrance on the left), and he directed many of his works here. Today, the Estates Theater (part of the National Theater group) continues to produce *The Marriage of Figaro, Don Giovanni,* and occasionally *The Magic Flute.*

• *Backtrack a few steps to Celetná street, turn right, and head about 50 yards to the...*

❾ Powder Tower

The big, black, 500-year-old Powder Tower was the main gate of the old town wall. It also housed the city's gunpowder—hence the name. This is the only surviving bit of the wall that was built to defend the city in the 1400s. (Though you can go inside, it's not worth paying to tour the interior.)

Prague: The Queen of Art Nouveau

Prague is Europe's best city for Art Nouveau. That's the style of art and architecture that flourished throughout Europe around 1900. It was called "nouveau"—or new—because it was associated with all things modern: technology, social progress, and enlightened thinking. Art Nouveau was neo-nothing, but instead a fresh answer to all the revival styles of the late-19th century, and an organic response to the Eiffel Tower art of the Industrial Age.

By taking advantage of recent advances in engineering, Art Nouveau liberated the artist in each architect. Notice the curves and motifs expressing originality—every facade is unique. Artists such as Alfons Mucha believed that the style should apply to all facets of daily life. They designed everything from buildings and furniture to typefaces and cigarette packs.

Prague's three top Art Nouveau architects are Jan Koula, Josef Fanta, and Osvald Polivka (whose last name sounds like the Czech word for "soup"). Think "Cola, Fanta, and Soup"—easy to remember and a good way to impress your local friends.

Though Art Nouveau was born in Paris, it's in Prague where you'll find some of its greatest hits: the Municipal House and nearby buildings, Grand Hotel Evropa (on Wenceslas Square), the exuberant facades of the Jewish Quarter, the Jerusalem Synagogue, and—especially—the work of Prague's own Alfons Mucha. You can see his stained-glass window in St. Vitus Cathedral (at Prague Castle—page 106), and the excellent Mucha Museum (near Wenceslas Square—page 88). Mucha's masterpiece, *The Slav Epic,* is out of the country on a world tour through 2019.

• Pass regally through the Powder Tower. In so doing, you're leaving the Old Town. You emerge into a big, busy intersection. To your left is the Municipal House, a cream-colored building topped with a green dome. Find a good spot where you can view the facade.

❿ Municipal House (Obecní Dům)

The Municipal House, which celebrated its centennial in 2011, is the "pearl of Czech Art Nouveau." Art Nouveau flourished during the same period as the Eiffel Tower and Europe's great Industrial Age train stations.

The same engineering prowess and technological advances that went into making those huge erector-set rigid buildings were used by artistic architects to create quite the opposite effect: curvy, organically flowing lines, inspired by vines and curvaceous women. Art Nouveau was a reaction against the sterility of modern-age construction. Look at the elaborate wrought-iron balcony —flanked by bronze Atlases hefting their lanterns—and the lovely stained glass (like in the entrance arcade).

Mosaics and sculptural knickknacks (see the faces above the windows) made the building's facade colorful and joyous. Study the bright mosaic above the balcony, called *Homage to Prague.* A symbol of the city, the goddess Praha presides over a land of peace and high culture—an image that stoked cultural pride and nationalist sentiment. On the balcony is a medallion showing the three-tower castle that is the symbol of Prague.

The Municipal House was built in the early 1900s, when Czech nationalism was at a fever pitch. Having been ruled by the Austrian Habsburgs for the previous 300 years, the Czechs were demanding independence. This building was drenched in patriotic Czech themes. Within a few short years, in 1918, the nation of Czechoslovakia was formed—and the independence proclamation was announced to the people right here, from the balcony of the Municipal House.

The interior of the Municipal House has perhaps Europe's finest Art Nouveau decor. It's free to enter and wander the public areas. While to really appreciate the building you must attend a concert here or take one of the excellent tours offered throughout the day, any visit here gets a sweet dose of Art Nouveau (for tour details and more about the interior, see page 89).

• *Now head west down Na Příkopě (to the left as you face the Powder Tower) toward the Metro station about 200 yards away. Enjoy the sights of...*

⓫ Na Příkopě, the Old City Wall

The street called Na Příkopě was where the old city wall once stood. More specifically, the name Na Příkopě means "On the Moat," and you're walking along what was once the moat outside the wall. To your right is the Old Town. To the left, the New. Look at your city map and conceptualize medieval Prague's smart design: The city was protected on two sides by its river, and on the other two sides by its walls (marked by the modern streets called Na Příkopě, Revoluční, and Národní Třída). The only river crossing back then was the fortified Charles Bridge.

• *Continue up Na Příkopě—passing the Museum of Communism (de-*

scribed on page 89)—to an intersection (and nearby Metro stop) called Můstek. To your left stretches the vast expanse of the wide boulevard called...

⑫ Wenceslas Square

Wenceslas Square—with the National Museum and landmark statue of St. Wenceslas at the very top—is the centerpiece of Prague's New Town. This square was originally founded as a thriving horse market. Today it's a modern world of high-fashion stores, glitzy shopping malls, fine old facades (and some jarringly modern ones), fast-food restaurants, and sausage stands. (For a self-guided walk through Wenceslas Square, see page 81.)

• *Let's plunge back into the Old Town and return to the Old Town Square. Turn about face, and head downhill (north) on the street called Na Můstku—"along the bridge" that crossed the moat (příkopě) we've been following until now.*

Walk down Na Můstku. After one touristy block, it jogs slightly to the left and becomes Melantrichova. A block farther along, on the left, is...

⑬ Havelská Market

This open-air market, offering crafts and produce, was first set up in the 13th century for the German trading community. Though

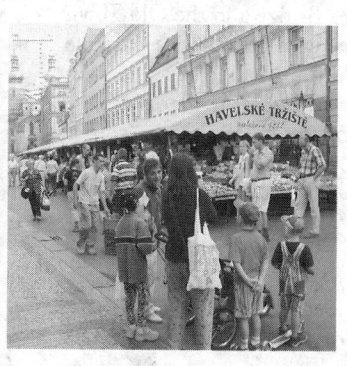

heavy on souvenirs these days (especially on weekends), the market—worth ▲—still feeds hungry locals and vagabonds cheaply. Lined with inviting benches, it's an ideal place to enjoy a healthy snack—and merchants are happy to sell a single vegetable or piece of fruit. The market is also a fun place to browse for crafts. It's a homegrown, homemade kind of place; you'll often be dealing with the actual artist or farmer. The many cafés and little eateries circling the market offer a relaxing vantage point from which to view the action.

• *Continue along Melantrichova street. Eventually—after passing increasingly tacky souvenir shops and a "museum of sex machines"—Melantrichova curves right and spills out at the Old Town Square, right by the Astronomical Clock. At the clock, turn left down Karlova street. The rest of our walk follows Karlova (though the road twists and turns a bit) to the Charles Bridge, where our tour ends. Begin by heading along the top of the Small Market Square (Malé Náměstí, with lots of outdoor tables), then follow Karlova's twisting course—Karlova street signs keep you on track, and* Karlův Most *signs point to the bridge. Or just follow the crowds.*

⑭ Karlova Street

Although traffic-free, Karlova street is utterly jammed with tourists as it winds toward the Charles Bridge. But the route has plenty of historic charm if you're able to ignore the contemporary tourism. As you walk, look up. Notice historic symbols and signs of shops, which advertised who lived there or what they sold. Cornerstones, designed to protect buildings from careening carriages, also date from centuries past. The touristy feeding-frenzy of today's Prague is at its ugliest along this commercial gauntlet. Obviously, you'll find few good values on this drag.

Keep walking toward Charles Bridge. After the street jogs right to cross Husova, many of the buildings you'll see on your right are associated with Prague's **Charles University.** Behind the souvenir stalls lie venerable classrooms and lecture halls. For example, the **Klementinum** (which once housed the university's library) is the large building that borders Karlova street on the right. Just past the intersection with Liliová, where the street opens into a little square, turn right through the archway (at #1) and into a tranquil courtyard that feels an eternity away from the touristy hubbub of Karlova. Locals enjoy using this courtyard as the key link of a less-crowded shortcut between Charles Bridge and the Old Town Square. You can also visit the Klementinum's impressive Baroque interior on a guided tour.

• *Karlova street leads directly to a tall medieval tower that marks the start of Charles Bridge. But before entering the bridge, stop on this side of the river. To the right of the tower is a little park with a great view of both the bridge and the rest of Prague across the river. While it's officially called Křižovnické Náměstí, I think of it as...*

⑮ Charles IV Square

Start with the statue of the bridge's namesake, **Charles IV** (1316-1378). Look familiar? He's the guy on the 100-koruna bill. Charles was the Holy Roman Emperor who ruled his vast empire from Prague in the 14th century—a high-water mark in the city's history. The statue shows one of Charles' many accomplishments: He holds a contract establishing Charles University, the first in central Europe. The women around the pedestal symbolize the school's four traditional subjects: theology, the arts, law, and medicine.

Charles was the preeminent figure in

Sightseeing Strategies

Crowd-Beating Tips Visit Prague Castle either first thing in the morning (be at St. Vitus Cathedral right at 9:00—except Sun morning, when it's closed for Mass) or midafternoon (closes at 17:00 in summer, 16:00 in winter). Hiring your own guide for a historic walk is relatively cheap and allows you to choose a time (evening or early morning) and route to avoid crowds.

Evening Activities Prague Castle's grounds stay open until 24:00 and provide a fanciful people-free zone to wander in the evening. Concerts in the National Theater, Smetana Hall at the Municipal House, and Rudolfinum feature superb artists at bargain prices (see "Entertainment in Prague," later).

Europe in the Late Middle Ages, and the father of the Prague we enjoy today. His domain encompassed the modern Czech Republic, and parts of Germany, Austria, and the Low Countries.

Charles was cosmopolitan. Born in Prague, raised in Paris, crowned in Rome, and inspired by the luxury-loving pope in Avignon, Charles returned home bringing Europe's culture with him. Besides founding Charles University, he built Charles Bridge, Charles Square (where you're standing), much of Prague Castle and St. Vitus Cathedral, and the New Town (modeled on Paris). His Golden Bull of 1356 served as Europe's constitution for centuries (and gave anti-Semite Charles first right to the property of Jews). Power-hungry, he expanded his empire through networking and shrewd marriages, not war. Charles traded ideas with the Italian poet Petrarch and imported artists from France, Italy, and Flanders (inspiring the art of the Museum of Medieval Art—see page 81). Under Charles, Prague became the most cultured city in Europe. Seemingly the only thing Charles did not succeed in was renaming Prague: He wanted it to be called "New Jerusalem."

Now look up at the **bridge tower.** Built by Charles, it's one of the finest Gothic gates anywhere. The statuary shows the 14th-century hierarchy of society: people at street level, above them kings, and bishops above the kings. Speaking of hierarchy, check out Charles' statue from near the street. From this angle, some think the emperor looks like he's peeing on the tourists. Which reminds me, public toilets are nearby.

• *Stroll to the riverside, belly up to the bannister, and take in the...*

⓰ View from the River

Before you are the Vltava River and Charles Bridge. Across the river, atop the hill, is Prague Castle topped by the prickly spires of St. Vitus Cathedral. **Prague Castle** has been the seat of power in this region for over a thousand years, since the time of Wenceslas. By some measures, it's the biggest castle on earth.

The **Vltava River** is better known by its German name, Moldau. It bubbles up from the Šumava Hills in southern Bohemia and runs 270 miles through a diverse landscape, like a thread connecting the Czech people. As we've learned, the Czechs have struggled heroically to carve out their identity while surrounded by mightier neighbors—Austrians, Germans, and Russians. The Vltava is their shared artery. The name "Prague" comes from the word "threshold," because the city was born at a convenient place to cross the wide river and enter a new place.

The **view of Charles Bridge** from here is photogenic to the max. The historic stone bridge, commissioned in 1342, connects the Old Town with the district called the Little Quarter at the base of the castle across the river. The bridge is almost seven football fields long, lined with lanterns and 30 statues, and bookmarked at each end with medieval towers.

You can climb either of the **bridge towers.** The tower on the **Old Town side** of the river (Staroměstská Mostecká Věž) is the one looming above you. Climbing its 138 steps rewards you with some of Prague's best views: a stunning vista of the bridge itself, jammed with people heading for the castle; and 180 degrees away, a perfect panorama that reminds you why Prague is called the "Golden City of a Hundred Spires." Across the bridge on the **Little Quarter side** (Malostranská Mostecká Věž), you can huff up 146 steps for fine views of the bridge, the Little Quarter rooftops, and the castle. If you're trying to decide which to climb, consider that for snapping photos, the light is better if you climb the Old Town tower early in the day, and the Little Quarter tower late in the day (90 Kč to climb each tower, daily 10:00-22:00, March and Oct until 20:00, Nov-Feb until 18:00).

• *Now wander onto the bridge. Make your way slowly across the bridge, checking out several of the statues, all on the right-hand side.*

❼ Charles Bridge

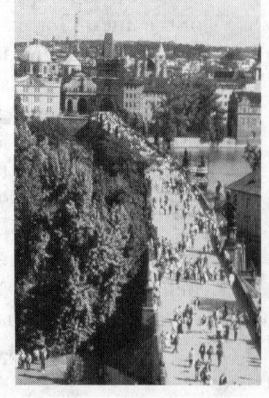

Among Prague's defining landmarks, this much-loved bridge offers one of the most pleasant and entertaining strolls in Europe and is worth ▲▲▲. Musicians, artisans, and a constant parade of people make it a festival every day. You can come back and back to this bridge enjoying its charms differently at various times of day. Early and late, it can be enchantingly lonely. It's a photographer's delight during that "magic hour," when the sun is low in the sky. The impressively expressive statues on either side of the bridge depict saints. Partway along the bridge, on your right, find a small **brass relief** showing a cross with five stars embedded in the wall of the bridge (it's just below the little grate that sits on top of the stone bannister). The relief depicts a figure floating in the river, with a semicircle of stars above him. This marks the traditional spot where St. John of Nepomuk, the national saint of the Czech people, is believed to have been tossed off the bridge and into the river.

For the rest of that story, continue two more statue groups to the bronze Baroque statue of **St. John of Nepomuk,** with the halo of five golden stars encircling his head. This statue always draws a crowd. John was a 14th-century priest to whom the queen confessed all her sins. According to a 17th-century legend, the king

PRAGUE

wanted to know his wife's secrets, but Father John dutifully refused to tell. The shiny plaque at the base of the statue shows what happened next: John was tortured and eventually killed by being thrown off the bridge. The plaque shows the heave-ho. When he hit the water, five stars appeared, signifying his purity. Notice the date on the inscription—1683. This oldest statue on the bridge was unveiled on the supposed 300th anniversary of the martyr's death. Traditionally, people believe that touching the St. John plaque will make a wish come true. But you get only one chance in life to make this wish, so think carefully before you commit.

• *A good way to end this walk is to enjoy the* ⓲ *city and river view from near the center of the bridge. From here, you can continue across the bridge to the Little Quarter (Kampa Island, on your left as you cross the bridge, is a tranquil spot to explore; for more on sights in this area, see page 94). Across the bridge and a 10-minute walk to the right is the Malostranská stop for the Metro or for the handy tram #22. You can also hike (or ride tram #22) up to the castle from here. Or retrace your steps across the bridge to enjoy more time in the Old Town.*

Sights in the Old Town (Staré Město)

I've arranged Prague's sights by neighborhood for handy sightseeing. Remember that Prague started out as four towns—the Old Town and New Town on the east side of the river, and the Castle Quarter and Little Quarter on the west—and it's still helpful for sightseers to think of the city that way.

My Prague Old Town Walk, earlier, covers the main sights in this area, including the **Old Town Square** and its many monuments—the **Týn Church** (see page 62) and the **Old Town Hall/Astronomical Clock** (page 63)—along with the **Church of St. James** (page 65) and the **Charles Bridge** (page 72). It also points out key landmarks, including the **Ungelt** courtyard (page 64), **House of the Black Madonna** (page 65), and **Powder Tower** (page 66).

Here are some additional sights in the Old Town. ∩ My Prague City Walk audio tour covers sights in both the Old Town and New Town.

▲▲▲JEWISH QUARTER (JOSEFOV)

Prague's Jewish Quarter is Europe's most accessible sight for learning about an important culture and faith that's interwoven with the fabric of Central and Eastern Europe. Within a three-block radius, several original synagogues, cemeteries, and other landmarks survive, today collected into one big, well-presented museum—the Jewish Museum in Prague. It can get crowded here, so time your visit carefully (early or late is best). For background on typical synagogue architecture, see the sidebar on page 297.

Jewish Museum in Prague (Židovské Muzeum v Praze)

The "museum" consists of four synagogues, a ceremonial hall, and a cemetery—each described later and covered by the same ticket. To avoid lines, buy your ticket at a less-crowded sight (such as the Klausen or Spanish synagogues) instead of a more crowded one (such as the Pinkas Synagogue). You can also buy tickets at the Information Center at Maiselova 15 (near the intersection with Siroka street).

Cost and Hours: 300 Kč, covered by 480-Kč "Jewish Town of Prague" combo-ticket with Old-New Synagogue; April-Oct Sun-Fri 9:00-18:00, Nov-March until 16:30, closed year-round on Sat—the Jewish Sabbath—and on Jewish holidays; their website lists closures; 300-Kč audioguide is overkill; tel. 222-317-191, www.jewishmuseum.cz.

Getting There: The Jewish Quarter is an easy walk from Old Town Square, up delightful Pařížská street (next to the green-domed Church of St. Nicholas). The Staroměstská Metro stop is just a couple of blocks away.

Avoiding Lines: The Pinkas Synagogue can be packed, especially 9:30-12:00, so be there right as it opens or later in the day. To save time in line, buy your ticket in advance at the other less-crowded locations.

Dress Code: Men are expected to cover their heads when entering a synagogue or cemetery. While you'll see many visitors

Prague's Jewish Quarter

Sights
1. Maisel Synagogue
2. Pinkas Synagogue
3. Old Jewish Cemetery
4. Ceremonial Hall
5. Klausen Synagogue
6. Old-New Synagogue
7. Spanish Synagogue

Other
8. Info/Ticket Office
9. Robert Guttmann Gallery
10. Kafka Statue
11. Franz Kafka Society Bookstore
12. Wittmann Tours

Eateries
13. Kolkovna
14. Kolonial
15. Rest. u Knihovny
16. Dinitz Kosher
17. King Solomon

ignoring this custom, it's respectful to borrow a museum-issued yarmulke.

Visiting the Museum: Your ticket comes with a map that locates the sights and lists admission appointments—the times you'll be let in if it's very busy. (Ignore the times unless it's extremely crowded.) You'll notice plenty of security, which can slow down entry.

You can see the sights in any order. I recommend the order listed below, but you can rearrange it to avoid crowds.

Maisel Synagogue (Maiselova Synagóga): This newly renovated pastel-colored Neo-Gothic synagogue was built as a private place of worship for a wealthy family. It now houses an interactive exhibit on Jewish history in the Czech lands and a few precious objects. During Nazi occupation, this building became a warehouse for a vast collection of Judaica, which Hitler planned to turn into a "Museum of the Extinct Jewish Race"...perhaps explaining why these items, and the Jewish Quarter itself, managed to survive through those dark days.

Inside, the interactive exhibit retraces a thousand years of Jewish history in Bohemia and Moravia. Well-explained in English, topics include the origin of the Star of David, Jewish mysticism, the Golem legend, the history of discrimination, and the creation of Prague's ghetto. Pre-WWII photographs of small-town synagogues from the region are projected on a large screen. Notice the eastern wall, with the holy ark containing a precious Torah mantel. Look for the banner of the Prague Jewish Butchers' Guild, the emblem of the Cobblers' Guild, a medieval seal ring, and the bema grillwork from Prague's demolished Zigeuner Synagogue.

Pinkas Synagogue (Pinkasova Synagóga): For many visitors, this house of worship—today used as a memorial to the Holocaust victims—is the most powerful of the Jewish Quarter sights.

Enter and go down the steps leading to the **main hall** of this small Gothic synagogue. Notice the old stone-and-wrought-iron bema in the middle, the niche for the ark at the far end, the crisscross vaulting overhead, and the Art Nouveau stained glass filling the place with light.

But the main focus of this synagogue is its walls, inscribed with the handwritten **names** of 77,297 Czech Jews sent to the gas chambers at Auschwitz and other camps. Czech Jews were especially hard hit by the Holocaust. More than 155,000 of them passed through the nearby Terezín camp alone. Most died with no grave marker, but they are remembered here. The names are carefully organized: Family names are in red, followed in black by the individual's first name, birthday, and date of death (if known) or date of deportation. You can tell by the dates that families often perished together. The names are gathered in groups by hometowns (listed in gold, as well as on placards at the base of the wall). As you ponder this sad sight, you'll hear the somber reading of the names alternating with a cantor singing the Psalms.

On your way out, watch on the right for the easy-to-miss stairs up to the small **Terezín Children's Art Exhibit.** Well-described in English, these drawings were made by Jewish children imprisoned at Terezín, 40 miles northwest of Prague. This is where the Nazis shipped Prague's Jews for processing before transporting them east to death camps. Thirty-five thousand Jews died at Terezín, and many tens of thousands more died in other camps. (Terezín makes an emotionally moving day trip from Prague; see page 169.)

Old Jewish Cemetery (Starý Židovský Hřbitov): Hiding behind a wall and sitting above the street level, this is where Prague's Jews buried their dead. A stroll through the crooked tombstones is a poignant experience.

Enter one of the most wistful scenes in Europe and meander along a path through 12,000 evocative tombstones. They're old, eroded, inscribed in Hebrew, and leaning this way and that. A few of the dead have larger ark-shaped tombs. Most have a simple epitaph with the name, date, and a few of the deceased's virtues.

PRAGUE

From 1439 until 1787, this was the only burial ground allowed for the Jews of Prague. Over time, the graves had to be piled on top of each other—seven or eight deep—so there are actually closer to 85,000 dead here. Graves were never relocated because of the Jewish belief that, once buried, a body should not be moved. Layer by layer, the cemetery grew into a small plateau. Tune into the noise of passing cars outside, and you realize that you're several feet above the modern street level—which is already high above the medieval level.

People place pebbles on honored tombstones. This custom, a sign of respect, shows that the dead have not been forgotten and recalls the old days, when rocks were placed upon a sandy gravesite to keep the body covered. Others leave scraps of paper that contain prayers and wishes.

Ceremonial Hall (Obřadní Síň): This rustic stone tower (1911), sitting at the edge of the cemetery, was a mortuary house used to prepare the body and perform purification rituals before burial. The inside is painted in fanciful, flowery Neo-Romanesque style. It's filled with a worthwhile exhibition on Jewish medicine, death, and burial traditions.

Klausen Synagogue (Klauzová Synagóga): This 17th-century synagogue is devoted to Jewish religious practices. The ground-floor displays touch on Jewish holidays. Upstairs, exhibits illustrate the rituals of everyday Jewish life. It starts at birth. There are good-luck amulets to ensure a healthy baby, and a wooden cradle that announces, "This little one will become big." The baby is circumcised (see the knife) and grows to celebrate a coming-of-age Bar or Bat Mitzvah around age 12 or 13. Marriage takes place under a canopy, and the couple sets up their home—the exhibit ends with some typical furnishings.

Note that the Spanish Synagogue—described next—is a few

Prague's Jewish Quarter

Jews first came to Prague in the 10th century. The least habitable, marshy area closest to the bend was allotted to the Jewish community. The Jewish Quarter's main intersection (Maiselova and Široká streets) was the meeting point of two medieval trade routes. For centuries, Jews coexisted—at times tensely—with their non-Jewish Czech neighbors.

During the Crusades in the 12th century, the pope declared that Jews and Christians should not live together. Jews had to wear yellow badges, and their quarter was walled in and became a ghetto (minority neighborhood). In the 16th and 17th centuries, Prague had one of the biggest ghettos in Europe, with 11,000 inhabitants. Within its six gates, Prague's Jewish Quarter was a gaggle of 200 wooden buildings.

Faced with institutionalized bigotry and harassment, Jews relied mainly on profits from moneylending (forbidden to Christians) and community solidarity to survive. While their money bought them protection (the kings taxed Jewish communities heavily), it was often also a curse. Throughout Europe, when times got tough and Christian debts to the Jewish community mounted, entire Jewish communities were evicted or killed. The worse pogroms were in 1096 and in 1389, when around 3,000 Jews were killed.

In 1781, Emperor Josef II, motivated more by economic concerns than by religious freedom, eased much of the discrimination against Jews. In 1848, the Jewish Quarter's walls were torn down, and the neighborhood—named Josefov in honor of the emperor who provided this small measure of tolerance—was incorporated as a district of the Old Town.

In 1897, ramshackle Josefov was razed and replaced by a new modern town—the original 31 streets and 220 buildings became 10 streets and 83 buildings. They leveled the medieval-era buildings (except the synagogues) and turned this into perhaps Europe's finest Art Nouveau neighborhood, boasting stately facades with gables, turrets, elegant balconies, mosaics, statues, and all manner of architectural marvels. By the 1930s, Prague's Jewish community was prospering.

But then World War II hit. Of the 55,000 Jews living in Prague in 1939, just 10,000 survived the Holocaust to see liberation in 1945. And in the communist era—when the atheistic regime was also anti-Semitic—recovery was slow.

Today there are only 3,000 "registered" Jews in the Czech Republic, and of these, only 1,700 are in Prague. (There are probably more Jewish people here, but after their experiences with the Nazis and communists, it's understandable that many choose not to register.) In spite of their tiny numbers, the legacy of Prague's Jewish community lives on. While today's modern grid plan has replaced the higgledy-piggledy medieval streets of old, Široká ("Wide Street") remains the main street. A few Jewish-themed shops and restaurants add extra ambience to this (otherwise modern) neighborhood.

blocks away from the core of the Jewish Quarter. Before heading over there, consider visiting the nearby **Old-New Synagogue** (described at the end of this section).

Spanish Synagogue (Španělská Synagóga): Called "Spanish" though its design is Moorish (which was all the rage when this was built in the 19th century), this has the most opulently decorated interior of all the synagogues. It marked a time of relative wealth and importance for Prague's Jews, who in this era were increasingly welcome in the greater community and (in many cases) chose to adopt a more reformed approach to worship. Exhibits explain the lives of Czech Jews in the 19th and early 20th centuries, when they believed to be living their best days yet...unaware that the Holocaust was looming.

The decor is exotic and awe-inspiring. Intricate interweaving designs (of stars and vines) cover every inch of the red-gold and green walls and ceiling. A rose window with a stylized Star of David graces the ark.

The new synagogue housed a new movement within Judaism—a Reform congregation—which worshipped in a more modern way. The bema has been moved to the front of the synagogue, so the officiant faces the congregation. There's also a prominent organ (upper right) to accompany the singing.

Displays of Jewish history bring us through the 18th, 19th, and tumultuous 20th centuries to today. In the 1800s, Jews were increasingly accepted and successful in the greater society. But tolerance brought a dilemma—was it better to assimilate within the dominant culture or to join the growing Zionist homeland movement? To reform the religion or to remain orthodox?

Upstairs, the **balcony exhibits** focus on Czech Jews in the 1900s. Start in the area near the organ, which explains the modern era of Jewish Prague, including the late 19th-century development of Josefov. Then work your way around the balcony, with exhibits on Jewish writers (Franz Kafka), philosophers (Edmund Husserl), and other notables (Freud). This intellectual renaissance came to an abrupt halt with World War II and the mass deportations to Terezín (see more sad displays on life there, including more children's art and a box full of tefillin prayer cases). The final displays bring it home: After 2,000 years of living away from their Holy Land roots, the Jewish people had a homeland—the modern nation of Israel. Finish your visit across the landing in the **Winter Synagogue,** showing a trove of silver—Kiddush cups, Hanukkah lamps, Sabbath candlesticks, and Torah ornaments.

Old-New Synagogue (Staronová Synagóga)

The oldest surviving and most important building in the Jewish Quarter, the Old-New Synagogue goes back at least seven cen-

PRAGUE

turies. While the exterior is simple compared to ornate neighboring townhouses, the interior is atmospherically 13th-century.

Cost and Hours: 200 Kč, or 480-Kč combo-ticket with Jewish Museum of Prague, Sun-Thu 9:00-18:00, off-season until 17:00, Fri closes one hour before sunset, closed Sat and on Jewish holidays, admission includes worthwhile 10-minute tour, tel. 222-317-191, www.synagogue.cz.

Visiting the Synagogue: Built in 1270, this is the oldest synagogue in Eastern Europe (and some say the oldest still-working synagogue in all of Europe). The name likely comes because it was "New" when built, but became "Old" when other, newer synagogues came on the scene. The exterior is simple, with a unique saw-tooth gable. Standing like a bomb-hardened bunker, it feels as though it has survived plenty of hard times.

As you enter, you descend a few steps below street level to 13th-century street level and the medieval world.

The **interior** is pure Gothic—thick pillars, soaring arches, and narrow lancet windows. If it looks like a church, well, the architects were Christians. The stonework is original, and the woodwork (the paneling and benches) is also old. This was one of the first Gothic buildings in Prague.

Seven centuries later, it's still a working synagogue. There's the stone bema in the middle where the Torah is read aloud, and the ark at the far end, where the sacred scrolls are kept. To the right of the ark, one chair is bigger, with a Star of David above it. This chair always remains empty out of respect for great rabbis of the past. Where's the women's gallery? Here, women worshipped in rooms that flanked the hall, watching the service through those horizontal windows in the walls.

Before leaving, check out the **lobby** (the long hall where you show your ticket). It has two fortified old lockers—in which the most heavily taxed community in medieval Prague stored its money in anticipation of the taxman's arrival.

NORTH OF THE OLD TOWN SQUARE, NEAR THE RIVER

Stray just a couple of blocks north of the Old Town Square and you'll find a surprisingly tourist-free world of shops and cafés, pastel buildings with decorative balconies and ornamental statues, winding lanes, cobblestone streets, and mosaic sidewalks. It's also home to this fine, underrated museum.

PRAGUE

**▲▲Museum of Medieval Art
(Středověké umění v Čechách a Střední Evropě)**

Prague flourished in the 14th century, and the city has amassed an impressive collection of altarpieces and paintings from that age. Today this art is housed in the former Convent of St. Agnes, which was founded in the 13th century by a Czech princess-turned-nun as the first hospital in Prague. A visit here is a sightseeing twofer: Enjoy the well-presented art in a refreshingly uncrowded setting, and savor the tranquil corridors and cloisters.

Cost and Hours: 220-Kč, 500-Kč combo-ticket also covers Sternberg Palace and Schwarzenberg Palace, plus two others; valid 7 days; convent buildings are free; open Tue-Sun 10:00-18:00, closed Mon; two blocks northeast of Spanish Synagogue, along the river at Anežská 12, tel. 224-810-628, www.ngprague.cz.

PRAGUE

Sights in the New Town (Nové Město)

Enough of pretty, medieval Prague—let's leap into the modern era. The New Town, with Wenceslas Square as its focal point, is today's urban Prague. This part of the city offers bustling boulevards and interesting neighborhoods. Even today, the New Town is separated from the Old Town by a "moat" (the literal meaning of the street called Na Příkopě). As you cross bustling Na Příkopě, you leave the glass and souvenir shops behind, and enter a town of malls and fancy shops that cater to locals and visitors alike. The New Town is one of the best places to view Prague's remarkable Art Nouveau art and architecture, and to learn more about its communist past.

∩ My Prague City Walk audio tour covers sights in both the Old Town and New Town.

WENCESLAS SQUARE AND NEARBY

These sights are on or within a few blocks of the elongated main square of the New Town.

▲▲Wenceslas Square (Václavské Náměstí)

More a broad boulevard than a square, this city landmark is named for St. Wenceslas, whose equestrian statue overlooks the square's top end. Wenceslas Square functions as a stage for modern Czech history: The creation of the Czechoslovak state was celebrated here in 1918; in 1968, the Soviets suppressed huge popular demonstrations (called the Prague Spring) at the square; and, in 1989, more than 300,000 Czechs and Slovaks converged here to demand their freedom (in the Velvet Revolution). Today it's a busy thoroughfare of commerce.

◆ Self-Guided Walk: For a taste of Prague's 20th-century

The Prague Spring and Its Fall

In January 1968, the Slovak politician Alexander Dubček replaced the aging apparatchiks at the helm of the Communist Party of Czechoslovakia. Handsome and relatively youthful, Dubček's brand was that of a smiling playboy; he appeared on magazine covers in his speedo, about to dive into a swimming pool. Young Czechs and Slovaks embraced Dubček as a potential hero of liberalization.

In April, Dubček introduced his "Action Program," designed to tiptoe away from strict and stifling Soviet communism and forge a more moderate Czechoslovak variation. Censorship eased, travel restrictions were relaxed, state companies began forming joint ventures with Western firms, money poured into the sciences, and a newspaper called "Tomorrow" (rather than "Today") became the most popular in the country. Plays put on at the Semafor Theater (in today's Světozor mall) lampooned Brezhnev and his ilk. During this so-called "Prague Spring," optimism soared.

But then, around midnight on August 20, 1968, the thundering sound of enormous airplanes ripped across the floodlit rooftops of Prague. The Soviets had dispatched over 200,000 Warsaw Pact troops to invade Czechoslovakia, airlifting tanks right into the capital city. Dubček and his team were arrested and taken to Moscow. Czechs and Slovaks—now living in a police state—were terrified as they took to the streets, boycotting and striking. Tanks rolled through Wenceslas Square, spraying protesters with bullets...some of which are still embedded in the National Museum's pillars. Over the course of the occupation, 72 Czechs and Slovaks were killed.

Dubček stepped down and went into internal exile, and his successor—the hardliner Gustáv Husák—immediately pursued a policy of "normalization." People who refused to sign a petition commending the "Russian Liberation" were fired from their jobs, and forced to find worse ones. Some protesters—including Jan Palach—set themselves on fire to protest against the regime. Tens of thousands of Czechs and Slovaks reluctantly emigrated to the West, fearing what might come next.

While the ill-fated tale of the Prague Spring is pessimistic, it provides an insightful bookend to what happened 21 years later: The children of the generation that suffered Czechoslovakia's bitterest disappointment brought about its greatest success.

history, take a stroll beginning at the top of the square. (To get here quickly, ride the Metro to the Muzeum stop.)

• *Begin at the big...*

Statue of Duke Wenceslas I: The "Good King" of Christmas-carol fame was actually a wise and benevolent 10th-century duke. Václav I (as he's called by locals) united the Czech people, back

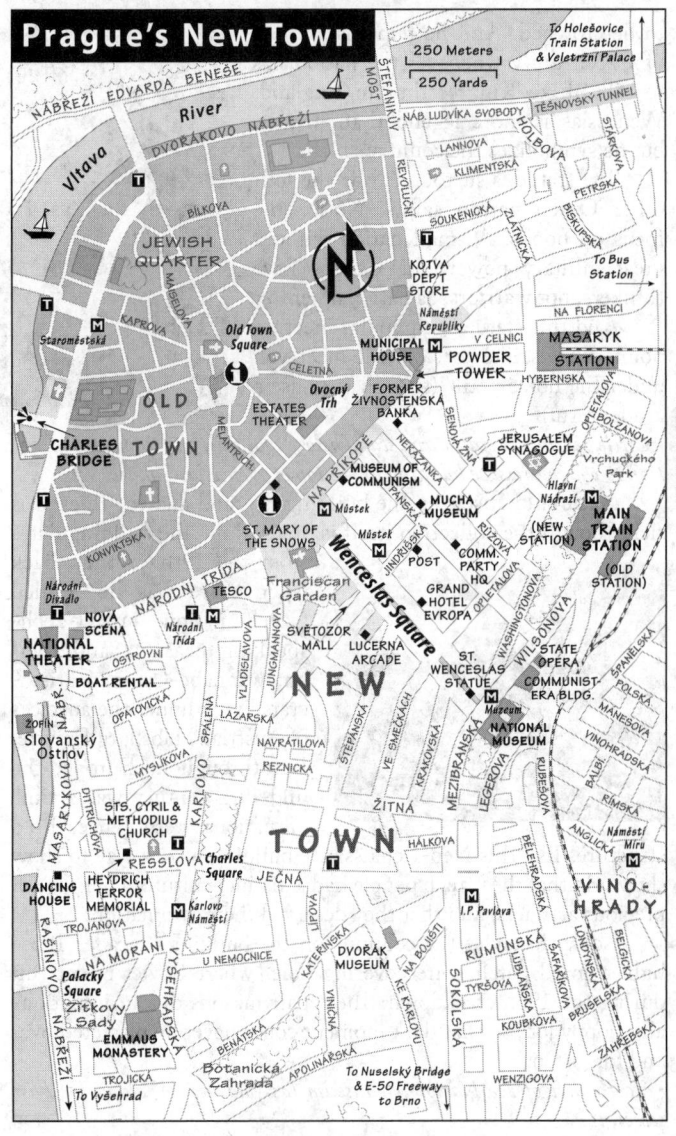

when this land was known as Bohemia. A rare example of a well-educated and literate ruler, Wenceslas Christianized and lifted the culture. He astutely allied the powerless Czechs with the Holy Roman Empire. And he began to fortify Prague's castle as a center of Czech government. After his murder in 929, Wenceslas was canonized as a saint. He became a symbol of Czech nationalism (and appears on the 20-Kč coin). Later kings knelt before his tomb to be crowned. And he remains an icon of Czech unity whenever the nation has to rally. Like King Arthur in England, Wenceslas is more legend than history, but he symbolizes the country's birth.

The statue is surrounded by the four other Czech patron saints. Notice the focus on books. A small nation without great military power, the Czechs have thinkers, not warriors, as national heroes.

And this statue is a popular meeting point. Locals like to say, "I'll meet you under the horse's tail" (though they use a cruder term).

• *Circle behind the statue and stand below that tail, and turn your attention to the impressive building at the top of Wenceslas Square.*

National Museum: The building is grand and the interior is rich, though the collection itself is pretty dull. The building dates

from the 19th century, back when there was no unified Czech nation—just Czech-speaking peasants and two-bit, wannabe-German aristocrats living under the auspices of Austria's Habsburg Empire. But throughout Europe, the mid-19th century was a time of national resurgence. Bold structures like this Neo-Renaissance building were a way to show the world that the Czech people had a distinct culture, a heritage of precious artifacts, and that they deserved their own nation.

Look closely at the columns on the building's facade. Those light-colored patches are covering holes where Soviet bullets hit during the 1968 crackdown. The repair masons did an intentionally sloppy job, so that dark moment could never be plastered over and forgotten.

• *To the left of the National Museum (as you face it), along the busy street, is a...*

Communist-Era Building: This ugly, modern structure once housed the rubber-stamp Czechoslovak Parliament back when it voted in lock-step with Moscow. Between 1994 and 2008, this building was home to Radio Free Europe. After communism fell, RFE lost some of its funding and could no longer afford its Munich headquarters. In gratitude for its broadcasts—which had kept the people of Eastern Europe in touch with real news—the Czech government offered this building to RFE for 1 Kč a year. But as RFE energetically beamed its American message deep into the Muslim world from here, it drew attention—and threats—from Al-Qaeda. In 2009, RFE moved to a new fortress-like headquarters at an easier-to-defend locale farther from the center. Now this is an annex of the National Museum.

• *Start walking down Wenceslas Square. Pause about 30 yards along, at the little patch of bushes. In the ground on the downhill side of those bushes is a...*

Memorial to the Victims of 1969: After the Russian crackdown of 1968, a group of patriots wanted to stand up to the power-

ful Soviet occupation. One was a young philosophy student named Jan Palach. He decided that the best way to stoke the flame of independence was to set himself on fire. On January 16, 1969, Palach stood on the steps of the National Museum and ignited his body for the cause of Czech freedom. He died a few days later in a hospital ward. A month later, another student did the same thing, followed by another. Czechs are keen on anniversaries, and—20 years after Palach's brave and patriotic act, in 1989—Czechs gathered here for a huge demonstration. A sense of new possibility swept through the city, and 10 months later, the communists were history.

• *Continue down Wenceslas Square until you reach the median in front of Grand Hotel Evropa. It's the ornate, yellow building about 300 yards down Wenceslas Square, on the right.*

Architecture Along Wenceslas Square: As you walk, notice the architecture. Unlike the historic Old Town, nearly everything here is from the past two centuries. Wenceslas Square is a showcase of Prague's many architectural styles: You'll see Neo-Gothic, Neo-Renaissance, and Neo-Baroque from the 19th century. There's curvaceous Art Nouveau from around 1900. And there's the modernist response to Art Nouveau—Functionalism from the mid-20th century, where the watchword was "form follows function" and beauty took a back seat to practicality. You'll see what's nicknamed "Stalin Gothic" from the 1950s communist era; a good example of that is the Hotel Jalta building, halfway downhill on the right (the sandy facade with lots of balconies). And there are forgettable glass-and-steel buildings of the 1970s.

The Velvet Revolution: Opposite Grand Hotel Evropa (that is, on the left side of the square), find the Marks & Spencer building, which has a **balcony** on it (partly obscured by tree branches).

Picture the scene on this square on a cold November night in 1989. Czechoslovakia had been oppressed for the previous 40 years by communist Russia. But now the Soviet empire was beginning to crumble, jubilant Germans were dancing on top of the shattered Berlin Wall, and the Czechs were getting a whiff of freedom.

Czechoslovakia's revolution began with a bunch of teenagers, who—following a sanctioned gathering—decided to march on Wenceslas Square (see sidebar). After they were surrounded and beaten by the communist riot police, their enraged parents, friends, and other members of the community began to pour into this square to protest. Night after night, this huge square was filled with more than 300,000 ecstatic Czechs and Slovaks who believed freedom was at hand. Each night they would jangle their key chains in the air as if saying to their communist leaders, "It's time for you to go home now." Finally they gathered and found that their communist overlords had left—and freedom was theirs.

On that night, as thousands filled this square, a host of famous people appeared on that balcony to greet the crowd. There was a well-known priest and a rock star famous for his rebellion against authority. There was Alexander Dubček, the hero of the Prague Spring reforms of 1968. And there was Václav Havel, the charismatic playwright who had spent years in prison, becoming a symbol of resistance—a kind of Czech Nelson Mandela. Now he was free. Havel's voice boomed over the gathered masses. He proclaimed the resignation of the Politburo and the imminent freedom of the Republic of Czechoslovakia. He pulled out a ring of keys and jingled it. Thousands of keys jingled back in response. It was their symbolic way of saying: The communists have packed up and left, and now we're free to unlock our chains.

In previous years, the communist authorities would have sent in tanks to crush the impudent masses. But by 1989, the Soviet empire was collapsing, and the Czech government was shaky. Locals think that Soviet head of state Mikhail Gorbachev (mindful of the Tiananmen Square massacre a few months before) might have made a phone call recommending a nonviolent response. Whatever happened, the communist regime was overthrown with hardly any blood being spilled. It was done through sheer people power—thanks to the masses of defiant Czechs who gathered here peacefully in Wenceslas Square, and Slovaks doing the same in Bratislava. They called it "The Velvet Revolution."

• *A block from the bottom of Wenceslas Square, look for the gate tucked behind the Jungmann statue on Jungmannovo Náměstí. Head through to find the...*

Franciscan Garden: Ahhh! This garden's white benches and

The Velvet Revolution of 1989

On the afternoon of November 17, 1989, 30,000 students gathered in Prague's New Town to commemorate the 50th anniversary of the suppression of student protests by the Nazis, which had led to the closing of Czech universities through the end of World War II. Remember, this was just a few weeks after the fall of the Berlin Wall, and the Czechs were feeling the winds of change blowing across Central Europe. The 1989 demonstration—initially planned by the Communist Youth as a celebration of the communist victory over fascism—spontaneously turned into a protest *against* the communist regime. "You are just like the Nazis!" shouted the students. The demonstration was supposed to end in the National Cemetery at Vyšehrad (the hill just south of the New Town). But when the planned events concluded in Vyšehrad, the students decided to march on toward Wenceslas Square...and make some history.

As they worked their way north along the Vltava River toward the New Town's main square, the students were careful to keep their demonstration peaceful. Any hint of violence, the demonstrators knew, would incite brutal police retaliation. Instead, as the evening went on, the absence of police became conspicuous. (In the 1980s, the police never missed a chance to participate in any demonstration...preferably outnumbering the demonstrators.) At about 20:00, as the students marched down Národní Třída toward Wenceslas Square, three rows of policemen suddenly blocked the demonstration at the corner of Národní and Spálená streets. A few minutes later, military vehicles with fences on their bumpers (having crossed the bridge by the National Theater) appeared behind the marching students. This new set of cops compressed the demonstrators into the stretch of Národní Třída between Voršilská and Spálená. The end of Mikulandská street was also blocked, and policemen were hiding inside every house entry. The students were trapped.

At 21:30, the "Red Berets" (a special anti-riot commando force known for its brutality) arrived. The Red Berets lined up on both sides of this corridor. To get out, the trapped students had to run through the passageway as they were beaten from the left and right. Police trucks ferried captured students around the corner to the police headquarters (on Bartolomějská) for interrogation.

The next day, university students throughout Czechoslovakia decided to strike. Actors from theaters in Prague and Bratislava joined the student protest. Two days later, the students' parents—shocked by the attacks on their children—marched into Wenceslas Square. Sparked by the events of November 17, 1989, the wave of peaceful demonstrations ended later that year on December 29, with the election of Václav Havel as the president of a free Czechoslovakia.

spreading rosebushes are a universe away from the fast beat of the city, which throbs behind the buildings corralling this little oasis. The peacefulness reflects the purpose of its Franciscan origin. St. Francis, the founder of the order, thought God's presence could be found in nature. In the 1600s, Prague became an important center for a group of Franciscans from Ireland. Enjoy the herb garden, children's playground, and public WC. The park is a popular place for a discreet rendezvous; it's famous among locals for kicking off romances.

• *Exit the garden at the opposite corner from where you entered (past the little yellow gardening pavilion—which now houses a design boutique—and the herb garden). Continue straight ahead to reach the Old Town, or visit the nearby Museum of Communism, Mucha Museum, or Municipal House. For places farther afield, you can hop on the Metro at Můstek. The rest of Prague is yours to enjoy.*

▲▲Mucha Museum (Muchovo Museum)

This enjoyable little museum features a small selection of the insistently likeable art of Alfons Mucha (MOO-khah, 1860-1939), a founding father of the Art Nouveau move-ment (and creator of Prague's most famous artwork, the *Slav Epic,* a huge 20-canvas ode to his nation and its history that's currently on a world tour). It's all crammed into a too-small space, some of the art is faded, and the admission price is steep—but there's no better place to gain an understanding of Mucha's talent, his career, and the influence he's had on the world art scene. And the museum, partly overseen by Mucha's grandson, gives you a peek at some of the posters that made Mucha famous. You'll learn how these popular patriotic banners, filled with Czech symbols and expressing his people's ideals and aspirations, aroused the national spirit. Enjoy decorative posters from his years in Paris, including his celebrated ads for the French actress Sarah Bernhardt. Check out the photographs of his models, which Mucha later re-created in pencil or paint, and be sure to see the 30-minute film on the artist's life.

Cost and Hours: 240 Kč, daily 10:00-18:00, good English descriptions, two blocks off Wenceslas Square at Panská 7, tel. 224-233-355, www.mucha.cz. Peruse the well-stocked gift shop.

ALONG NA PŘÍKOPĚ

At the bottom of Wenceslas Square, the street running to the right is called Na Příkopě. This street is a showcase of Art Nouveau: Be sure to keep your eyes up as you stroll here. City tour buses leave from along this street, which also offers plenty of shopping temptations.

▲Museum of Communism (Muzeum Komunismu)

Tucked away upstairs in a cramped and creaky old mansion, this humble but engaging museum traces the story of communism in Prague: the origin, dream, reality, and nightmare; the cult of personality; and, finally, the Velvet Revolution. Along the way, it gives a thought-provoking review of the Czech Republic's 40-year stint with Soviet economics, "in all its dreariness and puffed-up glory." You'll find propaganda posters and busts of communist All-Stars (Marx, Lenin, and others), and re-created slices of communist life. While dated and faded (like its subject), and lacking high-tech flair, the museum's clever displays and English descriptions evoke the time well—making this Prague's most accessible sight relating to its communist era.

Cost and Hours: 190 Kč, daily 9:00-21:00, Na Příkopě 10, tel. 224-212-966, www.muzeumkomunismu.cz.

Nearby: If you're curious to see communism outside of a museum, take a five-minute walk to the present-day **Headquarters of the Communist Party of Bohemia and Moravia (KSČM).** From the museum, hook around the corner (to the right) and head up Panská street a long block and a half—passing the Mucha Museum—to find Politických Vězňů 9 (on the left). The building—which sits on "Political Prisoners Street" (no joke)—is painted an appropriately peachy shade of red, and protesters have spilled red paint on its threshold. Step inside (go ahead—the door's open) to pick up some propaganda brochures and see party leadership and candidate photos of today's midlevel apparatchiks in bad suits... who seem oblivious to the political (and fashion) changes since 1989. They've swapped the red star with a cheerier symbol—a pair of bright-red cherries, as if voting Communist is like playing a slot machine. Despite heavy public pressure to outlaw this artifact of a hated-by-most era, the Communist Party still commands between 10 and 15 percent of the national Czech vote—mostly from aging, nostalgic voters more concerned about predictability than freedom. More pragmatic Czechs say they're glad the Communists have their own party—it keeps them marginalized, rather than being a vocal fringe that hijacks the agenda of a larger, more influential party.

▲▲Municipal House (Obecní Dům)

The cultural and artistic leaders who financed this Art Nouveau masterpiece (1905-1911) wanted a ceremonial palace to reinforce self-awareness of the Czech nation. While the exterior is impressive (and described on page 67 of my Prague Old Town Walk), the

PRAGUE

highlight is the interior—and it's free. To extend your Art Nouveau bliss, take a guided tour or attend a concert here.

Cost and Hours: The entrance halls and public spaces are free to enter and explore, open daily 10:00-18:00. For an in-depth look at all the sumptuous halls and banquet rooms, take advantage of the daily one-hour English **tours** (290 Kč, usually 3/day, departures 11:00-17:00; limited to 35 people—buy your ticket online or as soon as you can from the ground-floor shop where tours depart; Náměstí Republiky 5, tel. 222-002-101, www.obecnidum.cz).

Concerts: Performances are held regularly in the lavish Smetana Hall (schedule on website). Note that many concerts brag they are held in the Municipal House, but are performed in a smaller, less impressive hall in the same building.

Visiting the Municipal House: Don't be timid about poking around the interior, which is open to the public. Having lunch or a drink in one of the eateries is a great way to experience the decor, but you can also just glimpse them from the doorway (as you "check out the menu").

Enter under the green, wrought-iron arcade. In the **rotunda,** admire the mosaic floor, stained glass, the woodwork doorway, and the lighting fixtures. To the left is the **café** *(kavárna)*—a harmony of woodwork, marble, metal, and glittering chandeliers. Opposite the café is the equally stunning **restaurant** (both described on page 141).

From the rotunda, step into the **lobby,** where you can look up the staircase that leads up to the main concert hall (no tourist access upstairs). Also in the lobby is the box office selling concert tickets and guided English tours of the building.

Facing the staircase, go right and head **downstairs**—yes, tourists are welcome there. Admire the colorful tiles in the stairwell, and more colorful tiles in the downstairs main room. Look for the plaster model of this building and the adjacent Powder Tower, which shows how the angled facade conceals a surprisingly large performance space. Also check out the **American Bar** (salute the US flags above the bar) and the **Plzeňská Restaurant** (with its dark-wood booths and colorful tile scenes of happy peasants).

Finish your tour by going back upstairs to find the **Modernista shop** (tucked to the left as you face the main staircase)—full of fancy teacups and jewelry.

Also upstairs, you may find **temporary exhibits** (usually around 150 Kč), typically about Art Nouveau. This style was heavy on the applied arts (as opposed to fine arts like painting), so you'll see elegant lamps, chairs, prints, and clothes. The period celebrated new technologies, which allowed high-quality objects to be mass-produced for the average Jan and Jana. They're functional and minimal in design, but always beautiful. To reach this space, you're allowed to ascend the main staircase, pass by the guard, and glimpse into the stylish Smetana Hall along the way.

NEAR THE VLTAVA RIVER

I've listed these sights from north to south, beginning at the grand, Neo-Renaissance National Theater, which is five blocks south of the Charles Bridge and stands along the riverbank at the end of Národní Třída.

National Theater (Národní Divadlo)

Opened in 1883 with Smetana's opera *Libuše,* this theater was the first truly Czech venue in Prague. From the very start, it was nick-

named the "Cradle of Czech Culture." The building is a key symbol of the Czech National Revival that began in the late 18th century. In 1800, "Prag" was predominantly German. The Industrial Revolution brought Czechs from the countryside into the city, their new urban identity defined by patriotic teachers and priests. By 1883, most of the city spoke Czech, and the opening of this theater represented the birth of the modern Czech nation. It remains an important national icon: The state annually pours more subsidies into this theater than into all of Czech film production. It's the most beautiful venue in town for opera and ballet, often with world-class singers (for more details on performances, see page 126).

• *A 10-minute walk (or one stop on tram #17) south from the National Theater, beyond the islands, is Jirásek Bridge (Jiráskův Most), where you'll find the…*

Dancing House (Tančící Dům)

If ever a building could get your toes tapping, it would be this one, nicknamed "Fred and Ginger" by American architecture buffs. This metallic samba is the work of Frank Gehry (who designed the equally striking Guggenheim Museum in Bilbao, Spain, and Seattle's Museum of Pop Culture).

PRAGUE

Eight-legged Ginger's wispy dress and Fred's metal mesh head are easy to spot. Some Czechs prefer to think that the two "figures" represent the nation's greatest 20th-century heroes, Jozef Gabčík and Jan Kubiš (see "The Assassination of Reinhard Heydrich" sidebar). A contemporary art gallery occupies unused office space throughout the building (90 Kč, daily 11:00-19:00). The building's top-floor restaurant, **$$$ Céleste,** is a fine place for a fancy French meal. Whether you go up for lunch (reasonable, 12:00-14:30), a drink (16:00-18:00), or an expensive dinner, you'll be a louse in the Gehry haircut (tel. 221-984-160).

• *Two blocks up Resslova street is the Sts. Cyril and Methodius Church, which contains in its crypt the...*

▲National Memorial to the Heroes of the Heydrich Terror (Národní Památník Hrdinů Heydrichiády)

In 1942, WWII paratroopers Jozef Gabčík and Jan Kubiš assassinated the SS second-in-command Reinhard Heydrich, who controlled the Nazi-occupied Czech lands and was one of the main architects of the Holocaust. In the weeks following his assassination, the two paratroopers hid, along with other freedom fighters, in the crypt of the Greek Orthodox Sts. Cyril and Methodius Church on Resslova street. Today, a modest exhibition in the church's crypt retells their story, along with the history of the Czech resistance movement. Outside, notice the small me-morial, including bullet holes, plaque, and flowers on the street. Around the corner is the entry into the museum and the crypt.

Cost and Hours: 75 Kč, Tue-Sun 9:00-17:00, closed Mon, full history explained in small 25-Kč booklet, 2 blocks up from the Dancing House at Resslova 9A, tel. 224-916-100.

Prague's Embankment

Much of the city's Vltava-front embankment—especially the stretch between Palacký Square and Vyšehrad—has been gorgeously renovated in recent years, and has become a particularly fine (and untouristy) place to wander. Al fresco cafés and restaurant barges enliven the riverbank on sunny days, and a farmers market bustles on Saturday morning (8:00-14:00).

The Assassination of Reinhard Heydrich

Visitors to the Sts. Cyril and Methodius Church are reminded of a fascinating slice of Nazi-era intrigue.

In September 1941, Reinhard Heydrich—the SS second-in-command, Hitler's personal favorite, and one of the architects of the Holocaust, became the governor of the occupied Czech lands.

At the same time, the Czechoslovak government-in-exile was suffering a crisis of legitimacy in Britain's eyes. Following the British signing of the Munich Pact (an act of appeasement that would annex Czechoslovakia's Sudetenland area to the Nazis), thousands of Czechs and Slovaks went abroad to fight, and few of those left in the occupied lands were cut out for underground resistance.

It was under these circumstances that two paratroopers, Jozef Gabčík and Jan Kubiš, were chosen by British Special Operations and trained in Scotland for a secret and—as they were made to understand from the start—potentially suicidal mission to eliminate Heydrich.

On the morning of May 27, 1942, Heydrich was coming down Kobylisy hill on his daily commute. Just as the unaccompanied open car slowed down at a hairpin turn, Gabčík jumped in front of the car and pointed his Sten machine gun at Heydrich, and pulled the trigger. But the gun jammed. Heydrich, ordering his driver to stop, pulled out his revolver. At that moment, Kubiš, coming in from behind, threw a handmade grenade that missed and exploded outside the car. But the explosion was enough to wound Heydrich, who was transported to a nearby hospital, where he died a few days later. At his funeral—the Nazis' most elaborate funeral ceremony ever—Hitler appeared genuinely distressed, and Heydrich was eulogized as the model for all SS men.

The Nazi response in the Protectorate was brutal. Martial law was declared, two villages were summarily razed to the ground, and in the ensuing months, 5,000 individuals were executed. A reward was announced for tips leading to the capture of the assassins. Karel Čurda, a member of another paratrooper unit, betrayed his comrades. On June 18, at 4:15 in the morning, the Gestapo surrounded the Sts. Cyril and Methodius Church on Resslova street, where the two paratroopers were hiding. After a two-hour battle, Kubiš, on guard in the nave of the church, was killed along with two other defenders. Gabčík and three other paratroopers committed suicide in the crypt below.

Days after the assassination, the British government revoked its signature on the Munich Pact, recognizing Czechoslovakia's prewar boundaries; the French followed two months later. Heydrich—whose elimination was one of the most significant acts of resistance in occupied Europe—remains the highest-ranked Nazi official killed while in office.

PRAGUE

Sights in the Little Quarter (Malá Strana)

Huddled under the castle on the west bank of the river, this neighborhood is pleasant, though low on blockbuster sights. The most enjoyable approach from the Old Town is across the Charles Bridge. From the end of the bridge (TI in tower), Mostecká street leads two blocks up to the Little Quarter Square (Malostranské Náměstí) and the huge Church of St. Nicholas. But before you head up there, consider a detour to Kampa Island.

BETWEEN CHARLES BRIDGE AND LITTLE QUARTER SQUARE

Kampa Island

One hundred yards from the castle end of the Charles Bridge, stairs on the left lead down to the main square of Kampa Island (mostly created from the rubble of the Little Quarter, which was destroyed in a 1540 fire). The island features relaxing pubs, a breezy park, hippies, lovers, a fine contemporary art gallery, and river access. From the main square, Hroznová lane (on the right) winds around to a little bridge. The high-water mark at the end of the bridge dates from 1890. The **old**

water wheel is the last survivor of many mills that once lined the canal here. Each mill had its own protective water spirit *(vodník)*.

• *Fifty yards beyond the bridge (on the right, under the trees) is the...*

Lennon Wall (Lennonova Zeď)

While V. I. Lenin's ideas hung like a water-soaked trench coat upon the Czech people, rock singer John Lennon's ideas gave many locals hope and a vision. When Lennon was killed in 1980, a large wall was spontaneously covered with memorial graffiti. Night after night, the police would paint over the "All You Need Is Love" and "Imagine" graffiti. And day after day, it would reappear. Until independence came in 1989, travelers, freedom lovers, and local hippies gathered here. Silly as

it might seem, this wall is remembered as a place that gave hope to locals craving freedom. Even today, while the tension and danger associated with this wall are gone, people come here to imagine. *"John žije"* is Czech for "John lives."

• *From here, continue up to the Little Quarter Square.*

ON OR NEAR LITTLE QUARTER SQUARE

The focal point of this neighborhood, the Little Quarter Square (Malostranské Náměstí), is split into an upper and lower part by the domineering Church of St. Nicholas and its adjacent Jesuit college. A Baroque plague column oversees the upper square. Note that there's a handy Via Musica ticket office across from the plague column (on the uphill side).

Church of St. Nicholas (Kostel Sv. Mikuláše)

When the Jesuits came to Prague, they found the perfect piece of real estate for their church and its associated school—right on Little Quarter Square. The church (built 1703-1760) is the best example of High Baroque in town.

Cost and Hours: 70 Kč, daily 9:00-17:00, Nov-Feb until 16:00, opens at 8:30 for prayer.

Visiting the Church: The church's interior is giddy with curves and illusions. Stand directly under the tallest dome and look up. Spin slowly around, greeting four giant statues—the fathers of the Eastern Church. Pan up and see the earthly world merging with heaven above.

The **altar** features a lavish gold-plated Nicholas, flanked by the two top Jesuits: the founder, St. Ignatius Loyola, and his missionary follower, St. Francis Xavier.

Climb up the **gallery** through the staircase in the left transept for a close-up look at a collection of large canvases and illusionary frescoes by Karel Škréta, who is considered the greatest Czech Baroque painter. Notice that at first glance the canvases are utterly dark, but as sunbeams shine through the window, various parts of the painting brighten up. Like a looking glass, the image reflects the light, creating a play of light and dark. This painting technique represents a central Baroque belief: The world is full of darkness, and the only hope that makes it come alive emanates from God. The church walls seem to nearly fuse with the sky, suggesting that happenings on earth are closely connected to heaven.

Tower Climb: For a good look at the city and the church's 250-foot dome, climb 215 steps up the bell tower. Closed to the public during the communist times, the deck was used by the secret police to spy on the activities at the nearby embassies of the US, Britain, and West Germany (90 Kč, daily 10:00-22:00, shorter hours in winter, tower entrance is outside the right transept).

Concerts: The church is also an evening concert venue; tickets

PRAGUE

Prague's Little Quarter

are usually on sale at the door (490 Kč, generally nightly at 18:00 except Tue, www.stnicholas.cz).

• *From here, you can hike 10 minutes uphill to the castle (and 5 more minutes to the Strahov Monastery). If you're walking up to the castle, consider going via...*

Nerudova Street

This steep, cobbled street, leading from Little Quarter Square to the castle, is named for Jan Neruda, a gifted 19th-century journalist (and somewhat less-talented fiction writer). It's lined with old buildings still sporting the characteristic doorway signs (such as the lion, three violinists, and house of the golden suns) that once served as street addresses. The surviving signs are carefully restored and protected by law. They represent the family name, the occupation, or the various passions of the people who once inhabited the houses. (If you were to replace your house number with a symbol, what would it be?) In the 1770s, in order to collect taxes more effectively, Habsburg empress Maria Theresa decreed that numbers be used instead of these quaint house names. This neighborhood is filled with old noble palaces, now generally used as foreign embassies and as offices of the Czech Parliament.

SOUTH OF LITTLE QUARTER SQUARE
Church of St. Mary the Victorious
(Kostel Panny Marie Vítězné)

This otherwise ordinary Carmelite church displays Prague's most worshipped treasure, the Infant of Prague (Pražské Jezulátko). Kneel at the banister in front of the tiny lost-in-gilded-Baroque altar, and find the prayer in your language (of the 13 in the folder). Brought to Czech lands during the Habsburg era by a Spanish noblewoman who came to marry a Czech nobleman, the Infant has become a focus of worship and miracle tales in Prague and Spanish-speaking countries. South Americans come on pilgrimage to Prague just to see this one statue. An exhibit upstairs shows tiny embroidered robes given to the Infant, including ones from Habsburg Empress Maria Theresa of Austria (1754) and the country of Vietnam (1958), as well as a video showing a nun lovingly dressing the doll-like sculpture.

Cost and Hours: Free, Mon-Sat 9:30-17:30, Sun 13:00-18:00, English-language Mass Sun at 12:00, Karmelitská 9, www.pragjesu.cz.

▲Petřín Hill (Petřínské Sady)

This hill, topped by a replica of the Eiffel Tower, features several unusual sights. The sculptural figures of this poignant **Monument to Victims of Communism** (Pomník Obětem Komunismu), representing victims of the totalitarian regime, gradually atrophy as they range up the hillside steps. They do not die but slowly disappear, one limb at a time. The statistics inscribed on the steps say it all: From 1948 until 1989, in Czechoslovakia alone, 205,486 people were imprisoned, 248 were executed, 4,500 died in prison, 327 were shot attempting to cross the border, and 170,938 left the country.

To the left of the monument is the **Hunger Wall** (Hladová Zed'). This medieval defense wall was Charles IV's 14th-century equivalent of FDR's work-for-food projects. The poorest of the poor helped build this structure just to eke out a bit of income.

On the right (50 yards away) is the base of a handy **funicular**—hop on to reach Petřín Tower (uses tram/Metro ticket, runs daily every 10-15 minutes 8:00-22:00).

The summit of Petřín Hill is considered the best place in Prague to take your date for a romantic city view. Built for an exhibition in 1891, the 200-foot-tall **Petřín Tower**—an elegant pure Art Nouveau steel-and-wood structure—is one-fifth the height of its Parisian big brother, which was built two years earlier. But, thanks to this hill, the top of the tower sits at the same elevation as the real Eiffel Tower. Before you climb up, appreciate the tower's sinuous curves. Climbing the 400 steps rewards you with amazing views of the city. A **mirror maze** next door to the tower is fun for a quick wander if you're already here. Next to the maze, in front of the cupola-topped observatory, notice the statue of **Milan Rastislav Štefánik** (1880-1919), the charismatic Slovak astronomer and patriot who brought home tens of thousands of Czech and Slovak freedom fighters left stranded in Siberia by the Bolshevik Revolution (tower—105 Kč, mirror maze—75 Kč, both daily 10:00-22:00, shorter hours off-season).

Sights in the Castle Quarter (Hradčany)

Looming above Prague, dominating its skyline, is the Castle Quarter. Prague Castle and its surrounding sights are packed with Czech history, as well as with tourists. In addition to the castle, I enjoy visiting the nearby Strahov Monastery, which has a fascinating old library and beautiful views over all of Prague.

GETTING TO THE CASTLE QUARTER
You have three options: taxi, walk, or tram.

By **taxi,** take it to the top of Nerudova street, just below Castle Square. To **walk** up, figure 20 minutes uphill from Charles Bridge, along cobbled Nerudova street. After about 10 minutes, a steep lane on the right leads to Castle Square; or, if you continue straight, Nerudova becomes Úvoz and climbs to the Strahov Monastery.

For the **tram,** catch tram #22 at one of three convenient stops: the Národní Třída stop (between Wenceslas Square and the National Theater in the New Town); in front of the National Theater (Národní Divadlo, on the riverbank in the New Town); and at Malostranská (the Metro stop in the Little Quarter).

After rattling up the hill, tram #22 makes three **stops** near the castle:

Královský Letohrádek allows a scenic but slow approach through the Royal Gardens to the bridge near the castle's northern entrance; **Pražský Hrad** offers the quickest commute to the castle—from the tram stop, simply walk along U Prašného Mostu and over the bridge, past the stonefaced-but-photo-op-friendly guards at the northern entrance, and into the castle's Second Courtyard; and **Pohořelec** is best if you'd like to start with the Strahov Monastery, then hike down to the castle. After getting off at the Pohořelec tram stop, follow the tracks for 50 yards, take the pedestrian lane that rises up beside the tram tracks, and enter the fancy gate on the left near the tall red-brick wall. You'll see the twin spires of

Prague Castle Overview

the monastery; the library entrance is on the little square with the monastery church.

AVOIDING CROWDS

Prague Castle is one of the city's most crowded sights. Huge throngs of tourists turn the grounds into a sea of people during peak times (9:30-12:30, especially May-Sept). The most cramped area is the free-to-enter vestibule inside St. Vitus Cathedral; any sight that you pay to enter—including other parts of the cathedral—will be less jammed.

Early-Bird Visit: Leave your hotel no later than 8:00 (earlier is even better). Ride tram #22 up to the Pražský Hrad stop (or leave yourself time to walk through the Royal Gardens, and get off at Královský Letohrádek), then use the northern entrance to the complex's Second Courtyard and buy your tickets. See **Castle Square,** and most important, be sure that you're standing at the front door

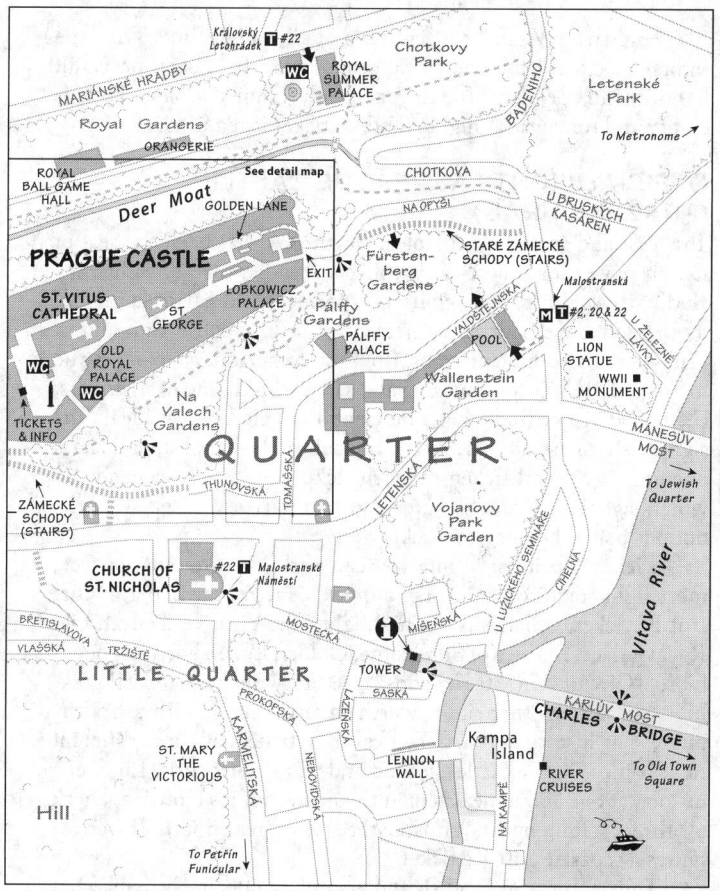

of **St. Vitus Cathedral** when it opens at the stroke of 9:00. For 10 minutes, you'll have the sacred space to yourself...then, on your way out, you'll pass a noisy human traffic jam of multinational tour groups clogging the entrance. Visit the rest of the castle sights at your leisure: the Old Royal Palace, the Basilica of St. George, and the Golden Lane. To see the **Strahov Monastery** and/or **Loreta Church** after your castle visit, backtrack uphill (either by foot, or by hopping back on tram #22 at a lower stop—near the castle, or even from the Malostranská stop near the river).

Afternoon Visit: Ride tram #22 to the Pohořelec stop. Tour the Strahov Monastery, then drop by Loreta Church on your way to Castle Square. By the time you hit the sights, the crowds should be thinning out (if St. Vitus is jammed, circle back later). The only risk here is running out of time to enter all the sights (which close at 17:00 in summer, or 16:00 in winter); in summer, I'd start at Strahov no later than 14:00.

Nighttime Visit: Least crowded of all is nighttime. True, the sights are closed, but the castle grounds are free, safe, peaceful, floodlit, and open late. The tiny, normally jammed Golden Lane is empty and romantic at night—and no ticket is required.

OFFICIAL SIGHTS AT PRAGUE CASTLE (PRAŽSKÝ HRAD)

This vast and sprawling complex, worth ▲▲, has been the seat of Czech power for centuries. It collects a wide range of sights, including the country's top church, its former royal palace, a higgledy-piggledy lane, and an assortment of history and art museums. (These are listed here in order, from top to bottom, starting at the main gate.) While it's imposing and a bit intimidating to sightseers, the casual visitor finds that a quick and targeted visit is ideal. The sights listed here are part of the official castle complex, and share opening hours and tickets. Which ticket you choose depends on which sights you want to enter—so familiarize yourself with the options before buying your ticket.

Ticket Options: While you can enter the grounds for free, most sights require tickets. For a quick visit, get the 250-Kč "Circuit B" ticket, which hits the highlights (St. Vitus Cathedral, Old Royal Palace, Basilica of St. George, Golden Lane). For a few bucks more, "Circuit A" (350 Kč) adds "The Story of Prague Castle" exhibit and a few other sights worthwhile for those with a healthy interest in history and art. You can buy tickets at three different ticket offices in the castle's second and third courtyards. Lines can be long at one and nonexistent at the next, so if it's crowded, check all three. Climbing St. Vitus Cathedral's Great South Tower requires a separate 150-Kč ticket.

Tours: Tours in English and an audioguide are available, but I'd skip both in favor of this book's self-guided tour (tours-100 Kč plus entry ticket, covers only the cathedral and Old Royal Palace; audioguide-350 Kč plus 500-Kč deposit).

Hours: Castle sights—daily 9:00-17:00, Nov-March until 16:00; castle grounds—daily 5:00-24:00; castle gardens—daily 10:00-18:00 in summer, closed off-season. St. Vitus Cathedral is closed Sunday mornings for Mass, and can be closed unexpectedly at other times. The Great South Tower of St. Vitus Cathedral is open daily 10:00-18:00, until 16:00 in winter, www.hrad.cz.

❷ Self-Guided Tour

· *Begin your visit to the castle complex at...*

Castle Square (Hradčanské Náměstí)

You're standing at the tip of the medieval iceberg called Prague Castle. It's a 1,900-foot-long series of courtyards, churches, and palaces, covering 750,000 square feet—by some measures, the largest castle on earth. In the center of the complex sits St. Vitus Cathedral (the two prickly steeples you see rising above the buildings).

You can't miss the **main entrance:** a gateway with a golden arch, guarded by two fighting-giant statues and two real-life soldiers in their blue-and-white guardhouses. The stoic **guards** make a great photo-op, as does the changing of the guard (on the hour from 5:00-23:00). In fact, there's a guard-changing ceremony at every gate: top, bottom, and side. The best ceremony and music occurs at noon, at the top gate.

Now turn around and survey the broad expanses of Castle Square. Enjoy the awesome city view and the entertaining bands

that play regularly at the gate. (If the Prague Castle Orchestra is playing, say hello to friendly, mustachioed Josef, and consider buying the group's CD—it's terrific.) From the square, stairs lead down to the Little Quarter.

Castle Square was the focal point of medieval power. The archbishop lived (and still lives) in the **Archbishop's Palace**—the ornate, white-and-yellow Rococo palace on the right. The portal on the left leads to the **Sternberg Palace** art museum, with European paintings.

On the left side of the square, the building with a step-gable roofline is **Schwarzenberg Palace,** where the aristocratic families of Český Krumlov "humbly" stayed when they were visiting from their country estates. Notice the envelope-shaped patterns stamped on the exterior. These Renaissance-era adornments etched into wet stucco—called sgraffito—decorate buildings throughout the castle, all over Prague, and across the Czech Republic. Today the castle is an art museum with a collection of Baroque-era Czech paintings and sculpture.

The black Baroque sculpture in the middle of the square is a **plague column.** Erected as a token of gratitude to Mary and the saints for saving the population from epidemic disease, these columns are an integral part of the main squares of many Habsburg towns.

Closer to you, near the overlook, the statue of a man in a business suit (marked *TGM*) honors the father of modern Czechoslovakia: **Tomáš Garrigue Masaryk** (1850-1937). At the end of World War I, Masaryk—a former university prof and pal of Woodrow Wilson—united the Czechs and the Slovaks into one nation and

PRAGUE

Prague Castle Detail

To Pražský Hrad Tram Stop — SECURITY CHECK

ROYAL BALL GAME HALL

RIDING SCHOOL

Royal Gardens

CASTLE

CASTLE

Deer Moat

NORTHERN ENTRANCE

ST. VITUS CATHEDRAL

St. George Courtyard

ROYAL PALACE EXIT

PRAGUE STORY

CAFE

Bastion Gardens

TICKET OFFICES

Second Courtyard

INFO & TICKET OFFICE

CZECH PRESIDENT'S OFFICE

TOWER

CHURCH RUINS

WC

GOLDEN GATE

TOWER ENTRANCE

ST. GEORGE

Third Courtyard

WC

OLD ROYAL PALACE

BULL STAIRCASE

MAIN ENTRANCE & SECURITY CHECK

POST

First Courtyard

EXIT ONLY

MATTHIAS GATE

CHAPEL OF THE HOLY CROSS

PAVILION

ARCH-BISHOP'S PALACE

Castle Square

MASARYK STATUE

TOUR BEGINS

Paradise Gardens

To Strahov Monastery & Pohořelec Tram Stop

GARDENS EXIT ONLY

ZÁMECKÉ SCHODY (STAIRS)

THUNOVSKÁ

KE HRADU

LITTLE

became its first president. He was the only 20th-century leader to live in Prague Castle.

• *Let's enter the castle. Veer left through the security checkpoint and emerge into the **Second Courtyard**. Two **ticket offices** (with information desks) are diagonally across from the Chapel of the Holy Cross. If the line isn't too long, buy a ticket now. Straight ahead as you enter is the...*

St. Vitus Treasury in the Chapel of the Holy Cross

This pricey-to-view collection shows off the accumulated wealth of the cathedral's ecclesiastical gear. The highlight, dating from Charles IV's reign (1360s), is a golden reliquary in the shape of a cross; used during coronation ceremonies, the cross contains what are supposedly the actual thorns, nails, sponge, rope, and fragments of the cross from Jesus' Crucifixion. You'll also see reliquary busts in the shape of saints (Vitus, Wenceslas, and Adalbert); monstrances slathered in diamonds and other precious stones; chalices; and icons. It's a fine collection, but it's outrageously overpriced. Skip it unless you're a monstrance aficionado.

Cost and Hours: 300 Kč, includes torturously dull audioguide; buy ticket at entrance—not at castle ticket office, which sells only a combo-ticket that adds another museum; daily 10:00-18:00, last entry one hour before closing, tel. 224-372-432.

• From the Second Courtyard, proceed into the **Third Courtyard.** You'll be face-to-face with...

▲▲▲St. Vitus Cathedral (Katedrála Sv. Víta)

This towering house of worship—with its flying buttresses and spiny spires—is the top church of the Czech people. Many VIPs from this nation's history—from saints to statesmen—are buried here. You can step into the very congested entry vestibule for a peek at the interior, but it's worth paying for a ticket that lets you go deeper, leave some of the crowds behind, and explore.

Visiting the Cathedral: The two soaring towers of this Gothic wonder rise 270 feet up. The ornate **facade** features pointed arches, elaborate tracery, Flamboyant pinnacles, a rose window, a dozen statues of saints, and gargoyles sticking their tongues out.

So what's up with the four guys in modern suits carved into the stone, as if supporting the big round window on their shoulders?

They're the architects and builders who finished the church six centuries after it was started. Even though church construction got underway in 1344, wars, plagues, and the reforms of Jan Hus conspired to stall its completion. Finally, fueled by a burst of Czech nationalism, Prague's top church was finished in 1929 for the 1,000th Jubilee anniversary of St. Wenceslas. The entrance facade and towers were the last parts to be finished.

• *Enter the cathedral. If it's not too crowded in the free entrance area, work your way to the middle of the church for a good...*

View down the Nave: The church is huge—more than 400 feet long and 100 feet high—and flooded with light. Notice the intricate "net" vaulting on the ceiling, especially at the far end. It's the signature feature of the church's chief architect, Peter Parler (who also built the Charles Bridge).

• *Now make your way through the crowds and pass through the ticket turnstile (left of the roped-off area). The third window on the left wall is worth a close look.*

Mucha Stained-Glass Window: This masterful 1931 Art Nouveau window was designed by Czech artist Alfons Mucha and executed by a stained-glass craftsman (if you like this, you'll love the Mucha Museum in the New Town—see page 88).

Mucha's window was created to celebrate the birth of the

Czech nation and the life of Wenceslas. The main scene (in the four central panels) shows Wenceslas as an impressionable child kneeling at the feet of his Christian grandmother, St. Ludmila. She spreads her arms and teaches him to pray. Wenceslas would grow up to champion Christianity, uniting the Czech people.

Above Wenceslas are the two saints who first brought Christianity to the region: Cyril (the monk in black hood holding the Bible) and his older brother, Methodius (with beard and bishop's garb). They baptize a kneeling convert.

PRAGUE

Follow their story in the side panels, starting in the upper left. Around A.D. 860 (back when Ludmila was just a girl), these two Greek missionary brothers arrive in Moravia to preach. The pagan Czechs have no written language to read the Bible, so (in the next scene below), Cyril bends at his desk to design the necessary alphabet (Glagolitic, which later developed into Cyrillic), while Methodius meditates. In the next three scenes, they travel to Rome and present their newly translated Bible to the pope. But Cyril falls ill, and Methodius watches his kid brother die.

Methodius carries on (in the upper right), becoming bishop of the Czech lands. Next, he's arrested for heresy for violating the pure Latin Bible. He's sent to a lonely prison. When he's finally set free, he retires to a monastery, where he dies mourned by the faithful.

But that's just the beginning of the story. At the bottom center are two beautiful (classic Mucha) maidens, representing the bright future of the Czech and Slovak peoples.

• *Continue circulating around the church, following the one-way, clockwise route.*

The Old Church: Just after the transept, notice there's a slight incline in the floor. That's because the church was constructed in two distinct stages. You're entering the older, 14th-century Gothic section. The front half (where you came in) is a Neo-Gothic extension that was finally completed in the 1920s (which is why much of the stained glass has a modern design). For 400 years—as the nave was being extended—a temporary wall kept the functional altar area protected from the construction zone.

• *In the choir area (on your right), soon after the transept, look for the big, white marble tomb surrounded by a black iron fence.*

Royal Mausoleum: This contains the remains of the first Habsburgs to rule Bohemia, including Ferdinand I, his wife Anne,

Tomáš Garrigue Masaryk (1850-1937)

Tomáš Masaryk was the George Washington of Czechoslovakia. He founded the first democracy in Eastern Europe at the end of World War I, uniting the Czechs and the Slovaks to create Czechoslovakia. Like Václav Havel 70 years later, Masaryk was a politician whose vision extended far beyond the mountains enclosing the Bohemian basin.

Masaryk, from a poor servant family in southern Moravia, earned his Ph.D. in sociology in Vienna, studied in Leipzig, then became a professor of philosophy at Charles University of Prague. By then, he was married to American Charlotta Garrigue, a social revolutionary from a prominent New York family. (The progressive Tomáš took her family name as part of his own.) Through Charlotta, Masaryk was introduced to America's high society, including a young Princeton professor named Woodrow Wilson.

Masaryk was greatly impressed with America, and his admiration for its democratic system became the core of his evolving political creed. He traveled the world and served in the Vienna parliament. At the outbreak of World War I, while most other Czech politicians stayed in Prague and supported the Habsburg Empire, 64-year-old Masaryk went abroad in protest and formed a highly original plan: to create an independent, democratic republic of Czechs and Slovaks. Masaryk and his supporters recruited an army of 100,000 Czech and Slovak soldiers who were willing to fight with the Allies against the Habsburgs, establishing a strong case to put on his friend Woodrow Wilson's Oval Office desk.

On the morning of October 28, 1918, news of the unofficial capitulation of the Habsburgs reached Prague. Supporters of Masaryk's idea quickly took control of the city and proclaimed the free republic. As the people of Prague tore down double-headed eagles (a symbol of the Habsburgs), the country of Czechoslovakia was born.

On November 11, 1918, four years after he had left the country as a political unknown, Masaryk arrived in Prague as the greatest Czech hero since the revolutionary priest Jan Hus. The dignified old man rode through the masses of cheering Czechs on a white horse. He told the jubilant crowd, "Now go home—the work has only started." Throughout the 1920s and 1930s, Masaryk was Europe's most vocal defender of democratic ideals against the rising tide of totalitarian ideologies.

Masaryk is one of only three foreign leaders (along with Gandhi and Churchill) to have a statue in Washington, DC.

and Maximilian II. The tomb dates from 1590, when Prague was a major Habsburg city.

• *Just after the choir, as you begin to circle around the back of the altar, watch on your right for the fascinating, carved-wood...*

Relief of Prague: This depicts the aftermath of the Battle of White Mountain, when the Protestant King Frederic escaped over the Charles Bridge (before it had any statues). Carved in 1630, the relief gives you a peek at old Prague. Find the Týn Church (far left) and St. Vitus Cathedral (far right), which was half-built at that time. Back then, the Týn Church was Hussite, so the centerpiece of its facade is not the Virgin Mary (more of a Catholic figure), but a chalice, a symbol of Jan Hus' ideals. The old city walls—now replaced by the main streets of the city—stand strong. The Jewish Quarter is the flood-prone zone along the riverside below the bridge on the left—land no one else wanted. The weir system on the river—the wooden barriers that help control its flow—survives to this day.

• *Circling around the high altar, you'll see various...*

Tombs in the Apse: Among the graves of medieval kings and bishops is that of **St. Vitus,** shown as a young man clutching a book and gazing up to heaven. Why is this huge cathedral dedicated to this rather obscure saint, who was martyred in Italy in A.D. 303 and never set foot in Bohemia? A piece of Vitus' arm bone (a holy relic) was supposedly acquired by Wenceslas I in 925. Wenceslas built a church to house the relic on this spot, attracting crowds of pilgrims. Vitus became quite popular throughout the Germanic and Slavic lands, and revelers danced on his feast day. (He's now the patron saint of dancers.) At the statue's feet is a rooster, because the saint was thrown into a boiling cauldron along with the bird (the Romans' secret sauce)...but he miraculously survived.

A few steps farther, the big silvery tomb with the angel-borne canopy honors **St. John of Nepomuk.** Locals claim it has more than a ton of silver (for more on St. John of Nepomuk and his halo of stars, see page 73).

Just past the tomb, on the wall of the choir (on the right), is another finely carved, circa-1630 **wood relief** depicting an event that took place right here in St. Vitus: Protestant nobles trash the cathedral's Catholic icons after their (short-lived) victory.

Ahead on the left, look up at the **royal oratory,** a box supported by busy late-Gothic, vine-like ribs. This private box, connected to the king's apartment by a corridor, let the king attend Mass in his jammies. The underside of the balcony is morbidly decorated with dead vines and tree branches, suggesting the pessimism common in the late Gothic period, when religious wars and Ottoman invasions threatened the Czech lands.

• *From here, walk 25 paces and look left through the crowds and door to see the richly decorated chapel containing the tomb of St. Wenceslas. Two roped-off doorways give visitors a look inside. The best view is from the second one, around the corner and to the left, in the transept.*

Wenceslas Chapel: This fancy chapel is the historic heart of the church. It contains the tomb of St. Wenceslas, patron saint of the Czech nation; it's where Bohemia's kings were crowned; and it houses (but rarely displays) the Bohemian crown jewels. The chapel walls are paneled with big slabs of precious and semiprecious stones. The jewel-toned stained-glass windows (from the 1950s) admit a soft light. The chandelier is exceptional. The place feels medieval.

The tomb of St. Wenceslas is a colored-stone coffin topped with an ark. Above the chapel's altar is a statue of Wenceslas, bearing a lance and a double-eagle shield. He's flanked by (painted) angels and the four patron saints of the Czech people. Above Wenceslas are portraits of Charles IV (who built the current church) and his beautiful wife. On the wall to the left of the altar, frescoes depict the saint's life, including the episode where angels arrive with crosses to arm the holy warrior. (For more on Wenceslas, see page 82.)

For centuries, Czech kings were crowned right here in front of Wenceslas' red-draped coffin.

• *Leave the cathedral, turn left (past the public WC), and survey the…*

Third Courtyard

The **obelisk** was erected in 1928—a single piece of granite celebrating the 10th anniversary of the establishment of Czechoslovakia and commemorating the soldiers who fought for its independence. It was originally much taller, but broke in transit—an inauspicious start for a nation destined to last only 70 years.

From here, you get a great look at the sheer size of St. Vitus Cathedral and its fat green **tower** (325 feet tall). Up there is the Czech Republic's biggest **bell** (16.5 tons, from 1549), nicknamed "Zikmund." You can view the bell as you climb up the 287 steps of the tower to the observation deck at the top (buy ticket and enter near sculpture of St. George—a 1960s replica of the 13th-century original).

It's easy to find the church's **Golden Gate** (for centuries the cathedral's main entry)—look for the glittering 14th-century mosaic of the Last Judgment. The modern, cosmopolitan, and ahead-of-his-time Charles IV commissioned this monumental decoration in 1370 in the Italian style. Jesus oversees the action, as some go to heaven and some go to hell. The Czech king and queen kneel directly beneath Jesus and six patron saints. On coronation day, royalty would walk under this arch, a reminder to them (and their subjects) that even those holding great power are not above God's judgment. See the grilled windows above this entryway? That's where the royal crown and national jewels are stashed.

Across from the Golden Gate, in the corner, notice the copper, scroll-like **awning** supported by bulls. This leads to a fine garden just below the castle. The stairway, garden, and other features around the castle were designed by the Slovene architect Jože Plečnik (see page 748). Around the turn of the 20th century, Prague was considered the cultural standard-bearer of the entire Slavic world—making this a particularly prestigious assignment.

• In the corner of the Third Courtyard, near the copper awning, is the…

▲Old Royal Palace (Starý Královský Palác)

The traditional seat of Czech power, this feels like a mostly empty historical shell. But its oversized Vladislav Hall—big enough for

horseback jousting competitions or bustling markets—is impressive. The smaller, adjoining rooms called the "Czech Office" was the site of a famous defenestration—the Czech way of dealing with unwanted politicians: In 1618, angry Czech Protestant nobles poured into these rooms and threw the two Catholic governors out the window. An old law actually permits this act—called defenestration—which usually targets bad politicians. An old print on the glass panel shows the second of Prague's many defenestrations. The two governors landed—fittingly—in a pile of horse manure. Even though they suffered only broken arms and bruised egos, this event kicked off the huge and lengthy Thirty Years' War. The palace also comes with a balcony offering fine views of the surrounding hillsides, and assorted other royal portraits and bric-a-brac.

• The next sight requires the "Circuit A" ticket; if you don't have one, skip down to the next stop.

Otherwise, as you exit the Royal Palace, hook left around the side of the building and backtrack a few steps uphill to find stairs leading down to…

PRAGUE

**The Story of Prague Castle Exhibit
(Příběh Pražského Hradu)**

For those wanting to dig deeper into the history of Prague and its castle, this exhibit features well-described historical artifacts from the very first Czechs through the imported Habsburg monarchy of the 17th century. As this is the main addition to the pricier "Circuit A" ticket, visit here only if you have a bigger-than-average appetite for history.

▲Basilica and Convent of St. George (Bazilika Sv. Jiří)

The oldest-feeling place at the castle, this atmospheric, dimly lit, stripped-down Romanesque chapel offers a subdued contrast to the big and bombastic spaces elsewhere.

The church was founded by Wenceslas' dad around 920, and the present structure dates from the 12th century. (Its Baroque facade came later.) Inside, the place is beautiful in its simplicity. Notice the characteristic thick walls and rounded arches. In those early years, building techniques were not yet advanced enough to use those arches for the ceiling—it's made of wood instead.

This was the royal burial place before St. Vitus was built, so the tombs here contain the remains of the earliest Czech kings. Climb the stairs that frame either side of the altar to study the area around the apse. St. Wenceslas' grandmother, Ludmila, was reburied here in 925. Her stone tomb is in the space just to the right of the altar. Inside the archway leading to her tomb, look for her portrait. Holding a branch and a book, she looks quite cultured for a 10th-century woman.

• *As you exit, notice the building across the lane from the basilica (with the columned and curved portico)—this was Maria Theresa's* **Institute for Noblewomen,** *created in the 1750s to empower and educate aristocratic but impoverished ladies.*

Now continue walking downhill on that lane. You'll see the basilica's Romanesque nave and towers—a strong contrast to the pretty Baroque facade. Farther down, to the left, were the residences of soldiers and craftsmen, and to the right, tucked together, were the palaces of Catholic nobility who wanted both to be close to power and able to band together should the Protestants grab the upper hand. The next street on the left leads up to the popular Golden Lane. As you pass through the entry turnstiles, the crowds turn right, but don't overlook the sights to your left (including a tiny café).

▲Golden Lane (Zlatá Ulička)

Named for the goldsmiths who likely worked here, this medieval merchant street retains its historic aura. When uncrowded, this atmospheric lane—lined with endearing little exhibits on the commerce and customs of a bygone era—is fun to explore. When busy, as it typically is, it's miserable.

• *Leaving the Castle Complex: Directly below the Golden Lane are two worthwhile sights that are not part of the castle complex—the **Toy Museum** and **Lobkowicz Palace**, both described later.*

Exit the complex through a fortified door at the bottom end of the castle. A scenic rampart just below the lower gate offers a commanding view of the city. From there, you can head to the nearest Metro/tram station, Strahov Monastery, Little Quarter, or Castle Square.

*To reach **Malostranská Station:** Follow the 700-some steps down the steep lane called Staré Zámecké Schody ("Old Castle Stairs") directly back to the riverbank. Alternatively, for a gentler descent, start heading down the steep lane. About 40 yards below the castle exit, a gate on the left leads you through a scenic vineyard and past the recommended Villa Richter restaurants to the station.*

*To reach the top of the **Little Quarter** or **Castle Square/Strahov Monastery,** as you leave the castle gate, take a hard right and stroll through the long, delightful park (free, daily 10:00-18:00 or later, closed Nov–March). Along the way, notice the Modernist layout of the Na Valech Gardens, designed by the 1920s court architect, Jože Plečnik of Slovenia. Halfway through the long park is a viewpoint overlooking the terraced Pálffy Gardens (80 Kč, same hours as park). You can zigzag down through these gardens into the Little Quarter. Or, if you want to walk to Castle Square, continue uphill along the castle wall and through the garden to the square. You can hike up to the Strahov Monastery from here.*

BELOW THE CASTLE

Extend your visit by dropping by a nobleman's palace and a toy museum with an entire floor devoted to the Barbie doll. These sights require separate admission tickets; they're not included in any castle tickets.

▲▲Lobkowicz Palace (Lobkowiczký Palác)

This palace, at the bottom of the castle complex, displays the private collection of a prominent Czech noble family, including paintings, ceramics, and musical scores. The Lobkowiczes' property was confiscated twice in the 20th century: first by the Nazis at the beginning of World War II, and then by the communists in 1948. In 1990, William Lobkowicz, then a Boston investment banker, returned to Czechoslovakia to fight a legal battle to reclaim his family's property and, eventually, to restore the castles and palaces to their former state. A conscientious host, William Lobkowicz himself narrates the delightful, included audioguide. While the National Gallery may seem a more logical choice for the art enthusiast, the obvious care that went into creating this museum, the collection's variety, and the personal insight that it opens into the past and present of Czech nobility make the Lobkowicz worth an hour of your time.

Cost and Hours: 275 Kč, includes audioguide, daily 10:00-18:00, tel. 233-312-925, www.lobkowicz.cz.

Eating: The Lobkowicz Palace Café, by the exit, has a creative, cosmopolitan menu and stunning panoramic views of the city (daily 10:00-18:00). The charming young man you may see selling ice cream out front is William's son, Will.

Toy Museum (Muzeum Hraček)
Across the street from Lobkowicz Palace, a courtyard and a long wooden staircase lead to two entertaining floors of old toys and dolls, thoughtfully described in English. You'll see a century of teddy bears, some 19th-century model train sets, old Christmas decor, and an incredible Barbie collection. Find the buxom 1959 first edition, and you'll understand why these capitalistic sirens of material discontent weren't allowed here until 1989.

Cost and Hours: 70 Kč, 120-Kč family ticket, daily 9:30-17:30, WC next to entrance.

ABOVE THE CASTLE
The Strahov Monastery, with its landmark domes, sits above the castle. Remember: If you'd like to combine the monastery with your castle visit, it's easy to ride tram #22 up to the Pohořelec stop (beyond the castle), visit the monastery, enjoy the views, then walk 10 minutes down to Castle Square—passing Loreta Church on the way. (However, if you're rushing to beat the morning crowds at the castle, it's better to head straight for St. Vitus Cathedral in the castle complex, then backtrack to Strahov later.) To locate these sights, see the map on page 104.

▲Strahov Monastery and Library (Strahovský Klášter a Knihovna)
Medieval monasteries were a mix of industry, agriculture, and education, as well as worship and theology. In its heyday, Strahov Monastery had a booming economy of its own, with vineyards, a brewery, and a sizable beer hall—all open once again. You can

explore the monastery complex, check out the beautiful old library, and even enjoy a brew (no longer monk-made, but still refreshing).

Cost and Hours: Grounds—free and always open; library—100 Kč, extra 50 Kč to take photos—strictly enforced, daily 9:00-12:00 & 13:00-17:00, www.strahovskyklaster.cz. A pay WC is just to the right of the monastery entrance.

Visiting the Monastery and Library: The monastery's **main church,** dedicated to the Assumption of St. Mary, is an originally Romanesque structure deco-rated by the monks in textbook Baroque (usually closed, but look through the gate inside the front door to see its interior). Notice the grand effect of the Baroque architecture—both rhythmic and theatric. Go ahead, inhale. That's the scent of Baroque.

Buy your ticket in the adjacent building, and head up the stairs to the **library,** offering a peek at how enlightened thinkers in the 18th century influenced learning. The **display cases** in the library gift shop show off illuminated manuscripts, described in English. Some are in old Czech, but because the Enlightenment promoted the universality of knowledge (and Latin was the universal language of Europe's educated elite), there was little place for regional dialects—therefore, few books here are in the Czech language.

Two rooms (seen only from the doors) are filled with 10th- to 17th-century books, shelved under elaborately painted ceilings. The theme of the first and bigger hall is **philosophy,** with the history of Western man's pursuit of knowledge painted on the ceiling. The second hall—down a hallway lined with antique furniture—focuses on **theology.** As the Age of Enlightenment began to take hold in Europe at the end of the 18th century, monasteries still controlled the books. Notice the gilded, locked case containing the *libri prohibiti* (prohibited books) at the end of the room, above the mirror. Only the abbot had the key, and you had to have his blessing to read these books—by writers such as Nicolas Copernicus, Jan Hus, Jean-Jacques Rousseau, and even including the French encyclopedia.

The **hallway** connecting the two library rooms was filled with cases illustrating the new practical approach to natural sciences.

In the crowded area near the philosophy hall, find the dried-up elephant trunks (flanking the narwhal or unicorn horn) and one of the earliest models of an electricity generator.

Nearby: That hoppy smell you're enjoying in front of the monastery is the recommended **Klášterní Pivovar,** where they brew beer just as monks have for centuries (in the little courtyard directly across from the library entrance; described on page 143).

Tucked in another courtyard across from the Strahov Monastery, the **Museum of Miniatures** (Muzeum Miniatur) displays 40 teeny exhibits—each under a microscope—crafted by an artist from a remote corner of Siberia. Yes, you could fit the entire museum in a carry-on-size suitcase, but good things sometimes come in very, very small packages—it's fascinating to see minutiae such as a padlock on the leg of an ant (100 Kč, kids-50 Kč, daily 9:00-17:00, Strahovské Nádvoří 11, tel. 233-352-371).

Just below the monastery, don't miss the **garden terrace** (look for the aptly named Bellavista Restaurant), with exquisite views over the domes and spires of Prague. The area just below the restaurant tables is free and open to visitors.

• *After enjoying the views, head through the small hole in the wall near the Museum of Miniatures, and go down the street to* **Loretánská street.** *Turning right, follow Loretánská to the castle, by way of...*

Loreta Church

This church has been a hit with pilgrims for centuries, thanks to its dazzling bell tower, peaceful yet plush cloister, sparkling treasury, and much-venerated Holy House. In the middle of the cloister courtyard, you'll find what's considered by some pilgrims to be part of Mary's actual home in Nazareth. You'll also see one of Prague's most beautiful Baroque churches, a fine treasury collection (upstairs), and—in a tiny chapel in one corner—"St. Bearded Woman," the patron saint of unhappy marriages.

Cost and Hours: 150 Kč, daily April-Oct 9:00-17:00, Nov-March 9:30-16:00, audioguide-150 Kč, tel. 220-516-740, www.loreta.cz.

Nearby: The parking-lot square in front of the Loreta Church has a statue of **Edvard Beneš,** the second president of Czechoslovakia (in the 1930s and 1940s), who led the government-in-exile during the Nazi occupation. His forced relocation of Sudetenland Germans following World War II has left him with a controversial legacy; notice the slumping posture and look of worry on his face. (For more on Beneš, see the sidebar on page 192.)

Facing the church from across the square is the **Černín Palace,** a civic building that was the unfortunate site of a modern-day defenestration. In the spring of 1948, soon after the communists took over, an extremely popular Czechoslovak politician (Jan Masaryk, the son of the first president of Czechoslovakia) was found dead in this building's courtyard, below the bathroom window—an apparent suicide. When the official secret-police files were unsealed after 1989, they revealed that Masaryk had been assassinated by Russian agents.

ROYAL SUMMER PALACE AND ROYAL GARDENS

These minor sights, above Prague Castle, are only worth visiting if you get off tram #22 at Královský Letohrádek (the Royal Summer Palace is across the street from this stop, WC at gate).

Royal Summer Palace (Královský Letohrádek)

This gift of love is like a Czech Taj Mahal, presented by Emperor Ferdinand I to his beloved Queen Anne. It's the purest Renaissance building in town. You can't go inside, but the building's detailed reliefs are worth a close look.

• *From here, set your sights on the cathedral's lacy, black spires marking the castle's entrance. Stroll through the...*

Royal Gardens (Královská Zahrada)

Once the private grounds and residence (you'll see the building) of the communist presidents, these were opened to the public with the coming of freedom under Václav Havel. Walk through these gardens (with lovely views of St. Vitus Cathedral) to the gate, which leads you over the moat and into Castle Square, the entrance to the vast castle complex.

Cost and Hours: Free, April-Oct daily 10:00-18:00, closed Nov-March.

Shopping in Prague

Prague's entire Old Town seems designed to bring out the shopper in visitors. Puppets, glass, crystal, and garnets (deep-red gemstones) are traditional; these days, fashion and design (especially incorporating the city's rich Art Nouveau heritage) are also big business. Most shops are open on weekdays from 9:00 until 17:00 or 18:00—and often longer, especially for tourist-oriented shops. Some close on Saturday afternoons and/or all day Sunday.

SHOPPING STREETS IN THE CENTER

If you'd like to simply window-shop in the tourist zone, consider the following streets.

Ungelt, the courtyard tucked behind the Týn Church just

off of the Old Town Square, is packed with touristy but decent-quality shops. Material has a fine selection of contemporary-style bead jewelry, and Botanicus is an excellent herbal cosmetics shop. Fajans Majolica has traditional blue-and-white Czech pottery and two stores sell marionettes: V Ungeltu and Hračky, Loutky ("Toys, Puppets").

Michalská, a semihidden lane right in the thick of the tourist zone, has a variety of shops (from the Small Market Square/Malé Náměstí near the Astronomical Clock, go through the big stone gateway marked *459*).

On **Havelská** street, you can browse the open-air Havelská Market, a touristy but enjoyable place to shop for inexpensive handicrafts and fresh produce (daily 9:00-18:00, two long blocks south of the Old Town Square; see page 69).

Celetná, exiting the Old Town Square to the right of Týn Church, is lined with big stores selling all the traditional Czech goodies. Tourists wander endlessly here, mesmerized by the window displays.

Na Příkopě, the mostly pedestrianized street following the former moat between the Old Town and the New Town, has the city center's handiest lineup of modern shopping malls. The best is Slovanský Dům ("Slavic House," at #22), where you'll wander past a 10-screen multiplex deep into a world of classy restaurants and designer shops surrounding a peaceful, parklike inner courtyard. Černá Růže ("Black Rose," at #12) has a great Japanese restaurant around a small garden; Moser's flagship crystal showroom is also here. The Galerie Myslbek, directly across the street, has fancy stores in a space built to Prague's scale. Na Příkopě street opens up into Republic Square (Náměstí Republiky)—boasting Prague's biggest mall, Palladium, hidden behind a pink Neo-Romanesque facade. Across the square is the communist-era brown steel-and-glass 1980s department store Kotva ("Anchor"), an obsolete beast on the verge of extinction.

Národní Třída (National Street), which continues past Na Příkopě in the opposite direction (toward the river), is less touristy and lined with some inviting stores. **Karlova,** the tourist-clogged drag connecting the Old Town Square to the Charles Bridge, should be avoided entirely. Shops along here sell made-in-China trinkets at too-high prices to lazy and gullible tourists.

SOUVENIR IDEAS

Czech Puppets: It takes a rare artist to turn pieces of wood into nimble puppets, and prices for the real deal can reach into the thousands of dollars. But given that puppets have a glorious past and vibrant present in the Czech Republic, even a simple jester, witch, or Pinocchio can make a thoughtful memento of your Czech adventure. You'll see cheap trinket puppets at souvenir stands across town. Buying a higher-quality keepsake is more expensive (starting in the $100 range). Here are a few better options to consider:

Marionety Truhlář, near the Little Quarter end of Charles Bridge (U Lužického Semináře 5); **Galerie Michael,** just a few doors down (U Lužického Semináře 7, www.marionettesmichael.cz); the no-name **loutky** ("Puppets") shop at the top of Nerudova (at #51, www.loutky.cz); and, in the Ungelt Courtyard, **Hračky, Loutky** ("Toys, Puppets").

Glass and Crystal: Legally, to be called "crystal" (or "lead crystal"), it must contain at least 24 percent lead oxide, which lends the glass that special, prismatic sparkle. The lead also adds weight, makes the glass easier to cut, and produces a harmonious ringing when flicked. ("Crystal glass" has a smaller percentage of lead.)

Well-respected sources for Czech glass and crystal include **Moser,** the most famous Czech brand—and one of the most expensive (flagship store at the Černá Růže shopping mall at Na Příkopě 12, plus another branch on the Old Town Square www.moser-glass.com); **Artěl,** with a small but eye-pleasing selection of Art Nouveau- and Art Deco-inspired glassware (for locations, see listing later, under "Art Nouveau Design Shops"); and **Blue,** a chain specializing in sleek, modern designs—many of them in the namesake hue (several locations, including Malé Náměstí 13, Pařížská 3, Melantrichova 6, Celetná 2, and Mostecká 24, and at the airport; www.bluepraha.cz). **Celetná street** is lined with touristy glass shops, some with a wide selection suitable for a surgical strike for a crystal souvenir.

For a unique, experiential take on Czech glass, visit Antonin Manto-Mrnka's **Galerie GOF+FA** (on the Small Market Square at Malé Náměstí 6, www.mantogallery.com).

Bohemian Garnets *(Granát):* These blood-colored gemstones have unique refractive—some claim even curative—properties. If you buy garnet jewelry, shop around, use a reputable dealer, and ask for a certificate of authenticity to avoid buying a glass imitation (these are common). Of the many garnet shops in Prague's shopping districts, **Turnov Granát Co-op** has the largest selection. It's

Shopping Streets & Areas
1. Ungelt Courtyard
2. Michalská
3. Celetná
4. Na Příkopě
5. Národní Třída

Puppets
6. Marionety Truhlář & Galerie Michael
7. To Loutky

Glass & Crystal
8. Moser (2)
9. Artěl Glass (3)
10. Blue (5)
11. More Crystal Shops
12. Galerie GOF+FA

Jewelry
13. Turnov Granát Co-op (3)
14. Studio Šperk
15. More Garnet Shops (3)
16. To Koralky

Shopping in Prague

PRAGUE

Cosmetics/Gifts
17 Manufaktura (5)

Fashion/Design
18 Pařížská Street
19 Eliška Krásnohorské St.
20 Dlouhá Street
21 Baťa Shoes
22 Tribu
23 Benediktská Street
24 Futurista Universum

25 Modernista (3)
26 To Modernista Pavilon
27 Kubista

Books/Maps/Posters
28 Shakespeare & Sons
29 Franz Kafka Society
30 Kiwi Map Store
31 ProVás Posters

Outdoor Markets
32 Havelská Market
33 Republic Square Market

refreshingly unpretentious, with a vaguely retro-communist vibe (shops at Dlouhá 28, Panská 1, and inside the Pánská Pasáž at Na Příkopě 23; www.granat.eu). **J. Drahoňovský's Studio Šperk** is a more upscale-feeling shop with more creative designs (Dlouhá 19, www.drahonovsky.cz). Additional shops specializing in Turnov garnets are at Dlouhá 1, Celetná 8, and Maiselova 3.

Costume Jewelry and Beads: You'll see *bižutérie* (costume jewelry) advertised all over town. Round, glass beads—sometimes called Druk beads—are popular, and can range from large marble-sized beads to minuscule "seed beads." The biggest producer of glass beads is Jablonex, from the town of Jablonec nad Nisou. A handy spot to check out some stylish, modern pieces is **Material,** in the Ungelt courtyard behind Týn Church. They have a fun selection of seed beads, as well as some finer pieces (www.i-material. com). **Koralky,** one of the best-supplied bead shops in Prague, is a bit farther out; take the Metro's green line to the Jiřího z Poděbrad stop (Vinohradská 76, www.koralky.cz).

Organic Cosmetics and Handmade Gifts: Manufaktura is your classy, one-stop shop for good-quality Czech gifts, from organic cosmetics to handicrafts—all handmade in the Czech Republic. You'll find many branch locations in Prague, including several near the Old Town Square (at Melantrichova 17, Celetná 12, and Karlova 26); at Republic Square (in the Palladium mall); near the Little Quarter end of the Charles Bridge (Mostecká 17); in the main train station; and even along Prague Castle's Golden Lane (www.manufaktura.cz). **Botanicus** is similar but smaller, (in the Ungelt courtyard behind Týn Church, www.botanicus.cz).

Fashion and Design: Czechs have a unique sense of fashion. One popular trend is garments that are adorned with embroidery, leather, beads, hand-painted designs, or other flourishes—all handmade and therefore unique. Shops selling these come and go, and in many cases several small designers work together and share a boutique—look for an "atelier." Vintage clothes are also as popular among young Czech hipsters as they are with their American counterparts.

The Jewish Quarter's **Pařížská street** has the highest concentration of big-name international designers, but for something more local, focus on some of the side-streets that run parallel to Pařížská. One block over, **Elišky Krásnohorské street** has the most engaging lineup of unpretentious local fashion. A block farther east, more boutiques line **Dušní street.** A short walk away, **Dlouhá street**—which exits the Old Town Square near the Jan Hus statue—offers more Czech designers.

On and Near Wenceslas Square: Fashionistas are sometimes surprised to learn that the famous and well-respected **Baťa** shoe brand is not Italian, but Czech. Their seven-story flagship store, on Wenceslas Square (at #6), is nirvana for shoe lovers. Nearby, one of the pavilions inside the Franciscan Garden (hiding just off of Wenceslas Square) houses **Tribu,** a fun and youthful fashion boutique with clothes, jewelry, and other unique pieces (www.tribu.cz).

Funky Hipster Design: Benediktská, a tiny street tucked in a quiet corner of the Old Town, has a little cluster of creative boutiques.

Art Nouveau Design Shops: Prague is Europe's best Art Nouveau city—and several shops give you a chance to take home some of that eye-pleasing style, in the form of glasswear, home decor, linens, posters, and other items. **Artěl**—a chain owned by an American (Karen Feldman) who fell in love with Prague and its unique sense of style—is thoughtfully curated. There are three locations (one directly behind the Municipal House at Celetná 29, and shops near either end of the Charles Bridge—on the Old Town side at Platnéřská 7, and on the Little Quarter side at U Lužického Semináře 7; www.artelglass.com). Other good design shops include **Futurista Universum,** (shares an entrance with the recommended Klub Architektů restaurant at Betlémské Náměstí 5a, www.futurista.cz), **Modernista** (downstairs inside the Municipal House, plus a flagship store in a sleek, gorgeously restored former train station in the Vinohrady neighborhood at Vinohradská 50, www.modernista.cz), and **Kubista,** in the House of the Black Madonna (Ovocný Trh 19, www.kubista.cz).

BOOKS, MAPS, POSTERS, AND MUSIC

Try **Shakespeare and Sons** (with a big selection in the Little Quarter) or **Franz Kafka Society** (with a smaller selection in the Jewish Quarter), both open daily and described on page 45. **Kiwi Map Store,** near Wenceslas Square, is Prague's best source for maps and travel guides (Jungmannova 23).

ProVás is a poster shop stocking a wide array of unique posters—originals, reprints, and lots of vintage ads from the 1920s (closed Sat-Sun, Rybná 21, www.agenturaprovas.cz).

What Not to Buy: Many Prague souvenir shops sell non-Czech (especially Russian) items to tourists who don't know better. Amber may be pretty, but—considering it's found along the Baltic Sea coast—obviously doesn't originate from this landlocked country. Stacking dolls, fur hats, and vodka flasks also fall into this category.

Entertainment in Prague

Prague booms with live and inexpensive theater, classical music, jazz, and pop entertainment. Everything is listed in several monthly cultural events programs (free at TIs).

Buying Tickets: You'll be tempted to gather fliers as you wander through town. Don't bother. To really understand all your options (the street Mozarts are pushing only their own concerts), drop by a **Via Musica** box office. There are two: One is next to Týn Church on the Old Town Square (daily 10:30-19:30, tel. 224-826-969), and the other is in the Little Quarter across from the Church of St. Nicholas (daily 10:30-18:00, tel. 257-535-568). A posted event schedule clear-

ly shows everything that's playing today and tomorrow, including tourist concerts, Black Light Theater, and marionette shows, with photos of each venue and a map (www.viamusica.cz). If you don't see a posted list of today's events, just ask for it.

Ticketpro sells tickets for the serious concert venues and most music clubs (English-language reservations tel. 296-329-999, www.ticketpro.cz). Ticketpro has several outlets: at Rytířská 31 (daily 8:00-12:00 & 12:30-16:30, between Havelská Market and Estates Theater); in the Lucerna Arcade (daily 9:30-18:00, on Wenceslas Square, opposite Grand Hotel Evropa); and in the privately run Tourist Center at Rytířská 12 (Mon-Fri 11:00-19:00, closed Sat-Sun). As with most ticket box offices, you'll pay about 30 Kč extra per ticket.

Dress Code: Locals dress up for the more "serious" concerts, opera, and ballet, but many tourists wear casual clothes—as long as you don't show up in shorts, sneakers, or flip-flops, you'll be fine.

BLACK LIGHT THEATER

A kind of mime/modern dance variety show, Black Light Theater has no language barrier and is, for some, more entertaining than a classical concert. Unique to Prague, Black Light Theater originated in the 1960s as a playful and mystifying theater of the absurd. These days, aficionados and critical visitors lament that it's becoming a cheesy variety show, while others are uncomfortable with the sexual flavor of some acts. Still, it's an unusual theater experience that many enjoy. Shows last about an hour and a half. Avoid the first four rows, which get you so close that it ruins the illusion. Each of these four theaters has its own spin on what Black Light is supposed to be. (The other Black Light theaters advertised around town aren't as good.)

Ta Fantastika tries to be poetic, with haunting puppetry and a little artistic nudity, but it's less "fun" than some of the others. Of these choices, it takes itself perhaps the most seriously (680 Kč, *Aspects of Alice* nightly at 18:00 and 21:30, reserved seating, near east end of Charles Bridge at Karlova 8, tel. 222-221-366, www.tafantastika.cz).

Image Theater has more mime and elements of the absurd, and tries to incorporate more dance along with the illusions. They offer the most diverse lineup of programs, including a "best of" and several short-term, themed shows—recent topics have been African safari and outer space. Some find Image's shows to be a bit too slapsticky for their tastes (480 Kč, nightly at 20:00, open seating—arrive early to grab a good spot, just off Old Town Square at Pařížská 4, tel. 222-314-448, www.imagetheatre.cz).

Laterna Magika, in the big, glassy building next to the National Theater, mixes Black Light techniques with film projection, dance, and other elements into a multimedia performance that draws Czech audiences. Because the theater is used for other types of performances as well, this Black Light show is staged less frequently than some of the others—but if they have a performance while you're in town, they're well worth considering (680 Kč; *Wonderful Circus, Legends of Magic, Graffiti;* typically 3-4 nights a week at 20:00, tel. 224-931-482, www.laterna.cz).

Srnec Theater is an ensemble run by founder Jiří Srnec (credited with inventing the Black Light Theater concept in 1961) and his son. Fittingly, this is the most "back-to-basics" option—while narratively simplistic, it revels in the childlike, goofy wonder of the effects. Their primary show, *Anthology,* traces the development of the art over the past 50 years; they also plan additional shows in the future (380-680 Kč, generally weekly at 20:00, in the same courtyard as the Museum of Communism and the McDonald's at Na Příkopě 10, mobile 774-574-475, www.srnectheatre.com).

CLASSICAL CONCERTS

Each day, six to eight classical concerts designed for tourists fill delightful Old World halls and churches with music of the crowd-pleasing sort: Vivaldi, Best of Mozart, Most Famous Arias, and works by the famous Czech composer Antonín Dvořák. Concerts typically cost 400-1,000 Kč, start anywhere from 13:00 to 21:00, and last about an hour. Typical venues include two buildings on the Little Quarter Square (the Church of St. Nicholas and the Prague Academy of Music in Liechtenstein Palace), the Klementinum's Chapel of Mirrors, the Old Town Square (in a different Church of St. Nicholas), and the stunning Smetana Hall in the Municipal House. Musicians vary from excellent to amateurish.

To ensure a memorable venue and top-notch musicians, choose a concert in one of three places—the Municipal House's Smetana Hall, the Rudolfinum, or the National Theater—featuring Prague's finest ensembles (such as the Prague Symphony Orchestra or Czech Philharmonic).

The **Prague Symphony Orchestra** plays in the gorgeous Art Nouveau Municipal House. Their ticket office is on the right side of the building, on U Obecního Domu street opposite Hotel Paris (Mon-Fri 10:00-18:00, tel. 222-002-336, www.fok.cz). A smaller selection of tickets is sold in the information office inside the Municipal House.

The **Czech Philharmonic** performs in the classical Neo-Renaissance Rudolfinum in the Jewish Quarter. Their ticket office is on the right side of the Rudolfinum, under the stairs (250-1,000 Kč, open Mon-Fri 10:00-18:00, and until just before the show starts on concert days, on Palachovo Náměstí on the Old Town side of Mánes Bridge, tel. 227-059-352, www.ceskafilharmonie.cz).

Both orchestras perform in their home venues about five nights a month from September through June. Most other nights these spaces are rented to agencies that organize tourist concerts of varying quality for double the price. Check first whether your visit coincides with either ensemble's performance.

You'll find tickets for tourist concerts advertised and sold on the street in front of these buildings. Although the music may not be the finest, these concerts do allow you to experience music in one of Prague's best venues on the night of your choice. This is especially worth considering if you want to enjoy classical music in the Municipal House when the Symphony Orchestra isn't in town (but make sure your concert takes place in the building's Smetana Hall rather than in the much smaller Grégr Hall).

OPERA AND BALLET

A handy ticket office for the three following theaters is in the little square (Ovocný Trh) behind the Estates Theater, next to a pizzeria.

The **National Theater** (Národní Divadlo), on the New Town side of Legií Bridge, is best for opera and ballet. Enjoy its Neo-Renaissance interior (300-1,000 Kč, shows from 19:00, tel. 224-912-673, www.narodni-divadlo.cz).

The **Estates Theater** (Stavovské Divadlo) is where Mozart premiered and personally directed many of his most beloved works (see page 66). *Don Giovanni, The Marriage of Figaro,* and *The Magic Flute* are on the program a couple of times each month (800-1,400 Kč, shows from 20:00, between the Old Town Square and the New Town on a square called Ovocný Trh, tel. 224-214-339, www.narodni-divadlo.cz).

The **State Opera** (Státní Opera), formerly the German Theater, is less architecturally rewarding than the National Theater. Operas by non-Czech composers are typically performed here (400-1,200 Kč, at 19:00 or 20:00, 101 Wilsonova, on the busy street between the main train station and Wenceslas Square—see map on page 83, tel. 224-227-693, www.narodni-divadlo.cz).

OTHER MUSIC

Young locals keep Prague's many music clubs in business. Most clubs—from rock to folk to jazz—are neighborhood institutions with decades of tradition, generally holding only 100-200 people. Most charge a cover for the music.

In the Old Town: Roxy, a few blocks from the Old Town Square, features live bands from outside the country twice a week—anything from Irish punk to Balkan brass—and experimental DJs other nights. (Dlouhá 33, www.roxy.cz).

Agharta Jazz Club, which showcases some of the best Czech and Eastern European jazz, is just steps off the Old Town Square in a cool Gothic cellar. (Železná 16, www.agharta.cz).

In the New Town: Lucerna Music Bar is popular for its '80s and '90s video parties on Friday and Saturday nights (Vodičkova 36—in the basement of Lucerna Arcade, www.musicbar.cz). The small **Reduta Jazz Club** launches you straight into the 1960s-era classic jazz scene (when jazz provided an escape for trapped freedom lovers in communist times). The top Czech jazzmen—Stivín and Koubková—regularly perform. President Bill Clinton once played the sax here (on Národní street next to Café Louvre, www.redutajazzclub.cz).

In the Little Quarter: Malostranská Beseda—with its tight, steamy, standing-room-only space—is the only club in the center with daily live performances (Malostranské Náměstí 21, see map on page 144, www.malostranska-beseda.cz).

Sleeping in Prague

Peak months for hotels in Prague are May, June, and September. Easter and New Year's are the most crowded times, when prices are jacked up a bit. Here I've assigned rankings based on peak season pricing. But, if you're traveling in July or August, you'll find rates generally 15 percent lower, and from November through March, about 30 percent lower. For tips on hotel rates and deals, making reservations, and other accommodation options—including apartments and other short-term rentals—see page 1071.

Sleep Code

Hotels are classified based on the average price of a standard double room with breakfast in high season. I've given *very* rough conversions to dollars using 25 Kč = $1.

$$$$ **Splurge:** Most rooms over 3,400 Kč (roughly $135)
 $$$ **Pricier:** 2,600-3,400 Kč ($105-135)
  $$ **Moderate:** 1,800-2,600 Kč ($70-105)
   $ **Budget:** 1,000-1,800 Kč ($40-70)
   ¢ **Backpacker:** Under 1,000 Kč ($40)
 RS% **Rick Steves discount**

Unless otherwise noted, credit cards are accepted, hotel staff speak basic English, and free Wi-Fi is available. Comparison-shop by checking prices at several hotels (on each hotel's own website, on a booking site, or by email). For the best deal, *book directly with the hotel.* Ask for a discount if paying in cash; if the listing includes **RS%,** request a Rick Steves discount.

OLD TOWN HOTELS AND PENSIONS

You'll pay higher prices to stay in the Old Town, but for many travelers, the convenience is worth the expense. These places are all within a 10-minute walk of the Old Town Square.

$$$$ **Hotel Metamorphis** is a splurge, with solidly renovated rooms in Prague's former caravanserai (hostel for foreign merchants in the 12th century). Its breakfast room is in a spacious medieval cellar with modern artwork. Some of the street-facing rooms, located above two popular bars, are noisy at night (Malá Štupartská 5, tel. 221-771-011, www.hotelmetamorphis.cz, hotel@metamorphis.cz).

$$$$ **Hotel Maximilian** is a sleek, mod, 71-room place with Art Deco black design; big, plush living rooms; and all the business services and comforts you'd expect in a four-star hotel. It faces a church on a perfect little square just a short walk from the action (Haštalská 14, tel. 225-303-111, www.maximilianhotel.com, reservation@maximilianhotel.com).

$$$$ **Design Hotel Jewel Prague** (U Klenotníka), with 11 modern, comfortable rooms in a plain building, is three blocks off the Old Town Square (RS%, no elevator, Rytířská 3, tel. 224-211-699, www.hoteljewelprague.com, info@jewelhotel.cz).

$$$ **Brewery Hotel u Medvídků** ("By the Bear Cubs") has 43 comfortable rooms in a big, rustic, medieval shell with dark wood furniture. Upstairs, you'll find lots of beams—or, if you're not careful, they'll find you (RS%, "historical" rooms cost slightly more, apartment available, Na Perštýně 7, tel. 224-211-916, www.umedvidku.cz, info@umedvidku.cz, manager Vladimír). The pension runs a popular beer-hall restaurant with live music most Fri-

Hotels in Prague's Old Town

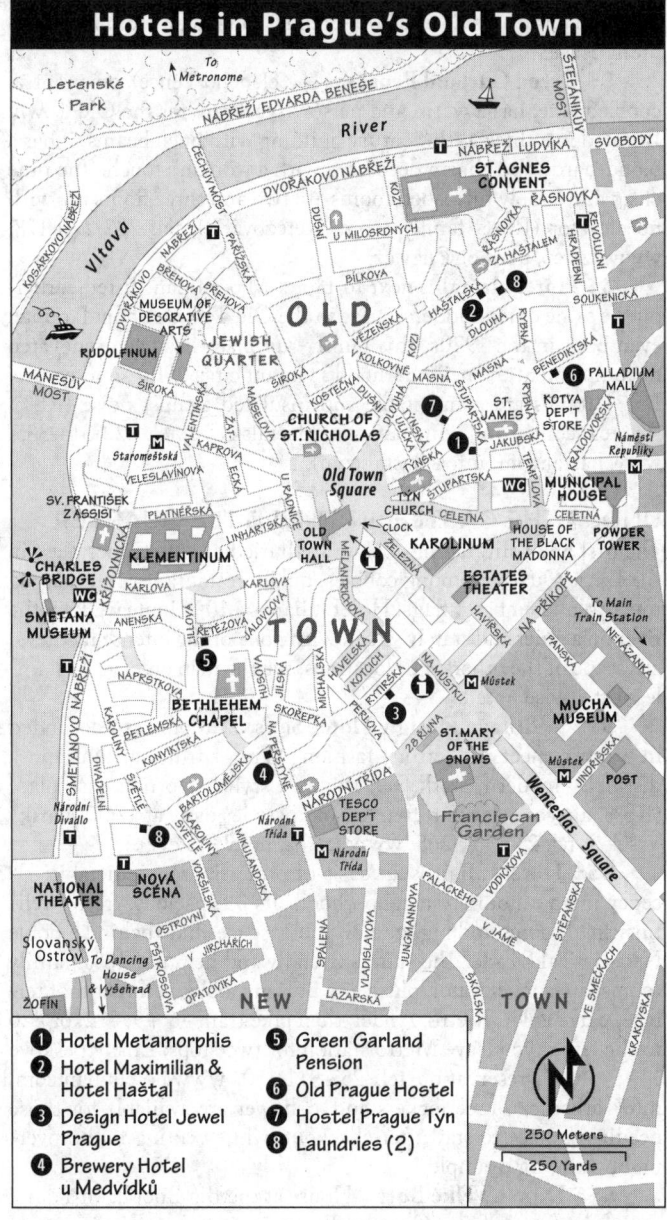

PRAGUE

1 Hotel Metamorphis
2 Hotel Maximilian & Hotel Haštal
3 Design Hotel Jewel Prague
4 Brewery Hotel u Medvídků
5 Green Garland Pension
6 Old Prague Hostel
7 Hostel Prague Týn
8 Laundries (2)

days and Saturdays until 23:00—request an inside room for maximum peace.

$$ Green Garland Pension (U Zeleného Věnce), on a central cobbled lane, has a warm and personal feel rare for the Old Town. Located in a thick 14th-century building with open beams, it has a blond-hardwood charm decorated with a woman's touch. The nine clean and simply furnished rooms are two and three floors up, with no elevator (RS%, family room, Řetězová 10, tel. 222-220-178, www.uzv.cz, pension@uzv.cz).

$$ Hotel Haštal is next to Hotel Maximilian (listed earlier) on the same quiet, hidden square in the Old Town. A popular hotel even back in the 1920s, this family-run place has been renovated to complement the neighborhood's vibrant circa-1900 architecture. Its 31 rooms are comfortable and insulated against noise (RS%, free tea, coffee, and wine, air-con, Haštalská 16, tel. 222-314-335, www.hastal.com, info@hastal.com).

UNDER THE CASTLE, IN THE LITTLE QUARTER

The first and third listings below are buried on quiet lanes deep in the Little Quarter, among cobbles, quaint restaurants, rummaging tourists, and embassy flags. Hotel Julián is a 10-minute walk up the river on a quiet and stately street, with none of the intense medieval cityscape of the others. For locations, see the map on page 144, unless otherwise noted.

$$$$ Vintage Design Hotel Sax's 22 rooms are decorated in a retro, meet-the-Jetsons fashion. With a fruity atrium and a distinctly modern, stark feel, this is a stylish, no-nonsense place (RS%, air-con, elevator, free tea and pastries daily at 17:00, Jánský Vršek 3, tel. 257-531-268, www.sax.cz, hotel@sax.cz).

$$$ Hotel Julián is an oasis of professional, predictable decency in an untouristy neighborhood. Its 33 spacious, fresh, well-furnished rooms and big, homey public spaces hide behind a noble Neoclassical facade. The staff is friendly and helpful (RS%, family rooms, air-con, elevator, plush and inviting lobby, summer roof terrace, parking lot; Metro: Anděl, then take tram #6, #9, #12, or #20 to the left as you leave Metro station for two stops; Elišky Peškové 11, Praha 5, reservation tel. 257-311-150, www.hoteljulian.com, info@julian.cz). Free lockers and a shower are available for those needing a place to stay after checkout (while waiting for an overnight train, for example).

$$$ Dům u Velké Boty ("House at the Big Boot"), on a quiet square in front of the German Embassy, is the rare quintessential family hotel in Prague: homey, comfy, and extremely friendly. Charlotta, Jan, and their two sons treat every guest as a (thirsty) friend, and the wellspring of their stories never runs dry. Each of their 12 rooms is uniquely decorated, most in a tasteful, 19th-century Biedermeier style (RS%, cheaper rooms with shared bath, family rooms, cash only, children up to age 10 sleep free—toys provided, Vlašská 30, tel. 257-532-088, www.dumuvelkeboty.cz, info@dumuvelkeboty.cz). There's no hotel sign on the house—look for the splendid geraniums that Jan nurtures in the windows.

$$ Residence Thunovská, just below the Italian embassy on a relatively quiet staircase leading up to the castle, rents six rooms in a house that once belonged to the Mannerist artist Bartholomeus Sprangler. The all-renovated rooms are historic and equipped with kitchenettes and Italian furniture. The original chimney that runs through the house is inscribed with the date 1577, and the rest of the house is not much younger. The manager, Dean, a soft-spoken American who married into Prague, treats his guests as trusted friends (RS%, breakfast extra—served in the next-door café, Thunovská 19, look for the Consulate of San Marino sign, reception open 9:00-19:00, otherwise on-call, tel. 257-531-189, mobile 721-855-880, www.prague-apartments.org, thunovska@volny.cz).

HOSTELS IN THE CENTER

It's tough to find a double for less than 2,500 Kč in the old center. But Prague has an abundance of fine hostels—each with a distinct personality, and each excellent in its own way for anyone wanting a cheap dorm bed or an extremely simple twin-bedded room for a reasonable price. For travelers seeking low-priced options, keep in mind that hostels are no longer the exclusive domain of backpackers. The first two hostels below are centrally located, but lack care and character; the last two are found in workaday neighborhoods and have atmospheric interiors.

¢ Old Prague Hostel is a small, well-worn place on the second and third floors of an apartment building on a back alley near the Powder Tower. The spacious rooms were once apartment bedrooms, so it feels less institutional than most hostels, but the staff can be indifferent and older travelers might feel a bit out of place. The TV lounge/breakfast room is a good hangout (private rooms available, in summer reserve 2 weeks ahead for doubles, a few days ahead for bunks; Benediktská 2, see map on page 129 for location, tel. 224-829-058, www.oldpraguehostel.com, info@ oldpraguehostel.com).

¢ Hostel Prague Týn—quiet, mature, and sterile—is hidden in a silent courtyard two blocks from the Old Town Square. The management is very aware of its valuable location, so they don't have to bother being friendly (private rooms available, reserve one week ahead, Týnská 19, see map on page 129 for location, tel. 224-808-301, www.hostelpraguetyn.com, info@hostelpraguetyn.com).

Eating in Prague

A big part of Prague's charm is found in wandering aimlessly through the city's winding old quarters, marveling at the architecture, watching the people, and sniffing out fun restaurants. In addition to meat-and-potatoes Czech cuisine, you'll find trendy, student-oriented bars and lots of fine ethnic eateries. For ambience, the options include traditional, dark Czech beer halls; elegant Art Nouveau dining rooms; and hip, modern cafés.

Generally, if you walk just a few minutes away from the tourist flow, you'll find better value, atmosphere, and service. The more touristy a place is, the more likely you'll pay too much—either in inflated prices or because waiters pad the bill. It's smart to closely examine your itemized bill and understand each line.

I've listed eating and drinking establishments by neighborhood. Most of the options—and highest prices—are in the Old Town. For a light meal, consider one of Prague's many cafés (see page 146).

Unlike most European countries, the Czech Republic permits smoking in restaurants and cafés. I've noted those that are either more or less smoky than the norm. For general advice on eating and tipping, see page 1078.

Fun, Touristy Neighborhoods: Several areas are pretty and well-situated for sightseeing, but lined only with touristy restaurants. While these places are not necessarily bad values, I've listed only a few of your many options—just survey the scene in these spots and choose whatever looks best. **Kampa Square,** just off the Charles Bridge, feels like a small-town square. **Havelská Market** is surrounded by colorful little eateries, any of which offer a nice perch for viewing the market scene while you munch. The massive **Old Town Square** is the place to nurse a drink or enjoy a meal while watching the tide of people, both tourists and locals, sweep back and forth. There's often some event on this main square, and its many restaurants provide tasty and relaxing vantage points.

Traditional Czech Places: It's getting difficult to find a truly Czech pub in the historic city center, as many cheap student pubs have been replaced by shops and hotels that make more money. Most Czechs no longer go to "traditional" eateries, preferring the cosmopolitan taste of the world to the mundane taste of sauerkraut. As a result, ancient institutions with "authentic" Czech ambience have become touristy—but they're still great fun, a good value, and respected by locals. Expect wonderfully rustic spaces, smoke, surly service, and reasonably good, inexpensive food. Understand every line on your bill. I've listed several of these characteristically Czech eateries.

Dining with a View: For great views, consider these options,

Restaurant Price Code

I've assigned each eatery a price category, based on the average cost of a typical main course. Drinks, desserts, and splurge items (steak and seafood) can raise the price considerably. I've given *very* rough conversions to dollars using 25 Kč = $1.

$$$$ **Splurge:** Most main courses over 500 Kč (roughly $20)

  $$$ **Pricier:** 250-500 Kč ($10-20)

   $$ **Moderate:** 120-250 Kč ($5-10)

    $ **Budget:** Under 120 Kč ($5)

In the Czech Republic, a pub, basic sit-down eatery, and less-touristy café or teahouse is **$**; a typical restaurant—or a fancy café with coffee over 50 Kč and tea over 100 Kč—is **$$**; an upscale restaurant is **$$$**; and a swanky splurge is **$$$$**.

all described in detail in the following pages: **Hotel u Prince's terrace** (rooftop dining above a fancy hotel, completely touristy but with awesome views); **Villa Richter** (next to Prague Castle, above Malostranská Metro stop); **Bellavista Restaurant** at the Strahov Monastery; **Petřínské Terasy** and **Nebozízek** (next to the funicular stop halfway up Petřín Hill); and **Čertovka** in the Little Quarter (superb views of the Charles Bridge).

Cheap-and-Cheery Sandwich Shops: All around town you'll find modern little sandwich shops (like the Panería chain) offering inexpensive fresh-made sandwiches (grilled if you like), pastries, salads, and drinks. You can get the food to go, or eat inside at simple tables.

Groceries and Farmers Markets: Ask your hotelier for the location of the nearest grocery store; it'll probably be small, stocked with what you need, and close by. Or check out the farmer-supplied grocery called **Grunt,** which offers lots of fresh products (in the Old Town at Národni 21).

Farmers markets crop up around the city and tantalize picnickers. Apart from vegetables, you'll find quality cheeses, juices, cakes, coffee, and more (www.farmarsketrziste.cz). The most central and touristy is the **Havelská Market** in the Old Town (also has handicrafts, daily 9:00-18:00, see page 69). The most scenic is the **Náplavka** ("River Landing") market on the Vltava embankment, just south of the Palacký Bridge; the original and biggest market is on **Vítězné Náměstí** at the Dejvická Metro stop (both Sat 8:00-14:00). A smaller farmers market enlivens the heart of the trendy **Žižkov** neighborhood on Wednesday, Friday, and Saturday mornings (at Metro stop Náměstí Jiřího z Poděbrad—you could combine a visit with a trip up the nearby Žižkov TV tower). And another is on **Republic Square** (Náměstí Republiky) from

PRAGUE

1. Restaurace u Provaznice
2. U Medvídků Beer Hall
3. U Zlatého Tygra Pub
4. Restaurace u Betlémské Kaple
5. Česká Kuchyně
6. Restaurace Mlejnice
7. Lokál Restaurant
8. Country Life Vegetarian Restaurant
9. Beas Cafeteria
10. Klub Architektů
11. Chez Marcel
12. Amici Miei Restaurant
13. Ariana Afghan Restaurant
14. Indian Jewel
15. James Joyce Irish Pub
16. La Casa Blů
17. Hotel/Restaurant u Prince Terasa
18. Restaurace u Pinkasů

Prague Restaurants in Old & New Towns

PRAGUE

19 Hospoda u Nováka
20 To Pivovarský Dům
21 Havelská Market
22 Le Patio & Café Louvre
23 Pasha Kebab Turkish Restaurant
24 Brasserie La Gare
25 Kavárna Muzeum Café
26 Municipal House Eateries
27 Kavárna Slavia
28 Grand Café Orient
29 Café Café
30 Café Montmartre & Ebel Coffee House
31 Dobrá Čajovna Teahouse
32 Čajový Klub

Tuesdays through Fridays, at the entrance to the Old Town (www. farmarsketrhyprahy1.cz).

IN THE OLD TOWN
Traditional Czech

$$ Restaurace u Provaznice ("By the Ropemaker's Wife") has all the Czech classics, peppered with the story of a once-upon-a-time-faithful wife. (Check the menu for details of the gory story.) Natives congregate under bawdy frescoes for the famously good "pig leg" with horseradish and Czech mustard (daily 11:00-24:00, a block into the Old Town from the bottom of Wenceslas Square at Provaznická 3, tel. 224-232-528).

$$ U Medvídků ("By the Bear Cubs") started out as a brewery in 1466 and is now a flagship beer hall of the Czech Budweiser. The one large room is bright, noisy, touristy, and a bit smoky (daily 11:30-23:00, a block toward Wenceslas Square from Bethlehem Square at Na Perštýně 7, tel. 224-211-916). The small beer bar next to the restaurant (daily 16:00 until late) is used by university students during emergencies—such as after most other pubs have closed.

$ U Zlatého Tygra ("By the Golden Tiger") has long embodied the proverbial Czech pub, where beer turns strangers into kindred spirits, who cross the fuzzy line between memory and imagination as they tell their hilarious life stories to each other. Today, "The Tiger" is a buzzing shrine to one of its longtime regulars, the writer Bohumil Hrabal, whose fictions immortalize many of the colorful characters that once warmed the wooden benches here. Only regulars have reserved tables. To get a spot, arrive around opening time (daily 15:00-23:00, just south of Karlova at Husova 17, tel. 222-221-111).

$ Restaurace u Betlémské Kaple, behind Bethlehem Chapel, is not "ye olde" Czech. It has light wooden decor, cheap lunch deals, and fish specialties that attract natives and visitors in search of a good Czech bite for good Czech prices (daily 11:00-23:00, Betlémské Náměstí 2, tel. 222-221-639).

$ Česká Kuchyně ("Czech Kitchen") is a blue-collar cafeteria serving steamy old Czech cuisine. It's fast, practical, cheap, and traditional as can be. Pick up your tally sheet as you enter, grab a tray, point to whatever you'd like, and keep the paper to pay as you exit. It's extremely cheap...unless you lose your paper. As you enter, you'll come across serving stations in this order: salads, fruit dumplings and sweets, soups, main dishes, and finally, drinks (daily 9:00-20:00, very central, across from Havelská Market at Havelská 23, tel. 224-235-574).

$$ Restaurace Mlejnice ("The Mill") is a fun little pub strewn with farm implements and happy eaters, located just out of the tourist crush two blocks from the Old Town Square. They serve hearty traditional and modern Czech plates. Reservations are smart in the evening (daily 11:00-24:00, between Melantrichova and Železná at Kožná 14, tel. 224-228-635, www.restaurace-mlejnice.cz/en).

$$ Lokál ("The Neighborhood Dump") is a hit with residents for its good-quality Czech classics. Filling a long, arched space, the restaurant plays on customers' nostalgia: The stark interior is a deliberate 1980s retro design, and the waiters have been instructed to be curt (but not impolite)—just as if they were serving in one of Prague's notorious train station "dumps." Reservations are smart (daily 11:00 until late, ask for English menu at the front by the tap, Dlouhá 33, tel. 222-316-265, www.lokal-dlouha.ambi.cz/en). The same group has a smaller branch, **Lokál u Bílé Kuželky,** in the Little Quarter (see listing later).

Vegetarian and Modern

These hip and trendy places have a fun, youthful vibe.

$$ Country Life Vegetarian Restaurant is a bright, easy, nonsmoking cafeteria with a well-displayed buffet of salads and hot veggie dishes. It's midway between the Old Town Square and the bottom of Wenceslas Square. They're serious about their vegetarianism, serving only plant-based, unprocessed, and unrefined food. Its quiet dining area is elegant for a cafeteria, with a few tables outside in the courtyard (pay by weight, Sun-Thu 9:00-20:30, Fri 9:00-17:00, closed Sat, through courtyard at Melantrichova 15/Michalská 18, tel. 224-213-366).

$$ Beas Cafeteria, a little vegetarian restaurant, is ruled by a Punjabi chef. Diners grab a steel tray and scoop up whatever looks good, typically various choices of *dal* (lentils) and *sabji* (vegetables) with rice or *chapati* (pancakes). The food is sold by weight—you'll likely spend 130 Kč for lunch. Tucked away in a courtyard behind the Týn Church, this place is popular with university students and young professionals (Mon-Fri 11:00-20:00, Sat-Sun from 12:00, Sun until 18:00, Týnská 19, mobile 608-035-727).

$$$ Klub Architektů, next to Bethlehem Chapel, is a modern hangout in a cave-like medieval cellar that also has straw-chair seating outside. The fun menu includes excellent original dishes, hearty salads, Moravian wines, and Slovak beer (daily 11:30-24:00, Betlémské Náměstí 169, tel. 224-248-878).

Beware that two popular Prague vegetarian restaurants, **Lehká Hlava** ("Clear Head") and **Maitrea** (a.k.a. "Buddha of the Future"), are owned by Antonín Koláček, a former manager of a state-controlled brown coal company (and more recently a Buddhist philanthropist) who was convicted in 2013 in a Swiss court as the mastermind behind a 1990s fraudulent privatization scheme that robbed the country of at least three billion crowns.

Ethnic Eateries and Bars

Dlouhá, the wide street leading away from the Old Town Square behind the Jan Hus Memorial, is lined with ethnic restaurants catering mostly to cosmopolitan locals. Within a couple of blocks, you can eat your way around the world. From Dlouhá, wander the Rámová/Haštalská/Vězeňská area to survey a United Nations of eateries: You'll find French (**Chez Marcel** at Haštalská 12); Italian (the expensive **Amici Miei** at Vězeňská 5, which prides itself on fresh *pesci* and *frutti di mare*); and Afghan (**Ariana** at Rámová 6).

These places deserve special consideration:

Indian: $$$ Indian Jewel, in the Ungelt courtyard behind the Týn Church, is the best place in Prague to find a full Indian menu that actually tastes Indian. Located in a pleasant, artfully restored courtyard, this is my choice for outdoor dining, with seriously executed sub-Continental classics and good-value lunch specials (daily specials, daily 11:00-23:00, Týn 6, tel. 222-310-156).

Irish: $ James Joyce Irish Pub may seem like a strange recommendation in Prague—home of some of the world's best beer—but it has the kind of ambience that locals (and few tourists) seek out. Expats have favored this pub (formerly known as Molly Malone's) for Guinness ever since the Velvet Revolution enabled the Celts to return to one of their homelands. Worn wooden floors, dingy walls, and the Irish manager transport you right into the heart of blue-collar Dublin—a popular place for young Czechs to seek jobs in the high-tech industry before the recession (daily 11:00 until late, U Obecního Dvora 4, tel. 224-818-851).

Latin American: $$ La Casa Blů, with cheap lunch specials, Mexican plates, Staropramen beer, and greenish mojitos, is your own little pueblo in Prague. It's one of the last student bastions in the Old Town. Painted in warm oranges and reds, energized by upbeat music, and guarded by creatures from Mayan mythology, La Casa Blů attracts a fiesta of happy eaters and drinkers (Mon-Sat 11:00-23:00, Sun 14:00-23:00, nonsmoking, on the corner of Kozí and Bílkova, tel. 224-818-270).

In the Jewish Quarter

These eateries are well-placed to break up a demanding tour of the Jewish Quarter—all within two blocks of each other on or near Široká (see map on page 75). Also consider the nearby ethnic eateries listed above.

$$$ Kolkovna, the flagship restaurant of a chain allied with Pilsner Urquell, is big and woody yet modern, serving a fun mix of Czech and international cuisine—ribs, salads, cheese plates, and beer. It feels a tad formulaic...but not in a bad way (a bit overpriced, daily 11:00-24:00, across from Spanish Synagogue at V Kolkovně 8, tel. 224-819-701).

$$ Kolonial ("Bicycle Place"), across the street from the Pinkas Synagogue, has a modern interior playing on the bicycle theme, six beers on tap, and an imaginative menu drawing from Czech, French, Italian, and Spanish cuisine (daily specials, daily 9:00-24:00, Široká 6, tel. 224-818-322).

$ Restaurace u Knihovny ("By the Library"), situated steps away from the City and National libraries as well as the Pinkas Synagogue, is a favorite lunch spot for locals who work nearby. The cheap daily lunch specials consist of seven variations on traditional Czech themes. The service is friendly, and the stylish red-brick interior is warm (daily 11:00-23:00, nonsmoking at lunch, on the corner of Veleslavínova and Valentinská, mobile 732-835-876).

$$$ Dinitz Kosher Restaurant, around the corner from the Spanish Synagogue, is the most low-key and reasonably priced of the kosher restaurants in the Jewish Quarter (Shabbat meals by prepaid reservation only, Sun-Thu 11:30-22:30, Fri 11:30-14:30, Bílkova 12, tel. 222-244-000, www.dinitz.cz). For Shabbat meals, the fancier **$$$ King Solomon Restaurant** is a better value (Široká 8, tel. 224-818-752, www.kosher.cz).

Dining with an Old Town Square View

The **$$$$ Hotel u Prince Terasa,** atop the five-star hotel facing the Astronomical Clock, is designed for foreign tourists. A sleek elevator takes you to the rooftop terrace, where every possible inch is used to serve good food (international with plenty of fish) from their open-air grill. The view is arguably the best in town—especially at sunset. The menu is a fun but overpriced mix, with photos that make ordering easy. Being in such a touristy spot, rude waiters are experts at nicking you with confusing menu charges; don't be afraid to confirm exact prices before ordering. This place is also great for a drink at sunset or late at night (fine salads, daily until 24:00, brusque staff, outdoor heaters, Staroměstské Náměstí 29, tel. 224-213-807, no reservations possible).

IN THE NEW TOWN
Traditional Czech

$$ Restaurace u Pinkasů, founded in 1843, is known among locals as the first place to serve Pilsner beer. You can sit in its traditional interior, in front to watch the street action, or out back in a garden shaded by the Gothic buttresses of the St. Mary of the Snows Church. While the prices are straightforward, some of the waiters could win the rudest-service award (daily 9:00-24:00, near the bottom of Wenceslas Square, between the Old Town and New Town, Jungmannovo Náměstí 16, tel. 221-111-150).

$ Hospoda u Nováka, behind the National Theater, is emphatically Czech, with few tourists. It takes good care of its regulars (you'll see the old monthly beer tabs in a rack just inside the door). Nostalgic communist-era signs are everywhere. During that time, pubs like this were close-knit communities where regulars escaped from the depression of daily life. Today, the U Nováka is a bright and smoky hangout where you can still happily curse whatever regime you happen to live under. While the English menu lists the well-executed Czech classics, it doesn't list the cheap daily specials—ask (daily 10:00-23:00, V Jirchářích 2, tel. 224-930-639).

$$ Pivovarský Dům ("The Brewhouse"), on the corner of Ječná and Lípová, is popular with locals for its rare variety of fresh beers (yeast, wheat, and fruit-flavored), fine classic Czech dishes, and an inviting interior that mixes traditional and modern (daily 11:00-23:00, reservations recommended in the evenings, variety of beer mugs sold; walk up Štěpánská street from Wenceslas Square for 10 minutes, or take tram #22 for two stops from Národní to Štěpánská; Lípová 15, tel. 296-216-666, www.pivovarskydum. com).

Modern and Ethnic

$$$ Le Patio, on the big and busy Národní Třída, has a hip, continental feel. But for a place that also sells furniture (head straight back and down the stairs), it definitely needs comfier dining chairs. Hanging lanterns and live music (Fri-Sat) contribute to the pleasant atmosphere. Dishes are from India, France, and points in between, and a serious vegetarian option is always available (daily 8:00-23:00, Národní 22, tel. 224-934-375).

$ Pasha Kebab Turkish Restaurant, near the bottom of Wenceslas Square, has American fast-food-chain ambience, good ingredients, and wonderful, authentic, ready-to-eat Turkish dishes (daily 10:00-22:00, a block from Můstek Metro stop, just beyond Franciscan garden at Jungmannova 27, tel. 224-948-481).

$$ Brasserie La Gare, just off Republic Square (Náměstí Republiky), opened with the mission to prove to Czechs that French food can be simple and inexpensive. The menu includes such classics as *escargots de Bourgogne* and coq au vin. The red-hued, modern interior also contains a French bakery and a deli (lunch specials, daily 11:00-24:00, V Celnici 3, tel. 222-313-712).

$ Kavárna Muzeum, in the former communist parliament building (now part of the National Museum) at Wenceslas Square, offers daily menus, freshly roasted coffee, soups, and sandwiches in a pleasant, kid-friendly setting (daily 10:00-19:00, Vinohradská 1, tel. 224-284-511).

Art Nouveau Splendor in the Municipal House

The Municipal House (Obecní Dům), the sumptuous Art Nouveau concert hall, has three restaurants: a café, a French restaurant, and

a beer cellar (all at Náměstí Republiky 5). The dressy café, **$$$ Kavárna Obecní Dům,** is drenched in chandeliered, Art Nouveau elegance and offers the best value and experience here. Light, pricey meals and drinks come with great atmosphere and bad service (daily 7:30-23:00, live piano or jazz trio 16:00-20:00, tel. 222-002-763). The fine and formal **$$$$ French restaurant** in the next wing oozes Mucha elegance (daily 12:00-16:00 & 18:00-23:00, tel. 222-002-777). The **beer cellar** is overpriced and touristy (daily 11:30-23:00).

PRAGUE

IN THE LITTLE QUARTER

These characteristic eateries are handy for a bite before or after your Prague Castle visit.

$$ Malostranská Beseda, in the impeccably restored former Town Hall, weaves together an imaginative menu of traditional Czech dishes (both classic and little known), vegetarian fare, and fresh fish. It feels a bit sterile and formulaic, but that follows a local trend. You can choose among three settings: the nonsmoking ground-floor restaurant on the left; the café on the right (serves meals, but it's OK to have only coffee or cake); or the packed beer hall downstairs, where Pilsner Urquell is served well (daily 11:00-23:00, Malostranské Náměstí 21, tel. 257-409-112). The restaurant has a recommended music club upstairs.

$$ Lokál u Bílé Kuželky ("By the White Bowling Pin"), a branch of the Old Town's recommended Lokál restaurant, is the best bet for quick, cheap, well-executed Czech classics on this side of the river (Mon-Fri 11:30-24:00, Sat-Sun 12:00-22:00, nonsmoking section, Míšeňská 12; from the Charles Bridge, turn right around the U Tří Pštrosů Hotel just before the Little Quarter gate; tel. 257-212-014).

$$ Lo Veg Restaurant, on the top two floors and a tiny terrace of a narrow medieval house, serves vegan variations on Czech classics as well as Asian fare. The setting is a tasteful mix of Renaissance roof beams, Balinese art, and gorgeous vistas (daily 11:30-22:00, Nerudova 36, mobile 702-901-060).

$$ Green Spirit Vegetarian Bistro and Café, on a quiet walnut tree-shaded patio next to the Gothic walls of St. Lawrence Church, is a snug, family-run place with an eclectic menu including burritos, pizzas, cakes, and salads (Mon-Fri 10:00-20:00, Sat-Sun from 11:00, Hellichova 14, tel. 257-317-459).

$$ Pastař ("The Pasta Maker"), across the bridge from the National Theater, is serious about freshly made pasta, pickled vegetables, and fresh-squeezed juices. It's part of a larger Czech trend of relying on small producers "with a story." Their deli bistro, with its cheeses and olives, can stock you up for a boating or riverside picnic (daily 11:30-23:00, Malostranské Nábřeží 558, mobile 777-009-108).

$ U Zavěšenýho Kafe a Divadlo Pokračuje ("By the Hanging Coffee" and "The Show Goes On"), just below Loreta Square on the way to the castle, is a creative little pub/restaurant that has attracted a cult following among Prague's cognoscenti. You can "hang" a coffee here for a local vagabond by paying for an extra coffee on your way out (daily 11:00-24:00, Loretánská 13, mobile 605-294-595).

$ U Hrocha ("By the Hippo"), a small authentic pub with tar dripping from its walls, is packed with beer drinkers. Expect simple, traditional meals—basically meat starters with bread. Just below the castle near Little Quarter Square (Malostranské Náměstí), it's actually the haunt of many members of parliament, which is around the corner (daily 12:00-23:00, chalkboard lists daily meals in English, Thunovská 10, tel. 257-533-389).

$$ Vinograf Wine Bar is a small, intimate place with just eight tables. It's run by Czech wine-lover Karel, who enjoys helping visitors appreciate his wines. He prepares a daily list of Czech wines available by the glass and serves meat-and-cheese plates for wine tasters who'd like a light meal (daily 16:00-24:00, a few steps off the end of Charles Bridge at Míšeňská 8, next to Lokál, tel. 603-116-085).

$$$$ Čertovka, down an alley so narrow that it requires a signal to regulate foot traffic, offers outdoor seating on two small terraces right on the water, with some of the best views of the Charles Bridge. Given the location, the prices are reasonable, but waiters don't bother being nice (daily 11:30-23:30, off the little square at U Lužického Semináře 24, no reservations taken, arrive early to claim a spot, tel. 257-534-524).

$$ Cukrkávalimonáda ("Sugar, Coffee, Lemonade") is part restaurant and part patisserie, serving big salads, ciabatta sandwiches, artful pastries, and freshly squeezed juice in a setting mixing old and new decor. The bistro—an oasis just a block away from the tourist crush—is 50 yards down the first street to the left after you exit the Charles Bridge (Mon-Sat 9:00-23:00, Sun 9:00-19:00, Lázeňská 7, tel. 257-225-396).

$$$ Restaurant Savoy, at the foot of the Legií Bridge, is the closest you'll get to Parisian food culture in Prague—with exquisite dishes, thoughtful service, and elegant Art Deco surroundings (lunch specials, Mon-Fri 8:00-22:30, Sat-Sun 9:00-22:30, Vítězná 5, tel. 257-311-562).

Near the Funicular, on Petřín Hill: These two places are near the funicular stop halfway up Petřín Hill, and offer great views over the city. **$$$ Petřínské Terasy** has woody seating indoors, or outside on the terrace (daily 12:00-23:00; Petřín 393, tel. 257-320-688), while **$$$$ Nebozízek** is more modern, with glassed-in seating (cash only, daily 11:00-23:00, Petřín 411, tel. 257-315-329).

IN THE CASTLE QUARTER

$$$ Bellavista Restaurant is in the garden of the Strahov Monastery, where the abbot himself would come to meditate in a peaceful garden setting. You'll pay for the amazing city views, but if the weather's nice, this is a good value, with traditional grilled meats, pasta, and salads (daily 11:00-24:00, tel. 220-517-274).

Villa Richter, at the end of the castle promontory (closest to the river) and surrounded by newly replanted vineyards, consists of three classy restaurants, each with killer Prague views. Forty yards below the lower castle gate, you'll see a gate leading to a vineyard. Stroll downhill through the vineyard and you'll come upon three distinct restaurants (all open daily 10:00-23:00, tel. 257-219-079). At **$$$ Panorama Pergola,** a string of outdoor tables lines a vineyard terrace overlooking the city (wine, sandwiches, cold plates, and hot views). **$$$$ Piano Nobile** is more pretentious, with Italian and French dishes and romantic white-linen tables indoors and out—it's the perfect place to propose (three-course meals). **$$$ Piano Terra** serves more affordable Czech dishes.

$$ Klášterní Pivovar ("Monastery Brewery"), founded by an abbot in 1628 and reopened in 2004, has two large rooms and a pleasant courtyard. This is the place, though touristy, to taste a range of unpasteurized beers brewed on the premises, including amber, wheat, and IPA. The wooden decor and circa-1900 newspaper clippings (including Habsburg Emperor Franz Josef's "Proclamation to My Nations," announcing the beginning of the First World War) evoke the era when Vienna was Europe's artistic capital, Prague was building its faux Eiffel Tower, and life moved much slower. To accompany the beer, try the strong beer-flavored cheese served on toasted black-yeast bread (daily 10:00-22:00, Strahovské Nádvoří 301, tel. 233-353-155). It's directly across from the entrance to the Strahov Library (don't confuse it with the enormous, tour group-oriented Klášterní Restaurace next door, to the right).

$$$ Host Restaurant is hidden in the middle of a staircase that connects Loretánská and Úvoz streets. This spot, which boasts super views of the Little Quarter and Petřín Hill, has a modern black-and-white design and an imaginative menu. For a good deal,

Restaurants & Hotels in the Little Quarter & Castle Quarter

PRAGUE

CASTLE QUARTER

BRUSNICE

JELENÍ

PATOČKOVA

KEPLEROVA

KANOVNICKÁ

STERNBERG PALACE

Castle Square

U KASÁREN

LORETA CHURCH

SCHWARZENBERG PALACE

KE HRADU

ČERNÍN PALACE

Loreta Square

LORETÁNSKÁ

Pohořelec

PARLÉŘOVA

POHOŘELEC

ÚVOZ

VLAŠSKÁ

Petřín

STRAHOV MONASTERY

CITY WALLS

PETŘÍN TOWER

Petřín

Eateries & Entertainment

1. Malostranská Beseda Restaurant & Club
2. Lokál U Bílé Kuželky & Vinograf Wine Bar
3. Lo Veg Restaurant
4. Green Spirit Vegetarian Bistro & Café
5. Pastař Restaurant
6. U Zavěšenýho Kafe a Divadlo Pokračuje
7. U Hrocha Pub
8. Čertovka
9. Cukrkávalimonáda Bistro
10. Restaurant Savoy
11. Petřínské Terasy Restaurant
12. Nebozízek Restaurant
13. Bellavista Restaurant
14. Villa Richter Eateries
15. Klášterní Pivovar
16. Host Restaurant
17. Hostinec u Černého Vola Pub
18. Malý Buddha Veggie Rest.
19. U Labutí Restaurant
20. Café Salmovský Palác
21. Kavárna ve Šternberském Paláci
22. Kavárna Nový Svět
23. Lobkowicz Palace Café

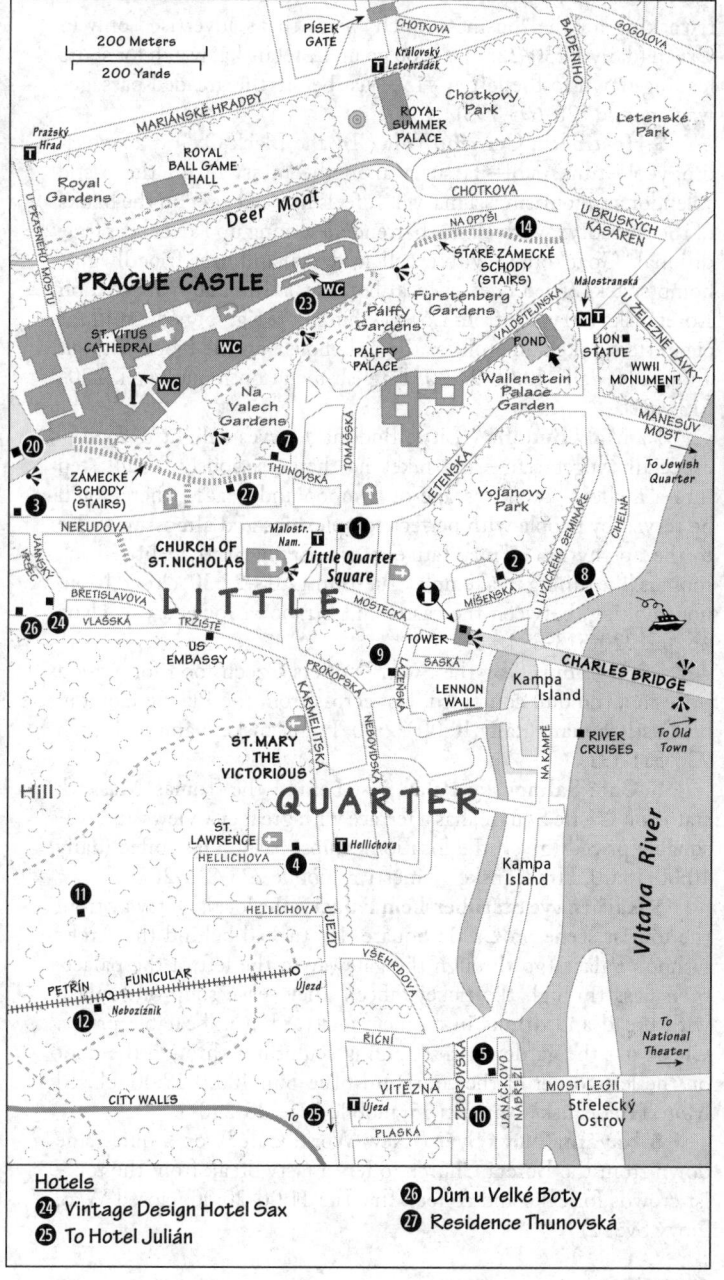

Hotels

㉔ Vintage Design Hotel Sax

㉕ To Hotel Julián

㉖ Dům u Velké Boty

㉗ Residence Thunovská

try asking for the "business lunch" *menu* that's advertised only in Czech (daily 11:30-22:00, as you go up Loretánská, watch for stairs leading down to the left at #15—just before the arcaded passageway, mobile 728-695-793).

$ Hostinec u Černého Vola ("By the Black Ox") is a smoky, dingy old-time pub—its survival in the midst of all the castle splendor and tourism is a marvel. It feels like a kegger on the banks of the river Styx, with classic bartenders serving up Kozel beer (traditional "Goat" brand with excellent darks) and beer-friendly gutbomb snacks (fried cheese, local hot dogs). The pub is located on Loretánská (50 yards from Loreta Church, no sign outside, sniff for cigarette smoke and look for the only house on the block without an arcade, daily 10:00-22:00, English menu on request, tel. 220-513-481).

$$ Malý Buddha ("Little Buddha") serves delightful food—especially vegetarian—and takes its theme seriously. You'll step into a mellow, low-lit escape of bamboo and peace, where you'll be served by people with perfect complexions and almost no pulse to the no-rhythm of meditative music. Eating in their little back room is like dining in a temple (Tue-Sun 12:00-22:30, closed Mon, nonsmoking, between the castle and Strahov Monastery at Úvoz 46, tel. 220-513-894).

$$ U Labutí ("By the Swans") offers Czech food for a good price in a tranquil courtyard, just across from the Plague Column on Castle Square (daily 10:00-22:00, Hradčanské Náměstí 11, tel. 220-511-191).

$ Café Salmovský Palác, just behind the Tomáš Masaryk statue on Castle Square, has a terrace with great city views and reasonably priced (given the location) soups, pasta, and coffee (daily 10:00-18:00, Hradčanské Náměstí 1, mobile 725-816-267).

$ Kavárna ve Šternberském Paláci is the locals' getaway from the tourist scene on Castle Square. It's tucked behind the Archbishop's Palace (go through the gateway to the left of the palace, then pass through the ticket office). They serve soup or goulash with bread and drinks in a quiet courtyard at unbeatable prices. Check out the garden with stunning sculptures through the door on the left corner of the courtyard (Tue-Sun 10:00-18:00, closed Mon, Hradčanské Náměstí 15, mobile 721-138-290).

$ Kavárna Nový Svět ("New World Café"), on a quiet lane down from the Loreta Church, offers a tasty break from the tourist crowds for cake and coffee (Thu-Tue 11:00-20:00, closed Wed, Nový Svět 2).

CAFÉS

Dripping with history, these places in the Old Town and New Town are as much about the ambience as they are about the coffee.

Most cafés also serve sweets and light meals. For locations, see the map on page 135.

$$ Kavárna Slavia, across from the National Theater (facing the Legií Bridge on Národní street), is a fixture in Prague, famous as a hangout for its literary elite. Today, it's tired and clearly past its prime, with an Art Deco interior, lousy piano entertainment, and celebrity photos on the wall. But its iconic status makes it a fun stop for a coffee—skip the food (daily 8:00-23:00, sit as near the river as possible, Smetanovo Nábřeží 2, tel. 224-218-493). Notice the *Drinker of Absinthe* painting on the wall (and on the menu)—with the iconic Czech writer struggling with reality.

$$ Grand Café Orient is only one flight up off busy Celetná street, yet a world away from the crush of tourism below. Located in the Cubist House of the Black Madonna, the café is upstairs and fittingly decorated with a Cubist flair. With its stylish, circa-1910 decor toned to dark green, this space is full of air and light—and a good value as well. The café takes its Cubism seriously: Traditionally round desserts are served square (sandwiches, salads, vanilla squares and other desserts, great balcony seating, Mon-Fri 9:00-22:00, Sat-Sun from 10:00, Ovocný Trh 19, at the corner of Celetná near the Powder Tower, tel. 224-224-240).

$$ Café Café, just off to the right from the main drag connecting the Old Town and Wenceslas Square, serves salads, sandwiches, and cakes in a fancy setting (daily 9:00-23:00, Rytířská 10, tel. 224-210-597).

$$ Café Montmartre, on a small street parallel to Karlova, combines Parisian ambience with unbeatable Czech prices for coffee (no food served). Dreamy Czech minds found their quiet asylum here after Kavárna Slavia (listed earlier) and other longtime favorites either closed down or became stuck in their past. The main room is perfect for discussing art and politics; the intimate room behind the courtyard is where you recite poetry to your partner (Mon-Fri 9:00-23:00, Sat-Sun from 12:00, Řetězová 7, tel. 222-221-244).

$ Ebel Coffee House, next door to Café Montmartre, prides itself on its wide assortment of fresh brews from every coffee-bean-growing country in the world, inviting cakes, sandwiches, and colorful setting that delights the mind as much as the caffeine (daily 9:00-22:00, Řetězová 3, tel. 224-895-788).

$$ Café Louvre is a longtime elegant favorite (opened in 1902 and maintaining its classic atmosphere) that still draws an energetic young crowd that's crazy about their cheesecake and hot chocolate. From the big and busy Národní street, you walk upstairs into a venerable world of newspapers (including in English) on sticks and waiters in vests and aprons. The back room has long been the place for billiard tables (100 Kč/hour). An English flier tells its history (two-course lunch offered 11:00-15:00, good gluten-free options, open daily 8:00-23:30, Národní 22, tel. 224-930-949).

TEAHOUSES

Many Czechs are bohemian philosophers at heart and prefer the mellow, smoke-free environs of a teahouse to the smoky, traditional beer hall. Young Czechs are much more interested in traveling to exotic destinations like Southeast Asia, Africa, or Peru than to Western Europe, so the Oriental teahouses set their minds in vacation mode. For locations, see the map on page 135.

While there are teahouses all over Prague, a fine example in a handy New Town locale is Prague's original one, established in 1991—just after freedom. **$ Dobrá Čajovna** ("Good Teahouse"), only a few steps off the bustle of Wenceslas Square, takes you into a very peaceful world that elevates tea to an almost religious ritual. You'll be given an English menu—which lovingly describes each tea—and a bell. The menu lists a world of tea (very fresh, prices by the small pot), "accompaniments" (such as Exotic Miscellany), and light meals "for hungry tea drinkers." When you're ready to order, ring your bell to beckon a tea monk—likely a member of the Lovers of Tea Society (Mon-Fri 10:00-21:30, Sat-Sun 14:00-21:30, near the base of Wenceslas Square, opposite McDonald's at Václavské Náměstí 14, tel. 224-231-480).

For a taste of tea from Prague's newly emerging Chinese middle class (rather than from some Czech's vision of Asia), head to **$ Čajový Klub** ("Tea Club"), just down the street from the Jerusalem Synagogue. Creatively run by a man from Beijing, here you'll find red cherry-wood decor, expertly served tea, and the freshest green leaves in town (Mon-Sat 10:00-21:00, closed Sun, Jeruzalémská 10, tel. 222-721-072).

Prague Connections

BY TRAIN

Prague's **main train station** (Hlavní Nádraží; "Praha hl. n." on schedules) serves all international trains; most trains within the Czech Republic, including high-speed SC Pendolino trains; and buses to and from Nürnberg and Munich. Trains serving Berlin also stop at the secondary **Holešovice station** (Nádraží Holešovice, located north of the river). Both stations have ATMs (best rates) and exchange bureaus (rotten rates). You'll find handy Czech train and bus schedules at www.idos.cz.

To get a better geographical picture, remember that the Czech Republic is a country of landlocked, would-be sailors (recall the greeting *"ahoj"*). Accordingly, the four main international rail lines connect Prague to the closest ports on the four seas: the

North Sea Line to Hamburg (7 hours) via Dresden and Berlin; the **Baltic Line** to Gdańsk (11 hours, one change) via Warsaw; the **Black Sea Line** to Varna (40 hours, one change) via Budapest and Belgrade; and the **Adriatic Line** to Split (20 hours, two changes) via Vienna and Zagreb.

MAIN TRAIN STATION (HLAVNÍ NÁDRAŽÍ)

The station is a busy hive of shops and services; posted maps help you find your way. Three parallel tunnels connect the tracks to the arrival hall. Taking any of these, you'll first reach a low-ceilinged corridor with several services: To the right are an exchange office with Internet booths, a variety of handy picnic-supply shops, and the "official" taxi stands (avoid these rip-off cabbies—explained later).

Continuing straight past this corridor, you'll reach the waste-of-space main hall, where you'll find four Metro entrances in the center (two for each direction; see "Getting from the Main Station to Your Hotel," later). One **ATM** is along the right wall; two more are in front of the ticketing area under the central stairs. **Lockers** are in the corner under the stairs on the right and a **Billa supermarket** is in the corner under the stairs to the left.

The **Touristpoint** office—at the left end of the main hall (as you face the tracks)—offers a last-minute room-finding service, books car rentals, and sells maps, international phone cards, sightseeing tours, and adrenaline experiences (daily 8:00-22:00, tel. 224-946-010, www.touristpoint.cz, info@touristpoint.cz). Perhaps most importantly, they're willing to call you a taxi to avoid the "official" crooks out front: The driver will meet you at the desk.

Buying Tickets: For most trains, head for the **Czech Railways (České Dráhy) ticket office**—marked *ČD Centrum*—in the middle of the main hall under the stairs. The regular ticket desks are faster if you already know your schedule and destination, but not all attendants speak good English. For more in-depth questions, look for the tiny **ČD Travel** office, on the left as you enter the main office, which sells both domestic and international tickets, and is more likely to provide help in English (Mon-Fri 9:00-18:00, Sat until 14:00, closed Sun, shorter hours in winter, tel. 972-241-861, www.cd.cz/en).

The **RegioJet travel office,** with desks at both sides of the main ticket office, sells international train tickets from the DB (Deutsche Bahn—German railways) system and offers various DB deals and discounts. RegioJet also runs its own trains to Olomouc and Košice, Slovakia, and sells a variety of domestic (e.g., to Český Krumlov) and international (Vienna) bus tickets without a commission (Mon-Fri 5:00-19:45, Sat-Sun from 6:45, tel. 539-

000-511, www.regiojet.cz). Despite its name, RegioJet does not sell plane tickets.

The **Leo Express ticket office,** across the hall from the ČD Centrum, sells tickets for its new Swiss-made trains to Olomouc and Košice (www.le.cz).

Bus Stops: To reach the bus stops for the AE bus to the airport and the DB buses to Nürnberg and Munich, simply find your way up to the Art Nouveau hall (explained later) and head outside.

Deciphering Schedules: Platforms are listed by number and—confusingly—sometimes also by letter. *S (sever)* means "south"—the corridor to the left as you face the tracks; *J (jih)* means "north"—the corridor to the right. But in practice, you can take any corridor and walk along the platform to your train. Also on schedules, *B1* means the bus platform (upstairs and out front), while *1B*—used by Leo Express trains—is the shorter track at the far-right end of platform 1.

A Bit of History: If you have time to kill waiting for a train, go exploring. First named for Emperor Franz Josef, the station was later renamed for President Woodrow Wilson (see the commemorative **plaque** in the main exit hall leading away from the tracks, and the large bronze **statue** in the park in front of the station). The

Czechs appreciate Wilson's promotion of self-determination after World War I, which led to the creation of the free state of Czechoslovakia in 1918. Under the communists (who weren't big fans of Wilson), it was bluntly renamed Hlavní Nádraží—"Main Station." They enlarged the once-classy Art Nouveau station and painted it the compulsory dreary gray with reddish trim.

For a glimpse at the station's genteel precommunist times, find your way up into its original **Art Nouveau Hall** (from the main concourse, look for up escalators with *Historical Building of the Station* signs). You'll emerge to stand under a grandly restored dome with elaborate decorations, providing an almost shocking contrast to the businesslike aura of the rest of the station.

Getting from the Main Station to Your Hotel

Even though the main train station is basically downtown, getting to your hotel can be a little tricky.

On Foot: Most hotels I list in the Old Town are within a 20-minute walk of the train station. Exit the station into a small park, walk through the park, and then cross the street on the other side. Head down Jeruzalémská street to the Jindřišská Tower and

PRAGUE

tram stop, walk under a small arch, then continue slightly to the right down Senovážná street. At the end of the street, you'll see the Powder Tower—the grand entry into the Old Town—to the left. Alternatively, Wenceslas Square in the New Town is a 10-minute walk—exit the station, cross the park, and walk to the left along Opletalova street.

By Metro: The Metro is easy. The entrance is right inside the station's main hall—look for the red *M* with two directions: *Háje* or *Letňany*. To purchase tickets from the machine by the Metro entrance, you'll need Czech coins (get change at the change machine in the corner near the luggage lockers, or break a bill at a newsstand or grocery). Validate your ticket in the yellow machines *before* you go down the stairs to the tracks. To get to hotels in the Old Town, catch a Háje-bound train to the Muzeum stop, then transfer to the green line (direction: Dejvická) and get off at either Můstek or Staroměstská; these stops straddle the Old Town. The next stop, Malostranská, is handy for hotels in the Little Quarter. For details on Prague's public transit, see page 48.

Taxi: The fair metered rate into the Old Town is about 200 Kč; if your hotel is farther out or across the river, it should be no more than 300 Kč. Avoid the "official" taxi stand that's marked inside the station: These thugs routinely overcharge arriving tourists (and refuse to take locals, who know the going rate and can't be fooled). Instead, to get an **honest cabbie,** exit the station's main hall through the big glass doors, then cross 50 yards through a park to Opletalova street. A few taxis are usually waiting there in front of Hotel Chopin, on the corner of Jeruzalémská street. Alternatively, the Touristpoint office, described earlier, can call a taxi for you (AAA Taxi—tel. 222-333-222; City Taxi—tel. 257-257-257). Before getting into a taxi, always confirm the maximum price to your destination, and make sure the driver turns on the meter. For more pointers on taking taxis, see page 51.

By Tram: The nearest tram stop is to the right as you exit the station (about 200 yards away). Tram #9 (headed away from railway tracks) takes you to the neighborhood near the National Theater and the Little Quarter, but isn't useful for most Old Town hotels.

Holešovice Train Station (Nádraží Holešovice)

This station, slightly farther from the center, is suburban mellow. The main hall has the same services as the main train station, in a more compact area. On the left are international and local ticket windows (open 24 hours) and an information office. On the right is an uncrowded café with Internet access (daily 8:00-19:30). Two ATMs are just outside the first glass doors, and the Metro is 50 yards to the right (follow signs toward *Vstup*, which means "entrance"; it's three stops to Hlavní Nádraží—the main station—or four stops to the city-center Muzeum stop). Taxis and trams are outside to the right (allow 300 Kč for a cab to the center).

Train Connections

All international trains pass through the main station (Hlavní Nádraží); some also stop at Holešovice (Nádraží Holešovice).

Direct overnight trains connect Prague to Vienna, Budapest, Kraków, and Warsaw. For tips on rail travel, see Practicalities.

From Prague's Main Station to Domestic Destinations: Konopiště Castle (train to Benešov, 2/hour, 1 hour, then 1.5-mile walk to castle), **Kutná Hora** (11/day, 1 hour, more with change in Kolín; to reach Kutná Hora's town center or bone church, you'll need to transfer to a local train), **Terezín** (train to Bohušovice, nearly hourly, 1-1.5 hours, then 5-minute taxi or bus ride—the direct bus from near Holešovice station is better), **Český Krumlov** (8/day, 1/day direct, 3.5 hours—bus is faster and cheaper, but may be booked up), **České Budějovice** (almost hourly, 2.5 hours), **Olomouc** (at least hourly, 2-3 hours), **Brno** (every 2 hours direct, 2.5 hours, more with changes).

From Prague's Main Station to International Destinations: Berlin (6/day direct, 4.5-5 hours), **Dresden** (every 2 hours, 2 hours), **Nürnberg** (1/day with change in Cheb, 5 hours, bus is better—see below), **Munich** (3/day direct, 6 hours; bus is better—see below), **Frankfurt** (3/day, 7-8 hours, 2 changes, more options with bus to Nürnberg), **Cologne** (bus to Nürnberg or Mannheim, then change to train, 7.5-9 hours total), **Vienna**—Vídeň in Czech (6/day direct, 4 hours, more with 1 change; 1 night train, 7 hours), **Paris** (5/day, 10.5-12 hours; 1 direct bus, 16 hours), **Budapest** (5/day direct, 7 hours; more with change in Vienna; 1 night train, 8 hours), **Kraków** (1/day with change to bus in Ostrava, 4/day with 1-2 changes, 7.5-8.5 hours, plus night train, 9 hours), **Warsaw** (2/day direct, including 1 night train, more with change in Ostrava, 8-9.5 hours).

By Bus

Prague's main bus station is at Florenc, east of the Old Town (Metro: Florenc). But some connections use other stations, including Roztyly (Metro: Roztyly), Na Knížecí (Metro: Anděl), Holešovice (Metro: Nádraží Holešovice), Hradčanská (Metro: Hradčanská), or the main train station (Metro: Hlavní Nádraží). Be sure to confirm which station your bus uses.

From Prague by Bus to: Terezín (hourly, 1 hour, departs from Holešovice), **Český Krumlov** (10/day, 3.5 hours, some from Florenc, others leave from Na Knížecí or Roztyly), **Břeclav** (with connections to **Mikulov Wine Region;** 1-2/hour from Florenc, fewer on weekends, 5-6 hours, train is better—see above), **Brno** (2/hour from Florenc, 2.5 hours), **Nürnberg,** Germany (6/day via IC Bus, 3.75 hours, covered by rail passes, departs in front of main train station), **Munich,** Germany (4/day via ExpressBus, 5 hours, covered by rail passes, departs from main train station), **Budapest** (1-4/day via Orange Ways, not covered by rail passes, 6.5-7.5 hours, www. orangeways.com).

BY PLANE
Václav Havel Airport

Prague's modern, tidy, user-friendly Václav Havel Airport (formerly Ruzyně Airport) is located 12 miles (about 30 minutes) west of the city center. Terminal 2 serves destinations within the EU except for Great Britain (no passport controls); Terminal 1 serves Great Britain and everywhere else. The airport has ATMs (avoid the change desks), desks promoting transportation services (such as city transit and shuttle buses), kiosks selling city maps and phone cards, and a TI (airport code: PRG, airport tel. 220-113-314, operator tel. 220-111-111, www.prg.aero/en).

Getting from the Airport to Your Hotel

Getting between the airport and downtown is easy. Leaving either airport terminal, you have four options, listed below from cheapest to priciest:

Dirt Cheap: Take bus #119 to the Nádraží Veleslavín stop (10 minutes), then take the Metro into the center (another 10 minutes, 32 Kč, buy tickets at info desk in airport arrival hall). This is also fastest as it avoids traffic jams.

Budget: Take the airport express (AE) bus to the main train station, or to the Masarykovo Nádraží Station near Republic Square—Náměstí Republiky (50 Kč, runs every half-hour daily 5:46-21:16, 40 minutes, look for the *AE* sign in front of the terminal and pay the driver, www.cd.cz/en). From either station, you can take the Metro, hire a taxi, or walk to your hotel. The Masarykovo Nádraží stop is slightly closer to downtown.

Moderate: Take the Čedaz minibus shuttle (from exit F at Terminal 1 or exit E at Terminal 2) to the Náměstí Republiky (Republic Square) station, at the entrance to the Old Town. The shuttle stop is on V Celnici street, across the street from Hotel Marriott and near the recommended Brasserie La Gare (pay 130 Kč directly to driver, daily 7:30-19:00, 2/hour, 30 minutes, info desk in arrival hall).

Expensive: Catch a taxi. Cabbies wait at the curb directly in front of the arrival hall. Or book a yellow AAA taxi through their office in the airport hall—you'll get a 50 percent discount coupon for the trip back (book your return trip by calling 222-333-222). AAA taxis wait in front of exit D at Terminal 1 and exit E at Terminal 2 (metered rate, generally 500-600 Kč to downtown).

BY PRIVATE CAR SERVICE

Mike's Chauffeur Service is a reliable, family-run company with fair and fixed rates around town and beyond. Friendly Mike's motto is, "We go the extra mile for you." If Mike is busy, he'll send one of his colleagues—all of whom speak English (round-trip fares, with waiting time included, prices valid through 2018 with this book: Český Krumlov-3,800 Kč, Terezín-1,900 Kč, Karlštejn-1,700 Kč, Karlovy Vary and Pilsner Urquell brewery in Plzeň-3,800 Kč, 4 percent surcharge for credit-card payment; these prices for up to 4 people, minibus for up to 8 also available; tel. 241-768-231, mobile 602-224-893, www.mike-chauffeur.cz, mike.chauffeur@cmail.cz). On the way to Český Krumlov, Mike will stop at no extra charge at Hluboká Castle and/or České Budějovice, where the original Bud beer is made. Mike can also arrange a local guide for your time in many of these places. And for day trips from Prague, Mike can bring bicycles along and will pedal with you.

Mike also offers "Panoramic Transfers" to **Vienna** (7,000 Kč, depart Prague at 8:00, arrive Český Krumlov at 10:00, stay up to 5 hours, 1-hour scenic Czech riverside-and-village drive, then a 2-hour autobahn ride to your Vienna hotel, maximum 4 people); **Budapest** (9,500 Kč via Bratislava or Český Krumlov, 6 hours); and **Kraków** (9,300 Kč direct, or 9,800 Kč with a stop at Auschwitz; these prices include all road taxes). Mike can also pick you up in any of these cities, and bring you to Prague. Check Mike's website for special deals on last-minute transfers, including super-cheap "deadhead" rides when you travel in the opposite direction of a full-fare client.

NEAR PRAGUE

Kutná Hora • Terezín Memorial • Konopiště Castle

Prague has plenty to keep a traveler busy, but don't overlook the interesting day trips in the nearby Bohemian countryside. Within a short bus or train ride of Prague (in different directions), you'll find a variety of worthwhile stopovers.

Kutná Hora

Kutná Hora (KOOT-nah HO-rah) is a refreshingly authentic, yet

unmistakably gorgeous town that sits on top of what was once Europe's largest silver mine. In its heyday, the mine was so productive that Kutná Hora was Bohemia's "second city" after Prague. Much of Europe's standard coinage was minted here, and the king got a 12 percent cut of every penny. In addition to financing much of Prague's grand architecture, these precious deposits also paid for Kutná Hora's particularly fine cathedral. But by about 1700, the mining and minting petered out, and the city slumbered.

Once rich, then ignored, Kutná Hora is now appreciated by tourists looking for a handy side-trip from Prague. While most visitors come here primarily for the famous, offbeat Sedlec Bone Church, the delightful town itself trumps it—with one of the finest Czech churches outside of Prague (St. Barbara's Cathedral), a breathtaking promenade

NEAR PRAGUE

Day Trips

overlooking the valley, a fascinating silver mine, and a cute, cobbled town center with pretty pastel houses.

All in all, underrated Kutná Hora makes a strong case for the title of "best Czech stop outside of Prague." Unlike dolled-up Český Krumlov, Kutná Hora is a typical Czech town. The shops on the main square cater to locals, and the factory between the Sedlec Bone Church and the train station—since the 1930s, the biggest tobacco processor in the country—is now Philip Morris' headquarters for Central Europe. Kutná Hora is about as close to quintessential Czech life as you can get.

GETTING TO KUTNÁ HORA

The town is 45 miles east of Prague. Direct trains from Prague stop at Kutná Hora's main train station, two miles from the town center (11/day, 1 hour; other trains are slower and require change in Kolín). From the main station, a local train shuttles visitors in just a few minutes to Sedlec Station (near the Sedlec Bone Church), then to the central Město Station (near the rest of the sights). After getting off at the main station, follow the passage beneath the tracks to the cute little yellow local train. For train schedules, see www.jizdnirady.idnes.cz.

In Prague, make sure to buy a ticket to "Kutná Hora Město" rather than "Kutná Hora hl. n." (the main station)—the price is nearly the same, and this gives you the flexibility to get off and on at any of the three Kutná Hora stations.

PLANNING YOUR TIME

For the most efficient visit, head to the Sedlec Bone Church first, then explore the town center of Kutná Hora. Kutná Hora is quiet on Sundays, when most shops are closed.

Here's my suggested plan: At Kutná Hora's main train station, transfer to the local train. Get off at its first stop (Kutná Hora Sedlec), and walk five minutes to the Bone Church. After your visit, head to St. Barbara's Cathedral in the town center via tourist minivan, taxi, or public bus. After touring the cathedral, follow my self-guided walk to the Czech Museum of Silver and take an English-language mine tour (consider booking ahead online or by phone, or simply drop by in advance to sign up). At the end of the day, walk to Město Station (about 15 minutes) to catch the train back to Kutná Hora's main train station, where you'll transfer to a train back to Prague.

Orientation to Kutná Hora

For a relatively small town (about 20,000 people), Kutná Hora is tricky to navigate: It's long and skinny, with a spaghetti of lanes spilling across the summit of a promontory that stretches from the main train station, past the Bone Church, to the historical center.

TOURIST INFORMATION

The main TI is on **Palacký Square** (Palackého Náměstí), housed in the same building as the Alchemy Museum (April-Sept daily 9:00-18:00; Oct-March Mon-Fri until 17:00, Sat-Sun until 16:00; tel. 327-512-378, www.kutnahora.cz). It offers Internet access and also rents bicycles (220 Kč/day, mobile 605-802-874).

A small TI kiosk, with handy WCs, is in front of the **cathedral;** you can also hire a local guide here. Reserve ahead if you can (500 Kč/hour Tue-Sun, no tours Mon, tel. 327-516-710, mobile 736-485-408, infocentrum@kh.cz).

Kutná Hora

ARRIVAL IN KUTNÁ HORA

The **Kutná Hora Sedlec Station** is a short walk from the Bone Church. From the station, head one block down the street perpendicular to the tracks, passing a large church on your right (a cathedral that predates the mine and the town). Cross the main street and find the small Bone Church in the middle of the cemetery directly ahead.

If you're skipping the Bone Church (or not visiting it first), stay on the train to the **Kutná Hora Město Station** in the valley. From there, hike up to St. Barbara's Cathedral (about 20 minutes) to find the start of my self-guided Kutná Hora walk.

1. Hotel u Vlašského Dvora
2. Hotel Garni & Restaurace Donna-U Žlutého Kola
3. Pivnice Dačický Restaurant
4. Dobrá Čajovna Teahouse
5. Piazza Navona Restaurant

Kutná Hora Walk

This self-guided walk connects virtually all of the sights in the historical center in a near-loop (Kutná Hora's most famous attraction—the Bone Church—is on the outskirts of town, and listed on page 163). Before you get too far into the walk, call or drop by the Czech Museum of Silver to book a spot on the 1.5-hour, claustrophobic mine tour. No stop on this walk is more than 10 minutes from the museum, so you can bail out and head for your tour at any point and easily resume the walk later.

• *Begin in the inviting park surrounding the cathedral.*

St. Barbara's Cathedral and Park: Rising like three pointy tents from a forest of buttresses, St. Barbara's strikes an exquisite Gothic profile. This culmination of Czech Gothic architecture was funded with a "spare no expense" attitude by a town riding the crest of a wave of mining wealth. Be sure to tour the **cathedral's interior**

(see listing, later)—but also take the time to do a slow lap around the pristine park that surrounds it.

Behind the church's apse, belly up to the **viewpoint** for an orientation to the city. From left to right, visually trace the historical center that perches along the promontory's crest: The long former Jesuit College now houses a modern art museum. The big, gray building that plunges down the cliff is the town's "little castle" *(Hrádek)*, with the Czech Museum of Silver. And the spire to the right of that bookends this walk. Surveying this scene, think about the history of a town made very, very rich by the glittering deposits it sits upon. Wealthy as it was, this was still an industrial town: The river below was so polluted they called it "Stink" in Czech. Notice the vineyards draping the hill. Kutná Hora is closer to Moravia (the eastern

Czech Republic) than it is to Prague—here, you're beginning to see the transition from beer country in Bohemia to the wine country of Moravia.

• *After circling the church, walk along the grand...*

Terrace: Just before you head along the panoramic promenade, notice the handy TI in the little house on the left. Then stroll regally along the stately white building, which now houses the modern and contemporary **GASK** art collection (see listing, later). The statues of saints that line the terrace are a reminder of the building's Jesuit past. The Jesuits arrived here in 1626 with a mission: to make the Protestant population Catholic again. These chubby sandstone figures, just like those on the Charles Bridge in Prague, were initially commissioned as Counter-Reformation propaganda pieces.

Near the end of the terrace, continue following the broad cobbled footpath downhill...and keep an eye out for an army of white-jacketed, white-helmeted miners trudging up the hill for their daily shift. Or maybe they're tourists, about to explore the former silver mine at the **Czech Museum of Silver,** which occupies the big building on your right (see listing, later).

• *At the little park in front of the museum, take the left (level) fork, following* Stone Fountain *signs. When you hit the bigger street (with lots of parked cars), turn left (uphill, on Rejskova), and bear left around the big drab building. You'll emerge into a little square (Rejskovo Náměstí), with a big and impressive...*

Stone Fountain (Kamenná Kašna): The intensive mining under Kutná Hora released arsenic and other toxins, poisoning the water supply. This means that the city struggled with obtaining

clean drinking water, which had to be brought to town by a sophisticated system of pipes, then stored in large tanks. At the end of the
15th century, the architect Rejsek built a 12-sided, richly decorated
Gothic structure over one of these tanks. Although no longer functioning, the fountain survives unchanged—the only structure like
it in Bohemia.

• *Facing the fountain, hook right around the corner and head down
Husova street. On the left, you'll pass the stately town library (Městská
Knihovna), then the gorgeous late-Baroque/Rococo Church of St. John of
Nepomuk (named for the ever-popular Czech patron saint). Turn left up
the street after this church (Lierova). At the top of the street, turn right
on Václavské Náměstí (Kutná Hora's own Wenceslas Square). On your
left, you'll spot the frilly decorations on the...*

Stone House (Kamenný Dům): Notice the meticulous detail
in the grape leaves, branches, and animals on this house's facade
and up in its gable. Talented Polish craftsmen delicately carved the
brittle stone into what was considered a marvel of its time. Skip the
boring museum of local arts and crafts inside.

• *Continue past the house as the street opens up into a leafy and inviting
square. For a slice of authentic Czech life, continue straight when the
street narrows again; a half-block down on your right, under the* tržnice
sign, is the town's humble...

Market: This double row of stalls selling fake Nike shoes and
cheap jeans is as much a part of Czech urban life today as farmers markets were in the past. Many of the stalls are run by Vietnamese immigrants, the Czech Republic's third-largest minority
(after Slovaks and Poles). Many came here in the 1970s as part of
a communist solidarity program that sent Vietnamese workers to
Czech textile factories. They learned the language, adapted to the
environment, and, after 1989, set off on a road to entrepreneurial
success that allowed them to bring over friends and relatives (Mon-
Fri 7:30-16:45, shorter hours Sat, closed Sun).

• *Backtrack a few steps uphill, then turn left to walk down through the
postcard-perfect Šultysova street, with a towering plague column at its
center. Turn left at the street past the column, enjoying the pretty, colorful arcades. You'll emerge into the lively main square.*

Palacký Square (Palackého Náměstí): Beautiful but still
somehow local, this square enjoys colorful facades, tempting al
fresco restaurant tables, and generous public benches. Across the
square on the left, notice the **TI**; inside the same building is the
Alchemy Museum (described later).

• *Exit the square at the far-right corner, following the traffic-free street
(in the gap between buildings, toward the green house). You'll enter...*

Havlíček Square (Havlíčkovo Náměstí): The monuments on
this leafy, parklike square are a Who's Who of important Czech
patriots.

Straight ahead, the stone statue with his arm outstretched is **Karel Havlíček** (1821-1856), the founder of Czech political journalism (and the square's namesake). From Kutná Hora, Havlíček ran an influential magazine highly critical of the Habsburg government. In 1851, he was forced into exile and detained for five years in the Tirolean Alps under police surveillance. His integrity is reflected by the quote inscribed on the statue: "You can try to bribe me with favors, you can threaten me, you can torture me, yet I will never turn a traitor." His motto became an inspiration for generations of Czech intellectuals, most of whom faced a similar combination of threats and temptations. Havlíček (whose name means "little Havel") was much revered in the 1970s and 1980s, when the *other* Havel (Václav) was similarly imprisoned for his dissent.

Below and to the right, the bronze, walrus-mustachioed statue in front of the big building honors the founder of Czechoslovakia, **Tomáš Garrigue Masaryk** (1850-1937; see sidebar on page 108). Circle around behind the pedestal to see the brief inscription tracing the statue's up-and-down history, which parallels the country's troubled 20th-century history: erected by Kutná Hora townspeople on October 27, 1938 (the eve of Czechoslovakia's 20th birthday); torn down in 1942 (by occupying Nazis, who disliked Masaryk as a symbol of Czech independence); erected again on October 27, 1948 (by freedom-loving locals, a few months after the communist coup); torn down again in 1957 (by the communists, who considered Masaryk an enemy of the working class); and erected once again on October 27, 1991. Notice that the Czechs, ever practical, have left a blank space below the last entry.

Masaryk stands in front of the **Italian Court** (Vlašský Dvůr). Step inside its fine courtyard. This palace, located on the site where Czech currency was once made, became Europe's most important mint and the main residence of Czech kings in the 1400s. It's named for the Italian minters who came to Kutná Hora to teach the locals their trade. Most of the present-day building is a 19th-century reconstruction. Today, it hosts a moderately interesting museum on minting and local history. While the main Gothic hall (now a wedding chamber) and the Art Nouveau-decorated St. Wenceslas Chapel are interesting, you can visit them only with a 40-minute guided tour (rarely in English; Czech tour comes with English handout; April-Sept daily 9:00-18:00, shorter hours Oct-March).

Exiting the courtyard of the Italian Court, turn right and watch on the wall to your right for a small bronze tablet showing a hand flashing a peace sign, covered with barbed wire. This is an unassuming little **memorial** to the victims of the communist regime's misrule and torture.

Continue straight down the steps into a little park, and then turn right to reach a great **viewpoint.** It overlooks the distinctive roof of the cathedral and the scenic valley below.

• *Your walk is finished. If you're headed for your tour at the **Czech Museum of Silver**, take this scenic route: Walk back up to Havlíček Square, circle around the Italian Court, curl along the downhill side of St. James' Church, and enjoy the views. Eventually the view terrace dead-ends at a little lane that bends right and uphill, depositing you at the museum.*

*If you're headed back to Prague, it takes about 15 minutes to walk to the **Kutná Hora Město train station** from Havlíček Square. Head downhill past the park, which funnels you between two buildings. Take the first left on Roháčova, then the first right on Sokolská. When you reach the wide cross-street (Nádražní), turn left and follow the train tracks to the little pink station.*

Sights in Kutná Hora

For sightseeing efficiency, start with the Bone Church on the outskirts, then return to the center of town (with the cathedral, silver mine/museum, and my self-guided walk).

ON THE OUTSKIRTS
▲▲Sedlec Bone Church (Kostnice v Sedlci)

Located about a mile and a half outside of the town's historical center, the Sedlec Bone Church sits in a serene graveyard and looks

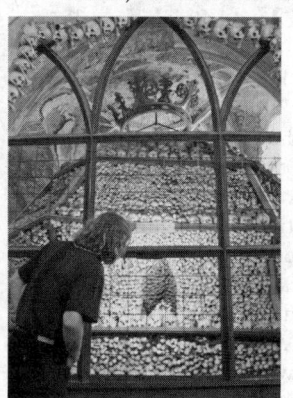

unassuming from the outside. But inside, it's filled with the bones of 40,000 people—stacked into neat, 20-foot-tall pyramids decorating the walls and ceilings. The 14th-century plagues and 15th-century wars provided all the raw material necessary for the monks who made these designs.

Cost and Hours: 90 Kč, daily April-Sept 8:00-18:00, March and Oct 9:00-17:00, Nov-Feb 9:00-16:00, good 40-Kč audioguide adds 15 minutes of commentary to make it more meaningful, tel. 327-561-143, www.kostnice.cz.

Visiting the Church: Stand outside the church. This is a place of reflection. The cemetery here was "seeded" with holy earth brought from Jerusalem, which made this sacred ground. Demand was high, and corpses that could no longer pay the rent (i.e., those who lacked surviving relatives with enough disposable income for postmortem real estate) were "evicted." What to do with the bones? Recycle them as church decorations with a message.

The monks, who first placed these bones 400 years ago, were guided by the belief that in order to live well, one must constantly remember death (*memento mori*—"what we are now, someday you shall be"). They also wanted to remind viewers that the earthly church was a community of both the living and the dead, a countless multitude that would one day stand before God. Later bone stackers were more interested in design than theology...as evidenced by the many show-off flourishes you'll see around the church.

Approach the church. Ignore the dull upper chapel, and head down below (look for the *kostnec* sign). Flanking the stairwell are two giant chalices made of bones (a symbol of Jan Hus' egalitarian approach to worship).

Downstairs, on either side are giant stacks of bones, reaching up to the top of the Gothic vaults (there are six such bone-pyramids in this small chapel). The skulls are neatly arranged on top, in the belief that this closeness to God would serve them well when Jesus returns to judge the living and the dead. Straight ahead dangles a chandelier, which supposedly includes at least one of every bone in the human body. In the glass case on the right (by the pillar), see the skulls with gnarly holes and other wounds. These belonged to soldiers who died fighting in the Hussite Wars—a boom time for this cemetery.

Finally, head into the left wing of the church, where you'll find a giant coat of arms of the aristocratic Schwarzenberg family—decorated with the skull of an Ottoman invader (a fearsome foe of the time), whose "eye" is being pecked out by a raven made of human bones.

Your visit is over. Go outside and head into town, thankful all of your limbs are intact.

Getting from the Church to Town: The Bone Church runs a **tourist minivan** that can shuttle you from the church to sights in town (35 Kč/person, 3-person minimum or pay the entire 105-Kč fee, April-Sept 9:00-18:00, Oct-March until 17:00, inquire at the desk, mobile 731-402-307). Ask the shuttle bus to drop you off at the park surrounding St. Barbara's Cathedral.

If the shuttle is on a break, church staff can call a **taxi,** which costs no more than 150 Kč to the cathedral. Another option is public **bus** #F01 (on weekdays) or #F07 (on weekends), which runs from near the Bone Church to a stop near the cathedral (12 Kč, pay driver, 2/hour Mon-Fri, 1/hour Sat-Sun, 20 minutes).

IN THE CENTER
▲▲St. Barbara's Cathedral (Chrám Sv. Barbory)

The cathedral was founded in 1388 by miners, who dedicated it to their patron saint. The dazzling interior celebrates the town's sources of wealth, with frescoes featuring mining and minting. This church was a stunning feat of architecture by two Gothic geniuses of Prague, Matyáš Rejsek and Benedict Ried. And, like Prague's cathedral, it sat unfinished and sealed off for centuries, until it was finally completed in the early 20th century.

Cost and Hours: 60 Kč, daily 9:00-18:00, shorter hours Nov-March, audioguide-40 Kč, tel. 327-515-796, www.khfarnost.cz.

Visiting the Cathedral: While this tour covers the highlights, you can ask to borrow slightly more detailed info sheets at the ticket desk or rent the more in-depth audioguide.

Head inside, walk to the middle of the main nave, and just take it all in. Intricate, lacy vaulting decorates an impossibly high ceiling that's also decorated with the coats of arms of local miners. This is the epitome of Gothic: a mind-bogglingly tall nave supported by flying buttresses that create space for not one, but two levels of big windows; pointed arches where the columns converge; and an overall sense of verticality and light.

Take in the gorgeous **high altar**—a Last Supper scene of carved and painted wood. Then circle clockwise around the apse, past

Baroque altars. Tune into the fine **stained-glass windows** (throughout the church) by František Urban, a somewhat less talented contemporary of Alfons Mucha, who nevertheless employs a similarly eye-pleasing Art Nouveau flair to illustrate scenes from church history. (A tiny version of this church's distinctive triple-pointed roofline appears in the background of several windows.)

Continue around the apse. The second-to-last chapel, called the **Smíšek Chapel,** is an artistic highlight. The late-Gothic frescoes—*The Arrival of the Queen of Sheba, The Trial of Trajan,* and especially the fresco under the chapel's window depicting two men with candles—are the only remaining works of a Dutch-trained master in Gothic Bohemia. The final chapel, called the **St. Wenceslas Chapel,** has frescoes under the windows showing miners going about their daily labor.

Continue up the side nave. Midway along, look for the **miner statue** on a pillar on your right. He's wearing a typical white miner's coat. White fabric was the cheapest option (as it required no dyes), and was easier to see in the dark. The leather mat wrapped around his waist made it easier for him to slide down chutes inside the mine. Most miners were healthy, unattached men in their 20s. An average of five miners died each day—from cave-ins, collapsing scaffolding, built-up poisonous gases, fires, and so on. At the back wall of the long chapel on your left, notice the precious frescoes from 1463 showing two people minting coins.

Loop around the back of the church, coming back up the left nave. You'll pass finely carved wooden **choir benches** that blend in perfect Gothic harmony with the church's architecture.

Art Gallery of the Central Bohemian Region (GASK)

The huge, former Baroque Jesuit college—which stretches from the cathedral all the way to the castle—was recently restored and converted into an art museum. It boasts the second-biggest exhibition space in the country (after the National Gallery in Prague), filled with ever-changing temporary exhibits of 20th- and 21st-century art.

Cost and Hours: Combo-ticket for all exhibits-200 Kč, single exhibit-80 Kč, April-Dec Tue-Sun 10:00-18:00, March Tue-Sun until 17:00, closed Mon year-round and Jan-Feb, Barborská 51, www.gask.cz.

▲Hrádek Castle and the Czech Museum of Silver (České Muzeum Stříbra)

Located in Kutná Hora's 15th-century Hrádek ("little castle"), the Czech Museum of Silver offers a fascinating look at the primary source of local wealth and pride. Over the centuries, this mine produced some 2,500 tons of silver, copper, and zinc. Today you can visit the facility only with a 1.5-hour tour, which lets you do some spelunking in the former miners' passages that run beneath the entire town center. Note that the tour involves some tight squeezes and may be overwhelming if you're claustrophobic. Also bring some warm clothing—mines are cold.

Cost and Tours: The English tour of the mine (Route II) costs 120 Kč; Route I, which includes only the aboveground museum, is pointless. You can book tours online only two or more days in advance. Better yet, call ahead (the day before or the morning of your visit) to ask when English tours are scheduled—wait through the Czech recording and ask to speak to someone in English. Without advance reservations, drop by the museum soon after you arrive in Kutná Hora to find out the schedule and reserve. Tel. 327-512-159, www.cms-kh.cz.

Hours: May-Sept Tue-Sun 10:00-18:00, April and Oct Tue-Sun until 17:00, Nov Tue-Sun until 16:00, closed Mon year-round and Dec-March.

Visiting the Museum and Mine: First, your guide takes you to see an intriguing horse-powered winch that once hoisted 2,000 pounds of rock at a time out of the mine. You'll learn the two methods miners used to extract the precious ore: either by hammering with a chisel or pick, or by setting a fire next to a rock—heating it until it naturally cracked.

Then you'll don a miner's coat and helmet, grab a bulky communist-era flashlight, and walk like the Seven Dwarves through the town center to a secret doorway. It's time to climb deep into the mine for a wet, dark, and claustrophobic tour of the medieval shafts that honeycomb the rock beneath the town—walking down 167 steps, traversing 900 feet of underground passages (but it feels even longer), then walking back up 35 steps.

Along the way, you'll see white limestone deposits in the form of mini-stalagmites and stalactites, and peer down into a 26-foot-deep pool of crystal-clear water. Squeezing through very tight passages, you'll feel like (fill in your own childbirth joke here). The mine holds a steady, year-round temperature of 54 degrees Fahrenheit while fat drops of condensation fall continually from the ceiling thanks to the nearly 100 percent humidity.

Prepare for the moment when all the lights go out, plunging you into a darkness as total as you'll ever experience. You'll understand why miners relied on their other senses. For instance, when silver was struck, it made a telltale sound and smelled faintly like garlic.

Finally, ascending to ground level, your guide will explain safety mechanisms at the surface, and walk you through the smelting and minting processes that turned those raw deposits into coins for an entire continent.

Alchemy Museum (Muzeum Alchymie)

The only one of its kind in the Czech Republic, situated in the surprisingly deep medieval cellars of this otherwise unassuming house, this museum features a laboratory dedicated to the pursuit of *prima materia* (primal matter). The English descriptions do a good job explaining the goals and methods of alchemy and the fate of its failed practitioners. The rare Gothic tower in the rear of the house is set up as an alchemist's study (complete with ancient books), looking much as it did when a prince used this vaulted space in his quest to purify matter and spirit.

Cost and Hours: 60 Kč, daily 9:00-18:00, Oct-March until 17:00, on the main square in the same building as the TI, tel. 327-512-378.

Sleeping and Eating in Kutná Hora

($$$$ = Splurge, $$$ = Pricier, $$ = Moderate, $ = Budget)
Sleeping: Although one day is enough for Kutná Hora, staying overnight saves you money (hotels are much cheaper here than in

Prague) and allows you to better savor the atmosphere of a small Czech town.

$ Hotel u Vlašského Dvora and **Hotel Garni** are two renovated townhouses run by the same management. Furnished in a mix of 1930s and modern style, the hotels come with access to a fitness center and sauna. Hotel Garni is slightly nicer (a few steps off main square at Havlíčkovo Náměstí 513, tel. 327-515-773, www.vlasskydvur.cz).

Eating: $$ Pivnice Dačický has made a theme of its namesake, a popular 17th-century author. Solid wooden tables rest under perky illustrations of medieval town life, and a once-local brew, also named after Dačický, flows from the tap. They serve standard Czech fare, as well as excellent game and fish. While its regulars still come here for the cheap lunch specials, during tourist season the crowd is mostly international. Service can be slow when a group arrives (daily 11:00-23:00, Rakova 8, tel. 327-512-248, mobile 603-434-367, www.dacicky.com).

$$ Dobrá Čajovna Teahouse also offers the chance to escape—not to medieval times, but to a Thai paradise. Filled with tea cases, water pipes, and character, this place is an ideal spot to dawdle away the time that this ageless town has reclaimed for you. On weekdays, they serve vegetarian lunch specials (Mon-Fri 11:00-22:00, Sat-Sun from 14:00, Havlíčkovo Náměstí 84, mobile 777-028-481).

$ Restaurace Donna-U Žlutého Kola ("Yellow Wheels") serves the fastest, tastiest Czech dishes in town, attracting a local crowd. There's a long menu in English, but the lunch specials are only listed on a separate sheet in Czech. When the weather's nice, sit in the shady courtyard behind the restaurant (daily, lunch specials until 15:00, on Havlíčkovo Náměstí, right above Hotel Garni, tel. 327-512-749).

$$ Piazza Navona features irritating English-language advertising ("the only true Italian restaurant in town"), but it still draws loyal customers thanks to its decent food and superb location on the main square (daily, Palackého Náměstí 90, tel. 327-512-588).

Kutná Hora Connections

To return to Prague, hop on a local train from Kutná Hora Město Station, near the historical center (or Kutná Hora Sedlec Station if you end your day at the Bone Church), and take it to the Kutná Hora main station for your train transfer to Prague. Note that the best Prague connection runs only about every two hours, so check schedules carefully; other options require an additional change and take much longer.

Terezín Memorial

Terezín (TEH-reh-zeen), an hour by bus from Prague, was originally a fortified town named after Habsburg Empress Maria Theresa (it's called "Theresienstadt" in German). It was built in the 1780s with state-of-the-art, star-shaped walls designed to keep out the Prussians. In 1941, the Nazis removed the town's 7,000 inhab-

itants and brought in 58,000 Jews, creating a horribly overcrowded ghetto. Ironically, the town's medieval walls, originally meant to keep Germans out, were later used by Germans to keep the Jews in. As the Nazis' model "Jewish town" for deceiving Red Cross inspectors, Terezín fostered the illusion that its Jewish inmates lived relatively normal lives—making the sinister truth all the more cruel.

Compared to other such sights in Eastern and Central Europe (such as Auschwitz or Mauthausen), Terezín (worth ▲▲) feels different: First, it focuses less on the Nazis' ruthless and calculated methods, and instead celebrates the arts and culture that thrived here despite the conditions—imbuing the place with a tragic humanity. Second, the various museums, memorials, and points of interest are spread over a large area in two distinct parts: a drab grid of a town and the original fortress (across the river, a short walk away). This means you're largely on your own to connect the dots and flesh out the story (use my self-guided tour to help).

GETTING THERE

The camp is about 40 miles northwest of Prague. It's most convenient to visit Terezín by **bus** (described next) or **tour bus** (various tour companies in Prague offer full-day tours to Terezín, including Wittman Tours, www.wittmann-tours.com; see page 56).

Buses to Terezín leave about hourly from Prague's Holešovice train station (Nádraží Holešovice, on Metro line C). When you get off the Metro (coming from the city center), head toward the front of the train, go upstairs, turn right, and walk to the end of the corridor. You'll see bus stands directly ahead, outside the station. The Terezín bus departs from platform 7 (direction: Litoměřice, pay driver). You'll arrive in Terezín an hour later at the public bus stop on the main square, across from the TI and around the corner from the Museum of the Ghetto. Some buses also stop earlier, by the Small Fortress. The driver and fellow passengers may tell you to get off there, but my self-guided tour works best if you begin at the stop in town (after the bus passes a field of crosses on your right and travels across the river).

Two different companies (Busline and Kavka) run this route; for schedules that include both companies, see www.jizdnirady.idnes.cz—you want "Terezín LT" (be sure to check the return schedule, too; for details on getting back to Prague, see "Terezín Connections," later).

PLANNING YOUR TIME

Because the sights are scattered, plan on lots of walking, and give yourself plenty of time: Three hours is barely enough for a minimal visit (and requires skipping some sights); allow at least four hours to quickly see everything, and more like six to really delve in. Your understanding of Terezín becomes immeasurably deeper with the help of a local guide (for a list of Prague-based guides, see page 53).

With more time, stop in the nearby attractive town of Litoměřice for lunch before returning to Prague.

ORIENTATION TO TEREZÍN

Cost: The 210-Kč combo-ticket includes all parts of the camp.

Hours: Most sights, including the Museum of the Ghetto, Magdeburg Barracks, and Hidden Synagogue, are open daily 9:00-18:00, Nov-March until 17:30. The Columbarium and Crematorium are closed Sat. The Crematorium is open daily 10:00-18:00, Nov-March until 16:00; the Small Fortress is open daily 8:00-18:00, Nov-March until 16:30.

Tours: Guided tours in English are offered if enough people request them; call ahead to get the schedule and reserve a spot (included in entry).

Information: Terezín's town **TI,** in the corner of the town hall that faces the Prague bus stop, has staff that are helpful and speak English (Sun 9:00-15:00, Mon-Thu 8:00-17:00, Fri 8:00-13:30, closed Sat, Náměstí ČSA 179, tel. 416-782-616, www.terezin.cz). In their window, you'll find handy information (such as the Prague bus schedule and directions to town landmarks). Museum information—tel. 416-782-225, mobile 606-632-914, www.pamatnik-terezin.cz.

Eating: Avoid the stale sandwiches in the **Museum of the Ghetto**'s dingy basement cafeteria, where most tour guides inexplicably bring their clients. The **Small Fortress** has a $ cafeteria.

   In Terezín town, **$$ Pizzeria Na Obzoru** ("On the Horizon") serves pasta, steaks, and creamy risottos on its pastel-colored, sailor-themed ground floor or in a brick-and-stone vaulted cellar (daily 11:00-22:00, one block up the street from the hidden synagogue at Dlouhá 24, mobile 731-771-841). **$ Atypic Restaurant** offers Czech canteen classics popular with students and employees of the museum, served on an airy terrace or in the cramped interior with a peek into the kitchen (daily 9:30-21:00, Máchova 91, tel. 416-782-780).

BACKGROUND

Terezín was the Nazis' model "Jewish town," a concentration camp dolled up for propaganda purposes. Here, in a supposedly "self-governed Jewish resettlement area," Jewish culture seemed to thrive, as "citizens" put on plays and concerts, published a magazine, and raised their families. But it was all a carefully planned deception, intended to convince Red Cross inspectors that Jews were being treated well. The Nazis even coached prisoners on how to answer the inspectors' anticipated questions.

The Nazi authorities also used Terezín as a place to relocate elderly and disabled Jews from throughout the Third Reich—so the ghetto was filled with prisoners not only from the Czech lands, but from all over Europe.

In the fall of 1944, the Nazis began transporting Jews from Terezín to even more severe death camps (especially Auschwitz) in large numbers. Virtually all Terezín's Jews (155,000 over the course of the war) ultimately ended up dying—either here (35,000) or in extermination camps farther east.

One of the notable individuals held at Terezín was Viennese artist Friedl Dicker-Brandeis. This daring woman, a leader in the Bauhaus art movement, found her life's calling in teaching children freedom of expression. She taught the kids in the camp to distinguish between the central things—trees, flowers, lines—and peripheral things, such as the conditions of the camp. In 1944, Dicker-Brandeis volunteered to be sent to Auschwitz after her husband was transported there; she was killed a month later.

Of the 15,000 children who passed through Terezín from 1942 to 1944, fewer than 100 survived. The artwork they created at Terezín is a striking testimony to the cruel horror of the Holocaust. In 1994, Hana Volavková, a Terezín survivor and the director of the Jewish Museum in Prague, collected the children's artwork and poems in the book *I Never Saw Another Butterfly*. Selections of the Terezín drawings are also displayed and well-described in English in Prague's Pinkas Synagogue (described on page 76).

Of the cultural activities that took place at Terezín, the best known was the children's opera *Brundibár*. Written just before the war, the antifascist opera premiered secretly in Prague at a time when Jewish activities were no longer permitted. From 1943 to 1944, the play, performed in Czech, ran 55 times in the camp. After the war it was staged internationally, and was rewritten and published in the US in 2003 as a children's book by Tony Kushner and Maurice Sendak (whose version later appeared on Broadway).

NEAR PRAGUE

NEAR PRAGUE

To Litoměřice

FORMER DEUTSCHES REICH

FORMER PROTECTORATE OF BOHEMIA & MORAVIA

To Ústí nad Labem

TEREZÍN TOWN

PRAŽSKÁ

MÁCHOVA

HUSOVA

FUČÍKOVA

19

16

5 KVĚTNA

FORMER BORDER OF SUDETENLAND

8

17

1

9

Main Square

WATER GATE

18

28 ŘÍJNA

DLOUHÁ

PALACKÉHO

VODÁRENSKÁ

TYRŠOVA

3

FORTRESS WALLS

N

BOHUŠOVICE GATE

4

5

COLUMBARIUM

200 Meters

200 Yards

6

To Bohušovice

Vegetable Plots

To 7

◑ SELF-GUIDED TOUR

The Terezín experience consists of two parts: the walled town of Terezín, which became a Jewish ghetto under Hitler; and (a half-mile walk east, across the river) the Small Fortress, which was a Gestapo prison camp for mostly political prisoners of all stripes (including non-Jewish Czechs). The complete tour involves about four miles of walking (including the walk from the town to the Small Fortress, then back again to catch your return bus to Prague). Pace yourself. If you want to cut it short, I've suggested sections that you could skip.

Terezín Town

• *The bus from Prague drops you off at Terezín town's spacious...*

Main Square (Náměstí Československé Armády): Today Ter-

Terezín

FORTRESS WALLS

SMALL FORTRESS

⑮

⑪ ⑫ ⑭

⑳ ⑬

⑩

To Prague

New Ohře River

NEAR PRAGUE

<u>Sights</u>
❶ Main Square
❷ Museum of the Ghetto
❸ Magdeburg Barracks
❹ Railway Tracks
❺ Columbarium
❻ Memorial Halls
❼ To Crematorium, Cemeteries & Memorial to Soviet Soldiers
❽ Hidden Synagogue
❾ Dry Moat
❿ National Cemetery
⓫ Gatehouse

⓬ Model Prison Cells, Washroom & Gavrilo Princip's Cell
⓭ History & Art Museum
⓮ Fourth Courtyard
⓯ Execution Ground & Mass Grave

<u>Other</u>
⓰ Bus to/from Prague
⓱ Bus to/from Litoměřice
⓲ Pizzeria Na Obzoru
⓳ Atypic Restaurant
⓴ Cafeteria

ezín feels like a workaday, if unusually tidy, Czech town, with a tight grid plan hemmed in by its stout walls. And for much of its

history, that's exactly what it was. But when Hitler annexed Czechoslovakia, he evicted the residents to create a ghetto for Jews forcibly transplanted here from Prague and elsewhere. Because it started out as a pretty town, rather than a gloomy prison or custom-built concentration camp, the Nazi authorities cultivated Terezín as a "model" to illustrate to the outside world how good the Jews had it here. (For more details, see "Background," earlier.)

Begin your tour by mentally filling the (now mostly empty)

Petr Ginz, Young Artist and Writer

Born in 1928 to a Jewish father and non-Jewish mother, Prague teenager Petr Ginz excelled at art and was a talented writer who penned numerous articles, short stories, and even a science-fiction novel. Petr was sent to the concentration camp at Terezín in 1942, where he edited the secret boys' publication *Vedem (We Are Ahead),* writing poetry and drawing illustrations, and paying contributors with food rations he received from home.

Some of Petr's artwork and writings were preserved by Terezín survivors and archived by the Jewish Museum in Prague. In 2003, Ilan Ramon, the first Israeli astronaut and the son of a Holocaust survivor, took one of Petr's drawings—titled *Moon Country*—into space aboard the final, doomed mission of the space shuttle *Columbia.*

The publicity over the *Columbia*'s explosion and Petr's drawing spurred a Prague resident to come forward with a diary he'd found in his attic. It was Petr's diary from 1941 to 1942, hidden decades earlier by Petr's parents and chronicling the year before the teen's deportation to Terezín. *The Diary of Petr Ginz* has since been published in more than 10 languages.

In the diary, Petr matter-of-factly documented the increasing restrictions on Jewish life in occupied Prague, interspersing the terse account with dry humor. In the entry for September 19, 1941, Petr wrote, "They just introduced a special sign for Jews" alongside a drawing of the Star of David. He continued, "On the way to school I counted 69 'sheriffs,'" referring to people wearing the star.

Petr spent two years at Terezín before being sent to Auschwitz, where he died in a gas chamber. He was 16.

square with thousands of Jewish inmates, all wearing their yellow *Juden* Star of David patches. Picture the giant circus tent and barbed-wire fence that stood on this square for two years during the war. Inside, Jewish workers boxed special motors for German vehicles being used on the frigid Soviet front. As part of year-long preparations for the famous Red Cross visit (which lasted all of six hours on June 23, 1944), the tent and fence were replaced by flower beds (which you still see on the square today) and a pavilion for outdoor music performances.

• *The helpful little TI is across the street from the bus stop. Just around the corner—in the yellow former schoolhouse that faces the adjacent square—is the...*

Museum of the Ghetto: This modern, concise, well-presented museum, with artifacts and insightful English descriptions, sets the stage for your Terezín visit. You can buy the Terezín combo-ticket here (and ask about the day's film schedule—explained next page). You'll find two floors of **exhibits** about the development of the Nazis' "Final Solution." The ground floor includes some evocative memorials (such as a stack of seized suitcases and a list of Terezín's victims). The exhibit upstairs illuminates life in the ghetto with historical documents (including underground publications and letters—inmates were allowed to mail one per month), items belonging to inmates, and video footage of survivors' testimonies. In the stairwell are large illustrations of ghetto life, drawn by people who lived here.

In the basement is a theater showing four excellent **films.** One film documents the history of the ghetto (31 minutes), offering a helpful, if dry, overview of the sights you'll see. Two others (14 and 20 minutes) focus on children's art in the camp, and the last is a 10-minute montage of clips from *Der Führer schenkt den Juden eine Stadt (The Führer Gives a City to the Jews),* by Kurt Gerron. Gerron, a Berlin Jew, was a 1920s movie star who appeared with Marlene Dietrich in *Blue Angel.* Deported to Terezín, Gerron in 1944 was asked by the Nazis to produce a propaganda film. The resulting film depicts healthy (i.e., recently arrived) "Jewish settlers" in Terezín happily viewing concerts, playing soccer, and sewing in their rooms—yet an unmistakable, deadly desperation radiates from their pallid faces. The only moment of genuine emotion comes toward the end, when a packed room of children applauds the final lines of the popular anti-Nazi opera *Brundibár:* "We did not let ourselves down, we chased the nasty Brundibár away. With a happy song, we won it all." Even the Nazis were not fooled: Gerron and his wife were shipped to Auschwitz, and the film was never shown in public.

• *To learn more about living conditions in the camp, return to the main square and continue straight past it, along Tyršova street. A few blocks down, just before the wall, on the left you'll find the...*

Magdeburg Barracks: Peek inside the large courtyard (you'll recognize it as the "soccer stadium" in Gerron's film), then con-

tinue upstairs and follow the one-way, counterclockwise loop. First you'll see a meticulously restored dormitory, complete with three-tiered beds, suitcases, eyeglasses, dolls, chessboards, sewing kits... and utterly no privacy. After Terezín's residents were evicted and Jews were imported in huge numbers, every available space was converted from single-family apartments to outrageously cramped slumber mills like this. Jaunty music lures you around the corner to the first of several rooms celebrating the arts here at Terezín. You'll see exhibits on composers, artists, and writers, who expressed their creativity even in these horrifying conditions. These include profiles of individuals (such as young Petr Ginz—see sidebar) and a wide variety of stirring art illustrating life in the ghetto. Near the end is a room reproducing the camp cabaret stage, where inmates entertained each other.

• *With limited time or energy, consider skipping the next several stops, which take a long, if poignant, detour outside the walls. Jump ahead to the moat (see "Dry Moat," later) by leaving the barracks, turning right, and walking 100 yards to a brick gate. (If you do decide to skip the following stops, you can easily fit in the Hidden Synagogue at the end, before hopping on your bus back to Prague, as it's one block from the main square.)*

To continue the full tour, exit the barracks, turn left, and walk until you dead-end at the city wall. Turn right and walk along the inside of the stout wall to the far corner. Slicing through the hole in the wall are the remnants of...

Railway Tracks: In the early years of the camp, Jews arrived at the train station in the nearby town of Bohušovice and then had to walk the remaining 1.5 miles to Terezín. This was too public a display for the Nazis, who didn't want townspeople to observe the transports and become suspicious (or to try to interact with the inmates in any way). So the prisoners were forced to construct a railway line that led right to Terezín...and then back out again to Auschwitz.

• *Follow the tracks outside the wall.*

Columbarium and Memorial Halls: Exiting the wall, on the left is a Columbarium, where the Nazis deposited cardboard boxes containing the ashes of dead prisoners. The Germans originally promised that the remains would be properly buried after the war, but in 1945, to erase evidence, the ashes of Terezín victims were dumped into the Ohře River. Farther along, past the little pension/café and across the bridge, on the right you will find Jewish and Christian ceremonial halls and the main morgue.

• *When the main road swings right, take the left turn (marked Krematorium) and walk past bucolic vegetable plots and fruit gardens, and along a driveway lined with pointy poplar trees, to reach the...*

Crematorium and Cemeteries: The low-lying yellow building (to the left of the monumental menorah) is the **crematorium,** where Nazis would burn the bodies of those who died here. Step inside to see a small exhibit on death and burial in the ghetto (explaining that, over time, single graves in coffins gave way to mass graves, then to simply burning bodies en masse and dumping the ashes in the river). Then head into the chilling main chamber, where four ovens were kept busy cremating bodies.

Outside, surrounding the crematorium is a **Jewish cemetery** with the bodies of those who died before cremation became the norm. Farther to the right (as you face the crematorium) is a **Russian cemetery** and a **Memorial to Soviet Soldiers.** The Soviets liberated Terezín without a fight as the Nazis retreated, on May 8, 1945. But just days before, an epidemic of typhus had spread through the camp. In the weeks after the war ended, scores of Soviet soldiers and medical workers who tried to contain the epidemic died, along with hundreds of former prisoners.

• *Retrace your steps back through the wall, and continue straight ahead past the train tracks, up Dlouhá street. After three blocks, watch on the left for the low-profile green house at #17. Ring the bell to be admitted to the fascinating...*

Hidden Synagogue: Inside you'll find a courtyard; the bakery that used to be here hid the synagogue behind it. This is the only one of the camp's eight hidden synagogues that survived. The atmospheric space is still inscribed with two Hebrew captions, which are translated as "May my eyes behold, how You in compassion return to Sinai," and "If I forget Jerusalem, may my tongue rot and my right arm fall off." These words indicate that the prayer room belonged to a congregation of Zionists (advocates of a Jewish state), who, one would expect, were specifically targeted by the Nazis.

Upstairs, a few prisoners lived in a tight attic space. Even though the cramped rooms (reconstructed with period items) seem impossibly small, they were a far better accommodation than the mass housing in which most prisoners were interned. It's thought that a group of craftsmen who labored in a nearby workshop were "lucky" enough to live here.

• *Leaving the synagogue house, turn right, and at the corner, turn left to pop out at the main square. To proceed to the Small Fortress, head down Tyršova as if you're going to the Magdeburg Barracks. Before you get there, turn left along the park, then continue one block up Palackého to the brick gate. You'll cross a bridge over a...*

Dry Moat: Imagine this moat filled with plots of vegetables, grown by starving Jews for well-fed SS officers. Turn left and walk along the moat. The top of the fortification walls on the other side were once equipped with benches and pathways.

• When you reach the main road, turn right across the New Ohře River (the original course of the river was diverted here when Terezín was built). After about five minutes, you'll come to a blocked-off, tree-lined driveway and the prison camp.

Terezín Prison Camp

• On the right side of the driveway is the wedge-shaped...

National Cemetery: The remains of about 10,000 victims of Terezín (including 2,386 individual graves; the rest were moved here from mass graves elsewhere) fill this cemetery, which was created after the war's end. The sea of headstones powerfully illustrates the scope of the crime that took place here. Notice that, in addition to the giant Star of David (closer to the fortress), a cross towers over the cemetery. This is a reminder that we've left the Jewish ghetto and are about to enter a very different part of the Terezín complex. From 1940 to 1945, this fortress functioned as a Gestapo prison, through which 32,000 inmates passed (of whom nearly 10 percent died here)—chiefly members of the Czech resistance and communists. While the majority of the camp's victims weren't Jewish, the 1,500 Jews interned here were treated with particular severity.

• Now head under black-and-white-striped gate.

Gatehouse: Inside the gate, on the left, is a modest museum about the pre-WWII history of this fortress. If you need a break before continuing, you could pause at the handy cafeteria. The wood-and-metal chandeliers inside were produced by Jewish workers for the SS officers who once dined in these two rooms.

• Continuing into the central part of the fortress, watch on the left for a turnstile into a long, skinny side courtyard. Go in and head to the end of the courtyard, under the notorious Arbeit Macht Frei *sign painted above an arched gate (a postwar replica of the viciously sarcastic "Work will set you free" sign that was displayed at all camps). Go under this gate to reach a courtyard ringed with...*

Model Prison Cells: Step into some of the barracks on the right side of the courtyard to see tight, triple-decker bunks where prisoners were essentially stacked at bedtime. Halfway down the courtyard, under the *Block-A* sign, peek into the medical cell.

At the far end, the washroom in the right-hand corner (by #15) was built solely for the purpose of fooling Red Cross inspectors. Go ahead, turn the faucets: No pipes were ever installed to bring in water.

The shower room two doors to the left, on the other hand, was used to fool the Jews. Here they got used to the idea of communal bathing, so they wouldn't be suspicious when they were later taken to similar-looking installations at Auschwitz. (There were no gas chambers at Terezín—most of the deaths here were caused by malnutrition, disease, and, to a lesser extent, execution.)

Before the Nazis, the Austrian monarchy used the Small Fortress as a prison. In the little side courtyard next to the shower room, look for a ghostly doorway with a plaque that recalls the most famous prisoner from that time, Bosnian Serb **Gavrilo Princip,** whose assassination of Archduke Franz Ferdinand and his wife Žofie in 1914 sparked World War I (see sidebar on page 183). Princip died here in 1918 of tuberculosis; of the six Sarajevo conspirators imprisoned here, only two survived.

• *Return through the* Arbeit Macht Frei *gate, then back out into the fortress' central yard. Turn left and continue deeper into the complex. The large building on your right is marked by* Muzeum *signs.*

Museum: The ground floor of this building features an exhibit about the Nazi-era history of the Small Fortress. Photographs and brief descriptions identify many of the individuals who were imprisoned—and in many cases, executed. Upstairs is a gallery of paintings by prominent Czech artists, mostly focusing on themes of camp life (and a few about the Spanish Civil War).

• *Back out in the main yard, continue straight ahead, through two gateways in a row. You'll emerge into the wide, eerie...*

Fourth Courtyard: Here you'll have more opportunities to step into former prison cells that flank the yard; some of these house temporary exhibits. At the far end, you'll find a plaque in the ground listing the 17 countries whose citizens perished at Terezín.

• *Returning to the fortress' main yard once more, turn right and follow the long buildings. Turn right to find the...*

Execution Ground and Mass Grave: This is where firing squads executed somewhere between 200 and 300 of Hitler's enemies. Many of Terezín's victims were buried in mass graves along the fortress ramparts. After the war, these remains were moved to the National Cemetery we saw on the way into the fortress.

• *Our tour ends here. As you ponder Terezín, remember the message of all such memorials: Never again.*

TEREZÍN CONNECTIONS

The bus for **Prague** leaves from Terezín's main square (hourly, 1 hour, pay driver). To continue from Terezín to **Dresden,** Germany, take a taxi or bus (3/hour, 5 minutes, pay driver) from Terezín's main square to the Bohušovice station, then take the local train from Bohušovice to Ústí (2/hour, 30 minutes), where you can catch the international express train (every 1-2 hours, 1 hour). For bus and train schedules, see www.idos.cz.

Konopiště Castle

Konopiště (KOH-noh-peesh-tyeh) was the Neo-Gothic residence of the Archduke Franz Ferdinand d'Este—the heir to the Austro-Hungarian Empire, whose assassination sparked World War I. Located 30 miles south of Prague, it's workable either as a day trip or on the way to Český Krumlov. While it's the least visually arresting of the castles near Prague, its interior has some captivating stories to tell about its former in-

habitants. Enjoyable for anyone, Konopiště is worth ▲ for most. But it's a must for Habsburg aficionados—historians find it worth ▲▲▲.

Construction of the castle began in the 14th century, but today's exterior and furnishings date from about 1900, when Franz Ferdinand, renovated his new home. As one of the first castles in Europe to have an elevator, a WC, and running water, Konopiště shows "modern" living at the turn of the 20th century.

Those who lived at Konopiště played a role in one of the most important moments in European history: Franz Ferdinand's assassination in Sarajevo (chillingly illustrated by items displayed inside the castle). The shooting eventually meant the end of the age of hereditary, divine-right, multiethnic empires—and the dawn of a Europe of small, nationalistic, democratic nation-states. Historians get goose bumps at Konopiště, where if you listen closely, you can almost hear the last gasp of Europe's absolute monarchs.

The castle interior is only viewable via a guided tour. There are several tour options, but the best is Route 3 (limited space, so call ahead to reserve; explained later, under "Orientation to Konopiště").

GETTING THERE

By Train: Trains from Prague's main station drop you in Benešov (2/hour, 1 hour, www.idos.cz); a well-marked trail goes from the station to the castle (1.5 miles). To walk to the castle, as you exit the Benešov train station, turn left and walk along the street parallel to the railroad tracks. Turn left at the first bridge you see crossing over the tracks. Along the way you'll see trail markers on trees, walls, and lampposts—one yellow stripe between two white stripes. Follow these markers. As you leave town, watch for a marker with an arrow pointing to a path in the woods. Take this path to bypass the castle's enormous parking lot, which is clogged with souvenir shops and bus fumes.

By Car: Konopiště is about a 45-minute drive from Prague and a two-minute detour off of the main route to Český Krumlov (head east toward Brno on the D-1 expressway; take exit #21 toward *Benešov/České Budějovice/Linz;* after about 15 kilometers, watch for the Konopiště turnoff on the right). Bypass the first, giant parking lot (ringed by restaurants); a bit farther along, on the left near the lake, is a smaller lot that's closer to the castle. From either lot, hike uphill about 10-15 minutes to Konopiště.

ORIENTATION TO KONOPIŠTĚ

Cost and Tours: The recommended Route 3 is 320 Kč (described later, under "Visiting the Castle"); Routes 1 and 2 are 220 Kč apiece; all three cost 690 Kč. Space on Route 3 is limited to eight people per hour: It's best to reserve a spot in advance by calling one day ahead or on the morning of your visit (worth the 20-Kč extra charge). All tickets are 30 percent cheaper if you join a Czech-speaking tour (but renting the English audioguide costs 50 Kč—effectively negating most of your savings). Tel. 317-721-366, www.zamek-konopiste.cz.

Hours: May-Aug Tue-Sun 9:00-12:30 & 13:00-17:00; Sept Tue-Fri 9:00-16:00, Sat-Sun until 17:00; April and Oct Tue-Fri until 15:00, Sat-Sun until 16:00; closed Mon year-round and Nov-March.

VISITING THE CASTLE

While there are three different tour options, **Route 3** is the most intimate and interesting. It takes you through the rooms where Franz Ferdinand, his Czech bride Žofie, and their three kids lived while waiting for Uncle Franz Josef to expire. When the communists took over, they simply threw drop cloths over the furniture and let the place sit, untouched, for decades. Now everything has been meticulously restored (with the help of 1907 photographs)—launching you right into a turn-of-the-20th-century time capsule.

The tour takes you through halls upon halls of hunting trophies (each one marked with the place and date of the kill), paintings of royal relatives (including an entire wall of Italian kings—relations of Franz Ferdinand's Neapolitan mother), and photographs of the many places they traveled and the three kids as they grew up. The tour includes Franz Ferdinand's dressing room (with his actual uniform and his travel case all packed up and ready to go); his private study (which feels like he just stepped away from his desk for a cup of coffee); the living room (with 1,180 pairs of antlers on the walls); the private dining room (with the table set for an intimate family dinner for five); the master bedroom (with its huge bed); the children's bedrooms, playrooms, and classroom (with their toys and books still on the shelves); three bathrooms with running water and flushing toilets; and—in the final room—a glass display case containing the dress Žofie was wearing that fateful day in Sarajevo (including her still-bloodstained corset). Down the hall are the royal couple's death masks, Franz Ferdinand's bloody suspenders, and the actual bullet that ended Žofie's life.

Route 2—which covers the oldest wing of the castle—is also worth considering, and provides the most comprehensive look into the castle, its history, and celebrated collections. You'll see the oversized elevator (with a couch to make the family comfortable on the 45-second ride upstairs), the library, and the staggeringly large armory collection. **Route 1,** covering some other rooms, the hunting hall, and the balcony, is the least interesting.

Other Sights at the Castle: Your tour ticket includes two quirky additional sights that are worth poking into. **Franz Ferdinand's Shooting Range,** just off of the castle courtyard, offers a quick glimpse at the emperor-in-waiting's elaborate system of moving targets; a video demonstrates how the various targets would move around to keep his skills sharp. The **Museum of St. George,** tucked beneath the long terrace (around the side of the palace),

Archduke Franz Ferdinand (1863-1914)

Archduke Franz Ferdinand was born to the brother of the Habsburg emperor (Franz Josef) and a Neapolitan princess. After his cousin died under "mysterious circumstances," Franz Ferdinand was thrust into the role of heir apparent to the throne of the Austro-Hungarian Empire—one of the biggest realms Europe has ever seen. But he had to be patient: His Uncle Franz Josef took the throne in 1848 and would hold onto it for nearly 70 years. In fact, he outlived his nephew.

While he waited, Franz Ferdinand kept himself busy by spending time at his bachelor pad in Konopiště. At a ball in Vienna, he met a gorgeous but low-ranking Czech countess, Žofie Chotková (also known by her German name, Sophie). The couple danced all night. After long years of a secret courtship, Franz Ferdinand announced his intentions to make Žofie his wife. His uncle was displeased—Žofie was "only" aristocratic, and the expected path for the heir apparent would be to marry a Western European princess. He insisted on a morganatic marriage so that Žofie could never be an empress and none of the children could inherit the throne. These family squabbles cemented Franz Ferdinand and Žofie's preference for living at Konopiště.

While waiting for a succession that would never arrive, Franz Ferdinand threw himself into his hobbies with an obsessive-compulsive zeal. He traveled around the world twice—partly for diplomatic reasons, but largely to pursue his passion for exotic hunting. Shooting at anything in sight—deer, bears, tigers, elephants, and crocodiles—he killed about 300,000 animals in all, a few thousand of whom stare morbidly at you from the walls at Konopiště. Franz Ferdinand and Žofie were also devoted parents, raising three children: young Žofie, Max, and Ernesto.

In the Kaiser's Pavilion on the grounds of Konopiště, Franz Ferdinand met with German Kaiser Wilhelm and tried to talk him out of plotting a war against Russia. Wilhelm argued that a war would work to the mutual benefit of Germany and Austria: Germans wanted colonies, and the Austro-Hungarian Empire—crippled by the aspirations of its many nationalities—could use a war to divert attention from its domestic problems. But Franz Ferdinand foresaw that war would be suicidal for Austria's overstretched monarchy.

Soon after, Franz Ferdinand and Žofie went to Sarajevo, in the Habsburg-annexed territories of Bosnia and Herzegovina. On that trip, young Gavrilo Princip, a Bosnian Serb separatist, shot the Habsburg archduke who so loved shooting, as well as Žofie. Franz Ferdinand's assassination ironically gave the Germans (and their pro-war allies in the Austro-Hungarian administration) the pretext for starting the war against Serbia and its ally, Russia. World War I soon broke out. The event Franz Ferdinand had tried to prevent was, in fact, sparked by his death.

NEAR PRAGUE

displays Franz Ferdinand's collection of hundreds of sculptures and paintings of St. George slaying the dragon...taking a theme to an extreme.

While the stretch between the parking lot and the castle entrance is overrun by tour groups, the **gardens** and the **park** are surprisingly empty. In the summer, the flowers and goldfish in the rose garden are a big hit with visitors. The peaceful 30-minute walk through the woods around the lake (wooden bridge at the far end) offers fine castle views.

Tucked away in the bushes behind the pond is a pavilion coated with tree bark, a perfect picnic spot. This simple structure, nicknamed the **Kaiser's Pavilion,** was the site of a fateful meeting between the German Kaiser Wilhelm and the Archduke Franz Ferdinand (see the sidebar on page 183).

Eating at Konopiště Castle: Three touristy restaurants sit under the castle, and a café and restaurant are in the castle courtyard, but I'd rather bring picnic supplies from Prague (or buy them at the grocery store by the Benešov train station). While the crowds wait to pay too much for lousy food in the restaurants, you'll enjoy the peace and thought-provoking ambience of a **picnic** in the shaded Kaiser's Pavilion. Or eat cheaply on Benešov's main square (try **$ U Zlaté Hvězdy**—"The Golden Star").

ČESKÝ KRUMLOV

Krummau

Surrounded by mountains, lassoed by its river, and dominated by its castle, this enchanted town mesmerizes visitors. When you see its awe-inspiring castle, delightful Old Town of cobbled lanes and shops, and easy canoeing options, you'll understand why having fun is a slam-dunk here. Romantics are floored by its spectacular setting; you could spend all your time doing aimless laps from one end of town to the other.

The sharp bends in the Vltava provide natural moats, so it's no wonder Český Krumlov has been a choice spot for eons. Celtic tribes settled here a century before Christ. Then came Germanic tribes. The Slavic tribes arrived in the ninth century. The Rožmberks (Rosenbergs)—Bohemia's top noble family—ran the city from 1302 to 1602. You'll spot their rose symbol all over town.

The 16th century was the town's Golden Age, when Český Krumlov hosted artists, scientists, and alchemists from across Europe. In 1588, the town became home to an important Jesuit college. In 1602, the Rožmberks ran out of money to fund their lavish lifestyles, so they sold their territory to the Habsburgs—who ushered in a more Germanic period. After that, as many as 75 percent of the town's people were German—until 1945, when most Germans were expelled (for more on this era and its repercussions, see the sidebar on page 192).

Český Krumlov's rich mix of Gothic, Renaissance, and Baroque buildings is easy to miss. As you wander, be sure to look up...notice the surviving details in the fine stonework and pretty gables. Step into shops. Snoop into back lanes and tiny squares. Gothic buildings curve with the winding streets. Many precious Gothic and Renaissance frescoes were whitewashed in Baroque times (when the colorful trimmings of earlier periods were way out of style). Today, these frescoes are being rediscovered and restored.

Český Krumlov is a huge tourist magnet, which makes things colorful and easy for travelers. At times it can feel like a medieval theme park—but fortunately there are still hidden nooks and sleepy back alleys to make the place feel genuine.

PLANNING YOUR TIME

It's easy to enjoy Český Krumlov without ever paying to enter a sight (morning and evening are best for strolling without crowds). But a tour of the Baroque Theater at the castle is worth considering: If you want to join an English tour, sign up first thing in the morning (call ahead or visit in person), then build your day around your visit time. While you're at it, consider booking an English tour of the castle interior. Those who hate planning ahead on vacation can join a Czech tour of the theater or castle anytime (English information sheets provided). And visits to the newly restored synagogue and Seidel Photo Studio Museum bring more recent history alive.

A paddle down the river to Zlatá Koruna Abbey is a highlight (three hours), and a 20-minute walk up to the Křížový Vrch (Hill of the Cross) rewards you with a fine view of the town and its unforgettable riverside setting.

Many sights are closed on Monday, though the major attraction—the town itself—is always open. Evenings are for atmospheric dining and drinking.

Orientation to Český Krumlov

Český Krumlov (CHESS-key KROOM-loff) means, roughly, "Czech Bend in the River." Calling it "Český" for short sounds silly to Czech speakers (since dozens of Czech town names begin with "Český")—rather, they call it "Krumlov."

The city is extremely easy to navigate. The twisty Vltava River, which makes a perfect S through the town, ropes the Old Town into a tight peninsula. Above the Old Town is the Castle Town. Český Krumlov's one main street starts at the isthmus and winds through the peninsula, crossing a bridge before snaking through the Castle Town, the castle complex (a long series of courtyards), and the castle gardens high above. I've narrated this route on my self-guided walk. The main square, Náměstí Svornosti—with the TI, ATMs, and taxis—dominates the Old Town and marks the center of the peninsula. All recommended restaurants, hotels, and sights are within a few minutes' walk of this square.

TOURIST INFORMATION

The helpful TI is on the **main square** (daily 9:00-18:00, June-Aug until 19:00, shorter hours in winter, tel. 380-704-622, www.ckrumlov.info). The 129-Kč *City Guide* book includes a fine town and castle map. The TI has a baggage-storage desk and can check train and bus schedules. Ask about concerts, city walking tours in English, and canoe trips on the river. They rent an audioguide featuring a self-guided town walk (100 Kč, one hour). A second, less-crowded TI—actually a private business—is in the lowest courtyard of the **castle** (daily 9:00-18:00, tel. 380-725-110).

Český Krumlov Card: This 200-Kč card, sold at the TI and participating sights, covers entry to the Round Tower, Castle Museum (but not castle tours), Museum of Regional History, and Seidel Photo Studio Museum. Do the math to decide if it makes sense for you.

ARRIVAL IN ČESKÝ KRUMLOV

By Train: The train station is a 20-minute walk from town (turn right out of the station, then walk downhill onto a steep cobbled path leading to an overpass into the town center). Taxis are standing by to zip you to your hotel (about 100 Kč), or call 602-113-113 to summon one.

By Bus: The bus station is just three blocks away from the Old Town. To walk from the bus-station lot to the town center, follow the "walking man" signs out of the lot to *Centrum,* veer right and downhill on the small road, and cross the main road past the Co-op grocery. Figure on 60 Kč for a taxi from the station to your hotel.

By Car: Parking lots ring the town center, each one marked by a blue *P* sign. If your hotel is in the mostly traffic-free center, you'll be allowed to drive in (gingerly passing hordes of tourists) and park on the main square just long enough to drop off your bags and get directions to one of the outer lots. The flow of traffic is one-way: Enter at the east end of town, on Horní street, then exit across two bridges at the south end of town, on Linecká street (get details from your hotel before you arrive).

HELPFUL HINTS

Exchange Rate: 25 Kč = about $1

Country Calling Code: 420 (see page 1086 for dialing instructions)

Festivals: Locals drink oceans of beer and celebrate their medieval roots at big events such as the Celebration of the Rose

(Slavnosti Růže), where blacksmiths mint ancient coins, jugglers swallow fire, mead flows generously, and pigs are roasted on open fires (late June, www.ckrumlov.info). The summer also brings a top-notch international music festival, with performances in pubs, cafés, and the castle gardens (mid-July–mid-Aug, www.festivalkrumlov.cz). During St. Wenceslas celebrations, the square becomes a medieval market and the streets come alive with theater and music (late Sept). Reserve a hotel well in advance if you'll be in town for these events.

Bike Rental: You can rent bikes at the **train station** (150 Kč/day with train ticket, prices slightly higher otherwise, tel. 380-715-000), **Vltava Sport Service** (see listing under "Canoeing and Rafting the Vltava" on page 201), and the recommended **Hostel 99.**

Tours in Český Krumlov

Walking Tours

Since the town itself, rather than its sights, is what it's all about here, taking a guided walk is the key to a meaningful visit. The TI sells tickets for several different guided walks. No reservations are necessary—just meet in front of the TI on the main square and pay the guide. Confirm times when you visit, as schedules can change. The **Old Town Tour** offers the best general town introduction (300 Kč, daily at 12:30, 1.5 hours); in peak season, this tour extends to include the castle exteriors (490 Kč, April-Oct daily at 14:30). There's also a nighttime version (departing between 19:30 and 20:30, depending on the season). For a self-guided town walk, consider the TI's audioguide (see "Tourist Information," earlier).

Local Guides

Oldřiška Baloušková studied in California before starting a family back in her hometown, which she knows through and through (500 Kč/hour, mobile 737-920-901, oldriskab@gmail.com). **Jiří (George) Václavíček,** a gentle and caring man who perfectly fits mellow Český Krumlov, is a joy to share this town with (500 Kč/hour, mobile 603-927-995, www.krumlovguide.com, jiri.vaclavicek@gmail.com). **Karolína Kortušová** is an enthusiastic, experienced guide with great organizational skills. Her company, Krumlov Tours, can set you up with a good local tour guide, palace and theater admissions, river trips, and more (guides-500 Kč/hour, mobile 723-069-561, http://krumlovtours.com, info@krumlovtours.com).

Český Krumlov Walk

The town's best sight is its cobbled cityscape, surrounded by a babbling river and capped by a dramatic castle. Most of Český Krum-

lov's modest sights are laced together in this charming self-guided walk from the top of the Old Town, down its spine, across the river, and up to the castle. The walk begins at a fine viewpoint...and ends at an even better one. I've divided it into two parts: downhill, through the Old Town to the river; then uphill, ascending through the castle complex on the other side. You can also do the two parts on different days. The second half of the walk makes a useful spine for organizing a visit to the castle quarter.

THE OLD TOWN

• *Start at the bridge over the isthmus, which was once the fortified grand entry gate to the town (see map on page 190). For the best view, step down to the little terrace in front of the restaurant gate.*

Horní Bridge: From this "Upper Bridge," note the natural fortification provided by the tight bend in the river. Trace the river to your right, where it curves around the last building in town, with a smokestack. This is the Eggenberg Brewery, makers of Český Krumlov's very own hometown brew (with daily tours—see page 200). Behind that, on the horizon, is a pile of white apartment high-rises—built in the last decade of the communist era to solve a housing shortage (many homes were demolished after their German owners were forced out at the end of World War II—see sidebar). To the left of the brewery stands a huge monastery (with the pointy red steeple; not generally open to the public). Behind that, on Kleť Mountain—the highest hilltop—stands a TV tower and a world-class astronomical observatory and research center.

Head back up to the middle of the bridge. Look down and left, then down and right. Notice how the Vltava wraps entirely around the town center. Rafters take about a half-hour to circle around the Old Town peninsula, beginning and ending under this bridge.

• *Head into town on...*

Horní Street: As you step off the bridge, Český Krumlov's aptly named "Upper Street" passes the **Museum of Regional History** on the right (see page 200). Just past the museum, a little garden overlook affords a fine castle view.

Immediately across the street (on the left), notice the Renaissance facade of **Hotel Růže:** This former Jesuit college hides a

Český Krumlov

1. Castle View Apartments
2. Hotel Konvice
3. Hotel Mlýn
4. Pension Olšakovský
5. Pension Danny
6. Hotel Garni Myší Díra & Maleček Boat Rental
7. Pension Teddy
8. Pension Anna
9. Pension Gardena
10. Pension U Kapličky
11. To Pension Kříž
12. Hostel 99 & Hospoda 99 Rest.
13. Krumlov House Hostel
14. Na Louži Restaurant
15. Cikánská Jizba
16. Krčma u Dwau Maryí
17. Laibon Restaurant
18. Kolektiv
19. Rybářská Restaurace
20. Krčma v Šatlavské
21. Restaurace Barbakán
22. Krumlovská Picka & CK Shuttle Office
23. Dobrá Čajovna Teahouse
24. Coffee Roasting Company
25. Vltava Sport Service
26. Start Quickie River Float
27. End Quickie River Float & Start Abbey/Boršov Floats

beautiful courtyard, now filled with artistic vendor stands. Pop inside to shop or just admire its decoration of faux sgraffito "bricks," made by scratching into an outer layer of one color of plaster to reveal a different color beneath. This style was all the rage during the town's boom time, and we'll be seeing several more examples on this walk.

• *Walk another block down the main drag, until you reach steps on the left leading to the...*

Church of St. Vitus: Český Krumlov's main church was built as a bastion of Catholicism in the 15th century, when the Roman

Catholic Church was fighting the Hussites. The 17th-century Baroque high altar shows a totem of religious figures: the Virgin Mary (crowned in heaven); St. Vitus (above Mary); and, way up on top, St. Wenceslas, the patron saint of the Czech people—long considered their ambassador in heaven. The canopy in the back, though empty today, once supported a grand statue of a Rožmberk atop a horse. The statue originally stood at the high altar. (Too egotistical for Jesuits, it was later moved to the rear of the nave, and then lost for good.) Notice the empty organ case.

While the main organ is out for restoration, the cute little circa-1716 Baroque beauty is getting plenty of use (photos of the restoration work on the far wall; generally open daily 8:30-16:30, Sunday Mass at 9:30, daily Mass at 17:00 in the winter chapel; tel. 724-937-121).

• *Continuing on Horní street, you'll come to the...*

Main Square (Náměstí Svornosti): Lined with a mix of Renaissance and Baroque homes of burghers (all built on 12th-century Gothic foundations), the main square has a grand charm. The Town Hall (the crenellated white building, on the right) flies both the Czech flag and the town flag, which shows the rose symbol of the Rožmberk family, who ruled the town for 300 years.

Imagine the history that this square has seen: In the 1620s, the town was held by the (very Catholic) Habsburgs, just as Lutheran Protestantism was rising to threaten Catholic Europe. Krumlov was a seat of Jesuit power and learning, and the intellectuals of the Roman church allegedly burned books on this square. Later, when there was a bad harvest, locals blamed witches—and burned them, too. Every so often, terrible plagues rolled through the countryside. In a nearby village, all but two residents were killed by a plague.

But the plague stopped before devastating the people of Český Krumlov, and in 1715—as thanks to God—they built the plague monument that stands on the square today (on the left). Much later,

ČESKÝ KRUMLOV

The Expulsion of Ethnic Germans from Czechoslovakia

For seven centuries, Czech- and German-speaking people jointly inhabited and cultivated the lands of Bohemia, Moravia, and Silesia. Then, during the 19th century, the growing importance of ethnic identity resulted in tensions between these communities and fierce competition between their institutions. Running up to World War I, animosity rose so high that Czech and German soccer clubs from Prague refused to compete against each other. This charged situation was made worse by the German- and Hungarian-dominated Habsburg monarchy, which treated local Slavs (Poles, Slovaks, Croats, Slovenes, and Serbs) as second-class citizens.

The end of World War I handed the Slavs an unprecedented opportunity to claim the land for themselves. The principle that gave countries such as Poland, Czechoslovakia, and Yugoslavia independence was called "self-determination": Each nation had the right to its own state within the area in which its people formed the majority. But the peoples of Eastern Europe had mixed over the centuries, making it impossible to create functioning states based purely on ethnicity. In the case of Bohemia—which became Czechoslovakia—the borders were drawn along historical boundaries. While the country was predominantly Slavic, areas with overwhelming German majorities remained.

Ethnic Germans in Czechoslovakia were never wholehearted supporters of the newly centralized, Slavic-majority democracy. While politically engaged in the new country, Nazi propaganda appealed to them amidst Hitler's rise to power and an economic downturn that was particularly harsh for their communities. In 1935, 63 percent of Germans in Czechoslovakia voted for the Sudeten Nazi Party, enabling Hitler to appeal to international powers on their behalf, using the principle of self-determination. The 1938 Munich Agreement ceded the German-speaking areas of Czechoslovakia to the Third Reich, and ethnic Czechs were forced to leave those areas.

Over the course of World War II, many Czechs came to believe that peaceful coexistence with Germans in a single state would be impossible. As the war wound down, Czechoslovakia's exiled president Edvard Beneš traveled to Washington and Moscow, securing backing for a state-organized expulsion of more than 2.2 million ethnic Germans still living in Czechoslovakia. Throughout 1945 and 1946, Czechoslovak soldiers carried out the

ČESKÝ KRUMLOV

"transfer" orders: They would typically enter a German-speaking town or village, take a few prisoners, and then threaten to execute the hostages unless everyone of German descent left. The expulsions sometimes turned violent: In June 1945, an army captain and a head of a revolutionary unit ordered their men to execute 2,000 ethnic German civilians, including children, near the town of Saatz.

While Beneš and most Czechs at the time considered the expulsion of ethnic Germans as just revenge for the war and historical injustices, the communists saw an opportunity for the future: The emptied region was to become a revolutionary laboratory. Ironically, the Czechs regained "their" land, but in the process eroded their freedom; meanwhile the Germans lost the land in which their ancestors lay buried, but gained a chance to build a prosperous democracy in their new home.

For the next 40 years, the "transfer" of ethnic Germans was a taboo subject, as the communist anti-Nazi propaganda machine continued as if the war had never ended. After 1989, the issue was reluctantly broached by politicians on both sides of the border, as it threatened to derail the otherwise excellent relations between the Czech and German governments. Toward 2004, tensions again rose, as Czech politicians resisted demands for reparations from Sudeten Germans in Berlin and Brussels, who held that such repayment should be a precondition to Czech entry into the European Union.

Over the last decade, the subject finally became depoliticized. Former German residents have continued to visit their old homes, sharing the stories of their trauma with young Czechs, who—having grown confident in their freedom—are able to take a more nuanced view of their country's history. In 2015, the Sudeten German Association stepped back from its support for repatriates' legal claims. A year later, the Czech Minister of Culture Daniel Herman delivered a speech at the annual Sudeten German convention in Nürnberg, addressing the audience as "dear compatriots" and expressing regret over the events of 1945 and 1946. An act that would have amounted to a political suicide just ten years earlier was positively received by the Czech public. Seventy years after a traumatic divorce, a door to reconciliation finally opened.

in 1938, Hitler stood right here before a backdrop of long Nazi banners to celebrate the annexation of the Sudetenland. And in 1968, Russian tanks spun their angry treads on the roads to this square to intimidate locals who were demanding freedom. Today, thankfully, this square is part of an unprecedented time of peace and prosperity for the Czech people.

• *From the main square, walk down Radniční street (on the right, just past the Town Hall) and cross the...*

Barber's Bridge (Lazebnický Most): This wooden bridge, decorated with two 19th-century statues, connects the Old Town and the Castle Town. On the right side stands a statue of St. John of Nepomuk, who's also depicted by a prominent statue on Prague's Charles Bridge. Among other responsibilities, he's the protector against floods. In the great floods in August 2002, the angry river submerged the bridge (but removable banisters minimized the damage). Stains just above the windows of the adjacent building show how high the water rose.

• *The second part of the walk involves lots of uphill hiking—but it's worth it to see the castle courtyards and dramatic views.*

KRUMLOV CASTLE

Big and imposing, the town castle boasts several fine courtyards, spectacular viewpoints, and gorgeous gardens—all of which are open to the public, free to enter, and fun to roam (though some areas may be closed on Mon). This part of the walk focuses on those public spaces, leading you from Barber's Bridge, through the heart of the castle, and up to a picturesque viewpoint just before the gardens. The castle also has several individual sights (Round Tower, Castle Museum, Upper Castle, Baroque Theater) that can be laced into this walk but require paid admission and/or a reserved tour (for details, see listings under "Sights in Český Krumlov," later).

• *Cross the bridge and head up shop-lined Latrán street, which bends to the right. Just after that bend, look for the stairs on your left (in front of the gray-and-white building). Head up, passing under a stone arch with the wood-carved rose symbol of the Rožmberk family. You'll emerge into the castle's...*

First (Lower) Courtyard: This is just the first of many courtyards that bunny-hop up through the castle complex. This was the site for workers and industry (stables, smithy, brewery, pharmacy, and so on)—convenient for aristocratic needs, but far enough away to keep noises and smells at bay.

Looking up, you can't miss the strikingly colorful **Round Tower** that marks the location of the first castle, built here to guard the medieval river crossing. With its 16th-century Renaissance paint job colorfully restored, it looks exotic, featuring fancy astrological decor, terra-cotta symbols of the zodiac, and a fine arcade.

• *Head up to the former drawbridge. Look over the sides of the bridge. Spot any bears?*

Bear Pits (Medvědí Příkop): These hold a family of European brown bears, as they have since the Rožmberks added bears to their coat of arms in the 16th century to demonstrate their (fake) blood relation to the distinguished Italian Orsini family (whose name means "bear-like"). Featured on countless coats of arms, bears have long been totemic animals for Europeans. Pronouncing the animal's real name was taboo in many cultures, and Czechs still refer to bears only indirectly. For example, in most Germanic languages the word "bear" is derived from "brown," while the Slavic *medvěd* literally means "honey eater."

Near the top of the bridge, notice the gently worded sign suggesting that—rather than toss down your junk-food leftovers—you add a few coins in the collection slot to finance "more varied meals and delicacies" for the bears.

• *Continue through the gateway into the...*

Second Courtyard: Here you'll spot more of the sgraffito (Renaissance faux features scraped into wet plaster) that decorates much of the castle. To your left, at the bottom of the courtyard, is the entrance to the **tower climb** and the **Castle Museum.** Farther up on the left is the **ticket office** for castle tours, including the Baroque Theater—stop in now (if you haven't already) to see about a tour.

• *From here, things get steep as we enter the...*

Heart of the Castle Complex: Head up the bridge, noticing the little view terrace on the left—the first of several along here. You'll emerge into the **Third Courtyard,** then (after a corridor) the **Fourth Courtyard.** Nicely preserved paintings enliven their blocky facades. Wrapped around these courtyards is the castle proper, a mighty Renaissance building sometimes called the Upper Castle (interiors open to visitors—notice the meeting points for various tour options). Continuing straight out through the end of the Fourth Courtyard, you'll cross the breathtaking **Cloak Bridge**—a triple-decker, statue-lined, covered bridge spanning a vast gorge and connecting the castle firmly with the gardens that sprawl behind it. Enjoy the views—but believe it or not, even better ones are coming up.

Notice the **Baroque Theater,** at the far end of the bridge, which still uses traditional methods for moving scenery and producing sound effects. Aspects of this back-in-the-day stagecraft

ČESKÝ KRUMLOV

still survive on Broadway today. This is one of only two such original theaters in Europe.

• *After the bridge, continue uphill through the...*

Fifth Courtyard: Really more of a pathway, this connects the castle to its gardens. Walk along the white wall—with peekaboo windows—until you are almost at the gate up top. High on the wall to the right, notice the **sundial.** Check the time: It's dead-on... except for Daylight Savings Time, which was unknown to medieval timekeepers. Notice that the sundial cuts into one of the faux windows, painted on the lower level of the building to create Renaissance symmetry.

Now step through the low-profile door directly across from the sundial. You'll emerge at a spectacular **viewpoint** that takes in the entire town, its curving river, and even the colorful tower and most of the castle complex you just came through. Jockey your way through the selfie-snapping crowd and drink it in. (Or literally drink, at the little adjacent bar.)

• *Our walk is finished. But if you still have stamina, you can consider exploring the **castle gardens**—they're just uphill, through the gate from the Fifth Courtyard. (While the castle exterior is open all the time, the garden is open daily 8:00-19:00, with shorter hours off-season.)*

Sights in Český Krumlov

KRUMLOV CASTLE COMPLEX (KRUMLOVSKÝ ZÁMEK)

No Czech town is complete without a castle—and now that the nobles are gone, their mansions are open to us common folk. Český Krumlov is no different. Its immense Krumlov Castle complex, one of the largest in Central Europe, perches on a rock promontory overlooking the Vltava River and the town. The original Gothic castle took shape here in the 13th century, and eventually the Rožmberk, Eggenberg, and Schwarzenberg families each in-

herited it in turn. In successive waves of additions and renovations, they built it into the splendid Renaissance/Baroque property you see today.

The following sights are listed in the order you'll reach them as you climb up through the complex (ideally following my self-guided walk, earlier). The Round Tower and Castle Museum can be visited at your leisure, while other castle interiors—including the excellent Baroque Theater—can only be seen with a guided tour (see next). On a quick visit, the only sight I'd bother paying admission for is the theater.

Reservations for Baroque Theater and Upper Castle: It's worth the 10 Kč reservation fee to hold a slot on an English tour of the Upper Castle interior or the Baroque Theater (the theater is the castle attraction most likely to sell out). To book ahead, stop by the ticket office in person, or call 380-704-721 to check English tour times and reserve a space. No other castle sights require (or accept) reservations.

Information: Tel. 380-704-711, www.castle.ckrumlov.cz.

▲Round Tower (Zâmecká Věž) and Castle Museum (Hradní Muzeum)

These two sights share a ticket office at the bottom of the castle's middle courtyard. While neither is a must, both are worth considering if you want a peek inside the castle without committing to a guided tour. These are also the only castle sights open on Mondays (in peak season).

Colorfully impressive from the outside, the **tower** is also fun to climb. Twist up the 163 well-worn wood and stone steps to the top, where you'll be rewarded with grand, 360-degree views over the town, the rest of the castle complex, and happy boaters floating on the river.

The exhibits at the **Castle Museum** focus on key moments in the lives of the town's various ruling families: Rožmberks, Eggenbergs, and Schwarzenbergs. Be sure to pick up the good, included audioguide as you enter. You'll see a hall of aristocratic portraits; the offices, bedrooms, and dining rooms of the various inhabitants; and a modest religious treasury, armory, and musical instruments collection. At the end you can sit in old-timey cinema seats and watch archival footage of the castle's residents from the 1920s and 1930s.

Cost and Hours: Tower-50 Kč, museum-100 Kč, comboticket for both-130 Kč; both open daily 9:00-17:00, June-Aug until 18:00, closed Mon in Nov-March; last entry one hour before closing.

▲Upper Castle (Horní Hrad)

While the Upper Castle grounds are free to explore, you'll need to take a tour to access the interiors. Two different tour routes give you a glimpse of the places where the Rožmberks, Eggenbergs, and Schwarzenbergs dined, studied, worked, prayed, entertained, and slept. (By European standards, the castle's not much, and the tours move slowly.) Imagine being an aristocratic guest here, riding the dukes' assembly line of fine living: You'd promenade through a long series of elegant spaces and dine in the sumptuous dining hall before enjoying a concert in the Hall of Mirrors, which leads directly to the Baroque Theater (described next). After the play, you'd go out into the château garden for a fireworks finale.

Cost and Hours: Choose from Tour I (Gothic and Renaissance rooms, of the most general interest) or Tour II (19th-century castle life). Tours run June-Aug Tue-Sun 9:00-12:00 & 13:00-18:00, spring and fall until 17:00, closed Mon and Nov-March. Tours in Czech cost 150 Kč, leave regularly, and include an adequate flier in English that contains about half the information imparted by the guide. English tours are preferable, but cost more (250 Kč), run less frequently, and are often booked solid. Pay to reserve a slot in advance; see "Reservations for Baroque Theater and Upper Castle," earlier, for details. You'll be issued a ticket with your tour time printed on it. Be in the correct courtyard at that time, or you'll be locked out.

▲▲Baroque Theater (Zámecké Divadlo)

Europe once had several hundred Baroque theaters. Using candles for light and fireworks for special effects, most burned down. Today, only two survive in good shape and are open to tourists: one at Stockholm's Drottningholm Palace; and one here, at Krumlov Castle. During the 45-minute tour, you'll sit on benches in the theater and then go under the stage to see the wood-and-rope contraptions that enabled scenes to be scooted in and out within seconds (while fireworks and smoke blinded the audience). It's a lovely little theater with an impressive 3-D effect that makes the stage look deeper than it really is, but don't bother with the tour unless you can snare a spot on an English one. The theater is used only once a year for an actual performance, attended by Baroque theater enthusiasts.

Cost and Hours: 300 Kč for English tour, 250 Kč for Czech tour, tours Tue-Sun May-Oct, no tours Mon and Nov-April; English departures at 10:00, 11:00, 13:00, 14:00, and 15:00. Due to the theater's fragility, groups are limited to 20 people, and English tours generally sell out. Reserve ahead—see "Reservations for Baroque Theater and Upper Castle," earlier.

ČESKÝ KRUMLOV

Castle Gardens (Zámecká Zahrada)

This lovely, 2,300-foot-long garden crowns the castle complex. It was laid out in the 17th century, when the noble family would have it lit with 22,000 oil lamps, torches, and candles for special occasions. The lower part is geometrical and symmetrical—French garden-style. The upper part is wilder—English garden-style. Both are delightful.

Cost and Hours: Free, open May-Sept Tue-Sun 8:00-19:00, April and Oct until 17:00, closed Mon and Nov-March.

OTHER SIGHTS IN TOWN

▲Seidel Photo Studio Museum (Museum Fotoatelier Seidel)

This fully preserved, meticulously renovated 1905 Art Nouveau villa featuring original furnishings, a garden, and 100-year-old photo equipment offers a welcome respite from the crowds and the ubiquitous Middle Ages. The museum, set in the home and studio of Josef Seidel (1859-1935) and his son František (1908-1997), features more than 100,000 of their original photographs of life in this mountainous region—the Böhmerwald (Bohemian Forest)—between 1880 and 1950. Josef Seidel was unique among his contemporaries in focusing on just one region, and was the first in the country to use autochrome. Allowed to remain in Český Krumlov during and after World War II when many Germans in the country were evicted (see sidebar on page 192), František continued his father's photography business, remaining here until his death in 1997. After his wife died in 2003, the town bought the house and converted it into a delightful museum and a cultural center for cross-border understanding. Restored, functional equipment offers hands-on experience with the process of photography during the late 19th and early 20th centuries. You can literally smell the history.

Cost and Hours: 130 Kč, includes English audioguide; daily May-Sept 9:00-18:00, shorter hours off-season; Linecká 272, across the river south of Old Town, mobile 736-503-871, www.seidel.cz.

Synagogue

Completed in 1910 in a mixture of architectural styles, this synagogue served the small Jewish community of Český Krumlov and neighboring villages. In 1938, there were 200 congregants here, but only two members of the area's Jewish community came back after World War II. Terribly run-down for decades after the war, the synagogue was restored to its former glory in 2015 by the Prague Jewish community, with funding from the European Union and

German and Austrian sponsors. It contains an exhibit on its history, and hosts concerts and contemporary art exhibits.

Cost and Hours: 50 Kč, daily 10:00-18:00, Za Soudem 282, across the river south of Old Town, mobile 601-590-213, www.synagoga-krumlov.cz.

Eating: The **$ Café Synagoga,** with an assortment of cakes, occupies the former basement residence of the rabbi's family and an adjacent peaceful garden.

Museum of Regional History (Regionální Muzeum v Českém Krumlově)

This small museum gives you a quick look at regional costumes, tools, and traditions. When you pay, pick up the English translation of the displays (it also includes a lengthy history of Krumlov). Start on the top floor, where you'll see a Bronze Age exhibit, old paintings, a glimpse of noble life, and a look at how the locals rafted lumber from the Bőhmerwald mountains all the way to Vienna (partly by canal). Don't miss the fun-to-study ceramic model of Český Krumlov in 1800 (note the extravagant gardens high above the town). The lower floor comes with fine folk costumes and domestic art.

Cost and Hours: 50 Kč, Tue-Sun 9:00-12:00 & 12:30-17:00, July-Aug until 18:00, closed Mon, Horní 152, tel. 380-711-674, www.muzeumck.cz.

▲Eggenberg Brewery Tour

This may be one of the most intimate and accessible brewery tours in this land that so loves its beer. Tucked into a river bend on the edge of town, Eggenberg's spunky little brewery has an authenticity that can't be matched by the big, soulless corporate breweries (such as Pilsner Urquell, in Plzeň, or the Czech Budweiser, in nearby České Budějovice). This is your chance to learn about the beer-making process at a facility where they're still using the same giant copper vats from 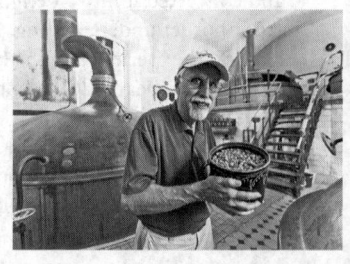 1915. While some of the facility has recently been modernized (and ongoing works may reroute the tour a bit), you'll still see lots of vintage equipment, including the original brew house (still in service), the fermentation vats, the cellars used for aging, and the bottling plant. Your tour ends with a visit to the pub, where you can sample some brews, including a "smoky" dark beer (Nakouřený Švihák), made with malt that tastes like salami, then aged for 100 days.

Cost and Hours: 100 Kč for the tour only, 130 Kč for tour and two tastes in the pub, 170 Kč for tour and four-pack of your choice of bottled beers to take away, 200 Kč includes everything; one-hour English tours daily at 11:00 year-round, also at 14:00 in May-Oct, tel. 380-711-426, www.eggenberg.cz.

Getting There: It's just a short stroll up Nové Město street from the main drag below the castle. During ongoing reconstruction, you may instead have to loop around town to the back entrance on Pivovarska—about a 10-minute walk.

ACTIVITIES

Český Krumlov lies in the middle of a valley popular for canoeing, rafting, hiking, and horseback riding. Boat-rental places are convenient to the Old Town, and several hiking paths start right in town. Serious hikers should consider a hike up the mushroom- and blueberry-filled Kleť mountain.

▲▲▲Canoeing and Rafting the Vltava

Splash a little river fun into your visit by renting a rubber raft or fiberglass canoe for a quick 30-minute spin around Český Krum-

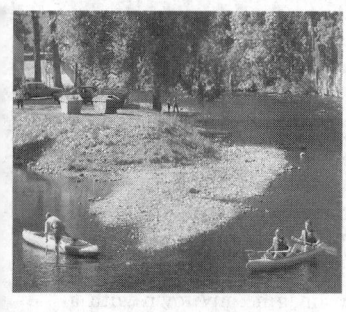

lov. Or go for a three-hour float and paddle through the Bohemian forests and villages of the nearby countryside. You'll end up at Zlatá Koruna Abbey (described later), from where rafting companies will shuttle you back to town—or provide you with a bicycle to pedal back on your own along a bike path. This is a great hot-weather activity. Though the river is far from treacherous, be prepared to get wet.

You'll encounter plenty of inviting pubs and cafés for breaks along the way. There's a little whitewater, but the river is so shallow that if you tip, you can simply stand up and climb back in. (When that happens, pull the canoe up onto the bank to empty it, since you'll never manage to pour the water out while still in the river.)

Choose from a kayak, a canoe (faster, less work, more likely to tip), an inflatable raft (harder rowing, slower, but very stable), or a retro-style raft made of logs. Prices are per boat (2-6 people) and include a map, a waterproof container, and transportation to or from the start and end points. Here are your options:

Quickie Circle-the-Town Float: The easiest half-hour experience is to float around the city's peninsula, starting and ending on opposite sides of the tiny isthmus. Heck, you can do it twice (500 Kč for 2 people in a canoe or raft).

Three-Hour Float to Zlatá Koruna Abbey: This is your best basic trip, with pastoral scenery, a riverside pub about two hours down on the left, and a beautiful abbey as your destination (about 9 miles, 800 Kč for 2 people including pick-up). From there you can bike back or catch a shuttle bus home—simply arrange a return plan with the rental company.

Full-Day Float to Boršov: This takes you another four hours past the Zlatá Koruna Abbey, floating lazily through a pristine valley below the ruined Dívčí Kámen Castle (about 16 miles, 1,200 Kč for 2 people including pick-up).

Rental Companies: Several companies offer this lively activity. The handiest and also busiest are **Půjčovna Lodí Maleček Boat Rental** (long hours daily April-Oct, closed Nov-March, at recommended Pension Myší Díra, Rooseveltova 28, tel. 380-712-508, www.malecek.cz, lode@malecek.cz) and **Vltava Sport Service** (daily April-Sept 9:00-17:00, closed Oct-March, Hradební 60, tel. 380-711-988, www.ckvltava.cz). **Expedicion** offers similar services, plus airport transfers and car rental, with fewer crowds (Soukenická 33, mobile 720-107-171, http://expedicion.cz). Vltava and Expedicion also rent mountain bikes (300 Kč/day) and can bring a bike to the abbey for you to ride back.

Hiking

For an **easy 20-minute hike** to the Křížový Vrch (Hill of the Cross), walk to the end of Rooseveltova street, cross at the traffic light, then head straight for the first (empty) chapel-like Station of the Cross. Turning right, it's easy to navigate along successive Stations of the Cross until you reach the white church on the hill (closed), set in the middle of wild meadows. Looking down into the valley at the medieval city nestled within the S-shaped river, framed by the rising hills, it's hard to imagine any town with a more powerful *genius loci* (spirit of the place). The view is best at sunset.

For a **longer hike,** start at the trailhead by the bear pits below the castle. Red-and-white trail markers guide you on an easy six-mile hike around the neighboring slopes and villages. The green-and-yellow stripes mark a five-mile hiking trail up Kleť Mountain—with an altitude gain of 1,800 feet. At the top, you'll find the Kleť Observatory, the oldest observatory in the country (and still a leading astronomical center). On clear days, you can see the Alps (observatory tours-50 Kč, hourly July-Aug Tue-Sun 10:30-15:30, April-June Sat-Sun only, closed Sept-March and Mon year-round, www.hvezdarna.klet.cz).

Horseback Riding

Head about a mile out of town, beyond the Křížový Vrch (Hill of the Cross), for horseback rides and lessons at Slupenec Horseback Riding Club.

ČESKÝ KRUMLOV

Roma in Eastern Europe

Numbering 12 million, the Roma people constitute a bigger European nation than the Czechs, Hungarians, or the Dutch. (The term "Gypsies," previously the common name for this group, is now considered derogatory and inaccurate.)

Descended from several low north-Indian castes, the Roma began to migrate through Persia and Armenia into the Ottoman Empire a thousand years ago. Known for their itinerant lifestyle, expertise in horse trading, skilled artisanship, and flexibility regarding private property, the Roma were both sought out and suspected in medieval Europe.

The Industrial Revolution threatened the Roma's traditional livelihoods, making their wandering lifestyle difficult to sustain. In the 1940s, Hitler sent hundreds of thousands of Roma to the gas chambers. In the occupied Protectorate of Bohemia and Moravia (Czechoslovakia minus the Sudetenland that had been annexed to Germany), Hitler had the help of Czech policemen who ran the two Roma "transfer" camps in Lety and Hodonín, where hundreds died even before being transported to Auschwitz. Only 10 percent of the protectorate's 5,000-strong prewar Roma population survived.

After the war, tens of thousands of Roma from eastern Slovakia were relocated into the Sudetenland. At this time, the communist governments in Eastern Europe required Roma to speak the country's major language, settle in towns, and work in new industrial jobs. Rather than producing well-adjusted citizens, the result was an erosion of time-honored Roma values, as the policy shattered traditionally cohesive communities. It left the new Roma generation prone to sexual, alcohol, and drug abuse, and filled state-run orphanages with deprived Roma toddlers.

When the obligation and right to work disappeared with the communist regimes in 1989, rampant unemployment and dependence on welfare joined the list of Roma afflictions. As people all over Eastern Europe found it difficult to adjust to the new economic realities, they again turned on the Roma as scapegoats. Many Roma now live in segregated ghettos. Those who make it against the odds and succeed in mainstream society typically do so by turning their backs on their Roma heritage.

In this context, the Roma in Český Krumlov are a surprising success story. The well-integrated, proud Roma community here (numbering 1,000, or 5 percent of the town's population) is considered a curious anomaly even by experts. Their success could be due to a number of factors: the legacy of the multicultural Rožmberks, the fact that almost everyone in Český Krumlov is a relative newcomer, or maybe it's how local youngsters, regardless of skin color, tend to resolve their differences over a beer in the local "Gypsy Pub" (Cikánská Jizba), with a trendy Roma band setting the tune.

ČESKÝ KRUMLOV

Cost and Hours: 300 Kč for one hour outdoors or in the ring, 2,200 Kč for all-day ride, Tue-Sun 10:00-15:00, closed Mon, helmets provided, Slupenec 1, worth a taxi trip, tel. 723-832-459, www.jk-slupenec.cz.

Shopping

In recent years, Krumlov has become a shopping heaven, with a continuous line of gifts, toys, and handicrafts shops along its main street and spilling into the back alleys. The arts market in the renaissance courtyard of the Hotel Růže near the main square is the most scenic and fun to delve into.

NEAR ČESKÝ KRUMLOV

Zlatá Koruna Abbey (Klášter Zlatá Koruna)

This Cistercian abbey was founded in the 13th century by a Bohemian king to counter the growing influence of the Vítek family, the ancestors of the mighty Rožmberks. As you enter the grounds, notice the magnificent central linden tree, with its strange, cape-like leaves; it's said to have been used by the anti-Catholic Hussites when they hanged the monks. The one-hour tour takes you through the rare two-storied Gothic Chapel of the Guardian Angel, the main church, and the cloister, while a 10-minute tour takes you to the abbot's chapel with the original Gothic Zlatá Koruna Madonna, the most treasured painting in the region. After the order was dissolved in 1785, the abbey functioned briefly as a village school, before being turned into a factory during the Industrial Revolution. Damage from this period is visible on the cloister's crumbling arches. The Gothic interiors adjacent to the ticket office serve as exhibition space for Český Krumlov's school of the arts, displaying the imaginative creations of the school's 6- to 18-year-old students (free).

Cost and Hours: 100 Kč—one-hour tour in Czech, generally runs every half-hour, pick up English leaflet; 20 Kč—10-minute Madonna tour, April-Oct Tue-Sun 9:00-16:00, June-Aug until 17:00, closed Mon and Nov-March, call 380-743-126 to arrange English tour, www.klaster-zlatakoruna.eu.

Getting There: Drivers can reach the abbey in about 10 minutes from Český Krumlov (head north out of town and follow route #39). But it's more fun to get there by raft or canoe—the abbey is directly above the river at the end of a three-hour float (see "Canoeing and Rafting the Vltava," earlier).

Sleep Code

Hotels are classified based on the average price of a standard double room with breakfast in high season. I've given *very* rough conversions to dollars using 25 Kč = $1.

$$$$ **Splurge:** Most rooms over 3,400 Kč (roughly $135)
$$$ **Pricier:** 2,600-3,400 Kč ($105-135)
$$ **Moderate:** 1,800-2,600 Kč ($70-105)
$ **Budget:** 1,000-1,800 Kč ($40-70)
¢   **Backpacker:** Under 1,000 Kč ($40)
RS%   **Rick Steves discount**

Unless otherwise noted, credit cards are accepted, hotel staff speak basic English, and free Wi-Fi is available. Comparison-shop by checking prices at several hotels (on each hotel's own website, on a booking site, or by email). For the best deal, *book directly with the hotel.* Ask for a discount if paying in cash; if the listing includes **RS%,** request a Rick Steves discount.

Sleeping in Český Krumlov

Krumlov is filled with small pensions and hostels. Summer is busy all around. While you can generally find a room in a modern pension in the outskirts upon arrival, book months ahead to stay in the heart of town.

IN THE OLD TOWN

$$$ Castle View Apartments rents seven diverse apartments. These are the best-equipped rooms I found in town—the bathroom floors are heated, all come with kitchenettes, and everything's done just right. Their website describes each stylish apartment; the "view" ones really do come with eye-popping vistas (RS%, apartment sleeps up to 6, breakfast at a nearby hotel, Šatlavská 140, mobile 731-108-677, www.castleview.cz, info@castleview.cz).

$$ Hotel Konvice is run by a German couple—and their three children—with a personal touch. Each room is uniquely decorated (a block above the main square at Horní 144, tel. 380-711-611, www.boehmerwaldhotels.de, info@stadthotel-krummau.de).

BELOW THE MAIN SQUARE

Secluded Parkán street, which runs along the river below the square, has a hotel and a row of small pensions. These places have a family feel and views of the looming castle above.

$$$ Hotel Mlýn, at the end of Parkán, is a tastefully furnished hotel with more than 30 rooms and all the amenities (elevator, pay parking, Parkán 120, tel. 380-731-133, www.hotelmlyn.eu, info@hotelmlyn.eu).

$ Pension Olšakovský, which has a delightful breakfast area on a terrace next to the river, treats visitors as family guests (free parking, Parkán 114, mobile 604-430-181, www.olsakovsky.cz, info@olsakovsky.cz).

AT THE BASE OF THE CASTLE

A quiet, cobbled pedestrian street (Latrán) runs below the castle just over the bridge from the Old Town. Lined with cute shops, it's a 10-minute walk downhill from the train station.

$ Pension Danny is a funky little place, with homey rooms and a tangled floor plan above a restaurant (in-room breakfast, Latrán 72, tel. 603-210-572, www.pensiondanny.cz, recepce@ pensiondanny.cz).

BETWEEN THE BUS STATION AND THE OLD TOWN

Rooseveltova street, midway between the bus station and the Old Town (a four-minute walk from either), is lined with several fine little places, each with easy, free parking. The key here is tranquility—the noisy bars of the town center are out of earshot.

$$ Hotel Garni Myší Díra ("Mouse Hole") hides 11 bright and woody Bohemian contemporary rooms overlooking the Vltava River just outside the Old Town (prices include transfer to/ from bus or train station, Rooseveltova 28, tel. 380-712-853, www. hotelmysidira.com). The no-nonsense reception, which closes at 20:00, runs the recommended boat rental company (Půjčovna Lodí Maleček, at the same address), along with a similar pension with comparable prices, **Villa Margarita,** farther along Rooseveltova.

$ Little **Pension Teddy** offers three deluxe rooms that share a balcony overlooking the river and have original 18th-century furniture. Or stay in one of four modern-style rooms, some of which also face the river (cash only, staff may be unhelpful, pay parking, Rooseveltova 38, tel. 777-713-277, mobile 724-003-981, www. pensionteddy.cz, info@pensionteddy.cz).

$ Pension Anna is well-run, with two doubles, six apartments, and a restful little garden. Its apartments are spacious suites, with a living room and stairs leading to the double-bedded loft. The upstairs rooms can get stuffy during the summer (pay parking, Rooseveltova 41, tel. 380-711-692, www.pensionanna-ck.cz, pension. anna@quick.cz). If you book a standard double and they bump you up to an apartment, don't pay more than the double rate.

OUTSIDE THE CITY CENTER

$ Pension Gardena has 16 spacious, airy rooms in two adjacent, tactfully renovated historical buildings. A family business with a garden, it's on the way into town from the bus station just a hundred yards above Horní Bridge (Kaplická 21, tel. 380-711-028, mobile 607-873-974, www.pensiongardena.com, gardena@seznam.cz).

$ Pension U Kapličky, on a quiet street adjacent to a chapel and a city park, consists of two artistically designed apartments in an unusually-shaped medieval house. Jitka, a teacher of stone carving at the local arts academy and one of the last old-timers to still call central Český Krumlov home, lives downstairs and bakes pastries for breakfast (reserve months ahead, Linecká 60, mobile 606-434-090, www.ckrumlov.cz/ck/ukaplicky, ukaplicky@ckrumlov.cz).

$ Pension Kříž, with five rooms in a new, tastefully decorated house, is tucked away in a quiet, modern villa district under the Křížový Vrch (Hill of the Cross), just a five-minute walk from Horní Bridge (Křížová 71, mobile 775-421-012, www.penzion-kriz.cz, ubytovani@penzion-kriz.cz)

HOSTELS

Of the hostels in town, Hostel 99 (closest to the train station) is clearly the high-energy, youthful party place. Krumlov House (closer to the bus station) is more mellow. Both are well-managed, and each is a five-minute walk from the main square.

¢ Hostel 99's picnic-table terrace looks out on the Old Town. While the gentle sound of the river gurgles outside your window late at night, you're more likely to hear a youthful international crowd having a great time. The hostel caters to its fun-loving young guests, offering a day-long river rafting and pub crawl, with a free keg of beer each Wednesday (private rooms available, laundry, use the lockers, no curfew or lockout, recommended Hospoda 99 restaurant, 10-minute downhill walk from train station or two bus stops to Spicak, Vezni 99, tel. 380-712-812, www.hostel99.cz, hostel99@hotmail.com).

¢ Krumlov House Hostel is take-your-shoes-off-at-the-door, shiny, hardwood-with-throw-rugs mellow. Efficiently run by a Canadian/American couple, it has a hip and trusting vibe and feels welcoming to travelers of any age (private rooms and apartments available, breakfast July-Aug only, well-stocked guest kitchen, laundry, Rooseveltova 68, tel. 380-711-935, www.krumlovhostel.com, info@krumlovhostel.com). The hostel sponsors "Write-Away," a literary retreat for traveling writers (http://writeaway.literarybohemian.com).

Eating in Český Krumlov

Krumlov, with a huge variety of creative little restaurants, is a fun place to eat. In peak season the good places fill up fast, so make reservations or eat early.

$$ Na Louži seems to be everyone's favorite Czech bistro,

Restaurant Price Code

I've assigned each eatery a price category, based on the average cost of a typical main course. Drinks, desserts, and splurge items (steak and seafood) can raise the price considerably. I've given *very* rough conversions to dollars using 25 Kč = $1.

$$$$ Splurge: Most main courses over 500 Kč (roughly $20)
  $$$ Pricier: 300-500 Kč ($10-20)
    $$ Moderate: 100-300 Kč ($5-10)
      $ Budget: Under 100 Kč ($5)

In the Czech Republic, a pub, basic sit-down eatery, and less-touristy café or teahouse is **$**; a typical restaurant—or a fancy café with coffee over 50 Kč and tea over 100 Kč—is **$$**; an upscale restaurant is **$$$**; and a swanky splurge is **$$$$**.

---

with 40 seats (many at shared tables) in one 1930s-style room decorated with funky old advertisements. They serve good, inexpensive, unpretentious local cuisine and hometown Eggenberg beer on tap (daily 10:00-23:00, Kájovská 66, tel. 380-711-280).

$$ Cikánská Jizba ("Gypsy Pub") is a Roma tavern filling one den-like, barrel-vaulted room. The Roma staff serves Slovak-style food (most of the Czech Republic's Roma population came from Slovakia). While this rustic little restaurant—which packs its 10 tables under a mystic-feeling Gothic vault—won't win any culinary awards, you never know what festive and musical activities will erupt, particularly on Friday nights, when Milan's son's band, Cindži Renta ("Wet Rag"), performs here (daily 13:00-24:00; off-season Mon-Sat 17:00-24:00, closed Sun; 2 blocks toward castle from main square at Dlouhá 31, tel. 380-717-585).

$$ Krčma u Dwau Maryí ("Tavern of the Two Marys") is a characteristic old place with idyllic riverside picnic tables, serving ye olde Czech cuisine and drinks. The fascinating menu explains the history of the house and makes a good case that the food of the poor medieval Bohemians was tasty and varied. Buck up for buckwheat, millet, greasy meat, or the poor-man's porridge (daily 11:00-23:00, Parkán 104, tel. 380-717-228).

$$ Laibon, while still a top choice for a filling vegetarian meal, has a chef who is evidently not inclined to calibrate her spices or rely exclusively on fresh ingredients (beware of canned pea soup). Settle down in the meditative inside or head out onto the castle-view river terrace and observe the raft-and-canoe action while you eat (daily 11:00-23:00, Parkán 105).

$$ Kolektiv tries to inject some modern sophistication into this olde town. It has a stark minimalist interior, a chalkboard menu, well-executed light café fare with some international flavors, a good cocktail selection, and stylish—if stuffy—service (daily

8:00-20:00, Fri-Sat until 21:00, Latrán 13, across from the castle stairs, tel. 776-626-644).

$$ Rybářská Restaurace ("Fisherman's Restaurant") doesn't look particularly inviting from the outside, but this is *the* place in town to taste fresh carp and trout. Choose between indoor tables under fishnets or riverside picnic benches outside, and ask about their cheap daily specials that feed the floating Czech crowds (daily 11:00-22:00, on the island by the millwheel, mobile 723-829-089).

$$$ Krčma v Šatlavské is an old prison gone cozy, with an open fire, big wooden tables under a rustic old medieval vault, and tables outdoors on the pedestrian lane. It's great for a late drink or roasted game (cooked on an open spit). *Medovina* is hot honey wine (daily 12:00-24:00, on Šatlavská, follow lane leading to the side from TI on main square, mobile 608-973-797).

$$$ Restaurace Barbakán is built into the town fortifications, with a terrace hanging high over the river. It's a good spot for old-fashioned Czech cooking and beer, at the top of town and near the recommended Rooseveltova street accommodations (open long hours daily, reasonable prices, Horní 26, tel. 380-712-679).

$$ Hospoda 99 Restaurace serves good, cheap soups, salads, and meals. It's the choice of hostelers and locals alike for its hamburgers, vegetarian food, Czech dishes, and cheap booze (meals served 10:00-22:00, bar open until 24:00, at Hostel 99, Vezni 99, tel. 380-712-812). This place is booming until late, when everything else is hibernating.

$ Krumlovská Picka, a tiny, atmospheric place on the island by the millwheel, offers takeout pizza and freshly baked-and-filled baguettes. Cuddle near the oven inside or picnic on the outside terrace (daily 12:00-23:00, Dlouhá 97).

$ Dobrá Čajovna is a typical example of the quiet, exotic-feeling teahouses that flooded Czech towns in the 1990s as alternatives to smoky, raucous pubs. Though directly across from the castle entrance, it's a world away from the tourist hubbub. As is so often the case, if you want to surround yourself with locals, don't go to a traditional place...go ethnic. With its meditative karma inside and a peaceful terrace facing the monastery out back, it provides a relaxing break (daily 13:00-22:00, Latrán 54, mobile 777-654-744).

$ Coffee Roasting Company, on the corner of Linecká just past the Seidel Photo Studio Museum, is a tiny local place far away from the crowds and dead serious about the quality of its cakes and fair-trade brews (daily 10:00-19:00).

Český Krumlov Connections

BY PUBLIC TRANSPORTATION

Almost all trains to and from Český Krumlov require a change in the city of **České Budějovice,** a transit hub just to the north. Buses, on the other hand, are direct. Bus and train timetables are available at www.idos.cz.

If you have time in České Budějovice between connections, consider a visit to the town's gigantic medieval main square, Náměstí Přemysla Otakara II (about a six-block walk from the station). Store your bags in lockers at the train station, then exit the station to the right, cross the street at the crosswalk, and head straight down Lannova třída (which becomes Kanovnická street) to the square.

By Train

From Český Krumlov by Train to: České Budějovice (6/day, 45 minutes), **Prague** (8/day, 1/day direct, 3.5 hours; bus is faster and cheaper, but may be booked and doesn't allow a stopover in Budějovice), **Vienna** (6/day with changes in Budějovice and Linz, 5 hours), **Budapest** (6/day with changes in Budějovice and Linz, 7 hours).

By Bus

The Český Krumlov bus station, a five-minute walk out of town, is just a big parking lot with numbered stalls for various buses (bus info tel. 380-711-190). The Student Agency (www.studentagency.cz) and Leo Express (www.le.cz) have online reservation and ticket systems, the newest buses, and a free drink for passengers.

From Český Krumlov by Bus to: Prague (10/day, 3.5 hours; tickets can be bought at the Český Krumlov TI), **České Budějovice** (transit hub for other destinations; hourly, 40 minutes).

BY SHUTTLE SERVICE

From Český Krumlov to Austria and Beyond: Several companies offer handy shuttle service. The best of the bunch is CK Shuttle, with free Wi-Fi on board and affordable fares: 800 Kč per person one-way to **Vienna** (4/day, 3.5 hours), **Salzburg** (4/day, 3 hours), **Hallstatt** (3/day, 3 hours), or **Prague** (3/day, 2.5 hours). They can also take you to Linz (where you can hop on the speedy east-west main rail line through Austria), Budapest, Munich, and other places. They offer door-to-door service to and from your hotel, and once you book on their website and receive a confirmation, your departure is guaranteed (office at Dlouhá 95, www.ckshuttle.cz). Another reliable option is Sebastian Tours (higher prices, mobile 607-100-234 or 608-357-581, www.sebastianck-tours.com, sebastiantours@hotmail.com).

POLAND
Polska

POLAND

Polska

Poland is a land of surprises. Many people imagine Poland as a backwards, impoverished land of rusting factories, smoggy cities, and gloomy natives. But these people are left speechless when they step into Kraków's vibrant main square, Gdańsk's colorful Royal Way, or Warsaw's lively Old Town. While parts of the country still do feel like a time warp, today's Poland also has a vibrant urbanity, an enticing food and design culture, dynamic history, and kindhearted natives.

The Poles are a proud people—as moved by their spectacular failures as by their successes. Their quiet elegance has been tempered by generations of abuse by foreign powers. You'll find fewer scams and con artists here than in other Eastern European countries.

In a way, there are two Polands: lively, cosmopolitan urban centers, and countless tiny farm villages in the countryside. A societal tension exists between city-dwelling progressives and what they call the "simple people" of Poland: hardworking small-town Poles descended from generations of farmers, who still live an uncomplicated, agrarian lifestyle. There's a large contingent of these salt-of-the-earth folks, who like things the way they are and tend to be politically conservative and staunchly Euroskeptic.

Poland is arguably Europe's most devoutly Catholic country. Their profound faith has united the Poles through many tough times. Squeezed between Protestant Germany (originally Prussia) and Eastern Orthodox Russia, Poland wasn't even a country for generations (1795-1918)—but its Catholicism helped keep its spirit alive. Under communism, Poles found their religion a source of strength as well as rebellion—they could express dissent against the atheistic regime by going to church. Be sure to step into some serene church interiors. These aren't museums—you'll almost certainly see locals in prayer.

(Be careful to show the proper respect: Maintain silence, keep a low profile, and if you want to snap pictures, do so discreetly.)

Much of Poland's story is a Jewish story. Before World War II, 80 percent of Europe's Jews lived in Poland. Warsaw was the world's second-largest Jewish city (after New York), with 380,000 Jews (out of a total population of 1.2 million). Poland was a magnet for Jewish refugees because of its relatively welcoming policies. Still, Jews were forbidden from owning land; that's why they settled mostly in the cities. But the Holocaust (and a later Soviet policy of sending "troublemaking" Jews to Israel) decimated the Jewish population. This tragic chapter, combined with postwar border shifts and population movements, made Poland one of Europe's most ethnically homogeneous countries. Today, virtually everyone in the country is an ethnic Pole, and only a few thousand Polish Jews remain.

Poland has long been extremely pro-America. Of course, their big neighbors (Russia and Germany) have been their historic enemies. And when Hitler invaded in 1939, the Poles felt let down by their supposed European friends (France and Britain), who declared war on Germany but provided virtually no military support to the Polish resistance. America, meanwhile, is seen as the big ally from across the ocean—and the home of the largest population of Poles outside of Poland. In 1989, when Poland finally won its freedom, many Poles half-joked that they should apply to become the 51st state.

On my first visit to Poland, I had a poor impression of Poles, who seemed brusque and often elbowed ahead of me in line. I've since learned that all it takes is a smile and a cheerful greeting—preferably in Polish—to break through the thick skin that helped

Poland Almanac

Official Name: Rzeczpospolita Polska (Republic of Poland), or Polska for short.

Snapshot History: This thousand-year-old country has been dominated by foreigners for much of the past two centuries, finally achieving true independence (from the Soviet Union) in 1989.

Population: 38.5 million people, slightly more than California. About 97 percent are ethnic Poles who speak Polish (though English is also widely spoken). Three out of every four Poles are practicing Catholics. The population is younger than most European countries, with an average age of 39 (Germany's is 46).

Latitude and Longitude: 52°N and 20°E (similar latitude to Berlin, London, and Edmonton, Alberta).

Area: 121,000 square miles, the same as New Mexico (or Illinois and Iowa put together).

Geography: Because of its overall flatness, Poland has been a corridor for invading armies since its infancy. The Vistula River (650 miles) runs south-to-north up the middle of the country, passing through Kraków and Warsaw, and emptying into the Baltic Sea at Gdańsk. Poland's climate is generally cool and rainy—40,000 storks love it.

Biggest Cities: Warsaw (the capital, 1.7 million), Kraków (757,000), and Łódź (747,000).

Economy: The Gross Domestic Product recently surpassed $1 trillion, with a GDP per capita of $26,500. The 1990s saw an aggressive and successful transition from state-run socialism to privately-owned capitalism. Still, Poland's traditional potato-and-pig-farming society is behind the times, with 16 percent of the country's workers producing less than 3 percent of its GDP. About one in ten Poles is unemployed, and nearly one in five lives in poverty. Poland weathered the economic crisis better than most European countries; some believe it's thanks to their relatively primitive economic model.

POLAND

these kind people survive the difficult communist times. With a friendly *Dzień dobry!,* you'll turn any grouch into an ally.

It may help to know that, because of the distinct cadence of Polish, Poles speaking English sometimes sound more impatient, gruff, or irritated than they actually are. Part of the Poles' charm is that they're not as slick and self-assured as many Europeans: They're kind, soft-spoken, and quite shy. On a recent train trip in Poland, I offered my Polish seatmate a snack—and spent the rest of trip enjoying a delightful conversation with a new friend.

Currency: 1 złoty (zł, or PLN) = 100 groszy (gr) = about 25 cents; 4 zł = about $1.

Government: Poland's mostly figurehead president selects the prime minister and cabinet, with legislators' approval. They govern along with a two-house legislature (Sejm and Senat) of 560 seats. Prime Minister Beata Szydło—already Poland's third female PM in less than 30 years of democracy—represents the majority political party, the right-wing Law and Justice (Prawo i Sprawiedliwość). President Andrzej Duda, formerly of the Law and Justice party (but currently a conservative-leaning independent), began his five-year term in 2015. (For more on Polish politics, see page 226.)

Flag: The upper half is white, and the lower half is red—the traditional colors of Poland. Poetic Poles claim the white represents honor, and the red represents the blood spilled by the Poles to honor their nation. The flag sometimes includes a coat of arms with a crowned eagle (representing Polish sovereignty). Under Poland's many oppressors (including the Soviets), the crown was removed from the emblem, and its talons were trimmed. On regaining its independence, Poland coronated its eagle once more.

Not-so-Average Poles: Poland's three big airports offer a rundown of just a few of the country's biggest names: St. John Paul II (in Kraków), Fryderyk Chopin (in Warsaw), and Lech Wałęsa (in Gdańsk). And, despite the many "Polack jokes" you've heard (and maybe repeated), you're already familiar with many other famous Polish intellectuals—you just don't realize they're Polish. The "Dumb Polack" Hall of Fame includes Mikołaj Kopernik **(Nicolas Copernicus),** scientist **Marie Curie** (née Skłodowska), writer Teodor Józef Korzeniowski (better known as **Joseph Conrad,** author of *Heart of Darkness*), filmmaker **Roman Polański** (*Chinatown, The Pianist),* **Daniel Libeskind** (the master architect for redeveloping the 9/11 site in New York City)...and one of this book's co-authors.

POLAND

HELPFUL HINTS

Restroom Signage: To confuse tourists, the Poles have devised a secret way of marking their WCs. You'll see doors marked with *męska* (men) and *damska* (women)—but even more often, you'll simply see a triangle (for men) or a circle (for women). A sign with a triangle, a circle, and an arrow is directing you to the closest WCs.

Pay to Pee: Many Polish bathrooms charge a small fee (around 1 zł). Don't be surprised if you're even charged at a restaurant where you're paying to dine.

Train Station Lingo: "PKP" is the abbreviation for Polish National Railways ("PKS" is for buses). In larger towns with sev-

Top 10 Dates that Changed Poland

A.D. 966: The Polish king, Mieszko I, is baptized a Christian, symbolically uniting the Polish people and founding the nation.

1385: The Polish queen (called a "king" by sexist aristocrats of the time) marries a Lithuanian duke, starting the two-century reign of the Jagiełło family.

1410: Poland defeats the Teutonic Knights at the Battle of Grunwald, part of a Golden Age of territorial expansion and cultural achievement.

1572: The last Jagiellonian king dies, soon replaced by bickering nobles and foreign kings. Poland declines.

1795: In the last of three Partitions, the country is divvied up by its more-powerful neighbors: Russia, Prussia, and Austria.

1918: Following World War I, Poland gets back its land and sovereignty.

1939: The Free City of Gdańsk (then called Danzig) is invaded by Nazi Germany, starting World War II. At war's end, the country is "liberated" (i.e., occupied) by the Soviet Union.

1980: Lech Wałęsa leads a successful strike, demanding more freedom from the communist regime.

1989: Poland gains independence under its first president—Lech Wałęsa. Fifteen years later, Poland joins the European Union.

2010: President Lech Kaczyński and 95 other high-level government officials are killed in a plane crash in Russia.

eral train stations, you'll normally use the one called Główny (meaning "Main"—except in Warsaw, where it's Centralna). *Dworzec główny* means "main train station." Most stations have several platforms *(peron)*, each of which has two tracks *(tor)*. Departures are generally listed by the *peron*, so keep your eye on both tracks for your train. Arrivals are *przyjazdy*, and departures are *odjazdy*. Left-luggage counters or lockers are marked *przechowalnia bagażu*. *Kasy* are ticket windows. These can be marked (sometimes only in Polish) for specific needs—domestic tickets, international tickets, and so on; ask fellow travelers to be sure you select the right line. The line you choose will invariably be the slowest one—leave plenty of time to buy your ticket. On arriving at a station, to get into town, follow signs for *wyjście* (sometimes followed by *do centrum* or *do miasta*).

Transit Route Planner: For a good public transit route planner for most Polish cities, try www.jakdojade.pl.

Busy May: Be prepared for crowds and closures in the month of

May. May 1 is May Day and May 3 is Constitution Day, so the entire country gets closed up for several days. Later in the month, younger kids get out of school, so families go on vacation (and Kraków is one of the most popular domestic destinations).

Telephones: Remember these Polish prefixes: 800 is toll-free, and 70 is expensive (like phone sex). Many Poles use mobile phones (which come with the prefix 50, 51, 53, 60, 66, 69, 72, 78, 79, or 88). For details on how to dial, see page 1086.

POLISH HISTORY

Poland is flat. Take a look at a topographical map of Europe, and you'll immediately appreciate the Poles' historical dilemma: The

path of least resistance from northern Europe to Russia leads right through Poland. Over the years, many invaders—from Genghis Khan to Napoleon to Hitler—have taken advantage of Poland's strategic location. The country is nicknamed "God's playground" for the many wars that have rumbled through its territory. Poland has been invaded by Soviets, Nazis, French, Austrians, Russians, Prussians, Swedes, Teutonic Knights, Tatars, Bohemians, Magyars—and, about 1,300 years ago, Poles.

Medieval Greatness

The first Poles were the Polonians ("people of the plains"), a Slavic band that arrived here in the eighth century. In 966, Mieszko I, Duke of the Polonian tribe, adopted Christianity and founded the Piast dynasty (which would last for more than 400 years). Centuries before Germany, Italy, or Spain first united, Poland was born.

Poland struggled against two different invaders in the 13th century: the Tatars (Mongols who ravaged the south) and the Teutonic Knights (Germans who conquered the north—see page 502). But despite these challenges, Poland persevered. The last king of the Piast dynasty was also the greatest: Kazimierz the Great, who famously "found a Poland made of wood and left one made of brick and stone," and helped bring Poland (and its then-capital, Kraków) to international prominence (see page 257). The progressive Kazimierz also invited Europe's much-persecuted Jews to settle here, establishing Poland as a haven for the Jewish people, which it would remain until the Nazis arrived.

Kazimierz the Great died at the end of the 14th century without a male heir. His grand-niece, Princess Jadwiga, became

"king" (the Poles weren't ready for a "queen") and married Lithuanian Prince Władysław Jagiełło, uniting their countries against a
common enemy, the Teutonic Knights. Their marriage marked the
beginning of the Jagiellonian dynasty and set the stage for Poland's
Golden Age.

During this time, Poland expanded its territory, the Polish nobility began to acquire more political influence, Italy's Renaissance
(and its architectural styles) became popular, and the Toruń-born
astronomer Nicholas Copernicus shook up the scientific world with
his bold new heliocentric theory. Up on the Baltic coast, the port
city of Gdańsk took advantage of its Hanseatic League trading
partnership to become one of Europe's most prosperous cities.

Foreign Kings and Partitions

When the Jagiellonians died out in 1572, political power shifted
to the nobility. Poland became a republic of nobles governed by its
wealthiest 10 percent—the *szlachta*, who elected a series of foreign
kings. In the 16th and 17th centuries—with its territory spanning from the Baltic Sea to the Black Sea—the Polish-Lithuanian
Commonwealth was the largest state in Europe.

But over time, many of the elected kings made poor diplomatic decisions and squandered the country's resources. To make matters worse, the nobles' parliament (Sejm) introduced the concept of
liberum veto (literally "I freely forbid"), whereby any measure could
be vetoed by a single member of parliament. This policy, which effectively demanded unanimous approval for any law to be passed,
paralyzed the Sejm's waning power.

Sensing the Commonwealth's weakness, in the mid-17th century forces from Sweden rampaged through Polish and Lithuanian
lands in the devastating "Swedish Deluge." While Poland eventually reclaimed its territory, a third of its population was dead. The
Commonwealth continued to import self-serving foreign kings,
including Saxony's Augustus the Strong and his son, who drained
Polish wealth to finance vanity projects in their hometown of Dresden.

By the late 18th century, the Commonwealth was floundering...and surrounded by three land-hungry empires (Russia, Prussia, and Austria). The Poles were unaware that these neighbors had
entered into an agreement now dubbed the "Alliance of the Three
Black Eagles" (since all three of those countries, coincidentally,
used that bird as their symbol); they began to circle Poland's white
eagle like vultures. Stanisław August Poniatowski, elected king
with Russian support in 1764, would be Poland's last.

Over the course of less than 25 years, Russia, Prussia, and
Austria divided Polish territory among themselves in a series of
three Partitions. In 1772 and again in 1790, Poland was forced into

ceding large chunks of land to its neighbors. Desperate to reform their government, Poles enacted Europe's first democratic constitution (and the world's second, after the US Constitution) on May 3, 1791—still celebrated as a national holiday. This visionary document protected the peasants, dispensed with both *liberum veto* and the election of the king, and set up something resembling a modern nation. But the constitution alarmed Poland's neighbors, who swept in soon after with the third and final Partition in 1795. "Poland" disappeared from Europe's maps, not to return until 1918.

Even though Poland was gone, the Poles wouldn't go quietly. As the Partitions were taking place, Polish soldier Tadeusz Kościuszko (also a hero of the American Revolution) returned home to lead an unsuccessful military resistance against the Russians in 1794.

Napoleon offered a brief glimmer of hope to the Poles in the early 19th century, when he marched eastward through Europe and set up the semi-independent "Duchy of Warsaw" in Polish lands. But that fleeting taste of freedom lasted only eight years; with Napoleon's defeat, Polish hopes were dashed. The Congress of Vienna, which again redistributed Polish territory to Prussia, Russia, and Austria, is sometimes called (by Poles) the "Fourth Partition." In a classic case of "my enemy's enemy is my friend," the Poles still have great affection for Napoleon for how fiercely he fought against their mutual foes.

The Napoleonic connection also established France as a safe haven for refugee Poles. After another failed uprising against Russia in 1830, many of Poland's top artists and writers fled to Paris—including pianist Fryderyk Chopin and Romantic poet Adam Mickiewicz (whose statue adorns Kraków's main square and Warsaw's Royal Way). These Polish artists tried to preserve the nation's spirit with music and words; those who remained in Poland continued to fight with swords and fists. By the end of the 19th century, the image of the Pole as a tireless, idealistic insurgent emerged. During this time, some Romantics—with typically melodramatic flair—dubbed Poland "the Christ of nations" for the way it was misunderstood and persecuted by the world, despite its nobility.

Poles didn't just flock to France during the Partitions. Untold numbers of Polish people uprooted their lives to pursue a better future in the New World. About 10 million Americans have Polish ancestry, and most of them came stateside from the mid-19th to early 20th centuries. Because the sophisticated and educated tended to remain in Poland, these new arrivals were mostly poor farmers who were (at first) unschooled and didn't speak English, placing them on a bottom rung of American society. It was during this time that the tradition of insulting "Polack jokes" emerged. Some claim these originated in Chicago, which was both a national trendsetter in humor and a magnet for Polish immigrants. Others suggest that German immigrants to America imported insulting stereotypes of their Polish neighbors from the Old World. Either way, the jokes only became more vicious through the 20th century, until the Polish government actually lobbied the US State Department to put a stop to them.

As the map of Europe was redrawn following World War I, Poland emerged as a reborn nation, under the war hero-turned-head of state, Marshal Józef Piłsudski. The newly reformed "Second Polish Republic," which patched together the bits and pieces of territory that had been under foreign rule for decades, enjoyed a diverse ethnic mix—including Germans, Russians, Ukrainians, Lithuanians, and an enormous Jewish minority. A third of Poland spoke no Polish.

This interwar period was a time of particular flourishing for the Jewish culture. Jews were, for the first time, legally protected citizens of Poland, with full voting rights. Cities like Warsaw, Kraków, and Wilno (today's Vilnius, Lithuania)—where Jews made up a quarter to a third of the population—saw the blossoming of a rich Jewish culture.

Meanwhile, the historic Baltic port city of Gdańsk—which was bicultural (German and Polish)—was granted the special "Free City of Danzig" status to avoid dealing with the prickly issue of whether to assign it to Germany or Poland. But the peace was not to last.

World War II

On September 1, 1939, Adolf Hitler began World War II by attacking Danzig to bring it into the German fold. Before the month was out, Hitler's forces had overrun Poland, and the Soviets had taken over a swath of eastern Poland (today still part of Ukraine, Belarus, and Lithuania).

The Nazis considered the Poles *slawische Untermenschen,* "Slavic sub-humans" who were useful only for manual labor. And Poland was also home to a huge population of Jewish people. Nazi Germany annexed Polish regions that it claimed historic ties to, while the rest (including "Warschau" and "Krakau") became a puppet state ruled by the *Generalgouvernement* and Hitler's handpicked governor, Hans Frank. The Nazis considered this area *Lebensraum*— "living space" that wasn't nice enough to actually incorporate into Germany, but served perfectly as extra territory for building things that Germans didn't want in their backyards...such as the notorious death camp, Auschwitz-Birkenau.

The Poles anxiously awaited the promised military aid of France and Britain; when help failed to arrive, they took matters into their own hands, forming a ragtag "Polish Home Army" and staging incredibly courageous but lopsided battles against their powerful German overlords (such as the Warsaw Uprising—see page 419). Throughout the spring of 1945, as the Nazis retreated from their failed invasion of the Soviet Union, the Red Army gradually "liberated" the rubble of Poland from Nazi oppression—guaranteeing it another four decades of oppression under another regime.

During World War II, occupied Poland had the strictest laws in the Nazi realm: This was the only place where, if you were caught trying to help Jews escape, your entire family could be executed. And yet, many Poles risked their lives to help escapees.

With six million deaths over six years—including both Polish Jews and ethnic Poles—Poland suffered the worst per-capita WWII losses of any nation. By the war's end, one out of every five Polish citizens was dead—and 90 percent of those killed were civilians. While the human and infrastructure loss of World War II was incalculable, that war's cultural losses were also devastating—for example, some 60,000 paintings were lost.

At the war's end, the victorious Allies shifted Poland's borders significantly westward—folding historically German areas into Polish territory and appropriating previously Polish areas for the USSR. This prompted a massive movement of populations—which today we'd decry as "ethnic cleansing"—as Germans were forcibly removed from western Poland, and Poles from newly Soviet territory were transplanted to Poland proper. Entire cities were repopulated (such as the formerly German metropolis of Breslau, which was renamed Wrocław and filled with refugee Poles from Lwów, now Lviv, in Ukraine). After millions died in the war, millions more were displaced from their ancestral homes. When the dust settled, Poland was almost exclusively populated by Poles.

Saddle on a Cow: Poland Under Communism

Poland suffered horribly under the communists. A postwar intimidation regime was designed to frighten people "on board" and coincided with government seizure of private property, rationing, and food shortages. The country enjoyed a relatively open society under Premier Władysław Gomułka in the 1960s, but the impractical, centrally planned economy began to unravel in the 1970s. Stores were marked by long lines stretching around the block.

The little absurdities of communist life—which today seem almost comical—made every day a struggle. For years, every elderly woman in Poland had hair the same strange magenta color. There was only one color of dye available, so if you had dyed hair, the choice was simple: Let your hair grow out (and look clownishly half red and half white), or line up and go red.

During these difficult times, the Poles often rose up—staging

The Heritage of Communism

Poland has been free, democratic, and capitalist since 1989, but some adults carry lots of psychological baggage from living under communism. While the vast majority of Poles much prefer the current system to the old one, even the gloomiest memories are tinged with nostalgia. A friend who was 13 in 1989 recalled those days this way:

"My childhood is filled with happy memories. Under communism, life was family-oriented. Careers didn't matter. There was no way to get rich, no reason to rush, so we had time. People always had time.

"But there were also shortages—many things were 'in deficit.' We stood in line not knowing what would be for sale. We'd buy whatever shoes were available and then trade. At grocery stores, vinegar and mustard were always on the shelf, along with plastic cheese to make it seem less empty. Milk and bread were very low quality—it wasn't unusual to find a cigarette butt in your loaf. We had to carry ration coupons, which we'd present when buying a staple that was in short supply. They'd snip a corner off the coupon after making the sale. We didn't necessarily buy what we needed—just anything that could be bartered on the black market. I remember my mother and fa-

major protests in 1956, 1968, 1970, and 1976. Stalin famously noted that introducing communism to the Poles was like putting a saddle on a cow.

When an anticommunist Polish cardinal named Karol Wojtyła was elected pope in 1978, then visited his homeland in 1979, it was a sign to his countrymen that change was in the air. (For more on St. John Paul II, see page 266.) In 1980, Lech Wałęsa, an electrician at the shipyards in Gdańsk, became the leader of the Solidarity movement, the first workers' union in communist Eastern Europe. After an initial 18-day strike at the Gdańsk shipyards, the communist regime gave in, legalizing Solidarity (for more on Solidarity, see page 463).

But the union grew too powerful, and the communists felt their control slipping away. On Sunday, December 13, 1981, Poland's head of state, General Wojciech Jaruzelski, declared martial law in order to "forestall Soviet intervention." (Whether the Soviets actually would have invaded remains a hotly debated issue.) Tanks ther had to 'organize' for special events...somehow find a good sausage and some Coca-Cola.

"Instead of a tidy roll of toilet paper, bathrooms came with a wad of old newspapers. Sometimes my uncle would bring us several toilet paper rolls, held together with a string—absolutely the best gift anyone could give.

"Boys in my neighborhood collected pop cans. Since drinks were very limited in Poland, cans from other countries represented a world of opportunities beyond our borders. Parents could buy their children these cans on the black market, and the few families who were allowed to travel returned home with a treasure trove of cans. One boy up the street from me went to Italy, and proudly brought home a Pepsi can. All of the boys in the neighborhood wanted to see it—it was a huge status symbol. But a month later, communism ended, you could buy whatever you wanted, and everyone's can collections were worthless.

"We had real chocolate only for Christmas. The rest of the year, for treats we got something called 'chocolate-like product,' which was sweet, dark, and smelled vaguely of chocolate. And we had oranges from Cuba for Christmas, too. Everybody was excited when the newspapers announced, 'The boat with the oranges from Cuba is just five days from Poland.' We waited with excitement all year for chocolate and those oranges. The smell of Christmas was so special. Now we have that smell every day. Still, my happiest Christmases were under communism."

ominously rolled through the streets of Poland on that snowy December morning, and the Poles were terrified.

Martial law lasted until 1983. Each Pole has his or her own chilling memories of this frightening time. During riots, the people would flock into churches—the only place they could be safe from the ZOMO (riot police). People would go for their evening walks during the 19:30 government-sanctioned national news as a sign of protest. But Solidarity struggled on, going underground and becoming a united movement of all demographics, 10 million members strong (more than a quarter of the population).

In July of 1989, the ruling Communist Party agreed to hold open elections (reserving 65 percent of representatives for themselves). Their goal was to appease Solidarity, but the plan backfired: Communists didn't win a single contested seat. These elections helped spark the chain reaction across Eastern Europe that eventually tore down the Iron Curtain. Lech Wałęsa became Poland's first postcommunist president. (For more on Lech Wałęsa, see page 466.)

Poland in the 21st Century

When 10 new countries joined the European Union in May 2004, Poland was the most ambivalent of the bunch. After centuries of being under other empires' authority, the Poles were hardly eager to relinquish some of their hard-fought autonomy to Brussels. Many Poles thought that EU membership would make things worse (higher prices, a loss of traditional lifestyles) before they got better. But most people agreed that their country had to join to survive in today's Europe. Today most Poles begrudgingly acknowledge that the benefits of EU membership have outweighed the drawbacks.

The most obvious initial impact of EU membership was the droves of job-seeking young Poles who migrated to other EU countries (mostly Britain, Ireland, and Sweden, which were the first to waive visa requirements for Eastern European workers). Many found employment at hotels and restaurants. Visitors to London and Dublin noticed a surprising language barrier at hotel front desks, and Polish-language expat newspapers joined British gossip rags on newsstands. Those who remained in Poland were concerned about the "brain drain" of bright young people flocking out of their country. But with the economic crisis, quite a few Polish expats returned home. And the 2016 Brexit vote has placed UK-Polish relations in doubt, likely prompting another wave of returnees. For more on this phenomenon, see "The Polish Plumber Syndrome" sidebar on page 1070.

Poland is by far the most populous of the recent EU members, with nearly 39 million people (about the same as Spain, or about half the size of Germany). This makes Poland the sixth-largest of the 26 EU member states—giving it serious political clout, which it has already asserted...sometimes to the dismay of the EU's more established powers.

On the American political spectrum, Poland may be the most "conservative" country in Europe. Poles are phobic when it comes to "big government"—likely because they've been subjugated and manipulated by so many foreign oppressors over the centuries. For most of the 2000s, the country's right wing was represented by a pair of twin brothers, Lech and Jarosław Kaczyński. (The Kaczyński brothers were child actors who appeared in several popular movies together.) Their conservative Law and Justice Party is pro-tax cuts, fiercely Euroskeptic (anti-EU), and very Catholic. In the 2005 presidential election, Lech Kaczyński emerged as the victor; several months later, he took the controversial step of appointing his identical twin brother Jarosław as Poland's prime minister.

The political pendulum swung back toward the center in October of 2007, when the Kaczyński brothers' main political rival, the pro-EU Donald Tusk, led his Civic Platform Party to victory in the parliamentary elections. The name Kaczyński loosely means

Polish Jokes

Through the dreary communist times, the Poles managed to keep their sense of humor. A popular target of jokes was the riot police, called the ZOMO. Here are just a few of the things Poles said about these unpopular cops:

- It's better to have a sister who's a whore than a brother in the ZOMO.
- ZOMO police are hired based on the 90-90 principle: They have to weigh at least 90 kilograms (200 pounds), and their I.Q. must be less than 90.
- ZOMO are dispatched in teams of three: one who can read, one who can write, and a third to protect those other two smart guys.
- A ZOMO policeman was sitting on the curb, crying. Someone came up to him and asked what was wrong. "I lost my dog!" he said. "No matter," the person replied. "He's a smart police dog. I'm sure he can find his way back to the station." "Yes," the ZOMO said. "But without him, I can't!"

The communists gave their people no options at elections: If you voted, you voted for the regime. Poles liked to joke that in some ways, this made communists like God—who created Eve, then said to Adam, "Now choose a wife." It was said that communists could run a pig as a candidate, and it would still win; a popular symbol of dissent became a pig painted with the words "Vote Red."

There were even jokes about jokes. Under communism, Poles noted that there was a government-sponsored prize for the funniest political joke: 15 years in prison.

"duck"—so the Poles quipped that they were led by "Donald and the Ducks."

Tragically, the levity wasn't to last. On April 10, 2010, a plane carrying President Lech Kaczyński crashed in a thick fog near the city of Smolensk, Russia. All 96 people on board—including top government, military, and business officials, high-ranking clergy, and others—were killed, plunging the nation into a period of stunned mourning. Poles wondered why, yet again, an unprecedented tragedy had befallen their nation. (Ironically, the group's trip was intended to put a painful chapter of Poland's history to rest: a commemoration of the Polish officers and enlisted men killed in the Soviet massacre at Katyń.)

Meanwhile, Poland's economy has kept chugging along, even as the rest of Europe and much of the world were bogged down by the economic crisis. More than a quarter of Poland's trade is with neighboring Germany—another of Europe's healthiest economies—and Poland was the only European Union country that didn't have a recession in 2009. Why? Poland is a big,

Bar Mleczny (Milk Bar)

When you see a "bar" in Poland, it doesn't mean alcohol—it means cheap grub. Eating at a bar mleczny (bar MLECH-neh) is an essential Polish sightseeing experience. These cafeterias, which you'll see all over the country, are an incredibly cheap way to get a good meal...and, with the right attitude, a fun cultural experience.

In the communist era, the government subsidized the food at milk bars, allowing workers to enjoy a meal out. The name comes from the cheese cutlets that were sold here, back in a time when good meat was rare. The tradition continues today, as milk-bar prices remain astoundingly low: My bill for a filling meal usually comes to about $5. And, while communist-era fare was gross, today's milk-bar cuisine is usually quite tasty.

Milk bars usually offer many of the traditional tastes listed in the "Polish Food" section. Common items are soups (like żurek and barszcz), a variety of cabbage-based salads, kotlet (fried pork chops), pierogi (like ravioli, with various fillings), and naleśniki (pancakes). You'll see glasses of juice and (of course) milk, but most milk bars also stock bottles of water and Coke.

There are two types of milk bars: updated, modern cafeterias that cater to tourists (English menus), add some modern twists to their traditional fare, and charge about 50 percent more; and time-machine dives that haven't changed for decades. At truly traditional milk bars, the service is aimed at locals, which means no English menu and a confusing ordering system.

Every milk bar is a little different, but here's the general procedure: Head to the counter, wait to be acknowledged, and point to what you want. Handy vocabulary: to (sounds like "toe") means "this"; i (pronounced "ee") means "and."

If the milk-bar lady asks you any questions, you have three options: Nod stupidly until she just gives you something; repeat one of the things she just said (assuming she's asked you to choose between two options, like meat or cheese in your pierogi); or hope that a kindly English-speaking Pole in line will leap to your rescue. If nothing else, ordering at a milk bar is an adventure in gestures. Smiling seems to slightly extend the patience of milk-bar staffers.

Once your tray is all loaded up, pay the cashier, do a double-take when you realize how cheap your bill is, then find a table. After the meal, bus your own dishes to the little window.

self-sustaining, insular economy. In recent years, Poland's relatively weak currency ("cheaper" than the euro, yet also shielded from euro volatility) and robust economy are luring foreign investment, paradoxically threatening the very autonomy that has buffered it so far.

In recent years, the political pendulum has just kept on swinging, as key governmental posts have gone back and forth between the two dominant parties—the Civic Platform and Law and Justice. It seems the Poles are getting the hang of this whole democracy thing.

POLISH FOOD

Polish food is hearty and tasty. Because Poland is north of the Carpathian Mountains, its weather tends to be chilly, limiting the kinds of fruits and vegetables that flourish here. As in other northern European countries (such as Russia or Scandinavia), dominant staples include potatoes, dill, berries, beets, and rye. Much of what you might think of as "Jewish cuisine" turns up on Polish menus (gefilte fish, potato pancakes, chicken soup, and so forth)—which makes sense, given that Poles and Jews lived in the same area for centuries.

Polish soups are a highlight. The most typical are *żurek* and *barszcz*. *Żurek* (often translated as "sour soup" on menus) is a light-colored soup made from a sourdough base, usually containing a hard-boiled egg and pieces of *kiełbasa* (sausage). *Barszcz*, better known to Americans as borscht, is a savory beet soup that you'll see in several varieties: *Barszcz czerwony* (red borscht) is a thin, flavorful broth with a deep red color, sometimes containing dumplings or a hard-boiled egg. *Barszcz ukraiński* (Ukrainian borscht) is thicker, with cream and vegetables (usually cabbage, beans, and carrots). In summer, try the "Polish gazpacho"—*chłodnik*, a savory cream soup with beets, onions, and radishes that's served cold. I never met a Polish soup I didn't like...until I was introduced to *flaki* (sometimes *flaczki*)—tripe soup.

Another familiar Polish dish is pierogi. These ravioli-like dumplings come with various fillings. The most traditional are minced meat, sauerkraut, mushroom, cheese, and blueberry; many restaurants also experiment with more exotic fillings. Pierogi are often served with specks of fatty bacon to add flavor. Pierogi are a budget traveler's dream: Restaurants serving them are everywhere, and they're generally cheap, tasty, and very filling.

Bigos is a rich and delicious sauerkraut stew cooked with

meat, mushrooms, and whatever's in the pantry. *Gołąbki* is a dish of cabbage leaves stuffed with minced meat and rice in a tomato or mushroom sauce. *Kotlet schabowy* (fried pork chop)—once painfully scarce in communist Poland—remains a local favorite to this day. *Kaczka* (duck) is popular, as is freshwater fish: Look for *pstrąg* (trout), *karp* (carp, beware of bones), and *węgorz* (eel). On the Baltic Coast (such as in Gdańsk), you'll also see *łosoś* (salmon), *śledź* (herring), and *dorsz* (cod). Poles eat lots of potatoes, which are served with nearly every meal. Look for *placki ziemniaczane*—potato pancakes.

Several foods—both new and old—are popular in today's Poland. Herring-and-vodka bars are extremely trendy, many following the "4/8 model"—4 zł for a shot of vodka, 8 zł for a herring snack. The Polish street food *zapiekanka*—a toasted baguette with melted cheese, rubbery mushrooms from a can, and a drizzle of ersatz ketchup—began life as a "hardship food" under communism, as a pale imitation of pizza. But these days it has been reborn as a foodie staple, with *zapiekanka* vendors topping them with a world of creative flavors. The bagel-like rings you'll see sold on the street, *obwarzanki* (singular *obwarzanek*), are also cheap, and usually fresh and tasty. And, as throughout Europe, gourmet hamburgers are in—including a trend for vegan burgers.

Poland has good pastries—look for a *cukiernia* (pastry shop). The classic Polish treat is *pączki*, glazed jelly doughnuts. They can have different fillings, but most typical is a wild-rose jam. *Szarlotka* is apple cake—sometimes made with chunks of apples (especially in season), sometimes with apple filling. *Sernik* is cheesecake, and *makowiec* is poppy-seed cake. *Winebreda* is an especially gooey Danish. *Babeczka* is like a cupcake filled with pudding. And *Napoleonka* is a French-style treat with layers of crispy wafers and custard.

Lody (ice cream) is popular. The tall, skinny cones of soft-serve ice cream are called *świderki*, sometimes translated as "American ice cream." The most beloved traditional candy is *ptasie mleczko* (birds' milk), which is like a semisour marshmallow covered with chocolate. E. Wedel is the country's top brand of chocolate, with outlets in all the big cities (see page 429).

Thirsty? *Woda* is water, *woda mineralna* is bottled water (*gazowana* is with gas, *niegazowana* is without), *kawa* is coffee, *herbata* is tea, *sok* is juice, and *mleko* is milk. Żywiec, Okocim, and Lech are the best-known brands of *piwo* (beer).

Wódka (vodka) is a Polish staple—the word means, roughly, "precious little water." Żubrówka, the most famous brand of vodka, comes with a blade of grass from the bison reserves in eastern Poland (look for the bottle with the bison). The bison "flavor" the grass...then the grass flavors the vodka. Poles often mix Żubrówka with apple juice, and call this cocktail *szarlotka* ("apple cake"); it also goes by the name *tatanka* (a Native American word for "bison"). For "Cheers!" say, *"Na zdrowie!"* (nah ZDROH-vyeh).

Unusual drinks to try if you have the chance are *kwas* (a cold, fizzy, Ukrainian-style nonalcoholic beverage made from day-old rye bread) and *kompot* (a hot drink made from stewed berries). Poles are unusually fond of carrot juice (often cut with fruit juice); Kubuś is the most popular brand.

"Bon appétit" is *"Smacznego"* (smatch-NEH-goh). To pay, ask for the *rachunek* (rah-KHOO-nehk).

POLISH LANGUAGE

Polish is closely related to its neighboring Slavic languages (Slovak and Czech), with the biggest difference being that Polish has lots of fricatives (hissing sounds—"sh" and "ch"—often in close proximity).

Polish intimidates Americans with long, difficult-to-pronounce words. But if you take your time and sound things out, you'll quickly develop an ear for it. One rule of thumb to help you out: The stress is always on the next-to-last syllable.

Polish has some letters that don't appear in English, and some letters and combinations are pronounced differently than in English:

ć, ci, and **cz** all sound like "ch" as in "church"
ś, si, and **sz** all sound like "sh" as in "short"
ż, ź, zi, and **rz** all sound like "zh" as in "leisure"
dż and **dź** both sound like the "dj" sound in "jeans"
ń and **ni** sound like "ny" as in "canyon"
ę and **ą** are pronounced nasally, as in French: "en" and "an"
c sounds like "ts" as in "cats"
ch sounds like "kh" as in the Scottish "loch"
j sounds like "y" as in "yellow"
w sounds like "v" as in "Victor"
ł sounds like "w" as in "with"

So to Poles, "Lech Wałęsa" isn't pronounced "lehk wah-LEH-sah," as Americans tend to say—but "lehkh vah-WEHN-sah."

The Polish people you meet will be impressed and flattered if you take the time to learn a little of their language. To get started, check out the selection of Polish survival phrases on the following pages.

As you're tracking down addresses, these words will help: *miasto* (mee-AH-stoh, town), *plac* (plahts, square), *rynek* (REE-nehk, big market square), *ulica* (OO-leet-sah, road), *aleja* (ah-LAY-yah, avenue), and *most* (mohst, bridge). And that long word you see everywhere—*zapraszamy*—means "welcome."

Polish Survival Phrases

Keep in mind a few Polish pronunciation tips: **w** sounds like "v," **ł** sounds like "w," **ch** is a back-of-your-throat "kh" sound (as in the Scottish "loch"), and **rz** sounds like the "zh" sound in "pleasure." The vowels with a tail (**ą** and **ę**) have a slight nasal "n" sound at the end, similar to French.

English	Polish	Pronunciation
Hello. (formal)	*Dzień dobry.*	jehn **doh**-brih
Hi. / Bye. (informal)	*Cześć.*	cheshch
Do you speak English? (asked of a man)	*Czy Pan mówi po angielsku?*	chih pahn **moo**-vee poh ahn-**gyehl**-skoo
Do you speak English? (asked of a woman)	*Czy Pani mówi po angielsku?*	chih **pah**-nee **moo**-vee poh ahn-**gyehl**-skoo
Yes. / No.	*Tak. / Nie.*	tahk / nyeh
I (don't) understand.	*(Nie) rozumiem.*	(nyeh) roh-**zoo**-myehm
Please. / You're welcome. / Can I help you?	*Proszę.*	**proh**-sheh
Thank you (very much).	*Dziękuję (bardzo).*	jehn-**koo**-yeh (**bard**-zoh)
Excuse me. / I'm sorry.	*Przepraszam.*	psheh-**prah**-shahm
(No) problem.	*(Żaden) problem.*	(**zhah**-dehn) **proh**-blehm
Good.	*Dobrze.*	**dohb**-zeh
Goodbye.	*Do widzenia.*	doh veed-**zay**-nyah
one / two / three	*jeden / dwa / trzy*	**yeh**-dehn / dvah / tzhih
four / five / six	*cztery / pięć / sześć*	**chteh**-rih / pyench / sheshch
seven / eight	*siedem / osiem*	**shyeh**-dehm / **oh**-shehm
nine / ten	*dziewięć / dziesięć*	**jeh**-vyench / **jeh**-shench
hundred / thousand	*sto / tysiąc*	stoh / **tih**-shants
How much?	*Ile?*	**ee**-leh
local currency	*złoty (zł)*	**zwoh**-tih
Write it.	*Napisz to.*	**nah**-peesh toh
Is it free?	*Czy to jest za darmo?*	chih toh yehst zah **dar**-moh
Is it included?	*Czy jest to wliczone?*	chih yehst toh vlee-**choh**-neh
Where can I find / buy...?	*Gdzie mogę dostać / kupić...?*	guh-**dyeh moh**-geh **doh**-statch / **koo**-peech
I'd like... (said by a man)	*Chciałbym...*	**khchaw**-beem
I'd like... (said by a woman)	*Chciałabym...*	**khchah**-wah-beem
We'd like...	*Chcielibyśmy...*	**khchehl**-ee-bish-mih
...a room.	*...pokój.*	**poh**-kooey
...a ticket to ___.	*...bilet do ___.*	**bee**-leht doh ___
Is it possible?	*Czy jest to możliwe?*	chih yehst toh mohzh-**lee**-veh
Where is...?	*Gdzie jest...?*	guh-**dyeh** yehst
...the train station	*...dworzec kolejowy*	**dvoh**-zhehts koh-leh-**yoh**-vih
...the bus station	*...dworzec autobusowy*	**dvoh**-zhehts ow-toh-boos-**oh**-vih
...the tourist information office	*...informacja turystyczna*	een-for-**maht**-syah too-ris-**titch**-nah
...the toilet	*...toaleta*	toh-ah-**leh**-tah
men / women	*męska / damska*	**mehn**-skah / **dahm**-skah
left / right / straight	*lewo / prawo / prosto*	**leh**-voh / **prah**-voh / **proh**-stoh
At what time...?	*O której godzinie...?*	oh kuh-**too**-ray gohd-**zhee**-nyeh
...does this open / close	*...będzie otwarte / zamknięte*	**bend**-zheh oht-**vahr**-teh / zahm-**knyehn**-teh
Just a moment.	*Chwileczkę.*	khvee-**letch**-keh
now / soon / later	*eraz / niedługo / później*	**teh**-rahz / nyed-**woo**-goh / **poozh**-nyey
today / tomorrow	*dzisiaj / jutro*	**jee**-shigh / **yoo**-troh

In a Polish Restaurant

English	Polish	Pronunciation
I'd like to reserve... (said by a man)	Chciałbym zarezerwować...	**khchaw**-beem zah-reh-zehr-**voh**-vahch
I'd like to reserve... (said by a woman)	Chciałabym zarezerwować...	**khchah**-wah-beem zah-reh-zehr-**voh**-vahch
We'd like to reserve...	Chcielibyśmy zarezerwować...	**khchehl**-ee-bish-mih zah-reh-zehr-**voh**-vahch
...a table for one person / two people.	...stolik na jedną osobę / dwie osoby.	**stoh**-leek nah **yehd**-now oh-**soh**-beh / dvyeh oh-**soh**-bih
Is this table free?	Czy ten stolik jest wolny?	chih tehn **stoh**-leek yehst **vohl**-nih
Can I help you?	W czym mogę pomóc?	vchim **moh**-geh **poh**-moots
The menu (in English), please.	Menu (po angielsku), proszę.	**meh**-noo (poh ahn-**gyehl**-skoo) **proh**-sheh
service (not) included	usługa (nie) wliczona	oos-**woo**-gah (nyeh) **vlee**-choh-nah
cover charge	wstęp	vstenp
"to go"	na wynos	nah **vih**-nohs
with / without	z / bez	z / behz
and / or	i / lub	ee / loob
milk bar (cheap cafeteria)	bar mleczny	bar **mletch**-nih
fixed-price meal (of the day)	zestaw (dnia)	**zehs**-tahv (dih-**nyah**)
specialty of the house	specjalność zakładu	speht-**syahl**-nohshch zah-**kwah**-doo
half portion	pół porcji	poow **ports**-yee
daily special	danie dnia	**dah**-nyeh dih-**nyah**
appetizers	przystawki	pshih-**stahv**-kee
bread	chleb	khlehb
cheese	ser	sehr
sandwich	kanapka	kah-**nahp**-kah
soup	zupa	**zoo**-pah
salad	sałatka	sah-**waht**-kah
meat / poultry	mięso / drób	**myehn**-soh / droob
fish / seafood	ryba / owoce morza	**rih**-bah / oh-**voht**-seh **moh**-zhah
fruit / vegetables	owoce / warzywa	oh-**voht**-seh / vah-**zhih**-vah
dessert	deser	**deh**-sehr
(tap) water	woda (z kranu)	**voh**-dah (**skrah**-noo)
mineral water	woda mineralna	**voh**-dah mee-neh-**rahl**-nah
carbonated / not carbonated	gazowana / niegazowana	gah-zoh-**vah**-nah / **nyeh**-gah-zoh-vah-nah
milk	mleko	**mleh**-koh
(orange) juice	sok (pomarańczowy)	sohk (poh-mah-rayn-**choh**-vih)
coffee / tea	kawa / herbata	**kah**-vah / hehr-**bah**-tah
wine	wino	**vee**-noh
red / white	czerwone / białe	chehr-**voh**-neh / bee-**ah**-weh
sweet / dry / semi-dry	słodkie / wytrawne / półwytrawne	**swoht**-kyeh / vih-**trahv**-neh / poow-vih-**trahv**-neh
glass / bottle	szklanka / butelka	**shklahn**-kah / boo-**tehl**-kah
beer	piwo	**pee**-voh
vodka	wódka	**vood**-kah
Cheers!	Na zdrowie!	nah **zdroh**-vyeh
Enjoy your meal.	Smacznego.	smatch-**neh**-goh
More. / Another.	Więcej. / Inny.	**vyehnt**-say / **ee**-nih-nih
The same.	Taki sam.	**tah**-kee sahm
the bill	rachunek	rah-**khoo**-nehk
I'll pay.	Ja płacę.	yah **pwaht**-seh
tip	napiwek	nah-**pee**-vehk
Delicious!	Pyszne!	**pish**-neh

KRAKÓW

Kraków is easily Poland's best destination: a beautiful, old-fashioned city buzzing with history, enjoyable sights, tourists, and college students. Even though the country's capital moved from here to Warsaw 400 years ago, Kraków remains Poland's cultural and intellectual center. Of all the Eastern European cities laying claim to the boast, "the next Prague," Kraków is for real.

What's so special about it? First off, Kraków is simply charming; more than any town in Europe, it seems made for aimless strolling. And its historic walls and former moat corral an unusually full range of activities and interests: bustling university life; thought-provoking museums; breathtaking churches that evoke a powerful faith (and include many sights relating to Poland's favorite son, St. John Paul II); sprawling parks that invite you to just relax; vivid Jewish heritage sights; a burgeoning foodie and nightlife scene; and compelling side-trips to the most notorious Holocaust site anywhere (Auschwitz-Birkenau), a communist-planned workers town, and a mine filled with salty statues. With so many opportunities to learn, to have fun, or to do both at once, it's no surprise that Kraków has become the darling of Polish tourism.

PLANNING YOUR TIME

Don't skimp on your time in Kraków. It takes a minimum of two days to experience the city, and a third or fourth day lets you dig in and consider a world of fascinating side-trips.

Almost everyone coming to Kraków also visits the Auschwitz-Birkenau Concentration Camp Memorial—and should. As it's about an hour and a half away, this demands the better part of a

Kraków: A Snapshot History

Kraków grew wealthy from trade in the late 10th and early 11th centuries. Traders who passed through were required to stop here for a few days and sell their wares at a reduced cost. Local merchants turned around and sold those goods with big price hikes...and Kraków thrived. In 1038, it became Poland's center.

Tatars invaded in 1241, leaving the city in ruins. Krakovians took this opportunity to rebuild their streets in a near-perfect grid, a striking contrast to the narrow, mazelike lanes of most medieval towns. The destruction also paved the way for the spectacular Main Market Square—still Kraków's best attraction.

King Kazimierz the Great sparked Kraków's Golden Age in the 14th century (see page 257). In 1364, he established the university that still defines the city (and counts Copernicus and St. John Paul II among its alumni).

But Kraków's power waned as Poland's political center shifted to Warsaw. In 1596, the capital officially moved north. At the end of the 18th century, three neighboring powers—Russia, Prussia, and Austria—partitioned Poland, annexing all of its territory and dividing it among themselves. Warsaw ended up as a satellite of oppressive Moscow, and Kraków became a poor provincial backwater of Vienna. After Napoleon briefly reshuffled the map of Europe in the early 19th century, Kraków was granted the status of a relatively independent city-state for about 30 years. The feisty Free City of Kraków, a tiny sliver wedged between three of Europe's mightiest empires, enjoyed an economic boom that saw the creation of the Planty park, the arrival of gas lighting and trams, and the construction of upscale suburbs outside the Old Town. Only after the unsuccessful Kraków Uprising of 1846 was the city forcefully brought back into the Austrian fold. But despite Kraków's reduced prominence, Austria's comparatively liberal climate allowed the city to become a haven for intellectuals and progressives (including a young revolutionary thinker from Russia named Vladimir Lenin).

day to fully appreciate (either as a round-trip from Kraków, or en route to or from another destination). Visiting Auschwitz requires a reservation, which can be hard to get. For all the details, see the next chapter.

If you have only two full days (the "express plan"), start off with my self-guided walk through the Old Town and a quick stroll up to Wawel Castle, then head over to the Schindler's Factory Museum and wind down your day in Kazimierz. Your second day is for a side-trip to Auschwitz. This plan gives you an enticing once-over-lightly, but leaves almost no time for entering the sights.

More time buys you the chance to relax, enjoy, and linger: Tackle the Old Town and Wawel Castle on the first day, Kazimi-

The Nazis overran Poland in September of 1939, installing a ruling body called the *Generalgouvernement,* headed by former attorney Hans Frank. Germany wanted to quickly develop "Krakau" (as they called it) into the German capital of the nation. They renamed the Main Market Square "Adolf-Hitler-Platz," tore down statues of Polish figures (including the Adam Mickiewicz statue that dominates the Main Market Square today), and invested heavily in construction and industrialization (opening the door for Oskar Schindler to come and take over a factory from its Jewish owners). The German overlords imposed a "New Order" that included seizing businesses, rationing, and a strict curfew for Poles and Jews alike. A special set of "Jewish laws" targeted, then decimated, Poland's huge Jewish population.

Kraków's cityscape—if not its people—emerged from World War II virtually unscathed. But when the communists took over, they decided to give intellectual (and potentially dissident) Kraków an injection of good Soviet values—in the form of heavy industry. They built Nowa Huta, an enormous steelworks and planned town for workers, on Kraków's outskirts, thereby dooming the city to decades of smog. Thankfully, Kraków is now much cleaner than it was 20 years ago.

St. John Paul II was born (as Karol Wojtyła) in nearby Wadowice and served as archbishop of Kraków before being called to Rome. Today, the hometown boy-turned-saint draws lots of pilgrims and is, for many, a big part of the city's attraction. Saintly ties aside, Kraków might be the most Catholic town in Europe's most Catholic country; be sure to visit a few of its many churches.

The story of Kraków continues to play out. In recent years, its Kazimierz district has come back to life—both with Jewish-themed cultural sights, and with some of Eastern Europe's best bars, food trucks, and restaurants. This mingling of the historic with the contemporary typifies a city that always has been, and continues to be, Poland's heartbeat.

erz and museums of your choice on the second day, and Auschwitz (and other side-trips) with additional days. If you have a special interest, you could side-trip to the St. John Paul II pilgrimage sights on the outskirts of town, or to the communist architecture of the Nowa Huta suburb. Wieliczka Salt Mine is another crowd-pleasing, half-day option.

Regardless of how long you stay, your evening choices are many and varied: Savor the Main Market Square over dinner or a drink, take in a jazz show, do a pub crawl through the city's many youthful bars and clubs (best in Kazimierz), or enjoy traditional Jewish music and cuisine (also in Kazimierz).

Kraków's Old Town Sights

- OLD MARKET
- BAŁOKEGO
- ŁOBZOWSKA
- AŚNYKA
- DŁUGA
- PADEREWSKIEGO
- WALK BEGINS
- BARBICAN
- FLORIAN GATE
- CZARTORYSKI MUSEUM
- KARMELICKA
- GARBARSKA
- DUNAJEWSKIEGO
- Planty
- PIJARSKA
- SŁAWKOWSKA
- ŚW. MARKA
- ŚW. JANA
- FLORIAŃSKA
- SZPITALNA
- KRUPNICZA
- #24 Teater Bagately
- PODWALE
- SZCZEPAŃSKA
- SZEWSKA
- OLD
- SZOŁAYSKI HOUSE
- Main Market Square
- ŚW. TOMASZA
- STUDENSKA
- ŚW. ANNY
- JAGIELLOŃSKA
- CLOTH HALL
- ST. MARY'S
- COLLEGIUM MAIUS
- MICKIEWICZ STATUE
- Small Market Square
- JABŁONOWSKICH
- GOŁĘBIA
- TOWN HALL TOWER
- SIENNA
- OLSZEWSKIEGO
- ARCH-BISHOP'S MANSION
- PASAŻ 13 MALL
- GRODZKA
- SIENNA
- PIŁSUDSKIEGO
- BRACKA
- STOLARSKA
- DOMINICAN CHURCH
- WC
- To Airport, Auschwitz & Kościuszko Mound
- SMOLENSK
- FRANCISZKAŃSKA
- #8 plac Wszystkich Świętych
- DOMINIKAŃSKA
- TOWN
- ST. FRANCIS
- WYSPIAŃSKI PAVILION
- Planty
- POSELSKA
- MILK BAR
- SENACKA
- MILK BAR
- STRASZEWSKIEGO
- Mary Mag. Square
- STS. PETER & PAUL
- FELICJANEK
- ZWIERZYNIECKA
- BISHOP ERAZM CIOŁEK PALACE
- ARCHDIOCESAN MUSEUM
- WALK ENDS
- KANONICZA
- ST. ANDREW'S
- JOHN PAUL II CENTER
- SAREGO
- POWIŚLE
- PODZAMCZE
- CATHEDRAL
- INNER COURTYARD
- ŚW. IDZIEGO
- ŚW. GERTRUDY
- Vistula River
- WAWEL HILL
- LOST WAWEL MUSEUM
- DRAGON STATUE
- BERNARDYŃSKA
- ST. BERNARDINO'S
- STRADOMSKA
- KONOPNICKIEJ
- KOLETEK

KRAKÓW

Sights

1 John Paul II Wawel Cathedral Museum
2 Sandomierska Tower
3 Gallery of 19th-Century Polish Art (Entrance)
4 Rynek Underground Museum
5 Kraków City Museum Visitors Center
6 Wieliczka Promotion Office

Services & Other

7 Massolit Books
8 Frania Café/Laundry
9 Betty Clean Laundry
10 Kraków Bike Tours & Rental
11 KRK Bike Rental
12 Trams #3 & #24 to/from Kazimierz (3)

Orientation to Kraków

Kraków (Poles say KROCK-oof, but you can say KRACK-cow; it's sometimes spelled "Cracow" in English) is mercifully compact, flat, and easy to navigate. While the urban sprawl is big (with 757,000 people), the tourist's Kraków feels small—from the main square, you can walk to just about everything of interest in less than 15 minutes. Just to the south is Poland's main river, the Vistula (Wisła, VEES-wah).

Most sights—and almost all recommended hotels and restaurants—are in the **Old Town** (Stare Miasto, STAH-reh mee-AH-stoh), which is surrounded by a greenbelt called the Planty (PLAHN-tee). In the center of the Old Town lies the Main Market Square (Rynek Główny, REE-nehk GWOHV-nee)—it's such an important landmark, I call it simply "the Square." At the Old Town's northeast corner, just outside the ring road, is the main train station. And at the southern end of the Old Town, on the riverbank, is the hill called **Wawel** (VAH-vehl)—with a historic castle, museums, and Poland's national church.

About a 20-minute walk (or quick tram/taxi ride) southeast of the Square is the neighborhood called **Kazimierz** (kah-ZHEE-mehzh)—with Jewish landmarks and Holocaust sites (including the Schindler's Factory Museum) and the city's best foodie and nightlife area.

A few more attractions are just beyond the core, including the St. John Paul II pilgrimage sights (in the Łagiewniki neighborhood), the communist-planned town of Nowa Huta, Wieliczka Salt Mine, and the Kościuszko Mound.

TOURIST INFORMATION

Kraków has many helpful TIs, called InfoKraków (www. infokrakow.pl). Five branches are in or near the Old Town (all open daily May-Sept 9:00-19:00, Oct-April 9:00-17:00, unless otherwise noted):

• In the **Planty** park, between the main train station and Main Market Square (in round kiosk at ulica Szpitalna 25, tel. 12-354-2720)

• On **ulica Św. Jana,** just north of the Main Market Square (specializes in concert tickets, daily year-round 9:00-19:00, at #2, tel. 12-354-2725)

• In the **Cloth Hall** right on the Main Market Square (tel. 12-354-2716)

• In the **Wyspiański Pavilion,** just south of the Square on ulica Grodzka (daily 9:00-17:00, plac Wszystkich Świętych 3, not at the window but inside the building, tel. 12-616-1886)

• Just west of **Wawel Hill** (also covers the entire region, Powiśle 11, tel. 12-354-2710)

Other TI branches are in **Kazimierz** (daily 9:00-17:00, ulica Józefa 7, tel. 12-354-2728) and the **airport** (daily 9:00-19:00, tel. 12-285-5341).

Note that the TIs sell tickets *only* for one walking-tour company, See Kraków; for additional options, see "Tours in Kraków," later, and look around online.

Sightseeing Pass: The TI's **Kraków Tourist Card** includes admission to 40 city museums (basically everything except the Wawel Hill sights and Wieliczka Salt Mine)—but admissions are so cheap, it's unlikely you'd save money with the card. Given how walkable Kraków is, the version that does not include public transit (70 zł/3 days) is a better value for most people than the one that does (100 zł/2 days, 120 zł/3 days).

Warning: Many private travel agencies, room-booking services, and tour operators masquerade as TIs, with deceptive blue-and-white *i* signs. If I haven't listed them in this section, they're not a real TI.

Kraków City History Museum's Visitor Center: Tucked in the Cloth Hall (on the quiet western side) is a little information office operated by the Kraków City History Museum, where you can book tickets, without a line, for the popular Schindler's Factory Museum. If you anticipate crowds at the Schindler museum, drop by this office to book an entry time (daily 10:00-19:00, until 20:00 in summer, at #1).

ARRIVAL IN KRAKÓW
By Train

Kraków's main train station (called "Kraków Główny," KROCK-oof GWOHV-nee) sits just northeast of the Old Town, adjoining the sprawling Galeria Krakowska shopping mall. The station and the mall face a broad plaza (plac Dworcowy) across the ring road from the Planty park and Old Town. My recommended Old Town hotels are within about a 15-minute walk, or a quick tram or taxi ride. (If you're staying in the Old Town, the tram doesn't save you much time, but could cut down on how far you have to haul your bags. If you're staying in Kazimierz—a 30-minute walk away—the tram is definitely worthwhile.)

Whether you're arriving or departing, get oriented to the station's layout. The main concourse has all of the amenities: ATMs, lockers (under the big schedule board between the ticket windows), WCs, takeaway coffee, a handy Biedronka minisupermarket, and a shopping mall. From this area, five numbered escalators lead up to the corresponding train platforms. Tucked under these escalators, find a long row of numbered ticket windows (some for do-

KRAKÓW

mestic tickets only, others for domestic and international—check signs before you line up; a few are marked with UK flags to denote English-speaking staff). In the middle of the row of ticket windows (between #11 and #12) is the PKP Passenger Service Center, which may have a longer wait but is more likely to have staff who speak English (no extra fee).

Getting Between the Station and Downtown: The easiest option is to take a **taxi** (they wait in the parking lot on the station's rooftop—go up the stairs or elevator from your platform). The usual metered rate to downtown is a reasonable 10-15 zł; only take a taxi marked with a company name and telephone number. You can also summon an **Uber,** which is often cheaper (for more on Uber, see "Getting Around Kraków," later).

If you prefer to walk or take a tram, you first must navigate the Galeria Krakowska shopping mall. Begin by following *Exit to the City* signs. Once inside the mall, continue straight ahead. To **walk,** follow *Old Town* signs, which eventually route you to the left. You'll pop out at a big plaza where you'll continue straight, taking the broad ramp down into a pedestrian underpass beneath the ring road. Emerging at the other side, bear right up the ramp into the Planty. The Main Market Square is straight ahead (you'll see the twin spires of St. Mary's Church).

If you'd rather take a **tram,** continue straight ahead through the mall, following signs to *Pawia street.* Emerging here, you'll see the Dworzec Główny Zachód tram stop. Buy a ticket from the machine and hop on tram #3 in the direction of Nowy Bieżanów. This tram stops at the eastern edge of the Old Town (Poczta Główna stop) before continuing to Kazimierz (Miodowa stop). (Note: Avoid the tram stop you'll see signposted inside the station—this is served only by trams that don't go anywhere near the Old Town or Kazimierz.)

There is a **shortcut** to avoid going through the sprawling and sometimes congested mall: The modern train station is attached to the old station (the yellow building facing the big plaza, now hosting art exhibitions) by a sidewalk under a green canopy. This can save you a little walking (and a lot of shopping temptations). It's tricky to find from inside the station: Go behind the Biedronka supermarket, near track 1, and exit toward Lubicz street. Walk up the ramp and follow the green canopy to the plaza.

To get **from town to the station** (or to the bus station behind it), head to the northeast corner of the Planty, take the underpass beneath the ring road, walk across the plaza and into the Galeria Krakowska mall, and once inside, follow signs to *Railway Station* and *Station Hall.*

By Bus

The bus station is directly behind the main train station. When arriving by bus, it's easiest to get into town by first heading into the train station, then continuing through it, following the above directions.

To get *to* the bus station from the Old Town (such as to catch a bus to Auschwitz), follow the directions above, then walk all the way through to the far end of the train station area (past platform 5, exit marked for *bus station*). Exiting the train station, escalate up to the bus terminal (marked *MDA Dworzec Autobusowy*). Inside are the standard amenities (lockers and WCs), domestic and international ticket windows, and an electronic board showing the next several departures. Some bus departures, marked on the board with a *G*, leave from the upper *(gorna)* stalls, which you can see out the window. Other bus departures, marked with a *D*, leave from the lower *(dolna)* stalls; to find these, use the stairs or the elevator right in the middle of the bus terminal. Note that some minibuses, such as those to Auschwitz, also leave from, or near, this station (though the buses and minibuses that go to the Wieliczka Salt Mine leave from nearby streets—see page 317).

By Car

Centrum signs lead you into the Old Town—you'll know you're there when you hit the ring road that surrounds the Planty park. Parking garages surround the Old Town. Your hotelier can advise you on directions and parking.

By Plane

The modern **John Paul II Kraków-Balice Airport** is about 10 miles west of the center (airport code: KRK, airport info: tel. 12-295-5800, www.krakowairport.pl). The easiest way downtown is to hop on the slick and speedy **train** (follow signs to the platform across the street from the arrivals area, 8 zł, buy ticket from machine or from conductor on board, 2/hour, 18 minutes to Kraków's main train station—see arrival instructions earlier, under "By Train"). Alternatively, **public bus** #208 or (at night) #902 leaves from right in front of the arrivals area (*Kolej do Centrum* signs, 4 zł, goes to main bus station—see arrival instructions earlier, under "By Bus," 50-minute trip depending on traffic). There's also a **taxi** stand in front of the terminal (ask about the fare up front—rates vary, but official cabs should not exceed 90 zł, more expensive at night, about 30 minutes). You can also request an Uber, or arrange a taxi transfer in advance (such as with recommended driver Andrew Durman, listed later, under "Tours in Kraków").

Many budget flights—including those on Wizz Air and Ryanair—use the **International Airport Katowice in Pyrzowice**

KRAKÓW

(Międzynarodowy Port Lotniczy Katowice w Pyrzowicach, airport code: KTW, www.katowice-airport.com). This airport is about 18 miles from the city of Katowice, which is about 50 miles west of Kraków. Direct buses run sporadically between Katowice Airport and Kraków's main train station area (50 zł, trip takes 1.75 hours, generally scheduled to meet incoming flights). You can also take the bus from Katowice Airport to Katowice's train station (hourly, 50 minutes), then take the train to Kraków (hourly, 1.5 hours). Wizz Air's website is useful for figuring out your connection: www.wizzair.com.

HELPFUL HINTS

Exchange Rate: 1 złoty (zł, or PLN) = about 25 cents; 4 zł = about $1.

Country Calling Code: 48 (see page 1086 for dialing instructions)

Sightseeing Schedules: Some sights are closed on Monday (including the Gallery of 19th-Century Polish Art, Szołayski House, and a few museums in Kazimierz), but many sights are open (including the churches and Jagiellonian University Museum, and in Kazimierz, all of the Jewish-themed sights). On Saturday, most of Kazimierz's Jewish-themed sights are closed. Before heading out, check the "Kraków at a Glance" sidebar on page 248. Also be aware of days that certain sights are free: On Sunday, the National Museum branches (including the Gallery of 19th-Century Polish Art in the Cloth Hall) are free, but some are open limited hours. And on Monday, Schindler's Factory Museum is free (and especially crowded), as are two of the sights at Wawel Castle (but open only in the morning April-Oct).

Post Office: The main post office (Poczta Główna) is at the intersection of Starowiślna and the Westerplatte ring road, a few blocks east of the Main Market Square (Mon-Fri 8:30-20:30, Sat 8:00-15:00, closed Sun). In summer, look for a kitschy postal wagon on the Main Market Square, where you can mail postcards.

Bookstore: For an impressive selection of new and used English books, try **Massolit Books,** just west of the Old Town. They also have a café with drinks and light snacks, and a good children's section (Sun-Thu 10:00-20:00, Fri-Sat 10:00-21:00, ulica Felicjanek 4, tel. 12-432-4150, www.massolit.com).

Laundry: Frania Café, halfway between the Old Town and Kazimierz, is an inviting café/pub with ample washers and dryers, relaxing ambience, free Wi-Fi, a full bar serving espresso drinks and laundry-themed hard drinks, long hours, and a friendly staff (21 zł/load self-service, 29 zł for them to do it for you in 2-3 hours—consider dropping it off on your way to

Kazimierz and picking it up on the way back, likely open daily 10:30-24:00, ulica Starowiślna 26, mobile 783-945-021).

Betty Clean is a full-service laundry that's slightly closer to the Old Town, but pricey (about 13 zł/shirt, 22 zł/pants, takes 24 hours, 50 percent more for express 3-hour service, Mon-Fri 7:30-19:30, Sat 8:00-15:30, closed Sun, just outside the Planty park at ulica Zwierzyniecka 6, tel. 12-423-0848).

GETTING AROUND KRAKÓW

Kraków's top sights and best hotels are easily accessible by foot. You'll need wheels only if you're going to outlying areas (Kazimierz, Nowa Huta, John Paul II pilgrimage sights, and so on).

By Public Transit

Trams and buses zip around Kraków's urban sprawl. The same tickets work system-wide and can be purchased at most kiosks, or at the machines you'll see at most stops (these accept coins and small bills). You can also buy tickets on board—most trams have machines (coins only); otherwise, you'll buy your ticket from the driver and pay a bit more. For a good route planner, see www.jakdojade.pl.

A *bilet jednoprzejazdowy*, which covers any single journey (including transfers), costs 3.80 zł. However, many journeys you're likely to take—such as between the Old Town and Kazimierz—are likely to be brief, so you'll save a bit by buying a 20-minute ticket *(20-minutowy)* for 2.80 zł. You can also get longer-term tickets for 24 hours (15 zł), 48 hours (24 zł), and 72 hours (36 zł)—though unless your accommodations are a tram ride away from the sights, you're unlikely to need these. These prices are for a "one-zone" ticket, which covers almost everything of interest in Kraków (including Nowa Huta, the St. John Paul II pilgrimage sights, and the Kościuszko Mound)—unless you're headed for the airport or Wieliczka Salt Mine, which are beyond the city limits and require a slightly more expensive *aglomeracyjny* ticket (4 zł for a single journey). Always validate your ticket when you board the bus or tram (24-, 48-, and 72-hour tickets must be validated only the first time you use them).

Tram #3 is particularly handy. It goes from the side of the train station (Dworzec Główny Zachód) to the ring road in front of the station (Dworzec Główny), then stops at the eastern edge of the Old Town (Poczta Główna, at the main post office) before continuing to Kazimierz (Miodowa is at the north end, near ulica Szeroka; Św. Wawrzyńca is at the south end, near the old tram depot) and Podgórze, near Schindler's Factory Museum (plac Bohaterow Getta). **Tram #24** is also handy: It stops at the western edge of the Old Town (Teatr Bagately), then loops around the northern edge to stop near the Barbican (Stary Kleparz) before meeting up with

KRAKÓW

tram #3 in front of the train station (Dworzec Główny) and continuing on to Kazimierz and Podgórze (same stops as listed above).

By Taxi or Uber

Only take cabs that are clearly marked with a company logo and telephone number. Kraków taxis start at 7 zł and charge about 3 zł per kilometer. Rides generally cost less than 20 zł, but can take longer than you'd expect: Due to the Old Town's many traffic restrictions and pedestrian zones, a "short ride across town" may require looping all the way around the ring road. You're more likely to get the fair metered rate by calling or hailing a cab, rather than taking one waiting at tourist spots. To call a cab, try **Radio Taxi** (tel. 19191).

If you're comfortable using **Uber** back home, try it here. As in the US, Uber is typically cheaper than official taxis (though prices can spike during busy "surge" periods). In my experience, Polish Uber drivers (and their cars) are a bit less polished and professional than back home—but they're cheap. When requesting a ride on your app, you can choose between the basic UberPop and the more professional UberSelect for a few zlotys more.

By Bike

The riverfront bike path is enticing on a nice day; the Planty park, while inviting, can be a bit crowded for biking. **Kraków Bike Tours** rents a wide variety of new, good-quality bikes (10 zł/first hour, cheaper per hour for longer rentals, 50 zł/day, 60 zł/24 hours, daily 9:00-19:00, until 20:00 in summer, just off the Square at Grodzka 2; see listing later, under "Tours in Kraków"). Nearby, **KRK Bike Rental** rents basic, cheaper bikes (9 zł/hour, 50 zł/24 hours, April-Oct daily 9:00-21:00, less in bad weather, closed Nov-March, ulica Św. Anny 4, mobile 509-267-733, www.krkbikerental.pl).

Tours in Kraków

Local Guides

Hiring a guide in Kraków is fun and affordable, and makes a huge difference in your experience. I've enjoyed working with three in particular, any of whom can show you the sights in Kraków and also have cars for day-tripping into the countryside: **Tomasz Klimek** (350 zł/half-day, 500 zł/day, slightly more with a car, mobile 605-231-923, tomasz.klimek@interia.pl); **Marta Chmielowska** (350 zł/4 hours, 500 zł/day, same prices by foot or car, can be more for larger groups and for long-distance trips, mobile 603-668-008, martachm7@gmail.com); and **Anna Bakowska** (same prices as Marta, mobile 604-151-293, www.leadertour.eu, leadertour@wp.pl). I wouldn't bother hiring a guide for the trip to Auschwitz (which generally costs 600-700 zł)—only official Auschwitz guides can legally give tours onsite, so you'll wind up joining one of the tours once there; instead, it's a better value to hire a driver (like Andrew, listed next).

Drivers

Since Kraków is such a useful home base for day trips, it can be handy to splurge on a private driver for door-to-door service. **Andrew (Andrzej) Durman,** a Pole who lived in Chicago and speaks fluent English, is a gregarious driver, translator, miracle worker, and all-around great guy. While not an officially licensed tour guide, Andrew is an eager conversationalist and loves to provide lively commentary while you roll. Although you can hire Andrew for a simple airport transfer or an Auschwitz day trip, he also enjoys tackling more ambitious itineraries, from helping you track down your Polish roots to taking you on multiple-day journeys around Poland and beyond (prices are for up to 4 people if you book directly: 400 zł to Auschwitz, 250 zł to Wieliczka Salt Mine, 80 zł for transfer from Kraków-Balice Airport, 500 zł for transfer from Katowice Airport, 600 zł for an all-day trip into the countryside—such as into the High Tatras or to track down your Polish roots near Kraków, more to cover gas costs for trips longer than 100 km one-way; long-distance transfers for up to 4 people to Prague, Budapest, Vienna, or Berlin for 1,800 zł—or 200 zł extra if he picks you up there; also available for multiday trips—price negotiable, all prices higher for bigger van, tel. 12-411-5630, mobile 602-243-306, www.tour-service.pl, andrew@tour-service.pl). If he's busy, Andrew may send you with one of his English-speaking colleagues, Bartek or Matthew.

Local guide Marta Chmielowska's husband, **Czesław** (a.k.a. Chester), can also drive you to nearby locations (300 zł for all-day trip to Auschwitz for 1-2 people, 350 zł for 3-8 people; 220 zł to Wieliczka Salt Mine, including waiting time, or a very long day combining Wieliczka and Auschwitz for 550 zł; 1,700 zł for a transfer to Prague; to book, see Marta's contact information, earlier).

Walking Tours

Various companies run daily city walking tours in English in summer. Most do a three-hour tour of the Old Town as well as a three-hour tour of Kazimierz, the Jewish district (most charge about 50 zł per tour, depending on company). Three people can hire their own great local guide for about the same amount of money. Because the scene is continually evolving, it's best to pick up local fliers (the TI works exclusively with one company, See Kraków, but hotel reception desks generally have more options), then choose the one that fits your interests and schedule. You'll also see ads for

Kraków at a Glance

▲▲▲**Main Market Square** Stunning heart of Kraków and a people magnet any time of day. **Hours:** Always open. See page 257.

▲▲▲**Schindler's Factory Museum** Historic building where Oskar Schindler saved more than 1,000 Jewish workers, now filled with engaging exhibit about Kraków's WWII experience. **Hours:** April-Oct Mon 10:00-16:00 (closes at 14:00 first Mon of month), Tue-Sun 9:00-20:00; Nov-March Mon 10:00-14:00, Tue-Sun 10:00-18:00. See page 306.

▲▲**Planty** Once a moat, now a scenic park encircling the city. **Hours:** Always open. See page 252.

▲▲**St. Mary's Church** Landmark church with extraordinary wood-carved Gothic altarpiece. **Hours:** Mon-Sat 11:15-17:45, Sun 14:00-17:45. See page 255.

▲▲**Cloth Hall** Fourteenth-century market hall with 21st-century souvenirs. **Hours:** Summer Mon-Fri 9:00-18:00, Sat-Sun 9:00-15:00, sometimes later; winter Mon-Fri 9:00-16:00, Sat-Sun 9:00-15:00. See page 260.

▲▲**St. Francis Basilica** Lovely Gothic church with some of Poland's best Art Nouveau. **Hours:** Daily 6:00-19:45. See page 263.

▲▲**Wawel Cathedral** Poland's splendid national church, with tons of tombs, a crypt, and a climbable tower. **Hours:** April-Sept Mon-Sat 9:00-17:00, Sun 12:30-17:00; Oct-March daily until 16:00. See page 270.

▲▲**Wawel Castle Grounds** Historic hilltop with views, castle, cathedral, courtyard with chakras, and a passel of museums. **Hours:** Grounds open daily 6:00 until dusk, but many of the museums closed Mon, and Sun in winter. See page 274.

▲▲**Gallery of 19th-Century Polish Art** Worthwhile collection of paintings by should-be-famous artists, upstairs in the Cloth Hall. **Hours:** Tue-Sun 10:00-18:00, closed Mon. See page 281.

"free" tours—which are, of course, not really free (the guide gets paid only if you tip generously).

Food Tours

In this stealth-foodie city, you have multiple good options. **Eat Polska**—which does a marvelous job of connecting food to culture and history, making the experience equal parts informative and

▲▲**Rynek Underground Museum** Super-modern exhibit on medieval Kraków filling excavated cellars beneath the Main Market Square. **Hours:** Mon 10:00-20:00 (closed second Mon of each month), Tue 10:00-16:00, Wed-Sun 10:00-22:00, shorter hours in winter. See page 288.

▲▲**Old Jewish Cemetery** Poignant burial site in Kazimierz, with graves from 1552 to 1800. **Hours:** Sun-Fri 9:00-16:00, sometimes until 18:00 May-Sept, closes earlier in winter and by sundown on Fri, closed Sat. See page 295.

▲**Czartoryski Museum** Varied collection, with European paintings and Polish armor, handicrafts, and decorative arts. **Hours:** Likely closed for restoration, otherwise Tue-Sun 10:00-16:00, closed Mon. See page 286.

▲**Jagiellonian University Museum Collegium Maius** Proud collection of historic university, surrounding a tranquil courtyard where medieval professors lived. **Hours:** Entry by guided tour; 30-minute version—Mon-Fri 10:00-14:20, Sat 10:00-13:20, until 17:20 Tue and Thu in April-Oct, no tours Sun; one-hour version in English—usually Mon-Fri at 13:00, no tours Sat-Sun. See page 289.

▲**New Jewish Cemetery** Graveyard with tombs from after 1800, partly restored after Nazi desecration. **Hours:** Sun-Fri 8:00-18:00, winter until 16:00, closed Sat. See page 303.

▲**Ethnographic Museum** Traditional rural Polish life on display. **Hours:** Tue-Sun 10:00-19:00, closed Mon. See page 301.

▲**Pharmacy Under the Eagle** Small Podgórze exhibit about the Holocaust in Kraków, including three evocative historic films. **Hours:** Mon 10:00-14:00, Tue-Sun 9:00-17:00; closed the second Tue of each month. See page 305.

▲**Museum of Contemporary Art in Kraków** Today's thought-provoking art, displayed in renovated old warehouses behind Schindler's Factory Museum. **Hours:** Tue-Sun 11:00-19:00, closed Mon. See page 311.

KRAKÓW

delicious—does top-notch, insightful food tours (at 13:00, 290 zł, 4 hours) and vodka tours with food pairings (at 17:00, 260 zł, 3.5 hours; for details on either, see www.eatpolska.com). **Urban Adventures,** a bit more casual, does evening food walks that basically assemble a full meal with a little sightseeing thrown in (at 18:00, 310 zł, 3 hours, www.urbanadventures.com).

Crazy Guides

This irreverent company offers tours to the communist suburb of Nowa Huta and other outlying sights. For details, see page 319.

Bike and Segway Tours

Kraków Bike Tours is a well-established operation that runs daily four-hour bike tours in English, with 25 stops in the Old Town, Kazimierz, and Podgórze (90 zł, May-Sept daily at 10:00 and 15:00, spring and fall only 1/day at 12:00, confirm schedule and meet tour at their office down the passage at Grodzka 2—right at the bottom of the Square, mobile 510-394-657, www.krakowbiketour.com). They also offer Segway tours.

Bus Tours to Auschwitz or Wieliczka

As Kraków is so easily enjoyed on foot, taking a bus tour doesn't make much sense in town. But they can be handy for reaching outlying sights. Various tour companies run big-bus itineraries to Auschwitz (6 hours), Wieliczka Salt Mine (4 hours), and other regional side-trips (each itinerary around 120-180 zł).

Given the difficulty of reserving your own appointment at Auschwitz (explained in the next chapter), one of these bus tours—which include a guided tour of the camp—may be your most convenient option. **See Kraków** (which has a monopoly at the TI, www.seekrakow.com) and **Discover Cracow** (www.discovercracow.com) both use smaller 19-seat minibuses. They sometimes offer hotel pick-up, which seems convenient, but you'll waste a lot of time driving around the city to other hotels. **Cracow City Tours** (www.cracowcitytours.com) uses larger 50-seat buses with a central pick-up point (on plac Matejki, across the ring road from the Barbican, at the north end of the Old Town).

At any company, the on-bus guiding is hit-or-miss but largely irrelevant anyway—since you'll be handed off to an official Auschwitz guide once at the camp. Note that the many tour offices and faux-TIs you'll see around town simply sell tickets for these companies. If you waited too long to reserve at Auschwitz and are desperate to get in at short notice, try dropping in to various agencies around town to see if any of these outfits has space.

Buggy Tours

You'll see (and hear) horse-drawn buggies that trot around Kraków from the Main Market Square. The going rate is a hefty 100 zł for a 30-minute tour. After dark, they're all lit up like fanciful Cinderella coaches—a memorable scene, all lined up in front of St. Mary's Church.

Golf-Cart Tours

Several outfits around town (including on the Square) offer tours on a golf cart with recorded commentary. Given the limits on car traffic in the old center, this can be a handy way to connect the sights for those with limited mobility. Generally you'll pay about 160 zł for a 45-minute tour around the Old Town; to extend the trip to Kazimierz, it's 300 zł; and adding the Podgórze former Jewish ghetto and Schindler's Factory Museum costs a total of 380 zł (these prices are for the entire golf cart, up to 5 people). Some outfits also do point-to-point transfers within town for 50 zł.

Tour Packages for Students

Andy Steves (Rick's son) runs Weekend Student Adventures (WSA Europe), offering 3-day and 10-day budget travel packages across Europe including accommodations, skip-the-line sightseeing, and unique local experiences. Locally guided and DIY unguided options are available for student and budget travelers in 12 of Europe's most popular cities, including Kraków (guided trips from €199, see www.wsaeurope.com for details).

Kraków's Royal Way Walk

Most of Kraków's major sights are conveniently connected by this self-guided walk. This route is known as the "Royal Way" because the king used to follow this same path when he returned to Kraków after a journey. After the capital moved to Warsaw, most kings still used Wawel Cathedral for important events. In fact, from 1320 to 1795, nearly every Polish king traversed Kraków's Royal Way at least twice: on the day he was crowned and on the day he was buried. You could sprint through this walk in about an hour and a half (less than a mile altogether), but it's much more fun if you take it like the kings did...slowly.

• *Begin just outside the main gate (the Florian Gate) at the north end of the Old Town.*

▲Barbican (Barbakan) and City Walls

Tatars—those mysterious and terrifying invaders from Central Asia—destroyed Kraków in 1241. To better defend their city, Krakovians built this wall. The original rampart had 47 watchtowers and eight gates. (You can see a bronze model of the wall just to the right of the tower.)

The big, round defensive fort standing outside the wall is the **Barbican**—built to provide extra fortification to weak sections—namely, the gates. Imagine how it looked in 1500, when the Barbican stood outside the town moat with a

KRAKÓW

long bridge leading to the Florian Gate—the city's main entryway. Today you can pay to scramble along the passages and fortifications of the Barbican, though there's little to see inside, other than a small but good exhibit giving you a sense of how the walls were designed (8 zł, April-Oct daily 10:30-18:00, closed Nov-March). The same ticket also lets you climb up onto the surviving stretch of Old Town walls flanking the Florian Gate (entry from inside walls).

• *The greenbelt in which the Barbican sits is called the...*

▲▲Planty

By the 19th century, Kraków's no-longer-necessary city wall had fallen into disrepair. As the Austrian authorities were doing all over their empire, they decided to tear down what remained, fill in the moat, and plant trees. (The name comes not from the English "plant," but from the Polish *plantovac,* or "flat"—because they flattened out this area to create it.) Today, the Planty is a beautiful park that stretches 2.5 miles around the entire perimeter of

Kraków's Old Town. To give your Kraków visit an extra dimension, consider a quick bike ride around the Planty (best early in the morning, when it's less crowded) with a side-trip along the parklike riverbank near Wawel Castle; you'll see bike-rental places around the Old Town, including the two mentioned on page 246.

Circle around the left side of the Barbican. On your left, keep an eye out for a unique monument depicting an elderly, bearded man in the corner of a huge frame. This honors **Jan Matejko,** arguably Poland's most beloved painter, who specialized in giant-scale epic historical scenes that would easily fill this frame. We'll hear Matejko's name several more times on this walk.

As you continue around the Barbican, look down to see the much lower ground level around its base—making it easy to imagine that the Planty was once anything but flat.

• *Across the busy street from the Barbican, standing in the middle of the long park, is the...*

Grunwald Monument

This memorial honors one of the most important battles in the history of a nation that has seen more than its share: the Battle of Grunwald on July 15, 1410, when Polish and Lithuanian forces banded together to finally defeat the Teutonic Knights, who had been running roughshod over the lands along the Baltic. (For more on the battle and the knights, see page 502.) Lying dramatically slain at the base of this monument, like a toppled Goliath, is the defeated Grand Master of the Teutonic Knights—German crusaders who had originally been brought to Poland as mercenaries. It's easy to see this vanquished statue as a thinly veiled metaphor for one of Poland's powerful, often domineering neighbors that the Poles stood up to—and defeated. When the Nazis took power here, this statue was one of the first things they tore down. When they left, it was one of the first things the Poles put back up.

• *If you'd like to see a slice of Krakovian life, side-trip one block to the left of the monument, to the local farmers market.*

The Old Market (Stary Kleparz)

The colorful Old Market offers a refreshing dash of today's Kraków that has nothing to do with history or tourism. It's just lots of hardscrabble people selling what they grow or knit, and lots of others buying. Wander around as if on a cultural scavenger hunt. Find the freshest doughnuts *(pączki),* the most popular bakery, the villager selling slippers she knitted, and the old man with the smoked cheese (Mon-Sat 7:00-18:00—but busiest and most interesting in the morning, closed Sun).

• *Now retrace your steps to the Barbican, and enter the Old Town by walking through the...*

Florian Gate (Brama Floriańska)

As you approach the gate, look up at the **crowned white eagle**—representing courage and freedom—the historic symbol of the Polish people.

Inside the gate, notice the little chapel on the right with a replica of the famous **Black Madonna of Częstochowa,** probably the most important religious symbol among Polish Catholics. The original, located in Częstochowa (70 miles north of Kraków), is an

Eastern Orthodox-style icon of mysterious origin with several mystical legends attached to it. After the icon's believed role in protecting a monastery from Swedish invaders in the mid-17th century, it was named "Queen and Protector of Poland."

Once through the gate, look back at it. High above is **St. Florian,** patron of the fire brigade. As fire was a big concern for a wooden city of the 15th century, Florian gets a place of honor.

You'll often see traditionally clad **musicians** near the gate, performing their lilting folk melodies for tips.

KRAKÓW

• *You're standing at the head of Kraków's historic (and now touristic) gamut...*

▲Floriańska Street (Ulica Floriańska)

Hanging on the inside of the city wall in both directions is a make-shift **art gallery,** where—traditionally—starving students hawk

the works they've painted at the Academy of Fine Arts (across the busy street from the Barbican). These days, the art is so kitschy, this stretch of the town's fortification is nicknamed "The Wailing Wall." The entrance to get on top of the wall—covered by the Barbican ticket—is at the end of this starving artists' gallery. If you detoured even farther along the wall, soon you'd reach the eclectic Czartoryski Museum, home to a rare Leonardo da Vinci oil painting (see page 280).

Now begin strolling down **Floriańska street** (floh-ree-AHN-skah). Notice that all over town, storefronts advertising themselves as "tourist information" offices are actually tourist sales agencies (legitimate TIs are listed on page 240). And money-exchange counters can be thieves with an address. (Do the arithmetic—the buying and selling rates should be within 6 percent or so, and there should be no fee.) Along with the fast-food joints, also notice some uniquely Polish snacks: The various pizza and kebab windows also sell *zapiekanki*—a toasted baguette with toppings, similar to a French bread pizza. Or, for an even quicker bite, buy an *obwarzanek* (ring-shaped, bagel-like roll, typically fresh) from a street vendor; many still use their old-fashioned blue carts.

About halfway down the first block, on the left (at #45, round green sign), look for **Jama Michalika** ("Michael's Cave"). This

dark, atmospheric café, popular with locals for its coffee and pastries, began in 1895 as a simple bakery in a claustrophobic back room. Around the turn of the 20th century, this was a hangout of the Młoda Polska (Young Poland) movement—the Polish answer to Art Nouveau (explained on page 259). The walls are papered with sketches from poor artists—local bohemians who couldn't pay their tabs. In 1915, this was home to the first Polish cabaret. Today that stage is used by a folk troupe that performs traditional music and dance with dinner many evenings (pick up the flier; also see listing under "Entertainment in Kraków," page 328). Poke around inside this circa-1900 time warp and appreciate this unique art gallery. Consider having coffee and dessert here, or a cigar in the charming smokers' bar in front.

About a block farther down, at #20 (on the right), **Staropolskie Trunki** ("Old Polish Drinks") offers an education in vodka—with as much tasting as you'd like. It's a friendly little place with a long bar and countless local vodkas and liquors—all open and ready to be tasted. Best of all, there's a cheery local barista to talk you through the experience (four tastes for 10 zł with a fun explanation that amounts to a private tour, buy a bottle and the tastes are free, daily 10:00-24:00).

• Continue into the Main Market Square, where you'll run into…

▲▲St. Mary's Church (Kościół Mariacki)

A church has stood on this spot for 800 years. The original church was destroyed by the first Tatar invasion in 1241, but all subsequent versions—including the current one—have been built on the same foundation. You can look down the sides to see how the Main Market Square has risen about seven feet over the centuries.

How many church towers does St. Mary's have? Technically, the answer is one. The shorter tower belongs to the church; the taller one is a municipal watchtower, from which you'll hear a bugler playing the hourly *hejnał* song. According to Kraków's favorite legend, during that first Tatar invasion, a town watchman saw the enemy approaching and sounded the alarm. Before he could finish the tune, an arrow pierced his throat—which is why, even today, the *hejnał* stops suddenly partway through. Today's buglers—12 in all—are firemen first, musicians second. Each one works a 24-hour shift up there, playing the *hejnał* four times on the hour—with one bugle call for each direction. (It's even broadcast on national Polish radio at noon.) While you're in Kraków, you'll certainly hear one of these tiny, hourly, broken performances.

To see one of the most finely crafted Gothic altarpieces anywhere, it's worth paying admission to enter the church. The front door is open 14 hours a day and is free to those who come to pray, but tourists use the door around the right side (buy your ticket across the little square from this door).

Cost and Hours: 10 zł, Mon-Sat 11:15-17:45, Sun 14:00-17:45 (these are last-entry times). The famous wooden altarpiece is open between noon and 18:00; try to be here by 11:50 for the ceremonial opening (Mon-Sat) or at 18:00 for the closing (except on Sat, when it's left open for the service on Sun).

Visiting the Church: Inside, you're struck by the lavish decor. This was the church of the everyday townspeople, built out of a spirit of competition with the royal high church at Wawel Castle. At the altar is one of the best medieval woodcarvings in existence—the exquisite, three-part **altarpiece** by German Veit Stoss (Wit Stwosz in Polish). Carved in 12 years and completed in 1489, it's packed with emotion rare in Gothic art. Get as close as you can and study the remarkable details. Stoss used oak for the struc-

tural parts and linden trunks for the figures. When the altar doors are closed, you see scenes from the lives of Mary and Jesus. The open altar depicts the Dormition (death—or, if splitting theological hairs, heavenly sleep) of the Virgin. The artist catches the apostles around Mary, reacting in the seconds after she collapses. Mary is depicted in three stages: life leaving her earthly body, being escorted to heaven by Jesus, and (at the very top) being crowned in heaven. The six scenes on the sides are the Annunciation, birth of Jesus, visit by the Three Magi, Jesus' Resurrection, his Ascension, and Mary becoming the mother of the apostles at Pentecost.

There's more to St. Mary's than the altar. While you're admiring this church's art, notice the flowery Neo-Gothic painting covering the choir walls. Stare up into the starry, starry blue ceiling. As you wander around, consider that the church was renovated a century ago by three Polish geniuses from two very different artistic generations: the venerable positivist Jan Matejko and his Art Nouveau students, Stanisław Wyspiański and Józef Mehoffer (we'll learn more about these two later on our walk). The huge silver bird under the organ loft in back is that symbol of Poland, the crowned white eagle.

Tower Climb: You may be able to climb up the 239 stairs to the top of the taller tower to visit the *hejnał* fireman. While it's a huff—with some claustrophobic stone stairs, followed by some steep, acrophobic wooden ones—the view up top is the best you'll find of the Square (15 zł, pay at the ticket office for the church, departs at :10 and :40 past each hour, April-Oct Mon-Sat 9:30-11:10 & 13:10-17:40, closed Sun, usually closed Nov-March).

Kazimierz the Great (1333-1370)

Out of the many centuries of Polish kings, only one earned the nickname "great," and he's the only one worth remembering: Kazimierz the Great.

K. the G., who ruled Poland from Kraków in the 14th century, was one of those larger-than-life medieval kings who left his mark on all fronts—from war to diplomacy, art patronage to womanizing. His scribes bragged that Kazimierz "found a Poland made of wood, and left one made of brick and stone." He put Kraków on the map as a major European capital. He founded many villages (some of which still bear his name—including one that's an important neighborhood of Kraków) and replaced wooden structures with stone ones (such as Kraków's Cloth Hall). Kazimierz also established the Kraków Academy (today's Jagiellonian University), the second-oldest university in Central Europe. And to protect all these new building projects, he heavily fortified Poland by building a series of imposing forts and walls around its perimeter. If you have a 50-zł note, take a look at it: That's Kazimierz the Great on the front, and on the back you'll see his capital, Cracovia, and the most important town he founded, Casmirus.

Most of all, Kazimierz is remembered as a progressive, tolerant king. In the 14th century, other nations were deporting—or even interning—their Jewish subjects, who were commonly scapegoated for anything that went wrong. But the enlightened Kazimierz created policies that granted Jews more opportunities (often related to banking and trade) and allowed them a chance for higher social standing—establishing the country as a safe haven for Jews in Europe.

Kazimierz the Great was the last of Poland's long-lived Piast dynasty. Although he left no male heir—at least, no legitimate one—Kazimierz's advances set the stage for Poland's Golden Age (14th-16th centuries). After his death, Poland united with Lithuania (against the common threat of the Teutonic Knights), the Jagiellonian dynasty was born, and Poland became one of Europe's mightiest medieval powers.

KRAKÓW

• *Leaving the church, notice the neck clamps dangling from the exterior walls near the side door. If you were leaving Mass in centuries past, there would be locals chained here for public humiliation. You'd spit on them before turning right and stepping into one of the biggest market squares anywhere.*

▲▲▲Main Market Square (Rynek Główny), a.k.a. "The Square"

Kraków's marvelous Square, one of Europe's most gasp-worthy public spaces, bustles with street musicians, colorful flower stalls, cotton-candy vendors, loitering teenagers, the local breakdancing troupe, businesspeople commuting by foot, gawking tourists, soap-balloon-blowers, and the lusty coos of pigeons. The Square is where Kraków lives. It's often filled with various special events, markets, and festivals. The biggest are the seasonal markets before Easter and Christmas, but you're likely to stumble on something special going on just about any time of year (especially June through Aug).

The Square was established in the 13th century, when the city had to be rebuilt after being flattened by the Tatars. At the time, it was the biggest square in medieval Europe. It was illegal to sell any-thing on the street, so everything had to be sold here on the Main Market Square. It was divided into smaller markets, such as the butcher stalls, the ironworkers' tents, and the still-standing Cloth Hall (de-scribed later).

Notice the modern **fountain** with the glass pyramid at this end of the Square. A major excava-tion of the surrounding area created a museum of Kraków's medi-eval history that literally sprawls beneath the Square (for more on the recommended **Rynek Underground Museum,** see page 288).

The statue in the middle of the Square is a traditional meeting place for Krakovians. It depicts Romantic poet **Adam Mickiewicz** (1789-1855), who's considered the "Polish Shakespeare." His epic masterpiece, *Pan Tadeusz*, is still regarded as one of the greatest works in Polish literature. A wistful, nostalgic tale of Polish-Lith-uanian nobility, *Pan Tadeusz* stirred patriotism in a Poland that had been dismantled by surrounding empires.

If you survey the Square from here, you'll notice that the Old Town was spared the bombs of World War II. The Nazis consid-ered Kraków a city with Germanic roots and wanted it saved. But they were quick to destroy any symbols of Polish culture or pride. The statue of Adam Mickiewicz, for example, was pulled down immediately after occupation.

Near the end of the Square, you'll see the tiny, cubical, cop-per-domed **Church of St. Adalbert,** one of the oldest churches in Kraków (10th century). This Romanesque structure predates the Square. Like St. Mary's (described earlier), it seems to be at an angle because it's aligned east-west, as was the custom when it was built. (In other words, the churches aren't crooked—the Square is. Any other "crooked" building you see around town predates the 13th-century grid created during the rebuilding of Kraków.)

Drinks are reasonably priced at cafés on the Square (most around 10-15 zł). Find a spot where you like the view and the chairs, then sit and sip. Order a coffee, Polish *piwo* (beer, such

The Młoda Polska (Young Poland) Art Movement

Polish art in the late 19th century was ruled by positivism, a school with a very literal, straightforward focus on Polish history (Jan Matejko led the charge; see page 402). But when the new generation of Kraków's artists came into their own in the early 1900s, they decided that the old school was exactly that. Though moved by the same spirit and goals as the previous generation— evoking Polish patriotism at a time when their country was being occupied—these new artists used very different methods. They were inspired by a renewed appreciation of folklore and peasant life. Rather than being earnest and literal (an 18th-century Polish war hero on horseback), the new art was playful and highly symbolic (the artist frolicking in a magical garden in the idyllic Polish countryside). This movement became known as Młoda Polska (Young Poland)—Art Nouveau with a Polish accent.

Stanisław Wyspiański (vees-PAYN-skee, 1869-1907) was the leader of Młoda Polska. He produced beautiful artwork, from simple drawings to the stirring stained-glass images in Kraków's St. Francis Basilica. Wyspiański was an expert at capturing human faces with realistic detail, emotion, and personality. The versatile Wyspiański was also an accomplished stage designer and writer. His patriotic play *The Wedding*— about the nuptials of a big-city artist and a peasant girl—is regarded as one of Poland's finest dramas. You'll find excellent examples of Wyspiański's art in Kraków's St. Francis Basilica and Szołayski House, and in Warsaw's National Museum.

Józef Mehoffer (may-HOH-fehr), Wyspiański's good friend and rival, was another great Młoda Polska artist. Mehoffer's style is more expressionistic and abstract than Wyspiański's, often creating an otherworldly effect. See Mehoffer's work in Kraków's St. Francis Basilica and at the artist's former residence (see the Józef Mehoffer House, page 288); and in Warsaw, at the National Museum.

Other names to look for include Jacek Malczewski (mahl-CHEHV-skee), who specialized in self-portraits, and Olga Boznańska (bohz-NAHN-skah), the movement's only prominent female artist. Both are featured in Warsaw's National Museum; Malczewski's works also appear in Kraków's Gallery of 19th-Century Polish Art.

as Żywiec, Okocim, or Lech), or a shot of *wódka* (Żubrówka is a good brand; for more on Polish drinks, see page 230). For a higher vantage point, the Cloth Hall's **Café Szał terrace**—overlooking the Square and St. Mary's Church—offers one of the best views in town (open daily until 24:00, affordable drinks, some light meals, enter through Gallery of 19th-Century Polish Art entrance).

As the Square buzzes around you, imagine this place before 1989. There were no outdoor cafés, no touristy souvenir stands, and no salesmen hawking cotton candy or neon-lit whirligigs. The communist government shut down all but a handful of the businesses. They didn't want people to congregate here—they should be at home, resting, because "a rested worker is a productive worker." The buildings were covered with soot from the nearby Lenin Steelworks in Nowa Huta. The communists denied the pollution, and when the student "Green Brigades" staged a demonstration in this Square to raise awareness in the 1970s, they were immediately arrested. How things have changed.

• *The huge, yellow building right in the middle of the Square is the...*

▲▲Cloth Hall (Sukiennice)

In the Middle Ages, this was the place where cloth sellers had their market stalls. Kazimierz the Great turned the Cloth Hall into a permanent structure in the 14th century. In 1555, it burned down and was replaced by the current building. The crowned letter *S* (at the top of the gable above the entryway) stands for King Sigismund the Old, who commissioned this version of the hall. As Sigismund fancied all things Italian (including women—he married an Italian princess), this structure is in the Italianate Renaissance style. Sigismund kicked off a nationwide trend, and you'll still see Renaissance-style buildings like this one all over the country, making the style as typically Polish as it is typically Italian. We'll see more works by Sigismund's imported Italian architects at Wawel Castle.

The Cloth Hall is still a functioning market—selling mostly souvenirs, including wood carvings, chess sets, jewelry (especially amber), painted boxes, and trinkets (summer Mon-Fri 9:00-18:00, Sat-Sun 9:00-15:00, sometimes later; winter Mon-

Fri 9:00-16:00, Sat-Sun 9:00-15:00). Cloth Hall prices are slightly inflated, but still cheap by American standards. You're paying a little extra for the convenience and the atmosphere, but you'll see locals buying gifts here, too.

Pay WCs are at each end of the Cloth Hall. The upstairs of the Cloth Hall is home to the excellent **Gallery of 19th-Century Polish Art** (enter behind the statue of Adam; for a self-guided tour, see page 281).

• *Browse through the Cloth Hall passageway. As you emerge into the sleepier half of the Square, the big tower on your left is the...*

Town Hall Tower

This is all that remains of a town hall building from the 14th century—when Kraków was the powerful capital of Poland. After the 18th-century Partitions of Poland, Kraków's prominence took a nosedive. By the 19th century, Kraków was Nowheresville. As the town's importance crumbled, so did its town hall. It was cheaper to tear down the building than to repair it, and all that was left standing was this nearly 200-foot-tall tower. In summer, you can climb the tower, stopping along the way to poke around an exhibit on Kraków history, but the views from up top are disappointing. However, you can step into the entryway for a free look at a model of an earlier version of the building, with a fanciful, Prague-style, multispired tower.

Cost and Hours: 9 zł, free on Mon, open April-Oct daily 10:30-18:00, closed Nov-March.

Nearby: The **gigantic head** at the base of the Town Hall Tower is a sculpture by contemporary artist Igor Mitoraj, who studied here in Kraków. Typical of Mitoraj's works, the head is an empty shell that appears to be wrapped in cloth. While some locals enjoy having a work by their fellow Krakovian in such a prominent place, others disapprove of its sharp contrast with the Square's genteel Old World ambience. Tourists enjoy playing peek-a-boo with the head's eyes—a fun photo op.

• *When you're finished on the Square, we'll head toward Wawel Hill. The official Royal Way makes a beeline for the castle, but we'll take a scenic detour to see some less touristy back streets, visit Kraków's historic university and one of its best churches, and go for a quick walk through the Planty park.*

Exit the square at the corner nearest the Town Hall Tower, down ulica Św. Anny. After two short blocks, turn left onto Jagiellońska street. Enter the courtyard of the big, red-brick building on your right.

Jagiellonian University and the Collegium Maius

Kraków had the second university in Central Europe (founded in 1364, after Prague's). Over the centuries, Jagiellonian U. has

boasted such illustrious grads as Copernicus and St. John Paul II. And today, the city's character is still defined largely by its huge student population (numbering around 150,000). Many of the university buildings fill the area to the west of the Old Town, so you'll see more students (and fewer tourist traps) in this part of town than elsewhere.

This building—called the Collegium Maius—is the historic heart of Kraków's university culture. It dates from the 15th century. In the Middle Ages, professors were completely devoted to their scholarly pursuits. They were unmarried and lived, ate, and slept here in an almost monastic environment. They taught downstairs and lived upstairs. In many ways, this building feels more like a monastery than a university. While this courtyard is the most interesting part, you can also tour the interior (for details, see page 289).

The university also comes with some chilling history. On November 6, 1939, the occupying Nazis called all professors together for a meeting. With 183 gathered unknowingly in a hall, they were suddenly loaded into trucks and sent to their deaths in concentration camps. Hitler knew: If you want to decapitate a culture, you kill its intelligentsia.

Before you leave, if you're a fan of rich, thick hot chocolate, enjoy a cup at **Kawiarnia U Pęcherza** (down the stairs near the entrance)—widely regarded as the best in town.

Head down the *sgraffito*-lined passage on the side of the courtyard (it's the first door on your left as you entered the courtyard—just past the little security office). You'll emerge into the **Professors' Garden,** a tranquil space filled with red brick, ivy, stony statues, and inviting benches (open daily 9:00-18:30 or until dusk).

• *Exit the garden and turn right on Jagiellońska. Spot any students? You'll follow this for two more blocks, passing the much larger and newer, but still red-brick,* **Collegium Novum** *building—the modern administrative headquarters of Jag U., built in the late 19th century to commemorate the 500th anniversary of the building we just left.*

Jagiellońska dead-ends at a dynamic statue on a pillar. Turn left into the inviting **Planty**—*the ring park we saw at the start of this walk.*

You'll stroll about five minutes through the Planty, with the Old Town buildings on your left and the ring road through the park on your right. When you reach a street with tram tracks, cross it and turn left. Pause in the park just before the church, and take note of the light-yellow building on the left (across the street), with a picture of St. John Paul II smiling down from above the stone doorway.

Archbishop's Palace

This building was St. John Paul II's residence when he was the archbishop of Kraków. And even after he became Pope, it remained

his home-away-from-Rome for visits to his hometown. After a long day of saying formal Mass during his visits to Kraków, he'd wind up here. Weary as he was, before going to bed he'd stand in the window above the entrance for hours, chatting casually with the people assembled below—about religion, but also about sports, current events, and whatever was on their minds.

In 2005, when the Pope's health deteriorated, this street filled with his supporters, even though he was in Rome. For days, somber locals focused their vigil on this same window, their eyes fixed on a black crucifix

that had been placed here. At 21:37 on the night of April 2, 2005, the Pope passed away in Rome. Ten thousand Krakovians were on this street, under this window, listening to a Mass broadcast on loudspeakers from the church. When the priest announced the Pope's death, every single person simultaneously fell to their knees in silence. For the next several days, thousands of the faithful continued to stand on this street, staring intently at the window where they last saw the man they considered to be the greatest Pole.

• *Now go through the back door of one of Kraków's finest churches...*

▲▲St. Francis Basilica (Bazylika Św. Franciszka)

This beautiful Gothic church, which was St. John Paul II's home church while he was archbishop of Kraków, features some of Po-

land's best Art Nouveau in situ (in the setting for which it was intended). After an 1850 fire, it was redecorated by the two leading members of the Młoda Polska (Young Poland) movement: Stanisław Wyspiański and Józef Mehoffer. The glori-

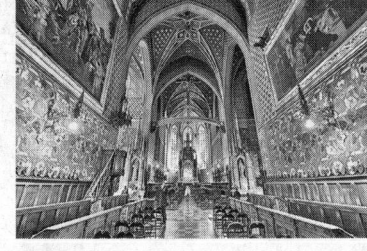

ous decorations inside this church are the result of their great rivalry run amok.

Cost and Hours: Free, daily 6:00-19:45—but frequent services, so be discreet.

● Self-Guided Tour: Step through the door and let your eyes adjust to the low light. Take a few steps up the nave, pausing at the third pew on the left. Notice the **silver plate** labeled "Jan Paweł II"—marking JPII's favorite place to pray when he lived in the Archbishop's Palace across the street.

Now walk another 20 feet down the nave, and notice the painting on the right, with an orange-and-blue background. This depicts **St. Maksymilian Kolbe,** the Catholic priest who sacrificed his own life to save a fellow inmate at Auschwitz in 1941 (notice the *16670*—his concentration camp number—etched into the background; read his story on page 360). Kolbe is particularly beloved here, as he actually served at this church.

Now turn around and look up above the door you entered. There, in all its glory, is the stained-glass window titled *God the Father Let It Be,* created by the great Art Nou- veau artist Stanisław Wyspiański—and regarded by some as his finest masterpiece. (For more on Wyspiański, see page 259.) The colors beneath the Creator change from yellows and oranges (fire) to soothing blues (water), depending on the light. Wyspiański was supposedly inspired by Michelangelo's vision of God in the Sistine Chapel, though he used a street beggar to model God's specific features. Wyspiański also painted the delightful floral stained-glass windows that line the nave, high up—fitting for a church dedicated to a saint so famous for his spiritual connection to nature.

Now turn back around to face the main altar, and head into the **chapel** on the left (marked *Całun Turyński*). This important chapel houses a replica of the Shroud of Turin— which, since it touched the original shroud, is also considered a holy relic. At the main altar in this chapel, notice the plaques honoring Michała Tomaszek and Zbigniew Strzałkowski. These two Polish priests traveled to Peru as missionaries. There, they (along with an Italian priest) were murdered by communist guerrillas calling themselves the Shining Path. Today they are considered martyrs. Nearby, look for photos of Pope Francis (who, like this church and these missionaries, is Franciscan) praying at this altar.

Before leaving this chapel, look high on the walls at the glorious Stations of the Cross. These are painted by **Józef Mehoffer**—a friend and rival of Wyspiański—as a response to Wyspiański's work.

Now head back into the nave, turn left, and walk toward the main altar. (If a service is going on, you may not be able to get very far—just look from here.) On the walls, notice Wyspiański's gorgeous Art Nouveau floral patterns.

Up in the apse, take a moment to appreciate the Wyspiański-designed **stained-glass windows** flanking the high altar. On the right is St. Francis, the church's namesake. On the left is the Blessed Salomea—a medieval Polish woman who became queen of Hungary, but later returned to Poland and entered a convent after her husband's death. Notice she's dropping a crown—repudiating the earthly world and giving herself over to the simple, stop-and-smell-God's-roses lifestyle of St. Francis. Salomea (who's buried in a side chapel) founded this church. Notice also the Mucha-like paintings by Wyspiański on the pilasters between the windows... yet one more sumptuous Art Nouveau detail in this church that's so rich with them.

• *Head back outside. If no services are going on, you can slip out the side door, to the left of the altar. Otherwise, head back out the way you came and hook right. Either way, you're heading to the right along Franciszkańska street. After passing a few monuments and a tram stop, turn right down busy...*

Grodzka Street

Now you're back on the Royal Way proper. At the corner of Grodzka street stands the modern, copper-colored **Wyspiański Pavilion.** Step inside (daily 9:00-17:00), past the little TI, to see three new stained-glass windows based on designs Wyspiański once submitted for a contest to redecorate Wawel Cathedral. Although these designs were rejected back then, they were finally realized on the hundredth anniversary of his death (in 2007). Visible from inside the building during the day, and gloriously illuminated to be seen outside the building at night, they represent three Polish historical figures: the gaunt St. Stanisław (Poland's first saint), the skeletal Kazimierz the Great (in the middle), and the swooning King Henry the Pious.

If you're not churched out, you can dip into the **Dominican Church**—just a block away, to your left (described on page 290).

Now continue down Grodzka street. This lively thoroughfare, connecting the Square with Wawel, is teeming with shops—and

KRAKÓW

Karol Wojtyła (1920-2005): The Greatest Pole

The man who became St. John Paul II began his life as Karol Wojtyła, born to a humble family in the town of Wadowice near Kraków on May 18, 1920. Karol's mother died when he was a young boy. When he was a teenager, he moved with his father to Kraków to study philosophy and drama at Jagiellonian University. Young Karol was gregarious and athletic—an avid skier, hiker, swimmer, and soccer goalie. During the Nazi occupation in World War II, he was forced to work in a quarry. In defiance of the Nazis, he secretly studied theology and appeared in illegal underground theatrical productions. When the war ended, he resumed his studies, now at the theology faculty.

After graduating in 1947, Wojtyła swiftly rose through the ranks of the Catholic Church hierarchy. By 1964, he was archbishop of Kraków, and just three years later, he became the youngest cardinal ever. Throughout the 1960s, he fought an ongoing battle with the regime when they refused to allow the construction of a church in the Kraków suburb of Nowa Huta. After years of saying Mass for huge crowds in open fields, Wojtyła finally convinced the communists to allow the construction of the Lord's Ark Church in 1977. A year later, Karol Wojtyła was called to the papacy—the first non-Italian pope in more than four centuries. In 1979, he paid a visit to his native Poland. In a series of cautiously provocative speeches, he demonstrated to his countrymen the potential for mass opposition to communism.

Imagine you're Polish in the 1970s. Your country was devastated by World War II and has struggled under an oppressive regime ever since. Food shortages are epidemic. Lines stretch around the block even to buy a measly scrap of bread. Life is bleak, oppressive, and hopeless. Then someone who speaks your language—someone you've admired your entire life, and one of the only people you've seen successfully stand up to the regime—becomes one of the world's most influential people. A Pole like you is the leader of a billion Catholics. He makes you believe that the impossible can happen. He says to you again and again: "Nie

some of Kraków's best restaurants (see "Eating in Kraków," later). Survey your options now, and choose (and maybe reserve) your favorite for dinner tonight. This street is also characterized by its fine arcades over the sidewalks. While this might seem like a charming Renaissance feature, the arcades were actually added by the Nazis after they invaded in 1939; they wanted to convert Kraków into a city befitting its status as the capital of their Polish puppet state.

This is also a good street to find some of Kraków's **milk bars** (two are listed on page 345). The most traditional one is about two blocks down, on the right (at #45), with a simple *Bar Mleczny* sign.

lękajcie się"—"Have no fear." And you begin to believe it.

From his bully pulpit, the Pope had a knack for cleverly challenging the communists—just firmly enough to get his point across, but stopping short of jeopardizing the stature of the Church in Poland. Gentle but pointed wordplay was his specialty. The inspirational role he played in the lives of Lech Wałęsa and the other leaders of Solidarity emboldened them to rise up; it's no coincidence that the first successful trade-union strikes in the Soviet Bloc took place shortly after John Paul II became pope. Many people (including Mikhail Gorbachev) credit John Paul II for the collapse of Eastern European communism.

Even as John Paul II's easy charisma attracted new worshippers to the Church (especially young people), his conservatism on issues such as birth control, homosexuality, and female priests pushed away many Catholics. Under his watch, the Church struggled with pedophilia scandals. Many still fault him for turning a blind eye and not putting a stop to these abuses much earlier.

By the end of his papacy, John Paul II's failing health and conservatism had caused him to lose stature in worldwide public opinion.

And yet, approval of the Pope never waned in Poland. His countrymen—even the relatively few atheists and agnostics—saw John Paul II both as the greatest hero of their people...and as a member of the family, like a kindly grandfather. When Pope John Paul II died on April 2, 2005, the mourning in his homeland was particularly deep and sustained. Musical performances of all kinds were canceled, and the irreverent MTV-style music channel simply went off the air out of respect.

A speedy nine years after his death, Karol Wojtyła became St. John Paul II in April of 2014. Out of 265 popes, only two have been given the title "great." There's already talk in Rome of increasing that number to three. Someday soon we may speak of this man as "St. John Paul the Great." His countrymen already do.

These government-subsidized cafeterias are the locals' choice for a quick, cheap, filling, lowbrow lunch. Prices are deliriously cheap (soup costs about a dollar), and the food isn't bad. For more on milk bars, see page 228.

• *One more block ahead, the small square on your right is...*

Mary Magdalene Square
(Plac Św. Marii Magdaleny)

This square offers a great visual example of Kraków's deeply religious character. In the Middle Ages, Kraków was known as "Small

Rome" for its many churches. Today, there are 142 churches and monasteries within the city limits (32 in the Old Town alone)—more per square mile than anywhere outside of Rome. You can see several of them from this spot: The nearest, with the picturesque white facade and row of saints out front, is the **Church of Saints Peter and Paul** (Poland's first Baroque church, and a popular tourist concert venue). The statues lining this church's facade are the 11 apostles (minus Judas), plus Mary Magdalene, the square's namesake. The next church to the right, with the twin towers, is the Romanesque **St. Andrew's** (now with a Baroque interior). Dating from the rough-and-tumble 11th century, it was designed to double as a place of last refuge—notice the arrow slits around the impassable lower floor. According to legend, a spring inside this church provided water to citizens who holed up here during the Tatar invasions. The church was spared, but that didn't save the rest of Kraków from being overrun by marauding armies. Imagine this stone fortress of God being the only building standing amid a smoldering and flattened Kraków after the 13th-century destruction.

If you look farther down the street, you can see three more churches. And even the square next to you used to be a church, too—it burned in 1855, and only its footprint survives.

• *Go through the square and turn left down...*

Kanonicza Street (Ulica Kanonicza)

With so many churches around here, the clergy had to live somewhere. Many lived on this well-preserved street—supposedly the oldest street in Kraków. As you walk, look for the cardinal hats over three different doorways. The **Hotel Copernicus,** on the left at #16, is named for a famous guest who stayed here five centuries ago. Directly across the street at #17, the **Bishop Erazm Ciołek Palace** hosts a good exhibit of medieval art and Orthodox icons. Next door, the yellow house at #19 is where Karol Wojtyła lived for 10 years after World War II—long before he became St. John Paul II. Today this building houses the **Archdiocesan Museum,** which is the top spot in the Old Town to learn about Kraków's favorite son. Both of these sights are described later, under "Sights in Kraków."

• *This marks the end of Kanonicza street—and the end of our self-guided walk. But there's still much more to see. Across the busy street, a ramp leads up to the most important piece of ground in all of Poland: Wawel (described next).*

KRAKÓW

Sights in the Old Town

WAWEL HILL: THE HEART AND SOUL OF POLAND

Wawel (VAH-vehl), a symbol of Polish royalty and independence, is sacred territory to every Polish person. A castle has stood here

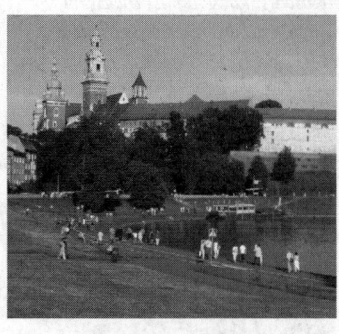

since the beginning of Poland's recorded history. Today, Wawel—awash in tourists—is the most visited sight in the country. Crowds and an overly complex admissions system for the hill's many historic sights can be exasperating. Thankfully, a stroll through the cathedral and around the castle grounds requires no tickets, and—with the help of the following commentary—is enough. I've described these sights in the order of a handy self-guided walk. The many museums on Wawel (all described in this section) are mildly interesting, but can be skipped (grounds open daily from 6:00 until dusk, inner courtyard closes 30 minutes earlier). In May and June, it's mobbed with students, as it's a required field trip for Polish school kids.

Wawel Sights: The sights you'll enter at Wawel are divided into two institutions: church and castle, each with separate tickets. Tickets for the castle sights are sold at two points (at the long line at the top of the ramp, or with no line at the top of the hill, across the central square). The most important church sight—the cathedral—is mostly free, but to enter the paid sights inside (or the museum), get a ticket at the office across from the cathedral entrance.

• *From Kanonicza street—where my self-guided walk ends—head up the long ramp to the castle entry.*

Entry Ramp

Huffing up this ramp, it's easy to imagine how this location—rising above the otherwise flat plains around Kraków—was both strategic and easy to defend. When Kraków was part of the Habsburg Empire in the 19th century, the Austrians turned this castle complex into a fortress, destroying much of its delicate beauty. When Poland regained its independence after World War I, the castle was returned to its former glory. The bricks you see on your left as you climb the ramp bear the names of Poles from around the world who donated to the cause.

The jaunty equestrian statue ahead is **Tadeusz Kościuszko** (1746-1817), a familiar name to many Americans. Kościuszko was a hero of the American Revolution and helped design West

Point. When he returned to his native Poland, he fought bravely but unsuccessfully against the Russians (during the Partitions that would divide Poland's territory among three neighboring powers). Kościuszko also gave his name to several American towns, a county in Indiana, a brand of mustard from Illinois, and the tallest mountain in Australia.

• *Hiking through the Heraldic Gate next to Kościuszko, you pass the ticket office (if you'll be going into the museums, use the other ticket office, with shorter lines, on the top of the hill—see "Tickets and Reservations," later). As you crest the hill and pass through the stone gate, on your left is...*

▲▲Wawel Cathedral

Poland's national church is its Westminster Abbey. While the history buried here is pretty murky to most Americans, to Poles, this church is *the* national mausoleum. It holds the tombs of nearly all of Poland's most important rulers and greatest historical figures.

Cost and Hours: It's usually free to walk around the main part of the church. You must buy a 12-zł ticket to climb up the tallest tower; visit the crypt, the royal tombs, and some of the lesser chapels; and tour the John Paul II Wawel Cathedral Museum. Buy this ticket at the house across from the cathedral entry—marked *KASA*—where you can also rent an audioguide (7 zł). The cathedral is open April-Sept Mon-Sat 9:00-17:00, Sun 12:30-17:00, Oct-March daily until 16:00 (tel. 12-429-9516, www.katedra-wawelska.pl). Note that the cathedral's museum (described later) is closed on Sunday.

Cathedral Exterior

Before entering, go around to the far side of the cathedral to take in its profile. This uniquely eclectic church is the product of centuries of haphazard additions...yet somehow, it works. It began as a simple, stripped-down Romanesque church in the 12th century. (The white base of the nearest tower is original. Anything at Wawel that's made of white limestone like this was probably part of the earliest Romanesque structures.) Kazimierz the Great and his predecessors gradually surrounded the cathedral with some 20 chapels, which were further modified over the centuries, making this beautiful church a happy hodgepodge of styles. To give you a sense of the historical sweep, scan the chapels from left to right: 14th-century Gothic, 12th-century Romanesque (the base of the tower), 17th-century Baroque (the inside is Baroque, though the exterior is a copy of its Renaissance neighbor), 16th-century Renaissance, and 18th- and 19th-century Neoclassical. (This variety in styles is even more evident in the chapels' interiors, which we'll see soon.)

Pay attention to the two particularly interesting domed chapels to the right of the tall tower. The gold one is the Sigismund Chapel, housing memorials to the Jagiellonian kings—including Sigismund the Old, who was responsible for Kraków's Renaissance renovation in the 16th century. The Jagiellonian Dynasty was a high point in Polish history. During that golden 16th century, Poland was triple the size it is today, stretching all the way to the Ottoman Empire and the Black Sea. Poles consider the Sigismund Chapel, made with 80 pounds of gold, to be the finest Renaissance chapel north of the Alps. The copper-domed chapel next to it, home to the Swedish Vasa dynasty, resembles its neighbor (but it's a copy built 150 years later, and without all that gold).

Go back around and face the church's **front entry** for more architectonic extravagance. The tallest tower, called the Sigismund

Tower, has a clock with only an hour hand. Climbing a few steps into the entry, you see Gothic chapels (with pointy windows) flanking the door, a Renaissance ceiling, lavish Baroque decoration over the door, and some big bones (a simple whale rib). In the Middle Ages, these were thought to have been the bones of the mythic Wawel dragon, and put here as an oddity to be viewed by the public. (Back then, there were no museums, so notable items like these were used to lure people to the church.) It's said that as long as the bones hang here, the cathedral will stand. The door is the original from the 14th century, with fine wrought-iron work. The *K* with the crown stands for Kazimierz the Great. The black marble frame is made of Kraków stone from nearby quarries.

Cathedral Interior

The cathedral interior is slathered in Baroque memorials and tombs, decorated with tapestries, and soaked in Polish history. The ensemble was designed to help keep Polish identity strong through the ages. It has...and it still does.

Visiting the Cathedral: After you step inside, you'll follow the one-way, clockwise route that leads you through the choir, then around the back of the apse, then back to the entry.

At the entry, look straight ahead to see the silver tomb under a **canopy,** inspired by the one in St. Peter's Basilica at the Vatican. It contains the remains of the first Polish saint, Stanisław (from the 11th century). In front of the canopy, look for a metallic reliquary that's shaped like a book with its pages being ruffled by the wind (labeled, in Latin, *Sanctus Johannes Paulus II*). The glass capsule in the reliquary holds a drop of St. John Paul II's blood. It takes this shape because of what believers consider a highly significant moment during his memorial service: Before a crowd of thousands on St. Peter's Square in Rome, a book was placed on John Paul II's simple wooden coffin. As the service processed, its pages were ruffled back and forth by the wind, until they were finally slammed shut...as if the Holy Spirit were "closing the book" on his life.

Go behind this canopy into the ornately carved **choir** area. For 200 years, the colorful chair to the right of the high altar has been the seat of Kraków's archbishops, including Karol Wojtyła, who served here for 14 years before becoming pope. It's here that Polish royal coronations took place.

Now you'll continue into the left aisle. From here, if you have a ticket, you can enter two of the optional attractions: Seventy claustrophobic wooden stairs lead up to the 11-ton **Sigismund Bell** and pleasant views of the steeples and spires of Kraków. Then, to the left (closer to where you entered), descend into the little **crypt** (with a rare purely Romanesque interior), which houses the remains of Adam Mickiewicz, the Romantic poet whose statue dominates the Main Market Square, and another beloved Romantic poet and playwright, Juliusz Słowacki. You'll also find a white marble monument to Fryderyk Chopin (who's buried in Paris), put here on the 200th anniversary of his birth in 2010.

Now continue around the apse (behind the main altar). After curving around to the right, look for the red-marble tomb (on the right) of The Great One—**Kazimierz,** of course. Look for *Kazimierz Wielki*—at his feet you can see a little beaver. This is an allusion to a famous saying about Kazimierz, the nation-builder: He found a Poland made of wood, and left one made of brick and stone.

You may notice that there's one VIP (Very Important Pole) who's missing...Karol Wojtyła, a.k.a. John Paul II. Even so, a few more steps toward the entrance, on the left, is the **Chapel of St. John Paul II.** The late pontiff left no specific requests for his body, and the Vatican controversially (to Poles, at least) chose to entomb him in Vatican City, instead of sending him back home to Wawel. While Karol Wojtyła's remains are in St. Peter's Basilica, this chapel was recently converted to honor him—with a plaque in the floor and an altar with his picture. Someday, Poles hope, he may be moved here (but, the Vatican says, don't hold your breath).

Directly opposite the chapel, you'll see the rusty funeral regalia (orb and scepter) of **St. Jadwiga;** ten steps farther is her white sarcophagus (with a dog at her feet). This 14th-century "king" of Poland advanced the fortunes of her realm by partnering with the king of Lithuania. The resulting Jagiellonian dynasty fought off the Teutonic Knights, helped Christianize Lithuania, and oversaw a high-water mark in Polish history. (Despite the queen's many contributions, the sexism of the age meant that she was considered a "king" rather than a "queen.") All the flowers here demonstrate how popular she remains among Poles today; she was sainted by Pope John Paul II in 1997.

Across from Jadwiga, peek into the gorgeous 16th-century **Sigismund Chapel,** with its silver altar (this is the gold-roofed chapel you just saw from outside). Locals consider this the "Pearl of the Polish Renaissance" and the finest Renaissance building outside Italy.

Just beyond is a door leading back outside. If you don't have a ticket, your tour is finished—head out here. But those with a ticket can keep circling around.

Next, look into the **Vasa Chapel:** Remember that its exterior matches the restrained, Renaissance style of the Sigismund Chapel, but the interior is clearly Baroque, slathered with gold and silver—quite a contrast.

To the left of the main door, take a look at the Gothic **Holy Cross Chapel,** with its seemingly Orthodox-style 14th-century frescoes.

In the back corner of the church—on the other side of the main door—is the entrance to the **royal tombs.** (You'll exit outside the church, so be sure you're done in here first.) Once downstairs, the first big room, an original Romanesque space called St. Leonard's Crypt, houses Poland's greatest war heroes: Kościuszko (of American Revolution fame), Jan III Sobieski (who successfully defended Vienna from the Ottomans; he's in the simple black coffin with the gold inscription *J III S*), Sikorski, Poniatowski, and so on. Poles consider this room highly significant as the place where St. John Paul II celebrated his first Mass after becoming a priest (in November of 1946). Then you'll wander through several rooms of second-tier Polish kings, queens, and their kids. Head down more stairs to find the plaque honoring the Polish victims of the Katyń massacre in the USSR during World War II. Stepping into the next room, you'll see the cathedral's newest tomb: President Lech Kaczyński and his wife Helena, who were among the 96 Polish politicians killed in a tragic 2010 plane crash—which was delivering those diplomats to a ceremony memorializing the Katyń massacre. Up a few stairs is the final grave, belonging to Marshal Józef Piłsudski, the WWI hero who later seized power and was the de facto ruler of Poland from 1926 to 1935. His tomb was moved here so the rowdy soldiers who came to pay their respects wouldn't disturb the others.

• *Nearby (and covered by the same ticket as the tower and crypt) is the cathedral's museum.*

John Paul II Wawel Cathedral Museum

This small museum, up the little staircase across from the cathedral entry, was recently spiffed up and re-dedicated to Kraków's favorite archbishop. It fills four rooms with artifacts relating to both the cathedral and St. John Paul II.

Downstairs is the Royal Room, with vestments, swords, regalia, coronation robes, and items that were once buried with the kings, as well as early treasury items (from the 11th through 16th centuries).

Upstairs is the "Papal Room" with items from St. John Paul II's life: his armchair, vestments, caps, shoes, and miter (pointy pope hat), plus souvenirs from his travels. (If you're into papal memorabilia, the collection at the nearby Archdiocesan Museum—described later—is better.) The adjoining room holds a later treasury collection (17th through 20th centuries).

Cost and Hours: Admission to this museum is included with your ticket to the cathedral's special options (Sigismund Bell tower, plus crypt and royal tombs); open April-Sept Mon-Sat 9:00-17:00, Oct-March until 16:00, closed Sun year-round; tel. 12-429-3321.

• *When you're finished with the cathedral sights, stroll around the...*

▲▲Wawel Castle Grounds

In the rest of the castle, you'll uncover more fragments of Kraków's history and have the opportunity to visit several museums. I consider the museums skippable, but if you want to visit them, buy tickets before you enter the inner courtyard. Read the descriptions on page 277 to decide which museums appeal to you.

○ Self-Guided Tour: This guided stroll, which doesn't enter any of the admission-charging attractions, is plenty for most visitors.

• *For a historical orientation, stand with the cathedral to your back, and survey the empty field between here and the castle walls.*

Field of History: This hilltop has seen lots of changes over the years. Kazimierz the Great turned a small fortress into a mighty Gothic castle in the 14th century. But that original fortress burned to the ground in 1499, and ever since, Wawel has been in flux. For example, in the grassy field, notice the foundations of two Gothic churches that were destroyed when the Austrians took over Wawel in the 19th century and needed a parade ground for their troops. (They built the red-brick hospital building beyond the field, now used by the Wawel administration.)

• *Facing the cathedral, look right to find a grand green-and-pink entryway. Go through here and into the palace's dramatically Renaissance-style...*

Inner Courtyard: If this space seems to have echoes of Florence, that's because it was designed and built by young Florentines after Kazimierz's original castle burned down. Notice the three distinct levels: The ground floor housed the private apartments of the higher nobility (governors and castle administrators); the middle level held the private apartments of the king; and the top floor—much taller, to allow more light to fill its large spaces—were the public state rooms of the king. The ivy-covered wing to the right of where you entered is Fascist in style, built as the headquarters of the notorious Nazi governor of German-occupied Poland, Hans Frank. (He was tried and executed in Nürnberg after the war.) At the far end of the courtyard is a false wall, designed to create a pleasant Renaissance symmetry, and also to give the illusion that the castle is bigger than it is. Looking through the windows, notice that there's nothing but air on the other side. When foreign dignitaries visited, these windows could be covered to complete the illusion. The entrances to most Wawel museums are around this courtyard, and some believe that you'll find something even more special: chakra.

Adherents to the Hindu concept of **chakra** believe that a powerful energy field connects all living things. Some believe that, mirroring the seven chakra points on the body (from head to groin), there are seven points on the surface of the earth where this energy is most concentrated: Delhi, Delphi, Jerusalem, Mecca, Rome, Velehrad...and Wawel Hill—specifically over there in the corner (immediately to your left as you enter the courtyard—the stretches of wall flanking the door to the baggage-check room). Look for peaceful people (here or elsewhere on the castle grounds) with their eyes closed. One thing's for sure: They're not thinking of Kazimierz the Great. The smudge marks on the wall are from people pressing up against this corner, trying to absorb some good vibes from this chakra spot.

The Wawel administration seems creeped out by all this. They've done what they can to discourage this ritual (such as putting up information boards right where the power is supposedly most focused), but believers still gravitate from far and wide to hug the wall. Give it a try...and let the chakra be with you. (Just for fun, ask a Wawel tour guide about the chakra, and watch her squirm—they're forbidden to talk about it.)

• *If you want to visit some of the **castle museums** (you can enter four of the five from this courtyard), you'll first need to buy tickets elsewhere. Stick with me for a little longer to finish our tour of the grounds, and we'll wind up near a ticket office.*

Head downhill through the square, across to the gap in the buildings beyond the field, to the...

Viewpoint over the Vistula: Belly up to the wall and enjoy the panorama over the **Vistula River** and Kraków's outskirts. The "Polish Mississippi"—which runs its entire course in Polish lands—is the nation's artery for trade and cultural connection. It stretches 650 miles from the foothills of the Tatra Mountains in southern Poland, through most of the country's major cities (Kraków, Warsaw, Toruń), before emptying into the Baltic Sea in Gdańsk.

From this viewpoint, you can see some unusual landmarks, including the odd wavy-roofed building just across the river (which houses the Manggha Japanese art gallery) and the biggest conference center in Poland (opened in 2015, to the left of the wavy building). A bit farther to the left is an eyesore of a communist concrete department store, now used as a billboard. In the summer, you'll see a popular and very cool "beach bar" filling the field in front of the building (the Forum Przestrzenie, described on page 332). To the right, the suspiciously symmetrical little bulge that tops the highest hill on the horizon is the artificial Kościuszko Mound (see page 321). And on a particularly crisp day, far in the distance (beyond the wavy building), you can see the Tatra Mountains marking the border of Slovakia.

Now look directly below you, along the riverbank, to find a fire-belching monument to the **dragon** that was instrumental in the founding of Kraków. Once upon a time, a prince named Krak founded a town on Wawel Hill. It was the perfect location—except for the fire-breathing dragon who lived in the caves under the hill and terrorized the town. Prince Krak had to feed the dragon all of the town's livestock to keep the monster from going after the townspeople. But Krak, with the help of a clever shoemaker, came up with a plan. They stuffed a sheep's skin with sulfur and left it outside the dragon's cave. The dragon swallowed it, and before long, developed a terrible case of heartburn. To put the fire out, the dragon started drinking water from the Vistula. He kept drinking and drinking until he finally exploded. The town was saved, and Kraków thrived. Today visitors enjoy watching the dragon blow fire into the air (about every four minutes, but can vary from a big plume to a tiny puff).

If you want to head down to see the Vistula and the dragon close up, take a shortcut through the nearby **Dragon's Den** (Smocza Jama, enter at the little copper-roofed brick building, at the far right of this viewpoint plaza). It's just a 135-step spiral staircase and a few underground caverns—worthwhile only as a quick way to get from the top of Wawel down to the banks of the Vistula (3 zł, pay at machine—coins only, daily 10:00-17:00, July-Aug until 18:00, closed Nov-March).

If you'd like a higher viewpoint on the riverfront, you can pay 4 zł to climb 137 stairs to the top of **Sandomierska Tower**

(at the far end of the hill, past the visitors center, no elevator). But I'd skip it—disappointingly, the view from up top is only through small windows (daily 10:00-18:00, June-Aug until 19:00, Oct Sat-Sun only 10:00-17:00, closed Nov-April).

• *Our Wawel tour is finished. If you'd like to explore some of the museums, you can buy your tickets in the nearby visitors center (head back into the main Wawel complex—with the empty field—and turn right); here you'll also find WCs, a café, a gift shop, and other amenities. Or go down to the riverfront park: Walk downhill (through the Dragon's Den, or use the main ramp and circle around the base of the hill) to reach the park—one of the most delightful places in Kraków to simply relax, with beautiful views back on the castle complex.*

Wawel Castle Museums

There are five museums and exhibits in Wawel Castle (not including the cathedral and Cathedral Museum, the Dragon's Den, or Sandomierska Tower—all described above). A sixth exhibit, featuring Leonardo da Vinci's masterful painting *Lady with an Ermine*, may be on display here at the castle, or it could be at the Czartoryski Museum, if it's reopened (see page 286).

Remember: While the following sights are fascinating to Poles, casual visitors often find that the best visit is simply to enjoy the exteriors and the cathedral (following my self-guided tour, described earlier). Each sight has its own admission and slightly different hours (tel. 12-422-5155, ext. 219, www.wawel.krakow. pl). English descriptions are posted, and you can rent an audioguide for 20 zł that covers some of the sights. If you're visiting all of the sights, start with the Royal State Rooms and/or Royal Private Apartments (which share an entrance), then—on your way back down—see the Leonardo exhibit (if it's still here), the Oriental Art exhibit, and the Crown Treasury and Armory. Then head back out into the outer courtyard for the Lost Wawel exhibit.

Tickets and Reservations: Each sight has separate tickets (prices listed below), which you'll buy at one of two ticket windows. Most people line up at the top of the entry ramp, but it's faster to buy tickets at the visitors center at the far corner of the castle grounds (across the field from the cathedral, near the café). You generally can't buy tickets at the door of each sight, so decide in advance which ones you want to see and buy all your tickets at the start of your visit. A limited number of tickets are sold for each sight; boards count down the number of tickets available for each one on the day you're there. Tickets come with an assigned entry time (though you can usually sneak in before your scheduled appointment). In the summer, ticket lines can be long, and sights can sell out by midmorning. You can make a free reservation for some of the sights (tel. 12-422-1697, extra fee applies), but frankly, the sights aren't worth all the fuss—if they're sold out, you're not missing much.

Hours: Unless otherwise noted, the museums are open April-Oct Tue-Fri 9:30-17:00, Sat-Sun 10:00-17:00, closed Mon; Nov-March Tue-Sat 9:30-16:00, closed Sun-Mon. The last ticket is sold 1.25 hours before closing, and the last entry is one hour before closing.

Exceptions: In summer (April-Oct), Lost Wawel and the Crown Treasury and Armory are free and open on Mondays (9:30-13:00). Off-season (Nov-March), everything is closed on Monday and most are closed on Sunday except Lost Wawel, the Royal State Rooms, and the Leonardo exhibit (Jan-March only).

Eating: Various light eateries circle the castle courtyard, but if you just want a drink, it's hard to beat the affordable self-service café next to the Lost Wawel entrance, with fine views across to the cathedral.

▲Royal State Rooms (Komnaty Królewskie)

While precious to Poles, these rooms are mediocre by European standards. Still, this is the best of the Wawel museums. First, climb up to the top floor and wander through some ho-hum halls with paintings and antique furniture. Along the way, you'll walk along the outdoor gallery (enjoying views down into the courtyard). Finally, you'll reach the Throne Room, with 30 carved heads in the ceiling. According to legend, one of these heads got mouthy when the king was trying to pass judgment—so its mouth has been covered to keep it quiet. Continue into some of the palace's finest rooms, with 16th-century Brussels tapestries (140 of the original series of 300 survive), remarkably decorated wooden ceilings, and gorgeous leather-tooled walls. Wandering these halls (with their period furnishings), you get a feeling for the 16th- and 17th-century glory days of Poland, when it was a leading power in Eastern Europe. The Senate Room, with its throne and elaborate tapestries, is the climax.

Cost and Hours: 18 zł, see hours listed earlier, plus Nov-March also open—and free—Sun 10:00-16:00, enter through courtyard.

Royal Private Apartments (Prywatne Apartamenty Królewskie)

The rooms, which look similar to the State Rooms, can only be visited with a guided (and included) 45-minute tour. As spaces are strictly limited, these tend to sell out the fastest (on busy days, they may already be booked up by around 10:00).

Cost and Hours: 25 zł, request English tour when buying your ticket—they depart 3/hour, see hours listed earlier, enter through courtyard.

Oriental Art (Sztuka Wschodu)

Though small, this exhibit displays swords, carpets, banners, vases, and other items dating from the 1683 Battle of Vienna, in which the Ottoman army attempted to capture the Austrian capital. These are trophies of Jan III Sobieski, the Polish king who led a pan-European army to victory in that battle.

Cost and Hours: 8 zł, see hours listed earlier, enter through courtyard; don't miss entry on your way back downstairs from Royal State Rooms.

Crown Treasury and Armory (Skarbiec i Zbrojownia)

This is a decent collection of swords, saddles, and shields; ornately decorated muskets, crossbows, and axes; and cannons in the basement. Off in a smaller side room are some of the most precious items. Look for the regalia given to Jan III Sobieski as thanks for his defeat of the Ottoman invaders in the Battle of Vienna: giant swords consecrated by the pope and the mantle (robe) of the Order of the Holy Ghost from France's King Louis XIV. Nearby is the

13th-century coronation sword of the Polish kings and some gorgeously inlaid rifles.

Cost and Hours: 18 zł, see hours listed earlier, plus April-Oct also open—and free—Mon 9:30-13:00, enter through courtyard.

▲▲Leonardo da Vinci's *Lady with an Ermine*

The single best and most famous painting in Kraków is normally displayed at the Czartoryski Museum. But while that space is closed for renovation (likely through 2017, and possibly longer), you'll most likely find the canvas at Wawel Castle. It's well worth the price of entry to view this rare, small (21 x 16 inches), but magnificently executed portrait of a teenage girl—a rare surviving work by one of history's greatest minds. (If you have your heart set on seeing this painting, make sure it's here before making the trip—it may be on loan or in storage.)

Cost and Hours: 10 zł, see hours listed earlier, plus Jan-March also open Sun 10:00-16:00, enter through courtyard.

Visiting the Museum: Spend some time lingering over the canvas (dating from 1489 or 1490). The girl is likely Cecilia Gallerani, the young mistress of Ludovico Sforza, the duke of Milan and Leonardo's employer. The ermine (white during winter) suggests chastity (thus bolstering Cecilia's questioned virtue), but is also a naughty reference to the duke's nickname, Ermellino—notice that his mistress is sensually, um, "stroking the ermine."

Painted before the *Mona Lisa*, the portrait was immediately recognized as revolutionary. Cecilia turns to look at someone, her gaze directed to the side. Leonardo catches this unguarded, informal moment, an unheard-of gesture in the days of the posed, front-facing formal portrait. Her simple body language and faraway gaze speak volumes about her inner thoughts and personality. Leonardo tweaks the generic Renaissance "pyramid" composition, turning it to a three-quarters angle, and softens it with curved lines that trace from Cecilia's eyes and down her cheek and sloping shoulders before doubling back across her folded arms. The background—once gray and blue—was painted black in the 19th century.

In a recent high-tech analysis using special lights and cameras, conservators were able to virtually peel back layers of paint to see earlier "drafts" of the painting (Leonardo was known to tinker with his works over time). They've revealed that the ermine was likely not included in the original version. Perhaps Leonardo added it later as a nod to the duke.

Lady with an Ermine is one of only three surviving oil paintings by Leonardo. It's better preserved than her famous cousin in Paris *(Mona Lisa)*, and—many think—simply more beautiful. Can we be sure it's really by the enigmatic Leonardo? Yep—the master's fingerprints were found literally pressed into the paint (he was known to work areas of paint directly with his fingertips).

▲Lost Wawel (Wawel Zaginiony)

This exhibit traces the history of the hill and its various churches and castles. Begin by viewing the model of the entire castle complex in the 18th century (pre-Austrian razing). From here, the one-way route leads through scarcely explained excavations of a 10th-century church. The collection includes models of the cathedral at various historical stages (originally Romanesque—much simpler, before all the colorful, bulbous domes, chapels, and towers were added—then Gothic, and so on). Circling back to the entrance, find the display of fascinating decorative tiles from 16th-century stoves that once heated the place.

Cost and Hours: 10 zł, see hours listed earlier, plus April-Oct also open—and free—Mon 9:30-13:00; Nov-March also open—and free—Sun 9:30-13:00; enter near snack bar across from side of cathedral.

NATIONAL MUSEUM BRANCHES

Kraków's National Museum (Muzeum Narodowe) is made up of a series of small but interesting collections scattered throughout the city (www.muzeum.krakow.pl). I've listed the best of the National Museum's branches below. A 35-zł **combo-ticket** covers the permanent collections in all of these museums (good for your entire stay)—worth considering if you'll be visiting more than three of them. National Museum branches are free to enter on Sunday (but some have reduced hours).

▲▲Gallery of 19th-Century Polish Art
(Galeria Sztuki Polskiej XIX Wieku)

This small and surprisingly enjoyable collection of works by obscure Polish artists fills the upper level of the Cloth Hall. While you probably won't recognize any of the Polish names in here—and this collection isn't quite as impressive as Warsaw's National Gallery—many of these paintings are just plain delightful. It's worth a visit to see some Polish canvases in their native land, and to enjoy views over the Square from the hall's upper terraces.

Cost and Hours: 16 zł, free on Sun, Tue-Sun 10:00-18:00, closed Mon, dry 7-zł audioguide, entrance on side of Cloth Hall facing Adam Mickiewicz statue, tel. 12-424-4600.

Background: Keep in mind that during the 19th century—when every piece of art in this museum was created—there was no "Poland." The country had been split up among its powerful neighbors in a series of three Partitions, and would not appear again on the map of Europe until after World War I. Meanwhile, the 19th century was a period of national revival throughout Europe, when

KRAKÓW

various previously marginalized ethnic groups began to take pride in what made them different from their neighbors. So the artists you see represented here were grappling with trying to forge a national identity at a time when they didn't even have a nation. You'll sense a pessimism that comes from a country that feels abused by foreign powers, mingled with a resolute spirit of national pride.

⊘ Self-Guided Tour: The collection fills just four rooms: Two small rooms in the center and two big halls on either side. On a quick visit, focus on the highlights in the big halls I mention here.

Entering the Cloth Hall, buy your ticket and head up the stairs—pausing on the first floor to peek out onto the inviting **café terrace** for a fine view of the Square and St. Mary's. Then continue up to the main exhibit, on the second floor.

The first two small rooms don't feature much of interest. You enter **Room I** (Bacciarelli Room), with works from the Enlightenment; straight ahead is **Room II** (Michałowski Room), featuring Romantic works from 1822 to 1863. The larger, twin halls on either side merit a linger.

Siemiradzki Room (Room III, on the right): This features art of the Academy—that is, "conformist" art embraced by the art critics of the day. Entering the room, turn right and survey the canvases counterclockwise. The space is dominated by the works of Jan Matejko, a remarkably productive painter who specialized in epic historical scenes that also commented on his own era (for more on Matejko, see page 402).

• *Circling the room, look for these paintings.*

1. Jan Matejko—*Wenyhora:* The first big canvas is Matejko's depiction of Wenyhora, a late-18th-century Ukrainian soothsayer who, according to legend, foretold Poland's hardships—the three Partitions, Poland's pact with Napoleon, and its difficulties regaining nationhood. Like many Poles of the era, Matejko was preoccupied with Poland's tragic fate, imbuing this scene with an air of inevitable tragedy.

2. Jacek Malcezewski—*Death of Ellenai:* A similar gloominess is reflected in this canvas. The main characters in a Polish Romantic poem, Ellenai and Anhelli, have been exiled to a remote cabin in Siberia (in Russia, one of the great powers occupying Poland). Just when they think things can't get worse...Ellenai dies. Anhelli sits immobilized by grief.

• *A few canvases down, dominating the right side of the hall, is...*

3. Jan Matejko—*Tadeusz Kościuszko at Racławice:* One of the heroes of the American Revolution, now back in his native

Poland fighting the Russians, doffs his hat after his unlikely victory at the Battle at Racławice. In this battle (which ultimately had little bearing on Russia's drive to overtake Poland), a ragtag army of Polish peasants defeated the Russian forces. Kościuszko is clad in an American uniform, symbolizing Matejko's respect for the American ideals of democracy and self-determination.

• *Dominating the far wall is...*

4. Henryk Siemiradzki—*Nero's Torches:* On the left, Roman

citizens eagerly gather to watch Christians being burned at the stake (on the right). The symbolism is clear: The meek and downtrodden (whether Christians in the time of Rome, or Poles in the heyday of Russia and Austria) may be persecuted now, but we have faith that their noble ideals will ultimately prevail.

• *On the next wall, find...*

5. Pantaleon Szyndler—*Bathing Girl:* This piece evokes the orientalism popular in 19th-century Europe, when romanticized European notions of the Orient (such as harem slave girls) were popular artistic themes. Already voyeuristic, the painting was originally downright lewd until Szyndler painted over a man leering at the woman from the left side of the canvas.

• *The huge canvas on this wall is...*

6. Jan Matejko—*The Prussian Homage:* The last Grand Master of the fearsome Teutonic Knights swears allegiance to the Polish king in 1525. This historic ceremony took place in the Main Market Square in Kraków, the capital at the time. Notice the Cloth Hall balustrade and the spires of St. Mary's Church in the background. Matejko has painted his own face on one of his favorite historical figures, the jester Stańczyk at the foot of the throne (for more on Stańczyk, see page 403).

• *Continue the rest of the way around the room. Keep an eye out for Tadeusz Ajdukiewicz's portrait of Helena Modrzejewska, a popular actress of the time, attending a party in this very building. Finally, backtrack through Room I and continue into the...*

Chełmoński Room (Room IV): Featuring works of the late 19th century, this section includes Realism and the first inklings of Symbolism and Impressionism. Just as elsewhere in Europe (including Paris, where many of these artists trained), artists were beginning to throw off the conventions of the Academy and embrace their own muse.

• *As you turn right and proceed counterclockwise through the room, the first stretch of canvases features landscapes and genre paintings. Among these, a particularly fine canvas is...*

1. Wladyslaw Malecki—*A Gathering of Storks:* The majestic birds stand under big willows in front of the setting sun. Even seemingly innocent wildlife paintings have a political message: Storks are particularly numerous in Poland, making them a subtle patriotic symbol.

• *A few canvases down, find...*

2. Józef Brandt—*A Meeting on a Bridge:* This dramatic painting shows soldiers and aristocrats pushing a farmer into a ditch—a comment on the state of the Polish people at that time. Just to the right, see Brandt's *Fight for a Turkish Standard.* This artist specialized in battle scenes, frequently involving a foe from the East—as was often the reality here along Europe's buffer zone with Asia.

• *Just to the left of Brandt's works is...*

3. Samuel Hirszenberg—*School of Talmudists:* Young Jewish students pore over the Talmud. One of them, deeply lost in thought, may be pondering more than ancient Jewish law. This canvas suggests the inclusion of Jews in Poland's cultural tapestry during this age. While still subject to pervasive bigotry here, many Jewish refugees found Poland to be a relatively welcoming, tolerant place to settle on a typically hostile continent.

• *Dominating the end of the room is...*

4. Józef Chełmoński—*Four-in-Hand:* In this intersection of worlds, a Ukrainian horse-man gives a lift to a pipe-smoking nobleman. Feel the thrilling energy as the horses charge directly at you through splashing puddles.

• *Heading back toward the entrance, on the right wall, watch for...*

5. Witold Pruszkowski—*Water Nymphs:* Based on Slavic legends (and wearing traditional Ukrainian costumes), these mischievous, siren-like beings have just taken one victim (see his hand in the foreground) and are about to descend on another (seen faintly in the upper-right corner). Beyond this painting are some travel pictures from Italy and France (including some that are very Impressionistic, suggesting a Parisian influence).

• *Flanking the entrance/exit door are two of this room's best works. First, on the right, is...*

6. Władysław Podkowiński—*Frenzy:* This gripping painting's title *(Szał)*, tellingly, has been translated as either *Ecstasy* or *Insanity*. A pale, sensuous woman—possibly based on a socialite for whom the artist fostered a desperate but unrequited love—clutches an all-fired-up black stallion, who's frothing at the mouth. This sexually charged painting caused a frenzy indeed at its 1894 unveiling, leading the unbalanced artist to attack his own creation with a knife (you can still see the slash marks in the canvas).

• *And finally, on the other side of the door is...*

7. Jacek Malczewski—*Introduction:* A young painter's apprentice on a bench contemplates his future. Surrounded by nature and with his painter's tools beside him, it's easy to imagine this as a self-portrait of the artist as a young man...wondering if he's choosing the correct path. Malczewski was an extremely talented Młoda Polska artist who tends to be overshadowed by his contemporary, Wyspiański. Viewing this canvas—and others by him—makes me feel grateful that he decided to stick with painting.

Szołayski House (Kamienica Szołayskich)

This restored mansion, just one block from the Main Market Square, features high-quality temporary exhibits, most often featuring artists from the early 20th century; one recent exhibit honored the French sculptor Auguste Rodin, and many others have showcased Art Nouveau works by the Młoda Polska movement (for more on this movement and its members, see page 259). In the past, the museum featured that movement's prodigiously talented headliner, Stanisław Wyspiański—and in the future, he may be back here. But in the meantime, find out what's on, and if the artist or theme interests you, check it out.

Cost and Hours: Price depends on exhibits, may be free on Sun, open Tue-Sat 10:00-18:00, Sun 10:00-16:00, closed Mon, one block northwest of the Square at plac Szczepański 9, tel. 12-433-5450.

Nearby: The charming and stately square that Szołayski House faces, **plac Szczepański,** is a hub for youthful, cutting-edge, artistic types. Tucked in a corner of the Old Town, just away from the Square, it's a strange and wonderful little oasis of urban sophistication. In addition to Szołayski House itself, the square has several bohemian cafés (including the recommended Charlotte). If you follow Szczepańska street one more block out to the Planty, then turn left, you'll find **Bunker Sztuki,** an art gallery that fills an unfortunate communist-era building that really does feel like a bunker. But this conformist architecture is filled with quite the opposite: changing exhibitions of contemporary art (12 zł, free on Tue, open Tue-Sun 11:00-19:00, closed Mon, http://bunkier.art.pl). The gallery's fine café, under a delightfully airy canopy facing the Planty, has a Parisian ambience—a great place to escape the crowds and/or rain (see "Eating in Kraków," later).

Bishop Erazm Ciołek Palace (Pałac Biskupa Erazma Ciołka)

This branch of the National Museum features two separate art collections. Upstairs, the extensive "Art of Old Poland" section shows off works from the 12th through the 18th centuries, with room after room of altarpieces, sculptures, paintings, and more. The "Orthodox Art of the Old Polish Republic" section on the ground floor offers a taste of the remote Eastern reaches of Poland, with icons and other ecclesiastical art from the Orthodox faith. You'll see a sizeable section of the iconostasis (wall of icons) from the town of Lipovec. Both collections are covered by the same ticket and are very well-presented in a modern facility. Items are labeled in English, but there's not much description.

Cost and Hours: 9 zł, free on Sun, Tue-Sat 10:00-18:00, Sun 10:00-16:00, closed Mon, audioguide-7 zł, Kanonicza 17, tel. 12-424-9371.

▲Czartoryski Museum (Muzeum Czartoryskich)

This eclectic collection, displaying armor, handicrafts, decorative arts, and paintings, is one of Kraków's best-known (and most overrated) museums. It's wrapping up a multiyear renovation; during your visit, some or all of its collection may already be open again. But the painting gallery—with its top pieces (a Leonardo and a Rembrandt)—may take longer to reopen. Likely through at least 2017, its undisputed highlight, Leonardo's *Lady with an Ermine,* will be displayed instead at Wawel Castle. Before visiting this museum, get the latest from a TI about how much is open.

Cost and Hours: If museum is open—around 12 zł, free on Sun, open Tue-Sun 10:00-16:00 or possibly until 18:00, closed

Mon, 2 blocks north of the Main Market Square at ulica Św. Jana 19, tel. 12-422-5566, www.czartoryski.org.

Background: The museum's collection came about, in part, thanks to Poland's 1791 constitution (Europe's first), which inspired Princess Izabela Czartoryska to begin gathering bits of Polish history and culture. She fled with the collection to Paris after the 1830 insurrection, and 45 years later, her grandson returned it to its present Kraków location. When he ran out of space, he bought part of the monastery across the street, joining the buildings with a fancy passageway. The Nazis took the collection to Germany, and although most of it has been returned, some pieces are still missing.

The museum owns two undisputed masterpieces, which are in varying states of accessibility. Art lovers will want to ask around for the scoop on their latest locations. While the museum is closed, its top painting—**Leonardo da Vinci's** *Lady with an Ermine*—can likely be found at Kraków's Wawel Castle (described on page 280). **Rembrandt van Rijn's** *Landscape with the Good Samaritan* (1638) may be on display in another city (or possibly in Kraków).

The museum technically owns a third masterpiece, **Raphael's** *Portrait of a Young Man,* but its whereabouts are unknown. Arguably one of the most famous and most valuable stolen paintings of all time, it's quite likely a self-portrait (but possibly a portrait of Raphael by another artist), depicting a Renaissance dandy, clad in a fur coat, with a self-satisfied smirk. Painted (perhaps) by the Renaissance master in 1513 or 1514, and purchased by a Czartoryski prince around the turn of the 19th century, the work was seized by the occupying Nazis during World War II. Along with the paintings by Leonardo and Rembrandt, this Raphael decorated the Wawel Castle residence of Nazi governor Hans Frank. But when Frank and the Nazis fled the invading Red Army at the end of the war, many of their pilfered artworks were lost—including the Raphael. For decades, this canvas was synonymous with art theft—the (literal) poster boy for Nazi crimes against culture. Then, dramatically, a Polish news site announced in 2012 that the priceless painting had been found, safe and sound (in a bank vault in an undisclosed location). Unfortunately, this was a misinterpretation of remarks made by government officials. But authorities are still hopeful the painting "will surface sooner or later" and that the "Czartoryski Raphael," as it's called, will be returned to this museum.

Visiting the Museum: If the museum is open, you'll wander through rooms of ornate armor (including a ceremonial Turkish tent from the 1683 siege of Vienna, plus feathered Hussar armor), tapestries, treasury items, majolica pottery, and Meissen porcelain figures. Rounding out the exhibits are painting galleries (including

KRAKÓW

Italian, French, and Dutch High Renaissance and Baroque, as well as Czartoryski family portraits) and ancient art (mostly sculptures and vases).

More National Museum Branches

While less interesting than the branches listed above, the National Museum's **Main Branch** (Gmach Główny) is worth a visit for museum completists. It features 20th-century Polish art and temporary exhibits (11 zł, a few blocks west of the Main Market Square at aleja 3 Maja 1). In 2017 (and beyond), they are planning a big retrospective exhibit on the works of Stanisław Wyspiański—the founder of the Młoda Polska (Art Nouveau) movement—which would easily be worth ▲, or more for art lovers. Check their website to see what's on (www.muzeum.krakow.pl).

The National Museum has yet more branches: The **Europeum** collection, housed in a restored granary, features works by European masters, including Breughel and Veneziano, along with a range of lesser-known artists (just west of the Old Town at plac Sikorskiego 6). You can also check out the museum of Wyspiański's friend and rival, the **Józef Mehoffer House** (Dom Józefa Mehoffera, 6 zł, ulica Krupnicza 26, tel. 12-421-1143), and the former residence of their mentor, the **Jan Matejko House** (Dom Jana Matejki, 8 zł, ulica Floriańska 41, tel. 12-422-5926).

OTHER OLD TOWN ATTRACTIONS
▲▲Rynek Underground Museum (Podziemia Rynku)

Recent work to renovate the Square's pavement unearthed a wealth of remains from previous structures. Now you can do some urban spelunking with a visit to this high-tech medieval-history museum, which is literally underground—beneath all the photo-snapping tourists on the Square above.

Cost and Hours: 19 zł, free on Tue, open Mon 10:00-20:00 (but closed second Mon of each month), Tue 10:00-16:00, Wed-Sun 10:00-22:00, shorter hours Nov-March; last entry 1.25 hours before closing, enter at north end of Cloth Hall near the fountain, Rynek Główny 1, tel. 12-426-5060, www.podziemiarynku.com.

Visiting the Museum: You'll enter through a door near the north end of the Cloth Hall (close to the fountain, facing St. Mary's). Climb down a flight of stairs, buy your ticket, then follow the numbered panels—1 to 70—through the exhibit (all in English). Cutting-edge museum technology illuminates life and times in medieval Kraków: Touchscreens let you delve into topics that intrigue you, 3-D virtual holograms resurrect old buildings, and video clips illustrate everyday life on unexpected surfaces (such as a curtain of fog).

All of this is wrapped around large chunks of early structures that still survive beneath the Square; several "witness columns" of rock and dirt are accompanied by diagrams helping you trace the layers of history. Interactive maps emphasize Kraków's Europe-wide importance as an intersection of major trade routes, and several models, maps, and digital reconstructions give you a good look at Kraków during the Middle Ages—when the Old Town looked barely different from today. You'll see a replica of a blacksmith's shop and learn how "vampire prevention burials" were used to ensure that the suspected undead wouldn't return from the grave. In the middle of the complex, look up through the glass of the Square's fountain to see the towers of St. Mary's above. Under the skylight is a model of medieval Kraków. While it looks much the same as today, notice a few key changes: the moat ringing the Old Town, where the Planty is today; and the several smaller market halls out on the Square.

Deeper in the exhibit, explore the long corridors of ruined buildings that once ran alongside the length of the Cloth Hall. There are many intriguing cases showing artifacts that shops would have sold (jewelry, tools, amber figurines, and so on). Also in this area, you'll find a corridor with images of the Square all torn up for the recent renovation, plus a series of five modern brick rooms, each showing a brief, excellent film outlining a different period of Kraków's history. These "Kraków Chronicles" provide a big-picture context to what otherwise seems like a loose collection of cool museum gizmos, and also help you better appreciate what you'll see outside the museum's doors.

▲Jagiellonian University Museum: Collegium Maius

Kraków's historic university building can be toured with a student guide. While the courtyard itself (described earlier in "Kraków's Royal Way Walk") is the best part, the musty interior is mildly interesting. You'll choose between two different guided tours: 30 minutes (very popular) or one hour. It's smart to call ahead to find out when the shorter tour is scheduled in English, and to reserve for either tour (tel. 12-663-1307 for advance reservations,

KRAKÓW

or tel. 12-663-1521 for same day, www.maius.uj.edu.pl). The building is two short blocks west of the Main Market Square, at ulica Jagiellońska 15.

The **30-minute tour** covers the "main exhibition" route: the library, refectory (with a gorgeously carved Baroque staircase), treasury (including Polish filmmaker Andrzej Wajda's honorary Oscar), assembly hall, and some old scientific instruments (12 zł, a few tours per day in English, 20 people maximum, leaves every 20 minutes Mon-Fri 10:00-14:20, Tue and Thu until 17:20 in April-Oct, Sat 10:00-13:20, these are the last tour times, no tours Sun). On Tuesday afternoons, you can see the route on your own, for free (15:00-17:20, shorter hours in winter).

The **one-hour tour** adds some more interiors, room after room of more old scientific instruments, medieval art (mostly church sculptures), a Rubens, a small landscape from the shop of Rembrandt, and Chopin's piano (16 zł, usually in English Mon-Fri at 13:00, no tours Sat-Sun).

Dominican Church, a.k.a. Holy Trinity Church (Bazylika Trójcy Świętej)

In most towns, this would be something special. In church-crazy Kraków, it's an also-ran. Still, it's convenient (just a couple of blocks south of the Square) and worth a peek.

Cost and Hours: Free but donation requested, daily 6:30-13:00 & 16:00-20:00, facing plac Dominikański at Stolarska 12.

Visiting the Church: Inside, you'll find a Neo-Gothic space that was rebuilt after a devastating 1850 fire. You may be approached and offered an audioguide to tour the church, in exchange for a donation; it's a good little tour and worth doing, if you have the time. Or, for a quick visit, tune in to just a few details: The unique metal chandeliers are one of many modern flourishes added during the late-19th-century restoration of the church. Climb the staircase in the left aisle to reach the chapel of St. Hyacinth. Locally known as St. Jacek, this early Dominican leader—called the "Apostle of the North"—is also the patron saint of pierogi (stuffed dumplings, similar to ravioli). During a famine, St. Jacek supposedly invented pierogi and—in a loaves-and-fishes-type miracle—produced plateful after plateful, feeding the desperate locals. His image adorns Kraków's annual Pierogi Cup contest, and to this day, when old-fashioned Poles are surprised, they might exclaim, "*Święty Jacek* *z pierogami!*" ("St. Hyacinth and his pierogi!"). Back down in the main part of the church, stroll slowly past the gorgeously carved wooden seats of the choir area (behind the altar); then, at the main altar, identify the three parts of the Trinity: Jesus (short beard), God (long beard), and Holy Spirit (beardless dove).

Archdiocesan Museum (Muzeum Archidiecezjalne)

This museum, in a building where St. John Paul II lived both as a priest and as a bishop, is the best place in town to learn more about Kraków's favorite son (without making the trip to the St. John Paul II Sanctuary on the outskirts—described later). You'll head up-stairs and tour the rooms where JPII actually lived, both as a priest and (later) as a bishop. You'll see John Paul II's personal effects, including clothes, handwritten notes, travel gear, bike, kayak, and skis—reminding visitors that he was one sporty pope. Then you'll tour the lavish private apartments where he lived from 1958 until 1967, as archbishop of Kraków. Throughout the collection are many portraits and photographs of the late pontiff—making his cult of personality almost palpable.

Cost and Hours: 5 zł, Tue-Fri 10:00-16:00, Sat-Sun 10:00-15:00, closed Mon, Kanonicza 19-21, tel. 12-421-8963, www.muzeumkra.diecezja.pl.

Sights in Kazimierz

The neighborhood of Kazimierz (kah-ZHEE-mehzh), 20 minutes by foot southeast of Kraków's Old Town, is the historic heart of

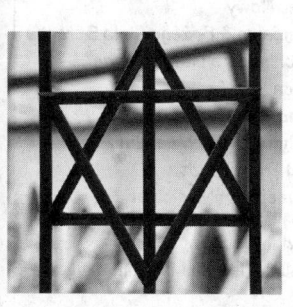

Kraków's once-thriving Jewish commu-nity. After years of neglect, the district began a rejuvenation in the early 2000s. Today, while not quite as slick and pol-ished as Prague's Jewish Quarter, Kazimi-erz's assortment of synagogues, cemeter-ies, and museums helps visitors appreciate the neighborhood's rich Jewish history. At the same time, Kazimierz also happens to be the city's edgy, hipster culture center—jammed with colorful bars, creative eat-eries, and designer boutiques. This unlikely combination—where somber synagogues coexist with funky food trucks—makes Ka-zimierz a big draw for travelers both young and old.

When To Go: Try to visit any day except Saturday, when most Jewish-themed sights are closed (except the Old Synagogue, High Synagogue, and Galicia Jewish Museum). Monday comes with a few closures: the Ethnographic Museum, Museum of Contem-porary Art in Kraków, and Museum of Municipal Engineering.

KRAKÓW

Kazimierz Walk

① Kazimierz Monument
② Old Jewish Cemetery & Jan Karski Statue
③ Old Shop Fronts
④ Hamsa Rest. & Jarden Bookshop
⑤ Klezmer-Hois Restaurant
⑥ New Jewish Cemetery
⑦ Rubinstein Birthplace
⑧ Popper Synagogue
⑨ Old Synagogue
⑩ Food Trucks
⑪ Isaac Synagogue
⑫ Plac Nowy
⑬ Meiselsa & Bożego Ciała Streets
⑭ "Schindler's List Passage"
⑮ Ulica Józefa
⑯ Plac Wolnica
⑰ Ethnographic Museum
⑱ Old Tram Depot
⑲ Museum of Municipal Engineering
⑳ Judah Square
㉑ Galicia Jewish Museum

On Monday, the Schindler's Factory Museum is free, but it's open shorter hours and is more crowded than usual. For more suggestions of what to do in Kazimierz, see the Shopping, Entertainment, Sleeping, and Eating sections.

Etiquette: To show respect, men cover their heads while visiting a Jewish cemetery or synagogue. Most sights offer loaner yarmulkes, or you can wear your own hat.

Getting to Kazimierz: From the Old Town, it's about a

20-minute **walk.** From the Main Market Square, head down ulica Sienna (near St. Mary's Church) and through the Planty park. When you hit the busy ring road, bear right and continue down Starowiślna for 15 more minutes. The **tram** shaves off a few minutes: Find the stop along the ring road, on the left-hand side of ulica Sienna (across the street from the Poczta Główna, or main post office). Catch tram #3 or #24, and ride two stops to Miodowa. Walking or by tram, at the intersection of Starowiślna and Miodowa, you'll see a small park across the street and to the right. To reach the heart of Kazimierz—ulica Szeroka—cut through this park. The same trams continue to the sights in Podgórze (including the Schindler's Factory Museum).

To return to the Old Town, catch tram #3 or #24 from the intersection of Starowiślna and Miodowa (kitty-corner from where you got off the tram).

Information: An official **TI** is just a few blocks off the bottom of ulica Szeroka, at ulica Józefa 7 (daily 9:00-17:00, tel. 12-422-0471).

▲KAZIMIERZ WALK

This self-guided walk is designed to help you get your bearings in Kazimierz, connecting both its Jewish sights (mostly in "Part 1") and its eclectic other attractions, from trendy bars to underrated museums ("Part 2"). Allow about an hour for the entire walk, not counting museum visits along the way. From the end of the walk, you can easily cross the river to this area's biggest sight, the Schindler's Factory Museum.

Part 1: Jewish Heritage on Ulica Szeroka

• *We'll start on ulica Szeroka ("Broad Street")—the center of the neighborhood, which feels like more of an elongated square than a "street." Begin at the bottom (southern) edge of the small, grassy park, near the strip of restaurants. In the park, look for the low-profile, stone...*

Kazimierz Monument

You're standing in the historical heart of Kraków's Jewish community. In the 14th century, King Kazimierz the Great enacted policies that encouraged Jews fleeing other kingdoms to settle in Poland—including in Kraków. He also founded this town, which still bears his name. Originally, Jews lived in the Old Town, but they were scapegoated after a 1495 fire and forced to relocate to Kazimierz. Back then, Kazimierz was still a separate town, divided by a wall into Christian (west) and Jewish (east) neighborhoods. Ulica Szeroka was the main square of the Jewish community. Over time, Jews were more or less accepted into the greater community, and Jewish culture flourished here.

All that would change in the mid-20th century. The **monument** honors the "65 thousand Polish citizens of Jewish nationality from Kraków and its environs"—more than a quarter of the city's pre-WWII population—who were murdered by the Nazis during the Holocaust. When the Nazis arrived, they immediately sent most of Kraków's Jews to the ghetto in the eastern Polish city of Lublin. Soon after, they forced Kraków's remaining 15,000 Jews into a walled ghetto at Podgórze, across the river. The Jews' cemeteries were defiled, and their buildings were ransacked and destroyed. In 1942, the Nazis began transporting Kraków's Jews to death camps (including Płaszów, just on Kraków's outskirts, and Auschwitz).

Only a few thousand Kraków Jews survived the war. During the communist era, this waning population was ignored or mistreated. After 1989, interest in Kazimierz's unique Jewish history was faintly rekindled. But it was only when Steven Spielberg chose to film *Schindler's List* here in 1993 that the world took renewed interest in Kazimierz. (A local once winked to me, "They ought to build a statue to Spielberg on that square.") Although the current Jewish population in Kraków numbers only 200, Kazimierz has become an internationally known destination for those with an interest in Jewish heritage.

• *Facing the park, look to the left. The arch with the Hebrew characters marks the entrance to the...*

▲▲Old Jewish Cemetery (Stary Cmentarz)

This small cemetery was used to bury members of the Jewish community from 1552 to 1800. With more than a hundred of the top

Jewish intellectuals of that age buried here, this is considered one of the most important Jewish cemeteries in Europe.

Cost and Hours: 10 zł includes cemetery and attached Remu'h Synagogue; sporadic hours according to demand—especially outside peak season—but generally open Sun-Fri 9:00-16:00, can be open until 18:00 May-Sept, closes earlier off-season and by sundown on Fri, closed Sat year-round, ulica Szeroka 40.

Visiting the Cemetery: Walk under the arch, pay the admission fee, step into the cemetery, and survey the tidy rows of headstones. This early Jewish resting place (later replaced by the New Cemetery, described later) was desecrated by the Nazis during the Holocaust. In the 1950s, it was discovered, excavated, and put back together as you see here. Shattered gravestones form a mosaic wall around the perimeter. As in all Jewish cemeteries, you'll see many small stones stacked on the graves. The tradition comes from placing stones—representing prayers—over desert graves to cover the body and prevent animals from disturbing it. Behind the little synagogue to the left, the tallest tombstone next to the tree belonged to Moses Isserles (a.k.a. Remu'h), an important 16th-century rabbi. He is believed to have been a miracle worker,

KRAKÓW

and his grave was one of the only ones that remained standing after World War II. Notice the written prayers crammed into the cracks and crevices of the tombstone.

Near the gate to the cemetery, step into the tiny **Remu'h Synagogue** (c. 1553, covered by cemetery ticket). Tight and cozy, this has been carefully renovated and is fully active. Notice the original 16th-century frescoed walls and ceilings, and the donation box at the door. For more on typical synagogue architecture, see the sidebar.

• *Back outside, turn left and continue up to the top of...*

Ulica Szeroka

Just above the cemetery gate, notice a bronze statue of a gentleman seated on a bench. This is a tribute to **Jan Karski** (1914-2000), a Catholic Pole and resistance fighter who published his eyewitness account *The Story of a Secret State* about the Holocaust in 1944. Karski—the ultimate whistleblower—was one of the first people who spoke out about Nazi atrocities, at a time when even many world leaders had only an inkling about what was happening in Hitler's realm. Karski's message, so shocking as to be literally unbelievable to many, went ignored by some key leaders—arguably extending the horrors of the Holocaust.

Just above that, at the top corner of the square, notice the side street with a row of rustic old Jewish **shop fronts,** which evoke the bustle of prewar Kazimierz. The Jewish names—Rattner, Weinberg, Nowak, Holcer—stand testament to the lively soul of this neighborhood in its heyday. This lane leads to Miodowa street, which you can follow left to reach two of Kazimierz's lesser-known synagogues (Tempel and Kupa, both described later).

The building at the top of the square houses the recommended **Hamsa** restaurant (with modern Israeli food) and **Jarden Bookshop,** which serves as an unofficial information point for the neighborhood and sells a wide variety of fairly priced books on Kazimierz and Jewish culture in the region (Mon-Fri 9:00-18:00, Sat-Sun 10:00-18:00, ulica Szeroka 2).

Kitty-corner from the bookshop, notice **Klezmer-Hois**—one of many restaurants offering live traditional Jewish klezmer music nightly in summer (for more on klezmer music, and details on your options, see page 331).

The **New Jewish Cemetery**—less touristed and a striking contrast to the Old Jewish Cemetery we just saw—is a worthwhile detour, about a five-minute walk away (see description on page 303).

The Synagogue

A synagogue is a place of public worship, where Jews gather to pray, sing, and read from the Torah. Most synagogues have similar features, though they vary depending on the congregation.

The synagogue generally faces toward Jerusalem (so in Kraków, worshippers face east). At the east end is an alcove called the ark, which holds the Torah. These scriptures (the first five books of the Old Testament) are written in Hebrew on scrolls wrapped in luxuriant cloth. The other main element of the synagogue is the bema, an elevated platform from which the Torah is read aloud (the equivalent of a pulpit in a Christian church). In traditional Orthodox synagogues, the bema is near the center of the hall, and the reader stands facing the same direction as the congregation. In other branches of Judaism, the bema is at the front, and the reader faces the worshippers. Orthodox synagogues have separate worship areas for men and women, usually with women in the balcony.

The synagogue walls might be decorated with elaborate patterns of vines or geometric designs, but never statues of people, which could be considered idol worship. A lamp above the ark is always kept lit, as it was in the ancient temple of Jerusalem, and candelabras called menorahs also recall the temple. Other common symbols are the two tablets of the Ten Commandments given to Moses, or a Star of David, representing the Jewish king's shield.

At a typical service, the congregation arrives at the start of Sabbath (Friday evening). As a sign of respect toward God, men don yarmulkes (small round caps). As the cantor leads songs and prayers, worshippers follow along in a book of weekly readings. At the heart of the service, everyone stands as the Torah is ceremoniously paraded, unwrapped, and placed on the bema. Someone—the rabbi, the cantor, or a congregant—reads the words aloud. The rabbi ("teacher") might give a commentary on the Torah passage.

KRAKÓW

To get there, cut through the grassy little lot between Jarden Bookshop and Klezmer-Hois, turn right, cross the busy street, then go through the railway underpass.

When you're ready to move on, do a 180 and head back downhill on ulica Szeroka. You'll pass the little park again, then come to a row of lively, mostly Jewish-themed **restaurants** with outdoor tables. Several places along here (especially Ester Hotel, at the bottom of the row) feature outdoor klezmer music in good weather—allowing you to get a taste of this unique musical form before committing to a full meal.

Halfway down this side of the square, the green house at #14 is where **Helena Rubinstein** was born in 1870. At age 31, she emigrated to Australia, where she parlayed her grandmother's traditional formula for hand cream into a cosmetics empire. Many cosmetics still used by people worldwide today were invented by Rubinstein, who died at age 92 in New York City as one of the most successful businesswomen of all time—just one of many illustrious Jewish residents of Kazimierz.

Two doors past the Rubinstein house, notice the round arch marking the courtyard of the **Popper Synagogue,** a popular venue for klezmer concerts.

Continue past the restaurants to the very bottom of ulica Szeroka, and pause at the steps before heading down into the sunken area around the Old Synagogue. To the synagogue's left, notice a short, reconstructed stretch of Kazimierz's 14th-century **town wall.** This is a reminder that medieval Kazimierz was a separate city from Kraków. It's easy to read some history into a map of Kazimierz (you'll find one on the big panel in front of the Old Synagogue): Today's Starowiślna and Dietla streets—which frame off Kazimierz in a triangle of land hemmed in by the riverbank—were once canals (Kazimierz was built on an island). When King Kazimierz the Great—who reportedly didn't care much for Krakovians—founded this district in 1335, he envisioned it as a separate town to rival Kraków. It wasn't until around 1800 that the two towns merged.

• *Turn your attention to the bottom of the square, with the...*

Old Synagogue
(Stara Synagoga)

The oldest surviving Jewish building in Poland (15th century) sits eight steps below street level. Jewish structures weren't allowed to be taller than Christian ones—and so, in order to have the proper proportions, the synagogue's "ground floor"

had to be underground. Today the synagogue houses a good three-room museum on local Jewish culture, with informative English descriptions and a well-preserved main prayer hall (9 zł, free on Mon; April-Oct Mon 10:00-14:00, Tue-Sun 9:00-17:00; shorter hours off-season; good 50-stop audioguide-10 zł; ulica Szeroka 24, tel. 12-422-0962).

• *A few more Jewish sights can be found in the surrounding streets; I'll point these out in "Part 2," though the rest of this walk focuses on a more recent chapter.*

Part 2: Contemporary Kazimierz

• *Stand with your back to the Old Synagogue and turn left, heading up the little alley next to Szeroka 28—called Lewkowa.*

Hipster Kazimierz

Follow Lewkowa between some old buildings. When you pop out into an open area, jog right, then continue straight along ulica Ciemna. Soon you'll hit an inviting little **pod of food trucks** (described on page 346). Pause here—perhaps while nursing an açaí smoothie, an artisanal kielbasa, or a taco—and ponder the explosion of youthful culture that's taken place in Kazimierz over the last generation.

At the end of World War II, Kazimierz was badly damaged and depopulated. And so it remained for generations, as the communist authorities brushed Jewish heritage under the rug. By the early 2000s, Kazimierz's artistically dilapidated buildings, low rents, and easy proximity to the Old Town became enticing to creative young people. A variety of artsy entrepreneurs took root here, beginning with a cluster of ramshackle, rustic bars (inspired partly by Budapest's "ruin pub" scene). Today the district has the city's (and probably Poland's) highest concentration of trendy food trucks, cafés, bars, restaurants, and design shops—several of which we'll see as we continue.

• *From the food trucks, continue straight ahead (on Izaaka street). This leads you around the left side of...*

Isaac Synagogue (Synagoga Izaaka)

One of Kraków's biggest synagogues, this was built in the 17th century. Inside, the walls in the prayer hall are decorated with giant paintings of prayers for worshippers who couldn't afford to buy books (with translations posted below). The synagogue also serves as the local center for the Hasidic Jewish group Chabad, with a kosher restaurant and a library (7 zł; April-Oct Sun-Thu 8:30-20:00, Fri 8:30-14:30, closed Sat year-round, shorter hours off-season; ulica Kupa 18, tel. 12-430-2222). In addition to its Sabbath services, this is Kraków's only synagogue that has daily prayers (at 8:30). They also host klezmer music concerts many evenings at 18:00 (60 zł).

• *Just past Isaac Synagogue is the heart of Kazimierz's nightlife zone (also bustling by day). Dive in, passing some characteristic cafés (on your left) and the chic Taawa nightclub (on your right). Then jog right at the glitzy Plac Nowy 1 beer hall to reach...*

Plac Nowy

Kazimierz's endearing "new" market square, plac Nowy (plats NOH-vee), retains much of the gritty flavor of the district before tourism and gentrification. The circular brick building in the center is a slaughterhouse where Jewish butchers would properly kill livestock, kosher-style. Today its windows are filled with little stand-up eateries ranging from burgers and ice cream to the traditional local pizza-like *zapiekanki*. Circle the market hall and browse for a snack (for more on the plac Nowy scene, see "Eating in Kraków," later). Good Lood has Kraków's best artisanal ice cream—if you don't mind the long line. This square is also ringed by several fun and funky bars—enjoyable by day, but hopping at night (see page 329).

• *Leave plac Nowy along Meiselsa street (to the left from where you entered, past the yellow Jewish Cultural Center). After one block, pause at the intersection of...*

Meiselsa and Bożego Ciała Streets

The Holocaust was a dark chapter that dominates Kazimierz's history. But this intersection is a reminder that, up until the Nazis arrived, Kazimierz was a place where Jews and Christians lived side-by-side, in relative harmony. Notice the street names, which mix Jewish and Catholic namesakes: ulica Meiselsa ("Meisels Street"—honoring a deeply respected 19th-century rabbi) and ulica Bożego Ciała ("Corpus Christi Street"—named for the 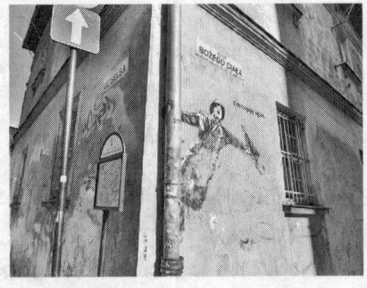 towering brick church you can see just ahead). As if to celebrate the ecumenism of this intersection, a street artist has painted a graffiti Gene Kelly on the wall...very "happy again" indeed that Kazimierz is blossoming and full of life.

• *Backtrack a few steps up Meiselsa and duck into the courtyard on the right, under the dilapidated arch (labeled Stajnia).*

"Schindler's List **Passage"**

This courtyard is a popular tourist spot thanks to its brush with fame, as a location for some key scenes in *Schindler's List* (find the back-and-white stills from the movie partway down on the right, just before the arch). Spielberg connection aside, this is a particularly evocative setting to nurse a relaxing drink at one of the atmospheric cafés.

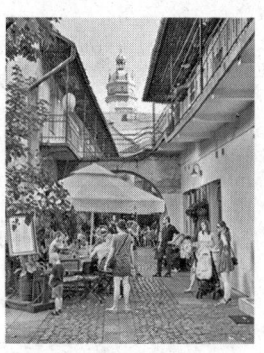

• *Carry on all the way through the passage. You'll pop out at...*

Ulica Józefa: Design Street

This street has Kazimierz's highest concentration of funky, one-off boutiques: jewelry, fashion, housewares, and more. For a rundown of the best options along here, see page 324. There's also a TI just across the street.

• *When you're ready to move along, take ulica Józefa a few steps to the intersection with ulica Bożego Ciała, turn left, and follow it a long block. You'll pass Corpus Christi Church on your left, then arrive at...*

Plac Wolnica

Remember that Kazimierz was originally a separate town from Kraków. This was its main market square, designed to one-up its crosstown rival—right down to the dramatic, red-brick Catholic church on the corner (Corpus Christi).

The former Kazimierz town hall at the far end of the square houses an unusually good **Ethnographic Museum** (Muzeum Etnograficzne)—worth ▲. If you're interested in Polish folk culture, it's worth a visit. On the ground floor, you'll find models of traditional rural Polish homes, as well as musty replicas of the interiors (like an open-air folk museum moved inside). The exhibit continues upstairs, where each in a long lineup of traditional Polish folk costumes is identified by specific region. Follow the one-way route through exhibits on village lifestyles, rustic tools, and musical instruments (including a Polish bagpipe). A highlight is the explanation of traditional holiday celebrations—from elaborate crèche scenes at Christmas, to a wall of remarkably painted Easter eggs. Some items are labeled in English, but it's mostly in Polish. The top floor features temporary exhibits (13 zł, free on Sun, open Tue-Sun 10:00-19:00, closed Mon, ulica Krakowska 46, tel. 12-430-6023, www.etnomuzeum.eu).

• *There's more to see in Kazimierz. But if you're pooped, you could catch tram #6, #8, #10, or #13 back to Wawel Castle, then on to the plac Wszystkich Świętych stop in the heart of the Old Town (catch tram from along Krakowska street, behind the Ethnographic Museum).*

KRAKÓW

To continue the walk from plac Wolnica, head up ulica Św. Wawrzyńca (at the corner where you entered the square, with the Corpus Christi Church on your left).

Ulica Św. Wawrzyńca: Industrial Kazimierz

By the late 19th century, Kazimierz was not just a Jewish cultural hotspot, but also a center of local industry. (It's no coincidence that Oskar Schindler had his factory near here.) After the church, on your left, look for the glass-and-steel arched roof of the Industrial Age **old tram depot,** which now houses a recommended brewpub. In sunny summer weather, the pebbly courtyard is filled with happy drinkers.

Across the street, notice the many tram tracks leading in to a courtyard with several more storage sheds for local trams. This gorgeously restored complex now houses the **Museum of Municipal Engineering** (Muzeum Inżynierii Miejskiej). Exhibits include a history of the town's public-transit system (including several antique trams), old Polish-made cars and motorcycles (among them the tiny commie-era Polski Fiat), typography and historical printing presses, and a hands-on area for kids called "Around the Wheel" (10 zł, family ticket-29 zł, includes English audioguide, free on Tue; open Tue-Sun 10:00-16:00; Tue, Thu, and Sun until 18:00 in June-Sept; closed Mon year-round; Św. Wawrzyńca 15, tel. 12-421-1242, www.mimk.com.pl).

Continue along ulica Św. Wawrzyńca a few more steps. At the intersection with Wąska, **Judah Square** (Skwer Judah) is a vacant lot with a gaggle of enticing food carts watched over by a giant mural. Commissioned for Kraków's Jewish Cultural Festival in 2013, the illustration was painted by Israeli street artist Pilpeled. It shows a young boy who feels small and scared, but lionhearted nevertheless—a poignant

symbol for the Holocaust survivors of Kazimierz. If you're ready for a meal or snack, you'll find several good options here.

• A half-block farther down ulica Św. Wawrzyńca is another place for refreshment, the recommended Craftownia (Polish microbrews on tap, on the left at #22). Next you'll reach the intersection with Dajwór street. Turn left here and walk a few steps up the street; on the right, you'll find the...

Galicia Jewish Museum (Galicja Muzeum)

This museum, worth ▲ and housed in a restored Jewish furniture factory, focuses on the present rather than the past. The permanent "Traces of Memory" photographic exhibit shows today's remnants of yesterday's Judaism in the area around Kraków (a region known as "Galicia"). From abandoned synagogues to old Jewish gravestones flipped over and used as doorsteps, these giant postcards of Jewish artifacts (with good English descriptions) ensure that an important part of this region's heritage won't be forgotten. Good temporary exhibits complement this permanent collection (15 zł, daily 10:00-18:00, 1 block east of ulica Szeroka at ulica Dajwór 18, tel. 12-421-6842, www.galiciajewishmuseum.org). The museum also serves as a sort of cultural center, with a good bookstore and café.

• *Notice yet another cluster of food trucks across the street from the museum.*

Our Kazimierz orientation walk is finished. From here, you have several options. To **return to ulica Szeroka,** *where we began, walk up Dajwór street past the museum, then angle left through the park at the reconstructed chunk of town wall—you'll wind up at the Old Synagogue.*

For the next two options, you'll first head back down to ulica Św. Wawrzyńca, turn left, and walk one more block to the intersection with Starowiślna street. Just to the left on Starowiślna, look for the tram stops. The tram stop on the far side of the street takes you **back to the Old Town** *(tram #3 or #24). From the tram stop on the near side of the street, tram #3 or #24 zips you to the* **sights in Podgórze**—*including Ghetto Heroes' Square and the Schindler's Factory Museum (both described later). You can also reach the Podgórze sights on foot by turning right on Starowiślna and crossing the bridge (about a 10-minute walk).*

MORE JEWISH SIGHTS IN KAZIMIERZ

In addition to the sights connected by the walk above, here's another cemetery and a few more synagogues to round out your Jewish Kazimierz experience.

▲New Jewish Cemetery (Nowy Cmentarz)

This burial place—much larger than the Old Jewish Cemetery—has graves of those who died after 1800. It was vandalized by the

Nazis, who sold many of its gravestones to stonecutters and used others as pavement in their concentration camps. Many have since been cemented back in their original positions, while others—which could not be replaced—have been used to create the moving mosaic wall and Holocaust monument (on the right as you enter). Most gravestones are in one of four languages: Hebrew (generally the oldest, especially if there's no other language, though some are newer "retro" tombstones); Yiddish (sounds like a mix of German and Hebrew and uses the Hebrew alphabet); Polish (Jews who assimilated into the Polish community); and German (Jews who assimilated into the German community). The earliest graves are simple stones, while later ones imitate graves in Polish Catholic cemeteries—larger, more elaborate, and with a long stone jutting out to cover the body. Notice that some new-looking graves have old dates. These were most likely put here well after the Holocaust (or even after the communist era) by relatives of the dead.

Cost and Hours: Free, Sun-Fri 8:00-18:00, winter until 16:00, closed Sat. It's tricky to find: Go under the railway tunnel at the east end of ulica Miodowa, and jog left as you emerge. The cemetery is to your right (enter through gate with small *cmentarz żydowski* sign).

Synagogues

In addition to the three synagogues mentioned on the Kazimierz Walk (Old Synagogue, Isaac, and Remu'h), others also welcome visitors. Each of these charges a small admission fee and is closed Saturdays (unless noted). The **High Synagogue**—so called because its prayer room is upstairs—displays changing exhibits, most of which focus on the people who lived here before the Holocaust (daily, ulica Józefa 38). **Tempel Synagogue** (Synagoga Templu) has the grandest interior—big and dark, with elaborately deco-rated, gilded ceilings and balconies (corner of ulica Miodowa and ulica Podbrzezie). The **Jewish Community Centre** next door of-fers activities both for members of the local Jewish community and for tourists (lectures, genealogical research, Friday-night Shabbat meals, Hebrew and Yiddish classes, and so on; www.jcckrakow.org). Nearly across the street, the smaller **Kupa Synagogue** (Syna-goga Kupa)—clean and brightly decorated—sometimes hosts tem-porary exhibits (Miodowa 27).

NEAR KAZIMIERZ: PODGÓRZE

The neighborhood called Podgórze (POD-goo-zheh), directly across the Vistula from Kazimierz, has one of Kraków's most fa-mous sights: Schindler's Factory Museum. I've listed these sights in the order you'll reach them as you come from Kazimierz or the Old Town.

Background: This is the neighborhood where the Nazis forced Kraków's Jews into a ghetto in early 1941. (*Schindler's List* and the films in the Pharmacy Under the Eagle museum depict the sad scene of the Jews loading their belongings onto carts and trudging over the bridge into Podgórze.) Non-Jews who had lived here were displaced to make way for the new arrivals. The ghetto was surrounded by a wall with a fringe along the top that resembled

Jewish gravestones—a chilling premonition of what was to come. A short section of this wall still stands along Lwowska street. The tram continued to run through the middle of Podgórze, without stopping—giving Krakovians a chilling glimpse at the horrifying conditions inside the ghetto.

Getting There: To go directly to Ghetto Heroes' Square, continue through Kazimierz on tram #3 or #24 (described earlier, under "Getting to Kazimierz") to the stop called plac Bohaterow Getta. Or you can ride the tram or walk 10 minutes across the bridge from the end of my Kazimierz Walk.

Ghetto Heroes' Square (Plac Bohaterow Getta)

This unassuming square is the focal point of the visitor's Podgórze. Today the square is filled with a monument consisting of 68 empty

metal chairs—representing the 68,000 people deported from here. This is intended to remind viewers that the Jews of Kazimierz were forced to carry all of their belongings—including furniture— to the ghetto on this side of the river. It was also here that many Jews waited to be sent to extermination camps. The small, gray building at the river end of Ghetto Heroes' Square feels like a train car inside, evocative of the wagons that carried people from here to certain death.

▲Pharmacy Under the Eagle (Apteka pod Orłem)

This small but good museum, on Ghetto Heroes' Square, tells the story of Tadeusz Pankiewicz, a Polish Catholic pharmacist who chose to remain in Podgórze when it became a Jewish ghetto. During this time, the pharmacy was an important meeting point for the ghetto residents, and Pankiewicz and his staff heroically aided and hid Jewish victims of the Nazis. (Pankiewicz survived the war and was later acknowledged by Israel as one of the "Righteous Among the Nations"—non-Jews who risked their lives to help the Nazis' victims during World War II. You'll see his medal on display in the white memorial room at the end of the museum.) Today the pharmacy hosts an exhibit about the Jewish ghetto. You'll enter into the re-created pharmacy, where the "windows" are actually screens that show footage from the era. Push buttons, pull out drawers, answer the phone—it's full of interactive opportunities to better understand what ghetto life was like. You'll learn about people who worked in the pharmacy (including riveting interviews with eye-witnesses—some in English, others subtitled) and hear Pankiewicz telling stories about that tense time. You'll also learn a bit about the pharmacy business from that period.

Cost and Hours: 10 zł; if you're also going to the Schindler's Factory Museum, buy the 23-zł combo-ticket, free on Mon, open Mon 10:00-14:00, Tue-Sun 9:00-17:00, closed the second Tue of each month, plac Bohaterow Getta 18, tel. 12-656-5625, www. mhk.pl/branches/eagle-pharmacy.

▲▲▲Schindler's Factory Museum (Fabryka Emalia Oskara Schindlera)

One of Europe's best museums about the Nazi occupation fills some of the factory buildings where Oskar Schindler and his Jewish employees worked. While the museum tells the story of Schindler and his workers, it broadens its perspective to take in the full experience of all of Kraków during the painful era of Nazi rule—making it the top WWII museum in this country so profoundly affected by that war. It's loaded with in-depth information (all in English), and touchscreens invite you to learn more and watch eyewitness interviews. Scattered randomly between the exhibits are replicas of everyday places from the age—a photographer's shop, a tram car, a hairdresser's salon—designed to give you a taste of 1940s Kraków. Throughout the museum are calendar pages outlining wartime events and giving a sense of chronology. Note that you'll see nothing of the actual factory or equipment, as the threat of the advancing Red Army forced Schindler to move his operation lock, stock, and barrel to Nazi-occupied Czechoslovakia in 1944.

Cost and Hours: 21 zł, 24-zł combo-ticket with next-door Museum of Contemporary Art, 23-zł "Memory Trail" combo-ticket with Pharmacy Under the Eagle; free on Mon; open April-Oct Mon 10:00-16:00 (except closes at 14:00 first Mon of month), Tue-Sun 9:00-20:00; Nov-March Mon 10:00-14:00, Tue-Sun 10:00-18:00; last entry 1.5 hours before closing, tel. 12-257-1017, www.mhk.pl/branches/oskar-schindlers-factory.

Crowd-Beating Tips: Crowds can be a real problem at this popular sight—especially on Mondays (when it's free, and many other museums are closed), during the summer holidays (June-Aug), and midday (usually worst 11:00-16:00). At busy times, you may have to wait in a long line—an hour or more—just to buy a ticket. And then, once inside, congestion can make it challenging to fully appreciate the place. If you anticipate crowds, you can book tickets for no extra fee up to three days before your

KRAKÓW

visit (www.bilety.mhk.pl); or you can buy tickets anytime (even for later the same day) at the Kraków City Museum Visitors Center in the Cloth Hall on the Main Market Square (see "Tourist Information," page 241). But even if you avoid the ticket line, it could still be jammed inside. The best strategy is to arrive early (9:00 or soon after on most days) or late (in summer, arriving by 18:00 gives you two hours to tour the exhibits)—but be warned that if you're arriving late, it's possible on very busy days that all tickets could be sold out.

Getting There: It's in a gloomy industrial area a five-minute walk from Ghetto Heroes' Square (plac Bohaterow Getta): Go up Kącik street (use the pedestrian underpass, then head to the left of the big, glass skyscraper), go under the railroad underpass, and continue two blocks, past MOCAK (the Museum of Contemporary Art in Kraków, described later) to the second big building on the left (ulica Lipowa 4). Look for signs to *Emalia*.

Visiting the Museum: You'll begin on the ground floor, where you'll buy your ticket and have the chance to tour the special exhibits. There's also a "film café" (interesting for fans of the movie) with refreshments. Then head upstairs to the first floor.

First Floor: The 35-minute **film,** called *Lipowa 4* (this building's address), sets the stage with interviews of both Jews and

non-Jews describing their wartime experience (find it just off of the museum's first, circular room; subtitled in English, it runs continuously). From here, the one-way route winds through the permanent exhibit, called **"Kraków Under Nazi Occupation 1939-1945."** First, while idyllic music plays, "stereoscopic" (primitive 3-D) photos of prewar Kraków capture an idyllic age when culture flourished and the city's Jews (more than one-quarter of the population) blended more or less smoothly with their Catholic-Pole neighbors. But then, a video explains the Nazi invasion of Poland in early September of 1939: It took them only a few weeks to overrun the country (which desperately awaited the promised-for help of their British and French allies, who never arrived). Through the next several rooms, watch the film clip of SS soldiers marching through the Main Market Square—renamed "Adolf-Hitler-Platz"—and read stories about how the Nazis' *Generalgouvernement* attempted to reshape the life of its new capital, "Krakau." (Near the tram car, look for the decapitated head of the Grunwald monument—described on page 252—which had been a powerful symbol of a Polish military victory over German forces.)

Oskar Schindler (1908-1974) and His List

Steven Spielberg's instant-classic, Oscar-winning 1993 film, *Schindler's List,* brought the world's attention to the inspiring story of Oskar Schindler, the compassionate German business-man who did his creative best to save the lives of the Jewish work-ers at his factory in Kraków. Spielberg chose to film the story right here in Kazimierz, where the historical events actually unfolded. Today the Schindler's Factory Museum gives visitors the chance to learn not just about the man and his workers, but about the historical context of their story: the Nazi occupation of Poland.

Oskar Schindler was born in 1908 in the Sudetenland (cur-rently part of the Czech Republic, then predominantly German). Early on, he displayed an idiosyncratic interpretation of ethics that earned him both wealth and enemies. As Nazi aggressions escalated, Schindler (who was very much a Nazi) carried out es-pionage against Poland; when Germany invaded the country in 1939, Schindler smelled a business opportunity. Early in the Nazi occupation of Poland, Schindler came to Kraków and lived in an apartment at ulica Straszewskiego 7 (a block from Wawel Cas-tle, but unmarked and not available for tours). He took over the formerly Jewish-owned Emalia factory at ulica Lipowa 4, which produced metal pots and pans that were dipped into protec-tive enamel; later the factory also began producing armaments for the Nazi war effort. The factory was staffed by about 1,000 Jews from the nearby Płaszów Concentration Camp, which was managed by the ruthless SS officer Amon Göth (depicted in *Schindler's List*—based on real events—shooting at camp inmates for sport from his balcony).

At a certain point, Schindler began to sympathize with his Jewish workers, and gradually did what he could to protect them and offer them better lives. Schindler fed them far better than most concentration-camp inmates and allowed them to sell some of the pots and pans they made on the black market to make money. After he saw many of his employees and friends murdered

You'll see the story of a newly German-owned shop selling Nazi propaganda and learn how professors at Kraków's Jagiellonian University were arrested to prevent them from fomenting rebel-lion among their students. During this time, even Polish secondary schools were closed—effectively prohibiting learning among Poles, whom the Nazis considered inferior. But Polish students continued to meet clandestinely with their teachers. You'll also see images of Hans Frank—the hated puppet ruler of Poland—moving into the country's most important symbol of sovereignty, Wawel Castle. The exhibit also details how early Nazi policies targeted Jews with roundups, torture, and execution. (Down the staircase is an eerie simulation of a cellar prison.) As the Nazis ratcheted up their genoduring an SS raid in 1943, he ramped up these efforts. He would come up with bogus paperwork to classify those threatened with deportation as "essential" to the workings of the factory—even if they were unskilled. He sought and was granted permission to build a "concentration camp" barracks for his workers on the factory grounds, where they lived in far better conditions than those at Płaszów. These lucky few became known as Schindlerjuden—"Schindler's Jews."

As the Soviet army encroached on Kraków in October of 1944, word came that the factory would need to be relocated west, farther from the front line. While Schindler could easily have simply turned his workers over to the concentration-camp system and certain death—as most other industrialists did—he decided to bring them with him to his new factory at Brünnlitz (Brněnec, in today's Czech Republic). He assembled a list of 700 men and 300 women who worked with him, along with 200 other Jewish inmates, and at great personal expense, moved them to Brünnlitz. At the new factory, Schindler and the 1,200 people he had saved produced grenades and rocket parts—virtually all of them, the workers later claimed, mysteriously defective.

After the war, Schindler—who had spent much of his fortune protecting his Jewish workers—hopped around Germany and Argentina, repeatedly attempting but failing to break back into business (often with funding from Jewish donors). He died in poverty in 1974. In accordance with his final wishes, he was buried in Jerusalem, and today his grave is piled high with small stones left there by appreciative Jewish visitors. He has since been named one of the "Righteous Among the Nations" for his efforts to save Jews from the Holocaust. Thomas Keneally's 1982 book *Schindler's Ark* brought the industrialist's tale to a wide audience that included Steven Spielberg, who vaulted Schindler to the ranks of a pop-culture icon.

cidal activities, troops swept through Kraków on March 3, 1941, forcing all the remaining Jews in town to squeeze into the newly created Podgórze ghetto. At the bottom of the stairs, look for the huge pile of plunder—Jewish wealth stolen by the Nazis.

Second Floor: Climb upstairs using the long **staircase,** which was immortalized in a powerful scene in *Schindler's List.* At the top of the stairs on the right is a small room that served as "Schindler's office" for the film; more recently, it's been determined that his actual office was elsewhere (we'll see it soon).

You'll walk through a corridor lined by a replica of the wall that enclosed the **Podgórze ghetto** and see poignant exhibits about the horrific conditions there (including a replica of the cramped living quarters). The Nazis claimed that Jews had to be segregated here, away from the general population, because they "carried diseases."

Continue into the office of Schindler's secretary, with exhibits about Schindler's life and video touchscreens that play testimonial

footage of Schindler's grateful employees. Then proceed into the actual **Schindler's office.** The big map (with German names for cities) was uncovered only in recent years when the factory was being restored. Because Schindler's short tenure here was the only time in the factory's history that these Polish place names would appear in German, it's believed that this map was hung over his desk. Facing the map is a giant monument of enamel pots and pans, like those that were made in this factory. There are 1,200 pots—one for each Jewish worker that Schindler saved. Inside the monument, the walls are lined with the names on Schindler's famous list. The creaky floorboards are intentional: a reminder that the Nazis knew every step you took.

Proceeding through the exhibit, you'll learn more about everyday life—both for ghetto dwellers and for everyday non-Jewish

Krakovians, including the Polish resistance (see the Home Army's underground print shop). More eyewitness accounts relate the terrifying days of March 13 and 14, 1943, when the Podgórze ghetto was liquidated, sending survivors to the nearby Płaszów Concentration Camp. The replica of the Płaszów quarry, where inmates were forced

to work in unimaginably difficult conditions, provides a poignant memorial for those who weren't fortunate enough to wind up on Schindler's list.

Now head all the way back down to the ground floor.

Ground Floor: Exhibits here capture the uncertain days near the end of the war in the summer of 1944, when Nazis arrested between 6,000 and 8,000 suspected saboteurs after the Warsaw Uprising, and sent them to Płaszów (see the replica of a basement hideout for 10 Jews who had escaped the ghetto); and later, when many Nazis had fled Kraków, leaving residents to await the Soviet Union's Red Army (see the replica air-raid shelters). The Red Army arrived here on January 18, 1945—at long last, the five years, four months, and twelve days of Nazi rule were over. The Soviets caused their own share of damage to the city before beginning a whole new occupation that would last for generations...but that's a different museum.

Finally, walk along the squishy floor—evoking how life for anyone was unstable and unpredictable during the Nazi occupation—into the **Hall of Choices.** The six rotating pillars tell the stories of people who chose to act—or not to act—when they witnessed atrocities. Think about the ramifications of the choices they made...and what you would have done in their shoes. The final room holds two books: a white book listing those who tried to help, and a black book listing Nazi collaborators. Exiting the museum, notice the portraits of Oscar Schindler's workers who lived long and happy lives after the war.

Nearby: Before heading back to downtown Kraków, consider paying a visit to the superb—and very different—**art museum** that fills the buildings on the factory grounds, behind this main building (described next). Or, for a glass of wine, head just a few doors down from the museum to find the delightful **Krakó Slow Wines** (marked *Lipowa 6F*). This mellow, inviting wine bar and shop is well-stocked with wines mostly from Central and Eastern Europe (daily 10:00-22:00, mobile 669-225-222, www.krakoslowwines.pl).

▲Museum of Contemporary Art in Kraków (Muzeum Sztuki Współczesnej w Krakowie)

Called "MOCAK" for short, this museum exhibits a changing array of innovative and thought-provoking works by contempo-

rary artists, often with heavy themes tied to the surrounding Holocaust sites. With the slogan *Kunst macht frei* ("Art will set you free"—a pointed spin on the Nazis' *Arbeit macht frei* concentration-camp motto), the museum occupies warehouse buildings once filled by Schindler's workers. Now converted to wide-open, bright-white halls, the buildings house many temporary exhibits as well as two permanent ones (the MOCAK Collection in the basement, and the library in the smaller side building). Pick up the floor plan as you enter. It's all well-described in English, and engaging even for those who don't usually like modern art.

Cost and Hours: 10 zł, 24-zł combo-ticket with next-door Schindler's Factory Museum, free on Tue, open Tue-Sun 11:00-

KRAKÓW

19:00, closed Mon, last entry one hour before closing, Lipowa 4, tel. 12-263-4001, www.mocak.pl.

Sights Outside of Kraków

Along with the St. John Paul II pilgrimage sights (best suited for believers), there are other interesting sights outside of town—an impressive salt mine, a purpose-built communist town, and an unusual earthwork. All require a bus or tram ride to reach.

ST. JOHN PAUL II AND PILGRIMAGE SIGHTS

Pilgrims coming to Kraków eager to walk in the footsteps of St. John Paul II are sometimes disappointed by the low number of actual museums relating to the man in the city center (though the churches affiliated with him are dazzling). However, there are worthwhile sights outside the city: the John Paul II Sanctuary on the outskirts of Kraków; and the John Paul II Family Home Museum in the town of Wadowice, an hour's drive away (and covered later).

Sanctuaries in Kraków

The two biggest, most impressive JPII destinations are about four miles south of Kraków's Old Town, in the Łagiewniki neighborhood. While the main attraction here for pilgrims is the John Paul II Sanctuary, historically and geographically you'll come first to the Divine Mercy Sanctuary—so I've covered that first. The sights aren't worth the trek for the merely curious, but they offer a glimpse of the powerful reverence and deep faith that characterizes the Polish people. If you're a pilgrim—or think you might be one—visiting these sights can be worthwhile; to make the most of your time, consider hiring a driver or a local guide with a car (see page 246).

Getting There: Public transportation from central Kraków is workable, but not ideal. (As these connections are still in flux, it's smart to ask about the best connection at the TI before making the trip.) The easiest public-transit route is to take **tram #8** (which loops around the Old Town, including stops next to St. Francis Basilica at plac Wszystkich Świętych, and near Wawel Castle) to the Divine Mercy Sanctuary (Sanktuarium Bożego Miłosierdzia stop)—about 30 minutes. From the tram stop, you'll huff a few minutes uphill along the wall to find the entrance to the complex. After touring the Divine Mercy sights, you can cross a footbridge to the St. John Paul II Sanctuary. A **taxi** or **Uber** from downtown costs around 30-40 zł one-way and takes 20-30 minutes.

Divine Mercy Sanctuary
(Sanktuarium Bożego Miłosierdzia)

This complex, built around a humble red-brick convent, honors the early-20th-century St. Faustina, who saw a miraculous vision of Jesus that became a powerful religious symbol for many Catholics. Today, pilgrims from around the world come here to revere the relics both of Faustina and of John Paul II (who advocated for her sainthood), and to learn more about her story from the convent's present-day sisters—many of whom speak English.

Background: One cold and blustery evening in 1931, Sister Faustina Kowalska (1905-1938) answered the convent doorbell to find a beggar asking for some food. Faustina brought some soup to the man, who revealed his true nature: a figure of Jesus Christ clad in a white robe, with one hand raised in blessing, and the other touching his chest. Emanating from his chest were twin beams of light: red (representing blood, the life of souls) and white (water, which through baptism washes souls righteously clean). Transformed by her experience, Faustina worked with an artist to create a painted version of the image—called the Divine Mercy—which has been embraced by Polish Catholics as one of the most important symbols of their faith.

Always frail in health, Faustina died at 33—the same age as Jesus. The story of Faustina deeply moved a young Karol Wojtyła. When he became pope, he dedicated the first Sunday after Easter as the day of Divine Mercy worldwide. In 2000, he made his fellow Krakovian the first Catholic saint of the third millennium. To properly revere the newly important St. Faustina, a bold, futuristic church and visitors center was built alongside her original convent.

Cost and Hours: All three parts of the complex—the smaller original chapel, a replica of Faustina's cell, and the huge, modern church, with its soaring bell tower—are free to enter, but donations are happily accepted. Each one has slightly different hours (listed later).

Visiting the Complex: Entering the complex through the side gate, you'll come up a **walkway** with flags from around the world, and plaques translating the Divine Mercy's message—"Jesus, I trust in you"—in dozens of languages.

Just before entering the **original chapel,** look up and to the right—the window with the flowers marks the cell where Faustina died. Inside the chapel (daily 6:00-21:15), the altar to the left of the

KRAKÓW

main altar displays an early copy of Faustina's Divine Mercy painting. Her relics are in the white case just below; in the white kneeler just in front of the chapel, notice the little reliquary holding one of her bones (which worshippers can embrace as they pray).

Leaving the chapel, turn left and go to the far end of the accommodations building. Enter the door on the right (follow signs for *Cela Św. Siostry Faustyny*) to find the **replica of Faustina's cell.** While this is a newer building, here they've created Faustina's convent cell, including many of her personal effects. Drop a coin in the slot for an evocative headphone description of these items, and of the vision of Jesus that put her convent on the map (usually open daily 8:30-18:00).

Dominating the campus is the futuristic, glass-and-steel **main church.** Consecrated by Pope John Paul II on his final visit to Poland in 2002, this building has several parts (daily 7:00-20:00). The lower level has a variety of small chapels, each one donated by Catholic worshippers in a different country (Germany, Hungary, Slovakia, and so on)—and each with a dramatically different style. The central chapel on this level has a modern altar and another bone of St. Faustina. Upstairs, the main sanctuary is a sleek cylindrical space with wooden sunbeams sharply radiating from the altar area. That altar—framed by the gnarled limbs of windblown trees, representing the suffering of human existence—contains a replica of the Divine Mercy painting, flanked by the woman who saw the vision (Faustina, on the right) and the Polish pope who made it a worldwide phenomenon (John Paul II, on the left).

Head back out to the terrace surrounding the church. The bold **tower**—as tall as St. Mary's on Main Market Square, and with a statue of John Paul II at the bottom—has an elevator that you can ride up to a glassed-in viewpoint offering panoramas over the Divine Mercy campus, the adjacent John Paul II Sanctuary complex, and—on the distant horizon—the spires of Wawel Cathedral and Kraków's Old Town. Near the base of the tower is a **canopy** where Mass is said on Divine Mercy Sunday each year, before a crowd of 100,000 who fill the fields below.

From here, it's about a 15-minute walk to the next sight (you'll pay a small fee to cross the "Bridge of Mercy," which spans a scenic gorge).

John Paul II Sanctuary (Sanktuarium Jana Pawła II)

This new complex, funded entirely by private donors, celebrates the life and sainthood of Kraków's favorite son. Construction is ongoing, but for now there are at least two sections of the complex worth visiting: the sanctuary and museum.

Cost and Hours: Sanctuary—free, daily 7:30-19:00, until 18:00 in winter, www.sanktuariumjp2.pl; museum—7 zł, Wed-Sat 10:00-16:00, Sun 10:00-15:00, closed Mon-Tue.

Sanctuary of St. John Paul II: This hypermodern church is big and splendid. In the **downstairs** area, the central chapel features paintings of JPII's papal visits to various pilgrimage sites, both in Poland (Częstochowa) and abroad (Fátima, Lourdes). Most of the chapels ringing the outside have different depictions of the Virgin Mary. Find the chapel that's a replica of the St. Leonard's Crypt under Wawel Cathedral—where a young priest named Karol Wojtyła celebrated his first Mass. In this chapel, you'll see JPII's empty papal tomb from the crypt beneath St. Peter's Basilica at the Vatican. (When he became a saint, his remains—which, controversially, are kept in Rome rather than his homeland—were moved up into the main part of the church, and this simple grave marker was donated to this church.) You'll also see a reliquary in the shape of a book with fluttering pages, holding a small amount of John Paul II's blood (for the story of the book, see page 271). This blood was kept in secret by JPII's personal secretary, only revealed after his death, when it was divvied up among a select few churches. In another chapel, you'll find the tombs of a few recent cardinals; as they're running out of space below Wawel Cathedral, this chapel is poised to handle the overflow. And in yet another chapel, you'll see finely executed reliefs in rock salt, in the style of Wieliczka Salt Mine.

Head upstairs to the sleek, modern **main sanctuary.** The concrete structure supports large walls, providing a canvas for dynamic

mosaics of Bible stories. Above the main altar, in the middle, you'll see the Three Kings delivering their gifts to the Baby Jesus and the Virgin Mary—with St. John Paul II serenely overlooking the scene. In the back-left corner, a smaller chapel focuses on a painting of St. John Paul II; in the hazy background, you can see the dome of St. Peter's at the Vatican (left) and the twin spires of St. Mary's in Kraków (right)—driving home the point that although John Paul II belonged to the world, first and foremost he's considered a son of Kraków and of Poland.

KRAKÓW

The sanctuary anchors a sprawling complex of conference facilities and other attractions for pilgrims. Poke around. The museum, described next, is the sight most worth visiting.

St. John Paul II Museum: This collects the many gifts bestowed on the beloved pope (African carved masks and ivory tusks; Latin American tapestries; the key to the city of Long Branch, New Jersey; and a pair of glass doves of peace given to him—perhaps with a touch of irony—by US Vice President Dick Cheney); ornate worship aids (chalices, crosses, and so on); and modern art that celebrates the modern pope and his life's work. There are also personal items, from his papal ski gear to the place settings from his Vatican dinner table to his stylish red leather shoes. You'll also see the throne from his last visit to Poland in 2002, and a replica of the humble room across the street from St. Francis Basilica where he stayed on visits back to his homeland.

John Paul II Sights in Wadowice

Karol Wojtyła was born and lived up until age 18 in Wadowice (VAH-doh-veet-seh), about 30 miles (a one-hour drive) southwest of Kraków. As it's roughly in the same direction as Auschwitz, a local guide or driver can help you connect both places for one busy day of contrasts. Visiting by public bus or minibus is possible (about 1.25 hours one-way); ask the TI for details.

The lovely town of Wadowice (about 20,000 people) has a quaint and beautifully restored main square with a pretty Baroque steeple. John Paul II pilgrims find it worth a visit to see the **John Paul II Family Home Museum,** which fills four floors of the tenement building where his family lived through his adolescence. You'll explore a multimedia overview of the life and times of one of the newest Catholic saints, including rooms of the family home, a collection of clothing and other articles that belonged to JPII, photographs and video clips of his life and of the tumultuous period in which he lived, and plenty of interactive displays to bring the entire story to life. Admission is limited, and you'll be accompanied the entire time. Ideally, time your visit to go with an English guide (typically 2/day, likely at 11:00 and 14:00—but confirm online or by phone); otherwise, you'll join the Polish tour. Either way, the tour can be a bit rushed, with less time to linger over the exhibits than you might like (20 zł with a Polish guide, or 30 zł with English guide, free and crowded on Tue; open daily May-Sept 9:00-19:00, April and Oct 9:00-18:00, Nov-March 9:00-16:00, closed the last Tue of each month, last entrance 1.5 hours before closing, across the street from the town church at ulica Kościelna 7, tel. 33-823-2662, www.homejp2.com).

MORE SIGHTS OUTSIDE OF KRAKÓW
▲▲Wieliczka Salt Mine (Kopalnia Soli Wieliczka)

Wieliczka (veel-EECH-kah), a salt mine 10 miles southeast of Kraków, is beloved by Poles. Deep beneath the ground, the mine is filled with sculptures that miners have lovingly carved out of the salt. You'll explore this unique gallery—learning both about the art and about medieval mining tech-niques—on a required tour. Though the sight is a bit overrated, it's unique and practically obligatory if you're in Kraków for a few days. In my experi-ence with tour groups, about half the people love Wieliczka, while half feel it's a waste of time—but it can be hard to predict which half you're in. Read the description here carefully before you decide. And expect a lot of walk-ing.

Cost and Hours: The standard "tourist route" costs 84 zł and is by guided tour only. The mine is open April-Oct 7:30-18:00, Nov-March 9:00-17:00 (these are last tour times). English-language tours leave every 30 minutes in the morning (10:00-13:00) and all day in summer (June-Sept), and otherwise depart hourly. They also have other routes that are more in-depth (such as the interactive "Miner's Route," where visitors wear coveralls and helmets and actually operate some of the old equipment); for details on these, see the website. The mine is in the town of Wieliczka at ulica Daniłowicza 10 (tel. 12-278-7302, www.kopalnia.pl).

You'll pay an extra 10 zł for permission to use your camera—but be warned that flash photos often don't turn out, thanks to the irregular reflection of the salt crystals. Dress warmly—the mine is a constant 57 degrees Fahrenheit. Before entering, you'll have to check large bags and go through a security checkpoint.

Your ticket includes a dull **mine museum** at the end of the tour. It adds an hour to the mine tour and is discouraged by locals ("1.5 miles more walking, colder, more of the same"). Make it clear when you buy your ticket that you're not interested in the museum.

You can buy your tickets—and an appointed entry time—at the **Wieliczka Promotion Office,** in Kraków's Old Town (Mon-Fri 9:00-17:00, closed Sat-Sun, Wiślna 12a).

Getting There: The salt mine is 10 miles from Kraków. By far the easiest option is to hop on the **train** at Kraków's main train station (track 3, 2/hour, 3 zł, takes 20 minutes, get off at Wieliczka Rynek-Kopalnia and walk 5-10 minutes to the mine). In a pinch,

KRAKÓW

you can take **bus #304** (at Kurniki stop across from church near Galeria Krakowska mall) or a **minibus,** but these take longer (40 minutes)—get details at the TI. **Private drivers** also make this trip (see page 247).

Background: Wieliczka Salt Mine has been producing salt since at least the 13th century. Under Kazimierz the Great, one-third of Poland's income came from these precious deposits. Wieliczka miners spent much of their lives underground, leaving for work before daybreak and returning after sundown, rarely emerging into daylight. To pass the time, and to immortalize their national pride and religiosity in art, 19th-century miners began to carve figures, chandeliers, and eventually even an elaborate chapel out of the salt. Until a few years ago, the mine still produced salt. Today's miners—about 400 of them—primarily work on maintaining the 200 miles of chambers. This entire network is supported by wooden beams (because metal would rust).

Visiting the Mine: From the lobby, your guide leads you 380 steps down a winding staircase. From this spot you begin a 1.5-mile stroll, generally downhill (more than 800 steps down altogether), past 20 of the mine's 2,000 chambers (with signs explaining when they were dug), finishing 443 feet below the surface. When you're done, an elevator beams you back up.

The tour shows how the miners lived and worked, using horses who spent their whole adult lives without ever seeing the light of day. It takes you through vast underground caverns, past subterranean lakes, and introduces you to some of the mine's many sculptures (including one of Copernicus—who actually visited here in the 15th century—as well as an army of salt elves, and this region's favorite son, St. John Paul II). Your jaw will drop as you enter the enormous **Chapel of St. Kinga,** carved over three decades in the early 20th century. Look for the salt-relief carving of

the Last Supper (its 3-D details are astonishing, considering it's just six inches deep). You'll end your visit with a five-minute multimedia show.

While advertised as two hours, your tour finishes in a deep-down shopping zone 1.5 hours after you started (they hope you'll hang out and shop). Note when the next elevator departs (just 3/hour), and you can be outta there on the next lift. Zip through the shopping zone in two minutes, or step over the rope and be immediately in line for the great escape (you'll be escorted quite some distance to the elevator, into which you'll be packed like mine workers).

Nearby: Near the parking lot, you'll see the **"Graduation Tower,"** a modern fort-like structure with a wooden walkway up top. The tower is designed to evaporate and then condense the supposedly very healthy brine from deep underground. The resulting moist, salty air is used to treat patients with lung problems. While locals are actually prescribed visits here, for most tourists it's not worth the extra money.

▲Nowa Huta

Nowa Huta (NOH-vah HOO-tah, "New Steel Works"), an enormous planned workers' town, offers a glimpse into the stark, grand-scale aesthetics of the communists. Because it's five miles east of central Kraków and a little tricky to see on your own, skip it unless you're determined—it can be tricky to appreciate. But architects and communist sympathizers may want to make a pilgrimage here.

Getting There: Tram #4 goes from near Kraków's Old Town (catch the tram on the ring road near Kraków's main train station, at the Dworzec Główny stop) along John Paul II Avenue (aleja Jana Pawła II) to Nowa Huta's main square, plac Centralny (about 30 minutes total), then continues a few minutes farther to the main gate of the Tadeusz Sendzimir Steelworks—the end of the line. From there it returns to plac Centralny and back to Kraków.

Tours: True to its name, Mike Ostrowski's **Crazy Guides** is a loosely run operation that takes tourists to Nowa Huta in genuine communist-era vehicles (mostly Trabants and Polski Fiats). If you've got an interest in the history—and would enjoy spending the day careening around the streets of Kraków in a car that feels like a cardboard box with a lawnmower engine—hire one of their laid-back hipster guides (139 zł/person for 2.5-hour "communism tour" of Nowa Huta; 179 zł/person for 4-hour "communism deluxe" tour

that also includes lunch at a milk bar and a visit to their period-decorated communist apartment; other options available—described on website, mobile 500-091-200, www.crazyguides.com, info@crazyguides.com). If you're already hiring a **local guide** in Kraków, consider paying a little extra to add a couple of hours for a short side-trip by car to Nowa Huta.

Background: Nowa Huta was the communists' idea of paradise. It's one of only three towns outside the Soviet Union that were custom-built to showcase socialist ideals. (The others are Dunáu-

KRAKÓW

jváros—once called Sztálinváros—south of Budapest, Hungary; and Eisenhüttenstadt—once called Stalinstadt—near Brandenburg, Germany.) Completed in just 10 years (1949-1959), Nowa Huta was built primarily because the Soviets felt that smart and sassy Kraków needed a taste of heavy industry. Farmers and villagers were imported to live and work in Nowa Huta. Many of the new residents, who weren't accustomed to city living, brought along their livestock (which grazed in the fields around unfinished buildings). For commies, it was downright idyllic: Dad would cheerily ride the tram into the steel factory, mom would dutifully keep house, and the kids could splash around at the man-made beach and learn how to cut perfect red stars out of construction paper. But Krakovians had the last laugh: Nowa Huta, along with Lech Wałęsa's shipyard in Gdańsk, was one of the home bases of the Solidarity strikes that eventually brought down the regime. Now, with the communists long gone, Nowa Huta remains a major suburb of Poland's cultural capital, with a whopping 200,000 residents.

Touring Nowa Huta: Nowa Huta's focal point used to be known simply as **Central Square** (plac Centralny), but in a fit of poetic justice, it was recently renamed for the anticommunist Ronald Reagan. A map of Nowa Huta looks like a clamshell: a semicircular design radiating from Central/Reagan Square. Numbered streets fan out like spokes on a wheel, and trolleys zip workers directly to the immense factory.

Believe it or not, the inspiration for Nowa Huta was the Renaissance (which, thanks to the textbook Renaissance design of the Cloth Hall and other landmarks, Soviet architects considered typically Polish). Notice the elegantly predictable arches and galleries that would make Michelangelo proud. The settlement was loosely planned on the gardens of Versailles (comparing aerial views of those two very different sites—both with axes radiating from a central hub—this becomes clear). When first built (before it was layered with grime), Nowa Huta was delightfully orderly, primly painted, impeccably maintained, and downright beautiful... if a little boring. It was practical, too: Each of the huge apartment blocks is a self-contained unit, with its own grassy inner courtyard, school, and shops. Driveways (which appear to dead-end at underground garage doors) lead to vast fallout shelters.

Today's Nowa Huta—while gentrifying—is a far cry from its glory days. Wander around. Poke into the courtyards. Reflect on what it would be like to live here. It may not be as bad as you imagine. Ugly as they may seem from the outside, these buildings are packed with happy little apartments filled with color, light, and warmth.

The wide boulevard running northeast of Central/Reagan Square, now called Solidarity Avenue (aleja Solidarności, lined with tracks for tram #4), leads to the **Tadeusz Sendzimir Steelworks.** Originally named for Lenin, this factory was supposedly built using plans stolen from a Pittsburgh plant. It was designed to be a cog in the communist machine—reliant on iron ore from Ukraine, and therefore worthless unless Poland remained in the Soviet Bloc. Down from as many as 40,000 workers at its peak, the steelworks now employs only about 10,000. Today there's little to see other than the big sign, stern administration buildings, and smokestacks in the distance. Examine the twin offices flanking the sign—topped with turrets and a decorative frieze inspired by Italian palazzos, these continue the Renaissance theme of the housing districts.

Another worthwhile sight in Nowa Huta is the **Lord's Ark Church** (Arka Pana, several blocks northwest of Central/Reagan

Square on ulica Obrońców Krzyża). Back when he was archbishop of Kraków, Karol Wojtyła fought for years to build a church in this most communist of communist towns. When the regime refused, he insisted on conducting open-air Masses before crowds in fields—until the communists finally capitulated. Consecrated on May 15, 1977, the Lord's Ark Church has a Le Corbusier–esque design that looks like a fat, exhausted Noah's Ark resting on Mount Ararat—encouraging Poles to persevere through the floods of communism. While architecturally interesting, the church is mostly significant as a symbol of an early victory of Catholicism over communism.

▲Kościuszko Mound (Kopiec Kościuszki)

On a sunny day, the parklands west of the Old Town are a fine place to get out of the city and commune with Krakovians at play. On the outskirts of town is the Kościuszko Mound, a nearly perfectly conical hill erected in 1823 to honor Polish and American military hero Tadeusz Kościuszko. The mound incorporates soil that was brought here from battlefields where the famous general fought, both in Poland and in the American Revolution. Later, under Habsburg rule, a citadel with a chapel was built around the mound, which provided a fine lookout over this otherwise flat terrain. And more recently, the hill was reinforced with steel and cement to prevent it from eroding away. You'll pay to enter the walls and walk to the top—up a curlicue path that makes the mound resemble a giant soft-serve cone—and inside you'll find a modest Kościuszko museum. While not too exciting, this is a pleasant place for an excursion on a nice day.

Cost and Hours: 12 zł, includes museum, mound open daily 9:00-dusk, Fri-Sun until 23:00 in May-Sept, museum open daily 9:30-18:30—less off-season, café, tel. 12-425-1116, www.kopieckosciuszki.pl.

Getting There: Ride tram #1 or #6 (from in front of the Wyspiański Pavilion or the main post office) to the end of the line, called Salvator. From here, you can either follow the well-marked path uphill for 20 minutes, or hop on bus #100 to the top (runs at :10 past each hour).

Shopping in Kraków

Two of the most popular Polish souvenirs—amber and pottery—come from areas far from Kraków. You won't find any great bargains on those items here, but several shops specializing in them are listed below. Somewhat more local are the many wood carvings you'll see.

The **Cloth Hall,** smack-dab in the center of the Main Market Square, is the most convenient place to pick up any Polish souvenirs. It has a great selection at respectable prices (summer Mon-Fri 9:00-18:00, Sat-Sun 9:00-15:00, sometimes later; winter Mon-Fri 9:00-16:00, Sat-Sun 9:00-15:00).

Here are some other souvenir ideas, and neighborhoods or streets that are particularly enjoyable for browsing.

Jewelry

The popular **amber** *(bursztyn)* you'll see sold around town is found on northern Baltic shores; if you're also heading to Gdańsk, wait until you get there (for more on amber, see page 458). One unique alternative that's a bit more local is **"striped flint"** *(krzemień pasiasty)*, a stratified stone that's polished to a high shine. It's mined in a very specific subregion near Kraków, and has become popular recently among Hollywood celebrities. Each piece has its own unique wavy, sandy patterns.

Jewelry shops abound in the Old Town. For a good selection of striped flint, amber, and other jewelry, try the no-name shop on **plac Mariacki,** the little square facing the side entrance of St. Mary's Church; they also have a selection of Polish folk costumes in the basement (at #9). A few more jewelry and design shops cluster along Sławkowska street, which runs north from the Main Market Square. **Galeria Skarbiec** ("Treasury"), two blocks south of the Main Market Square, is another good choice, with a stylish, upscale vibe (Grodzka 35).

Polish Pottery

"Polish pottery," with distinctive blue-and-white designs, is made in the region of Silesia, west of Kraków (mostly in the town of

Bolesławiec). But, assuming you won't be going there, you can browse one of the shops in Kraków. **Ceramika Bolesławiecka,** on a busy urban street between the Old Town and Kazimierz, has a tasteful, affordable selection of pottery that's oriented more for locals than tourists (closed Sun, Starowiślna 37). In the Old Town—and with inflated prices to match—two places face each other across Sławkowska street, just a block north of the Square: **Dekor Art** at #11 and **Mila** at #14.

Foods, Drinks, and Cosmetics

Krakowski Kredens is a handy, well-curated shop for overpriced but good-quality traditional foods from Kraków and the surrounding region, Galicia. While the deli case in the back is a pricey place to shop for a picnic (head for a supermarket instead), this is a good chance to stock up on souvenir-quality Polish foods for the folks back home. They have several locations around Kraków—and elsewhere in Poland—but one handy branch is just steps south of the Main Market Square down Grodzka, at #7 (www.krakowskikredens.pl).

Szambelan, a block south of the Main Market Square, is a fun concept for vodka lovers: Peruse the giant casks of three dozen different flavored vodkas, buy an empty bottle, and they'll fill and seal it to take home (Gołębia 2 at the corner with Bracka).

Mydlarnia u Franciszka, with a few locations around Kraków (including a handy one just south of the Main Market Square at Gołębia 2), sells a variety of fragrant local soaps, lotions, shampoos, and other cosmetics, some produced locally.

T-Shirts

Two creative shops in the Old Town sell souvenir T-shirts that are a step up in quality (and price) from the generic shops on the square. **Chrum** specializes in locally themed ironic T-shirts (closed Sun, across the street from the Barbican at plac Matejki 3, www.chrum.com), while **Red is Bad** sticks with tasteful, classic Polish eagles and flags on quality materials (just west of the Square at Szewska 25, www.redisbad.pl).

Stolarska Street

The relatively undiscovered, traffic-free Stolarska street—just a block off of the Main Market Square—is a fine place to stroll day or night, and to browse for gifts. (For more on this street, see page 342 in "Eating in Kraków.") Wander the street from north (Small Market Square) to south (Dominican Church) and window-shop. A few fun places are in the covered arcade on the left, after the Herring Embassy. One of the most interesting is **Galeria Plakatu Kraków,** a print, poster, and postcard shop with a wide variety of engaging images, from commie-retro to contemporary arts to

KRAKÓW

unique Polish variations on American movie posters (closed Sun, Stolarska 8-10). Nearby are an antique bookstore and a pottery art gallery.

Designer Shops along Ulica Józefa, in Kazimierz

As the epicenter of Kraków's hipster scene, Kazimierz is the best place in town to browse one-off boutiques (both design and fashion). Several good options line up along ulica Józefa, mostly concentrated along a two-block stretch. Head just one block south from plac Nowy on Estery street, turn right, and keep an eye out for these options (mostly on the left side of the street): **Blazko,** at #11, has some modern, colorful jewelry, handmade right on the premises. A few doors down **Galerie d'Art Naïf** features fascinating works by untrained artists, and (next door) **Deccoria Galeria** feels like a junk shop, cluttered with handmade jewelry, art, accessories, and vintage clothes. Next are **Panon Nonchalant,** with Polish fashion, and a vintage shop. **Art Factory,** at #9, is worth a browse for colorful jewelry, accessories, and housewares by local designers. **Pracownia** ("Lab"), farther down and also at #9, sells handmade art, jewelry, and clothes. And more clothes by Polish designers are across the street at **Nuumi Boutique** (#14).

A couple of blocks away, just off plac Wolnica, is another great spot for local design, housewares, jewelry and casual fashion (i.e., creative T-shirts): **Idea Fix** and **The Hive Store,** which share a storefront at Bocheńska 7 (daily).

Shopping Malls

Two enormous shopping malls lie just beyond the tourist zone. The gigantic **Galeria Krakowska,** with 270 shops, shares a square with the train station (Mon-Sat 9:00-22:00, Sun 10:00-21:00, has a kids' play area upstairs from the main entry). Only slightly smaller is **Galeria Kazimierz** (Mon-Sat 10:00-21:00, Sun until 20:00, just a few blocks east of the Kazimierz sights, along the river at Podgórska 24). A small but swanky mall called **Pasaż 13** is a few steps off the southeast corner of the Main Market Square, where Grodzka street enters the Square. Enter the mall under the balcony marked *Pasaż 13.* You'll find a cool brick-industrial interior, with upscale international chains...and not much that's Polish (Mon-Sat 11:00-21:00, Sun until 17:00).

Entertainment in Kraków

As a town full of both students and tourists, Kraków has plenty of fun options, especially at night.

IN THE OLD TOWN

For locations of the following places, see the map on page 326.

Main Market Square

Intoxicating as the Square is by day, it's even better at night...pure enchantment. Have a meal or nurse a drink at an outdoor café, or just grab a bench and enjoy the scene. There's often live al fresco music coming from somewhere (either at restaurants, at a temporary stage set up near the Town Hall Tower, or from talented buskers). You could spend hours doing slow laps around the Square after dark, and never run out of diversions. For a great view over the Square at twilight, nurse a drink at **Café Szał**—on the Cloth Hall's upper terrace (long hours, enter through Gallery of 19th-Century Polish Art).

Concerts

You'll find a wide range of musical events, from tourist-oriented Chopin concerts and classical "greatest hits" selections in quaint old ballrooms and churches, to folk-dancing shows, to serious philharmonic performances. Several companies offer competing concerts; some of the best-established include www.cracowconcerts. com, www.newculture.pl, www.facebook.com/orkiestrasm, and www.orfeusz.eu. The free, monthly *Karnet* cultural-events book lists everything (also online at www.karnet.krakow.pl). Because the offerings change from week to week, inquire locally about what's on during your visit. Hotel lobbies are stocked with fliers, but to get all of your options, visit the TI north of the Square on ulica Św. Jana, which specializes in cultural events (they can book tickets for most concerts with no extra fee, and can tell you how to get tickets for the others).

Popular Classical Concerts: The three main choices are organ concerts in churches (usually at 17:00); orchestral or chamber music; or Chopin (either can happen anytime between 18:00 and 20:00). The going rate for any concert is 60 zł. Many are held in churches (such as **Sts. Peter and Paul** on ulica Grodzka, **St. Adalbert** on the Square, **St. Bernadino's/Bernardynów** near Wawel Castle, **St. Idziego/Giles** near Wawel Castle, or the **Piarist Church of the Transfiguration** at the northern end of the Old Town). You'll also find concerts in fancy mansions on or near the Main Market Square (including the **Polonia House/Dom Polonii** at #14, near ulica Grodzka; the **Chopin Gallery**—also billed as the **Royal Chamber Orchestra Hall**—just up Sławkowska street from the Square at #14; and the **Bonerowski Palace** near the top of the Square at ulica Św. Jana 1). Occasionally in summer, they're also held in various gardens around town (July-Aug only, as part of a festival).

Folk Music: Two different venues present dinner shows in the old center. At both, a small, hardworking ensemble of colorfully costumed Krakovian singers, dancers, and musicians put on a fun

KRAKÓW

Kraków's Old Town Shopping & Entertainment

OLD MARKET

PADEREWSKIEGO

DŁUGA

BARBICAN

FLORIAN GATE

20

CZARTORYSKI MUSEUM

SŁAWKOWSKA

PIJARSKA

ŚW. MARKA

23

29

ŚW. JANA

FLORIAŃSKA

SZPITALNA

ŚW. TOMASZA

KARMELICKA

GARBARSKA

ŁOBZOWSKA

ASNYKA

DUNAJEWSKIEGO

Planty

200 Meters
200 Yards

KRUPNICZA

#24 Teater Bagately

T

SZCZEPAŃSKA

OLD

6

5

P

SZOŁAYSKI HOUSE

22

Main Market Square

25

ST. MARY'S

Small Market Square

28

STUDENSKA

JABŁONOWSKICH

PILSUDSKIEGO

SMOLENSK

To Airport, Auschwitz & Kościuszko Mound

PODWALE

SZEWSKA

ŚW. ANNY

JAGIELLOŃSKA

10

COLLEGIUM MAIUS

26

CLOTH HALL

1

MICKIEWICZ STATUE

17

27

2

TOWN HALL TOWER

21

15

7

SIENNA

SIENNA

OLSZEWSKIEGO

GOŁĘBIA

8

WIŚLNA

BRACKA

GRODZKA

ARCH-BISHOP'S MANSION

#8 plac Wszystkich Świętych

11

DOMINICAN CHURCH

WC

DOMINIKAŃSKA

TOWN

FRANCISZKAŃSKA

T

ST. FRANCIS

WYSPIAŃSKI PAVILION

3

MILK BAR

SENACKA

POSELSKA

Planty

STRASZEWSKIEGO

ZWIERZYNIECKA

FELICJANEK

Mary Mag. Square

BISHOP ERAZM CIOŁEK PALACE

ARCHDIOCESAN MUSEUM

WIŚLNA

GRODZKA

STS. PETER & PAUL

16

ST. ANDREW'S

JOHN PAUL II CENTER

19

ŚW. GERTRUDY

SAKEGO

24

FOWISLE

PODZAMCZE

CATHEDRAL

WAWEL HILL

LOST WAWEL MUSEUM

INNER COURTYARD

ŚW. IDZIEGO

18

ST. BERNARDINO'S

STRADOMSKA

BERNARDYŃSKA

Vistula River

DRAGON STATUE

KONOPNICKIEJ

KOLETEK

To 30

Shopping

1. Cloth Hall
2. Plac Mariacki Jewelry
3. Galeria Skarbiec
4. Ceramika Bolesławiecka
5. Dekor Art
6. Mila & Chopin Gallery/Royal Chamber Orchestra Hall
7. Krakowski Kredens
8. Szambelan & Mydlarnia u Franciszka
9. Chrum
10. Red is Bad
11. Galeria Plakatu Kraków
12. To Ulica Józefa Shops
13. Galeria Krakowska
14. Galeria Kazimierz
15. Pasaż 13 Mall

Entertainment

16. Sts. Peter and Paul Church
17. St. Adalbert Church
18. St. Bernadino's/Bernardynów
19. St. Idziego/Giles Church
20. Piarist Church of the Transfiguration
21. Polonia House/Dom Polonii
22. Bonerowski Palace
23. Jama Michalika
24. Hotel Royal (bus to Skansen Smaków)
25. Jazz Club u Muniaka
26. Harris Piano Jazz Bar
27. Buddha Nightclub
28. Vodka Café Bar
29. Staropolskie Trunki (Vodka Tasting)
30. To Forum Przestrzenie

KRAKÓW

little folk show. While the food, the space, and the clientele are all quite tired, it's a nice taste of Polish folk traditions—and the performers try hard to involve members of the audience in the polkas and circle dances. One option is in the historic **Jama Michalika,** with its dusty old Art Nouveau interior right along Floriańska street (85 zł includes dinner; Wed, Fri, and Sun at 19:00; Floriańska 45, mobile 604-093-570, www.cracowconcerts.com). A similar option is in the more modern **Tradycyja Restaurant,** right on the Main Market Square (at #15; 60 zł for just the show, or 120 zł to add dinner; Sat at 19:00; mobile 602-850-900, www.newculture.pl).

For a more serious folk music performance—and to really make an evening of it—consider a show in a more rustic setting just outside of town. The restaurant **Skansen Smaków,** filling a log cabin-like building, has shows each Thursday night. You'll meet the bus at the Hotel Royal near Wawel Castle at 18:30, ride to the restaurant, have a traditional Polish feast during the show, then be brought back home to the Old Town at 22:00 (100 zł, book ahead, tel. 600-349-429, www.skansensmakow.pl).

Jazz

Kraków has a surprisingly thriving jazz scene. Several popular clubs hide on the streets surrounding the Main Market Square (open nightly, most shows start around 21:30, sometimes free or a cover of 10-25 zł for better shows). **Jazz Club u Muniaka** is the most famous and best for all-around jazz in a sophisticated cellar environment (ulica Floriańska 3, tel. 12-423-1205). **Harris Piano Jazz Bar,** right on the Square (at #28), is more casual and offers a mix of traditional and updated "fusion" jazz, plus blues (tel. 12-421-5741, www.harris.krakow.pl).

Nightlife in the Old Town

The entire Old Town is crammed with nightclubs and discos pumping loud music on weekends. On a Saturday, the pedestrian streets can be more crowded at midnight than at noon. However, with the exception of the jazz clubs mentioned earlier, most of the nightspots in the Old Town are garden-variety dance clubs, completely lacking the personality and creativity of the Kazimierz nightspots described next. Worse, to save money, young locals stand out in front of nightclubs to drink their own booze (BYOB), rather than pay high prices for the drinks inside—making the streets that much more crowded and noisy. For low-key hanging out, people choose a café on the Square; otherwise, they head for Kazimierz.

In addition to the Harris Piano Jazz Bar (listed earlier), two places on the Square worth checking out are near the southeast corner. At #6, head into the passage to find the **Buddha** nightclub, with comfy lounge sofas under awnings in an immaculately restored old courtyard. For something funkier and even more local, go down the passage at #12, which runs a surprisingly long distance through the block. Soon you'll start to see tables for the **Herring Embassy;** you'll eventually emerge at **Stolarska street,** a still-enjoyable but far less touristy scene (for more on the Herring Embassy and Stolarska, see page 342).

If you have (or would like to cultivate) an appreciation for vodka, stop by the **Vodka Café Bar,** serving more than 100 types of vodkas, liquors, and hard drinks. You can buy a tasting flight board with six small shots; they'll help you narrow down your options (usually around 30 zł for the flight, more for top-shelf vodkas). It's a mellow, uncluttered space that lets you focus on the vodka and the company (Mon-Thu 15:00-24:00, Fri-Sun 13:00-24:00, Mikołajska 5).

IN KAZIMIERZ

Aside from the Old Town's gorgeous Square, Kraków's best area to hang out after dark is Kazimierz. Although this is also the former Jewish quarter, the Jewish Sabbath has nothing to do with the bar scene here. You can, however, still hear traditional Jewish music called klezmer. For tips on enjoying a concert of klezmer music, see the sidebar.

Bars and Clubs

Squeezed between centuries-old synagogues and cemeteries are wonderful hangouts running the full gamut from sober and tasteful to wild and clubby. The classic recipe for a Kazimierz bar: Find a dilapidated old storefront, fill it with ramshackle furniture, turn the lights down low, pipe in old-timey jazz music from the 1920s, and sprinkle with alcohol. Serves one to two dozen hipsters. After a few clubs of this type caught on, a more diverse cross-section of nightspots began to move in, including some loud dance clubs. The whole area is bursting with life—it's the kind of place where people just spontaneously start dancing.

On and near Plac Nowy: The highest concentration of bars ring the plac Nowy market square. While most of these are nondescript, a few stand out. Fronting the square, **Kolory** has a pleasant Parisian brasserie ambience (Estery 10). Circling to the right, you'll spot **Plac Nowy 1,** which specializes in Polish microbrews and up-market pub grub in a bright, sleek (and arguably "un-Kazimierz") setting. Spinning about 90 more degrees to the right, look for a branch of the Poland-wide **Pijalnia Wódki i Piwa** chain—part of the trend for 4/8 bars (that's 4 zł for a shot of vodka, 8 zł for a bar snack such as herring). Tucked in the corner just to the right of that is the easy-to-miss entrance for **Atelier,** which hides a relaxed, minimalist, art-gallery interior with cushy sofas and a hidden garden (plac Nowy 7 1/2). **Le Scandale** is all black leather and serves

KRAKÓW

Kazimierz Entertainment & Nightlife

(#3 & 24 from Old Town)

(#3 & 24 to Old Town)

New Cemetery

NEW CEMETERY ENTRANCE

POST

TEMPEL SYNAGOGUE

KUPA SYNAGOGUE

Old Cemetery

REMU'H SYNAGOGUE

Ulica Szeroka

Plac Nowy

ISAAC SYNAGOGUE

WALL

OLD SYNAGOGUE

GALICIA JEWISH MUSEUM

HIGH SYNAGOGUE

To Wawel Hill

UL. JÓZEFA

CORPUS CHRISTI CHURCH

MUSEUM OF MUNICIPAL ENGINEERING

KAZIMIERZ

Plac Wolnica

ETHNO-GRAPHIC MUSEUM

(#6, 8, 10 & 13 to Castle & Old Town)

100 Meters
100 Yards

Vistula River

NADWIŚLAŃSKA

PIWNA

JÓZEFIŃSKA

STAROMOSTOWA

WĘGIERSKA

BOLESŁAWA LIMANOWSKIEGO

100 Meters
100 Yards

① Klezmer-Hois Restaurant
② Hotel Ester
③ Awiw Restaurant
④ Kolory
⑤ Plac Nowy 1 Bar
⑥ Pijalnia Wódki i Piwa
⑦ Atelier
⑧ Le Scandale
⑨ Miejsce
⑩ Mleczarnia & Stajnia
⑪ Nova Resto Bar & Taawa
⑫ Singer
⑬ Eszeweria

tapas, Italian fare, and cocktails; don't miss the big garden in the back (plac Nowy 9). And at the end of this block, **Alchemia,** one of the first—and still one of the best—bars in Kazimierz, is candlelit, cluttered, and claustrophobic, with cave-like rooms crowded with rickety old furniture, plus a cellar used for live performances (Estery 5, www.alchemia.com.pl).

Just around the corner, on Estery street, Alchemia has its

Klezmer Music in Kazimierz

On a balmy summer night, Kazimierz's main square, ulica Szeroka, is filled with the haunting strains of klezmer—traditional Jewish music from 19th-century Poland, generally with violin, string bass, clarinet, and accordion. Skilled klezmer musicians can make their instruments weep or laugh like human voices. There are two main ways to enjoy some klezmer music: at a restaurant or at a concert.

Restaurants: Several eateries on ulica Szeroka offer klezmer music, typically starting between 19:00 and 20:00. The musicians move from room to room, and the menus tend to be a mix of traditional Jewish and Polish cuisine (which are quite similar). But don't come here just for the food—it's an afterthought to the music. While most places claim to do concerts "nightly year-round," they can be canceled anytime it's slow (especially off-season)—confirm ahead.

Some old-school restaurants offer reasonably priced food, but charge 30 zł per person for the music. Probably your best choice is the well-established **$$$ Klezmer-Hois,** filling a venerable former Jewish ritual bathhouse and making you feel like you're dining in a rich grandparent's home (daily 8:00-22:00, at #6, tel. 12-411-1245, www.klezmer.pl).

A newer trend is for restaurants with outdoor seating on ulica Szeroka to offer "free" al fresco klezmer music for customers (though the food tends to be that much more expensive). Because the music is free, anybody (at neighboring restaurants, or simply strolling past) can enjoy a taste of klezmer. Just show up, comparison-shop music and menus, and—if you like what you hear—pick a place for dinner or a drink. Eateries offering this option include **$$ Hotel Ester** (at #20, with relatively reasonable prices, and live music that begins in the early afternoon rather than evening) and **$$$ Awiw** (at #13, overpriced food).

Concerts: To really focus on klezmer as an art form, pay a bit more to attend a concert. Popular options include the Jascha Lieberman Trio, which performs most summer nights at 20:00 in the Popper Synagogue (65 zł, ulica Szeroka 16, www.jaschalieberman.com); or a performance in arguably the most powerful space, the giant old prayer hall of Isaac Synagogue (60 zł, Sun-Mon and Wed-Thu at 18:00, Kupa 18, www.sibelia.pl). For the latest lineup, check for fliers around town, or ask at any TI.

Don't worry too much about seeking out a particular musician—they are equally good, and each brings a unique style to the music. Many venues share musicians, so on any given night it's hard to predict who's performing where. Bottom line: If you're interested in klezmer music, you can't go wrong in Kazimierz.

own restaurant (described later, under "Eating in Kazimierz"). Hiding just a half-block beyond that is **Miejsce** ("The Place"), which is bright and minimalist, with stripped-down walls and carefully chosen Scan-design old furniture—it's run by the owners of a design firm specializing in decor from the 50s, 60s, and 70s (Estery 1).

Late at night, the little windows in the plac Nowy **market hall** do a big business selling *zapiekanki* (baguette with toppings) to hungry bar-hoppers.

On Rabina Meiselsa street, just a half-block off plac Nowy, two places share a long courtyard: **Mleczarnia,** a top-notch beer garden with rickety tables squeezed under the trees and its cozy old-fashioned pub across the street (at #20); and **Stajnia,** at the far end of the courtyard, where scenes from *Schindler's List* were filmed (see photos on wall at inner arch). Its interior feels like a Polish village drenched in red light and turned into a dance hall.

Near Isaac Synagogue: A block east of plac Nowy, a few more places cluster on the wide street in front of Isaac Synagogue. The huge **Nova Resto Bar** dominates the scene with a long covered terrace, a vast interior, and seating in their courtyard—all with a cool-color-scheme Las Vegas polka-dot style. This feels upscale and a bit pretentious compared to many of the others, but it's *the* place to be seen (25-40-zł meals, Estery 18). Upstairs is the similarly trendy music club **Taawa** (http://taawa.pl). Facing this double-decker wall of style are some smaller, more accessible options: **Singer** is classy and mellow, with most of its tables made of old namesake sewing machines (Estery 20), while **Warsztat** has an exploding-instruments-factory ambience (Izaaka 3; also recommended later, under "Eating in Kraków").

On Józefa Street: More good bars are just a short block south. Along Józefa, you'll find a pair of classic Kazimierz joints: **Eszeweria,** which wins the "best atmosphere" award, feels like a Polish speakeasy that's been in mothballs for the last 90 years—a low-key, unpretentious, and inviting hangout (Józefa 9). A block up, look for **Kolanko No. 6,** with a cozy bar up front, a pleasant beer garden in the inner courtyard, and a fun events hall in back (Józefa 17, www. kolanko.net; also recommended later, under "Eating in Kraków").

In Podgórze: If you run out of diversions in the heart of Kazimierz, head south. With the construction of a new pedestrian bridge over the river just south of this area, Kazimierz's nightlife scene is spreading to Podgórze, just across the river. Here in this fast-evolving zone, prices are a bit lower.

Beach Bar on the Riverbank

South of the river, roughly between Kazimierz and Wawel Castle, **Forum Przestrzenie** fills a dilapidated concrete department store—a mostly abandoned dinosaur from communist times, today used primarily as an extra-large billboard. But in recent years, the ground floor has been taken over by a lively hipster bar—especially appealing in the balmy summer months, when comfy low-slung chairs sprawl across a tidy lawn and a pebbly "beach" with views across the Vistula to Wawel Castle. They serve coffee, wine, beer, summery cocktails, and cheap bar snacks. A few artists and designers also have boutiques here (open daily in good weather 10:00-late, skip the trip if it's not nice out, ulica Marii Konopnickiej 28, mobile 515-424-724, www. forumprzestrzenie.com).

Sleeping in Kraków

Kraków is popular, with lots of accommodations options. Healthy competition keeps Kraków's prices reasonable and makes choosing a hotel fun rather than frustrating. Splurge dollars go a long way here—accommodations are inexpensive, and moving up a price class buys you a lot more luxury. Rates are soft; hoteliers don't need much of an excuse to offer you 10 to 20 percent off, especially on weekends or off-season. I've focused my accommodations in two areas: in and near the Old Town; and in Kazimierz, a local-style, more affordable neighborhood that is home to both the old Jewish quarter and a thriving dining and nightlife zone.

The Old Town is jam-packed with discos that thump loud music on weekend nights to attract roving gangs of rowdy students, backpackers, and obnoxious "stag parties" of drunken louts from the UK in town for a weekend of carousing. The "quiet after 22:00" law is flagrantly ignored. Kazimierz is also home to various hip dance clubs. Because of all these clubs, virtually all of my accommodations come with some risk of noise; to help your odds, always ask for a quiet room when you reserve...and bring earplugs.

KRAKÓW

IN AND NEAR THE OLD TOWN

Most of my listings are inside (or within a block or two of) the Planty park that rings the Old Town. Sleeping inside the Old Town comes with pros (maximum atmosphere; handy location for sightseeing and dining) and cons (high prices; the potential for noise—especially on weekends—as noted earlier). Places just outside the Old Town are still handy, but quieter. If you need a room in a pinch, several slick, international chains (Ibis, Mercure, Puro) have branches near the train station.

Sleep Code

Hotels are classified based on the average price of a standard double room with breakfast in high season.

$$$$	**Splurge:** Most rooms over 550 zł
$$$	**Pricier:** 400-550 zł
$$	**Moderate:** 250-400 zł
$	**Budget:** 100-250 zł
¢	**Backpacker:** Under 100 zł
RS%	**Rick Steves discount**

Unless otherwise noted, credit cards are accepted, hotel staff speak basic English, and free Wi-Fi is available. Comparison-shop by checking prices at several hotels (on each hotel's own website, on a booking site, or by email). For the best deal, *book directly with the hotel.* Ask for a discount if paying in cash; if the listing includes **RS%**, request a Rick Steves discount.

Guest Houses

These good-value pensions come with lots of stairs (no elevators) and are located in the heart of the Old Town along busy pedestrian streets, many without air-conditioning—so they can be noisy with the windows open in the summer, especially on weekends. Don't expect a 24-hour reception desk; it's always smart to tell them your arrival time, especially if it's late in the day.

$$ Tango House, run by dance instructor Marcin Miszczak, is in a well-located building with an ancient-feeling stairwell decorated with faded Art Nouveau paintings. Its eight long, skinny, retro-stylish rooms have parquet floors (ask for quieter courtyard room to avoid rowdy street noise on weekends, ulica Szpitalna 4, tel. 12-429-3114, www.tangohouse.pl, info@tangohouse.pl).

$$ Globtroter Guest House offers 17 basic, somewhat stuffy, rustic-feeling rooms with high ceilings and big beams around a serene garden courtyard. Jacek (Jack), who really understands and respects travelers, conscientiously focuses on value—keeping prices reasonable by not offering needless extras (RS%, 2 people can cram into a single to save money, family rooms, breakfast at nearby café extra, pay laundry service, fun 700-year-old brick cellar lounge down below, go down passageway at #7 at the square called plac Szczepański, tel. 12-422-4123, www.globtroter-krakow.com, globtroter@globtroter-krakow.com).

$$ La Fontaine B&B, run by a French-Polish family, offers 11 rooms and 13 apartments just off the Main Market Square. Tastefully decorated with French flair, it's cute as a poodle. Each room has a little lounge with a microwave and fridge—most in the hall, some inside the room. If you don't mind huffing up lots of stairs, this is a fine value (air-con in some rooms, low slanted ceilings in some rooms, guest kitchen, pay laundry service, ulica Sławkowska 1, tel. 12-422-6564, www.bblafontaine.com, biuro@ bblafontaine.com).

$ Golden Lion Guest House is cheap and basic but well-located, with 11 smallish, dated rooms on a bustling pedestrian street a block off the Main Market Square (ask for quieter room in back, air-con in some rooms, guest kitchen, no parking, ulica Szewska 19, mobile 501-066-958, tel. 12-422-9323, www.goldenlion. pl, reservation@goldenlion.pl, Łodziński family).

Outside of the Old Town: $$ Cracowdays is the farthest of my listings from the center of town, about a 15-minute walk away (a tram can cut a few minutes off the trek). But it's also a notch more refined than the guest houses listed previously. It sits in a pleasant residential neighborhood west of the Main Market Square, with six beautifully decorated and thoughtfully tended rooms, all sharing a central kitchen (stand-alone studio apartment in another building, breakfast extra, air-con, Grabowskiego 7, mobile 666-971-478, www.cracowdays.com, reservation@cracowdays.com).

Hotels

$$$$ Donimirski Boutique Hotels, with four different locations in or near Kraków's Old Town, set the bar for splurge hotels in Kraków (www.donimirski.com). All Donimirski hotels come with friendly staff, discounts for my readers, and classy little extras that add up to a memorable hotel experience. **Hotel Polski Pod Białym Orłem,** conveniently located near the Florian Gate just inside the Old Town walls, has 60 luxurious rooms (RS%, apartments available, air-con, elevator, ulica Pijarska 17, tel. 12-422-1144, hotel. polski@donimirski.com). **Hotel Gródek** offers 23 rooms a three-minute walk behind St. Mary's Church, on a quiet dead-end street overlooking the Planty park (RS%, pay parking, Na Gródku 4, tel. 12-431-9030, grodek@donimirski.com). **Hotel Maltański** has 16 rooms in the beautifully renovated former royal stables, facing the Planty park just two blocks from Wawel Castle (RS%, no elevator but only 2 floors, pay parking, ulica Straszewskiego 14, tel. 12-431-0010, maltanski@donimirski.com). And **Hotel Pugetów,** with seven small but plush rooms, is in the workaday neighborhood between the Main Market Square and Kazimierz (RS%, air-con, pay parking, ulica Starowiślna 15A, tel. 12-432-4950, pugetow@ donimirski.com).

$$$$ Hotel Senacki is a business-class place renting 20 comfortable rooms between Wawel Castle and the Main Market Square. The location is handy, but it can be noisy on weekends—ask for a quieter back room. The staff is warm, professional, and conscientious. Top-floor "attic" rooms have low beams, skylight windows, and a flight of stairs after the elevator (air-con, eleva-

Kraków's Old Town Hotels & Restaurants

OLD MARKET

PADEREWSKIEGO

DŁUGA

KARMELICKA

To 5

ŁOBZOWSKA

ASNYKA

GARBARSKA

Planty

PIJARSKA

BARBICAN

FLORIAN GATE

SŁAWKOWSKA

ŚW. MARKA

14

DUNAJEWSKIEGO

2

OLD

ZARTORYSKI MUSEUM

6

23

ŚW. JANA

23

200 Meters

200 Yards

SZCZEPAŃSKA

P

33

26

FLORIAŃSKA

16

KRUPNICZA

28

27

SZOŁAYSKI HOUSE

SZPITALNA

STUDENSKA

PODWALE

#24 Teater Bagately

T

4

SZEWSKA

3

i

ŚW. TOMASZA

35

1

PODWALE

ŚW. ANNY

Main Market Square

ST. MARY'S

31

JABŁONOWSKICH

COLLEGIUM MAIUS

JAGIELLOŃSKA

39

CLOTH HALL

MICKIEWICZ STATUE

Small Market Square

32

7

TOWN HALL TOWER

i

ST. ADALBERT'S

25

SIENNA

PIŁSUDSKIEGO

GOŁĘBIA

11

22

29

OLSZEWSKIEGO

ARCH-BISHOP'S MANSION

13

21

GRODZKA

17

STOLARSKA

DOMINICAN CHURCH

WC

WIŚLNA

P

#8 plac Wszystkich Świętych

34

FRANCISZKAŃSKA

T

38

DOMINIKAŃSKA

ST. FRANCIS

12

TOWN

ZWIERZYNIECKA

STRASZEWSKIEGO

WYSPIAŃSKI PAVILION

i

18

20

Planty

To Airport, Auschwitz & Kościuszko Mound

SMOLENSK

FELICJANEK

Planty

37

8

POSELSKA

SENACKA

Mary Mag. Square

10

STS. PETER & PAUL

SAREGO

BISHOP ERAZM CIOŁEK PALACE

GRODZKA

ST. ANDREW'S

ARCHDIOCESAN MUSEUM

KANONICZA

19

JOHN PAUL II CENTER

ŚW. GERTRUDY

POWIŚLE

PODZAMCZE

i

CATHEDRAL

30

24

ŚW. IDZIEGO

WAWEL HILL

INNER COURTYARD

Vistula River

LOST WAWEL MUSEUM

BERNARDYŃSKA

ST. BERNARDINO'S

STRADOMSKA

DRAGON STATUE

KONOPNICKIEJ

KOLETEK

KRAKÓW

Map Labels

KURNIKI

🏥

B Kurniki

#3 🚊
Dworzec
Główny
Zachód

**Plac
Matejki**

GALERIA
KRAKOWSKA
MALL

**TRAIN
STN.**

B
**BUS
STATION**

ZACISZE

#24 🚊
B A S Z T O W A

PAWIA

**Plac Jana
Jeroziorańskiego**

POST
OFFICE

LUBICZ

BOSACKA

To Nowa
Huta

ℹ️

**SŁOWACKI
THEATER**

PEDESTRIAN
UNDERPASS

#3 & 24 🚊
Dworzec
Główny

🏥

ŚW. KRZYŻA

Planty

WESTERPLATTE

RADZIWIŁŁOWSKA

36

MIKOŁAJSKA

🏥

KOPERNIKA

ZYBLIKIEWICZA

#3 & 24 🚊
Poczta Główna

BLICH

**MAIN POST
OFFICE**

WIELOPOLE

15

STAROWIŚLNA

9

DIETLA

#3 & 24 🚊
Dietta

ŚW. SEBASTIANA

See Kazimierz map

ŚW. SEBASTIANA

B. JOSELEWICZA

K A Z I M I E R Z

DIETLA

PODBRZEZIE

MIODOWA

#3 & 24 🚊
Miodowa

**Old
Cemetery**

POST

STAROWIŚLNA

DAJWOR

**REMU'H
SYNAGOGUE**

**Plac
Nowy**

**MARKET
HALL**

**GALERIA
KAZIMIERZ**

To Podgórze &
Wieliczka Salt Mine

KRAKÓW

Accommodations

❶ Tango House
❷ Globtroter Guest House
❸ La Fontaine B&B
❹ Golden Lion Guest House
❺ To Cracowdays
❻ Hotel Polski Pod Białym Orłem
❼ Hotel Gródek
❽ Hotel Maltański
❾ Hotel Pugetów
❿ Hotel Senacki & Bar Grodzki
⓫ Wentzl Hotel
⓬ Hotel Wawel
⓭ Bracka 6
⓮ Hotel Amber
⓯ Hotel Wielopole
⓰ Kraków City Apartments
⓱ Kraków for You Apartments

Eateries

⓲ Restauracja pod Aniołami
⓳ Pod Nosem
⓴ Miód Malina
㉑ Marmolada
㉒ Wesele
㉓ U Babci Maliny (2)
㉔ Pod Baranem
㉕ Szara
㉖ Ed Red
㉗ Charlotte
㉘ Café Bunkier
㉙ Ambasada Śledzia
㉚ Pod Wawelem Beer Hall
㉛ Cyklop Pizza & Jadłodajnia "U
Stasi"
㉜ Moa Burger
㉝ Krowarzywa
㉞ Lajkonik Sandwiches
㉟ Milkbar Tomasza
㊱ Academy of Music Café
㊲ Bar Mleczny
㊳ Restauracja Samoobsługowa
Polakowski
㊴ Chimera Cafeteria

tor—but doesn't go to "attic" rooms, ask about nearby pay parking, ulica Grodzka 51, tel. 12-422-7686, www.hotelsenacki.pl, senacki@hotelsenacki.pl).

$$$$ Wentzl Hotel is your splurge-right-on-the-Square option, with 18 rooms. The decor is over-the-top-classy Old World with modern touches, like state-of-the-art TVs and bathrooms. When reserving, request either a room with a view on the Square—which can be noisy, especially on weekends—or one of the three quieter back rooms (air-con, elevator, Rynek Główny 19, tel. 12-430-2664, www.wentzl.pl, hotel@wentzl.pl).

$$$ Hotel Wawel has 39 rooms on a well-located street that's quieter than the Old Town norm. It's colorful and feels plush for the price; above the swanky marble lobby are hallways creatively painted with the history of the building and images from around Kraków. Out back, a fountain gurgles in a cute little courtyard (air-con, elevator—but doesn't go to top floor, steam room and whirlpool bath extra, ulica Poselska 22, tel. 12-424-1300, www.hotelwawel.pl, hotel@hotelwawel.pl).

$$$ Bracka 6, wonderfully located just one short block off the Main Market Square, is a sort of a hybrid between a hotel and an apartment house. The 16 stylish rooms—with sleek lines, lots of glass, and exposed brick—each have a kitchen, so breakfast is extra. It's on the second and third floors with no elevator, and the reception is open limited hours (daily 8:00-22:00 or so)—but the lack of full hotel amenities keeps the prices affordable for this level of modern elegance (air-con, Bracka 6, tel. 12-341-4011, www.bracka6.pl, info@bracka6.pl).

$$$ Hotel Amber sits on a dreary urban street just outside the Planty park, but still less than a 10-minute walk from the Square. The staff is proud of their attentive service (and circulates a handy little informative newsletter daily). The hotel has two parts: 18 perfectly fine, if smallish, rooms in the original building; and 20 slightly more upscale rooms in the newer "design" section. While a bit overpriced, both parts share a small gym, sauna, and garden in back (air-con, elevator, Garbarska 8-10, tel. 12-421-0606, www.hotel-amber.pl, office@hotel-amber.pl).

$$ Hotel Wielopole sits a block outside of the Planty, on the way to the lively Kazimierz district. Its 35 tight rooms are tucked down a (relatively) quiet side street just past the main post office, facing a big Holiday Inn. Run by the same company as Hotel Amber (described above), it has an equally pleasant emphasis on welcoming service (air-con, elevator, vegetarian restaurant in cellar, Wielopole 3, tel. 12-422-1475, www.wielopole.pl, office@wielopole.pl).

Apartments

Apartments aren't just for long stays—these places welcome even one-nighters. As reception times are limited, be sure to clearly communicate your arrival time. A wide variety of apartments are easy to find at online booking sites, but both of these places have a reception desk that manages several units, making them a bit more hotelesque than the norm. Still, you're on your own for breakfast, and don't expect your room to be cleaned during your stay.

$$ Kraków City Apartments, conscientiously run by Andrzej and Katarzyna, has 14 straightforward, modern apartments tucked away in a quiet courtyard at the corner of the Old Town (2-bedroom apartments available for up to 6 people, nonsmoking, elevator to all rooms except studios, reception open daily 9:00-20:00, ulica Szpitalna 34, reception mobile 507-203-050, Andrzej's mobile 504-235-925, www.krakowapartments.info, info@krakowapartments.info).

$$ Kraków for You Apartments offers 12 modern, well-decorated studios and one- and two-bedroom units around a courtyard along one of Kraków's most happening streets, just a few steps off the Main Market Square (reception open daily 10:00-20:00, request quieter courtyard room, lots of stairs with no elevator, go down the passage at Grodzka 4, tel. 12-421-4835, mobile 660-541-085, www.krakowforyou.com, info@krakowforyou.com, Mikołaj).

IN KAZIMIERZ

Kazimierz is both Kraków's Jewish heart and soul, and its trendiest eating and nightlife zone. Sleeping here puts you in close proximity to both synagogues and klezmer concerts, and to food trucks and hip nightclubs (expect some noise, especially on weekends). Keep in mind that, while pleasant in its own right, Kazimierz is a 20-minute walk or a 5-minute tram ride from Kraków's atmospheric old center (for details on getting to Kazimierz from the Old Town, see page 292). For locations, see the map on page 292.

$$$$ Metropolitan Boutique Hotel is an upscale refuge, just a block before the heart of Kazimierz (just off the busy road on the way to Kraków's Old Town). Its 39 rooms—with exposed brick and slick modern style—sit along a somewhat dreary but conveniently located side street (air-con, elevator, gym, Joselewicza 19, tel. 12-442-7500, www.hotelmetropolitan.pl).

$$$ Rubinstein Residence sits right in the middle of ulica Szeroka—surrounded by klezmer restaurants and synagogues, in the heart of the neighborhood. It fills a painstakingly restored old townhouse (parts of it dating to the 15th century) with heavy wood beams and 30 swanky rooms—some of them palatial suites that incorporate old features like frescoes and pillars. The rooftop terrace—with views over Kazimierz and to the Old Town—sets this

place above (air-con, elevator, Szeroka 12, tel. 12-384-0000, www.
rubinstein.pl, recepcja@rubinstein.pl).

$$ Karmel Hotel, with 11 rooms above an Italian restaurant,
sits on a pleasant side street near the heart of Kazimierz. It offers
elegance at a reasonable price (some rooms have air-con, upstairs
with no elevator, some night noise on weekends, ulica Kupa 15,
tel. 12-430-6697, www.karmel.com.pl, hotel@karmel.com.pl).

$ Tournet Guest House, well-run by friendly Piotr and Syl-
wia Działowy, is your cheap-and-cheery option, offering 18 col-
orful, overly perfumed rooms near the edge of Kazimierz toward
Wawel Castle (elevator plus a few stairs, reception open 7:00-
22:00, ulica Miodowa 7, tel. 12-292-0088, www.nocleg.krakow.pl,
tournet@nocleg.krakow.pl).

¢ Hostel Momotown is a smidge more institutional and less
party-oriented than your average hostel, but it's still loose and
friendly. Run by Paweł Momot, it has 77 dorm beds, some private
rooms, and a fun garden for hanging out (ulica Miodowa 28, tel. 12-
429-6929, www.momotownhostel.com, info@momotownhostel.
com). Two blocks away, they also rent 14 basic but cheap **$ pri-
vate rooms** that share a kitchenette, overlooking Kazimierz's main
square, ulica Szeroka.

Eating in Kraków

Kraków has a wide array of great restaurants—for every one I've
listed, there are two or three nearly as good. As the restaurant scene
changes constantly, I've chosen places that are well-established and
have a proven track record for reliably good food. In my listings,
you'll find a mix of old-school Polish places and modern foodie
alternatives (which are still rooted in the local tradition). You could
also consider a **food tour** (described under "Tours in Krakow," page
248).

IN THE OLD TOWN

Kraków's Old Town is loaded with dining options. Prices are rea-
sonable even on the Main Market Square. And a half-block away,
they get even better. All of these eateries (except the milk bars) are
likely to be booked up on weekends—always reserve ahead.

$$$ Restauracja pod Aniołami ("Under Angels") offers
a dressy, candlelit atmosphere on a wonderful covered patio, or
in a deep, steep, romantic cellar with rough wood and medieval
vaults. Peruse the elaborately described menu of medieval noble-
men's dishes. The cuisine is traditional Polish, with an emphasis on
grilled meats and trout (on a wood-fired grill). Every meal begins
with *smalec* (spread made with lard, fried onion, bacon, and apple).
Don't go here if you're in a hurry—only if you want to really slow

---

Restaurant Price Code

I've assigned each eatery a price category, based on the average cost of a typical main course. Drinks, desserts, and splurge items (steak and seafood) can raise the price considerably.

$$$$	**Splurge:** Most main courses over 60 zł
$$$	**Pricier:** 45-60 zł
$$	**Moderate:** 25-45 zł
$	**Budget:** Under 25 zł

In Poland, a milk bar or takeout spot is **$**; a basic sit-down eatery is **$$**; a casual but more upscale restaurant is **$$$**; and a swanky splurge is **$$$$**.

---

down and enjoy your dinner. Reservations are smart (daily 13:00-24:00, ulica Grodzka 35, tel. 12-421-3999, www.podaniolami.pl).

$$$ Pod Nosem ("Under the Nose") is a smart choice for refined, updated Polish cuisine in a sophisticated, less touristy atmosphere. It's tucked at the far end of sleepy Kanonicza lane, just beyond the tourists and before Wawel Castle. In a tight dining room that skips the kitsch, they offer an extensive wine list and a short menu of artfully executed Polish dishes (daily 12:00-22:00, Kanonicza 22, tel. 12-376-0014, www.kanonicza22.com).

$$$ Miód Malina ("Honey Raspberry") is a delightful, acceptably kitschy Polish-Italian fusion restaurant filled with the comforting aroma of its wood-fired oven. The menu is mostly Polish, with a few Italian dishes thrown in. Sit in the cozy, warmly painted interior, or out in the courtyard (reservations smart, daily 12:00-23:00, ulica Grodzka 40, tel. 12-430-0411, www.miodmalina.pl). The same people run two other restaurants a bit closer to the Square, with similar atmosphere and equally good food, but are more focused on Polish fare: **$$ Marmolada** (Grodzka 5) and **$$$ Wesele,** with outdoor tables right on the Square (at #10).

$$ Pod Baranem ("Under the Ram") is a solid midrange bet for traditional Polish food without being tacky or pretentious. Well-respected by locals, it sits just outside of the tourist chaos, quietly facing the Planty near Wawel Castle. Several cozy rooms—tasteful but not stuffy—sprawl through a homey old building (daily 12:00-22:00, lighter meals before 19:00, Św. Gertrudy 21, tel. 12-429-4022, www.podbaranem.com).

Splurging on the Main Market Square: You'll find plenty of expensive, tourist-oriented restaurants on the Square. Though all of them have rich interiors, there's not much point in paying a premium to dine here unless you're sitting outside. It's difficult to recommend any specific places here, but options with good reputations and relatively decent value include **$$$ Szara** (at #6) and **$$$ Wesele** (at #10; related to Miód Malina, above). Even the best of these places is overpriced. To enjoy the same experience more affordably, have just a drink on the square and dine elsewhere.

Steak House: $$$ Ed Red, by acclaimed local chef Adam Chrząstowski, serves up the best steaks in Kraków. He carefully sources his beef from Poland, and dry-ages it himself (21 or 45 days). A short walk from the Main Market Square, the space is classy but not stuffy, with exposed brick, leather benches, and a busy open kitchen. While it's a splurge by local standards, you can get a top-quality steak for under $20—a bargain anywhere else—as well as a short menu of affordably priced alternatives. Reservations are smart (daily 12:00-23:00, Sławkowska 3, mobile 690-900-555, www.edred.pl).

Youthful Style at Plac Szczepański: While seemingly every corner of the Old Town is jammed with tourists, the pleasant square called plac Szczepański feels more like the terrain of university students—a carefully protected bastion of the local upscale art culture. While just two blocks from the Square, this small array of cafés and galleries has a vibe that's more Warsaw-urbane than ye olde Kraków. **$ Charlotte** is a winner—it's a classy, French-feeling bakery/café/wine bar. They make their own breads and pastries in the basement (with lots of seating—you can watch the bakers work if you come early enough in the morning), cultivate a stay-awhile coffee-house ambience upstairs, and throw in a few square-facing sidewalk tables to boot. And it's affordable, serving up sandwiches, pastries, and salads. While the food is light café fare rather than a filling dinner, after 18:00 they redecorate to give it a more sophisticated flair (Mon-Fri 7:00-24:00, Sat 9:00-24:00, Sun 9:00-22:00, plac Szczepański 2, tel. 12-431-5610). Just around the corner, facing the Planty park, is the delightful **$$ Café Bunkier.** It belongs to the hulking Bunkier Sztuki contemporary art gallery, but—in contrast to that building's concrete vibe—the café sits under a glass canopy that faces the lush greenbelt, with well-worn wooden tables and an almost Parisian ambience. While it's not the place for a filling meal, it's worth coming here for some light food and drinks while enjoying Kraków's greenery. It's especially cozy on a rainy day (daily 9:00-24:00, food from 12:00, plac Szczepański 3a, tel. 12-431-0585).

On Stolarska Street: Stolarska street, a neatly pedestrianized, oddly untrammeled "embassy row" just a block away from the Main Market Square, is worth exploring for a meal or a drink. Stolarska has a fun variety of more locals-oriented bars and cafés. Begin at the Small Market Square (Maly Rynek) behind St. Mary's Church and head south. On the left, look for the ridiculously long sign that perfectly identifies the business: Pierwszy Lokal Na Stolarskiej Po Lewej Stronie Idąc Od Małego Rynku ("The first pub on the left side of Stolarska coming from the Small Market Square"). Notice that this once-sleepy street is lined with embassies and consulates—it's easy to spot the flags of Germany, the US, and France. On the left, in the stretch of cafés under canopies, you'll see the **$ Ambasada Śledzia** ("Herring Embassy"), with a divey, youthful atmosphere and a "Polish tapas" approach: A dozen different types of herring and other light meals, plus a variety of vodka to wash it down, are posted on the menu. You'll order at the bar, then find a table, or take it to go (open long hours daily, Stolarska 8). Nearly across the street, the Pasaż Bielaka (look for the low-profile stone doorway at #5) runs through the middle of the block all the way out to the Main Market Square (emerging at Rynek Główny #12); partway along is another sprawling branch of the Herring Embassy.

Beer Hall: $$ Pod Wawelem ("Under Wawel") is a rollicking Czech-style beer hall right on the Planty park near Wawel Castle. It's packed with locals seeking big, sloppy, greasy portions of meaty fare, with giant mugs of various beers on tap (including Polish and Bavarian). Choose between the bustling interior or the outdoor terrace right on the Planty. Locals come here not for a romantic dinner, but for a rowdy evening out with friends (different specials every day—such as giant schnitzel, pork ribs, or roasted chicken; daily 12:00-24:00, ulica Św. Gertrudy 26-29, tel. 12-421-2336).

Pizza: $ Cyklop, with 10 tables wrapped around the cook and his busy oven, has good wood-fired pizzas and a cozy, charming ambience (daily 11:00-23:00, near St. Mary's Church at Mikołajska 16, tel. 12-421-6603).

Burgers (and Vegan Burgers): Gourmet hamburgers are all the rage in Poland these days. One of the best options in the center is **$ Moa Burger,** with a dozen different types of big, sloppy, "New Zealand-style" hamburgers. Order at the counter, then find a seat at a shared table (daily 11:00-23:00, Mikołajska 3, tel. 12-421-2144). Another fad is vegan "burgers"; a handy place in the center is **$ Krowarzywa** (a pun roughly meaning both "Cow Alive" and "Cow Vegetable")—with a hip atmosphere and an enticing menu of meatless options (daily 12:00-23:00, Sławkowska 8, mobile 531-777-136).

Quick Sandwich: If you need a break from milk bars (described next), but want to grab a sandwich on the go, stop by **$ Lajkonik,** a modern bakery/coffee shop *(piekarnia i kawiarnia)* that sells fresh takeout sandwiches (Mon-Fri 7:00-21:00, Sat 8:00-21:00, Sun 8:00-22:00, handy location right in front of the Dominican Church at Dominikański 2, others are just outside of the Old Town).

Milk Bars and other Quick, Cheap, Traditional Eats

Kraków is a good place to try the cheap cafeterias called "milk bars." For pointers on eating at a milk bar, review the sidebar on page 228.

$ Milkbar Tomasza is an updated, upgraded milk bar popular with local students. Modern and relatively untouristy, it has a hipster ambience and serves big, splittable portions of high-quality food—often with some international flourishes—plus breakfast dishes all day (cheap soup and salad deals, great big salads, Tue-Sun 8:00-20:00, closed Mon, ulica Tomasza 24, tel. 12-422-1706).

$ Jadłodajnia "U Stasi" is a throwback that makes you feel like you're in on Kraków's best-kept secret. Its hidden location—tucked at the far end of the passage with the recommended Cyklop pizzeria—attracts a wide range of loyal local clientele, from hard-scrabble seniors to politicians, artists, and actors. They're all here for well-executed, unpretentious, home-style Polish lunch grub. There can be a bit of a language barrier, so go with the flow: Pick up the English menu as you enter, find a table, wait for them to take your order, enjoy your meal, then pay as you leave. This is an excellent value and a real, untouristy Polish experience. The short menu changes every day—and when they're out, they're out (Mon-Fri 12:00-17:00, closed Sat-Sun, Mikołajskiej 16).

$ U Babci Maliny ("Granny Raspberry"), with a grinning Granny on the sign, is another well-established and popular milk bar. One location, frequented almost entirely by Krakovians, is designed for university students and staff and is tucked into an inner courtyard of the Science Academy. Find the door at Sławkowska 17, then make your way into the inner courtyard, with an entrance to a rustic cellar where it looks like a kitschy cottage bomb went off (Mon-Fri 11:00-21:00, Sat-Sun 12:00-21:00). Another location is across the street from the National Theater building at Szpitalna 38. The main floor, also done up in a kitschy cottage style, is self-service and budget-priced, while the cellar—with a drawing-room vibe—has table service and is about 20 percent more expensive (daily 11:00-23:00). Both locations have walls of photos of the owner posing with bodybuilders and ultimate fighters...not quite in keeping with the country theme.

The **$ Academy of Music Café** (a.k.a. Restauracja U Romana) is a no-frills student cafeteria that enjoys a restful, top-floor perch with views over the back of St. Mary's Church and the rooftops of Kraków. It has a short, basic menu of food and drinks; come here not for high cuisine, but for high-up cuisine. You'll enter the Academy of Music at Św. Tomasza 43—using the heavy metal door opposite Hotel Campanile—then angle left inside to find the elevator in the stairwell and ride it to floor 6. Order at the counter, get your food, then head out to the tranquil terrace (mid-Sept-June Mon-Fri 9:00-18:00, Sat 9:00-16:00, closed Sun and July-mid-Sept).

Throwback Milk Bars on Grodzka Street: Just a couple of

blocks south of the Main Market Square, on busy ulica Grodzka, two classic milk bars somehow survive the onslaught of the modern world. First, at the corner with Senacka, is the remarkably basic and traditional milk bar, with a sign reading simply **$ Bar Mleczny** ("Milk Bar"; a low-profile sign over the door gives the eatery's name, *Restauracja "pod Temidą"*). The next best thing to a time machine to the communist era, this place has grumpy monolingual service, a mostly local clientele, and cheap but good food (daily 9:00-21:00). A few more steps down, also on the right (just before the two churches), **$ Bar Grodzki** is a single tight little room with

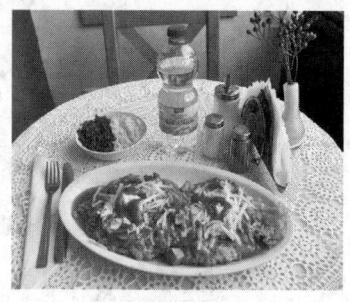

shared tables. They specialize in tasty potato pancake dishes *(placki ziemniaczane)*. Order high on the menu and try the rich and hearty "Hunter's Delight"—potato pancake with sausage, beef, melted cheese, and spicy sauce. The English menu posted by the counter makes ordering easy. Order, sit, and wait to be called to fetch your food (daily 9:00-19:00).

$ Restauracja Samoobsługowa Polakowski is a glorified milk bar with country-kitchen decor and cheap, tasty Polish fare. The tongue-twisting *samoobsługowa* simply means "self-service"— as at other milk bars, you'll order at the counter and bus your dishes when done. Curt service...cute hats (daily 11:00-22:00, facing St. Francis Basilica and the Wyspiański Pavilion at plac Wszystkich Świętych 10).

$ Chimera Cafeteria, just off the Main Market Square, is a handy spot for a quick lunch in the center. It serves fast traditional meals to a steady stream of students. You'll order at the counter— choose a big plate (6 items) or medium plate (4 items), and select from an array of salads and main dishes by pointing to what looks good. Then eat outside on their quiet garden courtyard (good for vegetarians, daily 9:00-22:00, near university at ulica Św. Anny 3). I'd skip their expensive full-service restaurant (in the basement), which shares an entryway.

IN KAZIMIERZ

The entire district is bursting with lively cafés and bars—it's a happening night scene. And, beyond the Jewish-themed places along ulica Szeroka (see the sidebar on page 331), Kazimierz's restaurants are less touristy and more diverse than the Old Town's. For locations, see the map on the next page.

KRAKÓW

Kazimierz Hotels & Restaurants

New Cemetery

NEW CEMETERY ENTRANCE

(#3 & 24 from Old Town)

To ❶

(#3 & 24 to Old Town)

POST

TEMPEL SYNAGOGUE

Old Cemetery

KUPA SYNAGOGUE

REMU'H SYNAGOGUE

Ulica Szeroka

Plac Nowy

ISAAC SYNAGOGUE

WALL

HIGH SYNAGOGUE

OLD SYNAGOGUE

GALICIA JEWISH MUSEUM

To Wawel Hill

CORPUS CHRISTI CHURCH

MUSEUM OF MUNICIPAL ENGINEERING

KAZIMIERZ

Plac Wolnica

ETHNO-GRAPHIC MUSEUM

100 Meters
100 Yards

Vistula River

(#6, 8, 10 & 13 to Castle & Old Town)

Accommodations
❶ To Metropolitan Boutique Hotel
❷ Rubinstein Residence
❸ Karmel Hotel
❹ Tournet Guest House
❺ Hostel Momotown

Eateries
❻ Judah Square Food Trucks
❼ Isaac Synagogue Food Trucks
❽ Dajwór 21 Food Trucks
❾ Plac Nowy Eateries
❿ Nova Krova
⓫ Good Lood

⓬ Pod Ursa Major
⓭ Bagelmama
⓮ Stara Zajezdnia
⓯ Craftownia
⓰ Studio Qulinarne
⓱ Bottiglieria 1881
⓲ Hamsa Restaurant
⓳ Alchemia & Alchemia od Kuchni
⓴ Kolanko No. 6
㉑ Satori Café/Bistro
㉒ Warsztat (3)
㉓ Lody Tradycyjna Receptura
㉔ Ciastkarnia Bakery

KRAKÓW

Fast and Cheap

Kazimierz has some great carry-out and street food—handy for a lunch break from daytime sightseeing here, or for an affordable dinner break from bar-hopping.

$ Food Trucks: Kazimierz has three vacant lots filled with fun-to-browse food trucks—most open daily for lunch and dinner. Each one comes with about a half-dozen entirely different options. The first and best is at **Judah Square.** Named for its big graffiti mural (by an Israeli street artist), it's tucked at the southern fringe of the tourists' Kazimierz, near the old tram depot (corner of Św. Wawrzyńca and Wąska). Mainstays here include the Big Red Bustaurant (fish-and-chips sold from a double-decker London bus); Belgian-style fries; Andrus (super-decadent and gooey roasted pork sandwiches); Boogie Truck burgers; Pan Kumpir baked potatoes; and the beloved Chimney Cake Bakery, which rotisserie-roasts dough and sugar into a sweet and crunchy cake, then fills it with ice cream and other toppings. Right in the heart of the tourist zone, another food truck pod fills a vacant lot **behind Isaac Synagogue,** just steps from ulica Szeroka. Here you'll find painted-wooden-palate furniture, hammocks, twinkle lights, and a mellow vibe. You'll see Walenty Kania, who does one thing and does it well: kielbasa (Polish sausage), with options made of sheep, deer, horse, goat, and, of course, ham. There's also a Mexican burrito truck, an açaí smoothie place, a Thai ice cream stand, and—of course—more chimney cakes. Finally, a third, newer, and less interesting pod of food trucks is at **Dajwór 21,** across the street from the Galicia Jewish Museum. Note that any and all of these could reshuffle their carts—or be gone entirely, replaced by a ritzy new building—at any moment. But it's clear that, in general, Kazimierz's food-truck scene is here to stay.

Polish Fast Food on Plac Nowy: The centerpiece of the plac Nowy market is a circular brick slaughterhouse, which has recently been taken over by Kazimierz foodies. Each of the shop windows—which once housed butchers and basic Polish grub—is now operated by a different pop-up eatery, from burgers to kebabs to Belgian fries to sushi hand rolls. But the real specialty here is the Poles' beloved *zapiekanki*—a toasted baguette with cheese, ketchup, and a bewildering array of other toppings. You can take a spin around the building to survey your options—noting where the lines are longest (locals know which *zapiekanki* is best). For dessert, line up at Good Lood, top-quality ice cream that's made fresh each morning and available until it's sold out (this is an outpost of the main branch a few blocks away on plac Wolnica—see next).

Foodie Favorites on Plac Wolnica: The big main square of Kazimierz (a couple of blocks south of plac Nowy) has a few locally beloved eateries. **$ Nova Krova** ("New Cow") sells entirely vegan and organic "burgers" and other sandwiches in a hip, woody atmosphere (Mon-Thu 12:00-21:00, Fri-Sat 12:00-23:00, Sun 10:00-21:00, at #12). And just kitty-corner, on hot days you'll see a long line at **Good Lood** (a pun on *lody*—ice cream), with scoops of fresh and flavorful homemade ice cream (daily 11:00-22:00 or until the flavors run out—since it's made fresh daily, at #11). **Pod Ursa Major**—highly respected by local beer lovers—is a microbrew pub serving the six types of beer they brew in the mountains southeast of Kraków (long hours daily, at #10).

Creative Bagels: $ Bagelmama, run by an American named Nava (who has worked as a private chef for tennis star John McEnroe), is a casual bagel shop that's popular with expats and locals. The bagels come dressed with a wide variety of spreads, and they also sell sandwiches, soups, salads, desserts, and fresh juices. You can eat in or get it to go (daily 9:00-17:00, ulica Dajwór 10, tel. 12-346-1646).

Beer: Beer lovers find two different experiences along Św. Wawrzyńca. **$$ Stara Zajezdnia** ("Old Tram Depot") fills exactly that—a cavernous old industrial hall—with tables and happy drinkers, draining huge mugs of the five different types of beer brewed on the premises. (You can also order a sampler.) In good weather, the vast courtyard out front becomes an idyllic beer garden filled with relaxing lounge chairs. Both zones have table service and basic pub grub (Św. Wawrzyńca 12, mobile 664-323-988). For craft beer lovers, **Craftownia** has 18 Polish microbrews on tap (and many more by the bottle) in a nondescript setting (Mon-Thu 14:00-late, Fri-Sun 12:00-late, Św. Wawrzyńca 22, mobile 515-010-565).

Dining in Kazimierz

For a good-quality sit-down meal, consider these options.

$$$$ Studio Qulinarne is a big, glassy, industrial-mod space with a trendy vibe and a fine-dining menu. With artfully prepared, seasonal cuisine and a long wine list, it's a good choice for an upscale splurge—still affordable by international standards—that feels removed from the rollicking Kazimierz bustle (Mon-Fri 12:00-14:30 & 18:00-22:00, Sat 18:00-22:00 only, closed Sun, Gazowa 4, tel. 12-430-6914, www.studioqulinarne.com).

$$$ Bottiglieria 1881 is a chic, sophisticated wine bar tucked unassumingly just off plac Wolnica. The cellar is stocked with wines from all over the world (with an emphasis on Italian), all complemented by the short, seasonal, thoughtfully designed menu with modern Polish and international dishes. Come for a glass or for a full meal (Tue-Sat 12:00-23:00, Sun 12:00-20:00, closed Mon, Bochenska 5, mobile 660-661-756).

$$ Hamsa, with a prime location at the top of ulica Szeroka, offers "hummus and happiness," with an updated take on Israeli food (that's Middle Eastern, not traditional Jewish fare). Don't come here for matzo balls and klezmer music, but for an enticing menu of *mezes* (small plates, like hummus and various dips) and grilled meat dishes in a modern, hip atmosphere (daily 9:00-24:00, ulica Szeorka 2, mobile 515-150-145).

Kazimierz Bars and Cafés with Food

Some of my favorite atmospheric Kazimierz bars also serve food. It's not high cuisine—the food is an afterthought to the busy bar.

$$ Alchemia od Kuchni is an inviting little subway-tiled street-food restaurant—a sleek space around the corner from the ramshackle main branch. You can order at the counter for a bite to go, or opt for table service (daily 8:00-23:00, Estery 5).

$$ Kolanko No. 6 is a great spot for classic Kazimierz atmosphere. The bar up front is filled with old secondhand furniture. Walking toward the back, you discover an inviting garden with tables and, beyond that, a hall where they host events. They serve light meals, specializing in crêpes, toasted sandwiches, salads, and international dishes (daily 10:00-24:00, Józefa 17, tel. 12-292-0320).

$ Satori is a relaxing eddy of a café/bistro, which rests just outside of the Kazimierz tourist chaos. With an artfully mismatched-furniture atmosphere that encourages lingering, this is a good choice either for a coffee or an affordable full meal (homemade pastas and salads, daily 11:00-22:00, Sun until 21:00, Józefa 25, mobile 660-508-840).

$$ Warsztat ("Workshop") is littered with musical instruments: The bar is a piano, and the tight interior is crammed with other instruments and rakishly crooked lampshades. The menu is an odd hybrid of Italian, Middle Eastern, and Polish cuisine, and the portions are big (salads, pizzas, pastas, and meats; daily 9:00-24:00, Izaaka 3, tel. 12-430-1451). They also have two other locations: a small one (focusing on Polish dishes) by the front door of the Tempel Synagogue, and a bigger one on Bożego Ciała street.

Kazimierz Desserts

Ice Cream: Lody Tradycyjna Receptura has, true to its name, some of the best "ice cream from a traditional recipe" in Kraków—if not in Poland. The straightforward, seasonal flavors—just a few varieties—are made fresh each morning and sold until they run out. Locals line up here—and if you have a sweet tooth, you should, too (daily 9:00-19:00, Starowiślna 83). **Good Lood,** a newer version offering essentially the same concept, has an equally loyal following at its two locations—one on plac Wolnica, and the other in the plac Nowy market hall (both described earlier).

Cakes: Ciastkarnia ("Confectionery") is a cute little bakery with top-quality but still affordable cakes from traditional recipes, and a few pleasant tables facing a little park (daily 9:00-20:00, shorter hours off-season, Brzozowa 13, mobile 602-790-988).

KRAKÓW

Kraków Connections

For getting between Kraków and **Auschwitz,** see page 368 in the next chapter. To confirm rail journeys, check specific times online (www.rozklad-pkp.pl) or at the main train station.

From Kraków by Train to: Warsaw (hourly, about 2.5 hours, slick EIC express train, requires seat reservation), **Gdańsk** (6/day direct, 5.5 hours on EIC express, plus night train, 10 hours), **Toruń** (7/day, 5.5 hours, transfer at Warsaw's Zachodnia station), **Prague** (4/day with 1-2 changes, 7.5-8.5 hours; plus night train, 9 hours), **Berlin** (2/day, 7.5 hours with change at Warsaw's Zachodnia station, more options with multiple changes; plus 1 direct and handy Deutsche Bahn IC bus, 8 hours, www.bahn.com), **Budapest** (2/day, 10-11 hours, change in Katowice, Poland, and Břeclav, Czech Republic; plus night train, 11 hours; faster by infrequent Orange Ways bus: 4/week, 7 hours, www.orangeways.com), **Vienna** (2/day, 7 hours, change in Katowice; plus night train, 9 hours).

By Bus: Though train connections are typically faster, buses can be less expensive and make sense for some trips. Polski Bus prides itself on offering buses with Wi-Fi and electrical outlets (www.polskibus.com). However, some of my readers have reported hot, crowded, uncomfortable rides on these buses—you get what you pay for.

AUSCHWITZ-BIRKENAU

The unassuming regional capital of Oświęcim (ohsh-VEENCH-im) was the site of one of humanity's most unspeakably horrifying tragedies: the systematic murder of at least 1.1 million innocent people. From 1941 until 1945, Oświęcim was the home of Auschwitz, the biggest, most notorious concentration camp in the Nazi system. Today, Auschwitz is the most poignant memorial anywhere to the victims of the Holocaust.

"Auschwitz" (OWSH-vits) actually refers to a series of several camps in Poland—most importantly Auschwitz I, in the village of Oświęcim (50 miles west of Kraków), and Auschwitz II, a.k.a. Birkenau (about 1.5 miles west of Oświęcim). Those visiting Auschwitz generally see both parts, starting with Auschwitz I, then riding a shuttle bus to Birkenau. **Auschwitz I,** where public transportation from Kraków arrives, has the main museum building, the *Arbeit Macht Frei* gate, and indoor museum exhibits in former prison buildings. **Birkenau** (BEER-keh-now) is on a much bigger scale and mostly outdoors, with the infamous guard tower, a vast field with ruins of barracks, a few tourable rough barracks, the notorious "dividing platform," a giant monument flanked by remains of destroyed crematoria, and a prisoner processing facility called "the Sauna."

A visit here is obligatory for Polish 14-year-olds; students usually come again during their last year of school, as well. You may see Israeli high school groups walking through the grounds wearing Star of David emblems. Many visitors leave flowers and messages. One of the messages—from a German visitor—reads, "Nations who forget their own history are sentenced to live it again."

GETTING THERE

To reach Auschwitz from Kraków, it's easiest to join a package tour or hire a private guide or driver (75-minute drive each way). But the trip is also doable by public transportation (1.75-2.5 hours, depending on the type of transit). For details, see "Auschwitz Connections," at the end of this chapter.

Orientation to Auschwitz

Cost: Entrance to the grounds is free (though donations are gladly accepted). However, during busy times (April-Oct 10:00-15:00), you'll need to pay 45 zł to join a required organized tour at Auschwitz I. (Alternatively, you could opt to join a more in-depth, six-hour "study tour" for 70 zł, or you could hire your own guide—see sidebar.) At other times, you're allowed to visit Auschwitz I on your own—though the tour is still well worth considering. Any time of year, the grounds at Birkenau can be toured without a guide, though you'll likely need to be accompanied by a guide if you want to climb the guard tower.

Mandatory Reservations: With a million and a half visitors each year, Auschwitz struggles with crowd control. Reservations are required—whether visiting on your own or with a tour. It's free to reserve, but spaces book up very early. As soon as your dates are set—ideally weeks, or even months, in advance—visit http://visit.auschwitz.org. Select "Visit for individuals," then select a date, and choose between "General Tour 3,5 h" (for the 45-zł, 3.5-hour guided tour—be sure to select one

Why Visit Auschwitz?

Why visit a notorious concentration camp on your vacation?

 Auschwitz-Birkenau is one of the most moving sights in Europe, and certainly the most important of all the Holocaust memorials. Seeing the camp can be difficult: Many visitors are overwhelmed by a combination of sadness and anger over the tragedy, as well as inspiration at the remarkable stories of survival. Auschwitz survivors and victims' families want tourists to come here and experience the scale and the monstrosity of the place. In their minds, a steady flow of visitors will ensure that the Holocaust is always remembered—so nothing like it will ever happen again.

Auschwitz isn't for everyone. But I've never met anyone who toured Auschwitz and regretted it. For many, it's a profoundly life-altering experience—at the very least, it will forever affect the way you think about the Holocaust.

in English) or "Tour for individuals without an educator" (to visit on your own, for free—not possible between 10:00 and 15:00 in summer). After you fill out the form, you'll receive an eticket. Print this out and bring it along when you visit the memorial. If you hire a local guide or driver to bring you here from Kraków, they can usually handle making a reservation for you—but be very clear on the details, as this can take some coordination.

Available time slots can fill up quickly—particularly at popular times, such as May and June, when school groups flood the site. If an English tour isn't available for your dates, consider booking one in a **foreign language,** then splitting off and using this chapter's self-guided tour. If you arrive in Poland without reservations, there are a couple of last-minute options: **Book a day tour** through a private company in Kraków, which includes both transportation and a tour of the camp (see sidebar); or consider taking your chances and **just showing up.** A white booth in front of the main building (facing the parking lot, opens at 8:00) lists spaces available on upcoming tours that day. You may luck out and get a tour right away...or, on busy days, you could wait hours. (You can pass any wait time by first going to Birkenau, which has less strict timing requirements.) If you anticipate crowds, try to arrive early (get there at 9:00 or 9:30); the later you arrive, the longer you may have to wait.

Hours: The museum opens every day at 8:00, and closes June-Aug at 19:00, April-May and Sept at 18:00, March and Oct at 17:00, Feb at 16:00, Jan and Nov at 15:00, and Dec at 14:00. These are "last entry" times; the grounds at Auschwitz I stay open 1.5 hours later (though many buildings—including the national memorials—close promptly at these times). The grounds at Birkenau, where many groups end their visits, may stay open even later.

Information: Tel. 33-844-8100, www.auschwitz.org.

Getting from Auschwitz I to Birkenau: Buses shuttle visitors two miles between the camps (free, about 4/hour in peak season, less off-season, times posted at the bus stop outside the main building of each site, timed to correspond with tours). Taxis are also standing by (about 15 zł). Many visitors, rather than wait for the next bus, decide to walk the 30 minutes between the camps, offering a much-needed chance for reflection. Along the way, you'll pass the Judenrampe, an old train car like the ones used to transport prisoners, explained by an informational sign.

Services: Auschwitz I's main building has a helpful information desk, bookshops, exchange offices, baggage storage (large bags aren't allowed on site), WCs, and basic eateries. You'll also find maps of the camp (posted on the walls) and a theater that shows the film described below. The guard tower at Birkenau has another bookshop and more WCs.

Film: The 17-minute movie (too graphic for children) was shot by Ukrainian troops days after the Red Army liberated the camp (4 zł, schedule for showings in English varies—ask when you arrive).

Photography: Because the philosophy of the camp is to spread the story of Auschwitz, taking photographs of anything outdoors is encouraged. However, to ease the movement of visitors, photography is not allowed inside certain museum buildings (when it *is* allowed, don't use a flash or tripod).

Eating: A café and decent cafeteria are at the main Auschwitz building. More options are in the commercial complex across the street.

Expect Changes: Various parts of the Auschwitz museum are continually maintained and updated. Some things may be different than described here, but everything is always well-signposted.

Etiquette: The camp encourages visitors to remember that Auschwitz is the place where more than a million people lost their lives. Behave and dress here as you would at a cemetery.

Guided Tours at Auschwitz

Visiting Auschwitz on your own works well, given the abundance of English descriptions (and this chapter's self-guided tour). However, due to crowd-control issues, from May through October individual visitors are not allowed to enter the Auschwitz I part of the complex on their own between the peak times of 10:00 and 15:00. Instead, you're required to either join one of the museum's organized tours or reserve your own private museum guide. Note that even during these busy times, individuals may enter Birkenau without a guide.

Organized Museum Tours: The Auschwitz Museum's excellent guides are serious and frank historians, who feel a strong sense of responsibility about sharing the story of the camp. The regularly scheduled 3.5-hour English tour covers Auschwitz, Birkenau, and the film (45 zł). These tours must be pre-booked at http://visit.auschwitz.org. There are usually several English tours each day—check availability on the website. Due to crowd concerns, arrive for your scheduled tour 30 minutes early.

Private Official Museum Guides: If you have a special interest, a small group, or just want a more personalized visit, it's affordable and worthwhile to hire one of the museum's guides for a private tour. Choose between the basic 3.5-hour tour of the camp (300 zł) or a longer "study tour" (480 zł/6 hours, 570 zł/8 hours—possible all in one day, or spread over two days; all rates are higher for more than 10 people). Because English-speaking guides are limited, try to reserve as far ahead as possible (ideally several months) at http://visit.auschwitz.org.

Tours from Kraków: Various Kraków-based companies sell round-trip tours from Kraków to Auschwitz, which include a guided tour of the camp (typically around 150 zł). I wouldn't normally recommend these, but they can be handy if you're trying to book a time slot on your own and everything is sold out. The main outfits are **See Kraków** (www.seekrakow.com), **Discover Cracow** (www.discovercracow.com), and **Cracow City Tours** (www.cracowcitytours.com)—for details, see page 250.

Local Guides and Drivers from Kraków: For hassle-free transportation to the camp, you can hire a Kraków-based guide or driver to bring you to Auschwitz; I've listed my favorites on page 247 (drivers) and 246 (guides). However, since they're not officially registered museum guides, they technically aren't allowed to show you around the site. Instead, they'll help you book a slot on an organized English tour (which can be handy, as it saves you having to deal with the website). While it's pricey, some travelers consider hiring a driver/guide to be a worthwhile splurge, since you'll have door-to-door service to the camp and three hours in the car with a local expert.

Auschwitz Tour

AUSCHWITZ I

• *From the entrance building, step out and look over the grassy field to get oriented.*

Before World War II, this camp was a base for the Polish army. When Hitler occupied Poland, he took over these barracks and

turned it into a concentration camp for his Polish political enemies. The location was ideal, with a nearby rail junction and rivers providing natural protective boundaries. An average of 14,000 prisoners were kept at this camp at one time. (Birkenau could hold up to 100,000.) In 1942, Auschwitz became a death camp for the extermination of European Jews

and others whom Hitler considered "undesirable." By the time the camp was liberated in 1945, at least 1.1 million people had been murdered here—approximately 960,000 of them Jewish.

• *Go closer to the camp entrance, approaching the notorious...*

"Arbeit Macht Frei" Gate

Although this gate imparts the message "Work Sets You Free," the only way out of the camp for the prisoners was through the crematorium chimneys. Note that the "B" was welded on upside down by belligerent inmates, who were forced to make this sign (and much of the camp). This is actually a replica; the original was stolen one night in December of 2009, then recovered two days later, cut up into several pieces. The original is now safely in the museum's possession, but no longer displayed in public.

Just inside the gate and to the right, the camp orchestra (made up of prisoners) used to play marches; having the prisoners march made them easier to count.

• *From the gate, proceed straight up the "main street" of the camp.*

You'll pass two rows of barracks. The first one holds a variety of national memorials. We'll circle back here later, if you'd like to enter some of them. But these are of less general interest than the second row of barracks, which hold the main museum exhibitions. Blocks 4 and 5 focus on how Auschwitz prisoners were killed. Blocks 6, 7, and 11 explore the conditions for prisoners who survived here a little longer than most. In each block, arrows send you on a one-way route from numbered room to numbered room; in many cases, there are also exhibits downstairs and upstairs—don't miss these.

• *Start with...*

Auschwitz I

❶ Arbeit Macht Frei Gate
❷ Extermination (Block 4)
❸ Material Evidence (Block 5)
❹ Everyday Life (Block 6)
❺ Camp Conditions (Block 7)
❻ Execution Courtyard
❼ "Death Block" (Block 11)
❽ All Jews (Block 27)
❾ Netherlands (Block 21)
❿ Belgium & France (Block 20)
⓫ Hungary (Block 18)
⓬ Austria & Former Yugoslavia (Block 17)
⓭ Czech & Slovak (Block 16)
⓮ Poland (Block 15)
⓯ Russia (Block 14)
⓰ Roma/Gypsy (Block 13)
⓱ Crematorium
⓲ Gallows
⓳ Camp Commander's Home
⓴ Theater (Graphic Film)
㉑ Shuttle Bus to Birkenau

Block 4: Extermination

In Room 1, a map identifies the countries from which Auschwitz prisoners were brought—as far away as Norwegian fjords and Greek isles. In an alcove along the side of the room is an urn filled with ashes, a symbolic memorial to all of the camp's victims.

Room 2 shows photographs of Jewish ghettos from all over Europe being "liquidated"—that is, its residents assembled and deported to various concentration camps. Thanks to its massive occupancy, Auschwitz was a common destination for many.

Room 3 displays rare photos of scenes inside the camp, taken by arrogant SS men. To prevent a riot, the Nazis claimed at first that this was only a transition camp for resettlement in Eastern Europe. At the far end of Room 3, a helpful orientation map for visitors shows the town of Oświęcim, Auschwitz I, Auschwitz II (Birkenau), and other parts of the camp network.

Upstairs in Room 4 is a model of a Birkenau crematorium. People entered on the left, then got undressed in the underground rooms (hanging their belongings on numbered hooks and encouraged to remember their numbers to retrieve their clothes later). They then moved into the "showers" and were killed by Zyklon-B gas (hydrogen cyanide), a German-produced cleaning agent that is lethal in high doses. This efficient factory of murder took about 20 minutes to kill 8,000 people in four gas chambers. Elevators brought the bodies up to the crematorium. Members of the *Sonderkommand*—Jewish inmates who were kept isolated and forced by the Nazis to work here—removed the corpses' gold teeth and shaved off their hair (to be sold) before putting the bodies in the ovens. It wasn't unusual for a *Sonderkommand* worker to discover a wife, child, or parent among the dead. A few of these workers committed suicide by throwing themselves at electric fences; those who didn't were systematically executed by the Nazis after a two-month shift. Across from the model of the crematorium are canisters of Zyklon-B.

Across the hall in the dimly lit Room 5 is one of the camp's most powerful exhibits: a wall of actual victims' hair—4,400 pounds of it. Also displayed is cloth made of the hair, used to make Nazi uniforms. The Nazis were nothing if not efficient...nothing, not even human body parts, could be wasted.

Back downstairs in Room 6 is an exhibit on the plunder of victims' personal belongings. People being transported here were encouraged to bring luggage—and some victims had even paid in advance for houses in their new homeland. After they were killed, everything of value was sorted and stored in warehouses that prisoners named "Canada" (after a country they associated with great wealth). Although the Canada warehouses were destroyed, you can see a few of these items in the next building.

• *Head next door.*

Chilling Statistics:
The Holocaust in Poland

The majority of people murdered by the Nazis during the Holocaust were killed right here in Poland. For centuries, Poland was known for its relative tolerance of Jews, and right up until the beginning of World War II, Poland had Europe's largest concentration of Jews: 3,500,000. Throughout the Holocaust, the Nazis murdered 4,500,000 Jews in Poland (many of them brought in from other countries) at camps, including Auschwitz, and in ghettos such as Warsaw's.

By the end of the war, only 300,000 Polish Jews had survived—less than 10 percent of the original population. Many of these survivors were granted "one-way passports" (read: deported) to Israel, Western Europe, and the US by the communist government in 1968 (following a big student demonstration with a strong Jewish presence). Today, only about 10,000 Jews live in all of Poland.

Block 5: Material Evidence of the Nazis' Crimes

The exhibits in this block consist mostly of piles of the victims' goods, a tiny fraction of everything the Nazis stole. As you wander through the rooms, you'll see eyeglasses; fine Jewish prayer shawls; crutches and prosthetic limbs (the first people the Nazis exterminated were mentally and physically ill German citizens); and a pile of pots and pans. Then, upstairs, you'll witness a seemingly endless mountain of shoes; children's clothing; and suitcases with names of victims—many marked *Kind,* or "child." Visitors often wonder if the suitcase with the name "Frank" belonged to Anne, one of the Holocaust's most famous victims. After being discovered in Amsterdam by the Nazis, the Frank family was transported here to Auschwitz, where they were split up. Still, it's unlikely this suitcase was theirs. Anne Frank and her sister Margot were sent to the Bergen-Belsen camp in northern Germany, where they died of typhus shortly before the war ended. Their father, Otto Frank, survived Auschwitz and was found barely alive by the Russians, who liberated the camp in January of 1945.

• *Proceed to the next block.*

Block 6: Everyday Life

Although the purpose of Auschwitz was to murder its inmates, not all of them were killed immediately. After an initial evaluation, some prisoners were registered and forced to work. (This did not mean they were chosen to live—just to die later.) This block shows various aspects of daily existence at the camp.

The halls are lined with photographs of victims, each one

St. Maksymilian Kolbe (1894-1941)

Among the many inspirational stories of Auschwitz is that of a Polish priest named Maksymilian Kolbe. Before the war, Kolbe traveled as a missionary to Japan, then worked in Poland for a Catholic newspaper. While he was highly regarded for his devotion to the Church, some of his writings had an unsettling anti-Semitic sentiment. But during the Nazi occupation, Kolbe briefly ran an institution that cared for refugees—including Jews.

In 1941, Kolbe was arrested and interned at Auschwitz. When a prisoner from Kolbe's block escaped in July of that year, the Nazis punished the remaining inmates by selecting 10 of them to be put in the Starvation Cell until they died—based on the Nazi "doctrine of collective responsibility." After the selection had been made, Kolbe offered to replace a man who expressed concern about who would care for his family. The Nazis agreed. (The man Kolbe saved is said to have survived the Holocaust.)

All 10 of the men—including Kolbe—were put into Starvation Cell 18. Two weeks later, when the door was opened, only Kolbe had survived. The story spread throughout the camp, and Kolbe became an inspiration to the inmates. To squelch the hope he had given the others, Kolbe was executed by lethal injection.

In 1982, Kolbe was canonized by the Catholic Church. Some critics—mindful of his earlier anti-Semitic rhetoric—still consider Kolbe's sainthood controversial. But most Poles feel he redeemed himself for his earlier missteps through this noble act at the end of his life.

identified with a name, birthdate, occupation, date of arrival at Auschwitz, date of death, and camp registration number. Examining these dates, it's clear that those registered survived here an average of two to three months. (Flowers are poignant reminders that these victims are survived by loved ones.) Similar photographs hang in several other museum buildings, as well; as with the plundered items in the last block, keep in mind that these represent only a tiny fraction of the masses of people murdered at Auschwitz.

19472
DĄBROWSKI JAN
ur. 8.2.1920 r., robotnik
przybył 30.7.1941, zginął wrzesień 1942.

Room 1 (on the left as you enter the front door) displays drawings of the arrival process. After the initial selection, those chosen to work were showered, shaved, and photographed. After a while, photographing each prisoner got to be too expensive, so prisoners were tattooed instead (see photographs): on the chest, on the arm, or—for children—on the leg. A display shows the symbols that prisoners had to wear to show their reason for internment—Jew, Roma (Gypsy), homosexual, political prisoner, and so on. At the end of the room, a display case holds actual camp uniforms.

Across the hall, Room 4 shows the starvation that took place here. The 7,500 survivors that the Red Army found when the camp was liberated were essentially living skeletons (the "healthier" inmates had been forced to march to Germany). Of those liberated, 20 percent died soon after of disease and starvation.

In Room 5, you can see scenes from the prisoner's workday (sketched by survivors after liberation). Prisoners worked as long as the sun shone—eight hours in winter, up to twelve hours in summer—mostly on farms or in factories.

Room 6 is about Auschwitz's child inmates, 20 percent of the camp's victims. Blond, blue-eyed children were either "Germanized" in special schools or, if younger, adopted by German families. Dr. Josef Mengele conducted gruesome experiments here on children, especially twins and triplets, ostensibly to find ways to increase fertility for German mothers. Also in this room, look for a display of the prisoners' daily ration (in the glass case): a pan of tea or coffee in the morning; thin vegetable soup in the afternoon; and a piece of bread (often made with sawdust or chestnuts) for dinner. This makes it clear that Auschwitz was never intended to be a "work camp," where people were kept alive, healthy, and efficient to do work. Rather, people were meant to die here—if not in the gas chambers, then through malnutrition and overwork.

• *Block 7 shows living and sanitary conditions at the camp, which you'll see in more detail later at Birkenau. Blocks 8-10 are vacant (medical experiments were carried out in Block 10). And Block 11 was the most notorious of all.*

Block 11: The Death Block

Step into the walled-in **courtyard** between Blocks 10 and 11. The wall at the far end is where the Nazis shot several thousand political cal prisoners, leaders of camp resistance, and religious leaders. Notice that the windows are covered, so that nobody could witness the executions. Also take a close look at the memorial—the back of it is made of a material designed by Nazis to catch the bullets without a ricochet. Inmates were shot at short range—about three feet. The pebbles represent prayers from Jewish visitors.

Now head into the **"Death Block"** (#11), from which nobody ever left alive. Death here required a "trial"—but it was never a fair trial. Room 2 (on the left as you enter) is where these sham trials were held, lasting about two minutes each. In Room 5, you can see how prisoners lived in these barracks—three-level bunks, with three prisoners sleeping in each bed (they had to sleep on their sides so they could fit). In Room 6, people undressed before they were executed.

In the **basement,** you'll see several different types of cells. The Starvation Cell (#18) held prisoners selected to starve to death when a fellow prisoner escaped; Maksymilian Kolbe spent two weeks here to save another man's life (see sidebar on Kolbe). In the Dark Cell (#20), which held up to 30, people had only a small window for ventilation—and if it became covered with snow, the prisoners suffocated. In the Standing Cells (#22), four people would be forced to stand together for hours at a time (the bricks went all the way to the ceiling then).

Upstairs, you'll find gallows and a bench used for administering lashes. Filling this floor are exhibits on various forms of punishment, mostly focusing on resistance within the camp, escapees, and local Poles who were executed—either for trying to assist the prisoners, or for fighting with Nazi officers.

• *Leaving Block 11, proceed straight ahead, between the buildings, to the other row of barracks. Several of these blocks house...*

National Memorials

These exhibits were created not by museum authorities, but by representatives of the home countries of the camps' victims. As these memorials overlap with the general exhibits, and are designed for Europeans to learn more about the victims from their own home countries, most visitors skip this part of the site. On the other hand, while the main museum exhibits await renovation and modernization, the displays in these national memorials tend to be slicker and better-presented than the ones we just saw. (Some of these may be works in progress, as old exhibits are routinely upgraded.) As you walk along this street toward our next stop (the crematorium), consider stepping into the ones that interest you.

The first one you see is the memorial to **Jewish** victims (Block 27). It's compelling and thoughtfully presented, relying heavily on video clips, evocative music, and sound effects.

Most of the other national memorials are on the right side of the street. Across from the Jewish memorial, Block 21 honors **Dutch Jews;** it begins with a quote by perhaps the most famous

Dutch victim of the concentration camps, Anne Frank (whose story is also told—among many others'—throughout the exhibit).

Block 20, a former hospital block, is shared by **Belgium** and **France.** A room near the entrance explains how some prisoners were killed by lethal injection, with portraits and biographical sketches of victims. Upstairs is the powerful Belgium exhibit, with a room featuring victims' portraits. Block 18 holds a very modern, conceptual exhibit about **Hungary**'s victims, with an eerie heartbeat sound pervading the space. Block 17, which is likely a work in progress, is intended to memorialize victims from **Austria** and the **former Yugoslavia.** Across from this block, notice the long gallows used for mass hangings. Block 16 contains a new and well-presented exhibit about **Czech** and **Slovak** victims.

Block 15 honors victims from **Poland,** focusing on the 1939 Nazi invasion of the country, which resulted in the immediate internment of Polish political prisoners. Exhibits explain the process of "Germanization"—such as renaming Polish streets with German names—and (upstairs) the underground resistance that fought to get back some control over Poland.

Block 14 is the **Russian** national memorial. However, this one's a bit controversial: While Russia claims to have lost "Russian" Jews to the Holocaust, virtually all of them were technically Polish Jews who had been living within Russia. (They spoke Polish, not Russian.) To sidestep the hot topic of how to identify these victims, this memorial focuses not on victims, but on the Russian liberation of the camp.

Block 13 houses the **Roma (Gypsy)** exhibit. You'll learn that the Roma, along with the Jews, were considered no better than "rats, bedbugs, and fleas," and explore elements of the so-called *Zigeunerfrage*—the "Gypsy question" about what to do with this "troublesome" population.

• *At the end of this row of barracks, you reach a guard tower and a barbed-wire fence. Jog a few steps to the right, through the hole in the fence, then angle left toward the earthen mound with the giant, ominous brick chimney. The entrance is at the far end of the building.*

Crematorium

Up to 700 people at a time could be gassed here. People undressed outside, or just inside the door. As you enter, bear right and find your way into the big "shower room." Look for the vents in the ceiling—this is where the SS men dropped the Zyklon-B. In the adjacent room is a replica of the furnace. This facility could burn 340 bodies a day—so it took two days to burn all of the bodies from one round of executions. (The Nazis didn't like this inefficiency, so they built four more huge crematoria at Birkenau.)

• *Turning left as you exit the crematorium takes you back to the entrance building. But first, circle around to the opposite side of the crematorium for the closest thing this story has to a happy ending.*

Shortly after the war, camp commander Rudolf Höss was tried, convicted, and sentenced to death. Survivors requested that he be executed at Auschwitz, and in 1947, he was hanged here. The **gallows** are preserved behind the crematorium (about a hundred yards from his home where his wife—who is said to have loved her years here—raised their children in a villa maintained by slaves and furnished with possessions of the dead).

• *Take your time with Auschwitz I. When you're ready, continue to the second stage of the camp—Birkenau (see "Getting from Auschwitz I to Birkenau" on page 354).*

AUSCHWITZ II—BIRKENAU

In 1941, realizing that the original Auschwitz camp was too small to meet their needs, the Nazis began a second camp in some nearby farm fields. The original plan was for a camp that could hold 200,000 people, but at its peak, Birkenau (Brzezinka) held only about 100,000. They were still adding onto it when the camp was liberated in 1945.

• *Train tracks lead past the main building and into the camp. The first sight that greeted prisoners was the...*

Guard Tower

If you've seen *Schindler's List,* the sight of this icon of the Holocaust—shown in stirring scenes from the movie—may make you queasy.

Climb to the top of the entry building (also houses WCs and bookstore) for an overview of the massive camp. As you look over the camp, you'll see a vast field of chimneys and a few intact wooden and brick barracks. Some of the barracks were destroyed by Germans. Most were dismantled to be used for fuel and building materials shortly after the war. But the first row has been reconstructed (using components from the original structures). The train tracks lead straight back to the dividing platform, and then dead-end at the ruins of the crematorium and camp monument at the far side.

• *Descend the tower, enter the camp, turn right, and walk through the barbed-wire fence to reach the...*

Wooden Barracks

The first of these barrack buildings was the **latrine:** The front half

Auschwitz II – Birkenau

MONUMENT

Creek

CREMATORIA

FORMER RAIL LINE

FORMER

BARRACKS

GUARD TOWER

200 Meters
200 Yards

TOUR BEGINS

To Auschwitz I & Oświęcim Town

TOUR ENDS

CREMATORIA

"The Sauna"

Foundations

Existing Buildings

① Guard Tower, Viewpoint, WC & Bookstore
② Latrine & Restored Barracks
③ Dividing Platform
④ Brick Barracks
⑤ Crematoria Ruins (4)
⑥ Monument
⑦ "The Sauna"
⑧ "Canada" Foundations
⑨ Shuttle Bus to Auschwitz I

of the building contained washrooms, and the back was a row of toilets. There was no running water, and prisoners were in charge

of keeping the latrine clean. Because of the resulting unsanitary conditions and risk of disease, the Nazis were afraid to come in here—so the latrine became the heart of the black market and the inmates' resistance movement.

The third barrack was a **bunkhouse.** Each inmate had a personal number, a barrack number, and a bed number. Inside, you can see the beds (angled so that more could fit). An average of 400 prisoners—but up to 1,000—would be housed in each of these buildings. These wooden structures, designed as stables by a German company (look for the horse-tying rings on the wall), came in prefab pieces that made them cheap and convenient. Two chimneys connected by a brick duct provided a little heat. The bricks were smoothed by inmates who sat here to catch a bit of warmth.

• *Return to the train tracks, and follow them toward the monument about a half-mile away, at the back end of Birkenau. At the intersection of these tracks and the perpendicular gravel road (halfway to the monument)—now marked by a lonely train car—was the gravel pitch known as the...*

Dividing Platform

A Nazi doctor would stand facing the guard tower and evaluate each prisoner. If he pointed to the right, the prisoner was sentenced to death, and trudged—unknowingly—to the gas chamber. If he pointed to the left, the person would be registered and live a little longer. It was here that families from all over Europe were torn apart forever.

• *Photographs near the wooden building—on the left-hand side as you face the back of the camp complex—show the sad scene. Just beyond that building is a field with some...*

Brick Barracks

Enter one of these buildings. The supervisors lived in the two smaller rooms near the door. Farther in, most barracks still have the wooden bunks that held about 700 people per building. Four or five people slept on each bunk, including the floor—reserved for new arrivals. There were chamber pots at either end of the building. After a Nazi doctor died of typhus, sanitation improved, and these barracks got running water.

Now head back to the train tracks. As you walk along the camp's only road, which leads along the tracks to the crematorium, imagine the horror of this place—no grass, only mud, and all the barracks packed with people, with smoke blowing in from the busy crematoria. This was an even worse place to die than Auschwitz I.

• *The train tracks lead to the camp memorial and crematorium. At the end of the tracks, go 50 yards to the left and climb the three concrete steps to view the ruin of the...*

Crematorium

This is one of four crematoria here at Birkenau, each with a capacity to cremate more than 4,400 people per day. At the far-right end of the ruins, see the stairs where people entered the rooms to undress.

They were given numbered lockers, conning them into thinking they were coming back. (The Nazis didn't want a panic.) Then they piled into the "shower room"—the underground passage branching away from the memorial—and were killed. Their bodies were burned in the crematorium (on the left), giving off a scent of sweet almonds (from the Zyklon-B). Beyond the remains of the crematorium is a hole—once a gray lake where tons of ashes were dumped. This efficient factory of death was destroyed by the Nazis as the Red Army approached, leaving the haunting ruins you see today.

When the Soviets arrived on January 27, 1945, the nightmare of Auschwitz-Birkenau was over. The Polish parliament voted to turn these grounds into a museum, so that the world would understand, and never forget, the horror of what happened here.

• *At the back of the camp stands the...*

Monument

Built in 1967 by the communist government in its heavy "Socialist Realism" style, this monument represents gravestones and the chimney of a crematorium. The plaques, written in each of the languages spoken by camp victims (including English, far right), explain that the memorial is "a cry of despair and a warning to humanity."

• *With more time, you could continue deeper into...*

The Rest of the Camp

There's much more to see for those who are interested—Birkenau sprawls for a frightening distance. One place worth seeing is the

reception and disinfection building that prisoners called **"the Sauna"** (the long building with four tall chimneys). It was here that prisoners would be forced to strip and be deloused; their belongings were seized and taken to the "Canada" warehouses (described earlier) to be sorted. Walking through here (on glass floors designed to protect the original structure below), you'll see artifacts of the grim efficiency with which prisoners were "processed"—their heads were shaved, they were tattooed with a serial number, and they were assigned uniforms and wooden clogs to wear. Portraits at the end of the building humanize those who passed through here. Look for the cart, which was used to dispose of ashes. In front of the Sauna is a field of foundations of the **"Canada" warehouses.** Nearby are the other two destroyed **crematoria.**

Auschwitz Connections

The Auschwitz Museum is in the town of Oświęcim, about 50 miles west of Kraków. By bus or minibus, the journey takes 1.75 hours each way (longer by train); driving shaves off about 10-20 minutes.

FROM KRAKÓW TO AUSCHWITZ

The easiest way to reach Auschwitz is with a **package tour** (figure around 150 zł per person) or **private guide or driver** (300-500 zł for the carload); both of these options are described on page 246. While the package tours are more convenient than going on your own, three people can hire their own driver for less and have a more intimate experience.

If you're using public transportation, here are your choices (each one of these costs around 10-15 zł):

The most comfortable public-transit option is to take one of the frequent **buses,** mostly run by PKS Oświęcim (at least hourly, 1.75 hours, get the most recent schedule at any Kraków TI, buses depart from Kraków's main bus station behind the train station). Buy a one-way ticket from the bus-station ticket office or from the driver to leave your options open for getting home. Look for buses to "Oświęcim" (not necessarily "Auschwitz"). Note that these buses can be full, and because most come from other towns, there's no way to reserve a seat—so line up early (generally about 15 minutes ahead). If you don't get on a bus, you'll have to wait for the next one (or, if there's a minibus leaving sooner, you can take one of those instead—described next). Once in the town of Oświęcim, buses from Kraków stop first at the train station, then continue on to one of two stops near the museum: About half of the buses go directly into the parking lot at the museum itself, while the rest use a low-profile bus stop on the edge of the Auschwitz camp grounds (you'll see a small *Muzeum Auschwitz* sign on the right just before the stop, and a blue *Oświęcim Muzeum PKS* sign at the stop itself). From this bus stop, follow the sign down the road and into the parking lot; the main museum building is across the lot on your left. Note that since some buses don't actually go into the museum's parking lot, the Auschwitz stop can be easy to miss—don't be shy about letting your driver know where you want to go: *"Muzeum?"*

Several **minibuses** from Kraków head for Auschwitz (sporadic departures—generally 1-2/hour, 1.75 hours). Like the buses, some go directly to the museum, while others use the bus stop at the edge of camp. These generally depart from the lower platform of the main bus station (but confirm the departure point at the TI). Some of my readers report that the minibuses are a bit more cramped

On the Way to Auschwitz: The Polish Countryside

You'll spend about an hour gazing out the window as you drive or ride to Auschwitz. This may be your only real look at the Polish countryside. Ponder these thoughts about what you're passing...

The small houses you see are traditionally inhabited by three generations at the same time. Nineteenth-century houses (the few that survive) often sport blue stripes. Back then, parents announced that their daughters were now eligible by getting out the blue paint. Once they saw these blue lines, local boys were welcome to come a-courtin'.

Big churches mark small villages. Like in the US, tiny roadside memorials and crosses indicate places where fatal accidents have occurred.

Polish farmers traditionally had small lots that were notorious for not being very productive. These farmers somewhat miraculously survived the communist era without having to merge their farms. For years, they were Poland's sacred cows: producing little, paying almost no tax, and draining government resources. But since Poland joined the European Union in 2004, they're being forced to get up to snuff...and, in many cases, collectivize their farms after all.

Since most people don't own cars, bikes are common and public transit is excellent. There are lots of bus stops, as well as minibuses that you can flag down anywhere for a 2-zł ride. The bad roads are a legacy of communist construction, exacerbated by heavy truck use and brutal winters.

Poland has more than 2,000 counties, or districts, each with its own coat of arms; you'll pass several along the way. The forests are state-owned, and locals enjoy the right to pick berries in the summer and mushrooms in the autumn (you may see people—often young kids—selling their day's harvest by the side of the road). The mushrooms are dried and then boiled to make tasty soups in the winter.

than the buses and, while intended for local commuters, can be crammed with tourists. But they work fine in a pinch.

You could ride the **train** to Oświęcim, but it's less convenient than the bus because it leaves you at the train station, farther from the museum (nearly hourly, fewer Sat-Sun, 2-2.5 hours). If you do wind up at the Oświęcim train station, it's about a 20-minute walk to the camp (turn right out of station, go straight, then turn left at roundabout, camp is several blocks ahead on left). Or you can take a taxi (around 15 zł).

RETURNING FROM AUSCHWITZ TO KRAKÓW

Upon arrival at Auschwitz I, plan your departure by visiting the information window inside the main building. They can give you a schedule of departures and explain where the bus or minibus leaves from. (If you'll be staying late into the afternoon, make a point of figuring out the last possible bus or train back to Kraków, and plan accordingly.) Remember to allow enough time to make it from Birkenau back to Auschwitz I to catch your bus.

Although most minibuses and a few buses back to Kraków leave from the camp parking lot itself, if you're taking the bus, you'll most likely catch it from the stop on the edge of the Auschwitz I grounds. To reach this bus stop, leave the Auschwitz I building through the main entry and walk straight along the parking lot, then turn right on the road near the end of the lot. At the T-intersection, cross the street to the little bus stop with the blue *Oświęcim Muzeum PKS* sign. Don't be distracted by the ads for a nearby travel agency—you can buy tickets on board.

There's no public transportation back to Kraków from Birkenau, where most people end their tours; you'll have to take the shuttle bus back to Auschwitz I first.

WARSAW

Warszawa

Warsaw (Warszawa, vah-SHAH-vah in Polish) is Poland's capital and biggest city. It's huge, famous, and important...but not particularly romantic. If you're looking for Old World quaintness, head for Kraków. If you're tickled by spires and domes, get to Prague. But if you want to experience a truly 21st-century city, Warsaw's your place.

Not that long ago, the city was dreary and uninviting, but things have changed here—fast. Today, Warsaw's residents—Varsovians—are chic and sophisticated. Young professionals dress and dine as well as Parisians or Milanese do, and they have mastered the art of navigating an urban jungle in heels or a man bun. And from an infrastructure perspective, you can almost feel Warsaw peeling back the layers of communist grime as it replaces potholed highways with pedestrian-friendly parks. Today's Warsaw has gleaming new office towers and street signs, cutting-edge shopping malls, swarms of international businesspeople, hipster culture as vivid as anything in Brooklyn, and a gourmet coffee shop or designer pastry store on every corner.

Stroll down revitalized boulevards that evoke the city's glory days, pausing at an outdoor café to sip coffee and nibble at a *pączek* (the classic Polish jelly doughnut). Drop by a leafy park for an al fresco Chopin concert, packed with pensive Poles. Commune with the soul of Poland at the city's many

Warsaw History: Ebbs and Flows

Warsaw has good reason to be a city of the future: The past hasn't been very kind. Since becoming Poland's capital in 1596, Warsaw has seen wave after wave of foreign rulers and invasions—especially during the last hundred years. But in this horrific crucible, the enduring spirit of the Polish people was forged. As one proud Varsovian told me, "Warsaw is ugly because its history is so beautiful."

The city's Golden Age was between the World Wars, when Poland—newly reconstituted after a century and a half of foreign rule under the Partitions—was proudly independent and looking to the future. Interwar Warsaw saw a flourishing of commerce, construction, and the arts almost unmatched in Europe at that time.

Sadly, this age of unbridled optimism was cut brutally short by the city's darkest days, as the Nazis occupied the city (and all of Poland) at the outbreak of World War II. First, its Jewish residents were forced into a tiny ghetto. They rose up... and were slaughtered (the Ghetto Uprising—see page 412). Then, in the war's waning days, its Polish residents rose up... and were slaughtered (the Warsaw Uprising—see page 419). Fed up with the troublesome Varsovians, Hitler sent word to systematically demolish the entire city, block by block. At the war's end, Warsaw was virtually gone. An estimated 800,000 residents were dead—nearly two out of every three.

The Poles almost gave up on what was then a pile of rubble, planning to build a brand-new capital city elsewhere. But ultimately they decided to rebuild, creating a city of contrasts: painstakingly restored medieval lanes, retrofitted communist apartment blocks (*bloki* in Polish), and sleek skyscrapers. Between the buildings, you'll find fragments of a complex, sometimes tragic, and often inspiring history.

state-of-the-art museums focusing on Poland's artists (at the National Museum), its favorite composer (at the Chopin Museum), its dramatic history (at the Warsaw Historical Museum and Warsaw Uprising Museum), its dedication to the sciences (at the Copernicus Science Center), and its Jewish story (at the Museum of the History of Polish Jews). You can also dig into one of Europe's most affordable—and most interesting—foodie scenes, where a world of wildly creative chefs open new restaurants all the time. If you picture a dreary metropolis, think again. Warsaw is full of surprises.

PLANNING YOUR TIME

One day is the absolute minimum to get a quick taste of Warsaw. The city can easily fill two or three days, and even then you'll need to be selective. No matter how long you're staying, get your bearings by taking a stroll through Polish history on the Royal Way, using my self-guided walk from Palm Tree Circle to the Old Town. Then visit other sights according to your interests and time: Jewish history, the Warsaw Uprising, Polish artists, royalty, hands-on science gizmos, hipster hangouts, or Chopin. To slow down and take a break from the city, relax in Łazienki Park. For dinner, buck the tourist trend by leaving the overpriced Old Town and riding a tram, taxi, or Uber to the hip Śródmieście district, which has the highest concentration of quality eateries.

Orientation to Warsaw

Warsaw sprawls with 1.7 million residents. Everything is on a big scale—it seems to take forever to walk just a few "short" blocks. Get

comfortable with public transportation (or taxis or Uber), and plan your sightseeing to avoid backtracking.

The tourist's Warsaw blankets a mild hill on the west bank of the Vistula River (in Polish: Wisła, VEES-wah). To break things into manageable chunks, I think of the city as three major zones (from north to south):

The **Old Town and Royal Way,** at Warsaw's northern edge, is the most touristy area. Here you'll find the Old Town (Stare Miasto, STAH-reh mee-AH-stoh), the adjacent and nearly-as-old New Town (Nowe Miasto, NOH-vay mee-AH-stoh), the Royal Castle on Castle Square (Plac Zamkowy, plahts zahm-KOH-vee), and the historical artery called the Royal Way (Szlak Królewski, shwock kroh-LEHV-skee). This bustling strip has fine boulevards, genteel cafés, expansive squares and parks, and lots of stately landmarks both historic and faux-historic (much of this area was rebuilt after World War II).

"Palm Tree Circle" is my nickname for the center of the city, near the traffic circle with a fake palm tree—where busy Jerusalem Avenue (aleja Jerozolimskie, ah-LAY-uh yeh-ro-zoh-LIM-skyeh) crosses the shopping street called Nowy Świat (NOH-vee SHVEE-aht). Nearby are some good accommodations, trendy upscale eateries, pedestrianized shopping streets and glitzy malls, the National Museum (Polish art), the Palace of Culture and Science (communist-era landmark skyscraper), and the central train station (Warszawa Centralna).

The **Śródmieście** (SHROD-myesh-cheh, "Downtown") district, to the south, is a mostly-residential zone with the city's best restaurant and nightlife scene and some good accommodations.

The only real sight here is lush Łazienki Park, with its summertime al fresco Chopin concerts.

In sprawling Warsaw, many more sights—including some major ones—lie outside these three areas, but all are within a long walk or a short ride on public transit. These include the Museum of the History of Polish Jews and Warsaw Uprising Museum (to the west) and the Copernicus Science Center (to the east, along the river).

TOURIST INFORMATION

Warsaw's helpful, youthful TI has three branches: on the **Old Town Market Square** (daily May-Sept 9:00-20:00, Oct-April until 18:00), at the **Palace of Culture and Science** (enter on the side facing the train station, on Emilii Plater; daily May-Sept 8:00-19:00, Oct-April until 18:00), and at **Chopin Airport** (daily 9:00-19:00). The general information number for all TIs is 22-19115. All branches offer advice on live music and have piles of free, useful brochures ("city breaks," Jewish heritage, Chopin, mermaids, St. John Paul II, and so on). Everything is also available online (www.warsawtour.pl).

Busy sightseers might consider the **Warsaw Pass,** which covers public transportation, admission to several major sights, and free passage on the best hop-on, hop-off bus tour (119 zł/24 hours, 159 zł/48 hours, 189 zł/72 hours, sold at the TI). If your museum-going plans are ambitious, do the math.

ARRIVAL IN WARSAW
By Train

Most trains arrive at the **central train station** (Warszawa Centralna, vah-SHAH-vah tsehn-TRAHL-nah), a renovated commu-nist-era monstrosity. (Don't get off at Warszawa Zachodnia, which is far from the tourist area.) Arriving at Warszawa Centralna, it can be tricky to get your bearings: Three parallel concourses run across the tracks, accessed by three different sets of escalators from each plat-form, creating a subterranean maze (with well-signed lockers, ticket windows, and lots of shops and eateries). Be patient: To get your bearings, ride up on your platform's middle escalator, then look for signs to the vast, open **main hall** (follow signs for *main hall/hala główna*). Here you'll find a row of ticket windows, a railroad service center, a supermarket, eateries, waiting areas (upstairs), and (from outside, near the taxi stand) views of the adjacent Palace of Culture

Warsaw Overview

1. Hotel Rialto
2. H15 Boutique Hotel
3. Autor Rooms
4. Plac Zbawiciela Eateries
5. Dyspensa & Słodki Słony
6. Beirut & other Poznańska Eateries
7. Mokotowska Street (Shopping)

CYTADELA

GDAŃSKI BRIDGE

Vistula River

SŁOMIŃSKIEGO

WYBRZEŻE

PRAGA

See the Central Warsaw map

KONWIKTORSKA SANGUSZKI

BONIFRATERSKA

FRANCISZKAŃSKA

FRETA

New Town Square

NEW TOWN

DEFENSIVE WALL

Old Town Square

WYBRZEŻE HELSKIE

JAGIELLOŃSKA

To Mus. of Hist. of Polish Jews & Former Ghetto

ŚWIĘTOJERSKA

BARBICAN

OLD TOWN

ŚLĄSKO-DĄBROWSKI BRIDGE

WYBRZEŻE

ROYAL CASTLE

Krasiński Garden

GEN. ANDERSA

DŁUGA

MIODOWA

Castle Square

ST. ANNE'S

SZCZECIŃSKA

ROYAL WAY

Ratusz

SOLIDARNOŚCI

NATIONAL THEATER & OPERA

WIERZBOWA

KRAKOWSKIE PRZEDMIEŚCIE

RADZIWIŁŁ PALACE

KARKOWA

BROWARNA

DOBRA

To National Stadium

ORLA

SENATORSKA

Saxon Garden

Piłsudski Square

HOTEL BRISTOL

COPERNICUS SCIENCE CENTER

ŚWIĘTOKRZYSKI BRIDGE

PTASIA

KRÓLEWSKA

WARSAW UNIVERSITY

CZACKIEGO

Centrum Nauki Kopernik

GRZYBOWSKA

HOLY CROSS

OBOŻNA

To Warsaw Uprising Museum

Świętokrzyska

ŚWIĘTOKRZYSKA

Nowy Świat-Uniwersytet

TAMKA

CHOPIN MUSEUM

GALERIA CENTRUM MALL

NOWY ŚWIAT

FOKSAL

PONIATOWSKIEGO BRIDGE

PALACE OF CULTURE & SCIENCE

CHMIELNA

SMOLNA

JERUSALEM AVE.

E. PLATER

ZŁOTA

WIDOK

Centrum

JEROZOLIMSKIE

PALM TREE CIRCLE

NATIONAL MUSEUM

LUDNA

CENTRAL TRAIN STATION

AL.

NOWOGRODZKA

ŻURAWIA

Three Crosses Square

CHAŁUBIŃSKIEGO

WSPÓLNA

POZNAŃSKA

MARSZAŁKOWSKA

HOŻA

WILCZA

KRUCZA

ROYAL WAY

ROZBRAT

AL. NIEPODLEGŁOŚCI

KOSZYKOWA

MOKOTOWSKA

AL. UJAZDOWSKIE

AL. PIĘKNA

ŚRÓDMIEŚCIE

Constitution Square

Plac Zbawiciela

NOWOWIEJSKA

AL. ARMII LUDOWEJ

Politechnika

Łazienki Park

WAWELSKA

N

0.5 Kilometer

0.5 Mile

ROYAL WAY

To Wilanów Palace

CHOPIN MONUMENT & CONCERTS

PALACE ON THE WATER

BELWEDER

and Science and Złota 44 skyscrapers. If you have a little time to kill, walk across the street to the super-modern Złote Tarasy Shopping Mall (described on page 409).

Getting into Town: To reach the tourist zone and most of my recommended hotels, a taxi/Uber is the easiest choice, while the bus is more economical (but more challenging to find).

Taxis wait outside the main hall. Many are dishonest—look for one with a company logo and telephone number, and ask for an estimate up front (the fare should be no more than about 20-30 zł for most of my recommended hotels). You can also request an **Uber.**

From the station, **bus #175** or **#128** takes you to the Royal Way and Old Town in about 10 minutes (see "Getting Around Warsaw," later). You can catch either bus in front of the skyscraper with the Hotel Marriott (across busy Jerusalem Avenue from the station). From the corridors under the main hall, carefully track *Aleje Jerozolimskie* signs to find the pedestrian underpass. Several different exits are marked this way, but look for signs to *Śródmieście Station*, and then—near the end of that corridor—*Hotel Marriott*. Both buses terminate just off Piłsudski Square, a five-minute walk from the Old Town. **Bus #160** also goes to the Old Town (though not via the Royal Way), but it departs from the opposite side of the station: To find its stop from the main hall, go out the side door toward *ul. Emilii Plater*. Before boarding any bus, buy a ticket from the machine near the stop—or get one in the underground zone, at any kiosk marked *RUCH*.

Buying Train Tickets: Lining one wall of the main arrival hall *(hala główna)* are 16 **ticket windows.** A more user-friendly **passenger service center** is in the opposite corner (daily 9:10-20:30). While it can be slower to buy tickets or make reservations here (take a number as you enter), staff members are more likely to speak English and have patience for clueless tourists. Additional ticket windows are in the maze of corridors under the station. Allow yourself plenty of time to wait in line to buy tickets. Remember: Even if you have a rail pass, a reservation is still required on many express trains (including EIC trains to Kraków or Gdańsk). If you're not sure, ask. To get to your train, first find your way to the right platform *(peron,* as noted on schedules), then keep an eye on both tracks *(tor)* for your train. Train info: Tel. 19436 (22-19436 from outside Warsaw), www.rozklad-pkp.pl.

By Plane

Warsaw's **Fryderyk Chopin International Airport** (Port Lotniczy im. Fryderyk Chopina, airport code: WAW) is about six miles southwest of the center. The airport has just one terminal (Terminal A), which is divided into five check-in areas split between two zones: the southern hall (areas A and B) and the northern hall (areas C, D, and E). The airport is small and manageable; outside the arrivals area, you'll find a TI, ATMs, car-rental offices, and exchange desks *(kantor)*. Airport info: tel. 22-650-4220, www. lotnisko-chopina.pl.

You can take the train or bus into town (similar prices, around 5 zł). The train is faster, but the bus makes more stops in the city center and may get you closer to your hotel. From the arrivals area, just follow signs to either option, and buy your ticket at the red machine before you board.

The **train** departs about every 15 minutes and takes 20-30 minutes. The route is operated by two different companies (SKM and KM)—take the one that's departing first. Be ready for your stop: Half the trains make fewer stops and take you to Centralna station; the others make a few more stops and use the Warszawa Śródmieście station—which feeds into the same underground passages as Centralna (these trains also continue one more stop to the Warszawa Powiśle station, which is a bit closer to Nowy Świat and can be more convenient to some hotels). Whether arriving at Centralna station or Warszawa Śródmieście, see the "By Train" arrival instructions, earlier.

Bus #175 departs every 15-20 minutes and runs into the city center (Centralna station, the Royal Way, and Piłsudski Square near the Old Town, 30-45 minutes depending on traffic).

For a **taxi,** head to the official taxi stand (avoid random hucksters offering you a ride out front). The trip to most hotels shouldn't cost more than 40-50 zł. It takes about 30 minutes, but potentially much longer during rush hour. You can also request an **Uber,** which is typically less expensive (except at very busy times).

Modlin Airport (airport code: WMI), about 21 miles northwest of the city center, primarily serves budget airlines (especially Ryanair). The most direct option for getting to downtown Warsaw is by shuttle bus—**ModlinBus** and **OKbus** both connect the airport to downtown (33 zł, 2/hour, 1-hour trip, cheaper if you book ahead online—www.modlinbus.com or www.okbus.pl). An alternative is the well-coordinated **bus-plus-train connection:** Take a shuttle bus to Modlin's main train station, then hop on a train to Warszawa Centralna station (17 zł, hourly, 1-1.5 hours total, www. mazowieckie.com.pl). If you want to ride a **taxi** all the way into Warsaw, the maximum legitimate fare is 200 zł (or 250 zł at night). Airport info: www.modlinairport.pl.

GETTING AROUND WARSAW

By Public Transit: In this big city, it's essential to get a handle on public transportation. You'll rely mostly on buses and trams, but the Metro can be useful for reaching a few sights. Everything is covered by the same ticket. A single ticket costs 4.40 zł (called *bilet*

Warsaw at a Glance

▲▲▲**Museum of the History of Polish Jews** Exceptional, expansive exhibit on the full Jewish experience through Polish history. **Hours:** Mon and Thu-Fri 10:00-18:00, Wed and Sat-Sun 10:00-20:00, closed Tue. See page 411.

▲▲**Royal Castle** Warsaw's best palace, rebuilt after World War II, but retaining its former opulence and many original furnishings. **Hours:** May-Sept Mon-Sat 10:00-18:00, Thu until 20:00, Sun 11:00-18:00; Oct-April Tue-Sat 10:00-16:00, Sun 11:00-16:00, closed Mon. See page 394.

▲▲**Old Town Market Square** Re-creation of Warsaw's glory days, with lots of colorful architecture. **Hours:** Always open. See page 398.

▲▲**National Museum** Collection of mostly Polish art, with unknown but worth-discovering works by Jan Matejko and the Młoda Polska (Art Nouveau) crew. **Hours:** Tue-Sun 10:00-18:00, Thu until 21:00, closed Mon. See page 401.

▲▲**Warsaw Uprising Museum** State-of-the-art space tracing the history of the Uprising and celebrating its heroes. **Hours:** Mon and Wed-Fri 8:00-18:00, Thu until 20:00, Sat-Sun 10:00-18:00, closed Tue. See page 417.

▲▲**Copernicus Science Center** Spiffy new science museum with well-explained, hands-on exhibits in English; Warsaw's best family activity. **Hours:** Tue-Fri 9:00-18:00, Sat-Sun 10:00-19:00, closed Mon. See page 406.

jednorazowy, good for one trip up to 75 minutes). But most trips should last no longer than 20 minutes, so you can save a zloty by buying a 3.40-zł "20-minute city travelcard" *(bilet 20-minutowy).* A 24-hour travelcard *(bilet dobowy)*—which pays for itself if you take at least five trips—costs 15 zł. Ticket machines, which are at most major stops and on board some trams, are easy to use. Or you can buy tickets at any kiosk with a *RUCH* sign. Be sure to validate your ticket as you board by inserting it in the little yellow box. Transit info: www.ztm.waw.pl.

Most of the city's major attractions line up on a single axis, the Royal Way, which is served by several different buses (but no trams). **Bus #175**—particularly useful on arrival—links Chopin Airport, the central train station, the Royal Way, and Old Town (it terminates at Piłsudski Square, about a five-minute walk from Castle Square). Once you're in town, the designed-for-tourists **bus**

▲**Castle Square** Colorful spot with whiffs of old Warsaw—Royal Castle, monuments, and a chunk of the city wall—and cafés just off the square. **Hours:** Always open. See page 393.

▲**Łazienki Park** Lovely, sprawling green space with Chopin statue, peacocks, and Neoclassical buildings. **Hours:** Always open; wonderful outdoor Chopin concerts mid-May-late Sept Sun at 12:00 and 16:00. See page 420.

Chopin Museum Elegant old mansion featuring slick exhibits but not much substance about Chopin; occasional piano concerts worthwhile. **Hours:** Tue-Sun 11:00-20:00, closed Mon. See page 405.

Warsaw Museum Glimpse of the city before and after World War II, with excellent movie in English. **Hours:** Closed until at least mid-2017; when open: Museum—likely Tue-Sun 10:00-20:00, off-season until 18:00, closed Mon year-round; Movie—likely Tue-Fri at 10:00 and 12:00; Sat-Sun at 12:00 and 14:00. See page 399.

Palace of Culture and Science Huge "Stalin Gothic" skyscraper with a more impressive exterior than interior, housing theaters, multiplex cinema, observation deck, and more. **Hours:** Observation deck—daily 10:00-20:00, may be open later in summer. See page 408.

Jewish Ghetto: Path of Remembrance Pilgrimage from Ghetto Heroes Square to the infamous Nazi "transfer spot" where Jews were sent to death camps. **Hours:** Always open. See page 416.

#180 conveniently connects virtually all the significant sights and neighborhoods: the former Jewish Ghetto and Museum of the History of Polish Jews, Castle Square/Old Town, the Royal Way, Łazienki Park, and Wilanów Palace (south of the center). This particularly user-friendly bus lists sights in English on the posted schedule inside (other buses don't). Buses #175 and #180, as well as buses **#116, #128,** and **#222,** go along the most interesting stretch of the Royal Way (between Jerusalem Avenue and the Old Town area). **Bus #178** conveniently connects Castle Square to the Warsaw Uprising Museum. Bus routes beginning with "E" (marked in red on schedules) are express, so they go long distances without stopping (these don't run July-Aug).

Note that on Saturdays and Sundays in summer (June-Sept), the Nowy Świat section of the Royal Way is closed to traffic, so the above routes detour along a parallel street.

Trams can be particularly useful for reaching the trendy Śródmieście district in the south. Several trams (including #4, #15, #18, and #35) run along the north-south Marszałkowska corridor, with stops at plac Konstytucji (Constitution Square, the heart of the Śródmieście) and at plac Zbawiciela (with the highest concentration of eateries).

Warsaw's two-line **Metro** system is handy for commuters, but less so for visitors. Still, it can be useful for some trips. Line 1 runs roughly parallel to the river and Royal Way, several blocks to the west; the most useful stops for tourists are Centrum (near the Palace of Culture and Science) and Świętokrzyska (where it crosses line 2). Line 2—which runs east to west, crossing deep under the river—is more practical; handy stops are Rondo Daszyńskiego (near the Warsaw Uprising Museum); Świętokrzyska (a transfer station between the two lines); Nowy Świat-Uniwersytet (in the middle of the Royal Way, near the Copernicus Monument); Centrum Nauki Kopernik (on the riverbank, near the Copernicus Science Center); and Stadion Narodowy (National Stadium).

By Taxi: As in most big Eastern European cities, it's wise to use only cabs that are clearly marked with a company logo and telephone number (or call your own: Locals like City Taxi, tel. 19459; MPT Radio Taxi, tel. 19191; or Ele taxi, tel. 22-811-1111). All official taxis have similar rates: 8 zł to start, then 3 zł per kilometer (4.50 zł after 22:00 or in the suburbs). The drop fee may be higher if you catch the cab in front of a fancy hotel. Note that **Uber** is active in Warsaw—if you're comfortable using it back home, it works the same way here, and is often cheaper.

Tours in Warsaw

Walking Tours

Each year, new companies crop up offering walking tours in Warsaw. These tend to have one of two approaches: A "free" tour of the main sights (with generous tipping expected); or communism-themed tours, often with a ride to a gloomy apartment-block area for a taste of the Red old days. The options change often, so survey the latest ones, do some homework (check online reviews), and pick a tour that suits your interests. The TI and most hotels have brochures.

Private Guides

Having a talented local historian as your guide in this city, with such a complex and powerful story to tell, greatly enhances your experience. I've worked with two excellent young guides: the smart and charming **Monika Oleśko** (320 zł/3 hours, 480 zł/5.5 hours, more for larger groups; by bike or by car; mobile 784-832-718, warsawteller.wordpress.com, olesko.monika@gmail.com) and the professorial **Hubert Pawlik** (660 zł for 5 hours on foot or with his car, or 115 zł per person for a walking tour, mobile 502-298-105, www.warsaw-citytours.com). Hubert's big, comfy SUV can fit a small group. Both Monika and Hubert can do theme tours or tailor the time to your interests.

Food Tours

Eat Polska does excellent food and vodka tours around this fast-emerging foodie mecca. A top-quality guide will take your small group (maximum 6 people for the food tours, 12 for the vodka tours) to a variety of restaurants and bars around the city, with tasting samples at each one. The guides do an exceptional job of providing insightful context about what you're tasting, making this educational about both Polish cuisine and Polish culture in general. If you have a serious interest in food, this is the most worthwhile tour in town (food tours typically daily at 13:00, 290 zł, 4 hours; vodka tours with food pairings daily at 17:00, 260 zł, 3.5 hours; contact to arrange details, www.eatpolska.com).

Bus Tours

Warsaw's spread-out landscape makes it a natural for a hop-on, hop-off bus—although heavy traffic may make you wish you'd taken a tram or the Metro instead. Two competing companies offer tours around Warsaw (60 zł/24 hours, 80 zł/48 hours): City-Sightseeing, with red buses, has two routes and generally better frequency; I'd skip City-Tour (with yellow buses), which runs only once hourly.

Warsaw's Royal Way Walk

The Royal Way (Szłak Królewski) is the six-mile route that the kings of Poland used to travel from their main residence (at Castle Square in the Old Town) to their summer home (Wilanów Palace, south of the center and not worth visiting). This self-guided walk covers a one-mile section of the Royal Way in the heart of the city—from Palm Tree Circle to the castle. This is a busy, mostly-pedestrian boulevard with two different names: At the south end, vibrant **Nowy Świat** offers shops, restaurants, and a good glimpse of urban Warsaw; to the north, and ending at the Old Town, **Krakowskie Przedmieście** is lined with historic landmarks and is better for sightseeing. Not counting sightseeing stops, figure about 30 minutes to walk along Nowy Świat ("Part 1"), then another 30 minutes along Krakowskie Przedmieście to the Old Town ("Part 2").

PART 1: PALM TREE CIRCLE AND NOWY ŚWIAT

• *Start this walk at the traffic circle officially named for Charles de Gaulle, but colloquially known as...*

Palm Tree Circle

This is one of the city's main intersections, marked by the quirky and now iconic palm tree. Stand near the communist-era monument under the spruce trees (on the curb, kitty-corner from the biggest building) and get oriented.

You're standing at the intersection of two major boulevards: **Nowy Świat** (where we're heading next) and **Jerusalem Avenue** (aleja Jerozolimskie, which heads from Warszawa Centralna station across the river). This street once led to a Jewish settlement called New Jerusalem. Like so much else in Warsaw, it's changed names many times. Between the World Wars, it became "May 3rd Avenue," celebrating Poland's 1791 constitution (Europe's first). But this was too nationalistic for the occupying Nazis, who called it simply Bahnhofstrasse ("Train Station Street"). Then the communists switched it back to "Jerusalem," strangely disregarding the religious connotations of that name. (Come on, guys—what about a good, old-fashioned "Stalin Avenue"?) The strikingly wide boulevards were part of the city's post-WWII Soviet rebuilding. Communist urban planners felt that eight- to twelve-lane roads were ideal for worker pageantry like big May Day parades...and, when the workers aren't happy, for Soviet tanks to thunder around, maintaining order.

You can't miss the giant **palm tree** in the middle of Jerusalem Avenue. When a local artist went to the real Jerusalem, she was struck by the many palm trees—and wanted to erect one along Warsaw's own little stretch of "Jerusalem." This artificial palm tree went up in 2002 as a temporary installation. It was highly controversial, dividing the neighborhood. One snowy winter day, the pro-palm tree faction—who appreciated the way the tree spiced up this otherwise dreary metropolis—camped out here in bikinis and beachwear to show their support. They prevailed, and the tree is now a permanent fixture.

The big, blocky building across the street (behind statue of de Gaulle) was the **headquarters of the Communist Party,** built in 1948. *Nowy Świat* translates as "New World," inspiring a popular communist-era joke: What do you see when you turn your back on the Communist Party? A "New World." Ironically, when the economy was privatized in 1991, this building became home to Poland's stock exchange. And then the country's only dealership for

Ferraris—certainly not an automobile for the proletariat—moved in downstairs.

On the corner in front of the former Communist Party HQ, a statue of **Charles de Gaulle** strides confidently up the street. A gift from the government of France, this celebrates the military tactician who came to Warsaw's rescue when the Red Army invaded from the USSR after World War I.

To the left of the Communist Party building is the vast **National Museum**—a good place for a fascinating lesson in Polish art (see the self-guided tour on page 401).

Before walking down Nowy Świat, notice the small but powerful **monument** near you. In 1956, this was dedicated to the "Poles who fought for People's Poland"—with a strong communist connotation. In a classic example of Socialist Realism, the communists appropriated a religious theme that Poles were inclined to embrace (this *pietà* composition)...and politicized it. But in 2014, the statue was rededicated to the "*partyzantom* who fought for free Poland in World War II." "Partisan" was a bad word in the 1950s, when it was used to describe the soldiers of the Polish Home Army—which fought against both the Nazis and the Soviets.

• *From here, turn your back to the Communist Party building and head into a new world—down Nowy Świat—to the first intersection. As you stroll, notice how massive and intense Warsaw suddenly becomes more intimate and accessible.*

Nowy Świat

This charming shopping boulevard is lined with boutiques, cafés, and restaurants—it's the most upscale, elegant-feeling part of the city. Before World War II, Nowy Świat was Warsaw's most popular neighborhood. And today, once again, rents are higher here than anywhere else in town. While most tourists flock into the Old Town, Varsovians and visiting businesspeople prefer this zone and farther south. The city has worked hard to revitalize this strip with broader, pedestrian-friendly sidewalks, flower boxes, and old-time lampposts.

Look down the street and notice the consistent architecture. In the 1920s, this was anything but cohesive: an eclectic and decadent strip of Art Deco facades, full of individualism. Rather than rebuild in that "trouble-causing" style, the communists used an idealized, more conservative, Neoclassical style, which feels more like the 1820s than the 1920s.

Ulica Chmielna, the first street to the left, is an appealing pedestrian boutique street leading to Emil Wedel's chocolate heaven (a five-minute walk away; described later, under "Eating in Warsaw"). Between here and the Palace of Culture and Science stretches one of Warsaw's top shopping neighborhoods (culminat-

WARSAW

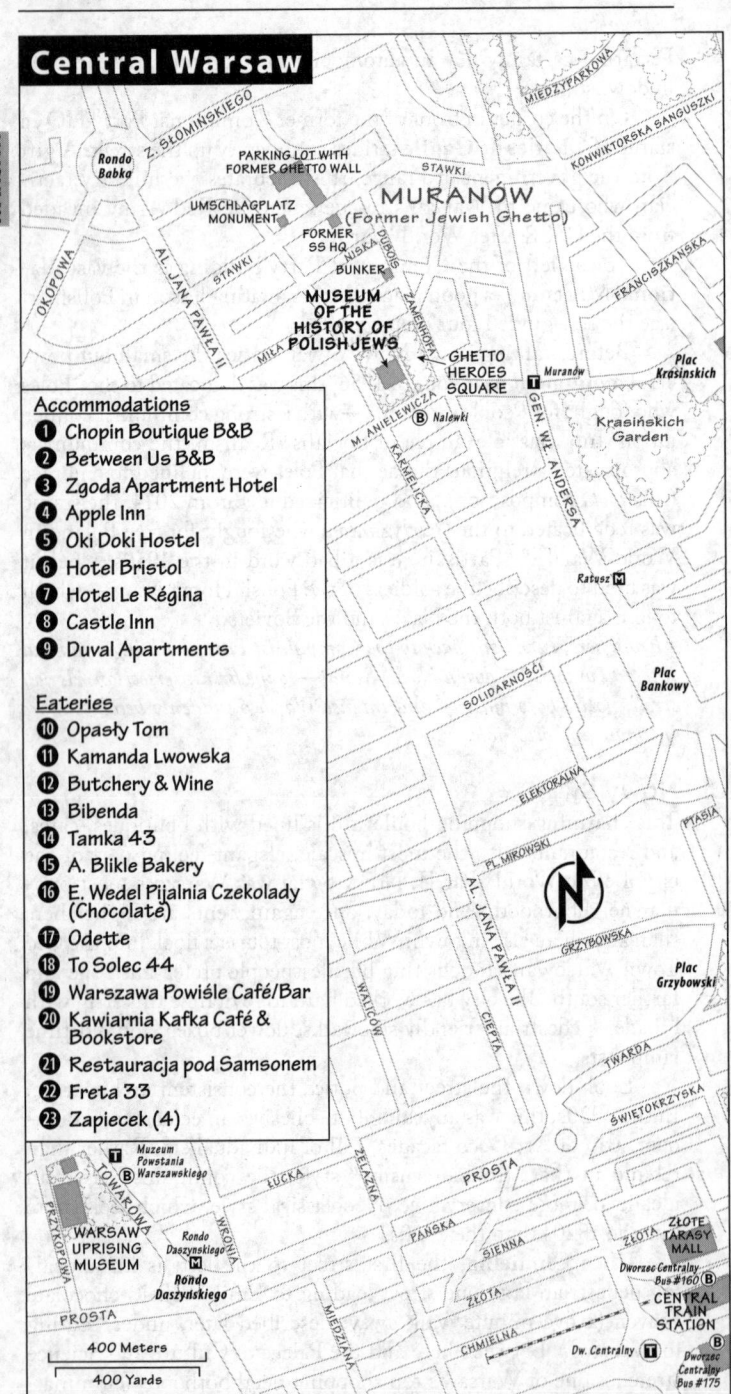

Central Warsaw

MURANÓW (Former Jewish Ghetto)

Rondo Babka

Z. SŁOMIŃSKIEGO

PARKING LOT WITH FORMER GHETTO WALL

STAWKI

KONWIKTORSKA SANGUSZKI

UMSCHLAGPLATZ MONUMENT

FORMER SS HQ

NISKA DUBOIS

BUNKER

MUSEUM OF THE HISTORY OF POLISH JEWS

ZAMENHOFA

MIŁA

M. ANIELEWICZA

GHETTO HEROES SQUARE

Muranów

Plac Krasińskich

FRANCISZKAŃSKA

Krasińskich Garden

KARMELICKA

Nalewki

GEN. WŁ. ANDERSA

OKOPOWA

AL. JANA PAWŁA II

STAWKI

Ratusz

Plac Bankowy

SOLIDARNOŚCI

ELEKTORALNA

PTASIA

PL. MIROWSKI

AL. JANA PAWŁA II

GRZYBOWSKA

Plac Grzybowski

WAŁÓW

CIEPŁA

TWARDA

ŚWIĘTOKRZYSKA

Accommodations

1. Chopin Boutique B&B
2. Between Us B&B
3. Zgoda Apartment Hotel
4. Apple Inn
5. Oki Doki Hostel
6. Hotel Bristol
7. Hotel Le Régina
8. Castle Inn
9. Duval Apartments

Eateries

10. Opasły Tom
11. Kamanda Lwowska
12. Butchery & Wine
13. Bibenda
14. Tamka 43
15. A. Blikle Bakery
16. E. Wedel Pijalnia Czekolady (Chocolate)
17. Odette
18. To Solec 44
19. Warszawa Powiśle Café/Bar
20. Kawiarnia Kafka Café & Bookstore
21. Restauracja pod Samsonem
22. Freta 33
23. Zapiecek (4)

Muzeum Powstania Warszawskiego

TOWAROWA

PRZYKOPOWA

WARSAW UPRISING MUSEUM

Rondo Daszyńskiego

WRONIA

Rondo Daszyńskiego

ŁUCKA

ŻELAZNA

PROSTA

PANSKA

KROCHMALNA

SIENNA

MIEDZIANA

ZŁOTA

CHMIELNA

ZŁOTE TARASY MALL

Dworzec Centralny Bus #160

CENTRAL TRAIN STATION

Dw. Centralny

Dworzec Centralny Bus #175

PROSTA

400 Meters

400 Yards

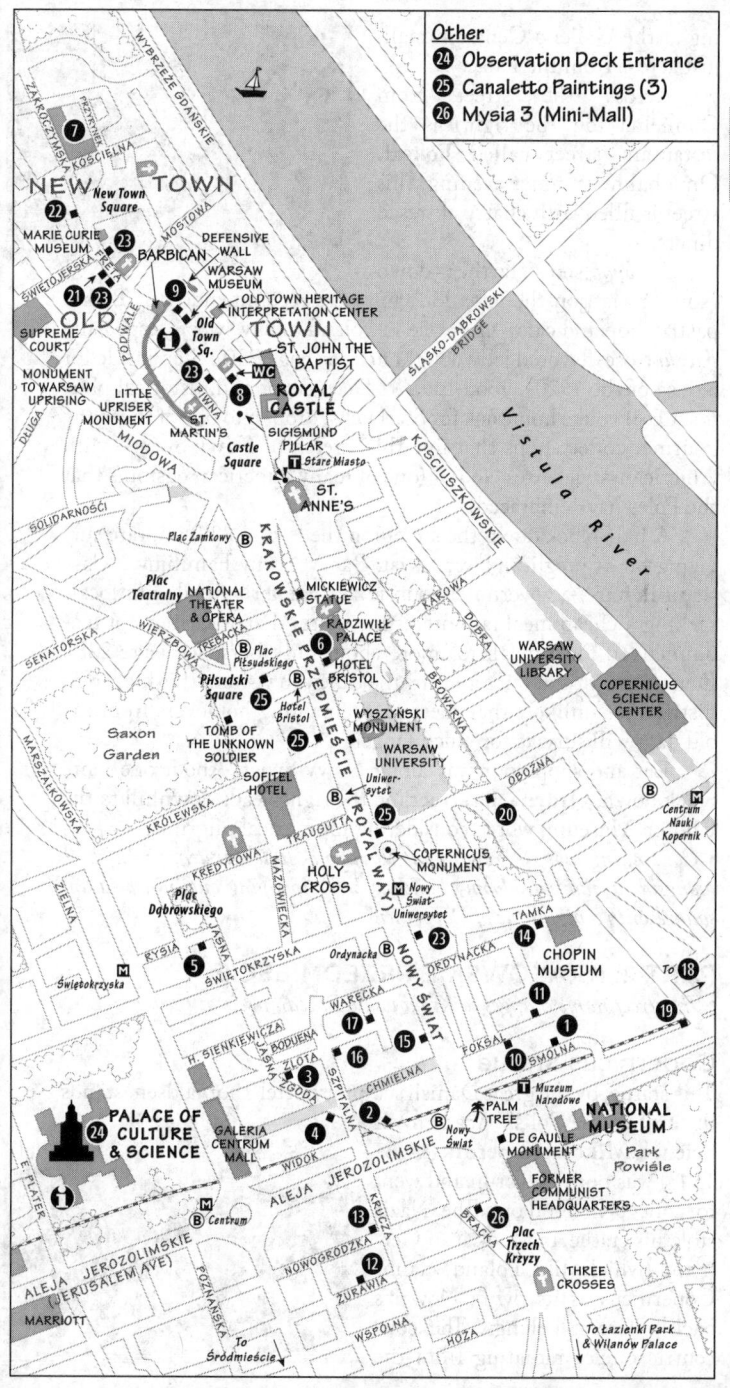

ing at the Galleria Centrum mall, just across from the Palace).

Across the street from Chmielna (on the right) is the restaurant street called **Foksal.** On a balmy summer evening, this street is filled with chatty al fresco diners.

A few steps farther down Nowy Świat, on the left, don't miss the recommended **A. Blikle** pastry shop and café—*the* place in Poland to buy sweets, especially *pączki* (rose-flavored jelly doughnuts; see page 230). Step inside for a dose of the 1920s: good-life Art Deco decor and historical photos. Or, if you're homesick for Starbucks, drop in to one of the many gourmet coffee shops that line this stretch of Nowy Świat—with American-style lattes "to go" (one of many American customs that the Poles have embraced).

A half-block down the street (on the left, at #39) is a rare surviving bit of preglitz Nowy Świat: Bar Mleczny Familijny, a classic **milk bar**—a government-subsidized cafeteria filled with locals seeking a cheap meal (an interesting cultural artifact, but not recommended for a meal; for more about milk bars, see page 228). Don't be surprised if it's gone by the time you visit; in this high-rent district, it's unlikely that these few remaining holdovers from the old days will survive for much longer.

Eat and shop your way along Nowy Świat. About one more block down, **Ordynacka street** (on the right) leads downhill to the Chopin Museum, worth considering for musical pilgrims.

• *Continuing along Nowy Świat through a duller stretch, you'll walk alongside a hulking, gloomy building before popping out in a pleasant square with a big statue of Copernicus.*

PART 2: KRAKOWSKIE PRZEDMIEŚCIE

• *The street name changes to Krakowskie Przedmieście at the big...*

Copernicus Statue

This statue, by the great Danish sculptor Bertel Thorvaldsen, stands in front of the Polish Academy of Science. **Mikołaj Kopernik** (1473-1543) was born in Toruń and went to college in Kraków. The Nazis stole his statue and took it to Germany (which, like Poland, claims Copernicus as its own). Now it's back where it belongs. The concentric circles radiating from the front of the statue represent the course of the planets' orbits, from Mercury to Saturn.

Just to Copernicus' left is a low-profile, black-marble **Chopin bench**—one of many scattered around the center. These benches mark points related to his life (in this case, his sister lived across the street). Each of these benches plays Chopin's music with the push of a button (though because of passing traffic, this one is tough to hear).

Directly in front of the statue, in the glass case, find a replica of a **Canaletto painting** of this same street scene in 1778, and compare it to today's reality. As the national archives were destroyed, city builders referred to historic paintings like these for guidance after WWII. You'll see other Canaletto replicas like this one scattered around the city.

• *Across from Copernicus, the Church of the Holy Cross is worth a look.*

Church of the Holy Cross (Kościół Św. Krzyża)

We'll pass many churches along this route, but the **Church of the Holy Cross** is unique (free entry). Composer Fryderyk Chopin's

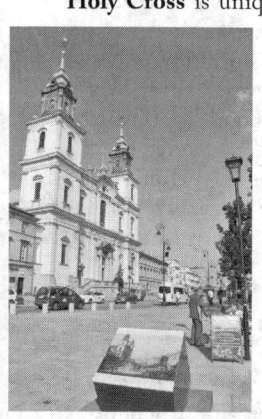

heart is inside one of the pillars of the nave (first big pillar on the left, look for the marker). After two decades of exile in France, Chopin's final wish was to have his heart brought back to his native Poland after his death. During World War II, the heart was hidden away in the countryside for safety. Check out the bright gold chapel, located on the left as you face the altar, near the front of the church. It's dedicated to a saint whom Polish Catholics believe helps them with "desperate and hopeless causes." People praying here are likely dealing with some tough issues. The beads draped from the altarpieces

help power their prayers, and the many little brass plaques are messages of thanks for prayers answered.

In the back-left corner (as you face the altar) is a chapel dedicated to Poland's favorite son, St. John Paul II. His ghostly image appears out of the wall; beneath him is a rock inscribed with the words *Tu es Petrus* (Latin for "You are Peter"—what Jesus said when he made St. Peter the first-ever pope), embedded with a capsule containing JPII's actual blood. Just opposite, in the back-right corner, behind the giant barbed wire, is a memorial to the 22,000 Polish POWs—mostly officers and prominent civilians—massacred by Soviet soldiers in 1940 near Katyń, a village in today's Russia. Stalin was determined to decapitate Poland's military intelligentsia in a ruthless mass killing, which Poles have never forgotten.

• *Leaving the church, imagine how locals would relate to the 19th-century, bronze-and-granite...*

Statue of Christ Bearing the Cross

In front, a placard reads, "Lift up your hearts." Even as Warsaw bore the burden of Russian occupation, this statue inspired them to be strong and not lose hope. It was one of many crosses they bore: a Catholic nation pinched between Orthodox Russians and Protestant Germans.

• *Cross the street (appreciating how pedestrian-friendly it is—crossing here used to be a game of Frogger), and continue left.*

Warsaw University

A long block up the street on the right, you'll see the gates (marked *Uniwersytet*) to the main campus of **Warsaw University,** founded in 1816. This lively student district has plenty of bookstores and cafeterias.

The 18th century was a time of great political decline for Poland, as a series of incompetent foreign kings mishandled crises and squandered funds. But ironically, it was also Warsaw's biggest economic boom time. Along this boulevard, aristocratic families of the period built **mansions**—most of them destroyed during World War II and rebuilt since. Some have curious flourishes (just past the university on the right, look for the doorway supported by four bearded brutes admiring their overly defined abs). Over time, many of these families donated their mansions to the university.

• *The bright-yellow church a block up from the university, on the right, is the...*

Church of the Nuns of the Visitation
(Kościół Sióstr Wizytek)

This Rococo confection from 1761 is the only church on this walk that survived World War II, and is notable because Chopin was briefly the organist here.

The monument in front of the church commemorates **Cardinal Stefan Wyszyński,** who was the Polish primate (the head of the Polish Catholic Church) from 1948 to 1981. He took this post soon after the arrival of the communists, who opposed the Church, but also realized it would be risky for them to shut down the churches in such an ardently religious country. The Communist Party and the Catholic Church coexisted tensely in Poland, and when Wyszyński protested a Stalinist crackdown in 1953, he was arrested and imprisoned. Three years later, in a major victory for the Church, Wyszyński was released. He continued to fight the communists, becoming a great hero of the Polish people in their struggle against the regime.

Across the street is another then-and-now Canaletto illustration.

• *Farther up (on the right, past the park) is the elegant, venerable...*

Hotel Bristol

A striking building with a round turret on its corner, the Hotel Bristol was used by the Nazis as a VIP hotel and bordello, and survived World War II. If you wander

through any fancy Warsaw lobby... make it this one. Step in like you're staying here and explore its fine public spaces, with fresh Art Deco and Art Nouveau flourishes. The café in front retains its Viennese atmosphere, but the *pièce de résistance* is the stunning Column Bar deeper in, past the dramatically chandeliered lounge.

• *Leave the Royal Way briefly here to reach Piłsudski Square (a block away, up the street opposite Hotel Bristol).*

Piłsudski Square
(Plac Marszałka Józefa Piłsudskiego)

The vast, empty-feeling **Piłsudski Square** (pew-SOOD-skee) has been important Warsaw real estate for centuries, constantly changing with the times. In the 1890s, the Russians who controlled this part of Poland began construction of a huge and magnificent Orthodox cathedral on this spot. But soon after it was completed, Poland regained its independence, and anti-Russian sentiments ran hot. So in the 1920s, just over a decade after the cathedral went up, it was torn down. During the Nazi occupation, this square took the name "Adolf-Hitler-Platz." Under the communists, it was Zwycięstwa, meaning "Victory" (of the Soviets over Hitler's fascism). When the regime imposed martial law in 1981, the people of Warsaw silently protested by filling the square with a giant cross made of flowers. The huge **plaque** in the ground near the road (usually marked by flowers) commemorates two monumental communist-era Catholic events on this square: John Paul II's first visit as pope to his homeland on June 2, 1979; and the May 31, 1981 funeral of Cardinal Stefan Wyszyński, whom we met across the street. The cross nearby also honors the 1979 papal visit, with one of his most famous and inspiring quotes to his countrymen: "Let thy spirit descend, let thy spirit descend, and renew the face of the earth—of *this* earth" (meaning Poland, in a just-barely-subtle-enough dig against the communist regime that was tolerating his visit). More recently, on April 17, 2010, more than 100,000 Poles convened on this square for a more solemn occasion: a memorial service for President Lech Kaczyński, who had died in a tragic plane crash in Russia.

Stand in the center, near the giant plaque, with the Royal Way at your back, for this quick spin-tour orientation: Ahead are the Tomb of the Unknown Soldier and Saxon Garden (explained later); 90 degrees to the right is the old National Theater, eclipsed by a modern business center/parking garage; another 90 degrees to the right is a statue of Piłsudski (which you passed to get here—described later); and 90 more degrees to the right is the Sofitel—formerly the Victoria Hotel, the ultimate plush, top-of-the-top hotel where all communist-era VIPs stayed. To the right of the hotel, on the horizon, you can see Warsaw's newly emerging skyline. The imposing Palace of Culture and Science, which once stood alone over the city, is now joined by a cluster of brand-new skyscrapers, giving Warsaw a Berlin-esque vibe befitting its important role as a business center of Eastern Europe.

Walk to the fragment of colonnade by the park that marks the **Tomb of the Unknown Soldier** (Grób Nieznanego Żołnierza). The colonnade was once part of a much larger palace built by the Saxon prince electors (Dresden's Augustus the Strong and his son), who became kings of Poland in the 18th century. After the palace was destroyed in World War II, this fragment was kept to memorialize Polish soldiers. The names of key battles over 1,000 years are etched into the columns, the urns contain dirt from major Polish battlefields, and the two soldiers are pretty stiff. Every hour on the hour, they do a crisp Changing of the Guard—which, poignantly, honors those who have perished in this country, so shaped by wars against foreign invaders.

Just behind the Tomb is the stately **Saxon Garden** (Ogród Saski), inhabited by genteel statues, gorgeous flowers, and a spurting fountain. This park was also built by the Saxon kings of Poland. Like most foreign kings, Augustus the Strong and his son cared little for their Polish territory, building gardens like these for themselves instead of investing in more pressing needs. Poles say that foreign kings such as Augustus did nothing but "eat, drink, and loosen their belts" (it rhymes in Polish). According to Poles, these selfish absentee kings were the culprits in Poland's eventual decline. But they do appreciate having such a fine venue for a Sunday stroll.

Walk back out toward the Royal Way, stopping at the statue you passed earlier. In 1995, the square was again renamed—this time for **Józef Piłsudski** (1867-1935), the guy with the big walrus moustache. With the help of a French captain named Charles de Gaulle (whom we met earlier), Piłsudski forced the Russian Bolsheviks out of Poland in 1920 in the so-called Miracle on the Vistula. Piłsudski is credited with creating a once-again-independent Poland after more than a century of foreign oppression, and he essentially ran Poland as a virtual dictator after World War I. Of course, under the communists, Piłsudski was swept under the rug. But since 1989, he has enjoyed a renaissance as many Poles' favorite prototype anticommunist hero. His name adorns streets, squares, and bushy-mustachioed monuments all over the country.

WARSAW

• *Return to Hotel Bristol, turn left, and continue your Royal Way walk.*

Radziwiłł Palace

Next door to the hotel, you'll see the huge **Radziwiłł Palace.** The Warsaw Pact was signed here in 1955, officially uniting the Soviet satellite states in a military alliance against NATO. This building has also, from time to time, served as the Polish "White House."

• *Beyond Radziwiłł Palace, on the right, you'll reach a park with a...*

Statue of Adam Mickiewicz

Poland's national poet, Adam Mickiewicz spearheaded Poland's cultural survival during more than a century when the country disappeared from maps—absorbed by Austria, Prussia, and Russia. This was an age when underdog nations (and peoples without nations) all over Europe had their own national revival movements. The statue was erected in 1898 with permission from the Russian czar, as long as the people paid for it themselves. It's still an important part of community life: Polish high school students have a big formal ball (like a prom) 100 days before graduation. After the ball, if students come here and hop around the statue on one leg, it's supposed to bring them good luck on their finals. Mickiewicz, for his part, looks like he's suffering from a heart attack—perhaps in response to the impressively ugly National Theater and Opera a block in front of him.

• Continue to the end of the Royal Way, marked by the big pink palace. Just before the castle, on your right, is...

St. Anne's Church

This church is Rococo, with playful capitals inside and out and a fine pulpit shaped like the prow of a ship—complete with a big anchor. The richly ornamented apse, behind the altar, survived World War II. This church offers organ concerts nearly daily in summer (see "Entertainment in Warsaw," later).

For a scenic finale to your Royal Way stroll, climb the 150 steps of the **view tower** by the church (5 zł, generally open daily 10:00-18:00, later in summer, closed in bad winter weather). You'll be rewarded with excellent views—particularly of Castle Square and the Old Town. From up top, visually retrace your steps along the Royal Way, and notice the emerging skyline surrounding the Palace of Culture and Science. The tower also affords a good look at the Praga district across the river, where the Red Army waited for the Nazis to level Warsaw during the uprising. Help was so close at hand...but stayed right where it was.

• Just across from the view tower entrance, look for another Chopin bench. From St. Anne's Church, it's just another block to Castle Square, the TI, and the start of the Old Town.

Sights in Warsaw

THE OLD TOWN

In 1945, not a building remained standing in Warsaw's "Old" Town (Stare Miasto). Everything you see is rebuilt, mostly finished by 1956. Some think the Old Town seems artificial and phony, in a Disney World kind of way. For others, the painstaking postwar reconstruction feels just right, with Old World squares and lanes charming enough to give Kraków a run for its money. Before 1989, stifled by communist repression and choking on smog, the Old Town was an empty husk of its historic self. But now, the outdoor restaurants and market stalls have returned, and tourists (and a few Varsovians) are out strolling.

These sights are listed in order from south to north, and linked with walking directions, beginning at Castle Square and ending at the New Town.

▲Castle Square (Plac Zamkowy)

This lively square is dominated by the big, pink Royal Castle that is the historic heart of Warsaw's political power.

After the second great Polish dynasty—the Jagiellonians—died out in 1572, it was replaced by the Republic of Nobles (about 10 percent of the population), which elected various foreign kings to their throne. The guy on the 72-foot-tall **pillar** is Sigismund III, the first Polish king from the Swedish Vasa family (Waza in Polish). In 1596, he relocated the capital from Kraków to Warsaw. This move made sense, since Warsaw was closer to the center of 16th-century Poland (which had expanded to the east), and because the city had gained political importance over the past 30 years as the meeting point of the Sejm, or parliament of nobles.

Along the right side of the castle, notice the two previous versions of this pillar lying on a lawn. The first one, from 1644, was falling apart and had to be replaced in 1887 by a new one made of granite. In 1944, a Nazi tank broke this second pillar—a symbolic piece of Polish heritage—into the four pieces (still pockmarked with bullet holes) that you see here today. As Poland rebuilt, its citizens put Sigismund III back on his pillar. Past the pillars are views of Warsaw's red-and-white National Stadium across the river—built for the Euro Cup soccer tournament in 2012.

Across the square from the castle, you'll see the partially reconstructed **defensive wall.** This rampart once enclosed the entire Old Town. Like all of Poland, Warsaw has seen invasion from all sides.

Explore the café-lined lanes that branch off Castle Square. Street signs indicate the year that each lane was originally built.

The first street is **ulica Piwna** ("Beer Street"), where you'll find **St. Martin's Church** (Kościół Św. Martina, on the left). Run by Franciscan nuns, this church has a simple, modern interior. Walk up the aisle and find the second pillar on the right. Notice the partly destroyed crucifix—it's the only church artifact that survived World War II. Across the street and closer to Castle Square, admire the carefully carved doorway of the house called *pod Gołębiami* ("Under Doves")—dedicated to the memory of an old woman who fed birds amidst the Old Town rubble after World War II.

Back on Castle Square, find the white **plaque** on the wall (at plac Zamkowy 15). It explains that 50 Poles were executed by Nazis on this spot on September 2, 1944. You'll see plaques like this all over the Old Town, each one commemorating victims or opponents of the Nazis. The brick planter under the plaque is often filled with fresh flowers to honor the victims.

• *Turn your attention to the...*

▲▲Royal Castle (Zamek Królewski)

A castle has stood here since the Mazovian dukes built a wooden version in the 14th century. It has grown through the ages, being rebuilt and remodeled by many different kings. When Warsaw became the capital in 1596, this massive building served a dual purpose: It was both the king's residence and the meeting place of the parliament (Sejm). It reached its peak under Stanisław August Poniatowski—the final Polish king—who imported artists and architects to spiff up

the interior, leaving his mark all over the place. Luftwaffe bombs destroyed it in World War II (only one wall remained standing). Rebuilding stalled because Stalin considered it a palace for the high-class elites. It was finally rebuilt in the more moderate 1970s, funded by local donations.

Warsaw's Royal Castle has a gorgeous interior—the most opulent I've seen in Poland. Many of the furnishings are original (hidden away when it became clear the city would be demolished in World War II). A visit to the castle is like perusing a great Polish history textbook. In fact, you'll likely see grade-school classes sitting cross-legged on the floors. Watching the teachers quizzing eager young history buffs, try to imagine what it's like to be a young Pole growing up in a country with such a tumultuous history.

Cost and Hours: 23 zł, free on Sun; open May-Sept Mon-Sat 10:00-18:00, Thu until 20:00, Sun 11:00-18:00; Oct-April Tue-Sat 10:00-16:00, Sun 11:00-16:00, closed Mon; last entry one hour before closing; plac Zamkowy 4, tel. 22-355-5170, www.zamek-krolewski.pl. A public WC is on the courtyard just around the corner of the castle.

Tours: The castle has a well-produced audioguide (17 zł, worth the extra cost) and good English information posted throughout. For the basics, use my commentary to follow the one-way route through the castle.

Visiting the Castle: Because the castle visitor route often changes, it's possible you won't see these rooms in this order; if that happens, match the labels in each room to the corresponding text below.

Entering the courtyard, go to the right to buy tickets, then cross to the opposite side to tour the interior. (If you want an audioguide, go downstairs to rent it first.) Head up the stairs and follow *Castle Route* signs.

Start in the Oval Gallery, then head into the **Council Chamber,** where a "Permanent Council" consisting of the king, 18 senators, and 18 representatives met to chart Poland's course. Next is the **Great Assembly Hall,** heavy with marble and chandeliers. The statues of Apollo and Minerva flanking the main door are modeled after King Stanisław August Poniatowski and Catherine the Great of Russia, respectively. (The king enjoyed a youthful romantic dalliance with Catherine on a trip to Russia, and never quite seemed to get over her...much to his wife's consternation, I'm sure.)

The **Knights' Hall** features the Polish Hall of Fame, with paintings of great events and busts and portraits of VIPs—Very Important Poles. The statue of Chronos—god of time, with the globe on his shoulders—is actually a functioning clock, though now it's stopped at 11:15 to commemorate the exact time in 1944 when the Nazis bombed this palace to bits. Just off this hall is the **Marble Room,** with more portraits of Polish greats ringing the top of the room. Above the fireplace is a portrait of Stanisław August Poniatowski.

Continuing through the Knights' Hall, you'll wind up in the remarkable **Throne Room.** Notice the crowned white eagles, the

symbol of Poland, decorating the banner behind the throne. The Soviets didn't allow anything royal or aristocratic, so postwar restorations came with crownless eagles. Only after 1989 were these eagles crowned again. Peek into the **European Monarchs' Portrait Rooms,** where you'll meet the likes of Russia's Catherine the Great, England's George III, and France's Louis XVI—in whose esteemed royal league Stanisław August Poniatowski liked to consider himself.

After four more grand rooms (including the King's Bedroom, with a gorgeous silk canopy over the bed), you'll enter the **Canaletto Room,** filled with canvases of late-18th-century Warsaw painted in exquisite detail by this talented artist. (This Canaletto, also known for his panoramas of Dresden, was the nephew of another more famous artist with the same nickname, known for painting Venice's canals.) Paintings like these helped post-WWII restorers resurrect the city from its rubble. To the left, on the lower wall, the biggest canvas features the view of Warsaw from the Praga district across the river; pick out the few landmarks that are still standing (or, more precisely, have been resurrected). The castle you're standing in dominates the center of the painting, overlooking the river. Notice the artist's self-portrait in the lower left. Opposite, on the right side of the room, is Canaletto's depiction of the election of Stanisław August Ponia-towski as king, in a field outside Warsaw (notice the empty throne in the middle of the group). Among the assembled crowd, each flag represents a different Polish province.

From here, head left of the big "view of Warsaw" painting into the **side chapel,** reserved for the king. In the box to the left of the altar is the heart of Tadeusz Kościuszko, a hero of both the American Revolution and the Polish struggle against the Partitions (for more about the Partitions, see page 220).

As you cross over to the other part of the castle, you'll pass through the **Four Seasons Gallery** (with some fine but faded Gobelin tapestries) before entering a few rooms occupied by the houses of parliament—a reminder that this "castle" wasn't just the king's house, but also the meeting place of the legislature. In the **New Deputies' Chambers,** notice the maps showing Poland's constantly in-flux borders—a handy visual aid for the many school groups that visit here.

After several rooms, you'll reach the grand **Senators' Chamber,** with the king's throne, surrounded by different coats of arms. Each one represents a region that was part of Poland during its Golden Age, back when it was united with Lithuania and its territory stretched from the Baltic to the Black Sea (see the map on the wall). In this room, Poland adopted its 1791 constitution (notice the replica in the display case to the left of the throne). It was the first in Europe, written soon after America's and just months before France's. And, like the Constitution of the United States, it was very progressive, based on the ideals of the Enlightenment. But when the final Partitions followed in 1793 and 1795, Poland was divided between neighboring powers and ceased to exist as a country until 1918—so the constitution was never fully put into action.

Next, the **Crown Prince's Room** features paintings by Jan Matejko that capture the excitement surrounding the adoption of this ill-fated constitution (for more on Matejko, see page 402). The next room has another Matejko painting: King Stefan Batory negotiating with Ivan the Terrible's envoys to break their siege of a Russian town. Notice the hussars—fearsome Polish soldiers wearing winged armor. Finally, you'll wind through more rooms with yet more paintings of great historical events and portraits of famous Poles.

Other Castle Sights: Sharing an entrance lobby with the main castle interiors, the **Gallery of Paintings, Sculpture, and Decorative Arts** isn't worth the 21-zł extra admission fee for most visitors; save your time and money for the National Museum instead. But art lovers may be interested to see the 36 paintings of the gallery's Landkroński Collection. These originally belonged to Stanisław August Poniatowski, who sold them to an aristocratic family that eventually presented them to Poland as a gift. The prize of the gallery are two canvases by Rembrandt (both from 1641). *Girl in a Picture Frame* is exactly that—except that she's "breaking the frame" by resting her hands on a faux frame that Rembrandt has painted inside the real one...shattering the fourth wall in a way that was unusual for the time. The other, *A Scholar at His Writing Table,* shows the hirsute academic glancing up from his notes. Circle around behind the canvases to see X-rays of the paintings, which have helped experts better understand the master's techniques. The rest of the gallery consists of roomfuls of portraits and a fine cabinet of silver and crystal.

Consider a detour to the **Kubicki Arcades** (Arkady Kubiciego), the impressively excavated arcades deep beneath the castle. From the entrance lobby, head downstairs to the area with the cloakroom, bathrooms, and bookshop, then find the long escalator that takes you down to the arcades. It's free to wander the long, cavernous, and newly clean and gleaming space, made elegant by grand drapes.

The castle has a vast collection, which it organizes into various exhibitions—some permanent and some temporary. The extensive **oriental carpet collection** in the "Tin-Roofed Palace" (Pałac pod Blachą) is sparsely described and skippable for most; the same building also features seven unimpressive apartments of Prince Józef Poniatowski, the king's brother (15 zł for both, free on Sun, same hours as castle, around the right side of the castle as you face it—past the two fallen columns, buy ticket at main ticket desk).

• *When you're ready to resume exploring the Old Town, leave the square at the far end, on* **St. John's Street** *(Świętojańska). On the plaque under the street name sign, you can guess what the dates mean, even if you don't know Polish: This building was constructed from 1433 to 1478, destroyed in 1944, and rebuilt from 1950 to 1953.*

Partway down the street on the right, you'll come to the big brick...

WARSAW

Cathedral of St. John the Baptist (Katedra Św. Jana Chrzciciela)

This cathedral-basilica is the oldest (1370) and most important church in Warsaw. Superficially unimpressive, the church's own archbishop admitted that it was "modest and poor"—but "the historical events that took place here make it magnificent" (much like Warsaw itself). Poland's constitution was consecrated here on May 3, 1791. Much later, this church became the final battle-ground of the 1944 Warsaw Uprising—when a Nazi "tracked mine" (a huge bomb on tank tracks—this one appropriately named *Goliath*) drove into the church and exploded, massacring the rebels. You can still see part of that tank's tread hanging on the outside wall of the church (through the passage on the right side, between the buttresses near the end of the church).

Cost and Hours: Free, crypt-5 zł, good guidebook-5 zł, open to tourists daily 10:00-13:00 & 15:00-17:30, closed during services and organ concerts. The cathedral hosts organ concerts in summer (see "Entertainment in Warsaw," later).

Visiting the Cathedral: Head inside. Typical of brick church-es, it has a "hall church" design, with three naves of equal height. Look for the crucifix ornamented with real human hair (chapel left of high altar). The high altar holds a copy of the Black Ma-donna—proclaimed "everlasting queen of Poland" after a victory over the Swedes in the 17th century. The original Black Madon-na is in Częstochowa (125 miles south of Warsaw)—a mecca for Slavic Catholics, who visit in droves in hopes of a miracle. In the back-left corner, find the chapel with the tomb of Cardinal Stefan Wyszyński—the great Polish leader who, as Warsaw's archbishop, morally steered the country through much of the Cold War. (No-tice the request to pray for his beatification, as Poles would love to see him become a saint.) The crypt holds graves of several impor-tant Poles, including Stanisław August Poniatowski (the last Polish king) and Nobel Prize-winning author Henryk Sienkiewicz.

• *Continue up the street and enter Warsaw's grand...*

▲▲Old Town Market Square (Rynek Starego Miasta)

For two centuries, this was a gritty market square. Sixty-five years ago, it was a pile of bombed-out rubble. And today, like a phoenix from the ashes, it's risen to remind residents and tourists alike of the prewar glory of the Polish capital.

Head to the **mermaid fountain** in the middle of the square.

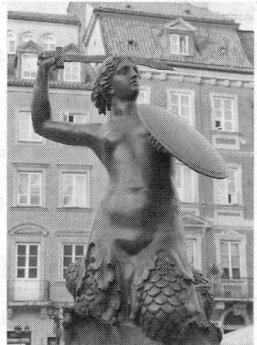

The mermaid is an important symbol in Warsaw—you'll see her everywhere. Legend has it that a mermaid *(syrenka)* lived in the Vistula River and protected the townspeople. While this siren supposedly serenaded the town, she's most appreciated for her strength (hence the sword). This square seems to declare that life goes on in Warsaw, as it always has. Children frolic here, oblivious to the turmoil their forebears withstood. When the fountain gurgles, the kids giggle.

Each of the square's four sides is named for a prominent 18th-century Varsovian: Kołłątaj, Dekert, Barss, and Zakrzewski. These men served as "Presidents" of Warsaw (mayors, more or less), and Kołłątaj was also a framer of Poland's 1791 constitution. Take some time to explore the square. Enjoy the colorful architecture. Notice that many of the buildings were intentionally built to lean out into the square—to simulate the higgledy-piggledy wear and tear of the original buildings.

History Museums near the Square

If you'd like to learn more about Warsaw's history, two good museums are located nearby.

• *First, on the Dekert (north) side of the square is the...*

Warsaw Museum (Muzeum Warszawy): When this museum's lengthy and long-delayed restoration is complete (possibly as early as mid-2017), it promises to provide an insightful look at the turbulent history of this city—particularly the Old Town. The exhibits are an afterthought to the museum's best feature: a poignant 20-minute film (in English) tracing the tragic WWII experience of this city—from a thriving interwar metropolis, to a bombed-out wasteland, to the focus of a massive rebuilding effort (may be covered by a separate ticket). For the latest, see www.muzeumwarszawy.pl.

• *The other museum—focusing on the Old Town's history and reconstruction—is behind the buildings on the river side of the square (behind the mermaid's back). Walk one block, and turn left to find the...*

Old Town Heritage Interpretation Center: This fine little visitors center displays lots of before-and-after photos and videos of the Old Town—there are even glass floors looking down onto original fragments of the neighborhood (5 zł, Tue-Sun 10:00-19:00, closed Mon, ulica Brzozowa 11, www.muzeumwarszawy.pl).

• *When you're ready to move on, exit the square on Nowomiejska (at the mermaid's 2 o'clock, by the second-story niche sculpture of St. Anne). After a block, you'll reach the...*

Barbican (Barbakan)

This defensive gate of the Old Town, similar to Kraków's, protected the medieval city from invaders.

• *Once you've crossed through the barbican, you're officially in Warsaw's...*

New Town (Nowe Miasto)

This 15th-century neighborhood is "new" in name only: It was the first part of Warsaw to spring up outside the city walls (and is therefore slightly newer than the Old Town). The New Town is a fun place to wander: only a little less charming than the Old Town, but with a more real-life feel—people live and work here. Its centerpiece is the **New Town Square** (Rynek Nowego Miasta), watched over by the distinctive green dome of St. Kazimierz Church.

Scientists might want to pay homage at the museum (and birthplace) of Warsaw native **Marie Skłodowska-Curie,** a.k.a. Madame Curie (1867-1934); it's along the street between the New Town Square and the barbican. This Nobel Prize winner was the world's first radiologist—discovering both radium and polonium (named for her native land) with her husband, Pierre Curie. Since she lived at a time when Warsaw was controlled by oppressive Russia, she conducted her studies in France. The museum—with photos, furniture, artifacts, and a paucity of English information—is a bit of a snoozer, best left to true fans (overpriced at 11 zł, Tue-Sun 9:00-16:30, closed Mon, ulica Freta 16, tel. 22-831-8092, www.muzeum-msc.pl).

From the New Town to Castle Square

You can backtrack the way you came, or, to get a look at the Old Town's back streets, consider this route from the big, round barbican gate (where the New Town meets the Old): Go back through the barbican and over the little bridge, turn right, and walk along the houses that line the inside of the wall. You'll pass a leafy garden courtyard on the left—a reminder that people actually live in the tourist zone within the Old Town walls. Just beyond the garden on the right, look for the carpet-beating rack, used to clean rugs (these are common fixtures in people's backyards). Go left into the square called Szeroki Dunaj ("Wide Danube") and look for another mermaid (over the Thai restaurant). Continue through the square and turn right at Wąski Dunaj ("Narrow Danube"). After about 100 yards, you'll pass the city wall. Just to the right (outside the wall), you'll see the monument to the **Little Upriser** of 1944, a child wearing a grown-up's helmet and too-big boots, and carrying a machine gun. Children—especially Scouts (Harcerze)—played a key role in the resistance against the Nazis. Their job was mainly carrying messages and propaganda.

Now continue around the wall (the upper, inner part is more pleasant). Admire more public art as you head back to Castle Square.

NEAR PALM TREE CIRCLE

These sights are in the city center, near Palm Tree Circle—where Jerusalem Avenue crosses Nowy Świat.

East of the Royal Way (Toward the River)
▲▲National Museum (Muzeum Narodowe)

A celebration of underrated Polish artists, this museum offers a surprisingly engaging and—if you follow my tour—concise overview of this country's impressive painters (many of whom are unknown outside their home country). A modern, state-of-the-art exhibition space allows these unsung canvases to really belt it out. Polish and other European artists are displayed side by side, as if to assert Poland's worthiness on the world artistic stage. After seeing a few of the masterpieces here, you won't disagree.

Cost and Hours: 15 zł, includes audioguide, more for temporary exhibits, permanent collection free on Tue; open Tue-Sun 10:00-18:00, Thu until 21:00, closed Mon, last entry 45 minutes before closing; one block east of Nowy Świat at aleja Jerozolimskie 3, tel. 22-629-3093, www.mnw.art.pl.

❍ **Self-Guided Tour:** The collection fills several separate galleries. The museum's strongest point—and the bulk of this tour—is its 19th-century Polish art. But before diving in, consider some of the other collections.

Overview: To get your bearings, pick up a floor plan as you enter. On the ground floor are Ancient Art (from Greek pieces to artifacts left by early Polish tribes); Gallery Faras (highlighting the museum's fine collection of archaeological findings from that ancient Egyptian city); and a good collection of Medieval Art, which gathers altarpieces from churches around Poland—organized both chronologically and geographically—and displays some of the most graphic crucifixes and *pietàs* I've seen.

Upstairs is the excellent Gallery of 19th-Century Art (described next), which flows into the Old Polish and European Portrait Gallery (as interesting as somebody else's yearbook). Nearby, through the gift shop, is the worthwhile 20th- and 21st-Century Art collection, with an impressive array of Modern and Postmodern Polish artists, including photographers and filmmakers. The underwhelming Old European Painting collection—pre-19th-century canvases arranged by theme and juxtaposed to highlight

Jan Matejko (1838-1893)

Jan Matejko (yawn mah-TAY-koh) is Poland's most important painter, period. In the mid- to late-19th century, the nation of Poland had been dissolved by foreign powers, and Polish artists struggled to make sense of their people's place in the world. Rabble-rousing Romanticism seemed to have failed (inspiring many brutally suppressed uprisings), so Polish artists and writers turned their attention to educating the people about their history, with the goal of keeping their traditions alive.

Matejko was at the forefront of this so-called positivist movement. Matejko saw what the tides of history had done to Poland and was determined to make sure his countrymen learned from it. He painted two types of works: huge, grand-scale epics depicting monumental events in Polish history; and small, intimate portraits of prominent Poles. Polish schoolchildren study history from books with paintings of virtually every single Polish king—all painted by the incredibly prolific Matejko.

Matejko is admired not for his technical mastery (he's an unexceptional painter) or for the literal truth of his works—he was notorious for fudging historical details to give his canvases a bit more propagandistic punch. But he is revered for the emotion behind—and inspired by—his works. His paintings are utilitarian, straightforward, and dramatic enough to stir the patriot in any Pole. The intense focus on history by Matejko and other positivists is one big reason why today's Poles are still so in touch with their heritage.

You'll see Matejko's works in Warsaw's National Museum and Royal Castle, as well as in Kraków's Gallery of 19th-Century Polish Art (above the Cloth Hall). You can also visit his former residence in Kraków.

the differences between southern and northern European art—is split up among all three floors.

To cut to the chase, focus on the **Gallery of 19th-Century Art.** We'll start with the granddaddy of Polish art, Jan Matejko.

• *From the entrance lobby, head up the left staircase, then turn left across the mezzanine and enter the collection. Matejko is hiding at the far end of this wing: Entering the collection, angle right, then head all the way to the room at the far end, which is dominated by a gigantic battlefield canvas. (If you get lost, ask the attendants, "mah-TAY-koh?")*

Jan Matejko: While not the most talented of artists—he's a fairly conventional painter, lacking a distinctive, recognizable style—Matejko more than made up for it with vision and productivity. His works—often on oversized canvases—are steeped in proud Polish history. Matejko's biggest work here—in fact, the biggest canvas in the whole building—is the enormous ***Battle***

of Grunwald. This epic painting commemorates one of Poland's high-water marks: the dramatic victory of a Polish-Lithuanian army over the Teutonic Knights, who had been terrorizing north-ern Poland for decades (for more on the Teutonic Knights, see page 502). On July 15, 1410, some 40,000 Poles and Lithuanians (led by the sword-waving Lithuanian in red, Grand Duke Vytautas) faced off against 27,000 Teutonic Knights (under their Grand Master, in white) in one of the medieval world's bloodiest battles. Matejko plops us right in the thick of the battle's climax, painting life-size figures and framing off a 32-foot-long slice of the actual two-mile battle line.

In the center of the painting, the Teutonic Grand Master is about to become a shish kebab. Duke Vytautas, in red, leads the final charge. And waaaay up on a hill (in the upper-right corner, on horseback, wearing a silver knight's suit) is Władysław Jagiełło, the first king of the Jagiellonian dynasty...ensuring his bloodline will survive another 150 years.

Matejko spent three years covering this 450-square-foot canvas in paint. The canvas was specially made in a single seam-less piece. This was such a popular work that almost as many fans turned out for its unveiling as there are figures in the painting. On the TV nearby, you can see how the vast painting was recently restored.

From Poland's high point in the *Battle of Grunwald,* look on the right wall for another, much smaller Matejko canvas, *Stańczyk,* to see how Poland's fortunes shifted drastically a century later. This more intimate portrait depicts a popular Polish figure: the court jester Stańczyk, who's smarter than the king, but not allowed to say so. This complex character, representing the national conscience, is a favorite symbol of Matejko's. Stańczyk slumps in gloom. He's just read the news (on the table beside him) that the city of Smolensk has fallen to the Russians after a three-year siege (1512-1514). The jester had tried to warn the king to send more troops, but the king was too busy partying (behind the curtain). The painter Matejko—who may have used his own features for Stańczyk's face—also blamed the nobles of his own day for fiddling while Poland was partitioned.

More Matejkos fill this room. Just to the right of *Stańczyk* is a self-portrait of the gray-bearded artist (compare their features), then a painting of the hoisting of the Sigismund Bell to the ca-thedral tower in Kraków (it's still there). Farther right, you'll see Matejko's portraits of his children and his wife.

On the final wall is a smaller but very dramatic scene, *The Sermon of Piotr Skarga.* In the upper-right corner, this charis-matic, early-17th-century Jesuit priest waves his arms to punctuate his message: Poland's political system is broken. Skarga is addressing fat-cat nobles and the portly King Sigismund II Vasa (seated and wearing a ruffled collar), who were acting in their own self-interests instead of prioritizing what was best for Poland. Notice that Skarga's audience isn't hearing his ravings—they seem bored, bugged, or both. The king is even taking a nap. They should have listened: Poland's eventual decline is often considered the fault of its unworkable political system. After the Partitions, the ahead-of-his-time Skarga was rehabilitated as a visionary who should have been heeded. Notice that, like Stańczyk, Skarga is a self-portrait of Matejko.

• *Leaving Matejko, we'll pass through several more rooms of lesser-known Polish painters to the opposite wing, where we'll meet several of Matejko's students—each of whom developed his own style and left his mark on the Polish art world. But on the way, I'll point out a few canvases that may be worth pausing at.*

Other Polish Painters: First, head back down the long corridor the way you came (passing some Matejko copycats), cutting through a corner of the Portrait Gallery. When you reach the door you came in, bear right to stay inside the gallery. At the end of that first, large room, you'll find some battle scenes by **Józef Brandt**—the only painter who rivaled Matejko in capturing epic warfare on canvas. Many of Brandt's scenes focus on confronting an enemy from the east, which was Poland's lot for much of its history. His biggest work here, *Rescue of Tatar Captives*, is typical of his scenes.

Continue straight into the next room, with some fine landscape scenes. This room (the partition in the middle) also has works by the talented **Józef Chełmoński:** *Indian Summer* and (around back) *Storks*—a young boy and his grandfather look to the sky, as a formation of storks flies overhead.

Turn right and go through one more long room (watching, on the left wall, for **Aleksander Gierymski**'s small, evocative, personality-filled *Jewish Woman Selling Oranges*).

• *You'll emerge into a big room that kicks off the collection of...*

Młoda Polska: Matejko's pupils took what he taught them and incorporated the Art Nouveau styles that were emerging around Europe to create a new movement called "Young Poland" (see page 259). This room features works by two of the movement's big names. On the left wall are paintings by **Jacek Malczewski,** some of them depicting the goateed, close-cropped artist in a semisurrealistic, Polish countryside context. Malczewski painted more or less realistically, but enjoyed incorporating one or two subtle, symbolic elements evocative of Polish folkloric tradition—like magical realism on canvas. *The Death of Ellenai* (1907) shows the pivotal scene in Juliusz Słowacki's epic 1838 poem, *Anhelli*, in which a young nobleman exiled from Poland during the Partitions is forced to make his way through the wastelands of Siberia. When his young and idealistic travel companion, Ellenai, perishes, Anhelli kisses her feet and abandons all hope.

Most of the works on the opposite wall are by **Józef Mehoffer,** who paints with brighter colors in a more stylized form, with more abstraction. This creates dreamlike scenes that are, consequently, somehow less poignant than Malczewski's. Mehoffer's hypnotic *Strange Garden* is a bucolic vision of blue-clad Mary Poppinses, nude cherubs, lots of flowers...and a gigantic, hovering, golden dragonfly that places the otherwise plausible scene in the realm of pure fantasy. In the middle of the room, the small version of Auguste Rodin's *The Kiss* reminds us how this emotion-conveying style, called Symbolism, was also finding expression elsewhere in Europe.

The next room, at the end of the hall, features some lesser-known painters from the age. Among these, **Olga Boznańska's** works are worth lingering over: gauzy, almost Impressionistic portraits that skillfully capture the humanity of each subject.

Head back into the Malczewski/Mehoffer room and find the small, darkened adjoining rooms. The first one features additional Malczewski paintings; the second is a treasure trove of works by the founder and biggest talent of Młoda Polska, **Stanisław Wyspiański.** The specific items in this room are subject to change—as Kraków, which owns the best collection of hometown boy Wyspiański, is shuffling its works in and out of special exhibitions—but you'll likely see both paintings and pastel works by this Art Nouveau juggernaut. Wyspiański also designed stage sets and redecorated some important churches; some of the large pastel-on-paper works you may see here were used as studies for those projects. And you'll likely see some self-portraits and portraits of his wife and children. Pondering the works here—and throughout the museum—think about how such a talented artist from a small country can be left out of textbooks across the ocean.

Chopin Museum (Muzeum Fryderyka Chopina)

The reconstructed Ostrogski Castle houses this slick museum honoring Poland's most famous composer. You'll see manuscripts, letters, and original handwritten compositions by the composer. Unfortunately, the museum's high-tech gadgetry does more to distract from this rich collection of historic artifacts than to bring it to life. While Chopin devotees may find it riveting, those with only a passing familiarity with the composer may leave feeling like they still don't know much about this Polish cultural giant.

Cost and Hours: 22 zł, free on Sun, open Tue-Sun 11:00-20:00, closed Mon, last entry 45 minutes before closing, 3 blocks east of Nowy Świat at ulica Okólnik 1, tel. 22-441-6251, www. chopin.museum. Because the museum is highly interactive, only 70 visitors are allowed per hour. But, except for rare occasions, just dropping in should be no problem.

Visiting the Museum: Buy your ticket at the adjacent building, then enter the mansion that houses the exhibit. You'll be given an electronic card; tap it against glowing red dots to access additional information. You'll proceed more or less chronologically through the composer's life, with various opportunities to hear his compositions. You'll see a replica of Chopin's drawing room in Paris, and his last piano, which he used for composing during the final two years of his life (1848-1849). Exhibits here trace themes of the composer's life, such as the women he knew (including his older sister Ludwika, his mother, and George Sand—the French author who took a male pseudonym in order to be published, and who was romantically linked with Chopin). The exhibit ends in the basement, where you can nurture your appreciation of Chopin by listening to his music.

Concerts: Under the palace is a new **concert hall,** which hosts performances by students (call museum to ask for concert schedule and to reserve a space—only 70 seats available; usually Oct-July Thu at 18:00, and typically free).

Eating: The recommended **Tamka 43**—with affordable lunch deals downstairs and top-end fine dining (with a menu inspired by dishes Chopin enjoyed) upstairs—is in the glassy building that faces the museum.

Other Chopin Sight: The composer's tourable **birth house** is in a park in Żelazowa Wola, 34 miles from Warsaw. While interesting to Chopin devotees, it's not worth the trek for most. On summer weekends, the Chopin Museum sometimes runs a handy bus to the house—ask at the museum (departs from Marszałkowska street, 30 minutes each way; 7 zł for the bus, 7 zł for the park, 23 zł for the park and birth house, 39 zł also includes museum in Warsaw; birth house open Tue-Sun 9:00-19:00, Oct-March until 17:00, closed Mon year-round, tel. 46-863-3300).

▲▲Copernicus Science Center (Centrum Nauki Kopernik)

This facility, a wonderland of completely hands-on scientific doo-dads that thrill kids and adults alike, is a futuristic romper room. Filling two floors of an industrial-mod, purpose-built space, this is Warsaw's best family activity. Exhibits are grouped more or less thematically and described in both Polish and English.

Cost and Hours: 27 zł, 18 zł for kids 19 and under, 72-zł family ticket for up to 4 people; open Tue-Fri 9:00-18:00, Sat-Sun 10:00-19:00, closed Mon, last entry one hour before closing; Wybrzeże Kościuszkowskie 20, tel. 22-596-4100, www.kopernik.org.pl.

Crowd-Beating Tips: This popular attraction can get crowded—especially on weekends and school holidays, when the line can be long. (A webcam on their website shows the current line; you can also book tickets in advance online, but the center's website is in Polish only.) On weekdays, it's generally no problem to walk right in.

Getting There: It's an easy downhill walk from Warsaw's Royal Way, but the hike back up is fairly steep. Near the modern bridge, you'll find a Metro stop and a bus stop (both called Centrum Nauki Kopernik). From here, bus #102 goes to Nowy Świat, then up the Royal Way (Uniwersytet and Zachęta stops) before heading west to the Warsaw Uprising Museum. Metro line 2 connects the science center to the National Stadium, the Royal Way (near the Copernicus statue), and the Warsaw Uprising Museum.

Visiting the Center: Your ticket is a plastic card that you can insert into certain interactive exhibits. On the ground floor, the

"Roots of Civilization" features working models of various tools and machines, demonstrating how humanity has mastered the mechanics of physics. You can play archaeologist in a sandbox, listen to *Ode to Joy* while tuning into different instruments, and see a small "fire tornado" (every bit as cool as it sounds). A playroom for toddlers, called **"Buzzz!,"** has a nature theme. Meanwhile, **"RE: Generation"** targets teens and adults with computer touchscreens that investigate the biological underpinnings of emotion—from what makes you laugh to what grosses you out—and examines how cultures around the world are both similar and different.

The **"Heavens of Copernicus" planetarium** requires a separate ticket (19 zł, 14 zł for kids 19 and under, in Polish with English headset, show starts at the top of each hour—ask for schedule at ticket desk).

The fun continues upstairs, where **"Humans and the Environment"** illuminates the human body (find out just how long your intestines are, identify and place the organs, and see how various joints work like hinges). In the exercise arena, you can compete against various virtual animals (can you jump as high as a kangaroo or hang like a chimp?). The **"Lightzone"** illustrates how light travels in waves, lets you try out an old-fashioned (but still impressive) camera obscura, and use prisms and lenses to play a game of "light billiards." **"On the Move"** features fascinating hands-on physics demos, including an earthquake simulator, an air cannon, and a tube that lets you harness sound waves to make water vibrate. New exhibits are added (and old ones refreshed) all the time—be sure to pick up the brochure at the entry to understand your options.

Nearby: The **Discovery Park** surrounding the museum was created when the busy riverfront highway was rerouted into an underground tunnel, creating this delightful people zone. From here you have good views of the modern Holy Cross Bridge (Most Świętokrzyski, from 2000) and the National Stadium, proudly wrapped in the patriotic red and white of the Polish flag. These riverbanks are a popular hangout by day and after dark; in the summer, a stroll along here reveals a world of picnics, family outings, and impromptu parties.

Two short blocks inland from the science center is the architecturally innovative **Warsaw University Library** (Biblioteka Uniwersytecka w Warszawie, or BUW), with its distinctive oxidized-copper-colored facade decorated with open books from various cultures. The facade is fun to ogle, and the rooftop holds a huge and inviting garden.

West of the Royal Way (near Centralna Station)
Palace of Culture and Science
(Pałac Kultury i Nauki, or PKiN)

This massive skyscraper, dating from the early 1950s, is the tallest building between Frankfurt and Moscow (760 feet with the spire, though several new buildings are threatening to eclipse that peak). While you can ride the lift to its top for a commanding view, the highlight is simply viewing it up close from ground level.

Viewing the Skyscraper: This building was a "gift" from Stalin that the people of Warsaw couldn't refuse. Varsovians call it "Stalin's Penis"...using cruder terminology than that. (There are seven such "Stalin Gothic" erections in Moscow.) If it feels like an Art Deco Chicago skyscraper, that's because the architect was inspired by the years he spent studying and working in Chicago in the 1930s. Because it was to be "Soviet in substance, Polish in style," Soviet architects toured Poland to absorb local culture before starting the project. Notice the frilly decorative friezes that top each level—evocative of Poland's many Renaissance buildings (such as Kraków's Cloth Hall). The clock was added in 1999 as part of the millennium celebrations. Since the end of communism, the younger generation doesn't mind the structure so much—and some even admit to liking it for the way it enlivens the predictable glass-and-steel skyline springing up around it.

Everything about the Pałac is big. Approach it from the east side (facing the busy Marszałkowska street and the slick Galeria Centrum shopping mall). Stand in front of the granite tribune where communist VIPs surveyed massive May Day parades and pageantry on the once-imposing square, which today is a sloppy parking lot. From there, size up the skyscraper—its grand entry flanked by massive statues of Copernicus on the right (science) and the great poet Mickiewicz on the left (culture). It's designed to show off the strong, grand-scale Soviet aesthetic and architectural skill. The Pałac contains various theaters (the culture), museums of evolution and technology (the science), a congress hall, a multiplex (showing current movies), an observation deck, and lots of office space. With all this Culture and Science under one Roof, it's a shame that only the ground-floor lobby (which feels like stepping into 1950s Moscow and is free to enter) and the 30th-floor observatory deck are open to the public.

Observation Deck: You can zip up to the "XXX Floor" in 20 seconds on the retrofitted Soviet elevators—but the trip is overpriced and the view's a letdown (20 zł, daily 10:00-20:00, may be open later in summer, enter through main door on east side of Pałac—opposite from Centralna station, tel. 22-656-7600, www.pkin.pl).

Złote Tarasy Shopping Mall

Tucked behind Centralna station, "Golden Terraces" is a supermodern shopping mall with a funky, undulating glass-and-steel roof. Yes, you didn't come all the way to Poland to visit a shopping mall. But if you're at the station, crossing the street to peek in here offers a taste of Poland's race into the future.

Hours: Mon-Sat 9:00-22:00, Sun 9:00-21:00, lots of designer shops, food court on top level, www.zlotetarasy.pl.

Złota 44

This skyscraper, with its dramatic swooping lines rising high from the Złote Tarasy shopping mall, was designed by world-renowned architect Daniel Libeskind (who also redeveloped the 9/11 site in New York City). Born in Poland, at a very young age Libeskind emigrated with his family to the US, returning only recently to embark on this project. Its shape evokes an eagle (a symbol for Poland) just beginning to take flight. Of all the shiny new towers popping up in Warsaw's skyline, this is the most architecturally interesting—and offers a striking counterpoint to the Stalinist Palace of Culture and Science nearby. (For more on the building, visit www. zlota44.com/en.)

JEWISH WARSAW

In the early 1600s, an estimated 80 percent of all Jews lived in Poland—then the largest country in Europe. But after centuries of dwelling in relative peace in tolerant and pragmatic Poland, Warsaw's Jews suffered terribly at the hands of the Nazis. Several sights in Warsaw commemorate those who were murdered, and those who fought back. Because the Nazis leveled the ghetto, there is literally nothing left except the street plan, some monuments, and the heroic spirit of its former residents. However, the top-notch Museum of the History of Polish Jews—which opened in 2014—has rejuvenated the area, making it even more of a magnet for those interested in this chapter of Polish history.

Getting There: To reach Ghetto Heroes Square and the museum from the Old Town, you can hop a **taxi** or **Uber** (10 zł) or take a **bus** (to the Nalewki-Muzeum stop; bus #180 is particularly useful; bus #111 reaches this stop from farther south—Piłsudski Square, the university, and the National Museum). You can also **walk** there in about 15 minutes: Go through the barbican gate two blocks into the New Town, turn left on Świętojerska, and walk straight 10 minutes—passing the green-glass Supreme Court building. En route, at the corner of Świętojerska and Nowiniarska, watch for the pattern of bricks in the sidewalk, marking *Ghetto Wall 1940-1943*.

▲Ghetto Heroes Square (Plac Bohaterow Getta)

The square is in the heart of what was the Jewish ghetto—now surrounded by bland Soviet-style apartment blocks. After the uprising, the entire ghetto was reduced to dust by the Nazis, leaving the communists to rebuild to their own specifications. The district is called Muranów ("Rebuilt") today.

The **monument** in the middle of the square commemorates those who fought and died "for the dignity and freedom of the Jewish Nation, for a free Poland, and for the liberation of humankind." The statue features heroic Jewish men who knew that an inglorious death at the hands of the Nazis awaited them. Flames in the background show Nazis burning the ghetto. The opposite side features a sad procession of Jews trudging to concentration camps, with subtle Nazi bayonets and helmets moving things along.

As you face the monument, look through the trees to the right to see a seated statue. **Jan Karski** (1914-2000) was a Catholic Pole and resistance fighter who traveled extensively through Poland during the Nazi occupation, collected evidence, and then reported on the Warsaw Ghetto and the Holocaust to the leaders of the Western Allies (including a personal meeting with FDR). In 1944, while the Holocaust was still going on, Karski published his eye-witness account, *The Story of a Secret State* (which you can see on this statue's armrest). After the war he became a US citizen, and in 2012 President Barack Obama awarded him a posthumous Presidential Medal of Freedom.

• *The huge, glassy building facing the monument from across the square is the...*

▲▲▲Museum of the History of Polish Jews (Muzeum Historii Żydów Polskich, a.k.a. POLIN)

This world-class attraction thoughtfully traces the epic, millennium-long story of Jews in Poland. This is not a "Holocaust mu-

seum;" it provides stirring documentation of the full and very rich Polish Jewish experience across the centuries. In-depth, engaging, vividly illustrated, and eloquently presented, the exhibits present a powerful context for the many Jewish cultural sites around Poland—offering insights both for people familiar with the story and for beginners. The museum is at once expansive and intimate, with ample descriptions, videos, and touchscreens; you could spend all day here, but two hours is the absolute minimum. It wins my vote for the best museum in Poland, and it's easily Europe's best Jewish museum—and a strong contender for the best European historical museum, period. The building also hosts cultural events and temporary exhibits.

Cost and Hours: Core exhibition-25 zł, Mon and Thu-Fri 10:00-18:00, Wed and Sat-Sun 10:00-20:00, closed Tue, essential audioguide-10 zł, last entry 2 hours before closing, Anielewicza 6, cafeteria, tel. 22-471-0300, www.jewishmuseum.org.pl.

Visiting the Museum: Before entering, view the building's striking **exterior** (designed by Finnish architect Rainer Mahlamäki). You'll enter (and go through a security checkpoint) at the large,

Warsaw's Jews and the Ghetto Uprising

From the Middle Ages until World War II, Poland was a relatively safe haven for Europe's Jews. While other kings were imprisoning and deporting Jews in the 14th century, the progressive king Kazimierz the Great welcomed Jews into Poland, even granting them special privileges (see page 257).

By the 1930s, there were more than 380,000 Jews in Warsaw—nearly a third of the population (and the largest concentration of Jews in any European city). The Nazis arrived in 1939. Within a year, they had pushed all of Warsaw's Jews into one neighborhood and surrounded it with a wall, creating a miserably overcrowded ghetto (crammed with an estimated 460,000 people, including many from nearby towns). There were nearly 600 such ghettos in cities and towns all over Poland.

By the summer of 1942, more than a quarter of the Jews in the ghetto had either died of disease, committed suicide, or been murdered. The Nazis started moving Warsaw's Jews (at the rate of 5,000 a day) into what they claimed were "resettlement camps." Most of these people—300,000 in all—were actually murdered at Treblinka or Auschwitz. Finally the waning population—now about 60,000—began to get word from concentration camp escapees about what was actually going on there. Spurred by this knowledge, Warsaw's surviving Jews staged a dramatic uprising.

On April 19, 1943, the Jews attacked Nazi strongholds and had some initial success. The overwhelming Nazi war machine—which had rolled over much of Europe—imagined they'd be able to put down the rebellion easily. Instead, they struggled for a month to finally crush the Ghetto Uprising. The ghetto's residents and structures were "liquidated." About 300 of Warsaw's Jews survived, thanks in part to a sort of "underground railroad" of courageous Varsovians.

Warsaw's Jewish sights are emotionally moving, but even more so if you know some of their stories. You may have heard of **Władysław Szpilman,** a Jewish concert pianist who survived the war with the help of Jews, Poles, and even a Nazi officer. Szpilman's life story was turned into the highly acclaimed, Oscar-winning film *The Pianist,* which powerfully depicts events in Warsaw during World War II.

Less familiar to non-Poles—but equally affecting—is the story of Henryk Goldszmit, better known by his pen name, **Janusz Korczak.** Korczak wrote imaginative children's books that are still enormously popular among Poles. He worked at an orphanage in the Warsaw ghetto. When his orphans were sent off to concentration camps, the Nazis offered the famous author a chance at freedom. Korczak turned them down, choosing to die at Treblinka with his children.

asymmetrical hole in the side of the building. Once you're inside, the symbolism becomes clear: This represents Moses parting the Red Sea. (While the main exhibit covers the thousand years of Jews in Poland, this sets the stage by going back even further—to the Jewish origin story.)

Buy your tickets for the core exhibition and rent the invaluable 60-stop audioguide, which helps provide a concise structure for your exploration of the sprawling exhibitions. Then head downstairs and follow the one-way route. In this high-tech, interactive space, exhibits in eight galleries mingle with actual artifacts to bring history to life.

You'll begin by passing through a simulated forest—evocative of legends about the Jews' arrival in Poland—to reach the **First Encounters** exhibit. Here you'll learn how Jewish merchants made their way to Poland in the 10th century (with maps of their trade routes and samples of what they sold). The story is told partly from the perspective of Ibrahim ibn Jakub, a Sephardic Jew who penned early travelogues about Europe. In 1264, Duke Bolesław the Pious—the first of many tolerant Polish rulers—gave Jews rights, including minting coins; you'll see an example dating from the 13th century and marked with a Hebrew character. In the next room (on the left wall) are illustrations of the leading Polish cities of the time and (on the right wall) Polish medieval monarchs, with in-depth explanations of each one's policies toward their Jewish subjects.

Next, the **Paradisus Iudaeorum** explains how, as Jews became more established in Polish society in the 15th and 16th centuries, they enjoyed better and better living conditions. (Meanwhile, anti-Semites bitterly complained that Poland was becoming a "Jewish Paradise"—the name of this exhibit.) The centerpiece here is a gigantic, interactive model of Kraków and its Jewish quarter, Kazimierz. In the library section, you can flip through virtual pages of books from the era.

Continuing into the next area, you'll enter a dark hallway that explains the Khmelnytsky Uprising—a mid-17th-century Cossack rebellion against the Polish lords and the Jews who served them. This brought a new wave of pogroms and 10,000 Jewish deaths.

After the uprising, Polish lords invited Jews to privately owned market towns—called *shtetls*—to help re-establish the economy. **The Jewish Town** offers a fascinating look at different walks of life in a typical Jewish community: the market, where Jews and Christians could mingle at the tavern; the home, where a family would live, work, eat, and sleep in a single room; the cemetery (touchscreens invite you to learn about the symbolism of Jewish tombstones); and the synagogue, with a gloriously colorful replica of a ceiling and bema (prayer platform) from a wooden synagogue from the village of Gwoździec—dripping with symbolism that's explained on nearby touchscreens. An exhibit also traces the mid-18th-century rise of Hasidism—a mystical branch of Judaism—in the eastern Polish lands (today's Ukraine).

With the Partitions of the late 18th century (when Polish territory was divided among neighboring powers), Polish Jews found themselves split among three different empires—symbolized by a room with giant portraits of the rulers of Prussia, Russia, and Austria, all facing the Polish throne. **Encounters with Modernity** examines how Jews in different parts of the Polish lands had very different experiences. You'll see a replica salon of a wealthy Jewish family who mingled with elites, and learn about the debate at that time of what the role of Jews in society should be (illustrated by a fine collection of items from Jewish ceremonies commemorating rites of passage). You'll also learn about the competing movements within Judaism that emerged during this era: Hasidism, led by charismatic Tzadiks who promised a closer spiritual connection to God, and the more reform-minded Haskalah, an intellectual approach inspired by the Enlightenment. A riveting, painterly film follows a day in the life of a young student at a *yeshiva* (school). A railway station represents the Industrial Revolution, when the world got smaller and brought a new world of opportunities...and of threats. You'll learn how some Jews worked hard to integrate with their dominant cultures (such as the painter Maurycy Gottlieb). This period also saw the emergence of modern anti-Semitism, including a brutal pogrom in Warsaw in 1881. As Jews sought to define a modern Jewish identity in the late 19th century, many emigrated—some to North or South America, and still others to the Holy Land (the beginnings of Zionism).

All of this sets the stage for World War I, when Jews were drafted into various armies—and often forced to fight one another. But at war's end, Poland was reconstituted as an independent nation. You'll step out onto **The Street,** which re-creates an interwar shopping street from a Jewish community. ("The Jewish Street" was also slang for the Jewish world in general.) It was between the World Wars—when a newly independent Poland extended full citizenship and voting rights to its Jewish citizens—that Jewish cultural life flourished as never before. One-third of Poland's population was Jewish—that's three million people. You'll see re-created Warsaw sites relating to newspapers, cinema, writers, and artists; you'll learn about Jewish tourism of the era (when middle-class Jews would travel around Poland and Europe to visit Jewish cultural sites); and you'll see exhibits about education and reform—including bilingual schooling (Yiddish and Polish), the beloved educator and author Janusz Korczak, and the debate over "ghetto benches" (segregated seating areas in schools). However, this was also a time of rising anti-Semitism, segregation, boycotts, and anti-Jewish quotas; during this period, some 140,000 Jews emigrated to the Holy Land.

After one more nostalgic stroll down "The Street," you come to September 1, 1939, when the Nazis invaded Poland. They stripped Jews of their rights and possessions; humiliated, tortured, and executed them; and eventually implemented the **Holocaust.** The exhibit traces, step by step, the escalation of the Nazis' "Final Solution," with a focus on events here in Warsaw: Forcing Jews into a ghetto (you'll walk across a platform representing the bridge that connected the two parts of the ghetto, offering Jewish people fleeting glimpses of "normal" life going on outside their walls); the liquidation of the ghetto and the movement of Warsaw's Jews to the death camp at Treblinka; and the Ghetto Uprising, a desperate last stand in which the dwindling number or Warsaw's Jews put up a valiant, but ultimately failed, fight. Making these stories personal are contemporaneous diaries, documents, and photographs. The exhibit poses difficult questions about how Poles helped—or did not help—the Jews who were gradually disappearing from their cities. And it explains how a sort of "underground railroad" worked hard and at great peril to save as many Jews as possible—as depicted in the movie *The Pianist.* (Look for the chess set carved by a Jew in hiding.) All told, 9 out of every 10 Polish Jews were murdered in the Holocaust. Only about 300,000 survived.

Finally, **The Postwar Years** follows Holocaust survivors in the years just after the war, when, astonishingly, they were scapegoated for war crimes. About 150,000 more (half the total survivors) fled to the newly-created state of Israel, and those who remained had to navigate an unfriendly, anti-Semitic communist regime. In 1968, the communists launched an "anti-Zionist" campaign; eventually around 15,000 Polish Jews lost their citizenship and left for Israel, Western Europe, and the US. Not until the fall of communism could the rest finally enter a world of new possibilities. The creation of this museum—the first time that the full story of the Jews of Poland has ever been told in such a mainstream way, and in all its epic scope—represents a critical milestone in celebrating a culture that has survived a harrowing history.

Ghetto Walking Tour

For a poignant stroll through what was the ghetto, with faint echoes of a tragic history, take this brief, lightly guided walk for a few blocks. Facing the monument with the museum behind you, head left (with the park on your left) and walk along Zamenhofa—which, like many streets in this neighborhood, is named for a hero of the Ghetto Uprising. From the monument, you'll follow a series of three-foot-tall, black stone memorials to uprising heroes—the **Path of Remembrance.** Like Stations of the Cross, each recounts an event of the uprising. Every April 19th (the day the uprising began), huge crowds follow this path.

In a block, just beyond the corner of Miła (partly obscured by some bushes), you'll find a **bunker** where about 100 organizers of the uprising hid (and where they committed suicide when the Nazis discovered them on May 8, 1943).

Continue following the black stone monuments up Zamenhofa (which becomes Dubois), then turn left at the corner, onto broad and busy Stawki. The ugly gray building on your left (a half-block down at #5, near the tram stop) was the **headquarters of the SS** within the ghetto. This is where the transportation of Warsaw's Jews to concentration camps was organized.

Using the crosswalk at the tram stop, cross Stawki and proceed straight ahead into the gap between the two buildings. At the back of this parking lot is a surviving part of the red-brick **ghetto wall,** with a few remaining scraps of 1940s barbed wire.

Farther up Stawki street, on the right, you can stop at the **Umschlagplatz** monument—shaped like a cattle car. That's German for "transfer place," and it marks the spot where the Nazis brought Jewish families to prepare them to be loaded onto trains bound for Treblinka or Auschwitz. This was the actual site of the touching scene in the film *The Pianist* where the grandfather shares bits of chocolate with his family before being forever separated. In the walls of the monument are inscribed the first names of some of the victims.

WARSAW UPRISING SIGHTS

While the 1944 Warsaw Uprising is a recurring theme in virtually all Warsaw sightseeing, two sights in particular—one a monument, the other a museum—are worth a visit for anyone with a special interest. Neither is right on the main tourist trail; the monument is closer to the sightseeing action, while the museum is a subway, tram, or taxi ride away.

Warsaw Uprising Monument

The most central sight related to the Warsaw Uprising is the monument at plac Krasińskich (intersection of ulica Długa and Miodowa,

one long block and about a five-minute walk northwest of the New Town). Larger-than-life soldiers and civilians race for the sewers in a desperate attempt to flee the Nazis. Just behind the monument is the oxidized-copper facade of Poland's Supreme Court.

▲▲Warsaw Uprising Museum (Muzeum Powstania Warszawskiego)

Thorough, modern, and packed with Polish field-trip groups, the museum celebrates the heroes of the uprising. It's a bit cramped, and finding your way through the exhibits can be confusing, but it helps illuminate this complicated chapter of Warsaw's history. The location is inconvenient (a 10-minute tram or bus ride west of Centralna station) and, because it eats up several hours to visit, may not be worth the trek for those with a casual interest. But history buffs find it worthwhile.

Cost and Hours: 18 zł, free on Sun (but you'll pay 2 zł for the good *City of Ruins* movie—buy ticket at cashier before entering museum), Mon and Wed-Fri 8:00-18:00, Thu until 20:00, Sat-Sun 10:00-18:00, closed Tue, tel. 22-539-7947, www.1944.pl.

Audioguide: The informative, two-hour audioguide is ideal if you really want to delve into the whole story (10 zł, rent it in the gift shop). But the museum is so well-described, you can just wander aimlessly and be immersed in the hellish events.

Eating: The museum's café is oddly pleasant, serving drinks and light snacks amidst genteel ambience from interwar Warsaw. In summer you can dine on a peaceful terrace.

Getting There: The museum is on the western edge of downtown—a long, dull walk through urban gloom—at ulica Przyokopowa 28. While it's easiest to reach by taxi or Uber (figure about 20 zł from the Royal Way), you can get close on public transit. The nearest tram/bus stop is called Muzeum Powstania Warszawskiego, which you can reach on tram #22 or #24 (from Centralna station, or the street in front of the National Museum), bus #178 (from Castle Square), bus #105 (from the Uniwersytet stop on the Royal Way), or bus #109 (from in front of Centralna station). From the stop, you'll see the back of the museum (with its tower); circle around to find the entrance. Only a little farther from the museum is the Metro stop called Rondo Daszyńskiego.

⊘ Self-Guided Tour: Buy your ticket at the little house on the left (marked *kasa*), then head into the main hall. The high-tech **main exhibit** sprawls across three floors. It tells the story of the uprising chronologically, with a keen focus on military history. The exhibit covers several topics, but doesn't provide a big-picture narrative; to fully understand the context of what you're seeing, read the sidebar before your visit.

The **children's area** (to the right as you enter) reminds visitors that Varsovian kids played a role in the Warsaw Uprising, too.

The **ground floor** sets the stage with Germany's invasion and occupation of Poland. The Generalgouvernement (Nazi puppet government of occupied Poland, ruled by Hans Frank in Kraków) wasted no time in asserting its control over the Poles; you'll learn how they imprisoned and executed priests, professors, and students. You'll also hear the story of the earlier, smaller uprisings that preceded the Warsaw Uprising, including the Poland-wide Operation Tempest (Burza) in 1943. During those earliest rebellions, Warsaw was intentionally left out of the fray...but only for the time being.

To keep with the chronological flow, skip the middle floor for now, and ride the elevator to the **top floor** (#2), which covers the main part of the uprising. You'll meet some of the uprising's heroes and learn about their uniforms, weapons, and methods. The "Kino Palladium" movie screen shows fascinating Home Army newsreel footage from the period (with English subtitles). To the right of the screen, you'll walk through a simulated sewer, reminiscent of the one that many Home Army soldiers and civilians used to evade the Germans. Imagine terrified troops quietly traversing a sewer line like this one more than a mile long (but with lower ceilings)— and doing it while knee-deep in liquid sewage. At the end of the "sewer," stairs lead down to the middle floor.

The **middle floor** focuses on the grueling aftermath of the uprising. The later days of the uprising are outlined, battle by battle. A chilling section describes how Warsaw became a "city of graves," with burial mounds and makeshift crosses scattered everywhere. One room honors the Field Postal Service, which, at great personal risk, continued mail delivery of both military communiqués and civilian correspondences. Many of these brave "mailmen" were actually Scouts who were too young to fight. Nearby, another room re-creates a clandestine radio broadcast station set up in a living room.

If you need a break, look for the red corridor leading through the USSR section to the **café** and WC.

End your visit by walking down the stairs into the **main hall,** which is dominated by two large-scale exhibits: a replica of an RAF Liberator B-24 J, used for airborne surveillance of wartime Warsaw; and a giant movie screen showing more newsreels assembled by the Home Army's own propaganda unit during the uprising.

The Warsaw Uprising

By the summer of 1944, it was becoming clear that the Nazis' days in Warsaw were numbered. The Red Army drew near, and by late July, Soviet tanks were within 25 miles of downtown Warsaw.

The Varsovians could simply have waited for the Soviets to cross the river and force the Nazis out. But they knew that Soviet "liberation" would also mean an end to Polish independence. The Polish Home Army numbered 400,000—30,000 of them in Warsaw alone—and was the biggest underground army in military history. The uprisers wanted Poland to control its own fate, and they took matters into their own hands. The resistance's symbol was an anchor made up of a P atop a W (which stands for Polska Walcząca, or "Poland Fighting"—you'll see this icon all around town). Over time, the Home Army had established an extensive network of underground tunnels and sewers, which allowed them to deliver messages and move around the city without drawing the Nazis' attention. These tunnels gave the Home Army the element of surprise.

On August 1, 30,000 Polish resistance fighters launched an attack on their Nazi oppressors. They poured out of the sewers and caught the Nazis off guard. The ferocity of the Polish fighters stunned the Nazis, who thought they'd put down the uprising within hours. But the Nazis regrouped, and within a few days, they had retaken several areas of the city—murdering tens of thousands of innocent civilians as they went. In one notorious incident, some 5,500 Polish soldiers and 6,000 civilians who were surrounded by Nazis in the Old Town were forced to flee through the sewers; many drowned or were shot. (This scene is depicted in the Warsaw Uprising Monument on plac Krasińskich.)

Two months after it had started, the Warsaw Uprising was over. The Home Army called a cease-fire. About 18,000 Polish uprisers had been killed, along with nearly 200,000 innocent civilians. An infuriated Hitler ordered that the city be destroyed—which it was, systematically, block by block, until virtually nothing remained.

Through all this, the Soviets stood still, watched, and waited. When the smoke cleared and the Nazis left, the Red Army marched in and claimed the wasteland that was once called Warsaw. After the war, General Dwight D. Eisenhower said that the scale of destruction here was the worst he'd ever seen. The communists later tracked down the surviving Home Army leaders, killing or imprisoning them.

Depending on whom you talk to, the desperate uprising of Warsaw was incredibly brave, stupid, or both. As for the Poles, they remain fiercely proud of their struggle for freedom. The city of Warsaw has recently commemorated this act of bravery with the new Warsaw Uprising Museum.

Under the screen, behind the black curtains, an exhibit tells the story of Germans in Warsaw, along with another, more claustrophobic walk-through sewer.

Also in the main hall, look for the entrance to the seven-minute 3-D film *City of Ruins*, with virtual aerial footage of the postwar devastation. This gives you a look at the reality of the thousand people (nicknamed "Robinson Crusoes") who lived in bombed-out Warsaw immediately after the war. It's worth waiting in line to see this powerful film.

The **park** surrounding the building features several thought-provoking sights. A Chevy truck armored by the Home Army is both a people's tank and an example of how outgunned they were. Along the back is the Wall of Memory, a Vietnam War Memorial-type monument to soldiers of the Polish Home Army who were killed in action. You'll see their rank and name, followed by their code name, in quotes. The Home Army observed a strict policy of anonymity, forbidding members from calling each other by anything but their code names. The bell in the middle is dedicated to the commander of the uprising, Antoni Chruściel (code name "Monter").

SOUTH OF THE CENTER
▲Łazienki Park (Park Łazienkowski)

The huge, idyllic Łazienki Park (wah-ZHYEN-kee) is where Varsovians go to play. The park is sprinkled with fun Neoclassical buildings, strutting peacocks, and young Poles in love. It was built by Poland's very last king (before the final Partition), Stanisław August Poniatowski, to serve as his summer residence and provide a place for his citizens to relax.

On the edge of the park (along Belwederska) is a **monument to Fryderyk Chopin.** The monument, in a rose garden, is flanked by platforms, where free summer piano **concerts** of Chopin's music

are given weekly (mid-May-late Sept only, generally Sun at 12:00 and 16:00—confirm at TI). The statue shows Chopin sitting under a wind-blown willow tree. Although he spent his last 20 years and wrote most of his best-known music in France, his inspiration came from wind blowing through the willow trees of his native land, Poland. The Nazis were quick to destroy this statue, which symbolizes Polish culture. They melted the original (from 1926) down for its metal. Today's copy was recast after World War II. Savor this spot; it's great in summer, with roses wildly in bloom, and in autumn, when the trees provide a golden backdrop for the black, romantic statue.

Venture down into the ravine and to the center of the park, where (after a 10-minute hike) you'll find King Poniatowski's strik-

ing **Palace on the Water** (Pałac na Wodzie)—literally built in the middle of a river. Nearby, you'll spot a clever amphitheater with seating on the riverbank and the stage on an island. The king was a real man of the Enlightenment, hosting weekly Thursday dinners here for artists and intellectuals. But Poland's kings are long gone, and proud peacocks now rule this roost.

Łazienki Park is also slated to be the future home of the state-of-the-art **Museum of Polish History,** which is being built along the Łazienkowska highway (near Ujazdów Castle, at the northeastern edge of the park). While it likely won't open until at least 2018, this museum will be yet another big draw for visitors (to check on the progress, see www.en.muzhp.pl).

Getting There: The park is just south of the city center on the Royal Way. Buses #116 and #180 run from Castle Square in the Old Town along the Royal Way directly to the park (get off at the stop called Łazienki Królewskie, by Belweder Palace—you'll see Chopin squinting through the trees on your left). Maps at park entrances locate the Chopin monument, Palace on the Water, and other park attractions.

Shopping in Warsaw

You'll notice that many Varsovians are chic, sophisticated, and very well-dressed. To see where they outfit themselves, go shopping. **Mysia 3** is a super-hip mini mall with three concise floors dedicated to mostly Polish fashion designers, but also has cutting-edge housewares and decor (Mon-Sat 10:00-20:00, Sun 12:00-18:00, across Jerusalem Avenue from Nowy Świat, inside the former communist propaganda office at Mysia 3, www.mysia3.pl). Warsaw's main "fashion row" is a bit farther south, in the Śródmieście district. **Mokotowska street,** which angles northeast from trendy plac Zbawiciela, is lined with literally dozens of chichi boutiques, jew-

WARSAW

elry shops, shoe stores, designer pastry shops, hair salons, and hipster barbers. The highest concentration is a few short blocks north of plac Zbawiciela, north of Piękna. Along here, Mokotowska 48 is a small shopping complex of local fashionistas. If you enjoy this zone, the area immediately to the west—along Wilcza and Poznańska streets—has more of the same.

Entertainment in Warsaw

Warsaw fills the summer with live music options. In addition to more serious options (opera, symphony, etc.), consider these crowd-pleasing choices.

CHOPIN

My favorite Warsaw music option is to enjoy a Chopin performance. There's nothing like hearing Chopin's compositions passionately played by a teary-eyed Pole who really feels the music. The best option is the outdoor concert in front of the big Chopin statue in **Łazienki Park,** but it is held only one day a week in summer (free, mid-May-late-Sept Sun at 12:00 and 16:00, www.lazienki-krolewskie.pl; for more on this option, see the Łazienki Park listing on page 420).

If you're not in town on a Sunday, the next best thing is the **Chopin Salon.** Jarek Chołodecki, who runs the recommended Chopin Boutique B&B, hosts an intimate piano concert in his delightful salon nightly at 19:30. The performance can cover a range of musical styles and composers—but generally there are piano pieces featuring Chopin. The concert lasts from 45 minutes to more than an hour and is followed by wine, homemade cakes, and social time. A small group of locals and travelers gathers around Jarek's big shiny Steinway grand to hear great music by talented young artists in a great city (50 zł, ulica Smolna 14, reservations required, tel. 22-829-4801, www.bedandbreakfast.pl). Jarek is also involved in the **Warsaw House of Music**—described later—which also presents Chopin concerts and other music.

The **Chopin Museum** has a concert series where music academy students recommended by their professors perform an hour-long concert. These are free and typically take place October through July each Thursday at 18:00—but they can be cancelled, so it's smart to confirm (tel. 22-441-6100, www.en.chopin.nifc.pl; no concerts Aug-Sept).

Additionally, various **touristy Chopin concerts** are popping up all over the city; figure 60 zł for a piano performance set in a drawing room or small theater. This is a fast-changing scene; options include Time for Chopin (in the Old Town, www.timeforchopin.com) or Warsaw Classical Experience (in the House of Literature, facing Castle Square, www.waclaex.eu). Ask your hotel or the TI for the latest fliers.

OTHER MUSIC

Warsaw House of Music (also called Nowy Świat Muzyki—"New World of Music")—in a refurbished town house along the Royal Way—hosts an even wider range of musical events, both for locals and for out-of-towners. The lineup does include some Chopin, but goes beyond touristy cliches to delve into other historical musical forms from Warsaw, including Jewish klezmer music, interwar Polish cabaret songs, Slavic folk songs, and traditional and contemporary jazz (Nowy Świat 63, tel. 22-692-4824, www.warsawhouseofmusic.pl).

Two big, opulent churches in and near the Old Town put on 30-minute **organ concerts** most days through the summer. Choose between the Cathedral of St. John the Baptist, with lots of history and a pretty, plain brick interior, right in the heart of the Old Town (10 zł, Aug-late Oct Mon-Sat at 14:00, no concerts Sun); or the frilly, Rococo St. Anne's Church, with a more sumptuous interior, just outside the Old Town (10 zł, May-early Oct Mon-Sat at 12:00, no concerts Sun). Both are run by the same company (mobile 501-158-477, www.kapitula.org).

Free outdoor **jazz concerts** take place each Saturday in summer right on the Old Town Square (July-Aug at 19:00).

LIVELY HANGOUT ZONES

The Old Town and New Town are totally for tourists. To find some more interesting areas to explore and hang out after dark, your first stop should be **plac Zbawiciela** in the Śródmieście and the surrounding streets (see page 431). Locals also enjoy spending a balmy afternoon or evening on the **Vistula riverbanks.** Long ignored by Varsovians, the left (west) bank has undergone a dramatic renovation, with beautiful parklike embankments ideal for strolling. Meanwhile, the right (east) bank is still rugged and undeveloped, with forests and natural beaches—the biggest being around the eastern base of the Poniatowski Bridge (where Jerusalem Avenue crosses the river, just past Palm Tree Circle).

Sleeping in Warsaw

Because Warsaw is a major business destination, its hotel rates fluctuate from day to day. I've categorized them based on estimated prices during busy times, but you may find them much higher or much lower depending on what's happening in town. Regardless, you'll find Warsaw affordable for a European capital—for what you'd spend on a basic room in Rome or Amsterdam, you can get a palatial room in a top-end hotel here. That said, two of my Warsaw favorites—Chopin Boutique B&B and Duval Apartments—are both affordable and characteristic, making them excellent choices.

I've arranged my listings by neighborhood. Keep in mind that in the Old Town, you'll rarely see a local, while in Śródmieście, you'll rarely see a tourist. Choose your Warsaw experience.

NEAR PALM TREE CIRCLE (NOWY ŚWIAT AND JERUSALEM AVENUE)

Considering how spread out Warsaw is, this is a convenient location for reaching various sights around the city. While comfortable inside, these hotels are in big buildings on uninspiring urban streets.

$$ Chopin Boutique B&B offers more comfort and class than a hotel twice its price, in a beautifully renovated and well-located old building near the Na-tional Museum. Jarek Chołodecki, who lived near Chicago for many years, returned to Warsaw and converted apartments into this wonderful bed-and-breakfast with 24 rooms. It's a friendly, casual, stylish place, creatively decorated and impeccably maintained. You'll feel like you're staying with your Warsaw sophisticate cousin—quirky, charismatic Jarek loves to chat with his guests, many of whom return and become his good friends. Each morning, conversation percolates at the big, family-style breakfast table over a morning meal made mostly from organic and locally-sourced foods. The garden courtyard is a nice escape from the city, and the drawing room plays host to nightly music concerts—see "Entertainment in Warsaw," earlier (RS%, breakfast extra, elevator, ulica Smolna 14, tel. 22-829-4801, www.bedandbreakfast.pl, office@bedandbreakfast.pl).

$$ Between Us B&B is an ideal home-away-from-home for hipsters in Warsaw. Beata rents three trendy rooms above a youthful café centrally located in downtown Warsaw. As this place books up early, reserve far ahead (on second floor, no elevator, check in at Między Nami café downstairs, Bracka 20, tel. 22-828-5417, mobile 603-096-701, www.between-us.eu, info@between-us.eu).

$$ Zgoda Apartment Hotel, impersonal but comfortable, has 51 apartments designed for business travelers on a tight budget (breakfast extra or use the kitchenette, air-con, elevator, Zgoda 6, tel. 22-553-6200, www.desilva.pl, zgoda@desilva.pl).

$$ Apple Inn, with seven tight rooms in the attic of a hulking, central building, is your cheap-and-cheery option in the center

---

Sleep Code

Hotels are classified based on the average price of a standard double room with breakfast in high season.

$$$$	**Splurge:** Most rooms over 550 zł
$$$	**Pricier:** 400-550 zł
$$	**Moderate:** 250-400 zł
$	**Budget:** 100-250 zł
¢	**Backpacker:** Under 100 zł
RS%	**Rick Steves discount**

Unless otherwise noted, credit cards are accepted, hotel staff speak basic English, and free Wi-Fi is available. Comparison-shop by checking prices at several hotels (on each hotel's own website, on a booking site, or by email). For the best deal, *book directly with the hotel.* Ask for a discount if paying in cash; if the listing includes **RS%,** request a Rick Steves discount.

(breakfast extra, shared kitchen and library, sometimes unstaffed—clearly communicate your arrival time, Chmielna 21, unit 22B—ride elevator to fourth floor, mobile 601-746-006, www.appleinn.pl, Miki).

¢ Oki Doki Hostel, on a pleasant square a few blocks in front of the Palace of Culture and Science, is colorful, creative, and easygoing. Each of its 37 rooms was designed by a different artist with a special theme—such as Van Gogh, Celtic spirals, heads of state, or Lenin. It's run by Ernest—a Pole whose parents loved Hemingway—and his wife Łucja, with help from their sometimes-jaded staff (private rooms available, plac Dąbrowskiego 3, tel. 22-826-5112, 22-828-0122, www.okidoki.pl, okidoki@okidoki.pl).

IN ŚRÓDMIEŚCIE ("DOWNTOWN")

Foodies, people who hate tourists, and travelers who really want to disappear into Warsaw choose to sleep in Śródmieście. A 10- to 15-minute walk (or quick tram ride) south of Jerusalem Avenue, it feels urban-residential and very local. And if trendy restaurants are on your agenda, sleeping near the culinary hotspots in Śródmieście is an efficient strategy. Compared to most of my other Warsaw listings, these feel a bit chic and trendy...just right for the neighborhood.

$$$ Hotel Rialto is a professional-feeling boutique hotel with Art Deco flair—both inside (in the lobby, respected restaurant, and 44 rooms) and out. It feels sophisticated, but without pretense (air-con, elevator, Wilcza 73, nearest tram/bus stop at Koszykowa, tel. 22-584-8700, www.rialto.pl, info@rialto.pl).

$$$ H15 Boutique Hotel feels posh for its price range, with a show-off lobby, a sleek black-and-white color scheme, and 46 rooms—ranging from simple doubles to expansive apartments. It tries very hard to be stylish—to the point of being a bit pretentious—but its handy location (surrounded by great restaurants) and reasonable rates make it worth considering (air-con, elevator, pay on-site parking, Poznańska 15, nearest tram/bus stop at Hoża, tel. 22-553-8700, www.h15boutiqueapartments.com, reservations@h15ab.com).

$$$ Autor Rooms is classy and intimate—a third-floor apartment with four rooms (each one different) and a shared breakfast table. It's off a busy street in an urban jungle just off Constitution Square, but once you're settled in, it's a handy home base (air-con, elevator, Lwowska 17, nearest tram/bus stop at plac Konstytucji, mobile 797-992-737, www.autorrooms.pl, hello@autorrooms.pl, Kaja).

IN OR NEAR THE OLD TOWN

The Old Town area has some fine splurges and easy access to the romantic, rebuilt historic core. But it's less handy to Warsaw's trendier side.

$$$$ Hotel Bristol is Warsaw's top splurge—as much a landmark as a hotel (see description on page 389), this classic address on the Royal Way is where you're likely to spot visiting dignitaries and celebrities. (Just inside the round entrance on the corner, find the wall of brass knobs identifying past VIP guests—from Pablo Picasso to Kelly Osborne.) The public spaces are palatial, with sumptuous Art Deco lounges, bars, and coffee shops that make you want to dress up just to hang out. And the 206 rooms are fresh, elegant, and well-equipped. If you like a posh home base, check the rates here first—you may be surprised at how affordable opulence can be (air-con, classy old vintage elevator, gym, swimming pool, sauna, Krakowskie Przedmieście 42, tel. 22-551-1000, www.hotelbristolwarsaw.pl, bristol@luxurycollection.com).

$$$$ Hotel Le Régina is another tempting splurge, buried in the quiet and charming New Town (just beyond the Old Town). From its elegant public spaces to its 61 top-notch rooms, everything here is done with class (pricey breakfast, elevator, exercise room, pool, Kościelna 12, tel. 22-531-6000, www.leregina.com, reception.leregina@mamaison.com).

$$$ Castle Inn, sitting on Castle Square at the entrance to the Old Town, is the next rung up the ladder for youth hostelers who've outgrown the grungy backpacker scene. Run by the owners of Oki Doki Hostel (described earlier), it has 22 creative and colorful rooms, each with different decor (breakfast extra, lots of stairs and no elevator, can be noisy—request quiet room, Świętojańska 2, tel. 22-425-0100, www.castleinn.pl, castleinn@castleinn.pl).

$$ Duval Apartments, named for a French woman who supposedly had an affair with the Polish king in this building, offers four beautifully appointed rooms above a restaurant and teahouse (called Same Fusy) a few steps off the square in the Old Town. Each spacious room has a different theme: traditional Polish, Japanese, glass, or retro. Offering B&B comfort with hotel anonymity, this is an excellent value and one of my Warsaw favorites (lots of stairs with no elevator, breakfast extra, some restaurant noise—light sleepers should request a quiet room, Nowomiejska 10, mobile 608-679-346, www.duval.net.pl, duval@duval.net.pl). Arrange a meeting time with Agnieszka or Marcin when you reserve.

Eating in Warsaw

Tourists are drawn to the Old Town, where prices are sky-high and quality is rock-bottom. But once you get outside that zone, Warsaw

is one of Eastern Europe's best foodie cities. For a memorable experience, don't be shy about exploring some more local neighborhoods. Prices are low, so even a "splurge" restaurant lets you experience high-end experimental cuisine for a fraction of the cost of a similar place in a Western European capital. For this reason—and to take full advantage of the city's exciting food scene—my recommendations here skew to fancier foodie options. Eat "ye olde" in Kraków and Prague, if you must—but in Warsaw, be adventurous.

Wherever you dine, most restaurants are open until the "last guest," which usually means about 23:00 (sometimes later in summer)—but can be earlier than expected on slow nights. If dining late, call ahead.

NEAR PALM TREE CIRCLE (NOWY ŚWIAT AND JERUSALEM AVENUE)

These practical options are right in the middle of your sightseeing plans—handy for lunch on the go, or worth going out of your way for to enjoy a memorable dinner. The clientele is a mix of local yuppies, savvy business travelers, and casual tourists smart enough to steer clear of Old Town restaurants.

$$$ Opasły Tom ("Bursting Tome"), a tidy, literary-themed restaurant by respected chef Agata Wojda, serves reasonably priced, modern cuisine inspired by Polish roots and ingredients. Reserve ahead at this dressy place (daily 12:00-22:00, Foksal 17, tel. 22-621-1881, http://kregliccy.pl/opaslytom). The area near Opasły Tom, along **Foksal street,** is lined with several lively, contemporary eateries where diners enjoy the al fresco tables.

Restaurant Price Code

I've assigned each eatery a price category, based on the average cost of a typical main course. Drinks, desserts, and splurge items (steak and seafood) can raise the price considerably.

$$$$	**Splurge:** Most main courses over 60 zł
$$$	**Pricier:** 45-60 zł
$$	**Moderate:** 25-45 zł
$	**Budget:** Under 25 zł

In Poland, a milk bar or takeout spot is **$**; a basic sit-down eatery is **$$**; a casual but more upscale restaurant is **$$$**; and a swanky splurge is **$$$$**.

$$$ Kamanda Lwowska is the best spot in Warsaw for traditional Polish cooking. It's named for the former Polish city that's now in Ukraine (Lwow, a.k.a. Lviv). It has a few outdoor seats and a charming, cluttered old cellar with just a touch of kitsch. The friendly and fun staff serves up well-executed Polish classics (daily 10:00-24:00, Foksal 10, tel. 22-828-1031).

$$$$ Butchery & Wine, in an unassuming location on a drab urban street, is a pocket of chic international cuisine in the heart of Warsaw. The waiters, smartly dressed in pinstripe aprons, serve upscale comfort food (specializing in steaks) to a small, lively room of business travelers. The wine list is extensive, and reservations are smart (Mon-Sat 12:00-22:00, Sun until 20:00, Żurawia 22, tel. 22-502-3118, www.butcheryandwine.pl).

$$ Bibenda is a super-trendy bar with cocktails and an enticing seasonal menu of Polish fusion dishes—using Polish classics as a starting point, then jazzing them up with elements borrowed from corresponding dishes in other cultures. For example, you might see fried chicken (a Polish staple), marinated in buttermilk (from the American south), with a raspberry/chipotle glaze (from Mexico). Or perhaps a *gołąbki* (Polish cabbage roll) done in the style of a Turkish *dolma* (stuffed grape leaves). It's trendy and affordable, and the food is delicious. Reservations are wise at dinnertime (Tue-Sun 12:00-late, closed Mon, Nowogrodzka 10, mobile 502-770-303, www.bibenda.pl.

Tamka 43, in a sleek but unpretentious modern space facing the Chopin Museum, has two parts: The main floor is an affordable **$$ café/wine bar,** handy for a quick lunch or glass of wine near the museum. Upstairs is a fine-dining **$$$$ restaurant,** with a menu based on historical research of Chopin's favorite dishes and a prizewinning wine list (reservations are smart). Both areas have lunch specials—which are a particularly good deal if you want to try the nice restaurant (daily 12:00-22:00, Tamka 43, tel. 22-441-6234, www.tamka43.pl).

Uniquely Polish Treats

These places are on or close to the busy Nowy Świat boulevard.

A. Blikle, Poland's most famous pastry shop, serves a wide variety of delicious treats. This is where locals shop for cakes when they're having someone special over for coffee. The specialty is *pączki* (PONCH-kee), the quintessential Polish doughnut, filled with rose-flavored jam. You can get your goodies "to go" in the shop, or pay double to enjoy them with coffee in the swanky, classic café with indoor or outdoor seating (daily 9:00-21:00, Nowy Świat 35, tel. 22-828-6601). They also have a sit-down restaurant, but I come here only for the *pączki*.

E. Wedel Pijalnia Czekolady thrills chocoholics. Emil Wedel made Poland's favorite chocolate, and today, his former residence houses this chocolate shop and genteel café. This is the spot for delicious pastries and a *real* hot chocolate—*czekolada do picia* ("drinking chocolate"), a cup of actual melted chocolate, not just hot chocolate milk. The staff describes it as, "True Wedel ecstasy for your mouth that will take you to a world of dreams and desires." Or, if you fancy chocolate mousse, try *pokusa* ("Wedel Temptation"). Wedel's was *the* Christmas treat for locals under communism. Cadbury bought the company when Poland privatized, but they kept the E. Wedel name, which is close to all Poles' hearts...and taste buds (Mon-Fri 8:00-22:00, Sat 9:00-22:00, Sun 9:00-21:00, between Palace of Culture and Science and Nowy Świat at ulica Szpitalna 8, tel. 22-827-2916, www.wedelpijalnie.pl/en).

Odette, tucked in a sleek, new, mixed-use complex a short walk from the main tourist zone and from Wedel, is a good choice for updated treats: pristinely executed designer cakes at reasonable prices. Look through the glass door to the kitchen (Tue-Sun 10:00-20:00, Mon 13:00-20:00, Wojciecha Górskiego 6, unit 7, mobile 604-745-444). These upscale dessert shops are all the rage—keep an eye out for them all over the city (such as Słodki Słony, described later).

In Powiśle, near the Riverbank

The low-lying Powiśle neighborhood—squeezed in the little canyon between the Royal Way and the river—is newly trendy, thanks partly to its proximity to the inviting riverbank parks. Solec 44 is worth going out of your way for to enjoy a memorable dinner, while the others are simply fun hangout cafés if you're in the area. To reach this area by foot, you can walk through the steep Beyera Park (behind the Chopin Museum), or go down Jerusalem Avenue toward the bridge, enter the rail station, go down the stairs, walk all the way along *peron* (platform) 1 to the end, then go down the stairs at the far end. You'll pop out right at Warszawa Powiśle, a short walk from Solec 44. Alternatively, you can walk partway across the bridge at Jerusalem Avenue, then go down the stairs at the first tower.

$$$ Solec 44 epitomizes Warsaw's foodie melding of old and new. They are deeply engaged with Polish culinary roots: They source traditionally-made, artisanal sausages and cheeses, and have a big wall of shelves (which looks like a bizarre culinary experiment) where they ferment various vegetables in the traditional manner. And yet, the food itself is modern, creative, and daring. It fills a once-deteriorating, communist-era cultural center, tucked unassumingly behind a kebab stand on an overgrown embankment. The rustic-chic interior and the outdoor deck (rich with the aroma of their busy smoker) are both inviting and unpretentious. A meal here gives you a good understanding of where Polish food has come from, and where it's heading in the next generation...and the cocktails are great, too. Reserve ahead (Tue-Sun 12:00-late, Mon 16:00-late, Solec 44, mobile 798-363-996, www.solec.waw.pl).

$ Warszawa Powiśle is a café/bar occupying the old, communist-style ticket office for the suburban train station of the same name. Tucked along a picturesque bike lane beneath the towering legs of a bridge, its sidewalk is jammed with cool Varsovians and in-the-know visitors (light sandwiches, daily 9:00 until late, Kruczkowskiego 3B, tel. 22-474-4084).

$ Kawiarnia Kafka combines a used bookstore (with books sold by weight) with a hip, creative café. Inside you'll find comfy chairs, stay-awhile tables, and checkerboard tiles; outside, on the lawn across from the café, guests lounge in slingback chairs (Mon-Fri 9:00-22:00, Sat-Sun 10:00-22:00, Obožna 3, tel. 22-826-0822).

IN ŚRÓDMIEŚCIE ("DOWNTOWN")

Warsaw's Śródmieście district is the epicenter of Polish hipster/foodie culture—where you'll find young Varsovian foodies digging into affordable dishes at the trendiest new places. This area is a 15-minute walk south of Jerusalem Avenue, and also well-served by public transportation (for example, trams #4, #15, #18, and #35 run frequently along the main north-south Marszałkowska corridor to plac Zbawiciela; of these, tram #4 stops in the middle of the road below Castle Square, where the Royal Way meets the Old Town). Listed next are a few different restaurant-hunting zones, with some specific recommendations for each one. For locations, see the map on page 375.

On Plac Zbawiciela

Named "Holiest Savior Square" for the looming church, this is a dizzying six-way intersection with a big traffic circle ringed by el-

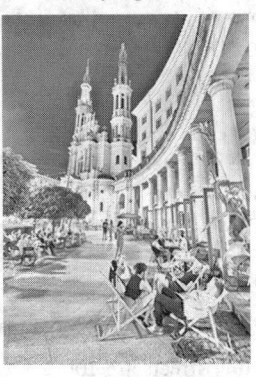

egant old colonnades. To get a quick taste of the Śródmieście scene, come here first and just do a slow loop around the circle, surveying your options. Starting to the right of the steeple and moving clockwise, here are a few options you'll see: **$$ Izumi Sushi**, **$ Karma** coffee shop, and **$$ Tuk Tuk** Thai street food are all popular, with great seating out on the square. Continuing two crosswalks around the circle, the Italian-themed **Pini Café & Vino** has nice outdoor tables across from the church. Farther around, just down Mokotowska from the circle, look for the line of people at **Sucré,** an unpretentious hole-in-the-wall serving all-natural, homemade ice cream. In the next section, **$$ Charlotte** designer bakery and wine bar is another popular choice, with homemade treats and tables spilling out all over the square. Up above, **Plan B** is a hipster dive bar with drinks, snacks, and views down over the square; this is where revelers head at 2 in the morning, after the restaurants are closed (find the graffiti-slathered staircase up, just past Charlotte).

Nearby, on Mokotowska ulica: This street, stretching north from plac Zbawiciela (past Sucré ice-cream shop), has more options. **$$$$ Dyspensa** is a good place for a serious sit-down meal in a dressy but not stuffy environment. They serve a thoughtfully selected menu of updated Polish cuisine, plus a few international options, as well as a handwritten list of daily specials. Reservations are smart (daily 12:00-23:00, Mokotowska 39, tel. 22-629-9989, www.dyspensa.pl). A half-block up the street is the mellower **$$ Słodki Słony** ("Sweet Salty"), at the casual end of the scale of Polish celebrity chef Magda Gessler's restaurant empire. Up front is a big, tempting display case bursting with over-the-top decadent desserts; farther in is a cozy dining area where you can dig into sandwiches, salads, and other light fare (daily, Mokotowska 45, tel. 22-622-4934, www.slodkislony.pl).

On and near Poznańska Street

A few short blocks west of plac Zbawiciela, this street is also lined with trendy and youthful eateries (especially around the intersection with Wilcza street; the nearest tram/bus stop is Hoża, and it's also not far from plac Konstytucji). Strolling this strip, you'll find several enticing options: **$$ Kaskrut** (a pun on *casse-croûte*) has a variety of well-executed minimalist dishes, including vegan options, a tight interior, and casual sidewalk tables (closed Mon, Poznańska 5). **$$$$ Nolita** is one of Warsaw's top splurges—top-end, white-tablecloth fine dining—but still affordable on a European scale (closed Sat lunch and all day Sun, Wilcza 46, www.nolita. pl). **$$$ Wilcza 50** is a big, glitzy, crank-'em-out place offering international fare in a modern and spacious setting (daily, Wilcza 50). And **$$ Tel Aviv** has gluten-free and vegan Middle Eastern food (daily, Poznańska 11). A favorite in this area is **$$ Beirut,** a gregariously crowded bar serving up excellent Middle Eastern food. The hummus bar, on the left, has a wide variety of *mezes* (small plates) and grilled meats, while the "Kraken Rum Bar" on the right has fish dishes (portions are modest—plan to share a few, order at the counter then find a table, Poznańska 12).

IN OR NEAR THE OLD TOWN

The restaurants in the Old Town and surrounding streets are 100 percent for tourists. Dining right on the Old Town Market Square is exorbitantly expensive, but could be worth it for those who treasure a romantic memory. Still, I'd rather walk a block or two to one of these options, which are as good as it gets in this area. For locations, see the map on page 384.

$$ Restauracja pod Samsonem ("Under Samson") is a quirky throwback and a sentimental favorite. The menu is affordable, well-executed, unfussy Jewish and Polish comfort food. The outdoor seating, on the New Town's main drag just outside the barbican, is enjoyable in good weather. And the staff is old-school: gruff, playfully opinionated, and stingy (you'll have to pay to check your coat or use the bathroom—yes, even if you're dining here). But nostalgic locals appreciate this as a stubborn remnant of the old days—a time before service with a smile, fine dining for business travelers, and hipster fusion restaurants (daily 10:00-23:00, Freta 3, tel. 22-831-1788).

$$ Freta 33—a block deeper into the New Town, facing the serene New Town Square—has decent international fare (such as pastas), fine outdoor seating, and a contemporary subway-tile interior (daily 12:00-23:00, Freta 33, tel. 22-635-0931).

$$ Zapiecek, with a half-dozen locations in and near the Old Town, is a kitschy chain serving up cheap and cheery traditional Polish dishes. But the prices are reasonable, and the food (especially the pierogi) is better and more authentic than it ought to be, given its tourist-trap vibe (handiest location faces the Cathedral of St. John the Baptist at Świętojańska 13, others are on the main drag through the New Town at Freta 1 and Freta 18, yet another on the Royal Way at Nowy Świat 64, all open long hours daily).

Warsaw Connections

Almost all trains into and out of Warsaw go through hulking Warszawa Centralna station (described earlier, under "Arrival in Warsaw," including ticket-buying tips). If you're heading to Gdańsk, note that the red-brick Gothic city of Toruń and the impressive Malbork Castle are on the way, but are on separate train lines, making it difficult to do both en route (see the Gdańsk and Pomerania chapters). Also be aware that EIC and IC express trains to many destinations—including Kraków and Gdańsk—require seat reservations, even if you have a rail pass.

To confirm rail journeys, check specific times online (www.rozklad-pkp.pl) or at Centralna station.

From Warszawa Centralna Station by Train to: Kraków (hourly, about 2.5 hours), **Gdańsk** (hourly, 3 hours), **Malbork** (hourly, 2.5 hours), **Toruń** (every 2 hours direct, 2.5 hours on express IC train), **Prague** (2/day direct, including 1 night train, more with change in Ostrava, 8-9.5 hours), **Berlin** (4/day direct, 6 hours, no direct night train), **Budapest** (1/day direct, 10 hours; 1/day overnight, 11.5 hours; also 2/day with change in Břeclav, Czech Republic, 10 hours), **Vienna** (2/day direct, 7 hours; plus 1 night train, 10 hours).

By Bus: PolskiBus—described on page 350—runs bus routes throughout Poland (www.polskibus.com).

GDAŃSK & THE TRI-CITY

Gdańsk (guh-DAYNSK) is a true find on the Baltic Coast of Poland. You may associate Gdańsk with dreary images of striking dock-workers from the nightly news in the 1980s—but there's so much more to this city than shipyards, Solidarity, and smog. It's surprisingly easy to look past the urban sprawl to find one of northern Europe's most historic and picturesque cities. Gdańsk is second only to Kraków as Poland's most appealing destination.

Exploring Gdańsk is a delight. The gem of a Main Town boasts block after block of red-brick churches and narrow, colorful, ornately decorated Hanseatic burghers' mansions. The riverfront embankment, with its trademark medieval crane, oozes salty maritime charm. Gdańsk's history is also fascinating—from its 17th-century Golden Age to the headlines of our own generation, big things happen here. You might even see ol' Lech Wałęsa still wandering the streets. And yet Gdańsk is also looking to its future, steadily repairing some of its WWII damage after a long communist hibernation. Over the past decade, whole swaths of the city have been remade with a bold new modernity...but always with a respect for the past.

Gdańsk and two nearby towns (Sopot and Gdynia) together form an area known as the "Tri-City," offering several day-trip opportunities north along the coast (see page 487). The once-faded, now-revitalized elegance of the seaside resort of Sopot beckons to tourists, while the modern burg of Gdynia sets the pace for today's Poland. Beyond the Tri-City, the sandy Hel Peninsula is a popular spot for summer sunbathing.

PLANNING YOUR TIME

This region merits two days to make the trip here worthwhile. Gdańsk's major sights can be seen in a day, but a second day allows you to see everything in town at a more relaxing pace, and take your pick from among several possible side-trips.

Gdańsk sightseeing has two major components: the Royal Way (historic main drag with good museums) and the modern shipyard where Solidarity was born (with a fascinating museum). With just one day, do one of these activities in the morning, and the other in the afternoon. With two days, do one each day, and round out your time with other attractions: Art lovers enjoy the National Museum (with a stunning altar painting by Hans Memling), history buffs make the pilgrimage to Westerplatte (where World War II began), and church and pipe-organ fans might visit Oliwa Cathedral in Gdańsk's northern suburbs (on the way to Sopot).

If you have more time, consider the wide variety of side-trips. The most popular option is the half-day round-trip to Malbork Castle (30-45 minutes each way by train, plus two or three hours to tour the castle—see next chapter). It only takes a quick visit to enjoy the resort town of Sopot (25 minutes each way by train), but on a sunny day, the town's beaches may tempt you to laze around longer. Consider a sprint through Gdynia to round out your take on the Tri-City. If you have a full day and great weather, and you don't mind fighting the crowds for a patch of sandy beach, go to Hel.

Gdańsk gets busy in late June, when school holidays begin, and it's crowded with (mostly German, Norwegian, and Swedish) tourists from July to mid-September—especially during St. Dominic's Fair (Jarmark Św. Dominika, three weeks from late July to mid-Aug), with market stalls, concerts, and other celebrations.

Several Gdańsk museums are closed Monday—especially outside summer. Monday is a good day to visit churches or the European Solidarity Center, or to take a side-trip to Sopot (but not to Malbork Castle, which is also closed Mon).

Orientation to Gdańsk

With 460,000 residents, Gdańsk is part of the larger urban area known as the Tri-City (Trójmiasto, total population of 1 million). But the tourist's Gdańsk is compact, welcoming, and walkable—virtually anything you'll want to see is within a 20-minute stroll of everything else.

Focus on the Main Town (Główne Miasto), home to most of

the sights described, including the spectacular Royal Way main drag, ulica Długa. The Old Town (Stare Miasto) has a handful of old brick buildings and faded, tall, skinny houses—but the area is mostly drab and residential, and not worth much time. Just beyond the northern end of the Old Town (about a 20-minute walk from the heart of the Main Town) is the entrance to the Gdańsk Shipyard, with the excellent European Solidarity Center and its top-notch museum. From here, shipyards sprawl for miles.

The second language in this part of Poland is German, not English. As this was a predominantly German city until the end of World War II, German tourists flock here in droves. But you'll win no Polish friends if you call the city by its more familiar German name, Danzig. You'll also find that Gdańsk is becoming an increasingly popular cruise destination, with about 100 ships calling here each year (most dock at the nearby city of Gdynia, and passengers take a bus or train in). During summer daytime hours, the town is filled with little tour groups.

TOURIST INFORMATION

Gdańsk has two different TI organizations: The regional TI occupies the **Upland Gate,** facing the busy road that hems in the Main Town, at the start of my self-guided walk (May-Sept Mon-Fri 9:00-20:00, Sat-Sun 9:00-18:00; Oct-April daily 9:00-18:00; tel. 58-732-7041, www.pomorskie.travel). The city TI has three branches—one conveniently located at the bottom end of the main drag, at **Długi Targ 28** (just to the left as you face the river gate; daily 9:00-19:00, Oct-April until 17:00; tel. 58-301-4355, www.gdansk4u.pl), with satellite TIs at the **main train station** (in the underpass, tel. 58-721-3277) and at the **airport** (open 24/7, tel. 58-348-1368). Yet another handy tourist website is www.visitgdansk.com.

Sightseeing Card: Busy sightseers should consider the **Tourist Card,** which includes entry to several sights in Gdańsk, Gdynia, and Sopot, and discounts at others (such as 20 percent off the European Solidarity Center). Check the list of what's covered, and do the arithmetic (60 zł/24 hours, 90 zł/72 hours, pay more to add local transit, sold only at TIs).

ARRIVAL IN GDAŃSK

By Train: Gdańsk's main train station (Gdańsk Główny) is a pretty brick palace on the western edge of the old center. (To save money, architects in Colmar, France copied this exact design to build their city's station.)

GDAŃSK & THE TRI-CITY

Trains to other parts of Poland (marked *PKP*) use platforms 1-3; regional trains with connections to the Tri-City (marked *SKM*) use the shorter platforms 3-5 (for instructions on riding these regional SKM trains, see page 487).

Inside the terminal building, you'll find lockers, ATMs, and ticket windows. Outside, the pedestrian underpass by the McDonald's has a TI and leads you beneath the busy road (first set of exits: tram stop; end of corridor: shopping mall at the edge of the Old Town).

The easiest choice for reaching your hotel is to hop in a **taxi** or request an **Uber** (which shouldn't cost more than 15 zł to any of my recommended hotels). Or it's a 15-minute walk to the heart of the Main Town and many recommended hotels: Go through the underpass, exit to the right, circle around the right side of Cinema City, and follow the busy road until you see the brick towers on your left. Riding the **tram** can shave a few minutes off this walk (buy tickets in underpass, then head up to find stop in the middle of the road; ride tram #2, #3, #6, #8, or #11 just one stop to Brama Wyżynna).

By Plane: Gdańsk's airport, named for Lech Wałęsa, is about five miles west of the city center (airport code: GDN, tel. 58-348-1163, www.airport.gdansk.pl). The **train** zips you to the main train station in just 30 minutes (6 zł, direct trains run hourly; additional trains run 4/hour but require a transfer at the Gdańsk Wrzeszcz station, where you can switch to the regional SKM train line). Public **bus** #210 stops near the main train station and at Brama Wyżynna, near the heart of the Main Town (3.20 zł, buy ticket at machine at stop or buy on board for a bit more; 2/hour on weekdays, 1/hour on weekends, 40 minutes). The 25-minute **taxi** or **Uber** ride into town should cost no more than 60 zł.

GETTING AROUND GDAŃSK

Nearly everything is within easy walking distance of my recommended hotels, but public transportation can be useful for reaching outlying sights such as Oliwa Cathedral, Westerplatte, Sopot, Gdynia, and Hel (specific transportation options for these places are described in each listing).

By Public Transportation: Gdańsk's trams and buses work on the same tickets: Choose between a single-ride ticket (3.20 zł), one-hour ticket (3.80 zł), and 24-hour ticket (13 zł). Major stops have user-friendly ticket machines. Otherwise, buy tickets *(bilety)* at kiosks marked *RUCH* or *Bilety ZKM*, or pay a little more to buy tickets on board. In the city center, the stops worth knowing about are Plac Solidarnośći (near the European Solidarity Center), Gdańsk Główny (in front of the main train station), and Brama Wyżynna (near the Upland Gate and the new Gdańsk Śródmieście

Gdańsk at a Gdlance

▲▲▲**Royal Way/Ulica Długa Walk** Gdańsk's colorful showpiece main drag, cutting a picturesque swath through the heart of the wealthy burghers' neighborhood. See page 439.

▲▲▲**Solidarity Sights and Gdańsk Shipyard** Home to the beginning of the end of Eastern European communism, with a towering monument and excellent museum. **Hours:** Memorial and shipyard gate—always open. European Solidarity Center exhibit—daily 10:00-20:00, Oct-April until 18:00. See page 463.

▲▲**Main Town Hall** Ornate meeting rooms, town artifacts, and tower with sweeping views. **Hours:** Mid-June-mid-Sept Mon-Thu 9:00-16:00, Fri-Sat 10:00-18:00, Sun 10:00-16:00; mid-Sept-mid-June Tue 10:00-13:00, Wed-Sat 10:00-16:00, Thu until 18:00, Sun 11:00-16:00, closed Mon. See page 459.

▲▲**Artus Court** Grand meeting hall for guilds of Golden Age Gdańsk, boasting an over-the-top tiled stove. **Hours:** Same as Main Town Hall. See page 460.

▲▲**St. Mary's Church** Giant red-brick church crammed full of Gdańsk history. **Hours:** Mon-Sat 8:30-18:30, Sun 11:00-12:00 & 13:00-18:30; Oct-April daily until 17:00. See page 450.

▲**Amber Museum** High-tech exhibit of valuable golden globs of petrified tree sap. **Hours:** Same as Main Town Hall, above. See page 457.

▲**Uphagen House** Tourable 18th-century interior, typical of the pretty houses that line ulica Długa. **Hours:** Same as Main Town Hall. See page 459.

▲**National Maritime Museum** Sprawling exhibit on all aspects of the nautical life, housed in several venues connected by a ferry boat. **Hours:** July-Aug daily 10:00-18:00; Sept-Oct and March-June Tue-Sun 10:00-16:00, closed Mon; Nov-Feb Tue-Sun 10:00-15:00, closed Mon. See page 462.

Historical Zone of the Free City of Gdańsk Tiny museum examining Gdańsk's unique status as a "Free City" between the World Wars. **Hours:** Tue-Sun 12:00-18:00, Sept-April until 17:00, closed Mon year-round. See page 461.

Archaeological Museum Decent collection of artifacts from this region's past. **Hours:** July-Aug Tue-Fri 9:00-17:00, Sat-Sun 10:00-17:00; Sept-June Tue and Thu-Fri 8:00-16:00, Wed 9:00-17:00, Sat-Sun 10:00-16:00; closed Mon year-round. See page 462.

National Museum in Gdańsk Ho-hum art collection with a single blockbuster highlight: Hans Memling's remarkable Last Judgment altarpiece. **Hours:** May-Sept Tue-Sun 10:00-17:00 (Thu 12:00-19:00 in June-Aug); Oct-April Tue-Fri 9:00-16:00, Sat-Sun 10:00-17:00, closed Mon year-round. See page 474.

commuter train station). When buying tickets, don't confuse *ZKM* (Gdańsk city transit) with *SKM* (commuter trains).

One public bus worth knowing about is Gdańsk's **bus #100.** Every 20 minutes, this made-for-tourists minibus (designed to navigate the twisty streets of the town center) makes a loop through the Old Town and Main Town, with stops strategic for sightseeing (covered by regular transit ticket).

By Taxi: Taxis cost about 8 zł to start, then 2-3 zł per kilometer (a bit more at night). Find a taxi stand, or call a cab (try Neptun, tel. 19686 or 585-111-555; or Dajan, tel. 58-19628).

Tours in Gdańsk

Private Guides

Hiring a local guide is an exceptional value. **Agnieszka Syroka—** youthful, bubbly, and personable—is a wonderful guide (400 zł for up to 4 hours, more for all day, mobile 502-554-584, www. tourguidegdansk.com, asyroka@interia.pl or syroka.agnieszka@ gmail.com).

Gdańsk Walk

In the 16th and 17th centuries, Gdańsk was Poland's wealthiest city, with gorgeous architecture (much of it in the Flemish Man-

nerist style) rivaling that in the two historic capitals, Kraków and Warsaw. During this Golden Age, Polish kings would visit this city of well-to-do Hanseatic League merchants and gawk along the same route trod by tourists today.

The following self-guided walk (rated ▲▲▲) introduces you to the best of Gdańsk. It bridges the two historic centers (the Main Town and the Old Town), dips into St. Mary's Church (the city's most important church), and ends at the famous shipyards and Solidarity Square (where Poland began what ultimately brought down the USSR). I've divided the walk into two parts (making it easier to split up, if you like): The first half focuses on a loop through the Main Town (with most of the high-profile sights), while the second part carries on northward, through the less-touristy Old Town to the shipyards.

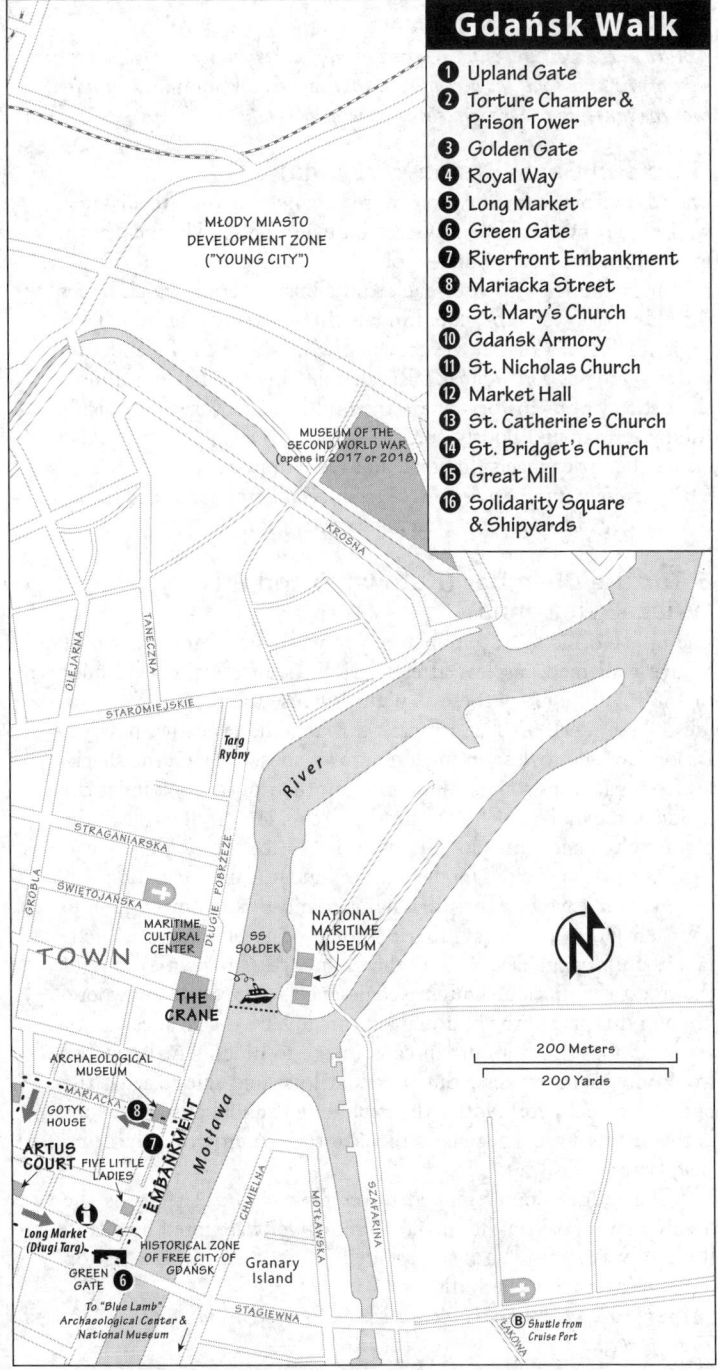

Gdańsk Walk

1. Upland Gate
2. Torture Chamber & Prison Tower
3. Golden Gate
4. Royal Way
5. Long Market
6. Green Gate
7. Riverfront Embankment
8. Mariacka Street
9. St. Mary's Church
10. Gdańsk Armory
11. St. Nicholas Church
12. Market Hall
13. St. Catherine's Church
14. St. Bridget's Church
15. Great Mill
16. Solidarity Square & Shipyards

MŁODY MIASTO DEVELOPMENT ZONE ("YOUNG CITY")

MUSEUM OF THE SECOND WORLD WAR (opens in 2017 or 2018)

KROSNA

OLEJARNIA

TANECZNA

STAROMIEJSKIE

Targ Rybny

River

STRAGANIARSKA

ŚWIĘTOJAŃSKA

GROBLA

DŁUGIE POBRZEŻE

MARITIME CULTURAL CENTER

SS SOŁDEK

NATIONAL MARITIME MUSEUM

TOWN

THE CRANE

ARCHAEOLOGICAL MUSEUM

MARIACKA

GOTYK HOUSE

8

ARTUS COURT   FIVE LITTLE LADIES

7

EMBANKMENT

Motława

Long Market (Długi Targ)

GREEN GATE   6

HISTORICAL ZONE OF FREE CITY OF GDAŃSK

Granary Island

To "Blue Lamb" Archaeological Center & National Museum

GDZIELNA

MOTŁAWSKA

SZAFARNIA

STĄGIEWNA

LASTADIA

B Shuttle from Cruise Port

200 Meters

200 Yards

N

PART 1: THE MAIN TOWN

• Begin at the west end of the Main Town, just beyond the last gate at the edge of the busy road (at a road sign that says Sztokholm...*a reminder that the car ferry to Sweden leaves from near here).*

❶ Upland Gate (Brama Wyżynna)

The Main Town's fortifications were expanded with a Renaissance wall bound by the Upland Gate (built in 1588). "Upland" refers to the hills you see beyond—considered high country in this flat region. Standing with your back to the busy arterial (which traces the old moat), study the gate. Find its three coats of arms (the black eagle for Royal Prussia, the crowned white eagle for Poland, and the two crosses for Gdańsk). Recall that this city has, for almost the entirety of its history before the mid-20th century, been bicultural: German and Polish, coexisting more or less peacefully. Also notice the little wheels that once hoisted a drawbridge.

• It's a straight line from here to the river. Walk through the arch (which houses a TI) to the next arch, just a few steps ahead.

❷ Torture Chamber (Katownia) and Prison Tower (Wieża Więzienna)

The tall, Gothic brick gate before you was part of an earlier protective wall made useless after the Renaissance walls were built in 1588. While today these structures house the Amber Museum (described later), it's free to walk through the evocative passage. Inside, find gargoyles (on the left, a town specialty) and the shackles from which prisoners were hung (on the right). Look up at the inside of the high gable to the headless man, identifying this as the torture chamber. This old jail—with its 15-foot-thick walls—was used as a prison even in modern times, under Nazi occupation.

As you leave the Torture Chamber and Prison Tower, look to your left (100 yards away) to see a long, brick building with four fancy, uniform gables. This is the **Armory** (Zbrojownia), one of the finest examples of Dutch Renaissance architecture anywhere. Though this part of the building appears to have the facades of four separate houses, it's an urban camouflage to hide its real purpose from potential attackers. But there's at least one clue to what the building is really for: Notice the exploding cannonballs at the tops of the turrets. (We'll get a better look at the Armory from the other side, later in this walk.)

The round, pointy-topped tower next to the Armory is the **Straw Tower** (Baszta Słomiana). Gunpowder was stored here, and the roof was straw—so if it exploded, it could easily blow its top without destroying the walls.

• Straight ahead, the final and fanciest gate between you and the Main Town is the...

❸ Golden Gate (Złota Brama)

While the other gates were defensive, this one's purely ornamental. The four women up top represent virtues that the people of

Gdańsk should exhibit toward outsiders (left to right): Peace, Freedom, Prosperity, and Fame. The gold-lettered inscription, a psalm in medieval German, compares Gdańsk to Jerusalem: famous and important. Directly above the arch is the Gdańsk coat of arms: two white crosses under a crown on a red shield. We'll see this symbol all over town. Photographers love the view of the Main Town framed in this arch. Inside the arch, study the old photos showing the 1945 bomb damage. On the left is the glorious view you just enjoyed...ravaged by war. And on the right is a heartbreaking aerial view of the city in 1945, when 80 percent of its buildings were in ruins.

• *Passing through the Golden Gate, you reach the Main Town's main drag.*

❹ The Royal Way

Before you stretches ulica Długa (cleverly called the "Long Street")—the main promenade of what, 600 years ago, was the biggest and richest city in Poland, thanks to its profitable ties to the Hanseatic League of merchant cities. This promenade is nicknamed the "Royal Way" because (just as in Warsaw and Kraków) the king would follow this route when visiting town.

Walk half a block, and then look back at the Golden Gate. The women on top of this side represent virtues the people of Gdańsk should cultivate in themselves (left to right): Wisdom, Piety, Justice, and Concord (if an arrow's broken, let's take it out of the quiver and fix it). The inscription—sharing a bit of wisdom as apropos today as it was in 1612—reads, "Concord makes small countries develop, and discord makes big countries fall." Gdańsk was cosmopolitan and exceptionally tolerant in the Middle Ages, attracting a wide range of people, including many who were persecuted elsewhere: Jews, Scots, Dutch, Flemish, Italians, Germans, and more. Members of each group brought with them strands of their culture, which they wove into the tapestry of this city—demonstrated by the eclectic homes along this street. Each facade and each gable were different, as nobles and aristocrats wanted to display their wealth. On my last visit, a traveler seeing this street for the first time gasped to me, "It's like stepping into a Fabergé egg."

During Gdańsk's Golden Age, these houses were taxed based on frontage (like the homes lining Amsterdam's canals)—so they were built skinny and deep. The widest houses belonged to the super-elite. Different as they are from the outside, every house had the same general plan inside. Each had three parts, starting with the front and moving back: First was a fancy drawing room, to show off for visitors. Then came a narrow corridor to the back rooms—often along the side of an inner courtyard. Because the houses had only a few windows facing the outer street, this courtyard provided much-needed sunlight to the rest of the house. The residential quarters were in the back, where the family actually lived: bedroom, kitchen, office. To see the interior of one of these homes, pay a visit to the interesting **Uphagen House** (at #12, on the right, a block and a half in front of the Golden Gate; described later).

This lovely street wasn't always so lively and carefree. At the end of World War II, the Royal Way was in ruins. That epic war actually began here, in what was then the "Free City of Danzig." Following World War I, nobody could decide what to do with this influential and multiethnic city. So, rather than assign it to Germany or Poland, it was set apart as its own little autonomous state-let. In 1939, Danzig was 80 percent German-speaking—enough for Hitler to consider it his. And so, on September 1 of that year, the Nazis seized it in one day with relatively minor damage (though the attack on the Polish military garrison on the city's Westerplatte peninsula lasted a week).

But six years later, when the Soviets arrived (March 30, 1945), the city was left devastated. This was the first traditionally German city that the Red Army took on their march toward Berlin. And, while it was easy for the Soviets to seize the almost empty city, the commander then insisted that it be leveled, building by building—in retaliation for all the pain the Nazis had caused in Russia. (Soviets didn't destroy nearby Gdynia, which they considered Polish rather than German.) Soviet officers turned a blind eye as their soldiers raped and brutalized residents. An entire order of horrified nuns committed suicide by throwing themselves into the river.

It was only thanks to detailed drawings and photographs that these buildings could be so carefully reconstructed. Notice the cheap plaster facades done in the 1950s—rough times under communism, in the decade after World War II. (Most of the town's medieval brick was shipped to Warsaw for a communist-sponsored "rebuild the capital first" campaign.) While the fine facades were restored, the buildings behind the facades were completely rebuilt to modern standards.

Just beyond Uphagen House, **Cukiernia Sowa** ("The Owl," on the right at #13) is *the* place for cakes and coffee. Directly across the street, **Grycan** (at #73) has been a favorite for ice cream here for generations.

Just a few doors down, on the left, are some of the most striking **facades** along the Royal Way. The blue-and-white house with the three giant heads is from the 19th century, when the hot style was eclecticism—borrowing bits and pieces from various architectural eras. This was one of the few houses on the street that survived World War II.

At the next corner on the right is the huge, blocky, red **post office,** which doesn't quite fit with the skinny facades lining the rest of the street. Step inside. With doves fluttering under an airy glass atrium, the interior's a class act. Directly across the street, the candy shop **(Ciuciu Cukier Artist)** is often filled with children clamoring to see lollipop-making demos. Step in and inhale a universal whiff of childhood.

A few doors farther down, on the left at #62, pop into the **Millennium Gallery** amber shop (which would love to give you an educational amber polishing demo) to see the fascinating collection of old-timey photos, letting you directly compare Gdańsk's cityscape before and after the WWII destruction.

Above the next door, notice the colorful **scenes.** These are slices of life from 17th-century Gdańsk: drinking, talking, buying, playing music. The ship is a *koga,* a typical symbol of Hanseatic ports like Gdańsk.

Across the street and a few steps down are the fancy facades of three houses belonging to the very influential medieval **Ferber family,** which produced many burghers, mayors, and even a bishop. On the house with the little dog over the door (#29), look for the heads in the circular medallions. These are Caesars of Rome. At the top of the building is Mr. Ferber's answer to the constant question, "Why build such an elaborate house?"—*PRO INVIDIA,* "For the sake of envy."

A few doors down, on the right, is Gdańsk's most scenically situated milk bar, the recommended **Bar Mleczny Neptun.** Back in communist times, these humble cafeterias were subsidized to give workers an affordable place to eat out. To this day, they offer simple and very cheap grub.

Next door (at #35) is the **Russian Culture Center,** with Russian movies and art exhibits. With a complicated history—and many Poles now siding with Ukraine in their stand against Vladimir Putin's incursion into Ukrainian territory—this is a poignant address.

Before you stands the **Main Town Hall** (Ratusz Głównego Miasta) with its mighty brick clock tower. Consider climbing its

Gdańsk History

Visitors to Gdańsk are surprised at how "un-Polish" the city's history is. In this cultural melting pot of German, Dutch, and Flemish merchants (with a smattering of Italians and Scots), Poles were only a small part of the picture until the city became exclusively Polish after World War II. However, in Gdańsk, cultural backgrounds traditionally took a back seat to the bottom line. Wealthy Gdańsk was always known for its economic pragmatism—no matter who was in charge, merchants here made money.

Gdańsk is Poland's gateway to the waters of Europe, where its main river (the Vistula) meets the Baltic Sea. The town was first mentioned in the 10th century, and was seized in 1308 by the Teutonic Knights (who called it "Danzig"; for more on the Teutonic Knights, see page 502). The Knights encouraged other Germans to settle on the Baltic coast, and gradually turned Gdańsk into a wealthy city. In 1361, Gdańsk joined the Hanseatic League, a trade federation of mostly Germanic merchant towns that provided mutual security. By the 15th century, Gdańsk was a leading member of this mighty network, which virtually dominated trade in northern Europe (and also included Toruń, Kraków, Lübeck, Hamburg, Bremen, Bruges, Bergen, Tallinn, Novgorod, and nearly a hundred other cities).

In 1454, the people of Gdańsk rose up against the Teutonic Knights, burning down their castle and forcing them out of the city. Three years later, the Polish king borrowed money from wealthy Gdańsk families to hire Czech mercenaries to take the Teutonic Knights' main castle, Malbork (described in the next chapter). In exchange, the Gdańsk merchants were granted special privileges, including exclusive export rights. Gdańsk now acted as a middleman for much of the trade passing through Polish lands, and paid only a modest annual tribute to the Polish king.

The 16th and 17th centuries were Gdańsk's Golden Age. Now a part of the Polish kingdom, the city had access to an enormous hinterland of natural resources to export—yet it maintained a privileged, semi-independent status. Like Amsterdam, Gdańsk became a progressive and booming merchant city. Its mostly Germanic and Dutch burghers imported Dutch, Flemish, and Italian architects to give their homes an appropriately Hanseatic flourish. At a time of religious upheaval in the rest of Europe, Gdańsk became known for its tolerance—a place that opened its doors to all visitors (many Mennonites and Scottish religious refugees emigrated here). It was also a haven for great thinkers, including philosopher Arthur Schopenhauer and scientist Daniel Fahrenheit (who invented the mercury thermometer).

Along with the rest of Poland, Gdańsk declined in the late 18th century and became part of Prussia (today's northern Germany) during the Partitions. But the people of Gdańsk—even those of German heritage—had taken pride in their independence and weren't enthusiastic about being ruled from Berlin. After World War I, in a unique compromise to appease its complex ethnic makeup, Gdańsk did not fall under German or Polish control, but once again became an independent city-state: the Free City of Danzig (populated by 400,000 ethnic Germans and 15,000 Poles). The city, along with the so-called Polish Corridor connecting it to Polish lands, effectively cut off Germany from its northeastern territory. On September 1, 1939, Adolf Hitler started World War II when he invaded Gdańsk in order to bring it back into the German fold. Later, nearly 80 percent of the city was destroyed when the Soviets "liberated" it from Nazi control.

After World War II, Gdańsk officially became part of Poland, and was painstakingly reconstructed (mostly replicating the buildings of its Golden Age). In 1970, and again in 1980, the shipyard of Gdańsk witnessed strikes and demonstrations that would lead to the fall of European communism. Poland's great anticommunist hero and first postcommunist president, Lech Wałęsa, is Gdańsk's most famous resident, and still lives here. When he flies around the world to give talks, he leaves from Gdańsk's "Lech Wałęsa Airport."

A city with a recent past that's both tragic and uplifting, Gdańsk celebrated its 1,000th birthday in 1997. Very roughly, the city has spent about 700 years as an independent entity, and about 300 years under Germanic overlords (the Teutonic Knights, Prussia, and the Nazis). But today, Gdańsk is decidedly its own city. And, as if eager to prove it, Gdańsk is making big improvements at a stunning pace: new museums (the European Solidarity Center and World War II Museum), cultural facilities (the Shakespeare Theater), sports venues (a stadium that resembles a blob of amber, built for the 2012 Euro Cup tournament), and an ongoing surge of renovation and refurbishment that has the gables of the atmospheric Hanseatic quarter gleaming once again.

observation tower and visiting its superb interior, which features ornately decorated meeting rooms for the city council (described later).

• *Just beyond the Main Town Hall, ulica Długa widens and becomes...*

❺ The Long Market (Długi Targ)

Step from the Long Street into the Long Market, and do a slow, 360-degree spin to appreciate the amazing array of proud architecture here in a city center that rivals the magnificent Grand Place in Brussels. The centerpiece of this square is one of Gdańsk's most important landmarks, the statue of **Neptune**—god of the sea. He's a fitting symbol for a city that dominates the maritime life of Poland. Behind him is another worthwhile museum, the **Artus Court.** Step up to the magnificent door and study the golden relief just above, celebrating the Vistula River (in so many ways the lifeblood of the Polish nation): Lady Vistula is exhausted after her heroic journey, and is finally carried by Neptune to her ultimate destination, the Baltic Sea. (This is just a preview of the ornate art that fills the interior of this fine building—described later.)

Midway down the Long Market (on the right, across from the Hard Rock Café) is a glass case with the **thermometer and barometer of Daniel Fahrenheit.** Although that scientist was born here, he did his groundbreaking work in Amsterdam.

• *At the end of the Long Market is the...*

❻ Green Gate (Zielona Brama)

This huge gate (named for the Green Bridge just beyond) was actually built as a residence for visiting kings...who usually preferred to stay back by Neptune instead (maybe because the river, just on the other side of this gate, stank). It might not have been good enough for kings and queens, but it's plenty fine for a former president: Lech Wałęsa's office is upstairs (see the plaque on the left side, *Biuro Lecha Wałęsy*). His windows, up in the gable, overlook the Long Market. A few steps down the skinny lane to the left is the endearing little **Historical Zone of the Free City of Gdańsk** museum, which explains the interwar period when "Danzig" was an independent and bicultural city-state (described later).

• *Now go through the gate, walk out onto the Green Bridge, anchor yourself in a niche on the left, and look downstream.*

❼ Riverfront Embankment

The Motława River—a side channel of the mighty Vistula—flows into the nearby Baltic Sea. This port was the source of Gdańsk's phenomenal Golden Age wealth. This embankment was jam-packed in its heyday, the 14th and 15th centuries. It was so crowded with boats that you would hardly have been able to see the water, and boats had to pay a time-based moorage fee for tying up to a post.

Look back at the Green Gate and notice that these bricks are much smaller than the locally-made ones we saw earlier on this walk. These bricks are Dutch: Boats from Holland would come here empty of cargo, but with a load of bricks for ballast. Traders filled their ships with goods for the return trip, leaving the bricks behind.

The old-fashioned **galleons** and other tour boats moored nearby depart hourly for a fun cruise to Westerplatte (where on September 1, 1939, Germans fired the first shots of World War II) and back. Though kitschy, the galleons are a fun way to get out on the water (details on page 486).

Across the river is **Granary Island** (Wyspa Spichrzów), where grain was stored until it could be taken away by ships. Before World War II, there were some 400 granaries here. Today, much of the island is still in ruins while developers make their plans. Recently, the city ringed the island with an inviting boardwalk, which offers a restful escape from the city and fine views across the narrow river to the embankment. In the summer, sometimes they erect a big Ferris wheel here. And someday there will be several more rebuilt granaries in this area (likely mixed with modern buildings) to match the ones you already see on either side of the bridge. The three rebuilt granaries downstream, in the distance on the next island, house exhibits for the National Maritime Museum (described later).

From your perch on the bridge, look down the embankment

(about 500 yards, on the left) and find the huge wooden **Crane (Żuraw)** bulging over the water. This monstrous 15th-century crane—a rare example of medieval port technology—was once used for loading and repairing ships...beginning a shipbuilding tradition that continued to the days of Lech Wałęsa. The crane mechanism was operated by several workers scrambling around in giant hamster wheels. Treading away to engage the gears and pulleys, they could lift 4 tons up 30 feet, or 2 tons up 90 feet.

• *Walk along the embankment about halfway to*

*the Crane, passing the lower embankment, with excursion boats heading to the Westerplatte monument. Pause when you reach the big brick building with green window frames and a tower. This red-brick fort houses the **Archaeological Museum** (described later). Its collection includes the five ancient stones in a small garden just outside its door (on the left). These are the **Prussian Hags**—mysterious sculptures from the second century A.D. (each described in posted plaques).*

Turn left through the gate in the middle of the brick building. You'll find yourself on the most charming lane in town...

❽ Mariacka Street

The calm, atmospheric "Mary's Street" leads from the embankment to St. Mary's Church. Stroll the length of it, enjoying the most romantic lane in Gdańsk. The **porches** extending out into the street, with access to cellars underneath, were a common feature in Gdańsk's Golden Age. For practical reasons, after the war, these were restored only on this street. Notice how the porches are bordered with fine stone relief panels and gargoyles attached to storm drains. If you get stuck there in a hard rainstorm, you'll understand why in Polish these are called "pukers." Enjoy a little amber comparison-shopping. As you stroll up to the towering brick St. Mary's Church, imagine the entire city like this cobbled lane of proud merchants' homes, with street music, delightful facades, and brick church towers high above.

Look up at the church tower viewpoint—filled with people who hiked 409 steps for the view. Our next stop is the church, which you'll enter on the far side under the tower. Walk around the left side of the church, appreciating the handmade 14th-century bricks on the right and the plain post-WWII facades on the left. (Reconstructing the Royal Way was better funded. Here, the priority was simply getting people housed again.) In the distance is the fancy facade of the Armory (where you'll head after visiting the church).

• *But first, go inside...*

❾ St. Mary's Church (Kościół Mariacki)

Of Gdańsk's 13 medieval red-brick churches, St. Mary's (rated ▲▲) is the one you must visit. It's the largest brick church in the world—with a footprint bigger than a football field (350 feet long and 210 feet wide), it can accommodate 20,000 standing worshippers.

Cost and Hours: 4 zł, 6 zł also includes tower climb—described later; Mon-Sat 8:30-18:30, Sun 11:00-12:00 & 13:00-18:30; Oct-April daily until 17:00; tower closed Dec-late March.

❿ **Self-Guided Tour:** Inside, sit directly under the fine carved and painted 17th-century Protestant pulpit, midway down the nave, to get oriented.

Overview: Built from 1343 to 1502 by the Teutonic Knights (who wanted a suitable centerpiece for their newly-captured main city), St. Mary's remains an important symbol of Gdańsk. The church started out Catholic, became Lutheran in the mid-1500s, and then became Catholic again after World War II. (Remember, Gdańsk was a Germanic city before World War II and part of the big postwar demographic shove, when Germans were sent west, and Poles from the east relocated here. Desperate, cold, and homeless, the new Polish residents moved into what was left of the German homes.) While the church was originally frescoed from top to bottom, the Lutherans whitewashed the entire place. Today, some of the 16th-century whitewash has been peeled back (behind the high altar—we'll see this area soon), revealing a bit of the original frescoes. The floor is paved with 500 gravestones of merchant families. Many of these were cracked when bombing sent the brick roof crashing down in 1945.

Most Gothic stone churches are built of stone in the basilica style—with a high nave in the middle, shorter aisles on the side,

and flying buttresses to support the weight. (Think of Paris' Notre-Dame.) But with no handy source of stone available locally, most Polish churches are built of brick, which won't work with the basilica design. So, like all Gdańsk churches, St. Mary's is a "hall church"—with three naves the same height and no exterior buttresses.

Also like other Gdańsk churches, St. Mary's gave refuge to the Polish people after the communist government declared martial law in 1981. When a riot broke out and violence seemed imminent, people flooded into churches, knowing that the ZOMO riot police wouldn't dare follow them inside.

Most of the church decorations are original. A few days before the Soviets arrived to "liberate" the city in 1945, locals—knowing what was in store—hid precious items in the countryside. Take some time now to see a few of the highlights.

• *From this spot, you can see most of what we'll visit in the church: As you face the altar, the astronomical clock is at 10 o'clock, the Ferber family medallion is at 1 o'clock, the Priests' Chapel is at 3 o'clock (under a tall, colorful window), and the magnificent 17th-century organ is directly behind you (it's played at each Mass and during free concerts on Fri in summer).*

Pulpit: For Protestants, the pulpit is important. Designed as an impressive place from which to share the Word of God in the people's language, it's located midnave, so all can hear.

• *Opposite the pulpit is the moving...*

Priests' Chapel: The 1965 statue of Christ weeping commemorates 2,779 Polish chaplains executed by the Nazis because they were priests. See the grainy black-and-white photo of one about to be shot, above on the right.

• *Head up the nave to the...*

High Altar: The main altar, beautifully carved in 1517, is a triptych showing the coronation of Mary. She is surrounded by the Trinity: flanked by God and Jesus, with the dove representing the Holy Spirit overhead. The church's medieval stained glass was destroyed in 1945. Poland's biggest stained-glass window, behind the altar, is from 1980.

• *Start circling around the right side of the altar. Look right to find (high on a pillar) the big, opulent family marker.*

Ferber Family Medallion: The falling baby (under the crown) is Constantine Ferber. As a precocious child, li'l Constantine leaned out his window on the Royal Way to see the king's processional come through town. He slipped and fell, but landed in a salesman's barrel of fish. Constantine grew up to become the mayor of Gdańsk.

• *As you continue around behind the altar, search high above you, on the walls to your right, to spot those restored pre-Reformation frescoes. Directly behind the altar, under the big window, is the...*

Empty Glass Case: This case was designed to hold Hans Memling's *Last Judgment* painting, which used to be in this church, but is currently being held hostage by the National Museum (described on page 474). To counter the museum's claim that the church wasn't a good environment for such a precious work, the priest had this display case built—but that still wasn't enough to convince the museum to give the painting back. (You'll see a small replica of the painting in the rear of this church.)

• *Now circle back the way you came to the area in front of the main altar, and proceed straight ahead into the transept. High on the wall to your right, look for the...*

Astronomical Clock: This 42-foot-tall clock is supposedly the biggest wooden clock in the world. Below it is an elaborate circular calendar that, like a medieval computer, calculates on which day each saint's festival day falls in different years (see the little guy on the left, with the pointer). Above are zodiac signs and the time (back then, the big hand was all you needed). Way up on top, Adam and Eve are naked and ready to ring the bell. Adam's been swinging his clapper at the top of the hour since 1473...but sadly, the clock is broken.

• *A few steps in front of the clock is a modern chapel with the...*

Memorial to the Polish Victims of the 2010 Plane Crash: The gold-shrouded Black Madonna honors the 96 victims of an air disaster that killed much of Poland's government—including the president and first lady—during a terrible storm over Russia. The main tomb is for Maciej Płażyński, from Gdańsk, who was leader of the parliament. On the left, the jagged statue has bits of the wreckage and lists each victim by name.

• *In a small chapel in the rear corner of the church—on the far right with your back to the high altar—you'll find the...*

Pietà and Memling Replica: The *pietà*, carved of limestone and painted in 1410, is by the Master of Gdańsk. In the same room is a musty old copy of Memling's *Last Judgment*—the exquisite original once graced this very chapel. If you're not planning to go see it at the National Museum, you could read the description on page 474 now.

• *Next door are stairs leading to the...*

Church Tower: You can climb 409 steps to burn off some pierogi and earn a grand city view. It's a long hike (and you'll know it—every 10th step is numbered). But because the viewpoint is surrounded by a roof, the views are distant and may not be worth the effort. The first third is up a tight, medieval spiral staircase. Then you'll walk through the eerie, cavernous area between the roof and the ceiling, before huffing up steep concrete steps that surround the square tower (as you spiral up, up, up around the bells). Finally you'll climb a little metal ladder and pop out at the viewpoint.

• *Leaving the church, angle left and continue straight up ulica Piwna ("Beer Street") toward the sprightly facade of the Armory.*

❿ The Gdańsk Armory (Zbrojownia)

The 1605 armory, which we saw from a distance at the start of this walk, is one of the best examples of Dutch Renaissance architecture in Europe. Athena, the goddess of war and wisdom, stands in the center, amid motifs of war and ornamental pukers.

• *If you want to make your walk a loop, you're just a block away from where we started (to the left). But there's much more to see. Facing the Armory, turn right and start the second half of this walk.*

PART 2: THROUGH THE OLD TOWN TO THE SHIPYARDS

• *From here, we'll work our way out of the Main Town and head into the Old Town, toward Solidarity Square and the shipyards. We'll be walking along this street (which changes names a couple of times) nearly all the way. Keep in mind that this part of the walk ends at the European Solidarity Center's fine museum. You'll want plenty of time to tour the museum and linger over its exhibits, so if you're already pooped or it's getting late in the day, consider finishing this walk another time.*

From the Armory, head down Kołodziejska, which quickly becomes Węglarska. After two blocks (that is, one block before the big market hall), detour to the right down Świętojańska and use the side door to enter the brick church.

⓫ St. Nicholas Church (Kościół Św. Mikołaja)

Near the end of World War II, when the Soviet army reached Gdańsk on its march westward, they were given the order to burn all the churches. Only this one survived—because it happened to be dedicated to Russia's patron saint. As the best-preserved church in town, it has a more impressive interior than the others, with lavish black-and-gold Baroque altars.

• *Backtrack out to the main street and continue along it, passing a row of seniors selling their grown and foraged edibles. Immediately after the church is Gdańsk's...*

⓬ Market Hall

Built in 1896 and renovated in 2005, Gdańsk's market hall is fun to explore. Appreciate the delicate steel-and-glass canopy overhead. This is a totally untouristy scene: You'll see everything from skintight *Polska* T-shirts, to wedding gowns, to maternity wear. The meat is downstairs, and the veggies are outside on the adjacent square. As this was once the center of a monastic community, the basement has the graves of medieval Dominican monks, which were exposed when the building was refurbished: Peer over the glass railing, and you'll see some of those scant remains.

Across the street from the Market Hall, a round, red-brick **tower,** part of the city's protective wall back in 1400, marks the end of the Main Town and the beginning of the Old Town.

• *Another block up the street, on the right, is the huge...*

⓭ St. Catherine's Church (Kościół Św. Katarzyny)

"Katy," as locals call it, is the oldest church in Gdańsk. In May of 2006, a carelessly discarded cigarette caused the church roof to burst into flames. Local people ran into the church and pulled everything outside, so nothing valuable was damaged; even the carillon bells were saved. However, the roof and wooden frame were totally destroyed. The people of Gdańsk were determined to rebuild this important symbol of the city. Within days of the fire, fundraising concerts were held to scrape together most of the money needed to raise the roof once more. Step inside. On the left side of the gate leading to the nave, photos show bomb damage. Farther in, on the left, are vivid photos of the more recent conflagration. The interior is evocative, with still-bare-brick walls that almost seem intentional—as if they're trying for an industrial-mod look.

• *The church hiding a block behind Katy—named for Catherine's daugh-*

ter Bridget—has important ties to Solidarity and is worth a visit. Go around the right side of Katy and skirt the parking lot to find the entrance.

⑩ St. Bridget's Church (Kościół Św. Brygidy)

This was the home church of Lech Wałęsa during the tense days of the 1980s. The church and its priest, Henryk Jankowski, were particularly aggressive in supporting the ideals of Solidarity. Jankowski became a mouthpiece for the movement. In gratitude for the church's support, Wałęsa named his youngest daughter Brygida.

Cost and Hours: 2 zł, daily 10:00-18:00.

Visiting the Church: Head inside. For your visit, start at the high altar, then circle clockwise back to the entry.

The enormous, unfinished **high altar** is made entirely of amber—more than a thousand square feet of it. Features that are already in place include the Black Madonna of Częstochowa, a royal Polish eagle, and the Solidarity symbol (tucked below the Black Madonna). The structure, like a scaffold, holds pieces as they are completed and added to the ensemble. The video you may see playing overhead gives you a close-up look at the amber elements.

The wrought-iron gate of the adjacent **Chapel of Fatima** (right of main altar) recalls great battles and events in Polish history from 966 to 1939, with important dates boldly sparkling in gold. Some say the Polish Church is too political. But it was only through a politically-engaged Church that this culture survived the Partitions of Poland over a century and a half, plus the brutal anti-religious policies of the communist period. The national soul of the Polish people—whether religious or not—is tied up in the Catholic faith.

Henryk Jankowski's tomb—a white marble box with red trim—is a bit farther to the right. Jankowski was a key hero dur-

ing Solidarity times; the tomb proclaims him *Kapelan Solidarności* ("Solidarity Chaplain"). But his public standing took a nosedive near the end of his life—thanks to ego-driven projects like his amber altar, as well as accusations of anti-Semitism and corruption. Forced to retire in 2007, Jankowski died in 2010. (An offering box is next to his tomb, if you'd like to donate to the amber altar project.)

In the rear corner, where a figure lies lifeless on the floor under a wall full of wooden crosses, is the tomb of Solidarity martyr **Jerzy Popiełuszko**. A courageous and famously outspoken Warsaw priest, in 1984 Popiełuszko was kidnapped, beaten, and murdered by the communist secret police. Notice that the figure's hands and feet are bound—as his body was found. The crosses are historic—each one was carried at various strikes against the communist regime. The communists believed they could break the spirit of the Poles with brutality—like the murder of Popiełuszko. But it only made the rebels stronger and more resolved to ultimately win their freedom. (Near the exit, on a monitor, a fascinating 12-minute video shows great moments of this church, with commentary by Lech Wałęsa himself.)

• *Return to the main street, turn right, and continue on. The big brick building ahead on the left, with the many windows, is the Great Mill. Walk past that and look down at the canal that once powered it.*

⓯ The Great Mill

This huge brick building dates from the 14th century. Look at the waterfalls and imagine standing here in 1400—with the mill's 18 wheels spinning 24/7, powering grindstones that produced 20 tons of flour a day. Like so much else here, the mill survived until 1945. Until recently it housed a shopping mall, but it may soon become home to one of the city's many museums.

The **park** just beyond the mill is worth a look. In the distance is the Old City Town Hall (Dutch Renaissance style, from 1595). The monument in the middle honors the 17th-century astronomer Jan Haweliusz. He's looking up at a giant, rust-colored wall with a map of the heavens. Haweliusz built the biggest telescopes of his era to better appreciate and understand the cosmos. Behind the mill stands the miller's home—its opulence indicates that, back in the Middle Ages, there was a lot of money in grinding. Just steps into the family-friendly park is a fountain that brings shrieks of joy to children on hot summer days.

• *To get to the **shipyards,** keep heading straight up Rajska. You'll pass the modern Madison shopping mall. After another long block, jog right, passing to the right of the big, ugly, and green 1970s-era skyscraper. On your right, marked by the famous red sign on the roof, is today's **Solidarity headquarters** (which remains the strongest trade union in Poland, with 700,000 members, and is also active in many other countries). Just in front of the Solidarity building, you may see two big chunks of **wall:** a piece of the Berlin Wall and a stretch of the shipyard wall that Lech Wałęsa scaled to get inside and lead the strike. The message: What happened behind one wall eventually led to the fall of the other Wall.*

From here, hike on (about 100 yards) to the finale of this walk.

⓰ Solidarity Square and the Shipyards

Three tall crosses mark Solidarity Square and the rust-colored European Solidarity Center (with an excellent museum). For the exciting story of how Polish shipbuilders set in motion events that led to the end of the USSR, turn to page 463.

Sights in Gdańsk

MAIN TOWN (GŁÓWNE MIASTO)

The following sights are all in the Main Town, listed roughly in the order you'll see them on the self-guided walk of the Royal Way.

Gdańsk Historical Museum

The Gdańsk Historical Museum has four excellent branches: the Amber Museum, Uphagen House, Main Town Hall, and Artus Court. Along with St. Mary's Church (described on page 450), these are the four most important interiors in the Main Town. All have the same hours, but you must buy a separate ticket for each.

Cost and Hours: 10 zł for Uphagen House and Artus Court, 12 zł for Amber Museum and Main Town Hall; hours fluctuate, but typically open mid-June-mid-Sept Mon-Thu 9:00-16:00, Fri-Sat 10:00-18:00, Sun 10:00-16:00; mid-Sept-mid-June Tue 10:00-13:00, Wed-Sat 10:00-16:00, Thu until 18:00, Sun 11:00-16:00, closed Mon.

Information: The museums share a phone number and website (central tel. 58-767-9100, www.mhmg.gda.pl).

▲Amber Museum (Muzeum Bursztynu)

Housed in a pair of connected brick towers (the former Prison Tower and Torture Chamber) just outside the Main Town's Golden

Gate, this museum has two oddly contradictory parts. One shows off Gdańsk's favorite local resource, amber, while the other focuses on implements of torture. You'll follow the one-way route through four exhibits on amber (with lots of stairs), and then walk the rampart to the other tower for a little torture (the 1.5-hour audioguide is overpriced at 25 zł). For a primer before you visit, read the "All About Amber" sidebar.

Visiting the Museum: The exhibit has four parts: First, head up to the **second floor** for a scientific look at amber. View inclusions (organic items trapped in resin) through a magnifying glass and microscope, and see dozens of samples showing the full rainbow of amber shades. Interactive video screens ex-

All About Amber

Poland's Baltic seaside is known as the Amber Coast. You can see amber (bursztyn) in Gdańsk's Amber Museum, in the collection at Malbork Castle (see the Pomerania chapter), and in shop windows everywhere. This fossilized tree resin originated here on the north coast of Poland 40 million years ago. It comes in as many different colors as Eskimos have words for snow: 300 distinct shades, from yellowish white to yellowish black, from opaque to transparent. (I didn't believe it either, until I toured Gdańsk's museum.) Darker-colored amber is generally mixed with ash and sand—making it more fragile, and generally less desirable. Lighter amber is mixed with gasses and air bubbles.

Amber has been popular since long before there were souvenir stands. Archaeologists have found Roman citizens (and their coins) buried with crosses made of amber. Almost 75 percent of the world's amber is mined in northern Poland, and it often simply washes up on the beaches after a winter storm. Some of the elaborate amber sculptures displayed at the museum are joined with "amber glue"—melted-down amber mixed with an adhesive agent. More recently, amber craftsmen are combining amber with silver to create artwork—a method dubbed the "Polish School."

Some Poles believe that, in addition to being good for the economy, amber is good for their health. A traditional cure for arthritis pain is to pour strong vodka over amber, let it set, and then rub it on sore joints. Other remedies call for mixing amber dust with honey or rose oil. It sounds superstitious, but users claim that it works.

plain the creation of amber. The **third-floor** exhibit explains the "Amber Route" (the ancient Celtic trade road connecting Gdańsk to Italy) and medicinal uses of the stuff, and displays a wide range of functional items made from amber—clocks, pipe stems, candlesticks, chandeliers, jewelry boxes, and much more. Take a whiff—what's that smell? It's a cathedral. Amber is an ingredient in incense. The **fourth floor** shows off more artistic items made of amber—sculptures, candelabras, beer steins, chessboards, and a model ship with delicate sails made of amber. At the **top floor,** you'll find a modern gallery showing more recent amber craftsmanship and displays about amber's role in fashion today.

Then, walking along the upper rampart level of the courtyard, you'll enter an exhibit about the building itself and the town's fortifications. This leads to the **Prison Tower** and the torture exhibit—with sound effects, scant artifacts, and mannequins helpfully demonstrating the grisly equipment.

▲Uphagen House (Dom Uphagena)

This interesting place, at ulica Długa 12, is your chance to glimpse what's behind the colorful facades lining this street. It's the only grand Gdańsk mansion rebuilt as it was before 1945. The model near the entry shows the three parts: dolled-up visitors' rooms in front, a corridor along the courtyard, and private rooms in the back. The finely decorated salon was used to show off for guests. Most of this furniture is original (saved from WWII bombs by locals who hid it in the countryside). Passing into the dining room, note the knee-high paintings of hunting and celebrations. Along the passage to the back, each room has a theme: butterflies in the smoking room, then flowers in the next room, then birds in the music room. In the private rooms at the back, the decor is simpler. Downstairs, you'll pass through the kitchen, the pantry, and a room with photos of the house before the war, which were used to reconstruct what you see today.

▲▲Main Town Hall (Ratusz Głównego Miasta)

This landmark building contains remarkable decorations from Gdańsk's Golden Age. You can also climb 293 concrete steps to

the top of the **tower** for commanding views (5 zł extra, mid-June-mid-Sept only).

Visiting the Main Town Hall: In the entry room, examine the photos showing this building at the end of World War II and ogle the finely-crafted spiral staircase. The ornately-carved wooden **door,** which we'll pass through in a minute, is all-original, from the 1600s. Above the door are two crosses under a crown. This seal of Gdańsk is being held—as it's often depicted—by a pair of lions. The felines are stubborn and independent, just like the citizens of Gdańsk. The surface of the door is carved with images of crops. Around the frame of the door are mermen, reminding us that this agricultural bounty, like so many of Poland's resources, is transported on the Vistula and out through Gdańsk.

Go through the door into the **Red Hall,** where the Gdańsk city council met in the summertime. (The lavish fireplace, with another pair of lions holding the coat of arms of Gdańsk, was just for show. There's no chimney.) City council members would sit in the seats around the room, debating city policy. Marvel at the 17th-century inlaid wood panels (just above eye level) showing slices of local life. Paintings on the wall above represent the seven virtues that the burghers meeting in this room should possess. And the exquisite ceiling—with 25 paintings in total—is all about theology.

Including both Christian and pagan themes, the ceiling was meant to inspire the decision-makers in this room to make good choices. Study the oval painting in the middle (from 1607)—the museum's highlight. It shows the special place Gdańsk occupies between God, Poland, and the rest of the world. In the foreground, the citizens of Gdańsk go about their daily lives. Above them, high atop the arch, God's hand reaches down (from within clouds of Hebrew characters) and grasps the Main Town Hall's steeple. The rainbow arching above also symbolizes God's connection to Gdańsk. Mirroring that is the Vistula River, which begins in the mountains of southern Poland (on the right), runs through the country, and exits at the sea in Gdańsk (on the left, where the rainbow ends).

Continue into the less-impressive **Winter Hall,** with another fireplace (this one actually hooked up to a chimney) and another coat of arms held by lions. Keep going through the next room, into a room with photos of **WWII damage.** The twist of wood is all that's left of the main support for the spiral staircase (today reconstructed in the room where you entered). Ponder the inspiring ability of a city to be reborn after the tragedy of war.

Upstairs are some temporary exhibits and several examples of **Gdańsk-style furniture.** These pieces are characterized by three big, round feet along the front, lots of ornamentation, and usually a virtually impossible-to-find lock (sometimes hidden behind a movable decoration). You can also see a coin collection, from the days when Gdańsk had the elite privilege of minting its own currency.

Then head upstairs, to a fascinating exhibit about Gdańsk's time as a **"free city"** between the World Wars—when, because of its delicate ethnic mix of Poles and Germans, it was too precarious to assign it to either country. You'll see border checkpoints, uniforms, signs in German (the predominant language of "Danzig"), and reconstructed rooms (homes and shops) from the era. Near the end of this room, you have the option to climb up to the top of the tower. Otherwise, you'll take stairs down—with huge photos at each landing showing the city in ruins after World War II, then triumphantly being rebuilt—and into the cellars, where you'll wander through some pointless subterranean chambers before emerging back into the courtyard where you started.

▲▲Artus Court (Dwór Artusa)

In the Middle Ages, Gdańsk was home to many brotherhoods and guilds (like businessmen's clubs). For their meetings, the city provided this elaborately decorated hall, named for King Arthur—a medieval symbol for prestige and power. Just as in King Arthur's Court, this was a place where powerful and important people came together. Of many such halls in Baltic Europe, this is the only original one that survives (skip the dry and too-thorough audioguide; in tall, white, triple-arched building behind Neptune statue at Długi Targ 43).

Visiting the Artus Court: In the grand hall, various **cupboards** line the walls. Each organization that met here had a place to keep its important documents and office supplies. Suspended from the ceiling are seven giant **model ships** that depict Baltic vessels, symbolic of the city's connection to the sea.

In the far-back corner is the museum's highlight: a gigantic **stove** decorated with 520 colorful tiles featuring the faces of kings, queens, nobles, mayors, and burghers—a mix of Protestants and Catholics, as a reminder of Gdańsk's religious tolerance. Almost all the tiles are original, having survived WWII bombs.

Notice the huge **paintings** on the walls above, with 3-D animals emerging from flat frames. Hunting is a popular theme in local artwork. Like minting coins, hunting was a privilege usually reserved for royalty, but it was extended in special circumstances to the burghers of special towns...like Gdańsk. These "paintings" are new, digitally-generated reproductions of the originals, which were damaged in World War II.

The next room—actually in the next building—is a typical **front room** of the burghers' homes lining ulica Długa. Ogle the gorgeously-carved wooden staircase. Upstairs is a hall of knights—once again evoking Arthurian legend. If you've rented an audioguide, take it back up front to return it; otherwise, you can exit through the back.

Other Museums in the Main Town
Historical Zone of the Free City of Gdańsk (Strefa Historyczna Wolne Miasto Gdańsk)

In a city so obsessed with its Golden Age and Solidarity history, this charming little collection illuminates a unique but often-overlooked chapter in the story of Gdańsk: The years between World Wars I and II, when—in an effort to find a workable compromise in this ethnically mixed city—Gdańsk was not part of Germany or Poland, but a self-governing "free city" *(wolne miasto)*. Like a holdover from medieval fiefdoms in modern times, the city-state of Gdańsk even issued its own currency and stamps. This modest museum earnestly shows off artifacts from the time—photos, stamps, maps, flags, promotional tourist leaflets, and other items from the free city, all marked with the Gdańsk symbol of two white crosses under a crown on a red shield. The brochure explains that four out of five people living in the free city identified themselves not as Germans or Poles, but as "Danzigers." While some might find the subject obscure, this endearing collection is a treat for WWII history buffs. Be sure to borrow the English translations at the entrance.

Cost and Hours: 8 zł, Tue-Sun 12:00-18:00, Sept-April until 17:00, closed Mon year-round, down the little alley just in front of the Green Gate at Warzywnicza 10A, tel. 58-320-2828, www. strefahistorycznawmg.pl.

Archaeological Museum (Muzeum Archeologiczne)

This recently-updated museum is worth a quick peek for those interested in archaeology. Highlights include distinctive urns with cute faces (which date from the Hallstatt Period and were discovered in slate graves around Gdańsk); Bronze and Iron Age tools; before-and-after photos of WWII Gdańsk; and a reconstructed 12th-century Viking-like Slavonic longboat. You can also climb the building's tower, with good views up Mariacka street toward St. Mary's Church.

Cost and Hours: Museum-8 zł (free on Sat), tower-5 zł; July-Aug Tue-Fri 9:00-17:00, Sat-Sun 10:00-17:00; Sept-June Tue and Thu-Fri 8:00-16:00, Wed 9:00-17:00, Sat-Sun 10:00-16:00; closed Mon year-round; ulica Mariacka 25, tel. 58-322-2100, www. archeologia.pl.

▲National Maritime Museum (Narodowe Muzeum Morskie)

Gdańsk's history and livelihood are tied to the sea. This collection, spread among several buildings on either side of the river, examines all aspects of this connection. Nautical types may get a thrill out of the creaky, sprawling museum, but most visitors find it little more than a convenient way to pass some time and enjoy a cruise across the river. The museum's lack of English information is frustrating; fortunately, some exhibits have descriptions you can borrow.

Cost and Hours: Each part of the museum has its own admission (6-8 zł; ask about combo-tickets). The Maritime Cultural Center is worth neither the time nor the money for grown-ups. It's open July-Aug daily 10:00-18:00; Sept-Oct and March-June Tue-Sun 10:00-16:00, closed Mon; Nov-Feb Tue-Sun 10:00-15:00, closed Mon; ulica Ołowianka 9, tel. 58-301-8611, www.cmm.pl.

Visiting the Museum: The exhibit has four parts. The first two parts—the Crane and Maritime Cultural Center—are on the Main Town side of the river. The landmark medieval **Crane** (Żuraw), Gdańsk's most important symbol, houses a humble exhibit on living in the city during its Golden Age (16th-17th centuries). For more on the Crane itself, see page 449.

The **Maritime Cultural Center,** a modern exhibit right next door to the Crane, is not worth the exercise unless you are leading a school group. For adults, the most interesting areas are on the third floor ("Working Boats," with examples of vessels from around the world) and the fourth floor (temporary exhibits).

The rest of the museum—the Old Granaries and the *Sołdek* steamship—is across the river on Ołowianka Island, which you can reach via the little **ferry** (named the *Motława,* like the river; 1.50 zł one-way). The ferry runs about every 15 minutes in peak season (during museum hours only), less frequently in shoulder season, and not at all in the winter.

Once on the island, visit the three rebuilt **Old Granaries** (Spichlerze). These make up the heart of the exhibit, tracing the history

of Gdańsk—particularly as it relates to the sea—from prehistoric days to the present. Models of the town and region help put things in perspective. Other exhibits cover underwater exploration, navigational aids, artifacts of the Polish seafaring tradition, peekaboo cross-sections of multilevel ships, and models of the modern-day shipyard where Solidarity was born. This place is home to more miniature ships than you ever thought you'd see, and the Nautical Gallery upstairs features endless rooms with paintings of boats.

Finally, crawl through the holds and scramble across the deck of a decommissioned steamship called the *Sołdek,* docked permanently across from the Crane (ship generally closed in winter). This was the first postwar vessel built at the Gdańsk shipyard. Below decks, you can see where the crew shoveled the coal; wander through a maze of pipes, gears, valves, gauges, and ladders; and visit the rooms where the sailors lived, slept, and ate. You can even play captain on the bridge.

SOLIDARITY (SOLIDARNOŚĆ) AND THE GDAŃSK SHIPYARD (STOCZNIA GDAŃSKA)

Gdańsk's single most memorable experience is exploring the shipyard that witnessed the beginning of the end of communism's stranglehold on Eastern Europe. Taken together, the sights in this area are worth ▲▲▲. Here in the former industrial wasteland that Lech Wałęsa called the "cradle of freedom," this evocative site tells the story of the brave Polish shipyard workers who took on—and ultimately defeated—an Evil Empire. A visit to the Solidarity sights has two main parts: Solidarity Square (with the memorial and gate in front of the shipyard), and the outstanding museum inside the European Solidarity Center.

GDAŃSK & THE TRI-CITY

Getting to the Shipyard: These sights cluster around Solidarity Square (Plac Solidarności), at the north end of the Old Town, about a 20-minute walk from the Royal Way. For the most interesting approach, follow "Part 2" of my self-guided walk (earlier), which ends here.

Background: After the communists took over Eastern Europe at the end of World War II, oppressed peoples throughout the Soviet Bloc rose up in different ways. The most dramatic uprisings—Hungary's 1956 Uprising (see page 578) and Czechoslovakia's 1968 "Prague Spring" (see page 82)—were brutally crushed under the treads of Soviet tanks. The formula for freedom that finally succeeded was a patient, nearly decade-long series of strikes and protests spearheaded by Lech Wałęsa and his trade union, called Solidarność—"Solidarity." (The movement also benefited from good timing, as it coincided with the *perestroika* and *glasnost* policies of Soviet premier Mikhail Gorbachev.) While some American politicians might like to take credit for defeating communism, Wałęsa and his fellow workers were the ones fighting on the front lines, armed with nothing more than guts.

Solidarity Square (Plac Solidarności) and the Monument of the Fallen Shipyard Workers

The seeds of August 1980 were sown a decade before. Since becoming part of the Soviet Bloc, the Poles staged frequent strikes, protests, and uprisings to secure their rights, all of which were put down by the regime. But the bloodiest of these took place in December of 1970—a tragic event memorialized by the **three-crosses monument** that towers over what's now called Solidarity Square.

The 1970 strike was prompted by price hikes. The communist government set the prices for all products. As Poland endured drastic food shortages in the 1960s and 1970s, the regime frequently announced what it called "regulation of prices." Invariably, this meant an increase in the cost of essential foodstuffs. (To be able to claim "regulation" rather than "increase," the regime would symbolically lower prices for a few select items—but these were always nonessential luxuries, such as elevators and TV sets, which nobody could afford anyway.) The regime was usually smart enough to raise prices on January 1, when the people were fat and happy after Christmas, and too hungover to complain. But on December 12, 1970, bolstered by an ego-stoking visit by West German Chancellor Willy Brandt, Polish premier Władysław

Gomułka increased prices. The people of Poland—who cared more about the price of Christmas dinner than relations with Germany—struck back.

A wave of strikes and sit-ins spread along the heavily industrialized north coast of Poland, most notably in Gdańsk, Gdynia, and Szczecin. Thousands of angry demonstrators poured through the gate of this shipyard, marched into town, and set fire to the Communist Party Committee building. In an attempt to quell the riots, the government-run radio implored the people to go back to work. On the morning of December 17, workers showed up at shipyard gates across northern Poland, and were greeted by the army and police. Without provocation, the Polish army opened fire on the workers. While the official death toll for the massacre stands at 44, others say the true number is much higher. The monument, with a trio of 140-foot-tall crosses, honors those lost to the regime that December.

Go to the middle of the **wall** behind the crosses, to the monument of the worker wearing a flimsy plastic work helmet, attempting to shield himself from bullets. Behind him is a list—pockmarked with symbolic bullet holes—of workers murdered on that day. *Lat* means "years old"—many teenagers were among the dead. The quote at the top of the wall is from St. John Paul II, who was elected pope eight years after this tragedy. The pope was known for his clever way with words, and this very carefully phrased quote—which served as an inspiration to the Poles during their darkest hours—skewers the regime in a way subtle enough to still be tolerated: "Let thy spirit descend, and renew the face of the earth—of *this* earth" (that is, Poland). Below that is the dedication: "They gave their lives so you can live decently."

Stretching to the left of this center wall are plaques representing labor unions from around Poland—and around the world (look for the Chinese characters)—expressing solidarity with these workers. To the right is an enormous Bible verse: "May the Lord give strength to his people. May the Lord bless his people with the gift of peace" (Psalms 29:11).

Inspired by the brave sacrifice of their true comrades, shipyard workers rose up here in August of 1980, formulating the "21 Points" of a new union called Solidarity. Their demands included the right to strike and form unions, the freeing of political prisoners, and an increase in wages. The 21 Points are listed in Polish on the panel at the far end of the right wall, marked *21 X TAK* ("21 times yes"). An unwritten precondition to any agreement was the right for the workers of 1980 to build a memorial to their comrades slain in 1970. The government agreed, marking the first time a communist regime ever allowed a monument to be built to honor its own victims. Wałęsa called it a harpoon in the heart of the com-

Lech Wałęsa

In 1980, the world was turned on its ear by a walrus-mustachioed shipyard electrician. Within three years, this seemingly run-of-the-mill Pole had precipitated the collapse of communism, led a massive 10-million-member trade union with enormous political impact, been named *Time* magazine's Man of the Year, and won a Nobel Peace Prize.

Lech Wałęsa was born in Popowo, Poland in 1943. After working as a car mechanic and serving two years in the army, he became an electrician at the Gdańsk Shipyard in 1967. Like many Poles, Wałęsa felt stifled by the communist government, and was infuriated that a system that was supposed to be for the workers clearly wasn't serving them.

When the shipyard massacre took place in December of 1970 (see page 464), Wałęsa was at the forefront of the protests. He was marked as a dissident, and in 1976, he was fired. Wałęsa hopped from job to job and was occasionally unemployed—under communism, a rock-bottom status reserved for only the most despicable derelicts. But he soldiered on, fighting for the creation of a trade union and building up quite a file with the secret police.

In August 1980, Wałęsa heard news of the beginnings of the Gdańsk strike and raced to the shipyard. In an act that has since become the stuff of legend, Wałęsa scaled the shipyard wall to get inside.

Before long, Wałęsa's dynamic personality won him the unofficial role of the workers' leader and spokesman. He negotiated with the regime to hash out the August Agreements, becoming a rock star-type hero during the so-called 16 Months of Hope... until martial law came crashing down in December 1981. Wałęsa was arrested and interned for 11 months in a country house. After

munists. The towering monument, with three crucified anchors on top, was designed, engineered, and built by shipyard workers. The monument was finished just four months after the historic agreement was signed.

• *Now continue to the gate and peer through into the birthplace of Eastern European freedom.*

Gdańsk Shipyard (Stocznia Gdańska) Gate #2

When a Pole named Karol Wojtyła was elected pope in 1978—and visited his homeland in 1979—he inspired his 40 million countrymen to believe that impossible dreams can come true. Prices being released, he continued to struggle underground, becoming a symbol of anticommunist sentiment.

Finally, the dedication of Wałęsa and Solidarity paid off, and Polish communism dissolved—with Wałęsa rising from the ashes as the country's first postcommunist president. But the skills that made Wałęsa a rousing success at leading an uprising didn't translate well to the president's office. Wałęsa proved to be a stubborn, headstrong politician, frequently clashing with the parliament. He squabbled with his own party, declaring a "war at the top" of Solidarity and rotating higher-ups to prevent corruption and keep the party fresh. He also didn't choose his advisors well, enlisting several staffers who wound up immersed in scandal. His overconfidence was his Achilles' heel, and his governing style verged on authoritarian.

Unrefined and none too interested in scripted speeches, Wałęsa was a simple man who preferred playing ping-pong with his buddies to attending formal state functions. Though lacking a formal education, Wałęsa had unsurpassed drive and charisma... but that's not enough to lead a country—especially during an impossibly complicated, fast-changing time.

Wałęsa was defeated at the polls, by the Poles, in 1995, and when he ran again in 2000, he received a humiliating one percent of the vote. Since leaving office, Wałęsa has kept a lower profile, but still delivers speeches worldwide. Many poor Poles grumble that Lech, who started life simple like them, has forgotten the little people. But his fans point out that he gives much of his income to charity. And on his lapel, he still always wears a pin featuring the Black Madonna of Częstochowa—the most important symbol of Polish Catholicism.

Poles say there are at least two Lech Wałęsas: the young, bombastic, working-class idealist Lech, at the forefront of the Solidarity strikes, who will always have a special place in their hearts; and the failed President Wałęsa, who got in over his head and tarnished his legacy.

continued to go up, and the workers continued to rise up. By the summer of 1980, it was clear that the dam was about to break.

In August, Anna Walentynowicz—a Gdańsk crane operator and known dissident—was fired unceremoniously just short of her retirement. This sparked a strike in the Gdańsk Shipyard (then called the Lenin Shipyard) on August 14, 1980. An electrician named Lech Wałęsa had been fired as an agitator years before and wasn't allowed into the yard. But on hearing news of the strike, Wałęsa went to the shipyard and climbed over the wall to get inside. The strike now had a leader.

These were not soldiers, nor were they idealistic flower children. The strike participants were gritty, salt-of-the-earth manual laborers: forklift operators, welders, electricians, machinists. Imagine being one of the 16,000 workers who stayed here for 18 days during the strike—hungry, cold, sleeping on sheets of Styrofoam, inspired by the new Polish pope, excited about finally standing up to the regime... and terrified that at any moment

you might be gunned down, like your friends had been a decade before. Workers, afraid to leave the shipyard, communicated with the outside world through this gate—wives and brothers showed up here and asked for a loved one, and those inside spread the word until the striker came forward. Occasionally, a truck pulled up inside the gate, with Lech Wałęsa standing atop its cab with a megaphone. Facing the thousands of people assembled outside the gate, Wałęsa gave progress reports on the negotiations and pleaded for supplies. The people of Gdańsk responded, bringing armfuls of bread and other food to keep the workers going. Solidarity.

During the strike, two items hung on the fence. One of them (which still hangs there today) was a picture of Pope John Paul II—a reminder to believe in your dreams and have faith in God (for more on the Pope and his role in Solidarity, see page 266). The other item was a makeshift list of the strikers' 21 Points—demands scrawled in red paint and black pencil on pieces of plywood.

• *Walk around the right end of the gate and enter the former shipyard.*

The shipyard churned out over a thousand ships from 1948 to 1990, employing 16,000 workers. About 60 percent of these ships were exported to the USSR—and so, when the Soviet Bloc broke apart in the 1990s, they lost a huge market. Today the facilities employ closer to 1,200 workers...who now make windmills.

Before entering the museum, take a look around. This part of the shipyard, long abandoned, is being redeveloped into a **"Young City"** (Młode Miasto)—envisioned as a new city center for Gdańsk, with shopping, restaurants, offices, and homes. Rusting shipbuilding equipment has been torn down, and old brick buildings are being converted into gentrified flats. The nearby boulevard called Nowa Wałowa will be the spine connecting this area to the rest of the city. Farther east, the harborfront will also be rejuvenated, creating a glitzy marina and extending the city's delightful waterfront people zone to the north (see www.ycgdansk.com). Fortunately, the shipyard gate, monument, and other important sites from the Solidarity strikes—now considered historical monuments—will remain.

• *The massive, rust-colored European Solidarity Center, which faces Solidarity Square, houses the museum where we'll learn the rest of the story.*

▲▲▲European Solidarity Center (Europejskie Centrum Solidarności)

Europe's single best sight about the end of communism is made even more powerful by its location: in the very heart of the place where those events occurred. Fill-

ing just one small corner of a huge, purpose-built educational facility, the permanent exhibition uses larger-than-life photographs, archival footage, actual artifacts, interactive touchscreens, and a state-of-the-art audioguide to eloquently tell the story of the end of Eastern European communism.

Cost and Hours: 17 zł, includes audioguide, daily 10:00-20:00, Oct-April until 18:00, last entry one hour before closing, Plac Solidarności 1, tel. 506-195-673, www.ecs.gda.pl.

⊘ Self-Guided Tour: First, appreciate the architecture of the **building** itself. From the outside, it's designed to resemble the rusted hull of a giant ship—seemingly gloomy and depressing. But step inside to find an interior flooded with light, which cultivates a surprising variety of life—in the form of lush gardens that make the place feel like a very expensive greenhouse. You can interpret this symbolism a number of ways: Something that seems dull and dreary from the outside (the Soviet Bloc, the shipyards themselves, what have you) can be full of brightness, life, and optimism inside.

In the lobby, buy your ticket and pick up the essential, included audioguide. The exhibit has much to see, and some of it is arranged in a conceptual way that can be tricky to understand without a full grasp of the history. I've outlined the basics in this self-guided tour, but the audioguide can illuminate more details—including translations of films and eyewitness testimony from participants in the history.

• *The permanent exhibit fills seven lettered rooms—each with its own theme—on two floors. From the lush lobby, head up the escalator and into...*

The Birth of Solidarity (Room A): This room picks up right in the middle of the dynamic story we just learned out on the square. It's August of 1980, and the shipyard workers are rising up. You step straight into a busy shipyard: punch clocks, workers' lockers, and—up on the ceiling—hundreds of plastic helmets. A big **map** in the middle of the room shows the extent of the shipyard in 1980. Inside the cab of the **crane,** you can watch an interview with spunky Anna Walentynowicz, whose firing led to the first round of strikes. Nearby stands a **truck;** Lech Wałęsa would stand on top of the cab of a truck like this one to address the nervous locals who had amassed outside the shipyard gate, awaiting further news.

In the middle of the room, carefully protected under glass, are those original **plywood panels** onto which the strikers scrawled their 21 demands, then lashed to the gate. Just beyond that, a giant wall of photos and a map illustrate how the strikes that began here spread like a virus across Poland. At the far end of the room, behind the partition, stand **two tables** that were used during the talks to end the strikes (each one with several actual items from that era, under glass).

After 18 days of protests, the communist authorities finally agreed to negotiate. On the afternoon of August 31, 1980, the Governmental Commission and the Inter-Factory Strike Committee (MKS) came together and signed the August Agreements, which legalized Solidarity—the first time any communist government permitted a workers' union. As Lech Wałęsa sat at a big table and signed the agreement, other union reps tape-recorded the proceedings and played them later at their own factories to prove that the unthinkable had happened. Take a moment to linger over the rousing **film** that plays on the far wall, which begins with the strike, carries through with the tense negotiations that a brash young Lech Wałęsa held with the authorities, and ends with the triumphant acceptance of the strikers' demands. Lech Wałęsa rides on the shoulders of well-wishers out to the gate to spread the good news.

• Back by the original 21 demands, enter the next exhibit...

The Power of the Powerless (Room B): This section traces the roots of the 1980 strikes, which were preceded by several far less successful protests. It all begins with a kiss: a giant photograph of Russian premier Leonid Brezhnev mouth-kissing the Polish premier Edward Gierek, with the caption **"Brotherly Friendship."** Soviet premiers and their satellite leaders really did greet each other "in the French manner," as a symbolic gesture of their communist brotherhood.

Working your way through the exhibit, you'll see the door to a **prison cell**—a reminder of the intimidation tactics used by the Soviets in the 1940s and 1950s to deal with their opponents as they exerted their rule over the lands they had liberated from the Nazis.

The typical **communist-era apartment** is painfully humble. After the war, much of Poland had been destroyed, and population shifts led to housing shortages. People had to make do with tiny spaces and ramshackle furnishings. Communist propaganda blares from both the radio and the TV.

A map shows **"red Europe"** (the USSR plus the satellites of Poland, Czechoslovakia, Hungary, and East Germany), and a **timeline** traces some of the smaller Soviet Bloc protests that led up to Solidarity: in East Germany in 1953, in Budapest and Poznań in 1956, the "Prague Spring" of 1968, and other 1968 protests in Poland.

In the wake of these uprisings, the communist authorities cracked down even harder. Peek into the **interrogation room,** with a wall of file cabinets and a lowly stool illuminated by a bright spotlight. (Notice that the white Polish eagle on the seal above the desk is missing its golden crown—during communism, the Poles were allowed to keep the eagle, but its crown was removed.)

The next exhibit presents a day-by-day rundown of the **1970 strikes,** from December 14 to 22, which resulted in the massacre of the workers who are honored by the monument in front of this building. A wall of mug shots gives way to exhibits chronicling the steady rise of dissent groups through the 1970s, culminating in the June 1976 protests in the city of Radom (prompted, like so many other uprisings, by unilateral price hikes).

• *Loop back through Room A, and proceed straight ahead into...*

Solidarity and Hope (Room C): While the government didn't take the August Agreements very seriously, the Poles did... and before long, 10 million of them—one out of every four, or effectively half the nation's workforce—joined Solidarity. So began what's often called the **"16 Months of Hope."** Newly legal, Solidarity continued to stage strikes and make its opposition known. Slick Solidarity posters and children's art convey the childlike enthusiasm with which the Poles seized their hard-won kernels of freedom. The communist authorities' hold on the Polish people began to slip. Support and aid from the outside world poured in, but the rest of the Soviet Bloc looked on nervously, and the Warsaw Pact army assembled at the Polish border and glared at the uprisers. The threat of invasion hung heavy in the air.

• *Exiting this room, head up the staircase and into...*

At War with Society (Room D): You're greeted by a wall of TV screens delivering a stern message. On Sunday morning, December 13, 1981, the Polish head of state, **General Wojciech Jaruzelski**—wearing his trademark dark glasses—appeared on national TV and announced the introduction of **martial law.** Solidarity was outlawed, and its leaders were arrested. Frightened Poles heard the announcement and looked out their windows to see Polish Army tanks rumbling through the snowy streets. (On the opposite wall, see footage of tanks and heavily armed soldiers intimidating their countrymen into compliance.) Jaruzelski claimed that he imposed martial law to prevent the Soviets from invading. Today, many historians question whether martial law was really necessary, though Jaruzelski remained unremorseful through his death in 2014.

Continuing deeper into the exhibit, you come to a **prisoner transport.** Climb up inside to watch chilling scenes of riots, demonstrations, and crackdowns by the ZOMO riot police. In one gruesome scene, a demonstrator is quite intentionally—and practically in slow motion—run over by a truck. From here, pass through a gauntlet of *milicja* riot-gear shields to see the truck crashing through a gate. Overhead are the uniforms of miners from the **Wujek mine** who were massacred on December 16, 1981 (their names are projected on the pile of coal below).

Martial law was a tragic, terrifying, and bleak time for the Polish people. It didn't, however, kill the Solidarity movement, which continued its fight after going underground. Passing prison cells, you'll see a wall plastered with handmade, underground posters and graffiti. Notice how in this era, **Solidarity propaganda** is much more primitive; circle around the other side of the wall to see several presses that were actually used in clandestine Solidarity print shops during this time. The outside world sent messages of support as well as supplies—represented by the big wall of cardboard boxes. This approval also came in the form of a Nobel Peace Prize for Lech Wałęsa in 1983; you'll see video clips of his wife accepting the award on his behalf (Wałęsa feared that if he traveled abroad to claim it, he would not be allowed back into the country).

• *But even in these darkest days, there were glimmers of hope. Enter...*

The Road to Democracy (Room E): By the time the Pope visited his homeland again in 1983, martial law had finally been lifted, and Solidarity—still technically illegal—was gaining momentum, gradually pecking away at the communists. Step into the small inner room with footage of the **Pope's third pilgrimage** to his homeland in 1987, by which time (thanks in no small part to his inspirational role in the ongoing revolution) the tide was turning.

Step into the room with the big, white **roundtable.** With the moral support of the pope and the entire Western world, the brave Poles were the first European country to throw off the shackles of communism when, in the spring of 1989, the "Roundtable Talks" led to the opening up of elections. (If you look through the view-finders of the TV cameras in the corners, you'll see footage of those meetings.) The government arrogantly called for parliamentary elections, reserving 65 percent of seats for themselves.

In the next room, you can see Solidarity's strategy in those **elections:** On the right wall are posters showing Lech Wałęsa with each candidate. Another popular "get out the vote" measure was the huge poster of Gary Cooper—an icon of America, which the Poles deeply respect and viewed as their friendly cousin across the Atlantic—except that, instead of a pistol, he's packing a ballot. Rousing reminders like this inspired huge voter turnout. The communists' plan backfired, as virtually every open seat went to Solidarity. It was the first time ever that opposition candidates had taken office in the Soviet Bloc. On the wall straight ahead, flashing a V-for-*wiktoria* sign, is a huge photo of Tadeusz Mazowiecki—an early leader of Solidarity, who became prime minister on June 4, 1989.

• *For the glorious aftermath, head into the final room.*

The Triumph of Freedom (Room F): This room is dominated by a gigantic **map of Eastern Europe.** A countdown clock on the right ticks off the departure of each country from communist clutches, as the Soviet Bloc "decomposes." You'll see how the success of Solidarity in Poland—and the ragtag determination of a scruffy band of shipyard workers right here in Gdańsk—inspired people all over Eastern Europe. By the winter of 1989, the Hungarians had opened their borders, the Berlin Wall had crumbled, and the Czechs and Slovaks had staged their Velvet Revolution. (Small viewing stations that circle the room reveal the detailed story for each country's own road to freedom.) Lech Wałęsa—the shipyard electrician who started it all by jumping over a wall—became the first president of postcommunist Poland. And a year later, in Poland's first true elections since World War II, 29 different parties won seats in the parliament. It was a free-election free-for-all.

In the middle of the room stands a white wall with **inspirational quotes** from St. John Paul II and Václav Havel—the Czech poet-turned-protester-turned-prisoner-turned-president—which are repeated in several languages. On the huge wall, the **Solidarity "graffiti"** is actually made up of thousands of little notes left behind by visitors to the museum. Feel free to grab a piece of paper and a pen and record your own reflections.

• *Finally, head downstairs and find the...*

St. John Paul II Room (Room G): Many visitors find that touring this museum—with vivid reminders of a dramatic and pivotal moment in history that took place in their own lifetimes and was brought about not by armies or presidents, but by everyday people—puts them in an emotional state of mind. Designed for silent reflection, this room overlooks the monument to those workers who were gunned down in 1970.

• *For an epilogue, if you're not already pooped, continue deeper into the former shipyard to see one more important landmark from 1980. The path leads to a low-profile, red-brick building, the...*

Sala BHP

This is the building where the communists sat down across the table from Lech Wałęsa and his team and worked out a compromise (as seen in the videos inside the European Solidarity Center). Entering, turn left to view a series of photos that illustrate Solidarity history; these are all the more poignant because they lack the bombastic presentation of the glitzy museum. The images speak for themselves. The other side of the building (right from the entrance) is the actual hall where those fateful meetings took place, with a long table set up on the stage.

Cost and Hours: Free, daily 10:00-18:00, Oct-April until 16:00, www.salabhp.pl.

NORTH OF THE MAIN TOWN
Museum of the Second World War

Since 2007, Gdańsk has been preparing this expansive, architecturally striking, world-class museum just east of the Solidarity shipyard. Collecting thousands of artifacts (from intimate belongings of wartime victims, to tanks and railway cars), it was originally designed to present an ambitiously global, yet personal, perspective on the war that began right at Gdańsk's doorstep. But as it neared completion, politicians from the nationalistic Law and Justice Party deemed it too pacifistic and "not Polish enough," demanding changes to make it more singularly patriotic. Political wrangling ensued to determine who controlled the museum's content. With this delay, it's unclear when the museum will open (likely in 2017 or 2018; for details, ask at the TI or see www.muzeum1939.pl). But when it does—and if its original design is preserved—it will likely be regarded one of Europe's definitive World War II museums.

SOUTH OF THE MAIN TOWN

A 10- to 15-minute walk south of the Main Town, these sights round out your Gdańsk experience. They're most worthwhile to those with a special interest in each one's subject matter: art, theater, and kids who love archaeology.

National Museum in Gdańsk
(Muzeum Narodowe w Gdańsku)

This art collection, housed in what was a 15th-century Franciscan monastery, is worth ▲▲ to art lovers for one reason: Hans Memling's glorious *Last Judgment* triptych altarpiece, one of the two most important pieces of art to be seen in Poland (the other is Leonardo da Vinci's *Lady with an Ermine*, usually in Kraków's Czartoryski Museum). If you're not a purist, you can settle for seeing the much smaller replica in St. Mary's Church. But if medieval art is your bag, make the 10-minute walk here from the Main Town.

Cost and Hours: 10 zł; May-Sept Tue-Sun 10:00-17:00 (Thu 12:00-19:00 in June-Aug); Oct-April Tue-Fri 9:00-16:00, Sat-Sun 10:00-17:00; closed Mon year-round; last entry 45 minutes before closing; walk 10 minutes due south from ulica Długa's Golden Gate, after passing the Shakespeare Theater take the pedestrian underpass beneath the big cross street, then continue down the busy street until you see signs for the museum; ulica Toruńska 1, tel. 58-301-7061, www.mng.gda.pl.

Visiting the Museum: From the entry, the **altarpiece by Hans Memling** (c. 1440-1494) is at the top of the stairs and to the right. The history of the painting is as interesting as the work itself. It was commissioned in the mid-15th century by the Medicis' banker in Florence, Angelo di Jacopo Tani. The ship delivering the painting from Belgium to Florence was hijacked by a Gdańsk pirate, who brought the altarpiece to his hometown to be displayed in St. Mary's Church. For centuries, kings, emperors, and czars admired it from afar, until Napoleon seized it in the early 19th century and took it to Paris to hang in the Louvre. Gdańsk finally got the painting back, only to have it exiled again—this time into St. Petersburg's Hermitage Museum—after World War II. On its return to Gdańsk in 1956, this museum claimed it—though St. Mary's wants it back.

Have a close look at Memling's well-traveled work. It's the end of the world, and Christ rides in on a rainbow to judge humankind. Angels blow reveille, waking the dead, who rise from their graves. The winged archangel Michael—dressed for battle and wielding the cross like a weapon—weighs the grace in each person, sending them either to the fires of hell (right panel) or up the sparkling-crystal stairway to heaven (left).

It takes all 70 square feet of paneling to contain this awesome scene. Jam-packed with dozens of bodies and a Bible's worth of symbolism, and executed with astonishing detail, the painting can keep even a nonart lover occupied. Notice the serene, happy expressions of the righteous, as they're greeted by St. Peter (with his giant key) and clothed by angels. And pity the condemned, their faces filled with terror and sorrow as they're tortured by grotesque devils more horrifying than anything Hollywood could devise.

Tune in to the exquisite details: the angels' robes, the devils' genetic-mutant features, the portrait of the man in the scale (a Medici banker), Michael's peacock wings. Get as close as you can to the globe at Christ's feet and Michael's shining breastplate: You can just make out the whole scene in mirror reflection. Then back up and take it all in—three panels connected by a necklace of bodies that curves downward through hell, crosses the earth, then rises up to the towers of the New Jerusalem. On the back side of the triptych are reverent portraits of the painting's patron, Angelo Tani, and his new bride, Catarina.

Beyond the Memling, the remainder of the collection isn't too thrilling. The rest of the upstairs has more Flemish and Dutch art, as well as paintings from Gdańsk's Golden Age and various works by Polish artists. The ground floor features a cavernous, all-white cloister filled with Gothic altarpiece sculptures, gold and silver wares, majolica and Delft porcelain, and characteristic Gdańsk-style furniture.

Gdańsk Shakespeare Theater (Teatr Szekspirowski)

Gdańsk has a long and proud tradition of staging plays by Shakespeare. As early as the 17th century, theater troupes from England would come to this cosmopolitan trading city to perform. In 1993, local actors revived the tradition with an annual Gdańsk Shakespeare Festival. And in 2014, the city built the state-of-the-art Gdańsk Shakespeare Theater to honor its connection to the Bard.

The building's minimalist, black-brick, blocky architecture—with a few symbolic faux-buttresses to echo the gables of the surrounding buildings—was criticized for not blending in very well with its surroundings. But the celebration of theater that takes place inside is welcomed by all. The main theater can be modified to create three different types of performance spaces (proscenium, thrust stage, and theater in the round)—and even has a retractable roof to wash the actors with direct sunlight.

If you want to take a peek, the building is on ulica Zbytki—just follow Pcztowa street south from the middle of ulica Długa.

Tours and Performances: Theater lovers can take a one-hour guided tour of the building for 15 zł. Call or check their website for details on the tour and upcoming performances (tel. 58-351-0101, www.teatrszekspirowski.pl).

Shakespeare contributes only a tiny piece of the theater's full lineup—it plays host to a wide variety of performances and festivals throughout the year. You're most likely to find Shakespeare performed in English during the annual Shakespeare Festival, which is typically in the summer (www.shakespearefestival.pl).

"Blue Lamb" Archaeological Education Center (Centrum Edukacji Archeologicznej "Błękitny Baranek")

Hiding far from the Main Town, on Granary Island, this kid-friendly exhibit re-creates the atmosphere of medieval Gdańsk. Occupying a rebuilt granary called the "Blue Lamb," its highlight is a full-scale replica of an atmospheric medieval street, populated by mannequins whose features are based on actual human remains. Also telling the tale are artifacts from the period, a selection of films (subtitled in English), and touchscreens that provide some background. Though information is a bit sparse (especially along the medieval street), the collection tries hard not to be just another fuddy-duddy, dusty old museum, making it popular with kids on field trips.

Cost and Hours: 10 zł, Tue-Sun 10:00-17:00, July-Aug until 18:00, closed Mon year-round, ulica Chmielna 53, tel. 58-320-3188, www.archeologia.pl.

OUTER GDAŃSK

These two sights—worthwhile only to those with a particular interest in them—are each within the city limits of Gdańsk, but they take some serious time to see round-trip.

Oliwa Cathedral (Katedra Oliwska)

The suburb of Oliwa, at the northern edge of Gdańsk, is home to this visually striking church. The quirky, elongated facade hides a surprisingly long and skinny nave. The ornately decorated 18th-century organ over the main entrance features angels and stars that move around when the organ is played. While locals are proud of this place, it's hard to justify the effort it takes to get out here. Skip it unless you just love Polish churches or you're going to a concert.

Concerts: The animated organ performs its 20-minute show frequently, especially in summer (in high season, concerts at the top of most hours—confirm schedule online or at Gdańsk TI before making the trip, www.archikatedraoliwa.pl). Note that on Sundays and holidays, there are no concerts before 15:00.

Getting There: Oliwa is about six miles northwest of central Gdańsk, on the way to Sopot and Gdynia. To reach Oliwa from Gdańsk's main train station, you have two options: Ride **tram #6** or **#12**, get off at Oliwski Park, and walk a few minutes through the park to the church (about 30 minutes total); or take an **SKM commuter train** to the Gdańsk Oliwa stop (15 minutes), then walk 15 minutes (or take a 10-zł taxi ride) to Oliwski Park and the cathedral.

Westerplatte

World War II began on September 1, 1939, when Adolf Hitler sent the warship *Schleswig-Holstein* to attack this Polish munitions depot, which was guarding Gdańsk's harbor. Though it may give serious WWII history buffs goosebumps, most visitors will find little to see here aside from a modest museum, a towering monument, and some old bunkers.

Getting There: The most enjoyable approach is on a cruise—either on a modern boat, or on the fun old-fashioned galleons (45 minutes each way; see page 486). You can also take **bus #138** from the main train station (about 30 minutes).

Shopping in Gdańsk

The big story in Gdańsk is amber *(bursztyn)*, a fossil resin available in all shades, shapes, and sizes (see the "All About Amber" sidebar, earlier). While you'll see amber sold all over town, the best place to browse and buy is along the atmospheric ulica Mariacka (between the Motława River and St. Mary's Church). This pretty street, with old-fashioned balconies and dozens of display cases, is fun to wander even if you're not a shopper. Other good places to buy amber are along the riverfront embankment and on ulica Długa. To avoid rip-offs—such as amber that's been melted and reshaped—always buy it from a shop, not from someone standing on the street. (But note that most shops also have a display case and salesperson out front, which are perfectly legit.) Prices everywhere are about the same, so instead of seeking out a specific place, just window shop until you see what you want. Styles range from gaudy necklaces with huge globs of amber, to tasteful smaller pendants in silver settings, to cheap trinkets. All shades of amber—from near-white to dark brown—cost about the same, but you'll pay more for inclusions (bugs or other objects stuck in the amber).

Gdańsk also has several modern shopping malls, most of them in the Old Town or near the main train station. The walk between the Main Town and the Solidarity shipyard goes past some of the best malls (see page 456).

Sleeping in Gdańsk

The high season is generally May through September; at all these places, you'll pay a bit less in the off-season (Oct-April). Many hotels are booked up (mostly with German tourists) in peak season (mid-June-mid-Sept)—reserve ahead.

ACROSS THE RIVER

These hotels are across the river from the Main Town. That puts you a bit farther from the sightseeing action, but it's a relatively short walk (no more than 10 minutes from any of these).

$$$$ Hotel Podewils is the top choice for a friendly splurge. Filling a storybook-cute house from 1728, overlooking the marina and across the river from a fine panorama of the Gdańsk embankment, it's classy. The public spaces and 10 rooms have all the modern amenities, but with plush, almost Baroque, decor (air-con, Szafarnia 2, tel. 58-300-9560, www.podewils.pl, gdansk@podewils.pl).

$$ Hotel Królewski, in a beautifully renovated red-brick granary, offers 30 stylish rooms sitting right along the river, facing classic Gdańsk embankment views. It's just beyond the three granaries of the National Maritime Museum, across the river from the Crane. The Polish Baltic Philharmonic is right next door, so you may be serenaded by a rehearsal or performance (apartments, try asking for a view room for no extra charge, elevator, good restaurant, ulica Ołowianka 1, tel. 58-326-1111, www.hotelkrolewski.pl, office@hotelkrolewski.pl). To get into town, hop on the ferry across the river offered by the Maritime Museum; if it's not run-

Sleep Code

Hotels are classified based on the average price of a standard double room with breakfast in high season.

$$$$	**Splurge:** Most rooms over 550 zł
$$$	**Pricier:** 400-550 zł
$$	**Moderate:** 250-400 zł
$	**Budget:** 100-250 zł
¢	**Backpacker:** Under 100 zł
RS%	**Rick Steves discount**

Unless otherwise noted, credit cards are accepted, hotel staff speak basic English, and free Wi-Fi is available. Comparison-shop by checking prices at several hotels (on each hotel's own website, on a booking site, or by email). For the best deal, *book directly with the hotel.* Ask for a discount if paying in cash; if the listing includes **RS%,** request a Rick Steves discount.

ning, it's a scenic 15-minute walk along the river, past the marina, and over the bridge into the Main Town.

$$ Willa Litarion, run by the Owsikowski family, sits on the back side of a charmingly restored row of colorful houses on the island just across the river from the main drag. It's tall and skinny, with no elevator, and faces a gloomy parking lot, but it's a handy location at a decent price. Each of the 13 small rooms is different, but all are artsy and mod (pay parking garage, ulica Spichrzowa 18, tel. 58-320-2553, www.litarion.pl, recepcja@litarion.pl). Several other, similar (but less appealing) "villas" line this same street—if you're in a pinch for a room, this is a handy place to go ringing doorbells.

At the Academy of Music: Two places hide in the back of the big Academy of Music building (Akademia Muzyczna), a 10-minute walk from the sights in a nondescript residential neighborhood. They're difficult to find at first, but the prices are worth the hunt. **$$ Dom Muzyka** rents 87 simple, tidy rooms. Their "deluxe" rooms, mostly twins, are bigger and overlook the quiet courtyard; most of the standard rooms face a busy street but have good windows and air-conditioning (apartments, elevator, popular with tour groups, good restaurant, free and easy parking, ulica Łąkowa 1, tel. 58-326-0600, www.dommuzyka.pl, biuro@dommuzyka.pl). In the same complex, **$ Dom Sonata** is a tempting budget option. Its 60 rooms—nearly as nice as at Dom Muzyka, but with fewer hotelesque amenities—house students for most of the year, but are rented out to tourists from July through September (breakfast extra, air-con, elevator, ulica Łąkowa 1, tel. 58-300-9260, www.domsonata.com.pl, domsonata@amuz.gda.pl). To get here from the Main Town's Green Gate, cross the two bridges, then walk a long block along the modern commercial building, and turn right just before the park (on Łąkowa, across from the big brick church). Walk to the end of this block, and before the busy road, go through the gate just before the big yellow-brick building on the right. Once inside the gate checkpoint, the hotel is around the back of the yellow building, the door farthest down. If you get lost, just ask people, "Hotel?"

IN THE MAIN TOWN

The Main Town is convenient for sightseeing, but can come with nighttime noise—particularly in summer, when loud bars and discos keep things lively. Request a quiet room...and pack earplugs.

$$$ Hotel Wolne Miasto ("Free City") offers rich, wood-carved public spaces with photos of old Gdańsk and 68 elegant rooms on the edge of the Main Town, just two blocks from the main drag. It's above a popular disco that gets noisy on weekends (Thu-Sat nights), so it's especially important to request a quieter room when you reserve (elevator, ulica Świętego Ducha 2, tel. 58-322-2442, www.hotelwm.pl, rezerwacja@hotelwm.pl).

$$$ Hotel Admirał is simply practical: a big, impersonal, business-class place with 44 nicely decorated rooms tucked in a quiet residential alley at the north end of the embankment, just a few steps off the old fish market. Their rates are soft, so this place is worth considering if you can get a good deal (air-con, elevator, Tobiasza 9, tel. 58-320-0320, www.admiralhotel.pl, recepcja@admiralhotel.pl).

$$ Gotyk House, a good value, is run with warmth and pride by the Rybicki family. Owner Andrzej is an energetic armchair historian who works hard to make his little hotel comfortable while still respecting the sanctity of what's supposedly Gdańsk's oldest house. The chimes from St. Mary's Church, next door, provide a pleasant soundtrack. The cellar houses a minuscule gingerbread museum and small shrine to Copernicus (whose longtime lover may have lived here). The seven straightforward rooms share a tiny breakfast room, so you'll have to tell them what time you'd like to eat (tight public spaces, ulica Mariacka 1, tel. 58-301-8567, mobile 516-141-133, www.gotykhouse.eu, reservation@gotykhouse.eu).

$$ Aparthotel Neptun lacks personality, but owns a great location—on a slightly dreary side street between delightful Mariacka and bustling Długi Targ ("Long Square"). While it's just a few steps to most of the town's big sights, it's just far enough away to avoid the crowds and the weekend noise. The 30 rooms and apartments are modern, efficient, well-equipped, and forgettable...but well-priced for the central location (breakfast extra, elevator, Grzaska 1, mobile 604-466-466, www.aparthotelgdansk.com, info@aparthotelgdansk.com).

¢-$$ Stay Inn, a self-declared "hostel with vibe," is fresh and young, but still feels practical. The location couldn't be more central—facing the side of St. Mary's Church, right in the heart of the Main Town—and though the street it's on is quieter than most, a downstairs pub can be noisy on weekends. It combines 29 beds in small 5- to 8-bed dorms with 10 private rooms that are as hotelesque as any in this price range. The dorm dwellers and fancier folks alike share the same kitchen/lounge/breakfast room. Everything feels tidy and well-designed; it lacks the grungy party personality of some hostels, so it's well worth considering even for nonhostelers (elevator, bike rental, Piwna 28, tel. 58-354-1543, www.stayinngdansk.com, booking@stayinngdansk.com).

GDAŃSK & THE TRI-CITY

Eating in Gdańsk

In addition to traditional Polish fare, Gdańsk has some excellent Baltic seafood. Herring *(śledź)* is popular here, as is cod *(dorsz)*. Natives brag that their salmon *(łosoś)* is better than Norway's. For a stiff drink, sample *Goldwasser* (similar to Goldschlager). This sweet and strong liqueur, flecked with actual gold, was supposedly invented here in Gdańsk. The following options are all in the Main Town, within three blocks of the Royal Way.

BUDGET RESTAURANTS IN THE CITY CENTER

These places are affordable, tasty, quick, and wonderfully convenient—on or very near the Royal Way (ulica Długa). They're worth considering even if you're not on a tight budget.

$ Bar pod Rybą ("Under the Fish") is nirvana for fans of baked potatoes *(pieczony ziemniak)*. They offer more than 20 varieties, piled high with a wide variety of toppings and sauces, from Mexican beef to herring to Polish cheeses. They also serve fish dishes with salad and potatoes, making this a cheap place to sample local seafood. The tasteful decor—walls lined with old bottles, antique wooden hangers, and old street signs—is squeezed into a single cozy room packed with happy eaters. In the summer, order inside, and they'll bring your food to you at an outdoor table (daily 10:00-22:00, ulica Piwna 61, tel. 58-305-1307).

$ Bar Mleczny Neptun is your handiest milk-bar option in the Main Town. A hearty meal, including a drink, runs about $5. This popular place has outdoor seating along the most scenic stretch of the main drag, and an upstairs dining room overlooking it all. The items on the counter are for display—point to what you want, and they'll dish it up fresh (Mon-Fri 7:30-19:30, Sat-Sun 10:00-19:00, may have shorter hours off-season, free Wi-Fi, ulica Długa 33, tel. 58-301-4988). For more on milk bars, see page 228.

$ Pijalnia Wódki i Piwa, part of a popular Polish chain, hides half a block behind the Hard Rock Café (on Kuśnierska). This little

GDAŃSK & THE TRI-CITY

Gdańsk Hotels & Restaurants

Accommodations
1. Hotel Podewils
2. Hotel Królewski
3. Willa Litarion
4. Dom Muzyka & Dom Sonata Hotels
5. Hotel Wolne Miasto
6. Hotel Admiral
7. Gotyk House
8. Aparthotel Neptun
9. Stay Inn

Eateries
10. Bar pod Rybą
11. Bar Mleczny Neptun
12. Pijalnia Wódki i Piwa
13. Bar Turystyczny
14. Baryłka, Kamienica Goldwasser & Sushi 77
15. Lao Thai
16. Targ Rybny/Fischmarkt
17. Restauracja Kubicki

Other
18. Galeon Lew & Czerna Perła Boats to Westerplatte
19. Żegluga Gdańska Boats to Westerplatte
20. ZTM "Ferry Trams" to Hel & Sopot

> ## Restaurant Price Code
>
> I've assigned each eatery a price category, based on the aver-
> age cost of a typical main course. Drinks, desserts, and splurge
> items (steak and seafood) can raise the price considerably.
>
> **$$$$** **Splurge:** Most main courses over 60 zł
> **$$$** **Pricier:** 45-60 zł
> **$$** **Moderate:** 25-45 zł
> **$** **Budget:** Under 25 zł
>
> In Poland, a milk bar or takeout spot is **$**; a basic sit-down eat-
> ery is **$$**; a casual but more upscale restaurant is **$$$**; and a
> swanky splurge is **$$$$**.

vodka-and-herring bar takes you back to the 1970s. Pop in to study
the retro decor: ads from the 1970s and photos of the lines that
people routinely endured. The place is literally wallpapered with
pages from the "Tribune of the Masses" newspaper infamous for its
propaganda that passed for news. They play pop hits from the last
years of communism. The menu is fun, accessible, and simple: 4 zł
for vodka or other drinks, and 8 zł for herring or other bar nibbles
(open daily 9:00-late).

$ Bar Turystyczny is misnamed—not just for tourists, it has
become beloved by locals as the central area's favorite milk bar.
Easy to miss on the way between the Main Town and the Solidarity sights, it's always jammed (Mon-Fri 8:00-18:00, Sat-Sun 9:00-
17:00, Szeroka 8, tel. 58/301-6013).

ON THE RIVERFRONT EMBANKMENT

Perhaps the most appealing dining zone in Gdańsk stretches along
the riverfront embankment near the Crane. On a balmy summer
evening, the outdoor tables here are
enticing. This area is popular—consider scouting a table during your
sightseeing, and reserve your choice
for dinner later that night. While
these places are mostly interchangeable, I've listed a few to consider, in
the order you'll reach them as you
walk north along the embankment.

$$ Baryłka ("Barrel") is a sim-
pler, more affordable alternative to
some of the pricier places along here. While the outdoor seat-
ing is enticing, the elegant upstairs dining room, with windows
overlooking the river, is also appealing (daily 9:00-24:00, Długie
Pobrzeże 24, tel. 58-301-4938).

$$$$ Kamienica Goldwasser offers high-quality Polish and international cuisine. Choose between cozy, romantic indoor seating on several levels, or scenic outdoor seating (daily 10:00-24:00, occasional live music, Długie Pobrzeże 22, tel. 58-301-8878).

$$$ Sushi 77, serving up a wide selection of surprisingly good sushi right next to the Crane, is a refreshing break from ye olde Polish food. Choose between the outdoor tables bathed in red light, or the mod interior (daily 12:00-23:00, Długie Pobrzeże 30, tel. 58-682-1823).

Past the Crane

About 100 yards past the Crane, near the old fish market (Targ Rybny), cluster several more options.

$$ Lao Thai is a modern space right along the embankment, selling surprisingly high-quality, yet still affordable, Thai cuisine (daily 12:00-22:00, ulica Targ Rybny 11, tel. 58/305-2525).

$$$ Targ Rybny/Fischmarkt ("The Fish Market") has less appealing outdoor seating that overlooks a park and parking lot. But the warm, mellow-yellow nautical ambience inside is pleasant, making this a good bad-weather option. It features classy but not stuffy service, and an emphasis on fish (daily 10:00-23:00, ulica Targ Rybny 6C, tel. 58-320-9011).

$$ Restauracja Kubicki, along the water just past the Hilton, has a long history (since 1918), but a recent remodel has kept the atmosphere—and its food—feeling fresh. This is a good choice for high-quality Polish and international cuisine in a fun, sophisticated-but-not-stuffy interior that's a clever mix of old and new (daily 12:00-23:00, Wartka 5, tel. 58-301-0050).

Gdańsk Connections

BY TRAIN

Gdańsk is well-connected to the Tri-City via the commuter SKM trains (explained later, under "Getting Around the Tri-City"). It's also connected to Warsaw and Kraków by the high-speed EIC line (which requires reservations). Given the distance between Gdańsk and other Polish destinations, also consider domestic flights: LOT has easy flights between Gdańsk and Kraków or Warsaw for about the same price as a train ticket.

From Gdańsk by Train to: Hel (town on Hel Peninsula, 3/day direct July-Aug only, 2 hours; otherwise about hourly with change in Gdynia), **Malbork** (2/hour, about half are express EIC trains that take 30 minutes, the rest are slower regional trains that take around 45 minutes), **Toruń** (4/day direct, 2.5 hours; more with a change in Bydgoszcz, 3 hours), **Warsaw** (hourly, 3 hours on express EIC train), **Kraków** (6/day direct, 5.5 hours, 1 more with change in

Warsaw; plus 10-hour night train), **Berlin** (1/day direct, 6 hours; 3/day, 7.5 hours, change in Poznań.

BY BOAT

Various boats depart from Gdańsk's embankment to nearby destinations, including **Westerplatte** (the monument marking where World War II started) and **Hel** (the beachy peninsula, described below). While boats also run sporadically to Sopot and Gdynia, the train is better for those trips (described under "Getting Around the Tri-City," later). As these boat schedules tend to change from year to year, confirm your plans carefully at the TI. All boat trips are weather permitting, especially the faster hydrofoils. In shoulder season (April-June and Sept-Oct), even though most boats stop running from Gdańsk, several routes still run between Sopot, Gdynia, and Hel. Boats generally don't run in winter (Nov-March).

To Westerplatte: To travel by boat to the monument at Westerplatte, you have three options. The most enjoyable one is to ride the replica **17th-century galleons,** either the *Galeon Lew* ("Lion Galleon") or the *Czarna Perła* ("Black Pearl"). These over-the-top, touristy boats depart hourly from the embankment just outside the Green Gate for a lazy 1.5-hour round-trip cruise to Westerplatte and back. (You can choose to get off at Westerplatte and take a later boat

back.) Both of them have English commentary on the way there and live nautical music on the return trip (if you've ever wanted to hear "What Shall We Do with a Drunken Sailor?" in Polish, here's your chance). It's not exactly pretty—you'll see more industry than scenery—but it's a fun excuse to set sail, even if you don't care about Westerplatte (40 zł round-trip, 30 zł one-way, the two boats take turns departing at the top of each hour 10:00-19:00 in July-Aug, fewer departures May-June and Sept, from the embankment near the Crane, mobile 601-629-191, www.galeony.pl). Two other, duller alternatives leave from right nearby: big, modern **Żegluga Gdańska** boats (www.zegluga.pl); or much cheaper but less frequent city-run **ZTM "ferry trams"** *(tramwaj wodny),* which depart from the embankment on the south side of the bridge (3-4/day).

To Hel: Various boats zip out to Hel in two hours during the summer. Though the specifics change from year to year, this route is most likely run by Żegluga Gdańska (May-June weekends only, July-Aug 3/day, 35 zł each way, www.zegluga.pl).

BY CRUISE SHIP

A few cruise ships (under 800 passengers) dock in **Gdańsk,** near the Westerplatte monument (described earlier; connected to the center by 45-minute pleasure-boat trip or 30-minute ride on bus #138). But most cruises advertising a stop in Gdańsk actually dock in the nearby town of **Gdynia.** For details on this town—and what to do if you arrive there—see page 491.

The Tri-City (Trójmiasto)

Gdańsk is the anchor of the three-part metropolitan region known as the Tri-City (Trójmiasto). The other two parts are as different as night and day: Sopot, a swanky resort town, and Gdynia, a practical, nose-to-the-grindstone business center. The Tri-City as a whole is home to bustling industry and a sprawling university, with several campuses and plenty of well-dressed, English-speaking students. Beyond the Tri-City, the long, skinny Hel Peninsula—a sparsely populated strip of fishing villages and fun-loving beaches—arches dramatically into the Baltic Sea.

Sopot—boasting sandy beaches, tons of tourists, and a certain elegance—is clearly the most appealing day-trip option. Gdynia offers a glimpse into workaday Poland, but leaves most visitors cold. Hel, which requires the better part of a day to visit, is worthwhile only if you've got perfect summer weather and a desire to lie on the beach.

GETTING AROUND THE TRI-CITY

Gdańsk, Sopot, and Gdynia are connected by regional commuter trains (*kolejka*, operated by SKM) as well as by trains of Poland's national railway (operated by PKP). Tickets for one system can't be used on the other. While trains for the two systems chug along the same tracks, they use different (but nearby) platforms/stations. For example, in Sopot, the SKM station is a few hundred feet before the PKP station. Regional SKM trains are much more frequent than long-distance PKP trains—they go in each direction about every 10-15 minutes (less frequently after 19:30). Trains to Hel are always operated by PKP.

In Gdańsk, two SKM train stations flank the major sights: the main train station ("Gdańsk Główny" on schedules, platforms 3-5) and, a few blocks south, Gdańsk Śródmieście (in the middle of the busy street in front of the National Museum). Buy tickets at the machine marked *SKM Bilety* (English instructions). Prices are based on the distance but are typically cheap (figure 6 zł one-way for the 35-minute trip from Gdańsk to Gdynia). Tickets purchased

Gdańsk Day Trips

from a machine come already validated, but if you buy one from a kiosk, you'll need to stamp it in the easy-to-miss yellow slots under the boards with SKM information.

Each city has multiple stops. Remember, in Gdańsk, use either Gdańsk Główny (the main station) or Gdańsk Śródmieście; for Sopot, use the stop called simply Sopot; and for Gdynia, it's Gdynia Główna (the main station).

For a more romantic—and much slower—approach, consider the boat (see "Gdańsk Connections," earlier).

Sopot

Sopot (SOH-poht), dubbed the "Nice of the North," was a celebrated haunt of beautiful people during the 1920s and 1930s, and it remains a popular beach getaway to this day.

Sopot was created in the early 19th century by Napoleon's doctor, Jean Georges Haffner, who believed Baltic Sea water to be therapeutic. By the 1890s, it had become a fashionable seaside resort. This gambling center boasted enough high-roller casinos to garner comparisons to Monte Carlo.

The casinos are gone, but the health resorts remain, and you'll still see more well-dressed people here per capita than just about anywhere else in the country. While it's not quite Cannes, Sopot feels relatively high class, which is unusual in otherwise unpretentious Poland. But even so, a childlike spirit of summer-vacation fun pervades this St-Tropez-on-the-Baltic, making it an all-around enjoyable place.

You can get the gist of Sopot in just a couple of hours. Zip in on the train, follow the main drag to the sea, wander the pier, get your feet wet at the beach, then head back to Gdańsk. Why not come here in the late afternoon, enjoy those last few rays of sunshine, stay for dinner, then take a twilight stroll on the pier?

Orientation to Sopot

The main pedestrian drag, Monte Cassino Heroes street (ulica Bohaterów Monte Cassino), leads to the Molo, the longest pleasure pier in Europe. From the Molo, a broad, sandy beach stretches in each direction. Running parallel to the surf is a tree-lined, people-filled path made for strolling.

Tourist Information: The TI is near the base of the Molo at Plac Zdrojowy 2 (daily 10:00-18:00, mobile 790-280-884, www.sopot.pl).

Arrival in Sopot: From the SKM station, exit to the left and walk down the street. After a block, you'll see the PKP train station on your left. Continue on to the can't-miss-it main drag, ulica Bohaterów Monte Cassino (marked by the big red-brick church steeple). Follow it to the right, down to the seaside.

Sights in Sopot

▲Monte Cassino Heroes Street (Ulica Bohaterów Monte Cassino)

Nicknamed "Monciak" (MOHN-chak) by locals, this in-love-with-life promenade may well be Poland's most manicured street (and is named in honor of the Polish soldiers who helped the Allies pry Italy's Monte Cassino monastery from Nazi forces during World War II). Especially after all the suburban and industrial dreck you passed through to get here, it's easy to be charmed by this pretty drag. The street is lined with happy tourists, trendy cafés, al fresco restaurants, movie theaters, and late-19th-century facades (known for their wooden balconies).

The most popular building along here (on the left, about half-way down) is the so-called **Crooked House** (Krzywy Domek), a trippy, Gaudí-inspired building that looks like it's melting. Hard-partying Poles prefer to call it the "Drunken House," and say that when it looks straight, it's time to stop drinking.

Molo (Pier)

At more than 1,600 feet long, this is Europe's longest wooden entertainment pier. While you won't find any amusement-park rides, you will be surrounded by vendors, artists, and Poles having the time of their lives. Buy a *gofry* (Belgian waffle topped with whipped cream and fruit) or an oversized cloud of *wata cukrowa* (cotton candy), grab your partner's hand, and stroll with gusto (7.50 zł, free Oct-April, open long hours daily, www.molo.sopot.pl).

Climb to the top of the Art Nouveau lighthouse for a waterfront panorama. Scan the horizon for sailboats and tankers. Any pirate ships? For a jarring reality check, look over to Gdańsk. Barely visible from the Molo are two of the most important sites in 20th-century history: the towering monument at Westerplatte, where World War II started, and the cranes rising up from the Gdańsk Shipyard, where Solidarity was born and European communism began its long goodbye.

In spring and fall, the Molo is a favorite venue for pole vaulting—or is that Pole vaulting?

The Beach

Yes, Poland has beaches. Nice ones. When I heard Sopot compared to places like Nice, I'll admit that I scoffed. But when I saw those stretches of inviting sand as far as the eye can see, I wished I'd packed my swim trunks. (You could walk from Gdańsk all the way to Gdynia on beaches like this.) The sand is finer than anything I've seen in Croatia...though the water's not exactly crystal-clear. Most of the beach is public, except for a small private stretch in front of the Grand Hotel Sopot. Year-round, it's crammed with locals. At these northern latitudes, the season for bathing is brief and crowded.

Overlooking the beach next to the Molo is the **Grand Hotel Sopot.** It was renovated to top-class status just recently, but its history goes way back. They could charge admission for room #226, a multiroom suite that has hosted the likes of Adolf Hitler, Marlene Dietrich, and Fidel Castro (but not all at the same time). With all the trappings of Sopot's belle époque—dark wood, plush upholstery, antique furniture—this room had me imagining Hitler sitting at the desk, looking out to sea, and plotting the course of World War II.

Gdynia

Compared to its flashier sister cities, straightforward Gdynia (guh-DIN-yah) has retained a more working-class vibe, still in touch with its salty, fishing-village roots. Gdynia is less historic than Gdańsk or Sopot, as it was mostly built in the 1920s to be Poland's main harbor after Gdańsk became a free city. Although nowhere as attractive as Gdańsk or Sopot, Gdynia has an authentic feel and a lovely waterfront promenade (www.gdynia.pl).

Gdynia is a major business center, and—thanks to its youthful, progressive city government—has edged ahead of the rest of Poland in transitioning from communism. It enjoys one of the highest income levels in the country. Many of the crumbling downtown buildings have been renovated, and Gdynia is becoming known for its top-tier shopping—all the big designers have boutiques here. If a local woman has been shopping on Świętojańska street in Gdynia, it means that she's got some serious zloty.

Because Gdańsk's port is relatively shallow, the biggest cruise ships must put in at Gdynia...leaving confused tourists to poke around town looking for some medieval quaintness, before coming to their senses and heading for Gdańsk. Gdynia is also home to a major military harbor and an important NATO base.

To get a taste of Gdynia, take the SKM train to the Gdynia Główna station, follow signs to *wyjście do miasta,* cross the busy street, and walk 15 minutes down Starowiejska. When you come to the intersection with the broad Świętojańska street, turn right (in the direction the big statue is looking) and walk two blocks to the tree-lined park on the left. Head through the park to the Southern Pier (Molo Południowe). This concrete slab—not at all as charming as Sopot's wooden-boardwalk version—features a modern shopping mall and a smattering of sights, including an aquarium and a pair of permanently moored museum boats.

The big sightseeing draw in Gdynia is at the fairly distant Nabrzeże Francuskie (French Quay, where cruise ships arrive—handy for cruisers but a taxi ride away for tourists coming on the train). Here you'll find the new **Emigration Museum,** telling the story of Poles who left through Gdynia to find a better life in the New World. High-tech, interactive exhibits help bring the story to life (10 zł, Tue 12:00-20:00, Wed-Sun 10:00-18:00, closed Mon, www.polska1.pl). To get here, you can ride bus #119, #133, #137, or #147 from along Władysława IV avenue (between the train station and the waterfront) to the Dworzec Morski/Muzeum Emigracji stop.

ARRIVING BY CRUISE IN GDYNIA

Many Northern European cruises include a stop at "Gdańsk"; most of these actually put in at Gdynia's sprawling port. And, while Gydnia's town center is relatively manicured and pleasant, its port area is the opposite—like a Soviet Bloc bodybuilder, it's muscular and hairy. Cruise ships are shuffled among hardworking industrial piers that make the area feel uninviting. Three of the port's many piers are used for cruises: Most ships—especially large ones—dock at **Nabrzeże Francuskie** (French Quay). Some smaller ships may use the distant **Nabrzeże Stanów Zjednoczonych** (United States Quay) or the very central **Nabrzeże Pomorskie** (Pomeranian Quay, part of the Southern Pier, an easy walk from the center). Port information: www.port.gdynia.pl.

Unfortunately, there are no **ATMs** or money-exchange options at or near the cruise-ship berths, but cash machines are plentiful in downtown Gdynia.

To get from your cruise ship to Gdańsk, the best option is a **shuttle bus-plus-train connection.** First, ride your cruise line's shuttle bus into downtown Gdynia (5-minute trip; price depends on the cruise line). The shuttle drops you off at Skwer Kościuski; from here, it's a 10-minute walk (gradually uphill) to the train station. Start by walking away from the water on the broad, parklike boulevard. After the street becomes ulica 10 Lutego (you'll pass the TI on your right), it curves to the right; once you're around the corner, use the crosswalk to reach the train station (marked *Dworzec Podmiejski*). From here you can ride the handy *kolejka* commuter train into Gdańsk (runs every 10-15 minutes, 35 minutes; for details on this train, see "Getting Around the Tri-City," earlier). You can either get off at the Gdańsk Główny stop (main train station—see "Arrival in Gdańsk—By Train," on page 436), or stay on one more stop to Gdańsk Śródmieście (a slightly shorter walk to the start of my self-guided walk). Returning on the train, you want the Gdynia Główna stop.

Taxi drivers line up to meet arriving cruise ships. Cabbies here tend to overcharge, but if they use the meter, these are the legitimate rates: 20 zł to Gdynia's train station (*Dworzec*, DVOH-zhets); 125 zł to Gdańsk's Main Town; and 60-80 zł to Sopot. Taxi drivers generally take euros, though their off-the-cuff exchange rate may not be favorable.

For more details on Gdynia's port—and several others on the Baltic, North Sea, and beyond—pick up the *Rick Steves Northern European Cruise Ports* guidebook.

Hel Peninsula (Mierzeja Helska)

Out on the edge of things, this slender peninsula juts 20 miles into the ocean, providing a sunny retreat from the big cities—even as it shelters them from Baltic winds. Trees line the peninsula, and the northern edge is one long, sandy, ever-shifting beach.

On hot summer days, Hel is a great place to frolic in the sun with Poles. Sunbathing and windsurfing are practically religions here. Small resort villages line Hel Peninsula: Władysławowo (at the base), Chałupy, Kuźnica, Jastarnia, Jurata, and—at the tip—a town also called Hel. Beaches right near the towns can be crowded in peak season, but you're never more than a short walk away from your own stretch of sand. There are few permanent residents, and the waterfront is shared by budget campgrounds, hotels hosting middle-class families, and mansions of Poland's rich and famous (former president Aleksander Kwaśniewski has a summer home here).

The easiest way to go to Hel—aside from coveting thy neighbor's wife—is by boat (see "Gdańsk Connections," earlier). Trains from Gdańsk also reach Hel (summer only), and from Gdynia, you can take a train, bus, or minibus. But overland transit is crowded and slow—especially in summer, when Hel is notorious for its hellish traffic jams.

POMERANIA

Malbork Castle • Toruń

The northwestern part of Poland—known as Pomerania (Pomorze)—has nothing to do with excitable little dogs, but it does offer two attractions worth singling out. Malbork, the biggest Gothic castle in Europe, is one of the best castles in Eastern Europe. Farther south, the Gothic town of Toruń—the birthplace of Copernicus, and a favorite spot of every proud Pole—holds hundreds of red-brick buildings...and, it seems, even more varieties of tasty gingerbread.

PLANNING YOUR TIME

Malbork works well as a side-trip from Gdańsk (frequent trains, 30-45 minutes each way), and it's also on the main train line from Gdańsk to Warsaw. While Toruń doesn't merit a long detour, it's worth a stroll or an overnight if you want to sample a smaller Polish city. Unfortunately, Toruń is on a different train line than Malbork—if you visit both in one day, it'll be a very long one. Ideally, if traveling round-trip from Warsaw, see one of these destinations coming to Gdańsk, and visit the other on the way back. Or do Malbork as a side-trip from Gdańsk, then visit Toruń on the way to or from Warsaw.

Malbork Castle

Malbork Castle is soaked in history. The biggest brick castle in the world, the largest castle of the Gothic period, and one of Europe's most imposing fortresses, it sits smugly on a marshy plain at the edge of the town of Malbork, 35 miles southeast of Gdańsk. This was the headquarters of the notorious Teutonic Knights, a Germanic band of ex-Crusaders who dominated northern Poland in the Middle Ages.

GETTING THERE

Malbork is on the train line between Gdańsk and Warsaw. Coming by train from Gdańsk, you'll enjoy views of the castle on your right as you cross the Nogat River. Store your luggage at the station's lockers and head into town.

To get from the station to the castle, consider taking a **taxi** (shouldn't cost more than about 10 zł, though corrupt cabbies charge twice that—ask for an estimate before you get in). Or you can **walk** 15 minutes to the castle: Leave the station to the right, walk straight, and go through the pedestrian underpass beneath the busy road (by the red staircase). When you emerge on the other side, follow the busy road (noticing peek-a-boo views on your right of the castle's main tower) and take your first right turn (onto Kościuszki, the main shopping street). On Kościuszki, you'll pass the fancy pink building housing the TI on the right. Near the bottom of Kościuszki, at the fountain and the McDonald's, jog right, then bear left over two moats to find the ticket office (marked *kasa*).

ORIENTATION TO MALBORK CASTLE

Cost and Hours: Mid-April-Sept—40 zł, open Tue-Sun 9:00-19:00; Oct-mid-April—30 zł, open Tue-Sun 10:00-15:00; closed Mon year-round; grounds stay open an hour later than the castle; tel. 55-647-0978, www.zamek.malbork.pl.

Tours: You are technically required to enter the castle with a three-hour **guided tour** or an audioguide, but this is rarely enforced—you can usually just walk in. (If they do enforce this rule, simply enter with a Polish group—tours leave from the ticket booth every 15 minutes—and split off on your own once inside.) My self-guided tour covers the basics.

Your ticket includes a good **audioguide**, but supply is limited—they often run out during peak times (11:00-15:00). Try to get one if you can—it lets you wander aimlessly through this fascinating place, keying in *audio-tour stop* numbers as you explore.

In the summer, ask about free **English tours** (often 2-3/

day). Any time of year, you can pay 210 zł for a private English tour (book a few days ahead, tel. 55-647-0978, kasa@zamek. malbork.pl). If you show up and there's no scheduled English tour, ask whether an English-speaking guide is available. Then take the initiative, play "tour organizer," and gather a group of frustrated English speakers to split the cost of a private tour.

Eating: Several cheap food stands cluster outside the castle (by the river). For a meal inside the castle complex, the **$$$ Gothic Café,** under the stairs to the armory in the Middle Castle, is a serious restaurant with a renowned chef. Dishing up traditional Polish food inspired by old dishes once served here, it's handy for its lunch deal that includes a main dish and soup. You can eat in the busy cellar or out in the garden (tel. 55-647-0889, www.gothic.com.pl).

Best Views: The views of massive Malbork are stunning—especially at sunset, when its red brick glows. Be sure to walk out across the footbridge over the Nogat River. The most scenic part of the castle is probably the twin-turreted, riverside Bridge Gate, which used to be connected by a bridge to the opposite bank.

BACKGROUND

When the Teutonic Knights were invited to Polish lands in the 13th century to convert neighboring pagans, they found the perfect site for their new capital here, on the bank of the Nogat River. Construction began in 1274. After the Teutonic Knights conquered Gdańsk in 1308, the order moved its official headquarters from Venice to Malbork, where they remained for nearly 150 years. They called the castle Marienburg, the "Castle of Mary," in honor of the order's patron saint.

At its peak in the early 1400s, Malbork was both the imposing home of a seemingly unstoppable army and Europe's final bastion of chivalric ideals. Surrounded by swamplands, with only one gate in need of defense, it was a tough nut to crack. Malbork Castle was never taken by force in the Middle Ages, though it had to withstand various sieges by the Poles during the Thirteen Years' War (1454-1466)—including a campaign that lasted more than three years. Finally, in 1457, the Polish king gained control of Malbork by buying off Czech mercenaries guarding the castle. Malbork became a Polish royal residence for 300 years. But when Poland was partitioned in the late 18th century, this region went back into

German hands. The castle became a barracks, windows were sealed up, delicate vaulting was damaged, bricks were quarried for new buildings, and Malbork deteriorated.

In the late 19th century, Romantic German artists and poets rediscovered the place. An architect named Konrad Steinbrecht devoted 40 years of his life to Malbork, painstakingly restoring the palace to its medieval splendor. A half-century later, the Nazis used the castle to house POWs. Hitler—who, like many Germans, had a soft spot for Malbork's history—gave the order to defend it to the last man. About half of it was destroyed by the Soviet army, who saw it as a symbol of long-standing German domination. But it was restored once again, and today Malbork has been returned to its Teutonic glory.

◉ SELF-GUIDED TOUR

The official tour of Malbork lasts about three hours. While there's plenty to see, my self-guided tour shows you the highlights at your own pace. Use the map on the next page to navigate and jump around as needed. The castle complex is a bit of a maze, with various entrances and exits for each room, often behind closed (but unlocked) doors. Don't be shy about grabbing a medieval doorknob and letting yourself in.

Lower Castle and Entrance Gate

Just past the ticket taker, step through the front gate and stand on the castle's drawbridge. Look up at one of Europe's most intimidating fortresses—home to the Grand Master, monks, and knights of the Teutonic Order.

Above the door to the brick gate is a sculpture of the Virgin Mary with Baby Jesus...next to a shield and helmet. The two messages to visitors: This castle is protected by Mary, and the Teutonic Knights are here to convert pagans—by force, if necessary.

From the drawbridge, look right to observe the formidable fortifications. The rooster-capped tower (which contains a toilet) is connected by a sky bridge to the fancy Gothic 14th-century facade of the brick infirmary—kept at a distance for disease control.

Pass through the gate, into the entry area. Imagine the gate behind you closing. Look up to see wooden chutes where archers are preparing to rain arrows down on you. Your last thought: Maybe we should have left the Teutonic Knights alone, after all.

Before you're pierced by arrows, read the castle's history in its walls: The foundation is made of huge stones brought from Sweden, which are rare in these marshy lands. But most of the castle, like so many other buildings in northern Poland, was built with handmade red brick. Throughout the castle, the darker-colored, rougher brick is original, and the lighter-colored, smoother brick

Malbork Castle

1 Amber Collection (downstairs)
2 Armory (upstairs) & Gothic Café (downstairs)
3 "Boiler Room" (downstairs) & Grand Refectory (upstairs)
4 Grand Master's Palace
5 Grand Master Statues
6 Well
7 Dansker Tower
8 St. Mary's Church

was used during later restorations (in the 19th century, and again after World War II). Marvel at the ironclad doors and the heavy portcullis.

Venture through two more enclosed spaces, watching for the holes in the wall (for more guards and soldiers). The Teutonic Knights connected nearby lakes to create a system of canals, forming a moat around the castle that could be crossed only by this drawbridge. Ponder the fact that you have to go through five separate, well-defended gates to reach the...

Middle Castle (Zamek Średni)

This part of Malbork, built at an uphill incline to make it even more imposing, was designed to impress. Knights and monks lived here.

Let's get oriented: To your left is the east wing, where visiting monks would sleep. Today this houses the Amber Collection (ground floor) and the armory (upstairs). To the right (west) as you enter the main courtyard is the Grand Refectory (closer to the entrance) and the Grand Master's Palace (the taller, squarer building at the far end).

• Before we move on, this is a good time to read up on the history of the Teutonic Knights (see sidebar). When you're ready to continue, enter the ground floor of the building on the left (at audio-tour stop #15; remember, don't be shy about opening closed doors), and visit the...

Amber Collection

This exhibit will make jewelry shoppers salivate. For a primer, read the "All About Amber" sidebar on page 458. You'll start 42 million years ago and follow the story of amber. Begin at the huge chunks of raw amber and the illuminated display of inclusions (bugs and other organic objects stuck in the amber, à la *Jurassic Park*). Some of the ancient amber artifacts displayed here are up to 3,000 years old. These were found in graves, put there by people who thought amber would help the deceased enter a better world. Wandering the hall, you'll see all manner of amber creations: boxes, brooches, necklaces, chess sets, pipes, miniature ships, wine glasses, and belts for skinny-waisted, fashion-conscious women. Look for two truly exquisite pieces: a small casket and an altar. Many of the finely decorated jewelry boxes and chests have ivory, silver, or shell inlays—better for contrast than gold. The portable religious shrines and altars allowed travelers to remain reverent on the road and still pack light. Find the amber crucifix. This is a small replica of a six-foot-tall amber and silver cross, presented to St. John Paul II by the people of Gdańsk. Another exhibit case contains necklaces displaying the full range of amber colors, from opaque white at the top, to transparent yellow in the middle, to virtually black at the bottom.

• *Go back outside and turn left, to the wooden staircase above the recommended Gothic Café. Go up that staircase, and several more inside, to the top-floor...*

Armory

This is a small armory for such a massive castle. In its two rooms you'll see an impressive array of swords, armor, and other armaments. Look for the 600-year-old "hand-and-a-half" swords—too big to be held in one hand. At the end, in the display of cannons, pikes, and spears, find the giant shield. These shields could be lined up to form a portable "wall" to protect the knights. Downstairs, the suit of armor from the Hussars—Polish horseback knights—came with wings, which created a terrifying sound when the horses were galloping.

• *Head back outside (noticing the handy and rare WC straight ahead). Cross the main courtyard going downhill and enter the smaller courtyard through the passage next to the stubby, dark-wood-topped tower. Find the dark, steep, and unlabeled steps down into the...*

"Boiler Room"

The Teutonic Knights had a surprisingly sophisticated method for heating this huge complex. You see a furnace down below and a holding area for hot rocks above. The radiant heat given off by the rocks spread through the vents without also filling them with smoke (illustrated by a chart on the wall). This is one of 11 such "boiler rooms" in the castle complex. As you tour the rest of the castle, keep an eye out for little saucer-sized heating vents in the floor.

• *Climb back up the stairs, take an immediate left through a tiny arch, and then go left again, up through the door labeled #5 (not down, which takes you out of the castle). This leads into the...*

Grand Master's Palace

This was one of the grandest royal residences in medieval Europe, used in later times by Polish kings and German *Kaisers.* (Today it's sometimes used for special exhibitions.)

• *Walk through the kitchen into the big and bright...*

Grand Refectory: With remarkable palm vaulting and grand frescoes, this dining hall hosted feasts for up to 400 people to celebrate a military victory or to impress visiting dignitaries. Notice the 36 heating vents—which are directly above the boiler room you just visited—designed to keep the VIPs warm.

• *From here, climb the stairs into the...*

Private Rooms of the Grand Master: Though the Teutonic Order dictated that the monks sleep in dormitories, the Grand Master made an exception for himself—with a suite of private rooms that came with his own toilet (with a river view) and his own chapel, dedicated to St. Catherine. Exploring the Top Knight's residence, appreciate the show-off decor (including some 15th-century original frescoes of wine leaves and grapes). His private bedroom was decorated with frescoes of four virgins—female martyrs. The passage outside the private rooms came with a washbasin, as anyone wanting an audience with the Grand Master had to wash both his hands and his feet.

Next, enter the private dining room, the **Winter Refectory,** with fewer windows (better insulation) and little manhole-like openings in the floor where the "central heating" entered the room. The adjacent **Summer Refectory** had big stained-glass windows. With all the delicate vaulting supported by a single pillar in the middle, this room was clearly not designed with defense in mind. In fact, medieval Polish armies focused their attacks on this room. On one legendary occasion, the attackers—tipped off by a spy—knew that an important meeting was going on here and fired a cannonball into the room. It just missed the pillar. (You can see where the cannonball hit the wall, just above the fireplace.) The ceiling eventually did collapse during World War II.

• *Back out in the courtyard, look for the four...*

Grand Master Statues

Though this was a religious order, these powerful guys look more like kings than monks. From left to right, shake hands with Hermann von Salza (who was Grand Master when the Teutonic Knights came to Poland); Siegfried von Feuchtwangen (who actually moved the T. K. capital from Venice to Malbork, and who conquered Gdańsk for the Knights—oops, can't shake his hand, which was supposedly chopped off by Soviet troops); Winrich von Kniprode (who oversaw Malbork's Golden Age and turned it into a castle fit for a king); and Markgraf Albrecht von Hohenzollern (the last Grand Master before the order dissolved and converted to Protestantism).

• *To the right of the statues, continue into the High Castle by passing over the...*

Drawbridge

As you cross, notice the extensive system of fortifications and moats protecting the innermost part of the castle just ahead. Check

POMERANIA

The Teutonic Knights

The Order of the Teutonic Knights began in the Holy Land in 1191, during the Third Crusade. These German militarized monks built hospitals and cared for injured knights. When the Crusades ended in the 12th century, the Knights returned to Europe and reorganized as a chivalric order of Christian mercenaries—pagan-killers for hire.

In 1226, a northern Polish duke called in the Teutonic Knights to subdue a tribe of pagans who had been attacking his lands. Clad in their white cloaks with skinny black crosses, the Teutonic Knights spent 60 years "saving" the pagans by turning them into serfs or brutally massacring them.

Job done, the Teutonic Knights decided to stick around. With the support of the pope and the Holy Roman Emperor (who were swayed by the Knights' religious zeal), the Knights built one of Europe's biggest and most imposing fortresses: Malbork. In 1308, they seized large parts of northern Poland (including Gdańsk), cutting off Polish access to the Baltic Sea. The Knights grew rich from Hanseatic trade, specializing in amber, grain, and timber. By the late 14th century, the Teutonic Knights had grown to become Europe's largest-ever monastic state and were threatening to overtake Lithuania.

Inspired by a mutual desire to oust the Teutonic Knights, the Poles and the Lithuanians teamed up. In 1386, Polish Princess Jadwiga married Lithuanian Prince Władysław Jagiełło, kick-starting a grand new dynasty: the Jagiellonians.

Every Pole knows the date July 15, 1410: the Battle of Grunwald. King Władysław Jagiełło and Lithuanian Grand Duke Vytautas the Great led a ragtag army of some 40,000 soldiers—Lithuanians, Poles, other Slavs, and even speedy Tatar horsemen—against 27,000 Teutonic Knights. At the end of the day, some 18,000 Poles and Lithuanians were dead—but so were half of the Teutonic Knights, and the other half had been captured. Poland and Lithuania were victorious.

The Battle of Grunwald marked the beginning of the end for the Teutonic Knights, who were finally defeated during the Thirteen Years' War (1454-1466). The order officially dissolved in 1575, when they converted to Protestantism and much of their land was folded into Prussia. Later, 19th-century Polish Romantics reimagined the Teutonic Knights as an early symbol of Germanic oppression—poignant among Poles, who suffered through a new round of German abuse in World War II. Some conspiracy theorists believe the Teutonic Knights are still very much active...but that's another story.

POMERANIA

out the cracks in the walls (on right)—an increasing threat to this ever-settling castle set on marshy, unstable terrain. On the left is a collection of stone catapult balls that were actually fired at this castle when it was under siege. (Look high above to see the dents such stones can make.) The passage ahead is lined with holes (for surveillance) and with chutes up above (to pour scalding water or pitch on unwanted visitors). It's not quite straight—so a cannon fired here would hit the side wall of the passage, rather than enter the High Castle and its central courtyard. Which is what you're about to do now.

High Castle (Zamek Wysoki)

This is the heart of the castle, and its oldest section. From this spot, the Teutonic Knights governed their vast realm—the largest monk-ruled territory in European history. As much a monastery as a fortress, the High Castle was off-limits to all but 60 monks of the Teutonic Order and their servants. (The knights stayed in the Middle Castle.) Here you'll find the monks' dormitories, chapels, church, and refectory. As this was the nerve center of the Teutonic Knights—the T. K. HQ—it was also their last line of defense. They stored enormous amounts of food here in case of a siege.

In the middle of the High Castle courtyard is a **well**—an essential part of any inner castle, especially one as prone to sieges as Malbork. At the top is a sculpture of a pelican. Because this noble bird was believed to kill itself to feed its young (notice that it's piercing its own chest with its beak), it was often used in the Middle Ages as a symbol for the self-sacrifice of Jesus.

• *Take some time to explore the...*

High Castle—Ground Floor

Work clockwise around the courtyard from where you entered. A door leads to the prison (with small "solitary confinement" cells near the entrance). Along the next wall of the cloister is a post-WWII photo of bombed-out Malbork. Just adjacent, hiding in the far corner, is an exhibit on stained-glass windows from the castle church. Somewhere around here, you should see a demonstration of how medieval money was made. The Teutonic Knights minted their own coins—and you can buy your very own freshly minted replica today.

• *Continuing around the courtyard, you'll find the...*

Kitchen: This exhibit—with a long table piled with typical ingredients from that time—really gives you a feel for medieval monastery life. The monks who lived here ate three meals a day, along with lots of beer (made here) and wine (imported from France, Italy, and Hungary). A cellar under the kitchen was used as a primitive refrigerator—big chunks of ice were cut from the frozen river in winter, stored in the basement, and used to keep food cool in summer. Behind the long table, see the big dumbwaiter (with five shelves for hot dishes), which connects this kitchen with the refectory upstairs. Step into the giant stove and look up the biggest chimney in the castle.

• *Now go back out into the courtyard and climb up the stairs near where you first entered.*

High Castle—Middle Floor

• *From the top of the stairs, the first door on the left (with the colorfully painted arch) leads to the most important room of the High Castle, the...*

Chapter Room: Monks gathered here after Mass, and it was also the site for meetings of Teutonic Knights from around the countryside. If a Grand Master was killed in battle, the new one would be elected here. Carvings above each chair indicated the status of the man who sat there. The big chair belonged to the Grand Master. Notice the little windows above his chair, connecting this room to the church next door. Ecclesiastical music would filter in through these windows; imagine the voices of 60 monks bouncing around with these acoustics.

While monks are usually thought to pursue simple lives, the elegant vaulting in this room is anything but plain. The 14th-century frescoes (restored in the 19th century) depict Grand Masters. In the floor are more vents for the central heating.

• *Leave the Chapter Room and walk straight ahead, imagining the monk-filled corridors of Teutonic times. The first door on the right is the...*

Treasury: As you explore the five rooms of the tax collector and the house administrator, notice the wide variety of safes and other lock boxes. Documents, amber, and coins were kept behind heavily armored and well-locked doors.

• *Continue around the cloister. At the end of the corridor, spot the little devil at the bottom of the vaulting (on the right, about eye level). He's pulling his beard and crossing his legs—pointing you down the long corridor leading about 50 yards away from the cloister to the...*

Dansker Tower: From the devil's grimace, you might have guessed that this tower houses the latrine. Four wooden toilet stalls filled this big room. Where one is missing, you can look down to see how the "toilets" simply dropped the waste into the moat. For obvious sanitary (and olfactory) reasons, this potty tower is set apart from the main part of the castle. The bins above the toilets were filled with cabbage leaves, to be used by the T. K. as TP (and as an organic form of Preparation H). This tower could also serve as a final measure of defense—it's easier to defend than the entire castle. Food was stored above, just in case. More info on this grand castle WC is on the wall.

• *Return down the long corridor. Before the end, on the right-hand side of the long passage, a door leads into the...*

Church Exhibition: Once dormitories for the monks, these three rooms now display a wide range of relics from the church. In the last room, on the far wall, is the artistic highlight of the castle: a finely carved and painted three-panel altarpiece from about 1500 featuring the coronation of Mary. Mary's face is mesmerizing. Characteristic of the late Gothic period, the robes seem to fly unrealistically (as if they were bent metal).

• *Back out in the main cloister, turn right, and continue to the end, arriving at the...*

Golden Gate: This elaborate doorway—covered in protective glass—marks the entrance to **St. Mary's Church.** Before en-

tering, examine this rare original door. Ringed with detailed carvings from the New Testament, and symbolic messages about how monks of the Teutonic Order should live their lives, it's a marvelous example of late-13th-century art. At the bottom-left end of the arch, find the five wise virgins who, having filled their lamps with oil and conserved it wisely, are headed to heaven. On the right, the five foolish virgins who overslept and used up all their oil are damned, much to their dismay. Step inside the church to appreciate a glorious Gothic interior—recently reopened after a lengthy restoration. The highlight is the dramatic 25-foot-tall Madonna.

• *Back outside, go through the narrow door next to the Golden Gate (on the right) and hike up the tight spiral staircase to the final set of exhibits.*

High Castle—Top Floor

Walk through an exhibit about the illustrious guests of the castle. At the end, descend into the monks' common room (left, at the

bottom of the stairs). Over the fireplace is a relief depicting the Teutonic Knights fighting the pagans. To the left and above (see the stone windows) is a balcony where musicians entertained the monks after a meal. The next, very long room, with seven pillars, is the refectory, where the monks ate in silence. Along the right-hand wall are lockable storage boxes for tableware. At the end of this room, just beyond another ornate fireplace, notice the grated hole in the wall. This is where the dumbwaiter comes up from the kitchen (which we saw below). Beyond this room is an exhibit about the architectural renovation of the castle.

• *Your Malbork tour ends here. You leave the way you came. En route, you can walk around terraces lining the inner moat, between the castle walls (stairs lead down off the drawbridge, by the catapult balls). It's hardly a must-see, but it's pleasant enough, with the Grand Master's garden, a cemetery for monks, and the remains of the small St. Anne's Chapel (with Grand Master tombs).*

MALBORK CONNECTIONS

From Malbork by Train to: Gdańsk (2/hour, about half are express EIC trains that take 30 minutes, the rest are slower regional trains that take around 45 minutes), **Toruń** (about every 2 hours, 2.5 hours, change in Iława), **Warsaw** (hourly, 2.5 hours).

Toruń

Toruń (TOH-roon) is a pretty, lazy Gothic town conveniently located about halfway between Warsaw and Gdańsk. It's worth a couple of hours to stroll the lively streets, ogle the huge red-brick buildings, and savor the flavor of perhaps Poland's most livable city.

With about 210,000 residents and 30,000 students (at Copernicus University), Toruń is a thriving burg. Like Kraków (and unlike most other Polish cities), Toruń escaped destruction during World War II and remains well-preserved today. Locals brag that their city is a "mini Kraków." But that sells both cities short. Toruń lacks Kraków's over-the-top romanticism, and its sights are quickly exhausted. On the other hand, Toruń may well be Poland's most user-friendly city: tidy streets with a sensible grid plan (and English signposts to keep you on track), wide pedestrian boulevards crammed with locals who greet each other like they're long-lost friends, and an easygoing ambience that seems to say, "Hey—relax." And, while it has its share of tourists, Toruń feels more off-the-beaten-path than the other Polish destinations in this book.

Toruń clings fiercely to its two claims to fame: It's the proud birthplace of the astronomer Copernicus (Mikołaj Kopernik), and home to a dizzying variety of gingerbread treats (*piernika*; pyer-NEE-kah).

Orientation to Toruń

Everything in Toruń worth seeing is in the walled Old Town, climbing up a gentle hill from the Vistula River. The broad, traffic-free main drag, ulica Szeroka (called Różana at the entrance of town) bisects the Old Town, running parallel to the river. The **TI** is on the main square, behind the Old Town Hall (closed Sun off-season, Rynek Staromiejski 25, tel. 56-621-0930, www.it.torun.pl).

ARRIVAL IN TORUŃ

Toruń's main train station (called Toruń Główny) is across the river from the Old Town, about a mile away. The main hall has ticket windows, an ATM, and lockers. (The TI also stores bags for a small fee.)

To reach the Old Town, you have two options: If you go out the door from the main hall, you'll spot **taxis** waiting to take you into town (the trip costs around 15-20 zł). To take the **bus,** buy a ticket from the *RUCH* kiosk, then take the pedestrian underpass outside (look for *wyjście do miasta* sign and bus icon) and find the bus stop for bus #22, #25, or #27. Take the bus to Plac Rapackiego, the first stop after the long bridge. To return to the station, catch bus #22, #25, or #27 across the busy road from where you got off.

Toruń Walk

This brief self-guided walk takes you through the heart of Toruń. With no stops, you could do it in less than 30 minutes.

• *From the Plac Rapackiego bus stop, head into town through the passageways under the colorful buildings. Within a block, you're at the bustling...*

Old Town Market Square (Rynek Staromiejski): This square is surrounded by huge brick buildings and outdoor restaurants buzzing with lively locals. The **Old Town Hall** (Ratusz Staromiejski) fills the middle of the square, as was often the case in medieval Hanseatic towns. Its fine museum and climbable tower are Toruń's main sights worth visiting (described later, under "Sights in Toruń"). The building with the pointy spires on the right (across from the Old Town Hall) is the **Artus Court,** where the medieval town council and merchants' guilds met. While the town was founded in 1231, the current building is Neo-Gothic, dating from the 19th century.

The guy playing his violin in front of the Old Town Hall is a

Toruń

- ETHNOGRAPHIC PARK
- To Main Bus Station
- LEONA SZUMANA
- WAŁY GEN WŁADYSŁAWA SIKORSKIEGO
- DOMINSKA
- WYSOKA
- PROSTA
- 100 Meters
- 100 Yards
- OLD
- PODMURNA
- CHEŁMINSKA
- SZEWSKA
- TOWN
- FRANCISZKAŃSKA
- CHURCH OF VIRGIN MARY
- KRÓL JADWIGI
- New Market Square
- PANNY MARII
- Old Town Market Square
- TOWN HALL MUSEUM & TOWER
- ULIKA SZEROKA
- WIELKE GARBARY
- CHURCH OF HOLY SPIRIT
- COPERNICUS STATUE
- UL. MOSTOWA
- PRZEDZAMCZE
- Plac Rapackiego
- RÓŻANA
- PIEKARY
- MIKOŁAJA KOPERNIKA
- PIERNIKI GINGERBREAD SHOP
- ZEGLARSKA
- UL. PODMURNA
- CIASNA
- CASTLE RUINS
- #22, 25 & 27
- WALK BEGINS
- GINGERBREAD MUSEUM
- TOWN WALLS
- RABIAŃSKA
- COPERNICUS HOUSE
- CATHEDRAL OF TWO ST. JOHNS
- BANKOWA
- TOILET TOWER
- ALEJA JANA PAWŁA II
- KLASZTORNA GATE
- BULWAR FILADELFIJSKI
- ŻEGLARSKA GATE
- RIVERSIDE PROMENADE
- MOSTOWA GATE
- River
- PIŁSUDSKIEGO BRIDGE
- Vistula
- To Main Train Station (Toruń Glowny)
- ❶ Hotel Karczma "Spichrz"
- ❷ Hotel Retman

POMERANIA

rafter *(retman)*—one of the medieval lumberjacks who lashed tree trunks together and floated them down the Vistula to Gdańsk. This particular rafter came to Toruń when the town was infested with frogs. He wooed them with his violin and marched them out of town. (Hmm...sounds like a certain pied piper....)

The bigger statue, at the other end of the Old Town Hall, depicts **Mikołaj Kopernik,** better known as Nicolaus Copernicus (1473-1543). This Toruń-born son of aristocrats turned the world on its ear when he suggested that the sun, not the earth, is the center of the universe (the "heliocentric theory"). Toruń is serious about this local boy done good—he's the town mascot, as well as the namesake of the local university. Among its fields of study, Copernicus U. has a healthy astronomy program. There's a planetarium in the Old Town (just past the far corner of the square) and a giant radio telescope on the town outskirts. Despite all the local fuss over Copernicus, there's some dispute about his ethnicity; he was born in Toruń, all right, but at a time when it was the predominantly German town of "Thorn." So is he Polish or German? (For more on Copernicus, visit his birth house—now a modest museum on the astronomer—just two blocks away and described later, under "Sights in Toruń".)

Copernicus faces a shiny donkey at the corner of **Szeroka** and Żeglarska streets. We'll venture down Żeglarska first, and then return to walk down Szeroka. By the way, that shiny donkey with a sharp ridge on his back, while happy today, recalls a humiliating punishment. Centuries ago, delinquents and petty criminals needing to be set straight would be forced to straddle this donkey—after townspeople had tied heavy stones to their feet, weighing them down painfully.

• *But you're on vacation and, rather than humiliation, you get gingerbread. Head down Żeglarska to #25 (on the right).*

Pierniki (**Gingerbread**) **Shop:** For Poles, Toruń is synonymous with **gingerbread** *(piernika)*—you'll smell its sweet scent all over town. This Toruń treat can be topped with different kinds of jams or glazes, and/or dipped in chocolate. This shop has a fun system: All the varieties cost the same, so you can create just the mix you like by pointing. *Róża* is rose, *malina* is raspberry, *czarna porzeczka* is black currant, *morela* is apricot, and—of course—*czekolada* is chocolate.

• *A few steps down and across the street is the...*

Cathedral of Two Saint Johns (Katedra Św. Jana Chrzciciela i Jana Ewangelisty): Dedicated in the 12th century to John the Baptist and John the Evangelist, this is the parish church of the Old Town. From the street, notice the architectural heaviness: This marshy land lacked big stones, so instead of flying buttresses, they designed a bulky and sturdy brick structure so they could build big. Stepping inside, you find pure Gothic architecture. The gravestones of big shots pave the floor. Each trade guild had its own chapel. To the left of the altar, notice the finely restored 13th-century *Last Judgment.* In the rear of the church (on the right) is the baptismal font where, in 1473, Copernicus was baptized.

• *Having satisfied your ginger tooth and seen the town's most important church, head back to the square and that painful donkey, turn right, and join the human stream down the appropriately named...*

Ulica Szeroka ("Wide Street"): This enjoyable pedestrian promenade leads through the heart of town. Embedded in the paving bricks are the coats of arms of Toruń's medieval trading partners. And on each side of the street is an eclectic commotion of fun facades.

About 30 yards before the road forks at the stately, white Empik building, look down narrow Przedzamcze street to the right to see fragments of the town wall. This marks the border between the Old Town and the New Town (chartered only about 30 years later—both in the 13th century). While these areas are collectively known today as the unified "Old Town," they were quite different in the Middle Ages—each with its own market square, and separated by a wall. (If you're curious to see the New Town Square and

Town Hall, take the left fork at the Empik building and walk two blocks up ulica Królowej Jadwigi.)

• *Turn right down Przedzamcze, bear left at the parking lot, and continue under the stubby, standalone brick gate to the...*

Toruń Castle Ruins: This castle, built by the Teutonic Knights who were so influential in northern Poland in the Middle Ages (see page 502), was destroyed in the 15th century by the locals—who, aside from a heap of bricks, left only the tower that housed the Teutonic toilets. The ruins have nothing much to offer, but what survives is one of the better toilet towers in Europe—which was connected to the castle by an elevated walkway and located far enough away to keep things hygienic. The old mill next to the toilet is now a hotel named 1231, for the date the Teutonic Order arrived here.

• *Our walk is over. You can backtrack the way you came and explore more of the city (including the sights listed next). Or you can take a quick riverside stroll: Go under the toilet tower and down to the Vistula River, turn right, and stroll along the castle and 14th-century city walls back to your starting point. The road is called Bulwar Filadelfijski—for Toruń's sister city in Pennsylvania.*

Sights in Toruń

Toruń is more about strolling than it is about sightseeing—the town's museums are underwhelming. Aside from its half-dozen red-brick churches (any of which are worth dropping into), the following attractions are worth considering on a rainy day.

▲City Hall Museum and Tower

Like Kraków's Cloth Hall, this building, dominating the town square, was a general market. It served as the heart of the city. Today it offers the only chance in town to see historic artifacts. It gives a good history of the Teutonic Knights, who first came to Toruń in 1231. You'll see intimate bits and pieces of history—from pewter tankards to old gingerbread molds—that show the richness of this traders' city. Another wing of the ground floor is filled with medieval church art saved from the region's churches. Much of it is pre-Reformation Catholic art, with lots of Marys (the patron of the Teutonic Order) and a close-up look at some 14th-century stained glass. The royal halls upstairs feature portraits and fine 17th-century inlaid wooden doors. The 130-foot-tall tower can be climbed (on narrow wooden steps) for great views over the city center.

Cost and Hours: 11 zł apiece for museum and tower, 17-zł combo-ticket for both, free on Wed; Tue-Sun 10:00-18:00, Oct-April until 16:00, closed Mon year-round; Rynek Staromiejski 1, tel. 56-660-5612, www.muzeum.torun.pl.

Gingerbread Museum (Muzeum Piernika)

This fun attraction—by far Toruń's liveliest—is an actual working gingerbread bakery of yore. Barefoot, costumed medieval bakers walk you through the traditional process of rolling, cutting out, baking, and tasting your own batch of gingerbread cookies (30-40 minutes, start to finish). After aging for 12 weeks to achieve the proper consistency, the dough bakes for only 12 minutes—or, according to the medieval bakers, about 50 Hail Marys.

Cost and Hours: 14 zł, daily 10:00-18:00, Polish tours start at the top of each hour, English demonstrations most likely at 13:00 and 16:00, can be crowded in peak times—call ahead to confirm schedule and reserve a spot, 2 blocks toward the river from Old Town Market Square at Rabiańska 9, tel. 56-663-6617, www.muzeumpiernika.pl.

Copernicus House (Dom Kopernika)

Filling a pair of beautiful, gabled brick buildings, this dull, overpriced little museum celebrates the hero of Toruń. As much about medieval Toruń as about the famous astronomer, and sprawling over several floors in the two buildings, the exhibits loosely explain Nicolaus Copernicus' life and achievements.

The displays are copies of important documents and paintings and models of his instruments. The second part of the exhibit is an 18-minute slideshow with recorded commentary about medieval Toruń, with a model of the city that lights up dramatically at appropriate moments (plays on the half-hour, in English by request).

Cost and Hours: Museum only-11 zł, model/slideshow only-13 zł, 20-zł combo-ticket for both, free on Wed; Tue-Sun 10:00-18:00, Oct-April until 16:00, closed Mon year-round; Kopernika 15, tel. 56-662-7038, www.muzeum.torun.pl.

Sleeping in Toruń

$$ Hotel Karczma "Spichrz" ("Granary") is a fresh, atmospheric hotel in a renovated old granary. Its 23 rooms and public spaces are a fun blend of old and new—with huge wooden beams around every corner and the aroma of the restaurant's wood-fired grill wafting through the halls. It's comfortable, central, well-priced, and a little kitschy (tall people may not appreciate low ceilings and beams, elevator, a block off the main drag toward the river at ulica Mostowa 1, tel. 56-657-1140, www.spichrz.pl, hotel@spichrz.pl). The restaurant is also good.

$ Hotel Retman ("Rafter") has 29 older but nicely appointed rooms over a restaurant just down the street from the Gingerbread Museum (ulica Rabiańska 15, tel. 56-657-4460, www.hotel-retman.pl, recepcja@hotelretman.pl).

Toruń Connections

Toruń is a handy stopover on the way between Warsaw and Gdańsk.

From Toruń by Train to: Warsaw (every 2 hours direct, 2.5 hours on express IC train), **Gdańsk** (4/day, 2.5 hours; additional options with a change in Bydgoszcz, 3 hours), **Malbork** (about every 2 hours, 2.5 hours, change in Iława), **Kraków** (1/day direct, 6.5 hours; better to change at Warsaw's Zachodnia station: 7/day, 6 hours), **Berlin** (4/day, 6 hours, change in Poznań).

POMERANIA

HUNGARY
Magyarország

HUNGARY

Magyarország

 Hungary is an island of Asian-descended Magyars in a sea of Slavs. Even though the Hungarians have thoroughly integrated with their Slavic and German neighbors in the millennium-plus since they arrived, there's still something about the place that's distinctly Magyar (MUD-jar). Here in quirky, idiosyncratic Hungary, everything's a little different from the rest of Europe—in terms of history, language, culture, customs, and cuisine—but it's hard to put your finger on exactly how.

Just a century ago, this country controlled half of one of Europe's grandest realms: the Austro-Hungarian Empire. Today, perhaps clinging to their former greatness, many Hungarians remain old-fashioned and nostalgic. With their dusty museums and bushy moustaches, they love to remember the good old days. Buildings all over the country are marked with plaques boasting *MŰEMLÉK* ("historical monument").

Thanks to this focus on tradition, the Hungarians you'll encounter are generally polite, formal, and professional. Hungarians have class. Everything here is done with a proud flourish. People in the service industry seem to wear their uniforms as a badge of honor rather than a burden. When a waiter comes to your table in a restaurant, he'll say, *"Tessék parancsolni"*—literally, "Please command, sir." The standard greeting, *"Jó napot kívánok,"* means "I wish you a good day." Women sometimes hear the even more formal greeting, *"Kezét csókolom"*—"I kiss your hand." And when your train or bus makes a stop, you won't be alerted by a mindless, blaring beep—but instead, by peppy music. (You'll be humming these contagious little ditties all day.) Perhaps thanks to this artful blending of elegance and formality, Hungarians have a cultural affinity for the French.

Hungarians are also orderly and tidy...in their own sometimes unexpected ways. Yes, Hungary has its share of litter, graffiti, and crumbling buildings, but you'll find great reason within the chaos. The Hungarian railroad has a long list of discounted fares—for seniors, kids, dogs...and monkeys. (It could happen.) My favorite town name in Hungary: Hatvan. This means "Sixty" in Hungarian...and it's exactly 60 kilometers from Budapest. You can't argue with that kind of logic.

This tradition of left-brained thinking hasn't produced many great Hungarian painters or poets who are known outside their homeland. But the Hungarians, who are renowned for their ingenuity, have made tremendous contributions to science, technology, business, and industry. Hungarians of note include Edward Teller (instrumental in creating the H-bomb), John von Neumann (a pioneer of computer science), András Gróf (who, as Andy Grove, emigrated to the US and founded Intel), George Soros (the billionaire investor famous—or notorious—for supporting left-wing causes), and László József Bíró (inventor of the ballpoint pen). A popular local joke claims that Hungarians are so clever that they can enter a revolving door behind you and exit in front of you.

Perhaps the most famous Hungarian "scientist" invented something you probably have in a box in your basement: Ernő Rubik, creator of the famous cube. Hungarians' enjoyment of a good mind-bending puzzle is also evident in their fascination with chess, which you'll see played in cafés, parks, and baths.

Like their Viennese neighbors, Hungarians know how to enjoy the good life. Favorite activities include splashing and soaking in their many thermal baths. "Taking the waters," Hungarian-style, deserves to be your top priority while you're here. Though public baths can sound intimidating, they're a delight. In the following chapters I recommend my three favorite baths in Budapest, a fine bath in Eger, and two more just outside of Eger. For each, I've included careful instructions to help you enjoy the

Hungary Almanac

Official Name: Magyarország (Hungary).

Snapshot History: Settled by the Central Asian Magyars in A.D. 896, Hungary became Catholic in the year 1000, and went on to become Christian Europe's front line in fighting against the Ottomans (Muslims from today's Turkey) in the 16th-17th centuries. After serving as co-capital of the vast Austro-Hungarian Empire and losing World Wars I and II, Hungary became a Soviet satellite until achieving independence in 1989.

Population: Hungary's 10 million people (similar to Michigan) are 85 percent ethnic Hungarians who speak Hungarian. One in 50 is Roma (Gypsy). About 40 percent of the populace is Catholic, with nearly 15 percent Protestant and around 30 percent listed as "other" or unaffiliated. Of the world's approximately 12 million ethnic Hungarians, one in six lives outside Hungary (mostly in areas of Romania, Slovakia, Serbia, and Croatia that were once part of Hungary).

Latitude and Longitude: 47°N and 20°E; similar latitude to Seattle, Paris, and Vienna.

Area: 36,000 square miles, similar to Indiana or Maine.

Geography: Hungary is situated in the Carpathian Basin, bound on the north by the Carpathian Mountains and on the south by the Dinaric Mountains. Though it's surrounded by mountains, Hungary itself is relatively flat, with some gently rolling hills. The Great Hungarian Plain—which begins on the east bank of the Danube in Budapest—stretches all the way to Asia. Hungary's two main rivers—the Danube and Tisza—run north-south through the country, neatly dividing it into three regions.

Biggest Cities: Budapest (the capital on the Danube, nearly 2 million), Debrecen (in the east, 205,000), and Miskolc (in the north, 165,000).

warm-water fun like a pro. (To allay your first fear: Yes, you can wear your swimsuit.)

Hungarians have also revived an elegant, Vienna-style café culture that was dismantled by the communists. Whiling away the afternoon at a genteel coffeehouse, as you nurse a drink or a delicate dessert, is a favorite pastime. (For the best options in Budapest, see "Budapest's Café Culture" on page 669.)

Classical music is revered in Hungary, perhaps as nowhere else outside Austria. Aside from scientists and businessmen, the best-known Hungarians are composers: Béla Bartók, Zoltán Kodály, and Franz Liszt.

While one in five Hungarians lives in Budapest, the country-side plays an important role in the country's economy—this has always been a highly agricultural region. The sprawling Great Hun-

Economy: The Gross Domestic Product is $260 billion, with a per-capita GDP of $26,200. Thanks to its progressive "goulash communism," Hungary had a head start on many other former Soviet Bloc countries and is now thriving, privatized...and large-ly foreign-owned. In the 1990s, many communist-era workers (especially women) lost their jobs. Today, the workforce is small (only 57 percent of eligible workers) but highly skilled. Grains, metals, machinery, and automobiles are major exports, and about one-quarter of trade is with Germany.

Currency: 275 forints (Ft, or HUF) = about $1 (though the exchange rate can fluctuate significantly).

Government: The single-house National Assembly (199 seats) is the only ruling branch directly elected by popular vote. The legislators in turn select the figurehead president (currently János Áder) and the ruling prime minister (Viktor Orbán); both belong to the right-wing, nationalistic Fidesz party.

Flag: Three horizontal bands, top to bottom: red (representing strength), white (faithfulness), and green (hope). It's identical to the Italian flag, but flipped 90 degrees counterclockwise. It often includes the Hungarian coat of arms: horizontal red-and-white stripes (on the left); the patriarchal, or double-barred, cross (on the right); and the Hungarian crown (on top).

The Average János: The typical Hungarian eats a pound of lard a week (they cook with it). The average family has three members, and spends almost three-fourths of its income on housing. According to a recent condom-company survey, the average Hungarian has sex 131 times a year (behind only France and Greece), making them Europe's third-greatest liars.

garian Plain (Puszta) that makes up a vast swath of Hungary is the country's breadbasket. You'll pass through fields of wheat and corn, but the grains are secondary to Hungarians' (and tourists') true love: wine. Hungarian winemaking standards plummeted under the communists, but many vintner families have reclaiming their land, returned to their precise traditional methods, and are making wines worthy of pride once more. (For details, see the "Hungarian Wines" sidebar, later.)

Somehow Hungary, at the crossroads of Europe, has managed to become cosmopolitan while remaining perfectly Hungarian. The Hungarians—like Hungary itself—are a cross-section of Central European cultures: Magyars, Germans, Czechs, Slovaks, Poles, Serbs, Jews, Ottomans, Romanians, Roma (Gypsies), and many others. Still, no matter how many generations removed they are from Magyar stock, there's something different about Hungarians—and not just the language. Look a Hungarian in the eye, and you'll see a glimmer of the marauding Magyar, stomping in from the Central Asian plains a thousand years ago.

HELPFUL HINTS

First Name Last: Hungarians list a person's family name first, and the given name is last—just as in many other Eastern cultures (think of Kim Jong Il and his son Kim Jong-un). So the composer known as "Franz Liszt" in German is "Liszt Ferenc" in his homeland. (To help reduce confusion, many Hungarian business cards list the surname in capital letters.)

Hello Goodbye: Hungarians have a charming habit of using the English word "hello" for both "hi" and "bye," just like the Italians use "ciao." You might overhear a Hungarian end a telephone conversation with a cheery "Hello!"

Telephones: The default emergency telephone number in Hungary is 112. You can also dial 107 for police, 104 for ambulance, or 105 for fire. For tips on how to dial, see page 1086. When it comes to dialing, Hungary is unique in two ways: First, to dial domestic long-distance from a landline, you have to dial 06, then the area code and number. And second, it can be tricky to call a Hungarian mobile number (generally beginning with +3620, +3630, +3631, or +3670). In this book, I have listed these numbers as you'll dial them from any international line or any mobile phone (including a Hungarian one), starting with +36. (You can also replace the "+" with 00 if calling from Europe, or 011 if calling from the US.) However, if you are dialing these numbers from a landline within Hungary, you'll need to replace the "+36" with "06." So, to call a local guide with the number +3620-926-0557, you'd dial exactly that if calling from your American phone or from a Hungarian mobile phone. But if calling from your Budapest hotel room, dial 0620-926-0557.

Toll Sticker: Driving on Hungarian expressways requires a toll sticker (*autópálya matrica*, also called a "vignette," 2,975 Ft/week, 4,780 Ft/month, www.motorway.hu). Ask about this when you rent your car (if it's not already included, you'll have to buy one).

HUNGARIAN HISTORY

The Hungarian story—essentially the tale of a people finding their home—is as epic as any in Europe. Over the course of a millennium, a troublesome nomadic tribe that was the scourge of Europe gradually assimilated with its neighbors and—through a combination of tenacity and diplomacy—found itself controlling a vast swath of Central and Eastern Europe. Locals toss around the names of great historical figures such as Kossuth, Széchenyi, and Nagy as if they're talking about old friends. Take this crash course so you can keep up.

The story begins long, long ago and far, far away...

Welcome to Europe

The land we call Hungary has long been considered the place—culturally and geographically—where the West (Europe) meets the East (Asia). The Roman province of Pannonia once extended to the final foothills of the Alps that constitute the Buda Hills, on the west side of the Danube. Across the river, Rome ended and the barbarian wilds began. From here, the Great Hungarian Plain stretches in a long, flat expanse all the way to Asia—hemmed in to the north by the Carpathian Mountains. (Geologists consider this prairie-like plain to be the westernmost steppe in Europe—resembling the terrain that covers much of Central Asia.) After Rome collapsed and Europe fell into the Dark Ages, Hungary became the territory of Celts, Vandals, Huns, and Avars...until some out-of-towners moved into the neighborhood.

The seven Magyar tribes, led by the mighty Árpád (and, according to legend, guided by the mythical Turul bird), thundered into the Carpathian Basin in A.D. 896. They were a rough-and-tumble nomadic people from Central Asia who didn't like to settle down in one place. And yet, after their long and winding westward odyssey, the Great Hungarian Plain felt comfortingly like home to the Magyars—reminiscent of the Asian steppes of their ancestors.

The Magyars would camp out in today's Hungary in the winters, and in the summers, they'd go on raids throughout Europe. They were notorious as incredibly swift horsemen, whose use of stirrups (an eastern innovation largely unknown in Europe at the time) allowed them to easily outmaneuver foes and victims. Italy, France, Germany's Rhine, the Spanish Pyrenees, all the way to Constantinople (modern-day Istanbul)—the Magyars had the run of the Continent.

For half a century, the Magyars ranked with the Vikings as the most feared people in Europe. To Europeans, this must have struck a chord of queasy familiarity: a mysterious and dangerous eastern tribe running roughshod over Europe, speaking a gibberish language, and employing strange, terrifying, relentless battle techniques. No wonder they called the new arrivals "Hun-garians."

Now planted in the center of Europe, the Magyars effectively drove a wedge in the middle of the sprawling Slavic populations of the Great Moravian Kingdom (basically today's "Eastern Europe"). The Slavs were split into two splinter groups, north and south—a division that persists today: Czechs, Slovaks, and Poles to the north; and Croats, Slovenes, Serbs, Bosniaks, and Bulgarians to the south. (You can still hear the division caused by the Magyars in the language: While Czechs and Russians call a castle *hrad,* Croats and Serbs call it *grad.*)

After decades of terrorizing Europe, the Magyars were finally defeated by a German and Czech army at the Battle of Augsburg in 955. Géza, Grand Prince of the Hungarians—realizing that if they were to survive, his people had to put down roots and get along with their neighbors—made a fateful decision that would forever shape Hungary's future: He adopted Christianity; baptized his son, Vajk; and married him to a Bavarian princess at a young age.

On Christmas Day in the year 1000, Vajk changed his name to István (Stephen) and was symbolically crowned by the pope (for more on István, see page 613). A Venetian missionary, Gellért, came to Buda to attempt to convert the Hungarians—and was martyred (and later sainted) for his efforts. The domestication of the nomadic Magyars was difficult, thanks largely to the resistance of István's uncles, but was ultimately successful. Hungary became a legitimate Christian kingdom, welcomed by its neighbors. Under kings such as László I, Kálmán "the Book Lover," and András II, Hungary entered a period of prosperity. Medieval Hungary ruled a vast empire—including large parts of today's Slovakia, Romania (Transylvania), Serbia (Vojvodina), and Croatia.

The Tatars, the Ottomans, and Other Outsiders
(A.D. 1000-1686)

One of Hungary's earliest challenges came at the hands of fellow invaders from Central Asia. Through the first half of the 13th century, the Tatars—initially led by Genghis Khan—swept into Eastern Europe from Mongolia. In the summer of 1241, Genghis Khan's son and successor, Ögedei Khan, broke into Hungarian territory. The Tatars sacked and plundered Hungarian towns, laying waste to the kingdom. It was only Ögedei Khan's death in early 1242—and the ensuing dispute about succession—that saved the Hungarians, as Tatar armies rushed home and the Mongolian Empire contracted. The Hungarian king at the time, Béla IV, was left to rebuild his ruined kingdom from the rubble—creating for the first time many of the stout hilltop castles that still line the Danube.

Each of Béla's successors left his own mark on Hungary, as the Magyar kingdom flourished. They barely skipped a beat when the original Árpád dynasty died out in 1301, as they imported French kings (from the Naples-based Anjou, or Angevin, dynasty) to continue building their young realm. King Károly Róbert (Charles Robert) won over the Magyars, and his son Nagy Lajos (Louis the Great) expanded Hungarian holdings).

This was a period of flux for all of Central and Eastern Europe, as the nearby Czech and Polish kingdoms also saw their long-standing dynasties expire. For a time, royal intermarriages juggled the crowns of the region between various ruling families. Most notably, for 50 years (1387-1437) Hungary was ruled by Holy Roman Emperor Sigismund of Luxembourg, whose holdings also included the Czech lands, parts of Italy, much of Croatia, and more.

For more than 150 years, Hungary did not have a Hungarian-blooded king. This changed in the late 15th century, when a short-

age of foreign kings led to the ascension to the throne of the enlightened King Mátyás (Matthias) Corvinus. The son of popular military hero János Hunyadi, King Matthias fostered the arts, sparked a mini-Renaissance, and successfully balanced foreign threats to Hungarian sovereignty (the Habsburgs to the north and west, and the Ottomans to the south and east). Under Matthias, Hungarian culture and political power reached a peak. (For more on this great Hungarian king, see page 609.)

(For more on this great Hungarian king, see page 609.)

But even before the reign of "good king Mátyás," the Ottomans (from today's Turkey) had already begun slicing their way through the Balkan Peninsula toward Central Europe. (It's ironic that the two greatest threats to the Magyar kingdom came in the form of fellow Asian invaders: Tatars and Turks. Or maybe it's not surprising, as these groups all found the steppes of Hungary so familiar and inviting.) In 1526, the Ottomans entered Hungary when Sultan Süleyman the Magnificent killed Hungary's King Lajos II at the Battle of Mohács. By 1541, they took Buda. The Ottomans would dominate Hungarian life (and history) until the 1680s—nearly a century and a half.

The Ottoman invasion divided Hungary into thirds: Ottoman-occupied "Lower Hungary" (more or less today's Hungary); rump "Upper Hungary" (basically today's Slovakia), with its capital at Bratislava (which they called "Pozsony"); and the loosely independent territories of Transylvania, ruled by Hungarian dukes. During this era, the Ottomans built some of the thermal baths that you'll still find throughout Hungary.

Ottoman-occupied Hungary became severely depopulated, and many of its towns and cities fell into ruins. While it was advantageous for a Hungarian subject to adopt Islam (for lower taxes and other privileges), the Ottomans rarely forced conversions—unlike the arguably more oppressive Catholics who controlled other parts of Europe at the time (such as the monarchs of Spain, who expelled the Jews and conducted the Spanish Inquisition). Ottoman rule meant that Hungary took a different course than other parts of Europe during this time. The nation fully enjoyed the Renaissance, but missed out on other major European historical events—both good (the Age of Discovery and Age of Reason) and bad (the devastating Catholic-versus-Protestant wars that plagued much of the rest of Europe).

Crippled by the Ottomans and lacking power and options, desperate Hungarian nobles offered their crown to the Austrian Habsburg Empire, in exchange for salvation from the invasion. The Habsburgs instead used Hungary as a kind of "buffer zone" between the Ottoman advance and Vienna. And that was only the beginning of a very troubled relationship between the Hungarians and the Austrians.

Habsburg Rule, Hungarian National Revival, and Revolution (1686-1867)

In the late 17th century, the Habsburg army, starting from Vienna, began a sustained campaign to push the Ottomans out of Hungary in about 15 years. They finally wrested Buda and Pest from the Ottomans in 1686. The Habsburgs repopulated Buda and Pest with Germans, while Magyars reclaimed the countryside.

The Habsburgs governed the country as an outpost of Austria. The Hungarians—who'd had enough of foreign rule—fought them tooth and nail. Countless streets, squares, and buildings throughout the country are named for the "big three" Hungarian patriots who resisted the Habsburgs during this time: Ferenc Rákóczi (who led the unsuccessful War of Independence in 1703-1711), István Széchenyi (a wealthy count who funded grand structures to give his Magyar countrymen something to take pride in), and Lajos Kossuth (who led the Revolution of 1848).

The early 19th century saw a thawing of Habsburg oppression. Here, as throughout Europe, "backward" country traditions began to trickle into the cities, gaining more respect and prominence. It was during this time of reforms that Hungarian (rather than German) became the official language. It also coincided with a Romantic Age of poets and writers (such as Mihály Vörösmarty and Sándor Petőfi) who began using Hungarian to create literature for the first time. By around 1825, the Hungarian National Revival was underway, as the people began to embrace the culture and traditions of their Magyar ancestors. Like people across Europe—from Ireland to Italy, and from Prague to Scandinavia—the Hungarians were rediscovering what made them a unique people.

In March of 1848, a wave of Enlightenment-fueled nationalism that began in Paris spread like wildfire across Europe, igniting a revolutionary spirit in cities such as Vienna, Milan...and Budapest. On March 15, the Revolution of 1848 began on the steps of the National Museum in Pest.

In the spring of 1849, the Hungarians mounted a bloody but successful offensive to take over a wide swath of territory, including Buda and Pest. But in June, Franz Josef enlisted the aid of his fellow divine monarch, the Russian czar, who did not want the Magyars to provide an example for his own independence-minded subjects. Some 200,000 Russian reinforcements flooded into Hungary, crushing the revolution by August. After the final battle, the Habsburgs executed 13 Hungarian generals, then celebrated by clinking mugs of beer. To this very day, clinking beer mugs is, for many traditional Hungarians, just bad style.

For a while, the Habsburgs cracked down on their unruly Hungarian subjects. After an important military loss to Bismarck's Prussia in 1866, Austria began to agree that it couldn't control its rebellious Slavic holdings all by itself. And so, just 18 years after crushing the Hungarians in a war, the Habsburgs handed them the reins. With the Compromise *(Ausgleich)* of 1867, Austria granted Budapest the authority over the eastern half of their lands, creating the so-called Dual Monarchy of the Austro-Hungarian Empire. Hungary was granted their much-prized "home rule," where most matters (except finance, foreign policy, and the military) were administered from Budapest rather than Vienna. The Habsburg emperor, Franz Josef, agreed to a unique "king and emperor" *(König und Kaiser)* arrangement, where he was emperor of Austria, but only king of Hungary. In 1867, he was crowned as Hungarian king in both Buda (at Matthias Church) and Pest (on today's March 15 Square). The insignia "K+K" *(König und Kaiser)*—which you'll still see everywhere—evokes these grand days.

HUNGARY

Pre-Trianon Hungary

Pre-Trianon Hungary (1920) — Current Hungarian Border

200 Kilometers / 200 Miles

POLAND · UKRAINE · CZECH. REP. · SLOVAKIA · MOLDOVA · Danube R. · Vienna · AUSTRIA · Budapest · TRANSYLVANIA · SLOVENIA · ROMANIA · ITALY · CROATIA · VOJVODINA · Adriatic Sea · BOSNIA-HERZ. · SERBIA · Danube R. · BULGARIA · Black Sea

Budapest's Golden Age (1867-1918)

The *Ausgleich* marked a precipitous turning point for the Hungarians, who once again governed their traditional holdings: large parts of today's Slovakia, Serbia, and Transylvania, and smaller parts of today's Croatia, Slovenia, Ukraine, and Austria. To better govern their sprawling realm, in 1873, the cities of Buda, Pest, and Óbuda merged into one mega-metropolis: Budapest.

Serendipitously, Budapest's new prominence coincided with the 1,000th anniversary of the Hungarians' ancestors, the Magyars, arriving in Europe...one more excuse to dress things up. Budapest's long-standing rivalry with Vienna only spurred them to build bigger and better. The year 1896 saw an over-the-top millennial celebration, for which many of today's greatest structures were created (see page 556).

This was Budapest's Golden Age. No European city grew faster in the second half of the 19th century than Budapest; in the last quarter of the 19th century alone, Budapest doubled in size, building on the foundation laid by Széchenyi and other patriots. By 1900, the city was larger than Rome, Madrid, or Amsterdam. But before long, the Hungarians began to make the same mistakes the Habsburgs had—trampling on the rights of their minorities, and enforcing a policy of "Magyarization" that compelled subjects from all ethnic backgrounds to adopt the Hungarian language and culture. Soon the Golden Age came crashing to an end, and Hungary plunged into its darkest period.

The Crisis of Trianon (1918-1939)

World War I marked the end of the age of divine monarchs, as the Romanovs of Russia, the Ottomans of Asia Minor, and, yes, the Habsburgs of Austria-Hungary saw their empires break apart. Hungary, which had been riding the Habsburgs' coattails for the past half-century, now paid the price. As retribution for their role on the losing side of World War I, the 1920 Treaty of Trianon (named for the palace on the grounds of Versailles where it was signed) reassigned two-thirds of Hungary's former territory and half of its population to Romania, Ukraine, Czechoslovakia, and Yugoslavia.

It is impossible to overstate the impact of the Treaty of Trianon on the Hungarian psyche—and on Hungarian history. Not unlike the overnight construction of the Berlin Wall, towns along the new Hungarian borders were suddenly divided down the middle. Many Hungarians found themselves unable to visit relatives or commute to jobs that were in the same country the day before. This sent hundreds of thousands of Hungarian refugees—now "foreigners" in their own towns—into Budapest, sparking a bittersweet boom in the capital.

To this day, the Treaty of Trianon is regarded as one of the greatest tragedies of Hungarian history. Like the Basques and the Serbs, the Hungarians feel separated from each other by circumstances outside their control. Today, more than two million ethnic Hungarians live outside Hungary (mostly in Romania)—and many Hungarians claim that these lands still belong to the Magyars. The sizeable Magyar minorities in neighboring countries have often been mistreated—particularly in Romania (under Ceauşescu), Yugoslavia (under Milošević), and Slovakia (under Mečiar). You'll see maps, posters, and bumper stickers with the distinctive shape of a much larger, pre-WWI Hungary...patriotically displayed by Magyars who feel as strongly about Trianon as if it happened yesterday. Some Hungarians see the enlargement of the European Union as a happy ending in the big-picture sense: They have finally been reunited with Slovakia, Romania, and Croatia.

After Trianon, the newly shrunken Kingdom of Hungary had to reinvent itself. The Hungarian crown sat unworn in the Royal Palace, as if waiting for someone worthy to claim it. The WWI hero Admiral Miklós Horthy had won many battles with the Austro-Hungarian navy. Though the new Hungary had no sea and no navy, Horthy retained his rank and ruled the country as a regent. A popular joke points out that during this time, Hungary was a "kingdom without a king" and a landlocked country ruled by a sea admiral. This sense of compounded deficiency pretty much sums up the morose attitude Hungarians have about those gloomy post-Trianon days.

A mounting financial crisis, and lingering resentment about the strict post-WWI reparations, made Hungary fertile ground for some bold new fascist ideas.

World War II and the Arrow Cross (1939-1945)

As Adolf Hitler rose to power in Germany, some other countries that had felt mistreated in the aftermath of World War I—including Hungary—saw Nazi Germany as a vehicle to greater independence. Admiral Horthy joined forces with the Nazis with the hope that they might help Hungary regain the crippling territorial losses of Trianon. In 1941, Hungary (somewhat reluctantly) declared war on the Soviet Union in June—and against the US and Britain in December.

Being an ally to the Nazis, rather than an occupied state, also allowed Hungary a certain degree of self-determination through the war. And, while Hungary had its own set of anti-Semitic laws, the vast majority of its sizeable Jewish population was spared from immediate deportation to Nazi concentration camps. Winning back chunks of Slovakia, Transylvania, and Croatia in the early days of World War II also bolstered the Nazis' acceptance in Hungary.

As Nazism took hold in Germany, the Hungarian fascist movement—spearheaded by the Arrow Cross Party (Nyilaskeresztes Párt)—gained popularity within Hungary. As Germany increased its demands for Hungarian soldiers and food, Admiral Horthy resisted...until Hitler's patience wore thin. In March of 1944, the Nazis invaded and installed the Arrow Cross in power. The Arrow Cross made up for lost time, immediately beginning a savage campaign to execute Hungary's Jews—not only sending them to death camps, but butchering them in the streets. As the end of the war neared, Hungarian Nazi collaborators resorted to desperate measures, such as lining up Jews along the Danube and shooting them into the river. To save bullets, they'd sometimes tie several victims together, shoot one, and throw him into the freezing Danube—dragging the others in with him. Hungary lost nearly 600,000 Jews to the Holocaust.

The Soviet Army eventually "liberated" Hungary, but at the expense of Budapest: A months-long siege, from Christmas of 1944 to mid-February of 1945, reduced the proud city to rubble. One in 10 Hungarian citizens perished in the war.

Communism...with a Pinch of Paprika (1945-1989)

After World War II, Hungary was gradually compelled to adopt Moscow's system of government. The Soviet-puppet hardliner premier, Mátyás Rákosi, ruled Hungary with an iron fist. Everyday people were terrorized by the KGB-style secret police (called the ÁVO and ÁVH) and intimidated into accepting the new regime. Non-Hungarians were deported, potential and actual dissidents disappeared into the horrifying gulag system of Siberia (and similar forced-work camps in Hungary), food shortages were epidemic, people were compelled to spy on their friends and families, and countless lives were ruined. Coming on the heels of Trianon and two devastating world wars, communist rule was a blow that Hungary is still recovering from.

Beginning on October 23, 1956, the Hungarians courageously staged a monumental uprising, led by Communist Party reformer

Imre Nagy. Initially, it appeared that one of the cells on the Soviet Bloc might win itself the right to semiautonomy. But Moscow couldn't let that happen. In a Tiananmen Square-style crackdown, the Soviets sent in tanks to brutally put down the uprising and occupy the city. When the dust settled, 2,500 Hungarians were dead, and 200,000 fled to the West. (If you know any Hungarian Americans, their families more than likely fled in 1956.) Nagy was arrested, given a sham trial, and executed in 1958. For more on these events, see the "1956" sidebar on page 578.

The Hungarians were devastated. They were frustrated that the Suez Canal crisis distracted the world from their uprising. Many felt betrayed that the US—which spoke so boldly against the Soviet Union—did not offer them military support (contrary to the promises of the American-operated Radio Free Europe). While the US and its Western allies understandably did not want to turn the Cold War hot, the Hungarians (also understandably) felt abandoned.

Weeks after the uprising came the now-legendary "Blood in the Water" match at the Melbourne Olympics. Soviet satellite states were often ordered to "throw" matches to allow the USSR's athletes to prevail. On December 6, 1956, Moscow issued such a decree to the Hungarian men's water polo team in their semifinal against the Soviet Union. The Hungarians refused and played their hearts out, much to the delight of their fans (and the rest of the world). The game turned violent, and in one indelible image, a Hungarian athlete emerged from the pool with blood pouring from a gash above his right eye. The Hungarians won, 4-0, and went on to take the gold.

After the uprising, the USSR installed János Kádár—a colleague of Nagy's who was loyal to Moscow—to lead Hungary. For a few years, things were bleak, as the secret police ratcheted up their efforts against potential dissidents. But in the 1960s, Kádár's reformist tendencies began to cautiously emerge. Seeking to gain the support of his subjects (and avoid further uprisings), Kádár adopted the optimistic motto, "If you are not against us, you are with us." While still mostly cooperating with Moscow, Kádár gradually allowed the people of Hungary more freedom than citizens of neighboring countries had—a system dubbed "goulash communism." The "New Economic Mechanism" of 1968 partly opened Hungary to foreign trade. People from other Warsaw Pact countries—Czechs, Slovaks, and Poles—flocked to Budapest's Váci utca to experience "Western evils" unavailable to them back home, such as Adidas sneakers and Big Macs. People half-joked that Hungary was the happiest barrack in the communist camp.

In the late 1980s, the Eastern Bloc began to thaw. And Hungary—which was always skeptical of the Soviets (or any foreign rule)—was one of the first satellite states that implemented real change. In February of 1989, the Hungarian communist parliament, with little fanfare, essentially voted to put an expiration date on their own regime. There were three benchmarks in that fateful year: May 2, when Hungary was the first Soviet Bloc country to effectively open its borders to the West (by removing its border fence with Austria); June 16, when communist reformer Imre Nagy and his comrades were given a proper, ceremonial reburial on Heroes' Square; and August 19, when, in the first tentative steps toward the reunification of Europe, Hungarians and Austrians came together in a field near the town of Sopron for the so-called "Pan-European Picnic." (Some 900 East Germans seized this opportunity to make a run for the border...and slipped into the West when Hungarian border guards refused orders to shoot defectors.) On October 23—the anniversary of the 1956 Uprising—the truly democratic Republic of Hungary triumphantly replaced the People's Republic of Hungary.

Hungary Today: Capitalism, Gyurcsány, and Orbán (1989-Present)

The transition from communism to capitalism has been rocky in Hungary. While many Hungarians were eager for the freedom to travel and pursue the interests that democracy allowed them, many others struggled to cope with the sudden reduction of government-provided services.

In 2004, Hungary joined the European Union. And in recent years, Hungary has often been in the international news, as its fitful transition to democracy has taken some attention-grabbing turns. The Hungarian Socialist Party (MSzP), which took control of parliament in 2002, stubbornly maintained and even extended some social programs, despite worries that mounting public debt would bankrupt the country. As a result, rampant inflation continued to wrack the country. In late 2008, with Prime Minister Ferenc Gyurcsány warning of "state bankruptcy" and a currency collapse, Hungary received a $25 billion bailout package from the EU, International Monetary Fund, and World Bank. Gyurcsány finally resigned in early 2009, acknowledging that he was getting in the way of Hungary's economic recovery.

Viktor Orbán, of the nationalistic, right-of-center Fidesz Party, became prime minister in a landslide in May of 2010. Fidesz—a strange hybrid of populist and authoritarian—stands for traditional Christian and Hungarian values, economic interventionism, and severe skepticism about immigration and European Union membership.

Orbán seized on his two-thirds majority to adopt a new, Fidesz-favorable constitution that stripped away checks and balances and entrenched party leaders in institutions that had previously been considered apolitical. Almost immediately, international observers—including the EU and US—grew concerned.

In early 2011, Orbán's party created a new FCC-like media authority with broad latitude for suppressing material that it considers inappropriate. Fidesz also extended Hungarian citizenship to people of Hungarian descent living in neighboring countries. This stoked century-old Hungarian resentment about the territorial losses from the post-World War I Treaty of Trianon. Orbán also insists on flying the flag of Transylvania (a part of Hungary that was lost in Trianon)—rather than the EU flag—above the Hungarian Parliament.

Fidesz has a penchant for reinterpreting Hungarian history—rehabilitating some figures (such as Miklós Horthy, who forged an alliance with Hitler's Nazi Germany), while brushing other, less Fidesz-friendly figures under the rug. The party went on a renaming binge—rechristening more than two dozen streets, squares, and other features of Budapest—and has been aggressive about tearing down old monuments and erecting new ones.

On a positive note, Fidesz has also been proactive about funneling European Union funds into public-works projects, and Budapest has made stunning progress in renovating formerly dreary streets and squares. But this always seems to come with a Fidesz-approved aesthetic that evokes the party's values. Some critics have described these new spaces—vast and bombastic, as if designed to trumpet historical greatness and host military parades—as "fascistic."

Other Orbán and Fidesz policies have also been controversial—from nationalizing the school system (the same Fidesz-approved textbooks are now used in every school in Hungary) to proposing a per-use Internet tax. (That last one resulted in enormous public protests in the fall of 2014, and Orbán quickly backpedaled.)

Outrageous as Fidesz seems to younger, EU-supporting, highly educated Hungarians, the party pleased its base enough to easily retain its power in the 2014 parliamentary elections. (Fidesz's control of the media didn't hurt its chances either.) Many international observers worry that Fidesz's success could be the death knell for true democracy in Hungary.

In the fall of 2015, Fidesz was in the international news once more, as Orbán took a particularly hard line against Syrian immigrants flooding through Eastern Europe on their way to a better life in wealthy Western European nations. The government erected barbed wire fences and dispatched an intimidating border defense squad to make it clear that refugees weren't welcome. While humanitarians condemned Orbán's actions—which violated the European Union's open-borders agreements, and left many desperate people with nowhere to go—his supporters touted his success in preventing unwanted refugees from flooding the country.

Fortunately, tourists visiting today's Hungary are scarcely aware of its political squabbles. The Hungarian people—relieved to be free of oppression, and allowed to pursue their lovably quirky customs with a renewed vigor—enthusiastically welcome and charm visitors. It's been a long road for the Hungarians from those distant, windblown steppes of Central Asia...but today they seem to be doing better than ever.

HUNGARIAN FOOD

Hungarian cuisine is the undisputed best in Central Europe. It delicately blends Magyar peasant cooking (with rich spices), refined by the elegance of French preparation, with a delightful smattering of flavors from the vast, multiethnic Austro-Hungarian Empire (including Germanic, Balkan, Jewish, and Carpathian). Everything is heavily seasoned: with paprika, tomatoes, and peppers of every shape, color, size, and flavor.

An *étterem* ("eatery") is a nice sit-down restaurant, while a *vendéglő* is usually more casual (similar to a tavern or an inn), and a *bisztró* is a trendy eatery with a concise but well-executed menu. A *söröző* ("beer place") is a pub that sells beer and pub grub. A *kávéház* ("coffeehouse"), or café, is where Hungarians gather to meet friends, get a caffeine fix...and sometimes to have a great meal. Other cafés serve only light food, or sometimes only desserts. But if you want a wide choice of cakes, look for a *cukrászda* (pastry shop—*cukr* means "sugar").

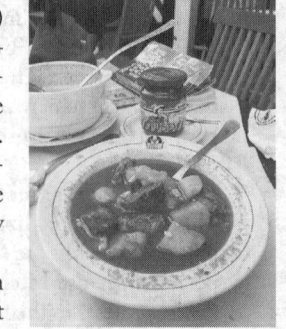

When foreigners think of Hungarian cuisine, what comes to mind is goulash. But tourists are often disappointed when "real Hungarian goulash" isn't the thick stew that they were expecting. The word "goulash" comes from the Hungarian *gulyás leves,* or "shepherd's soup"—a tasty, rustic, nourishing dish originally eaten by cowboys and shepherds on the Great Hungarian Plain. Here in its homeland, it's a clear, spicy broth with chunks of meat, potatoes, and other vegetables. Elsewhere (such as in the Germanic and Slavic countries that are Hungary's neighbors), the word "goulash" does describe a thick stew. The hearty Hungarian stew called *pörkölt* is probably closer to what most people think of as goulash.

Aside from the obligatory *gulyás,* make a point of trying another unusual Hungarian specialty: cold fruit soup *(hideg gyümölcs leves).* This sweet, cream-based treat—generally eaten before the meal, even though it tastes more like a dessert—is usually made with *meggy* (sour cherries), but you'll also see versions with *alma* (apples) or *körte* (pears). Other Hungarian soups *(levesek)* include *bableves* (bean soup), *zöldségleves* (vegetable soup), *gombaleves* (mushroom soup), *halászlé* (fish broth with paprika), and *húsleves* (meat or chicken soup). The ultimate staple of traditional Hungarian home-cooking, but rarely served in restaurants, is *főzelék*—a simple but tasty wheat flour-thickened stew that can be supplemented with various vegetables and meats).

Hungarians adore all kinds of meat. *Hús* or *marhahús* is beef, *csirke* is chicken, *borjú* is veal, *kacsa* is duck, *liba* is goose, *sertés* is pork, *sonka* is ham, *kolbász* is sausage, *szelet* is schnitzel (*Bécsi szelet* means Wiener schnitzel)—and the list goes on. One trendy ingredient you'll see on menus is *mangalica.* This uniquely Hungarian, free-range woolly pig (basically a domesticated boar) is high in unsaturated fat—which fits perfectly with the current foodie culture that elevates the mighty pig. *Libamáj* is goose liver, which shows up everywhere (anything prepared "Budapest style" is topped with goose liver). Lard is used extensively in cooking, making Hungarian cuisine very rich and filling.

Meat is often covered with delicious sauces or garnishes, from rich cream sauces to spicy pastes to fruit jam. For classic Hungarian flavors, you can't beat chicken or veal *paprikás* (described in the "Paprika Primer" sidebar).

Vegetarians have a tricky time in traditional Hungarian restaurants, many of which offer only a plate of deep-fried vegetables. A traditional Hungarian "salad" is composed mostly or entirely of pickled vegetables (pickles, cabbage, peppers, and others); even many modern restaurants haven't quite figured out how to do a good, healthy, leafy salad. Fortunately, the more modern, trendy eateries in the capital often offer excellent vegetarian options.

Starches *(köretek)*—which you'll sometimes order separate from the meat course—can include *nokedli* (small, boiled "drop noodles," a.k.a. *Spätzle*), *galuska* (noodles), *burgonya* (potatoes), *sült krumpli* (French fries), *krokett* (croquettes), or *rizs* (rice). *Kenyér* (bread) often comes with the meal. A popular snack—especially to accompany a wine-tasting—is a *pogácsa*, a savory doughnut.

Sometimes your main dish will come with steamed, grilled, or deep-fried vegetables. A common side dish is *káposzta* (cabbage, often prepared like sauerkraut). You may also see *töltött káposzta* (cabbage stuffed with meat) or *töltött paprika* (stuffed peppers). *Lecsó* (LEH-chew) is the Hungarian answer to ratatouille: a richly flavorful stew of tomatoes, peppers, and other vegetables.

Thin, crêpe-like pancakes *(palacsinta)* are usually a starter, but sometimes served as a main dish. A delicious traditional Hungarian dish is *Hortobágyi palacsinta* (Hortobágy pancakes, named for the Hungarian Great Plain where the dish originates). This is a savory crêpe wrapped around a tasty meat filling and drenched with creamy paprika sauce.

Pancakes also appear as desserts, stuffed and/or covered with fruit, jam, chocolate sauce, walnuts, poppy seeds, or whipped cream. Most famous is the *Gundel palacsinta*, named for *the* top-of-the-line Budapest restaurant—stuffed with walnuts and raisins in a rum sauce, topped with chocolate sauce, and flambéed.

Pastries are a big deal in Hungary. In the late 19th century, pastry-making caught on here in an attempt to keep up with the renowned desserts of rival Vienna. Today Hungary's streets are still lined with *cukrászda* (pastry shops) where you can simply point to whichever treat you'd like. Try the *Dobos torta* (a many-layered chocolate-and-caramel cream cake), *somlói galuska* (a dumpling with vanilla, nuts, and chocolate), anything with *gesztenye* (chestnuts), and *rétes*

(strudel with various fillings, including *túrós*, curds). And many *cukrászda* also serve *fagylalt* (ice cream, *fagyi* for short), sold by the *gombóc* (ball).

When the server comes to take your order, he might say *"Tessék"* (TEHSH-shayk), or maybe the more formal *"Tessék parancsolni"* (TEHSH-shayk PAW-rawn-chohl-nee)—"Please command, sir." When they bring the food, they will probably say, *"Jó étvág-*

Paprika Primer

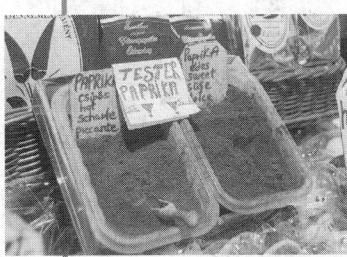

The quintessential ingredient in Hungarian cuisine is paprika. In Hungarian, the word *paprika* can mean both peppers (red or green) and the spice that's made from them. Peppers can be stewed, stuffed, sautéed, baked, grilled, or pickled. For seasoning, red shakers of dried paprika join the salt and pepper on tables.

Locals say paprika is best from the sunny south of Hungary. There are more than 40 varieties of paprika spice, with two main types: hot (*csípős* or *erős*) and sweet (*édesnemes* or simply *édes,* often comes in a white can; sometimes also called *csemege*—"delicate"). Hungarians typically cook with sweet paprika to add flavor and color. Then, at the table, they put out hot paprika so each diner can adjust the heat to his or her preferred taste. A can or bag of paprika is a handy and tasty souvenir of your trip.

On menus, anything cooked *paprikás* (PAW-pree-kash) comes smothered in a spicy, creamy red stew. Most often you'll see this option with *csirke* (chicken) or *borjú* (veal), and it's generally served with dumpling-like boiled egg noodles called *nokedli* (similar to German *Spätzle*). This dish is *the* Hungarian staple—if you sample just one dish in Hungary, make it chicken or veal *paprikás.*

To add even more kick to your food, ask for a jar of the bright-red paste called *Erős Pista* (EH-rewsh PEESH-taw). Literally "Spicy Steve," this Hungarian answer to Tabasco is best used sparingly. Or try *Édes Anna* (AY-desh AW-naw, "Sweet Anna"), a variation that's more sweet than spicy. You'll also see tubes of *Gulyáskrém* (a bright-orange, sweet-but-not-hot paste for jazzing up soups) and *Piros Arany* ("Red Gold," a deep-red, intensely flavorful, spicy paste).

yat!" (yoh AYT-vah-yawt)—"Bon appétit." When you're ready for the bill, you can simply say, *"Fizetek"* (FEE-zeh-tehk)—"I'll pay."

Drinks

Kávé (KAH-vay) and *tea* (TEH-aw) are coffee and tea. (Confusingly, *tej* is not tea—it's milk.) As for water (*víz,* pronounced "veez"), it comes as *szódavíz* (soda water, sometimes just carbonated tap water) or *ásványvíz* (spring water, more expensive).

Hungary is first and foremost a wine country. For the complete rundown on Hungarian wines, see the sidebar.

Hungarian Wines

Wine *(bor)* is an essential part of Hungarian cuisine. Whites *(fehér)* can be sweet *(édes)*, half-dry *(félszáraz)*, or dry *(száraz)*. Whites include the standards (riesling, chardonnay), as well as some wines made from more typically Hungarian grapes: *leányka* ("little girl"), a half-dry, fairly heavy, white table wine; *cserszegi fűszeres,* a spicy, light white that can be fruity; the half-dry, full-bodied *hárslevelű* ("linden leaf"); and the dry *furmint* and *kéknyelű* ("blue stalk").

Reds *(vörös)* include the familiar varieties (cabernet sauvignon, cabernet franc, merlot, pinot noir), and some that are less familiar. **Kekporto** is better known as *blauer Portugieser* in German-speaking countries. In Eger, don't miss **Bull's Blood,** a.k.a. Egri Bikavér, a distinctive blend of reds that comes with a fun local legend (described on page 691). The spicy, medium-body **kékfrankos** ("blue Frankish") supposedly got its name because when Napoleonic soldiers were here, they could pay either with valuable blue-colored bank notes or unstable white ones...and local vintners wanted the blue francs. (Like most wine origin legends, this story is untrue—*kékfrankos* wasn't cultivated here until after Napoleon's time.)

Probably the most famous Hungarian wine is **Tokaji Aszú,** a sweet, late-harvest, honey-colored dessert wine made primarily from *furmint* grapes. Known as the "wine of kings, and the king of

Hungary isn't particularly well-known for its beer (*sör*, pronounced "shewr"), but Dreher and Borsodi are two of the better brands. *Világos* is lager; if you prefer something darker, look for *barna* (brown).

Hungary is almost as proud of its spirits as its wines. The local firewater, *pálinka*, is a powerful schnapps made from various fruits (most often plum, *szilva;* or apricots, *barack*). Also look for the pear-flavored Vilmos brandy.

Unicum is a unique and beloved Hungarian bitter liquor made of 40 different herbs and aged in oak casks. Look for the round bottle with the red cross on the label. The flavor is powerfully unforgettable—like Jägermeister, but harsher. Unicum started out as a medicine and remains a popular digestif for easing an upset stomach (especially if you've eaten too much rich food—not an uncommon problem in Hungary). Purists claim it's better to drink it at room temperature (so you can fully appreciate its bouquet), but novices find it easier to slug back when chilled.

wines," Tokaji Aszú is a D.O.C. product, meaning that to have that name, it must be grown in a particular region. Tokaj is a town in northeastern Hungary, while *aszú* is a "noble rot" grape. The

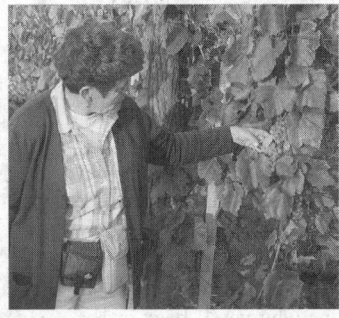

wine's unique, concentrated flavor is made possible by a fungus *(Botrytis cinerea)* that thrives on the grapes in the late fall. The grapes are left on the vine, where they burst and wither like raisins before they are harvested in late October and November. This sucks the water out of the grape, leaving behind very high sugar content and a deep golden color. Tokaji Aszú wines are numbered, from three to six, indicating how many eight-gallon tubs *(puttony)* of these "noble rot" grapes were added to the base wine—the higher the number, the sweeter the wine. Other variations on Tokaji can be less sweet. (This might sound like another bizarre Hungarian custom, but the French Sauterne and German Beerenauslese wines are also made from "noble rot" grapes. The similarly named French Tokay wine—which derives from the same word—is a different story altogether.)

Finally, note that, except for Bull's Blood and Tokaji Aszú, Hungarian wines are not widely available in the US. A bottle or two (transported in your checked luggage) is a unique souvenir.

HUNGARY

If the original Unicum overwhelms your palate, try one of the newer variations: Unicum Next, with more of a citrus flavor, and Unicum Szilva (with a golden plum on the label), which is aged in plums that cut some of the bitterness with a rich sweetness (www.zwack.hu).

If you're drinking with some new Magyar friends, impress them with the standard toast: *Egészségedre* (EH-gehs-shay-gehdreh; "to your health").

HUNGARIAN LANGUAGE

Even though Hungary is surrounded by Slavs, Hungarian is not at all related to Slavic languages (such as Polish, Czech, or Croatian). In fact, Hungarian isn't related to *any* European language, except for very distant relatives Finnish and Estonian. It isn't even an Indo-European language—meaning that English is more closely related to Hindi, Russian, and French than it is to Hungarian.

Hungarian is agglutinative: To create meaning, you start with a simple root word and then start tacking on suffixes—sometimes resulting in a pileup of extra sounds. The emphasis always goes on the first syllable, and the following syllables are droned in a kind of a monotone—giving the language a distinctive cadence that Hungary's neighbors love to tease about.

While the language can be overwhelming for tourists, one easy word is *"Szia"* (SEE-yaw), which means both hello and goodbye (like "ciao" or "aloha"). Confusingly, sometimes Hungarians simply say the English word "hello" to mean either "hi" or "bye." Another handy word that Hungarians (and people throughout Central Europe) will understand is *Servus* (SEHR-voos, spelled *Szervusz* in Hungarian)—the old-fashioned greeting from the days of the Austro-Hungarian Empire. If you draw a blank on how to say hello, just offer a cheery, *"Servus!"*

Hungarian pronunciation is straightforward, once you remember a few key rules. The trickiest: *s* alone is pronounced "sh," while *sz* is pronounced "s." This explains why you'll hear in-the-know travelers pronouncing Budapest as "BOO-daw-pesht." You might catch the *busz* up to Castle Hill—pronounced "boose." And "Franz Liszt" is easier to pronounce than it looks: It sounds just like "list." To review:

s sounds like "sh" as in "shirt"

sz sounds like "s" as in "saint"

Hungarian has a set of unusual palatal sounds that don't quite have a counterpart in English. To make these sounds, gently press the thick part of your tongue to the roof or your mouth (instead of using the tip of your tongue behind your teeth, as we do in English):

gy sounds like "dg" as in "hedge"

ny sounds like "ny" as in "canyon" (not "nee")

ty sounds like "tch" as in "itch"

cs sounds like "ch" as in "church"

As for vowels: The letter *a* almost sounds like o (aw, as in "hot"); but with an accent *(á)*, it brightens up to the more standard "ah." Likewise, while *e* sounds like "eh," *é* sounds like "ay." An accent *(á, é, í, ó, ú)* indicates that you linger on that vowel, but not necessarily that you stress that syllable. Like German, Hungarian has umlauts *(ö, ü)*, meaning you purse your lips when you say that vowel: roughly, *ö* sounds like "ur" and *ü* sounds like "ew." A long umlaut *(ő, ű)* is the same sound, but you hold it a little longer. Words ending in *k* are often plural.

Here are a few other letters that sound different in Hungarian than in English:

c and **cz** both sound like "ts" as in "cats"

zs sounds like "zh" as in "leisure"

j and **ly** both sound like "y" as in "yellow"

OK, maybe it's not *so* simple. But you'll get the hang of it...and Hungarians will appreciate your efforts.

For a complete list of Hungarian survival phrases, see the following pages. As you navigate, remember these key Hungarian terms: *tér* (pronounced "tehr," square), *utca* (OOT-zaw, street), *út* (oot, boulevard), *körút* (KUR-root, ring road), *híd* (heed, bridge), and *város* (VAH-rohsh, town). To better match what you'll see locally, in the following chapters I've mostly used these Hungarian terms (instead of the English equivalents).

Hungarian Survival Phrases

Remember, the letter *a* is pronounced "aw," while *á* is a brighter "ah." In the phonetics, *dj* is pronounced like the *j* in "jeans."

English	Hungarian	Pronunciation
Hello. (formal)	Jó napot kívánok.	yoh **nah**-poht **kee**-vah-nohk
Hi. / Bye. (informal)	Szia. / Hello.	**see**-yaw / "Hello"
Do you speak English?	Beszél angolul?	beh-**sayl** awn-goh-lool
Yes. / No.	Igen. / Nem.	**ee**-gehn / nehm
I (don't) understand.	(Nem) értem.	(nehm) **ayr**-tehm
Please.	Kérem.	**kay**-rehm
You're welcome.	Szívesen.	**see**-veh-shehn
Thank you (very much).	Köszönöm (szépen).	**kur**-sur-nurm (**say**-pehn)
Excuse me. / I'm sorry.	Bocsánat.	**boh**-chah-nawt
No problem.	Semmi gond.	**sheh**-mee gohnd
Good.	Jól.	yohl
Goodbye.	Viszontlátásra.	**vee**-sohnt-lah-tahsh-raw
one / two / three	egy / kettő / három	edj / **keh**-tur / **hah**-rohm
four / five / six / seven	négy / öt / hat / hét	**naydj** / urt / hawt / hayt
eight / nine / ten	nyolc / kilenc / tíz	nyolts / **kee**-lehnts / teez
hundred / thousand	száz / ezer	sahz / **eh**-zehr
How much?	Mennyi?	**mehn**-yee
local currency	forint (Ft)	**foh**-reent
Where is it?	Hol van?	hohl vawn
Is it free (no charge)?	Ingyen van?	een-**jehn** vawn
Where can I find / buy...?	Hol találok / vehetek...?	hohl **taw**-lah-lohk / veh-heh-tehk
I'd like / We'd like...	Kérnék / Kérnénk...	**kayr**-nayk / **kayr**-naynk
...a room.	...egy szobát.	edj **soh**-baht
...a ticket (to ___).	...egy jegyet (___-ig).	edj **yehdj**-eht (___-ig)
Is it possible?	Lehet?	leh-**heht**
Where is the ___?	Hol van a ___?	hohl vawn aw ___
big train station (in Budapest)	pályaudvar	**pah**-yood-vawr
small train station (elsewhere)	vasútállomás	**vaw**-shoot-ah-loh-mahsh
bus station	buszpályaudvar	**boos**-pah-yood-vawr
tourist information office	turista információ	**too**-reesh-taw **een**-for-maht-see-yoh
toilet	toalet / WC	**toh**-aw-leht / **vayt**-say
men / women	férfi / női	**fayr**-fee / **nur**-ee
left / right	bal / jobb	bawl / yohb
straight	egyenesen	**edj**-eh-neh-shehn
At what time...?	Mikor...?	**mee**-kor
...does this open / close	...nyit / zár	nyit / zahr
Just a moment.	Egy pillanat.	edj **pee**-law-nawt
now / soon / later	most / hamarosan / később	mohsht / **haw**-maw-roh-shawn / **kay**-shurb
today / tomorrow	ma / holnap	maw / **hohl**-nawp

In a Hungarian Restaurant

English	Hungarian	Pronunciation
I'd like to reserve a table for one / two people.	Szeretnék foglalni egy asztalt egy / két fő részére.	**seh**-reht-nayk **fog**-lawl-nee edj **aws**-tawlt edj / kayt few **ray**-say-reh
Is this table free?	Ez az asztal szabad?	ehz oz **aws**-tawl saw-**bawd**
Can I help you?	Tessék?	**tehsh**-shayk
The menu (in English), please.	Kérem az (angol), étlapot.	**kay**-rehm oz (**awn**-gohl) **ayt**-law-poht
service (not) included	a számla a felszolgálási díjat (nem) tartalmazza	aw **sahm**-law aw **fehl**-sohl-gah-lah-shee **dee**-yawt (nehm) **tawr**-tawl-maw-zaw
"to go"	elvitelre	**ehl**-vee-tehl-reh
with / without	___-val / nélkül	___-vawl / **nayl**-kewl
and / or	és / vagy	aysh / vawdj
fixed-price meal (of the day)	(napi) menü	(**naw**-pee) **meh**-new
daily special	napi ajánlat	**naw**-pee **aw**-yahn-lawt
main courses	főételek	**fur**-ay-teh-lehk
appetizers	előételek	**eh**-lur-ay-teh-lehk
bread / cheese	kenyér / sajt	**kehn**-yayr / shayt
sandwich	szendvics	**send**-veech
soup / salad	leves / saláta	**leh**-vehsh / **shaw**-lah-taw
meat / poultry	hús / szárnyasok	hoosh / **sahr**-nyaw-shohk
fish	halak	**haw**-lawk
seafood	tengeri halak	**tehn**-geh-ree **haw**-lawk
fruit / vegetables	gyümölcs / zöldség	**jewm**-urlch / **zulrd**-shayg
dessert	desszert	**deh**-sehrt
vegetarian	vegetáriánus	**veh**-geh-tah-ree-ah-noosh
(tap) water	(csap) víz	(chawp) veez
mineral water	ásványvíz	**ash**-vawn-veez
milk / (orange) juice	tej / (narancs) lé	**tay**ee / (**naw**-rawnch) lay
coffee / tea	kávé / tea	**kah**-vay / **teh**-aw
beer / wine	sör / bor	shohr / bohr
red / white	vörös / fehér	**vur**-rursh / **feh**-hayr
sweet / dry / semi-dry	édes / száraz / félszáraz	**ay**-dehsh / **sah**-rawz / **fayl**-sah-rawz
glass / bottle	pohár / üveg	**poh**-hahr / **ew**-vehg
Cheers!	Egészségedre!	**eh**-gehs-sheh-geh-dreh
More. / Another.	Még. / Máskikat.	mayg / **mah**-shee-kawt
The same.	Ugyanazt.	**oodj**-aw-nawst
Bill, please. (literally, "I'll pay.")	Fizetek.	**fee**-zeh-tehk
tip	borravaló	**boh**-raw-vaw-loh
Bon appétit!	Jó étvágyat!	yoh **ayt**-vah-yawt
Delicious!	Finom!	**fee**-nohm

BUDAPEST

Budapest (locals say "BOO-daw-pesht") is a unique metropolis at the heart of a unique nation. Here you'll find experiences like nothing else in Europe: Feel your stress ebb away as you soak in hundred-degree water, surrounded by opulent Baroque domes...and by Speedo- and bikini-clad Hungarians. Ogle some of Europe's most richly decorated interiors, which echo a proud little nation's bygone glory days. Perk up your ears with a first-rate performance at one of the world's top opera houses—at bargain prices. Ponder the region's bleak communist era as you stroll amid giant Soviet-style statues designed to evoke fear and obedience. Try to wrap your head around Hungary's colorful history...and your tongue around its notoriously difficult language. Dive into a bowl of goulash, the famous paprika-flavored peasant soup with a kick. Go for an after-dinner stroll along the Danube, immersed in a grand city that's bathed in floodlights.

Europe's most underrated big city, Budapest can be as challenging as it is enchanting. The sprawling Hungarian capital is a city of nuance and paradox—cosmopolitan, complicated, and tricky for the first-timer to get a handle on. Think of Budapest as that favorite Hungarian pastime, chess: It's simple to learn...but takes a lifetime to master. This chapter is your first lesson. Then it's your move.

PLANNING YOUR TIME

Budapest demands at least two full days—and that assumes you'll be selective and move fast. To slow down and really dig into the city, give it a third or fourth day. Adding more time opens up various day-trip options.

Budapest is quite decentralized: Plan your day ahead to minimize backtracking. Just about everything is walkable, but distances are far, and public transit can save valuable time.

When divvying your time between Buda and Pest, keep in mind that (aside from the Gellért and Rudas Baths) Buda's sightseeing is mostly concentrated on Castle Hill, and can easily be done in less than a day, while Pest deserves as much time as you're willing to give it. Save relatively laid-back Buda for when you need a break from the big city.

Below are some possible plans, depending on the length of your trip. Note that these very ambitious itineraries assume you want to sightsee at a speedy pace. In the **evening,** you have a wide range of options (detailed under "Entertainment in Budapest" on page 636, and "Nightlife in Budapest" on page 639): enjoying good restaurants, taking in an opera or concert, snuggling on a romantic floodlit river cruise, relaxing in a thermal bath, exploring the city's unique ruin pubs, or simply strolling the Danube embankments and bridges.

Budapest in Two Days

Spend Day 1 in Pest: Begin at the Parliament and stroll through Leopold Town, then walk through Pest town center to the Great Market Hall. From there, circle around the Small Boulevard to Deák tér; if you're not wiped out yet, walk up Andrássy út to Heroes' Square and City Park. Or, if you're exhausted already, just take the M1/yellow Metró line to Hősök tere, ogle the Heroes' Square statues and Vajdahunyad Castle, and reward yourself with a soak at Széchenyi Baths. (Note that this schedule leaves virtually no time for entering museums, though you might be able to fit in one or two big sights; the most worthwhile are the Parliament—for which you should book tickets ahead online—the Opera House, the Great Synagogue, or the House of Terror.)

On the morning of Day 2, tackle any Pest sights you didn't have time for yesterday (or take the bus out to Memento Park). After lunch, ride bus #16 from Deák tér to Buda's Castle Hill. Finally, head back to Pest for some final sightseeing and dinner.

Budapest in Three or Four Days

Your first day is for getting your bearings in Pest. Begin by strolling through Leopold Town (including a tour of the Parliament—book tickets ahead online). Next, walk up Andrássy út (including touring the Opera House and/or the House of Terror) to Heroes' Square and City Park. End your day with a soak at the Széchenyi Baths.

On Day 2, delve deeper into Pest, starting with a stroll through the town center. After visiting the Great Market Hall, you can cross the river to Buda for a soak at the Gellért or Rudas Baths, or circle around the Small Boulevard to see the National Museum and/or Great Synagogue.

On Day 3, use the morning to see any remaining sights, then ride from Deák tér out to Memento Park on the park's 11:00 direct bus. On returning, grab a quick lunch and take bus #16 from Deák tér to Castle Hill.

With a fourth day, spread the Day 1 activities over more time, and circle back to any sights you've missed so far.

Orientation to Budapest

Budapest is huge, with nearly two million people. Like Vienna, the city was built as the head of a much larger empire than it currently governs. But the city is surprisingly easy to manage once you get the lay of the land and learn the excellent public transportation network. Those who are comfortable with the Metró, trams, and buses have the city by the tail (see "Getting Around Budapest" on page 557).

The city is split down the center by the Danube River. On the east side of the Danube is flat **Pest** (pronounced "pesht"), and on the west is hilly **Buda**. A third part of the city, **Óbuda,** sits to the north of Buda.

Buda: Buda is dominated by **Castle Hill** (packed with tourists by day, dead at night). The pleasant **Víziváros** ("Water Town"; VEE-zee-vah-rohsh) neighborhood is between the castle and the river; nearby is the square called Batthyány tér (a handy hub for the Metró—M2/red line—plus tram lines and the HÉV suburban railway). To the south is the taller, wooded **Gellért Hill,** capped by the Liberation Monument, with a pair of thermal baths at its base—Gellért and Rudas.

Pest: Just across the river from Castle Hill, **"Downtown"** Pest is divided into two sections. The more polished northern half, called **Leopold Town** (Lipótváros), surrounds the giant Parliament building. This is the governmental, business, and banking district (sleepy after hours). The southern half, the grittier and more urban-

BUDAPEST

Budapest Neighborhoods

Not to Scale

To Óbuda

MARGARET ISLAND

SZÉCHENYI BATHS

City Park

NYUGATI (WESTERN) TRAIN STATION

MARG. BR.

GREAT

HOUSE OF TERROR

HEROES' SQUARE

OKTOGON

SZÉLL KÁLMÁN TÉR

VÍZI-VÁROS

Danube

PARLIAMENT

OPERA

LEOPOLD TOWN

ANDRÁSSY

BOUL

PEST

CASTLE HILL

SEVENTH DISTRICT

GREAT SYNAGOGUE

DÉLI (SOUTHERN) TRAIN STATION

CHAIN BRIDGE

ELIS. BRIDGE

TOWN CENTER

RÁKÓCZI

SMALL BLVD.

KELETI (EASTERN) TRAIN STATION

HEGYALJA ÚT

RUDAS BATHS

VÁCI UTCA

RÁDAY UTCA

ÜLLŐI ÚT

BUDA

LIBERTY BRIDGE

GREAT MARKET HALL

GELLÉRT HILL

GELLÉRT BATHS

River

To Memento Park

To Airport

DCH

feeling **Town Center** (Belváros, literally "Inner Town"), is a thriving shopping, dining, nightlife, and residential zone that bustles day and night. Major landmarks here include the vast Great Market Hall and the famous (and overrated) Váci utca shopping street.

Additional key sights lie along the **Small Boulevard** ring road (connected by trams #47 and #49), including—from north to south—the Great Synagogue (marking the start of the **Jewish Quarter,** which feels a bit rundown but features several Jewish sights, as well as the **Seventh District,** a hopping nightlife zone with cool "ruin pubs"), the National Museum, and the Great Market Hall. Even more points of interest are spread far and wide along the **Great Boulevard** ring road (circled by trams #4 and #6), including Margaret Island (the city's playground, in the middle of the Danube), the Nyugati/Western train station, the prominent Oktogon intersection (where it crosses Andrássy út), the opulent New York Café (with the Keleti/Eastern train station just up the street), and the intersection with Üllői út, near the Holocaust Memorial Center and Applied Arts Museum.

Roads: The Town Center is hemmed in by the first of Pest's four concentric **ring roads** *(körút)*. The innermost ring is called the Kiskörút, or "Small Boulevard." The next ring, several blocks farther out, is called the Nagykörút, or "Great Boulevard." These ring roads change names every few blocks, but they are always called *körút*. Arterial **boulevards,** called *út,* stretch from central Pest into the suburbs like spokes on a wheel. One of these boulevards, **Andrássy út,** begins near Deák tér in central Pest and heads out to Heroes' Square and City Park; along the way it passes some of the city's best eateries, hotels, and sights (Opera House, House of Terror).

Bridges: Buda and Pest are connected by a series of characteristic bridges. From north to south, there's the low-profile **Margaret Bridge** (Margit híd, crosses Margaret Island), the famous **Chain Bridge** (Széchenyi Lánchíd), the white and modern **Elisabeth Bridge** (Erzsébet híd), and the green **Liberty Bridge** (Szabadság híd). Four more bridges lie beyond the tourist zone: the Petőfi and Rákóczi bridges to the south, and Árpád and Megyeri bridges to the north.

Districts: Budapest uses a district system (like Paris and Vienna). There are 23 districts *(kerület)*, identified by Roman numerals. For example, Castle Hill is in district I, central Pest is district V, and City Park is in district XIV. Addresses often start with the district number (as a Roman numeral).

TOURIST INFORMATION

The city of Budapest runs several official TIs (www.budapestinfo. hu, tel. 1/438-8080). The main branch is at **Deák tér,** a few steps from the M2 and M3 Metró station (daily 8:00-20:00, free Wi-Fi, Sütő utca 2, near the McDonald's, district V). Other locations include **Heroes' Square** (in the ice rink building facing Vajdahunyad Castle, daily 9:00-19:00), in a small kiosk just inside the main entrance of the **Great Market Hall** (Mon 6:00-17:00, Tue-Fri 6:00-18:00, Sat 6:00-15:00, closed Sun), and in both terminals at the **airport** (TI at Terminal 2A open daily 8:00-22:00; TI at Terminal 2B open daily 10:00-22:00). In the busy summer months, TI "mobile info points" set up in highly trafficked areas (look for the teal-and-white umbrellas).

The helpfulness of Budapest's TIs can vary, but all offer a nice variety of free, useful publications, including a good city map, the information-packed *Budapest Guide* booklet, and various events planners. At any TI, you can collect a pile of other free brochures

BUDAPEST

Snapshot History of Budapest

Budapest is a rich cultural stew made up of Hungarians, Germans, Slavs, and Jews, with a dash of Turkish paprika, all simmered for centuries in a thermal bath. Each group has left its mark, but through it all, something has remained that is distinctly...Budapest.

Budapest sits on a thin layer of earth covering thermal springs. Those waters attracted the ancient Romans, who, two thousand years ago, established Aquincum just north of today's city center.

In A.D. 896, a nomadic group from Central Asia called the Magyars took over the Carpathian Basin (roughly today's Hungary). After running roughshod over Europe, the Magyars—the ancestors of today's Hungarians—settled down, adopted Christianity, and became fully European. The twin towns of Buda and Pest emerged as the leading cities of Hungary. Gradually Buda and Pest became both a de facto capital and a melting pot for the peoples of Central and Eastern Europe.

In the 16th century, the Ottomans invaded. They occupied Budapest (and much of Hungary) for nearly a century and a half. Finally the Habsburg monarchs from neighboring Austria liberated Hungary—and kept it for themselves.

After many decades of Hungarian uprisings, the Compromise of 1867 created the Austro-Hungarian Empire; six years later, the cities of Buda, Pest, and Óbuda merged to become Budapest, which governed a sizeable chunk of Eastern Europe. For the next few decades, Budapest boomed, and Hungarian culture blossomed. A flurry of construction surrounded the year 1896—Hungary's 1,000th birthday.

But with World War I, Budapest's fortunes reversed: Hungary lost the war, and two-thirds of its land. Hungary again backed a loser in World War II; the ruins of Budapest were claimed by the Soviets, who introduced communism to Hungary. Although a bold uprising in 1956 was brutally put down, a milder "goulash communism" eventually emerged here. Budapest became a place where other Eastern Bloc residents could experiment with "Western evils," from Big Macs to Nikes.

By the end of communism in 1989, the city's rich architectural heritage was in a shambles. Forever torn between a nostalgic instinct to cling to past glory days, and a modern drive to innovate, Budapest has reinvented its cityscape with a mix of old and new. The latest chapter in Budapest's history has been written by Prime Minister Viktor Orbán, who has overseen an unprecedented burst of urban renewal, but also a rise in authoritarianism and troubling nationalism.

Budapest's uniquely epic history—still a work in progress—has shaped a glorious metropolis that fascinates both Hungarians and tourists alike.

(for sights, bus tours, and more) and buy a Budapest Card. Be aware that many for-profit agencies masquerade as "TIs" or "info points" (such as in the train stations); these are unofficial, but some—such as the one in the white kiosk on Castle Hill, near the Matthias Church—can be helpful in a pinch.

Sightseeing Passes: The **Budapest Card** includes free use of all public transportation, free walking tours of Buda and Pest, free admissions to a handful of sights (including the National Museum, National Gallery, and Memento Park), and 10-50 percent discounts on many other major museums and attractions (4,900 Ft/24 hours, 7,900 Ft/48 hours, 9,900 Ft/72 hours; includes handy 100-page booklet with maps, updated hours, and brief museum descriptions; www.budapest-card.com). If you take advantage of the included walking tours, the Budapest Card can be a good value for a very busy sightseer—do the arithmetic.

Absolute Tour Center: This office, conveniently located near Andrássy út (behind the Opera House at Lázár utca 16) can also dispense tourist information questions. They also have free Wi-Fi, bike rental, secondhand books, and information on their walking, bike, and Segway tours—all described later, under "Tours in Budapest" (sporadic hours, usually open daily 9:00-20:00, until 19:00 Nov-March, tel. 1/269-3843, mobile +3620-929-7506, www.absolutetours.com).

ARRIVAL IN BUDAPEST
By Train
Budapest has three major train stations (*pályaudvar,* abbreviated *pu.*): Keleti ("Eastern") station, Nyugati ("Western") station, and Déli ("Southern") station. Before departing from Budapest, it's essential to carefully confirm which station your train leaves from.

The Keleti/Eastern train station and the Nyugati/Western train station are both cavernous, slightly rundown, late-19th-century Erector-set masterpieces in Pest. The Déli/Southern train station—behind Castle Hill in Buda—mingles its dinginess with modern, concrete flair.

All three stations are seedy and overdue for renovation. This makes them a bit intimidating—not the most pleasant first taste of Budapest. But once you get your bearings, they're easy to navigate. A few key words: *pénztár* or *jegypénztár* is ticket window, *vágány* is track, *induló vonatok* is departures, and *érkező vonatok* is arrivals. At all stations, access to the tracks is monitored: You might have to show your ticket to reach the platforms (though this is loosely enforced).

The taxi stands in front of each train station are notorious for ripping off tourists; it's better to call for a taxi (or, better yet, stick to public transit). For tips on this—and on using the Metró system

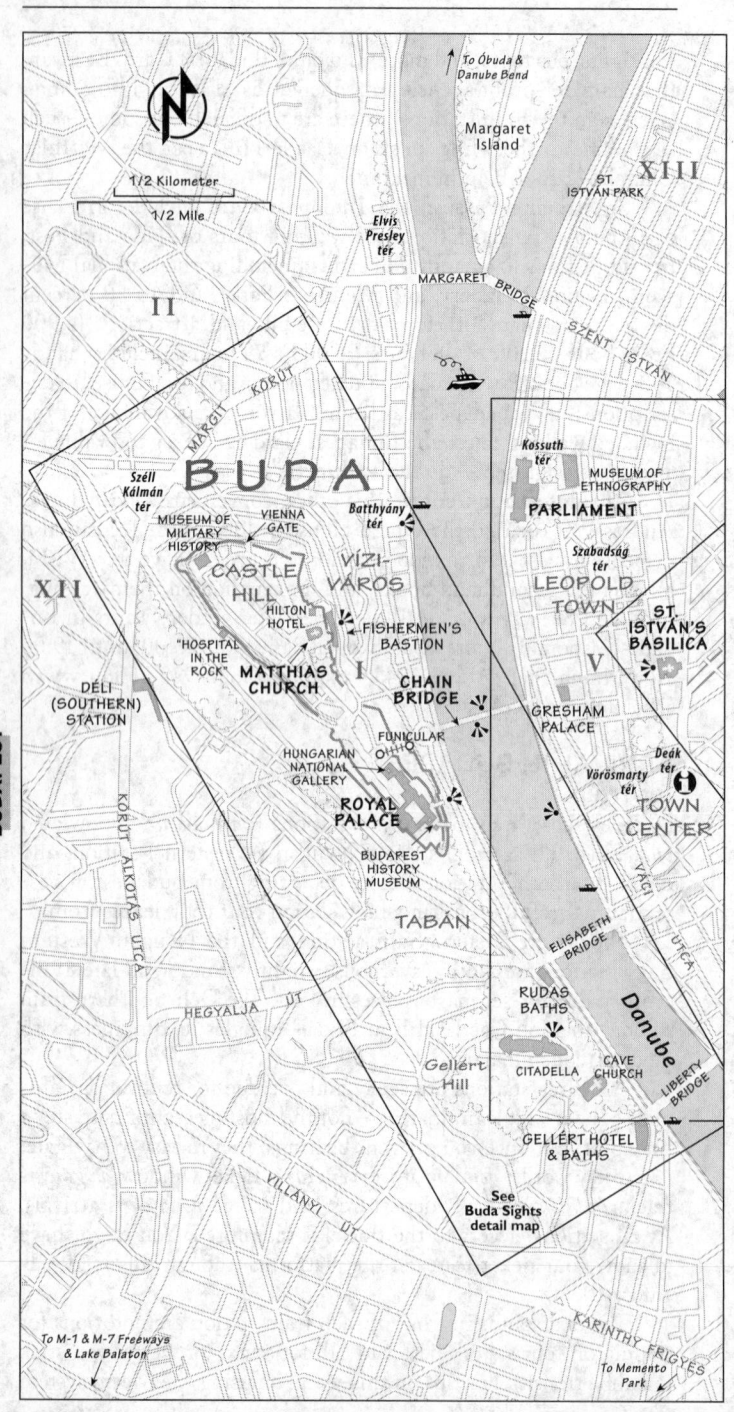

BUDAPEST

1/2 Kilometer

1/2 Mile

To Óbuda & Danube Bend

Margaret Island

XIII

ST. ISTVÁN PARK

Elvis Presley tér

MARGARET BRIDGE

SZENT ISTVÁN

II

BUDA

Kossuth tér

MUSEUM OF ETHNOGRAPHY

PARLIAMENT

Szabadság tér

LEOPOLD TOWN

ST. ISTVÁN'S BASILICA

MARGIT KÖRÚT

Széll Kálmán tér

MUSEUM OF MILITARY HISTORY

VIENNA GATE

Batthyány tér

VÍZI-VÁROS

CASTLE HILL

XII

HILTON HOTEL

FISHERMEN'S BASTION

"HOSPITAL IN THE ROCK"

MATTHIAS CHURCH

I

CHAIN BRIDGE

V

GRESHAM PALACE

DÉLI (SOUTHERN) STATION

FUNICULAR

Vörösmarty tér

TOWN CENTER

Deák tér

HUNGARIAN NATIONAL GALLERY

ROYAL PALACE

VÁCI UTCA

KÖRÚT ALKOTÁS UTCA

BUDAPEST HISTORY MUSEUM

TABÁN

ELISABETH BRIDGE

Danube

HEGYALJA ÚT

RUDAS BATHS

Gellért Hill

CITADELLA

CAVE CHURCH

LIBERTY BRIDGE

GELLÉRT HOTEL & BATHS

See Buda Sights detail map

VILLÁNYI ÚT

To M-1 & M-7 Freeways & Lake Balaton

KARINTHY FRIGYES

To Memento Park

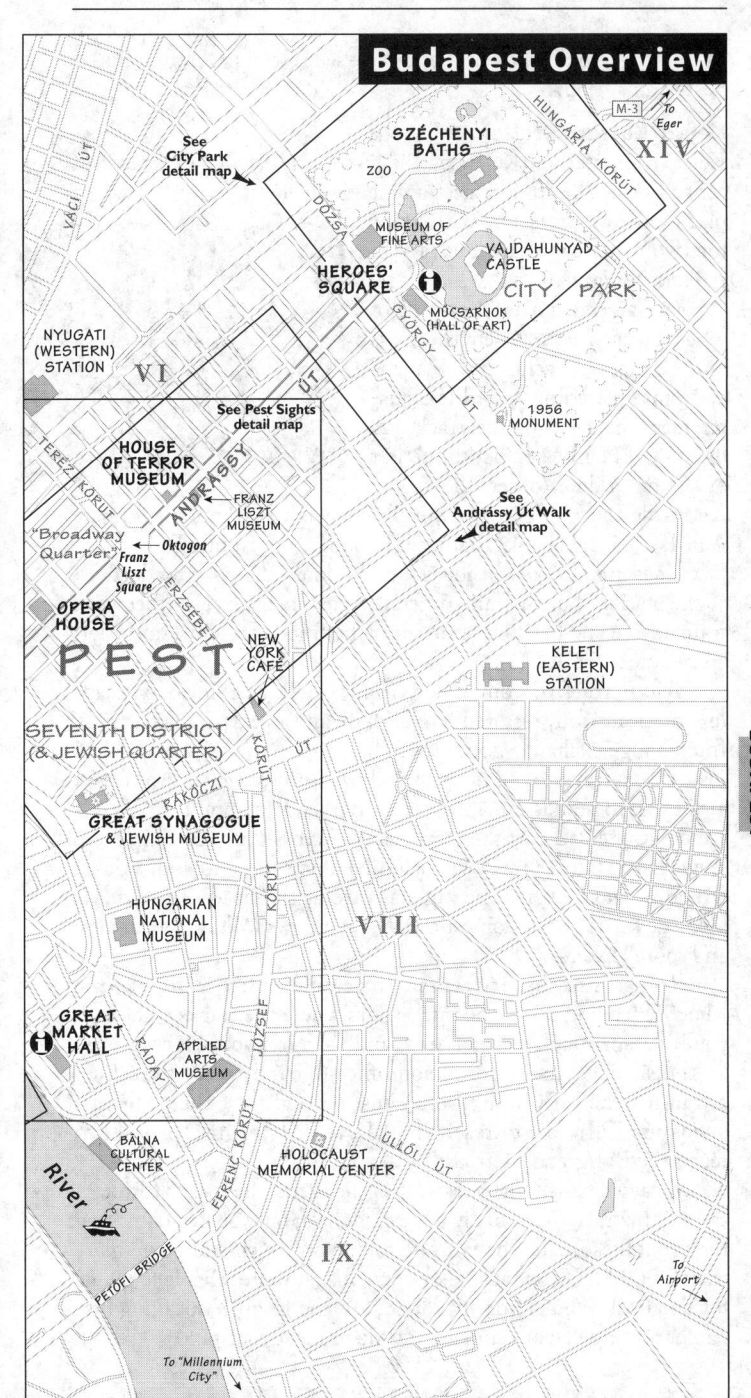

Budapest Overview

SZÉCHENYI BATHS

ZOO

See City Park detail map

MUSEUM OF FINE ARTS

HEROES' SQUARE

VAJDAHUNYAD CASTLE

MŰCSARNOK (HALL OF ART)

CITY PARK

M-3 To Eger

XIV

HUNGARIA KÖRÚT

DÓZSA

GYÖRGY

VÁCI ÚT

NYUGATI (WESTERN) STATION

VI

1956 MONUMENT

TERÉZ KÖRÚT

HOUSE OF TERROR MUSEUM

ANDRÁSSY ÚT

See Pest Sights detail map

FRANZ LISZT MUSEUM

"Broadway Quarter"

Oktogon

Franz Liszt Square

See Andrássy Út Walk detail map

ERZSÉBET KÖRÚT

OPERA HOUSE

PEST

NEW YORK CAFE

KELETI (EASTERN) STATION

SEVENTH DISTRICT (& JEWISH QUARTER)

RÁKÓCZI ÚT

KÖRÚT

GREAT SYNAGOGUE & JEWISH MUSEUM

HUNGARIAN NATIONAL MUSEUM

VIII

JÓZSEF KÖRÚT

GREAT MARKET HALL

APPLIED ARTS MUSEUM

RÁDAY

BÁLNA CULTURAL CENTER

HOLOCAUST MEMORIAL CENTER

ÜLLŐI ÚT

FERENC KÖRÚT

River

IX

To Airport

PETŐFI BRIDGE

To "Millennium City"

BUDAPEST

to connect into downtown Budapest—see "Getting Around Budapest" on page 557.

Keleti/Eastern Station

Keleti train station (Keleti pu.) is just south of City Park, east of central Pest. The station faces a pretty, split-level, newly renovated plaza called Baross tér, with stops for two different Metró lines (M2/red and M4/green).

On arrival, go to the front of long tracks 6-9 to reach the exits and services. Several travel agencies masquerading as TIs cluster near the head of the tracks. A handy OTP **ATM** is just to the left of the main door (other ATMs you see inside the station have rip-off rates—but two more legitimate ATMs are inside banks that face the square out front). Train ticket machines are also just inside the main door. There's no official TI at the station, but the railroad runs a customer service office with train advice and basic city info (near the front of track 9, in the left corner, near the ATM).

Along track 6, from back to front, you'll see a side door (leading to a beautifully restored arrivals hall, and an exit to a taxi stand), Interchange exchange booth (with bad rates—use the OTP ATM instead), international ticket windows *(nemzetközi jegypénztár),* grubby gyro stands, and the classy Baross Restaurant. Pay WCs are down the hall past the gyro places. Across the main hall, more services run **along track 9,** including domestic ("inland") ticket windows and lockers. The big staircase at the head of the tracks leads down to more domestic ticket windows, WCs, telephones, and more lockers.

To get **into the city center,** the easiest option is to take the Metró: Heading down the main stairs where the tracks dead-end, you'll pass through a ticket area, and then (on your right) a public transit ticket and information office (a handy place to pick up a transit ticket, if you need one). Just beyond that, the underpass opens up: Turn left to reach the M2/red Metró line, or right to reach the M4/green Metró line.

I'd avoid taxis—the ones waiting alongside the station (through the exit by track 6) are likely to be dishonest, but you can try asking for a rough estimate: the fair rate to downtown should be no more than 2,000 Ft. If you must take a taxi, it's far more reliable to phone for one (call 211-1111 or 266-6666, tell the English-speaking dispatcher where you are, and go outside to meet your taxi).

Nyugati/Western Station

Nyugati train station (Nyugati pu.) is the most central of Budapest's stations, facing the Great Boulevard on the northeast edge of
downtown Pest.

Most trains use the shorter
tracks 1-9, which are set back
from the main entrance. From
the head of these tracks, use the
stairs or escalator just inside the
doors to reach an underpass and
the Metró (M3/blue line). Or exit
straight ahead into a parking lot
with buses, taxis, and—around to
the right—the WestEnd City Center shopping mall. (The useful
trams around the Great Boulevard are outside the main door, at
the head of the longer tracks 10-13—see below.) Note that the taxi
drivers here are often crooked—it's far better to call for your own
cab (see instructions and taxi phone numbers described previously
for Keleti station).

The longer **tracks 10-13** extend all the way to the main entrance. Ticket machines line the tracks. Ticket windows are
through an easy-to-miss door by platform 13 (marked *jegypénztár* and *információ;* once you enter the ticket hall, international
windows are in a second room at the far end—look for *nemzetközi
jegypénztár*). Lockers are down the hall next to the international
ticket office, on the left. An **ATM** is just inside the main door, on
the right.

From the head of tracks 10-13, exit straight ahead out the
main entrance and you'll be on Teréz körút, the very busy Great
Boulevard ring road. In front of the building is the stop for the
handy trams #4 and #6 (which zip around the Great Boulevard); to
the right are stairs leading to an underpass (use it to avoid crossing
this busy intersection, or to reach the Metró's M3/blue line); and
to the left is the classiest Art Nouveau McDonald's on the planet,
filling the station's former waiting room. (Seriously. Take a look
inside.)

Déli/Southern Station

In the late 19th century, local newlyweds caught the train at Déli
train station (Déli pu.) for their honeymoon in Venice. Renovated
by the heavy-handed communists, today the station—tucked behind Castle Hill on the Buda side—is dreary, dark-stone, smaller,
and more modern-feeling than the other train stations. From the
tracks, go straight ahead into the vast, empty-feeling main hall,
with well-marked domestic and international ticket windows
at opposite ends. A left-luggage desk is outside beyond track 1.

Downstairs, you'll find several shops and eateries, and access to the very convenient M2/red Metró line, which takes you to several key points in town: Batthyány tér (on the Buda embankment, at the north end of the Víziváros neighborhood), Deák tér (the heart of Pest, with connections to two other Metró lines), and Keleti train station (where you can transfer to the M4/green Metró line).

By Plane

Budapest's **Liszt Ferenc Airport** is 10 miles southeast of the center (airport code: BUD, tel. 1/296-7000, www.bud.hu). Many Hungarians still call the airport by its former name, "Ferihegy." The airport's lone passenger terminal is called "Terminal 2" ("Terminal 1" closed in 2012). The terminal has two adjacent parts, which you can easily walk between in just a few minutes: the smaller Terminal 2A is for flights from EU/Schengen countries (no passport control required), while Terminal 2B is for flights from other countries. Both sections have ATMs and TI desks (open daily 8:00-23:00 in 2A, and daily 10:00-22:00 in 2B). Car rental desks are in the arrivals area for 2B.

Getting Between the Airport and Downtown Budapest: The fastest door-to-door option is to take a **taxi.** Főtaxi has a monopoly at the taxi stand out front; figure about 6,500 Ft to downtown, depending on traffic.

The **airport shuttle** minibus is cheaper for solo travelers, but two people will pay only a few dollars more to share a taxi (3,900 Ft/1 person, 4,900 Ft/2 people; minibus ride to any hotel in the city center takes about 30-60 minutes depending on hotel location, plus waiting time; tel. 1/550-0000, www.minibud.hu; if arranging a minibus transfer *to* the airport, call at least 24 hours in advance). Because they prefer to take several people at once, you may have to wait awhile at the airport for a quorum to show up (about 20 minutes in busy times, up to an hour when it's slow—they can give you an estimate).

Finally, there's the cheap but slow **public bus #200E.** This runs in about 25 minutes to the Kőbánya-Kispest station on the M3/blue Metró line; from there, take the Metró the rest of the way into town (entire journey covered by basic 530-Ft transit ticket, allow about an hour total for the trip to the center).

Getting Between the Airport and Eger: Eger makes an enjoyable small-town entry point in Hungary for getting over your jet lag. Unfortunately, there is no direct connection there from Budapest's airport. The easiest plan is to ride the airport shuttle minibus to Budapest's Keleti/Eastern train station, then catch the Eger-bound train from there. Or, to save a little money, you could take public bus #200E to Kőbánya-Kispest, ride the M3/blue Metró line to Deák tér, and transfer to the M2/red Metró line, which stops at both Keleti station (for the train to Eger) and Stadionok (for the bus to Eger).

By Car

Avoid driving in Budapest if you can—roads are narrow, and fellow drivers, bikes, and pedestrians make the roads feel like an obstacle course. Especially during rush hour (7:00-9:00 and 16:00-18:00), congestion is maddening, and since there's no complete expressway bypass, much of the traffic going through the city has to go *through* the city—sharing the downtown streets with local commuters. The recent wave of roadwork and other construction around Budapest only complicates matters. Signage can be confusing. Don't drive down roads marked with a red circle, or in lanes marked for buses; these can be monitored by automatic traffic cameras, and you could be mailed a ticket.

There are three concentric ring roads, all of them slow: the Small Boulevard (Kiskörút), Great Boulevard (Nagykörút), and outermost Hungária körút, from which highways and expressways spin off to other destinations. Farther out, the M-0 expressway makes a not-quite-complete circle around the city center, helping to divert some traffic.

Parking: While in Budapest, unless you're heading to an out-of-town sight (such as Memento Park), park the car at or near your hotel and take public transportation. Public street parking costs 175-525 Ft per hour (pay in advance at machine and put ticket on dashboard—watch locals and imitate). Within the Great Boulevard, it's generally free to park from 20:00 until 8:00 the next morning (farther out, it's free after 18:00). But in some heavily touristed areas, you may have to pay around the clock. Always check signs carefully, and confirm with a local (such as your hotelier) that you've parked appropriately. Also, be sure to park within the lines—otherwise, your car is likely to get "booted" (I've seen more than one confused tourist puzzling over the giant red brace on his wheel). A guarded parking lot is safer, but more expensive (figure 3,000-4,000 Ft/day, ask your hotel or look for the blue *P*s on maps). As rental-car theft can be a problem, ask at your hotel for advice.

HELPFUL HINTS

Exchange Rate: 275 Ft = about $1, €1 = about $1.10
Country Calling Code: 36 (see page 1086 for dialing instructions).
Rip-Offs: Budapest is quite safe, especially for a city of its size. Occasionally tourists run into con artists or pickpockets; as in any big city, wear a money belt and secure your valuables in touristy places and on public transportation.

Restaurants on the Váci utca shopping street are notorious for overcharging tourists. Anywhere in Budapest, avoid restaurants that don't list prices on the menu. Make a habit of checking your bill carefully. Most restaurants add a 10-12 percent service charge; if you don't notice this, you might accidentally double-tip (for more on tipping, see 1080). Also, at Váci utca and at train stations, avoid using the rip-off currency exchange booths (such as Interchange or Checkpoint). You'll do much better simply getting cash from an ATM associated with a major bank (including OTP, MKB, K&H, and various big international banks).

Budapest's biggest crooks? Unscrupulous cabbies. For tips on outsmarting them, see "Getting Around Budapest—By Taxi" on page 563. Bottom line: Locals *always* call for a cab, rather than hail one on the street or at a taxi stand. If you're not comfortable making the call yourself, ask your hotel or restaurant to call for you.

Sightseeing Tips: Budapest boomed in the late 19th century, after it became the co-capital of the vast Austro-Hungarian Empire. Most of its finest buildings (and top sights) date from this age. To appreciate an opulent interior—a Budapest experience worth ▲▲▲—prioritize touring either the Parliament or the Opera House, depending on your interests. The Opera tour is more crowd-pleasing, while the Parliament tour is grander and a bit drier (with a focus on history and parliamentary process). Seeing both is also a fine option. "Honorable mentions" go to the interiors of St. István's Basilica, the Great Synagogue, New York Café, and both the Széchenyi and the Gellért Baths.

The early 21st century is also a boom time in Budapest. The city is busy creating an ambitious Museum Quarter in City Park. The park itself is being renovated, along with many of its buildings (such as the Museum of Fine Arts and Vajdahunyad Castle). They're also erecting new, purpose-built homes for the National Gallery; Museum of Ethnography; Museum of Science, Technology, and Transport; and new House of Hungarian Music. Progress is ongoing, with the various buildings slated to open gradually over the course of 2018 and 2019. In the meantime, you'll likely see construction underway. For details, see www.ligetbudapest.org.

Medical Help: Near Buda's Széll Kálmán tér, **FirstMed Centers** is a private, pricey, English-speaking clinic (by appointment or urgent care, call first, Hattyú utca 14, 5th floor, district I, M2: Széll Kálmán tér, tel. 1/224-9090, www.firstmedcenters. com). Hospitals *(kórház)* are scattered around the city.

Pharmacies: The helpful **BENU Gyógyszertár** pharmacy is dead-center in Pest, between Vörösmarty and Széchenyi squares. Because they cater to clientele from nearby international hotels, they have a useful directory that lists the Hungarian equivalent of US prescription medicines (Mon-Fri 8:00-20:00, closed Sat-Sun, Dorottya utca 13, district V, M1: Vörösmarty tér, for location see map on page 653, tel. 1/317-2374). Each district has one 24-hour pharmacy (these should be noted outside the entrance to any pharmacy).

Monday Closures: Most of Budapest's museums are closed on Mondays. But you can still take advantage of plenty of other sights and activities: all three major baths, Memento Park, Great Synagogue and Jewish Quarter, Matthias Church on Castle Hill, St. István's Basilica, Parliament tour, Great Market Hall and Bálna Budapest, Opera House tour, City Park (and Zoo), Danube cruises, concerts, and bus, walking, and bike tours.

Train Tickets: Ticket-buying lines can be long at train stations, particularly for long-distance international trains. If you want to buy your ticket in advance, **MÁV** (Hungarian Railways) has a very convenient ticket office right in the heart of downtown Pest. They generally speak English and sell tickets for no additional fee (Mon-Fri 9:00-18:00, closed Sat-Sun, just up from the Chain Bridge and across from Erzsébet tér at József Attila utca 16, district V, M1: Vörösmarty tér, for location see map on page 653).

Post Offices: These are marked with a smart green *posta* logo (usually open Mon-Fri 8:00-18:00, Sat 8:00-12:00, closed Sun).

Laundry: Vajnóczki Tisztító Szalon, a block from the Oktogon, is a dry cleaner that also washes tourists' laundry (1,000 Ft/kg, next-day service, Mon-Fri 8:00-18:00, Sat until 13:00, closed Sun, Szófia utca 8, for location see map on page 648, tel. 1/342-3796). Two cheap self-service launderettes are in the Seventh District nightlife zone: **Laundry Budapest** has lots of machines (daily 9:00-24:00, last wash at 22:00, Dohány utca 37, near M2: Blaha Lujza tér, tel. 1/781-0098, www.laundrybudapest.hu). **Bazar Hostel** has just a few (open daily 24 hours, free Wi-Fi, closer to the Great Synagogue, at Dohány utca 22).

English Bookstore: Bestsellers has a fine selection of new books, mostly in English; it's near St. István's Basilica (Mon-Fri 9:00-18:30, Sat 11:00-18:00, Sun 12:00-18:00, Október 6 utca 11—see map on page 653, tel. 1/312-1295).

Bike Rental: Budapest—with lots of traffic congestion—isn't the easiest city for biking. But as the city adds more bike lanes and traffic-free zones, those comfortable with urban cycling may be tempted. You can rent a bike at **Yellow Zebra** (3,000 Ft/all day, 4,000 Ft/24 hours, see "Absolute Tour Center" listing on page 547).

BUDAPEST

Tonight We're Gonna Party Like It's 1896

Visitors to Budapest need only remember one date: 1896. For the millennial celebration of their ancestors' arrival in Europe, Hungarians threw a huge blowout party. In the thousand years between 896 and 1896, the Magyars had gone from being a nomadic Central Asian tribe that terrorized the Continent to sharing the throne of one of the most successful empires Europe had ever seen.

Budapest used its millennial celebration as an excuse to build monuments and buildings appropriate for the co-capital of a huge empire, including these landmarks:

- **Heroes' Square** and the **Millennium Monument**
- **Vajdahunyad Castle** (in City Park)
- The riverside **Parliament** building (96 meters tall, with 96 steps at the main entry)
- **St. István's Basilica** (also 96 meters tall)
- The M1/yellow Metró line, a.k.a. *Földalatti* ("Underground")—the first subway on the Continent
- The **Great Market Hall** (and four other market halls)
- **Andrássy út** and most of the fine buildings lining it
- The **Opera House**
- A complete rebuilding of **Matthias Church** (on Castle Hill)
- The **Fishermen's Bastion** decorative terrace (by Matthias Church)
- The green **Liberty Bridge** (then called Franz Josef Bridge, in honor of the ruling Habsburg emperor)

Ninety-six is the key number in Hungary—even the national anthem (when sung at the proper tempo) takes 96 seconds. But after all this fuss, it's too bad that the date was wrong: A commission—convened to establish the exact year of the Magyars' debut—determined it happened in 895. But city leaders knew they'd never make an 1895 deadline, and requested the finding be changed to 896.

Budapest also has a subsidized public bike network called **Bubi** (for "**Bu**dapest **Bi**kes"). Bike stations are scattered throughout the Town Center and adjoining areas; you can pick a bike up at any station, and drop it off at any other—making this handy for one-way trips. First, you buy a "ticket" at http://molbubi.bkk.hu or at a docking station (500 Ft/24 hours, 1,000 Ft/72 hours, 2,000 Ft/week, plus a 25,000-Ft deposit on your credit card for the duration of the ticket). Once you have a ticket, it's free to use a bike for 30 minutes or less, then costs 500 Ft for each additional 30 minutes. Ask at the TI if you need help figuring out the system.

Drivers: Friendly, English-speaking **Gábor Balázs** can drive you around the city or into the surrounding countryside (4,800 Ft/hour, 3-hour minimum in city, 4-hour minimum in countryside—good for a Danube Bend excursion, mobile +3620-936-4317, bgabor.e@gmail.com). **Zsolt Gál** is also available for transfers and side-trips, and specializes in helping people track down Jewish sites in the surrounding areas (mobile +3670-452-4900, forma111562@gmail.com). Note that these are drivers, not tour guides. For tour guides who can drive you to outlying sights, see "Tours in Budapest," later.

Best Views: Budapest is a city of marvelous vistas. Some of the best are from the Citadella fortress (high on Gellért Hill), the promenade in front of the Royal Palace and the Fishermen's Bastion on top of Castle Hill, and the embankments or many bridges spanning the Danube (especially the Chain Bridge). Don't forget the view from the tour boats on the Danube—particularly lovely at night.

GETTING AROUND BUDAPEST

Budapest sprawls. Connecting your sightseeing just on foot is tedious and unnecessary. It's crucial to get comfortable with the well-coordinated public transportation system: Metró lines, trams, buses, trolley buses, and boats. Budapest's transit system website, www.bkk.hu, offers a useful route-planner and a downloadable app for on-the-go transit info.

Tickets: The same tickets work for the entire system. Buy them at kiosks, Metró ticket windows, or machines (with English instructions). As it can be frustrating to find a ticket machine (especially when you see your tram or bus approaching), I generally invest in a multiday ticket to have the freedom of hopping on at will.

Your options are as follows:

• **Single ticket** (*vonaljegy*, for a ride of up to an hour on any means of transit; transfers allowed only within the Metró system)—350 Ft (or 450 Ft if bought from the driver)

• **Short single Metró ride** (*Metrószakaszjegy*, 3 stops or fewer on the Metró)—300 Ft

Budapest Transit

(Not to Scale)

--- Metró Line 1
— Metró Line 2
— Metró Line 3
--- Metró Line 4
Danube River

— Tram w/Route #'s
--- Bus w/Route #'s
HÉV Rail
Rail
Funicular
Public Riverboat

• **Transfer ticket** (*átszállójegy*—allowing up to 90 minutes, including one transfer between Metró and bus)—530 Ft

• **Pack of 10 single tickets** *(10 darabos gyűjtőjegy)*, which can be shared—3,000 Ft (that's 300 Ft per ticket, saving you 50 Ft per ticket; note that these must stay together as a single pack—they can't be sold separately)

• Unlimited multiday travel cards for Metró, bus, and tram, including a **24-hour travelcard** (*24 órás jegy*, 1,650 Ft/24 hours), **72-hour travelcard** (*72 órás jegy*, 4,150 Ft/72 hours), and **seven-day travelcard** (*hetijegy*, 4,950 Ft/7 days)

• **24-hour group travel card** (*csoportos 24 órás jegy*, 3,300 Ft), covering up to five adults—a great deal for groups of three to five people

• The **Budapest Card,** which combines a multiday ticket with sightseeing discounts (see page 547)

Always validate single-ride tickets as you enter the bus, tram, or Metró station (stick it in the elbow-high box). On older buses and trams that have little red validation boxes, stick your ticket in the black slot, then pull the slot toward you to punch holes in your ticket. Multiday tickets need be validated only once. The stern-looking people with burgundy armbands waiting as you enter or exit the Metró want to see your validated ticket. Cheaters are fined 8,000 Ft on the spot, and you'll be surprised how often you're checked—they seem to be stationed at virtually every Metró escalator. All public transit runs from 4:30 in the morning until 23:50; a few designated night buses and trams operate overnight.

New Transit Cards: Budapest plans to phase out paper tickets in favor of electronic pay-as-you-go cards (similar to London's Oyster card or New York's Metrocard). When this happens, passengers will load up a plastic card with credit, then "touch in" and "touch out" as they enter and exit the system. This may be implemented as early as 2017 or 2018. Ask around, or see www.bkk.hu for the latest.

Handy Terms: *Á ___ felé* means "in the direction of ___." *Megálló* means "stop" or "station," and *Végállomás* means "end of the line."

By Metró

Riding Budapest's efficient Metró, you really feel like you're down in the guts of the city. There are four working lines:

• **M1/yellow**—The first subway line on the Continent, this line runs just 20 steps below street level under Andrássy út from the center to City Park. Dating from 1896, "the Underground" *(Földalatti)* is so shallow that you must follow the signs on the street (listing end points—*ua Mexikói út felé* takes you toward City Park) to gauge the right direction, because there's no underpass for switching platforms. Though recently renovated, the M1 line retains its old-time atmosphere.

• **M2/red**—Built during the communist days, it's 115 feet deep and designed to double as a bomb shelter. Going under the Danube to Buda, the M2 connects the Déli/Southern train station, Széll

BUDAPEST

Kálmán tér (where you catch bus #16, #16A, or #116 to the top of Castle Hill), Batthyány tér (Víziváros and the HÉV suburban railway), Kossuth tér (behind the Parliament), Astoria (near the Great Synagogue on the Small Boulevard), and the Keleti/Eastern train station (where it crosses the M4/green line).

- **M3/blue**—This line makes a broad, boomerang-shaped swoop north to south on the Pest side. Its stations are noticeably older. Key stops include the Nyugati/Western train station, Ferenciek tere (in the heart of Pest's Town Center), Kálvin tér (near the Great Market Hall and many recommended hotels; this is also where it crosses the M4/green line), and Corvin-negyed (near the Holocaust Memorial Center).

- **M4/green**—The newest line (opened in 2014) runs from southern Buda to the Gellért Baths, under the Danube to Fővám tér (behind the Great Market Hall) and Kálvin tér (where it crosses the M3/blue line), then up to Rákóczi tér (on the Grand Boulevard) and the Keleti/Eastern train station (where it crosses the M2/red line). Many of its stations boast boldly modern, waste-of-space concrete architecture that's eye-opening to simply stroll through; the one at Gellért tér has a thermal spring-fed waterfall coursing past the main staircase.

The three original lines—M1, M2, and M3—cross only once: at the **Deák tér** stop (often signed as *Deák Ferenc tér*) in the heart of Pest, near where Andrássy út begins.

Aside from the historic M1 line, most Metró stations are at intersections of ring roads and other major thoroughfares. You'll usually exit the Metró into a confusing underpass packed with kiosks, fast-food stands, and makeshift markets. Directional signs (listing which streets, addresses, and tram or bus stops are near each exit) help you find the right exit. Or do the prairie-dog routine: Surface to get your bearings, then head back underground to find the correct stairs up to your destination.

Metró platforms are usually very well-signposted, with a list of upcoming stops on the wall behind the tracks. Digital clocks either count down to the next train's arrival, or count up from the previous train's departure; either way, you'll rarely wait more than a few minutes for the next train.

By HÉV

Budapest's suburban rail system, or HÉV (pronounced "hayv," stands for Helyiérdekű Vasút, literally "Railway of Local Interest"), branches off to the outskirts and beyond. On a short visit, it's unlikely that you'll need to use it, unless you're heading to the Óbuda neighborhood (for its museums), the charming Danube Bend town of Szentendre, or the royal palace at Gödöllő.

The HÉV line that begins at Batthyány tér in Buda's Víziváros neighborhood heads through Óbuda to Szentendre; from the station at Örs vezér tere, a different line runs east to Gödöllő. The HÉV is covered by standard transit tickets and passes for rides within the city of Budapest (such as to Óbuda). But if going beyond—such as to Szentendre or Gödöllő—you'll have to pay more. Tell the ticket-seller (or punch into the machine) where you're going, and you'll be issued the proper ticket.

By Tram

Budapest's trams are handy and frequent, taking you virtually anywhere the Metró doesn't. Here are some trams you might use (note that all of these run in both directions):

Tram **#2:** Follows Pest's Danube embankment, parallel to Váci utca. From north to south, it begins at the Great Boulevard (Jászai Mari tér, near Margaret Bridge) and stops on either side of the Parliament (north side near the visitors center/Országház stop, as well as south side near the Kossuth tér Metró stop), Széchenyi István tér and the Chain Bridge, Vigadó tér, and the Great Market Hall (Fővám tér stop).

Trams **#19** and **#41:** Run along Buda's Danube embankment from Batthyány tér (with an M2/red Metró station, and HÉV trains to Óbuda and Szentendre). From Batthyány tér, these trams run (north to south) through Víziváros, with several helpful stops: Clark Ádám tér (the bottom of the Castle Hill funicular, near the stop for bus #16 up to Castle Hill), Várkert Bazár (Castle Park with escalators and elevators up to the Royal Palace); Rudas Gyógyfürdő (Rudas Baths); then around the base of Gellért Hill to Szent Gellért tér (Gellért Baths and M4/green Metró station).

Trams **#4** and **#6:** Zip around Pest's Great Boulevard ring road (Nagykörút), connecting Nyugati/Western train station and the Oktogon with the southern tip of Margaret Island and Buda's Széll Kálmán tér (with M2/red Metró station). At night, this route is replaced by bus #6.

Trams **#47** and **#49:** Connect the Gellért Baths in Buda with Pest's Small Boulevard ring road (Kiskörút), with stops at the Great Market Hall (Fővám tér stop), the National Museum (Kálvin tér stop), the Great Synagogue (Astoria stop), and Deák tér (end of the line).

By Bus and Trolley Bus

I use the Metró and trams for most of my Budapest commuting. But some buses are useful for shortcuts within the city, or for reaching outlying sights. Note that the transit company draws a distinction between gas-powered "buses" and electric "trolley buses" (which are powered by overhead cables). Unless otherwise noted, you can assume the following are standard buses:

Buses **#16, #16A,** and **#116:** All head up to the top of Castle Hill (get off at Dísz tér, in the middle of the hill—the closest stop to the Royal Palace). You can catch any of these three at Széll Kálmán tér (M2/red Metró line). When coming from the other direction, bus #16 makes several handy stops in Pest (Deák tér, Széchenyi István tér), then crosses the Chain Bridge for more stops in Buda (including Clark Ádám tér, at Buda end of Chain Bridge on its way up to the castle).

Trolley buses **#70** and **#78:** Zip from near the Opera House (intersection of Andrássy út and Nagymező utca) to the Parliament (Kossuth tér).

Bus **#178:** Goes from Keleti/Eastern train station to central Pest (Astoria and Ferenciek tere Metró stops), then over the Elisabeth Bridge to Buda.

Bus **#26:** Begins at Nyugati/Western train station and heads around the Great Boulevard to Margaret Island, making several stops along the island.

Bus **#27:** Runs from either side of Gellért Hill to just below the Citadella fortress at the hill's peak (Búsuló Juhász stop).

Bus **#200E:** Connects Liszt Ferenc Airport to the Kőbánya-Kispest M3/blue Metró station.

Buses **#101B, #101E,** and **#150:** Run from Kelenföld (the end of the line for the M4/green Metró line) to Memento Park.

By Boat

Budapest's public transit authority operates a system of Danube riverboats (*hajójárat*, marked with a stylish *D* logo) that connect strategic locations throughout the city. The riverboat system has drawbacks: Frequency is sparse (1-2/hour on weekdays, hourly on weekends; off-season weekdays only, hourly), and it's typically slower than hopping on the Metró or a tram. But it's also a romantic, cheap alternative to pricey riverboat cruises, and can be a handy way to connect some sightseeing points.

A 750-Ft ticket covers any trip; on weekdays, it's also covered by a 24-hour, 72-hour, or seven-day travelcards (but not by the Budapest Card; on weekends, you have to buy a ticket regardless of your pass).

Lines **#D11** and **#D12** (on weekdays) and **#D13** (on weekends) run in both directions through the city, including these stops within downtown Budapest:

- **Népfürdő utca (Árpád híd),** at the northern end of Margaret Island (the weekend boat also makes several additional stops on the island);
- **Jászai Mari tér,** at the Pest end of Margaret Bridge;
- **Batthyány tér,** on the Buda embankment in Víziváros;
- **Kossuth Lajos tér,** near the Parliament on the Pest side;
- **Várkert Bazár,** at the base of the grand entrance staircase to Buda Castle;
- **Petőfi tér,** on the Pest embankment next to the Legenda Cruises riverboats (dock 8); and
- **Szent Gellért tér,** at the Buda end of Liberty Bridge, next to the Gellért Baths.

Some stops may be closed if the river level gets very low.

By Taxi

Budapest's public transportation is good enough that you probably won't need to take many taxis. But if you do, you may run into a dishonest driver. Arm yourself with knowledge: Budapest strictly regulates its official taxis, which must be painted yellow and have yellow license plates. These taxis are required to charge identical rates, regardless of company: a drop rate of 450 Ft, and then 280 Ft/kilometer, plus 70 Ft/minute for wait time. A 10 percent tip is expected. A typical ride within central Budapest shouldn't run more than 2,000 Ft. Despite what some slimy cabbies may tell you, there's no legitimate extra charge for crossing the river, and prices are per ride—not per passenger.

Instead of hailing a taxi on the street, do as the locals do and call a cab from a reputable company—it's cheaper and you're more likely to get an honest driver. Try **City Taxi** (tel. 1/211-1111), **Taxi 6x6** (tel. 1/266-6666), or **Fötaxi** (tel. 1/222-2222). Most dispatchers speak English, but if you're uncomfortable calling, you can ask your hotel or restaurant to call for you.

Many "cabs" you'd hail on the streets are there only to prey on rich, green tourists. Avoid unmarked taxis (nicknamed "hyenas" by locals)—especially those waiting at tourist spots and train stations. If you do wave down a cab on the street, be sure it has a yellow license plate; otherwise, it's not official. Ask for a rough estimate before you get in—if it doesn't sound reasonable, walk away. If you wind up being dramatically overcharged for a ride, simply pay what you think is fair and go inside. If the driver follows you (unlikely), your hotel receptionist will defend you.

Tours in Budapest

BY FOOT
▲▲▲Local Guides

Budapest has an abundance of enthusiastic, hardworking young guides who speak perfect English and enjoy showing off their city. Given the reasonable fees and efficient use of your time, hiring your own personal expert is an excellent value. While they might be available last-minute, it's better to reserve in advance by email.

I have three favorites, any of whom can do half-day or full-day tours, and can also drive you into the countryside: **Péter Pöl-**

czman is an exceptional guide who really puts you in touch with the Budapest you came to see (€110/half-day, €190/full day, mobile +3620-926-0557, www.budapestyourself.com, polczman@freestart.hu or peter@budapestyourself.com). **Andrea Makkay** has professional polish and a smart understanding of what visitors really want to experience (€110/half-day, €190/full day, mobile +3620-962-9363, www.privateguidebudapest.com, andrea.makkay@gmail.com—arrange details by email; if Andrea is busy, she can arrange to send you with another guide). And **George Farkas** is particularly well-attuned to the stylish side of this fast-changing metropolis (€120/half-day, €220/full day, mobile +3670-335-8030, www.mybudapesttours.hu, georgefarkas@gmail.hu).

Elemér Boreczky, a semiretired university professor, leads walking tours with a soft-spoken, scholarly approach, emphasizing Budapest's rich tapestry of architecture as "frozen music." Elemér is ideal if you want a walking graduate-level seminar about the easy-to-miss nuances of this grand city (€25/hour, mobile +3630-491-1389, www.culturaltours.mlap.hu, boreczky.elemer@gmail.com).

Péter, Andrea, George, and Elemér have all been indispensable help to me in writing and updating this book.

Walking Tours

Budapest's best-established walking-tour company is **Absolute Tours,** run by Oregonian Ben Frieday. Travelers with this book get a discount on any tour (15 percent if you book online—enter coupon code "RICK"—or 10 percent for tours booked in person). Their options include the 3.5-hour Absolute Walk, offering a good overview of Budapest; the Hammer & Sickle Tour, with a mini museum of communist artifacts and sites related to the 1956 Uprising; the Hungro Gastro Food and Wine Tasting, which includes a tour and tastings at the Great Market Hall and nearby specialty shops; the Night Stroll, which includes a one-hour cruise on the Danube; as well as nightlife tours, a Christmas Market tour (Dec only), and an "Alternative Budapest" tour that visits artsy, edgy, off-the-beaten-path parts of town. For prices and schedules, see www.absolutetours.com or contact the office (tel. 1/269-3843, mobile +3620-929-7506). Most tours depart from the Absolute Tour Center behind the Opera House (see the "Absolute Tour Center" listing on page 547); however, the food-and-wine tour meets at the Great Market Hall, and the "Alternative" tour departs from the blocky, green-domed Lutheran church at Deák tér, near the Metró station.

You'll also see various companies advertising **"free" walking tours.** While there is no set fee to take these tours, guides are paid only if you tip (they're hoping for 2,000 Ft/person). They offer a basic 2.5-hour introduction to the city, as well as itineraries focusing on the communist era and the Jewish Quarter. Because they're working for tips, the guides are highly motivated to impress their customers. But because the "free" tag attracts very large groups, these tours tend to be less intimate than paid tours, and (especially the introductory tours) take a once-over-lightly "infotainment" approach. As this scene is continually evolving, look for local fliers to learn about the options and meeting points.

BY BOAT
▲▲Danube Boat Tours

Cruising the Danube, while touristy, is a fun and convenient way to get a feel for the city's grand layout. The most established com-

pany, **Legenda Cruises,** is a class act that runs well-maintained, glassed-in panoramic boats day and night. All of their cruises include a free drink and romantic headphone commentary. By night, TV monitors show the interiors of the great buildings as you float by.

I've negotiated a special discount with Legenda for my readers—but you must book directly and ask for the Rick Steves price. By **day,** the one-hour "Duna Bella" cruise costs 3,120 Ft for Rick Steves readers; if you want, you can hop off at Margaret Island to explore on your own, then return after 1.5 hours on a later cruise (6/day April-Sept, 4/day March and Oct, 1/day Nov-Feb—but no Margaret Island stop in winter). By **night,** the one-hour "Danube Legend"

Budapest at a Glance

In Pest

▲▲▲**Széchenyi Baths** Budapest's steamy soaking scene in City Park—the city's single best attraction. **Hours:** Swimming pool—daily 6:00-22:00, thermal bath—daily 6:00-19:00. See page 602.

▲▲**Hungarian Parliament** Vast riverside government center with remarkable interior. **Hours:** English tours usually daily at 8:30 or 9:45, 10:00, 12:00, 13:00, 14:00, and 15:00; fewer on Mon off-season. See page 569.

▲▲**Great Market Hall** Colorful Old World mall with produce, eateries, souvenirs, and great people-watching. **Hours:** Mon 6:00-17:00, Tue-Fri 6:00-18:00, Sat 6:00-15:00, closed Sun. See page 585.

▲▲**Great Synagogue** The world's second-largest, with fancy interior, good museum, and memorial garden. **Hours:** March-Oct Sun-Thu 10:00-20:00, Fri 10:00-16:30; Nov-Feb Sun-Thu 10:00-16:00, Fri 10:00-14:00; always closed Sat and Jewish holidays. See page 587.

▲▲**Hungarian State Opera House** Neo-Renaissance splendor and affordable opera. **Hours:** Lobby/box office open Mon-Sat from 11:00 until show time—generally 19:00; Sun open 3 hours before performance—generally 16:00-19:00, or 10:00-13:00 if there's a matinee; English tours nearly daily at 14:00, 15:00, and 16:00. See page 591.

▲▲**House of Terror** Harrowing remembrance of Nazis and communist secret police in former headquarters/torture site. **Hours:** Tue-Sun 10:00-18:00, closed Mon. See page 594.

▲▲**Heroes' Square** Mammoth tribute to Hungary's historic figures, fronted by art museums. **Hours:** Square always open. See page 598.

▲▲**City Park** Budapest's backyard, with Art Nouveau zoo, Transylvanian Vajdahunyad Castle replica, amusement park, and Széchenyi Baths. **Hours:** Park always open. See page 600.

▲▲**Vajdahunyad Castle** Epcot-like replica of a Transylvanian castle and other historical buildings. **Hours:** Always viewable. See page 601.

▲▲**Holocaust Memorial Center** Excellent memorial and museum honoring Hungarian victims of the Holocaust. **Hours:** Tue-Sun 10:00-18:00, closed Mon. See page 602.

▲**St. István's Basilica** Budapest's largest church, with a saint's withered fist and great city views. **Hours:** Mon 9:00-16:30, Tue-Fri 9:00-17:00, Sat 9:00-13:00, Sun 13:00-17:00; panorama terrace daily June-Sept 10:00-18:30, March-May and Oct 10:00-17:30, Nov-Feb 10:00-16:30. See page 577.

▲**Hungarian National Museum** Expansive collection of fragments from Hungary's history. **Hours:** Tue-Sun 10:00-18:00, closed Mon. See page 586.

▲**Margaret Island** Budapest's traffic-free urban playground, with spas, ruins, gardens, a game farm, and fountains, set in the middle of the Danube. **Hours:** Park always open. See page 581.

▲**Vörösmarty Tér** Pest Town Center's main square, a hub for sightseeing and people watching **Hours:** Square always open. See page 583.

In Buda

▲▲**Matthias Church** Landmark Neo-Gothic church with gilded history-book interior and revered 16th-century statue of Mary and Jesus. **Hours:** Mon-Fri 9:00-17:00—possibly also 19:00-20:00 in summer, Sat 9:00-12:15, Sun 13:00-17:00. See page 610.

▲▲**Gellért Baths** Touristy baths in historic Buda hotel. **Hours:** Daily 6:00-20:00. See page 630.

▲▲**Rudas Baths** Half-millennium-old Turkish dome over a series of hot-water pools. **Hours:** Daily 6:00-20:00. See page 615.

▲▲**Memento Park** Larger-than-life communist statues collected in one park, on the outskirts of town. **Hours:** Daily 10:00-sunset. See page 616.

▲**Hungarian National Gallery** Top works by Hungarian artists, housed in the Royal Palace. **Hours:** Tue-Sun 10:00-18:00, closed Mon. See page 607.

▲**Hospital in the Rock** Fascinating underground network of hospital and bomb-shelter corridors from WWII and the Cold War. **Hours:** Daily 10:00-20:00. See page 613.

cruise (with no Margaret Island visit) costs 4,400 Ft for Rick Steves readers (4/day March-Oct, 1/day Nov-Feb). On weekends, it's smart to call ahead and reserve a spot for the evening cruises. Note: These special prices are for 2017, and may be slightly higher in 2018.

The Legenda dock is in front of the Marriott on the Pest embankment (find pedestrian access under tram tracks at downriver end of Vigadó tér, district V, M1: Vörösmarty tér, tel. 1/317-2203, www.legenda.hu). Competing river-cruise companies are nearby, but given the discount, Legenda offers the best value.

ON WHEELS
Bike and Segway Tours
The best option for tours by bike and Segway (a stand-up electric scooter) is **Yellow Zebra,** a sister company of Absolute Tours (bike tours—8,500 Ft, 3.5 hours, no tours Dec-Feb or in freezing temperatures; Segway tours—19,500 Ft, 2.5 hours, begins with 30-minute training). My readers get a 15 percent discount when booking online (www.yellowzebratours.com, enter coupon code "RICK"), or 10 percent off if booking in person. These tours meet at the Absolute Tour Center behind the Opera House (see page 547).

Bus Tours
Various companies run hop-on, hop-off bus tours, which make 12 to 16 stops as they cruise around town on a two-hour loop with headphone commentary (generally 5,000/24 hours, 6,000 Ft/48 hours). Most companies also offer a wide variety of other tours, including dinner boat cruises and trips to the Danube Bend. Pick up fliers about all these tours at the TI or in your hotel lobby.

RiverRide
This company offers a bus tour with a twist: Its amphibious bus can actually float on the Danube River, effectively making this a combination bus-and-boat tour. The live guide imparts dry English commentary as you roll (and float). While it's a fun gimmick, the entry ramp into the river (facing the north end of Margaret Island) is far from the most scenic stretch, and the river portion is slow-paced—showing you the same Margaret Island scenery twice, plus a circle in front of the Parliament. The Legenda Cruises boat tours, described earlier, give you more scenic bang for your buck (8,500 Ft, 2 hours, 4/day April-Oct, 3/day Nov-March, departs from Széchenyi tér near Gresham Palace, tel. 1/332-2555, www.riverride.com).

TOUR PACKAGES FOR STUDENTS
Andy Steves (Rick's son) runs Weekend Student Adventures (WSA Europe), offering 3-day and 10-day budget travel packages

across Europe including accommodations, skip-the-line sightseeing, and unique local experiences. Locally guided and DIY unguided options are available for student and budget travelers in 12 of Europe's most popular cities, including Budapest (guided trips from €199, see www.wsaeurope.com for details).

Sights in Pest

Most of Pest's top sights cluster in five neighborhoods: **Leopold Town** and the **Town Center** (together forming the city's "downtown"); the **Jewish Quarter,** just outside the inner ring road; along the grand boulevard **Andrássy út;** and at that boulevard's end, near **Heroes' Square and City Park.**

Several other excellent sights are not contained in these areas, and are covered in greater depth in this chapter: along the **Small Boulevard** (Kiskörút); along the **Great Boulevard** (Nagykörút); and along the boulevard called **Üllői út.**

LEOPOLD TOWN (LIPÓTVÁROS)

The Parliament building, which dominates Pest's skyline, is the centerpiece of the city's banking and business district. Called Lipótváros ("Leopold Town"), this snazzy "uptown" quarter features some of the best of Budapest's many monuments. Below, I've linked up the top sights in Leopold Town as a self-guided walk, starting at the grandiose Parliament building and ending at the Chain Bridge.

▲▲Hungarian Parliament (Országház)

With an impressive facade and an even more extravagant interior, the oversized Hungarian Parliament dominates the Danube riv-

erbank. A hulking Neo-Gothic base topped by a soaring Neo-Renaissance dome, it's one of the city's top landmarks. Touring the building offers the chance to stroll through one of Budapest's best interiors. While the guides can be hit-or-miss, the dazzling building speaks for itself.

Cost and Hours: 5,400 Ft, half-price for EU citizens if you show your passport. English tours are usually daily at 10:00, 12:00, 13:00, 14:00, and 15:00—but there are often more tours with demand (especially at 8:30 and/ or 9:45), or fewer for no apparent reason, so it's smart to reserve in advance. On Mondays when parliament is in session (generally Sept-May), there are no tours after 10:00.

BUDAPEST

Getting There: Ride tram #2 to the Országház stop, which is next to the visitors center entrance (Kossuth tér 1, district V). You can also ride the M2/red Metró line to Kossuth tér, then walk to the other end of the Parliament building to find the visitors center.

Getting Tickets: Tickets come with an appointed tour time and often sell out. To ensure getting a space, it's worth paying an extra 220 Ft per ticket to **book online** a day or two in advance at www.jegymester.hu. Select "Parliament Visit," then a date and time of an English tour, and be sure to specify "full price" (unless you have an EU passport). You'll have to create an account, but it's typically no problem to use a US address, telephone number, and credit card. Print out your eticket and show up at the Parliament visitors center at the appointed time (if you can't print it, show up early enough to have them print it out for you at the ticket desk—which can have long lines, especially in the morning).

If you didn't prebook a ticket, go to the **visitors center**—a modern, underground space at the northern end of the long Parliament building (look for the statue of a lion on a pillar)—and ask what the next available tour time is. The 10:00 English tour is almost always sold out online, but there may be space on an earlier tour (early risers should show up at 8:00 to try their luck). Afternoon tours are the most likely to have space. The visitors center and ticket desk are open daily 8:00-18:00 (sometimes closes earlier Mon), and only sell tickets for the same day—if booking in advance, you must use the ticket website.

Information: Tel. 1/441-4904, www.parlament.hu.

Background: The Parliament was built from 1885 to 1902 to celebrate the Hungarian millennium year of 1896 (see sidebar on page 556). Its elegant, frilly spires and riverside location were inspired by its counterpart in London (where the architect studied). When completed, the Parliament was a striking and cutting-edge example of the mix-and-match Historicist style of the day. Like the Hungarian people, this building is at once grandly ambitious and a somewhat motley hodgepodge of various influences—a Neo-Gothic palace topped with a Neo-Renaissance dome, which once had a huge, red communist star on top of the tallest spire. Fittingly, it's the city's top icon. The best views of the Parliament are from across the Danube—especially in the late-afternoon sunlight.

Visiting the Parliament: The visitors center has WCs, a café, a gift shop, and the Museum of the History of the Hungarian National Assembly. Once you have your ticket in hand, be at the airport-type security checkpoint inside the visitors center at least five minutes before your tour departure time.

On the 45-minute tour, your guide will explain the history and symbolism of the building's intricate decorations and offer a lesson in the Hungarian parliamentary system. You'll see dozens of bushy-mustachioed statues illustrating the occupations of worka-day Hungarians through history, and find out why a really good speech was nicknamed a "Havana" by cigar-aficionado parliamentarians.

To begin the tour, you'll climb a 133-step staircase (with an elevator for those who need it) to see the building's monumental entryway and 96-step grand staircase—slathered in gold foil and frescoes, and bathed in shimmering stained-glass light. Then you'll gape up under the ornate gilded dome for a peek at the heavily guarded Hungarian crown, which is overlooked by statues of 16 great Hungarian monarchs, from St. István to Habsburg Empress Maria Theresa. Finally, you'll walk through a cushy lounge—across one of Europe's largest carpets—to see the legislative chamber.

• *The vast square behind the Parliament is studded with attractions. Stay where you are for a quick...*

▲Kossuth Tér Spin-Tour

This square is sprinkled with interesting monuments and packed with Hungarian history. But it's gone through a lot of changes in the last few years, at the hands of architects and urban planners working under the steady guidance of the ruling Fidesz party, led by Viktor Orbán. A highly nationalistic, right-wing party, which swept to power after Hungarians grew weary of the bumblings of the poorly organized, shortsighted left-wing opposition party, Fidesz has exerted its influence over every walk of Hungarian life... beginning with the look of this building and square, and the monuments around it. The square itself used to be a more higgledy-piggledy mix of ragged asphalt, parks, monuments, and trees. But Fidesz wanted the mighty Parliament building to stand bold and unobstructed. Several older monuments (including, ironically, an "eternal" flame honoring victims of the communists) were swept away. Trees were cut down overnight, before would-be protesters could make a peep. And today the square has a scrubbed-clean look that some critics consider almost fascist.

Look to the right end of the Parliament. Poking up is a **pillar** topped by a lion being strangled and bitten by a giant snake (a typically heavy-handed Fidesz monument). This pillar marks the entrance to the Parliament visitors center; if you want to check on the availability of tours today, now's a good time (see details earlier).

Looking a bit farther to the right, at the end of the park you'll see another stony tribute, this one to the square's namesake, **Lajos Kossuth**, who led the 1848 Revolution against the Habsburgs. The street that leaves this square behind Kossuth's left shoulder is Falk Miksa utca, Budapest's **"antique row"**—a great place to browse for nostalgic souvenirs.

Panning right from the Kossuth statue, across the tram tracks

Pest Sights

1. Hungarian Parliament
2. Kossuth (Lajos) Tér
3. Museum of Ethnography
4. Szabadság Tér
5. St. István's Basilica
6. Gresham Palace
7. Chain Bridge
8. Great Market Hall
9. Hungarian National Museum
10. Great Synagogue
11. Orthodox Synagogue
12. Synagogue at Rumbach Street
13. Hungarian State Opera House
14. House of Terror
15. Franz Liszt Museum
16. New York Café
17. To Holocaust Memorial Center
18. Applied Arts Museum

BUDAPEST

you'll see the stately home of the **Museum of Ethnography.** While its collection of Hungarian folk artifacts is good (closed Mon), the building itself is also notable. The design was the first runner-up for the Parliament building, so they built it here, where it originally housed the Supreme Court. In a few years, the museum collection will move out to City Park, with plans for the Supreme Court to move back into its original home.

To the right, the **Ministry of Agriculture** was the second runner-up for the Parliament. Today it features a very low-profile, but poignant, monument to the victims of the 1956 Uprising against Soviet rule (see the "1956" sidebar): At the right end of the protruding arcade, notice that the walls are pockmarked with little metal dollops (you may have to walk closer to see these clearly). Two days into the uprising, on October 25, the ÁVH (communist police) and Soviet troops on the rooftop above opened fire on demonstrators gathered in this square—massacring many and leaving no doubt that Moscow would not tolerate dissent. In the monument, each of the little metal knobs represents a bullet.

Spin farther to the right, where a dramatic equestrian statue of **Ferenc Rákóczi** stands in the park. Rákóczi valiantly—but unsuccessfully—led the Hungarians in their War of Independence (1703-1711) against the Habsburgs. Although they lived more than a century apart, Rákóczi and Kossuth—who now face each other across this square—were aligned in their rebellion against the Habsburgs.

Complete your 360 and face the Parliament again. Every so often, costumed soldiers appear on the front steps for a brief **"changing of the guard"** ceremony set to recorded music...another very new, very patriotic custom, compliments of Fidesz.

In the wide sidewalk that runs in front of the Parliament, near the beautifully landscaped gardens, you'll see staircases leading to modest, hidden, subterranean museums (both free and open daily 10:00-18:00). These offer a cool break from the crowds and a glimpse into the heating and cooling tunnels beneath Kossuth tér. The (skippable) one on the right is the **lapidarium** *(kőtár)*, displaying old stone decorations from the Parliament—including gargoyle-like adornments from the spires.

More interesting (and on our way to the next stop) is the one on the left, marked *1956*. Heading down these stairs, you'll find a poignant memorial to the **1956 Uprising** that began on this very square (see sidebar). You'll see photos of the events, and video interviews of eyewitnesses to the massacre on this square on October 25, 1956 (as well as other government mass shootings around Hungary that fall). At the end of the hall is a memorial grave to the victims, and the symbol of the uprising: a tattered Hungarian flag with a hole cut out of the center.

• *Now let's take a quick...*

Monuments Stroll

Budapest is a city of great monuments, and some of the most vivid are on or near this square.

• *Circle around the left side of the giant Parliament building, passing another statue on a pillar, and walk all the way to the bannister overlooking a spectacular view of Buda. Walk along the banister to the left until you come upon a statue of a young man, lost deep in thought, gazing into the Danube.*

Attila József (1905-1937): This beloved modern poet lived a tumultuous, productive, and short life before he killed himself by jumping in front of a train at age 32. József's poems of life, love, and death—mostly written in the 1920s and 1930s—are considered the high point of Hungarian literature. His birthday (April 11) is celebrated as National Hungarian Poetry Day.

Here József re-enacts a scene from one of his best poems, "At the Danube." It's a hot day—his jacket lies in a heap next to him, his shirtsleeves are rolled up, and he cradles his hat loosely in his left hand. "As I sat on the bank of the Danube, I watched a watermelon float by," he begins. "As if flowing out of my heart, murky, wise, and great was the Danube." In the poem, József uses the Danube as a metaphor for life—for the way it has interconnected cities and also times—as he reflects that his ancestors likely pondered the Danube from this same spot. Looking into his profound eyes, you sense the depth of this artist's tortured inner life.

• *Walk down the steps next to József, and stand at the railing just above the busy road. If you visually trace the Pest riverbank to the left about 100 yards, just before the tree-filled, riverfront park, you can just barely see several low-profile dots lining the embankment. This is a...*

Holocaust Monument: Consisting of 50 pairs of bronze shoes, this monument commemorates the Jews who were killed when the Nazis' puppet government, the Arrow Cross, came to power in Hungary in 1944. While many Jews were sent to concentration camps, the Arrow Cross massacred some of them right here, shooting them and letting their bodies fall into the Danube.

• *If you'd like a closer look at the shoes, use the crosswalk (50 yards to your right) to cross the busy embankment road and follow the waterline.*

When you're ready to move on, turn your back to the Danube and walk inland, along the ugly building (with an entrance to the Metró), up to the back corner of Kossuth tér. Cross the street in a little park (at Vértanúk tere), where you'll see a monument to...

Imre Nagy (1896-1958): The Hungarian politician Imre Nagy (EEM-ray nodge), now thought of as an anticommunist hero, was actually a lifelong communist. In the 1930s, he allegedly worked for the Soviet secret police. When the 1956 Uprising broke out on

October 23, Imre Nagy was drafted (reluctantly, some say) to become the head of the movement to soften the severity of the communist regime. Because he was an insider, it briefly seemed that Nagy might hold the key to finding a middle path (represented by the bridge he's standing on) between the suffocating totalitarian model of Moscow and the freedom of the West. But the optimism was short-lived. The Soviets violently put down the uprising, arrested and sham-tried Nagy, executed him, and buried him disgracefully, face-down in an unmarked grave. The regime forced Hungary to forget about Nagy. Later, when communism

was in its death throes in 1989, the Hungarian people rediscovered Nagy as a hero. His body was located, exhumed, and given a ceremonial funeral at Heroes' Square. And today, thanks to this monument, Nagy keeps a watchful eye on today's lawmakers in the Parliament across the way.

• *Go up the short, diagonal street beyond Nagy, called Vécsey utca. After just one block, you emerge into...*

Szabadság Tér (Liberty Square)

One of Budapest's most genteel squares, this space is marked by a controversial monument to the Soviet soldiers who liberated Hungary at the end of World War II, and ringed by both fancy old apartment blocks and important buildings (such as the former Hungarian State Television headquarters, the US Embassy, and the National Bank of Hungary). A fine café, fun-filled playgrounds, statues of prominent Americans (Ronald Reagan and Harry Hill Bandholtz), and yet another provocative monument (to the Hungarian victims of the Nazis) round out the square's landmarks. Take a moment to tune into two of the more recent (and more divisive) monuments on the square.

• *The first person you'll see as you enter the square, striding confidently away from the Parliament, is an actor-turned-politician you may recognize...*

Ronald Reagan: When Fidesz took power in 2010, they quickly began rolling back previous democratic reforms and imposing alarming constraints on the media. Many international observers—including the US government—spoke out against what they considered an infringement on freedom of the press. In an effort to appease American concerns, Prime Minister Viktor Orbán erected this statue on one of his capital's main squares—and then, perhaps not quite grasping the subtleties of American politics, invited Secretary of State Hillary Clinton to the unveiling. It's fun to watch the steady stream of passersby (both Hungarians and tourists) do a double-take, chuckle, then snap a photo with The Gipper.

• *Now enjoy a slow stroll to the opposite end of the square, where you'll find the...*

Monument to the Hungarian Victims of the Nazis: This recent addition to the square—another heavy-handed Fidesz production—commemorates the German invasion of Hungary on March 19, 1944. Standing in the middle of a broken colonnade, an immaculate angel holds a sphere with a double cross (part of the crown jewels and a symbol of Hungarian sovereignty). Overhead, a mechanical-looking black eagle (symbolizing Germany) screeches in, its talons poised to strike.

Although offensive enough for its lack of artistry, this monument was instantly controversial for the way it whitewashes Hungarian history. Viewing this, you might imagine that Hungary was a peaceful land that was unwittingly caught up in the Nazi war machine. In fact, the Hungarian government was an ally of Nazi Germany for more than three years before this invasion. And there's no question that, after the invasion, many Hungarians enthusiastically collaborated with their new Nazi overlords.

Mindful of the old adage about people who forget their own history, locals have created a **makeshift counter-memorial** to the victims of the World War II-era Hungarians (not just Germans) in front of this official monument.

On a lighter note, the **fountain** that faces the monument is particularly entertaining. Sensors can tell when you're about to walk through the wall of water...and the curtain of water automatically parts just long enough for you to pass. Try it.

• *From the monument, continue two blocks straight ahead, up Hercegprímás utca. You'll emerge into a broad plaza in front of...*

▲St. István's Basilica (Szent István Bazilika)

Budapest's biggest church is one of its top landmarks. The grand interior celebrates St. István, Hungary's first Christian king. You can see his withered, blackened, millennium-old fist in a gilded reliquary in the side chapel. Or you can zip up on an elevator (or climb up stairs partway) to a panorama terrace with views over the rooftops of Pest. The skippable treasury has ecclesiastical items, historical exhibits, and artwork (reached by elevator, to the right as you face the church). The church also hosts regular organ concerts (advertised near the entry).

Cost and Hours: Interior—free but 200-Ft donation strongly suggested, open to tourists Mon 9:00-16:30, Tue-Fri 9:00-17:00, Sat 9:00-13:00, Sun 13:00-17:00, open slightly later for worshippers; panorama terrace—500 Ft, daily June-Sept 10:00-18:30, March-May and Oct 10:00-17:30, Nov-Feb 10:00-16:30; treasury-400 Ft,

1956

The year 1956 is etched into the Hungarian psyche. In that year, the people of Budapest staged the first major uprising against the communist regime. It also marked the first time that the Soviets implicitly acknowledged, in brutally putting down the uprising, that the people of Eastern Europe were not "communist by choice."

The seeds of revolution were sown with the death of a tyrant: Josef Stalin passed away on March 5, 1953. Suddenly the choke-hold that Moscow had held on its satellite states loosened. During this time of "de-Stalinization," Hungarian premier Imre Nagy presided over two years of mild reform, before his political opponents (and Moscow) became nervous and demoted him. (For more on Nagy, see page 575.)

In 1955, Austria declared its neutrality in the Cold War. This thrust Hungary to the front line of the Iron Curtain, and raised the stakes both for Hungarians who wanted freedom and for Soviets who wanted to preserve their buffer zone. When Stalin's successor, Nikita Khrushchev, condemned Stalin's crimes in a "secret speech" to communist leaders in February of 1956, it emboldened the Soviet Bloc's dissidents. A workers' strike in Poznań, Poland in October inspired Hungarians to follow their example.

On October 23, 1956, the Hungarian uprising began. A student union group gathered in Budapest at 15:00 to articulate a list of 16 demands against the communist regime. Then they marched toward Parliament, their numbers gradually swelling. One protester defiantly cut the Soviet-style insignia out of the center of the Hungarian flag, which would become the uprising's symbol.

By nightfall, some 200,000 protesters filled Kossuth tér behind Parliament, calling for Imre Nagy, the one communist leader they believed could bring change. Nagy finally appeared around 21:00. Ever the pragmatic politician, he implored patience. Following the speech, a large band of protesters took matters into their own hands, marched to City Park, and tore down the hated Stalin statue that stood there (see page 600).

Another group went to the National Radio building to read their demands on the air. The ÁVH (communist police) refused to let them do it, and eventually opened fire on the protesters. The peaceful protests evolved into an armed insurrection, as frightened civilians gathered weapons and supplies.

Overnight, Moscow decided to intervene. Budapesters awoke on October 24 to find Red Army troops occupying their city. That morning, Imre Nagy—who had just been promoted again to prime minister—promised reforms and tried to keep a lid on the simmering discontent.

The next day, October 25, a huge crowd gathered on Kossuth tér behind the Parliament to hear from Nagy. In the hubbub, shots rang out as Hungarian and Soviet soldiers opened fire on the (mostly unarmed) crowd. Of the victims, 72 deaths are known by name, but likely hundreds more were injured or perished.

The Hungarians fought back with an improvised guerilla resistance. They made use of any guns they could get their hands on, as well as Molotov cocktails, to strike against the Soviet occupiers. Many adolescents (the celebrated "Pest Youth") participated. The fighting tore apart the city, and some of the fallen were buried in impromptu graves in city parks.

Political infighting in Moscow paralyzed the Soviet response, and an uneasy ceasefire fell over Budapest. For 10 tense days, it appeared that the Soviets might allow Nagy to push through some reforms. Nagy, a firmly entrenched communist, had always envisioned a less repressive regime...but within limits. While he was at first reluctant to take on the mantle of the uprising's leadership, he gradually began to echo what he was hearing on the streets. He called for free elections, the abolishment of the ÁVH, the withdrawal of Soviet troops, and Hungary's secession from the Warsaw Pact.

But when the uprisers attacked and killed ÁVH officers and communist leaders in Budapest, it bolstered the case of the Moscow hardliners. On November 4, the Red Army launched a brutal counterattack in Budapest that left the rebels reeling. At 5:20 that morning, Imre Nagy's voice came over the radio to beg the world for assistance. Later that morning, he sought asylum at the Yugoslav Embassy across the street from City Park. He was never seen alive in public again.

János Kádár—an ally of Nagy's who was palatable to the uprisers, yet firmly loyal to Moscow—was installed as prime minister. The fighting dragged on for about another week, but the uprising was eventually crushed. By the end, 2,500 Hungarians and more than 700 Soviets were dead, and 20,000 Hungarians were injured. Communist authorities arrested more than 15,000 people, of whom at least 200 were executed (including Imre Nagy). Anyone who had participated in the uprising was blacklisted; fearing this and other forms of retribution, some 200,000 Hungarians fled to the West.

Though the 1956 Uprising met a tragic end, within a few years Kádár did succeed in softening the regime, and the milder, so-called "goulash communism" emerged. And today, even though the communists are long gone, the legacy of 1956 pervades the Hungarian consciousness. Some Budapest buildings are still pockmarked with bullet holes from '56, and many Hungarians who fled the country in that year still have not returned. October 23 remains Hungary's most cherished holiday.

BUDAPEST

same hours as terrace; music concerts Mon, Tue, and Thu—see page 639; Szent István tér, district V, M1: Bajcsy-Zsilinszky út or M3: Arany János utca.

Visiting the Church: The church is only about 100 years old—like most Budapest landmarks, it was built around the millennial celebrations of 1896. Head up the grand stairs to get oriented. To the right is the ticket desk, the elevator to the treasury, and the entrance to the church. To the left is the elevator to the panoramic tower.

The church's **interior** is dimly lit but gorgeously restored; all the gilded decorations glitter in the low light. You'll see not Jesus, but St. István (Stephen), Hungary's first Christian king, glowing above the high altar.

The church's main claim to fame is the **"holy right hand" of St. István.** The sacred fist—a somewhat grotesque, 1,000-year-old withered stump—is in a jeweled box in the chapel to the left of the main altar (follow signs for *Szent Jobb Kápolna,* chapel often closed). Pop in a 200-Ft coin for two minutes of light. Posted information describes the hand's unlikely journey to this spot (chapel open slightly shorter hours than church—look for signs).

On your way out, in the exit foyer, you'll find a small exhibit about the building's history.

• *From here, you're very close to the boulevard called* **Andrássy út,** *which leads to the Opera House, House of Terror, and City Park (all described starting on page 590). To get there, walk around the right side of the basilica, and turn right on busy Bajcsy-Zsilinszky út; Andrássy út begins across the street, on your left.*

But for now, we'll head to the Danube for a good look at the mighty Chain Bridge. Walk straight ahead from St. István's main staircase down **Zrínyi Utca.** *This recently pedestrianized people zone passes (on the right)* **Central European University,** *a graduate school largely funded by Hungarian-American George Soros, and its good bookshop. Later, after crossing Nádor utca, on the left you'll see* **Duna Palota,** *a venue and ticket office for Hungária Koncert's popular tourist shows (described on page 637).*

Zrínyi utca dead-ends at the big traffic circle called **Roosevelt tér.** *Turn left and walk a half-block to the entrance (on the left) of the...*

Gresham Palace

This was Budapest's first building in the popular Historicist style, and also incorporates elements of Art Nouveau. Budapest boomed in an era when architectural eclecticism—mashing together bits and pieces of different styles—was in vogue. But because much of the city's construction was compressed into a short window of time, even these disparate styles enjoy an unusual harmony. Damaged in World War II, the building was an eyesore for decades. (Reportedly, an aging local actress refused to move out, so developers had to wait for her to, ahem, vacate before they could reclaim the building.) In 1999, the Gresham Palace was meticulously restored to its former glory and converted to a luxury hotel. Even if you can't afford to stay here (see page 655), saunter into the lobby and absorb the gorgeous details (lobby open 24 hours daily, Széchenyi tér 5, district V, M1: Vörösmarty tér or M2: Kossuth tér).

• *Grandly spanning the Danube from this spot is Budapest's best bridge...*

▲Chain Bridge (Széchenyi Lánchíd)

One of the world's great bridges connects Pest's Széchenyi tér and Buda's Clark Ádám tér. This historic, iconic bridge, guarded by lions (symbolizing power), is Budapest's most enjoyable and convenient bridge to cross on foot.

Until the mid-19th century, only pontoon barges spanned the Danube between Buda and Pest. In the winter, the pontoons had to be pulled in, leaving locals to rely on ferries (in good weather) or a frozen river. People often walked across the frozen Danube, only to get stuck on the other side during a thaw, with nothing to do but wait for another cold snap.

Count István Széchenyi was stranded for a week trying to get to his father's funeral. After missing it, Széchenyi commissioned Budapest's first permanent bridge—which was also a major symbolic step toward another of Széchenyi's pet causes, the unification of Buda and Pest. The Chain Bridge was built by Scotsman Adam Clark between 1842 and 1849, and it immediately became an important symbol of Budapest. Széchenyi—a man of the Enlightenment—charged both commoners and nobles a toll for crossing his bridge, making it an emblem of equality in those tense times. Like all of the city's bridges, the Chain Bridge was destroyed by the Nazis at the end of World War II, but was quickly rebuilt.

• *As you look out to the Danube from here, to the right you can see the tip of...*

▲Margaret Island (Margitsziget)

In the Middle Ages, this island in the Danube (just north of the Parliament) was known as the "Isle of Hares." In the 13th century, a desperate King Béla IV swore that if God were to deliver

Hungary from the invading Tatars, he would dedicate his youngest daughter Margaret to the Church. When the Tatars left, Margaret was shipped to a nunnery here. Margaret embraced her new life as a castaway nun, and later refused her father's efforts to force her into a politically expedient marriage with a Bohemian king. As a reward for her faith, she became St. Margaret of Hungary.

Today, while the island officially has no permanent residents, urbanites flock here to relax in a huge, leafy park in the midst of the busy city...yet so far away. No cars are allowed on the island—just public buses. The island rivals City Park as the best spot in town for strolling, jogging, biking (you can rent a bike at Bringóhintó, with branches at both ends of the island), and people-watching. Rounding out the island's attractions are an iconic old water tower, the remains of Margaret's convent, a rose garden, a game farm, and a "musical fountain" that performs to the strains of Hungarian folk tunes.

Getting There: Bus #26 begins at Nyugati/Western train station, crosses the Margaret Bridge, then drives up through the middle of the island—allowing visitors to easily get from one end to the other (3-6/hour). **Trams** #4 and #6, which circulate around the Great Boulevard, cross the Margaret Bridge and stop at the southern tip of the island, a short walk from some of the attractions. You can also reach the island by **public riverboat**—weekday boats reach the two ends of the island, and weekend ones make several stops along the way. It's also a long but scenic **walk** between Margaret Island and other points in the city.

• If you'd like to head for the heart of Pest, Vörösmarty tér (and the sights listed next), it's just two long blocks away: Turn left out of the Gresham Palace, and walk straight on Dorottya utca.

PEST TOWN CENTER (BELVÁROS)

Pest's Belváros ("Inner Town") is its gritty urban heart—simultaneously its most beautiful and ugliest district. You'll see fancy facades, some of Pest's best views from the Danube embankment, richly decorated old coffeehouses that offer a whiff of the city's Golden Age, and a cavernous, colorful market hall filled with Hungarian goodies. But you'll also experience crowds, grime, and pungent smells like nowhere else in Budapest. Atmospherically shot through with the crumbling elegance of former greatness, Budapest is a place where creaky old buildings and sleek modern ones feel equally at home. Remember: This is a city in transition. Enjoy the rough edges while you can. They're being sanded off at a remarkable pace—and soon, tourists like you will be nostalgic for the "authentic" old days.

Below, I've linked the main landmarks in the Town Center

with a self-guided walk, starting at the square called Vörösmarty tér and ending at the Great Market Hall.

▲Vörösmarty Tér

The central square of the Town Center, dominated by a giant statue of the revered Romantic poet Mihály Vörösmarty and the vener-

able Gerbeaud coffee shop, is the hub of Pest sightseeing.

At the north end of the square is the landmark **Gerbeaud café** and pastry shop. Between the World Wars, the well-to-do ladies of Budapest would meet here after shopping their way up Váci utca. Today it's still *the* meeting point in Budapest...for tourists, at least.

Consider stepping inside to appreciate the elegant old decor, or for a cup of coffee and a slice of cake (but meals here are overpriced). Better yet, hold off for now—even more appealing cafés are nearby (and listed under "Budapest's Café Culture," on page 669).

The yellow **M1 Metró stop** in front of Gerbeaud is the entrance to the shallow *Földalatti*, or "underground"—the first subway on the Continent (built for the Hungarian millennial celebration in 1896). Today, it still carries passengers to Andrássy út sights, running under that boulevard all the way to City Park.

Walk to the far end of the square, and look up the street that's to your left. This traffic-free street (Deák utca)—also known as **"Fashion Street,"** with top-end shops—is the easiest and most pleasant way to walk to Deák tér and, beyond it, through Erzsébet tér to Andrássy út.

• *Extending straight ahead from Vörösmarty tér is a broad, bustling, pedestrianized shopping street. Look—but do not walk—down...*

Váci Utca

Dating from 1810-1850, **Váci utca** (VAHT-see OOT-zah) is one of the oldest streets of Pest. Váci utca means "street to Vác"—a town 25 miles to the north. This has long been the street where the elite of Pest would go shopping, then strut their stuff for their neighbors on an evening promenade. Today, the tourists do the strutting here—and the Hungarians go to American-style shopping malls.

This boulevard—Budapest's tourism artery—was a dreamland for Eastern Bloc residents back in the 1980s. It was here that they fantasized about what it might be like to be free, while drooling over Nikes, Adidas, and Big Macs before any of these "Western evils" were introduced elsewhere in the Warsaw Pact region. In fact, partway down the street (on the right, at Régi Posta utca) is the **first McDonald's behind the Iron Curtain,** where people from

BUDAPEST

all over the Eastern Bloc flocked to dine. Since you had to wait in a long line—stretching around the block—to get a burger, it wasn't "fast food"...but at least it was "West food."

Ironically, this street—once prized by Hungarians and other Eastern Europeans because it felt so Western—is what many Western tourists today mistakenly think is the "real Budapest." Visitors mesmerized by this people-friendly stretch of souvenir stands, tourist-gouging eateries, and upscale boutiques are likely to miss some more interesting and authentic areas just a block or two away. Don't fall for this trap. You can have a fun and fulfilling trip to this city without ever setting foot on Váci utca.

• *For a more appealing people zone than Váci utca, detour from Vörösmarty tér a block toward the river, to the inviting...*

Danube Promenade (Dunakorzó)

Some of the best views in Budapest are from this walkway facing Castle Hill—especially this stretch, between the white Elisabeth Bridge (left) and the iconic Chain Bridge (right). This is a favorite place to promenade *(korzó)*, strolling aimlessly and greeting friends.

Dominating this part of the promenade is the Neo-Romantic-style **Pesti Vigadó**—built in the 1880s, and recently restored. Charmingly, the word *vigadó*—used to describe a concert hall—literally means "joyous place." In front, the playful statue of **the girl with her dog** captures the fun-loving spirit along this drag. At the gap in the railing, notice the platform to catch **tram #2,** which goes frequently in each direction along the promenade—a handy and scenic way to connect riverside sights in Pest. (You can ride it to the right, to the Parliament; or to the left, to the Great Market Hall.)

About 30 more yards toward the Chain Bridge, find the little statue wearing a jester's hat. She's playing on the railing, with the castle behind her. The **Little Princess** is one of Budapest's symbols and a favorite photo-op for tourists. While many of the city's monuments have interesting backstories, more recent statues (like this one) are simply whimsical and fun.

• *Now walk along the promenade to the left (toward the white bridge). Directly in front of the corner of the Marriott Hotel, watch for the easy-to-miss stairs leading down under the tram tracks to a crosswalk that leads safely across the busy road to the riverbank. From the top of these stairs, look along the river.*

Lining the **embankment** are several long boats: Some are excursion boats for sightseeing trips up and down the Danube (especially pleasant at night), while others are overpriced (but scenic) restaurants. Kiosks along here dispense info and sell tickets for the various boat companies—look for Legenda Cruises (their dock is just downstream from here—go down the stairs, cross the road, then walk 100 yards left; for details, see page 565).

• *From here, both the promenade and Váci utca cut south through the Town Center. At the end of this zone is one of Budapest's top attractions.*

▲▲Great Market Hall (Nagyvásárcsarnok)

"Great" indeed is this gigantic marketplace. The Great Market Hall still keeps local shoppers happy, even as it has evolved into one of the city's top tourist attractions. Goose liver, embroidered tablecloths, golden Tokaji Aszú wine, pickled peppers, communist-kitsch T-shirts, savory *lángos* pastries, patriotic green-white-and-red flags, kid-pleasing local candy bars, and paprika of every degree of spiciness...if it's Hungarian, you'll find it here. Come to shop for souvenirs, to buy a picnic, or just to rattle around inside this vast, picturesque, Industrial Age hall.

Hours and Location: Mon 6:00-17:00, Tue-Fri 6:00-18:00, Sat 6:00-15:00, closed Sun, Fővám körút 1, district IX, M4: Fővám tér or M3: Kálvin tér.

Visiting the Market Hall: Step inside the market and get your bearings: The cavernous interior features three levels. The ground floor has produce stands, bakeries, butcher stalls, heaps of paprika, goose liver, and salamis. Upstairs are stand-up eateries and souvenirs. And in the basement are a supermarket, a fish market, and piles of pickles.

Stroll along the market's "main drag" (straight ahead from the entry), enjoying the commotion of produce stands and vendors selling authentic Hungarian products. About halfway along, you'll see paprika on both sides. Additional (and less touristy) stalls are down the little alley on the left. As you browse, remember that there are two types of paprika: sweet (*édes,* used for flavor) and hot (*csipős,* used sparingly to add some kick). While you're at it, pick up some spicy pastes (which hold their flavor better than the fast-degrading powders): the spicy *Erős Pista,* the sweet *Édes Anna,* the soup-enhancing *Gulyáskrém,* and the intensely spicy condiment called, simply, "Red Gold" *(Piros Arany).*

After you've worked your way to the far end of the hall, take the escalator to the upper level. You're immersed in a world of Hungarian **souvenirs** (for tips, see "Shopping in Budapest," page 645). If you're in the mood for some shopping, this is a convenient

BUDAPEST

place to look—with a great selection of souvenirs both traditional (embroidery) and not-so-traditional (commie-kitsch T-shirts). While there are no real bargains here, the prices are a bit better than out along Váci utca. The left wall (as you face the front) is lined with fun, cheap, stand-up, Hungarian-style fast-food joints and six-stool pubs. All along here are stands selling the deep-fried snack called *lángos* (LAHN-gohsh)—similar to elephant ears, but savory rather than sweet. The most typical version is *sajtos tejfölös*—with sour cream and cheese. You can also add garlic *(fokhagyma)*.

For a less glamorous look at the market, head down the escalators near the front of the market (below the restaurant) to the basement. It's pungent with tanks of still-swimming carp, catfish, and perch, and piles of pickles. Stop at one of the pickle stands and take a look. Hungarians pickle just about anything: peppers and cukes, of course, but also cauliflower, cabbage, beets, tomatoes, garlic, and so on.

Nearby: Along the river behind the Great Market Hall is the sleek, glass-roofed **Bálna Cultural Center,** a super-modern cultural center (with an extension of the Great Market Hall's vendors, an art gallery, and inviting public spaces). Completed in 2013, the complex was created by bridging a pair of circa-1881 brick warehouses with a swooping glass canopy that earns its name, "The Whale" (the meaning of *bálna;* free to enter, Sun-Thu 10:00-20:00, Fri-Sat 10:00-22:00, www.balnabudapest.hu).

ALONG THE SMALL BOULEVARD (KISKÖRÚT)

These two major sights are along the Small Boulevard, between the Liberty Bridge/Great Market Hall and Deák tér. (Note that the Great Market Hall, listed earlier, is also technically along the Small Boulevard.) The former Jewish Quarter, which sprawls behind the Great Synagogue, is also known as the Seventh District, one of Budapest's most happening nightlife zones, with a fun selection of "ruin pubs" (for details, see "Nightlife in Budapest," later).

▲Hungarian National Museum (Magyar Nemzeti Múzeum)

One of Budapest's biggest museums features all manner of Hungarian historic bric-a-brac, from the Paleolithic age to a more recent infestation of dinosaurs (the communists). Artifacts are explained by good, if dry, English descriptions. The museum adds substance to your understanding of Hungary's story—but it helps to have a pretty firm foundation first (read "Hungarian History" on page 518). The most engaging part is Room 20, where there are items from the communist period—including both pro- and anti-Party propaganda. The exhibit ends with video footage of the 1989 end of communism—demonstrations, monumental parliament votes, and a final farewell to the last Soviet troops leaving Hungarian soil. And the impressive Neoclassical building itself is historic: The 1848 Revolution against Habsburg rule was proclaimed from the front steps.

Cost and Hours: 1,600 Ft—but can change depending on temporary exhibits, audioguide available, Tue-Sun 10:00-18:00, closed Mon, near Great Market Hall at Múzeum körút 14, district VIII, M3: Kálvin tér, tel. 1/327-7773, www.hnm.hu.

▲▲Great Synagogue (Nagy Zsinagóga)

Also called the Dohány Street Synagogue, Budapest's gorgeous synagogue is the biggest in Europe and the second biggest in the world (after the Temple Emanu-El of New York). A visit here has three parts: touring its ornately decorated interior; exploring the attached museum, which offers a concise lesson in the Jewish faith; and lingering in the evocative memorial garden, with its weeping-willow *Tree of Life* sculpture and other poignant monuments.

Cost and Hours: 3,000 Ft, 500 Ft to take photos inside the synagogue. Open March-Oct Sun-Thu 10:00-20:00, Fri until 16:30; Nov-Feb Sun-Thu 10:00-16:00, Fri until 14:00; closed Sat year-round and Jewish holidays; Dohány utca 2, district VII, near M2: Astoria or the Astoria stop on trams #47 and #49, tel. 1/343-0420, www.dohany-zsinagoga.hu.

Tours: Guided tours depart regularly from the Great Synagogue ticket desk—see the posted schedule (last tour departs one hour before closing). Since these tours include admission, you're paying only a small price for the guiding. You have three options: A quick 45-minute tour combines the Great Synagogue and Memorial Garden (3,700 Ft). A longer 80-minute tour covers the above, plus a guided visit to the Hungarian Jewish Museum (3,950 Ft). The 100-minute version includes the Great Synagogue, Memorial Garden, and the nearby synagogue at Rumbach Street, plus free time in the museum (6,400 Ft).

❿ Self-Guided Tour: While the tours described above are worthwhile, the following commentary covers the basics.

Great Synagogue: The synagogue's striking **exterior** captures the rich history of the building and the people it represents: The synagogue was built in 1859 just outside what was then the city limits. Although Budapest's Jews held fast to their own faith, they also wished to demonstrate their worth and how well-integrated they were with the greater community. The two tall towers are not typical of traditional synagogues. These towers—along with the rosette (rose window)—helped the synagogue resemble Christian churches of the time. In fact, when it was built, the synagogue was dubbed by one cynic as "the most beautiful Catholic synagogue in the world."

Now step inside. Notice that the synagogue interior really feels like a church with the symbols switched—with a basilica floor plan, three naves, two pulpits, and even a pipe organ. The organ—which Franz Liszt played for the building's inauguration—is a clue that this synagogue belonged to the most progressive of the three branches of Judaism here at the time. (Orthodox Jews would never be permitted to do the "work" of playing an organ on the Sabbath.)

The Moorish-flavored decor is a sign of the Historicism of the time, which borrowed eclectic elements from past styles. Specifically, it evokes the Sephardic Jewish culture that flourished in Iberia; many Hungarian Jews are descended from that group, who fled here after being expelled from Spain in 1492.

In the ark, behind the white curtain, 25 surviving Torah scrolls are kept. Catholic priests hid these scrolls during World War II (burying them temporarily in a cemetery). The two-tiered balconies on the sides of the nave were originally for women, who worshipped separately from the men.

Ponder this building's recent history: Although it survived World War II, the Great Synagogue sat neglected for 40 years. But since the thawing of communism, Hungarian Jews have taken a renewed interest in preserving their heritage. In 1990, the Great Synagogue was painstakingly rebuilt, largely with financial support from the Hungarian-American cosmetics magnate Estée Lauder. Theodor Herzl, a pioneer of Zionism, was born in a house next door to the Great Synagogue (now gone). As you tour the place, think of all the other famous and influential people of Hungarian-Jewish descent from every walk of life: Harry Houdini (born Erich Weisz), Elie Wiesel, Joseph Pulitzer, Tony Curtis (and his daughter Jamie Lee), Goldie Hawn, Peter Lorre, and Eva and Zsa Zsa Gabor.

• *When you're finished inside, exit through the main doors, turn right, and go to the opposite end of the front courtyard. Here you'll find the entrance to the...*

Hungarian Jewish Museum (Magyar Zsidó Múzeum): This small but informative museum illuminates the Jewish faith, with artifacts and succinct but engaging English explanations. As this museum has undergone a thorough renovation, the specific details may vary. But look for the following topics.

One section explains **rituals and holidays,** from Rosh Hashanah and Yom Kippur to Passover and Chanukah. The exhibit also explains the symbolism of **objects** such as prayer shawls, the mezuzah, and so on.

Another exhibit focuses on **family life,** tracing the Jewish lifeline from birth to marriage to death. And yet another set of exhibits commemorates the **Holocaust.** You may see artifacts from this harrowing time: a set of drums made out of Torah scrolls; a bar of soap made of human fat (a grotesquely "efficient use of resources" from the Nazi concentration-camp system); and a menorah made by a resourceful inmate out of scraps of bread. You may also see exhibits honoring non-Jews who risked everything to rescue Jews during this dark time. For more about this tragic chapter of the Hungarian Jewish experience, don't miss the outstanding Holocaust Memorial Center (see page 602).

• *Exiting back into the front courtyard, go down the passageway between the synagogue and the museum (straight ahead from the security checkpoint).*

Tree of Life and Memorial Garden: As you walk alongside the Great Synagogue, notice the small **park** on your left. During the

Soviet siege that ended the Nazi occupation of Budapest in the winter of 1944-1945, many Jews in the ghetto here died of exposure, starvation, and disease. Soon after the Soviets liberated the city, a mass grave was dug here for an estimated 2,281 Jews. The trees and headstones (donated by survivors) were added later. The pillars you'll pass have historical photos of the synagogue and Jewish Quarter.

In the garden behind the synagogue is the *Tree of Life,* created by renowned artist Imre Varga. This weeping willow, cast in steel, was erected in 1990, soon after the fall of communism made it possible to acknowledge the Holocaust. The willow makes an upside-down menorah, and each of the 4,000 metal leaves is etched with the name of a Holocaust victim. New leaves are added all the time, donated by families of the victims.

In the center of the garden is a symbolic grave of **Raoul Wallenberg** (1912-1947). An improbable hero, this ne'er-do-well Swedish playboy from a prominent family was sent as a diplomat to Hungary because nobody else wanted the post. He was empowered by the Swedish government to do whatever he could—bribe, threaten, lie, or blackmail—to save as many Jews as possible from the Nazis. He surpassed everyone's low expectations by dedicating (and ultimately sacrificing) his life to the cause. By giving Swedish passports to Jews and admitting them to safe houses, he succeeded in rescuing tens of thousands of people from certain death. Shortly after the Soviets arrived, Wallenberg was arrested, accused of being a US spy, sent to a gulag...and never seen alive again. Russian authorities recently acknowledged he was executed, but have not revealed the details.

The grave is also etched with the names of other "righteous Gentiles" who went above and beyond to save Jews. According to the Talmud, "Whoever saves one life, saves the world entire."

Other Jewish Quarter Sights

In the area around the Great Synagogue are several other sights. The building just behind the memorial garden houses the Hungarian Jewish Archives. Its **Family Research Center** has birth, marriage, and death records for Jews from Budapest and much of Hungary. For 1,000 Ft, you're welcome to use their archives (ideally, let them know you're coming in advance—www.milev.hu, family@milev.hu). Upstairs is a small **virtual exhibition** about the Jewish Quarter.

The **Orthodox Synagogue** is located on a nondescript urban street two blocks from the Great Synagogue. Built in the Vienna-inspired Secession style in 1912, this temple stood damaged and deserted for decades after World War II until being renovated in 2006. Today it invites visitors to see its colorful, sumptuously decorated interior.

The **Synagogue at Rumbach Street** has a colorful but faded Moorish-style interior that survives from the Golden Age of Jewish culture in Budapest. The building may be closed during your visit for a much-needed restoration.

ANDRÁSSY ÚT

Connecting downtown Pest to City Park, Andrássy út is Budapest's main boulevard, lined with plane trees, shops, theaters, cafés, and locals living very well. Budapesters like to think of Andrássy út as the Champs-Elysées and Broadway rolled into one. While that's a stretch, it is a good place to stroll, get a feel for today's urban Pest, and visit a few top attractions (most notably the Opera House and the House of Terror) on the way to Heroes' Square and City Park.

I've arranged these sights in the order you'll reach them if you walk up the boulevard from where it begins, near Deák tér. The handy M1/yellow Metró line runs every couple of minutes just under the street, making it easy to skip several blocks ahead, or to backtrack (stops marked by yellow signs).

• *Three blocks up Andrássy út on the left is the...*

▲▲Hungarian State Opera House (Magyar Állami Operaház)

The Neo-Renaissance home of the Hungarian State Opera features performances (almost daily except during outdoor music season, late June-early Sept) and delight-

ful tours. The building dates from the 1890s, not long after Budapest had become co-capital of the Habsburg Empire. The Hungarians wanted to put their city on the map as a legitimate European capital, and that meant they needed an opera house. Emperor Franz Josef provided half the funds...on the condition that it be smaller than the opera house in his hometown of Vienna. And so, Miklós Ybl designed a building that would exceed Vienna's famous Staatsoper in opulence, if not in size. (Franz Josef was reportedly displeased.) It was built using almost entirely Hungarian materials. After being damaged in World War II, it was painstakingly restored in the early 1980s. Today, with lavish marble-and-gold-leaf decor, a gorgeous gilded interior slathered with paintings of Greek myths, and high-quality performances at bargain prices, this is one of Europe's finest opera houses.

You can drop in whenever the box office is open to ogle the ostentatious **lobby** (Mon-Sat from 11:00 until show time—generally 19:00, or until 17:00 if there's no performance; Sun open 3 hours before the performance—generally 16:00-19:00, or 10:00-13:00 if there's a matinee; Andrássy út 22, district VI, M1: Opera).

The 45-minute **tours** of the Opera House are a must for music lovers, and enjoyable for anyone, though the quality of the guides can be erratic: Most spout plenty of fun, if silly, legends, but others can be quite dry. You'll see the main entryway, the snooty lounge area, some of the cozy but plush boxes, and the lavish auditorium. You'll find out why clandestine lovers would meet in the cigar lounge, how the Opera House is designed to keep the big spenders away from the rabble in the nosebleed seats, and how to tell the difference between real marble and fake marble (2,990 Ft, 500 Ft extra to take photos; English tours nearly daily at 14:00, 15:00,

Andrássy Út Walk

SZINYEI MERSE

FELSŐ ERDŐSOR

BAJNOK

Kodály körönd

To
9

M Kodály körönd

SZIV

Lövölde tér

SZÍV

SZEGFŰ

SZALMÁS

RÓZSA

100 Meters

100 Yards

IZABELLA

ARADI

SZÖNDI

Vörösmarty utca

VÖRÖSMARTY

KIRÁLY

M PUPPET THEATER

VÖRÖSMARTY

PODMANICZKY

CSENGERY

HOUSE OF TERROR

Hunyadi tér

CSENGERY

DOB

EÖTVÖS

HÁRSFA

To
Nyugati/Western
Train Station

Tram #4 & #6

POST

SZÓFIA

To
New York
Café

JÓKAI

TERÉZ KÖRUT

Oktogon

ERZSÉBET KÖRUT

WEINER LEÓ

LOVAG

DESSEWFFY

Jókai tér

M Oktogon

Liszt Ferenc tér

KÚRT

KERTÉSZ

MOZSÁR

HEGEDŰ

AKÁCFA

NAGYMEZŐ

PAULAY EDE

CSÁNYI

BAJCSY - ZSILINSZKY

VADÁSZ

ZICHY JENŐ

"Broadway Quarter"

HAJÓS

OPERA HOUSE

Opera

M

DRESCHLER PALACE

VASVÁRI

KIS DIÓFA

KIRÁLY

ORTHODOX SYNAGOGUE

US EMBASSY

NAGY SÁNDOR

BANK

ABSOLUTE TOUR CENTER

NEW THEATER

SZÉKELY

KAZINCZY

POSTAL SAVINGS BANK

Ó UTCA

LÁZÁR

RÉVAY

M Arany János utca

CROSSWALK

KÁLDY GYULA

SEVENTH DISTRICT
(& Jewish Quarter)

HOLLÓ

DOB

NATIONAL BANK

GOZSDU UDVAR

Szabadság tér

HERCEGPRIMÁS

RUMBACH STREET SYNAGOGUE

ST. ISTVÁN'S BASILICA

M Bajcsy-Zsilinszky út

RUMBACH SEBESTYÉN

To Great Synagogue

ASBÓTH

AKVÁRIUM KLUB

ANKERHÁZ

KÁROLY KÖRÚT

Deák Ferenc tér

T

Deák tér

SEMMELWEIS

GERLÓCZY

BÉCSI

CITY HALL

COUNTY HALL

ISTVÁN

BÁRCZY

FEHÉRHAJÓ

VÁROSHÁZ

PILVAX

Vörösmarty tér

POST

PETŐFI SÁNDOR

DEÁK

VÁCI UTCA

PÁRIZSI

Ferenciek tere

M

1. Hungarian State Opera House
2. "Broadway Quarter"
3. Párisi Nagy Áruház Café
4. Franz Liszt Square
5. Franz Liszt Academy of Music
6. Oktogon
7. House of Terror
8. Former Academy of Music & Franz Liszt Museum
9. To Diplomatic Quarter, Heroes' Square & City Park

BUDAPEST

and 16:00; tickets are easy to get—just show up 10 minutes before the tour and head for the ticket desk in the lobby; mobile +3630-279-5677). You can pay 690 Ft extra to watch a five-minute performance of two arias after the tour—or you can hear the music just fine for free from the lobby.

To experience the Opera House in action, take in an excellent and affordable **performance** (see "Entertainment in Budapest," page 637).

• *The Opera House marks the beginning of an emerging dining-and-nightlife neighborhood dubbed the...*

"Broadway Quarter"

The next major cross-street, **Nagymező utca,** features a chic cluster of restaurants, bars, and theaters (especially on the left side of Andrássy). This is an enjoyable place to stroll on a summer evening. Many of my recommended restaurants described under "Eating in Budapest," later, are in this neighborhood.

A half-block down Andrássy út on the right (at #39) is a grand old early 20th-century building marked **Párisi Nagy Áruház** (Paris Department Store). One of the city's first department stores, this was a popular shopping stop for years, even through communism. But as was common in Budapest, the store closed down and sat deserted and glum for years. In the early 2000s, new owners totally restored

it, including the gorgeous upstairs Lotz Hall (which held a fine café). But unfortunately, that business, too, closed after a few years. As it's a gorgeous space and a historic building, hopefully it will re-open again soon...perhaps by the time you read this. If not, console yourself with a cocktail at Budapest's best rooftop terrace—the recommended 360 Bar (see page 644)—which you can enter through the door immediately to the right of the department store entrance.

• *Just after the end of the block is a popular outdoor-dining area.*

Franz Liszt Square (Liszt Ferenc Tér)

This leafy square is surrounded by hip, expensive cafés and restaurants. (The best is the recommended restaurant **Menza.**)

Strangely, neither the statue on this square nor the one facing it, across Andrássy út, is of Franz Liszt. But deeper in the park, you'll find a modern statue of Liszt energetically playing an imaginary piano. And at the far end of the square, fronting a gorgeous piazza, is the **Franz Liszt Academy of Music,** founded by and named for this half-Hungarian, half-Austrian composer who had a Hungarian name and passport. Liszt loved his family's Magyar heritage (though he didn't speak Hungarian) and spent his final six years in Budapest. His Academy of Music has been stunningly restored inside and out—step into the sumptuous lobby. This space, though smaller, gives the Opera House a run for its money...and speaking of money, the concerts here are even cheaper than at the already reasonably priced Opera (for details, see page 637).

• *One block up from Franz Liszt Square is the gigantic crossroads known as the...*

Oktogon

This vast intersection with its corners snipped off—where Andrássy út meets the Great Boulevard ring road (Nagykörút)—was called Mussolini tér during World War II, then November 7 tér in honor of the Bolshevik Revolution. Today kids have nicknamed it American tér for the fast-food joints littering the square and streets nearby.

From here, if you have time to delve into workaday Budapest, hop on tram #4 or #6, which trundle in both directions around the ring road. If you have time for a short detour to the most opulent coffee break of your life, head for the recommended **New York Café** (see page 670): Just hop on a tram to the right (tram #6 toward Móricz Zsigmond körtér or tram #4 toward Fehérvári út), and get off at the Wesselényi utca stop.

• *There's one more major sight between here and Heroes' Square. Walk two more blocks up Andrássy út to reach the...*

▲▲House of Terror (Terror Háza)

The building at Andrássy út 60 was home to the vilest parts of two destructive regimes: first the Arrow Cross (the Gestapo-like enforcers of Nazi-occupied Hungary), then the ÁVO and ÁVH secret police (the insidious KGB-type wing of the Soviet satellite government). Now re-envisioned as the "House of Terror," this building uses high-tech, highly conceptual, bombastic exhibits to document (if not proselytize about) the ugliest moments in Hungary's difficult

20th century. Enlightening and well-presented, it rivals Memento Park as Budapest's best attraction about the communist age.

Cost and Hours: 2,000 Ft, possibly more for special exhibits, Tue-Sun 10:00-18:00, closed Mon, audioguide-1,500 Ft, Andrássy út 60, district VI, M1: Vörösmarty utca—*not* the Vörösmarty tér stop, tel. 1/374-2600, www.terrorhaza.hu.

Tours: The 1,500-Ft English audioguide is good but almost too thorough, and can be difficult to hear over the din of Hungarian soundtracks in each room. You can't fast-forward through the dense and sometimes long-winded commentary. As an alternative, my self-guided tour covers the key points.

Background: In the lead-up to World War II, Hungary initially allied with Hitler—both to retain a degree of self-determination and to try to regain its huge territorial losses after World War I's devastating Treaty of Trianon (see page 524). But in March of 1944, the Nazi-affiliated Arrow Cross Party was forcibly installed as Hungary's new government. The Nazi surrogates deported nearly 440,000 Jewish people to Auschwitz, murdered thousands more on the streets of Budapest, and executed hundreds in the basement of this building. When the communists moved into Hungary after the war, they took over the same building as headquarters for their secret police (the ÁVO, later renamed ÁVH). To keep dissent to a minimum, the secret police terrorized, tried, deported, or executed anyone suspected of being an enemy of the state.

◑ Self-Guided Tour: Buy your ticket (and rent an audioguide, if you wish) and head into the museum.

The **atrium** features a Soviet T-54 tank, and a vast wall covered with 3,200 portraits of people who were murdered by the Nazis or the communists in this very building. The one-way exhibit begins two floors up, then spirals down to the cellar—just follow signs for Kiállítás/Exhibition. To begin, you can either take the elevator (to floor 2), or walk up the red stairwell nearby, decorated with old Socialist Realist sculptures from the communist days.

Upstairs, the first room gives an overview of the **Double Occupation.** The video by the entrance sets the stage for Hungary's 20th century: its territorial losses after World War I; its alliance with, then invasion by, the Nazis; and its "liberation," then occupation, by the USSR.

After passing through a room displaying uniforms and other gear belonging to Hungarian Nazis, you'll reach the room devoted to the **Gulag.** The word "gulag" refers to a network of secret Soviet prison camps, mostly in Siberia. These were hard-labor camps where potential and actual dissidents were sent in order to punish them, remove their dangerous influence from society, and make an example of those who would dare to defy the regime. On the carpet, a giant map of the USSR shows the locations of some of these camps, where an estimated 600,000 to 700,000 Hungarian civilians and prisoners of war were sent... about half of whom never returned.

The **Changing Clothes** room—with rotating figures dressed alternately in Arrow Cross and communist uniforms—satirizes the readiness of many Hungarians to align themselves with whomever was in power.

The room on **The Fifties** examines the gradual insinuation of the communist regime into the fabric of Hungary. Their methods ranged from already-marked ballots to glossy propaganda—such as the paintings celebrating the peasants of the "people's revolution" and romanticized depictions of communist leaders (look for Lenin as the brave sailor). Behind the distorted stage is the dark underbelly of the regime: the constant surveillance that bred paranoia among the people. The **Resistance** room—empty aside from three very different kitchen tables—symbolizes the way that resistance to the regime emerged in every walk of life.

The exhibition continues downstairs, where the **Resettlement and Deportation** section explains the ethnic cleansing—or, in the more pleasant parlance of the time, "mutual population exchange"—that took place throughout Central and Eastern Europe in the years following World War II. In Hungary alone, 230,000 Germans were uprooted and deported. Meanwhile, Hungarians who had become ethnically "stranded" in other nations after the Treaty of Trianon were sent to Hungary (100,000 from Slovakia, 140,000 from Romania, and 70,000 from Yugoslavia). Most have still not returned to their ancestral homes.

In **Surrender of Property and Land,** we learn that under communism, the Hungarian people had to survive on increasingly sparse rations. Enter the labyrinth of pork-fat bricks, which remind old-timers of the harsh conditions of the 1950s (lard on bread for dinner). Look for the ration coupons, which people had to present before being allowed to buy even these measly staples.

The next room examines the **ÁVO,** the communist secret police who intimidated the common people of Hungary—equivalent to the KGB in the Soviet Union. Before they were finished, the ÁVO/ÁVH imprisoned, abused, or murdered one person from every third Hungarian family. Their power came from enlisting untold numbers of civilians as informants.

After passing through the office of Gábor Péter (the first director of the ÁVO), you'll reach the **"Justice"** exhibit, which explores "show trials"—high-profile, loudly publicized, and completely choreographed trials of people who had supposedly subverted the regime. The burden of proof was on the accused, not on the accuser, and coerced confessions were fair game. From 1945 until the 1956 Uprising, more than 71,000 Hungarians were accused of political crimes, and 485 were executed.

Next you'll encounter another more upbeat method for controlling the people: bright, cheery communist **Propaganda.** The poster about the Amerikai Bogár warns of the threat of the "American Beetle" (from Kolorádó), which threatened Hungarian crops. When the communists collectivized traditional family farm plots, they tore down the trees and hedgerows that separated them—thereby removing birds that had kept pest populations in check. When a potato beetle epidemic hit, rather than acknowledging their own fault, the communists blamed an American conspiracy.

Rounding out this floor are sections on **"Hungarian Silver"** (actually aluminum—lampooning the lowbrow aesthetic of that era) and **Religion** (those who were publicly faithful were discriminated against, closely supervised by the secret police, and often arrested). Then you'll board an **elevator** that gradually lowers into the cellar. As it descends, you'll watch a three-minute video of a guard explaining the grotesque execution process. When the door opens, you're in the **Prison Cellar.** Wander through **former cells** used for different purposes. In the large room after the cells, you'll see a stool with a lamp; nearby are the **torture** devices: hot pads and electrical appliances. The bucket and hose were used to revive torture victims who had blacked out. After the torture room, a small room on the right contains a **gallows** that was used for executions (described earlier on your journey, in the elevator video).

The room commemorating the **1956 Uprising** features a symbol of that uprising—a Hungarian flag with a hole cut out of the middle (a hastily removed Soviet emblem) and the slogan *Ruszkik Haza!* ("Russkies go home!") For more on '56, see page 578.

After a sobering room that displays six symbolic gallows, the **Emigration** room features a wall of postcards. More than 200,000 Hungarians simply fled the country after the uprising. The **Hall of Tears** memorial commemorates all of the victims of the communists from 1945 to 1967 (when the final prisoners were released from this building). The **Room of Farewell** shows several color video clips that provide a (relatively) happy ending: the festive and exhilarating days in 1991 when the Soviets departed, making way for freedom; the reburial of the Hungarian hero, Imre Nagy, at Heroes' Square; and the dedication of this museum.

The chilling finale: walls of photographs of the **"Victimizers"** —members and supporters of the Arrow Cross and ÁVO, many of whom are still living and who were never brought to justice. The Hungarians have a long way to go to reconcile everything they lived through in the 20th century. For many of them, this museum is an important first step.

• *Across the street and a few steps up Andrássy út is the...*

Franz Liszt Museum

In this surprisingly modest apartment where the composer once resided, you'll find a humble but appealing collection of artifacts. A pilgrimage site for Liszt fans, it's housed in the former Academy of Music, which also hosts Saturday-morning concerts (see page 638).

Cost and Hours: 1,500 Ft; dry English audioguide with a few snippets of music-700 Ft, otherwise scarce English information—borrow the information sheet as you enter; Mon-Fri 10:00-18:00, Sat 9:00-17:00, closed Sun, Vörösmarty utca 35, district VI, M1: Vörösmarty utca—*not* Vörösmarty tér stop, tel. 1/322-9804, www.lisztmuseum.hu.

• *While you can walk from here to Heroes' Square (visible in the distance, about a 15-minute walk), there's less to see along the rest of Andrássy út. If you prefer, hop on the Metró here and ride it three stops to Hősök tere.*

HEROES' SQUARE AND CITY PARK

The grand finale of Andrássy út, at the edge of the city center, is also one of Budapest's most entertaining quarters. Here you'll find the grand Heroes' Square, dripping with history (both monumental and recent); the vast tree-filled expanse of City Park, dressed up with fanciful buildings that include an Art Nouveau zoo and a replica of a Transylvanian castle; and, tucked in the middle of it all, Budapest's finest thermal spa and single best experience, the Széchenyi Baths. If the sightseeing grind gets you down, take a minivacation from your busy vacation and relax the way Budapesters do: Escape to City Park.

▲▲Heroes' Square (Hősök Tere)

Built in 1896 to celebrate the 1,000th anniversary of the Magyars' arrival in Hungary, this vast square culminates at a bold **Millennium Monument.** Standing stoically in its colonnades are 14 Hungarian leaders who represent the whole span of this nation's colorful

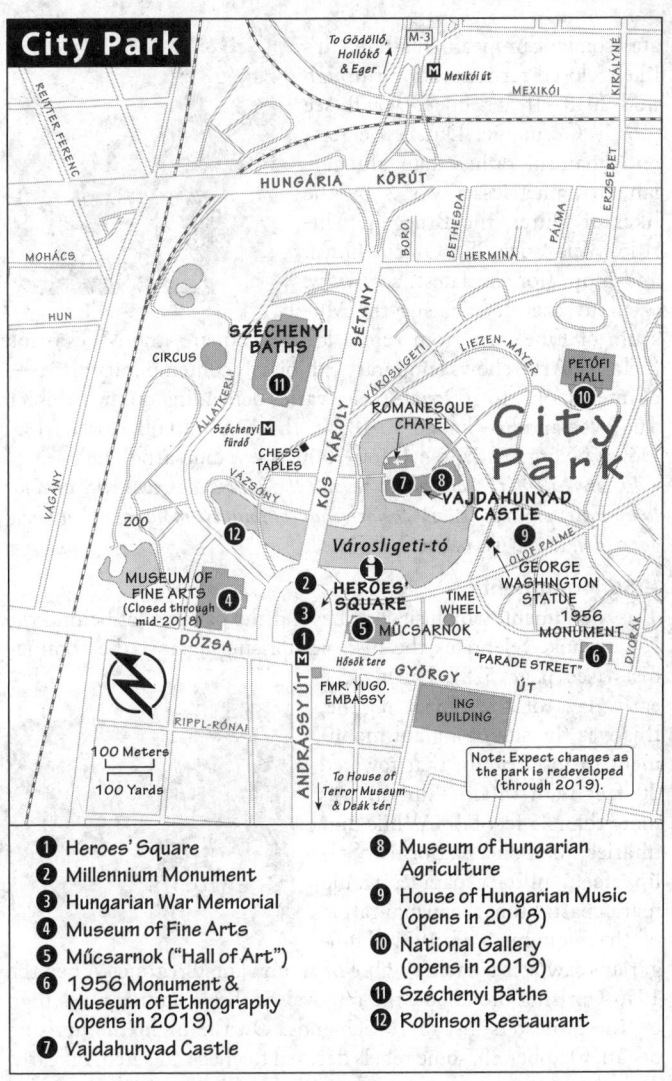

City Park

1 Heroes' Square
2 Millennium Monument
3 Hungarian War Memorial
4 Museum of Fine Arts
5 Műcsarnok ("Hall of Art")
6 1956 Monument & Museum of Ethnography (opens in 2019)
7 Vajdahunyad Castle
8 Museum of Hungarian Agriculture
9 House of Hungarian Music (opens in 2018)
10 National Gallery (opens in 2019)
11 Széchenyi Baths
12 Robinson Restaurant

Note: Expect changes as the park is redeveloped (through 2019).

BUDAPEST

and illustrious history. In front, at the base of a high pillar, are the seven original Magyar chieftains, the Hungarian War Memorial, and young Hungarian skateboarders of the 21st century. Look for names you may recognize: István, Béla IV, Mátyás Corvinus. The sculptures on the top corners of the two colonnades represent, from left to right: Work and Welfare, War, Peace, and the Importance of Packing Light. The square is also flanked by a pair of museums.

Museums on Heroes' Square: The **Museum of Fine Arts** (Szépművészeti Múzeum) is Budapest's best chance to appreciate some European masters. It's likely closed for renovation through mid-2018. If it's open, you'll see mostly Germanic, Dutch, Belgian, and Spanish, rather than Hungarian, art, plus lesser works by the likes of Dürer, the Bruegels, Murillo, Velázquez, El Greco, Goya, and more (for the latest, see www. szepmuveszeti.hu). Facing the Mu-

seum of Fine Arts from across Heroes' Square, the **Műcsarnok** ("Hall of Art") shows temporary exhibits by contemporary artists— of interest only to art lovers (price varies depending on the exhibits; Tue-Wed and Fri-Sun 10:00-18:00, Thu 12:00-20:00, closed Mon, Dózsa György út 37, tel. 1/460-7000, www.mucsarnok.hu).

• The area along the busy street beyond the Műcsarnok was once used for communist parades. While the original communist monuments are long gone, a new one has taken their place...

1956 Monument

This monument, which sits just beyond the parking lot behind the Műcsarnok, celebrates the historic uprising against the communists (see page 578). During the

early days of the Soviet regime, this was the site of a giant monument to Josef Stalin that towered 80 feet high (Stalin himself was more than 25 feet tall). While dignitaries stood on a platform at Stalin's feet, military parades would march past. From the inauguration of the monument in 1951, Hungarians saw it as a hated symbol of an unwanted regime. When the 1956 Uprising broke out, the removal of the monument was high on the protesters' list of 16 demands. On the night the uprising began, October 23, some rebels decided to check this item off early. They came here, cut off Stalin just below the knees, and toppled him from his platform. The current monument was erected in 2006 to commemorate the 50th anniversary of the uprising. Symbolizing the way Hungarians came together to attempt the impossible, it begins with scattered individuals at the back (rusty and humble), gradually coming together and gaining strength and unity near the front—culminating in a silver ship's prow boldly plying the ground.

▲▲City Park (Városliget)

Budapest's not-so-central "Central Park," which sprawls beyond Heroes' Square, was the site of the overblown 1896 Millennial

Exhibition, celebrating Hungary's 1,000th birthday. This particularly enjoyable corner of Budapest, which sprawls behind Heroes' Square, is endlessly entertaining. Explore the fantasy castle of Vajdahunyad (described next). Visit the animals and ogle the playful Art Nouveau buildings inside the city's zoo, or enjoy a circus under the big top. Go for a stroll, rent a rowboat, eat some cotton candy, or challenge a local Bobby Fischer to a game of chess. Or, best of all, take a dip in Budapest's ultimate thermal spa, the Széchenyi Baths (described later). This is a fine place to just be on vacation. Be aware that parts of the park may be torn up, as the city is rejuvenating the area as a new Museum Quarter.

▲▲Vajdahunyad Castle (Vajdahunyad Vára)

Many of the buildings for Hungary's Millennial Exhibition were erected with temporary materials, to be torn down at the end of the festival—as was the case for most world fairs at the time. But locals so loved Vajdahunyad Castle that they insisted it stay, so it was rebuilt in brick and stone. The complex actually has four parts, each representing a high point in Hungarian architectural style: Romanesque chapel, Gothic gate, Renaissance castle, and Baroque palace (free and always open to walk around the grounds).

From this direction, the **Renaissance castle** dominates the view. It's a replica of a famous castle in Transylvania that once belonged to the Hunyadi family (János and Mátyás Corvinus—both of whom are represented on Heroes' Square).

Cross over the bridge and through the **Gothic gateway.** Once inside the complex, on the left is a replica of a 13th-century Romanesque **Benedictine chapel.** Consecrated as an actual church, this is Budapest's most popular spot for weddings on summer weekends. Farther ahead on the right is a big Baroque mansion housing the **Museum of Hungarian Agriculture** (Magyar Mezőgazdasági Múzeum, www.mezogazdasagimuzeum.hu). It brags that it's Europe's biggest agriculture museum, but most visitors will find the lavish interior more interesting than the exhibits.

Facing the museum entry is a monument to **Anonymous**—

specifically, the Anonymous from the court of King Béla IV who penned the first Hungarian history in the Middle Ages.

• *The park's highlight is the big yellow building across the street from Vajdahunyad Castle...*

▲▲▲Széchenyi Baths (Széchenyi Fürdő)

My favorite activity in Budapest, the Széchenyi Baths are an ideal way to reward yourself for the hard work of sightseeing and call it a culturally enlightening experience.

Soak in hundred-degree water, surrounded by portly Hungarians squeezed into tiny swimsuits, while jets and cascades pound away your tension. Go for a vigorous swim in the lap pool, giggle and bump your way around the whirlpool, submerge yourself to the nostrils in water green with minerals, feel the bubbles from an underwater jet gradually caress their way up your leg, or challenge the locals to a game of Speedo-clad chess. And it's all surrounded by an opulent yellow palace with shiny copper domes. The bright blue-and-white of the sky, the yellow of the buildings, the pale pink of the skin, the turquoise of the water... Budapest simply doesn't get any better (for all the details, see "Experiences in Budapest," later).

NEAR ÜLLŐI ÚT

This museum is near the city center, on the boulevard called Üllői út. You could stroll there in about 10 minutes from the Small Boulevard ring road (walking the length of the Ráday utca café street gets you very close), or hop on the M3/blue Metró line to Corvinnegyed (just one stop beyond Kálvin tér).

▲▲Holocaust Memorial Center (Holokauszt Emlékközpont)

This sight honors the nearly 600,000 Hungarian victims of the Nazis...one out of every ten Holocaust victims. The impressive modern complex (with a beautifully restored 1920s synagogue as its centerpiece) is a museum of the Hungarian Holocaust, a monument to its victims, a space for temporary exhibits, and a research and documentation center of Nazi atrocities. Interesting to anybody, but essential to those interested in the Holocaust, this is Budapest's best sight about that dark time—and one of Europe's best, as well. While the exhibit sometimes acknowledges Roma (Gypsy) victims, its primary focus is on the fate of the Hungarian Jews.

Cost and Hours: 1,400 Ft, Tue-Sun 10:00-18:00, closed Mon, last entry one hour before closing, Páva utca 39, district IX, M3: Corvin-negyed, tel. 1/455-3333, www.hdke.hu.

Getting There: From the Corvin-negyed Métró stop, use the exit marked *Holokauszt Emlékközpont* and take the left fork at the exit. Walk straight ahead two long blocks, then turn right down Páva utca.

Visiting the Center: You'll pass through a security checkpoint to reach the courtyard. Once inside, a black marble wall is etched with the names of victims. Head downstairs to buy your ticket. The excellent permanent exhibit, called "From Deprivation of Rights to Genocide," traces in English the gradual process of disenfranchisement, marginalization, exploitation, dehumanization, and eventually extermination that befell Hungary's Jews as World War II wore on. The finale is the interior of the **synagogue,** now a touching memorial filled with glass seats, each one etched with the image of a Jewish worshipper who once filled it. Up above, on the mezzanine level, you'll find temporary exhibits and an information center that helps teary-eyed descendants of Hungarian Jews track down the fate of their relatives.

Nearby: A few blocks away (at Üllői út 33) is the fanciful, late-19th-century **Applied Arts Museum**—a green-roofed castle that's worth a quick lock (from the outside, at least) for architecture fans.

Sights in Buda

Nearly all of Buda's top sights are concentrated on or near its two riverside hills: Castle Hill and Gellért Hill.

CASTLE HILL (VÁRHEGY)

Once the seat of Hungarian royalty, and now the city's highest-profile tourist zone, Castle Hill is a historic spit of land looming above the Buda bank of the Danube. Scenic from afar, but (frankly) a bit soulless from up close, it's best seen quickly. This walk gives you the lay of the land and links up the hill's most worthwhile attractions and museums, including Matthias Church, the Fishermen's Bastion, the Hungarian National Gallery, and the WWII-era Hospital in the Rock. You'll also appreciate the bird's-eye views across the Danube to Pest. I've listed these sights in order from south to north, and linked them together with a self-guided walk.

When to Visit: Castle Hill is jammed with tour groups in the morning, but it's much less crowded in the afternoon. Since restaurants up here are touristy and a bad value, Castle Hill is an ideal after-lunch activity.

Buda Sights

B U D A

Castle Hill

VÍZI-VÁROS

TABÁN

Danube River

① Royal Palace
② Hungarian Nat'l Gallery
③ Budapest History Museum
④ Matthias Church
⑤ Fishermen's Bastion
⑥ Hospital in the Rock & Nuclear Bunker
⑦ Remains of St. Mary Magdalene Church
⑧ Museum of Military History
⑨ Citadella Fortress
⑩ Liberation Monument
⑪ Cave Church
⑫ Gellért Hotel & Baths
⑬ Rudas Baths

500 Meters
500 Yards

Getting There: The Metró and trams won't take you to the top of Castle Hill, but you have several other good options: a walk-escalator-elevator combo; a bus; or the funicular.

For a free and scenic approach, you can **walk** up through the castle gardens called Várkert Bazár (trams #19 and #41 stop right in front). From the monumental gateway facing the Danube embankment, head up the stairs into the park, then look right for the covered escalator. From its top, you can either turn left to hike the rest of the way up (on the switchbacked path), or you can carry on straight ahead to find an elevator (under a rust-colored canopy) that zips you right up to the view terrace in front of the Royal Palace. From here, you can begin the walk at the viewpoint in front of the palace, then see the Turul bird statue and funicular station on your way back across the hill later.

From Pest, it's usually fastest to hop on **bus #16,** with stops near the Deák tér Metró hub (on Harmincad utca alongside Erzsébet tér; use exit "E" from the station underpass) and at Széchenyi tér, at the Pest end of the Chain Bridge. (You can also catch it at Clark Ádám tér at the Buda end of the Chain Bridge—across the street from the lower funicular station, and much cheaper than the funicular.) Or you can go via Széll Kálmán tér (on the M2/red Metró line, or by taking tram #4 or #6 around Pest's Great Boulevard); from here, bus #16, as well as buses **#16A** and **#116,** head up to the castle. All of these buses stop at Dísz tér, at the crest of the hill, about halfway along its length (most people on the bus will be getting off there, too). From Dísz tér, cross the street and walk five minutes along the row of flagpoles toward the green dome, then bear left to find the big Turul bird statue at the start of this walk.

The **funicular** (*sikló*, SHEE-kloh) lifts visitors from the Chain Bridge to the top of Castle Hill (1,200 Ft one-way, 1,800 Ft round-trip, not covered by transit pass, daily 7:30-22:00, departs every 5-10 minutes, closed for maintenance every other Mon). It leaves you right at the Turul bird statue, where this walk begins. (If there's a long line at the lower funicular station, you can just hop on bus #16 across the roundabout—described above.)

To **leave the hilltop,** most visitors find it easiest just to walk down after their visit (see the end of this tour). But if you'll be taking the bus down, it's smart to buy tickets for the return trip before you ascend Castle Hill—the only place to buy them up top is at the post office near Dísz tér (Mon-Fri until 16:00, closed Sat-Sun).

• *Begin the walk at the big statue of the...*

Turul Bird

This mythical bird of Magyar folktales supposedly led the Hungarian migrations from the steppes of Central Asia in the ninth century. He dropped his sword in the Carpathian Basin, indicating that this was to be the permanent home of the Magyar people. While the Hungarians have long since integrated into Europe, the Turul remains a symbol of Magyar pride. During a surge of nationalism in the 1920s, a movement named after this bird helped revive traditional Hungarian culture. And today, the bird is invoked by right-wing nationalist politicians.

• *We'll circle back this way later. But for now, go through the monumental gateway by the Turul and climb down the stairs, then walk along the broad terrace in front of the...*

Royal Palace (Királyi Palota)

The imposing palace on Castle Hill barely hints at the colorful story of this hill since the day that the legendary Turul dropped his sword. It was once the top Renaissance palace in Europe...but that was several centuries and several versions ago. In the early 15th century, the Renaissance King Mátyás (Matthias) Corvinus—who we'll learn more about soon—converted a humble medi-

eval palace on this site into one of Europe's most extravagant residences, putting Buda and Hungary on the map. Just a few decades later, invading Ottomans occupied Buda and turned the palace into a military garrison. When the Habsburgs laid siege to the hill for 77 days in 1686, gunpowder stored in the cellar exploded, destroying the palace. The Habsburgs took the hill, but Buda was deserted and in ruins. The palace was rebuilt, then damaged again during the 1848 Revolution, then repaired again. As World War II drew to a close, Budapest became the front line between the Nazis and the approaching Soviets. The Red Army laid siege to the hill for

100 days. They eventually succeeded in taking Budapest...but the city—and the hill—were devastated.

The current palace—a historically inaccurate, post-WWII reconstruction—is a loose rebuilding of previous versions. It's big but soulless. The most prominent feature of today's palace—the green dome—didn't even exist in earlier versions. Fortunately, the palace does house some worthwhile museums (described later), and boasts the fine terrace you're strolling on, with some of Budapest's best views.

• *Behind the big equestrian statue is the main entrance to the...*

Hungarian National Gallery (Magyar Nemzeti Galéria)

While not quite a must-see, this museum is the best place in Hungary to appreciate the works of homegrown artists, and to get a peek into the often-morose Hungarian worldview. The collection—which is scheduled to move to a new home in City Park in 2019—includes a remarkable group of 15th-century, wood-carved altars from Slovakia (then "Upper Hungary"); piles of gloomy canvases dating from the dark days after the failed 1848 Revolution; several works by two great Hungarian Realist painters, Mihály Munkácsy and László Paál; and paintings by the troubled, enigmatic, and recently in-vogue Post-Impressionist Tivadar Csontváry Kosztka. The collection's highlights can be viewed quickly.

Cost and Hours: 1,800 Ft, may cost more for special exhibits, Tue-Sun 10:00-18:00, closed Mon, audioguide-800 Ft, required bag check for large bags, café, in the Royal Palace—enter from terrace by Eugene of Savoy statue, district I, mobile +3620-439-7325, www.mng.hu.

• *Head back outside and face the palace. Go through the passage to the right of the National Gallery entrance (next to the café). You'll emerge into a courtyard decorated with a gorgeous **fountain** dedicated to King Matthias Corvinus (see sidebar). Go around the right side of the fountain and through the passage, into the palace courtyard. At the far end of this too-big space is the entrance to the...*

Budapest History Museum (Budapesti Történeti Múzeum)

This earnest but dusty collection strains to bring the history of this city to life. If Budapest really intrigues you, this is a fine place to explore its history. Otherwise, skip it. The dimly-lit fragments of 14th-century sculptures, depicting early Magyars, allow you to see how Asian those original Hungarians truly looked. The "Light and Shadow" exhibit deliberately but effectively traces the union between Buda and Pest. Rounding out the collection are exhibits on prehistoric residents and a sprawling cellar that unveils fragments from the oh-so-many buildings that have perched on this hill over the centuries.

Cost and Hours: 2,000 Ft; March-Oct Tue-Sun 10:00-18:00,

Nov-Feb Tue-Sun until 16:00, closed Mon year-round; audioguide-1,200 Ft, some good English descriptions posted; district I, tel. 1/487-8800, www.btm.hu.

• *From the palace courtyard, it's time to...*

Walk to Matthias Church

Leaving the palace courtyard, walk straight up the slight incline. In good weather, you might see an opportunity to try your hand at shooting an old-fashioned bow and arrow. Then you'll pass under a gate with a raven holding a ring in its mouth (a symbol of King Matthias).

As you continue along the line of flagpoles, the big white building on your right (near the funicular station) is the **Sándor Palace,** the Hungarian president's office. This is where you can see the relatively low-key changing of the guard each hour on the hour, with a special show at noon. After Sándor Palace is the yellow former **Court Theater** (Várszínház), which has seen many great performances over the centuries—including a visit from Beethoven in 1800. Until recently, this housed the National Dance Theater. But current Hungarian Prime Minister Viktor Orbán (not known for humble gestures) grew jealous of the president's swanky digs, kicked out the dancers, and renovated this building as the prime minister's residence. In the field in the middle of this terrace, you'll notice the **ruins** of a medieval monastery and church. Along the left side (past the flagpoles) is the ongoing excavation of the medieval Jewish quarter—more reminders that most of what you see on today's Castle Hill has been destroyed and rebuilt many times over.

At the end of the field, passing the hulking former **Ministry of War** building, you'll reach **Dísz tér** (Parade Square). Here you'll see convenient bus stops for connecting to other parts of Budapest (bus #16, #16A, or #116 to Széll Kálmán tér; or bus #16 to the Pest side of the Chain Bridge).

On the left is a handy post office (bus tickets sold here Mon-Fri before 16:00, closed Sat-Sun). On the right, behind the low wall, is a courtyard with an open-air Hungarian **folk-art market.** While it's fun to browse, prices here are high (haggle away). The Great Market Hall has a better selection and generally lower prices (see page 585).

Continue straight uphill on **Tárnok utca** (noticing, on the left, the recommended Vár Bistro—a handy lunch cafeteria). This area often disappoints visitors. After being destroyed by Ottomans, it was rebuilt in sensible Baroque, lacking the romantic time-capsule charm of a medieval old town. But if you poke your head into some

Mátyás (Matthias) Corvinus: The Last Hungarian King

The Árpád dynasty—descendants of the original Magyar tribes—died out in 1301. For more than 600 years, Hungary would be ruled by elected foreign rulers...with one exception.

In the mid-15th century, the Hungarian military general János Hunyadi enjoyed great success on the battlefield against the Ottomans (including a pivotal victory in 1456's Battle of Belgrade). Meanwhile, Hungary's imported kings kept dying unexpectedly. Finally, the Hungarian nobility took a chance on a Hungarian-born ruler and offered the throne to Hunyadi's son, Mátyás (or Matthias in English). According to legend, they sent a raven with a ring in its mouth to notify Matthias, who was away in Prague. He returned to Buda, and took the raven both as his symbol and as his royal nickname: Corvinus (Latin for "raven").

Matthias Corvinus (r. 1458-1490) became the first Hungarian-descended king in more than 150 years. Progressive and well-educated in the Humanist tradition, Matthias Corvinus was the quintessential Renaissance king. A lover of the Italian Renaissance, he patronized the arts and built palaces legendary for their beauty. As a benefactor of the poor, he dressed as a commoner and ventured into the streets to see firsthand how the nobles of his realm treated his people.

A strong, savvy leader, Matthias created Central Europe's first standing army—30,000 mercenaries known as the Black Army. No longer reliant on the nobility for military support, Good King Matthias was able to drain power from the nobles—earning him the nickname the "people's king."

Matthias was also a shrewd military tactician. Realizing that skirmishing with the Ottomans would squander his resources, he made peace with the sultan to stabilize Hungary's southern border. Then he swept north, invading Moravia, Bohemia, and even Austria. By 1485, Matthias moved into his new palace in Vienna, and Hungary was enjoying a Golden Age.

But just five years later, Matthias died mysteriously at the age of 47, and his empire disintegrated. Before long the Ottomans flooded back into Hungary, and the country entered a dark period. It is said that when Matthias died, justice died with him. To this day, Hungarians rank him the greatest of all kings, and they sing of his siege of Vienna in their national anthem. They're proud that for a few decades they had a truly Hungarian king—and a great one at that.

courtyards, you'll almost always see some original Gothic arches and other medieval features.

As you continue along, ponder the fact that miles of **caves** were burrowed under Castle Hill—carved out by water, expanded by the Ottomans, and used by locals during the siege of Buda at the end of World War II. If you'd like to spelunk under Castle Hill and learn about how the caves were used during the 20th century, it's worth going on the lengthy Hospital in the Rock tour (described later). A block to your left is the entrance to the less interesting and skippable Labyrinth of Buda Castle.

On the left, the **Prima grocery store** sells reasonably priced cold drinks, and has a coffee shop upstairs (open daily). A good spot for dessert is just around the corner: **Rétesbár,** selling strudel *(rétes)* with various fillings (just down the little lane—Balta köz— next to the grocery store, daily 8:00-19:30).

Just beyond the grocery store, a warty plague column from 1713 marks **Szentháromság tér** (Holy Trinity Square), the main square of old Buda.

• *Dominating the square is...*

▲▲Matthias Church (Mátyás-Templom)

Arguably Budapest's finest church inside and out, this historic house of worship—with a frilly Neo-Gothic spire and gilded Hungarian historical motifs slathered on every interior wall—is Castle Hill's best sight. From the humble Loreto Chapel (with a tranquil statue of the Virgin that helped defeat the Ottomans), to altars devoted to top Hungarian kings, to a replica of the crown of Hungary, every inch of the church oozes history.

Cost and Hours: 1,500 Ft, Mon-Fri 9:00-17:00—possibly also open 19:00-20:00 in summer, Sat 9:00-12:15, Sun 13:00-17:00, Szentháromság tér 2, district I, tel. 1/488-7716, www.matyas-templom.hu.

Background: Budapest's best church has been destroyed and rebuilt several times in the 800 years since it was founded by King Béla IV. Today's version—renovated at great expense in the late 19th century and restored after World War II—is an ornately decorated lesson in Hungarian history. The church's unofficial namesake isn't a saint, so it can't be formally named for him. Its official name is the Church of Our Lady or the Coronation Church, but everyone calls it the Matthias Church, for Matthias Corvinus, the popular Renaissance king who got married here—twice.

❂ **Self-Guided Tour:** Examine the **exterior.** While the

BUDAPEST

nucleus of the church is Gothic, most of what you see outside—including the frilly, flamboyant steeple—was added for the 1896 millennial celebrations. At the top of the stone corner tower facing the river, notice the raven—the ever-present symbol of King Matthias Corvinus.

Buy your ticket across the square from the church's side door, at the ticket windows embedded in the wall. Then enter the church. The good English descriptions posted throughout will supplement this tour.

The sumptuous **interior** is wallpapered with gilded pages from a Hungarian history textbook. Different eras are represented by symbolic motifs. Entering the side door, turn left and go to the back end of the church. The wall straight ahead represents the Renaissance, with a giant coat of arms of beloved King Matthias Corvinus. (The tough guys in armor on either side are members of his mercenary Black Army, the source of his power.) Notice another raven, with a ring in its beak.

Work your way clockwise around the church. The first chapel (in the back corner, to the left as you face the closed main doors)—the **Loreto Chapel**—holds the church's prize possession: a 1515 statue of Mary and Jesus. Anticipating Ottoman plundering, locals walled over its niche. The occupying Ottomans used the church as their primary mosque—oblivious to the precious statue hidden behind the plaster. Then, a century and a half later, during the siege of Buda in 1686, gunpowder stored in the castle up the street detonated, and the wall crumbled. Mary's triumphant face showed through, terrifying the Ottomans. Supposedly this was the only part of town taken from the Ottomans without a fight.

Facing the doors, look to the top of the stout pillar on the right to see a **carved capital** showing two men gesturing excitedly at a book. Dating from 1260, these carvings are some of the earliest surviving features in this church, which has changed much over the centuries.

As you look down the **nave,** notice the banners. They've hung here since the Mass that celebrated Habsburg monarch Franz Josef's coronation at this church on June 8, 1867. In a sly political compromise to curry favor in the Hungarian part of his territory, Franz Josef was "emperor" *(Kaiser)* of Austria, but only "king" *(König)* of Hungary. (If you see the old German phrase "K+K"—still used today as a boast of royal quality—it refers to this *"König und Kaiser"* arrangement.) So, after F. J. was crowned emperor in Vienna, he came down the Danube and said to the Hungarians, "King me."

Now stand at the modern altar in the middle of the church, and look down the nave to the **main altar.** Mary floats above it all, and hovering over her is a full-scale replica of the Hungarian crown, which was blessed by St. John Paul II. More than a millennium after István, Mary still officially wears this nation's crown.

Climb the circular stone staircase (in the corner, near the chapel of László) up to the **gallery.** Walk along the royal oratory to a small room that overlooks the altar area. Here, squeezed in the corner between luxurious vestments, is another replica of the Hungarian crown (the original is under the Parliament's dome). Then you'll huff up another staircase for more views down over the nave, and an exhibit on the church's recent restoration, displaying original statues and architectural features. You'll exit back down into the nave.

• *Back outside, at the end of the square next to Matthias Church, is the...*

Fishermen's Bastion (Halászbástya)

Seven pointy domes and a double-decker rampart run along the cliff in front of Matthias Church. Evoking the original seven Magyar tribes, and built for the millennial celebration of their arrival, the Fishermen's Bastion is one of Budapest's top landmarks. This fanciful structure adorns Castle Hill like a decorative frieze or wedding-cake flowers. While some suckers pay for the views from here, parts of the rampart are free and always open. Or you can enjoy virtually the same view through the windows next to the bastion café for free. Note that the grand staircase leading down from the bastion offers a handy shortcut to the Víziváros neighborhood.

Cost and Hours: 800 Ft, buy ticket at ticket office along the park wall across the square from Matthias Church, daily mid-March-mid-Oct 9:00-19:00; after closing time and off-season, no tickets are sold, but bastion is open and free to enter; Szentháromság tér 5, district I.

• *Between the bastion and the church stands a statue of...*

St. István (c. 967-1038)

Hungary's first Christian king tamed the nomadic, pagan Magyars and established strict laws and the concept of private property. In the late 900s, Géza, Grand Prince of the Hungarians, lost a major battle against the forces of Christian Europe—and realized that he must raise his son Vajk (c. 967-1038) as a Catholic and convert his people, or they would be forcefully driven out of Europe. Vajk took the Christian name István (EESHT-vahn, "Stephen") and was baptized in the year 1000. The reliefs on this statue show the commissioners of the pope crowning St. István, bringing Hungary into the fold of Christendom. This put Hungary on the map as a fully European kingdom, forging alliances that would endure for centuries. Without this pivotal event, Hungarians believe that the Magyar nation would have been lost.

• *Head down the charming little street (named* **Szentháromság utca**) *that leads away from Matthias Church. Halfway down this street on the right, look for the venerable, recommended* **Ruszwurm** *café—the oldest in Budapest. Then continue out to the terrace and appreciate views of the* **Buda Hills**—*the "Beverly Hills" of Budapest, draped with orchards, vineyards, and the homes of the wealthiest Budapesters.*

If you go down the stairs here, then turn right up the street, you'll reach the entrance of the...

▲Hospital in the Rock and Nuclear Bunker (Sziklakórház és Atombunker)

Sprawling beneath Castle Hill is a 25,000-square-foot labyrinthine network of hospital and fallout-shelter corridors built during the mid-20th century. While pricey, this visit is a must for doctors, nurses, and World War II buffs. I enjoy this as a lively interactive experience to balance out an otherwise sedate Castle Hill visit.

Cost and Hours: 4,000 Ft for required one-hour tour, 10 percent discount with Matthias Church ticket, daily 10:00-20:00, English tours at the top of each hour, last tour departs at 19:00, gift shop like an army-surplus store, Lovas utca 4C, district I, mobile +3670-701-0101, www.sziklakorhaz.eu/en.

Getting There: To find the hospital, stand with your back to Matthias Church and the Fishermen's Bastion. Walk straight past the plague column and down the little street (Szentháromság utca), then go down the covered steps at the wall (or ride the elevator). At the bottom, turn right on Lovas utca, and walk 50 yards to the well-marked bunker entrance.

Visiting the Hospital and Bunker: First you'll watch a 10-minute movie (with English subtitles) about the history of the place. Then, on the tour, your guide leads you through the tunnels to see room after room of perfectly-preserved WWII and 1960s-era medical supplies and equipment, most still in working order.

More than 200 wax figures engagingly bring the various hospital rooms to life: giant sick ward, operating room, and so on. On your way to the fallout shelter, you'll pass the decontamination showers, and see primitive radiation detectors and communist propaganda directing comrades how to save themselves in case of capitalist bombs or gas attacks. In the bunker, you'll also tour the various mechanical rooms that provided water and ventilation to this sprawling underground city.

• *Our Castle Hill walk is finished. If you're ready to head back down to the river (and the Víziváros neighborhood), you can make a graceful exit down the big staircase below the Fishermen's Bastion.*

If you'd like to spend more time exploring Castle Hill, poke around the northern part of the hill, where you'll find several interesting sights. Next door to Matthias Church, the modern **Hilton Hotel** *is built around the fragments of a 13th-century Dominican church (to see them, go inside, find the lounge, and look out the window toward Pest). A few blocks farther north stand the remains of* **St. Mary Magdalene Church,** *destroyed during the Ottoman occupation but whose bell tower has been rebuilt. Around the corner is the dusty* **Museum of Military History.** *And along the tree-shaded terrace at the northern tip of the hilltop, look for the* **Turkish grave** *of a pasha (Ottoman ruler).*

From the northern end of the hill, you can head out through the Vienna Gate and follow the road downhill to bustling Széll Kálmán tér and its handy Metró stop (M2/red line).

GELLÉRT HILL (GELLÉRTHEGY) AND NEARBY

Gellért Hill rises from the Danube just downriver from the castle. When King István converted Hungary to Christianity in the year 1000, he brought in Bishop Gellért, a monk from Venice, to tutor his son. But some rebellious Magyars put the bishop in a barrel, drove long nails in from the outside, and rolled him down this hill...tenderizing him to death. Gellért became the patron saint of Budapest and gave his name to the hill that killed him. Today the hill

is a fine place to commune with nature on a hike or jog, followed by a restorative splash in its namesake baths.

Citadella

This strategic, hill-capping fortress was built by the Habsburgs after the 1848 Revolution to keep an eye on their Hungarian subjects. There's not much to do up here (no museum or exhibits), but it's a good destination for an uphill hike, and provides the best panoramic view over all of Budapest.

The hill is crowned by the **Liberation Monument,** featuring a woman holding aloft a palm branch. Locals call it "the lady with the big fish" or "the great bottle opener." A heroic Soviet soldier, who once inspired the workers with a huge red star from the base of the monument, is now in Memento Park.

Getting There: It's a steep hike up from the river to the Citadella. Bus #27 cuts some time off the trip, taking you up to the Búsuló Juhász stop (from which it's still an uphill hike to the fortress). You can catch bus #27 from either side of Gellért Hill. From the southern edge of the hill, catch this bus at the Móricz Zsigmond körtér stop (easy to reach: ride trams #19 or #41 south from anywhere along Buda's Danube embankment, or trams #47 or #49 from Pest's Small Boulevard ring road; you can also catch any of these trams at Gellért tér, in front of the Gellért Hotel).

▲▲Gellért Baths

Located at the famous and once-exclusive Gellért Hotel, right at the Buda end of the Liberty Bridge, this elegant bath complex has long been the city's top choice for a swanky, hedonistic soak. It's also awash in tourists, and the Széchenyi Baths beat it out for pure fun...but the Gellért Baths' mysterious thermal spa rooms, and its giddy outdoor wave pool, make it an enticing thermal bath option. For details, see "Experiences in Budapest," later.

Nearby: Burrowed into the cliff across the street from the Gellért Baths is the unique, tourable Cave Church.

▲▲Rudas Baths

Along the Danube toward Castle Hill from Gellért Baths, Rudas (ROO-dawsh) offers Budapest's most old-fashioned, Turkish-style bathing experience. The historic main pool of the thermal bath section sits under a 500-year-old Ottoman dome. Bathers move from pool to pool to tweak their body temperature. On weekdays, it's a nude, gender-segregated experience, while it becomes more accessible (and mixed) on weekends, when men and women put on swimsuits and mingle beneath that historic dome. For details, see "Experiences in Budapest," later.

Day Trips from Budapest

On a visit of a few days, Budapest will keep even the most avid sightseer busy. And after Budapest, Eger, covered in a chapter of its own, is one of the best Hungarian towns. But for a longer stay, a few outlying sights are worth knowing about. I've listed them here roughly in order of proximity to downtown Budapest.

▲▲Memento Park (a.k.a. Statue Park)

When regimes fall, so do their monuments...literally. Just think of all the statues of Stalin and Lenin that crashed to the ground in late 1989, when people throughout Eastern Europe couldn't wait to get rid of those reminders of their oppressors. But some clever entre-

preneur hoarded Budapest's, collecting them in a park in the countryside just southwest of the city—where tourists flock to get a taste of the communist era. Though it can be time-consuming to visit, this collection is worth ▲▲▲ for those fascinated by Hungary's commie past. You'll see the great figures of the Soviet Bloc—both international (Lenin, Marx, and Engels) and Hungarian (local bigwig Béla Kun)—as well as gigantic, stoic figures representing Soviet ideals. This stiff dose of Socialist Realist art, while time-consuming to reach, is rewarding for those curious for a taste of history that most Hungarians would rather forget.

Cost and Hours: 1,500 Ft, daily 10:00-sunset, tel. 1/424-7500, www.mementopark.hu.

Getting There: It's in the countryside, six miles southwest of city center, at the corner of Balatoni út and Szabadka út, in district XXII. The park runs a handy direct **bus** from Deák tér in downtown Pest to the park (April-Oct daily at 11:00, Nov-March Sat-Mon at 11:00—no bus Tue-Fri, round-trip takes 2.5 hours total, including a 1.5-hour visit to the park, 4,900-Ft round-trip includes park entry, book online for discount: www.mementopark.hu).

The **public transport** option requires a transfer: Ride the Metró's M4/green line to the end of the line at Kelenföld. Head up to street level and catch bus #101B or #101E, which takes you to Memento Park in about 15 minutes (second stop, runs every 10 minutes—but only on weekdays). On weekends, when bus #101B/#101E doesn't run, take bus #150, which takes longer but runs every day (2-4/hour, about 20 minutes). On either bus, be sure the driver knows where you want to get off.

Tours and Information: My self-guided tour gives you all the

Memento Park

BRICK WALL

20 Meters
20 Yards

LOOP VI
LOOP V
LOOP IV
LOOP III
LOOP II
LOOP I

BALATONI ÚT

B **B**
Public Bus Stop

7

TICKET OFFICE & GIFT SHOP

P

TRABANT CAR

1 ↑ **2**
ENTRY FACADE

B
Official/Direct Bus Stop

REPLICA OF BARRACKS

"Witness Square"

STALIN'S TRIBUNE →

SZABADKA ÚT

To Budapest

Note:
These numbers
correspond to the
official Memento
Park map. Numbers
filled in black are
described on this tour.

information you need. Alternatively, 50-minute English tours depart from the entrance (1,200 Ft, 40 percent discount if you book online; April-Oct daily at 11:45—shortly after direct bus arrives from Deák tér, additional tours in high season). The 1,500-Ft English guidebook, *In the Shadow of Stalin's Boots,* is very informative.

Background: Under the communists, creativity was discouraged. The primary purpose of art was to further the goals of the state, with creative expression only an afterthought. Promoting **Socialist Realist** art served to encourage complicity with the brave new world the communists were forging. It was also a break with the "decadent" bourgeois art that came before it (Impressionism, Post-Impressionism, and other modern -isms). From 1949 until 1956, Socialist Realism was legally enforced as the sole artistic style of the Soviet Bloc.

As propaganda was an essential weapon in the Soviet arsenal, the regime made ample use of Socialist Realist art. Aside from a few important figureheads, individuals didn't matter. Everyone was a cog in the machine—strong, stoic, and doing their jobs well and proudly for the good of the people. Individual characteristics and distinguishing features were unimportant; people were represented as automatons serving their nation. Artistic merit was virtually ignored. Most figures are trapped in stiff, unnatural poses that ignore the 3,000 years of artistic evolution since the Egyptians. Sculptures and buildings alike from this era were designed to evoke feelings of power and permanence.

❷ Self-Guided Tour: The numbers in the following tour match the statue labels in the park, the official park map, and the map in this chapter.

As you approach the park, you encounter the imposing red-brick Entry Facade featuring three of the Communist All-Stars: **❶ Vladimir Lenin,** a leader of Russia's Bolshevik Revolution; and **❷ Karl Marx** and **Friedrich Engels,** the German philosophers whose *Communist Manifesto* first articulated the principles behind communism in 1848. (These three figures weren't offensive enough to be destroyed, but very few statues survive anywhere of the biggest "star" of all, the hated Josef Stalin.) Like the rest of the park, the gate's design is highly conceptual: It looks impressive and monumental...but, like the rotted-out pomp of communism, there's nothing behind it. It's a glossy stage-set with no substance. If you try to go through the main, central part of the gate, you'll run into an always-locked door. Instead, as with the communist system, you have to find another way around (in this case, the side gate to the left).

Inside the gate, buy your ticket and head into the park. Survey the layout and note that the main road takes you confidently toward...a dead end (the brick wall). Once again, as with life under the communists, you'll have to deviate from this main axis to actually accomplish anything. Even so, notice that the six walkways branching off the main road all loop you right back to where you started—representing the endless futility of communism.

• *Work your way counterclockwise around the park.*

Liberation Monuments (Loop I): Dominating this loop is a **❸ giant soldier** holding the Soviet flag. This statue once stood at the base of the Liberation Monument that still overlooks the Danube from Gellért Hill (see page 614). Typical of Socialist Realist art, the soldier has a clenched fist (symbolizing strength) and a face that is inspired by his egalitarian ideology.

To the left of this soldier, see the **❹ two comrades** stiffly shaking hands: the Hungarian worker thrilled to meet the Soviet soldier—protector of the proletariat.

Beyond them is a ❺ **long wall,** with a triumphant worker breaking through the left end—too busy doing his job to be very excited. Just another brick in the wall.

• *Cross "main street" to a group of statues commemorating the key communist holiday of...*

April 4, 1945 (Loop II): On this date, the Soviets forced the final Nazi soldier out of Hungary. The tall panel nearest the entrance shows a Hungarian woman and a Soviet woman setting free the ❽ **doves of peace.** According to the inscription, "Our freedom and peace is founded upon the enduring Hungarian-Soviet friendship." (With friends like these...)

The ❾ **woman holding the palm leaf** is reminiscent of the Liberation Monument back on the Danube—which, after all, celebrates the same glorious day. Check out the size of that palm leaf: Seems like she's overcompensating...

At the back of the loop, the ❿ **Hungarian worker and Soviet soldier** (who appear to be doing calisthenics) are absurdly rigid

even though they're trying to be dynamic. (Even the statues couldn't muster genuine enthusiasm for communist ideals.)

• *Cross over and head up to the next loop to pay homage to...*

Heroes of the Workers' Movement (Loop III): Look for the ⓮ **bust** of the Bulgarian communist leader **Georgi Dimitrov** (ruled 1946-1949)—one of communist Hungary's many Soviet Bloc comrades. At the back of this loop are ⓰ three blocky portraits. The middle figure is the granddaddy of Hungarian communism: **Béla Kun.** To the left is one of the park's best-loved, most-photographed, and most artistic statues: ⓱ **Vladimir Lenin,** in his famous "hailing a cab" pose.

• *Cross over—passing the giant red star made of flowers—to meet...*

More Communist Heroes (Loop IV):

This group is dominated by a ㉔ dramatic, unusually emotive sculpture by a genuine artist, **Imre Varga.** Designed to commemorate the 100th anniversary of Béla Kun's birth, this clever statue accomplishes seemingly contradictory feats. On the one hand, it reinforces the communist message: Under the able leadership of Béla Kun (safely overlooking the fray from above), the crusty, bourgeois old regime of the Habsburg Empire (on the left, with the umbrellas and fancy clothes) was converted into the workers' fighting force of the Red Army (on the right, with the bayonets). And yet, those silvery civilians in back seem more appealing than the lunging soldiers in front. And notice the lamppost next to Kun: In Hungarian literature, a lamppost is a metaphor for the gallows. This reminds

viewers that Kun—in spite of his groundbreaking and heroic work for the communist movement in Hungary—was ultimately executed by communists in the Soviet Union during Stalin's purges of the late 1930s.

• *Zig and head up again, for a lesson in...*

Communist Concepts (Loop V):

Look for a rusty pair of ❸ **workers' hands** holding a sphere (which was once adorned with a red star). This represented the hard-won ideals of communism, carefully protected by the hands—but also held out for others to appreciate.

Dominating this group is a ❸❸ **communist worker** charging into the future, clutching the Soviet flag. Budapesters of the time had a different interpretation: a thermal bath attendant running after a customer who'd forgotten his towel. This is a favorite spot for goofy posed photos. To the left is a monument to the communist version of the Boy Scouts: the elementary-school-age ❸❹ **Little Drummers** and the older **Pioneers.** While these organizations existed

before the communists, they were slowly infiltrated and turned into propaganda machines by the regime. These kids—with their jaunty red and blue neckerchiefs—were sent to camp to be properly raised as good little communists; today, many of them have forgotten the brainwashing but still have fond memories of the socializing.

• *Now zag once more to learn about...*

More Communist Concepts (Loop VI): The ❸❼ long, **white wall** at the back of this section tells quite a story (from left to right): The bullet holes lead up to a jumbled, frightful clutter (reminiscent of Pablo Picasso's *Guernica*) representing World War II. Then comes the bright light of the Soviet system, and by the end everyone's properly regimented—striking *Charlie's Angels* poses—and looking boldly to the future (and enjoying a bountiful crop, to boot).

Next is a ❸❽ **fallen hero** with arm outstretched, about to collapse to the ground—mortally wounded, yet victorious. This mon-

BUDAPEST

ument to "the Martyrs of the Counter-Revolution" also commemorates those who died attempting to put down the 1956 Uprising.

• *Now continue down the main drag to, um, a....*

Dead End: The main path dead-ends at the wall, symbolizing life's frustrations under communism. Here stand statues of two Soviet officers who negotiated with the Nazis to end the WWII siege of Budapest. ❹ **Captain Miklós Steinmetz** (on the right) was killed by a Nazi land mine, while ❹ **Ilja Ostapenko** (on the left) was shot under mysterious circumstances as he returned from the successful summit. Both became heroes for the communist cause. Were they killed by wayward Nazi soldiers, as the Soviets explained—or by their own Red Army, to create a pair of convenient martyrs?

When you return to the entry gate, peruse the fun parade of communist kitsch at the **gift shop.** The stirring music may just move you to pick up the CD of *Communism's Greatest Hits*, and maybe a model of a Trabant (the classic two-stroke commie-mobile). A real **Trabant** is often parked just inside the gate.

• *Now head out across the parking lot to find...*

Stalin's Tribune: This section of the complex is a re-creation of the giant grandstand that once stood along "Parade Street." Hungarian and Soviet leaders stood here, at the feet of a giant Stalin statue, to survey military and civilian processions. But during the 1956 Uprising, protesters cut Stalin off at the knees...leaving only the boots. (The entire tribune was later dismantled, and Stalin disappeared without a trace.) If you circle around behind the tribune, you'll find stairs up top for a view over the park.

• *Flanking the lot in front of the tribune are replicas of...*

Barracks: These are reminiscent of the ramshackle barracks where political prisoners lived in communist-era work camps (sometimes called gulags, described on page 595). These hold special exhibits, often including a good explanation of "Stalin's Boots" (with a plaster replica, and photos of the original tribune) and the events of 1956. Sit down for the creepy film, *The Life of an Agent*—a loop of four training films (10-15 minutes each) that were actually used to teach novice spies about secret-police methods and policies.

BUDAPEST

• *Our tour is over. Now, inspired by the bold propaganda of your Hungarian comrades, march proudly into the dawn of a new day.*

Óbuda

"Old Buda," just north of Buda, is the oldest part of Budapest, with roots going back to Celtic and Roman times. It has various sights that cluster around the Szentlélek tér stop of the HÉV suburban train line (catch the HÉV from the Batthyány tér Metró stop in Buda). The most interesting museum displays works by Hungarian sculptor **Imre Varga,** who worked from the 1950s through the 1990s, and created many popular sculptures in Budapest and throughout Hungary. You'll also find a museum filled with eye-popping, colorful paintings by **Victor Vasarely,** the founder of Op Art. If you ride the HÉV farther north to the Aquincum stop, you'll reach an archaeological museum at the remains of the 2,000-year-old Roman town of **Aquincum** and its amphitheater. All of these sights are closed on Mondays.

Gödöllő Royal Palace

Holding court in an unassuming town on the outskirts of Budapest, this pink Baroque palace was once the residence of Habsburg Emperor Franz Josef and his wife, Empress Elisabeth—better known to her beloved Hungarian subjects as Sisi (see page 873). While the Habsburg sights in Vienna and near Prague are better, this is the best place in Hungary to learn about its former monarchs.

Cost and Hours: Permanent exhibit (main palace apartments)—2,500 Ft; April-Oct daily 10:00-18:00, last entry one hour before closing; Nov-March open only by guided tour at :30 past each hour Mon-Fri 10:30-14:30 (palace closes at 16:00), Sat-Sun 10:00-17:00; tel. 28/410-124, www.kiralyikastely.hu.

Getting There: Take the M2/red Metró line to Örs vezér tere, then catch the HÉV suburban train from to Gödöllő—figure about one hour each way from downtown Budapest.

The Danube Bend

This string of three river towns north of Budapest offers a convenient day-trip getaway for urbanites who want to commune with nature. While I find "the Bend" less than thrilling, it's undeniably convenient to reach from the capital by train or boat; these destinations make for handy stopovers if you're driving between Budapest and Bratislava or Vienna.

Szentendre is a colorful, "Balkans in miniature" artist colony. With a tidy main square, a few engaging art galleries, and several Orthodox churches built by the Serbs and Greeks who settled the town, it offers a relaxing escape from the city. This is the easiest pleasant small town to reach from Budapest—which means it's also deluged by tourists. To reach Szentendre, hop on the HÉV suburban train at Budapest's Batthyány tér Metró (the same one that goes to Óbuda, described above).

Visegrád offers a small riverside museum at the scant remains of a Renaissance palace built by King Mátyás Corvinus, and a dramatic hilltop castle with fine views over the Bend. While you can get here by boat or by train (to the Nagymaros-Visegrád station, then boat across the river), it's not worth the trip unless you're driving.

Esztergom Basilica is Hungary's biggest and most important church, built on the site where István, Hungary's first Christian king, was crowned in A.D. 1000. Packed with history, it looms grandly above the Danube (free, daily May-Aug 8:00-19:00, April and Sept-Oct until 18:00, Nov-March until 16:00, www.bazilika-esztergom.hu). The easiest way to reach it is by bus from Budapest's Újpest-Városkapu bus station (at the Metró stop of the same name); trains and other buses from Budapest take you to the far end of town, an inconvenient 45-minute walk to the basilica.

Experiences in Budapest

THERMAL BATHS (FÜRDŐ)

Splashing and relaxing in Budapest's thermal baths is the city's top attraction. Though it might sound daunting, bathing with the

Magyars is far more accessible than you'd think. The first two thermal baths I've described (Széchenyi and Gellért) are basically like your hometown swimming pool—except the water is 100 degrees, there are plenty of jets and bubbles to massage away your stress, and you're surrounded by scantily-clad Hungarians. If you want a more "authentic" and naked experience, I've also described one of those (Rudas, which also has a more modern and mixed "wellness" area).

All this fun goes way back. Hungary's Carpathian Basin is essentially a thin crust covering a vast reservoir of hot water. The word "Pest" comes from a Slavic word for "oven." The Romans named their settlement near present-day Budapest Aquincum—"abundant waters"—and took advantage of those waters by building many baths. Centuries later, the occupying Ottomans revived the custom. And today, thermal baths are as Hungarian as can be.

Locals brag that if you poke a hole in the ground anywhere in Hungary, you'll find a hot-water spring. Judging from Budapest, they could be right: The city has 123 natural springs and some two dozen thermal baths *(fürdő).* The baths, which are all operated by the same government agency, are actually a part of the health-care system. Doctors regularly prescribe treatments that include massage, soaking in baths of various heat and mineral compositions, and swimming laps. For these patients (who you might see carrying a blue ticket), a visit to the bath is subsidized.

But increasingly, there's a new angle on Hungary's hot water: entertainment. Adventure water parks are springing up all over the country, and even the staid old baths have some enjoyable jets and currents. Overcome your jitters, follow my instructions, and dive in...or miss out on *the* quintessential Budapest experience.

Taking the Waters

Some tourists feel squeamish at the thought of bathing with Speedo-clad, pot-bellied Hungarians. Relax! My readers almost unanimously report that the thermal baths were their top Hungarian experience. If you go into it with an easygoing attitude and a sense of humor, I promise you'll have a blast.

Dress Code: While Budapest has several mostly nude, gender-segregated Turkish baths (such as Rudas), my favorites—Széchenyi and Gellért—are less intimidating: Men and women are usually together, and you can keep your swimsuit on the entire time. But even at mixed baths, there generally are a few clothing-optional, gender-segregated areas, where locals are likely to be nude—or wearing a *kötény,* a loose-fitting loincloth.

What to Bring: If you have them, bring a swimsuit, towel, flip-flops, bottle of water, soap and shampoo for a shower afterward, comb or brush, swim cap (see later), plastic bag for your wet swimsuit, and maybe sunscreen and leisure reading. Hotels typically frown on guests taking their room towels to the baths; try asking nicely if they have some loaner towels just for this purpose. At Budapest's baths, you can usually rent a towel or swimsuit (for men, Speedos are always available, trunks sometimes). Rent your towel before you change, as you'll need cash (the rental fee plus the 2,000-Ft deposit per item). A swim cap is required in lap pools; you can rent or buy a flimsy one there, but if you know you'll be swimming laps, see if you can grab a shower cap from your hotel.

Entry Procedure: The baths may seem initially confusing, with long price lists and sometimes gruff staff. But the entry procedure has been streamlined in recent years and is easier than it might seem. Credit cards are accepted (but you'll need cash to rent towels). Don't bother with the "prepaid" tickets for the baths that are advertised in hotel lobbies around town; it's the same price to buy your tickets directly, and there's rarely a line.

All of Budapest's baths use the same easy system: When you pay, you'll be given a waterproof, wristwatch-like wristband. Put it on and keep it on. Touch it to the panel on the turnstile to enter, then again to be assigned a changing cabin, then again to unlock your cabin. At most baths (except Rudas), the door of your cabin should lock automatically when you close it (but test it to be sure). If you paid for a locker, just choose any empty one and lock it with your wristband; from then on, it can only be locked and unlocked with the same wristband. You can use your wristband to reopen your cabin or locker as often as you like. If you forget the number of your cabin, just touch your wristband to the panel, and it'll remind you. And when you exit, drop the wristband into a slot as you go through the turnstile.

Lockers and Cabins: The main choice when buying your ticket is locker or cabin. The locker price is slightly cheaper and gives you access to a gender-segregated, gymnasium-type locker room. A cabin offers more privacy for changing, and can be shared by a couple: One person pays the cabin rate, the other pays the locker rate, and both use the same cabin. As the cabins are tight, you may need to take turns...or get very cozy. I've found both cabins and lockers to be safe, but storing valuables here is at your own risk (if you're nervous, you can pay a few hundred forints to rent a safe).

Main Pools: Each bath complex has multiple pools, used for different purposes. Big pools with cooler water are for serious swimming, while the smaller, hotter thermal baths (*gyógyfürdő*, or simply *gőz*) are for relaxing, enjoying the jets and current pools, and playing chess. The water bubbles up from hot springs at 77° Celsius (170° Fahrenheit), then is mixed with cooler water to achieve the desired temperatures. Most pools are marked with the water temperature in Celsius (cooler pools are about 30°C/86°F; warmer pools are closer to 36°C/97°F or 38°C/100°F, about like the hot tub back home; and the hottest are 42°C/108°F...yowtch!). Locals hit the cooler pools first, then work their way up to the top temps.

Other Bath Features: Most thermal baths also have a dry sauna, a wet steam room, a cold plunge pool (for a pleasurable jolt when you're feeling overheated), and sunbathing areas (which may be segregated and clothing-optional). Some baths have fun flourishes: bubbles, whirlpools, massage jets, waterfalls, wave pools, and so on. Be aware that the various water features sometimes take turns running. If a particularly fun feature of the pool doesn't seem to be working, just give it a few minutes.

Sanitary Concerns: While the lap pools are chlorinated, most of the thermal baths are only lightly chlorinated, or not at all. Unlike swimming pools in the US—where the water is recycled back into the pool—water here is slowly drained out and replaced with fresh water from the hot springs. Locals figure this continuous natural flushing makes chemicals unnecessary. Still, total germophobes may not be entirely comfortable at the baths; either convince yourself to go with the flow, or skip the trip.

Massages: There are two basic choices. A **"relax massage"** or **"aroma massage"** is a restful rubdown, typically using oil (often scented). This is what's sometimes called a Swedish-style massage. The other option is a **"scrub massage"** or **"skin-firming massage."** Similar to a Turkish-style massage, this is (for some) less restful, as it's intended to exfoliate your skin and involves some very hard scrubbing. Remember that the spas are medical facilities, so the massage may be more functional and less serene than what you're used to back home. If you want a massage, you can pay and arrange a time when you're buying your ticket. On busy days (especially Mon, Fri, and Sat), you may have to wait an hour or two; at other times, you may be able to get your massage immediately (or whenever you want).

Yet another choice is a **Thai massage.** You'll lie on a mat as the masseuse uses her feet, knees, and elbows.

Key Terms: Here are some useful phrases:

English	Hungarian	Pronounced
Bath	*Fürdő*	FEWR-dur
Men	*Férfi*	FAYR-fee
Women	*Női*	NUR-ee
Changing cabin	*Kabin*	KAH-been
Locker	*Szekrény*	SEHK-rayn
Ticket office	*Pénztár*	PAYNZ-tar
Thermal bath	*Gyógyfürdő,*	JODGE-fewr-dur, gorz

The Baths

Of Budapest's two-dozen thermal baths, the three listed here are the best known, most representative, and most convenient for first-timers: The Széchenyi Baths are more casual and popular with locals; the Gellért Baths are touristy, famous, and genteel; and the Rudas Baths are old-school Turkish, with more nudity and less "fun" (unless you find public nudity fun…but that's a whole other book). Rudas also has a modern "wellness" section, offering an interesting contrast under one roof. To me, Széchenyi is second to none, but some travelers prefer the Gellért or Rudas experience. As they're all quite different, doing more than one is an excellent option. For more information on all of Budapest's baths, see www.spasbudapest.com.

▲▲▲Széchenyi Baths (Széchenyi Fürdő)

The big, yellow, copper-domed building in the middle of City Park, Széchenyi (SAY-chehn-yee) is the best of Budapest's many bath experiences. Magyars of all shapes and sizes stuff themselves into tiny swimsuits and strut their stuff. Housewives float blissfully in the warm water. Intellectuals and roly-poly elder statesmen stand in chest-high water around chessboards and ponder their next moves. This is Budapest at its best.

Cost: 4,900 Ft for locker (in gender-segregated locker room), 500 Ft more for personal changing cabin, 200 Ft more on weekends, cheaper if you arrive after 19:00. The price includes the outdoor swimming pool area and the indoor thermal bath and sauna (which closes earlier—see below).

Hours: Swimming pool (the best part, outdoors) open daily 6:00-22:00, indoor thermal bath and sauna open daily 6:00-19:00, last entry one hour before closing. On some summer weekends, the baths may be open later (see "Night Bathing," later).

Location and Entrances: In City Park at Állatkerti körút 11, district XIV, M1: Széchenyi fürdő (tel. 1/363-3210, www.szechenyibath.hu). The huge bath complex has three entrances. The **"thermal bath entrance"** is the grand main entry, facing south (roughly toward Vajdahunyad Castle). I prefer the **"swimming pool entrance,"** facing the zoo on the other side of the com-

plex—it's more user-friendly, has shorter lines, and is open later. A third, smaller **"medical entrance"** is between the other two (and near the Metró station). If there's a long line at one of the entrances, check the others.

Massage: In the lobby, an English menu lists a wide array of massages and other treatments. You can set up an appointment and pay at the office near the towel-rental desk (6,000 Ft/20 minutes, 12,000 Ft/50 minutes, expect 30-minute wait for your appointment when it's busy). Remember that these massages are more medicinal than hedonistic. But inside the complex are some more luxurious (and more expensive) options: a Thai massage parlor at the upper level of the complex (above the swimming pool entrance—just follow the signs) and a separate "information" desk just inside the swimming-pool entrance where you can book a "V.I.P. massage."

Night Bathing: The baths are a joy in the evening, when both the price and the crowds are reduced. In cool weather, or even rain or snow, the pools maintain their hot temperatures—making this a delightful after-hours activity. Busy sightseers can be extremely efficient by closing down the museums, then heading to the baths. The only caveat: The indoor (and less appealing) thermal bath sections close after 19:00.

Additionally, Széchenyi is open late into the night on weekends, for a "sparty" event, where the bath complex basically becomes one big hot-water dance club (around 12,000 Ft, tickets sell out so book online in advance, mid-Feb-Nov Sat 22:30-late, www.szecska.hu).

Entry Procedure: These instructions assume that you're using the swimming pool entrance. First, in the grand lobby, pay the cashier, then touch your wristband to the turnstile and enter. Pause to get oriented: Straight ahead is a row of private changing cabins. If you go **up the stairs,** you'll find more changing cabins; the Thai massage area; gender-segregated "solarium" sun terraces; a well-equipped fitness center; and a grandstand overlooking the main pool. It's worth heading upstairs just to snap some photos of the outdoor complex before you change. If you go **down the stairs,** you'll find the counter where you can rent a towel or swimsuit (towel-1,000 Ft plus refundable 2,000-Ft deposit; swimsuit-2,000 Ft plus refundable 2,000-Ft deposit). From here, a long hallway lined with hairdryers and mirrors leads to locker rooms at each end (remember, men are *férfi* and women are *női*).

When ready, report to the area that you paid for: If you paid for a **cabin,** look for an electronic panel on the wall, and hold your wristband against this panel for a few seconds—you'll automatically be assigned a number for a cabin. If you paid for a **locker,** you can head for the locker room and choose one.

Now that you've changed into your swimsuit and stored your belongings, let's have some fun.

Taking the Waters: The bath complex has two parts, outside and inside.

For most visitors, the best part is the swimming pool area **outside.** Orient yourself to the three pools (facing the main, domed building): The pool to the left is for **fun** (cooler water—30°C/86°F, warmer in winter, lots of jets and bubbles, lively and often crowded, includes circular current pool); the pool on the right is for **relaxation** (warmer water—38°C/100°F, mellow atmosphere, a few massage jets, chess); and the **main (lap) pool** in the center is all business (cooler water—28°C/82°F in summer, 26°C/79°F in winter, people doing laps, swim cap required). You get extra credit for joining the gang in a chess match. Stairs to saunas (with cold

Széchenyi Baths

ZOO CIRCUS ZOO

ÁLLATKERTI KŐRÚT

Fun Pool

Lap 5 Pool

Relaxation Pool

To Vörösmarty tér

M Széchenyi fürdő M

To Mexikói út

50 Meters
50 Yards

KÓS KÁROLY SÉTÁNY

← To Heroes' Square
To Vajdahunyad Castle
City Park

❶ Swimming Pool Entrance
❷ Thermal Bath Entrance
❸ Medical Entrance
❹ Fun Pool (whirlpool, bubbles)
❺ Lap Pool (cap required)
❻ Relaxation Pool (jets, chess)
❼ Changing Cabins (ground floor & upstairs) & Sun Terraces (upstairs)
❽ Locker Rooms & Towel Rental (downstairs)
❾ Grandstand, Fitness Center & Massage (upstairs)

BUDAPEST

plunge pools, cold showers, and even an ice maker) are below the doors to the indoor thermal bath complex.

If you're feeling waterlogged and need a break, it's fun simply to explore the sprawling complex. It's a bit of a maze...just poke around (but keep in mind that several areas—such as the locker rooms in the basement, and the solarium sun terraces up top—are clothing-optional; again, men are *férfi* and women are *női*). Go for a photo safari, and don't miss the grandstand up the stairs (see "Entry Procedure," earlier).

Inside the main building is the thermal bath section, a series of indoor pools; each of these is designed for a specific medical treatment. You'll notice each pool is labeled with the temperature (ranging from 28°C/82°F to 36°C/97°F to 38°C/100°F; you'll also find steam rooms with a 18°C/64°F cold plunge pool nearby). The pools also have varying types and amounts of healthy minerals—some of which can make the water quite green and/or stinky. Hungarians who use Széchenyi Baths medicinally are prescribed a specific regimen for moving from pool to pool. But if all of this smelly water is lost on you (as it is on many foreigners), it's totally fine to focus on the fun outdoor pools. (I've had many great visits to Széchenyi Baths without ever going inside.)

Leaving the Bath: When finished, continue your sightseeing...soggy, but relaxed. If you're heading to the **Metró,** the station is very close, but easy to miss: It's basically a pair of nondescript stairwells in the middle of the park, roughly toward Heroes' Square from the thermal bath entrance (look for the low-profile, yellow *Földalatti* sign; to head for downtown, take the stairwell marked *a Vörösmarty tér felé*).

▲▲Gellért Baths (Gellért Fürdő)

The baths at Gellért (GEH-layrt) Hotel cost a bit more than the Széchenyi Baths, and you won't run into nearly as many locals; this is definitely a more upscale, touristy, spa-like scene. If you want a soothing, luxurious bath experience in an elegant setting, this is the place: Its indoor thermal pools are Budapest's most atmospheric—with exquisite porcelain details and an air of mystery. Its outdoor zone—mostly for sunbathing—is less interesting than Széchenyi, with one exception: It has a deliriously enjoyable wave pool that'll toss you around like a queasy surfer (summer only).

Cost: 5,300 Ft for a locker, 400 Ft more for a personal changing cabin; 200 Ft extra on weekends.

Hours: Daily 6:00-20:00, last entry one hour before closing.

Location: It's on the Buda side of the green Liberty Bridge (M4: Szent Gellért tér; or take trams #47 and #49 from Deák tér in Pest, or trams #19 and #41 along the Buda embankment from

Víziváros below the castle, Gellért tér stop). The entrance to the baths is under the stone dome opposite the bridge, around the right side of the hotel (Kelenhegyi út 4, district XI, tel. 1/466-6166 ext. 165, www.gellertbath.com).

Entry Procedure: The grand entry hall is fully open to visitors, so feel free to poke around to get the lay of the land before buying your ticket (good views from the gallery up above). The entrance doors are flanked by ticket windows; just past those, on the right, is an information desk with English-speaking staff.

When buying a ticket, specify which changing area you want: with a "thermal bath ticket," you'll change in a large changing hall with wooden stalls separated by curtains, while a "swimming pool ticket" admits you to a mixed area with lockable cabins and gender-segregated locker rooms. I prefer the swimming pool section, which is more private and has real locks. Couples who want to share a cabin should ask for "swimming pool ticket, one cabin, one locker."

A dizzying array of **massages** and other treatment options are also sold at the ticket windows (5,500-12,000 Ft depending on type and duration; sort through your options and arrange a time when you buy your ticket). Upstairs, you can also book a Thai massage.

Buy your ticket (and, if you like, pay for a massage), put on your wristband, and glide through the swanky lobby. The indoor swim-

ming pool is on your right, about halfway down the main hall (look for Gate II). If you bought a swimming pool ticket, you'll enter here, go down the stairs, pass through a long corridor (with underwater windows into the main swimming pool), then climb up the stairs to the cabin areas and locker rooms (men/*férfi* on the left side of the complex, and women/*női* on the right). Use your wristband to find and lock your cabin (or choose your own locker), as explained earlier. If you have a thermal bath ticket, use Gate I (closer to the entrance) or Gate III (at the end of the hall).

If you want to rent a towel (1,000 Ft) or swimsuit (2,000 Ft; both with a 2,000-Ft deposit, cash only), look for the desk near the entrance to the changing cabin area.

Taking the Waters: Once you've changed, you can spend your time either indoors or out. From the locker room, look for signs *to the effervescent bath-pool* (for the indoor section) or *to the swimming-pool with artificial waves* (for the outdoor section).

Inside, the central, genteel-feeling hall is home to a cool-water swimming pool (swim cap required—you can buy a cheap one) and a crowded hot-water pool (36°C/97°F). This is used for swimming laps and for periodic water-exercise classes. On sunny days, they crank open the retractable roof; for nice views down onto the pool, find the stairs up near the locker rooms. Back toward the main hall are doors to the thermal baths (easy to miss—walk to the far end of the pool and

look for signs). These were once segregated into men's and women's sections, but they're now both open to everybody. These grand old halls are probably the most atmospheric part of the bath—slathered with colorful porcelain decorations. The former men's section is both hotter and more beautifully decorated than the women's section. (Hmmm...) I'd focus on the former men's section, which has big pools at either end: 36°C (97°F) and 38°C (100°F). Notice that these temperatures perfectly flank the normal temperature of the human body, allowing you to toggle your temp at will. At the far end of the bath are a steam room (45-50°C/113-122°F) and a cold plunge pool (18°C/64°F). Back out near the changing cabins is a dry sauna (a.k.a. "dry sweating rooms," 50-70°C/122-158°F). If you paid for a massage, report to the massage room in this section at your appointed time—or just show up and see if they can take you.

Outside, you'll find several sunbathing areas and a warm thermal pool, along with an atmospheric woody sauna and a big barrel-shaped plunge pool with cold water (all hiding up the stairs on the right). But the main attraction is the big, unheated wave pool in the center (generally closed Oct-April, weather-dependent). Not for the squeamish, this pool thrashes fun-loving swimmers around like driftwood. The swells in the deeper area are fun and easy to float on, but the crashing waves at the shallow end are vigorous, if not dangerous. If there are no waves, just wait around for a while (you'll hear a garbled message on the loudspeaker five minutes before the tide comes in).

▲▲Rudas Baths (Rudas Fürdő)

To get to the Turkish roots of Budapest's obsession with thermal baths, head for Rudas (ROO-dawsh). It's the most historic, local, and potentially intimidating of the three baths I list—but it may also be the most rewarding, as it offers the most variety. Rudas has three sections (covered by separate tickets): the Turkish-style thermal bath zone; the swimming pool area; and the wellness section. While the swimming pool is nothing special, the other two are strikingly different—and equally worthwhile. Read these quick descriptions before your visit to decide which area(s) you want to experience.

Rudas' **thermal section** feels more like the classic Turkish baths of yore: On most days, the main thermal bath section is men-only, and those men wander around nude or in flimsy loincloths under a 500-year-old dome first built by the Ottoman Turks. These baths are not about splashy fun—there are no jets, bubbles, or whirlpools. Instead, Rudas is about history, and about serious temperature modulation—stepping your body temperature up and down between very hot and very cold. While not for the skittish, Rudas offers adventurous travelers and bath connoisseurs another facet of the Budapest baths experience. Be aware that all of Budapest's single-sex, nude baths are (to varying degrees) a popular meeting point for the local gay community—though Rudas is less so than some others (such as Király Baths). Women have the thermal section to themselves only one day per week (Tue). Rudas becomes far more widely accessible to all visitors on weekends (Sat-Sun), when men and women mingle together in swimsuits under the fine old dome; then, at nighttime (Fri-Sat only), this old chamber becomes a modern nightclub until the wee hours.

The **wellness area**—with a handful of relaxing jet pools—is the modern, accessible yin to the thermal baths' antique yang. Both men and women (in swimsuits) have access to the wellness area every day. The main reason to visit this section is the rooftop terrace, where you can sunbathe or soak while looking out over sweeping views of the Budapest skyline. Imagine: You're up to your earlobes in hot water, looking out over commuters slogging across the city's clogged bridges...and feeling pretty happy to be on vacation.

Finally, Rudas' **swimming pool** is similar to, but far less elegant than, Gellért's, and is only worthwhile for those who want to swim laps.

Cost: The historic thermal bath alone costs 3,300 Ft on weekdays (3,700 Ft on weekends); the wellness center alone costs 3,100 Ft on weekdays (4,200 Ft on weekends); and the swimming pool can be added to either ticket for a few hundred extra forints. To enjoy the full scope of what Rudas offers, the best plan is to spring

BUDAPEST

for the **combo-ticket** that covers everything—thermal, wellness, and swimming pool (4,800 Ft weekdays/5,900 Ft weekends). If you're buying a ticket that includes the wellness area, you can save a few hundred forints if you use a locker instead of a cabin. Thermal bath tickets are discounted on weekday mornings (2,600 Ft, Mon-Fri 9:00-12:00).

Hours: Thermal bath open daily 6:00-20:00, wellness section daily 8:00-22:00, last entry one hour before closing. While the wellness area is mixed-gender every day, the thermal baths are open only to men Mon and Wed-Fri, only to women Tue, and to both men and women Sat-Sun. The night bathing (described later) is also mixed-gender.

Location: It's in a low-profile building at the foot of Gellért Hill, just south of the white Elisabeth Bridge (Döbrentei tér 9, district I, tel. 1/375-8373, www.rudasbaths.com). Trams #19 and #41, which run along the Buda embankment, stop right out front (Rudas Gyógyfürdő stop). Those trams also work from Szent Gellért tér, as do trams #56 and #56A or bus #7. From Pest, you can ride bus #7 from Astoria or Ferenciek tere to the Rudas Gyógyfürdő stop.

Night Bathing: The baths are open—to both men and women, in swimsuits—with a dance hall ambience Fri-Sat 22:00-late (4,800 Ft).

Entry Procedure: At the ticket desk, buy your ticket, and if you want, rent a towel (600 Ft for a "bath sheet," plus 1,500-Ft refundable deposit) or a swimsuit (1,300 Ft plus 1,500-Ft deposit). You can also book a massage—either a relaxing "aroma relax massage," or a rougher, exfoliating "water massage with soap" in a noisy, busy room (4,300-9,600 Ft depending on type and duration).

Use your plastic wristband to enter the turnstile and go into the changing area. If you paid to rent a towel or swimsuit, give your receipt to the attendant to claim it now. The thermal area has only cabins, while the swimming pool/wellness area also has lockers. As at other baths, you'll use your wristband to be assigned and unlock a cabin—but unlike other baths, you have to also use it to lock your cabin (it doesn't lock automatically).

Dress Code: In the wellness and swimming pool areas, you'll wear your swimsuit everywhere, every day. For the thermal bath area, if you're here on a mixed day (Sat-Sun), the dress code is swimsuits. On other days, bathers can go nude, and many of the men wear a flimsy loincloth called a *kötény* (issued as you enter). If you're a self-conscious, gawky tourist (it happens to the best of us), you can wear your swimsuit...although you might get some funny looks.

Taking the Waters: This historic complex has been thoroughly renovated, making the outer section feel almost institutional.

But the innermost section transports you half a millennium back in time.

Rudas' **thermal bath** area is all about modulating your body temperature—pushing your body to its limit with heat, then dousing off quickly with a bucket of cold water, then heating up again, and so on. The different temperatures are designed to let you do this as gradually or quickly as you like.

The central chamber, under an original 35-foot-high Turkish dome supported by eight pillars, is the historic core of the baths. The main, octagonal pool in the center is surrounded by four smaller pools, each in its own corner. Working clockwise from the right as you enter, the four corner pools get progressively hotter: 28°C (82°F), 30° C (86°F), 33°C (91°F), and 42°C (108°F). While the hottest pool feels almost scalding at first, you can ease your way into it, the same way you would into cold water. Conveniently, the largest, central pool—at 36°C (97°F)—is not too hot, not too cold...juuuust right.

Along one wall are entrances to the wet sauna (*nedves gőzkamra*, to the left), with 50°C (122°F) scented steam; and the dry sauna (*hőlégkamra*, to the right), with three progressively hotter rooms ranging from 45°C (113° F) to 72°C (161°F). Near the entrance to each one is a shower or—if you don't want to beat around the bush—a bucket of frigid water (if you're overheated, pull the rope for immediate relief).

Surrounding this central chamber are hallways with other areas: resting rooms, tanning beds (*szolarium*, costs extra), massage rooms, a cold plunge pool, and a scale to see how much sweat you've lost.

Float on your back for a while in the main octagonal pool, pondering the faintly glittering translucent tiles embedded in the old Turkish dome. You'll notice that the voices echoing around that dome are mostly Hungarian—there are very few tourists here. You might see people stretching, moving from pool to pool very purposefully, or even doing chin-ups from the metal supports; some are athletes in training.

When you're ready for a change of pace, head back through the lobby to the other half of the building. First you'll walk along the **swimming pool** (for laps), then enter the turnstile for the **wellness area.** The first room, with a huge window looking out over the busy embankment road, has three small pools of different temperatures (32°C/90°F, 36°C/97°F, and a sweltering 42°C/108°F), all with powerful massage jets. In the cold plunge pool (12-14°C/54-57°F), notice the ice maker that continually drops in a cube or two, every few seconds. Thirsty? Get a drink at the stately ram's-head tiled fountains that line the walls.

But the real highlight of the wellness area is upstairs: At the end of the room, find the staircase and head on up, passing the inviting restaurant (with loaner bathrobes and fine views across the Danube) on your way to the rooftop terrace. While other Budapest baths envelop you in opulent architecture, this is the only one that envelops you in Budapest itself. Whether soaking in rays on the sun deck, or taking a dip in the 36°C/97°F thermal pool, you're surrounded by the bustle of the city. Scanning the horizon, you'll see a workaday burg going about its business...oblivious to the swimsuit-clad barnacle clinging onto the base of Gellért Hill. Your solitude is broken only by the periodic rumble of trams trundling past on the road below you.

Exit Procedure: After changing, return your rental towel and swimsuit to the attendant and get your receipt; present this at the front desk (along with your original towel receipt) to get your deposit back. Then drop your wristband through the little slot at the turnstile, head out the door, and stumble along the Danube...as relaxed as you'll ever be.

Aaaaahhh.

Entertainment in Budapest

Budapest is a great place to catch a good—and inexpensive—musical performance. In fact, music lovers from Vienna often make the three-hour trip here just to take in a fine opera in a luxurious setting at a bargain price. Options range from a performance at one of the world's great opera houses to light, touristy Hungarian folk concerts. The tourist concerts are the simplest option—you'll see the fliers everywhere—but you owe it to yourself to do a little homework and find something that really appeals to you.

Various **helpful websites**—each with its own approach—offer current advice on cultural events and nightlife in Budapest: www.wherebudapest.hu (general), www.funzine.hu (general, with a younger bent), www.servus.hu.com (culture, also available in print), www.muzsikalendarium.hu (classical music), www.welovebudapest.com (general), and www.xpatloop.com. To buy **tickets,** I've given strategies for the top options (Opera House and Hungária Koncert). Resources such as *Budapest Panorama* usually explain how you can get tickets for specific performances. You can buy tickets for many Budapest events at www.jegymester.hu and www.kulturinfo.hu.

What's on can vary by **season.** Some of the best nightclubs and bars are partly or entirely outdoors, so they're far more enjoyable in the summer. Meanwhile, the Hungarian State Opera, Puppet Theater, and other indoor cultural events tend to take a summer break from late June into early September (though that's prime time for outdoor music and Hungária Koncert's touristy shows).

A Night at the Opera

Take in an opera by one of the best companies in Europe, in one of Europe's loveliest opera houses, for bargain prices. The Hun-garian State Opera performs almost nightly, both at the main Opera House (Andrássy út 22, district VI, M1: Opera, see page 591) and in the Erkel Színház theater (not nearly as impressive—described under "Other Venues," later). If you want classical opulence, be careful to get a performance in the Opera House—not the Erkel Színház. Note that there are generally no performances from late June into early September. Most performances are in the original language with Hungarian and English supertitles.

Ticket prices range from 1,500 to 18,000 Ft, but the best music deal in Europe may be the 600-Ft, obstructed-view tickets (easy to get, as they rarely run out—even when other tickets are sold out). If you buy one of these $2 opera tickets, you can choose whether to sit and see nothing, or stand and crane your neck to see about half the stage. Either way, you'll hear every note along with the big spenders.

To get tickets, book online (www.opera.hu or www.jegy.hu), print your eticket, and waltz right in. Or you can book by phone with a credit card (tel. 1/353-0170, phone answered daily 10:00-20:00), then pick up your ticket at the Opera House before the performance. Maybe best of all, just drop by in person and see what's available during your visit. There are often a few tickets for sale at the door, even if it's supposedly "sold out" (box office open Mon-Sat from 11:00 until show time—generally 19:00, or until 17:00 if there's no performance; Sun open 3 hours before the performance—generally 16:00-19:00, or 10:00-13:00 if there's a matinee). If you're desperate to attend a specific performance and it looks sold out online, don't give up: Try calling or stopping by the Opera House, or ask your hotelier. There's almost always a way to get a ticket.

Tourist Concerts by Hungária Koncert

Hungária Koncert offers a wide range of made-for-tourists performances of traditional music. These take place in the **Duna Palota** ("Danube Palace")—formerly the Budapest Ritz, three long blocks north of Vörösmarty tér in Pest (behind Széchenyi tér and the Gresham Palace at Zrínyi utca 5, district V, M1: Vörösmarty tér). Some performances may take place at the gorgeous **Pesti Vigadó** concert hall, right along the river in central Pest (see "Other Venues," below). In 2018, they may hold some performances in the newly renovated **Budai Vigadó** concert hall, on the Buda embankment near Batthyány tér.

While highbrow classical music buffs will want a more serious concert, these shows are crowd-pleasers. The most popular options are **Hungarian folk music-and-dance shows** by various interchangeable troupes (4,200-6,900 Ft, May-Oct Sun-Fri at 20:00, at Duna Palota) and the **Budapest Gala Concert,** mixing classical "greatest hits" with some folkloric music, ballet, and opera (7,900-9,900 Ft, May-Oct Sat at 20:00, can be at either theater). Or you can take in an **organ concert** at St. István's Basilica (see "Other Venues," next).

If you book directly, you'll get a 10 percent Rick Steves discount on anything they offer (must book in person, by phone, or by email; on their website, you can book the "student rate"; discount may not be honored if you buy your tickets through your hotel). The main office is in the Duna Palota at Zrínyi utca 5 (daily April-Dec 9:00-22:00, until 20:00 in winter, tel. 1/317-2754 or 1/317-1377, www.ticket.info.hu, hunkonc@ticket.info.hu). Hungária Koncert also offers lunch and dinner cruises on the Danube, in-depth tours of the Jewish Quarter, and (pointless) advance tickets for the baths.

Other Venues

Budapest has many other grand spaces for enjoying a performance. You can find details for each of these on their websites.

The most appealing is the **Franz Liszt Academy of Music** (Liszt Ferenc Zeneművészeti Egyetem, a.k.a. Zeneakadémia), on Franz Liszt Square, which hosts high-quality professional concerts every night. Recently restored to its stunning late-19th-century splendor, this venue rivals even the Opera House for opulence—if attending a concert, make sure it's in the Grand Hall, or Nagyterem (just off of Andrássy út at Liszt Ferenc tér 8, M1: Oktogon, www.zeneakademia.hu).

The **former Academy of Music** (Régi Zeneakadémia)—just up Andrássy út near the House of Terror—houses the Franz Liszt Museum and hosts performances on Saturday mornings at 11:00 (Vörösmarty utca 35, www.lfze.hu).

The **Pesti Vigadó** ("Pest Concert Hall"), gorgeously restored and sitting proudly on the Pest embankment, is another fine place for a concert in elegant surroundings (Vigadó tér 1, www.vigado.hu).

The city's two finest churches—both with sumptuous interiors—host tourist-oriented concerts. Most of the shows in

St. István Basilica are organ concerts, along with some by classical ensembles (www.organconcert.hu or www.concertsinbudapest. com). Up on Castle Hill, **Matthias Church** hosts a variety of touristy shows, from organ recitals to string orchestras (www.matyastemplom.hu).

The **National Dance Theater** (Nemzeti Táncszínház) puts on performances ranging from ballet to folk to contemporary at various venues around town, including the Palace of Arts (at the Millennium City Center—see below), the MOM Cultural Center (near the Great Synagogue, at Csörsz utca 18), and the Royal Garden Pavilion in the Várkert Bázár complex, along the Buda riverbank just below the Royal Palace (www.dancetheatre.hu).

The **Millennium City Center** complex, sitting on the Pest riverbank near the Rákóczi Bridge south of downtown (district IX, ride tram #2 south along the Pest embankment to the Millenniumi Kulturális Központ stop), is a state-of-the-art facility with multiple venues. The **Palace of Arts** (Művészetek Palotája) features art installations as well as musical performances in two venues: the 1,700-seat Béla Bartók National Concert Hall and the 460-seat Festival Theater (www.mupa.hu). The **National Theater** (Nemzeti Színház) presents mostly Hungarian-language drama and lectures (www.nemzetiszinhaz.hu).

Nightlife in Budapest

In addition to strolling the floodlit promenades, and taking an after-hours dip at a thermal bath (Széchenyi and Rudas are both partly open late—see "Experiences in Budapest," earlier), here are some ideas for after-hours fun.

YUPPIE DRINKING ZONES

The plaza in front of **St. István's Basilica** is Budapest's most fashionable locale for a glass of wine. Of the many upscale restaurants and bars in this area, DiVino—a bar with contemporary decor and a wide range of Hungarian wines by the glass—is a good choice (see page 662).

Franz Liszt Square (Liszt Ferenc tér), a leafy and inviting zone just off Andrássy út, is lined with mostly tourist-oriented bars (described on page 593). The pedestrianized **Ráday utca,** near Kálvin tér just north of the Great Market Hall, has a similar scene.

For something a bit more genteel—evocative of this city's late-19th-century Golden Age—locals pass their evenings sipping wine or nibbling dessert at a **café** (see "Budapest's Café Culture" on page 669).

RUIN PUBS

Budapest is becoming known worldwide as a nightlife destination. And that's thanks largely to the ruin-pub phenomenon. These lively pubs are filled with ramshackle secondhand furniture, a bohemian-junkyard vibe—and plenty of drinkers (both locals and tourists) having the time of their lives. Think of it as pretending you're a squatter for a few hours, before returning to the comfort of your hotel.

Each ruin pub *(romkocsma)* is different—from mellow hangouts to hopping dance clubs—so survey several to find your favorite. Most of the clientele are in their 20s or 30s, but hip oldsters feel perfectly welcome. To seek out your ideal ruin pub, know the terminology. A ruin pub may bill itself as a *mulató* (club, usually higher-energy) or a *kávézó* (coffeehouse, usually mellower). In good weather, the best part of a ruin pub is outdoors. Many have a *kert* ("garden"), filling deteriorating buildings' courtyards with strings of lights, hammocks, mismatched chandeliers, parachute-quilt awnings, lush houseplants, and artful graffiti. Others have a *tető* ("rooftop"), where you can get some fresh air and—often—views over the floodlit city. In winter or bad weather, find one with a cozy interior. For more on ruin pubs—including additional listings—see www.ruinpubs.com.

Ruin-Pub Crawl in the Seventh District

Budapest's Seventh District—the former Jewish Quarter, behind the Great Synagogue—has emerged as Budapest's prime nightlife zone for both locals and visitors. Why are so many of these funky bars concentrated in the Jewish Quarter? Because it's conveniently central, yet remained largely deserted and dilapidated after the communists took over—keeping rents very low and fostering just the right rickety-chic vibe for ruin pub purveyors.

I've connected several of Budapest's most interesting ruin pubs on this brief pub crawl, which is designed to give you your bearings in this buzzing area. As we make our way through the Seventh District, drop in on any places that appeal. But pace yourself—the first, best, and quintessential ruin pub is Szimpla, near the end of this walk. This area can be very lively any night of the week (especially in good weather), but it's best Thursday through Saturday. During the peak of summer (July-Aug), most Budapesters are out of town on holiday, making this scene a bit more touristy.

Begin by making your way to **Király utca** (it runs parallel to Andrássy út, two blocks south; for this tour, it's handiest to ride

Ruin Pubs in the Seventh District

1. Négyszáz
2. Mika Kert
3. Ellátó Kert
4. Kőleves
5. Rácskert
6. Hive
7. Szimpla Kert
8. Szimpla Kávézó
9. Street Food Karaván
10. El Rapido
11. Ramenka
12. Telep
13. Anker't
14. Gozsdu Sky Terrace

the M1 Metró line to the Opera stop, then walk south). Király utca itself is lined with a few bars and ruin-pub-type nightspots, but the best scene is just south and east of here.

From Király utca, head down **Kazinczy utca,** at the intersection with a little urban park made much bigger by a cheery parklands mural. Heading down Kazinczy, after one short block, poke down the unnamed alley on the right (after Piritós). This strip is lined with several enticing places, the best of which is probably **Négyszáz** ("400"), flanking the alley (officially at Kazinczy 52). Continuing straight ahead to the end of the lane, you can enter right into the middle of the long series of courtyards called **Gozsdu Udvar,** which is jammed with lively bars and cafés—and worth exploring in its own right, either now or later (for details, see page 666). Also in here (to the left, through the video arcade) is the entrance to **Gozsdu Sky Terrace,** a summer-only rooftop bar (described later).

Head back out to Kazinczy. Directly across the street from the alley is **Mika Kert** (Kazinczy 47), filling a vacant lot with happy drinkers. Across the street is **Ellátó Kert** ("Supplier," Kazinczy 48), a mostly-outdoor pub with mismatched furniture under tents, and with Latino flair and food. A bit farther down on the left (at #41), **Kőleves** ("Stone Soup") is another fine garden, with lazy hammocks and good food (see page 665).

Just after Kőleves, Kazinczy utca crosses Dob street. Consider detouring up or down a few steps along Dob to find a few good options. For example, left (north) on Dob, at #40, is **Rácskert,** with big water-tubs-turned-tables and multicolored light tubes. And right (south) on Dob, at #19, **Hive**—owned by a party hostel—is less ramshackle and hosts frequent live music. (Farther down past Hive, at #16, is one entrance to Gozsdu Udvar, mentioned earlier.)

When you're done with your Dob detours, simply continue straight along Kazinczy utca. You'll pass the Orthodox Synagogue (on your left), then cross Wesselényi utca. This next block is the home of the first—and still best—of the ruin pubs, Szimpla Kert (described next); but since Szimpla set the trend, several copycats have sprung up along the same street. Feel free to explore the other options, but first head for the top dog.

Szimpla Kert ("Simple Garden," on the right at #14) sprawls through an old building that ought to be condemned, and spills out into an equally shoddy courtyard. Surrounding the garden is a warren of tiny rooms—each one different. This place oozes nostalgia for young Budapesters who have fond memories of their communist-era childhoods. Even the snacks are communist kitsch, and along with a full range of alcohol, they serve the old commie soft drinks (such as grape-flavored Traubi *szóda* and sour cherry Meggymárka). Although it's on the route of the tourist pub-crawls, Szimpla is still mostly frequented by locals (www.szimpla.hu). This space also hosts a farmers market on Sunday mornings (9:00-14:00). They have a smaller, far-less-impressive café, **Szimpla Kávézó,** a few blocks north near the Franz Liszt Academy of Music (Kertész utca 48).

Need some street food to soak up all those ruin pub drinks? Along Kazinczy near Szimpla are a variety of street eats—from the handy **Street Food Karaván** food truck pod (see page 665) to **El Rapido,** a small ruin pub-slash-taquería with a bodega upstairs

> ## Escape Room Games
>
> If you enjoy haunted houses at Halloween, you'll love the latest trend in Budapest: "escape room games." Taking root in the fertile soil of the ruin-pub scene, dozens of local tour operators are setting up this fun (for some) and terrifying (for others) experience: Your small group is locked in a room in a spooky, derelict building. To escape, you must solve a series of clues and puzzles (in English) within the allotted time. Various hazards and hurdles pop up as you go, and you'll need to work together to achieve the goal. The escape room game concept—popular for team-building outings, but accessible to curious tourists—has taken off in a big way, and Hungary is now exporting the games to other European cities. Companies come and go, but well-established options include www.claustrophilia.hu, www.trap.hu, www.exitpointgames.hu, and www.parapark.hu. As the lineup is constantly changing and each outfit has its own personality, read some online reviews to find the one that suits your interests. Then book ahead, have fun...and good luck.

and a junk-crammed cellar (see *Taco on Grill* sign, at #11) to **Ramenka** (ramen noodles, across the street at #9).

If you're still vertical, head back to the place(s) that caught your eye. Or, to see a different side of the ruin-pub scene, venture to the options listed below; each one is within about a 10- to 15-minute walk from this area.

More Ruin Pubs

Telep ("Site") is a tumble-down secondhand bar incongruously located in a residential and office-block neighborhood just around the corner from the heart of the ruin-pub scene. There's an art gallery upstairs, often live music, and the semirowdy crowd out front gives this otherwise sleepy street a lively bustle (Madách Imre utca 8, just off Rumbach utca, http://telepgaleria.tumblr.com).

Anker't, a young, brash, and slightly snooty offshoot of a popular nightclub (Anker), has a minimalist charm. It's conveniently located a short block off Andrássy út—look for the |A| sign (across the street from the Opera House at Paulay Ede utca 33).

SUMMER TERRACES (TETŐ)

In addition to *kert* ("garden"), a key term for enjoying Budapest in the summer is *tető* ("roof"). Rooftop terraces offer laid-back scenery high above the congested city. Most roof terraces are open only in the summer (typically May-Sept; check websites to confirm), in good weather, and start serving drinks and light food around midafternoon. Several offer live music.

BUDAPEST

While this is an emerging scene, here are a few places worth checking out: **360 Bar,** my personal favorite, is on the roof of the old Párisi Nagy Áruház (enter at Andrássy út 39, www.360bar. hu). **Raqpart** owns a stunning setting on the Pest side of the Chain Bridge, overlooking the beautiful Buda panorama (in front of the Hotel InterContinental on Jane Haining rakpart, www.raqpart.hu). **High Note Sky Bar** has vivid yellow sofas and point-blank views of St. István's (atop the Aria Hotel at Hercegprímás utca 5, www.ariahotelbudapest. com). **Top Rum Sky & Bar** in Pest's Town Center overlooks University Square (atop Rum Hotel at Királyi Pál utca 4, www. hotelrumbudapest.com). **Gozsdu Sky Terrace** has an edgier vibe (tricky to find—from the video arcade in the Gozsdu Udvar passage, find the parking garage entrance and ride up to the 6th floor). **Corvintető,** one of the original roof terraces, has a techno-dance-club energy (on top of the old Corvin department store, across from New York Café at Blaha Lujza tér 1, enter on Somogyi Béla utca, www.corvinteto.hu).

Shopping in Budapest

While it's not quite a shopper's mecca, Budapest does offer some enjoyable opportunities to hunt for that perfect Hungarian souvenir.

For a look at local life and a chance to buy some mementos, Budapest's single best shopping venue is the **Great Market Hall** (described on page 585). In addition to all the colorful produce downstairs, the upstairs gallery is full of fiercely competitive souvenir vendors. There's also a **folk-art market on Castle Hill** (near the bus stop at Dísz tér), but it's generally more touristy and a little more expensive. And, while **Váci utca** has been Budapest's main shopping thoroughfare for generations, today it features the city's highest prices and worst values.

For something a bit less touristy, drop by the **Bálna ("Whale") Cultural Center,** which sits along the Danube just behind the Great Market Hall (described on page 586). You'll see some souvenir stands similar to what's upstairs in the Great Market Hall, as well as a few one-off designers. While it may be potluck for shoppers, it's worth exploring—and the architecture is interesting.

As a big, cosmopolitan capital, Budapest has its share of international fashion boutiques. Most of these are along or near **Deák utca** (called "Fashion Street," connecting Vörösmarty tér and Deák tér), or along the first stretch of **Andrássy út.** A few more big-ticket shops are along and near **Váci utca,** with an intriguing cluster along the cross-street **Irányi utca** (just south of Ferenciek tere, near the river in the Town Center). A block over, at Nyáry Pál utca 7, **Eventuell Gallery** displays and sells the works of local designers (www.eventuell.hu).

To see how Hungarian urbanites renovate their crumbling concrete flats, don't miss the home-improvement shops that line **Király utca,** which runs parallel to Andrássy út (two short blocks south). For a taste of the good old days—which somehow just feels right, here in nostalgic Budapest—wander up the city's **"antique row,"** Falk Miksa utca, just north of the Parliament.

Budapesters do most of their shopping in big, American-style **shopping malls**—three of which are downtown (most shops generally open Mon-Sat 10:00-21:00, Sun 10:00-18:00):

• **WestEnd City Center,** next door to Nyugati/Western train station (Váci út 1, district VI, M3: Nyugati pu., tel. 1/374-6573, www.westend.hu);

• **Mammut** ("Mammoth"), two separate malls a few steps from Buda's Széll Kálmán tér (Lövőház utca 2, district II, M2: Széll Kálmán tér, tel. 1/345-8020, www.mammut.hu); and

• **Arena Plaza,** near Keleti/Eastern train station (Kerepesi út 9, district XIV, M2: Keleti pu., tel. 1/880-7000, www.arenaplaza.hu).

SOUVENIR IDEAS

The most popular souvenir is that quintessential Hungarian spice, **paprika.** Sold in metal cans, linen bags, or porcelain vases—and often accompanied by a tiny wooden scoop—it's a nice way to spice up your cooking with memories of your trip. (But remember that only sealed containers will make it through customs on your way back home.) For details, see "Paprika Primer" on page 533.

Special drinks are a fun souvenir, though they're tricky to bring home (you'll have to wrap them very carefully and put them in your checked luggage—not permitted in carry-on; for customs regulations, see page 1068). Good choices include the unique Hungarian spirit **Unicum,** or a bottle of Hungarian **wine** (both described on page 534).

Another popular local item is a hand-embroidered **linen tablecloth.** The colors are often red and green—the national colors of Hungary—but white-on-white designs are also available (and classy). If the thread is thick and the stitching is very even, it was probably done by machine, and obviously is less valuable.

Other handicrafts to look for include **chess sets** (most from Transylvania) and **nesting dolls.** While these dolls have more to do with Russia than with Hungary, you'll see just about every modern combination available: from classic girl dolls, to Russian heads of state, to infamous terrorists, to American presidents. Tacky...but fun.

Fans of **communist kitsch** can look for ironic T-shirts that poke fun at that bygone era. But remember that the best selection is at the Memento Park gift shop, which also sells communist memorabilia and CDs of commie anthems.

For a wearable souvenir, **Tisza shoes** (Tisza Cipő) are retro and newly hip. The company dates from communist times, but went bust when Western brands became widely available. Recently, the brand was rescued by an investor with a renewed dedication to quality. They make both athletic and work shoes, as well as bags, shirts, and accessories. While you'll find Tisza products sold around the country, their flagship store is along the Small Boulevard near the Great Synagogue (at Károly körút 1, www.tiszacipo.hu).

HIPSTER DESIGN AND VINTAGE

Budapest is becoming a hipster mecca, and that means fun and idiosyncratic design, home decor, and vintage shops are popping up all around town. The fast-evolving scene makes it tricky to recommend a specific shop, but many intriguing boutiques have emerged in the **Seventh District/"Ruin Pub" zone.** Scout the possibilities on Király (with an emphasis on home decor), Dob, Rumbach, Dohány, Wesselényi, Kazinczy, and neighboring streets. **Printa,** a print shop and coffeehouse, is one reliable place to get a taste of the neighborhood's vendors; they may sell a map directing you to what's hot in the area right now (Rumbach 10, www.printa.hu). **Szimpla**—the original ruin pub—hosts a colorful farmers market each Sunday (9:00-14:00, Kazinczy utca 14, www.szimpla.hu).

Nearby, just across Andrássy út from the Seventh District, is a smattering of intriguing shops along **Hajós utca,** behind the Opera House. Check to see if you're in town for the **Wamp Design Fair.** One or two Sundays each month, dozens of local artists and designers gather to show off their products (free entry, 11:00-19:00, schedule at www.wamp.hu). In summer, this takes place in the city-center Elisabeth Square, while off-season it moves to Millenáris Park (on the Buda side, near M2: Széll Kálmán tér).

Sleeping in Budapest

Before choosing a hotel, consider the pros and cons of the neighborhood. Most travelers find staying in Pest more convenient than sleeping in Buda. Most sights worth seeing are in Pest, which also has a much higher concentration of Metró and tram stops, making it a snap to get around. Pest feels more lively and local than stodgy,

Sleep Code

Hotels are classified based on the average price of a standard double room with breakfast in high season. You can figure that €1 = about $1.10.

$$$$	**Splurge:** Most rooms over €170
$$$	**Pricier:** €130-170
$$	**Moderate:** €90-130
$	**Budget:** €50-90
¢	**Backpacker:** Under €50
RS%	**Rick Steves discount**

Unless otherwise noted, credit cards are accepted, hotel staff speak basic English, and free Wi-Fi is available. Comparison-shop by checking prices at several hotels (on each hotel's own website, on a booking site, or by email). For the best deal, *book directly with the hotel*. Ask for a discount if paying in cash; if the listing includes **RS%**, request a Rick Steves discount.

touristy Buda, but it's also much more urban. If you don't enjoy big cities, sleep in Buda instead.

In Budapest, most hotels quote their rates in euros (for the convenience of international guests), and I've followed suit. (Outside of the capital, hotels more often quote rates in forints.) However, most places prefer to be paid in forints (figured at the exchange rate on the day of payment). If you use a credit card and are given a choice of currencies, choose forints to avoid excessive conversion fees.

If you're on a tight budget, consider one of Budapest's many hostels or the good-value **Bellevue B&B** (page 658). At any hotel, three or four people can save money by requesting one big room.

PEST

I've arranged my listings by neighborhood, clustered around the most important sightseeing sectors.

Near Andrássy Út

Andrássy Boulevard is handy, local-feeling, and endlessly entertaining. With its ample restaurants, upscale-residential vibe, and easy connection to downtown (via the M1/yellow line), it's the neighborhood where I prefer to sleep. Most of the hotels listed here are within a two-block walk of this main artery.

$$$$ Hotel Moments—with 99 Art Deco rooms, a pristine atrium with iron railings, and a priceless location at the downtown end of Andrássy út—feels exclusive and understandably a bit snobby (air-con, elevator, free coffee bar, Andrássy út 8, district VI, M1: Bajcsy-Zsilinszky út, tel. 1/611-7000, www. hotelmomentsbudapest.hu, reservation@hotelmoments.hu).

Andrássy Út Hotels & Restaurants

Accommodations
1. Hotel Moments
2. K+K Hotel Opera
3. Kapital Inn
4. Casati Budapest Hotel
5. Butterfly Home Penthouse B&B
6. To Budapest B&B
7. EasyHotel
8. To Aventura Boutique Hostel
9. Home Made Hostel

Eateries & Other
10. Belvárosi Lugas Étterem
11. Menza Restaurant
12. Klassz Bistro
13. Pesti Disznó
14. Bock Bisztró
15. Két Szerecsen
16. Főzelékfaló Ételbár
17. Gerbeaud
18. Callas Café
19. Müvész Kávéház
20. Laundry
21. Absolute Tour Center

$$$ K+K Hotel Opera is wonderfully situated beside the Opera House in the fun "Broadway Quarter"—my favorite home-base location in Budapest. It has 200 classy rooms and helpful, professional service. The rates are variable, but you can often land a great value (air-con, elevator, pay parking garage, Révay utca 24, district VI, M1: Opera, tel. 1/269-0222, www.kkhotels.com, hotel.opera@kkhotels.hu).

$$ Kapital Inn is an upscale boutique B&B tucked behind the House of Terror. Its six rooms are pricey but perfectly stylish—there's not a pillow out of place. Albert, who lived in Boston, gives his B&B a sense of real hospitality. You'll enjoy the public spaces, from the restful, momentum-killing terrace to the giant kitchen, where Albert serves breakfast at a huge shared counter (cheaper room with shared bath, air-con, free communal minibar, pay laundry service, up several flights of stairs with no elevator, Aradi utca 30, district VI, M1: Vörösmarty utca, mobile +3630-915-2029, www.kapitalinn.com, kapitalinn@kapitalinn.com).

$$ Casati Budapest Hotel is a solid value, and conveniently located a block off Andrássy út (across the boulevard from the Opera House, then down a side street—just steps from the ruin-pub zone). This classy, Swiss-run hotel has 25 rooms in four different styles, ranging from "classic" to "cool" (all the same price—review your options online and choose your favorite). Many rooms surround a peaceful courtyard—in this potentially noisy neighborhood, it's worth requesting one of these (air-con, elevator, free sauna and fitness room, Paulay Ede utca 31, district VI, M1: Opera, tel. 1/343-1198, www.casatibudapesthotel.hu, info@casatibudapesthotel.com).

$ Butterfly Home Penthouse B&B—run with care by András (OHN-drash) and Timea—has three rooms near the Oktogon (air-con, elevator, Teréz körút 1, 4th floor, suite #2, buzzer #44, district VI, M1: Oktogon, mobile +3630-964-7287, www.butterflyhome.hu, info@butterflyhome.hu). The same people run **$ Budapest Bed and Breakfast,** with five simple but well-equipped rooms farther from the center—in the quiet diplomatic quarter halfway between the Oktogon and City Park (air-con, a long block off Andrássy út at Benczúr utca 3, district VI, M1: Kodály körönd, mobile +3630-964-7287, timea@butterflyhomebudapest.com). They also rent rooms in the Town Center, near the Great Market Hall (see "Butterfly Home Danube B&B," later).

The **$ EasyHotel** chain charges very little up front, then nickel-and-dimes you with optional extras (TV access, hairdryer, early check-in or late check-out, room-cleaning during your stay, etc.)—so you pay only for what you want. The 59 rooms feel popped out of a plastic mold, with a nauseating orange color scheme, sterile quasi-linoleum floors, and tiny prefab ship's-head bathrooms. But it's conveniently located (just a block off the busy Great Boulevard ring road and around the corner from the Oktogon), well-run by Zoltán, and the price is right...if you can resist the extras (no breakfast, air-con, elevator, two wheelchair-accessible rooms, Eötvös utca 25A, district VI, M1: Oktogon, tel. 1/411-1982, www. easyhotel.com, info@budapestoktogon.easyhotel.com).

Pest Town Center (Belváros), near Váci Utca

Most hotels on the very central and convenient Váci utca come with overly inflated prices. But these less-expensive options— just a block or two off Váci utca—offer some of the best values in Budapest.

$$ Gerlóczy Café & Rooms, which also serves good coffee and meals in its recommended café, is the best spot in central Budapest for affordable elegance. The 19 rooms, set around a classy old spiral-staircase atrium with a stained-glass ceiling, are thoughtfully and stylishly appointed. This gem is an exceptional value (breakfast extra, air-con, elevator, free minibar, some street noise, just off Városház utca at Gerlóczy utca 1, district V, M3: Ferenciek tere or M2: Astoria or M1/M2/M3: Deák tér, tel. 1/501-4000, www.gerloczy.hu, info@gerloczy.hu).

$$ Hotel Rum is a sleek retreat overlooking the rejuvenated University Square, in the heart of Pest's Town Center. Its 38 industrial-mod rooms come with concrete floors, subway tile, and ample style (air-con, elevator, Királyi Pál utca 4, district V, M3/M4: Kálvin tér, tel. 1/424-9060, www.hotelrumbudapest.com, hello@hotelrumbudapest.com). The top-floor bar, Top Rum—open even to nonguests—has great views over Pest's rooftops.

$ Butterfly Home Danube B&B, run by András (from the Butterfly Home Penthouse B&B, listed earlier), has five rooms and Danube views (air-con, elevator, Fővám tér 2, 2nd floor, suite #2, district V, M4: Fővám tér, mobile +3630-964-7287, www. butterflyhome.hu, info@butterflyhome.hu).

$ Loft V65 is a peaceful oasis of an apartment right on Váci utca. The large, well-appointed apartment has two double bedrooms, one-and-a-half baths, and a kitchen (sleeps up to 4 people). After you reserve, Gábor and András will arrange a meeting time to give you the keys (air-con, elevator, Váci utca 65, district V, M4: Fövám tér or M3: Ferenciek tere, in the mornings call András at mobile +3630-964-7287, in the afternoons call Gábor at US tel. 917-880-3656, www.LoftV65.com, LoftV65@gmail.com).

$ Katona Apartments, with five simple units just around the corner from busy Ferenciek tere, is conscientiously run by János and Virág. It's a family-friendly budget option in the very center of town (no breakfast but kitchenette, air-con in most units, elevator, Petőfi

Sándor utca 6, mobile +3670-221-1797, www.katonaapartments.hu, info@katonaapartments.hu).

$ Kálvin-Ház, a long block up from the Great Market Hall, is old but cheap. It has quirky management, a nice classic feel, and 36 big rooms with old-fashioned furnishings and squeaky parquet floors. The newer top-floor rooms have a bit less classic character, but are air-conditioned and tidier than the older rooms (elevator, Gönczy Pál utca 6, district IX, M4: Fövám tér, tel. 1/216-4365, www.kalvinhouse.hu, info@kalvinhouse.hu).

Near the National Museum
These two places are within a block or two of the National Museum, just across the Small Boulevard from the Town Center, near M3/M4: Kálvin tér (district VIII).

$$ Brody House, a hipster hangout with sprawling public spaces, began as an art gallery that provided a place for its guests to crash, and has evolved into a comfortable, full-service B&B. With a trendy, scuffed, ruin-pub vibe, it's classy yet ramshackle. It fills three spacious floors of a townhouse with eight rooms and three apartments that all ooze a funky, idiosyncratic style. Each room is named for an artist who once used it as a studio (breakfast extra, air-con in most rooms, two stories up with no elevator, Bródy Sándor utca 10, tel. 1/266-1211, www.brodyhouse.com, reception@brodyhouse.com).

$ Budapest Rooms is a great budget option, where the Boda family rents five simple but surprisingly stylish, nicely appointed rooms in a dull residential zone (family room, one room has private bathroom across the hall, Szentkirályi 15, tel. 1/630-4743, mobile +3620-569-9513, www.budapestrooms.eu, info@budapestrooms.eu).

The Seventh District
The Seventh District is one of Budapest's most happening nightlife zones, with ramshackle ruin pubs popping up all over. These options offer proximity to the fun—which means they come with some noise. (The area is also close to a very different chapter of Budapest's story, as this is also the former Jewish Quarter.)

$$ ROOMbach Hotel Budapest Center, tucked down a gloomy but central street facing the Rumbach Street Synagogue, has 51 sleek, basic, smallish rooms with a stylish industrial-mod design. Part of a good-value chain, it feels fresh and modern, and the triple-glazed windows work hard to keep out the ruin-pub noise (air-con, elevator, pay parking, Rumbach Sebestyén utca 14, tel. 1/413-0253, www.roombach.com, info@roombach.com).

$ At BudaBaB, thoughtful Americans Ryan and Ron rent two rooms in their apartment. You'll feel like you're a houseguest,

BUDAPEST

To Parliament & 11

To 21

20

24

15

To & 22 24

ACADEMY OF SCI. 16

To Heroes' Square & City Park

LEOPOLD

RÉVAY ÚT

NÁDOR

VIGYÁZÓ FER.

CENTRAL EUROPEAN UNIVERSITY

OKTÓBER 6

SAS

28

ST. ISTVÁN'S BASILICA

17

ZSILINSZKY

BAJCSY -

ANDRÁSSY

KÁLDY

SZÉKELY

Széchenyi István tér 9

ZRÍNYI

DUNA PÁLOTA

18

Bajcsy-Zsilinszky út

GYULA

GOZSDU UDVAR

HOLLÓ

CHAIN BRIDGE

Eötvös tér

GRESHAM PALACE 10

MÉRLEG

27

19

TOWN

RUMBACH STREET SYNAGOGUE

To Buda & Castle Hill

JÓZSEF ATTILA ÚT

BÉCSI

ASBÓTH

RUMBACH SEBESTYÉN

Tram #2

26

POST

József Nádor tér

Erzsébet tér

AKVÁRIUM KLUB

ANKERHÁZ

Deák Ferenc tér

DOROTTYA

WEKERLE S. U.

GERBEAUD CAFÉ

HARMINCAD

FERENC

Deák tér

T

KÁROLY

Vörösmarty tér M

Vörösmarty tér

FEHÉRHAJÓ ISTVÁN

KÁROLY

KÖRÚT

BELGRÁD

VIGADÓ

DEÁK

PESTI VIGADÓ

CSERE

PETŐFI SÁNDOR

CITY HALL

GERLÓCZA

SEMMELWEIS

Vigadó tér

TÖRR

ARANY

Kamermayer tér 1

COUNTY HALL

KAROSHÁZ

MAHART BOAT DOCK

RAKPART

JÁNOS

EGYPOSTI

HISTORIC MCDONALD'S

JUGENDSTIL BLDG. (#18)

PILVAX

FORMER PILVAX CAFÉ

VÁRMEGYE

KOSSUTH LAJOS UTCA

SZÉP

Danube

LEGENDA BOAT DOCK

PETŐFI

ADAMS

"SORRARAS" HISTORICISM BLDG. (#15)

VÁCI UTCA

TOWN 5

23

Ferenciek tere

FRANCISCAN CHURCH

REÁLTANODA

Petőfi tér

PIARISTA UTCA

KÍGYÓ

M

Petőfi tér

PIARISTA KÖZ

KLOTILD PALACES

KÁROLYI MIHÁLY

FERENCZY

Károlyi Park

Tram #19 & #41

SZABAD SAJTÓ ÚT

IKÁNYI 25

CENTER

Egyetem tér

24

Döbrentei tér

ELISABETH BRIDGE

Március 15 tér

P

IKÁNYI

T

VÁCI UTCA

PÁL

VERES PÁLNÉ

ELTE LAW FACULTY 2

NY. PÁL

12

RUDAS BATHS

T

Tram #2

BELGRÁD

NYÁRI

SÖRHÁZ

Serbian Church

SZERB

F. GYÖRGY

River

RAKPART

MOLNÁR

4

SERBIAN CHURCH

13

SZARKA

BÁSTYA

Gellért Hill

CITADELLA

SZT. GELLÉRT RAKPART

HAVAS

SÓ

T-KÖRÚT

CITADELLA

POST 3

Fővám tér

M

i

PIPA

SÉTÁNY

VÁMHÁZ

14

GREAT MARKET HALL

BUDA

CAVE CHURCH

VEREJTÉK

UNIV. OF ECONOMICS

SZÁJA

N

200 Meters

200 Yards

KELENHEGYI

LIBERTY BRIDGE

Szent Gellért tér

GELLÉRT HOTEL & BATHS

T

M

Szent Gellért tér

KEMENES

Pest Town Center Hotels & Restaurants

<u>Accommodations</u>
1. Gerlóczy Café & Rooms
2. Hotel Rum
3. Butterfly Home Danube B&B
4. Loft V65
5. Katona Apartments
6. Kálvin-Ház Hotel
7. Brody House
8. Budapest Rooms
9. Four Seasons Gresham Palace
10. Starlight Suiten
11. To GuestBed Budapest Apartments

<u>Eateries & Other</u>
12. Borssó Bistro
13. Halkakas Halbisztró
14. Great Market Hall
15. Café Kör
16. Mák Bistro
17. Belvárosi Lugas Étterem
18. DiVino Wine Bar
19. Borkonyha Wine Bar
20. Első Pesti Rétesház
21. To Hungarikum Bisztró
22. To St. Andrea Wine & Gourmet Bar
23. Főzelékfaló Ételbár & Jégbüfé Café
24. Hummus Bar (3)
25. Centrál Kávéház
26. BENU Gyógyszertár Pharmacy
27. MÁV Train Ticket Office
28. Bestsellers Bookstore

The Seventh District

Accommodations

1. ROOMbach Hotel Budapest Center
2. BudaBaB
3. GuestBed Budapest (Apt. Szukkot)

Eateries & Other

4. Mazel Tov
5. KönyvBár & Restaurant
6. Macesz Bistro
7. Kőleves
8. Soul Food
9. Street Food Karaván
10. DiVino Wine Bar & Gozsdu Udvar
11. Klauzál Market
12. Shalimar
13. Főzelékfaló Ételbár
14. Hummus Bar
15. New York Café
16. Laundry Budapest
17. Bazar Hostel (Laundry)

as everybody shares the bathrooms and the comfy living room; they appreciate conscientious guests. It's basic, cheap, and friendly (cash or prepay with PayPal for 3 percent surcharge, Akácfa utca 18, district VII, M2: Blaha Lujza tér, or tram #4 or #6 to Wesselényi stop, mobile +3670-315-8828, www.budabab.com, info@budabab.com).

Leopold Town, near the Chain Bridge

The first listing below is the city's most prestigious address; the next is a nicely located business-class option that is worth booking if you can get a discounted rate. Both are a short stroll from the delightful St. István tér/Zrínyi utca restaurant zone.

$$$$ Four Seasons Gresham Palace is Budapest's top hotel—and one of its most expensive. Stay here only if money is truly no object. You'll sleep in what is arguably Budapest's finest Art Nouveau building. Damaged in World War II, the Gresham Palace sat in disrepair for decades. Today it's sparkling from a recent head-to-toe renovation, and every detail in its lavish public spaces and 179 rooms is perfectly in place. Even if you're not sleeping here, dip into the lobby and café to soak in the elegance (air-con, elevator, top-floor spa, Széchenyi tér 5, district V, between M1: Vörösmarty tér and M2: Kossuth tér, tel. 1/268-6000, www.fourseasons.com/budapest, budapest.reservations@fourseasons.com). For more on the building's history, see page 580.

$$ Starlight Suiten has 54 spacious, good-value suites—each with a living room, bedroom, and kitchenette—on a sleepy, sterile street directly behind the Gresham Palace (air-con, elevator, free fitness room and sauna, Mérleg utca 6, district V, M1: Vörösmarty tér, tel. 1/484-3700, www.starlighthotels.com, reservation.starlight@cpihotels.com).

Apartments: $ GuestBed Budapest has a few apartments scattered around town (two in a mellow residential zone near the Margaret Bridge and the Great Boulevard, one more near St. István's Basilica, and another in the Seventh District—all well-described on their website). The straightforward apartments, all with full kitchens, are not luxurious, but you'll enjoy its welcoming and conscientious owners, János and József. They also rent a "B&B" room in their own apartment (sharing their bathroom)—you'll really feel like you're staying with local friends (Katona József utca 39, district XIII, tram #4/#6: Jászai Mari tér, mobile +3670-258-5194, www.guestbudapestapartment.com, budapestrentapartment@gmail.com).

Hostels

Budapest has seemingly dozens of apartments that have been taken over by young entrepreneurs, offering basic, rough-around-the-edges hostel charm. You'll buzz in at the door and climb up a creaky, dank, and smelly staircase to a funky little enclave of fellow backpackers. Most of these places have just three rooms (one double and two small dorms). As each fills a niche (party, artsy, communist-themed, etc.), it's hard to recommend just one—read reviews on a hostel site (such as www.hostelworld.com) and find one that suits your philosophy. For hostel locations, see the map on page 648.

¢ Aventura Boutique Hostel is a low-key, colorful, and stylish place in a dreary urban neighborhood near the Nyugati/Western train station. Well-run by friendly Ágnes, it's both homey and tastefully mod, with imaginatively decorated rooms (across the busy Great Boulevard ring road and a very long block from Nyugati train station at 12 Visegrádi utca, district XIII, M3: Nyugati pu., tel. 1/239-0782, www.aventurahostel.com, info@aventurahostel. com). They also rent several apartments—two nearby, the other near St. István's Basilica.

¢ **Home Made Hostel** is a fun-and-funky slumbermill artfully littered with secondhand furniture. With 20 beds in four rooms located near the Oktogon, it's managed and decorated with a sense of humor (Teréz körút 22, district VI, M1: Oktogon, tel. 1/302-2103, www.homemadehostel.com, info@homemadehostel.com).

BUDA
Víziváros

The Víziváros neighborhood—or "Water Town"—is the lively part of Buda squeezed between Castle Hill and the Danube, where fishermen and tanners used to live. Víziváros is the most pleasant and central area to stay on the Buda side of the Danube, with fine views across the river toward the Parliament building and bustling Pest. It's expensive and a little less convenient than Pest, but feels less urban.

The following hotels are in district I, between the Chain Bridge and Buda's busy Margit körút ring road. Trams #19 and #41 zip along the embankment in either direction. Batthyány tér, a few minutes' walk away, is a handy center with lots of restaurants (see page 667), a Metró stop (M2/red line), and the HÉV train to Óbuda and Szentendre.

$$$ Hotel Victoria, with 27 stylish, spotless, business-class rooms—each with a grand river view and attention to detail—is a class act. This tall, narrow place (three rooms on each of nine floors) is run with pride and attention to detail by on-the-ball manager Zoltán and his friendly staff (air-con, elevator, free sauna, free afternoon tea for guests 16:00-17:00, reserve ahead for pay parking garage, Bem rakpart 11, tel. 1/457-8080, www.victoria.hu, victoria@victoria.hu). The painstakingly restored 19th-century Hubay Palace behind the hotel (entrance next to reception) is used for concerts and other events. It feels like a museum, with inlaid floors, stained-glass windows, and stuccoed walls and ceilings.

$$ At Art'otel, every detail—from the breakfast dishes to the carpets to the good-luck blackbird perched in each room—was designed by American artist Donald Sultan. This stylish hotel has 165 rooms spread between two attached buildings: the new section fronting the Danube and, just behind it, a restored older house with views of the castle (breakfast extra, air-con, elevator, free sauna and

Buda Hotels & Restaurants

1. Hotel Victoria
2. Art'otel
3. Bellevue B&B
4. St. George Residence
5. Burg Hotel
6. Hotel Castle Garden
7. Vár Bistro
8. 21 Magyar Vendéglő
9. Baltazár
10. Batthyány tér Eateries
11. To Csalogány 26
12. ZONA
13. Ruszwurm Café
14. Prima Grocery

BUDAPEST

miniexercise room, bike rental, Bem rakpart 16, tel. 1/487-9487, www.artotels.com, budapest@artotels.com).

$ Bellevue B&B is one of Budapest's best deals. It hides in a quiet residential area on the Víziváros hillside just below the Fishermen's Bastion staircase. This gem is run by retired economists Judit (YOO-deet) and Lajos (LIE-yosh) Szuhay, who lived in Canada for four years and speak flawless English (Bálint helps out). The breakfast room and some of the six straightforward, comfortable rooms have views across the Danube to the Parliament and Pest. Judit and Lajos love to chat, and pride themselves on offering genuine hospitality and a warm welcome (let them know what time you're arriving). As this B&B is understandably popular, book ahead (cash only, air-con; M2: Batthyány tér plus a 10-minute uphill walk, or bus #16 from Deák, Széchenyi, or Clark Ádám squares to Dónati utca plus a 2-minute walk uphill, then downhill—they'll email you detailed directions; Szabó Ilonka utca 15/B, mobile +3630-370-8678 or +3630-951-5494, www.bellevuebudapest.com, judit@bellevuebudapest.com).

Castle Hill

Romantics may enjoy calling Castle Hill home (district I). These places couldn't be closer to the Castle Hill sights, but they're in a tourist zone—dead at night, and less convenient to Pest than other listings.

$$$ St. George Residence, just a couple of short blocks from Matthias Church, is historical and classy. They rent 24 elegant rooms—each one different, all with kitchenettes—around a restful garden courtyard (air-con, Fortuna utca 4, tel. 1/393-5700, www.stgeorgehotel.hu, info@stgeorgehotel.hu).

$$ Burg Hotel, with 26 overpriced rooms on Holy Trinity Square (Szentháromság tér), is simply efficient: concrete, spacious, and comfy, if a bit worn, with a professional staff. You'll find more conveniently located hotels for less money elsewhere, but if you simply *must* stay in a modern hotel across the street from Matthias Church, this is it (RS%, request view room for no extra charge, family rooms, no elevator, air-con, top-floor rooms are extremely long, Szentháromság tér 7, tel. 1/212-0269, www.burghotelbudapest.com, hotel.burg@mail.datanet.hu).

$ Hotel Castle Garden huddles above an Italian restaurant in a tranquil, parklike neighborhood just outside the castle's Vienna Gate (north end). As it's roughly on the way between the castle and Széll Kálmán tér, it's relatively handy, though still less convenient than the Víziváros listings. But its 39 tastefully appointed, contemporary rooms are a great value for the quality (air-con, elevator, pay parking garage, Lovas út 41, M2: Széll Kálmán tér; exit the castle through the Vienna Gate and turn left along the wall, or hike up from Széll Kálmán tér and turn right along the castle wall; tel. 1/224-7420, www.castlegarden.hu, hotel@castlegarden.hu).

Eating in Budapest

Budapest may be one of Europe's most underrated culinary destinations. Hungarian cuisine is delightful—rich, spicy, smooth, and delicious. And Budapest specializes in trendy restaurants that mix Hungarian flavors with international flair, making the food here even better. Best of all, the prices are reasonable, especially if you venture off the main tourist trail. Foodies might want to budget an extra day or two here, just to eat well. This is affordable sightseeing for your palate.

Thanks to Budapest's ever-evolving culinary scene, there's no shortage of places to dine. The food scene here is boom-and-bust: A place quickly acquires a huge and enthusiastic following, but soon falls from grace as an even more enticing competitor opens up shop. I've focused my listings on reliable standbys that have survived their initial spurt of fame.

International restaurants provide a break from Hungarian fare (in the unlikely event you need one). Budapest has abundant vegetarian, Italian, Indian, Chinese, and other non-Hungarian eateries; I've listed a few favorites. Once you leave the capital, these options are sparse, and the food gets even heartier and cheaper.

Most Hungarians dine between 19:00 and 21:00, peaking around 20:00; trendy zones such as St. István Square and Franz Liszt Square, which attract an after-work crowd, are lively earlier in the evening.

Check Your Bill: While most Hungarian restaurateurs are honest, rip-off joints abound in downtown Budapest's tourist zone—especially along the main walking street, Váci utca. (Frankly, I'd never eat on Váci utca, which practically guarantees bad food and service for high prices.) Avoid any place with a menu that doesn't list prices, and tune in to the fine print. For example, many Budapest restaurants automatically tack on a 10 to 12 percent service charge. Check for it as a line-item at the end of bill: Look for "service," "tip," *felszolgálási díj,* or *szervízdíj.* If you see this charge, an additional tip is not necessary for adequate service.

Lunch Specials: Many Budapest restaurants offer lunch specials, called *napimenü,* on weekdays. As these are designed for local office workers on their lunch breaks rather than for tourists, they're often not advertised in English—but if you see the magic word *napimenü,* ask about it. Even at trendy, otherwise pricey eateries, you'll generally pay around 1,000 Ft for a fixed menu (soup and main dish or main dish and dessert; no choices—take it or leave it).

PEST

I've listed these options by neighborhood, for easy reference with your sightseeing.

Pest's Town Center (Belváros), near Váci Utca

When you ask natives about good places to eat on Váci utca, they just roll their eyes. But wander a few blocks off the tourist route, and you'll discover alternatives with fair prices and better food. For locations, see the map on page 653.

$$$ Gerlóczy Café, tucked on a peaceful little square next to the giant City Hall, features French, Hungarian, and international

cuisine. The clientele is a mix of tourists and upscale-urban Buda-pesters, including local politicians and actors from nearby theaters. With a take-your-time ambience that's arguably more Parisian than Hungarian—and with live piano music on weekends after 19:00—this is a classy, particularly inviting

spot (good breakfasts, weekday lunch specials, good-value fixed-price dinners, daily 7:00-23:00, 2 blocks from Váci utca, just off Városház utca at Gerlóczy utca 1, district V, M3: Ferenciek tere, tel. 1/501-4000).

$$$$ Borssó Bistro, near University Square (Egyetem tér), is a trendy splurge offering small portions of delicately assembled modern French cuisine with a bit of Hungarian flair. The cozy two-story interior's ambience, like the cuisine, is an elegant yet accessible blend of old and new. They also have outdoor tables and occasional live music. Reservations are important (Tue 18:00-23:00, Wed-Sun 12:00-23:00, closed Mon, Király Pál utca 14, district V, M3/M4: Kálvin tér, tel. 1/789-0975, mobile +3620-807-7087, www.borsso.hu).

$ Halkakas Halbisztró ("Fishrooster Fish Bistro") is a tight, tidy, cheery, colorful bistro serving up mostly

Hungarian fish with a variety of sauces. In this landlocked country, that means fresh-water fish (catfish, carp, trout, and so on)—better than it sounds, and very local (Mon-Sat 12:00-22:00, closed Sun, Veres Pálné utca 33, district V, M4: Fővám tér or M3/M4: Kálvin tér, mobile +3630-226-0638).

Great Market Hall: At the far south end of Váci utca, you can eat a quick lunch on the upper floor of the Great Market Hall (Nagyvásárcsarnok). **$$ Fakanál Étterem—**

Restaurant Price Code

I've assigned each eatery a price category, based on the average cost of a typical main course. Drinks, desserts, and splurge items (steak and seafood) can raise the price considerably.

$$$$	**Splurge:** Most main courses over 4,500 Ft
$$$	**Pricier:** 3,000-4,500 Ft
$$	**Moderate:** 2,000-3,000 Ft
$	**Budget:** 2,000 Ft or less

In Hungary, takeout food or a cafeteria-type place is **$**; an unpretentious sit-down eatery is **$$**; an upmarket but still casual restaurant is **$$$**; and a swanky splurge is **$$$$**.

---

the glassed-in, sit-down cafeteria above the main entrance—is touristy, but offers good seating (Mon-Fri 10:00-17:00, Sat 10:00-14:00, closed Sun; live music most days 12:00-15:00). The sloppy, stand-up **$ stalls** along the right side of the building are cheaper, but quality can vary (grab a bar stool or you'll stand while you munch). A favorite treat is the heavy fry bread called *lángos* (like a savory elephant ear). Get the basic one—slathered with sour cream, cheese, and (if you dare) garlic—for about 1,000 Ft; order carefully, or they could add piles of toppings to triple or quadruple your bill. Or you can assemble a **picnic**—produce and butcher stands line the main floor, and an Aldi supermarket is in the basement (the end nearest Váci utca; market hall open Mon 6:00-17:00, Tue-Fri 6:00-18:00, Sat 6:00-15:00, closed Sun; supermarket open longer hours, Fővám körút 1-3, district IX, M4: Fővám tér).

Near St. István's Basilica

The streets in front of St. István's Basilica are jammed with upscale, dressy, yuppie-oriented eateries (district V, M1: Bajcsy-Zsilinszky út). Long popular with locals, it's now becoming quite touristy—but you'll still find a mixed clientele. Several options line Zrínyi utca (which stretches straight down to the Danube from the basilica's front door) and its cross streets. But the following choices are worth seeking out. For locations, see the map on page 653.

$$$ Café Kör ("Circle") is a reliable mainstay in this otherwise fast-evolving zone. This stylish but unsnooty eatery serves up mostly Hungarian and some Mediterranean fare in a tasteful, tight, one-room interior and at a few sidewalk tables. It prides itself on being friendly and providing a good value. Because it's beloved by local foodies, reservations are smart anytime—and essential on weekends (small portions available, good salads, daily specials, cash only, Mon-Sat 10:00-22:00, closed Sun, Sas utca 17, tel. 1/311-0053, www.cafekor.net).

$$$$ Mák Bistro is pricey but unpretentious, with a loyal fol-

BUDAPEST

lowing (reservations are smart, especially on weekends). It feels like a well-kept secret, tucked down a forgotten side street parallel to the bustling Zrínyi utca pedestrian drag. Inside, it has a lively brasserie ambience under white-painted brick vaults. The short, carefully selected seasonal menu is based on what's fresh. The good-value lunch specials are an affordable way to sample the fine cuisine (Tue-Sat 12:00-15:00 & 18:00-23:00, closed Sun-Mon, Vigyázó Ferenc 4, mobile +3630-723-9383, www.mak.hu).

$$ Belvárosi Lugas Étterem is your cheap-and-charming, no-frills option for straightforward, traditional Hungarian food. *Lugas* is a Hungarian word for a welcoming garden strewn with grape vines, and the cozy dining room—with a dozen tables under overhanging vines—captures that spirit. Or sit at one of their sidewalk tables outside on busy Bajcsy-Zsilinszky út, directly behind and across the street from the back of the basilica (daily 12:00-23:30, Bajcsy-Zsilinszky út 15, district VI, tel. 1/302-5393).

Wine-Focused Eateries: Two wine bars—one casual, the other upscale—have helped turn this neighborhood into a happening nightspot. **$$ DiVino** serves 130 types of exclusively Hungarian wines, listed by region on the chalkboard—all available by the glass or bottle. The well-versed staff can help introduce you to Hungary's underrated wines—just tell them what you like and let them guide you. While DiVino doesn't do flights or tastings per se, couples are encouraged to share glasses (many less than 1,000 Ft) to try several varieties. The interior has a hip atmosphere, and there's also inviting seating out on the square (daily 16:00-24:00, St. István tér 3, mobile +3670-935-3980; additional bigger location in the Gozsdu Udvar passage in the Seventh District. Just around the corner, **$$$$ Borkonyha** ("Winekitchen") serves up Hungarian cuisine ("Hungarian dishes—but less paprika, less fat"). And, as the name implies, they're evangelical about high-quality (and pricey) Hungarian wines—with about 45 types sold by the glass. The menu—especially the adventurous chalkboard specials—ventures into "nose-to-tail" cooking, using ingredients you won't find everywhere. The decor is sophisticated black, white, and gold—a dressy place where wine snobs feel at home—and they also have sidewalk seating out front. As this place has received a lot of international press—and, in 2014, its first Michelin star—reservations are essential (Mon-Sat 12:00-16:00 & 18:00-24:00, closed Sun, Sas utca 3, tel. 1/266-0835, www.borkonyha.hu).

Homemade Strudel: Első Pesti Rétesház is a favorite among fans of *rétes* (strudel). Step inside to watch them roll out the long, paper-thin sheets of dough, then wrap them around a variety of fillings. Get a piece to go at the takeaway counter, or sit and enjoy your *rétes* with a cup of coffee (also has a full food menu, daily 9:00-23:00, Október 6 utca 22, tel. 1/428-0134).

Near the Parliament

These restaurants are scattered in the blocks north of St. István Square, closer to the Parliament.

$$ Hungarikum Bisztró, tucked in an unassuming neighborhood between big government ministries, is the best place in Budapest for authentic, traditional Hungarian cuisine. Rather than gouging tourists, the youthful owners consider themselves ambassadors for the dishes their grandma raised them on. The mellow, unpretentious interior—with warm service and red-and-white-checked tablecloths—complements the strictly old-fashioned cuisine (daily 11:30-14:30 & 18:00-22:00, Steindl Imre utca 13, district V, M2: Kossuth Lajos tér, tel. 1/797-7177).

$$$ St. Andrea Wine & Gourmet Bar is a worthwhile pilgrimage for wine lovers. Located in the recently restored Eiffel Palace building (a long block in front of Nyugati/Western train station, along the Great Boulevard), this is the wine bar of the acclaimed St. Andrea winery in Egerszalók (see page 693). St. Andrea offers a great chance to try some of Hungary's best wines, paired with well-executed food, in a sophisticated setting (good-value lunch deals, affordable lighter menu before 18:00, open Mon-Fri 11:00-23:00, Sat 18:00-23:00, closed Sun, Bajcsy-Zsilinszky út 78, district V, M3: Nyugati pályaudvar, tel. 1/269-0130, www.standreaborbar.hu).

Near Andrássy Út and the Oktogon

For locations, see the map on page 648. Note that the Seventh District eateries (in the next section) are also nearby.

$$$ Menza (the old communist word for "School Cafeteria"), the only restaurant seriously worth considering on touristy Franz Liszt Square, wins the "Best Design" award. Recycling 1970s-era furniture and an orange-brown-gray color scheme, it's a postmodern parody of an old communist café—half kitschy-retro, half contemporary-stylish. When old-timers come in here, they can only chuckle and say, "Yep. This is how it was." With tasty and well-priced updated Hungarian and international cuisine, embroidered leather-bound menus, brisk but efficient service, breezy jazz on the soundtrack, and indoor or outdoor seating, it's a memorable spot (daily 10:00-24:00, halfway up Andrássy út at Liszt Ferenc tér 2, district VII, M1: Oktogon, tel. 1/413-1482, www.menza.co.hu). If you like the Franz Liszt Square scene, you'll find a similar energy on Kertész utca beyond the end of the square, and in the "Broadway Quarter" near the Opera House (on Hajós utca and Nagymező utca).

$$$ Klassz, right on Andrássy út, is a bistro with a similarly postmodern "eclectic-mod" aesthetic, both in its decor and its food. They serve reasonably priced, if hit-or-miss, international/nouvelle cuisine with Hungarian flair (daily 11:30-22:30, Andrássy út 41, district VI, between M1: Opera and M1: Oktogon, no reservations possible).

$$ Pesti Diszno ("Pest Pig"), set right in the "Broadway Quarter" along the liveliest stretch of theaters in town, celebrates the prized Hungarian hairy pig called *mangalica*. The menu ranges from well-executed classics to international fare to creative fusion dishes—like a *mangalica* hamburger. While the interior, with tall tables surrounding the open kitchen, is fine, I'd rather sit out under the red-and-white striped awnings facing the bright lights of Budapest's theater scene (daily 11:00-24:00, Nagymező 19, district VI, M1: Oktogon, tel. 1/951-4061, www.pestidiszno.hu).

$$$$ Bock Bisztró, run by a prominent vintner from Villány, offers traditional Hungarian staples presented with modern flourish—almost "deconstructed," but still recognizable. It has a wine-bar ambience, with cork-filled tables. Pricey and well-regarded, with a list of 250 wines (including 60 by the glass), it's a good opportunity to sample food and wine from around the country. The service can be a bit stuffy, but the food lives up to its reputation. Reservations are essential (Mon-Sat 12:00-24:00, closed Sun, in the Corinthia Grand Royal Hotel, a couple of blocks west of the Oktogon on the Great Boulevard, Erzsébet körút 43, district VII, M1: Oktogon, right by Király utca stop on trams #4 and #6, tel. 1/321-0340, www.bockbisztropest.hu).

$$ Két Szerecsen ("Two Saracens"), named for a historic coffee shop at this location a century ago that a trader filled with exotic goods, stays true to that eclectic spirit by featuring a wide variety of international cuisines—from Mediterranean to Asian. It has good indoor and outdoor seating, relatively small portions, and a menu that offers something for everyone (daily 9:00-24:00, a block off Andrássy út at Nagymező utca 14, district VI, M1: Opera, tel. 1/343-1984).

Seventh District (Ruin Pub Zone and Former Jewish Quarter)

Along with the recent rise of ruin pubs (see page 640), Budapest's Seventh District has seen the arrival of several good restaurants. While a few of these feature Jewish food (in a nod to this area's history as the former Jewish Quarter), others are more eclectic, catering to a younger clientele. As this is a fast-emerging scene, you could just explore here, but the following are some reliably good options. For locations, see the map on page 654.

$$$ Mazel Tov, one of Budapest's trendiest new eateries (reserve ahead), fills a dilapidated old building at the edge of the ruin-pub zone. Stepping across the tattered threshold, you emerge into a vine-strewn, bare-brick courtyard where twinkling lights are strung over the hardworking open kitchen. With a wink to this district's Jewish origins, they serve creative cocktails and Middle Eastern dishes like kebabs, shawarma, falafel, tabbouleh, and *shakshuka* (tomato-poached eggs). While the food can be hit-or-miss, the joyful atmosphere captures Budapest's thriving foodie energy (Mon-Fri 16:00-late, Sat-Sun 12:00-even later, food until 23:00, Akácfa utca 47, district VII, between M1: Opera and M2: Blaha Lujza tér, mobile +3670-626-4280, www.mazeltov.hu).

$$$ KönyvBár & Restaurant, just around the corner from Mazel Tov, is refined, mellow, and creative. The small dining room feels like a sleek, minimalist library, and the menu has a fun literary theme (*könyv* means "book"). Bibliophiles should reserve ahead for an appealing dining experience (Mon-Sat 12:00-24:00, closed Sun, Dob utca 45, district VII, between M1: Opera and M2: Blaha Lujza tér, mobile +3620-922-7027, www.konyvbar.hu).

$$$ Macesz Bistro is a Grandma's-dining-room-cozy corner restaurant serving traditional Jewish recipes with modern ingredients and technique. Reserve ahead (daily 12:00-16:00 & 18:00-23:00, Dob utca 26, district VII, M1: Opera, tel. 1/787-6164, http://maceszbistro.hu).

$$ Kőleves ("Stone Soup") runs a ruin-pub garden, but their restaurant feels upscale and put-together without being stuffy. The eclectic, international menu includes several Jewish (though not kosher) dishes. This is steps away from Macesz Bistro (listed above), and worth trying if that place is full (daily 12:00-24:00, Kazinczy utca 41, district VII, M1: Opera, mobile +3620-213-5999). Their adjacent garden courtyard serves cheap pub grub.

$ Soul Food is a casual Cajun- and creole-inspired eatery run by Attila, who's a well-traveled singer by profession and a chef by passion. It feels like a creative college dive: Create your own rice or noodle bowl, or order a sandwich or burger (daily 12:00-23:00, later on weekends, takeaway available, Kazinczy utca 32, district VII, M1: Opera, mobile +3670-313-8804).

Food Trucks: Just a couple of doors down from Szimpla (the oldest and best of the ruin pubs—see page 642), the **$ Street Food Karaván** fills a gravel lot with an enticing pod of creative food trucks and picnic tables. These trucks can be a way for bold new chefs to establish themselves, or for popular restaurants to reach more customers. For foodies—or just those seeking a break from their ruin-pub crawl—it's worth a browse (daily 11:30-late, Kazinczy utca 18, district VII, M1: Opera; for the latest rundown of food trucks see www.streetfoodkaravan.hu).

Gozsdu Udvar: This passage—which runs under apartment blocks through the busy epicenter of the ruin-pub zone—is jammed with bars and restaurants for a drink, snack, or meal. The place most worth considering is **\$\$ DiVino,** an outpost of the popular wine bar on St. István Square (see page 662)—with affordable glasses of good Hungarian wines and some light local dishes (nightly 16:00-late, mobile +3670-413-4899).

Market Hall with Cheap Eats: At the northern edge of the ruin-pub zone is the **\$ Klauzál Market,** a recently-renovated, 1897 neighborhood market hall. With soaring steel girders over pristinely restored food stalls and a handy Spar supermarket, it's a fine place to browse for a picnic or grab some street food (most vendors open until about 17:00; supermarket open Mon-Sat 6:30-21:00, Sun 7:00-18:00; Klauzál tér 6, runs through the block between Klauzál utca and Akácfa utca, district VII, between M1: Opera and M2: Blaha Lujza tér).

Indian: Hungarians seem to have an affinity for Indian cuisines, which, like Hungarian cuisine, smooth together powerful spices. **\$\$ Shalimar**'s high-ceilinged, nondescript dining room hides in a dreary neighborhood squeezed between the Seventh District ruin-pub zone and Franz Liszt Square. Everything about this place is unexceptional...except the food. I can never resist their *murg makhani,* and I'm never disappointed (cheaper half-portions available, daily 11:30-16:00 & 18:00-23:00, Dob utca 33, district VII, between M1: Opera and M2: Blaha Lujza tér, tel. 1/352-0305).

City Park

I wouldn't go out of my way to eat in City Park, but if you're enjoying a day here and would like a scenic meal, Robinson is a good option. For the location, see the map on page 599.

\$\$\$\$ Robinson, stranded on an island in City Park's lake, is a playful, mellow theme restaurant. With island-castaway ambience and more outdoor seating than indoor, it's made-to-order for lazing away a sunny afternoon at the park. The terrace and elegant, glassed-in dining room feature pricey but uneven international and Hungarian cuisine, and upstairs is a swanky steak house. In good weather, I'd come here for the terrace to just sip a coffee or have a slice of cake (daily 11:00-17:00 & 18:00-23:00, reserve ahead and ask for lakefront seating, Városligeti tó, district XIV, M1: Hősök tere, tel. 1/422-0222, www.robinsonrestaurant.hu).

For something quicker and more casual, closer to the end of the lake, look for the **\$ BRGR** burger stand.

BUDA

Eateries on Castle Hill are generally overpriced and touristy—as with Váci utca, locals never eat here. The Víziváros ("Water Town") neighborhood, between the castle and the river, is a bit better. Even if sleeping in Buda, try to dine in Pest—that's where you'll find the city's best restaurants. All of the restaurants listed here (except Szent Jupát) are in district I. For locations, see the map on page 657.

Castle Hill

For a quick bite, visit the handy, affordable **Prima** grocery store (Mon-Sat 7:00-20:00, Sun 9:00-18:00, on Tárnok utca near Szentháromság tér).

For coffee and cakes, try the historic **Ruszwurm** (described later, under "Budapest's Café Culture"). If you'd rather have a meal—and don't want to head down to Víziváros—try the following choices:

$ Vár Bistro is a convenient, affordable cafeteria that makes for an easy and quick way to grab a meal between sightseeing; best of all, it has delightful outdoor seating overlooking a pretty park (daily 8:00-20:00, Dísz tér 8, mobile +3630-237-0039).

$$$ 21 Magyar Vendéglő ("21 Hungarian Kitchen") features traditional Hungarian fare that's updated for the 21st century (hence the name). While the mod interior is pleasant, it's also fun to sit out on pretty Fortuna utca (near the north end of the hill). Most restaurants on Castle Hill are overpriced, and this is no exception—but the quality is good. This is a rare castle-zone eatery that really takes pride in its food rather than being a crank-'em-out tourism machine (daily 11:00-24:00, Fortuna utca 21, tel. 1/202-2113).

$$$ Baltazár, near the ruins of St. Mary Magdalene Church (a few short blocks from the main sights), is trying to inject some youthful liveliness into the staid, sleepy north end of Castle Hill. It's a fun choice, with bright, brash decor, pleasant outdoor seating, and a wood-fired charcoal grill that churns out smoky dishes. They also have an inviting beer garden just up the street, under the church tower (daily 7:30-24:00, Országház utca 31, tel. 1/300-7050).

Batthyány Tér and Nearby

This bustling square—the transportation hub for Víziváros (on the M2 line)—is overlooked by a recently renovated, late-19th-century market hall (today housing a big Spar supermarket and various shops). Several worthwhile, affordable eateries—nothing fancy, just practical—cluster around this square. Survey your options before settling in.

$ Nagyi Palacsintázója ("Granny's Pancakes")—just to the right of the market hall entrance—serves up cheap sweet and savory crêpes *(palacsinta)* to a local crowd (individual crêpes are small—order a combo for a filling meal, ask for English menu, open daily 24 hours, Batthyány tér 5).

As you face the market hall, go up the street that runs along its left side (Markovits Iván utca) to reach more good eateries: At the end of the block on the right is **$ Édeni Végan,** a self-service, point-and-shoot vegetarian cafeteria (daily 8:00-20:00, tel. 1/375-7575). And tucked behind the market hall is **$ Bratwursthäusle/ Kolbászda,** a fun little beer hall/beer garden with Bavarian specialties and blue-and-white checkerboard decor to match. Sit outside, or in the woody interior (daily 11:00-23:00, Gyorskocsi utca 6, tel. 1/225-3674).

Fine Dining near Batthyány Tér: $$$$ Csalogány 26 is a stylish, splurgy bistro a few short blocks from Batthyány tér in an otherwise dull urban neighborhood. Its modern international cuisine, served in a classy contemporary dining room, has earned it raves as one of the best eateries in this part of town—reserve ahead (Tue-Sat 12:00-15:00 & 19:00-22:00, closed Sun-Mon, Csalogány utca 26, tel. 1/201-7892, www.csalogany26.hu).

Trendy and Upscale near the Chain Bridge: $$$ ZONA feels sleek, hip, and central, just a few steps from the Chain Bridge on the Buda embankment. True to its name, it has two separate zones—a laid-back bar and a dressier dining room—both focused on the small portions of precisely executed food with an eclectic, international flair (daily 12:00-23:00, Lánchíd utca 7, mobile +3630-422-5981, www.zonabudapest.com).

SNACKS AND LIGHT MEALS

When you're in the mood for something halfway between a restaurant and a picnic meal, look for takeout food stands, bakeries (with sandwiches to go), grocers willing to make you a sandwich, and simple eateries for fast and easy sit-down restaurant food.

A popular snack is *lángos*—a savory deep-fried flatbread (similar to an elephant ear or Native American fry bread). Sold at stands on the street and upstairs in the Great Market Hall (see earlier), the most typical versions are spread with cheese and sour cream, and sometimes topped with garlic.

For quick, cheap, and very local grub, head for the chain called **$ Főzelékfaló Ételbár** (roughly, "Soup Slurper Eating Bar"). This self-service cafeteria dishes up basic fare to businesspeople on their lunch break. *Főzelék,* a simple soup that's thickened with roux and can be supplemented with various vegetables, is a staple of Hungarian home cooking. Go to the counter, select your *főzelék* soup, then choose from a variety of meat dishes (chicken, pork, meatballs, and more; some English spoken, but pointing also works). There are two locations in central Pest: One is just off Andrássy út in the "Broadway Quarter" (daily 9:00-22:00, Nagymező utca 22, a block north of the Opera House, district VI, M1: Opera); the other faces the busy highway at Ferenciek tere (Mon-Fri 10:00-20:00, Sat 12:00-20:00, closed Sun, Kossuth Lajos utca 2A, district V, M3: Ferenciek tere).

$ Hummus Bar, while not authentically Hungarian, is a popular expat-run chain that offers cheap Middle Eastern vegetarian meals (tasty falafel, sandwiches, and combination plates) to grateful backpackers and young locals. You can either eat in or get it to go. They have multiple locations, including in the Town Center on University Square (Egyetem tér, at Kecskeméti utca 1, district V, M3/M4: Kálvin tér); in Leopold Town (Alkotmány utca 20, district V, M2: Kossuth tér); between Liberty Square and St. István Square (Október 6 utca 19); and nestled among ruin pubs in the Seventh District (at the corner of Síp and Wesselényi). All are open roughly the same hours (Mon-Fri 10:00-22:00, Sat-Sun 12:00-22:00).

Sweets: For a fast and sweet snack, you have two good choices. Stands all over town sell *kürtőskalács*—a "chimney cake" pastry that's twisted around a spindle, rolled in sugar, and then slowly baked on a rotisserie until it's coated in a sweet, caramelized crust. They roll it in toppings (cinnamon, coconut, chocolate) and hand it over hot. Watch for vendors at the start of Andrássy út, in front of the Nyugati/Western train station, and elsewhere around town. For something a bit less exciting (but still delicious), you'll smell **Fornetti** stands everywhere (on street corners and Metró underpasses). This Hungary-based chain, which is becoming wildly popular across Central and Eastern Europe, sells small, tasty, freshly baked phyllo dough-based pastries by weight. They have both sweet and savory varieties. If you smell something heavenly in the Metró passages...it's probably a Fornetti.

BUDAPEST'S CAFÉ CULTURE

In the late 19th century, a vibrant café culture boomed here in Budapest, just as it did in Vienna and Paris. The *kávéház* ("coffeehouse") was a local institution. By 1900, Budapest had more than 600 cafés. In this crowded and fast-growing cityscape, a neighborhood café allowed urbanites to escape their tiny flats (or get a jolt of caffeine to power them through a 12-hour workday). Local people (many of whom had moved to the city from the countryside) didn't want to pay to heat their homes during the day. So instead, for the price of a cup of coffee, they could come to a café to enjoy warmth, companionship, and loaner newspapers.

Realizing that these neighborhood living rooms were breeding grounds for dissidents, the communists closed the cafés or converted them into *eszpresszós* (with uncomfortable stools instead of easy chairs) or *bisztrós* (stand-up fast-food joints with no chairs at all). Today, nostalgia is bringing back the *kávéház* culture—both as a place to get coffee and food, and as a social institution. While some serve only coffee and cakes, most serve light meals, and some serve full meals (as noted below).

While meals at some of these grand cafés are pricey, a budget alternative is to nurse an afternoon coffee and cake in opulent surroundings. Hungary has a proud tradition of cakes and pastries, which make liberal use of sweet cheese curds *(turós)* and poppy seeds *(mákszem)*. Here are a few Hungarian favorites to look for: The classic *Dobos torta* is a sponge-cake-and-buttercream concoction with alternating layers of chocolate and vanilla, all topped with caramelized sugar. *Rákóczi turós* is a dense cake of sweet cheese curds with jam on top. *Somlói galuska* is pieces of moist sponge cake soaked in rum, mixed with whipped cream, and drizzled with chocolate. *Krémes* is custard sandwiched between delicate wafers. And *flódni* has layers of apple, nuts, and poppy seeds.

On the Great Boulevard

$$$$ New York Café makes the others listed here look like Starbucks. Originally built in 1894 as part of the "New York Palace" (and it really is palatial), this fanciful, over-the-top explosion of Neo-Baroque and Neo-Renaissance epitomizes the "mix and match, but plenty of everything" Historicist style of the day. In the early 20th century, artists, writers, and musicians came here to sip overpriced coffee and bask in opulence. After decades of neglect, Italian investors completely restored it in 2006, and now it once again welcomes guests. You'll be met at the door and asked if you want a table; they'll typically let you gape at the inside for a few minutes if you ask nicely, but only paying customers may take photos. The food is drastically overpriced and disappointing—don't bother eating a meal here, but do consider coffee and cake. If you nurse your outrageously expensive latte for a while, it may actually be worth the hefty price tag. Be sure to read the fun history in the menu (daily 9:00-24:00, inside the Boscolo Hotel at Erzsébet körút 9, district VII, tel. 1/886-6167). Take the M2/red Metró line to Blaha Lujza tér, and exit toward *Erzsébet körút* and walk a block. You can also take tram #4 or #6 from the Oktogon (at Andrássy út) around the Great Boulevard to the Wesselényi utca stop. For location, see page 573.

Two Blocks Up from Váci Utca

$$$ Gerlóczy Café, listed as a restaurant on page 660, nicely recaptures Budapest's early-1900s ambience, with loaner newspapers on racks and a management that encourages loitering. Nearby, another good choice for coffee and cakes is the similarly old-fashioned **$$$ Centrál Kávéház.** While the food here is pricey and hit-or-miss (don't bother having a meal), it has an enjoyable and atmospheric two-story interior and a handy central location (daily 8:00-23:00, Károlyi Mihály utca 9, district V, M3: Ferenciek tere, tel. 1/266-2110). For location, see the map on page 653.

Near Ferenciek Tere

$ Jégbüfé is where locals get their quick, cheap, stand-at-a-counter fix of coffee and cakes. Inside you'll find display cases with desserts; outside, an ice-cream stand and popular Belgian waffle *(gofry)* window (Mon-Sat 7:00-21:30, Sun 8:00-21:30, Petőfi Sándor utca 3, district V, M3: Ferenciek tere—for location, see map on page 653).

On Vörösmarty Tér

$$$ Gerbeaud (zhehr-BOH) isn't just a café. It's a 150-year-old landmark, the most famous gathering place in Budapest. (For more on the café's history, see page 583.) While it feels faded and dull compared to the others listed here, Gerbeaud is a local institution. Skip the overpriced meals, but instead enjoy some people-watching over coffee and dessert--best on a sunny day from its outdoor tables (daily 9:00–21:00, for location see map on page 648, district V, M1: Vörösmarty tér, tel. 1/429-9000).

On Andrassy ut, near the Opera House

Two fine and very different cafés are within a block of the Opera (for locations, see map on page 649).

    $$$$ Callas features ideal outdoor seating facing the Opera House, and one of the finest Art Nouveau interiors in town, with gorgeous Jugendstil chandeliers. While their full meals are pricey, this is a wonderful spot on Andrássy út for a coffee break, a tasty

BUDAPEST

dessert, or breakfast (Mon-Sat 10:00-24:00, Sun until 20:00, Andrássy út 20, district VI, M1: Opera, tel. 1/354-0954).

$$$ Művész Kávéház ("Artists Coffee House"), across the street and a block toward the Oktogon, is a classic café with 19th-century elegance, a hoity-toity high-ceilinged interior, snobby staff, and fine outdoor seating on Andrássy út. True to its name, this institution in the "Broadway Quarter" is a favorite after-rehearsal haunt of locally famous actors and musicians (daily 9:00-22:00, Andrássy út 29, district VI, M1: Opera, tel. 1/333-2116).

In Buda, atop Castle Hill

$$ Ruszwurm lays claim to being Budapest's oldest café (since 1827). Tiny but classy, with old-style Biedermeier furnishings and fine sidewalk seating, it upholds its venerable reputation with pride. Its dead-central location—a block in front of Matthias Church in the heart of the castle district—means that it has become a popular tourist spot (though it remains dear to locals' hearts). Look for gussied-up locals chatting here after the 10:00 Sunday-morning Mass at the church (daily 10:00-19:00, Szentháromság utca 7, district I, for location see map on page 657, tel. 1/375-5284).

Budapest Connections

BY TRAIN

Hungary's train network is run by MÁV (Magyar Államvasutak). From centrally located Budapest, train lines branch out across Hungary. Most connections between outlying cities aren't direct—you often end up having to go back through Budapest. While Hungary's trains are generally good, many are old and fairly slow; major routes (especially those connecting to international destinations such as Bratislava or Vienna) use faster, newer, and slightly more expensive InterCity trains (marked with an "IC" or a boxed "R" on schedules). To ride an InterCity train, you must pay extra for a required reservation (which is printed on a separate ticket). Warning: Trains can be very crowded on weekends, when it's smart to book a reservation for any train trip.

For timetables, the first place to check is Germany's excellent all-Europe site, www.bahn.com. You can also check Hungary's own timetable website at http://elvira.mav-start.hu. For general rail information in Hungary, call 0640-494-949 (from outside Hungary, dial +36-1-444-4499).

It's best to buy your ticket in advance at the MÁV ticket office in downtown Pest (see page 555). Be aware that ticket lines can be very long at the train stations; if you're buying a ticket there, it's smart to arrive with plenty of time to spare.

Remember that Budapest has three major train stations (*pályaudvar,* abbreviated *pu.*): Keleti ("Eastern") station, Nyugati ("Western") station, and Déli ("Southern") station. The station used by a particular train can change from year to year. Before departing from Budapest, it's essential to carefully confirm which station your train leaves from.

From Budapest by Train to: Eger (every 2 hours direct, 2 hours, more with change in Füzesabony, usually from Budapest's Keleti/Eastern station), **Pécs** (every 2 hours direct, 3 hours; a few more connections possible with transfer at suburban Budapest-Kelenföld station), **Sopron** (every 2 hours direct, 2.5 hours, more with transfer at Budapest-Kelenföld), **Visegrád** (trains arrive at Nagymaros-Visegrád station, across the river—take shuttle boat to Visegrád; 1-2/hour, 40 minutes, from Budapest's Nyugati/Western station; a few slower but direct connections from Keleti/Eastern station), **Esztergom** (hourly, 1.5 hours, usually from Budapest's Nyugati/Western station; but Esztergom's train station is far from the basilica, making the bus—described later—a better option), **Kecskemét** (hourly, 1.5 hours), **Szeged** (hourly, 2.5 hours).

Bratislava (Pozsony in Hungarian, every 1-2 hours, 3 hours; more with changes); Vienna (Bécs in Hungarian, nearly hourly direct on express Railjet, 2.5 hours; more with changes), **Prague** (5/day direct, 7 hours, more with change in Vienna; plus 1 night train, 8.5 hours), **Kraków** (2/day, 10-11 hours, change in Katowice, Poland, and Břeclav, Czech Republic or Nové Zámky, Slovakia; plus night train, 11 hours), **Zagreb** (2/day direct, 6.5 hours), **Ljubljana** (1/day direct, 9 hours, other connections possible with 1-2 changes but complicated, no convenient night train), **Cluj-Napoca** (hub for Transylvania in Romania, 1/day direct, 7.5 hours), **Munich** (5/day by express RailJet, 7 hours, additional options with changes; 1 direct night train, 9.5 hours), **Berlin** (1/day direct, 11.5 hours, more with 1-3 changes; 1 night train, 13.5 hours).

BY BUS

Buses can be relatively inexpensive, but are typically slower and less convenient than trains. The only bus you you're likely to take is the one to **Eger** (2/hour, 2 hours), which leaves from the Stadionok bus station (at the M2/Métró red line stop of the same name). You can search bus schedules at the (Hungarian-only) website www.menetrendek.hu.

BY PLANE

For information about Budapest's Liszt Ferenc Airport, see "Arrival in Budapest—By Plane" on page 552.

ROUTE TIPS FOR DRIVERS

For pointers on driving into (and parking in) Budapest, see "Arrival in Budapest—By Car" on page 553. Remember, to use Hungary's expressways, you'll need to buy a toll sticker (see page 1098). To get out of town, here are some pointers.

To Eger and Other Points East: Head out of the city center on Andrássy út, circling behind Heroes' Square to access Kós Károly sétány through the middle of City Park. You'll pass Széchenyi Baths on the left, then (exiting the park) go over the Hungária körút ring road, before getting on M-3. This expressway zips you conveniently to Eger (exit #114 for Füzesabony; go north on road 33, then follow road 3, then road 25 into Eger).

To Bratislava, Vienna, and Other Points West: From central Pest, head over the Danube on the white, modern Elisabeth Bridge (Erzsébet híd). Once in Buda, the road becomes Hegyalja út; simply follow *Bécs-Wien* signs to get on M-1.

BY BOAT

In the summer, Mahart runs high-speed hydrofoils up the Danube to **Vienna.** It's not particularly scenic, and it's slower than the train, but it's a fun alternative for nautical types. The boat leaves Budapest at 9:00 and arrives in Vienna at 15:30; on the return trip, a boat leaves from Vienna at 9:00 and reaches Budapest at 14:30 (mid-May-Sept only, departs from Budapest Tue, Thu, and Sat; from Vienna Wed, Fri, and Sun). The trip costs €99 one-way between Budapest and Vienna (or €109 the other direction). To confirm times and prices, and to buy tickets, contact Mahart in Budapest (tel. 1/484-4010, www.mahartpassnave.hu) or DDSG Blue Danube in Vienna (Austrian tel. 01/58880, www.ddsg-blue-danube.at).

EGER

Eger (EH-gehr) is a county-seat town in northern Hungary, with about 60,000 people and a thriving teacher-training college. While you've probably never heard of Eger, the town has various claims to fame among Hungarians. Its powerful bishops have graced it with gorgeous churches. It has some of the best and most beloved spas in this hot-water-crazy country (including the excellent Salt Hill Thermal Spa in the nearby countryside). And, perhaps most of all, Eger makes Hungarians proud as the town that, against all odds, successfully held off the Ottoman advance into Europe in 1552. This stirring history makes Eger a field-trip mecca for Hungarian school kids. If the town is known internationally for anything, it's for the surrounding wine region (its best-known red wine is Bull's Blood, or Egri Bikavér).

And yet, refreshingly, enchanting Eger remains mostly off the tourist trail. Egerites go about their daily routines amidst lovely Baroque buildings, watched over by one of Hungary's most important castles. Everything in Eger is painted with vibrant colors, and even the communist apartment blocks seem quaint. The sights are few but fun, the ambience is great, and strolling is a must. It all comes together to make Eger an ideal introduction to small-town Hungary.

Eger

To Firefighters Museum

LENKEY J. U.
KOVÁCS J. U.
KNEZICH KÁROLY
DAJKA G. U.
VÉCSEY SÁNDOR U.
WAXWORKS
GOTHIC COURTYARD
CHURCH RUINS
HOSPITAL
MARKET HALL
MINARET
CASTLE
3D MOVIE
GÁRDONYI'S GRAVE
TICKETS
POST
CSIKY SÁNDOR U.
MACZKY V.
ZALÁR U.
DR. SÁNDOR MÁRKHOTH
KEPES INSTITUTE
BRÓDY SÁNDOR U.
ISTVÁN DOBÓ STATUE
Dobó Square
DOBÓ U.
DR. HIBAY K. U.
SYNAGOGUE GALLERY
MEKCSEY U.
ALMAGYAR
GÓLYA U.
SZENT JÁNOS U.
TOWN HALL
MINORITE CHURCH
FOGLÁR U.
SZÉCHENYI UTCA
ÉRSEK U.
JÓKAI U.
KOSSUTH LAJOS U.
ESZPERANTÓ SÉTÁNY
ARCHBISHOP'S PALACE
Bus Station
BAJ. ZSIL
BÁRKÓCZY U.
TÖRVÉNYHÁZ U.
CATHEDRAL
LYCEUM (CAMERA OBSCURA)
TÁRKÁNYI B. U.
ÉGÉSZSÉGHÁZ U.
SWIMMING POOL BY MAKOVECZ
TURKISH BATHS
FÜRDŐ U.
To Egerszalók & Sirens' Valley
TELEKESSY U.
ARANY JÁNOS U.
SÓHÁZ U.
SZVORÉNYI ÚT
GÁRDONYI SZINHÁZ (THEATER)
DEÁK FERENC
SZÁLLODA U.
KLAPKA GY. U.
Eger Creek
Bishop's Park (Érsekkert)
THERMAL BATHS
CSÁKÁNY U.
STADION U.
To Train Station

N

100 Meters
100 Yards

❶ Senator Ház Hotel & Rest.
❷ Imola Udvarház Rooms
❸ Offi Ház Hotel
❹ Szent János Hotel
❺ Dobó Vendégház Rooms
❻ HBH Restaurant
❼ Palacsintavár Rest.
❽ Szantofer Vendéglő Rest.
❾ Dobós Cukrászda Pastries
❿ Sárvári Cukrászda Pastries
⓫ Kürtőskalács Window
⓬ Bikavér Borház Wine Shop
⓭ Hist. Exhibition of Weapons
⓮ Palóc Folklore Museum
⓯ Town Under the Town
⓰ Castle Entrance

PLANNING YOUR TIME

Mellow Eger is a fine side-trip from Budapest. It's a doable round-trip in a single day (about two hours by train or bus each way), but it's much more satisfying and relaxing to spend the night.

A perfect day in Eger begins with a browse through the very colorful market and a low-key ramble on the castle ramparts. Then head to the college building called the Lyceum to visit its library and astronomy museum, and climb up to the thrillingly low-tech camera obscura. Take in the midday organ concert in the cathedral across the street from the Lyceum (mid-May-mid-Oct only). In the afternoon, unwind on the square or, better yet, at a thermal bath (in Eger, or at the Salt Hill Thermal Spa in nearby Egerszalók). If you need more to do, consider a drive into the countryside (including visits to local vintners—get details at TI). Round out your day with dinner on Little Dobó Square, or a visit to Eger's touristy wine caves in the Sirens' Valley.

In July and August (when Hungarians prefer to go to Lake Balaton), Eger is busy with international visitors; in September and October, around the wine harvest, most of the tourists are Hungarians.

Orientation to Eger

Eger Castle sits at the top of the town, hovering over Dobó Square (Dobó István tér). This main square is divided in half by Eger Creek, which bisects the town. Two blocks west of Dobó Square is the main pedestrian drag, Széchenyi utca, where you'll find the Lyceum and the cathedral. A few blocks due south from the castle (along Eger Creek) is Eger's thermal baths complex.

TOURIST INFORMATION

Eger's TI (TourInform) offers a town map, as well as piles of brochures about the city and region. They can help you find a room and are eager to answer your questions (mid-June-mid-Sept Mon-Fri 9:00-18:00, Sat-Sun until 13:00; mid-Sept-mid-June Mon-Fri 9:00-17:00, Sat until 13:00, closed Sun; Bajcsy-Zsilinszky utca 9, tel. 36/517-715, www.eger.hu).

ARRIVAL IN EGER

By Train: Eger's tiny train station is a 20-minute walk south of the center. The baggage-deposit desk is out along the platform by track 1, between the WCs (daily 7:00-19:00, attendant often waits in the adjacent *büfé*). For those in need of Hungarian cash, the closest ATM is at the Spar grocery store just up the street (turn left out of station, walk about 100 yards, and look for red-and-white supermarket on your right; the ATM is next to the main door, around front).

Taxis generally wait out front to take new arrivals into town (1,000-1,200 Ft). Even in little Eger, it's always best to take a taxi marked with a company name and number.

To catch the **bus** toward the center, go a block straight out of the station. Buses #11, #12, and #14 cut about 10 minutes off the walk into town (tickets are 300 Ft from driver or 240 Ft at train station newsstand facing track 1—ask for *helyijárat buszjegy*). Get off the bus when you reach the big yellow cathedral.

To **walk** all the way, leave the station straight ahead, walk one block, take the hard right turn with the road, and then continue straight (on busy Deák Ferenc utca) about 10 minutes until you run into the cathedral. With your back to the cathedral entry, the main square is two blocks ahead of you, then a block to the left.

By Car: In this small town, most hotels will provide parking or help you find a lot. For a short visit, the most central lots are behind the department store on Dobó Square, or in the square surrounding the Lyceum.

GETTING AROUND EGER

Everything of interest in Eger is within walking distance. But a taxi can be helpful to reach outlying sights, including the Sirens' Valley wine caves and the Salt Hill Thermal Spa in Egerszalók (taxi meter starts at 330 Ft, then around 280 Ft/km; try City Taxi, tel. 36/555-555, toll-free tel. 0680-622-622).

HELPFUL HINTS

Exchange Rate: 275 Ft = about $1, €1 = about $1.10

Country Calling Code: 36 (see page 1086 for dialing instructions).

Blue Monday: Note that the castle museums and the Kepes Institute are closed on Mondays, and the Lyceum is open on Monday only from May to August. But even on Mondays you can visit the cathedral (and enjoy its organ concert), swim in the thermal bath, explore the market, see the castle grounds, and enjoy the local wine.

Organ Concert: Daily from May through September, Hungary's second-biggest organ booms out a glorious 30-minute concert in the cathedral (800 Ft, Mon-Sat at 11:30, Sun at 12:45).

Tourist Train: A variety of hokey little tourist trains leave the main square regularly (at least at the top of each hour, and often at other times when it's busy). These trains do a 50-minute circuit around town, including a spin past the Sirens' Valley wine caves.

Sights in Eger

DOBÓ SQUARE AND DOBÓ UTCA

▲▲Dobó Square (Dobó István Tér)

Dobó Square is the heart of Eger. In most towns this striking, the main square is packed with postcard stalls and other tourist

traps. Refreshingly, Eger's square seems mostly packed with Egerites. Ringed by pretty Baroque buildings and watched over by Eger's historic castle, this square is one of the most pleasant spots in Hungary.

The statue in the middle is **István Dobó** (EESHT-vahn DOH-boh), the square's namesake and Eger's greatest hero, who defended the city—and all of Hungary—from an Ottoman invasion in 1552 (see his story in the sidebar). Next to Dobó is his co-commander, István Mekcsey. And right at their side is one of the brave women of Eger—depicted here throwing a pot down onto the attackers.

Dominating the square is the exquisitely photogenic **Minorite Church**—often said to be the most beautiful Baroque church in Hungary. The shabby interior is less interesting, but has some appealing details (free entry, daily 9:30-17:30). Notice that each of the hand-carved wooden pews has a different motif. Pay close attention to the side altars that flank the nave: The first set (left and right) are 3-D illustrations, painted to replicate the wood altars that burned in a fire; the next set are real. And look-ing up at the faded ceiling frescoes, you'll see (in the second one from the entrance) the church's patron: St. An-

thony of Padua, who's preaching God's word to the fishes after the townspeople refused to hear him. The green, arcaded building to the right of the Minorite Church is the Town Hall, next to an old-fashioned pharmacy.

Use the square to orient yourself to the town. Behind the stat-ue of Dobó is a bridge over the stream that bisects the city. Just be-fore you reach that bridge, look to the left and you'll see the north-ernmost Ottoman **minaret** in Europe—once part of a mosque, it's now a tourist attraction. Across the bridge is the charming **Little**

István Dobó and the Siege of Eger

In the 16th century, Ottoman invaders swept into Hungary. They easily defeated a Hungarian army—in just two hours—at the Battle of Mohács in 1526.

When Buda and Pest fell to the Ottomans in 1541, all of Europe looked to Eger as the last line of defense. István Dobó

and his second-in-command, István Mekcsey, were put in charge of Eger's forces. They prepared the castle (which still overlooks the square) for a siege and waited.

On September 11, 1552—after a summer spent conquering more than 30 other Hungarian fortresses on their march northward—40,000 Ottomans arrived in Eger. Only about 2,000 Egerites (soldiers, their wives, and their children) remained to protect their town. The Ottomans expected an easy victory, but the siege dragged on for 39 days. Eger's soldiers fought valiantly, and the women of Eger also joined the fray, pouring hot tar down on the Ottomans...everyone pitched in. A Hungarian officer named Gergely Bornemissza, sent to reinforce the people of Eger, startled the Ottomans with all manner of clever and deadly explosives. One of his brilliant inventions was a "fire wheel"—a barrel of gunpowder studded with smaller jars of explosives, which they'd light and send rolling downhill to wreak havoc until the final, deadly explosion. Ultimately, the Ottomans left in shame, Eger was saved, and Dobó was a national hero.

The unfortunate epilogue: The Ottomans came back in 1596 and, this time, succeeded in conquering an Eger castle guarded by unmotivated mercenaries. The Ottomans sacked the town and then controlled the region for close to a century.

In 1897, a castle archaeologist named Géza Gárdonyi moved from Budapest to Eger, where tales of the siege captured his imagination. Gárdonyi wrote a book about István Dobó and the 1552 Siege of Eger called *Egri Csillagok* ("Stars of Eger," translated into English as *Eclipse of the Crescent Moon,* available at local bookstores and souvenir stands). The book—a favorite of many Hungarians—is taught in schools, keeping the legend of Eger's heroes alive today.

EGER

Dobó Square (Kis-Dobó tér), home to the town's best hotels, its outdoor dining zone, and a handy and atmospheric opportunity to sample local wines at the Bikavér Borház wine shop (see page 691). Hovering above Little Dobó Square is Eger Castle; to get there, hang a right at the Senator Ház Hotel and go up Dobó utca. (All of these places are described later in more detail.)

Now face the opposite direction, with the castle at your back. On your right is a handy supermarket (with an ATM by the door). At the bottom end of this square, various pedestrian shopping lanes lead straight ahead two short blocks to Eger's main "walking street," Széchenyi utca (with the cathedral and the Lyceum at its left end).

▲Dobó Utca

This street, which leads from Little Dobó Square to the entrance of the castle, is lined with colorful shops and attractions. You'll encounter these sights in the following order from the main square (begin by heading up the street to the right of Senator Ház Hotel):

The **antique shop** (Régiségbolt, at #24) is worth a peek. If musty old things from the communist era—a painting of Lenin or a classic old radio—are cluttering your attic, you can sell them here.

The **wine-tasting courtyard** (#18) features a different local winery each week from May through October. Pop into the brightly lit, vaulted tasting room in the back to try a glass.

A few steps down Fazola Henrik (on the right), the **Historical Exhibition of Weapons** (Történi Tárház) features centuries of Eger armaments: clubs, rifles, and everything in between (closed Mon).

The **Palóc Folklore Museum** (#12) displays a handful of traditional tools, textiles, ceramics, costumes, and pieces of furniture (closed Mon and likely closed Oct-April; no English information).

▲EGER CASTLE (EGRI VÁR)

The great St. István—Hungary's first Christian king—founded a church on this hill a thousand years ago. The church was destroyed by Tatars in the 13th century, and this fortress was built to repel another attack. Most importantly, this castle is Hungary's Alamo, where István Dobó defended Eger from the Ottomans in 1552—as depicted in the relief just outside the entry gate. These days, it's usually crawling with field-tripping school-

EGER

children from all over the country. (Every Hungarian sixth grader reads *Eclipse of the Crescent Moon,* which thrillingly recounts the heroic siege of Eger.) For those of us who didn't grow up hearing the legend of István Dobó, the complex is hard to appreciate, and English information is sparse. Most visitors find that the most rewarding plan is simply to stroll up, wander the grounds, play "king of the castle" along the ramparts, and enjoy the sweeping views over Eger's rooftops.

Cost and Hours: While an 800-Ft "walking ticket" gets you into the castle grounds only, the 1,600-Ft ticket includes the big castle sights (history museum, art gallery, casements tour). The castle grounds are open daily (May-Sept 8:00-21:00, mid-March-April and Oct until 18:00, Nov-mid-March until 17:00). The castle museums have shorter hours (May-Sept Tue-Sun 10:00-18:00, Oct-April Tue-Sun until 16:00, closed Mon year-round).

Casements Tours: The underground casements and Heroes' Hall are only accessible by a one-hour tour in Hungarian (included in ticket price, tours depart frequently in summer, sporadically off-season).

Information: Tel. 36/312-744, www.egrivar.hu.

Getting There: To reach the castle from Dobó Square, cross the bridge toward Senator Ház Hotel, then jog right around the hotel, turning right onto Dobó utca (with its own set of attractions, described earlier). Take this street a few blocks until it swings down to the right; the ramp up to the castle is on your left.

Visiting the Castle: Buy your ticket at the lower gate, then hike up the entry ramp and through the inner gate into the main courtyard—with grassy fields, souvenir stands, and easy access to the ramparts. Straight ahead—through the corridor with the little information window—is a pink, Gothic-style courtyard, which contains two small museums. The **history museum** (in the top floor of the main building) is the best of its kind in town, with lots of artifacts and good English descriptions. The **picture gallery** (top floor of building to the left as you enter the courtyard) is worth a few minutes, with paintings giving you a look at traditional life in Hungary.

Exploring the **grounds,** you'll see the remains of a once-grand cathedral and a smaller rotunda dating from the days of St. István (10th or 11th century; at the far-right corner as you enter). The underground **casements** (tunnels through the castle walls, which include the Heroes' Hall with the symbolic grave of István Dobó) are accessible only by guided tour, but you can dip into the **dungeon** anytime with the museum ticket (to the left as you enter).

The *Eger 1552* **3-D movie** offers a fun little lesson in the town's history. Appropriately low-budget for this small town, the 10-minute film's graphics are closer to a retro video game than a blockbuster, but it does a fine job of re-creating the medieval townscape.

Other Castle Sights: The castle hosts a few privately run exhibits (with sporadic hours and prices).

The **waxworks,** or "Panoptikum" (500 Ft, daily April-Oct 9:00-17:00, shorter hours off-season; at far-left corner as you

enter)—while kind of silly—is fun for kids or those who never really grew up. Think of it as a very low-tech, walk-through *Ottomans of the Caribbean*. You'll see a handful of eerily realistic heroes and villains from the siege of Eger (including István Dobó himself and the leader of the Ottomans sitting in his colorful tent). Notice the exaggerated Central Asian features of the Egerites—a reminder that the Magyars were more Asian than European. A visit to the waxworks also lets you scramble through a segment of the tunnels that run inside the castle walls (a plus since it's not really worth it to wait around through the similar, Hungarian-language casements tour).

Additional sights include an **archery** exhibit (in summer, look for archers just to the right of the Gothic courtyard, and pay them for the chance to shoot old-fashioned bows and crossbows); and **temporary exhibits** in the ground floor of the Gothic courtyard. The castle also has a **café** and a **1552 Restaurant.**

ON SZÉCHENYI UTCA
▲▲Lyceum (Líceum)
In the mid-18th century, Bishop Károly Eszterházy wanted a university in Eger, but Habsburg Emperor Josef II refused to allow it.

Instead, Eszterházy built the most impressive teacher-training college on the planet, and stocked it with the best books and astronomical equipment that money could buy. The Lyceum still trains local teachers (enrollment: about 2,000). Tourists also roam the halls of the Lyceum; they come to visit its classic old library and its astronomy museum, which has a fascinating camera obscura. The library and museum are tucked away in the big, confusing building.

Cost and Hours: Library-800 Ft, museum-1,000 Ft; both open May-Aug daily 9:30-17:30; mid-March-April and Sept-Oct Tue-Sun 9:30-15:30, closed Mon; Nov-mid-March Tue-Sun 9:30-

EGER

13:30, closed Mon; Eszterházy tér 1, at south end of Széchenyi utca at intersection with Kossuth utca, enter through main door across from cathedral and buy tickets just inside and to the left.

Visiting the Lyceum: First, visit the old-fashioned **library** one floor up (from the main entry hall, cut through the middle of the courtyard, go up the stairs to the next floor, and look for Room 223, marked *Bibliothek*—it's on the right side of the complex as you face it from the entrance). This library houses 60,000 books (here and in the two adjoining rooms, with several stacked two deep). Dr. Erzsébet Löffler and her staff have spent the last decade cataloging these books. This is no easy task, since they're in over 30 languages—from Thai to Tagalog—and are shelved according to size, rather than topic. Only one percent of the books are in Hungarian—but half of them are in Latin. The ticket-taker can give you an English information sheet highlighting the collection's most prized pieces. The shelves are adorned with golden seals depicting some of the great minds of science, philosophy, and religion. Marvel at the gorgeous ceiling fresco, dating from 1778. To thank the patron of this museum, say *köszönöm* to the guy in the second row up, to the right of the podium (above the entry door, second from left, not wearing a hat)—that's Bishop Károly Eszterházy.

Turn right as you leave the library to find the staircase that leads up the **Astronomical Tower** (*Varázstorony*, follow signs several flights up) to the **Astronomical Museum.** Some dusty old stargazing instruments occupy one room, as well as a meridian line in the floor (a dot of sunlight dances along this line each day around noon). Across the hall is a fun, interactive **magic room,** where you can try out scientific experiments—such as using air pressure to make a ball levitate or sending a mini "hot-air balloon" up to the ceiling.

A few more flights up is the Lyceum's treasured **camera obscura**—one of just two originals surviving in Europe (the other is in Edinburgh). You'll enter a dark room and gather around a big, bowl-like canvas, where the guide will fly you around the streets of Eger (presentations about 2/hour, maybe more when busy). Fun as it is today, this camera must have astonished viewers when it was built in 1776—well before anyone had seen "moving pictures." It's a bit of a huff to get up here (nine flights of stairs, 302 steps)—but the camera obscura, and the actual view of Eger from the outdoor terrace just outside, are worth it.

▲▲Eger Cathedral

Eger's 19th-century bishops peppered the city with beautiful buildings, including the second-biggest church in Hungary. With

a quirky, sumptuous, Baroque-feeling interior, Eger's cathedral is well worth a visit.

Cost and Hours: 300-Ft donation requested (but you must buy ticket if visiting before an organ concert in the high season, 11:00-12:00), open Mon-Sat 8:30-18:00, Sun 13:00-18:00. The cathedral is the big, can't-miss-it yellow building at Pyrker János tér 1, facing the start of Széchenyi utca.

Visiting the Cathedral: Eger Cathedral was built in the 1830s by an Austrian archbishop who had previously served in Venice, and who thought Eger could use a little more class. The colonnaded Neoclassical **facade,** painted a pretty Habsburg yellow, boasts some fine Italian sculpture. As you walk up the main stairs, you'll pass Sts. István and László—Hungary's first two Christian kings—and then the Apostles Peter and Paul.

Enter the cathedral and walk to the first collection box, near the start of the nave. Then, turning back to face the door, look up at the ornate **ceiling fresco:**
On the left, it shows Hungarians in traditional dress; and on the right, the country's most important historical figures. At the bottom, you see this cathedral, celestially connected with St. Peter's in Rome (opposite). This symbol of devotion to the Vatican was a brave statement when it was

painted in 1950. The communists were closing churches in other small Hungarian towns, but the Eger archbishop had enough clout to keep this one open.

Continue to the transept, stopping directly underneath the main dome. The **stained-glass windows** decorating the north and south transepts were donated to the cathedral by a rich Austrian couple to commemorate the 1,000th anniversary of Hungary's conversion to Christianity—notice the dates: 1000 (when St. István converted the Magyars to Christianity), and 2000.

As you leave, notice the enormous **organ**—Hungary's second-largest—above the door. In the summer, try to catch one of the cathedral's daily half-hour organ concerts (800 Ft, May-Sept Mon-Sat at 11:30, Sun at 12:45, no concerts off-season).

Near the back-right corner, look for the statue of **Szent Rita,** a local favorite; the votive plaques that say *köszönöm* and *hálából* are offering "thanks" and "gratitude" for prayers answered.

Nearby: If you walk up Széchenyi utca from here, you'll see the fancy **Archbishop's Palace** on your left—still home to Eger's archbishop.

Just to the right of the steps leading up to the cathedral is the entrance to the **Town Under the Town** (Város a Város Alatt), a 45-minute guided tour of the archbishop's former wine-cellar network (1,000 Ft, generally departs at the top of each hour—schedule posted at door, 5-person minimum, you'll get a little English sprinkled in with the Hungarian; daily April-Sept 9:00-18:00, Oct-March until 17:00—these are last tour times, tel. 20/961-4019, www.varosavarosalatt.hu).

NORTH OF DOBÓ SQUARE
▲Market Hall (Piaccsarnok)

Wandering Eger's big indoor market will give you a taste of local life—and maybe some samples of local food, too. This ramshackle hall is a totally untouristy scene, with ugly plastic tubs piled high with an abundance of fresh local produce. Tomatoes and peppers of all colors and sizes are plentiful—magic ingredients that give Hungarian food its kick.

Hours: Opens daily at 6:00; while open weekday afternoons, it's best in the mornings.

Minaret

Once part of a mosque, this slender, 130-foot-tall minaret represents the century of Ottoman rule that left its mark on Eger and all of Hungary. The little cross at the top symbolizes the eventual Christian victory over Hungary's Ottoman invaders. You can climb the minaret's 97 steps for fine views of Eger, but it's not for those scared of heights or enclosed spaces. Because the staircase was designed for one man to climb to call the community to prayer, it's very tight. To avoid human traffic jams, they allow groups of visitors in about twice an hour.

EGER

Cost and Hours: 300 Ft, daily May-Sept 10:00-18:00, April and Oct until 17:00, closed Nov-March; if it's locked, ask around for the key.

Experiences in Eger

AQUA EGER

Swimming and water sports are as important to Egerites as good wine. They're proud that many of Hungary's Olympic medalists in aquatic events have come from the surrounding county. The men's water polo team took the gold for Hungary at three Olympiads in a row (2000-2008), Katinka Hosszú shattered records at the Rio games in 2016, and speed swimmer László Cseh spent much of his career winning silver medals just behind Michael Phelps. The town's Bitskey Aladár swimming pool—arguably the most striking building in this part of Hungary—is practically a temple to water sports.

Eger also has several appealing thermal bath complexes: one right in town, and two more a few miles away (near the village of Egerszalók). Budapest offers classier bath experiences, but the Eger options are more modern and a bit more accessible, and allow you to save your Budapest time for big-city sights. Before you go, be sure to read the "Taking the Waters" section in the Budapest chapter.

Baths and Pools in Eger

Note that you can't rent a swimsuit or a towel at either of these places; bring both with you, along with shower sandals for the locker room (if you've got them).

Bitskey Aladár Pool

This striking swimming pool was designed by Imre Makovecz, the father of Hungary's Organic architectural style. Some Eger tax-

payers resented the pool's big price tag, but it left the city with a truly distinctive building befitting its love of water sports. You don't need to be an architecture student to know that the pool is special. It's worth the five-minute walk from Dobó Square just to take a look. Oh, and you can swim in it, too.

Cost and Hours: 1,050 Ft, Mon-Fri 6:00-21:00, Sat-Sun 7:30-18:00, follow Eger Creek south from Dobó Square to Frank Tivadar utca, tel. 36/511-810, www.egertermal.hu.

▲Eger Thermal Bath (Eger Thermálfürdő)

For a refreshing break from the sightseeing grind, consider a splash at the spa. This is a fine opportunity to try a Hungarian bath: relatively accessible (men and women are clothed and together most of the time), but frequented mostly by locals.

Cost and Hours: 1,900 Ft (cheaper Mon-Fri after 16:00), 1,300 Ft extra gives you access to sauna and Turkish bath for two hours; June-Aug Mon-Wed 8:30-19:00, Thu-Fri 8:30-21:00, Sat 8:00-21:00, Sun 8:00-19:00; May and Sept Sun-Wed 9:00-19:00, Thu-Sat 9:00-21:00; Oct-April daily 9:00-19:00; Petőfi tér 2, tel. 36/510-558, www.egertermal.hu.

Getting There: It's easy to reach and within a 10-minute walk of most hotels. From Dobó Square, follow the stream four blocks south (look for signs for *Strand*), then into a park; halfway through the park, look for the bath's entrance on your left, over a bridge.

Entry Procedure: After you pay, show your wristband to an attendant to get a key to a locker (1,000-Ft deposit per key; private changing cabins available in the locker room for no extra charge). Change, stow your stuff, and join the fun.

Taking the Waters: There's a sprawling array of different pools, each one thoughtfully described in English and labeled with its depth and temperature. The best part is the green-domed, indoor-outdoor adventure bath, right at the side entrance. Its cascades, jets, bubbles, geysers, and powerful current pool will make you feel like a kid again. Exploring the complex, you'll also find big and small warm pools, a very hot sulfur pool (where Egerites sit peacefully, ignore the slight stink, and supposedly feel their arthritis ebb away), a kids' pool with splashy-slide fun, and a lap pool (some of these are closed off-season).

Turkish Bath: Eger's recently refurbished Turkish-style bath is closer to the main entrance (to the left as you face the main gate; you can't enter directly from the main part of the bath). It costs 1,300 Ft in combination with the main bath, or 2,200 Ft by itself (Mon-Tue 16:30-21:00, Wed-Thu 15:00-21:00, Fri 13:00-21:00, Sat-Sun 9:00-21:00).

Baths near Eger, in Egerszálok

Two more thermal baths—Salt Hill and Demjén—sit in the countryside outside of Eger, flanking a rocky hill between the villages of Egerszálok and Demjén. While these baths lack the old-fashioned

Hungary's Organic Architecture

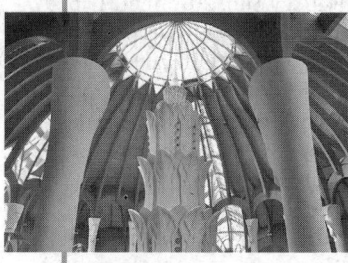

Hungary's postcommunist generation has embraced a unique, eye-catching style of architecture, called Organic, which was developed and championed by Imre Makovecz (1935-2011).

As a young architect, Makovecz pursued a flowing style that was quite intentionally at odds with the rigid right angles of communist architecture. He was inspired by the Hungarian Art Nouveau of a bygone and "decadent" Golden Age, and by pioneering Organic architects from other countries (including American Frank Lloyd Wright, who employed a more angular style but a similar aesthetic of making sure his works fit their surroundings).

After being blacklisted by the regime for his stubborn adherence to his architectural vision—and for his nationalistic politics—Makovecz ramped up his pursuit of something new. Because the authorities denied him access to modern building supplies, Makovecz made do with sticks, rocks, and other foraged building materials. He was also inspired by Transylvanian village architecture: whitewashed walls with large, overhanging mansard roofs to maximize attic space (resembling a big mushroom).

After the fall of the regime, Makovecz swiftly became Hungary's premier architect, but he still kept things simple. He believed that a building should be a product of its environment, rather than a cookie-cutter copy. Organic buildings use indigenous materials (especially wood) and take on unusual forms—often inspired by animals or plants—that blend in with the landscape. Organic buildings look like they're rising up out of the ground, rather than plopped down on top of it. You generally won't find this back-to-nature style in big cities like Budapest; Makovecz preferred to work in small communities such as Eger (see photo on page 687) instead of working for large corporations. Makovecz wanted his creations—from churches, thermal baths, and campgrounds to cultural centers, restaurants, and bus stations—to represent the civic pride of the local community. For more on Makovecz, visit www.makovecz.hu.

EGER

class of the Budapest options, they more than compensate with soggy fun.

Getting There: Both baths are about a mile outside the village of Egerszalók, which is itself about three miles from Eger. You can take a public **bus** from Eger's bus station to the baths (take bus going toward Demjén; for Salt Hill, get off at the *Egerszalók*

Gyógyfürdő stop—tell the bus driver "EH-gehr-sah-lohk FEWR-dur"—just after leaving the town of Egerszalók; for the Demjén Baths, get off at the entrance to Demjén village and walk back to the baths; bus runs 9/day Mon-Sat, only 4/day Sun, 20-minute trip, 400 Ft). Check the return bus information carefully (especially on weekends, when frequency plummets). Or you can take a **taxi** from Eger (about 3,000 Ft; tel. 36/555-555 for a return taxi from Egerszalók). Here's a fun and very hedonistic afternoon plan: Take the bus or taxi to the spa, taxi back to Eger's Sirens' Valley for some wine-cave hopping, then taxi back to your Eger hotel.

Nearby Wineries: The village of Egerszalók has several fine wineries, including the excellent **St. Andrea**—fun to combine with your bath visit. For details, see page 691.

▲▲Salt Hill Thermal Spa (at the Saliris Resort)

For decades, Egerites would come to this "salt hill" (a natural terraced formation caused by mineral-rich spring water running down the hillside) in the middle of nowhere and cram together to baste in pools of hot water. Then the developers arrived. Today, the gigantic Saliris Resort hotel and spa complex has been built near those original formations. With 12 indoor pools and five outdoor ones—many cleverly overlapping one another on several levels—these cutting-edge baths are worth the trip outside

of Eger. Take some time to explore the sprawling complex. Everything is labeled in English, and each pool is clearly marked with the depth and temperature. This complex uses the same system as at Eger's thermal baths: Press your wristband against a computer screen to be assigned a locker, change in the private cabin, then have fun.

Cost and Hours: 4,500 Ft all day, 2,100 Ft for up to 3 hours, all ticket prices are 1,000 Ft extra on busy "special days." You'll pay 1,500 Ft extra to access "sauna world," with five different saunas. Towel rental, massage, and other treatments are also available. Open June-Aug daily 10:00-20:00, likely shorter hours off-season—call ahead to check; tel. 36/688-500, http://salirisresort.hu.

Demjén Thermal Baths (Demjéni Termál Völgy)

Just over the hill from Salt Hill Thermal Spa, Demjén Baths is a less glitzy complex of nicely rustic wooden buildings and pools that are similarly nestled in hills (minus the terrace formations). Thanks to its low prices and long hours, these baths attract more locals. It also offers fewer amusements: Jets, fountains, and other "adventure bath"-type features are rare, and the goal here is simply stewing in pools of warm water. (The Aquapark section—open only in summer—does have waterslides and a diving pool, for an extra charge.) You'll pay, change in a cabin in the shared locker rooms, ask the attendant to assign you a locker (she'll tell you to remember your number, which you'll need to tell her when you're ready for her to unlock it for you), then go soak.

Cost and Hours: 1,700 Ft, plus 1,400 Ft for a "wellness" ticket that adds more saunas and spas, daily 9:00-24:00; Aquapark costs 1,900 Ft extra and open summers only until 20:00; mobile +3630-853-7419, www.demjengyogytermal.hu.

EGER WINE

Eger is at the heart of one of Hungary's best-known wine regions, internationally famous for its **Bull's Blood** (Egri Bikavér). You'll likely hear various stories as to how Bull's Blood got its name during the Ottoman siege of Eger. My favorite version: The Ottomans were amazed at the ferocity displayed by the Egerites, and wondered what they were drinking that boiled their blood and stained their beards so red...it must be potent stuff. Local merchants, knowing that the Ottomans were Muslim and couldn't drink alcohol, told them it was bull's blood. The merchants made a buck, and the name stuck.

Creative as these stories are, they're all bunk—the term dates only from 1851. Egri Bikavér is a blend (everyone has their own recipe), so you generally won't find it at small producers. Cabernet sauvignon, merlot, *kékfrankos*, and *kékoportó* are the most commonly used grapes.

But Bull's Blood is just the beginning of what the Eger wine region offers. Although Eger is better known for its reds, 42 of the 62 regional varieties are white. (For details, see "Hungarian Wines" on page 534.)

Tasting Local Wine: While it would be enjoyable to drive around the Hungarian countryside visiting wineries (and I've recommended one great choice, **St. Andrea,** later), the most accessible way to get a quick taste of local wine is at a wine shop in town. I like the Kenyeres family's **Bikavér Borház,** right on Little Dobó Square (across from Senator Ház Hotel). In addition to a well-stocked (if slightly overpriced) wine shop, they have a wine bar with indoor and outdoor seating (six tastings and two cheeses for around 2,000

EGER

Ft, wine also sold by the glass, some English spoken, menu lists basic English description for each wine, daily 10:00-22:00, possibly later in busy times, Kis-Dobó tér 10, tel. 36/413-262).

Sirens' Valley (Szépasszony-völgy)

When the Ottoman invaders first occupied Eger, residents moved into the valley next door, living in caves dug into the hillside. Eventually the Ottomans were driven out, the Egerites moved back to town, and the caves became wine cellars. (Most Eger families who can afford it have at least a modest vineyard in the countryside.) There are more than 300 such caves in the valley to the southwest of Eger, several of which are open for visitors.

The best selection of these caves (about 50) is in the Sirens' Valley (sometimes also translated as "Valley of the Beautiful Women"—or, on local directional signs, the less poetic "Nice Woman Valley"). While the valley can feel vacant and dead (even sometimes in the summer), if you visit when it's busy it can be a fun scene—locals showing off their latest vintage, with picnic tables and tipsy tourists spilling out into the street. At some places, you'll be offered free samples; others have a menu for tastes or glasses of wine. While you're not expected to buy a bottle, it's a nice gesture to buy one if you've spent a while at one cave (and it's usually very cheap). Most caves offer something light to eat with the wine, and you'll also see lots of independent, full-service restaurants. Some of the caves are fancy and finished, staffed by multilingual waiters in period costume. Others feel like a dank basement, with grandpa leaning on his moped out front and a monolingual granny pouring the wine inside. (The really local places—where the decor is cement, bottles don't have labels, and food consists of potato chips and buttered Wonder bread—can be the most fun.)

This experience is a strange mix of touristy and local, but not entirely accessible to non-Hungarian-speakers—it works best with a bunch of friends and an easygoing, sociable attitude. Hopping from cave to musky cave can make for an enjoyable evening, but be sure to wander around a bit to see the options before you dive in (cellars generally open 10:00-21:00 in summer, best June-Aug in the late afternoon and early evening, plus good-weather weekends in the shoulder season; it's sleepy and not worth a visit off-season, when only a handful of cellars remain open for shorter hours).

Getting to the Sirens' Valley: The valley is on the southwest outskirts of Eger. Figure no more than 1,000 Ft for a **taxi** between your hotel and the caves. During the summer, you can take a **tourist train** from Eger's main square to the caves (see "Helpful Hints" on page 678), then catch a later one back.

You can **walk** there in about 25 minutes: Leave the pedestrian zone on the street next to the cathedral (Törvényház utca), with the cathedral on your right-hand side. Take the first left just after the back end of the cathedral (onto Trinitárius utca), go one long block, then take the first right (onto Király utca). At the fork, bear to the left. You'll stay straight on this road—crossing busy Koháry István utca—for several blocks, passing through some nondescript residential areas (on Szépasszony-völgy utca). When you crest the hill and emerge from the houses, you'll see the caves (and tour buses) below you on the left—go left (downhill) at the fork to get there. First you'll come to a stretch of touristy restaurants; keep going past these, and eventually you'll see a big loop of caves on your left.

Wineries near the Baths in Egerszalók

The village of Egerszalók, near the Salt Hill and Demjén thermal baths (described earlier), has a variety of fun wineries. The most interesting, and well worth a visit for wine lovers, is **St. Andrea**. This slick, modern, Napa Valley-esque facility offers cellar tours and tastings of their excellent wines, which show up on fine restaurant menus across Hungary. They're evangelical both about their spirituality (hence the name) and their wine, and enjoy explaining everything in English. They make generous use of pinot noir grapes, and produce some good, pungent whites with volcanic qualities. While it may be possible to simply drop in for a tasting, it's better to call ahead and let them know you're coming (3,500 Ft/person, bottles for 2,500-5,500 Ft, Mon-Sat 10:00-18:00, closed Sun, Ady Endre út 88 in Egerszalók, mobile +3630-692-5860, www.standrea.hu). They also have a top-end wine bar in Budapest (see page 663). It's most practical with a car (or by taxi), but you can also walk there from the bus stop in Egerszalók's town center (about a half-mile; head down Ady Endre út, toward the baths).

Nightlife in Eger

Things quiet down pretty early in this sedate town. Youthful student bars and hangouts cluster along the main "walking street," Széchenyi utca (especially Fri and Sat nights). Older travelers feel more at home on Little Dobó Square, with schmaltzy live music until 21:00 or 22:00 in summer; the Bikavér Borház wine bar (described earlier) is the lively hub of activity here, and stays open later.

Sleeping in Eger

Eger is a good overnight stop. I've focused my listings on quaint, well-located hotels. Elevators are rare—expect to climb one or two flights of stairs to reach your room. Most of these hotels are in pedestrian zones, so get detailed driving and parking instructions

EGER

Sleep Code

Hotels are classified based on the average price of a standard double room with breakfast in high season. You can figure that €1 = about $1.10.

$$$$	**Splurge:** Most rooms over €170
$$$	**Pricier:** €130-170
$$	**Moderate:** €90-130
$	**Budget:** €50-90
¢	**Backpacker:** Under €50
RS%	**Rick Steves discount**

Unless otherwise noted, credit cards are accepted, hotel staff speak basic English, and free Wi-Fi is available. Comparison-shop by checking prices at several hotels (on each hotel's own website, on a booking site, or by email). For the best deal, *book directly with the hotel.* Ask for a discount if paying in cash; if the listing includes **RS%,** request a Rick Steves discount.

---

from your hotel; many offer free or cheap parking, but it's often a block or two away. Most hotels quote their rates in euros but prefer to be paid in forints.

$ Senator Ház Hotel is one of my favorite small, family-run hotels in Eastern Europe. Though the 11 rooms are a bit worn, this place is cozy and well-run by András and Csöpi Cseh and their right-hand man, Peter. With oodles of character, all the right quirks, and a picture-perfect location just under the castle on Little Dobó Square, it's a winner (RS%, air-con, Dobó István tér 11, tel. 36/411-711, www.senatorhaz.hu, info@senatorhaz.hu). The Cseh family also runs **$ Pátria Vendégház**— with two doubles and two luxurious apartments.

$ Imola Udvarház rents six spacious apartments—with kitchen, living room, bedroom, and bathroom—all decorated in modern Ikea style. They're pricey for this small town, but roomy and well-maintained, with a great location near the castle entrance. Their free on-site parking garage makes this a good choice for drivers (air-con, Tírodi Sebestyén tér 4, tel. 36/516-180, www. imolaudvarhaz.hu, info@imolaudvarhaz.hu).

$ Offi Ház Hotel shares Little Dobó Square with Senator Ház. Its five rooms are classy and romantic, but a bit tight, with slanted ceilings. Communication can be tricky (German helps), but the location is worth the hassle (air-con, Dobó István tér 5, tel.

36/518-210, www.offihaz.hu, offihaz@t-online.hu, Offenbächer family).

$ Szent János Hotel, less charming and more businesslike than the Senator Ház and Offi Ház, offers a good but less atmospheric location, 13 straitlaced rooms, and a pleasant winter garden to relax in. Choose between the newly renovated rooms, which face a busy pedestrian street and can be noisy on weekend nights, or the still-good older rooms, which face the quieter back side—both for the same price (air-con, a long block off Dobó Square at Szent János utca 3, tel. 36/510-350, www.hotelszentjanos.hu, hotelszentjanos@ hotelszentjanos.hu).

¢ Dobó Vendégház, run by warm Marianna Kleszo, has seven basic but colorful rooms just off Dobó Square. Marianna speaks nothing but Hungarian, but gets simple reservation emails translated by a friend (cash only, air-con in some upstairs rooms, Dobó utca 19, tel. 36/421-407, www.dobovendeghaz.hu, info@ dobovendeghaz.hu).

Eating in Eger

$$ HBH Restaurant (named for the Hofbräuhaus beer on tap) is doing its best to be classy in this small town. They offer traditional Hungarian dishes, either in a humdrum dining room or—better—at fine outdoor tables at the bottom of the main square (good wine list, daily 11:30-23:00, right at the bottom of Dobó Square at Bajcsy-Zsilinszky utca 19, tel. 36/515-516, www.hbh-eger.hu).

$$ Palacsintavár ("Pancake Castle"), near the ramp leading up to the castle, isn't your hometown IHOP. This cellar bar (which also has pleasant sidewalk seating) serves up inventive, artfully presented crêpe-wrapped main courses to a mostly student clientele. It's decorated with old cigarette boxes, and cutting-edge rock music plays on the soundtrack (Tue-Sun 12:00-23:00, closed Mon, Dobó utca 9, tel. 36/413-980, www.palacsintavar.hu).

$$ Restaurant Senator Ház, on Little Dobó Square, offers the best setting for al fresco dining in town, with good Hungarian and international food. Sure, you're paying a bit extra for the setting—but it's worth it for the postcard-perfect outdoor seating, from which you can survey the Little Dobó Square action (open daily 10:00-22:00, cheesy live music on summer evenings). Neighboring restaurants (such as Offi Ház) offer the same ambience.

$$ Szantofer Vendéglő serves traditional Hungarian food at local prices to both Egerites and tourists. The good, unpretentious, fill-the-tank grub is designed for the neighborhood gang (daily 11:30-22:00, Bródy Sándor utca 3, tel. 36/517-298).

Dessert: *Cukrászda* (pastry shops) line the streets of Eger. For deluxe, superdecadent pastries of every kind imaginable, drop by

---

Restaurant Price Code

I've assigned each eatery a price category, based on the average cost of a typical main course. Drinks, desserts, and splurge items (steak and seafood) can raise the price considerably.

$$$$ **Splurge:** Most main courses over 4,500 Ft
$$$ **Pricier:** 3,000-4,500 Ft
$$ **Moderate:** 2,000-3,000 Ft
$ **Budget:** 2,000 Ft or less

In Hungary, takeout food or a cafeteria-type place is **$**; an unpretentious sit-down eatery is **$$**; an upmarket but still casual restaurant is **$$$**; and a swanky splurge is **$$$$**.

Dobós Cukrászda (Mon-Sat 9:30-20:00, Sun 9:00-19:00, point to what you want inside and they'll bring it out to your table, Széchenyi utca 6, tel. 36/413-335). For a more local scene, find the tiny **Sárvári Cukrászda,** a block behind the Lyceum. Their pastries are good, but Egerites line up here for homemade gelato (Mon-Fri 7:00-19:00, Sat-Sun 10:00-19:00, Kossuth utca 1, between Jókai utca and Fellner utca). You'll spot several ice-cream parlors in this town, where every other pedestrian seems to be licking a cone. Another good option is the *kürtőskalács* **window** on Szent János utca, where you can step up and grab a piping-hot "chimney cake" that's slow-cooked on a rotisserie, then rolled in toppings (daily 9:00-19:30, Szent János utca 10).

Eger Connections

BY TRAIN

The only major destination you'll get to directly from Eger's train station is **Budapest** (every 2 hours direct to Budapest's Keleti/Eastern Station, 2 hours; more frequent and faster with a change in Füzesabony—see next). For other destinations, you'll connect through Füzesabony or Budapest.

Eger is connected to the nearby junction town of **Füzesabony** (FOO-zesh-ah-boyn) by frequent trains (13/day, 17 minutes). The very rustic Füzesabony station does not have lockers or an ATM; to find an ATM, exit straight from the station, walk about two blocks, and you'll find one on your right (just past the *Napcentrum*).

In Füzesabony, you can transfer to Budapest on either a slower milk-run train or a speedier InterCity train (a little pricier, as it requires an extra supplement, but gets you to Budapest in just under 2 hours total).

BY BUS

Eger's bus station (unlike its train station) is right in town, a five-minute uphill walk behind Eger's cathedral and the Archbishop's Palace: Go behind the cathedral and through the park, and look for the modern, green, circular building. Blue electronic boards in the center of the station show upcoming departures.

From Eger to Budapest: The direct Eger-Budapest bus service is about the same price as the train, and can be a bit faster (2/hour, tickets generally available just before departure). Express buses depart Eger at :15 after each hour and make the trip in one hour and 50 minutes; slower regular buses leave at :45 after each hour and take 20 minutes longer. While Eger's bus station is closer to the town center than its train station, this bus takes you to a less central point in Budapest (near Budapest's Stadionok bus station, on the M2/red Metró line).

To the Thermal Baths near Egerszalók: Buses from the same station also connect Eger to the thermal baths near Egerszalók (Salt Hill and Demjén; see "Getting There" on page 688). However, buses marked for *Egerszalók* do not actually go to the spa; instead, you need a bus going *beyond* Egerszalók, marked for *Demjén*.

EGER

SLOVENIA
Slovenija

SLOVENIA

Tiny, overlooked Slovenia is one of Europe's most unexpectedly charming destinations. At the intersection of the Slavic, German, and Italian worlds, Slovenia is an exciting mix of the best of each culture. Though it's just a quick trip away from the tourist throngs in Venice, Munich, Salzburg, and Vienna, Slovenia has stayed off the tourist track—making it a handy detour for in-the-know Back Door travelers. Be warned: Everyone I've met who has visited Slovenia wishes they'd allotted more time for this delightful, underrated land.

Today, it seems strange to think that Slovenia was ever part of Yugoslavia. Both in the personality of its people and in its landscape, Slovenia feels more like Austria. Slovenes are more industrious, organized, and punctual than their fellow former Yugoslavs...yet still friendly, relaxed, and Mediterranean. Locals like the balance. Visitors expecting minefields and rusting Yugo factories are pleasantly surprised to find Slovenia's rolling countryside dotted instead with quaint alpine villages and the spires of miniature Baroque churches, with snowcapped peaks in the distance.

Only half as big as Switzerland, Slovenia is remarkably diverse for its size. Travelers can hike on alpine trails in the morning and explore some of the world's best caves in the afternoon, before relaxing with a glass of local wine and a seafood dinner while watching the sun set on the Adriatic.

Though not unaffected by the recent economic crisis, Slovenia enjoys a prosperity unusual for a formerly communist country. The Austro-Hungarian Empire left it with a strong work ethic and an impressive industrial infrastructure, which the Yugoslav government expanded. By 1980, 60 percent of all Yugoslav industry was in little Slovenia (which had only 8 percent of Yugoslavia's population and 8 percent of its territory). Of the 13 new nations that have

Slovenia

AUSTRIA

HUNGARY

Murska Sobota

Klagenfurt

Villach

Drava River

Maribor

Ptuj

Jesenice

Solčava

Velenje

Varaždin

Mt. Triglav

LOGARSKA
DOLINA

Bovec

Bled

Luče

JULIAN
ALPS

Lake
Bled

Kranj

Velika
Planina

Ljubno

Celje

CROATIA

Kobarid

Soča
R.

Lake
Bohinj

Škofja
Loka

Kamnik

⊛**Ljubljana**

Sava

River

Zagreb
⊛

Idrija

SLOVENIA

Nova
Gorica

PREDJAMA
CASTLE

Novo
Mesto

Samobor

ITALY

LIPICA
STUD
FARM

POSTOJNA
CAVES

K A R S T

N

Trieste

ŠKOCJAN
CAVES

Crnomelj

50 Kilometers

Piran

Koper

CROATIA

50 Miles

Adriatic
Sea

I S T R I A

Opatija

Rijeka

joined the European Union since 2004, Slovenia was the only one rich enough to be a net donor (with a higher per-capita income than the average), and the first one to join the euro currency zone (it adopted the euro in January 2007). Thanks to its longstanding ties to the West and can-do spirit, Slovenia already feels more "Western" than any other destination in this book.

The country has a funny way of making people fall in love with it. Slovenes are laid-back, easygoing, stylish, and fun. They won't win any world wars (they're too well-adjusted to even try)... but they're exactly the type of people you'd love to chat with over a cup of coffee.

The Slovenian language is as mellow as the people. While Slovenes use Serb, German, and English curses in abundance, the worst they can say in their native tongue is, "May you be kicked by a horse." For "Darn it!" they say, "Three hundred hairy bears!" In bad traffic, they might mutter, "The street is white!"

Coming from such a small country, locals are proud of the few

things that are distinctly Slovenian, such as the roofed hayrack. Because of the frequent rainfall in the mountainous northwest, the hayracks are covered by a roof that allows the hay to dry thoroughly. The most traditional kind is the *toplar,* consisting of two hayracks connected by one big roof. It looks like a skinny barn

Slovenia Almanac

Official Name: Republika Slovenija, or simply Slovenija.

Snapshot History: After being dominated by Germans for centuries, Slovenian culture proudly emerged in the 19th century. In the aftermath of World War I, Slovenia merged with its neighbors to become Yugoslavia, then broke away and achieved independence for the first time in 1991.

Population: Slovenia's two million people (a count similar to Nevada's) are 83 percent ethnic Slovenes who speak Slovene, plus a smattering of Serbs, Croats, and Muslim Bosniaks. Almost 60 percent of the country is Catholic.

Latitude and Longitude: 46° N and 14° E (latitude similar to Lyon, France; Montreal, Canada; or Bismarck, North Dakota).

Area: At 7,800 square miles, it's about the size of New Jersey, but with one-fourth the population.

Geography: Tiny Slovenia has four extremely different terrains and climates: the warm Mediterranean coastline (just 29 miles long—about one inch per inhabitant); the snowcapped, forested alpine mountains in the northwest (including 9,400-foot Mount Triglav); the moderate-climate, central limestone plateau that includes Ljubljana and the cave-filled Karst region; and to the east, a corner of the Great Hungarian Plain (the Prekmurje region, near Maribor and Ptuj). If you look at a map of Slovenia and squint your eyes a bit, it looks like a chicken running toward the east.

Biggest Cities: Nearly one in five Slovenes lives in the two biggest cities: Ljubljana (the capital, pop. 270,000) and Maribor (in the east, pop. 158,000). Half of the population lives in rural villages.

Economy: Slovenia has a Gross Domestic Product of $60 billion and a GDP per capita of around $30,000. Slovenia's economy is based largely on manufactured metal products (trucks and machinery), which are traded with a diverse group of partners.

Currency: Slovenia uses the euro: €1 = about $1.10.

Government: The country is led by the prime minister (currently Miro Cerar), who heads the leading vote-getting party in legislative elections. He governs along with the figurehead president (Borut Pahor, who's up for re-election in 2017). Slovenia's relatively peaceful secession is credited largely to former president Milan Kučan, who remains a popular figure. The National Assembly consists of about 90 elected legislators; there's also a second house of parliament, which has much less power. Despite the country's small size, it is divided into some 200 municipalities—creating a lot of bureaucracy that locals enjoy complaining about.

Flag: Three horizontal bands of white (top), blue, and red. A shield in the upper left shows Mount Triglav, with a wavy-line sea below and three stars above.

The Average Slovene: The average Slovene skis in this largely alpine country, and is an avid fan of team handball (yes, handball). He or she lives in a 250-square-foot apartment, earns $1,400 a month, watches 16 hours of TV a week (much of it in English with Slovene subtitles), and enjoys a drink-and-a-half of alcohol every day.

Notable Slovenes: A pair of prominent Ohio politicians from the Cleveland area—perennial presidential candidate **Dennis Kucinich** and former senator **George Voinovich**—are each half-Slovene. (In 1910, Cleveland had the biggest Slovenian population of any city in the world—just ahead of Trieste and Ljubljana.) Classical musicians might know composers **Giuseppe Tartini** and **Hugo Wolf.** Even if you haven't heard of architect **Jože Plečnik** yet, you'll hear his name a hundred times while you're in Slovenia—especially in Ljubljana (see page 748). And most famous of all is US First Lady **Melania Trump** (born Melanija Knavs in the Slovenian city of Novo Mesto).

Sporty Slovenes: If you follow alpine sports or team handball, you'll surely know some world-class athletes from Slovenia. NBA fans might recognize basketball players **Primož Brezec** and **Bostjan Nachbar,** as well as some other less famous players. Slovenian hockey player **Anže Kopitar** plays in the NHL. The athletic Slovenes—perhaps trying to compensate for the minuscule size of their country—have accomplished astonishing feats: **Davo Karničar** has skied down from the "seven summits" (the highest points in each of the seven continents—that means the peaks of Everest, Kilimanjaro, McKinley, and so on). **Benka Pulko** became the first person ever to drive a motorcycle around the world—that is, all seven continents, including Antarctica, which is also the longest solo motorcycle journey by a woman (total trip: 111,856 miles in 2,000 days; for more, see www.benkapulko.com). **Dušan Mravlje** ran across all the continents. And ultramarathon swimmer **Martin Strel** has swum the entire length of several major rivers, including the Danube (1,775 miles), the Mississippi (2,415 miles), the Yangtze (3,915 miles), and the Amazon (3,393 miles; for more, see www.martinstrel.com).

with open, fenced sides. Hay hangs on the sides to dry; firewood, carts, tractors, and other farm implements sit on the ground inside; and dried hay is stored in the loft above. But these wooden *toplarji* are firetraps, and a stray bolt of lightning can burn one down in a flash. So in recent years, more farmers are moving to single hayracks *(enojni);* these are still roofed, but have posts made of concrete rather than wood. You'll find postcards and miniature wooden models of both kinds of hayracks (a fun souvenir).

Another uniquely Slovenian memento is a creatively decorated front panel from a beehive *(panjske končnice)*. Slovenia has a strong

beekeeping tradition, and beekeepers believe that painting the fronts of the hives makes it easier for bees to find their way home. Replicas of these panels are available at gift shops all over the country. (For more on the panels and Slovenia's beekeeping heritage, see page 800.)

Slovenia is also the land of polka. Slovenes claim that polka music was invented here, and singer/accordionist Slavko Avsenik—from the village of Begunje near Bled—cranked out popular oompah songs that made him bigger than the Beatles (and therefore, presumably, Jesus) in Germany. You'll see the Avsenik ensemble and other oompah bands on Slovenian TV, where hokey Lawrence Welk-style shows are an institution.

To really stretch your euros, try one of Slovenia's more than 400 farmhouse B&Bs, called "tourist farms" *(turistične kmetije)*—similar to *agriturismi* in Italy. These are actual working farms (often organic) that sell meals and/or rent rooms to tourists to help make ends meet. You can use a tourist farm as a home base to explore the entire country—remember, the farthest reaches of Slovenia are only a day trip away. A comfortable, hotelesque double with a private bathroom—plus a traditional Slovenian dinner and a hearty breakfast—costs as little as €50.

Most visitors to Slovenia are, in my experience, completely charmed by the place. With all it has going for it, it's hard to believe that Slovenia is not already overrun with tourists. Somehow, this little country continues to glide beneath the radar. Exploring its mountain trails, savoring its colorful capital, and meeting its friendly locals, you'll feel like you're in on a secret.

HELPFUL HINTS

Smoking Ban: Smoking is prohibited in public places, unless it's a specially designated (and well-ventilated) smoking room.

Larger hotels still have some smoking rooms, but smoking isn't allowed in public areas. Outdoors, all bets are off.

Telephones: Slovenian phone numbers beginning with 080 are toll-free; 090 and 089 denote expensive toll lines. Most mobile phone numbers begin with 03, 04, 05, or 07. For more tips on dialing, see page 1086.

Toll Sticker: To drive on Slovenia's expressways *(avtocesta)*, you'll need to display a toll sticker *(vinjeta,* veen-YEH-tah; €15/week, €30/month). If renting your car in Slovenia, it probably comes with a sticker (but make sure); if you're driving in from elsewhere, such as Austria or Hungary, you can buy one at a gas station, post office, or some newsstands (watch for *vinjeta* signs at gas stations as you approach the border). *Be warned:* This rule is taken very seriously. If you're found driving on expressways without the sticker, you'll immediately be fined €150.

SLOVENIAN HISTORY

Slovenia has a long and unexciting history as part of various larger empires. After Illyrian, Celtic, and Roman settlements came and went, this region became populated by Slavs—the ancestors of today's Slovenes—in the late sixth century. But Charlemagne's Franks conquered the tiny land in the eighth century, and, ever since, Slovenia has been a backwater of the Germanic world—first as a holding of the Holy Roman Empire and later, the Habsburg Empire. But even as the capital, Ljubljana, was populated by Austrians (who called the city Laibach), the Slovenian language and cultural traditions survived in the countryside.

Through the Middle Ages, much of Slovenia was ruled by the Counts of Celje (highly-placed vassals of the Habsburgs). In this era before modern nations—when shifting allegiances and strategic marriages dictated the dynamics of power—the Counts of Celje rose to a position of significant influence in Central and Eastern Europe. Celje daughters intermarried with some of the most powerful dynasties in the region: the Polish Piasts, the Hungarian Anjous, and the Czech Přemysls. Before long, the Counts of Celje had emerged as the Habsburgs' main rivals. In the 15th century, Count Ulrich II of Celje married into Serbia's ruling family and managed to wrest control of Hungary's massive holdings. Had he not been assassinated in 1456, this obscure Slovenian line—rather than an obscure Austrian one—may have emerged as the dominant power in the eastern half of Europe. (Instead, the Habsburgs consolidated their vanquished foe's fiefdoms into their ever-growing empire.) In homage, the three yellow stars of the Counts of Celje's seal still adorn Slovenia's coat of arms.

Soon after, with Slovenia firmly entrenched in the Counter-

Reformation holdings of the Habsburg Empire, the local Reformer Primož Trubar (1508-1586) strove both to put the Word of God into the people's hands, and to legitimize Slovene as a written language. This Slovenian answer to Martin Luther secretly translated the Bible into Slovene in Reformation-friendly Germany, then smuggled copies back into his homeland.

Over the next several centuries, much of Slovenia was wracked by Habsburg-Ottoman wars, as the Ottomans attempted to push north through this territory to reach Vienna. Slovenia also found itself caught in the crossfire between Austria and Venice. Seemingly exhausted by all of this warfare—and by their own sporadic, halfhearted, and unsuccessful uprisings against Habsburg rule—Slovenia languished as a sleepy backwater.

When the port city of Trieste (in Slovenian territory) was granted free status in 1718, it boosted the economy of Slovenian lands. The Enlightenment spurred a renewed interest in the Slovenian culture and language, which further flourished when Napoleon named Ljubljana the capital of his "Illyrian Provinces"—Slovenia's own mini-empire, stretching from Austria's Tirol to Croatia's Dalmatian Coast. During this brief period (1809-1813), the long-suppressed Slovene language was used for the first time in schools and the government. This kicked off a full-throated national revival movement—asserting the worthiness of the Slovenian language and culture compared to the dominant Germanic worldview of the time. Inspired by the patriotic poetry of France Prešeren (1800-1849), Slovenian pride surged.

The last century saw the most interesting chapter of Slovenian history. Some of World War I's fiercest fighting occurred at the Soča (Isonzo) Front in northwest Slovenia—witnessed by young Ernest Hemingway, who drove an ambulance (see sidebars on pages 815 and 830). During World War II, Slovenia was divided among Nazi allies Austria, Italy, and Hungary—and an estimated 20,000 to 25,000 Slovenes perished in Nazi- and Italian-operated concentration camps.

As Yugoslavia entered its Golden Age under war hero Marshal Tito, Slovenia's prime location where Yugoslavia meets Western Europe (a short drive from Austria or Italy)—and the diligent national character of the Slovenian people—made it a prime candidate for industrialization.

After Tito's death in 1980, the various Yugoslav republics struggled to redefine their role in the union. While many factions reverted to age-old, pre-Tito nationalistic fervor, the Slovenes grew increasingly focused on their own future...and began to press for real reforms of the communist system. Slovenia had always been Yugoslavia's smallest, northernmost, most prosperous republic.

Slovenes realized that Yugoslavia needed Slovenia much more than Slovenia needed Yugoslavia.

In 1988, the iconoclastic Slovenian magazine *Mladina* pushed the boundaries of Yugoslavia's nominally "free" press, publishing articles critical of the Yugoslav People's Army. Four young reporters (including Janez Janša, who would later become Slovenia's prime minister) were tried, convicted, and imprisoned, spurring outrage among Slovenes. A few months later, the Slovenian delegation defiantly walked out of the Yugoslav League of Communists Congress.

The first-ever free elections in Slovenia on April 8, 1990 ended communist rule and swept reformer Milan Kučan into the presidency. Kučan attempted to pursue a Swiss-style confederated relationship with his fellow Yugoslav republics, but met with resistance from his counterparts who were more focused on their own ethnic self-interests. Later that year, in a nationwide referendum, 88 percent of Slovenes voted for independence from Yugoslavia.

And so, concerned about the nationalistic politics of Serbian strongman Slobodan Milošević and seeking the opportunity for true democracy and capitalism, Slovenia seceded. Because more than 90 percent of the people here were ethnic Slovenes—and because Slovenia was careful to respect the rights of its minority populations—the break with Yugoslavia was simple and virtually uncontested. Its war for independence lasted just 10 days and claimed only a few dozen lives. (For more details, see "Understanding Yugoslavia" on page 1101.)

In May of 2004 Slovenia became the first of the former Yugoslav republics to join the European Union. The Slovenes have been practical about this move, realizing it's essential for their survival as a tiny nation in a modern world. But there are trade-offs, and "Euroskeptics" are down on EU bureaucracy. As borders disappear, Slovenes are experiencing more crime. Traditional farms are grappling with strict EU standards. Slovenian businesses are having difficulty competing with big German and other Western European firms. Before EU membership, only Slovenes could own Slovenian land, but now wealthy foreigners are buying property, driving up the cost of real estate. Still, overall, most Slovenes feel that EU membership was the right choice.

After independence, Slovenia impressed its European neighbors with its powerhouse economy and steady growth. However, the global financial crisis revealed that some of the affluence was deceptive: Many of Slovenia's biggest companies had been running up huge debts. As all of Europe's bubble burst in 2008, those corporate debts were assumed by Slovenia's big banks—devastating the economy and sparking financial worries.

In recent years, Slovenes have grown weary of a string of corrupt and incompetent politicians. Janez Janša, who became prime minister for the second time in 2011, was swept out of office amid a wave of protests and eventually sentenced to a prison term for corruption. His successor, Alenka Bratušek, resigned after just a year in office. One popular figure—at least in Ljubljana—is the visionary mayor Zoran Janković, who has reshaped the capital during his tenure (see page 732).

In the fall of 2015, Slovenia became the focal point of a Europe-wide debate when a flood of refugees from Syria and other nations showed up at its border. Like its neighbors Croatia and Hungary, Slovenia grappled with the challenge of caring for the new arrivals even as it facilitated their passage to wealthy northern European countries. News reports suggested that Slovenia responded to this humanitarian crisis with pragmatic compassion.

While many of the refugees expressed relief at what a friendly and competent place Slovenia was, those of us who already love the country were hardly shocked. The Slovenes are adjusting to the 21st century with their characteristic sense of humor and easygoing attitude, just as they've done throughout their history.

SLOVENIAN FOOD

Slovenes brag that their cuisine melds the best of Italian and German cooking—but they also embrace other international influences, especially French. Slovenian cuisine features many pan-Balkan elements: The savory phyllo-dough pastry *burek* is the favorite fast food here, and when Slovenes host a backyard barbecue, they grill up *čevapčiči* and *ražnjiči*, topped off with the eggplant-and-red-bell-pepper condiment *ajvar*. Slovenia enjoys Italian-style dishes, with a

pizza or pasta restaurant on seemingly every corner. Hungarian food simmers in the northeast corner of the country (where many Magyars reside). And in most of the country, traditional Slovenian food has a distinctly Germanic vibe—including the "four S's": sausages, schnitzels, strudels, and sauerkraut.

Traditional Slovenian meals come with a hearty helping of groats—a grainy mush made with buckwheat, barley, or corn. Buckwheat, which thrives in this climate, often appears on Slovenian menus. You'll also see plenty of *štruklji*, a dumpling-like savory layer cake that can be stuffed with cheese, meat, or vegetables. *Repa* is turnip prepared like sauerkraut. Among the hearty soups in Slovenia is *jota*—a staple for Karst peasants, made from *repa*, beans, vegetables, and often sausage.

Pršut

In Slovenia, Croatia, and Montenegro, *pršut* (purr-SHOOT) is one of the essential food groups. This air-cured ham (like Italian prosciutto) is soaked in salt and sometimes also smoked. Then it hangs in open-ended barns for up to a year and a half, to be dried and seasoned by the howling Bora wind. Each region produces a slightly different *pršut*. In Dalmatia, a layer of fat keeps the ham moist; in Istria, the fat is trimmed, and the *pršut* is dryer.

Since Slovenia joined the European Union, strict new standards have swept the land. Separate rooms must be used for the slaughter, preparation, and curing of the ham. While this seems fair enough for large producers, small family farms that want to produce just enough *pršut* for their own use—and maybe sell one or two ham hocks to neighbors—find they have to invest thousands of euros to be compliant.

The cuisine of Slovenia's Karst region (the arid limestone plain south of Ljubljana) is notable. The small farms and wineries of this region have been inspired by Italy's Slow Food movement—their owners believe that cuisine is meant to be gradually appreciated, not rushed. The Karst's tasty air-dried ham *(pršut)*, available throughout the country, is worth seeking out (see sidebar). Istria (the peninsula just to the south of the Karst, in southern Slovenia and Croatia) produces truffles that, locals boast, are as good as those from Italy's Piedmont region.

Voda is water, and *kava* is coffee. Radenska, in the bottle with the three little hearts, is Slovenia's best-known brand of mineral water—good enough that the word *Radenska* is synonymous with bottled water all over Slovenia and throughout the former Yugoslavia. It's not common to ask for (or receive) tap water, but you can try requesting *voda iz pipe*.

Adventurous teetotalers should forgo the Coke and sample Cockta, a Slovenian cola with an unusual flavor (which supposedly

comes from berry, lemon, orange, and 11 herbs). Originally called "Cockta-Cockta," the drink was introduced during the communist period, as an alternative to the difficult-to-get Coca-Cola. This local variation developed a loyal following...until the Iron Curtain fell, and the real Coke became readily available. Cockta sales plummeted. But in recent years—prodded by the slogan "The Taste of Your Youth"—nostalgic Slovenes are drinking Cockta once more.

The premier Slovenian brand of *pivo*

Slovenian Wines

It should come as no surprise that Slovenia produces excellent *vino* (wine). After all, this little country abuts well-respected wine-growing neighbors Italy and Hungary. In fact, Slovenia's winemaking tradition originated with its pre-Roman Illyrian and Celtic inhabitants, meaning that wine has been grown much longer here than in most other European countries. As in Hungary, wine standards plummeted with Yugoslav-era collectivization, but in recent years ambitious vintner families have been determined to bring quality back to Slovenian wines—with impressive results.

Slovenia's three main wine-growing regions are Primorska, Posavje, and Podravje.

The best-known is the **Primorska** region, in the southwest. With a Mediterranean climate (hence its name: "by the sea"), Primorska is best known for its reds. Primorska's Goriška Brda ("Hillsides of Gorica") shares the terroir of Italy's Friuli/Venezia Giulia region (and its much-vaunted, DOC-classified Collio Goriziano wines). This area produces some of Slovenia's most respected wines, made mostly with internationally-known grapes such as merlot and cabernet sauvignon. Goriška Brda also produces a good white using the *rebula* grape (also known by its Italian name, *ribolla gialla*). A bit farther south (and still within Primorska), the Karst grows lots of *refošk (refosco)* grapes, which thrive in iron-rich red soil *(terra rossa)*. The top product is the extremely full-bodied, "big" *teran*—infused with a high lactic acid content that supposedly gives the wine healing properties. Nearby coastal areas (around Koper) also grow *refošk,* along with the white *malvazija* grape that's also widely used in Croatian Istria.

To the northeast, near Hungary, is the **Podravje** region (the Drava River Valley), dominated by white grapes—especially *laški riesling* (known internationally as Welsh riesling) and *renski riesling* (what we'd call simply riesling). If you're visiting Ptuj or Maribor, you'll see local menus listing wines produced on the steeper right bank of the Drava River (Haloze) and the left bank (Slovenske Gorice, "Slovenian Hills").

And finally, a bit to the south of Podravje is the **Posavje** region (the Lower Sava River Valley, bordering Croatia). This area—which is still focused on quantity over quality—produces both white and red wines; it's known mostly for the light, russet-colored *cviček* wine (a blend of red and white grapes).

With any type of Slovenian wine, *vrhunsko* (premium) is a mark of quality, while *kakovostno* is a notch down, and *namizno* is a table wine. Other key terms are *suho* (dry), *sladko* (sweet), and *pol-* (half).

(beer) is Union (OO-nee-ohn), but you'll also see a lot of Laško (LASH-koh), whose mascot is the Zlatorog (or "Golden Horn," a mythical chamois-like animal). For the full story on Slovenian wines, see the sidebar.

Regardless of what you're drinking, to toast, say, *"Na ZD-ROW-yeh!"*—if you can't remember it, think of "Nice driving!"

Slovenia's national dessert is *potica,* a rolled pastry with walnuts and sometimes also raisins. While traditionally eaten at Christmas, it's available year-round. Slovenes eat it from the hard outer crust in, saving the nutty center for last. For more tasty treats, see the "Bled Desserts" sidebar on page 791. Locals claim that Ljubljana has the finest gelato outside of Italy—which, after all, is just an hour down the road.

SLOVENIAN LANGUAGE

Slovene is surprisingly different from the languages spoken in the other former Yugoslav republics. While Serbian and Croatian are mutually intelligible, Slovene is gibberish to Serbs and Croats. Most Slovenes, on the other hand, know Serbo-Croatian because, a generation ago, everybody in Yugoslavia had to learn it.

Linguists have identified some 46 official dialects of Slovene, and there are probably another 100 or so unofficial ones. Locals can instantly tell which city—or sometimes even which remote mountain valley—someone comes from by their accent.

The tiny country of Slovenia borders Italy and Austria, with important historical and linguistic ties to both. For self-preservation, Slovenes have always been forced to function in many different languages. All of these factors make them excellent linguists. Most young Slovenes speak flawless English effortlessly—then admit that they've never set foot in the United States or Britain, but love watching American movies and TV shows (which are always subtitled, never dubbed).

In Slovene, *c* is pronounced "ts" (as in "cats"). The letter *j* is pronounced as "y"—making "Ljubljana" easier to say than it looks (lyoob-lyee-AH-nah). Slovene only has one diacritical mark: the *strešica,* or "little roof." This makes *č* sound like "ch," *š* sound like "sh," and *ž* sound like "zh" (as in "measure"). The letter *v* is pronounced like "u"—so the Slovenian word *avto* sounds like "auto," and the mountain Triglav is pronounced "TREE-glau" (rhymes with "cow"). The only trick: As in English, which syllable gets the emphasis is unpredictable.

Learn some key Slovenian phrases (see the Slovenian survival phrases on the next page). You'll make more friends and your trip will go more smoothly.

Slovenian Survival Phrases

In the phonetics, ī sounds like the long i in "light," and bolded syllables are stressed. The vowel "eh" sometimes sounds closer to "ay" (depending on the speaker).

English	Slovenian	Pronunciation
Hello. (formal)	*Dober dan.*	**doh**-behr dahn
Hi. / Bye. (informal)	*Živjo.*	**zheev**-yoh
Do you speak English?	*Ali govorite angleško?*	ah-lee goh-voh-**ree**-teh ahn-**glehsh**-koh
Yes. / No.	*Ja. / Ne.*	yah / neh
I (don't) understand.	*(Ne) razumem.*	(neh) rah-**zoo**-mehm
Please. / You're welcome.	*Prosim.*	**proh**-seem
Thank you (very much).	*Hvala (lepa).*	**hvah**-lah (**leh**-pah)
Excuse me. / I'm sorry.	*Oprostite.*	oh-proh-**stee**-teh
problem	*problem*	proh-**blehm**
No problem.	*Ni problema.*	nee proh-**bleh**-mah
Good.	*Dobro.*	**doh**-broh
Goodbye.	*Na svidenje.*	nah **svee**-dehn-yeh
one / two	*ena / dve*	**eh**-nah / dveh
three / four	*tri / štiri*	tree / **shtee**-ree
five / six	*pet / šest*	peht / shehst
seven / eight	*sedem / osem*	**seh**-dehm / **oh**-sehm
nine / ten	*devet / deset*	deh-**veht** / deh-**seht**
hundred / thousand	*sto / tisoč*	stoh / **tee**-sohch
How much?	*Koliko?*	**koh**-lee-koh
local currency	*euro*	**ee**-oo-roh
Write it?	*Napišite?*	nah-**peesh**-ee-teh
Is it free?	*Ali je brezplačno?*	**ah**-lee yeh brehz-**plahch**-noh
Is it included?	*Ali je vključeno?*	**ah**-lee yeh vuk-**lyoo**-cheh-noh
Where can I find / buy...?	*Kje lahko najdem / kupim...?*	kyeh **lah**-koh nī-dehm / **koo**-peem
I'd / We'd like...	*Želel / Želeli bi...*	zheh-**lehl** / zheh-**leh**-lee bee
...a room.	*...sobo.*	**soh**-boh
...a ticket to ___.	*...vozovnico do ___.*	voh-**zohv**-neet-soh doh ___
Is it possible?	*Ali je možno?*	**ah**-lee yeh **mohzh**-noh
Where is...?	*Kje je...?*	kyeh yeh
...the train station	*...železniška postaja*	zheh-**lehz**-neesh-kah pohs-**tī**-yah
...the bus station	*...avtobusna postaja*	**ow**-toh-boos-nah pohs-**tī**-yah
...the tourist information office	*...turistično informacijski center*	too-**rees**-teech-noh een-for-maht-**see**-skee **tsehn**-tehr
...the toilet	*...vece (WC)*	**veht**-seh
men / women	*moški / ženski*	**mohsh**-kee / **zhehn**-skee
left / right / straight	*levo / desno / naravnost*	**leh**-voh / **dehs**-noh / nah-**rahv**-nohst
At what time...?	*Ob kateri uri...?*	ohb kah-**teh**-ree **oo**-ree
...does this open / close	*...se odpre / zapre*	seh ohd-**preh** / zah-**preh**
(Just) a moment.	*(Samo) trenutek.*	(sah-**moh**) treh-**noo**-tehk
now / soon / later	*zdaj / kmalu / pozneje*	zuh-**dī** / kuh-**mah**-loo / pohz-**neh**-yeh
today / tomorrow	*danes / jutri*	**dah**-nehs / **yoo**-tree

In a Slovenian Restaurant

English	Slovenian	Pronunciation
I'd like to reserve...	Rezerviral bi...	reh-zehr-**vee**-rahl bee
We'd like to reserve...	Rezervirali bi...	reh-zehr-**vee**-rah-lee bee
...a table for one / two.	...mizo za enega / dva.	**mee**-zoh zah **eh**-neh-gah / dvah
Is this table free?	Ali je ta miza prosta?	**ah**-lee yeh tah **mee**-zah **proh**-stah
Can I help you?	Izvolite?	eez-**voh**-lee-teh
The menu (in English), please.	Jedilni list (v angleščini), prosim.	yeh-**deel**-nee leest (vuh ahn-**glehsh**-chee-nee) **proh**-seem
service (not) included	postrežba (ni) vključena	post-**rehzh**-bah (nee) vuk-**lyoo**-cheh-nah
cover charge	pogrinjek	poh-**green**-yehk
"to go"	za s sabo	zah **sah**-boh
with / without	z / brez	zuh / brehz
and / or	in / ali	een / **ah**-lee
fixed-price meal (of the day)	(dnevni) meni	(duh-**new**-nee) meh-**nee**
specialty of the house	specialiteta hiše	speht-see-ah-lee-**teh**-tah **hee**-sheh
half portion	polovična porcija	poh-loh-**veech**-nah **port**-see-yah
daily special	dnevna ponudba	duh-**new**-nah poh-**nood**-bah
fixed-price meal for tourists	turistični meni	too-**rees**-teech-nee meh-**nee**
appetizers	predjedi	prehd-yeh-**dee**
bread	kruh	krooh
cheese	sir	seer
sandwich	sendvič	**send**-veech
soup	juha	**yoo**-hah
salad	solata	soh-**lah**-tah
meat / poultry	meso / perutnina	meh-**soh** / peh-root-**nee**-nah
fish / seafood	riba / morska hrana	**ree**-bah / **mor**-skah **hrah**-nah
fruit	sadje	**sahd**-yeh
vegetables	zelenjava	zeh-lehn-**yah**-vah
dessert	sladica	slah-**deet**-sah
(tap) water	voda (iz pipe)	**voh**-dah (eez **pee**-peh)
mineral water	mineralna voda	mee-neh-**rahl**-nah **voh**-dah
milk	mleko	**mleh**-koh
(orange) juice	(pomarančni) sok	(poh-mah-**rahnch**-nee) sohk
coffee	kava	**kah**-vah
tea	čaj	chī
wine	vino	**vee**-noh
red / white	rdeče / belo	ahr-**deh**-cheh / **beh**-loh
sweet / dry / semi-dry	sladko / suho / polsuho	**slahd**-koh / **soo**-hoh / **pohl**-soo-hoh
glass / bottle	kozarec / steklenica	koh-**zah**-rehts / stehk-leh-**neet**-sah
beer	pivo	**pee**-voh
Cheers!	Na zdravje!	nah **zdrow**-yeh
More. / Another.	Še. / Še eno.	sheh / sheh **eh**-noh
The same.	Isto.	**ees**-toh
Bill, please.	Račun, prosim.	rah-**choon proh**-seem
tip	napitnina	nah-peet-**nee**-nah
Delicious!	Odlično!	ohd-**leech**-noh

LJUBLJANA

Ljubljana (lyoob-lyee-AH-nah) is irresistible. With a lazy Old Town clustered around a castle-topped hill, Slovenia's capital is often likened to Salzburg. It's an apt comparison—but only if you inject a healthy dose of breezy Adriatic culture, add a Slavic accent, and replace favorite son Mozart with local architect Jože Plečnik.

Ljubljana feels smaller than its population of 270,000. With several clusters of good museums that try hard—but have only so much to say—it does its best to please sightseers. But ultimately, this town is all about ambience. The cobbled core of Ljubljana is an idyllic place that sometimes feels too good to be true. The cityscape is slathered with one-of-a-kind architecture, festivals fill the summer, and people enjoy a Sunday stroll any day of the week. Fashion boutiques and al fresco cafés jockey for control of the Old Town, while the leafy riverside promenade crawls with stylishly dressed students sipping *kava* and polishing their near-perfect English. Laid-back Ljubljana is the kind of place where graffiti and crumbling buildings seem elegantly atmospheric instead of shoddy. But more and more of those buildings have been getting a facelift recently, as a spunky mayor has been spiffing up the place and creating gleaming traffic-free zones left and right—making what was already an exceptionally livable city into a true pedestrians' paradise.

Batted around by history, Ljubljana has seen cultural influences from all sides—most notably Prague, Vienna, and Venice. This has left the city a happy hodgepodge of cultures. Being the midpoint between the Slavic, Germanic, and Italian worlds gives Ljubljana a special spice.

The Story of Ljubljana

In ancient times, Ljubljana was on the trade route connecting the Mediterranean (just 60 miles away) to the Black Sea. (Toss a bottle off the bridge here, and it can float to the Danube and, eventually, all the way to Russia.) Legend has it that Jason and his Argonauts founded Ljubljana when they stopped here for the winter on their way home with the Golden Fleece. Some stories say Jason slayed a dragon here, while according to others, it was St. George; either way, the dragon remains the city mascot to this day.

Some of the area's earliest known inhabitants during the Neolithic and Bronze ages lived in rustic houses on tall wooden piles in the marshy lands surrounding today's city center. They poled around the shallow lagoons in dugout canoes. Sometimes called "crannog dwellers" (after similar homes in the Scottish Highlands), these earliest Ljubljanans left behind precious few artifacts, save for half of a wooden wheel and axle that's 5,200 years old.

The area was later populated by the Illyrians and Celts, and was eventually Romanized (and called Emona) before being over-run by Huns, only to be resettled by Slavs—the ancestors of to-day's Slovenes.

In 1335, Ljubljana fell under the Habsburg emperors, who called it Laibach and steered its development for the next six centuries. Slovenian language and culture were considered back-wards, as most of Laibach's inhabitants spoke German and lived essentially Austrian lifestyles. This Austrian vibe persists today, thanks to abundant Austrian Baroque and Viennese Art Nouveau architecture.

Napoleon put Ljubljana on the map when he named it the capital of his Illyrian Provinces, a realm that stretched from the Danube to Dubrovnik, and from Austria to Albania (for just four short years, 1809-1813). For the first time, the Slovene language was taught in schools, awakening a newfound pride in Slovenian

PLANNING YOUR TIME

Ljubljana deserves at least a full day. Rather than checking off a list of museums, spend most of your time strolling the pleasant town center, exploring the many interesting squares and architectural gems, browsing the produce market, shopping at the boutiques, and sipping coffee at sidewalk cafés along the river.

Here's the best plan for a low-impact sightseeing day: Begin on Prešeren Square, the heart of the city. Cross the Triple Bridge and wander through the riverside produce market before joining the town walking tour at 10:00 (at 11:00 in Oct-March). Then wander south along the Ljubljanica River and through the Kra-kovo gardens to tour the Jože Plečnik House (closed Mon). In cultural heritage. People still look back fondly on this very brief era, which was the first (and probably only) time when Ljubljana rose to prominence on the world stage. (Despite spending more than 600 years as part of the Habsburg Empire, Ljubljana has no "Habsburg Square"...but it does have a "French Revolution Square.")

In the mid-19th century, the railway connecting Vienna to the Adriatic (Trieste) was built through town—and Ljubljana boomed. An earthquake hit the city in 1895, damaging many buildings. Locals cleverly exaggerated the impact (propping up buildings that were structurally sound, and even tearing down unwanted old houses that had been unharmed) in preparation for the visit of Emperor Franz Josef—who took pity on the city and invested generously in its reconstruction. Ljubljana was made over in the Art Nouveau style. A generation later, architect Jože Plečnik bathed the city in his distinctive, artsy-but-sensible, classical-meets-modern style.

In World War II, Slovenia was occupied first by the Italians, then by the Nazis. Ljubljana had a thriving resistance movement that the Nazis couldn't suppress—so they simply fenced off the entire city and made it a giant prison for three years, allowing in only basic food shipments. But the Slovenes—who knew their land far better than their oppressors did—continued to slip in and out of town undetected, allowing them to agitate through the end of the war.

In 1991, Ljubljana became the capital of one of Europe's youngest nations. Today the city is filled with university students, making it feel very youthful. Ljubljana is on the cutting edge when it comes to architecture, public art, fashion, and trendy pubs—a tendency embodied by its larger-than-life mayor, Zoran Janković (see page 732). And yet, Ljubljana's scintillating avant-garde culture has soft edges—hip, but also nonthreatening and user-friendly.

the afternoon, commit some quality time to people-watching at a riverside café, window-shop at some colorful boutiques (perhaps following my self-guided shopping walk in the Old Town), or do more sightseeing (good options include the City History Museum, near several Jože Plečnik landmarks downtown; the Serbian Orthodox Church and Tivoli Park, with the Contemporary History Museum, west of downtown; or the Slovenian Ethnographic Museum and other sights in Metelkova, north of downtown).

Ljubljana is sleepy on Sundays (virtually all shops are closed and the produce market is quiet, but museums are generally open, a modest flea market stretches along the riverfront, and the TI's walking tour still runs). The city is also relatively quiet in August, when the students are on break and many locals head to beach resorts. They say that in August, even homeless people go to the coast.

Orientation to Ljubljana

Ljubljana's central zone is compact, and with a little wandering, you'll quickly get the hang of it. The Ljubljanica River—lined with cafés, restaurants, and a buzzing outdoor market—bisects the city, making a 90-degree turn around the base of a castle-topped hill. Most sights are either along or just a short walk from the river. Visitors enjoy the distinctive bridges that span the Ljubljanica, including the landmark Triple Bridge (Tromostovje) and pillared Cobblers' Bridge (Čevljarski Most)—both designed by Jože Plečnik. Between these two is a plain bridge (with great views) called Brv (roughly, "simple footbridge"). The center of Ljubljana is Prešeren Square, watched over by a big statue of Slovenia's national poet, France Prešeren.

I've organized the sights in this chapter based on which side of the river they're on: the east (castle) side of the river, which is where Ljubljana began and has more medieval charm; and the west (Prešeren Square) side of the river, which has a more Baroque/Art Nouveau feel and most of the urban sprawl. At the northern edge of the tourist's Ljubljana is the train station and Metelkova museum and nightlife zone; at the southern edge are the garden district of Krakovo and the Jože Plečnik House; and at the western edge is Tivoli Park.

Ljubljana's Two Big Ps: You'll hear the following two easy-to-confuse names constantly during your visit. Mind your Ps, and your visit to Ljubljana becomes more meaningful: **Jože Plečnik** (YOH-zheh PLAYCH-neek, 1872-1957) is the architect who shaped Ljubljana, designing virtually all of the city's most important landmarks. For more information, see page 748. **France Prešeren** (FRAHN-tseh preh-SHAY-rehn, 1800-1849) is Slovenia's greatest poet and the namesake of Ljubljana's main square.

TOURIST INFORMATION

Ljubljana's helpful, businesslike TI has a useful website (www.visitljubljana.com) and two branches: at the **Triple Bridge,** across from Prešeren Square (daily June-Sept 8:00-21:00, Oct-May until 19:00, Stritarjeva 1, tel. 01/306-1215); and at the upper corner of the **market** (with bikes to rent and information about the rest of

Slovenia; June-Sept daily 8:00-21:00; Oct-May Mon-Fri 8:00-19:00, Sat-Sun 9:00-17:00; Krekov trg 10, tel. 01/306-4575). At either TI, pick up a pile of free resources, including the big city map, the *Tourist Guide,* and the monthly events guide.

The **Ljubljana Tourist Card,** which includes access to public transportation and covers entry to many city museums as well as the TIs' walking tours and boat trips, could save busy sightseers some money (€23/24 hours, €30/48 hours, €35/72 hours).

ARRIVAL IN LJUBLJANA

By Train: Ljubljana's modern, user-friendly train station (Železniška Postaja) is at the northern edge of the city center. Emerging from the passage up to track 1a, turn right and walk under the long canopy to find the yellow arrivals hall. Everything is well-signed in English, including the handy train-information office (with useful handouts outlining journeys to several domestic and international destinations), lockers, and—near the front of the station—a big **ticket office** with clearly marked ticket windows and an **ATM**. Arrivals are *prihodi,* departures are *odhodi,* and track is *tir.*

You can **walk** to any of my recommended hotels within about 20 minutes (often less). To reach Prešeren Square at the city's center, leave the arrivals hall to the right and walk a long block along the busy Trg Osvobodilne Fronte (or "Trg O.F." for short, with the bus station in the middle). After passing the bus stalls, turn left across Trg O.F. and go down Miklošičeva, at the building with the round, red-brick columns. This takes you past some of Ljubljana's most appealing architecture to Prešeren Square.

Unscrupulous **taxis** crouch in front of the station, waiting to spring on unsuspecting tourists. The fair metered rate to any of my recommended hotels is around €3 (maybe up to €4-5 in heavy traffic or after hours). But, because the city refuses to regulate taxi tariffs, train-station taxis uniformly charge exorbitant rates—generally around €3-5 per kilometer (plus an extra fee of around €2-3 for bags). Simply put, it's impossible to hail a taxi on the street in front of the station and get anything resembling a fair fare. To avoid giving these crooks the satisfaction, call for a taxi that charges fair rates (tel. 080-1190, 01/511-2314, or 01/520-9704). Taking just a few more minutes to wait for your cab could easily save you €10 or more. For more on taxis—and how to avoid rip-offs—see "Getting Around Ljubljana—By Taxi," later.

By Bus: Ljubljana's bus station (Autobusna Postaja) is a low-profile building (with ticket windows, a bakery, and newsstands) in the middle of Trg O.F., right in front of the train station. To get into the city center, see "By Train," earlier.

By Car: As you approach Ljubljana on the expressway, the toll

Ljubljana Hotels & Restaurants

To ② ②

⑧

To Contemporary History Museum

Tivoli Park

TIVOLSKA CESTA

GOSPOSVETSKA

SLOVENSKA CESTA

CIGALETOVA

SERBIAN ORTHODOX CHURCH

Ajdovščina Park

Miklošičev Park

NATIONAL GALLERY

ŠTEFANOVA ULICA

DALMATINOVA ULICA

MODERN ART MUSEUM

CANKARJEVA CESTA

③⑦

THE SKYSCRAPER

US EMBASSY

NATIONAL THEATER

SLOVENSKA CESTA

NAZORJEVA ULICA

GRAND HOTEL UNION

MIKLOŠIČEVA

SLOVENIAN NATIONAL MUSEUM & NATURAL HISTORY MUSEUM

TOMŠIČEVA ULICA

Trg Narodnih Herojev

ČOPOVA ULICA

POST

FRANCISCAN CHURCH

Prešeren Square

SUBIČEVA ULICA

PARLIAMENT

⑭

Square of the Republic

⑱

WOLFOVA

⑩ TRIPLE BRIDGE

ⓘ

ERJAVČEVA CESTA

Congress Square

②⑨ BRV BRIDGE

③③ Ribji Square

LJUBLJANSKA BANKA CESTA

P

④ River

⑦ OLD

PREŠERNOVA

GREGORČIČEVA ULICA

⑤

②④ ULICA

③①

SLOVENSKA CESTA

VEGOVA ULICA

②⓪

MESTNI

COBBLERS' BRIDGE

②⑧

IGRIŠKA ULICA

⑫

RIMSKA CESTA

②③

UNIVERSITY

Novi Trg

ŠTARI TRG

②⑤

BREG

REBER

⑨

French Revolution Square

NATIONAL & UNIVERSITY LIBRARY

Ljubljanica

LEVSTIKOV TRG

N.U.K. #2

P

GOSPOSKA

CITY MUSEUM

⑯

ROMAN CITY WALL

ZOISOVA CESTA

MIRJE

BARJANSKA CESTA

EMONSKA CESTA

KRAKOVO

②⑥

REČNA UL.

GRADAŠKA ULICA

PLEČNIK HOUSE

EIPPROVA ULICA

②⑦

Accommodations

1. Hotel Angel
2. Allegro Hotel
3. Antiq Hotel
4. Vander Urbani Resort
5. Cubo Hotel
6. Adora Hotel
7. Meščanka Rooms
8. Slamič B&B
9. Hotel Mrak
10. Hotel Emonec & Launderette
11. B&B Petra Varl
12. Penzion Pod Lipo
13. Hostel Celica

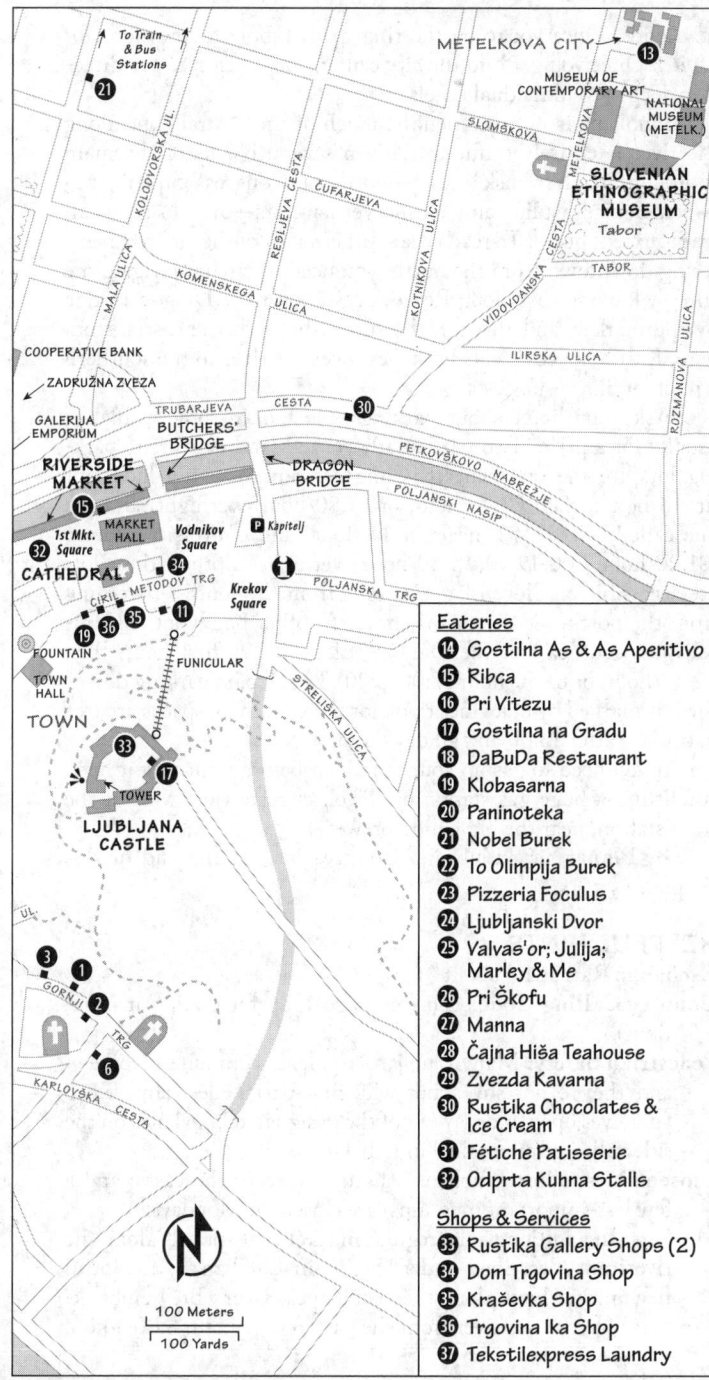

Eateries

14 Gostilna As & As Aperitivo
15 Ribca
16 Pri Vitezu
17 Gostilna na Gradu
18 DaBuDa Restaurant
19 Klobasarna
20 Paninoteka
21 Nobel Burek
22 To Olimpija Burek
23 Pizzeria Foculus
24 Ljubljanski Dvor
25 Valvas'or; Julija; Marley & Me
26 Pri Škofu
27 Manna
28 Čajna Hiša Teahouse
29 Zvezda Kavarna
30 Rustika Chocolates & Ice Cream
31 Fétiche Patisserie
32 Odprta Kuhna Stalls

Shops & Services

33 Rustika Gallery Shops (2)
34 Dom Trgovina Shop
35 Kraševka Shop
36 Trgovina Ika Shop
37 Tekstilexpress Laundry

road ends. Once you're on the ring road, simply follow signs for *Center*. Once you get into the city center, you'll begin to see directional signs to individual hotels.

Ljubljana is not car-friendly; much of the central zone along the river is entirely traffic-free. Even several blocks of the main thoroughfare, Slovenska cesta—north of Congress Square, between Šubičeva ulica and Gosposvetska cesta—are closed to all traffic except buses. To reach the southern part of the city when entering downtown from the north, you need to circumnavigate the core by looping east along Resljeva cesta, over the Dragon Bridge by the market, and through the tunnel beneath the castle; from here, Karlovška cesta cuts back west over the river to the southern stretch of Slovenska cesta.

Ask your hotel about parking—most have some available, usually for a price. Two particularly central (and expensive) parking lots are the one beneath **Congress Square** (€1.20/hour for first 3 hours, then €2.40/hour, or €1.80/hour overnight) and the one called **N.U.K. #2,** near the National and University Library (€1.20/hour 7:00-19:00, €1.80/hour overnight). Both of these lots are accessible on Slovenska cesta only from the south—if coming from the north, see directions above. Another handy lot is **Kapitelj,** just southeast of the Dragon Bridge (€1.90/first hour, then €2.40/hour, or €1.50/hour 18:00-6:00). Legal, paid parking downtown is marked by blue lines (look for meters); these spaces are free Saturdays after 13:00 and all day Sunday.

If you need to gas up your rental car before returning it here, you'll find a huge gas station on Tivolska cesta (just west of the train station, near the big Union brewery).

By Plane: See "Ljubljana Connections," at the end of this chapter.

HELPFUL HINTS

Exchange Rate: €1 = about $1.10

Country Calling Code: 386 (see page 1086 for dialing instructions).

Pedestrian Safety: Many Ljubljana residents commute by bike—and they're not shy about whizzing past pedestrians. Keep your eyes open and stay out of the designated bike lanes on the sidewalks (often marked in red).

Closed Days: Most Ljubljana museums (except the castle and a few less-important museums) are closed on Mondays.

Markets: In addition to the regular **market** that sprawls along the riverfront (described under "Sights in Ljubljana"), a colorful **flea market** hops along the Ljubljanica River's Breg embankment (across the river from the castle) every Sun 8:00-14:00.

On summer Saturdays, there's also a lively and colorful **arts and handicrafts market** in the same place (Sat 8:00-14:00).

Wi-Fi: The city's **WiFree** program—with Wi-Fi hotspots near Prešeren Square and along the river—lets you get online free for up to an hour. Pick up the brochure at the TI (you'll be texted a code to enter).

Post Office: The main post office *(pošta)* is in a beautiful yellow Art Nouveau building a block up Čopova from Prešeren Square, at the intersection with Slovenska cesta (Mon-Fri 8:00-19:00, Sat 8:00-12:00, closed Sun).

Laundry: The handiest option is **Emonec Launderette,** with self-service machines across the courtyard from the couldn't-be-more-central Hotel Emonec (described on page 756); this is a convenient spot to tumble-dry your undies while exploring (€5/load wash and dry, daily 6:00-20:00, Wolfova 12, tel. 01/200-1520). **Hostel Celica** also has self-service laundry—but it has only one machine, and hostel guests have priority (€8/load, not very central at Metelkova 8). For pricey full service, try **Tekstilexpress,** between the city center and Tivoli Park (€4.80/kilo, figure about €20-25 for a full load, takes 24 hours, Mon-Fri 7:00-19:00, Sat 9:00-13:00, closed Sun, Cankarjeva 10B, tel. 01/252-7354).

Car Rental: Handy options include **Hertz** (Trdinova 9, tel. 01/434-0147, www.hertz.si), **Europcar** (in City Hotel at Dalmatinova 15, mobile 031-382-052, www.europcar.si), **Avis** and **Budget** (both in Grand Hotel Union at Miklošičeva 3; Avis—tel. 01/241-7340, www.avis.si; Budget—tel. 01/421-7340, www.budget.si), and **Sixt** (at the train station, tel. 01/234-4650).

Best Views: The Skyscraper's observation deck offers the best views in town (see page 743). Views from the castle are nearly as good. At street level, my favorite views are from the bridge called Brv (between the Triple and Cobblers' bridges), especially at night. On sunny days, the colorful architecture on and near Prešeren Square pops, and you'll take photos like crazy along the river promenade.

GETTING AROUND LJUBLJANA

By Bus: Virtually all of Ljubljana's sights are easily accessible by foot. And using the buses is a bit of a headache: First, you have to buy a plastic "Urbana" card for €2, which you then load with credit to pay for rides (you can't pay the driver). A ride costs €1.20 (valid for up to 90 minutes, card shareable by up to three people). Buy the card at the TI, where you can return it to reclaim your €2 at the end of your trip. Transit info: www.lpp.si.

By Taxi: Always call for a cab, or you'll get ripped off. Because cabbies can legally charge whatever they want, even if they use the meter you'll still pay way too much. Legitimate taxis usually start at about €1.50, and then charge €1 per kilometer. But because city leaders refuse to regulate taxi tariffs, many unscrupulous cabbies (including all of those who wait at the train station) legally charge far more, and tack on bogus additional "surcharges." Crooked cabbies are a big problem in Ljubljana, but you can avoid this headache entirely by always calling a reputable taxi company instead of hailing one on the street. If you do this, Ljubljana is a fantastic taxi town with very affordable rates—a ride within the city center (such as from the station to a hotel) should run only a few euros, generally less than €5. Good companies include **Metro Taxi** (tel. 080-1190 or 041-240-200), **Laguna** (tel. 01/511-2314), or **Intertours** (tel. 01/520-9704). Don't be intimidated—dispatchers speak English, and your hotel, restaurant, or the TI can call a cab for you.

By Bike: Ljubljana is a cyclist's delight, with lots of well-marked bike lanes. It's easiest to rent bikes at the market square TI (€2/2 hours, €8/day; see "Tourist Information," earlier). Like many European cities, Ljubljana has a subsidized borrow-a-bike program (called BicikeLJ) with 30 locations around the city center. Once you register online with a credit card (€1 fee for a weekly subscription), rides are free or very cheap (free for the first hour, €1 for the second, €2 for the third, and so on). If you're planning on doing lots of biking, it's worth the hassle to sign up (http://en.bicikelj.si).

By Shuttle Bus: After Ljubljana pedestrianized much of its downtown core a few years back, the natives began to squawk about the hassle of getting around without a car. To mollify critics, the city subsidizes a network of green electric carts, called **Kavalir,** which anyone (even tourists) can flag down or call to take them anywhere within the pedestrian zone...for free. Just wave one down and tell them where you want to go (or phone them—April-Oct call 031-666-331 or 031-666-332; Nov-March call 031-666-299).

Tours in Ljubljana

To help you appreciate Ljubljana, taking a walking tour—either through the TI or by hiring your own local guide—is worth ▲▲.

Walking Tour

The TI organizes excellent two-hour guided town walks of Ljubljana in English, led by knowledgeable guides. In summer, the walk also includes either a trip up to the castle (by funicular or tourist train) or a 30-minute boat ride on the river. From April through September, there are three tours daily at 10:00, 14:00, and 17:00. From October through March, the walking tour goes daily at 11:00 (€10, or €9 if you pay at TI, meet at Town Hall around corner from Triple Bridge TI). They also offer a variety of other tours, including a food tour, a torchlight tour of Roman ruins, a Town Hall tour, and so on—get details at the TI.

Local Guides

Having an expert show you around his or her hometown for two hours for €70 has to be the best value in town. **Marijan Krišković,** who leads tours for me throughout Europe, is an outstanding guide (mobile 040-222-739, kriskovic@yahoo.com). **Barbara Jakopič,** thoughtful and extremely knowledgeable, also leads my tours (mobile 040-530-870, b_lucky2@yahoo.com). **Minka Kahrič,** who's traveled to the North Pole, also leads tours closer to home—including walks around Ljubljana and excursions into the country-side (€70/2-hour walking tour; driving: €100/up to 4 hours, €140/up to 8 hours; mobile 041-805-962, polarnimedo@yahoo.com). You can also book a guide through the TI (arrange at least 24 hours in advance).

Boat Cruise

Because Ljubljana is a small town that's easily seen on foot, a boat trip on the Ljubljanica River is more romantic than informative. You have two options for your one-hour cruise (weather permit-ting): with English commentary from a live guide (€10, 2/day in summer, departs from near the Triple Bridge—about one block along the embankment away from the market, get details from TI), or unguided (€8, may have audioguides, 2-3/hour in sum-mer 10:00-20:00, operated by various companies and from various docks—they'll approach you as you walk past).

Excursions from Ljubljana

Many worthwhile sights near Ljubljana are tricky to reach by pub-lic transportation. To hit several efficiently in one day, join an ex-cursion. Three relatively well-established outfits are **Roundabout** (their one-day "Karst and Coast Mystery" tour takes you to Pred-jama Castle, Škocjan Caves, Lipica, and Piran for €49 plus admis-sion to the caves and an optional wine tasting; www.roundabout. si; their "off the beaten track" tours delve deeper into local culture), **Slovenia Explorer** (their ambitious "Slovenia in 1 Day" trip visits Lake Bled, Postojna Caves, and Predjama Castle for €119; www.slovenia-explorer.com), and **Nature Adventures** (focused on active trips including rafting, paragliding, skydiving, and horseback rid-ing; www.adventures-nature.com). For multiday trips around the country, check out the **Loopyslovenia** hop-on, hop-off bus service (www.loopyslovenia.com).

Prešeren Square Spin Tour

The heart of Ljubljana is the people-friendly, traffic-free Prešeren Square (Prešernov trg, rated ▲▲), which is described in this self-guided spin tour.

The city's meeting point is the large **statue of France Prešeren,** Slovenia's greatest poet, whose works include the lyrics

to the Slovenian national anthem (and whose silhouette adorns Slovenia's €2 coin). The statue shows Prešeren, an important catalyst of 19th-century Slovenian nationalism, being inspired from above by a Muse. This statue provoked a scandal and outraged the bishop when it went up a century ago—a naked woman sharing the square with a church! To ensure that nobody could be confused about the woman's intentions, she's conspicuously depicted with typical Muse accessories: a laurel branch and a cloak. Even so, for the first few years citizens covered the scandalous statue with a tarp each night. And the model who posed for the Muse was so disgraced that no one in Slovenia would hire her—so she emigrated to South America and never returned.

Stand at the base of the statue to get oriented. The bridge crossing the Ljubljanica River is one of Ljubljana's top landmarks, Jože Plečnik's **Triple Bridge**

(Tromostovje). The middle (widest) part of this bridge already existed, but Plečnik added the two side spans to more efficiently funnel the six streets of traffic on this side of the bridge to the one street on the other side. The bridge's Venetian vibe is intentional: Plečnik recognized that Ljubljana, located midway between Venice and then-capital Vienna, is itself a bridge between the Italian and Germanic worlds. Across the bridge are the TI, WCs, ATMs, market and cathedral (to the left), and the Town Hall (straight ahead).

Now turn 90 degrees to the right, and look down the first street after the riverbank. Find the rose-colored woman in the picture frame on the second floor of the first yellow house. This is **Julija,** the unrequited love of Prešeren's life. Tour guides spin romantic tales about how the couple met. But the truth is far less exciting: He was a teacher in her father's house when he was in his 30s and she was 4. Later in life, she inspired him from afar—as she does now, from across the square—but they never got together. She may have been his muse, but when it came to marriage, she opted for wealth and status.

When Ljubljana was hit by an earthquake in 1895, locals took the opportunity (using an ample rebuilding fund from the

Austro-Hungarian Empire) to remake their city in style. Today Ljubljana—especially the streets around this square—is an architecture-lover's paradise. The **Hauptmann House,** to the right of Julija, was the only building on the square to survive the quake. A few years later, the owner redecorated it in the then-trendy Viennese Art Nouveau style you see today, using bright colors (since his family sold dyes). All that remains of the original structure is the little Baroque balcony above the entrance.

Just to the right of the Hauptmann House is a car-sized **model** of the city center—helpful for orientation. The street next to it (with the McDonald's) is **Čopova,** once the route of Ljubljana's Sunday promenade. A century ago, locals would put on their Sunday best and stroll from here to Tivoli Park, listening to musicians and dropping into cafés along the way. Plečnik called it the "lifeline of the city," connecting the green lungs of the park to this urban center. Through the 20th century, this route became less pedestrian-friendly, as Slovenska cesta and railroad tracks were both laid across it. Things are getting better with the closure of Slovenska to all traffic except buses, but Ljubljana's best evening *paseo* thrives along the river from the Triple Bridge all the way up the river.

Continue looking to the right, past the big, pink landmark Franciscan Church of St. Mary. Next door, the characteristic glass awning marks **Galerija Emporium**—the first big post-quake department store, today government-protected. At the top of the building is Mercury, god of commerce, watching over the square that has been Ljubljana's commercial heart since the city began. (If you look care-

fully, you can see the mustachioed face of the building's owner hiding in the folds of cloth by Mercury's left foot.) Since this area

Ljubljana at a Glance

▲▲▲**People-Watching** Ljubljana's single best activity is sitting at an outdoor café along the river and watching the vivacious, stylish, fun-loving Slovenes strut their stuff. **Hours:** 24/7.

▲▲**Riverside Market** Lively market area in the Old Town with produce, clothing, and souvenirs. **Hours:** Best in the morning, especially Sat; market hall open Mon-Fri 7:00-16:00, Sat 7:00-14:00, closed Sun. See page 730.

▲▲**Serbian Orthodox Church of Sts. Cyril and Methodius** Beautifully decorated house of worship giving insight into the Orthodox faith. **Hours:** Daily 8:00-19:00. See page 740.

▲▲**National and University Library** Jože Plečnik's pièce de résistance, with an intriguing facade, piles of books, and a bright reading room. **Hours:** Main staircase open Mon-Fri 8:00-20:00, Sat 9:00-14:00, closed Sun; student reading room open to the public only mid-July-mid-Aug Mon-Sat 14:00-18:00. See page 745.

▲▲**Jože Plečnik House** Final digs of the famed hometown architect who shaped so much of Ljubljana, explained by an enthusiastic guide. **Hours:** Tue-Sun 10:00-18:00, English tours begin at the top of each hour, last tour departs at 17:00, closed Mon. See page 747.

▲▲**Slovenian Ethnographic Museum** Engaging, well-presented collection celebrating Slovenian culture. **Hours:** Tue-Sun 10:00-18:00, closed Mon. See page 749.

▲**Cathedral** Italian Baroque interior and bronze doors with intricate, highly symbolic designs. **Hours:** Open long hours daily but closed 12:00-15:00. See page 733.

▲**Ljubljana Castle** Tower with good views and so-so 3-D film. **Hours:** Grounds open daily April-Sept 9:00-23:00, Oct-March 10:00-21:00; castle open daily June-Sept 9:00-21:00, April-May and Oct 9:00-20:00, Nov 10:00-19:00, Dec-March 10:00-18:00. See page 735.

▲**Contemporary History Museum** Baroque mansion in Tivoli Park, with exhibit highlighting Slovenia's last 100 years. **Hours:** Tue-Sun 10:00-18:00, closed Mon. See page 742.

▲**City Museum of Ljubljana** Modern, high-tech exhibit covering the city's history. **Hours:** Tue-Sun 10:00-18:00, Thu until 21:00, closed Mon. See page 744.

was across the river from medieval Ljubljana (beyond the town's limits...and the long arm of its tax collector), it was the best place to buy and sell goods. Today this sumptuously restored building houses a top-end fashion mall, making it the heart of Ljubljana's boutique culture. Step inside for a glimpse at the grand staircase.

The street between Galerija Emporium and the pink church is **Miklošičeva cesta,** which connects Prešeren Square to the train station. When Ljubljana was rebuilding after the 1895 earthquake, town architects and designers envisioned this street as a showcase of its new, Vienna-inspired Art Nouveau image.

Up Miklošičeva cesta and on the left is the prominent **Grand Hotel Union,** with a stately domed spire on the corner. When these buildings were designed, Prague was the cultural capital of the Slavic world. The new look of Ljubljana paid homage to "the golden city of a hundred spires" (and copied Prague's romantic image). The city actually had a law for several years that new corner buildings had to have these spires. Even the trees you'll see around town were part of the vision. When the architect Plečnik designed the Ljubljanica River embankments a generation later, he planted tall, pointy poplar trees and squat, rounded willows—imitating the spires and domes of Prague.

Detour a block up Miklošičeva cesta to see two more architec-tural gems of that era (across from the Grand Hotel Union): First is a Secessionist building—marked **Zadružna Zveza**—with classic red, blue, and white colors (for the Slo-venian flag). Next is the noisy, pink, zigzagged **Cooperative Bank.** The bank was designed by Ivan Vurnik, an ambitious Slovenian architect who wanted to invent a distinctive national style after World War I, when the Habsburg Empire broke up and Eastern Europe's nations were proudly emerging for the first time.

Prešeren Square is the perfect springboard to explore the rest of Ljubljana. Now that you're oriented, visit some of the areas listed next.

Sights in Ljubljana

Ljubljana is bursting with well-presented, we-try-harder museums celebrating Slovenian history and culture. These include the Slo-venian History Exhibition at the castle, the City Museum of Lju-bljana, and the Contemporary History Museum in Tivoli Park. As these are similar and largely overlapping, if you get museumed-out easily, just pick the one that's handiest to your sightseeing plan.

THE MARKET AND OLD TOWN

The castle (east) side of the river is the city's most colorful and historic quarter, packed with Old World ambience.

▲▲Riverside Market (Tržnice)

In Ljubljana's thriving Old Town market, big-city Slovenes enjoy buying directly from the producer. Prices go down as the day gets late and as the week goes on. The market, worth an amble anytime, is best on Saturday mornings, when the townspeople take their time wandering the stalls. In this tiny capital of a tiny country, you may even see the president searching for the perfect melon.

❍ **Self-Guided Walk:** Begin your walk through the market at the Triple Bridge (and TI). The riverside **colonnade,** which echoes the long-gone medieval city wall, was de-signed by (who else?) Jože Plečnik. This first stretch—nearest the Triple Bridge—is good for souvenirs: woodcarvings, replica painted frontboards from beehives, honey products (including honey brandy), and lots of color-ful candles (bubbly Marta will gladly paint a special message on your candle for no extra charge). For lots more shopping tips—here and nearby—see "Shopping in Ljubljana," later.

Farther in, the market is almost all local, and the colonnade is populated by butchers, bakers, fishermen, and lazy cafés. Peek down at the actual river and see how the architect wanted the town and river to connect. The lower arcade (which you can access directly from the Triple Bridge or by going down the spiral staircase by the beehive panels) is a people zone, with public WCs, inviting cafés, and a stinky fish market *(ribarnica)* offering a wide variety. The recommended restaurant just below, **Ribca,** serves fun fishy plates, beer, and coffee with great riverside seating.

Across from the stairs that lead down into the fish market, about where the souvenir stands end, you reach the first small mar-ket square. On your right, notice the 10-foot-tall concrete **cone.** Plečnik wanted to make Ljubljana the "Athens of the North" and imagined a huge cone-shaped national acropolis—a complex for government, museums, and culture. This ambitious plan didn't make it off the drawing board, but part of Plečnik's Greek idea came true: this marketplace, based on an ancient Greek *agora*.

Plečnik's cone still captures the Slovenes' imaginations...and adorns Slovenia's €0.10 coin.

At the top of this square, you'll find the 18th-century **cathedral** standing on the site of a 13th-century Romanesque church (check out its finely decorated doors—and, if they're open, go inside; for a complete description, see later).

The building at the end of the first market square is the seminary palace. In the basement is a **market hall** *(pokrita tržnica),* with vendors selling cheeses, meats, baked goods, dried fruits, nuts, and other goodies (Mon-Fri 7:00-16:00, Sat 7:00-14:00, closed Sun). This place is worth a graze—walk all the way through. Most merchants are happy to give you a free sample (point to what you want, and say *probat, prosim*—"a taste, please").

Leaving the market hall at the opposite end, turn left to reach the modern **Butchers' Bridge.** Jože Plečnik designed a huge roofed bridge to be built here, but—like so many of his designs—the plans were scuttled. Decades later, aware of Plečnik's newfound touristic currency, some town politicians dusted off the old plans and proposed building the bridge. The project stalled for years until the arrival of Mayor Zoran Janković, who swiftly constructed this modern version of the bridge. While it looks nothing like Plečnik's original plans, the bridge kept the old name and has been embraced by the community (there's a handy public WC down below on the lower level). The sculptures on the bridge, by local artist Jakov Brdar, were originally intended to be temporary—but people loved them, so they stayed. (The wild-eyed, wild-bearded Brdar often hangs out near the bridge, asking passersby how they like his creations.) Notice the mournful pose of the Adam and Eve statues (being evicted from the Garden of Eden) at the market end of the bridge. And don't miss the bizarre smaller sculptures along the railing—such as the ones that look like mischievous lizards breaking out of their eggs. Almost as soon as it was built, the bridge's railings were covered with padlocks—part of the recent Europe-wide craze for young couples to commemorate their love by locking a padlock to a bridge railing. But all those locks put too much strain on the railing—they are regularly cut off, soon to be replaced by new ones.

Sprawling up from the bridge is the **main market square,** packed with produce and clothing stands. (The colorful flower market hides behind the market hall.) The vendors in the row nearest the colonnade sell fruit from all over, but the ones located deeper in the market sell only locally-grown produce.

Zoran Janković

The latest chapter in Ljubljana's story has been written by its mayor, Zoran Janković. Sort of the Michael Bloomberg of Slovenia, this successful businessman transformed himself into a broadly supported mayor who is unafraid to pursue an ambitious civic agenda.

As chairman of the huge Mercator supermarket chain, Janković was famous for prowling around the front lines of his stores, micromanaging all the day-to-day business. After corporate political shuffling forced him out, Janković turned his attention to the municipal realm—and, in 2006, was elected mayor of Ljubljana in a landslide.

The people of this city had grown accustomed to well-intentioned but ineffectual leaders who would propose and then cancel ambitious projects. But Janković's no-nonsense follow-through finally made things happen. Project after project materialized, on time and under budget: the funicular to the castle, several new bridges (including the Butchers' Bridge at the market), the creation of quaintly cobbled traffic-free zones throughout almost the entire town center, the rejuvenation of miles of riverfront embankment for pedestrians, and closing a several-block stretch of one of Ljubljana's most heavily used downtown streets (Slovenska cesta) to all car traffic. The sweeping changes have had their critics, among them elderly people who can no longer easily drive to their homes in the now-traffic-free center. Janković has attempted to assuage them with free shuttle buses. Ultimately, most Ljubljanans are thrilled with the transformation of their city—he was reelected in another landslide in 2012. Janković embodies the ideal of how a progressive electorate can trust a capable leader to wisely invest public funds in urban-beautification projects that benefit the common good.

These producers go out of their way to be old-fashioned—a few of them still follow the tradition of pushing their veggies on wooden carts (called *cizas*) to the market from their garden patches in the suburbs. Once at the market, they simply display their goods on top of their cart, turning it into a sales kiosk. Tell the vendor what you want—it's considered rude for customers to touch the fruits and vegetables before they're bought. Over time, shoppers develop friendships with their favorite producers. On busy days, you'll see a long line at one stand, while the other merchants stand bored. Your choice is simple: Get in line, or eat subpar produce.

Near the market hall, look for the little **scales** in the wooden kiosks marked *Kontrolna Tehtnica*—allowing buyers to immediately check whether the producer cheated them (not a common problem, but just in case). The Habsburg days left locals with the old German saying, "Trust is good; control is better." Nearby, look for the innovative "Nonstop Mlekomat" stand, a vending machine that lets you buy a plastic bottle, then fill it with a liter of raw, unskimmed, farm-fresh milk for €1.

At the far end of the market—close to the Dragon Bridge—you may see a few **food trucks** selling roasted chicken and deep-fried seafood.

Two more sights are immersed in the market action (both described next); the cathedral sits at the top of the market area, near the Triple Bridge, while the Dragon Bridge spans the river just beyond the end of the market colonnade.

▲Cathedral (Stolnica)

Ljubljana's cathedral is dedicated to St. Nicholas, protector against floods and patron saint of the fishermen and boatmen who have long come to sell their catch at the market. While the interior is worth a peek, the intricately decorated doors—created for Pope John Paul II's visit here in 1996—are even more interesting.

Cost and Hours: Free, open long hours daily but closed 12:00-15:00.

Visiting the Cathedral: Begin outside, at the top of the small market square. Go under the high arch and take a close look at the cathedral's remarkable **main door.** Buried deeply in the fecund soil of the nation's ancient and pagan history, the linden tree of life sprouts with the story of the Slovenes. The ceramic pots represent the original Roman settlement here. Just to the left, above the tree, are the Byzantine missionaries Cyril and Methodius, who came here to convert the Slavs to Christianity in the ninth century. Just above, Crusaders and Ottomans do battle. Near the top, see the Slovenes going into the cave—entering the dark 20th century (World War I, World War II, and communism). At the top is Pope John Paul II (the first Slavic pontiff, who also oversaw the fall of communism). Below him are two men who are on track to becoming Slovenia's first saints; the one on the right is Frederic Baraga, a 19th-century bishop who became a missionary in Michigan and codified Chippewa grammar (notice the Native American relief on the book he's holding). In the upper right-hand corner is a sun, which has been shining since Slovenia gained its independence in 1991. Around back of the cathedral is a similar door, carved with images of the six 20th-century bishops of Ljubljana.

The cathedral's **interior** is stunning Italian Baroque. The transept is surrounded by sculptures of four bishops of Roman Ljubljana (when it was called Emona, or

Aemon). Left of the main altar, notice the distinctive chair. This was designed by the very religious Jože Plečnik, whose brother was a priest here. Look up over the nave to enjoy the recently restored, gorgeous ceiling fresco.

▲Dragon Bridge (Zmajski Most)

The dragon has been the symbol of Ljubljana for centuries, ever since Jason (of Argonauts and Golden Fleece fame) supposedly slew one in a nearby swamp. This is one of the few notable bits of Ljubljana architecture *not* by Plečnik (but by Jurij Zaninović, a fellow student of Vienna architect Otto Wagner). While the dragon is the star of this very photogenic Art Nouveau bridge, the bridge itself was officially dedicated to the 40th anniversary of Habsburg Emperor Franz Josef's

reign (see the dates on the side: 1848-1888). Tapping into the emp's vanity got new projects funded—vital as the city rebuilt after the 1895 earthquake. But the Franz Josef name never stuck; those dragons are just too darn memorable.

From the Dragon Bridge, it's an easy funicular ride or steep hike up to Ljubljana Castle (described later). Or you can head back through the market to reach the Town Square and Old Town (see next), where I've narrated a self-guided shopping tour.

▲Town Square (Mestni Trg) and the Old Town

Ljubljana's Town Square, just across the Triple Bridge and up the street from Prešeren Square, is home to the **Town Hall** (Rotovž), highlighted by its clock tower and pillared loggia. Step inside the Renaissance courtyard to see paintings, artifacts, and a map of late 17th-century Ljubljana. Studying this map, notice how the river, hill, and wall worked together to fortify the town. Courtyards like this (but humbler) are hidden throughout the city. As rent in these old places is cheap, many such courtyards host funky and characteristic little businesses. Be sure to get off the main drag and poke into Ljubljana's nooks and crannies.

In the square between the Town Hall and the cathedral is a recent replica of the **Fountain of Three Carniolan Rivers,** inspired in style and theme by Rome's many fountains. The figures with vases represent this region's three main rivers: Ljubljanica, Sava, and Krka. This is one of many works in town by Francesco Robba, an Italian who came to Ljubljana for a job, fell in love with a Slovene, and stayed here the rest of his life—decorating the city's churches with beautiful Baroque altars. At the nearby corner, check out the wild interior of the Nova KBM Bank, which looks more like a cutting-edge nightclub.

Now turn with your back to the fountain. You're staring down the single street that constitutes Ljubljana's Old Town. In the early 19th century, Ljubljana consisted mainly of this solitary main drag, running along the base of Castle Hill (plus a small "New Town" across the river). Stretching south from here are two other "squares"—Stari trg (Old Square) and Gornji trg (Upper Square)—which have long since grown together into one big, atmospheric promenade lined with quaint boutiques, great restaurants, and cafés. Virtually every house along this drag has a story to tell of a famous resident or infamous incident. As you walk, keep your eyes open for Ljubljana's mascot dragon—it's everywhere.

For a self-guided shopping stroll that runs the length of this delightful street—and highlights several fine shops en route—see "Shopping in Ljubljana," later.

▲Ljubljana Castle (Ljubljanski Grad)

The castle above town offers enjoyable views of Ljubljana and the surrounding countryside. There has probably been a settlement on this site since prehistoric times, though the first true fortress here was Roman. The 12th-century version was gradually added on to over the centuries, until it fell into disrepair in the 17th century. Today's castle—rebuilt in the 1940s and renovated in the 1970s—is a hollow-feeling replica, lacking any sense of real history. However, in recent years they've filled this shell with four worthwhile attractions and some respectable restaurants. It also offers a fine view, looking out over Ljubljana's rooftops and to the Alps on the horizon. The castle is home to the Ljubljana Festival, with concerts throughout the summer (tel. 01/306-4293, www.ljubljanafestival.si).

Cost and Hours: The grounds are free to visit and open daily April-Sept 9:00-23:00, Oct-March 10:00-21:00. Tickets and hours for the history exhibition, film, castle tower, and puppetry museum change from year to year. Most likely, you can pay €7.50 (or €10 with the round-trip funicular) for admission to all four. To add an audioguide or a guided tour (described next), you'll pay a total of €10 (or €12 with the funicular). The attractions are open daily June-Sept 9:00-21:00, April-May and Oct 9:00-20:00, Nov 10:00-19:00, Dec-March 10:00-18:00, tel. 01/232-9994, www.ljubljanskigrad.si.

"Time Machine" Tours: Guides dressed as historical figures lead one-hour tours of the castle (€10 combo-ticket with castle sights, or €12 to add funicular; July-Sept 4/day, May-June 2/day, Oct-April 2/day Sat-Sun only, confirm schedule at information office or funicular ticket desk, tours depart from castle information center).

Getting to the Castle: A slick **funicular** whisks visitors to the top in a jiff (€2.20 one-way, €4 round-trip, also included in combo-tickets described above, runs every 10 minutes, 1-minute ride, daily April-Sept 9:00-23:00, Oct-March 10:00-21:00, catch it at Krekov trg—across the street from the market square TI). From the top, you'll find free WCs and a few easy flights of stairs up into the heart of the castle complex (or take the elevator). Another sweat-free route to the top is via the **tourist train** that leaves at the top of each hour (or more frequently with demand) from the street in front of the Town Hall (€4 round-trip, daily in summer 9:00-21:00, shorter hours off-season, doesn't run in snow or other bad weather). There are also two handy **trails** to the castle. The steeper-but-faster route begins near the Dragon Bridge: Find Študentovska lane, just past the statue of Vodnik in the market. This lane dead-ends at a gravel path, which you'll follow up to a fork. Turn left to zigzag up the steepest and fastest route, which deposits you just below the castle wall; from here, turn left again and curl around the wall to reach the main drawbridge. Slower but a bit less steep is Reber, just off Stari trg, a few blocks south of the Town Hall: Walk up to the top of Reber, and, at the dead end, turn right and start climbing up the stairs. From here on out, keep bearing left, then go right when you're just under the castle (follow *Grad* signs).

Visiting the Castle: The castle's information office is on the courtyard above the top of the funicular. Across the way are the well-stocked Rustika gift shop and three eateries (the fancy Strelec; Gradska Kavana, the "castle café"; and the recommended Gostilna na Gradu, with traditional Slovenian cuisine). The upper floors house two wedding halls—Ljubljana's most popular places to get married (free for locals).

Most of the sights worth seeing at the castle are in the opposite wing, clustered around the base of the tallest tower. As you face the tower, the entrance to the history exhibit is to the left, while the "Virtual Castle" film and tower climb itself are to the right. The Museum of Puppetry is near the information office.

The **Slovenian History Exhibition** offers a concise but engaging overview of this little country's story. As you enter, ask to borrow the free audioguide, then head downstairs and work your way up. Dark display cases light up when you approach, revealing actual artifacts, video clips, and touchscreens with more information. A unique feature of the museum is that you're invited to touch replicas of important historic items (in many cases, the originals are in other Ljubljana museums). Don't miss the top floor of the exhibit (go up the glassed-in staircase), which is the most interesting—covering the tumultuous 20th century. You'll learn about topics ranging from the battlefields of World War I, to the creation of the first Yugoslavia, to the fascist occupation and harrowing Italian-run concentration camps of World War II, to the cult of personality around Partisan war hero-turned-Yugoslav president Tito, to Slovenia's bid for independence.

Entering the door to the right of the tower, you'll first find the small **penitentiary** exhibit, recalling the post-Napoleonic era, when the castle was converted to a prison. It saw the most action during World War I, when it housed political prisoners (including the beloved Slovenian writer Ivan Cankar) and POWs. Modest exhibits inside actual former cells describe the history and list the names of past inmates.

If you head downstairs from the entrance, you'll find a Gothic **chapel** with Baroque paintings of St. George (Ljubljana's patron saint, the dragon-slayer) and coats of arms of the various aristocratic families that have called this castle home.

Heading up the stairs, you'll find the informative, entertaining, and nicely animated **"Virtual Castle" film,** in which Ljubljana's mascot dragon describes this hill's layers of history (12 minutes, plays all day on the half-hour; often in English, but otherwise borrow English headset).

Finally, climb the 92 spiral steps up to the **castle tower,** with one of the best views in town.

Don't miss the oddly fascinating **Museum of Puppetry** (ride up the elevator inside the gift shop near the castle information office). This traces the history of puppetry as an art form, which flourished in the Modernist milieu of early-20th-century Ljubljana. You'll step into a surreal world of marionettes, shadow puppets, and other creations. This is not a goofy attraction for kids; in fact, some of the puppets are quite grotesque and disturbing. You'll see marionettes of Adolf Hitler and Partisan troops, watch grainy footage of famous puppet masters (including Milan Klemenčič, who pioneered the form here in 1910), then climb up to the mezzanine and put on a show of your own.

Eating: Combine your visit to the castle with a meal at the recommended **Gostilna na Gradu,** with the best traditional Slovenian food in town (in the castle courtyard; described later, under

"Eating in Ljubljana"). The pricey **Strelec** restaurant, while a bit pretentious, has a big-name chef and a growing reputation.

THE MUSEUM ZONE AND TIVOLI PARK

The Prešeren Square (west) side of the river is the heart of modern Ljubljana, and home to several prominent squares and fine museums. These sights are listed roughly in order from Prešeren Square and can be linked to make an interesting walk.

• *Leave Prešeren Square in the direction the poet is looking, bear to your left (up Wolfova, by the picture of Julija), and walk a block to...*

Congress Square (Kongresni Trg)

This grassy, tree-lined square hosts big events. It's ringed by some of Ljubljana's most important buildings: the University headquarters, the Baroque Ursuline Church of the Holy Trinity, a classical mansion called the Kazina, and the Philharmonic Hall. The green belt at the heart of the square, called Park Zvezda ("Star Park") for its radiating paths, is fronted by several inviting cafés and restaurants; the recommended **Zvezda Kavarna** is a top spot for its local cakes and ice cream.

At the top end of the square, by the entry to a pedestrian underpass, a Roman sarcophagus sits under a gilded statue of a **Roman citizen**—a replica of a Roman tomb sculpture from 1,700 years ago, when this town was called Emona. The busy street above you has been the site of the main trading route through town since ancient Roman times. Information boards tell you more.

Take a few steps into the underpass, and look left to find the easy-to-miss **Chopin Passage** (Chopinov Prehod), which displays exposed parts of the original Roman-era road and a model of Emona in ancient times.

• *Continue the rest of the way through the underpass beneath Slovenska cesta, then walk straight through the gap in the Maxi shopping mall into the...*

▲Square of the Republic (Trg Republike)

This unusual plaza is ringed by an odd collection of buildings. While hardly quaint, the Square of the Republic gives you a good taste of a modern corner of Ljubljana. And it's historic—this is where Slovenia declared its independence in 1991.

The **twin office towers** (with the world's biggest digital watch, flashing the date, time, and temperature) were designed by Plečnik's protégé, Edvard Ravnikar. As harrowing as these structures seem, imagine if the builders had followed the original plans—the towers would be twice as tall as they are now and connected by a bridge, representing the gateway to Ljubljana. These buildings were originally designed as the Slovenian parliament, but they were scaled back when Tito didn't approve (since it would have made Slovenia's parliament bigger than the Yugoslav parliament in Belgrade). Instead, the **Slovenian Parliament** is across the square, in the low-profile office building with the sculpted entryway. The carvings are in the Socialist Realist style, celebrating the noble Slovenian people conforming to communist ideals for the good of the entire society. Completing the square are a huge conference center (Cankarjev Dom, the white building behind the skyscrapers), a shopping mall, and some public art.

• *Just a block north, across the street and through the grassy park (Trg Narodni Herojev), you'll find the...*

Slovenian National Museum (Narodni Muzej Slovenije) and Slovenian Museum of Natural History (Prirodoslovni Muzej Slovenije)

These two museums share a single historic building facing a park behind the Parliament. They're both average but worth considering if you have a special interest or if it's a rainy day.

The **National Museum** occupies the ground floor, featuring a lapidarium with carved-stone Roman monuments and exhibits on Egyptian mummies. (Temporary exhibits are also on this level.) Upstairs and to the right are more exhibits of the National Museum, with archaeological findings ranging from old armor and pottery to the museum's two prized possessions: a fragment of a 45,000-year-old Neanderthal flute fashioned from a cave bear's femur—supposedly the world's oldest musical instrument; and the "figural situla," a beautifully decorated hammered-bronze bucket from the fifth century B.C. Embossed with scenes of everyday Iron Age life, this object has been a gold mine of information for archaeologists.

Upstairs and to the left is the **Natural History** exhibit, featuring the flora and fauna of Slovenia. You'll see partial skeletons of a mammoth and a cave bear, plenty of stuffed reptiles, fish, and birds, and an exhibit on "human fish" (*Proteus anguinus*—long, skinny, pale-pink, sightless salamanders unique to caves in this part of Europe).

Cost and Hours: €6 for National Museum, €4 for Natural History Museum, or €8.50 for both, some English descriptions, both open daily 10:00-18:00, Thu until 20:00, Prešernova 20, tel. 01/241-4400, www.nms.si and www.pms-lj.si.

• *At the far end of the building is a glassed-in annex displaying Roman stone monuments (free). Turning left around the museum building and walking one block, you'll see the...*

US Embassy

This pretty yellow chalet (with brown trim and a red roof, at Prešernova cesta 31) wins my vote for quaintest embassy building in the world. Resist the urge to snap a photo...those guards are all business.

• *Just up Prešernova cesta from the embassy are two decent but skippable art museums.*

National Gallery (Narodna Galerija)

This museum has three parts: European artists (in the new building), Slovenian artists (in the old building), and temporary exhibits. Find the work of Ivana Kobilca, a late 19th-century Slovenian Impressionist. Art lovers enjoy her self-portrait in *Summer*. If you're going to Bled, you can get a sneak preview with Marko Pernhart's huge panorama of the Julian Alps.

Cost and Hours: €5, special exhibits typically cost extra, permanent collection free first Sun of the month, open Tue-Sun 10:00-18:00, closed Mon; if main entrance at Cankarjeva 20 is closed for renovation, use the other entrance at the big glass box between two older buildings at Prešernova 24; tel. 01/241-5418, www.ng-slo.si.

Museum of Modern Art (Moderna Galerija Ljubljana)

Newly renovated, this museum has a permanent collection of modern and contemporary Slovenian artists, as well as temporary exhibits by both homegrown and international artists. To explore the "Continuities and Ruptures" permanent collection (aptly named for a place with such a fractured, up-and-down recent history), borrow the English floor plan and take a chronological spin through the 20th century. Unusual for a "modern" art museum is the room with Partisan art, with stiff, improvised, communist-style posters from the days when Tito and his crew were just a ragtag militia movement.

Cost and Hours: €5, ask about combo-ticket with contemporary branch at Metelkova—see page 751, Tue-Sun 10:00-18:00, Thu until 20:00 in July-Aug, closed Mon, Tomšičeva 14, tel. 01/241-6800, www.mg-lj.si.

• *By the busy road near the art museums, look for the distinctive Neo-Byzantine design (tall domes with narrow slits) of the...*

▲▲Serbian Orthodox Church of Sts. Cyril and Methodius

Ljubljana's most striking church interior isn't Catholic, but Orthodox. This church was built in 1936, soon after the Slovenes joined a political union with the Serbs. Wealthy Slovenia attracted its poorer neighbors from the south—so it built this church for that community. Since 1991, the Serb population continues to grow, as people from the struggling corners of the former Yugoslavia flock to prosperous Slovenia. Its gorgeous interior—which feels closer to Moscow than to Rome— offers visitors a taste of this important faith.

Cost and Hours: Free, daily 8:00-19:00; divine liturgy Sun at 11:00, other days services at 8:30 and 18:00; Prešernova cesta 35, www.spc-ljubljana.si.

Visiting the Church: Step inside for the best glimpse of the Orthodox faith this side of Dubrovnik. The church is colorfully decorated without a hint of the 21st century, mirroring a very conservative religion. Many of the church's colorful frescoes are copies of famous frescoes that decorate medieval Serbian Orthodox monasteries throughout the Balkans. On the balcony (at the back of the nave), you'll see Cyrillic script that explains the history of the church. Notice that there are no pews, because worshippers stand throughout the service. On the left, find the little room with tubs of water, where the faithful light tall, skinny beeswax candles (purchased at the little window in the back corner). The painted screen, or iconostasis, is believed to separate our material world from the spiritual realm behind it. Ponder the fact that several centuries ago, before the Catholic Church began to adapt to a changing world, all Christians worshipped this way. For more on the Orthodox faith, see the sidebar on page 1017).

• *On the other side of the busy street is...*

Tivoli Park (Park Tivoli)

This huge park, just west of the center, is where Slovenes relax on summer weekends. The easiest access is through the graffiti-covered underpass from Cankarjeva cesta (between the Serbian Orthodox Church and the Museum of Modern Art). As you emerge, the Neoclassical pillars leading down the promenade clue you in that this part of the park was designed by Jože Plečnik. Along this "main boulevard" of the park, various changing photographic exhibitions are displayed.

• *Aside from taking a leisurely stroll, the best thing to do in the park is visit the...*

▲Contemporary History Museum
(Muzej Novejše Zgodovine)

In a Baroque mansion (Cekinov Grad) in Tivoli Park, a well-done exhibit called "Slovenians in the 20th Century" traces the last hundred years of Slovenia—essentially from the end of World War I to independence in 1991. Out front is a T-55 Yugoslav tank that was commandeered by the Slovenes during their war for independence. Inside, the ground floor displays temporary exhibits, and upstairs you'll find several rooms using models, dioramas, light-and-sound effects, and English explanations to creatively tell the story of one of Europe's youngest nations. While it's a little difficult to fully appreciate, the creativity and the spunky spirit of the place are truly enjoyable.

Cost and Hours: €3.50, permanent exhibit free first Sun of the month, guidebook-€5, open Tue-Sun 10:00-18:00, closed Mon, in Tivoli Park at Celovška cesta 23, tel. 01/300-9610, www.muzej-nz.si.

Getting There: The museum is a 20-minute walk from the center, best combined with a wander through Tivoli Park. The fastest approach: As you emerge from the Cankarjeva cesta underpass into the park, climb up the stairs, then turn right and go straight ahead for five minutes. You'll continue straight up the ramp, then turn left after the tennis courts and look for the big pink-and-white mansion on the hill.

Visiting the Museum: The exhibit begins at the dawn of the 20th century, during Slovenia's waning days as part of the Austro-Hungarian Empire. You'll walk through a simulated trench from the Soča Front, then learn about the creation of the post-World War I Kingdom of Serbs, Croats, and Slovenes (or, as this exhibit pointedly puts it, "Kingdom of Slovenes, Croats, and Serbs").

Your footfalls echo loudly as you enter the room describing Slovenia's WWII experience (ask them to start the 12-minute "multivision" wrap-around slideshow, with music and sound effects). You'll learn how during that war, Slovenia was divided between neighboring fascist powers Germany, Italy, and Hungary. Each one tried (but failed) to exert linguistic and cultural control over the people, hoping to eradicate the Slovenian national identity. Video screens show subtitled interviews with people who lived through those war years.

Passing through the ballroom, you reach the "Slovenia 1945-1960" exhibit, outlining both the good (modernization) and the bad (prison camps and secret police) of the early Tito years. Despite his ruthless early rule, Tito remains popular here; under his stern bust, page through the photo album of Tito's visits to Slovenia. Find the display of the country's former currencies. Examining the Yugoslav dinar, notice that the figureheads on that communist currency were generic, idealized workers, farmers, and other members of the proletariat...except for a few notable individuals (including Tito). Meanwhile, Slovenia's short-lived post-Yugoslav currency, the *tolar* (1991-2006, R.I.P.), featured artists and scientists rather than heads of state and generals.

The most evocative room has artifacts from the Slovenes' brave declaration of independence from a hostile Yugoslavia in 1991. The well-organized Slovenes had only to weather a 10-day skirmish to gain their freedom. It's chilling to think that at one point bombers were en route to level this gorgeous city. The planes were called back at the last minute, by a Yugoslav People's Army officer with allegiances to Slovenia.

• *Hungry? Straight ahead and down the stairs from the museum, look for the "Hot Horse" food kiosk, selling €4 horseburgers (no joke). A local institution, this is a popular place to get together with friends and neighbors. The giant, modern, blocky, light-blue building across the busy road is the Pivovarna Union—the brewery for Ljubljana's favorite beer.*

On your way back to the center, you could stop by...

▲The Skyscraper (Nebotičnik)

This 1933 building was the first skyscraper in Slovenia, for a time the tallest building in Central Europe, and one of the earliest European buildings that was clearly influenced by American architecture. Art Deco inside and out, it's a thrill for architecture fans and anyone who enjoys a great view—the top floor, which hosts a pricey restaurant, café, and observation deck, offers the best panorama of Ljubljana's skyline. Zip up in the elevator just to take a peek, or stay for a drink or meal.

There are three levels: The best is floor #12, where you can sit outside (or, in bad weather, head up the spiral stairs to the glassed-in terrace) and enjoy a drink with unobstructed views over the city and castle (€3 beer/wine/coffee, €5-8 cocktails, €5-7 light food). One floor below (#11) is the indoor club/lounge, with a similar menu. And on the next floor down (#10) is the restaurant, with pricey food (€10-19 main courses) and less-impressive views. The good-value €8 lunch deals are available in either place. I'd skip the restaurant and the club, and just grab a drink or snack up on the terrace.

Cost and Hours: Free to ride the elevator up for a peek, but you should buy at least a drink if you want to stick around; terrace and club open daily 9:00-very late; restaurant open Mon-Sat 12:00-21:00, closed Sun; 2 blocks from Prešeren Square at Štefanova 1, tel. 040-601-787, www.neboticnik.si.

• *A few blocks south, near several Jože Plečnik sights (see next section) at the river end of French Revolution Square, you'll find the...*

▲City Museum of Ljubljana (Mestni Muzej Ljubljana)

This thoughtfully presented museum, located in the recently re-stored Auersperg Palace, offers a high-tech, in-depth look at the story of this city. Though everything is well-described in English (and touchscreens provide even more information), a student on the museum's staff might be able to show you around if it's not too busy—ask.

Cost and Hours: €6, Tue-Sun 10:00-18:00, Thu until 21:00, closed Mon, kid-friendly, Gosposka 15, tel. 01/241-2510, www.mgml.si.

Visiting the Museum: You'll begin your visit in the cellar, with Roman ruins (including remains of the original Roman road and sewer system, found right here) and layers of medieval artifacts. A model of the modern city—sitting upon footprints of the Roman (red) and medieval (blue) settlements—illustrates Ljubljana's many layers of history. If it's not traveling to other museums (as it usually is), you may see the world's oldest wooden wheel on an axle, dating from around 3200 B.C. and discovered in the Ljubljana marshlands. Upstairs are the mayor's room (with a few exhibits) and the ever-evolving permanent collection, called Faces of Ljubljana. Exhibits on economy and trade include communist-era advertisements, while another section explains how Ljubljana has belonged to 10 different states over the last 200 years, ranging from the genteel Habsburg Empire to the oppressive Nazi regime to membership in the benevolent EU. You'll also see an actual Fiat Zastava 750 car, the classic "Fičko" car that everyone owned—or wanted to own—in communist Yugoslavia (sort of a proto-Yugo). Rounding out the collection is a range of temporary exhibits.

Nearby: Your ticket includes admission to two archaeological sites nearby (summer only)—pick up a map at the front desk.

• *If visiting the museum, don't miss the nearby National and University Library and French Revolution Square—both described in the next section.*

JOŽE PLEČNIK'S ARCHITECTURE

Jože Plečnik is to Ljubljana what Antoni Gaudí is to Barcelona: a homegrown, amazingly prolific genius who shaped his town with a unique and beautiful vision. And Plečnik's mark on Ljubljana, much like Gaudí's on Barcelona, has a way of turning people who couldn't care less about architecture into fans. There's plenty to see. In addition to the Triple Bridge, the riverside market, and the sights listed here, Plečnik designed the embankments along the Ljubljanica and Gradaščica rivers in the Trnovo neighborhood; the rebuilt Roman wall along Mirje street, south of the center; the Church of St. Francis, with its classicist bell tower; St. Michael's

Church on the Marsh; Orel Stadium; Žale Cemetery; and many more buildings throughout Slovenia.

Some of the best Plečnik sights are near the river, just south of Congress and Prešeren squares. I've linked them into a short self-guided walk.

• *From Prešeren Square, stroll south along the river. After the plain bridge called Brv, you'll come to the...*

▲Cobblers' Bridge (Čevljarski Most)

Named for the actual cobblers who set up shop along the river in olden times, the bridge encapsulates Plečnik's style perhaps better

than any other structure: simple, clean lines adorned with classical columns. Ideal for people-watching (with the castle hovering scenically overhead), this is one of Ljubljana's most appealing spots.

• *Continue past Cobblers' Bridge on the right side of the river, past the fountain. After about a block, turn right up the parked-up street called Novi trg. At the top of this street, on the left, is a red-brick building embedded with gray granite blocks in an irregular checkerboard pattern. This is the...*

▲▲National and University Library
(Narodna in Univerzitetna Knjižnica, or NUK)

Widely regarded as Plečnik's masterpiece, this building is a bit underwhelming...until an understanding of its symbolism brings it to life.

Cost and Hours: Free, staircase open Mon-Fri 8:00-20:00, Sat 9:00-14:00, closed Sun. The quiet main reading room is officially open for visitors only mid-July-mid-Aug Mon-Sat 14:00-18:00.

Visiting the Library:
Begin by standing outside and surveying the **exterior.** On the surface, the red-and-gray color scheme evokes the red soil and chunks of granite of the Karst region, south of Ljubljana. But on a deeper level, the library's design conveys the theme of overcoming obstacles to attain knowledge. In the facade, the blocks of irregular size and shape represent a complex numerological pattern that suggests barriers on the path to enlightenment. The sculpture on the river

side is Moses—known for leading his people through 40 years of hardship to the Promised Land. On the right side of the building, find the horse-head doorknobs—representing the winged horse Pegasus (grab hold, and he'll whisk you away to new levels of enlightenment).

Step **inside**. The main staircase is dark and gloomy—modeled after an Egyptian tomb. But at the top, through the door marked *Velika Čitalnica,* is the bright, airy main reading room: the ultimate goal, a place of learning. The top-floor windows are shaped roughly like open books. Sadly, except for one month a year when the students are on summer break, you can't actually enter the reading room; you'll just have to look at postcards in the shop, and imagine young Ljubljanans hunched studiously over their books, surrounded by Plečnik's bookshelves, railings, and high windows.

Aside from being a great work of architecture, the building also houses the most important library in Slovenia, with more than two million books (about one per Slovene). The library is supposed to receive a copy of each new book printed in the country. In a freaky bit of bad luck, this was the only building in town damaged in World War II, when a plane crashed into it. But the people didn't want to see their books go up in flames—so hundreds of locals formed a human chain, risking life and limb to save the books from the burning building.

• *Directly behind the library is a mellow square with an obelisk in the middle. This is...*

French Revolution Square (Trg Francoske Revolucije)

Plečnik designed the **obelisk** in the middle of the square to commemorate Napoleon's short-lived decision to make Ljubljana the capital of his Illyrian Provinces. It's rare to find anything honoring Napoleon outside of Paris, but he was good to Ljubljana. Under his rule, Slovenian culture flourished, the Slovene language became widely recognized and respected for the first time, schools were established, and roads and infrastructure were improved. The monument contains ashes of the unknown French soldiers who died in 1813, when the region went from French to Austrian control.

The Teutonic Knights of the Cross established the nearby **monastery** (Križanke, ivy-capped wall and gate, free entry) in 1230. The adaptation of these monastery buildings into the Ljubljana Summer Theatre was Plečnik's last major work (1950-1956).

• *From here, it's a scenic 10-minute walk to the next sight. From the obelisk, walk down Emonska toward the twin-spired church. You'll pass (on the left) the delightful Krakovo district—a patch of green countryside in downtown Ljubljana. Many of the veggies you see in the riverside market come from these carefully tended gardens. When you reach the Gradaščica stream, head over the bridge (also designed by Plečnik) and go around the left side of the church to find the house.*

▲▲Jože Plečnik House (Plečnikova Zbirka)

One of Ljubljana's most interesting sights is the house of the architect who redesigned much of the city. Today the house is decorated exactly as it was the day Plečnik died, containing much of his equipment, models, and plans. The house can be toured only with a guide, whose enthusiasm brings the place to life. There are very few barriers, so you are in direct contact with the world of the architect. Still furnished with unique, Plečnik-designed furniture, one-of-a-kind inventions, and favorite souvenirs from his travels, the house paints an unusually intimate portrait of an artist. While the house initially underwhelms some visitors, it's a ▲▲▲ pilgrimage for those who get caught up in Ljubljana's idiosyncratic sense of style.

Cost and Hours: €6, Tue-Sun 10:00-18:00—last tour departs at 17:00, closed Mon, 45-minute English tours begin at the top of each hour, Karunova 4, tel. 01/280-1600, www.mgml.si.

Getting There: It's directly behind the twin steeples of the Trnovo Church. The 15-minute stroll from the center—the same one Plečnik took to work each day—is nearly as enjoyable as the house itself. You can either walk south along the river, then turn right onto Gradaška and stroll along the stream to the church; or, from French Revolution Square, head south on Emonska. Either way, you'll pass through the garden-patch district of Krakovo, where pea patches and characteristic Old World buildings gracefully cohabitate. On the way to or from the museum, it's enjoyable to get a meal in Krakovo (two great restaurants—Pri Škofu and Manna—are described later, under "Eating in Ljubljana").

Background: Ljubljana's favorite son lived here from 1921 until his death in 1957. He added on to an existing house, building a circular bedroom for himself and filling the place with bric-a-brac he designed, as well as artifacts, photos, and gifts from around the world that inspired him as he shaped Ljubljana. Living a simple, almost monastic lifestyle, Plečnik knew what he liked, and these tastes are mirrored in his house.

Visiting the House: While waiting for your tour to begin,

Jože Plečnik (1872-1957)

There is probably no other single architect who has shaped one city as Jože Plečnik (YOH-zheh PLAYCH-neek) shaped Ljubljana. From libraries, office buildings, cemeteries, and stadiums to landscaping, riverside embankments, and market halls, Plečnik left his mark everywhere.

Plečnik was born in Ljubljana to a cabinet maker. He worked as a furniture designer and dabbled as a self-trained architect, catching the eye of the great Secessionist architect Otto Wagner—who invited him to study in Vienna. Plečnik's first commissions, done around the turn of the 20th century in Vienna, were pretty standard Art Nouveau stuff. Then Tomáš Masaryk, president of the new nation of Czechoslovakia, decided that Prague Castle could use a new look. But he didn't want an Austrian architect; it had to be a Slav. In 1921, Masaryk chose Jože Plečnik, who sprinkled the castle grounds with his distinctive touches. By now, Plečnik had perfected his simple, eye-pleasing style, which mixes modern and classical influences, with lots of columns and pyramids—at once austere and playful.

By the time Plečnik finished in Prague, he had made a name for himself. His prime years were spent creating for the Kingdom of Yugoslavia (before the ideology-driven era of Tito). Plečnik returned home to Ljubljana and set to work redesigning the city, both as an architect and as an urban planner. He lived in a humble house (now a recommended museum) behind the Trnovo Church. On his walk to work every day, he pondered ways to make the city even more livable. As you wander through town, notice how thoughtfully he incorporated people, nature, the Slovenian heritage, town vistas, and symbolism into his works—it's feng shui on a grand urban scale.

For all of Plečnik's ideas that became reality, even more did not. After World War II, the very religious Plečnik fell out of favor with the new communist government. (It's fun to imagine how this city might look if Plečnik had always gotten his way.) After his death in 1957, Plečnik was virtually forgotten by Slovenes and scholars alike.

But in 1986, an exposition about Plečnik at Paris' Pompidou Center jump-started interest in the architect. Within a few years, Plečnik was back in vogue. Today, scholars laud him as a genius who was ahead of his time...while locals and tourists enjoy the elegant simplicity of his works.

explore the modest but engaging **museum,** offering biographical details about Plečnik. In one room, a model of Ljubljana locates the many structures he designed all around the city. You'll also see descriptions and photos of his greatest works, and large wooden models of two of his biggest "unrealized projects" that never made it off the drawing board: the cone-shaped national acropolis and the roofed Butchers' Bridge at the market.

The **tour** takes you through the actual rooms where Plečnik lived: kitchen, circular bedroom, sitting room, studio, and greenhouse. As you tour the place, be patient. Listen to its stories. Appreciate the subtle details. Notice how reverently your guide (and other Slovenes) speaks of this man. Contrast the humbleness of Plečnik's home with the dynamic impact he had on the cityscape of Ljubljana and the cultural heritage of Slovenia. Wandering Plečnik's hallways, it's hard not to be tickled by this man's sheer creativity and by the unique world he forged for himself to live in. As a visitor to his home, you're in good company. He invited only his closest friends here—except during World War II, when Ljubljana was occupied by Nazis and the university was closed, and Plečnik allowed his students to work with him here.

IN METELKOVA

Three museums face each other on a slick modern plaza next to the park called Tabor, about a 15-minute walk northeast of Prešeren Square in the dull but up-and-coming district of Metelkova. Nearby, you can explore the funky squatters' colony of Metelkova City (with Ljubljana's famous prison-turned-youth hostel).

▲▲Slovenian Ethnographic Museum (Slovenski Etnografski Muzej)

Housed in a state-of-the-art facility, this delightful museum is Ljubljana's most underrated attraction. With both permanent and temporary exhibits, the museum strives to explain what it is to be Slovene, with well-presented and well-described cultural artifacts from around the country. If you've caught the Slovenian folk culture itch, this is the place to scratch it.

Cost and Hours: €4.50, free first Sun of month, Tue-Sun 10:00-18:00, closed Mon, great café, Metelkova 2, tel. 01/300-8745, www.etno-muzej.si.

Visiting the Museum: The ground and first floors have good temporary exhibits, while upstairs you'll find two permanent exhibits.

The best exhibit, filling the third floor, is called **"Between Nature and Culture."** As you exit the elevator, turn left and find the shrunken head, which comes with a surprisingly frank exhibit that acknowledges the shortsighted tendency for museum curators—

including at this museum—to emphasize things that are foreign or different. Continue through collections of "Reflections of Distant Worlds" (non-European cultures) to reach the core of the collection, which focuses on Slovenia. A good but slow-moving film visits the country's four major regions. Another exhibit ponders how people half a world away—in Slovenia and in North America—simultaneously invented a similar solution (snowshoes) for a common problem. One display deconstructs Slovenian clichés (including this country's odd fascination with its traditional hayracks). The arrangement of the collection emphasizes the evolution of an increasingly complicated civilization, from basic farming tools to ceramics to modern technology. You'll see exhibits on traditional Slovenian beekeeping, blacksmithing, weaving, shoemaking, costumes and customs, pottery, furniture, and religious objects. The children's "Ethnoalphabet" area features an A-to-Ž array of engaging, hands-on activities.

The other permanent exhibit, on the second floor (from the elevator, turn left to find the entrance), is called "**I, We, and Others.**" A bit too conceptual for its own good, this heady exhibit ponders the notion of belonging. Designed for Slovenes more than foreigners (with very limited posted English information—borrow the free English audioguide from the ticket desk before heading up), it explores various aspects of how people define who they are, from individual and family to community and nation. Videos and sounds enhance the exhibits, and the curators neatly juxtapose well-known icons from different cultures (such as various national parliament buildings) in thought-provoking ways. While it's easy to get lost amid the navel-gazing, there is something particularly poignant about this topic here in the identity-obsessed Balkans.

Slovenian National Museum-Metelkova (Narodni Muzej Slovenije)

Next door to the Ethnographic Museum is this facility, where items from the Slovenian National Museum that were formerly tucked away in storage are now displayed on two floors. The very pretty historical bric-a-brac is neatly presented without much context—it's just an excuse to get a bunch of interesting stuff out into public view. Each room has a different collection: furniture, pottery and ceramics, church vestments, weapons and armor, and more. The painting gallery is nicely organized by century and style. The museum also features temporary exhibits. Everything's labeled in English, and a guide can show you around, if they're not too busy.

Cost and Hours: €6, Tue-Sun 10:00-18:00, closed Mon, Maistrova 1, tel. 01/230-7032.

Museum of Contemporary Art-Metelkova
(Muzej Sodobne Umetnosti Metelkova, MSUM)

This cutting-edge branch of the Museum of Modern Art opened in 2012 to showcase changing exhibitions of present-day, mostly Slovenian and Eastern European artists. In addition to temporary installations, it populates its permanent "The Present and Presence" exhibit with a variety of pieces from its collection. The modern space is at once sleek and playful, making this museum worth a visit for art lovers who appreciate works from the 1960s to the present.

Cost and Hours: €5, ask about combo-ticket with Museum of Modern Art, Tue-Sun 10:00-18:00, closed Mon, Maistrova 3, tel. 01/241-6825, www.mg-lj.si.

Metelkova City (Metelkova Mesto)

The heart of Slovenia's counterculture, this former military installation is now a funky, graffiti-and-wild-art-slathered squatter's colony, billed as an "autonomous cultural center." Built by the Habsburgs in the 1880s, the complex—with barracks, warehouses, and a prison—was used by a laundry list of later occupiers, from Italian fascists to Nazis to the Yugoslav People's Army. After Yugoslavia pulled its troops out of Slovenia (following the Ten-Day War), the cluster of buildings sat derelict and abandoned. In 1993, transient artists moved into the sprawling complex and set up galleries, theaters, bars, and nightclubs. While controversial at first, Metelkova City has gradually become accepted by most Ljubljanans, and the city (which owns the property) not only tolerates but, in subtle ways, encourages this hotbed of youthful artistic expression. While edgy, this place is fascinating to explore—it's sleepy by day and lively by night (www.metelkovamesto.org).

Anchoring the area is **Hostel Celica,** one of Europe's most unusual youth hostels, which fills a former prison building. Twenty artists were invited to decorate cells that have been turned into accommodations, and the ground floor features vibrant public spaces, a good and affordable restaurant (a nice place for a lunch or a light dinner), and a shoes-off "Oriental café." The message: Thoughtful art and architecture can transcend an ugly history. You can drop by to see the building anytime, and ask to borrow a flashlight to explore the dank and gloomy basement solitary confinement cells, with a small but interesting exhibition on the history of the building (and the various prisoners who have called it home—including Janez Janša, who did time here during communism and later became Slovenia's prime minister). But if you're interested in this place, make a point to visit at 14:00 for a free guided tour of the entire complex (tours run daily; you can also try calling to arrange a tour at other times, tel. 01/230-9700, www.hostelcelica.com).

LJUBLJANA

Shopping in Ljubljana

Ljubljana, with its easygoing ambience and countless boutiques, is made to order for whiling away an afternoon shopping. It's also a fun place to stock up on souvenirs. Popular items include wood carvings and models (especially of the characteristic hayracks that dot the countryside), different flavors of schnapps (the kind with a whole pear inside—cultivated to actually grow right into the bottle—is a particularly classy gift), honey mead brandy (*medica*—sweet and smooth), bars of soap wrapped in wool (good for exfoliating), and those adorable painted panels from beehives (described on page 800). Rounding out the list of traditional Slovenian items are wrought-iron products from Kropa, crystal from Rogaska, lace from Idrija, and salt from Piran.

There are two convenient areas in the city center that offer abundant shopping opportunities: at **Ciril-Metodov trg and near the market;** and, beginning a few steps away, the **Old Town** pedestrian lane that cuts through the downtown core. I've described options in both places below. (A third street worth exploring—with a bit more funky student style—is the graffiti-slathered **Trubarjeva cesta,** a block up from the river and easy to find from Prešeren Square.)

AT CIRIL-METODOV TRG AND NEAR THE MARKET

The most atmospheric trinket-shopping is in the first stretch of the **market colonnade,** along the riverfront next to the Triple Bridge (described earlier, under "Sights in Ljubljana").

If you're looking for serious handicrafts rather than trinkets, drop by the **Rustika** gallery, just over the Triple Bridge (on the castle side). In addition to beehive panels, they also have lace, painted chests and boxes, and other tasteful local-style mementos (daily 9:00-21:00, Stritarjeva 9, mobile 031-459-509). There's another Rustika location up at the castle courtyard. A somewhat more downscale souvenir shop with a wide variety is **Dom Trgovina,** across from the TI on the main market square (Mon-Sat 9:00-21:00, Sun 10:00-21:00, Ciril-Metodov trg 5).

Kraševka sells high-quality artisanal products (mostly foods) from the Karst region, and also acts as a sort of information office for that area (Mon-Fri 9:00-19:00, Sat 9:00-15:00, closed Sun, Ciril-Metodov trg 10, tel. 01/232-1445).

Trgovina Ika, a small artisan boutique with its own hip and idiosyncratic sense of style, is a delightful place to browse for truly authentic Slovenian stuff that goes beyond souvenirs. Its unique items by local designers—jewelry, hats, scarves, shoes, and so on—are modern and fashionable (Mon-Fri 10:00-19:30, Sat 9:00-18:00, Sun 10:00-14:00, Ciril-Metodov trg 13, tel. 01/123-21743).

IN THE OLD TOWN

Ljubljana's main Old Town street—which changes names from Mestni trg to Stari trg, then Gornji trg—is also lined with several characteristic shops, selling a few of the unique gift items produced in this proud little country. Here's a lightly narrated tour of this inviting street, from start to finish. Unless otherwise noted, all of these shops are open long hours on weekdays (often until 20:00); most close a bit earlier on Saturdays (around 17:00), and close in the early afternoon on Sundays (usually by 13:00 or 14:00).

○ Self-Guided Shopping Stroll: Begin in front of the Town Hall. Before you start the walk, take the opportunity to browse the shops along Ciril-Metodov trg, noted above (all of which are within a five-minute walk of here). When you're ready, head down the street.

First, on the left at Mestni trg 6, look for two fun shops: **Dvorec Trebnik** sells cosmetics and bath products handmade by people with disabilities; **Smile** is a colorful design/concept store. A few steps farther along at #7, **Honey House** sells products harvested by beekeeper Luka (closed Sun). For tips on browsing your honey options, see page 800.

Just beyond at #8, **Piranske Soline** sells products from the giant salt pans that sit just south of Piran on Slovenia's tiny coastline. You can pick up some locally harvested sea salt, or peruse their salt-based beauty products (bath salts, body milk, and other exfoliants, www.soline.si).

Across the street at #19, **Güjžina** highlights food, wines, and other products from the Hungarian-influenced region of Slovenia called Prekmurje (also called Pannonia). While the restaurant (on the left, €11-16 meals) is hit-or-miss, their wine bar (on the right) is a good place to learn more about the products of one of Slovenia's top wine-growing regions. If you want a dessert, this is a fine place to try the cake called *gibanica*—originating in Prekmurje, and beloved throughout Slovenia.

Back on the left, at #8, **La Chocolate** is the first of two artisanal *čokoladnice* (chocolate shops) along this strip (www.lachocolate.si).

Farther along, on the right (at #17), **Galerija Idrijske Čipke** shows off handmade lace from the town of Idrija (www.idrija-lace.com).

Continuing past various clothes boutiques, look for (on the left, at #11) another chocolate shop, Čokoladnica Cukrček. A bit pricier than La Chocolate, this shop is best known for its foil-wrapped "Prešeren Balls" chocolates—a clever and civic-minded

LJUBLJANA

takeoff on Salzburg's "Mozart Balls," replacing the composer with Slovenia's greatest poet (www.cukrcek.si).

Continue along the street (which here changes names from Mestni trg to Stari trg), passing more clothes shops. On the left, at Stari trg 3, look for **Cha** tea shop, which sells over 100 varieties of tea, plus porcelain teapots and cups from all over. It's attached to the recommended Čajna Hiša teahouse.

A few steps down on the left (at #5), **Cafetino** is the best place in town for coffee. They have more than 20 types available—espresso or Turkish-style, plus beans to take home.

Next door, follow the passage to reach **Za Popen't Pivoteka,** a "bottle shop" selling 200 kinds of beer in individual bottles. While they stock a few Slovenian beers, they focus on international microbrews—including several American brands. Even if it's not authentically Slovenian, this shop is a fun browse for beer lovers. The name is a play on words, loosely meaning "foamy goodness" (www.zapopent.si). In the same courtyard is the stylish **Formadoma** design shop, specializing in housewares (closed Sun, www.formadoma.eu).

Now you'll wade through a stretch of enticing restaurants with wonderful outdoor tables (for my recommendations here, see page 757). Notice Julija and Romeo, facing each other wistfully across the street.

After the little "restaurant row," the lineup of shops resumes. On the left at Stari trg 11A, look for **Patrizia** jewelry; a few doors down, **Wool Art Knitwear** has unique (and very well-insulated) Serbian-style clothing. Across the street at #18, **Babushka Boutique** sells creative prints and Pinteresty gifts (www.babushkaboutique.com).

From here, you'll pass a few more funky shops, as well as some rare books and antiques shops. On the right at #26, don't miss **Woodway,** with locally-made wooden jewelry, sunglasses, and phone cases, and cork handbags and wallets from Portugal (www.woodway.si).

The cobbled charm culminates at the square called **Gornji trg.** Look uphill and notice the village charms of some of the oldest buildings in town: four medieval houses with rooflines slanted at the ends, different from the others on this street.

Sleeping in Ljubljana

Ljubljana has good accommodations in all price ranges. I've focused my listings in or within easy walking distance of the city center. To get the best value, book ahead. The most expensive hotels raise their prices even more during conventions (Sept-Oct, and sometimes also June).

Sleep Code

Hotels are classified based on the average price of a standard double room with breakfast in spring and fall. Prices may go up in summer, and down in winter.

$$$$	**Splurge:** Most rooms over €150
$$$	**Pricier:** €110-150
$$	**Moderate:** €80-110
$	**Budget:** €50-80
¢	**Backpacker:** Under €50
RS%	**Rick Steves discount**

Unless otherwise noted, credit cards are accepted, hotel staff speak basic English, and free Wi-Fi is available. Comparison-shop by checking prices at several hotels (on each hotel's own website, on a booking site, or by email). For the best deal, *book directly with the hotel.* Ask for a discount if paying in cash; if the listing includes **RS%**, request a Rick Steves discount.

Boutique Hotels in the Old Town: Three similar (but unrelated) boutique hotels cluster idyllically on a cobbled square in Ljubljana's Old Town. While quite overpriced (catering to deep-pocketed business travelers), they offer Old World charm with upscale touches. All of these are in old buildings with period touches; expect lots of stairs and no elevators. **$$$$ Hotel Angel,** part of the Lesar group, is the plushest of the bunch. Its 12 rooms have crisp white decor (air-con, pay parking, Gornji trg 7, tel. 01/425-5089, www.angelhotel.si, info@angelhotel.si, warm Jovan). **$$$ Allegro Hotel** has a musical theme and 17 rooms with hardwood floors around a checkerboard-tiled garden courtyard (cheaper rooms with shared bath, air-con, prebook for pay parking, Gornji trg 6, mobile 059-119-620, www.allegrohotel.si, info@allegrohotel.si). The family-run **$$$ Antiq Hotel** is a bit older, with less polish and 16 idiosyncratically decorated rooms sprawling through two buildings with a mazelike floor plan (cheaper rooms with shared bath, air-con, some rooms have low beams and doorways, Gornji trg 3, tel. 01/421-3560, www.antiqhotel.eu, info@antiqhotel.eu).

$$$$ Vander Urbani Resort is a unique concept: Nestled central as can be just off the in-love-with-life riverfront embankment, it really does feel like an intensely hip resort in the city center—right down to the minuscule rooftop swimming pool and sundeck. The resort prides itself on the cutting-edge urban design of its 16 rooms, and tries to use Slovenian and organic products wherever possible (air-con, elevator, café, restaurant, champagne bar, Krojaška ulica 6-8, tel. 01/200-9000, www.vanderhotel.com, info@vanderhotel.com).

$$$$ Cubo Hotel is a jolt of trendy minimalism on Ljubljana's hotel scene. Its 26 rooms are the best place in town for sleek, mod elegance. Choose between streetside rooms, which enjoy castle views but get some traffic noise, or quieter courtyard rooms (air-con, elevator, Slovenska cesta 15, tel. 01/425-6000, www.hotelcubo.com, reception@hotelcubo.com).

$$$ Adora Hotel, on the other side of the church from the three boutique hotels described earlier, is a bit less charming, but also cheaper and very comfortable. Its 10 rooms have a restrained rustic style (air-con, elevator, free loaner bikes, pay parking, Rožna ulica 7, tel. 082-057-240, www.adorahotel.si, info@adorahotel.si).

$$ Meščanka ("City Woman") rents seven cozy, well-equipped rooms and apartments in a fantastic location right along the bustling riverfront promenade. The decor is mod, funky, and colorful, and the good windows work hard to provide silence (no breakfast, air-con, reception open 10:00-12:00 & 14:00-19:00—let them know if you're coming outside that time, Ključavničarska 4, mobile 051-880-044, www.mescanka.si, info@mescanka.si, Saša).

$$ Slamič B&B has 17 modern rooms with hardwood floors, tasteful decor, and absentee management. Over an appealing up-scale café in a nondescript but central neighborhood, this is a fine spot for affordable elegance (air-con, free parking, reception open daily 7:00-23:00, Kersnikova 1, tel. 01/433-8233, www.slamic.si, info@slamic.si).

$$ Hotel Mrak has 34 comfortable but overpriced rooms in a pleasant neighborhood near French Revolution Square. While it's a bit rough around the edges, this trusty old place is my sentimental favorite in Ljubljana (ground-floor and top-floor rooms have air-con, elevator, restaurant with terrace under an old vine, pay parking, Rimska 4, tel. 01/421-9650, www.hotelmrak.si, info@hotelmrak.si).

$ Hotel Emonec (eh-MOH-nets), with some of the most centrally located cheap beds in Ljubljana, hides just off Wolfova lane between Prešeren and Congress squares. Its 54 rooms—in two buildings across a courtyard from each other—feel like a cookie-cutter chain hotel, with tight bathrooms and a shoestring staff. But the price and ideal location make it worth considering (pay parking garage, they also run a handy self-service launderette—see page 723, Wolfova 12, tel. 01/200-1520, www.hotel-emonec.com, hotelemonec@siol.net).

$ B&B Petra Varl offers comfortable, affordable, nicely ap-pointed rooms on a courtyard across from the bustling riverside market. Petra, an artist who speaks good English, will help you feel at home. As this place is Ljubljana's top budget option, book early (includes kitchenette with basic do-it-yourself breakfast, cash only, air-con, go into courtyard at Vodnikov trg 5 and look for *B&B* sign at 5A, mobile 031-851-842, bb@varl.si).

$ Penzion Pod Lipo has 10 rooms above a restaurant in a mostly residential area about a 12-minute walk from Prešeren Square. While the rooms are old and simple, it's thoughtfully run by Marjan (breakfast extra, cash only, sometimes unstaffed—let them know when you'll arrive, nonsmoking, guest kitchen, putting green on terrace, tel. 01/251-1683, mobile 031-809-893, www.penzion-podlipo.com, info@penzion-podlipo.com).

¢ Hostel Celica, a proud, innovative, and lively place, is owned by the city and run by a nonprofit student organization. This former military prison's 20 cells *(celica)* have been converted into hostel rooms—each one unique and decorated by a different designer (free tours of the hostel daily at 14:00). The top floor features more typical hostel rooms (each with its own bathroom, for 4-12 people). The building also houses an art gallery, tourist information, self-service laundry, and a variety of eateries. For more on the history of this site, see page 751 (private rooms, active excursions around Slovenia, Metelkova 8, a dull 15-minute walk to Prešeren Square, 8 minutes to the train station, tel. 01/230-9700, www.hostelcelica.com, info@hostelcelica.com). The hostel hosts live music events one night a week until around 24:00, but otherwise maintains "quiet time" after 23:00. However, the surrounding neighborhood—a bit rundown and remote, but safe—is a happening nightlife zone, which can make for noisy weekends.

Eating in Ljubljana

At this crossroads of cultures (and cuisines), Italian and French flavors are just as "local" as meat-and-starch Slovenian food. This cosmopolitan city also dabbles in other cuisines; you'll find Thai, Indian, Chinese, Mexican, and more. Most places seem to offer a similar menu of Slovenian/Mediterranean fare with international flourishes. To locate these restaurants, see the map on page 720.

Lunch Deals: Ljubljana has many of the best restaurants in this book. However, they tend to be quite expensive. To stretch your budget, make a point to have your main meal at lunch, when most of Ljubljana's top eateries serve a high-quality three-course meal (starter, main, dessert) at a very affordable price—usually around €10, not including drinks. You won't have much choice (they may only have one or two options each day), but the quality is high and the value is outstanding. Some places offer these deals only on weekdays. After a big lunch, you can have a light dinner—picnic, *burek,* pizza, sandwich...or just gelato. Places I recommend that offer these lunch deals include Pri Vitezu, DaBuDa, Valvas'or, Julija, Marley & Me, Pri Škofu, Manna, and the restaurant at the top of The Skyscraper (I've noted "lunch special" where applicable below).

IN THE CITY CENTER

$$$$ Gostilna As ("Ace"), tucked into a courtyard just off Prešeren Square, offers fish lovers the best blowout in town. It's dressy, pricey, and pretentious (the service is deliberate, and waiters ignore the menu and recommend what's fresh). Everything is specially prepared each day and beautifully presented. It's loosely based on the Slow Food model: Servings are small, and you're expected to take your time and order two or three courses. The dining room is old-fashioned and a bit stuffy, but in good weather, their rooftop terrace is gorgeous (mostly fish and Italian dishes, daily 12:00-24:00, reservations smart, Čopova 5A, or enter courtyard with *As* sign near image of Julija on Wolfova, tel. 01/425-8822, www.gostilnaas.si). For cheaper food and drinks from the same kitchen, eat at the attached **$$$ As Aperitivo,** a much livelier, more casual spot. You'll sit in the leafy courtyard or the winter garden, with big windows that stay open in the summer (salads, sandwiches, pastas, and main courses, food served daily 12:00-24:00, longer hours for drinks, good gelato counter inside). The courtyard also has a couple of other fun eateries—and, in the summer only, live music.

$$ Ribca ("Fish") hides under the first stretch of market colonnade near the Triple Bridge. This is your best bet for a relatively quick and cheap riverside lunch. Choose between the two straightforward menus: grilled fillets or fried small fish. With the fragrant fish market right next door, you know it's fresh. If you just want to enjoy sitting along the river below the bustling market, this is also a fine spot for a coffee or beer (Mon 8:00-16:00, Tue-Sat 8:00-21:00, Sun 11:00-18:00, tel. 01/425-1544).

$$$$ Pri Vitezu is well-respected for its seasonal menu of classic Mediterranean dishes. It sits along the newly spiffed-up Breg embankment, just beyond Cobblers' Bridge; sit out on the pedestrian mall or in the Old World-elegant interior. Although a bit pretentious and quite expensive at dinner, this place is especially worthwhile for its good-value lunch special (Mon-Sat 11:00-23:00,

---

Restaurant Price Code

I've assigned each eatery a price category, based on the average cost of a typical main course. Drinks, desserts, and splurge items (steak and seafood) can raise the price considerably.

$$$$ **Splurge:** Most main courses over €14

$$$ **Pricier:** €10-14

$$ **Moderate:** €6-10

$ **Budget:** Under €6

In Slovenia, a takeout spot is **$**; a basic sit-down eatery is **$$**; a casual but more upscale restaurant is **$$$**; and a swanky splurge is **$$$$**.

---

closed Sun; shorter hours in winter and closed Sat-Sun; Breg 18-20, tel. 01/426-6058, www.privitezu.si).

$$ Friday Street Food: On good-weather Fridays from spring through fall, Ljubljana's outdoor market hosts the **Odprta Kuhna** ("Open Kitchen")—a sprawling al fresco food court where the country's newest and best chefs gather to showcase their creations. For the people of Ljubljana, this is both a culinary event and a social one. Foodies make this a priority (mid-March-mid-Oct Fri 10:00-21:00, until 23:00 in summer, can be canceled in bad weather, in the heart of the outdoor market zone—in front of the cathedral—at Pogačarjev trg, www.odprtakuhna.si).

Traditional Slovenian Food: Because Slovenes head into the countryside when they want traditional fare, Ljubljana isn't the best place to find authentic Slovenian grub. But if you'd like to try some, your best budget bet may be **$ Klobasarna,** listed below. For a more formal sit-down meal, head for **$$$ Gostilna na Gradu,** in the castle courtyard high above town—if you don't mind going up to the castle to get it (the handy funicular costs €4 round-trip). Run by a well-respected chef, it serves up a seasonal menu of traditional flavors with modern flair. The portions are small, but the prices are surprisingly affordable. Choose between the dull vaulted interior, the glassed-in arcade, or the outdoor tables. Reservations are recommended before you make the trip up here (Mon-Sat 10:00-24:00—food served until 22:00, Sun 9:00-18:00—food served until 17:00, Grajska Planota 1, mobile 031-301-777, www.nagradu.si).

Asian Fusion: $$ DaBuDa is the best spot in Ljubljana for Asian cuisine, featuring a well-described menu of good Thai dishes (salads, curries, wok meals, and noodles) in a very mod, dark-wood, split-level setting frequented by hip young professionals (lunch special, daily 12:00-23:00, also few outdoor tables, between Congress Square and Square of the Republic at Šubičeva 1A, tel. 01/425-3060).

Fast and Cheap: $ Klobasarna is a budget foodie option specializing in *kranjska klobasa*—traditional Carniolan sausage, from the Slovenian uplands. The menu is simple—one wiener or two, extra for *jota* (hearty turnip stew)—and delicious. They also serve the Slovenian dumplings called *štruklji* (Mon-Sat 10:00-23:00, Sun 10:00-15:00, Ciril-Metodov trg 15, mobile 051-605-017). **$ Paninoteka,** with wonderful outdoor seating overlooking Cobblers' Bridge and fine interior seating, has affordable and tasty sandwiches; their full menu is good, but much more expensive (daily 9:00-22:00, Jurčičev trg 3, mobile 040-349-329). *Burek*, the typical Balkan phyllo-dough snack, can be picked up at street stands around town. Most are open 24 hours and charge about €2-3 for a hearty portion. An easy choice is **$ Nobel Burek**, next to Miklošičeva cesta 30; but many locals prefer **$ Olimpija Burek**, around the corner at Pražakova 14 (across from the post office).

Pizzerias: $$ Pizzeria Foculus, tucked in a boring alleyway a few blocks up from the river, has a loyal local following, a happening atmosphere, an innovative leafy interior, a few outdoor tables, and Ljubljana's best pizza (over 50 types, daily 11:00-24:00, just off French Revolution Square across the street from Plečnik's National and University Library at Gregorčičeva 3, tel. 01/251-5643). **$$ Ljubljanski Dvor** enjoys the most convenient and scenic location of any pizzeria in town. On a sunny summer day, the outdoor riverside terrace is unbeatable; I'd skip the dull interior and the pricier pasta restaurant higher up (Mon-Sat 10:00-24:00, Sun 12:00-24:00, 50 yards from Cobblers' Bridge at Dvorni trg 1, tel. 01/251-6555). Ljubljanski Dvor also has a handy, cheap **$ take-out window** (go around back to the walk-up window on Congress Square). Enjoy a slice at one of their outdoor tables facing Congress Square, or get it to go and munch it along the river.

IN THE OLD TOWN

The main drag through the Old Town (which starts at the Town Hall and changes names as it goes: Mestni trg, then Stari trg, then Gornji trg) is lined with inviting eateries. Tables clutter the cobbled pedestrian street. If you're at a loss for where to eat in town, stroll here to survey your options, then pick your favorite menu and ambience. As many restaurants along here are uniformly good, no one place really has the edge.

Several popular options cluster in one particularly atmospheric stretch; all except Romeo offer a similar menu of Mediterranean-Slovenian cuisine and wonderful outdoor seating: **$$$$ Valvas'or,** the upscale option, has a dressy dining room and a posh gold color scheme (weekday lunch deal, Mon-Sat 12:00-22:00, closed Sun, Stari trg 7, tel. 01/425-0455). **$$$ Julija** features homey country-Slovenian decor inside (lunch deals, daily 12:00-22:00, Stari trg 9, tel. 01/425-6463). **$$ Romeo,** across the street, is a lowbrow bar serving unexceptional Mexican food...but the name sure is clever (get it? "Romeo and Julija"). And **$$$ Marley & Me** comes with a warm welcome from Matej (weekday lunch specials, daily 11:00-23:00, Stari Trg 9, tel. 08/380-6610). I've also enjoyed a great salad lunch at the nearby **$$ Čajna Hiša** teahouse (described later, under "Coffee, Tea, and Treats.")

IN KRAKOVO

The Krakovo district—just south of the city center, where garden patches nearly outnumber simple homes—is a pleasant area to wander. It's also home to two tasty restaurants. If the nearby Jože Plečnik House is open during your visit, you could combine your visit there with a meal at one of these options.

$$ Pri Škofu ("By the Bishop") is a laid-back, leafy place with appealing outdoor seating, a nondescript modern interior, and a focus on freshness, serving international cuisine with a Slovenian flair. This hidden gem is deliciously memorable; reserve ahead (creative soups, cheap lunches, homemade desserts, Mon-Fri 10:00-24:00—but may be closed on Mon, Sat-Sun 12:00-24:00, Rečna 8, tel. 01/426-4508).

$$$$ Manna, with artfully presented, seasonal Slovenian-Mediterranean fusion cuisine, sits along the pleasant Gradaščica canal. The interior is pure Secession—the Gustav Klimt-era, early 20th-century, gold-accented Viennese style that was so influential in Ljubljana. I prefer the more artistic, café-like downstairs to the stuffy upstairs dining room, but the seating out front is hard to beat on a nice day. This is another fine splurge that you can enjoy affordably through their lunch special (Mon-Sat 11:00-24:00, Sun 11:00-21:00, Eipprova 1A, tel. 05/992-2308, www.restaurant-manna.com).

COFFEE, TEA, AND TREATS

Riverfront Cafés: Enjoying a coffee, beer, or ice-cream cone along the Ljubljanica River embankment (between the Triple and Cobblers' bridges) is Ljubljana's single best experience—worth ▲▲▲. Tables spill into the street, and some of the best-dressed, best-looking students on the planet happily fill them day and night. (A common question from first-time visitors to Ljubljana: "Doesn't anybody here have a job?") This is some of the top people-watching in Europe. Just explore and find the spot with the breezy ambience you like best. When ordering, the easiest choice is a *bela kava* (white coffee)—a caffè latte.

Teahouse: If coffee's not your cup of tea, go a block inland to the teahouse **$$ Čajna Hiša.** They serve about 50 different types of tea, light food (including great salads and sandwiches), and desserts (Mon-Fri 8:00-22:00, Sat 8:00-15:00, Sun 10:00-14:00, on the atmospheric main drag in the Old Town a few steps from Cobblers' Bridge at Stari trg 3, tel. 01/421-2444). They also have an attached tea shop, **Cha** (described on page 754).

Cakes: Zvezda Kavarna, a trendy, central place at the bottom of Congress Square, is a local favorite for cakes, pastries, and ice cream. A nostalgic favorite here—once popular in communist times, and recently reintroduced to great acclaim—is the *emona kocka* (Emona cube), a layer cake with nuts, cake, and chocolate (Mon-Sat 7:00-23:00, Sun 10:00-20:00, a block up from Prešeren Square at Wolfova 14, tel. 01/421-9090). Their **Deli,** one door toward Prešeren Square, has takeaway coffee and smoothies, a wide variety of cakes to go, and some of the most decadent ice cream in town (same hours). And their **Bistro,** around the corner facing Congress Square, has a full menu.

Chocolates and Ice Cream: Rustika is a local chain that sells tasty homemade chocolates, cookies (including one kind with four different types of chocolate), and a wide variety of unusual and delicious artisanal ice cream flavors. The menu changes from day to day, but highlights can include balsamic vinegar with vanilla or strawberry, very dark chocolate, Kanada (with maple syrup and walnuts), and Greek yogurt with honey and nuts. The handiest location is about an eight-minute walk from Prešeren Square, and comes with a delightful stroll along colorful Trubarjeva cesta (ice cream available summer only, Mon-Fri 8:00-19:00, Sat 9:00-13:00, closed Sun, Trubarjeva cesta 44, mobile 059-935-730). Don't confuse this sweet shop with the Rustika gift shop.

More Ice Cream: Ljubljana is known for its Italian gelato-style ice cream. You'll see fine options all along the Ljubljanica River embankment, but many places serve ice cream only in summer. **Romantica,** just up the steps from the river, is the foodies' choice, with creative and delicious artisanal flavors (just uphill from Ljubljanksi Dvor pizzeria at Dvorni trg 1). **Fétiche Patisserie,** along the riverfront café embankment, is another good choice, with some unusual, pungent, Asian-themed flavors. Other favorites include **Rustika** and **Zvezda Kavarna** (both described earlier).

Ljubljana Connections

As Slovenia's transportation hub, Ljubljana is well-connected to both domestic and international destinations. When checking schedules, be aware of city name variations: In Slovene, Vienna is "Dunaj," Budapest is "Budimpešt," and Venice is "Benétke."

GETTING TO CROATIA'S ISTRIAN PENINSULA

To reach **Istria** (just south of Slovenia) by public transportation, you have two relatively straightforward options: In summer, direct buses depart Ljubljana for Rovinj each day (3-4/day late June-Aug, 1/day Sept, none Oct-late June). From late June through late September, there's also a train connection to Pula (1/day, change in Hrpelje-Kozina); once in Pula, you can connect by bus to other Istrian destinations. On off-season weekends, you might have to get creative (try connecting through Rijeka).

BY TRAIN

From Ljubljana by Train to: Lesce-Bled (roughly hourly, 40-60 minutes—but bus is better because it goes right to Bled town center), **Postojna** (nearly hourly, 1 hour), **Divača** (close to Škocjan Caves and Lipica, nearly hourly, 1.75 hours), **Sežana** (close to Lipica, nearly hourly, 2 hours), **Piran** (direct bus is better—see next; otherwise allow 4 hours, train to Koper, 4/day, 2.5 hours; then bus to Piran, 7/day, 30 minutes), **Maribor** (hourly, 2-3 hours, most with a change in Zidani Most), **Ptuj** (1/day direct, 2.5 hours, more with change in Pragersko and sometimes additional change in Zidani Most), **Zagreb** (4/day direct, 2.5 hours), **Rijeka** (2/day direct, 3 hours), **Pula** (1/day late June-late Sept, 5 hours, change in Hrpelje-Kozina), **Split** (1/day, 9 hours, change in Zagreb), **Vienna** (that's **Dunaj** in Slovene, 1/day direct, 6 hours; otherwise 7/day with change in Villach, Maribor, or Graz, 7 hours), **Budapest** (that's **Budimpešta** in Slovene; 1/day direct, 8 hours, other connections possible with 1-2 changes, 9 hours, no convenient night train), **Venice** (called **Benétke** in Slovene; fastest by bus—see next; otherwise 2/day with a change in Villach, 6 hours), **Salzburg** (2/day direct, 4-5 hours, an additional 2/day possible with change in Villach), **Munich** (2/day direct, 6 hours, including 1 night train; otherwise change in Salzburg). Train info: Toll tel. 01/291-3332, www.slo-zeleznice.si.

BY BUS

The bus station is a low-profile building in front of the train station. Buses depart from the numbered stalls in the middle of the street. For any bus, you have to buy tickets at the bus station ticket windows or at the automated e-kart kiosk (pay with credit card or cash), not from the driver. For bus information, pick up one of the blue phones inside the station to be connected to a helpful English-speaking operator. Bus info: www.ap-ljubljana.si, toll tel. 1991 (€1.50/call), from the US call 011-386-1-234-4600.

By Bus to: Bled (Mon-Sat hourly—usually at the top of each hour, fewer on Sun, 1.25 hours), **Postojna** (at least hourly, 1 hour), **Divača** (close to Škocjan Caves and Lipica, about every 2-3 hours, 1.5 hours), **Piran** (5/day Mon-Fri, 2/day Sat, 4/day Sun, 2.5 hours), over the **Vršič Pass** to **Bovec** (2/day July-Aug at 6:30 and 15:00, June and Sept Sat-Sun only at 6:30, 4.25 hours to Bovec, none Oct-May), **Kobarid** (1/day in July-Aug over Vršič Pass, 5 hours; otherwise faster but less scenic via Idrija, 3.5 hours), **Rijeka** (1/day in summer, none off-season, 2.5 hours), **Zagreb** (10/day, less on weekends, 2.5 hours). To reach Croatia's Istria—specifically **Rovinj**—the bus is your best option (3-4/day late June-Aug, 1/day Sept, none Oct-late June, 4-5.5 hours, buses also stop in **Piran** and **Poreč**; off-season: 2/week to **Poreč** or **Pula** and change there to Rovinj, generally Mon and Fri, departs at 16:00). DRD runs a handy direct bus from Ljubljana to the **Venice-Mestre** train station (on the mainland, with easy and frequent train connections to the island; 1/day each way, departs at 8:15, 3.75 hours).

BY SHARED SHUTTLE SERVICE

If bus and train schedules don't quite get you where you need to go, **GoOpti**—a company with an innovative business model for shared minibus transfers—can be a convenient and inexpensive option for somewhat flexible travelers. First, go to www.goopti. com and select your destination, date, and preferred time of arrival or departure. Then, 24 hours before departure, you'll get an update of the specific pickup time, based on the needs of other passengers. Prices can flex dramatically, but it's quite affordable (for example, an advance nonrefundable purchase from Ljubljana could be €17 to Piran, €20 to Venice, or €22 to Zagreb; for the best price, book two months ahead). For a few euros extra, they can pick you up at your hotel rather than the train or bus station. To lock in a specific time, you can pay extra for a "VIP" transfer ("VIP flex" is similar, but refundable).

GoOpti reaches destinations throughout Slovenia (including Ljubljana, the airport, Lake Bled, Lake Bohinj, Bovec in the Julian Alps, towns in the Karst such as Postojna and Sežana, and Piran and other Slovenian coastal destinations), but it's also handy for farther-flung international destinations—such as Venice or its airport, Trieste, various Austrian cities (Vienna, Salzburg, Klagenfurt, etc.), and Croatian cities such as Zagreb and Pula.

BY PLANE

Slovenia's only **airport** (airport code: LJU) is 14 miles north of Ljubljana, about halfway to Bled. Confusingly, the airport goes by three names: Ljubljana Airport (the international version); Brnik (for the town that it's near); and Jože Pučnik Airport (a politician for whom it was controversially renamed in 2007). Most flights are operated by Slovenia's national airline, Adria Airways (www.adria-airways.com), but additional flights are run by EasyJet (www.easyjet.com), Wizz Air (www.wizzair.com), and various national carriers (Air France, Turkish Airlines, Finnair, and so on). The airport is small and manageable. Morning flights tend to cluster around the same time frame (between 6:45 and 7:30); as the airport doesn't open until 5:00, there's no need to show up before then. If you need to kill time here, follow signs (around to the left as you exit the terminal) to *Razgledna Terasa* and *Terasa Avionček* and ride the elevator up to the rooftop terrace with a café (daily 9:00-19:00). Here you can sip a coffee while you watch planes land and take off. Airport info: tel. 04/206-1000, www.lju-airport.si.

Getting Between Downtown Ljubljana and the Airport: Two kinds of buses connect the airport with Ljubljana's bus station: **public bus** #28 (to the right as you exit the airport; Mon-Fri hourly until 20:00, only 7/day Sat-Sun, 45 minutes, €4.10), and a **minibus** (to the left as you exit the airport, scheduled to depart after various arriving flights—look for schedule posted near bus stop). Two different companies run the minibus transfers, which take about 30 minutes and cost €9 to downtown: Markun (mobile 041-792-865, www.prevozi-markun.com) and Marko Nowotny (mobile 040-771-771, www.mnj.si). I'd take whichever one is departing first. For a transfer *to* the airport, your hotel or any TI can make arrangements with one of these companies a day or so in advance (same price)—or you can try GoOpti, described earlier. Unfortunately, certain evening arrivals don't coordinate well with either the bus or the minibus, so you might have to wait a while or take a pricey **taxi** (figure €25-35 to the airport if you call a reputable company, but more like €42 *from* the airport—since you have to use the pricey taxi stand out front).

To Lake Bled: For tips on going from the airport directly to Lake Bled, see page 793.

Airport Alternatives: Ljubljana's airport—the only one in the country—charges high taxes and fees, and has limited connections to some European destinations. To save money (or to avoid a layover), many Slovenes fly in and out of relatively nearby airports in neighboring countries: **Zagreb** (2-hour drive from Ljubljana, see page 988); **Venice** (3-hour drive from Ljubljana); **Trieste** (2-hour drive from Ljubljana); and **Klagenfurt/Kärnten** (especially for those going to Lake Bled, from which it's a 2-hour drive). To get between these airports and your Slovenian destination, consider GoOpti, described earlier; this is typically cheaper than a taxi and more convenient than a bus or train connection.

LAKE BLED

Lake Bled—Slovenia's leading mountain resort—comes complete with a sweeping alpine panorama, a fairy-tale island, a cliff-hanging medieval castle, a lazy lakeside promenade, and the country's most sought-after desserts. And the charms of its glorious mountain vistas and traditional folk life only crescendo as you explore the surrounding areas. Taken together, there are few more enjoyable places to simply be on vacation.

Since the Habsburg days, Lake Bled (locals pronounce it "blayd") has been *the* place where Slovenes wow visiting diplomats. In the late 19th century, local aristocrats—who knew how to find a fine mountain resort—surrounded the humble lakefront village with classy villas. Tito also had one of his vacation homes here (today's Hotel Vila Bled), where he entertained illustrious guests. But above all, Lake Bled feels like a place that Slovenes enjoy alongside their visitors.

Lake Bled has plenty of ways to idle away an afternoon. While the lake's main town, also called Bled, is more functional than quaint, it offers postcard views of the lake and handy access to the region. Hike up to Bled Castle for intoxicating vistas. Make a wish and ring the bell at the island church. Wander or bike the dreamy path around the lake. Sit on a dock, dip your feet in the water, and feed some of the lake's resident swans. Then dive into some of Bled's famous cakes while you take in the view of Triglav, Slovenia's favorite mountain (see the "Mount Triglav" sidebar on page 813). Bled quiets down at night—there's no nightlife beyond a handful of pubs—giving hikers and other holiday-makers a chance to recharge.

Bled is also a great jumping-off point for a car trip through the

Julian Alps (see next chapter), and a wide variety of other worthwhile side-trips are right at its doorstep. These include the less developed lake named Bohinj, even deeper in the mountains; a spectacular (yet easy) hike in the nearby mountain gorge of Vintgar; and the pleasant Old Town of Radovljica, with its fascinating little beekeeping museum.

PLANNING YOUR TIME

Bled and its neighboring mountains deserve at least two days. With one day, spend it in and around Bled (or, spend a quick morning in Bled and an afternoon day-tripping). With a second day and a car, drive through the Julian Alps using the self-guided tour in the next chapter. The circular route takes you up and over the stunning Vršič Pass, then down the scenic and historic Soča River Valley. Without a car, skip the second day, or spend it doing nearby day trips: Bus or bike to Radovljica and its bee museum, hike to Vintgar Gorge, or visit Lake Bohinj (all described under "Near Lake Bled," at the end of this chapter).

Orientation to Lake Bled

The town of Bled is on the east end of 1.5-mile-long Lake Bled. The lakefront is lined with soothing parks and chunky resort hotels. A 3.5-mile path meanders around the lake. As no motorized boats are allowed, Lake Bled is particularly peaceful.

The tourists' center of Bled has two parts, which melt into each other: a ragtag village and a cluster of giant hotels. The main thoroughfare, called **Ljubljanska cesta,** leads out of Bled town toward Ljubljana and most other destinations. Just up from the lakefront is the modern **commercial center** (Trgovski Center Bled), with a supermarket, ATM, shops, and a smattering of lively cafés. Nicknamed "Gaddafi," the commercial center was designed for a city in Libya, but the deal fell through—so the frugal Slovenes built it here instead.

Bled's less-touristy Old Town, under the castle, has a web of tight streets and big but humble old houses surrounding the pointy spire of St. Martin's Church. Here you'll find the bus station, some good restaurants, a few hostels, and more locals than tourists.

The mountains poking above the ridge at the far end of the lake are the Julian Alps, crowned by the three peaks of Mount Triglav. The big mountain behind the town of Bled is Stol ("Chair"), part of the Karavanke range that defines the Austrian border.

Lake Bled

Ⓟ Pletna Boat Dock
Ⓡ Rowboat Rental

To Podhom &
Vintgar Gorge

CESTA V VINTGAR

To
Zasip

Rečica River

634

RECIŠKA CESTA

KOLODVORSKA CESTA

See Bled Town detail map

PREŠERNOVA CESTA

BLED TOWN

CASTLE   CHURCH

BLED JEZERO
STATION

To Lesce
(Train Station),
Radovljica &
Ljubljana

JUBLJANSKA CESTA

SWIMMING
POOL

ROWING
CENTER

Lake   Bled

COMMERCIAL
CENTER

Bled
Island

CHURCH
OF THE
ASSUMPTION

99
STEPS

SUMMER
LUGE

ALP
PENZION &
ESSENSE SPA

CAMP-
GROUND

▲ Mt. Straža

VILA
BLED

CESTA SVOBODE

MLINO

ADVENTURE
PARK

1 Kilometer

GARDEN VILLAGE
GLAMPGROUND

To Selo,
Tourist Farm Mulej &
Kralov Med Beehive

1/2 Mile

To Lake Bohinj   209

TOURIST INFORMATION

Bled's most central TI is in the long, lakefront casino building across the street from the big, white Hotel Park (as you face the lake, the TI is hiding around the front at the far left end, overlooking the lake). Pick up the map with the lake on one side and the whole region on the other and the free Bled information booklet, with up-to-date details on local attractions and transportation options. Get advice on hikes and day trips, confirm transit schedules, and if you're doing any serious hiking, spring for a good regional map. They also have free Wi-Fi and rent cars (July-Aug Mon-Sat 8:00-21:00, Sun 9:00-17:00; May-June and Sept-Oct Mon-Sat 8:00-19:00, Sun 11:00-17:00; Nov-April Mon-Sat 8:00-18:00, Sun 8:00-13:00; Cesta Svobode 10, tel. 04/574-1122, www.bled.si).

The TI's other branch is harder to reach for nondrivers—on the main road out of town—but it conveniently shares an office with the **Triglav National Park Information Center,** which offers lots of helpful advice for those heading into the mountains. The center, with free parking, is called "Triglavska Roža" (free information, bike rentals, maps and guidebooks for sale; daily mid-April-mid-Oct 8:00-18:00; off-season until 16:00; Ljubljanska cesta 27, tel. 04/578-0205, www.tnp.si).

ARRIVAL IN BLED

By Train: Two train stations have the name "Bled." The **Bled Jeze-ro** ("Bled Lake") Station is across the lake from Bled town and is used only by infrequent, slow, tourist-oriented trains into the mountains. You're much more likely to use the **Lesce-Bled** Station in the nearby village of Lesce (pronounced lest-SEH). The Lesce-Bled Station is on the main line and has far better connections to Ljubljana and international destinations. So if you're buying a train ticket or checking schedules, request "Lesce-Bled" rather than just "Bled." (This is so important, I'll remind you again later.)

The small **Lesce-Bled Station** is in Lesce, about 2.5 miles from Bled. The nearest ATM is upstairs in the shopping center across the street (at the Gorenjska Banka on the third floor, across the parking lot from Mercator supermarket). From the station in Lesce, you can take the bus into Bled town (2/hour, 10 minutes, catch it across the street from the train station); or pay about €14 for a taxi into town. If taking the train out of Lesce-Bled, you can buy tickets at this station or on the train—nobody in Bled town sells tickets.

By Bus: Bled's main bus station is just up from the lake in the Old Town. To reach the lake, walk straight downhill on Cesta Svobode. Note that many buses also stop on the way into town, along Ljubljanska cesta; it's good to ask if your bus driver is willing to do so because it's handier for walking to many of my recommended accommodations (for details, see "Sleeping in Bled," later).

By Car: Coming from Ljubljana, you'll wind your way into Bled on Ljubljanska cesta, which rumbles through the middle of town before swinging left at the lake. Parking is tricky; if you're sleeping in town, ask your hotel. But if you're only here for a quick visit (2-hour limit), you can try to find a spot in the short-term parking lot just above the commercial center (free for 1 hour; €2/2 hours), or along the lake (€2/hour). To stretch your visit, head for the underground lot between Hotel Krim and the ice rink (€2, 4-hour limit). If you're staying even longer, park at the lot by the Triglav National Park Information Center and TI, on the road into town (described earlier; €5/24 hours). A new Mercator commercial center at the top of town, scheduled to open in 2017, may have unlimited parking—ask. Also see "Route Tips for Drivers" under "Lake Bled Connections" on page 793.

By Plane: For details on getting from Ljubljana's airport to Bled, see "Lake Bled Connections," later.

HELPFUL HINTS

Exchange Rate: €1 = about $1.10

Country Calling Code: 386 (see page 1086 for dialing instructions).

Money: Bled town's handiest ATMs are at **SKB Banka** (upstairs in round building at commercial center), **Gorenjska Banka** (at far end of Hotel Park), and **NLB** (on the main road into town, at Pension Union).

Post Office: It's just above the commercial center on Ljubljanska cesta (Mon-Fri 8:00-19:00, Sat 8:00-12:00, closed Sun, July-Aug slightly longer, tel. 04/575-0200).

Laundry: Most hotels can do laundry for you, but it's expensive (priced by the piece). You'll get a better deal from a can-do local, **Anže Štalc.** Call Anže to arrange drop-off, and pick it up cleaned and folded 24 hours later (€15/load, €5 more for same-day express service, mobile 041-575-522).

Car Rental: The Julian Alps are ideal by car. Several companies have branches in Bled, including **Europcar** (mobile 031-382-055), **Budget** (mobile 041-578-0320), **Sixt** (mobile 030-645-350), **Hertz** (tel. 04/201-6999), and the local **Avantcar** (mobile 041-400-980); as the offices tend to move around, inquire in Bled about the current locations.

Massage: If you're here to relax, consider a massage at the **Essense** wellness center at the recommended Alp Penzion. This modern, classy facility—hiding in the countryside about a 15-minute walk or 5-minute taxi ride above the lake—offers a wide range of spa treatments, including pedicures and Thai massage. A standard 50-minute massage will run you about €45 (call first to arrange, Cankarjeva cesta 20A, tel. 04/576-7450, www.essense.si, info@essense.si). You'll also find wellness centers with massage, saunas, and whirlpools at a few of the newer big hotels, including the recommended **Hotel Lovec,** as well as **Hotel Astoria** and **Golf Hotel** (open to nonguests for an additional charge).

GETTING AROUND LAKE BLED (LITERALLY)

By Bike: You can rent a mountain bike at the TI (€3.50/hour, €6/3 hours, €8/half-day, €11/day). The TI also has electric bikes, which give you a much-appreciated boost once you get them moving (€5/1 hour, €10/4 hours, €15/8 hours). While walking around the lake is slo-mo bliss, biking it lets you fast-forward between the views of your choice. Biking is also a great way to reach Vintgar Gorge— about three mostly-level miles one-way, perfect for combining a countryside pedal with a walk immersed in nature. For a longer pedal, ask for the TI's excellent biking map, with various great bike trips clearly marked and described. The separated bike path to the nearby town of Radovljica (and its bee museum) is about four level miles one-way (get details at the TI).

By Horse and Buggy: Buggies called *fijakers* are the romantic, expensive, and easy way to get around the lake. Hire one along

LAKE BLED

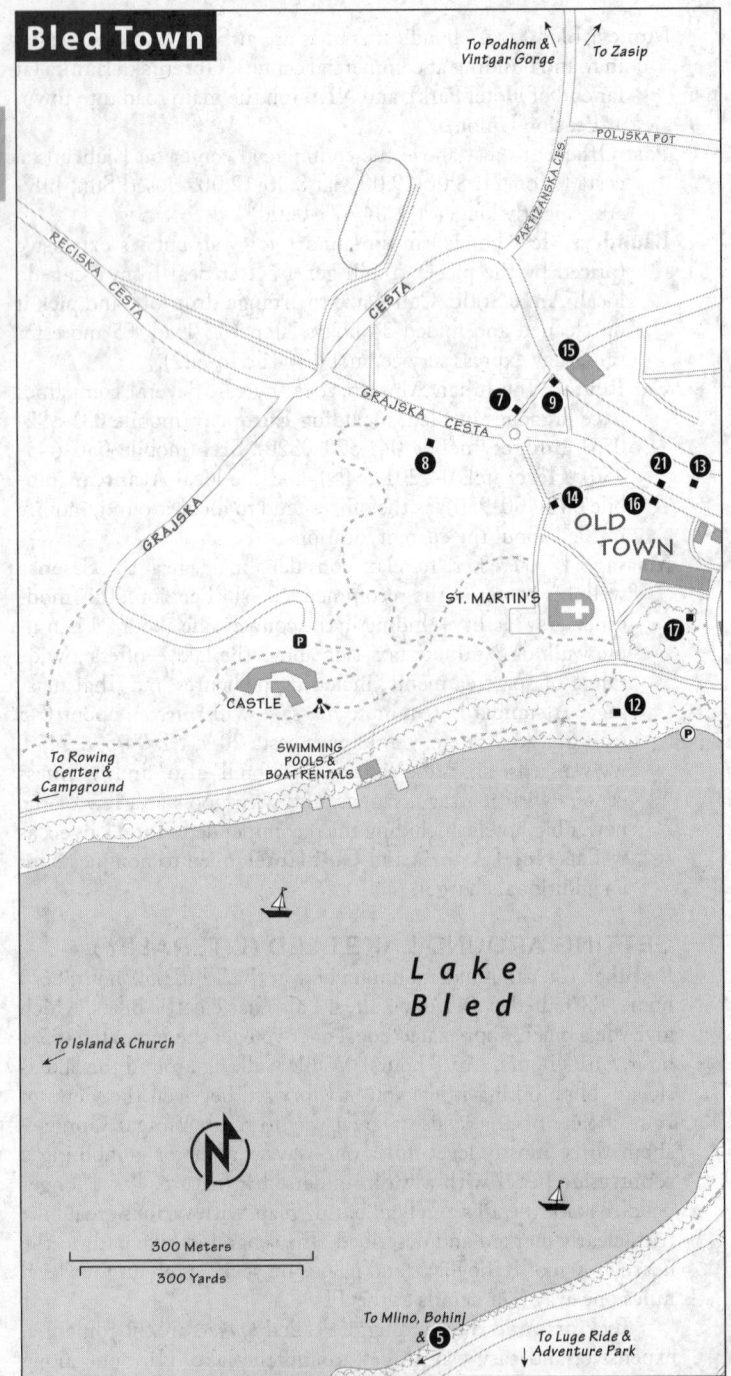

Bled Town

To Podhom & Vintgar Gorge

To Zasip

POLJSKA POT

PARTIZANSKA CES

REČIŠKA CESTA

CESTA

GRAJSKA CESTA

GRAJSKA

15

7

9

8

21 **13**

14 **16**

OLD TOWN

ST. MARTIN'S

17

CASTLE

P

12

P

SWIMMING POOLS & BOAT RENTALS

To Rowing Center & Campground

Lake Bled

To Island & Church

N

300 Meters

300 Yards

To Mlino, Bohinj & **5**

To Luge Ride & Adventure Park

LAKE BLED

1. Mayer Penzion, Hotel Berc, Penzion Berc & Penzion Kaps
2. Mija Sušnik Apts. & Vila Gorenka
3. Hotel Lovec & Okarina Restaurant
4. Grand Hotel Toplice
5. To Vila Istra, Garden Village & Tito's Vila Bled
6. Vila Alice
7. Apartmaji Mežan
8. Penzion Bledec
9. Travellers Haven
10. To Alp Penzion
11. Oštarija Peglez'n Rest. & Bled Pub
12. Vila Prešeren Restaurant
13. Gostilna Pri Planincu Restaurant & Pub
14. Pizzeria Rustika
15. Mercator Groceries (2)
16. Šmon Slaščičarna Pastries
17. Irish Pub
18. Art Café
19. Kult Bled & Devil
20. Fijakers (Horse Carriages)
21. Lifetrek Adventures

the lakefront between Hotel Park and the castle (see map on page 772 for location; around the lake–€40, one-way up to castle–€40, round-trip to castle with 30-minute wait time–€50, mobile 041-710-970).

By Tourist Train: A little train makes a circuit around the lake every 40 minutes in summer (€4, daily 9:00-21:00 in peak season, shorter hours off-season, weather-dependent, mobile 051-337-478).

By Tourist Bus: A handy but pricey shuttle bus passes through Bled daily in the summer. It starts from the main bus station, stops at a few hotels (including Grand Hotel Toplice), then goes up to the castle and on to the Vintgar Gorge entrance (€2.30 one-way to Vintgar, €1.80 just to the castle, departs at 10:00 June-Sept and also at 9:00 July-Aug, confirm schedule at TI or bus station or check www.alpetour.si).

A different summertime bus is designed to reach villages to the east that are otherwise poorly served by public transportation, along with some larger towns such as Radovljica. The bus runs only two days a week, with a different route each day (€4/day, July-Aug Tue and Thu only, ask for schedule at TIs or hotel receptions).

By Taxi: Your hotel can call a taxi for you. Or contact **Bled Tours,** run by friendly, English-speaking driver Sandi Demšar and his girlfriend Cvetka (€10 to the castle or to Lesce-Bled train station, €14 to Radovljica, €50 to Ljubljana airport, €120 to Klagenfurt airport in Austria, office in Hotel Krim, Ljubljanska cesta 7, mobile 031-205-611, www.bledtours.si, info@bledtours.si).

By Boat: For information on renting your own boat, see "Boating" on page 782. For details on riding the characteristic *pletna* boats, see listing for "The Island" (page 777).

Tours at Lake Bled

Local Guides

Tina Hiti and **Sašo Golub,** an energetic young couple, are both excellent guides who enjoy sharing the town and region they love with American visitors. Hiring one of them can add immeasurably to your enjoyment and understanding of Bled and the surrounding area (€45 for 2-hour tour of Bled, arrange several days in advance, info@pg-slovenia.com, Tina's mobile 040-166-554, Sašo's mobile 040-524-774, www.pg-slovenia.com). Tina and Sašo are especially handy for side-tripping into the countryside if you don't want to drive yourself. I've spent great days with both of them and was thankful they were behind the wheel. Their most popular trip is a day in the Julian Alps (€190 round-trip from Bled, €230 to pick up or drop off in Ljubljana, extra charge for 5 or more people, ask about adding a picnic lunch for a small extra charge). They also offer many other options, including all-day shore excursions from the cruise port in Koper (€300 for a day visiting Ljubljana and Bled, up to 3 people), food tours, airport transfers, and trips in the Slovenian countryside to research your roots. As Tina and Sašo both lead tours for me in Europe—and have two young kids—they may send you off with a well-trained substitute. Tina's father **Gorazd,** a former Yugoslav Olympian in ice hockey, brings the older generation's perspective to the trip; **Ervin** provides a younger view; and **Petra** is well-versed in mountain herbs.

Excursions

To hit several far-flung day-trip destinations in one go, consider a package tour from Bled. Destinations range from Ljubljana and the Karst region to the Austrian Lakes to Venice. For example, an all-day Julian Alps trip to the Vršič Pass and Soča Valley runs about €40 per person (sold by various agencies around town—ask the TI). This tour is handy, but two people can rent a car for the day for about the same price and do it at their own pace using the self-guided driving tour in the next chapter.

Adventure Trips

Various Bled-based companies specialize in taking tourists on active, outdoorsy excursions into the surrounding countryside and mountains. One popular, all-day trip is white-water rafting on the Soča River (around €90/person). Other options include canyoning, river tubing, mountain biking, paragliding, rock climbing, and more. Outfits include **Lifetrek Adventures** (near the bus station at Grajska 4, mobile 040-508-853, www.lifetrek-slovenia.com) and **TinaRaft** (based in Radovljica, mobile 041-646-255, www.tinaraft.si). Note that these companies tend to attract a young, sometimes-rowdy crowd that enjoys lubricating their adventures with alcohol.

Sightseeing Flights

If you have perfect weather and deep pockets, there's no more thrilling way to experience Slovenia's high-mountain scenery than from a small propeller plane soaring over the peaks. Flights depart from a grass airstrip near the village of Lesce, a 10-minute drive or taxi ride from Bled. Expensive...but unforgettable (€90 for 15-minute hop over Lake Bled only, €150 for 30-minute flight that also buzzes Lake Bohinj, €210 for deluxe 45-minute version around the summit of Triglav, arrange at least a day in advance, tel. 04/532-0100, www.alc-lesce.si, info@alc-lesce.si).

Sights at Lake Bled

Bled doesn't have many sights, but there are plenty of rewarding and pleasant activities.

▲▲▲Walk Around the Lake

Strolling the 3.5 miles around the lake is enjoyable, peaceful, and scenic. At a leisurely pace, it takes about an hour and a half...not

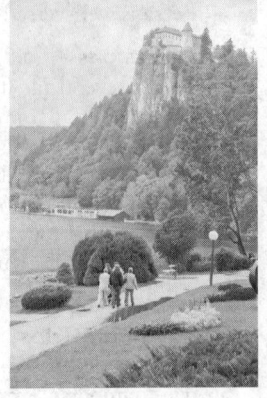

counting stops to snap photos of the ever-changing view. On the way, you'll pass some great villas, mostly from the beginning of the 19th century. The most significant one was a former residence of Marshal Tito—today the Hotel Vila Bled, a fine place to stop for a coffee and pretend Tito invited you over for a visit (described next). For the more adventurous, hiking paths lead up into the hills surrounding the lake (ask TI for details and maps; or hike to—and through—Vintgar Gorge, described on page 794).

▲Tito's Vila Bled

Before World War II, this villa on Lake Bled was the summer residence for the Yugoslav royal family. When Tito ran Yugoslavia, the part-Slovene communist leader took over the place and had it renovated using plans from the architect Jože Plečnik. During his heyday, Tito entertained international guests here (big shots from the communist and nonaligned world, from Indira Gandhi to Nikita Khrushchev to Kim Il Sung to Raúl Castro). Since 1984, it's been a classy hotel and restaurant, offering guests grand Lake Bled views and James Bond ambience. The garden surrounding the villa is filled with exotic trees, brought here by Tito's guests from distant lands.

The terrace has a restaurant that welcomes visitors to drop in for a meal, a piece of cake, or just a cup of coffee (reservations smart if you're dining; likely closed Nov-March). Tito fans might want to splurge for an overnight (www.vila-bled.si). But even if you're not a guest here, the hotel's staff is generally tolerant of curious tourists poking around the public areas inside.

In the marbled lobby, ask to see Tito's original desk (on the way to the bar)—with a rare photo of Tito in civilian clothes. Then head upstairs to gawk at the **Socialist Realist wall murals.** These murals, decorating the upper walls of a vast ballroom on the second floor, are a fascinating peek at the propaganda of the time. Follow the rousing story of the origins of postwar Yugoslavia, starting on the upper left as you enter: First you see the Nazi destruction of Belgrade in 1941, a dark moment that inspired the South Slavs to band together to fight these foreign occupiers. See Tito raising his ragtag army, then leading them into pivotal battles in Bosnia-Herzegovina (notice the minaret and the destroyed bridge over the Neretva River), followed by a winter spent enduring hardship. At the end of this long wall, Tito's victorious Partisans crush the final vestiges of the Nazis; in the upper-right corner, the spring blossoms represent a promising future for the people of Yugoslavia. The large panel at the end of the room trumpets the idealized postwar world that Tito envisioned: proud workers from all walks of life coming together for the betterment of Yugoslavia. In the shadow of a mighty factory—a symbol of heavy industry, which communists embraced as the way of the future—notice that the ironworker and the farmer are holding hands in unity. The room's focal point is the mother hoisting a young child with one arm, and the flag of the nascent Socialist Federal Republic of Yugoslavia with the other.

Getting There: The villa is a 20-minute lakeside walk from the town of Bled at Cesta Svobode 26 (it's the big, white villa with the long staircase at the southern end of the lake, just beyond the village of Mlino). You can also ask your *pletna* gondolier to drop you off here after visiting the island. Those hiking around the lake will pass the gate leading up through Tito's garden to the restaurant and lobby.

▲▲The Island (Blejski Otok)

Bled's little island—capped by a super-cute church—nudges the lake's quaintness level over the top. Locals call it simply "The Island" *(Otok)*. While it's pretty to look at from afar, it's also fun to visit.

The island has long been a sacred site with a romantic twist. On summer Saturdays, a steady procession of brides and grooms, cheered on by their entourages, heads for the island. Ninety-nine steps lead from the island's dock up to the Church of the Assumption on top. It's tradition for the groom to carry—or try to carry—his bride up these steps. About four out of five are successful (proving themselves "fit for marriage"). During the communist era, the church was closed and weddings were outlawed here. But the tradition reemerged—illegally—even before the regime ended, with a clandestine ceremony in 1989.

Cost and Hours: Free to visit island, church-€6, ticket includes tower climb, daily May-Sept 9:00-19:00, April and Oct until 18:00, Nov-March until 16:00.

Getting There: The most romantic route to the island is to cruise on one of the distinctive *pletna* boats (€12/person round-trip, includes 30-minute stay on the island; catch one at several spots around the lake—most convenient from in front of Grand Hotel Toplice or just below Hotel Park, might have to wait for more passengers to fill the boat; boats generally run from dawn, last boat leaves one hour before church closes; replaced by enclosed electric boats in winter—unless the lake freezes, in which case you can rent ice skates; mobile 031-316-575). Other places to catch a *pletna* include the village of Mlino, partway around the lake; the bottom of the grand staircase leading up to Vila Bled (it's a shorter trip from here, but the same cost); and at the campground. For more on these characteristic little vessels, see the "*Pletna* Boats" sidebar. Note that *pletna* boatmen stick close to the 30-minute waiting time on the island—which can go very fast. For more time, you can **rent your own boat** and row to the island (see Boating listing, later). It's even possible to **swim,** especially from the end of the lake nearest the island (see "Swimming" listing, later), but you're not allowed into the church in your swimsuit. Guess you'll just have to go in naked.

Visiting the Island: At the top of the stairs, the **Potičnica café** sells *potica*, the Slovenian nut-roll cake that's traditional at Christmastime but delicious any day of the year. The attached **souvenir shop** is the best in Bled, well-stocked with a variety of high-quality Slovenian gifts, trinkets, and keepsakes.

Upstairs in the same building is the worthwhile but easy-to-miss **art gallery,** which displays changing exhibits as well as a wonderful permanent exhibit commemorating Slovenia's member-

ship in the EU. Local sculptor Ladina Kurbor has created finely detailed clay figurines clad in the traditional national costume from each of the European Union member nations. The attached room houses figurines wearing traditional dress from various parts of Slovenia (identified on the map and explained by the posted descriptions).

The island's main attraction is the **church.** An eighth-century Slavic pagan temple dedicated to the goddess of love and fertility once stood here; the current Baroque version (with Venetian flair—the bell tower is separate from the main church) is the fifth to occupy this spot. Go inside and find the rope for the church bell, hanging in the middle of the aisle just before the altar. A local superstition claims that if you can get this bell to ring three times with one big pull of the rope, your dreams will come true. Worth a try—but be careful if you're slight of build, as the rope can take you for a ride.

If you're waiting for a herd of tourists to ring out their wishes, pass the time looking around the area in front of the altar. When the church was being renovated in the 1970s, workers dug up several medieval graves (you can see one through the glass under the bell rope). They also discovered Gothic frescoes on either side of the altar, including, above the door on the right, an unusual ecclesiastical theme: the *bris* (Jewish circumcision ritual) of Christ.

Your ticket also includes the **bell tower.** At 91 steps, it's a shorter climb than the one up from the boat dock. Up top, you'll find a restored pendulum mechanism from 1890 and fine lake views that are marred by a mesh covering that makes it impossible to snap a clear picture.

To descend by a different route, walk down the trail behind the church (around the right side), then follow the path around the island's perimeter back to where your *pletna* boat awaits.

▲Bled Castle (Blejski Grad)

Bled's cliff-hanging castle, dating in one form or another from 1,000 years ago, was the seat of the Austrian bishops of Brixen,

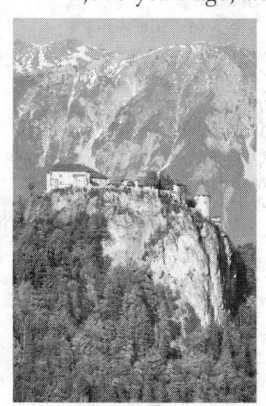

who controlled Bled in the Middle Ages. Today it's merely a fine tourist attraction with a little history and lots of big views. The various sights at the castle—a decent history museum, a frescoed chapel, an old-fashioned printing press, and a wine cellar—are more cute than interesting, but the real reason to come up here is to bask in the sweeping panoramas over Lake Bled and the surrounding mountainscapes.

Cost and Hours: €9, daily May-Oct 8:00-20:00, Nov-April 9:00-18:00, printing press and wine cellar close one hour earlier; tel. 04/572-9782, www.blejski-grad.si.

Getting There: To really earn those views, you can **hike** up the steep hill (20-30 minutes). The handiest trails are behind big St. Martin's Church: Walk past the front door of the church with the lake at your back, and look left after the first set of houses for the *Grad* signs marking the steepest route (follow the wooden stakes all the way up the steep switchback steps); or, for a longer

Pletna Boats

The *pletna* is an important symbol of Lake Bled. In addition to providing a pleasant way to reach the island, these boats also carry on a tradition dating back for generations. In the 17th century, Habsburg Empress Maria Theresa granted the villagers from Mlino—the little town along the lakefront just beyond Bled—special permission to ferry visitors to the island. (This provided a much-needed source of income for Mlino residents, who had very limited access to farmland.) They built their *pletna*s by hand, using a special design passed down from father to son for centuries—like the equally iconic gondolas of Venice. Eventually, this imperial decree and family tradition evolved into a modern union of *pletna* oarsmen, which continues to this day.

Today *pletna* boats are still hand-built according to that same centuries-old design. There's no keel, so the skilled oarsmen work hard to steer the flat-bottomed boat with each stroke—boats piloted by an inexperienced oarsman can slide around on very windy days. There are 21 official *pletna*s on Lake Bled, all belonging to the same union. The gondoliers dump all of their earnings into one fund, give a cut to the tourist board, and divide the rest evenly amongst themselves. Occasionally a new family tries to break into the cartel, underselling his competitors with a "black market" boat that looks the same as the official ones. While some see this as a violation of a centuries-old tradition, others view it as good old capitalism. Either way, competition is fierce.

but less steep route, continue past the church on the same street about five minutes, bearing uphill (left) at the fork, and find the *Grad 1* sign just after the Penzion Bledec hostel on the left. Once you're on this second trail, don't take the sharp-left uphill turn at the fork (instead, continue straight up, around the back of the hill). If you'd rather skip the hike, you can take the morning **tourist bus** (see "Getting Around Lake Bled," earlier), your **rental car**, a **taxi** (around €12), or—if you're wealthy and romantic—a **horse**

and buggy (€40, €10 extra for driver to wait 30 minutes and bring you back down). However, all of these options take you only to the parking lot, from which it's still a steep and slippery-when-wet five-minute hike up to the castle itself.

Eating: The **$$$$ restaurant** at the castle is pricey, but worth the splurge for the views and excellent menu featuring regional cuisine. Come for dinner while it's still light out and savor the setting. There's good seating inside, but it's even better on the outside terrace. Call ahead to book a view table—but do it soon, as this popular place books up quickly. If you have a reservation to dine here, it's free to enter the castle grounds (daily in summer 10:00-22:00, shorter hours off-season, tel. 04/579-4424, www.jezersek. si). Paupers can bring their own **picnic** to munch along the wall with million-dollar views over Lake Bled (buy sandwiches at the Mercator grocery store in the commercial center before you ascend—see page 791).

Visiting the Castle: After buying your ticket, go through the gate and huff the rest of the way up to the outer courtyard. We'll tour the castle clockwise, starting from here. As the castle is continually being spruced up, some details may be different than described.

Turning left at the entrance, you'll pass WCs, then the door to Mojster Janez's working replica of a **printing press** *(grajska tiskarna/manufaktura)* from Gutenberg's time. You can buy your own custom-made souvenir certificate using this very old technology. While this may seem like a tourist gimmick, there's actually some interesting history here. As in many lands, the printing press was a critical tool in the evolution of Slovenia's culture. Look above the press for a life-size mannequin of Primož Trubar (1508-1586), a Slovenian cross between Martin Luther and Johannes Gutenberg. In Trubar's time, Slovene was considered a crude peasants' language—not just unworthy of print, but actually illegal to print. So this Reformer went to Germany and, in 1550—using presses like this one—wrote and printed the first two books in the Slovene language: *Abecedarium* (an alphabet primer to teach illiterate Slovenes how to read) and *Catechismus* (a simplified version of the New Testament). Trubar smuggled his printed books back to Slovenia (hidden in barrels of playing cards) and, en route to Ljubljana, was briefly given refuge in this castle. (Trubar is still much-revered today, appearing on the Slovenian €1 coin.) Up the stairs is an exhibition in English about early printing methods and the importance of moveable type for advancing the Protestant Reformation, whose goal was to get the Word of God more easily into the hands of everyday people. You'll also see one of those first Trubar books—notice it was printed in Tübingen, Germany, an early enclave of the Reformation.

Just past the printing press is the castle's oldest tower—from the 11th century—and a **café terrace** offering pricey drinks with grand views.

Continue past the café and begin climbing the stairs up to grander and grander **views** over the lake. Reaching the terrace at the very top, you'll find the best vistas; the restaurant; a tiny chapel with 3-D frescoes that make it seem much bigger than it is (next to the museum entrance); a small shop selling iron items that are still forged the traditional way; and the well-presented castle **museum,** which strains to make the story of Bled, the castle, and the surrounding region of Carniola interesting. The ground floor has exhibits about geology, prehistoric artifacts, ironworking, and the seasonal life cycle of the region, while the upstairs has a cool 3-D model of the surrounding mountains, smaller models illustrating the growth of the building, more prehistory, and exhibits on the development of tourism at Lake Bled (including its many fine vacation villas). While video screens and some English information are helpful, there's only so much to say.

When you're done up here, head down the stairs between the museum and restaurant (passing WCs). Coming back down into the lower courtyard, turn left down the ramp to find the **wine cellar,** where you can pay a hefty €14-17 to bottle and cork your own souvenir bottle of wine (you're paying for the experience more than the wine). Slovenian wines are well-explained by one of two guys (both, coincidentally, named Andrej) who dress as monks, since winemaking was a monastic responsibility in the Middle Ages.

Before leaving the castle, climb the stairs up to the wooden **defensive gallery** for the best views in town of the mountains east of Bled. The biggest one is called Stol ("Chair"). In the foreground, you can see the steeple marking the town of Podhom; just to the left, the folds in the hills hide the dramatic Vintgar Gorge (see page 794). The gallery leads to the round tower, with an exhibit on a Bled tourism pioneer and a fun "multivision" presentation about nearby activities.

Boating

Bled is the rowing center of Slovenia. Town officials even lengthened the lake a bit so it would perfectly fit the standard two-kilometer laps, with 100 meters more for the turn (on maps, you can see the little divot taken out of the far end). Bled hosted its fourth world championship in August 2011. The town has produced many Olympic medalists, who've won gold in Sydney, silver in Athens, and bronze in London. Notice that local crew team members, whom you'll likely see running or rowing, are characters—with a tradition of wild and colorful haircuts. This dedication to rowing adds to Bled's tranquility, since no motorized boats are allowed on the lake.

If you want to get into the action, you'll find **rental rowboats** at various points around the lake (€10-20/hour). Look for them at Pension Pletna in the lakeside village of Mlino (a scenic 15-minute walk around the lake from Bled); at the swimming pool under the castle (the closest but priciest option); and in the modern building just before the campground on the far end of the lake.

Swimming

Lake Bled has several suitable spots for a swim. The swimming pools under the castle are filled with lake water and routinely earn

the "blue flag," meaning the water is top-quality (swim all day—€7, less for afternoon only, mid-June-Sept daily 8:00-19:00, closed Oct-mid-June and in bad weather, tel. 04/578-0528). Lake Bled's main beach is at the campground at the far end of the lake, though you can also swim near the village of Mlino. If you swim to the island, remember that you can't enter the church in your swimsuit.

Luge Ride (Poletno Sankanje)

Bled's "summer toboggan" luge ride, atop Mount Straža overlooking the lake, allows you to scream down a steep, curvy metal rail track on a little plastic sled. This is a really scary one—speedy, with lots of tight turns, and with great views over the lake—but it's quite pricey. A chairlift takes you to the top of the track, where you'll sit on your sled, take a deep breath, and remind yourself: Pull back on the stick to slow down, push forward on the stick to go faster. You'll drop 480 feet in altitude on the 570-yard-long track, speeding up to about 25 miles per hour as you race toward the lake.

Cost and Hours: €9/ride, cheaper for multiple rides, chairlift only—€4, weather-dependent—if it rains, you can't go. In summer, it's open daily (late June-Aug 10:00-20:00, early Sept 11:00-18:00). In shoulder season, it's Sat-Sun only (mid-April-late June generally 11:00-18:00, late Sept-mid-Oct 11:00-17:00). It's closed off-season (mid-Oct-early April).

Getting There: The base of the chairlift is on the hillside just south of town, beyond Grand Hotel Toplice and just behind the Hostel Vila Viktorija.

Adventure Park (Pustolovski Park)

Next to the luge at the top of Mount Straža, this park has a series of five high-ropes courses designed for everyone from five-year-olds to adults. You'll get rigged up in a safety harness and go through a training course, then be set loose on your choice of courses (with help from spotters on the ground); plan on spending about two hours to do all of them. It's a steep hike up the hill, or you can pay €4 to ride the chairlift for the luge ride (or pay more to ride the chairlift up and luge back down).

Cost and Hours: €20 for adults, €16 for kids 7-14, €10 for kids under 7, late June-Aug daily 10:00-20:00, first half of Sept daily 11:00-18:00, shorter hours and Sat-Sun only rest of season, closed late Oct-early April, last entry two hours before closing, mobile 031-761-661, www.pustolovski-park-bled.si.

▲Kralov Med Beehive Demonstration

Tucked in Selo village, a long walk or short drive from Bled, this fascinating countryside sight is worth ▲▲▲ (or zzz) for fans of the apicultural arts. (First, read up on beekeeping on page 800.) Local beekeeper Blaž Ambrožič has built an apiary (freestanding house of beehives) and teaches visitors all about this very Slovenian form of agriculture. First you'll see the painted panels, with bees buzzing in and out. Blaž's prize possession is a gigantic Winnie-the-Pooh-style hive that he transplanted from a tree trunk. He'll demonstrate how you can hold your hand within inches of the buzzing hive without getting stung, thanks to the peaceful nature of the indigenous Carniolan bee. Inside, you can watch through a big (and safe) window as Blaž pulls out the honeycomb frames from the hive and works with his bees. You can sample (and buy) different types of honey, along with other bee-related gifts. Outside is a perennial garden that demonstrates when various plants blossom, providing much-needed pollen for the bees.

Cost and Hours: €4/person, call or email a day ahead to arrange a time, demonstrations usually last an hour or more and may even run for just two people, Selo pri Bledu 26, tel. 041-657-120, www.kralov-med.si, blazambrozic@gmail.com.

Getting There: Blaž's beehives are in the village of Selo, a five-minute drive or taxi ride or 40-minute walk from Bled town. Head out of town along the lake (past Grand Hotel Toplice), then turn left (inland) at the village of Mlino. In the next village, Selo, look for the two colorful beehive apiaries along the main road, just above the recommended Tourist Farm Mulej.

Nightlife in Bled

BLED PUB CRAWL

Bled is quiet after hours. However, the town does have a few fun bars that are lively with a young crowd (all open nightly until late). Since many young people in Bled are students at the local tourism

LAKE BLED

school, they're likely to speak English...and eager to practice with a native speaker. Try a Smile, a Corona-type Slovenian lager. *Šnops* (schnapps) is a local specialty—popular flavors are plum *(slivovka)*, honey *(medica)*, blueberry *(borovničevec)*, and pear *(hruškovec)*.

Kick things off with the fun-loving local gang at **Gostilna Pri Planincu** near the bus station (described later, under "Eating in Bled"). Then head down Cesta Svobode toward the lake; just below Hotel Jelovica, you'll find the rollicking **Irish Pub** (a.k.a. "The Pub"), with Guinness and indoor or outdoor seating. For the hippest scene in town, duck across the street and wander a few more steps down toward the lake to find the **Art Café**, with a mellow ambience reminiscent of a Van Gogh painting. Around the lake near the commercial center, **Bled Pub** (a.k.a. "The Cocktail Bar" or "Troha"—for the family that owns it) is a trendy late-night spot where bartenders sling a dizzying array of mixed drinks to an appreciative, youthful crowd (between the commercial center and the lake, above the recommended Oštarija Peglez'n restaurant). If you're still standing, several other bars and cafés percolate in the commercial center, including **Kult Bled,** facing the main road. Slathered with iconic film images and neon colors, it attracts a thirtysomething crowd and occasionally hosts live music. **Devil** is open even later (also in the commercial center, near the ATM).

Sleeping in Bled

Bled has more hotel beds per capita than anywhere in Slovenia—and most of them are in big convention hotels. I prefer staying in smaller, more characteristic, pension-type accommodations on the town's fringe—most of them an easy walk from the lake. These quaint little family-run places book up early with Germans and Brits; reserve well ahead. For even cheaper beds, consider one of the many *sobe* (rooms in private homes) scattered around the lake; look for signs in the neighborhood just above Prešernova cesta.

ABOVE THE LAKE
These friendly, cozy, characteristic accommodations are Bled's best values. The only catch is that they're perched on a hilltop a 5- to 10-minute climb up from the lake (easier than it sounds). There are two ways to find these from the town center: Walk around the lake to Grand Hotel Toplice, then go up the stairs around the right side of the Hotel Jadran (on the hill across the street from Grand Hotel Toplice). Or, from the main road into town (Ljubljanska cesta), take the small service road just above the commercial center (in front of Hotel Lovec), and loop up around the big Kompas and Golf hotels. If arriving by bus, ask nicely if your driver will let you disembark along Ljubljanska cesta (just above the traffic light) to

Sleep Code

Hotels are classified based on the average price of a standard double room with breakfast in spring and fall. Prices may go up in summer, and down in winter.

$$$$	**Splurge:**	Most rooms over €150
$$$	**Pricier:**	€110-150
$$	**Moderate:**	€80-110
$	**Budget:**	€50-80
¢	**Backpacker:**	Under €50
RS%	**Rick Steves discount**	

Unless otherwise noted, credit cards are accepted, hotel staff speak basic English, and free Wi-Fi is available. Comparison-shop by checking prices at several hotels (on each hotel's own website, on a booking site, or by email). For the best deal, *book directly with the hotel.* Ask for a discount if paying in cash; if the listing includes **RS%,** request a Rick Steves discount.

avoid the long walk from the bus station. From this bus stop, you can walk down Ljubljanska cesta and take the road just above the post office, which leads up to this area. If you're sleeping up here, Penzion Berc and Mayer Penzion both have great restaurants (described later, under "Eating in Bled").

$$ Mayer Penzion, thoughtfully run by the Trseglav family, comes with 13 great-value rooms, a helpful staff, a tasty restaurant, an atmospheric wine-tasting cellar, and beautifully handcrafted Slovenian woodwork. They book up fast in summer with return clients, so reserve early (family deals, elevator, Želeška cesta 7, tel. 04/576-5740, www.mayer-sp.si, penzion@mayer-sp.si). They also rent a cute, newly restored two-story Slovenian farm cottage next door.

$$ Hotel Berc and **Penzion Berc** (pronounced "berts"), run by the Berc brothers, are next door to Mayer Penzion and flank a romantic outdoor restaurant. Both have cozy public spaces, balconies off every room, and free loaner bikes, and are worth reserving ahead (both cash only). The hotel building has 15 rooms with pleasantly woody decor (Pod Stražo 13, tel. 04/576-5658, www.berc-sp.si, hotel@berc-sp.si, run by Luka). The adjacent *penzion* offers 10 very sharp rooms (closed Nov-Christmas and sporadically off-season, Želeška cesta 15, tel. 04/574-1838, www.berc-sp.si, penzion@berc-sp.si; run by Miha, who also offers local excursions).

$$ Penzion Kaps, owned by Peter (whose father, Anton, is a great craftsman), has 13 comfortable rooms with balconies, modern bathrooms, and classic old wood carvings in a Shangri-La kind of place. The inviting breakfast room clusters around a giant ceramic stove (cash only, free loaner bikes, Želeška cesta 22, mobile 059-117-746, www.penzion-kaps.si, info@penzion-kaps.si).

$ Friendly **Mija Sušnik** rents out two comfortable apartments. Modern, tidy, and equipped with kitchens, these are a good budget choice for families (no breakfast, cash only, laundry service, free parking, Želeška cesta 3, tel. 04/574-1731, susnik@bled-holiday. com). It's just toward the lake from the bigger pensions, with a big crucifix out front. Her sister Ivanka also rents apartments, but they're farther from the lake.

¢ **Vila Gorenka** is your low-budget, no-frills option. The Žerovec family's old-fashioned house has eight faded and musty rooms; three of them have their own bathrooms, while the rest share two other bathrooms. Room #10 has a grand-view balcony (cash only, breakfast extra, closed Nov-Easter, just below the bigger pensions at Želeška cesta 9, mobile 040-958-624, http://freeweb. siol.net/mz2, vilagorenka@gmail.com, Janez).

ON OR NEAR THE LAKE

You'll pay a premium to be closer to the lake—but it's hard to argue with the convenience.

$$$$ **Hotel Lovec** (LOH-vets), a Best Western Premier, sits in a convenient (but nonlakefront) location just above the commercial center. Gorgeously renovated inside and out, and run by a helpful staff, it's professional yet welcoming and cheery. Its 60 plush rooms come with all the comforts and a respected restaurant (family rooms, delicious breakfast, elevator, indoor pool, free parking, Ljubljanska cesta 6, tel. 04/620-4100, www.lovechotel.com, reservations@kompas-lovec.com).

$$$$ **Grand Hotel Toplice** (TOHP-leet-seh) is the grande dame of Bled, with 87 high-ceilinged rooms, parquet floors, a genteel lakeview café/lounge, posh decor, all the amenities, and a long list of high-profile guests—from Madeleine Albright to Jordan's King Hussein to Slovene-by-marriage Donald Trump (ask to see their "wall of fame"). Once elegant, this place is a bit faded these days, but it's still a classic. Rooms in the back are cheaper, but have no lake views and overlook a noisy street—try to get one as high up as possible (air-con, elevator, free one-hour boat rental for guests, free parking, Cesta Svobode 12, tel. 04/579-1000, www. hotel-toplice.com, ghtoplice@hotelibled.com). The hotel's name—*toplice*—means "spa"; guests are free to use the hotel's swanky, natural-spring-fed indoor swimming pool (a chilly 72 degrees Fahrenheit).

$$$ **Vila Istra** is housed in a prominent and gorgeously re-

stored Art Nouveau villa from 1887. The remarkably spacious rooms include one double and five sprawling suites. Room furnishings gild the lily a bit, but respect the history of the building. It's a scenic 15-minute walk outside of the town center, almost to the village of Mlino (air-con, Cesta Svobode 35, mobile 059-080-808, www.vila-istra.info, booking@bled.net).

NEAR THE OLD TOWN

$$$ Vila Alice, a beautifully appointed option on a busy road in the sleepy upper part of town, offers seven rooms in a classy villa with elegant public spaces, a private garden, and a sauna (air-con in some rooms, free parking, reception open daily 7:00-22:00, convenient for drivers at Prešernova cesta 26, mobile 040-231-303, www.vila-alice.com, info@vila-alice.com).

¢ Apartmaji Mežan, run by welcoming Janez and Saša, has four family-friendly apartments in a modern home buried in the middle of town, just uphill from the church. As it's next to an old barn, it's technically a tourist farm (cash only, no breakfast, Riklijeva 6, mobile 041-210-290 or 041-516-688, www.apartmaji-mezan.si, sasa.mezan@gmail.com).

¢ Penzion Bledec (BLED-ets), a family-run, official IYHF hostel, is just below the castle at the top of the Old Town. Each of the 12 rooms has its own bathroom. They have dorms, private rooms, and great family rooms (full-service laundry for guests, restaurant, Grajska 17, tel. 04/574-5250, www.bledec.si, info@bledec.si).

¢ Travellers Haven is a low-key hostel run with a smile by Mirjam. The 31 beds fill eight rooms in a nicely renovated hundred-year-old villa in the Old Town. The lodgings are well maintained and the hangout areas are inviting, though the tight bathrooms offer little privacy (reception open 8:00-13:00 & 16:00-23:00, laundry machines, rental bikes, Riklijeva cesta 1, mobile 041-396-545, www.travellers-haven.si, travellers-haven@t-2.net).

OUTSIDE TOWN

The following listings are a bit farther out: Alp Penzion is a 20-minute walk from the lakefront, but still doable for nondrivers, while the tourist farm and "glampground" are best for drivers.

$$$$ Garden Village is very expensive...but very cool. Alternately billed as a "glampground" and a "green resort," this splurge combines the closeness to nature of camping with the amenities of a hip resort. From the main lodge, restaurant, and rustic pond/pool, the complex tumbles down a ravine toward a gushing river, connected by slippery plank walks. You can choose between the tree house (with a loft and netted hammock area up top for kids); the glamping tents, with canvas walls and nestled in an abundant produce garden; or the simpler pier tents, actually on stilts over the river. All of these include breakfast, Wi-Fi, and other amenities, but additional charges for cleaning and shorter stays can really add up (on the road toward Lake Bohinj, turn off on the left just before Vila Bled, Cesta Gorenjskega odreda 16, tel. 08/389-9220, www. gardenvillagebled.com, reservations@gardenvillagebled.com).

$ Alp Penzion makes the most of a peaceful countryside setting amid hayfields, within a 20-minute, partly uphill walk of the lake (better for drivers or for those who don't mind the walk). With 12 rooms (some with balconies), this kid-friendly place is enthusiastically run by the Sršen family, who offer lots of fun extras, including a summer barbecue grill/outdoor pub (family rooms, dinner possible in summer—ask when you book, air-con, free loaner bikes, Cankarjeva cesta 20A, for location see map on page 769, tel. 04/574-1614, www.alp-penzion.com, bled@alp-penzion.com). Just next door is the relaxing Essense spa (described earlier, under "Helpful Hints").

$ Tourist Farm Mulej, possible for hardy walkers but much better for drivers, is a new but traditional farmhouse in a tranquil valley about a half-mile from the lake (1.5 miles from Bled town). Damjana and Jože, who run this working farm (with 70 milk cows... and their smells), also rent out eight modern rooms and four apartments—all with balconies—and serve breakfasts and dinners made with food they produce. Be sure to see the udderly fascinating, fully automated cow-milking machine called Lely, who's practically a member of the family (cash only, family rooms, air-con, free loaner bikes, horseback riding free for experienced guests, Selo pri Bledu 42a, tel. 04/574-4617 or 04/022-4888, www.mulej-bled.com, info. mulej@gmail.com). It's in the farm village of Selo—drive along the lakeside road south from Bled, then turn off in Mlino toward Selo, and look for the signs (to the right) once in the village. For the location, see the map on page 769.

Eating in Bled

Bled has several good restaurants, but most everything is quite similar. For variety, wait for Ljubljana.

$$$$ Okarina, run by charming, well-traveled Leo Ličof (who may be retiring soon), serves a diverse array of cuisines, all of them well-executed: international fare, traditional Slovenian specialties (with an emphasis on game), and Indian (Himalayan) dishes. Leo has a respect for salads and vegetables and a passion for fish. Creative cooking, fine presentation, friendly service, and an atmosphere as tastefully eclectic as the food make this place a great splurge (Mon-Fri 12:00-15:00 & 18:00-23:00, Sat-Sun 12:00-

---

Restaurant Price Code

I've assigned each eatery a price category, based on the average cost of a typical main course. Drinks, desserts, and splurge items (steak and seafood) can raise the price considerably.

$$$$	**Splurge:** Most main courses over €14
$$$	**Pricier:** €10-14
$$	**Moderate:** €6-10
$	**Budget:** Under €6

In Slovenia, a takeout spot is **$**; a basic sit-down eatery is **$$**; a casual but more upscale restaurant is **$$$**; and a swanky splurge is **$$$$**.

23:00, closed Nov-mid-April, next to recommended Hotel Lovec at Ljubljanska cesta 8, tel. 04/574-1458).

$$$ Oštarija Peglez'n ("The Old Iron"), conveniently located on the main road between the commercial center and the lake, cooks up tasty Slovenian and Mediterranean meals, with an emphasis on fish and fun, family-style shareable plates. Choose between the delightful Slovenian cottage interior or the shady streetside terrace. Reservations are smart in summer (daily 12:00-23:00, Cesta Svobode 19A, tel. 04/574-4218).

$$$ Vila Prešeren is the best lakeside choice, featuring mod decor, good international cuisine (as well as some traditional Slovenian dishes), and tables on a giant terrace reaching down to the lakefront. This is a great spot to linger over a meal, a drink, or a classic Lake Bled dessert (daily 7:00-23:00, Veslaška promenada 14, tel. 04/575-2510).

In the B&B Zone Above Town: Just up the hill from the lakefront, two recommended B&Bs run restaurants ideal for dinner in a lovely setting. At either place, it's smart to reserve ahead—especially in summer. **$$$ Fine Food Berc** is a dreamy splurge restaurant (operated by the recommended Penzion Berc). You'll dine at white-tablecloth tables positioned just so on the lush lawn or in the cutesy interior—both come with live piano music. Reservations are smart (May-Sept daily 17:00-23:00, Želeška cesta 15, tel. 04/574-1838). Next door, **$$$ Mayer Penzion** runs a classy restaurant with fine traditional cooking and good seating inside and out. This is where a Babel of international tourists comes to swap hiking tips and day-trip tales (limited menu, Tue-Sun 18:00-24:00, closed Mon, Želeška cesta 7, tel. 04/576-5740).

$$ Gostilna Pri Planincu ("By the Mountaineers") is a homey, informal bar coated with license plates and packed with fun-loving and sometimes-rowdy natives. A larger dining area sprawls behind the small, local-feeling pub, and there's outdoor seating out front and on the side patio. The menu features huge portions of stick-to-

Bled Desserts

While you're in Bled, be sure to enjoy the town's specialty, a cream cake called **_kremna rezina_** (KRAYM-nah ray-ZEE-nah; often referred to by its German-derived name, **_kremšnita,_** KRAYM-shnee-tah). It's a layer of cream and a thick layer of vanilla custard artfully sandwiched between sheets of delicate, crispy crust. Heavenly. Slovenes travel from all over the country to sample this famous dessert. You may also see some newfangled strawberry and chocolate _kremšnita_ variations, but purists swear by the original.

Slightly less renowned—but just as tasty—is **_grmada_** (gur-MAH-dah, "bonfire"). This dessert was developed by Hotel Jelovica as a way to get rid of their day-old leftovers. They take yesterday's cake, add rum, milk, custard, and raisins, and top it off with whipped cream and chocolate syrup.

There's also _prekmurska gibanica_—or just **_gibanica_** (gee-bah-NEET-seh) for short. Originating in the Hungarian corner of the country, _gibanica_ is an earthy pastry filled with poppy seeds, walnuts, apples, and cheese, and drizzled with rum.

Yet another dessert is the very traditional **_potica_** (poh-TEET-seh), a walnut roll that's usually eaten at Christmastime. While it's rare to find this in bakeries, the café on the island in the lake sells several varieties.

Desserts are typically enjoyed with a lake-and-mountains view—the best spots are the terrace at Vila Prešeren, the Panorama restaurant by Grand Hotel Toplice, and the terrace across from Hotel Park (figure around €5 for cake and coffee at any of these places). For a more local but nonlakeview setting, consider the recommended Šmon Slaščičarna (only slightly cheaper).

your-ribs Slovenian pub grub, plus Balkan grilled-meat specialties. Look for their huge, home-style traditional daily specials. Upstairs is a timbered pizzeria dishing up wood-fired pies (daily 9:00-23:00, pizzeria open from 11:00, Grajska cesta 8, tel. 04/574-1613). The playful cartoon mural along the outside of the restaurant shows different types of mountaineers (from left to right): thief, normal, mooch ("gopher"), climber, and naked (...well, almost).

$$ Pizzeria Rustika, in the Old Town, offers wood-fired pizzas and salads. Its upstairs terrace is relaxing on a balmy evening (daily 12:00-23:00, service can be slow when it's busy, Riklijeva cesta 13, tel. 04/576-8900).

Supermarket: The **$ Mercator** grocery store, in the commercial center, has the makings for a bang-up picnic. They sell sandwiches to go for about €3, or will make you one to order (point to what you want). This is a great option for hikers and budget travelers (Mon-Fri 7:30-20:30, Sat 7:00-15:00, Sun 8:00-12:00). There's another location closer to the Old Town and castle (Mon-Sat 7:00-20:00, Sun 8:00-16:00).

Dessert: While tourists generally gulp down their cream cakes on a hotel restaurant's lakefront terrace, residents favor the desserts at **Slaščičarna Zima** (a.k.a. the "Brown Bear," for the bear on the sign). It's nicely untouristy, but lacks the atmosphere of the lakeside spots (daily 7:30-21:00, near bus station at Grajska cesta 3, tel. 04/574-1616).

Splurge Restaurant Near Bled

$$$$ Vila Podvin, in the village of Mošnje (about a 15-minute drive from Lake Bled, just past Radovljica), has gained a big culinary reputation in recent years. The talented celebrity chef, UrošŠ (who has hosted some popular Slovenian cooking shows), prides himself on melding traditional Slovenian recipes with modern techniques and flavors. The dressy but inviting interior and fine garden are equally enjoyable places to dine. Their lunch special—available until 15:00—is a nice way to affordably sample their menu. Reservations are smart (Tue-Sat 12:00-22:00, Sun 12:00-17:00, closed Mon, Mošnje 1, tel. 08/384-3470, www.vilapodvin.si). They also rent very sharp rooms and offer cooking classes (explained on their website).

Lake Bled Connections

The most convenient train connections to Bled leave from the Lesce-Bled Station, about 2.5 miles away (see details under "Arrival in Bled," earlier). Remember, when buying a train ticket to Lake Bled, make it clear that you want to go to the **Lesce-Bled Station** (not the Bled Jezero Station, which is poorly connected to the main line). No one in the town of Bled sells train tickets; buy them at the station just before your train departs (open Mon-Fri 5:30-21:00, Sat 7:00-15:00, Sun 14:30-19:30). If the ticket window there is closed, buy your ticket on board from the conductor (who will likely waive the surcharge).

Note that if you're going to **Ljubljana,** the bus (which leaves from Bled town itself) is better than the train (which leaves from the Lesce-Bled train station).

From Lesce-Bled by Train to: Ljubljana (roughly hourly, 40-60 minutes), **Salzburg** (3/day, 4 hours, some change in Villach, Austria), **Munich** (3/day, 5.5 hours, some change in Villach), **Vienna** (that's **Dunaj** in Slovene, 3/day, 5.25-6 hours, change in Villach), **Venice** (2/day with transfers in Villach—one partway by bus, 6-6.5 hours; instead consider a GoOpti minibus—described on page 764), **Zagreb** (4/day direct, 3-3.5 hours).

By Bus to: Ljubljana (Mon-Sat hourly—usually at :30 past the hour, fewer on Sun, 1.25 hours), **Radovljica** (Mon-Fri at least 2/hour, Sat hourly, Sun almost hourly, 15 minutes), **Lesce-Bled train station** (2/hour, 10 minutes), **Lake Bohinj** (hourly, 40 minutes to Bohinj Jezero stop, 50 minutes to Bohinj Vogel or Bohinj Zlatorog stop, 3/day in summer continue all the way to Savica Waterfall trailhead), **Podhom** (15-minute hike away from Vintgar Gorge, Mon-Fri 5/day in the morning, 1/day Sat, none Sun, 15 minutes), **Spodnje Gorje** (also 15-minute hike from Vintgar Gorge, take bus in direction of Krnica, hourly, 15 minutes). Confirm times at the TI or by using the schedules posted at the unstaffed Bled bus station. Buy tickets on the bus.

By Plane: Ljubljana Airport (airport code: LJU) is between Lake Bled and Ljubljana, about a 45-minute drive from Bled. Connecting by taxi costs around €60 (set price up front—since it's outside of town, they don't use the meter; be sure to use a Bled-based taxi because a Ljubljana-based taxi will likely be more expensive). The Zup Prevozi shuttle bus is a more affordable option at €13, but it runs only a few times each day (generally coordinated to meet EasyJet flights—see schedule at www.zup-prevozi.eu). Another option is to prearrange a shared shuttle service with either GoOpti (see description on page 764) or Zup Prevozi. The public bus connection from Bled to the airport is cheap (total cost: about €6) but complicated and time-consuming: First, go to Kranj (Mon-Fri 12/day, Sat-Sun 8/day, 35 minutes), then transfer to a Brnik-bound bus (at least hourly, 20 minutes). Many Bled residents prefer to fly from Klagenfurt, Austria. For details on both the Ljubljana and Klagenfurt airports, see page 765.

Route Tips for Drivers: Bled is less than an hour north of Ljubljana on the slick A-2 expressway. The exit is marked for *Lesce,* but you'll also see signs for *Bled,* which will lead you directly to the lake (where the road becomes Ljubljanska cesta).

To reach **Radovljica** (bee museum) or **Lesce** (train station), drive out of Bled on Ljubljanska cesta toward the expressway. Watch for the turnoff to *Lesce* on the right. They're on the same road: Lesce first (to reach train station, divert right when entering town), then Radovljica. (Signs to *Radovljica* will divert you out to the main road that parallels the expressway, then back down into Radovljica; instead, you could follow signs to Lesce, and drive through that town for the more direct route.)

Near Lake Bled

The countryside around Bled offers several day trips that can be done easily without a car (bus connection information is described in each section). The three trips listed here are the best (one small-town/museum experience, two hiking/back-to-nature options). They're more convenient than can't-miss, but each is worthwhile on a longer visit, and all give a good taste of the Julian Alps. For a self-guided driving tour through farther-flung (and even more striking) parts of the Julian Alps, see the next chapter.

Vintgar Gorge

For those seeking an easy yet spectacular walk, Vintgar (VEENT-gar), worth ▲▲, is one of my favorite low-impact hikes in Slovenia. Just north of Bled, the river Radovna has carved this mile-long, picturesque gorge into the mountainside. Boardwalks and bridges put you right in the middle of the magic in this "poor man's Plitvice." Shaded and relatively cool, this is a refreshing place for a walk on a hot day.

The gorge—easily reachable from Bled by bus or foot—works well for those who are itching for a hike but don't have a car. From the entrance, allow about 1.5 hours for a round-trip hike, including time for photos (and there will be photos). On sunny days, the gorge can be crowded (and less idyllic) after about 11:00—if you anticipate crowds, get an early start.

Cost and Hours: €4 to enter gorge, open daily April-Oct 8:00-19:00 or until dusk, June-Aug maybe until 20:00, closed Nov-March, tel. 04/572-5266.

Getting to Vintgar Gorge: The gorge is 2.5 miles north of Bled. To reach the gorge entrance, you can walk (takes at least one hour one-way), pedal a rental bike (about 30 minutes, easiest with an electric bike), take a bus (15-minute ride plus 15-minute walk, or 30-minute ride on summer tourist bus), or drive (less than 10 minutes).

Walkers and **cyclists** leave Bled on the road between the castle and St. Martin's Church and take the uphill (left) road at the fork. Just after the little yellow chapel, turn right on the road with the big tree, then immediately left at the Mercator grocery store. When the road swings left, continue straight onto Partizanska (marked for *Podhom* and a walking sign for *Vintgar;* ignore the bus sign for

Vintgar pointing left). At the fork just after the little bridge, go left for Podhom, then simply follow signs for *Vintgar*.

In summer, the easy **tourist bus** takes you right to the gorge entrance (only runs in the morning; see "Getting Around Lake Bled," page 771). Otherwise, you can take a **local bus** to one of two stops: Podhom (Mon-Fri 5/day in the morning, 1/day Sat, none Sun, 15 minutes) or Spodnje Gorje (take bus in direction of Krnica, hourly, 15 minutes). From either the Podhom or the Spodnje Gorje bus stop, it's a 15-minute walk to the gorge (follow signs for *Vintgar*).

Drivers follow signs to *Podhom*, then *Vintgar* (see walking/cycling instructions), and park for free right at the gorge entrance.

Gorge Hike: After buying your ticket, you'll hit the boardwalk trail (sometimes a bit slippery) and crisscross over the most dramatic and narrow stretch, tiptoeing over several waterfalls and marveling at the clarity of the water. Then the gorge—and the trail—flattens out and passes under a high stone footbridge and over a scenic dam. Finally, at the end of the gorge, you'll reach a footbridge over a plunging waterfall (next to a snack stand and WCs). For more views, continue on five minutes downhill (following the *Pod Slap* signs), then circle over the river again to reach a knoll where you can peer up at the waterfall and bridge you just crossed.

When finished, you can simply go back the way you came, or take a prettier return to Bled (described next).

Scenic Hike Back to Bled: If you still have energy once you reach the end of the gorge, consider this longer hike back with panoramic views. Behind the snack stand deep in the gorge, find the trail marked *Pod Katarina*. You'll go uphill for 25 strenuous minutes (following the red-and-white circles and arrows) before cresting the hill and enjoying beautiful views over Bled town and the region. Continue straight down the road 15 minutes to the typical, narrow old village of Zasip, then walk (about 30 minutes) or take the bus back to Bled.

Radovljica

The town of Radovljica (rah-DOH-vleet-suh, "Radol'ca" for short), perched on a plateau above the Sava River, has the charming Old Town that Bled lacks (refreshingly, it also lacks much of Bled's summer crowds). The traffic-free core of the town, once hemmed in by a stout wall (still faintly visible in some areas), is jammed with historic buildings that surround the long, skinny main square called Linhartov trg. While Radovljica's Old Town is a pleasant place to stroll or nurse a coffee, you can see it all in a few minutes. The main reason to visit here is to tour its small but strangely fascinating beekeeping museum—despite having only a few rooms, it still ranks as one of Europe's biggest on the apiarian arts. Skip the town on Mondays, when the museum is closed (and be aware that the museum has shorter hours off-season).

Tourist Information: The enthusiastic TI loves to help visitors appreciate the town of "Radol'ca" (May-Sept daily 9:00-19:00; Oct-April Mon-Fri 9:00-16:00, Sat-Sun 9:00-18:00; Linhartov trg 1, tel. 04/531-5112, www.radolca.si).

GETTING TO RADOVLJICA

Buses to Radovljica generally leave Bled every half-hour (fewer on weekends, buy ticket from driver, trip takes about 15 minutes). To reach the town center and the bee museum from the bus station, leave the station going straight ahead, cross the bus parking lot and the next street, then turn left down the far street (following brown sign for *Staro Mesto*). In five minutes, you'll reach the start of the pedestrianized Linhartov trg (with the TI—on the right—and the start of my "Old Town Stroll").

Drivers leave Bled on Ljubljanska cesta and follow the directions under "Route Tips for Drivers" on page 793. The road dead-ends at Radovljica's pedestrian zone, where you'll find a parking lot (by the rustic garage), the TI, and the start of my "Old Town Stroll."

A handy **bike** path scenically and peacefully connects Bled with Radovljica (about 4 miles, get details at TI).

Sights in Radovljica

Old Town Stroll

Whether arriving by bus or by car, you'll enter the Old Town next to the TI. If you curl around below the main road, you'll find the scant remains of the city's original **moat**—the only surviving one in Slovenia.

On the left, just as you enter the Old Town, **Vinoteka Sodček** offers a handy opportunity to sample Slovenian wines. Their €12 tasting includes five wines, plus cheese and *pršut* (air-dried ham)—it's best to call ahead to arrange this. You can also buy bottles of wine here for €10-15. Owner Aleš knows his stuff (Mon-Sat 9:00-21:00, closed Sun, Linhartov trg 8, tel. 04/531-5071).

Continuing into the Old Town, after a half-block you'll pass a fun little **secondhand shop** on the right—crammed with everything from beat-up modern appliances to genuine Slovenian antiques.

Beyond that, the street opens up into **Linhartov trg,** a charming square fronted by historic buildings. On the left is the **Magušarjeva Hiša,** a fine old Gothic house where potter Urban Magušar lives, has a studio and exhibition space, and teaches pottery classes—if you're curious, step into the courtyard and ask him if you can see the house (Trubarjeva 1, mobile 041-734-808).

The **Vidičeva Hiša** café serves great ice cream and cakes. Farther along is the traditional, recommended **Lectar** restaurant, with a "living museum" in the basement where you can watch bakers making traditional gingerbread ornaments (€1.50 entry).

Across the street is a monument with a student holding a big medallion image of **Josipina Hočevar,** a Radovljica native who later helped fund the town's water system (see the old well nearby) and a school and many important buildings in Krško, near Zagreb. Next to that is the **Šivičeva Hiša,** an atmospheric late-Gothic house that's open to the public. If you go a block down any street to the right, you'll come to a fine valley **viewpoint** emphasizing Radovljica's dramatic position on a long promontory.

Dominating the main part of the square is the big, yellow **town "castle"** (actually a mansion); upstairs you'll find the **Api-cultural Museum** (described next), the Linhart Museum, and the

Baroque Hall—once divided into 10 small offices, but recently restored to its previous grandeur.

Beyond the mansion (and connected to it by a gallery) is **St. Peter's Church;** to its right is its rectory, where you can dip into the pretty courtyard.

Circle all the way around the church, then go through the gate to the edge of the ravine. Burrowed into the hillside is a **WWII-era bunker** left behind by the Nazis. Peeking into the window of the bunker, you'll see it's been turned into a chapel dedicated to Edith Stein, a 20th-century Polish Jew who became a Carmelite nun but was arrested by the Nazis and executed at Auschwitz. She was later made a saint by Pope John Paul II (notice the menorah and Star of David inside the chapel, on the right). While she has no official ties to Radovljica, locals are inspired by Edith's example.

▲▲Apicultural Museum (Čebelarski Muzej)

This museum celebrates Slovenia's long and very proud beekeeping heritage. While the exhibits about the history of beekeeping are oddly fascinating, the highlight is the extensive collection of colorfully painted frontboard panels (used on the front of hives)—one of Slovenia's most cherished folk arts. Replicas of these panels are sold in souvenir shops nationwide, but these are the real deal.

Cost and Hours: €3, good English descriptions, €1.60 English guidebook is a nice souvenir; May-Oct Tue-Sun 10:00-18:00, closed Mon, shorter hours off-season, Jan-Feb closed Sat-Mon; clean and easy WCs, upstairs at Linhartov trg 1, tel. 04/532-0520, www.muzeji-radovljica.si.

Visiting the Museum: Everything is well-described in English, but this commentary will help you locate the highlights.

The **first room** of the museum traces the history of beekeeping, from the time when bees were kept in hollowed-out trees to the present day. The bust celebrates beekeeper extraordinaire Anton Janša. On the nearby wall, you'll see excerpts from his first-ever textbook on beekeeping, as well as documents from other VIBs (very important beekeepers).

In the **second room** are old-fashioned tools. When a new queen bee is born, the old queen takes half the hive's bees to a new location. Experienced beekeepers used the long, skinny instrument (a beehive stethoscope) to figure out when the swarm was working up a steady buzz, indicating they were ready to fly the coop. Then, once the bees had moved to a nearby tree, the beekeeper used the big spoons to retrieve the queen—surrounded by an angry ball of her subjects—from her new home before she could get settled in. The beekeeper transferred the furious gang into a man-made hive designed for easier, more sanitary collection of honey. You can also see the tools beekeepers used to create smoke, which makes bees less aggressive. Even today, some of Slovenia's old-fashioned bee-keepers simply light up a cigarette and blow smoke on any bees that get ornery. The life-size model of a man carrying a box on his back illustrates how dedicated beekeepers would trudge uphill with their hives to help them reach higher and higher blossoms as the summer wore on. You'll also see a variety of old beehives (and a press used to squeeze every last drop of honey out of that comb), as well as photos of apiaries—large, freestanding buildings that house multiple hives. The map on the wall shows how the Carniolan bee—favored by beekeepers for its relatively mellow personality and fast growth in springtime—has been exported far and wide throughout the world, thanks to its adaptability to new climates.

The **third room** features the museum's highlight: whimsically painted beehive frontboards (called *panjske končnice*). Beekeepers,

 believing these paintings would help the bees find their way home, developed a tradition of decorating their hives with religious, historical, and satirical folk themes. The oldest panel dates from 1758, but the practice really took off in the 19th century. Take your time perusing these delightful illustrations. The depiction of a hunter's funeral shows all the animals happy... except his dog. In another panel, animals shave the hunter—evoking an old Slovenian saying about "shaving the fool." Panels also reveal professional stereotypes of the time: One popular panel shows two farmers fighting over a cow, while a lawyer milks it. Another features a giant snail running over very slow-moving tailors (who were considered extremely lethargic in sewing new clothes). Historical panels include a bloody beheading during a local battle and several scenes of troublesome Turks. There's everything from portraits of Habsburg emperors, to a "true crime" sequence of a man murdering his family as they sleep, to proto-"Lockhorns" cartoons of marital strife, to awkward depictions of foreign lands (based on likely incomplete or faulty descriptions of the day), to 18th-century erotica (one with a woman showing some leg and another with a flip-up, peek-a-boo panel). A few panels blur the line between humorous and misogynistic: Look for the devil sharpening a woman's tongue on a wheel; the mill where old women are put in and young women are pulled out; or the man carrying a cross—and his wife—on his back. (Equal-opportunity offenders, beekeepers also painted scenes of drunk men being yanked out of bars and away from card

Slovenian Beekeeping

Since the days before Europeans had sugar, Slovenia has been a big honey producer. Slovenian farmer Anton Janša (1734-1773) is considered the father of modern beekeeping. Habsburg Empress Maria Theresa brought him to Vienna to become Europe's first official teacher of this art. And even today, beekeeping is considered a crucial part of Slovenian culture. The area around Lake Bled (Carniola) has about 6,000 inhabitants, including 65 beekeepers who manage 5,000 hives—the most bees per capita of any place in Europe.

Most Slovenian beekeepers maintain large buildings called apiaries, which hold banks of smaller hives (as opposed to beekeepers in North America, who tend to have a few separate large hives). This innovation—one of many by Janša—allows beekeepers to maximize efficiency. The front panel of each individual hive is painted in bright colors, often depicting creative folk scenes. This is designed to help both the bees and the beekeepers (who were, traditionally, often illiterate) distinguish the hives from each other. (While bees may not be able to tell a painting of a bear from one of a flower, they can distinguish enough patterns and colors to keep themselves from accidentally going to the wrong hive—in which case they'd be attacked as an outsider.)

Replicas of those characteristic **beehive panels** are available at shops in Bled and Ljubljana and make for appealing souvenirs. Basic reproductions of the beehive panels cost around €12-15, while better-quality, hand-painted ones run €20-30 or more. When perusing your options, it helps to know the stories behind each one (see page 799 for a rundown on some of the designs).

The other apian souvenir is **honey.** In 2013, Slovenian honey

games by their wives.) The life-size wooden statues were used to "guard" the beehives—and designed to look like fearsome Ottoman and Napoleonic soldiers.

The **fourth room** examines the biology of bees. In the summer only, look for the actual, functioning beehive. Try to find the queen—she's usually marked with a dot on her back. The surround-sound hive nearby lets you step inside to hear the noise of a buzzing queen. You'll also see bee-related products, including wax items, ornaments, and pastries. Another exhibit shows how bees—so respected here in Slovenia, and around the world—are a popular decorative motif, adorning everything from coins to buildings (in was designated as a unique product by the European Union—a certification that means only honey produced in a certain place and manner can carry that name. Taste can differ tremendously from hive to hive, and is determined by the specific flowers and blossoms a hive's bees gather pollen from. Ideally find a shop that will let you sample several. In general, honeys made from mixed flowers and linden blossoms (which tend to be cloudy from a natural crystallization process) have the sweetest, mildest flavor; those made from chestnut or pine trees can have a bitter after-taste. The honeys that appear creamy are infused with flavors and are most often eaten on bread or pancakes; plain honey is more versatile.

Besides honey, beekeepers also make money by raising new queen bees. Each hive has one, and they can't be bred—one of the larvae is simply fed special "royal jelly" that encourages her to become a leader. In the springtime, when bees are born, the beekeeper keeps a close eye on the hive to figure out whether there are any potential queens about to emerge. If he finds one, he'll move the old queen—who brings half the hive with her—to a new home (before she can find one on her own).

Slovenes still reserve an importance and affection for bees that's rare in modern times. For example, the Slovene language has two different words for "to give birth" and "to die": One they use exclusively for humans and bees, and a different one for all other animals. If a beekeeper dies, it's believed (with some pretty incontrovertible evidence) that the new beekeeper must formally "introduce" himself to the hive by going there and explaining to the bees what has happened; otherwise, they become confused and agitated, and often die themselves.

To learn more about Slovenian beekeeping, visit the insight-ful Apicultural Museum in Radovljica. For an even more vivid, practical experience, call Blaž at Kralov Med near Bled for a dem-onstration (see page 784). At either place, you'll get a sense for just how proud Slovenes are of their bees.

many cultures, diligent bees, who store their honey, are symbolic of banks).

The **final room** features a modern beekeeper's house, special exhibits, and a good but dry, detailed 14-minute film about the Carniolan bee.

Back at the entrance, the ticket desk sells a few choice souve-nirs, including hand-painted replicas of frontboards, honey brandy, candles, ornaments, and other bee products.

Nearby: Sharing a ticket desk with the bee museum, the skip-pable **Linhart Museum** celebrates one of Slovenia's leading En-lightenment thinkers: Radovljica-born Anton Linhart, the 18th-century politician and historian who wrote some of the first plays in the Slovenian language, setting the stage for France Prešeren (€5 combo-ticket with Apicultural Museum, same hours).

Eating in Radovljica

Several Radovljica restaurants near the bee museum have view terraces overlooking the surrounding mountains and valleys.

$$$ Lectar offers pricey, hearty Slovenian fare in a rural-feeling setting with a user-friendly, super-traditional menu. Its several heavily-decorated rooms are often filled with tour groups, but in good weather, don't miss the terrace out back. Come here if you want to linger over rustic Slovenian specialties—not if you're in a hurry. The restaurant is known for its heart-shaped gingerbread cookies (called *lect*), inscribed with messages of love. In the cellar is a "living museum" where you can pay a small fee to watch costumed bakers make and decorate these hearts according to the traditional recipe (Wed-Mon 12:00-22:00, closed Tue, family-friendly, Linhartov trg 2, tel. 04/537-4800).

$$ Gostilna Avguštin, across the street, is the simpler local alternative for unpretentious, stick-to-your-ribs Slovenian fare. Their terrace in back enjoys an even better view than Lectar's (daily 11:00-24:00, Linhartov trg 15, tel. 04/531-4163).

Lake Bohinj

The pristine alpine Lake Bohinj (BOH-heen), 16 miles southwest of Bled, enjoys a quieter scene and (in clear weather) even better vistas of Triglav and the surrounding mountains. This is a real back-to-nature experience, with just a smattering of hotels and campgrounds, rather than the well-oiled resort machine of Bled. Some people adore Bohinj; others are bored by it. While spectacular in clear, sunny weather, it's disappointing in the clouds (and, because of its position deep in the mountains, it can be socked-in here even when it's clear in Bled). But if the weather is great and you're finding Bled too touristy to allow you to really enjoy nature, go to Bohinj.

GETTING TO LAKE BOHINJ

From Bled, hourly **buses** head for Bohinj, stopping at three different destinations: Bohinj Jezero (the village of Ribčev Laz, 40 minutes), then Bohinj Vogel (a 10-minute walk from the base of the Vogel Mountain cable car, 50 minutes), and finally a few hundred yards more to Bohinj Zlatorog (Hotel Zlatorog and the one-hour hike to the Savica Waterfall trailhead, 50 minutes). In summer, a few buses continue all the way to the Savica Waterfall trailhead (see details under "Savica Waterfall," later). Off-season, there are fewer buses—confirm times before you depart.

Drivers leave Bled going south along the lakefront road, Cesta Svobode; in the village of Mlino, you'll peel off from the lake and follow signs to *Boh Bistrica* (a midsize town near Lake Bohinj). Once in the town of Bohinjska Bistrica, turn right, following *Boh Jezero* signs. The road takes you to the village of Ribčev Laz and along the lakefront road with all the attractions—the drive from Bled to the lake takes about 30 minutes. You can follow this road all the way to the Vogel cable-car parking lot; at the Vogel turnoff, you can continue straight ahead to reach the Savica Waterfall trailhead, or turn right and cross the bridge to curl around the far end of the lake and see the pristine river that feeds the lake (which flows out of the pool at the base of the Savica Waterfall).

Sights at Lake Bohinj

A visit to Bohinj has three parts: a village (offering boat trips on the lake), a cable car (and nearby cemetery), and a waterfall hike. I've listed them as you'll reach them along the main road from Bled, which runs along the south side of the lake. If you plan to do everything (boat trip, cable car, waterfall hike), ask at the TI in Ribčev Laz about a combo-ticket to save some money.

Ribčev Laz Village
Coming from Bled, your first views of Bohinj will be from the little village called Ribčev Laz (loosely translated as "Good Fishin' Hole") at the southeast corner of the lake. Here you'll find a TI, a handful of hotels and ice-cream stands, and the Bohinj Jezero bus stop.

On the way into town, on a small hill to the right, is a **monument** to the four Bohinj-area mountaineers who first summited Mount Triglav on August 26, 1778.

The town's main landmark is its picturesque lakefront church, **St. John the Baptist** (to your right as you face the lake, past the stone bridge; not open to visitors).

A five-minute stroll down the main lakefront road is a dock where you can catch an electric **tourist boat** to make a silent circuit around the lake (€10.50 round-trip, €7.50 one-way, daily 10:00-

18:00, runs hourly, less off-season). The boat stops at the far end of the lake, at Camp Zlatorog—a 10-minute walk from the Vogel cable car (see below).

Across from the Ribčev Laz dock is a fun concrete 3-D model of Triglav. Finally, a few more steps down the road, just beyond a boat rental dock, is a statue of **Zlatorog**, the "Golden Horn"—a mythical chamois-like creature native to the Julian Alps.

▲Vogel Mountain Cable Car

For a mountain perch without the sweat, take the cable car up to the top of Vogel Mountain, offering impressive panoramic views of Mount Triglav and the Julian Alps. On a clear day, this is the best mountain panorama you can get without wings (the light is best in the morning).

Cost and Hours: €13.50 round-trip, Dec-Oct daily 8:00-18:00, runs every 30 minutes in summer and continuously in winter, closed Nov, www.vogel.si.

Getting There: To reach the cable-car station, drivers follow signs to *Vogel* (to the left off the main lakefront road, marked *1915* and *1917*); by bus, get off at the Bohinj Vogel stop (request this stop from driver) and hike about 10 minutes up the steep road on the left (away from the lake).

Visiting the Summit: After you arrive at the top, savor the views from the metal platform where you exit the cable car...just don't look down. Walking up through the cable-car station (past the Viharnik snack bar, with basic food and far-from-basic views), you'll pop out at the summit, a ski-in-winter, hike-in-summer area with a pasture filled with grazing cows and smaller chairlifts to various recreation areas.

The first chairlift is designed for skiers and doesn't run in summer, but if you hike down into the little valley, you can take the second chairlift up the adjacent summit (Orlove Glave) for views into another valley on the other side. Then, from Orlove Glave, you can hike or ride the chairlift back to where you started. With plenty of time and very strong knees, you could even hike from Orlove Glave all the way back down to Lake Bohinj.

If you need a break near the cable-car station, the alpine hut Merjasec ("Wild Boar") offers tasty strudel and a wide variety of local brandies (including the notorious "Boar's Blood"—a concoction of several different flavors guaranteed to get you snorting).

World War I Cemetery

Back down below the cable car, on the main road just beyond the Bohinj Vogel bus stop, look for the metal gate on the left marking the final resting place for some WWI Soča Front soldiers (see sidebar on page 830). While no fighting occurred here (it was mostly on the other side of these mountains), injured soldiers were brought to a nearby hospital, and those who didn't recover ended up here. Notice that many of the names are not Slovenian, but Hungarian, Polish, Czech, and so on—a reminder that the entire multiethnic Austro-Hungarian Empire was involved in the fighting. If you're walking down from the cable-car station, the cemetery makes for a poignant detour on your way to the main road (look for it through the trees).

Savica Waterfall (Slap Savica)

Up the valley beyond the end of the lake is Bohinj's final treat, a waterfall called Slap Savica (sah-VEET-seh). Hardy hikers enjoy following the moderate-to-strenuous uphill trail (including 553 stairs) to see the cascade, which dumps into a remarkably pure pool of aquamarine snowmelt.

Cost and Hours: €2.50, daily in summer from 8:00 until dusk, allow up to 1.5 hours for the round-trip hike.

Getting There: Drivers follow the lakefront road to where it ends, right at the trailhead. Without a car, getting to the trailhead is a hassle. Boats on the lake, as well as most public buses from Bled, take you only as far as the Bohinj Zlatorog stop—the end of the line, and still a one-hour hike from the trailhead (from the bus stop, follow signs to *Slap Savica*). However, three buses a day (Mon-Sat July-Sept only, none Sun or off-season) run from Bled all the way to the Savica trailhead (likely departing Bled at 10:00, 14:20, and 16:20, about an hour to the trailhead, returning at 15:30 and 18:30—but confirm times locally before making the trip). Frankly, if the connections don't fit your itinerary, it's not worth worrying about.

Sleeping at Lake Bohinj

If you'd like to get away from it all and settle in at Bohinj, consider **$ Stare Pension** (STAH-reh). Well-run by mild-mannered Jože, it has 10 older, rustic-but-well-maintained rooms (five of them with balconies) in a pristine setting at the far end of the lake (Ukanc 128, mobile 040-558-669, www.impel-bohinj.si, info@impel-bohinj.si). They also rent an eight-person villa for longer stays (info@rent-villa-slovenia.com).

To get higher into the forested hills, you can head for **$ Penzion Resje,** which sits above Bohinjska Bistrica. Simple but cozy, it has 14 affordable rooms, a great restaurant, and an away-from-it-all local feel, nestled in a tiny village called Nemški rovt—"German road" (Nemški rovt 21A, tel. 04/572-1079, www.penzion-resje.si, resje21a@gmail.com, Jože).

THE JULIAN ALPS

Vršič Pass • Soča River Valley • Bovec • Kobarid

The countryside around Lake Bled is plenty spectacular. But to top off your Slovenian mountain experience, head for the hills. The northwestern corner of Slovenia—within yodeling distance of Austria and Italy—is crowned by the Julian Alps (named for Julius Caesar). Here, mountain culture has a Slavic accent.

The Slovenian mountainsides are laced with hiking paths, blanketed in deep forests, and speckled with ski resorts and vacation chalets. Beyond every ridge is a peaceful alpine village nestled around a quaint Baroque steeple. And in the center of it all is Mount Triglav—ol' "Three Heads"—Slovenia's national symbol and, at 9,396 feet, its tallest mountain.

The single best day in the Julian Alps is spent driving up and over the 50 hairpin turns of breathtaking Vršič Pass (vur-SHEECH, open May-Oct) and back down via the Soča (SOH-chah) River Valley, lined with offbeat nooks and Hemingway-haunted crannies. As you curl on twisty roads between the cut-glass peaks, you'll enjoy stunning high-mountain scenery, whitewater rivers with superb fishing, rustic rest stops, thought-provoking WWI sights, and charming hamlets.

A pair of Soča Valley towns watch over the region. Centrally situated Bovec is all about good times (it's the whitewater adventure-sports hub), while Kobarid has Old World charm and better restaurants, and attends to more serious matters (WWI history). Though neither is a destination in itself, both Bovec and Kobarid are pleasant, functional, and convenient home bases for lingering in this gloriously beautiful region.

PLANNING YOUR TIME

Most visitors do this area as a surgical strike on a full-day side-trip from Lake Bled or Ljubljana—and even that quick glimpse is very satisfying. But there's plenty here to make it worth slowing down and spending a night (or possibly more). If you'd like to take advantage of the Soča Valley's hiking trails and many adventure sports (especially whitewater rafting on the Soča River), give yourself more time.

GETTING AROUND THE JULIAN ALPS

The Julian Alps are best by **car.** Even if you're doing the rest of your trip by train, consider renting a car here for maximum mountain day-trip flexibility. I've included a self-guided driving tour that incorporates the best of the Julian Alps (Vršič Pass and the Soča Valley).

If you're without your own wheels, hiring a **local guide with a car** can be a great value, maximizing not only what you see, but what you learn. Or you can choose a cheaper but less personalized day-trip **excursion** from Bled. (Both options are explained under "Tours at Lake Bled," page 774.)

In the summer, a public **bus** follows more or less the driving-tour route over the Vršič Pass described below (departs Ljubljana daily July-Aug at 6:30 and 15:00, June and Sept Sat-Sun only at 6:30, 4.25 hours to Bovec, afternoon bus also continues to Kobarid in 5 hours total, road closed Oct-May). Additional Vršič Pass buses leave from Kranjska Gora at the foot of the mountains, which is also connected by bus to Ljubljana and Bled. (Yet another option is to take a direct bus from Ljubljana to Bovec that uses the somewhat-less-scenic southerly route via Idrija—but then you'd miss going over the Vršič Pass.) To check or confirm schedules, see www.ap-ljubljana.si.

If you lack the time or transport to reach the Vršič Pass and Soča Valley, you could stay closer to Bled, and get a taste of the Julian Alps with a more convenient day trip to the Vintgar Gorge or Lake Bohinj (reachable with easy and frequent bus connections; see "Near Lake Bled" in the previous chapter).

Julian Alps Driving Tour

This all-day, self-guided driving tour—rated ▲▲▲—takes you over the highest mountain pass in Slovenia, with stunning scenery and a few quirky sights along the way. From waterfalls to hiking trails, WWI history to queasy suspension bridges, this trip has something for everyone.

ORIENTATION TO THE JULIAN ALPS

Most of the Julian Alps are encompassed by Triglav National Park (Triglavski Narodni Park). This drive is divided into two parts: the

Vršič Pass and the Soča River Valley. While not for stick-shift novices, all but the most timid drivers will agree that the scenery is worth the many hairpin turns. Frequent pull-outs offer plenty of opportunities to relax, stretch your legs, and enjoy the vistas.

Planning Your Time: This drive can be done in a day, but consider spending the night along the way for a more leisurely pace. You can start and end in Bled or Ljubljana. You can return to your starting point, or do this trip one-way as a very scenic detour between these two destinations.

Length of This Tour: These rough estimates do not include stops: Bled to the top of Vršič Pass—1 hour; Vršič Pass to Trenta (start of Soča Valley)—30 minutes; Trenta to Bovec—30 minutes; Bovec to Kobarid—30 minutes; Kobarid to Ljubljana or Bled—2 hours (remember, it's an hour between Ljubljana and Bled). In other words, if you started and ended in Bled and drove the entire route without stopping, you'd make it home in less than five hours...but you'd miss so much. It takes at least a full day to really do the region justice.

Tourist Information: The best sources of information are the Bled TI (see page 769), the Triglav National Park Information Centers in Trenta (see page 816), and the TIs in Bovec and Kobarid (both listed in this chapter).

Maps: Pick up a good map before you begin (available at local TIs, travel agencies, and gas stations). The all-Slovenia *Autokarta Slovenija* or the TI's *Next Exit: Goldenhorn Route* map both include all the essential roads, but several more detailed options are also available. The 1:50,000 Kod & Kam *Posoče* map covers the entire Vršič Pass and Soča Valley (but doesn't include the parts of the drive near Bled and Ljubljana).

OK...let's ride.

PART 1: VRŠIČ PASS

From Bled or Ljubljana, take the A-2 expressway north, enjoying views of Mount Triglav on the left as you drive. About 10 minutes past Bled, you'll approach the industrial city of **Jesenice**, whose iron- and steelworks once filled this valley with multicolored smoke. The city, which was known as the "Detroit of Yugoslavia," plans to convert these old factories (most of which closed in the 1980s) into a sort of theme park.

Just after the giant smokestack with the billboards, the little gaggle of colorful houses on the right (just next to the freeway) is **Kurja Vas** ("Chicken Village"). This unassuming place is locally famous for producing hockey players: 18 of the 20 players on the 1971 Yugoslav hockey team—which went to the World Championships—were from this tiny hamlet.

As you zip past Jesenice, keep your eye out for the exit marked *Jesenice-zahod, Trbiž/Tarvisio, Kr. Gora,* and *Hrušica* (it's after the

To Klagenfurt ↗

The Julian Alps & Northwest Slovenia

① Pristava Lepena Resort
② Tourist Farm Pri Plajerju
③ Tourist Farm Kranjc
④ Hiša Franko Rest. & Rooms

See detail maps

(TUNNEL)

85

101

Mojstrana

HRUŠICA EXIT

Jesenice

Begunje

A-2

Bled Town

Lesce

Radovljica

Lake Bled

Bohinjska Bistrica

209

FINAL CAR TRAIN STATION

(TUNNEL)

Podbrdo

403

Kranj

⊕ Brnik

SLOVENIA

Škofja Loka

A-2

210

Gorenja Vas

• Želin

River

408   407

To Idrija ↓ & Ljubljana

Ljubljana

To Idrija ↓

JULIAN ALPS

gas station, just before the tunnel to Austria). When you exit, turn left toward *Trbiž/Tarvisio* and *Kranjska Gora* (yellow sign).

Just after the exit, the big blue building surrounded by tall lights was the former border station (the overpass you'll go under leads into Austria). Locals have fond memories of visiting Austria during the Yugoslav days, when they smuggled back forbidden Western goods. Some items weren't available at home (VCRs, Coca-Cola, designer clothes), while other goods were simply better in Austria (chocolate, coffee, dishwasher soap).

Slovenes brag that their country—"with 56 percent of the land covered in forest"—is Europe's second-greenest. As you drive toward Kranjska Gora, take in all this greenery...and the characteristic Slovenian hayracks (recognized as part of the national heritage and now preserved; see page 749). The Vrata Valley (on the left) is a popular starting point for climbing Mount Triglav. Paralleling the road on the left is a "rails-to-trails" bike path—converted from an old railway bed—that loops from here through Italy and Austria, allowing bikers to connect three countries in one day. On the right, watch for the statue of Jakob Aljaž, who actually bought Triglav—back when such a thing was possible (he's pointing at his purchase). Ten minutes later, in Gozd Martuljek, you'll cross a bridge and enjoy a great head-on view of Špik Mountain.

Kranjska Gora was once Yugoslavia's leading winter resort, and remains popular with Croatian skiers. As every Slovene and Croatian wants a ski bungalow here, it has some of the highest property values in the country. Entering Kranjska Gora, you'll see a turnoff to the left marked for *Bovec* and *Vršič*. This leads up to the pass, but winter sports fanatics may first want to take a 15-minute detour to see the biggest ski jump in the world, a few miles ahead (stay straight through Kranjska Gora, then turn left at signs for **Planica,** the last stop before the Italian border; you'll likely pay a small parking fee to drive in and see it, or you can park before the payment booth and walk in). Every few years, tens of thousands of sports fans flock here to watch the ski-flying world championships. This is where a local boy was the first human to fly more than 100 meters on skis. Today's competitors routinely set new world records (currently 784 feet—that's 17 seconds in the air). Nearby is a newly built **Nordic center,** used as a home base for a wide range of winter sports and related activities, from a ski museum and ski-jump simulator to an indoor cross-country ski training ground (www.planica.si). From the ski jump, you're a few minutes' walk from Italy or Austria. This region—spanning three nations—lobbied unsuccessfully under the name Senza Confini (Italian for "without borders") to host the 2006 Winter Olympics. This philosophy is in tune with the European Union's vision for a Europe of regions, rather than nations.

Back in Kranjska Gora, follow the signs for *Vršič*. Before long, you'll officially enter **Triglav National Park** and come to the first of this road's 50 hairpin turns (24 up, then 26 down)—each one numbered and labeled with the altitude in meters. Notice that the turns are cobbled to provide better traction. If the drive seems daunting, remember that 50-seat tour buses routinely conquer this pass...if they can do it, so can you. Better yet, imagine—and watch for—the bicyclists who regularly pedal to the top. The best can do it in less than 30 minutes—faster than driving.

After switchback #8, with the cute waterfall, park your car on the right and hike up the stairs on the left to the little **Russian**

Mount Triglav

Mount Triglav ("Three Heads") stands watch over the Julian Alps, and all of Slovenia. Slovenes say that its three peaks are

the guardians of the water, air, and earth. This mountain defines Slovenes, even adorning the nation's flag: You'll often see the national seal, with three peaks (the two squiggly lines under it represent the Adriatic). Or take a look at Slovenia's €0.50 coin.

From the town of Bled, you'll see Triglav peeking up over the ridge on a clear day. (You'll get an even better view from nearby Lake Bohinj.)

It's said that you're not a true Slovene until you've climbed Triglav. One native took these words very seriously and climbed the mountain 853 times...in one year. Climbing to the summit—at 9,396 feet—is an attainable goal for any hiker in decent shape. If you're here for a while and want to become an honorary Slovene, befriend a local and ask if he or she will take you to the top.

If mountain climbing isn't your style, relax at an outdoor café with a piece of cream cake and a view of Triglav. It won't make you a Slovene...but it's close enough on a quick visit.

chapel. This road was built during World War I by at least 10,000 Russian POWs of the Austro-Hungarian Empire to supply the

Soča Front. The POWs lived and worked in terrible conditions, and several hundred died of illness and exposure. On March 8, 1916, an avalanche thundered down the mountains, killing hundreds more workers. This chapel was built where the final casualty was found. Take a minute to pay your respects to the men who built the road you're enjoying today. It's a Russian Orthodox chapel—notice that the crosses topping the steeples have three crossbars. (For more on the Orthodox faith, see page 1017.)

Back on the road, after #17, look up as high as you can on the cliff face to see sunlight streaming through a **"window"** in the rock.

This natural formation, a popular destination for intrepid hikers, is big enough for the Statue of Liberty to crawl through.

After #22, at the pullout for Erjavčeva Koča restaurant, you may see tour-bus groups making a fuss about the mountain vista. They're looking for a ghostly face in the cliff wall, supposedly belonging to the mythical figure **Ajda.** This village girl was cursed by the townspeople after correctly predicting the death of the Zlatorog (Golden Horn), a magical, beloved, chamois-like animal. Her tiny image (with a Picasso nose) is just above the tree line, a little to the right—try to get someone to point her out to you (you can see her best if you stand at the signpost near the road).

After #24, you reach the **summit** (5,285 feet). Consider getting out of the car to enjoy the views (in peak season, you'll pay an attendant a €3 "ecological tax" to park here). Hike up to the hut for a snack or drink on the grand view terrace. On the right, a long gravel chute gives hikers a thrilling glissade. (From the pullout just beyond #26, it's easy to view hikers "skiing" down.) If you have time and energy to burn, consider hiking about 20 minutes uphill from the summit to

the Poštarski Dom ("Fifth Hut," with good food). Along the way, you'll see the ruins of a telpher cable-car line, which was used to run supplies between here and the valley floor during World War I. You'll also enjoy some of the best possible views of the Ajda face.

As you begin the descent, keep an eye out for old WWI debris. A lonely guard tunnel stands after #28, followed by a tunnel marked *1916* (on the left) that was part of the road's original path. Just after, watch for the turnoff at the right, at a little gravel parking lot with a picnic table. From the platform viewpoint, you can see mountain valleys formed in two different ways: To the left, the jagged V-shaped Soča Valley, carved by a raging river; and on the right, the gentle U-shaped Trenta Valley, gouged by a glacier.

Continuing down, you'll see abandoned checkpoints from when this was the border between Italy and the Austro-Hungarian Empire. At #48 is a statue of **Julius Kugy,** an Italian botanist who wrote books about alpine flora.

At #49, the road to the right (marked *Izvir Soče*) leads to the **source of the Soča River.** If you feel like stretching your legs after all that shifting, drive about five minutes down this road to a restaurant parking lot. From here, you can take a challenging 20-minute uphill hike (which includes some stretches where you'll cling to guide wires) to the Soča source. This is also the starting point for

Hemingway in the Julian Alps

It was against the scenic backdrop of the Slovenian Alps that a young man from Oak Park, Illinois, first came to Europe—the continent with which he would forever be identified. After graduating from high school in 1917 and working briefly as a newspaper reporter, young Ernest Hemingway wanted to join the war effort in Europe. Bad vision kept him out of the army, but he craved combat experience—so he joined the Red Cross Ambulance Corps instead.

After a short detour through Paris, Hemingway was sent to the Italian Front. On his first day, he was given the job of retrieving human remains—gruesomely disfigured body parts—after the explosion of a munitions factory. Later he came to the Lower Piave Valley, not far from the Soča Front. In July 1918, his ambulance was hit by a mortar shell. Despite his injuries, he saved an Italian soldier who was also wounded. According to legend, Hemingway packed his own wound with cigarette butts to stop the flow of blood.

Sent to Milan to recuperate, Hemingway fell in love with a nurse, but she later left him for an Italian military officer. A decade later, Hemingway wrote about Kobarid (using its Italian name, Caporetto), the war, and his case of youthful heartbreak in the novel *A Farewell to Arms*.

the well-explained, 12-mile Soča Trail (Soška Pot), which leads all the way to the town of Bovec.

Nearing the end of the switchbacks, follow signs for *Bovec*. Crossing the Soča River, you begin the second half of this trip.

PART 2: SOČA RIVER VALLEY

During World War I, the terrain between here and the Adriatic made up the Soča (Isonzo) Front. As you follow the Soča River south, down what's nicknamed the "Valley of the Cemeteries," the scenic mountainsides around you tell the tale of this terrible warfare. Imagine a young Ernest Hemingway driving his ambulance through these same hills (see sidebar).

But it's not all so gloomy. There are plenty of other diversions—interesting villages and churches, waterfalls and suspension bridges, and more. Perhaps most impressive is the remarkable clarity and milky-blue color of the Soča itself, which Slovenes proudly call their "emerald river."

After switchback #49, you'll cross a bridge, then pass a church and a botanical garden of alpine plants (Alpinum Juliana, summer only). Across the street from the garden (on the right) is the parking lot for the Mlinarica Gorge. While the gorge is interesting, the bridge leading to it was damaged in a severe storm and hasn't yet been rebuilt—so it's best left to hardy hikers.

The last Vršič switchback (#50) sends you into the village of **Trenta.** As you get to the cluster of buildings in Trenta's "downtown," look on the left for the **Triglav National Park Information Center,** which also serves as a regional TI (daily July-Aug 9:00-19:00, May-June and Sept-Oct 10:00-18:00, Dec-April 10:00-14:00, closed Nov, tel. 05/388-9330, www.tnp.si). The €5 museum here provides a look (with English explanations) at the park's flora, fauna, traditional culture, and mountaineering history. An AV show celebrates the region's forests, and a poetic 15-minute slide-

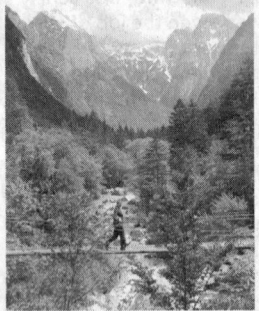

show explains the wonders and fragility of the park (included in museum entry, ask for English version as you enter).

After Trenta, you'll pass through a tunnel; then, on the left, look for a classic **suspension bridge.** Pull over to walk out for a bounce, enjoying the river's crystal-clear water and the spectacular mountain panorama.

About five miles beyond Trenta, in the town of Soča, is the **Church of St. Joseph** (with reddish-brown steeple, tucked behind the big tree on the right). Step inside to see some fascinating art. During World War II, an artist hiding out in the mountains filled this church with patriotic symbolism. The interior is bathed in Yugoslav red, white, and blue—a brave statement made when such nationalistic sentiments were dangerous. On the ceiling is St. Michael (clad in Yugoslav colors) with Yugoslavia's three WWII enemies at his feet: the eagle (Germany), the wolf (Italy), and the serpent (Japan). The tops of the walls along the nave are lined with saints, but these are Slavic, not Catholic. Finally,

look carefully at the Stations of the Cross and find the faces of hated Yugoslav enemies: a lederhosen-clad Hitler (pulling a rope to upright the cross; fourth from altar on left) and Mussolini (seated, as Herod; first from altar on right). Behind the church, the stylized cross on the hill marks a **WWI cemetery**—the final resting place of some 600 Austro-Hungarian soldiers who were killed in action.

For another good example of how the Soča River cuts like God's band saw into the land, stop about two minutes past the church at the small gravel lot (on the left) marked *Velika Korita Soče* **("Grand Canyon of Soča").** While the entire Soča Valley is dramatic, this half-mile, 30- to 50-foot deep stretch is considered the most impressive. Venture out onto the suspension bridge over the gorge…and bounce if you dare. If the water's high, notice the many side streams pouring into the churning river in a series of miniwaterfalls. For more views, cross over the bridge and hike down along the treacherously uneven and narrow, rocky path downstream to another bridge.

Just beyond the suspension bridge is the turnoff (on the left) to the Lepena Valley, home of the recommended Pristava Lepena ranch, with accommodations and Lipizzaner horses (described later, under "Sleeping in Bovec"). If you head up this valley, you'll find a big gravel pullout on the right (marked *Velika Korita*) that lets you cross another springy bridge over a particularly wide stretch of the river. This is a popular place for those who enjoy hiking up alongside the "Grand Canyon" we passed earlier (about 5 miles round-trip, uneven terrain).

Soon after the Lepena Valley turnoff, watch on the left for the large **barn** (marked *Žičnica Golobar*). Pull over here if you'd like a close look at one of the stations for a primitive, industrial telpher cable-car line, which was used mostly for logging.

Roughly five miles after the town of Soča, you exit the national park, pass a WWI graveyard (on the left), and come to a fork in the road. The main route leads to the left, through Bovec. But first, take a two-mile detour to the right (marked *Trbiž/ Tarvisio* and *Predel/Kluže*), where the WWI **Kluže Fort** keeps a close watch over the narrowest part of a valley leading to Italy (€3; July-Aug daily 9:00-20:00; June and

Sept Sun-Fri 9:00-17:00, Sat 9:00-18:00; May and Oct Sat-Sun 10:00-17:00, closed Mon-Fri; closed Nov-April; www.kluze.net). In the 15th century, the Italians had a fort here to defend against the Ottomans. Half a millennium later, during World War I, it was used by Austrians to keep Italians out of their territory. Notice the ladder rungs fixed to the cliff face across the road from the fort— allowing soldiers to quickly get up to the mountaintop.

Back on the main road, immediately after the Kluže turnoff, watch for the gravel pullout on the left with the little wooden hut (look for the green sign with old photos). To see some original **WWI-era fortifications,** pull over here and hike on the gravel path 10 minutes through the woods to reach the Ravelnik Outdoor Museum. Here you can see trenches dug into the dirt and rocks, abandoned pillboxes, rusty sheds, and other features of an evocative wartime landscape. While not entirely typical of Soča Front embattlements (remember, those were mostly high on the mountaintops and remain challenging to reach), Ravelnik offers a taste of those times.

Continue following the main road to **Bovec.** This town, which saw some of the most vicious fighting of the Soča Front, was hit hard by earthquakes in 1994 and 1998 (and by another tremor in 2004). Today, it's been rebuilt and remains the adventure-sports capital of the Soča River Valley—also known as the "Adrenaline Valley," famous for its whitewater activities. (Since the water comes from high-mountain runoff, the temperature of the Soča never goes above 68 degrees Fahrenheit.) For a good lunch stop in Bovec, turn right at the roundabout as you first reach the town; you'll pass Martinov Hram's inviting restaurant terrace on the right, and soon after, the Letni Vrt pizzeria (for details on both, see "Eating in Bovec," later). But if you're not eating or spending the night in Bovec, you could skip the town entirely and not miss much (continue along the main road to bypass the town center).

About three miles past Bovec, as you cross the bridge (with the yellow *Boka* sign), look carefully high up on the rock wall in the gorge to your right to spot the **Boka waterfall,** which carves a deep gouge into the cliff as it tumbles into the valley. (Hardy hikers can climb up for a better view of this fall—the trailhead is just after the bridge on the right—but it's an extremely strenuous hike.)

Head south along the river, with water somehow both perfectly clear and spectacularly turquoise. When you pass the intersection at the humble village of **Žaga,** you're just four miles from Italy. Continuing south, you'll pass a pullout (just before Srpenica) that is a popular put-in point for kayaking trips along the river. Keep an eye out for happy kayakers. Soon after, on the left, you'll pass the giant TKK caulk factory.

Soon you'll see signs for **Kobarid,** home to a sleepy main square and some fascinating WWI sights. Don't blink or you'll miss the Kobarid turnoff on the right—it lets you skirt into town past the highly recommended Kobarid Museum, which tells the tale of the WWI-era Soča Front. Farther along, you'll reach the tidy main square. Driving up to the Italian mausoleum hovering over the town is a must. (These sights are described later, under "Sights in Kobarid.")

Leaving Kobarid, continue south along the Soča to **Tolmin.** Before you reach Tolmin, decide on your preferred route back to civilization…

FINISHING THE DRIVE

While you could go back over the pass the way you came, there are various ways to make your trip a loop by circling through some more varied scenery. Which way you go depends on your final destination: Ljubljana or Bled.

To Ljubljana (or Southern Slovenia/Croatia)

From Tolmin, you have two possible driving routes to the capital. Either option brings you back to the A-1 expressway south of Ljubljana, and will get you to the city in about two hours (though the second route has fewer miles).

Nova Gorica Route: The option you'll encounter first (turnoff to the right before Tolmin) is the smoother, longer route southwest to Nova Gorica. Along this road, you'll pass a hydroelectric dam and go under a 1906 rail viaduct that once connected this area to the port of Trieste (now in Italy). In the charming town of Kanal, you'll cross over the Soča on a picturesque bridge that's faintly reminiscent of Mostar's (as in that city, young people stage a competition that involves jumping off this bridge into the raging river below). Farther along, the striking Solkan Bridge (another link in the Trieste rail line) is the longest single-span stone arch bridge in the world. Soon after, you arrive in Nova Gorica. This fairly dull city is divided in half by the Italian border (the Italian side is called "Gorizia"). Because Italians aren't allowed to gamble in their hometowns, Nova Gorica is packed with casinos catering to Italian gamblers. In fact, it's home to Europe's biggest casino. Rocks spell out the name "TITO" on a hillside above town—a strange relic of an earlier age. From Nova Gorica, you can hop on the H-4 expressway, which links easily to the main A-1 expressway. Also notice that the road from Nova Gorica to Ljubljana takes you through the heart of the Karst region—famous for its wineries and its caves.

Idrija Route: For a more off-the-beaten-path, ruggedly scenic approach, take this rural option: Continue through Tolmin, then head southeast through the hills back toward Ljubljana. Along the way, you could stop for a bite and some sightseeing at the town of Idrija (EE-dree-yah), known to all Slovenes for three things: its tourable mercury mine, fine delicate lace, and tasty *žlikrofi* (like ravioli). Back at the expressway (at Logatec), head north to Ljubljana.

To Bled

To reach Bled, you could follow either of the Ljubljana-bound routes outlined above, then carry on northward for another hour to Bled (allow about 3 hours total). But the following options are more direct.

Car Train: The fastest option is to load your car onto a "Car Train" (Autovlak) that cuts directly through the mountains. The train departs at 18:31 from Most na Soči (just south of Tolmin, along the Idrija route described above) and arrives at Bohinjska

Bistrica, near Lake Bohinj, at 19:09 (€14 for the car; afternoon departure late April-late Sept only, also departs year-round at 7:34 and 10:35, confirm schedule at the Bled TI before making the trip). No reservations are necessary, but arrive at the train station about 30 minutes before the scheduled departure to allow time to load the car. Note: This is a very old train that can be quite jerky and bumpy. You'll stay inside your car the entire time. If you're claustrophobic, prone to motion sickness, or both, consider giving this train a miss.

To get to the car train, drive through Tolmin, then Most na Soči (turning left for *Ljubljana*). About a mile out of Most na Soči, watch on the right for the big bridge over the river, marked for *Čepovan* and *železniška postaja* (train station). Crossing the bridge, turn right to find the train station; once there, go around the far-left side of the long station building and drive up the ramp to wait your turn to load. You'll buy your ticket, load on your car, pull your hand brake, and put the car in gear. Then you'll stay in the car and enjoy the scenery. Taking off, you'll cross a scenic viaduct, then twist through the mountains, going through multiple tunnels, including a final 10-minute passage from Podbrdo beneath the mountains to Bohinjska Bistrica, where you'll unload your car. From Bohinjska Bistrica, it's less than a half-hour drive back to Bled, or a 10-minute drive (in the opposite direction) to Lake Bohinj.

Through Italy via Predel Pass: Although this route requires some backtracking, it also includes a detour through Italy. From Kobarid, drive back the way you came (through Bovec), then turn off for the Kluže Fort (described on page 817), marked for *Predel* and Italy. In a few miles, after passing the fort, the road curves up through two small villages (first Log pod Mangartom, then Strmec na Predelu directly above it). Continue past the ruined fortress and cross the Italian border (there's no need to stop). Then curl down a few hairpin turns past the end of tranquil, scenic Lake Predel, and continue straight through the ghost city of Cave del Predil (a heavily industrialized former lead-mining town; overhead are the five rounded peaks of the Cinque Punte formation) and along the valley road, following signs for Slovenia. Approaching Tarvisio, turn right (continuing to follow signs for *Kranjska Gora* and Slovenia); from here, it's about a half-hour (10 miles) back across the Slovenian border to Kranjska Gora. This is where you first began your ascent of the Vršič Pass—just retrace your steps back to Bled.

Other Driving Routes: The fastest route (about 2 hours) essentially follows the car train route, but goes over rather than through the mountains. This route is partially on a twisty, rough, very poor-quality road (go through Tolmin, turn off at Bača pri Modreju to Podbrdo, then from Petrovo Brdo take a very curvy road through the mountains into Bohinjska Bistrica and on to

Bled). For timid drivers, it's more sane and not too much longer to start out on the Idrija route toward Ljubljana (described earlier), but turn off in Želin (before Idrija) toward Skofja Loka and Kranj, then continue on to Bled.

Bovec

The biggest town in the area, Bovec (BOH-vets) has a happening main square and all the tourist amenities. It's best known as a hub for whitewater adventure sports. While not exactly quaint, Bovec is pleasant enough to qualify as a good lunch stop or overnight home base. If nothing else, it's a nice jolt of civilization wedged between the alpine cliffs.

Orientation to Bovec

TOURIST INFORMATION
The helpful TI is on the main square (June-Sept daily 8:30-20:30, Oct-May daily 9:00-16:00 except closed Sat-Sun in Nov-April, Trg Golobarskih Žrtev 8, tel. 05/384-1919, www.bovec.si).

ARRIVAL IN BOVEC
The main road skirts Bovec, but you can turn off (watch for signs on the right) to take the road that goes through the heart of town, then rejoins the main road farther along. As you approach the city center, you can't miss the main square, Trg Golobarskih Žrtev, with the TI and a recommended restaurant.

HELPFUL HINTS
Exchange Rate: €1 = about $1.10

Country Calling Code: 386 (see page 1086 for dialing instructions).

Parking: You'll find a big free parking lot behind the **Mercator** supermarket (on the left on the way into town, just before the main square), and a few pay parking spaces on or near the square itself.

Activities in Bovec

As the de facto capital of Slovenia's "Adrenaline Valley," Bovec offers many opportunities to enjoy the nature all around it.

Adventure Sports
The main activity in the Soča Valley is getting out on the rushing, crystal-clear waters of the river. The main options are rafting, kaya-

king, and hydrospeeding (a masochistic variation on boogie boarding—lying face-down on a short surfboard and shooting headfirst toward the rapids). The official season is March 15 until October 31, but outside of summer, the frigid water is less appealing and fewer companies operate. From an adrenaline perspective, these activities are best in spring—when the water is highest—and tamer in summer. By fall, water levels are even lower.

When conditions are ideal, most **rafting** companies put in near the Boka waterfall (just downriver from Bovec), and pick up at the village of Trnovo ob Soči. (When water levels are low, companies put in near Sprenica instead.) Most rafting trips last about 2.5-3 hours, with about 1.5 hours actually on the river and extra time to swim.

Kayaking is available at various points along the river, which vary dramatically in level of difficulty; the TI's free *Water-Adventure-Sport* map outlines your options and notes areas that are unsafe. To get a glimpse of kayakers, hang out at Napoleon Bridge, just outside of Kobarid.

The most popular place for **canyoning**—a risky activity that involves wading and rappelling in rushing rivers—is in Canyon Sušec, about halfway between Bovec and Kobarid.

Other popular options include skydiving and paragliding; biking (Bovec Šport Centar rents electric mountain bikes); ziplines (there's a course above Bovec and another high in the Učja Valley); and even—gasp!—golf (Bovec has a 9-hole course, www.golfbovec.si). Of course, all of these activities come with some degree of risk (except, perhaps, golf); use common sense and investigate the safety record of any company that offers trips. The Bovec TI is a good source of information about any of these, and an ever-changing roster of local adventure travel companies run a variety of tours. Well-established outfits include Bovec Šport Centar (www.bovec-sc.si) and Soča Rafting (www.socarafting.si).

Sightseeing Flights
Aero Taxi runs scenic sightseeing flights from Bovec's little airport (€79/20-minute "introductory" flight, €140/30-minute mountain-scenery flight, longer itineraries available, prices are for up to 3 people, mobile 041-262-726, www.janezlet.si).

Fly Fishing
The Soča River is a popular spot for fishing, predominantly for the endemic marble trout. Only fly fishing is allowed; some areas are catch-and-release, and all areas require a permit. **Soča Fly** offers information, fly-fishing gear, and tours (mobile 031-705-552).

Sleep Code

Hotels are classified based on the average price of a standard double room with breakfast in spring and fall. Prices may go up in summer, and down in winter.

$$$$	**Splurge:** Most rooms over €150
$$$	**Pricier:** €110-150
$$	**Moderate:** €80-110
$	**Budget:** €50-80
¢	**Backpacker:** Under €50
RS%	**Rick Steves discount**

Unless otherwise noted, credit cards are accepted, hotel staff speak basic English, and free Wi-Fi is available. Comparison-shop by checking prices at several hotels (on each hotel's own website, on a booking site, or by email). For the best deal, *book directly with the hotel.* Ask for a discount if paying in cash; if the listing includes **RS%**, request a Rick Steves discount.

Sleeping in Bovec

Dobra Vila and Hotel Sanje ob Soči are situated near the turnoff from the main road into central Bovec (about a 10-minute walk into town). Martinov Hram and Stari Kovač are closer to the main square, in the town center.

$$$ Dobra Vila, run with class by brothers Juri and Matjaš, has 11 plush, boldly stylish yet classic rooms, and a generous rear terrace. You'll stay in a gorgeously restored former telephone office that feels like an enticing whisper of ages past (air-con, Mala vas 112, tel. 05/389-6400, www.dobra-vila-bovec.si, welcome@dobra-vila-bovec.si). They also have the most elegant restaurant in town (see "Eating in Bovec," later).

$$ Hotel Sanje ob Soči means "Dreams by the Soča"—which describes both what you'll do here and the vision that entrepreneurial owners Boštjan and Valentina have for their sleek, modern, spa-like lodgings. The 10 rooms and nine apartments fill a pine-clad, Scandinavian-feeling shell on the edge of Bovec. The rooms—all with terraces, and each one named for the mountain that dominates its view—are fairly simple and Ikea-furnished (air-con, children's play area, Mala vas 105a, tel. 05/389-6000, mobile 031-331-690, www.sanjeobsoci.com, info@sanjeobsoci.com).

$ Martinov Hram has 12 nice, modern rooms over a popular restaurant a few steps from Bovec's main square. While the rooms are an afterthought to the busy restaurant (reception at the bar), they're comfortable (rooms on sunny side have air-con, Trg Golobarskih Žrtev 27, tel. 05/388-6214, www.martinov-hram.si, sara.berginc@gmail.com).

$ Stari Kovač B&B is your basic budget option, with eight rooms in an old-feeling guesthouse a steep block downhill from the main square (kitchens in each room or pay extra for breakfast, cash only, Rupa 3, tel. 05/388-6699, mobile 041-646-427, www.starikovac.com, info@starikovac.com).

NEAR BOVEC

$$$ Pristava Lepena is a relaxing oasis hiding out in the Lepena Valley just north of Bovec. Well-run by Milan and Silvia Dolenc, this place is its own little village, with a series of rustic-looking cabins, a restaurant, a small exercise room, a kids' play area, a tennis court, an outdoor swimming pool, and a sauna/whirlpool. Milan and Silvia organize regular events for their guests (such as musical performances, a barbecue night, and activities for kids). Hiding behind the humble split-wood shingle exteriors is surprising comfort: 13 cozy rooms (with wood-burning stoves, TV, telephone, and all the amenities) that make you feel like relaxing. This place whispers "second honeymoon" (closed in winter, multinight stays preferred, lunch and dinner available for extra charge; just south of the village of Soča, exit the main road at the sign for *Lepena*, and follow the white horses to Lepena 2; tel. 05/388-9900, mobile 041-671-981, www.pristava-lepena.com, pristava.lepena@siol.net). Milan and Silvia also have three Welsh ponies and four purebred Lipizzaner horses that guests can ride for a fee (may also be available to nonguests—call ahead and ask). Kids love their mascot mountain goats.

$ Tourist Farm Pri Plajerju is on a picturesque plateau at the edge of Trenta (the first town at the bottom of the Vršič Pass road). Run by the Pretner family (gregarious Marko is a park ranger, shy Stanka is "the boss"), this organic farm raises sheep and rents five apartments in three buildings separate from the main house. As the Soča Valley doesn't have many tourist farms, this is one of your best options if you want to stay at one. However, its location deeper in the mountains makes it a bit less convenient for side-tripping—it's 30 minutes to Bovec and an hour to Kobarid (breakfast and dinner extra; watch for signs to the left after coming over the pass and going through the village of Trenta, Trenta 16a; tel. 05/388-9209, mobile 041-600-590, www.eko-plajer.com, info@eko-plajer.com).

Eating in Bovec

Inexplicably, little Bovec's restaurants tend to charge a cover of €1-1.50—a greedy practice otherwise rare in Slovenia, but perhaps influenced by the town's proximity to Italy.

$$$ Martinov Hram, run by the Berginc family (sisters Sara and Suzi), has an inviting outdoor terrace under a grape trellis.

Restaurant Price Code

I've assigned each eatery a price category, based on the average cost of a typical main course. Drinks, desserts, and splurge items (steak and seafood) can raise the price considerably.

$$$$ **Splurge:** Most main courses over €14
$$$ **Pricier:** €10-14
$$ **Moderate:** €6-10
$ **Budget:** Under €6

In Slovenia, a takeout spot is $; a basic sit-down eatery is $$; a casual but more upscale restaurant is $$$; and a swanky splurge is $$$$.

Inside, the nicely traditional decor goes well with regional specialties with a focus on lamb, delicious pancakes, and homemade bread (daily 10:00-23:00 except closed Mon in Oct-May; on the main road through Bovec, just before the main square on the right at Trg Golobarskih Žrtev 27; tel. 05/388-6214).

$$ Letni Vrt is big, with an outdoor terrace facing Bovec's main intersection, and sprawling indoor dining rooms—including a nice winter garden that's inviting on cold days. The menu is almost comically lengthy—I'd stick with the good and affordable pizzas (daily 11:00-23:00, Fri-Sun only in winter, Trg Golobarskih Žrtev 1, tel. 05/389-6383).

$$$$ Dobra Vila, also a recommended hotel, is the only place in town for an elegant, upscale meal of thoughtfully presented international cuisine with local flair. It's smart to call ahead (daily 19:00-22:00, see contact information earlier).

Bovec Connections

From Bovec by Bus to: Kobarid (4-6/day, 30 minutes), **Ljubljana** (direct over scenic Vršič Pass: 2/day July-Aug, 1/day Sat-Sun only June and Sept, none off-season, 4.25 hours; some additional buses may go over Vršič Pass to Kranjska Gora, where you can change to other destinations; otherwise less scenic via Idrija).

Kobarid

Kobarid (KOH-bah-reed) feels older, and therefore a bit more appealing, than its big brother Bovec. This humble settlement was immortalized by a literary giant, Ernest Hemingway, who drove an ambulance in these mountains during World War I. He described Kobarid as "a little white town with a campanile in a valley. It was a clean little town and there was a fine fountain in the square." Sounds about right. Even though Kobarid loves to tout its Hemingway connection, historians believe that Papa did not actually visit Kobarid until he came back after the war to research his book.

Aside from its brush with literary greatness, Kobarid is known as a hub of information about the Soča Front (with an excellent WWI museum, a hilltop Italian mausoleum, and walks that connect to surrounding sites). You won't find the fountain Hemingway wrote about—it's since been covered up by houses (though the town government hopes to excavate it as a tourist attraction). You will find a modern statue of Simon Gregorčič (overlooking the main intersection), the beloved Slovenian priest-slash-poet who came from and wrote about the Soča Valley.

Orientation to Kobarid

The main road, Gregorčičeva, cuts right through the heart of little Kobarid, bisecting its main square (Trg Svobode). The Kobarid Museum is along this road, on the left before the square. To reach the museum from the main square, simply walk five minutes back toward Bovec.

TOURIST INFORMATION

The TI has good information on the area, and free Internet access and Wi-Fi (July-Aug daily 9:00-20:00; May-June and Sept Mon-Fri 9:00-13:00 & 14:00-19:00, Sat-Sun 9:00-13:00 & 16:00-19:00; Oct-April Mon-Fri 9:00-13:00 & 14:00-16:00, Sat 10:00-14:00, closed Sun; on the main square at Trg Svobode 16—follow the white footprints behind the statue of Gregorčič, tel. 05/380-0490, www.dolina-soce.com).

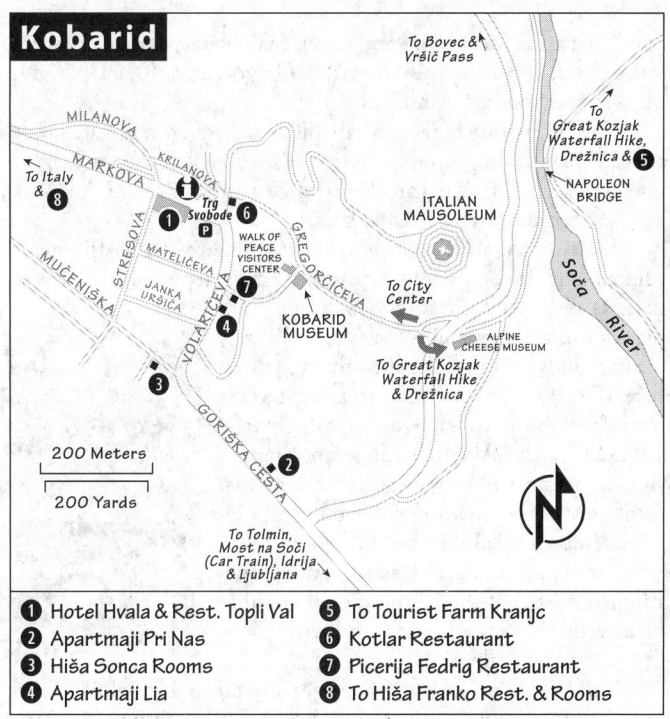

Kobarid

To Bovec & Vršič Pass

MILANOVA

MARKOVA

KRILANOVA

To Italy & 8

STRESOVA

MUČENIŠKA

JANKA URŠIČA

Trg Svobode

MATELIČEVA

VOLARIČEVA

GREGORČIČEVA

WALK OF PEACE VISITORS CENTER

KOBARID MUSEUM

To City Center

ITALIAN MAUSOLEUM

To Great Kozjak Waterfall Hike, Drežnica & 5

NAPOLEON BRIDGE

Soča River

ALPINE CHEESE MUSEUM

To Great Kozjak Waterfall Hike & Drežnica

GORIŠKA CESTA

200 Meters
200 Yards

To Tolmin, Most na Soči (Car Train), Idrija & Ljubljana

N

JULIAN ALPS

1 Hotel Hvala & Rest. Topli Val
2 Apartmaji Pri Nas
3 Hiša Sonca Rooms
4 Apartmaji Lia
5 To Tourist Farm Kranjc
6 Kotlar Restaurant
7 Picerija Fedrig Restaurant
8 To Hiša Franko Rest. & Rooms

ARRIVAL IN KOBARID

Driving into town from Bovec, watch carefully on the right for the poorly marked first turnoff into Kobarid (they want you to stay on the main road bypass around town; if you miss the turnoff, just continue on this, then turn right later to reach the main square). Turning into town, you could make a sharp left turn to reach the cheese factory (marked by the big modern tower), or continue straight ahead to pass the Kobarid Museum, then the main square. You'll find parking on the main square (free for up to 2 hours), from which it's an easy five-minute stroll to the museum.

Sights in Kobarid

▲▲Kobarid Museum (Kobariški Muzej)

This modest but world-class museum—worth ▲▲▲ for history buffs—offers a haunting look at the tragedy of the Soča Front. The tasteful exhibits, with fine English descriptions and a pacifist tone, take an even-handed approach to the fighting—without getting hung up on identifying the "good guys" and the "bad guys." The museum's focus is not on the guns and heroes, but on the big picture of the front and on the stories of the common people who fought and died here.

Cost and Hours: €6, good selection of books, daily April-Sept 9:00-18:00, Oct-March 10:00-17:00, Gregorčičeva 10, tel. 05/389-0000, www.kobariski-muzej.si.

Tours: History buffs can call ahead to arrange a private guide to lead them through the collection (€20/hour), or tour the sights outside (€25/hour). You can also arrange a guide through the Walk of Peace Visitors Center, listed later.

Visiting the Museum: The entry is lined with hastily-made cement and barbed-wire gravestones, flags representing all the nationalities involved in the fighting, and pictures of soldiers and nurses from diverse backgrounds who were brought together here (for example, the men wearing fezzes were from Bosnia-Herzegovina, which was annexed by the Austro-Hungarian Empire shortly before the war). The rooms in this front part of the museum show off typically good temporary exhibits about the war.

Buy your ticket and ask to watch the English version of the 19-minute film on the history of the Soča Front (informative but dry, plays on top floor).

The first floor up is divided into several rooms, which you'll tour counterclockwise. The White Room—filled with rusty crampons, wire-cutters, pickaxes, and shovels—explains wintertime conditions at the front. What looks like a bear trap was actually used to trap enemy soldiers. The Room of the Rear shows the day-to-day activities away from the front line, from supplying troops to more mundane activities (milking cows, washing clothes, getting a shave, lifting weights, playing with a dog). The Black Room is the museum's most somber, commemorating the more than one million casualties of the Soča Front. These heartbreaking exhibits honor the common people whose bodies fertilized the battlefields of Europe. Horrific images of war injuries are juxtaposed with a display of medals earned—prompting the question: Was it worth it? The little altar was purchased by schoolchildren, who sent it to the front to offer the troops some solace.

Through the door marked *The Krn Range Room* (also on the first floor up), pass the small model of the mountaintop war zone and find your way to the Kobarid Rooms, which trace the history of this region from antiquity to today. High on the wall, look for the timelines explaining the area's turbulent past. The one in the second room shows wave after wave of invaders (including Ottomans, Habsburgs, and Napoleon). In the next room, above a display case with military uniforms, another timeline shows the many flags that flew over Kobarid's main square during the 20th century alone.

On the top floor, across from the room where the film plays (described above), you'll see a giant model of the surrounding mountains, painstakingly tracing the successful Austrian-German *Blitzkrieg* attack during the Battle of Kobarid. Crawl into the small cave and press the button to hear a patriotic song about a soldier, who reads a letter he's written to his family about the conditions here.

▲▲Italian Mausoleum (Kostnica)

The 55 miles between here and the Adriatic are dotted with more than 75 cemeteries, reminders of the countless casualties of the

Soča Front. One of the most dramatic is this mausoleum, overlooking Kobarid. The access road, across Kobarid's main square from the side of the church, is marked by stone gate towers with the word *Kostnica*—one tower is topped with a cross and the other with a star for the Italian army.

Take the road up Gradič Hill—passing Stations of the Cross—to the mausoleum. Built in 1938 (when this was still part of Italy) around the existing Church of St. Anthony, this octagonal pyramid holds the remains of 7,014 Italian soldiers. The stark, cold Neoclassical architecture is pure Mussolini. Names are listed alphabetically, along with mass graves for more than 1,700 unknown soldiers *(militi ignoti)*.

Walk behind the church and enjoy the **view.** Scan the WWI battlements high on the mountain's rock face. Incredibly, the fighting was done on these treacherous ridges; civilians in the valleys only heard the distant battles. Looking up and down the valley, notice the "signal churches" evenly spaced on hilltops, each barely within view of the next—an ancient method for quickly spreading messages or warnings across long distances.

If the **church** is open, go inside and look above the door to see a brave soldier standing over the body of a fallen comrade, fending off enemies with nothing but rocks.

When Mussolini came to dedicate the mausoleum, local revolutionaries plotted an assassination attempt that they believed couldn't fail. A young man planned to suicide-bomb Mussolini as the leader came back into town from this hilltop. But as Mussolini's car drove past, the would-be assassin looked at his fellow townspeople around him, realized the innocent blood he would also spill, and had a last-minute change of heart. Mussolini's trip was uneventful, and fascism continued to thrive in Italy.

The Soča (Isonzo) Front

The valley in Slovenia's northwest corner—called Soča in Slovene and Isonzo in Italian—saw some of World War I's fiercest fighting. While the Western Front gets more press, this eastern border between the Central Powers and the Allies was just as significant. In a series of 12 battles involving 22 different nationalities along a 60-mile-long front, 300,000 soldiers died, 700,000 were wounded, and 100,000 were declared MIA. In addition, tens of thousands of civilians died. A young Ernest Hemingway, who drove an ambulance for the Italian army in nearby fighting, would later write the novel *A Farewell to Arms* about the battles here (see "Hemingway in the Julian Alps" sidebar on page 815).

On April 26, 1915, Italy joined the Allies. A month later, it declared war on the Austro-Hungarian Empire (which included Slovenia). Italy unexpectedly invaded the Soča Valley, quickly taking the tiny town of Kobarid, which it planned to use as a home base for attacks deeper into Austro-Hungarian territory. For the next 29 months, Italy launched 10 more offensives against the Austro-Hungarian army, which was encamped on higher ground on the mountaintops. All of these Italian offensives were unsuccessful, even though the Italians outnumbered their opponents three to one. This was unimaginably difficult warfare—Italy had to attack uphill, waging war high in the mountains, in the harshest of conditions. Trenches had to be carved into rock instead of mud. The fighting coincided with one of the most brutal winters in centuries; many unprepared conscripts—brought here from faraway lands and unaccustomed to the harsh winter conditions atop the Alps—froze to death. Some 60,000 soldiers were killed by avalanches.

Visitors take a look at this tight valley, hemmed in by seemingly impassible mountains, and wonder: Why would people fight so fiercely over such inhospitable terrain? At the time, Slovenia was the natural route from Italy to the Austro-Hungarian capitals at Vienna and Budapest. The Italians believed that if they could

▲Walk of Peace (Pot Miru)

This walking route—which extends more than 140 miles from these mountains all the way to the Adriatic—is designed to link museums, cemeteries, churches, and other sites related to the warfare of the Soča Front. But it also has a secondary purpose of celebrating and introducing visitors to all aspects of regional culture and natural sites. In addition to the excellent museum here in Kobarid, several other "outdoor museums" in the area let you get hold this valley and push over the mountains, Vienna—and victory—would be theirs. Once committed, they couldn't turn back, and the war devolved into one of attrition—who would fall first?

In the fall of 1917, Austro-Hungarian Emperor Karl appealed to his ally Germany, and the Germans agreed to assemble an army for a new attack to retake Kobarid and the Soča Valley. In an incredible logistical accomplishment, they spent just six weeks building and supplying this new army by transporting troops and equipment high across the mountaintops under cover of darkness...above the heads of their oblivious Italian foes dozing in the valley below.

On October 24, Austria-Hungary and Germany launched an attack that sent 600,000 soldiers down into the town of Kobarid. This crucial 12th battle of the Soča Front, better known as the Battle of Kobarid, was the turning point—and saw the introduction of battlefield innovations that are commonplace in the military today. German field commanders were empowered to act independently on the battlefield, reacting immediately to developments rather than waiting for approval. Also, for the first time ever, the Austrian-German army used elements of a new surprise-attack technique called *Blitzkrieg*. (One German officer, Erwin Rommel, made great strides in the fighting here, and later climbed the ranks to become famous as Hitler's "Desert Fox" in North Africa.)

The attack caught the Italian forces off-guard, quickly breaking through three lines of defense. Within three days, the Italians were forced to retreat. (Because the Italian military worked from the top down, the soldiers were sitting ducks once they were cut off from their commanders.) The Austrians called their victory the "Miracle at Kobarid." But Italy felt differently. The Italians see the battle of Caporetto (the Italian name for Kobarid) as their Alamo. To this day, when an Italian finds himself in a mess, he might say, "At least it's not a Caporetto."

A year later, Italy came back—this time with the aid of British, French, and US forces—and easily retook this area. On November 4, 1918, Austria-Hungary conceded defeat. After more than a million casualties, the fighting at Soča was finally over.

close to the places where the fighting actually occurred. Some are reachable by car, while others require a challenging mountain hike.

To learn more about all of these options, visit the **Walk of Peace Foundation Visitors Center,** across the street from the Kobarid Museum. They hand out good, free maps and booklets about these sites, and sell a fine guidebook to WWI sights in the area. Tour their engaging, state-of-the-art exhibition (free, July-Aug Mon-Fri 9:00-13:00 & 14:00-19:00, Sat-Sun 10:00-13:00 & 14:00-19:00, April-June and Sept-Oct slightly shorter hours, closed Nov-

March—but you can try knocking on weekdays, Gregorčičeva 8, tel. 05/389-0167, www.potmiru.si).

They also arrange **guides** to join you for part of the walk (€25/ hour). Contact them at least one day ahead to check their schedule and/or arrange a tour.

Kobarid Historical Walk
This shorter walk to WWI sights around Kobarid is well-explained by the free brochure available at the TI, museum, and information center (3 miles, mostly uphill, allow 3-5 hours; or you can just do a shorter, easier stretch along the river, 1-2 hours).

Alpine Cheese Museum
This humble exhibit, at the big Planika ("Edelweiss") dairy at the edge of town, examines the history of cheesemaking in this area since ancient times.

Cost and Hours: €2.50; May-Sept Mon-Sat 10:00-12:00 & 17:00-19:00, closed Sun except July-Aug 10:00-12:00; Oct shorter hours and closed Sun; closed Nov-April; Gregorčičeva 32, tel. 05/384-1013, www.mlekarna-planika.si/muzej. To get here, turn right into Kobarid, then take the sharp left turn that leads you down beneath the underpass to the cheese factory (marked by the tall modern tower).

Great Kozjak Waterfall (Veliki Kozjak) Hike
If you have time to kill in Kobarid and want to go for a sturdy hike, consider trekking to the Great Kozjak Waterfall—a dramatic cascade that flows through an extremely narrow gorge and plunges 50 feet into a beautiful pool. While local signs clock the hike at 30 minutes from the town center, plan on closer to 45 minutes each way. The trailhead is at the Bovec end of Kobarid: As you approach the town from Bovec, turn right into the town, then take an immediate and sharp left to go back under the main road, passing the cheese factory and following signs for *Kamp Koren*. Wind down to cross the Napoleon Bridge over the Soča (watch for kayakers), then turn left and head up the hill (you'll pass Kamp Koren). You can park in the big gravel lot across the street from the camp, or, to get closer to the trailhead, turn left just after Kamp Koren at the *Slap Kozjak* sign and follow the gravel road (park your car at the pullout after the multicolored beehives). Continue walking along the gravel path down into the ravine, passing views of a smaller waterfall. Go right at the fork, continue into the gorge, and take the high, narrow bridge over the stream (which has no railing—a little nerve-wracking for those afraid of heights). Finally, follow the boardwalk as it curls around a cliff for great views of the falls. A different, longer trail

follows the Soča River Valley, eventually looping up and around to Kozjak.

Sleeping in Kobarid

My first listing is right on the main square. The other three hide on side streets about a block off the main road through town, between the museum and the main square (about a three-minute walk).

$$$ Hotel Hvala is the only real hotel in town. Run by the Hvala family, its 32 contemporary rooms are comfortable, and the location can't be beat. The mural on the wall in the elevator shaft tells the story of the Soča Valley as you go up toward the top floor (closed parts of Feb and Nov, elevator, Trg Svobode 1, tel. 05/389-9300, www.hotelhvala.net, topli.val@siol.net).

$ Apartmaji Pri Nas ("Our Place") has six very stylish apartments in a pleasant suburban home along the main road that skirts the town center of Kobarid (no breakfast but kitchens in each unit, air-con, Goriška cesta 5, mobile 031-377-585, www.pri-nas.si, prinas.kobarid@gmail.com).

$ Hiša Sonca ("House of the Sun"), in a cheery, yellow family home along the main road, has two comfortable rooms and one big apartment that sleeps up to eight (breakfast extra, cash only, 2 blocks from main square at Mučeniška 1, mobile 031-664-253, www.apartma-hisasonca.com, hisasonca@gmail.com, Natalija).

¢ Apartmaji Lia, run by sweet Alenka Likar, has three tidy apartments in two buildings in the town center (cash only, no breakfast, air-con, main house at Volaričeva 9, mobile 041-953-366, www.apartmaji-lia.si, apartmajilia@gmail.com).

IN THE MOUNTAINS HIGH ABOVE KOBARID

One of my favorite Soča Valley accommodations hides in a tiny village a twisty 10-minute drive up from Kobarid's main square. **$ Tourist Farm Kranjc** is a remote but scenic, well-run working sheep farm with eight comfortable rooms, organic meals prepared with their own produce, and a huge shared-view terrace. While this farm—which feels traditional, but has modern style—is a bit less convenient to the sights, it's ideal if you want to really feel like you're huddled high in the mountains (dinner extra, air-con in attic rooms only, also ask about their "glamping" cots with private bathroom, Koseč 7, tel. 05/384-8562, mobile 041-946-088, www.turizem-kranjc.si, info@turizem-kranjc.si, Urška and the Kranjc family). It's in the village of Koseč, above Kobarid. From Kobarid, leave town by crossing the Napoleon Bridge (toward Kamp Koren and Great Kozjak Waterfall—see directions under

"Great Kozjak Waterfall Hike"). Just after that bridge, turn left and twist up to Drežnica, where you'll turn right to reach Koseč; once in the village, look for signs directing you up the steep road to the left.

Eating in Kobarid

Kobarid prides itself on its restaurants, hosting a few of the best-regarded eateries in the region. (The best of them all is Hiša Franko, just outside of town and described in the next section.) Kotlar and Topli Val serve up elegant, borderline-pretentious, overpriced but generally good meals that are worth the splurge. Picerija Fedrig is your budget alternative.

$$$ Kotlar Restaurant, on the main square, has a classy interior that sprawls around the prow of a faux sailboat. The emphasis is on seafood and locally-sourced meats (Mon 18:00-23:00, Thu-Sun 12:00-15:00 & 18:00-22:00, closed Tue-Wed, Trg Svobode 11, tel. 05/389-1110, www.kotlar.si). Kotlar also rents rooms if you're in a pinch.

$$$ Topli Val ("Heat Wave"), Hotel Hvala's restaurant, is pricey but good, with a menu that emphasizes fish and a lengthy list of Slovenian wines (Tue-Sun 12:00-15:00 & 18:00-23:00, closed Mon, Trg Svobode 1, tel. 05/389-9300).

$ Picerija Fedrig serves up good pizzas (Mon-Tue 17:00-22:00, Wed-Sun 12:00-22:00; closed Mon-Wed off-season; a block south of the main square at Volaričeva 11, tel. 05/389-0115).

Eating near Kobarid

$$$$ Hiša Franko, less than a five-minute drive outside of Kobarid, is becoming known as one of Slovenia's finest restaurants. Chef Ana Roš—who was profiled on the Netflix series *Chef's Table*—has a deep respect for locally-sourced ingredients and the Slovenian alpine culinary tradition. But she's also experimental, injecting international techniques and ingredients into her cooking. This is a sophisticated—yet welcoming and unpretentious—opportunity to try modern Slovenian cuisine at its best. Thanks to her ever-growing fame, you'll want to book as far ahead as possible (fixed-price meals only, Tue-Fri 19:00-23:00, Sat-Sun 12:00-15:00 & 19:00-23:00, closed Mon, also closed Tue off season, closed entirely Jan-March). They also rent 13 rooms—choose between the **$$$** modern rooms in the main building, or the **$$** simpler ones in the adjacent yellow house (Staro Selo 1, tel. 05/389-4120, www.hisafranko.com, info@hisafranko.com).

Getting There: To reach Hiša Franko, leave Kobarid following signs for *Italija* and *Robič* on the pleasant tree-lined road, and look for the restaurant's sign on the right.

Kobarid Connections

From Kobarid by Bus to: Bovec (4-6/day, 30 minutes), **Ljubljana** (1/day in July-Aug over Vršič Pass, 5 hours; otherwise faster but less scenic via Idrija, 3.5 hours).

AUSTRIA
Österreich

VIENNA

Wien

Vienna is the capital of Austria, the cradle of classical music, the home of the rich Habsburg heritage, and one of the world's most livable cities. The city center is skyscraper-free, pedestrian-friendly, dotted with quiet parks, and traversed by electric trams. Many buildings still reflect 18th- and 19th-century elegance, when the city was at the forefront of the arts and sciences. Compared with most modern European urban centers, the pace of life is slow.

For much of its 2,500-year history, Vienna (*Wien* in German—pronounced "veen") was on the frontier of civilized Europe. Located on the south bank of the Danube, it was threatened by Germanic barbarians (in Roman times), marauding Magyars (today's Hungarians, 10th century), Mongol hordes (13th century), Ottoman Turks (the sieges of 1529 and 1683), and encroachment by the Soviet Union after World War II.

The Habsburg dynasty ruled their great empire from Vienna, setting the stage for its position as an enduring cultural capital. Among the Hapsburgs, Maria Theresa in the late 1700s was famous for having 16 children and cleverly marrying many of them into royal families around Europe to expand the family's reach.

Vienna reached its peak in the 19th century, when it was on par with London and Paris in size and importance. Emerging as a cultural powerhouse, it was home to groundbreaking composers (Beethoven, Mozart,

Greater Vienna

Note: Only Selected U-Bahn, Tram & Bus Stops Shown

VIENNA

Brahms, Strauss), scientists (Doppler, Boltzmann), philosophers (Freud, Husserl, Schlick, Gödel, Steiner), architects (Wagner, Loos), and painters (Klimt, Schiele, Kokoschka). By the turn of the 20th century, Vienna was one of the world's most populous cities and sat on the cusp between stuffy Old World monarchism and subversive modern trends.

After the turmoil of the two world wars and the loss of Austria's empire, Vienna has settled down into a somewhat sleepy, pleasant place where culture is still king. Classical music is everywhere. People nurse a pastry and coffee over the daily paper at small cafés. It's a city of world-class museums, big and small. Anyone with an interest in painting, music, architecture, beautiful objects, or Sacher torte with whipped cream will feel right at home.

From a practical standpoint, Vienna serves as a prime gateway

Austria Almanac

Official Name: Republik Österreich ("Eastern Empire"), or simply Österreich.

Population: Of Austria's 8.6 million people, 91 percent are ethnic Austrians; 4 percent are from the former Yugoslavia. Three out of four Austrians are Catholic; about one in 20 is Muslim. German is the dominant language (though there are a few Slovene- and Hungarian-speaking villages in border areas).

Latitude and Longitude: 47°N and 13°E. The latitude is the same as Minnesota or Washington state.

Area: With 32,400 square miles, Austria is similar in size to South Carolina or Maine.

Geography: The northeast is flat and well-populated; the less-populated southwest is mountainous, with the Alps rising up to the 12,450-foot Grossglockner peak. The 1,770-mile-long Danube River meanders west-to-east through the upper part of the country, passing through Vienna.

Biggest Cities: One in five Austrians lives in the capital of Vienna (1.8 million in the city; 2.6 million in the greater metropolitan area). Other cities include Graz (275,000), Linz (200,000), and Innsbruck (150,000).

Economy: Austria borders eight other European countries and is well-integrated into the EU economy. The Gross Domestic Product is $403 billion (similar to that of Massachusetts). Its per-capita GDP of $47,500 is among Europe's highest. One of its biggest moneymakers is tourism. Austria produces wood, paper products (nearly half the land is forested)...and Red Bull Energy Drink. The country's aging population increasingly collects social security—a situation that will strain the national budget in years to come.

Government: Austria has been officially neutral since 1955, and its citizens take a dim view of European unity. Although right-leaning

city. Its central location is convenient to most major Eastern European destinations. Actually farther east than Prague, Ljubljana, and Zagreb, and just upstream on the Danube from Budapest and Bratislava, Vienna is an ideal launchpad for a journey into the East.

PLANNING YOUR TIME

For a big city, Vienna is pleasant and laid-back. Packed with sights, it's worth two days and two nights on even the speediest trip.

If you're visiting Vienna as part of a longer European trip, you could sleep on the train on your way in and out—Berlin, Prague, Kraków, Venice, Rome, and Cologne are each handy night trains away.

Palace Choices: The Hofburg and Schönbrunn are both world-class palaces, but seeing both is redundant if your time or parties made substantial gains in recent elections, the government continues to be a center-left coalition, currently headed by Chancellor Christian Kern (a Social Democrat) and Federal President Alexander Van der Bellen (Green Party). Austria is the only EU nation with a minimum voting age of 16.

Flag: Three horizontal bands of red, white, and red.

Cuisine: Austrian treats include Wiener schnitzel (breaded veal cutlet), *Knödel* (dumplings), *Apfelstrudel* (apple strudel), *Kaiserschmarrn* (fluffy pieces of caramelized crêpe served with fruit or nuts), and fancy desserts like the Sacher torte, Vienna's famous chocolate cake.

Language: Austria's official language is German. It's customary to greet people in the breakfast room and those you pass on the streets or meet in shops. The Austrian version of "Hi" is a cheerful *"Grüss Gott."* You'll get the correct pronunciation after the first volley—listen and copy. For German survival phrases, see the charts at the end of this chapter.

Gemütlichkeit: The Austrians are not Germans—and they cherish their distinct cultural and historical traditions. Austria is mellow and relaxed compared to Deutschland. *Gemütlichkeit* is the word most often used to describe this special Austrian cozy-and-easy approach to life. On the other hand, Austria feels relatively stiff and formal compared to most of Eastern Europe (except maybe Hungary).

The Average Austrian: A typical Austrian is 43 years old, has 1.41 children, and will live to be 81. He or she inhabits a 900-square-foot home, and spends leisure time with a circle of a few close friends. Chances are good that someone in that circle is a smoker—Austrians are among the highest consumers of cigarettes in Europe.

money is limited. If you're rushed and can fit in only one palace, make it the Hofburg. It comes with the popular Sisi Museum and is right in the town center, making for an easy visit. With more time, a visit to Schönbrunn—set outside town amid a grand and regal garden—is also a great experience.

Vienna in One to Four Days

Below is a suggested itinerary for how to spend your daytime sightseeing hours. The best options for **evenings** are taking in a concert, opera, or other musical event; enjoying a leisurely dinner (and people-watching) in the stately old town or atmospheric Spittelberg quarter; heading out to the *Heuriger* wine pubs in the foothills of the Vienna Woods; or touring the Haus der Musik interactive music museum (open nightly until 22:00). Plan your evenings based on the schedule of musical events. If you've downloaded my audio tours (see "Rick Steves Audio Europe" sidebar on page 14), the Vienna City Walk works wonderfully in the evening. Whenever you need a break, linger in a classic Viennese café.

Day 1

9:00	Take the 1.5-hour Red Bus City Tour, or circle the Ringstrasse by tram, to get your bearings.
10:30	Drop by the TI for planning and ticket needs.
11:00	Tour the Vienna State Opera (schedule varies, confirm at TI).
14:00	Follow my Vienna City Walk, including visits to the Kaisergruft and St. Stephen's Cathedral (nave closes at 16:30, or 18:30 June-Aug).

Day 2

9:00	Browse the colorful Naschmarkt.
11:00	Tour the Kunsthistorisches Museum.
14:00	Tour the Hofburg Palace Imperial Apartments and Treasury.

Day 3

10:00	Visit Belvedere Palace, with its fine Viennese art and great city views.
15:00	Tour Schönbrunn Palace to enjoy the imperial apartments and grounds.

Day 4

10:00	Enjoy (depending on your interests) the engaging Karlsplatz sights (Karlskirche, Wien Museum, Academy of Fine Arts, and the Secession).
14:00	Do some shopping along Mariahilfer Strasse, or rent a bike and head out to the modern Donau City "downtown" sector, Danube Island (for fun people-watching), and Prater Park (with its amusement park).

Orientation to Vienna

Vienna sits between the Vienna Woods (Wienerwald) and the Danube River (Donau). To the southeast is industrial sprawl. The Alps, which arc across Europe from Marseille, end at Vienna's wooded hills, providing a popular playground for walking and sipping new wine. This greenery's momentum carries on into the city. More than half of Vienna is parkland, filled with ponds, gardens, trees, and statue-maker memories of Austria's glory days.

Think of the city map as a target with concentric circles: The bull's-eye is St. Stephen's Cathedral, the towering spired church south of the Danube. Surrounding that is the old town, bound

tightly by the circular road known as the
Ringstrasse, marking what used to be
the city wall. The Gürtel, a broader, later
ring road, contains the rest of downtown.
Outside the Gürtel lies the uninteresting
sprawl of modern Vienna.

Much of Vienna's sightseeing—and
most of my recommended restaurants—
are located in the old town, inside the
Ringstrasse. Walking across this circular area takes about 30 minutes. St. Stephen's Cathedral sits in the center, at the
intersection of the two main (pedestrian-only) streets: Kärntner Strasse and the Graben.

Several sights sit along, or just beyond, the Ringstrasse: To the
southwest are the Hofburg and related Habsburg sights, as well as
the Kunsthistorisches Museum; to the south is a cluster of intriguing sights near Karlsplatz; to the southeast is Belvedere Palace. A
branch of the Danube River borders the Ring to the north.

As a tourist, concern yourself only with this compact old center. When you do, sprawling Vienna becomes easily manageable.

TOURIST INFORMATION

Vienna's main TI is a block behind the Vienna State Opera at Albertinaplatz (daily 9:00-19:00, free Wi-Fi, theater box office, tel.
01/211-140, www.vienna.info). It's a rare example of a TI in Europe that is really a service (possible because tourists pay for it with
a hotel tax). There are also TIs at the airport (daily 7:00-22:00) and
the train station (daily 9:00-19:00).

Look for the monthly program of concerts (called *Wien-
Programm*), the handy *Vienna from A to Z* booklet, the annual city
guide called *Vienna Journal*, and two good brochures: *Walks in Vienna* and *Architecture from Art Nouveau to the Present*. Ask about
their program of guided walks (€16 each), and consider buying a
Vienna Pass, which includes entry to many sights and lets you skip
lines (see page 867).

ARRIVAL IN VIENNA

For a comprehensive rundown on Vienna's various train stations
and its airport, as well as tips on arriving or departing by boat, see
"Vienna Connections," at the end of this chapter.

HELPFUL HINTS

Music Sightseeing Priorities: Be wary of Vienna's various music
    sights. Many "homes of composers" are pretty disappointing.
    My advice to music lovers is to take in a concert, tour the

Vienna

VIENNA

VIENNA

Vienna State Opera or snare cheap standing-room tickets to see a performance there, enjoy the Haus der Musik, or scour the wonderful Collection of Ancient Musical Instruments in the Hofburg's New Palace. If in town on a Sunday, don't miss the glorious music at the Augustinian Church Mass (see page 879).

Useful App: ∩ For free audio self-guided tours (Vienna City Walk, St. Stephen's Cathedral, Ringstrasse Tram Tour), get the **Rick Steves Audio Europe** app (for details, see page 14).

Post Offices: The main post office is near Schwedenplatz at Fleischmarkt 19 (open daily). Convenient branch offices are at the Hauptbahnhof (closed Sun), Westbahnhof (closed Sun), and near the opera house (closed Sat-Sun, Krugerstrasse 13).

English Bookstore: Stop by the woody and cool **Shakespeare & Co.,** in the historic and atmospheric Ruprechtsviertel district near the Danube Canal (Mon-Fri 9:00-21:00, Sat 9:00-20:00, closed Sun, north of Hoher Markt at Sterngasse 2, tel. 01/535-5053, www.shakespeare.co.at). See the map on page 869.

Laundry: Schnell & Sauber Waschcenter is big, has free Wi-Fi, and is conveniently located close to Mariahilfer Strasse accommodations and easily reached from downtown by U-Bahn (daily 6:00-24:00, Westbahnstrasse 60, U: Burggasse/Stadthalle, or take tram #49 to Urban-Loritz-Platz, see map on page 919, mobile 0660-760-4546, www.schnellundsauber.at).

Travel Agency: Conveniently located on Stephansplatz, **Ruefa** sells tickets for flights, trains, and boats to Bratislava. They'll waive the €8 service charge for train and boat tickets for my readers (Mon-Fri 9:00-18:30, closed Sat-Sun, Stephansplatz 10, tel. 01/513-4524, Gertrude and Sandra speak English).

Toll Sticker: Austria charges drivers to use its major roads. You'll need a *Vignette* sticker stuck to the inside of your rental car's windshield (buy at the border crossing, big gas stations near borders, or a rental-car agency; www.asfinag.at). The cost is €9 for 10 days, or €26 for two months. Not having one earns you a stiff fine.

GETTING AROUND VIENNA
By Public Transportation

Take full advantage of Vienna's efficient transit system, which includes trams, buses, U-Bahn (subway), and S-Bahn (faster suburban) trains. It's fast, clean, and easy to navigate.

I generally stick to the tram

to zip around the Ring (trams #1, #2, #D, and #O) and take the U-Bahn to outlying sights, hotels, and Vienna's train stations (see map on page 848). There are five color-coded U-Bahn lines: U-1 red, U-2 purple, U-3 orange, U-4 green, and U-6 brown. If you see a bus number that starts with *N* (such as #N38), it's a night bus, which operates after other public transit stops running. Transit info: tel. 01/790-9100, www.wienerlinien.at.

Tickets and Passes: Trams, buses, and the U-Bahn and S-Bahn all use the same tickets. Except on days spent entirely within the Ring, buying a single- or multiday pass is usually a good investment (and pays off if you take at least four trips). Many people find that once they have a pass, they end up using the system more.

Buy tickets from vending machines in stations (marked *Fahrkarten/Ticket*, easy and in English), from *Vorverkauf* offices in stations, or on trams or buses (single tickets only). You have lots of choices:

- Single tickets (€2.20, €2.30 on tram or bus, good for one journey with necessary transfers)
- 24-hour transit pass (€7.60)
- 48-hour transit pass (€13.30)
- 72-hour transit pass (€16.50)
- 7-day transit pass (*Wochenkarte*, €16.20—the catch is that the pass runs from Monday to Monday, so you may get less than seven days of use)
- 8-day "Climate Ticket" (*Acht-Tage-Klimakarte*, €38.40, can be shared—for example, four people for two days each).

Transit Tips: To get your bearings on buses, trams, the U-Bahn, and the S-Bahn, you'll want to know the end-of-the-line stop in the direction that you're heading. For example, if you're in the city center at Stephansplatz and you want to take the U-Bahn to the main train station (Hauptbahnhof), you'd take U-1 going in the direction "Reumannplatz."

You must stamp your ticket at the barriers in U-Bahn and S-Bahn stations, and in the machines on trams and buses (stamp multiple-use passes only the first time you board). Cheaters pay a stiff fine (about €100), plus the cost of the ticket.

On trams, stop announcements are voice-only and easy to miss—carry a map. Rookies miss stops because they fail to open the door. Push buttons, pull latches—do whatever it takes.

Before you exit a U-Bahn station, study the wall-mounted street map. Choosing the right exit—signposted from the moment you step off the train—saves lots of walking.

Cute little electric buses wind through the tangled old center (from Schottentor to Stubentor). Bus #1A is best for a joyride—hop on and see where it takes you.

VIENNA

Vienna's Public Transportation

VIENNA

By Taxi, Uber, or Private Driver

Vienna's comfortable, civilized, and easy-to-flag-down **taxis** start at €3.80 (higher rates at night). You'll pay about €10 to go from the opera house to the Hauptbahnhof. Pay only what's on the meter—the only legitimate surcharges are for calling a cab (€3) or for riding to the airport (€13).

If you like Uber, the ride service (and your app) works in Vienna just like it does in the US.

Consider the luxury of having your own **car and driver.** Johann (a.k.a. John) Lichtl is a gentle, honest, English-speaking cabbie who can take up to four passengers in his car (€27/1 hour, €25/hour for 2 hours or more, €27 to or from airport, mobile 0676-670-6750). Consider a custom-tailored city driving tour (2 hours), a day trip to the Danube Valley (€160), or a visit to the Mauthausen Memorial with a little Danube sightseeing en route (€240).

By Bike

With more than 600 miles of bike lanes (and a powerful Green Party), Vienna is a great city on two wheels. Consider using a rent-al bike for the duration of your visit (Pedal Power bike rental does hotel delivery and pickups; see next page). Just park your bike at the hotel, and you'll go anywhere in town faster than a taxi can take you. Biking (carefully) through Vienna's many traffic-free spaces is no problem. And bikes ride the U-Bahn for free (but aren't allowed during weekday rush hours).

The bike path along the Ring is wonderfully entertaining—you'll enjoy the shady parklike ambience of the boulevard while rolling by many of the city's top sights.

Besides the Ring, your best sightseeing by bike is through Stadtpark (City Park), across Danube Island, and out to the modern Donau City business district. These routes are easy to follow on the free tourist city map available from the TI (some routes can also be downloaded from the TI website). Red-colored pavement is the usual marking for bike lanes, but some bike lanes are marked just with white lines.

Borrowing a Free/Cheap Bike: Citybike Wien lets you borrow bikes from public racks all over town (toll tel. 0810-500-500, www.citybikewien.at). The three-speed bikes are heavy and clunky (with solid tires to discourage thieves)—and come with a basket, built-in lock, and ads on the side—but they're perfect for a short, practical joyride in the center (such as around the Ringstrasse).

The system is easy to use. Bikes are locked into more than 100 stalls scattered through the city center. To borrow one, register your credit card at the terminal at any rack, create a password (save it for future rentals), then unlock a bike (you can also register online at www.citybikewien.at). First-time registration is €1 (only one bike per credit card—couples must use two different cards). Since the bikes are designed for short-term use, it costs more per hour the longer you keep it (first hour-free, second hour-€1, third hour-€2, €4/hour after that). When you're done, drop off your bike at any stall.

Renting a Higher-Quality Bike: If you want to ride beyond the town center—or you simply want a better set of wheels—rent from **Pedal Power** (€6/hour, €19/4 hours, €30/24 hours, 10 percent discount with this book, daily May-Sept 8:30-18:00, shorter hours April and Oct, rental office near Prater Park, U: Praterstern, then walk 100 yards to Ausstellungsstrasse 3—see map on page 869, tel. 01/729-7234, www.pedalpower.at). For €5 extra they'll deliver a bike to your hotel and pick it up when you're done (service available year-round). They also organize bike tours (described later).

Tours in Vienna

∩ To sightsee on your own, download my free audio tours that illuminate some of Vienna's top sights and neighborhoods, including my Vienna City Walk and tours of St. Stephen's Cathedral and the Ringstrasse. The City Walk and Ringstrasse tram tour start at the opera house and work nicely in the evening as well as during the day. The cathedral tour can be spliced into the city walk for efficiency (for more on these audio tours, see the sidebar on page 14).

ON FOOT
TI Walking Tour
A basic 1.5-hour "Vienna at First Glance" introductory walk is offered daily throughout the summer (€16, leaves at 14:00 from in front of the main TI, just behind the opera house, in English and German, just show up, tel. 01/774-8901, www.wienguide.at).

Good Vienna Tours
This company offers a "pay what you like" 2.5-hour walk through the city center. While my Vienna City Walk is much more succinct, this can be an entertaining ramble with a local telling stories of the city. Reserve online or just show up (pay what you think it's worth at the end—no coins, paper only, daily departures at 10:00 and 14:00, maximum 35 people, meet at fountain at tip of Albertina across from TI, mobile 0664/554-4315, www.goodviennatours. eu).

ON WHEELS

Consider a bus tour, bike tour, or even one by horse-and-buggy.

Red Bus City Tours

Big convertible buses make a 1.5-hour loop around the city, hitting the highlights with a 20-minute shopping break in the middle. They cover the main attractions along with the entire Ringstrasse, and then zip through Prater Park, over the Danube for a glimpse of the city's Danube Island playground, and into the Donau City skyscraper zone. If the weather's good, the bus goes topless and offers great opportunities for photos (€15 ticket from driver, buses leave from Albertinaplatz 2, opposite the TI behind the opera house; hourly departures April-Oct 10:00-18:00, Nov-March at 11:00, 13:00, and 15:00; pretty good recorded narration in any language, tel. 01/512-4030, www.redbuscitytours.at, Gabriel).

Vienna Sightseeing

Their 3.5-hour city tour includes Schönbrunn Palace (€47, 2/day). They also run hop-on, hop-off bus tours with recorded commentary (three one-hour routes, €17/route, departs from opera house, www.viennasightseeing.at). If you just want a quick guided city tour, take the Red Bus tours recommended above.

Ring Tram Tour

One of Europe's great streets, the Ringstrasse is lined with many of the city's top sights. Take a tram ride around the ring with my free audio tour (see page 14), which gives you a fun orientation and a ridiculously quick glimpse of some major sights as you glide by. Neither tram #1 nor #2 makes the entire loop around the Ring, but you can see it all by making one transfer between them (at the Schwedenplatz stop). You can use a single transit ticket to cover the whole route, including the transfer (though you can't interrupt your trip, except to transfer). For more on riding Vienna's trams, see earlier, under "Getting Around Vienna."

The Vienna Ring Tram, a yellow made-for-tourists streetcar, is an easier though pricier option, running clockwise along the entire Ringstrasse (€9 for 30-minute loop, 2/hour 10:00-17:30, recorded narration, www.wienerlinien.at). The 25-minute tour starts every half-hour at Schwedenplatz. At each stop, you'll see a sign for this tram tour (look for *VRT Ring-Rund Sightseeing*). The schedule notes the next departure time.

Pedal Power

Tours cover the central district in three hours and go twice daily from May to September (€29/tour includes bike, €15 extra to keep bike for the day, ask about Rick Steves discount, English tours depart at 10:00 across the Ring from the opera house at Bösendorferstrasse 5, tel. 01/729-7234, www.pedalpower.at). They also rent bikes and offer Segway tours daily in summer.

Horse-and-Buggy Tour

These traditional horse-and-buggies, called *Fiaker*, take rich romantics on clip-clop tours lasting 20 minutes (Old Town—€55), 40 minutes (Old Town and the Ring—€80), or one hour (all the above, but more thorough—€110). You can share the ride and cost with up to five people. Because it's a kind of guided tour, talk to a few drivers before choosing a carriage, and pick someone who's fun and speaks English (tel. 01/401-060).

LOCAL GUIDES

Vienna becomes particularly vivid and meaningful with the help of a private guide. I've enjoyed working with these guides; any of them can set you up with another good guide if they are already booked.

Lisa Zeiler is a good storyteller with years of guiding experience (€150/2-3 hours, mobile 0699-1203-7550, lisa.zeiler@gmx.at). **Wolfgang Höfler,** a generalist with a knack for having psychoanalytical fun with history, enjoys the big changes of the 19th and 20th centuries. He'll take you around on foot or by bike (€160/2 hours, €50 for each additional hour, bike tours—€160/3 hours, mobile 0676-304-4940, www.vienna-aktivtours.com, office@vienna-aktivtours.com). **Adrienn Bartek-Rhomberg** offers themed walks in the city as well as Schönbrunn Palace tours (€150/3 hours, €300/full day, €280 "Panorama City Tour"—a minibus and walking tour for up to six people, mobile 0650-826-6965, www.experience-vienna.at, office@experience-vienna.at). **Gerhard Strassgschwandtner,** who runs the Third Man Museum (see page 912), is passionate about history in all its marvelous complexity (€160/2 hours, mobile 0676-475-7818, www.special-vienna.com, gerhard@special-vienna.com).

Vienna City Walk

This self-guided walk connects the top three sights in Vienna's old center: the Vienna State Opera, St. Stephen's Cathedral, and Hofburg Palace. These and many of the other sights you'll see along

Vienna at a Glance

▲▲▲**Hofburg Imperial Apartments** Lavish main residence of the Habsburgs. **Hours:** Daily 9:00-17:30, July-Aug until 18:00. See page 870.

▲▲▲**Hofburg Treasury** The Habsburgs' collection of jewels, crowns, and other valuables—the best on the Continent. **Hours:** Wed-Mon 9:00-17:30, closed Tue. See page 875.

▲▲▲**St. Stephen's Cathedral** Enormous, historic Gothic cathedral in the center of Vienna. **Hours:** Foyer and north aisle—daily 6:00-22:00 (from 7:00 on Sun); main nave—Mon-Sat 9:00-11:30 & 13:00-16:30, Sun 13:00-16:30, June-Aug until 18:30. See page 882.

▲▲▲**Vienna State Opera** Dazzling, world-famous opera house. **Hours:** By guided tour only, July-Aug generally Mon-Sat at the top of hour 10:00-16:00; fewer tours Sept-June and Sun. See page 887.

▲▲▲**Kunsthistorisches Museum** World-class exhibit of the Habsburgs' art collection, including works by Raphael, Titian, Caravaggio, Rembrandt, and Bruegel. **Hours:** Daily 10:00-18:00, Thu until 21:00, closed Mon Sept-May. See page 890.

▲▲▲**Schönbrunn Palace** Spectacular summer residence of the Habsburgs, rivaling the grandeur of Versailles. **Hours:** Daily 8:30-17:30, July-Aug until 18:30, Nov-March until 17:00. See page 903.

▲▲**Hofburg New Palace Museums** Uncrowded collection of armor, musical instruments, and ancient Greek statues, in the elegant halls of a Habsburg palace. **Hours:** Wed-Sun 10:00-18:00, closed Mon-Tue. See page 877.

▲▲**Albertina Museum** Habsburg residence with state apartments, world-class collection of graphic arts and modernist classics, and first-rate special exhibits. **Hours:** Daily 10:00-18:00, Wed until 21:00. See page 880.

▲▲**Kaisergruft** Crypt for the Habsburg royalty. **Hours:** Daily 10:00-18:00. See page 881.

▲▲**Haus der Musik** Modern museum with interactive exhibits on Vienna's favorite pastime. **Hours:** Daily 10:00-22:00. See page 887.

▲▲**Natural History Museum** Big, beautiful catalog of the natural world, featuring the ancient *Venus of Willendorf*. **Hours:** Wed 9:00-21:00, Thu-Mon 9:00-18:30, closed Tue. See page 894.

▲▲Belvedere Palace Elegant palace of Prince Eugene of Savoy, with a collection of 19th- and 20th-century Austrian art (including Klimt). **Hours:** Daily 10:00-18:00, Lower Palace until 21:00 on Wed. See page 898.

▲Spanish Riding School Prancing white Lipizzaner stallions. **Hours:** Performances nearly year-round, usually Sat-Sun at 11:00, plus training sessions generally Tue-Fri 10:00-12:00. See page 878.

▲St. Michael's Church Crypt Final resting place of about 100 wealthy 18th-century Viennese. **Hours:** By tour Mon-Sat at 11:00 and 13:00, no tours Sun. See page 882.

▲St. Peter's Church Beautiful Baroque church in the old center. **Hours:** Mon-Fri 7:00-20:00, Sat-Sun 9:00-21:00. See page 889.

▲Karlskirche Baroque church offering the unique chance to ride an elevator up into the dome. **Hours:** Mon-Sat 9:00-18:00, Sun 13:00-19:00. See page 895.

▲Wien Museum Karlsplatz City museum blending art and history to tell the story of Vienna's past. **Hours:** Tue-Sun 10:00-18:00, closed Mon. See page 896.

▲Academy of Fine Arts Painting Gallery Small but exciting collection by 15th- to 18th-century masters. **Hours:** Tue-Sun 10:00-18:00, closed Mon. See page 896.

▲The Secession Art Nouveau exterior and Klimt paintings in situ. **Hours:** Tue-Sun 10:00-18:00, closed Mon. See page 896.

▲Naschmarkt Sprawling, lively outdoor market. **Hours:** Mon-Fri 6:00-18:30, Sat until 17:00, closed Sun, closes earlier in winter. See page 897.

▲Museum of Military History Huge collection of artifacts tracing the military history of the Habsburg Empire. **Hours:** Daily 9:00-17:00. See page 900.

▲Kunst Haus Wien Museum Modern art museum dedicated to zany local artist Hundertwasser. **Hours:** Daily 10:00-18:00. See page 901.

▲Imperial Furniture Collection Eclectic collection of Habsburg furniture. **Hours:** Tue-Sun 10:00-18:00, closed Mon. See page 902.

VIENNA

this walk are covered in more detail elsewhere in this chapter (flip to "Sights in Vienna," later).

Length of This Walk: Allow one hour for the walk alone, and more time if you plan to stop at any major sights along the way.

When to Go: This walk works just as well in the evening as it does during the day, as long as you don't plan on touring some of the sights along the way.

Tours: ∩ Download my free Vienna City Walk audio tour. For efficiency, you can splice my St. Stephen's Cathedral audio tour into this walk.

◆ SELF-GUIDED WALK

• *Begin at the square outside Vienna's landmark opera house, home of the Vienna State Opera. (The entrance faces the Ringstrasse; we're starting at the busy pedestrian square that's to the right of the entrance as you're facing it.)*

❶ Opera House

If Vienna is the world capital of classical music, this building is its throne room, one of the planet's premier houses of music. It's typical of Vienna's 19th-century buildings in that it features a revival style—Neo-Renaissance—with arched windows, half-columns, and the sloping, copper mansard roof typical of French Renaissance *châteaux*.

Since the structure was built in 1869, almost all of the opera world's luminaries have passed through here. Its former musical directors include Gustav Mahler, Herbert von Karajan, and Richard Strauss. Luciano Pavarotti, Maria Callas, Placido Domingo, and many other greats have sung from its stage.

In the pavement along the side of the opera house (and all along Kärntner Strasse, the bustling shopping street we'll visit shortly), you'll find star plaques forming a Hollywood-style walk of fame. These represent the stars of classical music—famous composers, singers, musicians, and conductors.

Looking up at the opera, notice the giant outdoor screen onto which some live performances are projected (as noted in the posted schedules and on the screen itself).

If you're a fan, take a guided tour of the opera. Or consider springing for an evening performance (standing-room tickets are surprisingly cheap; see page 909). Regular opera tickets are sold at various points near here: The closest ticket office is the small one

Vienna City Walk

① Opera House
② Café Sacher
③ Albertinaplatz
④ Monument Against War & Fascism
⑤ Café Tirolerhof
⑥ Kärntner Strasse
⑦ Kaisergruft
⑧ Neuer Markt
⑨ Stephansplatz
⑩ Haas Haus
⑪ Graben
⑫ Holy Trinity Plague Column
⑬ St. Peter's Church
⑭ Loos' Loos (Public WCs)
⑮ Kohlmarkt
⑯ Demel Bakery & Manz Bookstore
⑰ Michaelerplatz & Hofburg Entrance
⑱ Imperial Apartments
⑲ Spanish Riding School
⑳ Treasury & Imperial Music Chapel
㉑ Heldenplatz
㉒ Maria Theresa Statue

just below the screen, while the main one is on the other side of the building, across the street on Operngasse. For information about other entertainment options during your visit, check in at the Wien Ticket kiosk in the booth on this square.

The opera house marks a busy intersection in Vienna, where Kärntner Strasse meets the Ring. The Karlsplatz U-Bahn station in front of the opera is an underground shopping mall with fast food, newsstands, and lots of pickpockets.

• *Walk behind the opera and across the street toward the dark-red awning to find the famous...*

❷ Café Sacher

This is the home of the world's classiest chocolate cake, the Sacher torte: two layers of cake separated by apricot jam and covered in dark-chocolate icing, usually served with whipped cream. It was invented in a fit of improvisation in 1832 by Franz Sacher, dessert chef to Prince Metternich (the mastermind diplomat who redrew the map of post-Napoleonic Europe). The cake became world famous when the inventor's son served it next door at his hotel (you may have noticed the fancy doormen). Many locals complain that the cakes here have gone downhill, and many tourists are surprised by how dry they are—you really need that dollop of *Schlagobers*. Still, coffee and a slice of cake here can be €8 well invested for the history alone (daily 8:00-24:00). While the café itself is grotesquely touristy, the adjacent Sacher Stube has ambience and natives to spare (same prices, daily 10:00-24:00). For maximum elegance, sit inside.

• *Continue past Hotel Sacher. At the end of the street is a small, triangular, cobbled square adorned with memorial sculptures.*

❸ Albertinaplatz

As you approach the square, to the right you'll find the **TI**.

On your left, the tan-and-white Neoclassical building with the statue alcoves marks the tip of the Hofburg Palace—the sprawling complex of buildings that was long the seat of Habsburg power (we'll end this walk at the palace's center). The balustraded terrace up top was originally part of Vienna's defensive rampart. Later, it was the balcony of Empress Maria Theresa's daughter Maria Christina, who lived at this end of the palace. Today, her home houses the **Albertina Museum,** topped by a sleek, controversial titanium canopy (called the "diving board" by critics). The museum's plush, 19th-century state rooms are the only Neoclassical (post-Rococo) palace rooms anywhere in the Habsburg realm. And the Batliner Collection of modernist paintings (Monet to Picasso) is a delight.

Albertinaplatz itself is filled with sculptures that make up the powerful, thought-provoking ❹ **Monument Against War and Fascism,** which commemorates the dark years when Austria came under Nazi rule (1938-1945).

The memorial has four parts. The split white monument, *The Gates of Violence,* remembers victims of all wars and violence. Standing directly in front of it, you're at the gates of a concentration camp. Then, as you explore the statues, you step into a montage of wartime images: clubs and WWI gas masks, a dying woman birthing a future soldier, victims of cruel medical experimentation, and chained slave laborers sitting on a pedestal of granite cut from the infamous quarry at Mauthausen concentration camp (located not far from Vienna). The hunched-over figure on the ground behind is a Jew forced to scrub anti-Nazi graffiti off a street with a brush. Of Vienna's 200,000 Jews, more than 65,000 died in Nazi concentration camps. The sculpture with its head buried in the stone is Orpheus entering the underworld, meant to remind Austrians (and the rest of us) of the victims of Nazism...and the consequences of not keeping our governments on track. Behind that, the 1945 declaration that established Austria's second republic—and enshrined human rights—is cut into the stone.

Viewing this monument gains even more emotional impact when you realize what happened on this spot: During a WWII bombing attack, several hundred people were buried alive when the cellar they were using as shelter was demolished.

Austria was led into World War II by Germany, which annexed the country in 1938 with disturbingly little resistance, saying Austrians were wannabe Germans anyway. But Austrians are not Germans (this makes for an interesting topic of conversation with Austrians you may meet). They're quick to proudly tell you that Austria was founded in the 10th century, whereas Germany wasn't born until 1870. For seven years just before and during World War II (1938-1945), there was no Austria. In 1955, after 10 years of joint occupation by the victorious Allies, Austria regained total independence on the condition that it would be forever neutral (and never join NATO or the Warsaw Pact). To this day, Austria is outside of NATO (and Germany).

Behind the monument is ❺ **Café Tirolerhof,** a classic Viennese café. Refreshingly air-conditioned, it's full of things that time has passed by: chandeliers, marble tables, upholstered booths, waiters in tuxes, and newspapers. For more on Vienna's cafés, see page 931.

This square is where many of the city's walking tours and bus tours start. You may see Red Bus City Tour buses, which offer a handy way to get a quick overview of the city (see "Tours in Vienna," earlier).

• From the café, turn right on Führichsgasse. Walk one block until you hit...

❻ Kärntner Strasse

This grand, traffic-free street is the people-watching delight of this in-love-with-life city. Today's Kärntner Strasse (KAYRNT-ner SHTRAH-seh) is mostly a crass commercial pedestrian mall—its famed elegant shops long gone. But locals know it's the same road Crusaders marched down as they headed off from St. Stephen's Cathedral for the Holy Land in the 12th century. Its name indicates that it leads south, toward the region of Kärnten (Carinthia, a province divided between Austria and Slovenia). Today it's full of shoppers and street musicians.

Where Führichsgasse meets Kärntner Strasse, note the city **Casino** (across the street and a half-block to your right, at #41)—once venerable, now tacky, it exemplifies the worst of the street's evolution. Turn left to head up Kärntner Strasse, going away from the opera house. As you walk along, be sure to look up, above the modern storefronts, for glimpses of the street's former glory. Near the end of the block, on the left at #26, **J & L Lobmeyr Crystal** ("Founded in 1823") still has its impressive brown storefront with gold trim, statues, and the Habsburg double-eagle. In the market for some $400 napkin rings? Lobmeyr's your place. Inside, breathe in the classic Old World ambience as you climb up to the glass museum (free entry, closed Sun).

• At the end of the block, turn left on Marco d'Aviano Gasse (passing the fragrant flower stall) to make a short detour to the square called Neuer Markt. Straight ahead is an orange-ish church with a triangular roof and cross, the Capuchin Church. In its basement is the...

❼ Kaisergruft

Under the church sits the Imperial Crypt, filled with what's left of Austria's emperors, empresses, and other Habsburg royalty. For centuries, Vienna was the heart of a vast empire ruled by the Habsburg family, and here is where they lie buried in their fancy pewter coffins. You'll find all the Habsburg greats, including Maria Theresa, her son Josef II (Mozart's patron), Franz Josef, and Empress Sisi. Before moving on, consider paying your respects here.

• *Stretching north from the Kaisergruft is the square called...*

❽ Neuer Markt

A block farther down, in the center of Neuer Markt, is the **four rivers fountain** showing Lady Providence surrounded by figures symbolizing the rivers that flow into the Danube. The sexy statues offended Empress Maria Theresa, who actually organized "Chastity Commissions" to defend her capital city's moral standards. The modern buildings around you were rebuilt after World War II. Half of the city's inner center was intentionally destroyed by Churchill to demoralize the Viennese, who were disconcertingly enthusiastic about the Nazis.

• *Lady Providence's one bare breast points back to Kärntner Strasse (50 yards away), where you'll turn left. Continuing down Kärntner Strasse, you'll find lots of shops filled with merchandise proven to entice tourists. Pass the U-Bahn station (which has WCs) where the street spills into Vienna's main square...*

❾ Stephansplatz

The cathedral's frilly spire looms overhead, worshippers and tourists pour inside the church, and shoppers buzz around the outside. You're at the center of Vienna.

The Gothic **St. Stephen's Cathedral** (c. 1300-1450) is known for its 450-foot south tower, its colorful roof, and its place in Viennese history. When it was built, it was a huge church for what was then a tiny town, and it helped put the fledgling city on the map. At this point, you may want to take a break from the walk to tour the church (for details on visiting the church, see page 882).

The red-and-white bricks embedded in the pavement in the square show where several earlier churches once stood. The 13th-century **Virgilkapelle,** with one of the best-preserved Gothic interiors in Vienna, actually survives underground and can be seen through a window just behind the WC in the subway station beneath your feet (escalator nearby).

Where Kärntner Strasse hits Stephansplatz, the grand, soot-covered building with red columns is the **Equitable Building** (filled with lawyers, bankers, and insurance brokers). It's a fine example of Neoclassicism from the turn of the 20th century—look up and imagine how slick Vienna must have felt in 1900.

Facing St. Stephen's is the sleek concrete-and-glass ❿ **Haas Haus,** a postmodern building by noted Austrian architect Hans Hollein (finished in 1990). The curved facade is supposed to echo the Roman fortress of Vindobona (its ruins were found near here). Although the Viennese initially protested having this stark modern tower right next to their beloved cathedral, since then, it's become a fixture of Vienna's main square. Notice how the smooth, rounded glass reflects St. Stephen's pointy architecture, providing a great photo opportunity—especially at twilight.

• *Exit the square with your back to the cathedral. Walk past the Haas Haus, and bear right down the street called the...*

⓫ Graben

This was once a *Graben,* or ditch—originally the moat for the Roman military camp. Back during Vienna's 19th-century heyday, there were nearly 200,000 people packed into the city's inner center (inside the Ringstrasse), walking through dirt streets. Today this area houses 20,000. The Graben was a busy street with three lanes of traffic until the 1970s, when the city inaugurated its new subway system and the street was turned into one of Europe's first pedestrian-only zones. Take a moment to absorb the scene—you're standing in an area surrounded by history, postwar rebuilding, grand architecture, fine cafés, and people enjoying life...for me, quintessential Europe.

Eventually, you reach Dorotheergasse, on your left, which leads (after two more long blocks) to the **Dorotheum** auction house. Consider poking your nose in here later for some fancy window shopping. Also along this street are two recommended eateries: the sandwich shop Buffet Trześniewski—one of my favorite places for lunch—and the classic Café Hawelka.

In the middle of the Graben pedestrian zone is the extravagantly blobby ⓬ **Holy Trinity plague column** *(Pestsäule).* The 60-foot pillar of clouds sprouts angels and cherubs, with the wonderfully gilded Father, Son, and Holy Ghost at the top (all protected by an anti-pigeon net).

In 1679, Vienna was hit by a massive epidemic of bubonic plague. Around 75,000 Viennese died—about a third of the city. Emperor Leopold I dropped to his knees (something emperors never did in public) and begged God to save the city. (Find Leopold about a quarter of the way up the monument, just above the brown banner. Hint: The typical inbreeding of royal families left him with a gaping underbite.) His prayer was heard by Lady Faith (the statue below Leopold, carrying a cross). With the help of a heartless little cupid, she tosses an old naked woman—symbolizing the plague—into the abyss and saves the city. In gratitude, Leopold vowed to erect this monument, which became a model for other cities ravaged by the same plague.

• *Thirty yards past the plague monument, look down the short street to the right, which frames a Baroque church with a stately green dome.*

⓭ St. Peter's Church

Leopold I ordered this church to be built as a thank-you for surviving the 1679 plague. The church stands on the site of a much older structure that may have been Vienna's first (or second) Christian church. Inside, St. Peter's shows Vienna at its Baroque best. Note that the church offers free organ concerts (advertised at the entry).

• *Continue west on the Graben, where you'll immediately find some stairs leading underground to...*

⓮ Loos' Loos

In about 1900, a local chemical maker needed a publicity stunt to prove that his chemicals really got things clean. He purchased two wine cellars under the Graben and had them turned into classy WCs in the Modernist style (designed by turn-of-the-20th-century architect Adolf Loos), complete with chandeliers and finely crafted mahogany. While the chandeliers are gone, the restrooms remain a relatively appealing place to do your business. Locals and tourists happily pay €0.50 for a quick visit.

• *The Graben dead-ends at the aristocratic supermarket Julius Meinl am Graben. From here, you could turn right into Vienna's "golden corner," with the city's finest shops. But we'll turn left. In the distance is the big green-and-gold dome of the Hofburg, where we'll head soon. The street leading up to the Hofburg is...*

⓯ Kohlmarkt

This is Vienna's most elegant and unaffordable shopping street, lined with Cartier, Armani, Gucci, Tiffany, and the emperor's palace at the end. Strolling Kohlmarkt, daydream about the edible window displays at ⓰ **Demel,** the ultimate Viennese chocolate shop (#14, daily 9:00-19:00). The room is filled with Art Nouveau boxes of Empress Sisi's choco-dreams come true: *Kandierte Veilchen* (candied violet petals), *Katzenzungen* (cats' tongues), and so on. The cakes here are moist (compared to the dry Sacher tortes). The enticing window displays change monthly, reflecting current happenings in Vienna.

Wander inside. There's an impressive cancan of Vienna's most beloved cakes—displayed to tempt visitors into springing for the €10 cake-and-coffee deal (point to the cake you want). Farther in, you can see the bakery in action. Sit inside, with a view of the cakemaking, or outside, with the street action (upstairs is less crowded). Shops like this boast "K.u.K."—signifying that during the Habsburgs' heyday, it was patronized by the *König und Kaiser* (king and emperor—same guy). If you happen to be looking through Demel's window at exactly 19:01, just after closing, you can witness one of the great tragedies of modern Europe: the daily dumping of its unsold cakes.

Next to Demel, the **Manz Bookstore** has a Loos-designed facade.

• *Kohlmarkt ends at the square called...*

⑰ Michaelerplatz

This square is dominated by the **Hofburg Palace.** Study the grand Neo-Baroque facade, dating from about 1900. The four heroic giants illustrate Hercules wrestling with his great challenges (Emperor Franz Josef, who commissioned the gate, felt he could relate). In the center of this square, a scant bit of **Roman Vienna** lies exposed just beneath street level.

Spin Tour: Do a slow, clockwise pan to get your bearings, starting (over your left shoulder as you face the Hofburg) with **St. Michael's Church,** which offers fascinating tours of its crypt. To the right of that is the fancy **Loden-Plankl shop,** with traditional Austrian formalwear, including dirndls. Farther to the right, across Augustinerstrasse, is the wing of the palace that houses the **Spanish Riding School** and its famous white Lipizzaner stallions. Farther down this street lies **Josefsplatz,** with the Augustinian Church, and the Dorotheum auction house. At the end of the street are Albertinaplatz and the opera house (where we started this walk).

Continue your spin: Two buildings over from the Hofburg (to the right), the modern **Loos House** (now a bank) has a facade featuring a perfectly geometrical grid of square columns and windows. Compared to the Neo-Rococo facade of the Hofburg, the stern Modernism of the Loos House appears to be from an entirely different age. And yet, both of these—as well as the Eiffel Tower and Mad Ludwig's fairy-tale Neuschwanstein Castle—were built in the same generation, roughly around 1900. In many ways, this jarring juxtaposition exemplifies the architectural turmoil of the turn of the 20th century, and represents the passing of the torch from Europe's age of divine monarchs to the modern era.

• *Let's take a look at where Austria's glorious history began—at the...*

Hofburg Imperial Palace

This is the complex of palaces where the Habsburg emperors lived out their lives (except in summer, when they resided at Schönbrunn Palace). Enter the Hofburg through the gate, where you immediately find yourself beneath a big rotunda (the netting is there to keep birds from perching). The doorway on the right is the entrance to the ❽ **Imperial Apartments,** where the Habsburg emperors once lived in chandeliered elegance. Today you can tour its lavish rooms, as well as a museum about Empress Sisi, and a porcelain and silver collection. To the left is the ticket office for the ❾ **Spanish Riding School.**

VIENNA

Continuing on, you emerge from the rotunda into the main courtyard of the Hofburg, called **In der Burg.** The Caesar-like statue is of Habsburg Emperor Franz II (1768-1835), grandson of Maria Theresa, grandfather of Franz Josef, and father-in-law of Napoleon. Behind him is a tower with three kinds of clocks (the yellow disc shows the phase of the moon tonight). To the right of Franz are the Imperial Apartments, and to the left are the offices of Austria's mostly ceremonial president (the more powerful chancellor lives in a building just behind this courtyard).

Franz Josef faces the oldest part of the palace. The colorful red, black, and gold gateway (behind you), which used to have a drawbridge, leads over the moat and into the 13th-century Swiss Court (Schweizerhof), named for the Swiss mercenary guards once stationed there. Study the gate. Imagine the drawbridge and the chain. Notice the Habsburg coat of arms with the imperial eagle above and the Renaissance painting on the ceiling of the passageway.

As you enter the Gothic courtyard, you're passing into the historic core of the palace, the site of the first fortress, and, historically, the place of last refuge. Here you'll find the ❷⓿ **Treasury**

(Schatzkammer) and the **Imperial Music Chapel** (Hofmusikka-pelle), where the Boys' Choir sings Mass. Ever since Joseph Hayden and Franz Schubert were choirboys here, visitors have gathered like groupies on Sundays to hear the famed choir sing.

Returning to the bigger In der Burg courtyard, face Franz and turn left, passing through the **tunnel,** with a few tourist shops and restaurants, to spill out into spacious ❹ **Heldenplatz** (Heroes' Square). On the left is the impressive curved facade of the **New Palace** (Neue Burg). This vast wing was built in the early 1900s to be the new Habsburg living quarters (and was meant to have a matching building facing it). But in 1914, the heir to the throne, Archduke Franz Ferdinand—while waiting politely for his long-lived uncle, Emperor Franz Josef, to die—was assassinated in Sara-jevo. The archduke's death sparked World War I and the eventual end of eight centuries of Habsburg rule.

Today the building houses the **New Palace museums,** an eclectic collection of weaponry, suits of armor, musical instru-ments, and ancient Greek statues. The two equestrian statues depict Prince Eugene of Savoy (1663-1736), who battled the Ot-toman Turks, and Archduke Charles (1771-1847), who battled Na-poleon. Eugene gazes toward the far distance at the prickly spires of Vienna's City Hall.

Spin Tour: Make a slow 360-degree turn, and imagine this huge square filled with people.

In 1938, 300,000 Viennese gathered here, entirely filling vast Heroes' Square, to welcome Adolf Hitler and celebrate their an-nexation with Germany—the *"Anschluss."* The Nazi tyrant stood on the balcony of the New Palace and stated, "Before the face of Ger-man history, I declare my former homeland now a part of the Third Reich. One of the pearls of the Third Reich will be Vienna." He never said "Austria," a word that was now forbidden.

When pondering why the Austrians—eyes teary with joy and vigorously waving their Nazi flags—so willingly accepted Hit-ler's rule, it's important to remember that Austria was already a fascist nation. Austrian Chancellor Engelbert Dollfuss, though pro-Catholic, pro-Habsburg, and anti-Hitler, was a fascist dicta-tor who silenced any left-wing opposition. Also, memories of the grand Habsburg Empire were still fresh in the collective psyche. The once vast and mighty empire of 50 million at its 19th-century peak came out of World War I a tiny landlocked country of six mil-lion that now suffered terrible unemployment. The opportunistic Hitler promised jobs along with a return to greatness—and the Austrian people gobbled it up.

Standing here, it's fascinating to consider Austrian aspirations for grandeur. In fact, the Habsburgs envisioned an ancient-Rome-inspired Imperial Forum stretching from here across the Ring-strasse.

• *Walk on through the Greek-columned passageway (the Äusseres Burg-tor), cross the Ringstrasse, and stand between the giant Kunsthistorisches and Natural History Museums, purpose-built in the 1880s to house the private art and scientific collections of the empire and to celebrate its culture and power. A huge statue of perhaps the greatest of the Habsburgs, Maria Theresa, stands in the center of it all.*

㉒ Maria Theresa Monument

Vienna's biggest monument shows the empress holding a scroll from her father granting the right of a woman to inherit his throne. The statues and reliefs surrounding her speak volumes about her reign: Her four top generals sit on horseback while her four top advisors stand. Behind them, reliefs celebrate cultural leaders of her day, including little Wolfie Mozart with mentor "Papa" Joseph Haydn (with his hand on Mozart's shoulder, facing the Natural History Museum). The moral of this propaganda: that a strong military and a wise ruler are prerequisites for a thriving culture—attributes that characterized the 40-year rule of the woman who was perhaps Austria's greatest monarch.

• *Our walk is finished. You're in the heart of Viennese sightseeing. Surrounding this square are some of the city's top museums. And the Hofburg Palace itself contains many of Vienna's best sights and museums. From the opera to the Hofburg, from chocolate to churches, from St. Stephen's to Sacher tortes—Vienna waits for you.*

Sights in Vienna

Vienna has a dizzying number of sights and museums, which cover the city's rich culture and vivid history through everything from paintings to music to furniture to prancing horses. Just perusing the list on your TI-issued Vienna city map can be overwhelming. To get you started, I've selected the sights that are most essential, rewarding, and user-friendly, and arranged them by neighborhood for handy sightseeing.

Passes and combo-tickets (described below) can save a few euros. Bring cash, as some sights don't take credit cards.

SIGHTSEEING PASSES AND COMBO-TICKETS

Avid sightseers should consider a pass or combo-ticket, which not only can save you money, but also time waiting in ticket lines. Note that those under 19 get in free to state-run museums and sights.

Passes: The **Vienna Pass** includes entry to the city's top 60 sights and unlimited access to Vienna Sightseeing's hop-on, hop-off tour buses (€60/1 day, €75/2 days, €90/3 days; purchase at TIs and

Vienna's City Center

VIENNA

1 Shakespeare & Co. Bookstore
2 Ruefa Travel Agency
3 Pedal Power Bike Rental
4 Red Bus City Tours
5 Opera Tour Entrance

several other locations around town—check at www.viennapass. com). It also lets you skip lines and step right up to the turnstile.

The much-promoted €25 **Vienna Card** (www.wienkarte.at) is not worth the mental overhead for most travelers. It gives you a 72-hour transit pass and minor discounts at the city's museums.

Combo-Tickets: The €29 **Sisi Ticket** covers the Hofburg Imperial Apartments (with its Sisi Museum and Porcelain Collection), Schönbrunn Palace's Grand Tour, and the Imperial Furniture Collection. At Schönbrunn, the ticket lets you enter the palace immediately, without a reserved entry time.

If you're seeing the **Treasury** (royal regalia and crown jewels) and the **Kunsthistorisches** (world-class art collection), the €20 combo-ticket is well worth it—and you get the **New Palace museums** as well (armory, old musical instruments, and statues from Ephesus).

The **Haus der Musik** (mod museum with interactive exhibits) has a combo deal with **Mozarthaus Vienna** (exhibits and artifacts about the great composer) for €18—saving a few euros for music lovers (though the Mozarthaus will likely disappoint all but the most die-hard Mozart fans).

HOFBURG PALACE AND RELATED SIGHTS

The imposing Imperial Palace, with 640 years of architecture, demands your attention. This first Habsburg residence grew with the family empire from the 13th century until 1913, when the last "new wing" opened. The winter residence of the Habsburg rulers until 1918, the Hofburg is still home to the Austrian president's office, 5,000 government workers, and several important museums.

Don't get confused by the Hofburg's myriad courtyards and many museums. Focus on three sights: the Imperial Apartments, the Treasury, and the museums at the New Palace (Neue Burg). With more time, consider the Hofburg's many other sights, covering various facets of the imperial lifestyle.

Eating at the Hofburg: Down the tunnel between the In der Burg courtyard and Heldenplatz is the tiny but handy **$ Hofburg Stüberl** sandwich bar—ideal for a cool, quiet sit and a drink or snack (open daily). The recommended **Soho Kantine,** off the Burggarten near the butterfly house, is also a cheap and practical option (see page 928).

▲▲▲Hofburg Imperial Apartments (Kaiserappartements)

These lavish, Versailles-type, "wish-I-were-God" royal rooms are the downtown version of the suburban Schönbrunn Palace. Palace visits are a one-way romp through three sections: a porcelain and silver collection, a museum dedicated to the enigmatic and troubled Empress Sisi, and the luxurious apartments themselves.

Vienna's Hofburg Palace

1 Imperial Apartments
2 Treasury & Imperial Music Chapel Entrances
3 New Palace Museums & National Library (Papyrus Museum)
4 Spanish Riding School Box Office
5 Spanish Riding School Morning Exercises
6 Augustinian Church
7 State Hall of the Austrian Nat'l Library
8 Butterfly House
9 Hofburg Stüberl (Snacks)
10 Soho Kantine (Cafeteria)
11 Café Restaurant Palmenhaus

VIENNA

The Imperial Apartments are a mix of Old World luxury and modern 19th-century conveniences. Here, Emperor Franz Josef I lived and worked along with his wife Elisabeth, known as Sisi. The Sisi Museum traces the development of her legend, analyzing her fabulous but tragic life as a 19th-century Princess Diana. You'll read bits of her poetic writing, see exact copies of her now-lost jewelry, and learn about her escapes, dieting mania, and chocolate bills.

Cost and Hours: €14, includes well-done audioguide; covered by Sisi Ticket; daily 9:00-17:30, July-Aug until 18:00, last entry one hour before closing; enter from under rotunda just off Michaelerplatz, through Michaelertor gate; tel. 01/533-7570, www.hofburg-wien.at.

Overview: Your ticket grants you admission to three separate exhibits, which you'll visit on a pretty straightforward one-way route. The first floor holds a collection of precious porcelain and silver knickknacks *(Silberkammer)*. You then go upstairs to the Sisi Museum, which has displays about her life. This leads into the 20 or so rooms of the Imperial Apartments *(Kaiserappartements)*, starting in Franz Josef's rooms, then heading into the dozen rooms where his wife Sisi lived.

If you listen to the entire audioguide, allow 40 minutes for the porcelain and silver collection, 30 minutes for the Sisi Museum, and 40 minutes for the apartments.

Visiting the Imperial Apartments: Your visit (and the excellent audioguide) starts on the ground floor.

Imperial Porcelain and Silver Collection: Browse the collection to gawk at the opulence and to take in some colorful Habsburg trivia. (Who'd have thunk that the court had an official way to fold a napkin—and that the technique remains a closely guarded secret?) Still, I wouldn't bog down here, as there's much more to see upstairs.

Once you're through all those rooms of dishes, climb the stairs—the same staircase used by the emperors and empresses who lived here. At the top is a timeline of Sisi's life. Swipe your ticket to pass through the turnstile, and enter the room with the **model of the Hofburg.** Circle to the far side to find where you're standing right now, near the smallest of the Hofburg's three domes. That small dome tops the entrance to the Hofburg from Michaelerplatz.

To the left of the dome (as you face the facade) is the steeple of the Augustinian Church. It was there, in 1854, that Franz Josef married 16-year-old Elisabeth of Bavaria, and their story began.

Sisi Museum: Empress Elisabeth (1837-1898)—a.k.a. "Sisi" (SEE-see)—was Franz Josef's mysterious, beautiful, and narcissistic wife. This museum traces her fabulous but tragic life. The exhibit starts with Sisi's sad end, showing her **death mask,** photos of her **funeral procession** (by the Hercules statues facing Michaelerplatz), and an **engraving** of a grieving Franz Josef. It was at her death that the obscure, private empress' legend began to grow.

Sisi was nearly 5'8" (a head taller than her husband), had a 20-inch waist (she wore very tight corsets), and weighed only about 100 pounds. (Her waistline eventually grew...to 21 inches. That was at age 50, after giving birth to four children.) A statue, a copy of one of 30 statues that were erected in her honor in European

Sisi (1837-1898)

Empress Elisabeth—Franz Josef's beautiful wife—was the 19th-century equivalent of Princess Diana. Known as "Sisi" since childhood, she became an instant celebrity when she married Franz Josef at 16.

Sisi's main goals in life seem to have been preserving her reputation as a beautiful empress, maintaining her Barbie-doll figure and tending to her fairy-tale, ankle-length hair. In the 1860s, she was considered one of the most beautiful women in the world. After turning 30, she refused to allow photographs or portraits, and was generally seen in public with a delicate fan covering her face (and bad teeth).

Complex and influential, Sisi was adored by Franz Josef, whom she respected. Although Franz Josef was supposed to have married her sister Helene (in an arranged diplomatic marriage), he fell in love with Sisi instead. It was one of the Habsburgs' few marriages for love.

Sisi's personal tragedy was the death of her son Rudolf, the crown prince, in an apparent suicide. Disliking Vienna and the confines of the court, Sisi traveled more and more frequently. As the years passed, the restless Sisi and her hardworking husband became estranged. In 1898, while visiting Geneva, Switzerland, she was murdered by an Italian anarchist.

cities, shows her holding one of her trademark fans. It doesn't show off her magnificent hair, however, which reached down as far as her ankles in her youth.

Imperial Apartments: These were the private apartments and public meeting rooms for the emperor and empress.

Franz Josef's apartments illustrate the lifestyle of the last great Habsburg ruler. In these rooms, he met with advisors and welcomed foreign dignitaries; hosted lavish, white-gloved balls and stuffy formal dinners; and raised three children. He slept (alone) on his austere bed while his beloved wife Sisi retreated to her own rooms. He suffered through the execution of his brother, the suicide of his son and heir, the murder of his wife, and the assassination of his nephew, Archduke Ferdinand, which sparked World War I and spelled the end of the Habsburg monarchy.

Among the rooms you'll see is the **audience room** where Franz Josef received commoners from around the empire. Imagine you've traveled for days to have your say before the emperor. You're

Emperor Franz Josef (1830-1916)

Franz Josef I—who ruled for 68 years (1848-1916)—was the embodiment of the Habsburg Empire as it finished its six-century-long ride. Born in 1830, Franz Josef had a stern upbringing that instilled in him a powerful sense of duty and—like so many men of power—a love of all things military.

His uncle, Ferdinand I, suffered from profound epilepsy, which prevented him from being an effective ruler. As the revolutions of 1848 rattled royal families throughout Europe, the Habsburgs forced Ferdinand to abdicate and put 18-year-old Franz Josef on the throne. He spent the first part of his long reign understandably paranoid, as social discontent continued to simmer.

Franz Josef was very conservative. But worse, he wrongly believed that he was a talented military tactician, leading Austria into catastrophic battles against Italy (which was fighting for its unification and independence) in the 1860s.

Wearing his uniform to the end, Franz Josef never saw what a dinosaur his monarchy was becoming. Franz Josef had no interest in democracy and pointedly never set foot in Austria's parliament building. His passion for low-grade paperwork earned him the nickname "Joe Bureaucrat." Mired in these petty details, he missed the big picture. In 1914, he helped start a Great War that ultimately ended the age of monarchs. The year 1918 marked the end of Europe's big royal families: Hohenzollerns (Prussia), Romanovs (Russia), and Habsburgs (Austria).

wearing your new fancy suit—Franz Josef required that men coming before him wear a tailcoat, women a black gown with a train. He'd stand at the **lectern** (far left) as the visiting commoners had their say (but for no more than two and a half minutes). On the lectern is a partial **list** of 56 appointments he had on January 3, 1910 (three columns: family name, meeting topic, and *Anmerkung*—the emperor's "action log").

Franz Josef's **study** evokes how seriously the emperor took his responsibilities as the top official of a vast empire. Famously energetic, Franz Josef lived a spartan life dedicated to duty; in his **bedroom,** notice his no-frills **iron bed.** He typically rose before dawn and started his day in prayer, kneeling at the **prayer stool** against the far wall. While he had a typical emperor's share of mistresses, his dresser was always well-stocked with **photos** of Sisi.

In **Sisi's bedroom,** refurbished in the Neo-Rococo style in 1854, there's a red carpet, covered with oriental rugs. The room always had lots of fresh flowers. Sisi not only slept here, but also lived here—the bed was rolled in and out daily—until her death in 1898. The **desk** is where she sat and wrote her letters and sad poems. In her **dressing/exercise room,** servants worked three hours a day on Sisi's famous hair. She'd exercise on the **wooden structure** and on the **rings** suspended from the doorway to the left. Afterward, she'd get a massage on the red-covered bed.

In the **small salon,** notice the portrait of **Crown Prince Rudolf,** Franz Josef's and Sisi's only son. On the morning of January 30, 1889, the 30-year-old Rudolf and a beautiful baroness were found shot dead in an apparent murder-suicide in his hunting lodge in Mayerling. The scandal shocked the empire and tainted the Habsburgs; Sisi retreated further into her fantasy world, and Franz Josef carried on stoically with a broken heart.

The tour ends in the **dining room.** It's dinnertime, and Franz Josef has called his extended family together. The settings are modest...just silver. Gold was saved for formal state dinners. Next to each name card was a menu listing the chef responsible for each dish. (Talk about pressure.) Franz Josef enforced strict protocol at mealtime: No one could speak without being spoken to by the emperor, and no one could eat after he was done. While the rest of Europe was growing democracy and expanding personal freedoms, the Habsburgs preserved their ossified worldview to the bitter end.

In 1918, World War I ended, Austria was created as a modern nation-state, the Habsburgs were tossed out...and Hofburg Palace was destined to become a museum.

▲▲▲Hofburg Treasury (Weltliche und Geistliche Schatzkammer)

One of the world's most stunning collections of royal regalia, the Hofburg Treasury shows off sparkling crowns, jewels, gowns, and assorted Habsburg bling in 21 darkened rooms. The treasures, well explained by an audioguide, include the crown of the Holy Roman Emperor, Charlemagne's saber, a unicorn horn, and more precious gems than you can shake a scepter at.

Cost and Hours: €12, €20 combo-ticket with Kunsthistorisches and New Palace museums; Wed-Mon 9:00-17:30, closed Tue; audioguide-€4 or €7/2 people, guided tours daily at 14:00 (€3); from the Hofburg's central courtyard pass through the black, red, and gold gate, then follow *Schatzkammer* signs to the Schweizerhof; tel. 01/525-240, www.kaiserliche-schatzkammer.at.

Visiting the Treasury: The Habsburgs saw themselves as the successors to the ancient Roman emperors, and they wanted crowns and royal regalia to match the pomp of the ancients. They used these precious objects for coronation ceremonies, official ribbon-cutting events, and their own personal pleasure. You'll see the prestigious crowns and accoutrements of the rulers of the Holy Roman Empire (a medieval alliance of Germanic kingdoms so named because it wanted to be considered the continuation of the Roman Empire).

Here's a rundown of the highlights (the audioguide is much more complete).

Room 2: The personal **crown of Rudolf II** (1602) occupies the center of the room along with its accompanying scepter and orb; a bust of Rudolf II (1552-1612) sits nearby. The crown's design symbolically merges a bishop's miter ("Holy"), the arch across the top of a Roman emperor's helmet ("Roman"), and the typical medieval king's crown ("Emperor").

Two centuries later (1806), this crown and scepter became the official regalia of Austria's rulers, as seen in the large **portrait of Franz I** (the open-legged guy behind you). Napoleon Bonaparte had just conquered Austria and dissolved the Holy Roman Empire. Franz (r. 1792-1835) was allowed to remain in power, but he had to downgrade his title from "Franz II, Holy Roman Emperor" to "Franz I, Emperor of Austria."

Rooms 3 and 4: These rooms contain some of the **coronation vestments and regalia** needed for the new Austrian (not Holy Roman) Emperor. There was a different one for each of the emperor's subsidiary titles, e.g., King of Hungary or King of Lombardy. So many crowns and kingdoms in the Habsburgs' vast empire!

Room 5: Ponder the **Cradle of the King of Rome,** once occupied by Napoleon's son, who was born in 1811 and made King of Rome. While pledging allegiance to democracy, Napoleon in fact crowned himself Emperor of France and hobnobbed with Europe's royalty. When his wife Josephine could not bear him a male heir, Napoleon divorced her and married into the Habsburg family.

Room 6: For Divine Right kings, even child-rearing was a sacred ritual that needed elaborate regalia for public ceremonies. The 23-pound **gold basin and pitcher** were used to baptize noble children, who were dressed in the **baptismal dresses** displayed nearby.

Room 7: These **jewels** are the true "treasures," a cabinet of wonders used by Habsburgs to impress their relatives (or to hock when funds got low).

Religious Rooms: Several rooms hold **religious objects**—crucifixes, chalices, mini-altarpieces, reliquaries, and bishops' vestments. Like the medieval kings who preceded them, Habsburg rulers mixed the institutions of church and state, so these precious religious accoutrements were also part of their display of secular power.

Regalia of the Holy Roman Empire: The next few rooms (11 and 12) contain some of the oldest and most venerated objects in the Treasury—the robes, crowns, and sacred objects of the Holy Roman Emperor.

The big red-silk and gold-thread **mantle,** nearly 900 years old, was worn by Holy Roman Emperors at their coronations. The collection's highlight is the 10th-century **crown of the Holy Roman Emperor.** It was probably made for Otto I (c. 960), the first king to call himself Holy Roman Emperor. The Imperial Crown swirls with symbolism "proving" that the emperor was both holy and Roman: The cross on top says the HRE ruled as Christ's representative on earth, and the jeweled arch over the top is reminiscent of the parade helmet of ancient Romans. The jewels themselves allude to the wearer's kinghood in the here and now. Imagine the impression this priceless, glittering crown must have made on the emperor's medieval subjects.

Nearby is the 11th-century **Imperial Cross** that preceded the emperor in ceremonies. Encrusted with jewels, it had a hollow compartment (its core is wood) that carried substantial chunks thought to be from *the* **cross** on which Jesus was crucified and *the* **Holy Lance** used to pierce his side (both pieces are displayed in the same glass case). Holy Roman Emperors actually carried the lance into battle in the 10th century. Look behind the cross to see how it was a box that could be clipped open and shut, used for holding holy relics. You can see bits of the "true cross" anywhere, but this is a prime piece—with the actual nail hole.

Another case has additional objects used in the coronation ceremony: The **orb** (orbs were modeled on late-Roman ceremonial objects, then topped with the cross) and **scepter** (the one with the oak leaves) were carried ahead of the emperor in the procession.

Now picture all this regalia used together. The **painting** (Room 12) shows the coronation of Maria Theresa's son Josef II as Holy Roman Emperor in 1764. Set in a church in Frankfurt (filled with the bigwigs—literally—of the day), Josef is wearing the same crown and royal garb that you've just seen.

More Hofburg Sights
▲▲Hofburg New Palace Museums
(Sammlungen in der Neuen Burg)

The New Palace (Neue Burg) houses three separate collections—an **armory** (with a killer collection of medieval weapons), historical **musical instruments,** and classical statuary from **ancient Ephesus.** Renting the audioguide brings the exhibits to life and lets you hear the collection's fascinating old instruments being played. An added bonus is the chance to wander alone, with almost no tourists, among the royal Habsburg halls, stairways, and painted ceilings.

Cost and Hours: €15 ticket covers all three collections and the Kunsthistorisches Museum across the Ring, €20 combo-ticket adds the Hofburg Treasury, Wed-Sun 10:00-18:00, closed Mon-Tue, audioguide-€3, tel. 01/525-240, www.khm.at.

VIENNA

▲Spanish Riding School (Spanische Hofreitschule)

This stately 300-year-old Baroque hall at the Hofburg Palace is the home of the renowned Lipizzaner stallions. The magnificent building was an impressive expanse in its day. Built without central pillars, it offers clear views of the prancing horses under lavish chandeliers, with a grand statue of Emperor Charles VI on horseback at the head of the hall.

Lipizzaner stallions are known for their noble gait and Baroque profile. These regal horses have changed shape with the tenor of the times: They were bred strong and stout during wars, and frilly and slender in more cultured eras. But they're always born black, fade to gray, and turn a distinctive white in adulthood.

Seeing the Horses and Buying Tickets: The school offers three ways to see the horses—performances, morning exercises, and guided tours of the stables (check the events list on the school's **website** at www.srs.at; enter your dates under "Event Search"). You can purchase tickets online or at the **box office** (opens at 9:00, located inside the Hofburg—go through the main Hofburg entryway from Michaelerplatz, then turn left into the first passage, tel. 01/533-9031). Photos are not allowed at any events, nor are children under age 3.

To **see the horses for free,** you can just walk by the stables at any time of day when the horses are in town. From the covered passageway along Reitschulgasse, there's a big window from where you can usually see the horses poking their heads out of their stalls.

Performances: The Lipizzaner stallions put on great 80-minute performances featuring choreographed moves to jaunty recorded Viennese classical music. The pricey seats book up months in advance, but standing room is usually available the same day (seats about €50-160, standing room about €25, prices vary depending on the show; Feb-mid-June and mid-Aug-Dec usually Sat-Sun at 11:00, no shows Jan and mid-June-mid-Aug). If buying tickets online, look for the tiny English flag at the top of the page when you're redirected to the ticket purchase page.

Morning Exercises: For a less expensive, more casual experience, morning exercises with music take place on weekday mornings in the same hall and are open to the public. Don't have high expectations, as the horses often do little more than trot and warm up. Tourists line up early at Josefsplatz (the large courtyard between Michaelerplatz and Albertinaplatz), at the door marked *Spanische Hofreitschule*. But there's no need to show up when the doors open at 10:00, since tickets never really "sell out" (€15, available at the door in high season—otherwise buy at visitors center on Michaelerplatz, family discounts, generally Tue-Fri 10:00-12:00, occasionally also on Mon, no exercises mid-June-July).

Guided Tours: One-hour guided tours in English are given almost every afternoon year-round. You'll see the Winter Riding School with its grand Baroque architecture, the Summer Riding School in a shady courtyard, and the stables (€18; tours usually daily at 14:00, 15:00, and 16:00; reserve ahead by emailing office@srs.at or calling the box office).

▲Augustinian Church (Augustinerkirche)

Built into the Hofburg, this is the Gothic and Neo-Gothic church where the Habsburgs got latched and dispatched (married and buried). Today, the royal hearts are in the church vault.

Cost and Hours: Church—free, open long hours daily; vault—€2.50 suggested donation, open to the public after Sunday Mass (at about 12:45), at Augustinerstrasse 3, facing Josefsplatz.

Visiting the Church: In the front (above the altar on the right), notice the windows, from which royals witnessed the Mass in private. Don't miss the exquisite, pyramid-shaped memorial (by the Italian sculptor Antonio Canova) to Maria Theresa's favorite daughter, Maria Christina. The hearts of 54 Habsburg nobles are in urns in a vault off the church's Loreto Chapel (on the right beyond the Maria Christina memorial).

The church's 11:00 Sunday Mass is a hit with music lovers. It's both a Mass and a concert, often with an orchestra accompanying the choir (acoustics are best in front). Pay by contributing to the offering plate and buying a CD afterward. Check posters by the entry or www.hochamt.at to see what's on—typically you'll hear one of Mozart or Haydn's many short Masses.

State Hall (Prunksaal) of the Austrian National Library

The National Library (Österreichische Nationalbibliothek) runs several museums in different parts of the Hofburg complex. The

most worthwhile is the State Hall (Prunksaal), a postcard-perfect Baroque library entered from Josefplatz, next to the Augustinian Church (see map on page 871). In this former imperial library, with a statue of Charles VI in the center, you'll find yourself whispering. The setting takes you back to 1730 and gives you the sense that, in imperial times, knowledge of the world was for the elite—and with that knowledge, the elite had power. More than 200,000 old books line the walls, but patrons go elsewhere to read them—the hall is just for show these days.

Cost and Hours: €7, daily 10:00-18:00, Thu until 21:00, tel. 01/53410, www.onb.ac.at.

Butterfly House (Schmetterlinghaus) in the Palace Garden (Burggarten)

The Burggarten greenbelt, once the backyard of the Hofburg and now a people's park, welcomes visitors to loiter on the grass. The iron-and-glass pavilion (c. 1910 with playful Art Nouveau touches) now houses the recommended Café Restaurant Palmenhaus and a small, fluttery butterfly exhibit.

Cost and Hours: €6.50; April-Oct daily 10:00-16:45, Sat-Sun until 18:15; Nov-March daily 10:00-15:45, www. schmetterlinghaus.at.

▲▲Albertina Museum

This impressive museum has three highlights: the imposing state rooms of the former palace, noteworthy collections of classic modernist paintings and European graphic arts, and excellent temporary exhibits.

The building, at the southern tip of the Hofburg complex (near the opera), was the residence of Maria Theresa's favorite daughter, Maria Christina, who was allowed to marry for love rather than political strategy. Her many sisters were jealous. (Marie-Antoinette had to marry the French king...and lost her head over it.) Maria Christina's husband, Albert of Saxony, was a great collector of original drawings and prints, which he amassed to cover all the important art movements from the late Middle Ages until the early 19th century (including prized works by Dürer, Rembrandt, and Rubens). As it's Albert and Christina's gallery, it's charmingly called the "Albertina."

Cost and Hours: €13, daily 10:00-18:00, Wed until 21:00, helpful audioguide-€4, overlooking Albertinaplatz across from the TI and opera, tel. 01/534-830, www.albertina.at.

Visiting the Museum: The entry level often houses photography exhibits. Climbing the stairs you reach the main attractions: the state rooms *(Prunkräume)* on your left on level 1, and the Batliner Collection on your right on level 2. Excellent special exhibitions, often featuring works from the Albertina's collections, are shown on level 2 and in the basement galleries.

State Rooms (level 1): Wander freely under chandeliers and across parquet floors through a handful of rooms of imperial splendor, unconstrained by velvet ropes. Many rooms are often closed for special functions, but even a few rooms give a good look at imperial Classicism—this is the only post-Rococo palace in the Habsburg realm.

Batliner Collection (level 2): This manageable collection sweeps you quickly through modern art history, featuring minor works by major artists (such as Monet, Degas, Munch, Klimt, Matisse, Kirchner, Nolde, and Bacon). Though the collection is permanent, what's on display rotates through about 100 works selected from the 300 in the archives.

Church Crypts near the Hofburg

Two churches near the Hofburg offer starkly different looks at dearly departed Viennese: the Habsburg coffins in the Kaisergruft and the commoners' graves in St. Michael's Church.

▲▲Kaisergruft (Imperial Crypt)

Visiting the imperial remains of the Habsburg family is not as easy as you might imagine. These original organ donors left their bodies—about 150 in all—in the unassuming Kaisergruft, their hearts in the Augustinian Church (viewable Sun after Mass), and their entrails in the crypt below St. Stephen's Cathedral. Don't tripe.

Cost and Hours: €5.50, daily 10:00-18:00, €0.50 map includes Habsburg family tree and a chart locating each coffin, crypt is in the Capuchin Church at Tegetthoffstrasse 2 at Neuer Markt; tel. 01/512-6853.

Visiting the Kaisergruft: Descend into a low-ceilinged crypt full of gray metal tombs. Start up the path, through tombs ranging from simple caskets to increasingly big monuments with elaborate metalwork ornamentation.

You soon reach the massive pewter tomb of **Maria Theresa** under the dome. The only female Habsburg monarch, she had to be granted special dispensation to rule. Her 40-year reign was enlightened and progressive. She and her husband, **Franz I**, recline Etruscan-style atop their fancy coffin, gazing into each other's eyes as a cherub crowns them with glory. They were famously in love (though Franz was less than faithful), and their numerous children were married off to Europe's royal houses. Maria Theresa outlived her husband by 15 years, which she spent in mourning. Old and fat, she installed a special lift to transport herself down into the Kaisergruft to visit her dear, departed Franz. At the four corners of the tomb are the Habsburgs' four crowns: the Holy Roman Empire, Hungary, Bohemia, and Jerusalem. At his parents' feet lies **Josef II,** the patron of Mozart and Beethoven. Compare the Rococo splendor of Maria Theresa's tomb with the simple coffin of Josef, who was known for his down-to-earth ruling style during the Age of Enlightenment.

Head on through the next room, and then down three steps,

to a room illustrating the Habsburgs' fading 19th-century glory. There's the appropriately austere military tomb of the long-reigning **Franz Josef** (see sidebar on page 874). Alongside is his wife, **Elisabeth**—a.k.a. Sisi (see page 873)—who always wins the "Most Flowers" award. Their son was Crown Prince **Rudolf.** Rudolf and his teenage mistress supposedly committed suicide together in 1889 at Mayerling hunting lodge...or was it murder? It took considerable ecclesiastical hair-splitting to win Rudolf this hallowed burial spot.

In the final room (with humbler copper tombs), you reach the final Habsburgs. **Karl I** (see his bust, not a tomb), the last of the Habsburg rulers, was deposed in 1918. His sons Crown Prince **Otto** and Archduke **Karl Ludwig** are entombed near their mother, **Zita.**

Today there are about 700 living Habsburg royals, mostly in exile. When they die, they will be buried in their countries of exile, not here.

▲St. Michael's Church Crypt (Michaelerkirche)

St. Michael's Church, which faces the Hofburg on Michaelerplatz, offers a striking contrast to the imperial crypt. Regular tours take visitors underground to see a typical church crypt, filled with the rotting wooden coffins of well-to-do commoners.

Cost and Hours: €7 for 45-minute tour, Mon-Sat at 11:00 and 13:00, no tours Sun, mostly in German but with enough English, wait at church entrance at the sign advertising the tour and pay the guide directly, mobile 0650-533-8003, www.michaelerkirche.at.

Visiting the Crypt: Climbing below the church, you'll see about a hundred 18th-century coffins and stand on three feet of debris, surrounded by niches filled with stacked lumber from decayed coffins and countless bones. You'll meet a 1769 mummy in lederhosen and a wig, along with a woman who is clutching a cross and has flowers painted on her high heels. You'll learn about death in those times, including how the wealthy—not wanting to end up in standard shallow graves—instead paid to be laid to rest below the church, and how, in 1780, Emperor Josef II ended the practice of cemetery burials in cities but allowed the rich to become the stinking rich in crypts under churches.

MORE SIGHTS WITHIN THE RING

▲▲▲St. Stephen's Cathedral (Stephansdom)

This massive Gothic church with the skyscraping spire sits at the center of Vienna. Its highlights are the impressive exterior, the view from the top of the south tower, a carved pulpit, and a handful of quirky sights associated with Mozart and the Habsburg rulers.

Cost and Hours: Church foyer and north aisle—free, daily 6:00-22:00 (from 7:00 on Sun); main nave—€4.50, Mon-Sat 9:00-

Empress Maria Theresa (1717-1780) and Her Son, Emperor Josef II (1741-1790)

Maria Theresa was the only woman to officially rule the Habsburg Empire in that family's 640-year reign. She was a strong and effective empress (r. 1740-1780), but Austrians are also quick to remember Maria Theresa as the mother of 16 children (10 survived into adulthood). Ponder the fact that the most powerful woman in Europe either was pregnant or had a newborn for most of her reign. Maria Theresa ruled after the Austrian defeat of the Ottomans, when Europe recognized Austria as a great power. (Her rival, the Prussian king, said, "When at last the Habsburgs get a great man, it's a woman.")

Maria Theresa's reign marked the end of the feudal system and the beginning of the era of the grand state. The first of the modern rulers of the Age of Enlightenment, she was a great social reformer. During her reign, she avoided wars and expanded her empire by skillfully marrying her children into the right families. For instance, after daughter Marie-Antoinette's marriage into the French Bourbon family (to Louis XVI), a country that had been an enemy became an ally. (Unfortunately for Marie-Antoinette, Maria Theresa's timing was off.)

To stay in power during an era of revolution, Maria Theresa had to be in tune with her age. She taxed the Church and the nobility, provided six years of obligatory education to all children, and granted free health care to all in her realm. Maria Theresa also welcomed the boy genius Mozart into her court.

The empress' legacy lived on in her son, Josef II, who ruled as emperor for a decade (1780-1790). He was an even more avid reformer, building on his mother's accomplishments. An enlightened monarch, Josef mothballed the too-extravagant Schönbrunn Palace, secularized the monasteries, established religious tolerance within his realm, freed the serfs, made possible the founding of Austria's first general hospital, and promoted relatively enlightened treatment of the mentally ill. Josef was a model of practicality (for example, he banned slow-to-decompose coffins and allowed no more than six candles at funerals)—and very unpopular with other royals. But his policies succeeded in preempting the revolutionary anger of the age, largely enabling Austria to avoid the anti-monarchist turmoil that shook so much of the rest of Europe.

11:30 & 13:00-16:30, Sun 13:00-16:30, June-Aug until 18:30; audioguide-€1; south and north towers, catacombs, and treasury have varying costs and hours—see below; English Mass each Sat at 19:00, tel. 01/515-523-526, www.stephanskirche.at.

Tours: The €5.50 tours in English are entertaining (daily at 10:30, check information board inside entry to confirm schedule; price includes main nave entry, minimum 5 people). The €1 audioguide is helpful.

🎧 Download my free St. Stephen's Cathedral audio tour.

Treasury: Consider riding the elevator (just inside the cathedral's entry) to the treasury, with precious relics, dazzling church art, a portrait of Rudolf IV (considered the earliest German portrait), and wonderful views down on the nave (€5.50 admission includes audioguide, daily 9:00-16:30, July-Aug until 17:30).

Catacombs: The catacombs are open to the public only by guided tour (€5.50, daily 10:00-11:30 & 13:30-16:30, tours generally depart on the half-hour and are in German and English). Just be at the stairs in the left/north transept to meet the guide—you'll pay at the end. You'll see a crypt for bishops and archbishops, and Crock-Pots of Habsburg guts filling dusty shelves.

Towers: The iconic **south tower** rewards a tough climb up a claustrophobic, 343-step staircase with dizzying views. You can reach it via the entrance outside the church, around the right as you face the west facade (€4.50, daily 9:00-17:30).

The shorter **north tower** holds the famous "Pummerin" bell, and you ascend via elevator (no stairs). But it's much lower, not as exciting, and has lesser views (€5.50, daily 9:00-17:30 & 19:00-21:30, entrance inside the church on the left/north side of the nave; you can access this elevator without buying a ticket for the main nave).

⊙ Self-Guided Tour: Before we go inside, let's look at the church's impressive exterior.

Cathedral Exterior: As you face the church's main entry, go to the right across the little square. From here, you can absorb the sheer magnitude of this massive church, with its skyscraping spire. The church we see today is the third one on this spot. (The red-and-white bricks embedded in the pavement mark the footprint of these earlier churches.) Today's church dates mainly from 1300 to 1450, when builders expanded on an earlier structure and added two huge towers at the end of each transept.

The impressive 450-foot **south tower**—capped with a golden orb and cross—took two generations to build (65 years) and was finished in 1433. The tower is a rarity among medieval churches in that it was completed before the Gothic style—and the age of faith—petered out.

The half-size **north tower** (223 feet), around the other side of the church, was meant to be a matching steeple. But around 1500, it was abandoned in midconstruction, when the money was needed to defend the country against the Ottomans rather than to build church towers.

The cathedral was heavily damaged at the end of World War II. Near where you are standing are **old photos** showing the destruction. In 1945, Vienna was caught in the chaos between the occupying Nazis and the approaching Soviets. Allied bombs sparked fires in nearby buildings, and the embers leapt to the cathedral rooftop. The original timbered Gothic roof burned, the cathedral's huge bell crashed to the ground, and the fire raged for two days. Civic pride prompted a financial outpouring, and the roof was rebuilt to its original splendor by 1952—doubly impressive considering the bombed-out state of the country at that time.

· *Now stand at the back of the square, across from the main entrance.*

The Romanesque-style main entrance is the oldest part of the church (c. 1240—part of a church that stood here before). Right behind you is the site of Vindobona, a Roman garrison town. Before the Romans converted to Christianity, there was a pagan temple here, and this entrance pays homage to that ancient heritage. Roman-era statues are embedded in the facade, and the two **octagonal towers** flanking the main doorway are dubbed the "heathen towers" because they're built with a few recycled Roman stones (flipped over to hide the pagan inscriptions and expose the smooth sides).

· *Enter the church.*

Cathedral Interior: Find a spot to peer through the gate down the immense nave—more than a football field long and nine stories tall. It's lined with clusters of slender pillars that soar upward to support the ribbed crisscross arches of the ceiling. Stylistically, the nave is Gothic with a Baroque overlay. It's a spacious, glorious venue that's often used for high-profile concerts (there's a ticket office outside the church, to the right as you face the main doorway).

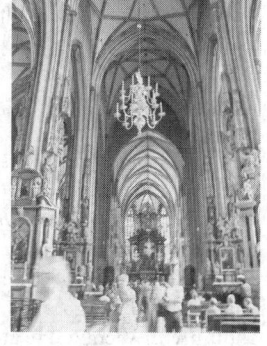

Over the main doorway is the choir loft, with the 10,000-pipe **organ,** a 1960 replacement for the famous one destroyed during World War II. This organ is also one of Europe's biggest, but it's currently broken and sits unused...too large to remove. Architects aren't sure whether it serves a structural purpose and adds support to the actual building.

Along the left wall is the **gift shop.** Step in to marvel at the 14th-century statuary decorating its wall—some of the finest carvings in the church. To the left of the gift shop is the gated entrance to the **Chapel of Prince Eugene of Savoy.** Prince Eugene (1663-1736), a teenage seminary student from France, arrived in Vienna in 1683 as the city was about to be overrun by the Ottoman Turks. He volunteered for the army and helped save the city, launching a brilliant career as a military man for the Habsburgs. His specialty was conquering the Ottomans. When he died, the grateful Austrians buried him here, under this chapel, marked by a tomb hatch in the floor.

• *Nearby is the entrance to the* **main nave.** *Buy a ticket and start down the nave toward the altar. At the second pillar on the left is the pulpit.*

This Gothic sandstone **pulpit** (c. 1500) is a masterpiece carved from three separate blocks (see if you can find the seams). A spiral stairway winds up to the lectern, surrounded and supported by the four church "fathers," whose writings influenced early Catholic dogma.

The pulpit is as crammed with religious meaning as it is with beautifully realistic carvings. The top of the stairway's railing swarms with lizards (animals of light) and toads (animals of darkness). The "Dog of the Lord" stands at the top, making sure none of those toads pollutes the sermon. Below the toads, wheels with three parts (the Trinity) roll up, while wheels with four spokes (the four seasons and four cardinal directions, symbolizing mortal life on earth) roll down.

Find the guy peeking out from under the stairs. This may be a **self-portrait** of the sculptor. In medieval times, art was done for the glory of God, and artists worked anonymously. But this pulpit was carved as humanist Renaissance ideals were creeping in from Italy—and individual artists were becoming famous. So the artist included what may be a rare self-portrait bust in his work. He leans out from a window, sculptor's compass in hand, to observe the world and his work.

• *Continue up to the gate that cuts off the front of the nave, turn right, and enter the south transept.*

Go all the way to the doors, then look left to find the **Mozart Plaque.** Wolfgang Amadeus Mozart (1756-1791) spent most of his adult life in Vienna. He attended Mass and was married in St. Stephen's, and two of his children were baptized here. He set up house in a lavish apartment a block east of the church (now the lackluster Mozarthaus museum). Mozart lived at the heart of Viennese society—among musicians, actors, and aristocrats. He played in a string quartet with Joseph Haydn. At church, he would have heard Beethoven's teacher playing the organ. (Mozart may have met the starstruck young Beethoven in Vienna—or maybe not; accounts vary.)

After his early success, Mozart fell on hard times. When he died at 35 (in 1791), his remains were dumped into a mass grave outside town. But he was honored with a funeral service in St. Stephen's—held in the Prince Eugene of Savoy Chapel, where they played his famous (but unfinished) *Requiem*.

• *Now head to the chapel at the front-right corner of the church.*

This imposing, red-marble **tomb of Frederick III** is like a big king-size-bed coffin with an effigy of Frederick lying on top (not visible—but there's a photo of the effigy on the left). The top of the tomb is decorated with his coats of arms, representing the many territories he ruled over. Frederick III (1415-1493) is considered the "father" of Vienna for turning the small village into a royal town with a cosmopolitan feel.

• *Walk to the middle of the church.*

The tall, ornate, black marble **high altar** (1641, by Tobias and Johann Pock) is topped with a statue of Mary that barely fits under the towering vaults of the ceiling. It frames a large painting of the stoning of St. Stephen, painted on copper. Stephen (at the bottom), having refused to stop professing his faith, is pelted with rocks by angry pagans. As he kneels, ready to die, he gazes up to see a vision of Christ, the cross, and the angels of heaven.

▲▲▲Vienna State Opera (Wiener Staatsoper)

The opera house, facing the Ring and near the TI, is a central point for any visitor. Vienna remains one of the world's great cities for classical music, and this building still belts out some of the finest opera, both classic and cutting-edge. While the critical reception of the building 130 years ago led the architect to commit suicide, and though it's been rebuilt since its destruction by WWII bombs, it's still a sumptuous place. The interior has a chandeliered lobby and carpeted staircases perfect for making the scene. The theater itself features five wraparound balconies, gold-and-red decor, and a bracelet-like chandelier. The only way to see the interior (besides attending a performance) is with a guided 45-minute tour.

Cost and Hours: Tours cost €7.50 and generally run at the top of each hour between 10:00 and 15:00, but because of rehearsals and performances, the schedule is different every day. Find the monthly schedule online, in the opera's *Prolog* magazine, or posted at the tour entrance (southwest corner of building); tel. 01/514-442-606, www.wiener-staatsoper.at.

▲▲Haus der Musik

Vienna's "House of Music" is a high-tech experience that celebrates this hometown forte. The museum, spread over several floors and well-described in English, is unique for its effective use of touch-screen computers and headphones to explore the physics of sound. One floor is dedicated to the heavyweight Viennese composers (Mozart, Beethoven, and company) who virtually created classical music as we know it. Really experiencing the place takes time. It's open late and is so interactive, relaxing, and fun that it can be

VIENNA

considered an activity more than a sight—an evening of joy for music lovers.

Cost and Hours: €13, half-price after 20:00, €18 combo-ticket with Mozarthaus, daily 10:00-22:00, two blocks from the opera house at Seilerstätte 30, tel. 01/513-4850, www.hdm.at. Your ticket includes a free app for added info as you visit.

Visiting the Museum: The first floor highlights the Vienna Philharmonic Orchestra, known the world over for their New Year's Eve concerts. (In a mini concert hall, a one-hour video—on a loop—lets you enjoy the event.) See Toscanini's baton, Mahler's cap, and well-used scores. Throw the dice to randomly "compose" a piece of music.

The second floor explores the physics of sound—wander through the "sonosphere" and marvel at the amazing acoustics. Interactive exhibits explore the nature of sound and music; I could actually hear what I thought only a piano tuner could discern. You can twist, dissect, and bend sounds to make your own musical language, merging your voice with a duck's quack or a city's traffic roar.

The third floor celebrates the famous hometown boys: Haydn, Mozart, Beethoven, Schubert, Strauss (father and son), Mahler, Schönberg, Webern, and Berg. (With the app, you can enjoy appropriate music in each room as you stroll.) Before leaving, pick up a virtual baton to conduct the Vienna Philharmonic.

▲Dorotheum Auction House (Palais Dorotheum)

For an aristocrat's flea market, drop by Austria's answer to Sotheby's. The ground floor has shops, an info desk with a schedule of upcoming auctions, and a few auction items. Some pieces are available for immediate sale (marked *VKP*, for *Verkaufpreis*— "sales price"), while others are up for auction (marked *DIFF. RUF*).

The first floor (above the mezzanine) has antique furniture and fancy knickknacks; the second floor has a showy antique gallery with fixed prices. Wandering through here, you feel like you're touring a museum with exhibits you can buy.

Cost and Hours: Free, Mon-Fri 10:00-18:00, Sat 9:00-17:00, closed Sun, classy little café on second floor, between the Graben pedestrian street and Hofburg at Dorotheergasse 17, tel. 01/51560, www.dorotheum.com.

▲St. Peter's Church (Peterskirche)

Baroque Vienna is at its best in this architectural gem, tucked away a few steps from the Graben. Admire the rose-and-gold, oval-shaped Baroque interior, topped with a ceiling fresco of Mary kneeling to be crowned by Jesus and the Father, while the dove of the Holy Spirit floats way up in the lantern. The church's sumptuous elements—especially the organ, altar painting, pulpit, and coat of arms (in the base of the dome) of church founder Leopold I—make St. Peter's one of the city's most beautiful and ornate churches.

Cost and Hours: Free, Mon-Fri 7:00-20:00, Sat-Sun 9:00-21:00; free organ concerts Mon-Fri at 15:00, Sat-Sun at 20:00; just off the Graben between the Plague Monument and Kohlmarkt, tel. 01/533-6433, www.peterskirche.at.

Mozarthaus Vienna Museum

In September 1784, 27-year-old Wolfgang Amadeus Mozart moved into this spacious apartment with his wife, Constanze, and their week-old son Karl. For the next three years, this was the epicenter of Viennese high life. It was here that Mozart wrote *Marriage of Figaro* and *Don Giovanni* and established himself as the toast of Vienna. Today, the actual apartments are pretty boring (mostly bare rooms), but the museum does flesh out Mozart's Vienna years with paintings, videos, and a few period pieces.

Cost and Hours: €11, includes audioguide, €18 combo-ticket with Haus der Musik, daily 10:00-19:00, a block behind the cathedral, go through arcade at #5a and walk 50 yards to Domgasse 5, tel. 01/512-1791, www.mozarthausvienna.at.

Jewish Museum Vienna (Jüdisches Museum Wien)

The museum operates two buildings a 10-minute walk apart. The **Jewish Museum Dorotheergasse** (near the Hofburg) fills a four-story downtown building with exhibits, a bookstore, and a small, reasonably priced café serving Middle Eastern fare. It documents Vienna's Jewish community from earliest times to the present.

The smaller, less interesting **Museum Judenplatz** (near Am Hof) was built around the scant remains of the medieval synagogue that served Vienna's 1,500 Jewish residents up until their massacre in 1420. Its main exhibit is an underground hall where you see the synagogue's foundations. The classy square above the ruins, called Judenplatz, is now dominated by a blocky **memorial** to the 65,000 Viennese Jews killed by the Nazis.

Cost and Hours: €10 ticket includes both museums; Dorotheergasse location, at #11—Sun-Fri 10:00-18:00, closed Sat, videoguide-€4; Judenplatz location, at #8—Sun-Thu 10:00-18:00, Fri until 17:00, closed Sat; tel. 01/535-0431, www.jmw.at.

Austrian Postal Savings Bank (Österreichische Postsparkasse)

Built between 1904 and 1912, the Postal Savings Bank was one of the key buildings in the development of modern architecture. Today it's a pilgrimage site for architects from all over the world (for whom it's a ▲▲▲ sight). It's still a bank, and you can enter the atrium for free. Hard-core Jugendstil fans may want to pay to visit the pleasant, small museum inside, which tells the building's story through plans, photos, and news reports, and preserves the original bank-teller counters.

Cost and Hours: Foyer and atrium—free, open Mon-Fri 7:00-17:30, closed Sat-Sun; museum—€8 (get tickets from counter 14 in atrium), open Mon-Fri 10:00-17:00, closed Sat-Sun; just inside the Ringstrasse at Georg-Coch-Platz 2, tel. 059-9053-3825, www.ottowagner.com.

MUSEUM DISTRICT

In the 19th century, the Habsburgs planned to link their palace and museum buildings with a series of arches across the Ringstrasse. Although that dream was never fully realized, the awe-inspiring museums still face off across Maria-Theresien-Platz, with a monument to Maria Theresa at its center (for more on this monument, see page 867).

▲▲▲Kunsthistorisches Museum

The Kunsthistorwhateveritis Museum—let's just say "Kunst" (koonst)—houses the family collection of Austria's luxury-loving Habsburg rulers. Their joie de vivre is re-

flected in this collection—some of the most beautiful, sexy, and fun art from two centuries (c. 1450-1650). At their peak of power in the 1500s, the Habsburgs ruled Austria, Germany, northern Italy, the Netherlands, and Spain—and you'll see a wide variety of art from all these places and beyond.

While there's little Viennese art here, you will find world-class European masterpieces galore (including canvases by Raphael, Caravaggio, Velázquez, Dürer, Rubens, Vermeer, Rembrandt, and a particularly exquisite roomful of Bruegels), all well displayed on one glorious floor, plus a fine display of Egyptian, classical, and applied arts.

Cost and Hours: €15 ticket also covers New Palace museums across the Ring, €20 combo-ticket adds the Hofburg Treasury; daily 10:00-18:00, Thu until 21:00, closed Mon in Sept-May;

audioguide-€4, on the Ringstrasse at Maria-Theresien-Platz, U: Volkstheater/Museumsplatz, tel. 01/525-240, www.khm.at.

Visiting the Museum: Of the museum's many exhibits, we'll tour only the highlights of the Painting Gallery (Gemäldegalerie) on the first floor. Italian-Spanish-French art is on one half of the floor, and Northern European art on the other. The museum seems to constantly move paintings from room to room, so be flexible.

Titian, *Danae* and *Ecce Homo:* In the long career of Titian the Venetian (it rhymes), he painted portraits, Christian Madonnas, and sexy Venuses with equal ease. Here, Titian captured Danae—a luscious nude reclining in bed—as she's about to be seduced. Zeus, the king of the gods, descends as a shower of gold to consort with her—you can almost see the human form of Zeus within the cloud. Danae is helpless with rapture, opening her legs to receive him, while her servant tries to catch the heavenly spurt with a golden dish. How could ultra-conservative Catholic emperors have tolerated such a downright pagan and erotic painting? Apparently, without a problem.

In the large canvas *Ecce Homo,* a crowd mills about, when suddenly there's a commotion. They nudge each other and start to point. Follow their gaze diagonally up the stairs to a battered figure entering way up in the corner. "Ecce Homo!" says Pilate. "Behold the man." And he presents Jesus to the mob.

Raphael, *Madonna of the Meadow:* Young Raphael epitomized the spirit of the High Renaissance, combining symmetry, grace, beauty, and emotion. This Madonna is a mountain of motherly love—Mary's head is the summit and her flowing robe is the base—enfolding Baby Jesus and John the Baptist. The geometric perfection, serene landscape, and Mary's adoring face make this a masterpiece of sheer grace—but then you get smacked by an ironic fist: The cross the little tykes play with foreshadows their gruesome deaths.

Correggio and Parmigianino: The Kunst displays excellent small canvases in the smaller side rooms. For example, in a room near Raphael, you may find Correggio's *Jupiter and Io,* showing Zeus seducing another female, this time disguised as a cloud. Parmigianino's *Self-Portrait in a Convex Mirror* depicts the artist gazing into a convex mirror and perfectly reproducing the curved reflection on a convex piece of wood. Amazing.

Arcimboldo, *Portraits of the Seasons:* These four cleverly deceptive portraits by the Habsburg court painter depict the four seasons (and elements) as people. For example, take *Summer*—a.k.a. "Fruit Face." With a pickle nose, pear chin, and corn-husk ears, this guy literally is what he eats. Its grotesque weirdness makes it typical of Mannerist art.

Caravaggio, *Madonna of the Rosary* and *David with the Head*

of Goliath: Caravaggio shocked the art world with brutally honest reality. Compared with Raphael's super-sweet *Madonna of the Meadow,* Caravaggio's *Madonna of the Rosary* (the biggest canvas in the room) looks perfectly ordinary, and the saints kneeling around her have dirty feet.

In *David with the Head of Goliath,* Caravaggio turns a third-degree-interrogation light on a familiar Bible story. David shoves the dripping head of the slain giant right in our noses. This David is not a heroic Renaissance Man like Michelangelo's famous statue, but a homeless teen that Caravaggio paid to portray God's servant. And the severed head of Goliath is none other than Caravaggio himself, an in-your-face self-portrait.

Velázquez, Habsburg Family Portraits: When the Habsburgs ruled both Austria and Spain, cousins kept in touch through portraits of themselves and their kids. Diego Velázquez was the greatest of Spain's "photojournalist" painters—heavily influenced by Caravaggio's realism, capturing his subjects without passing judgment, flattering, or glorifying them.

For example, watch little Margarita Habsburg grow up in three different portraits, from age two to age nine. Margarita was destined from birth to marry her Austrian cousin, the future Emperor Leopold I. Pictures like these, sent from Spain every few years, let her pen pal/fiancé get to know her.

Also see a portrait of Margarita's little brother, *Philip Prosper,* wearing a dress. Sadly, Philip was a sickly boy who would only live two years longer. The amulets he's wearing were intended to fend off illness. His hand rests limply on the back of the chair—above an adorable puppy who seems to be asking, "But who will play with me?"

Canaletto: Before leaving this wing, find paintings of the Habsburg summer palace, Schloss Schönbrunn, by Canaletto, one of which also shows the Viennese skyline in the distance. Then cross the stairwell and enter the part of the museum dedicated to Northern art.

Dürer, Landauer Altarpiece: Albrecht Dürer combined meticulous Northern detail with Renaissance symmetry. This altarpiece may initially look like a complex hog pile of saints and angels, but it's perfectly geometrical. The crucified Christ forms a triangle in the center, framed by triangular clouds and flanked by three-sided crowds of people—appropriate for a painting about the Trinity. Dürer practically invented the self-portrait as an art form, and he included himself, the lone earthling in this heavenly vision (bottom right), with a plaque announcing that he, Albrecht Dürer, painted this in 1511.

Peter Paul Rubens: In Rubens' *Self-Portrait*, admire the darling of Catholic-dominated Flanders (northern Belgium) in his prime: famous, wealthy, well-traveled, the friend of kings and princes, an artist, diplomat, man about town, and—obviously—confident. Rubens' work runs the gamut, from realistic portraits to lounging nudes, Greek myths to altarpieces, from pious devotion to violent sex. But, can we be sure it's Baroque? Ah yes, I'm sure you'll find a pudgy, winged baby somewhere.

How could Rubens paint all these enormous canvases in one lifetime? He didn't. He kept a workshop of assistants busy painting backgrounds and minor figures, working from his own small sketches. Then the master stepped in to add the finishing touches. For example, the giant canvas *The Miracles of St. Ignatius of Loyola* was painted partly by assistants, guided by Rubens' sketches (likely displayed nearby).

Jan Vermeer: In his small canvases, the Dutch painter Jan Vermeer quiets the world down to where we can hear our own heartbeat, letting us appreciate the beauty in common things.

The curtain opens and we see *The Art of Painting*, a behind-the-scenes look at Vermeer at work. He's painting a model dressed in blue, starting with her laurel-leaf headdress. The studio is its own little dollhouse world framed by a chair in the foreground and the wall in back. Then Vermeer fills this space with the few gems he wants us to focus on—the chandelier, the map, the painter's costume. Everything is lit by a crystal-clear light, letting us see these everyday items with fresh eyes.

Rembrandt van Rijn: Rembrandt became wealthy by painting portraits of Holland's upwardly mobile businessmen, but his greatest subject was himself. In the *Large Self-Portrait* we see the hands-on-hips, defiant, open-stance determination of a man who will do what he wants, and if people don't like it, tough.

In typical Rembrandt style, most of the canvas is a dark, smudgy brown, with only the side of his face glowing from the darkness. (Remember Caravaggio? Rembrandt did.) Unfortunately, the year this was painted, Rembrandt's fortunes changed.

Looking at the *Small Self-Portrait* from 1657, consider Rembrandt's last years. His wife died, his children died young, and commissions for paintings dried up as his style veered from the common path. He had to auction off paintings to pay his debts, and he died a poor man.

Pieter Bruegel the Elder: The undisputed master of the slice-of-life village scene was Pieter Bruegel the Elder (c. 1525-1569)—think of him as the Norman Rockwell of the 16th century. He celebrated their simple life, but he also skewered their weaknesses—not to single them out as hicks, but as universal examples of human folly.

The Peasant Wedding, Bruegel's most famous work, is less about the wedding than the food. It's a farmers' feeding frenzy, as the barnful of wedding guests scrambles to get their share of free eats. Two men bring in the next course, a tray of fresh porridge. Everyone's going at it, including a kid in an oversized red cap who licks the bowl with his fingers. In the middle of it all, look who's been completely forgotten—the demure bride sitting in front of the blue-green cloth. According to Flemish tradition, the bride was not allowed to speak or eat at the party, and the groom was not in attendance at all.

▲▲Natural History Museum (Naturhistorisches Museum)

The twin building facing the Kunsthistorisches Museum still serves the exact purpose for which it was built: to show off the Habsburgs' vast collection of plant, animal, and mineral specimens and artifacts. It's grown to become an exceptionally well-organized and enjoyable catalogue of the natural world, with 20 million objects, including moon rocks, dinosaur stuff, and the fist-sized *Venus of Willendorf* statuette (at 25,000 years old, it's the world's oldest sex symbol). Even though the museum has kept its old-school charm, nearly everything on display is presented and described well enough to engage any visitor, from kids to scientifically inclined grown-ups.

Cost and Hours: €10, Wed 9:00-21:00, Thu-Mon 9:00-18:30, closed Tue, €4 audioguide isn't necessary, on the Ringstrasse at Maria-Theresien-Platz, U: Volkstheater/Museumsplatz, tel. 01/521-770, www.nhm-wien.ac.at.

MuseumsQuartier

The vast grounds of the former imperial stables now corral a cutting-edge cultural center for contemporary arts and design. Among several impressive museums, the best are the Leopold Museum, specializing in 20th-century Austrian modernists (Schiele, Klimt, and Kokoschka, among others), and the Museum of Modern Art, Austria's leading gallery for international modern and contemporary art. For many, the MuseumsQuartier is most enjoyable as a spot to gather in the evening for a light, fun meal, cocktails, and people-watching.

Cost and Hours: Leopold Museum—€13, open daily 10:00-18:00, Thu until 21:00, closed Tue Sept-May, audioguide-€4 but not essential, tel. 01/525-700, www.leopoldmuseum.org; Museum of Modern Art—€11 (half-price Thu after 18:00), open Mon 14:00-19:00, Tue-Sun 10:00-19:00, Thu until 21:00, good audioguide-€3, tel. 01/52500, www.mumok.at. The main entrance/visitors center is at Museumsplatz 1 (ask about combo-tickets here if visiting more than just the Leopold and Modern Art museums; U: Volkstheater/Museumsplatz, tel. 01/525-5881, www.mqw.at).

KARLSPLATZ AND NEARBY

These sights cluster around Karlsplatz, just southeast of the Ringstrasse (U: Karlsplatz). If you're walking from central Vienna, use the U-Bahn station's passageway (at the opera house) to avoid crossing busy boulevards. Once at Karlsplatz, allow about 30 minutes' walking time to connect the various sights: Karlskirche, the Secession, and Naschmarkt.

Karlsplatz

This picnic-friendly square, with its Henry Moore sculpture in the pond, is the front yard of Vienna's Technical University. The massive, domed Karlskirche and its twin spiral columns dominate the square. The small green, white, and gold pavilions that line the street across the square from the church are from the late 19th-century municipal train system *(Stadtbahn).* With curvy iron frames, decorative marble slabs, and painted gold trim, these are pioneering works in the Jugendstil style, designed by the Modernist architect **Otto Wagner,** who influenced Klimt and the Secessionists. One of the pavilions has a sweet little exhibit on Wagner that illustrates the Art Nouveau lifestyle around 1900 (€5, Tue-Sun 10:00-18:00, closed Mon and Nov-March, near the Ringstrasse, tel. 01/5058-7478-5177, www.wienmuseum.at).

▲Karlskirche (St. Charles Church)

Charles Borromeo, a 16th-century bishop from Milan, inspired his

parishioners during plague times. This "votive church" was dedicated to him in 1713, when an epidemic spared Vienna. The church offers the best Baroque in the city, with a unique combination of columns (showing scenes from Borromeo's life, à la Trajan's Column in Rome), a classic pediment, an elliptical dome, and a terrific close-up look at its frescoes, thanks to a construction elevator that's open to the public. The dome's colorful 13,500-square-foot fresco—painted in the 1730s by Johann Michael Rottmayr—shows Signor Borromeo (in red-and-white bishop's robes) gazing up into heaven, spreading his arms wide, and pleading with Christ to spare Vienna from the plague.

Cost and Hours: €8, Mon-Sat 9:00-18:00, Sun 13:00-19:00, dome elevator runs until 17:30, audioguide-€2, www.karlskirche. at. The entry fee may seem steep, but remember that it helps to fund the restoration. There are often classical music concerts performed here on period instruments (usually Thu-Sat; ask about Rick Steves discount or €10 student discounts, generally given loosely—we're all still learning, right?; see www.concert-vienna.info).

▲Wien Museum Karlsplatz

This underappreciated city history museum walks you through the story of Vienna with well-presented artifacts and good English descriptions. While the museum gets few visitors, if you like history, it's excellent. A new building is being planned for the site, and the museum will likely close for several years sometime in 2018.

Cost and Hours: €10, free first Sun of the month, open Tue-Sun 10:00-18:00, closed Mon, Karlsplatz 8, tel. 01/505-8747, www.wienmuseum.at.

▲Academy of Fine Arts Painting Gallery (Akademie der Bildenden Künste Gemäldegalerie)

Few tourists make their way to Vienna's art academy to see its small but impressive collection of paintings, starring Botticelli, Guardi, Rubens, Van Dyck, and other great masters. The highlight is a triptych by the master of medieval surrealism, Hieronymus Bosch. The collection's location in a working art academy (it even smells like an art school) gives it a certain authenticity, and indeed, these paintings were left to the academy for teaching purposes.

The *Gemäldegalerie* is upstairs, on the school's first floor. Past the ticket desk, head to the left for the permanent collection (if you go right, you'll find free contemporary exhibits by local students).

Cost and Hours: €8, Tue-Sun 10:00-18:00, closed Mon; audioguide-€2, 3 blocks from the opera house at Schillerplatz 3, tel. 01/588-162-222, www.akbild.ac.at.

▲The Secession

This little building, strategically located behind the Academy of Fine Arts, was created by the Vienna Secession movement, a group of nonconformist artists led by Gustav Klimt, Otto Wagner, and friends.

Having turned their backs on the stuffy official art academy, the Secessionists used the building to display their radical art. The stylized trees carved into the exterior walls and the building's bushy "golden cabbage" rooftop are symbolic of a cycle of renewal. Today, the Secession continues to showcase contemporary cutting-edge art, and it preserves Gustav Klimt's famous *Beethoven Frieze*. A masterpiece of Viennese Art Nouveau, this 105-foot-long fresco was the multimedia centerpiece of a 1902 exhibition honoring Ludwig van Beethoven.

Cost and Hours: €9.50 includes special exhibits, Tue-Sun 10:00-18:00, closed Mon, audioguide-€3, Friedrichstrasse 12, tel. 01/587-5307, www.secession.at.

▲Naschmarkt

In 1898, the city decided to cover up its Vienna River. The long, wide square they created was filled with a lively produce market that still bustles most days (closed Sun). It's long been known as *the* place to get exotic faraway foods. In fact, locals say, "From here start the Balkans."

Hours and Location: Mon-Fri 6:00-18:30, Sat until 17:00, closed Sun, closes earlier in winter; between Linke Wienzeile and Rechte Wienzeile, U: Karlsplatz.

Visiting the Naschmarkt: The stalls of the Naschmarkt (roughly, "Nibble Market") stretch along Wienzeile street, just a

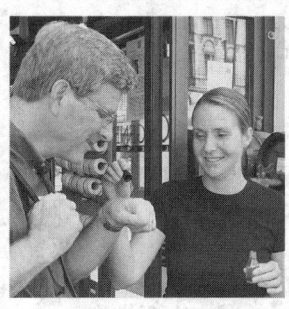

short stroll south of the opera house. This "Belly of Vienna" comes with two parallel lanes—one lined with fun and reasonable eateries, and the other featuring the town's top-end produce and gourmet goodies. This is where top chefs like to get their ingredients. At the gourmet vinegar stall, you can sample the vinegar as you would perfume—with a drop on your wrist (see photo). Farther from the center, the Naschmarkt becomes likably seedy, less expensive, and surrounded by sausage stands, Turkish *döner kebab* stalls, cafés, and theaters. At the market's far end is a line of buildings with fine Art Nouveau facades. Each Saturday, the Naschmarkt is infested by a huge flea market (sets up west of the Kettenbrückengasse U-Bahn station).

▲Mariahilfer Strasse Stroll

While there are more stately and elegant streets in the central district, the best opportunity to simply feel the pulse of workaday Viennese life is a little farther out, along Mariahilfer Strasse. The street has recently gone mostly pedestrian-only, and is fast becoming an attraction in itself. An easy plan is to ride the U-3 to the

Zieglergasse stop (see map on page 919), then stroll and browse your way downhill to the MuseumsQuartier U-Bahn station.

If you're interested in how Austria handles its people's appetite for marijuana, search out three interesting stops along this corridor: Bushplanet Headshop (at Esterhazygasse 32, near the Neubaugasse U-Bahn stop), Hemp Embassy Museum (next to Bushplanet Headshop—basically a display of big, sparkling marijuana plants), and Bushplanet Growshop (set back in a courtyard off Mariahilfer Strasse at #115, both Bushplanet locations open Mon-Fri 10:00-19:00, Sat until 18:00, closed Sun, www.bushplanet.at).

To add some fine-art culture to your stroll, drop in at the nearby Imperial Furniture Collection, where you'll see everything from Habsburg thrones to commodes (see page 902).

For a fine and free city view (along with reasonable eating), escalate to the top floor of the honeycombed Gerngross shopping center and find the Brandauer restaurant (at Mariahilfer Strasse #42; there's also a decent Akakiko Sushi place on the fifth floor—see listing on page 926).

Just off Mariahilfer Strasse #24 (near Capistrangasse) is a passageway (sometimes closed) leading to a chilling bit of WWII history: a Nazi flak tower built in 1944. Mighty towers like this, which housed antiaircraft guns and doubled as bomb shelters, survive in Hamburg, Berlin, and Vienna (where six still stand). This bomb shelter is connected by tunnel to today's Austrian government and still serves as a bunker of last resort.

SIGHTS BEYOND THE RING

The following museums and sights are located outside the Ringstrasse but inside the Gürtel, or outer ring road. For locations, see the map on page 844.

South of the Ring
▲▲Belvedere Palace (Schloss Belvedere)

This is the elegant palace of Prince Eugene of Savoy (1663-1736), the still much-appreciated conqueror of the Ottomans. Today you can tour Eugene's lavish palace, see sweeping views of the gardens and the Vienna skyline, and enjoy world-class art starring Gustav Klimt, French Impressionism, and a grab bag of other 19th- and early-20th-century artists. While Vienna's other art collections show off works by masters from around Europe, this has the city's best collection of homegrown artists.

The palace complex includes the Upper Palace (world-class art collection), smaller Lower Palace (historical rooms and temporary exhibits), the 21er Haus (modern pavilion mostly filled with contemporary art), and pleasantly beautiful Baroque-style gardens (free and fun to explore). For most visitors, only the Upper Palace is worth the entrance fee.

Cost and Hours: €14 for Upper Belvedere Palace only, €20 for Klimt Ticket covering Upper and Lower Palaces (and special exhibits), gardens free; daily 10:00-18:00, Lower Palace until 21:00 on Wed, grounds open until dusk; audioguide-€4 or €7/2 people, no photos allowed inside; entrance at Prinz-Eugen-Strasse 27, tel. 01/7955-7134, www.belvedere.at.

Eating at the Belvedere: There's a charming little café on the ground floor of the Upper Palace; in summer you can sit outdoors in the garden.

Getting There: The palace is a 15-minute walk south of the Ring. To get there from the center, catch tram #D at the opera house (direction: Hauptbahnhof). Get off at the Schloss Belvedere stop (just below the Upper Palace gate), cross the street, walk uphill one block, go through the gate (on left), and look immediately to the right for the small building with the ticket office.

Visiting the Belvedere: The two grand buildings of the Belvedere Palace are separated by a fine garden that slopes down from the Upper to Lower Palace. For our purposes, the Upper Palace is what matters. There are two grand floors, set around impressive middle halls.

From the entrance, climb the staircase to the first floor and enter the grand red-and-gold, chandeliered **Marble Hall.** This was Prince Eugene's party room. *Belvedere* means "beautiful view," and the view from the Marble Hall is especially spectacular. Look over the Baroque gardens, the Lower Palace, and the city.

Then head into the **east wing.** Alongside Renoir's ladies, Monet's landscapes, and Van Gogh's rough brushstrokes are similar works by their lesser-known Austrian counterparts. Around 1900, Austrian artists come to the fore, soaking up Symbolism, Expressionism, and other Modernist trends.

Sumptuous paintings by **Gustav Klimt** fill the rooms at the far end of the east wing. You can get caught up in his fascination with the beauty and danger he saw in women. To Klimt, all art was erotic art. He painted during the turn of the 20th century, when Vienna was a splendid laboratory of hedonism. Even fully clothed, his women have a bewitching eroticism in a world full of pollen and pistils.

The famous painting *Judith* (1901) shows no biblical heroine—Klimt paints her as a high-society Viennese woman with an ostentatious dog-collar necklace. With half-closed eyes and slightly parted lips, she's dismissive...yet mysterious and bewitching.

In what is perhaps Klimt's best-known painting, *The Kiss,* two lovers are wrapped up in the colorful gold-and-jeweled cloak of bliss. Klimt's woman is no longer dominating, but submissive, abandoning herself to her man in a fertile field and a vast universe.

Klimt nurtured the next generation of artists, especially **Egon Schiele.** While Klimt's works are seductive and otherworldly, Schiele's, tend to be darker and more introspective.

The **rest of the Upper Palace** collection goes through the whole range of 19th- and 20th-century art. In the first floor's west wing is the Belvedere's collection of Austrian Baroque art, including grotesquely grimacing heads by **Franz Xaver Messerschmidt** (1736-1783), a quirky 18th-century Habsburg court sculptor who went off to follow his own deranged muse.

▲Museum of Military History (Heeresgeschichtliches Museum)

A big part of Habsburg history is military. And this huge place, built about 1860 as an arsenal by Franz Josef, tells that story with a thoughtful motto (apparently learned from the school of hard knocks): "Wars belong in museums." This vast museum holds a rich collection of artifacts and historic treasures. The interesting 20th-century section includes exhibits devoted to Sarajevo in 1914, Chancellor Dollfuss and the pre-Hitler Austrian Fascist party, the Anschluss, and World War II.

Cost and Hours: €6, includes good audioguide, free first Sun of the month, open daily 9:00-17:00, small café on site, on Arsenalstrasse, tel. 01/795-610, www.hgm.at. It's a 10-minute walk from the Hauptbahnhof, or a 5-minute walk from the Quartier Belvedere tram/S-Bahn stop behind the Belvedere Palace (see map on page 844).

East of the Ring
Museum of Applied Arts
(Museum für Angewandte Kunst, a.k.a. MAK)

Facing the old town from across the Ring, the MAK, as it's called, is a design museum best known for its collection of furniture and decorative art from Vienna's artistic Golden Age, which is showcased in the permanent Vienna 1900 exhibit. The museum's unique gift shop also makes for a fun diversion.

Cost and Hours: €10, free Tue after 18:00; open Tue 10:00-22:00, Wed-Sun 10:00-18:00, closed Mon; multimedia guide-€2, classy restaurant with pleasant garden seating, Stubenring 5—take U-Bahn or tram #2 to Stubentor, tel. 01/711-360, www.mak.at.

▲Kunst Haus Wien Museum and Hundertwasserhaus

This "make yourself at home" museum and nearby apartment complex are a hit with lovers of modern art, mixing the work and philosophy of local painter/environmentalist Friedensreich Hundertwasser (1928-2000), a.k.a. "100H$_2$O."

The museum provides by far the best look at Hundertwasser, but for an actual lived-in apartment complex by the green master, walk 5 to 10 minutes to the one-with-nature Hundertwasserhaus (at Löwengasse and Kegelgasse). This complex of 50 apartments, subsidized by the government to provide affordable housing, was built in the 1980s as a breath of architectural fresh air in a city of boring, blocky apartment complexes. While not open to visitors, it's worth seeing for its fun and colorful patchwork exterior.

Cost and Hours: €11 for museum, €12 combo-ticket includes special exhibitions, open daily 10:00-18:00, extremely fragrant and colorful garden café, tel. 01/712-0491, www.kunsthauswien.com.

Getting There: It's located at Untere Weissgerberstrasse 13, near the Radetzkyplatz stop on trams #O and #1 (signs point the way). Take the U-Bahn to Landstrasse and either walk 10 minutes downhill (north) along Untere Viaduktgasse (a block east of the station), or transfer to tram #O (direction: Praterstern) and ride three stops to Radetzkyplatz.

▲Prater Park (Wiener Prater)

Since the 1780s, when the reformist Emperor Josef II gave his hunting grounds to the people of Vienna as a public park, this place has been Vienna's playground. For the tourist, the "Prater" is the sugary-smelling, tired, and sprawling amusement park (Wurstelprater). For locals, the "Prater" is the vast, adjacent green park with its three-mile-long, tree-lined main boulevard (Hauptallee). The park still tempts visitors with its huge 220-foot-tall, famous, and lazy Ferris wheel *(Riesenrad),* fun roller coasters, bumper cars, Lilliputian railroad, and endless eateries. Especially if you're traveling with kids, this is a fun place to share the evening with thousands of Viennese.

Cost and Hours: Park is free and always open; amusement

park—rides cost €2-€8 and run May-Oct roughly 10:00-22:00, but often later in good weather in summer, fewer rides open in off-season; U: Praterstern, www.prater.at. For a local-style family dinner, eat at Schweizerhaus (good food, great Czech Budvar—the original "Budweiser"—beer, classic conviviality).

North of the Ring
Sigmund Freud Museum

Freud enthusiasts (and detractors) enjoy seeing the apartment and home office of the man who fundamentally changed our understanding of the human psyche. Dr. Sigmund Freud (1856-1939), a graduate of Vienna University, established his practice here in 1891. For the next 47 years, he received troubled patients who hoped to find peace by telling him their dreams, life traumas, and secret urges. It was here that he wrote his influential works, including the landmark *Interpretation of Dreams* (1899). The museum is narrowly focused on Freud's life. If you're looking for a critical appraisal of whether he was a cocaine-addicted charlatan or a sincere doctor groping toward an understanding of human nature, you won't find it here.

Cost and Hours: €10, includes audioguide, daily 10:00-18:00, tiny bookshop, half-block from the Schlickgasse stop on tram #D, Berggasse 19, tel. 01/319-1596, www.freud-museum.at.

West of the Ring
▲Imperial Furniture Collection (Hofmobiliendepot)

Bizarre, sensuous, eccentric, or precious, this collection (on four fascinating floors) is your peek at the Habsburgs' furniture—from the empress's wheelchair ("to increase her fertility she was put on a rich diet and became corpulent") to the emperor's spittoon—all thoughtfully described in English. Evocative paintings help bring the furniture to life.

The Habsburgs had many palaces, but only the Hofburg was permanently furnished. The rest were done on the fly—set up and taken down by a gang of royal roadies called the "Depot of Court Movables" (Hofmobiliendepot). When the monarchy was dissolved in 1918, the state of Austria took possession of the Hofmobiliendepot's inventory—165,000 items. Now this royal storehouse is open to the public in a fine and sprawling museum.

Cost and Hours: €9.50, covered by Sisi Ticket, Tue-Sun 10:00-18:00, closed Mon, Mariahilfer Strasse 88, main entrance around the corner at Andreasgasse 7, U: Zieglergasse, tel. 01/5243-3570, www.hofmobiliendepot.at.

SIGHTS ON VIENNA'S OUTSKIRTS
▲▲▲Schönbrunn Palace (Schloss Schönbrunn)

Among Europe's palaces, only Schönbrunn rivals Versailles. This former summer residence of the Habsburgs is big, with more than 300 rooms in the main building alone. But don't worry—only 40 rooms are shown to the public. Of the plethora of sights at the vast complex, the highlight is a tour of the palace's Imperial Apartments— the chandeliered rooms where the Habsburg nobles lived. You can also stroll the gardens, tour the Imperial Carriage Museum, and visit a handful of lesser sights nearby.

Planning Your Time: Allow at least three hours (including transit time) for your excursion to Schönbrunn. The palace is sprawling and can be mobbed. To avoid lines, reserve your visit in advance, or use a Sisi Ticket (see "Reservations," next page). After viewing the Imperial Apartments, wander the gardens (most of which are free). With more time and energy, pick and choose among the other sightseeing options and buy tickets as you go.

Getting There: Schönbrunn is an easy 10-minute subway ride from downtown Vienna. Take U-4 (which conveniently leaves from Karlsplatz) to Schönbrunn (direction: Hütteldorf) and follow signs for *Schloss Schönbrunn*. Exit bearing right, then cross the busy road and continue to the right, to the far, far end of the long yellow building. There you'll find the visitors center, where tickets are sold.

Cost: Visits to the palace are by timed-entry tours. The Imperial Apartments offer two tour options: The best is the 40-room **Grand Tour** (€17.50, 50 minutes, includes audioguide, covered by Sisi Ticket), which includes both the rooms of Franz Josef and Sisi, as well as the (more impressive) Rococo rooms of Maria Theresa. The **Imperial Tour** (€14.20, 35 minutes, includes audioguide) covers only the less-interesting first 22 rooms. For €3 more you can visit with a real guide, but since these live tours are offered only a few times a day, I wouldn't bother.

If venturing beyond the apartments, consider a combo-ticket (available mid-March-Oct only): The €24 **Classic Pass** includes the Grand Tour, as well as the Gloriette viewing terrace, maze, orangery, and privy garden. The €55.50 **Gold Pass** adds on the rest of what's here—Imperial Carriage Museum, zoo, palm house, and desert house.

Hours: Imperial Apartments open daily 8:30-17:30, July-Aug until 18:30, Nov-March until 17:00; gardens generally open 6:30-20:00 but varies with season.

Reservations: In summer and on good-weather weekends, definitely make a reservation. Otherwise you'll likely have to stand in line at the ticket desk, and then you'll probably have to wait again for your assigned entry time—which could be hours later. To get right in, book your entry time in advance online (www.schoenbrunn.at); tickets can also be reserved by phone at least a half-hour ahead and picked up at the visitors center (tel. 01/8111-3239). Those with a Sisi Ticket can enter without a reserved entry time (see page 870 for details).

Other Crowd-Beating Tips: Even with a reserved entry time, the palace can be a jam-packed sauna of shoulder-to-shoulder mobs shuffling through. It's busiest from 9:30 to 12:00. Crowds start to subside after 14:00, so if you don't have a reservation, come late in the day. You can save some time in line by using one of the ticket machines (which sell only Grand Tour and Imperial Tour tickets). If you have time to kill before your entry time, spend it exploring the gardens or Imperial Carriage Museum.

Eating at Schönbrunn: Eating options at the palace range from sit-down restaurants to garden cafés.

▲▲▲Imperial Apartments

In the 1500s, the Habsburgs built a small hunting lodge near a beautiful spring *(schön-brunn),* and for the next three centuries, they made it their summer getaway from stuffy Vienna. The palace's exterior (late-1600s) is Baroque, but the interior was finished under Maria Theresa (mid-1700s) in let-them-eat-cake Rococo.

Visiting the Apartments: Your tour of the apartments, accompanied by an audioguide, follows a clearly signed one-way route. Think of the following minitour as a series of bread crumbs, leading you along while the audioguide fills in the details. Note that no photos are allowed in the Imperial Apartments.

Begin in the **guards' room,** where jauntily dressed mannequins of Franz Josef's bodyguards introduce you to his luxurious world. Continue through the Billiard Room to the **Walnut Room.** Wow. Rococo-style wood paneling and gilding decorate this room where Franz Josef—a hard-working modern monarch—received official visitors. Nearby is the **study**—Franz Josef (see his mustachioed portrait) worked at this desk, sometimes joined by his beautiful, brown-haired wife Sisi (see her portrait). In the **bedchamber,** where he died barely more than a century ago, a praying stool, iron bed, and little toilet all attest to Franz Josef's spartan lifestyle (though the paintings here remind us of the grand scale of his palace).

Empress Sisi's Study and Dressing Room: See her portrait in a black dress, as well as (a reconstruction of) the spiral staircase that once led down to her apartments. The long-haired mannequin and makeup jars in the dressing room indicate how obsessive Sisi was about her looks.

Franz Josef's and Sisi's Bedroom: The huge wood-carved double bed suggests marital bliss, but the bed is not authentic—and as for the bliss, history suggests otherwise. Nearby is **Sisi's salon.** Though this was Sisi's reception room, the pastel paintings show her husband's distinguished ancestors—the many children of Maria Theresa (including Marie-Antoinette, immediately to the left as you enter).

Follow along to the **dining room.** The whole family ate here at the huge table; today it's set with dinnerware owned by Maria Theresa and Sisi. Next is the **children's room,** with portraits of Maria Theresa (on the easel) and some of her 11 (similar-looking) daughters.

Hall of Mirrors: In this room, six-year-old Mozart performed for Maria Theresa and her family (1762). He amazed them by playing without being able to see the keys, he jumped playfully into the empress' lap, and he even asked six-year-old Marie-Antoinette to marry him.

Great Gallery: Imagine the parties they had here: waltzers spinning across the floor, lit by chandeliers reflecting off the mirrors, beneath stunning ceiling frescoes, while enjoying views of the gardens and the Gloriette monument (described below). When WWII bombs rained on Vienna, the palace was largely spared. It took only one direct hit—crashing through this ballroom—but, thankfully, that bomb was a dud.

More Fancy Rooms: It was in the **Blue Chinese Salon,** in 1918, that the last Habsburg emperor made the decision to relinquish power. Up next, the black-lacquer **Vieux-Laque Room** may convince you the Grand Tour ticket was worth the extra euros. Continue to the **Napoleon Room.** When Napoleon conquered Austria, he took over Schönbrunn and made this his bedroom. He dumped Josephine and took a Habsburg princess as his bride, and they had a son (cutely pictured holding a wreath of flowers).

Rich Bedchamber: This darkened room has what may have been Maria Theresa's wedding bed, where she and her husband Franz produced 16 children. Then comes their **study,** with a fitting end to this palace tour—a painting showing the happy couple who left their mark all over Schönbrunn.

▲▲Palace Gardens

The large, manicured grounds fill the palace's backyard, dominated by a hill-topping monument called the Gloriette. Unlike the gardens of Versailles, meant to shut out the real world, Schönbrunn's park was opened to the public in 1779 while the monarchy was in full swing. It was part of Maria Theresa's reform policy, making the garden a celebration of the evolution of civilization from autocracy into real democracy.

Today it's a delightful, sprawling place to wander—especially on a sunny day. You can spend hours here, enjoying the views and the people-watching. And most of the park is free, as it has been for more than two centuries (open daily sunrise to dusk, entrance on either side of the palace). Note that a number of specialty features in the gardens charge admission but are included in the Schönbrunn passes described earlier (under "Cost").

If the weather is good, huff up the zigzag path above the Neptune Fountain to the **Gloriette,** a purely decorative monument celebrating an obscure Austrian military victory. To gain access to the view terraces, you can pay for a pricey drink in the café or shell out for an admission ticket (€3.80)—but views are about as good from the lawn just in front of the monument.

Getting Around the Gardens: A tourist train makes the rounds all day, connecting Schönbrunn's many attractions (€7, 2/ hour in peak season, none Nov-mid-March, one-hour circuit).

Schönbrunn Zoo (Tiergarten Schönbrunn)

The world's oldest zoo, next door to the palace grounds, was built in 1752 by Maria Theresa's husband for the entertainment and education of the court. He later opened it up to the public—provided that they wore proper attire. Today, it's a modern A (anteater) to Z (zebra) menagerie that's especially appealing to families.

Cost and Hours: Adults-€18.50, kids-€9, daily 9:00-18:30, closes earlier off-season, www.zoovienna.at.

▲Imperial Carriage Museum (Kaiserliche Wagenburg)

The Schönbrunn coach museum is a 19th-century traffic jam of 50 impressive royal carriages and sleighs. It's overpriced (but worth the time if you've paid for the Schönbrunn Gold Pass). Highlights include silly sedan chairs, the death-black hearse carriage (used for Franz Josef in 1916, and most recently for Empress Zita in 1989), and an extravagantly gilded imperial carriage pulled by eight Cinderella horses.

Cost and Hours: €8, daily 9:00-17:00, Nov-April until 16:00, audioguide-€2, 200 yards from palace, walk through right arch as you face palace, tel. 01/525-243-470, www. kaiserliche-wagenburg.at.

Entertainment in Vienna

Vienna—the birthplace of what we call classical music—still thrives as Europe's music capital. On any given evening, you'll have your choice of opera, Strauss waltzes, Mozart chamber concerts, and lighthearted musicals. The Vienna Boys' Choir lives up to its worldwide reputation.

Besides music, you can spend an evening enjoying art, watching a classic film, or sipping Viennese wine in a village wine garden. Save some energy for Vienna after dark.

MUSIC

In Vienna, it's music *con brio* from September through June, reaching a symphonic climax during the Vienna Festival each May and June. Sadly, in summer (generally July and August), the Boys' Choir, opera, and many other serious music companies are—like you—on vacation. But Vienna hums year-round with live classical music; touristy, crowd-pleasing shows are always available.

For music lovers, Vienna is also an opportunity to make pilgrimages to the homes (now mostly small museums) of favorite composers. If you're a fan of Schubert, Brahms, Haydn, Beethoven, or Mozart, there's a sight for you. But I find these homes inconveniently located and generally underwhelming. The centrally located Haus der Musik (see page 887) is my favorite setting for celebrating the great musicians and composers who called Vienna home.

Venues: Vienna remains the music capital of Europe, with 10,000 seats in various venues around town mostly booked with classical performances. The best-known entertainment venues are the Staatsoper (State Opera House), the Volksoper (for musicals and operettas), the Theater an der Wien (opera and other performances), the Wiener Musikverein (home of the Vienna Philharmonic Orchestra), and the Wiener Konzerthaus (various events). Schedules for these venues are listed in the monthly *Wien-Programm* (available at TI). You can also check event listings at www.viennaconcerts.com.

Buying Tickets: Most tickets run from €45 to €60 (plus a stiff booking fee when purchased in advance by phone or online, or through a box office like the one at the TI). A few venues charge as little as €30; look around if you're not set on any particular concert. While it's easy to book tickets online long in advance, spontaneity is also workable, as there are invariably people selling their extra tickets at face value or less outside the door before concert time. If you call a concert hall directly, they can advise you on the availability of (cheaper) tickets at the door. Vienna takes care of its starving artists (and tourists) by offering cheap standing-room tickets to top-notch music and opera (generally an hour before each performance).

Vienna Boys' Choir (Wiener Sängerknaben)

The boys sing (from a high balcony, heard but not seen) at the 9:15 Sunday Mass from mid-September through June in the Hofburg's **Imperial Music Chapel** (Hofmusikkapelle). The entrance is at Schweizerhof; you can get there from In der Burg square or go through the tunnel from Josefsplatz.

Reserved seats must be booked in advance (€10-36; reserve by fax, email, or mail: fax from the US 011-431-533-992-775, send email to office@hofmusikkapelle.gv.at, or write Wiener Hofmusik-kapelle, Hofburg-Schweizerhof, 1010 Wien; call 01/533-9927 for information only—they can't book tickets at this number; www. hofmusikkapelle.gv.at).

Much easier, standing room inside is free and open to the first 60 who line up. Even better, rather than line up early, you can simply swing by and stand in the narthex just outside, where you can hear the boys and see the Mass on a TV monitor.

The Boys' Choir also performs at the **MuTh** concert hall on Fridays at 17:30 in September and October (€39-89, Am Augar-tenspitz 1 in Augarten park, U: Taborstrasse, tel. 01/347-8080, www.muth.at, tickets@muth.at).

They're talented kids, but, for my taste, not worth all the commotion. Remember, many churches have great music during Sunday Mass. Just 200 yards from the Hofburg's Boys' Choir chapel, the Augustinian Church has a glorious 11:00 service each Sunday (see page 879).

Opera
Vienna State Opera (Wiener Staatsoper)

The Vienna State Opera puts on 300 performances a year (in July and August the singers rest their voices or go on tour). Since there are different operas nearly nightly, you'll see big trucks out back and constant action backstage—all the sets need to be switched each day. The excellent "electronic libretto" translation screens help make the experience worthwhile for opera newbies.

Opera Tickets: Main-floor seats go for €120-200; bargain hunters get limited-view seats for €13-30. You can book tickets in advance by phone (tel. 01/513-1513, phone answered daily 10:00-21:00) or online (www.wiener-staatsoper.at). In person, head to one of the opera's two box offices: on the west side of the building (across Operngasse and facing the opera house), or the smaller one just under the big screen on the east side of the opera (facing Kärnt-ner Strasse; both offices open Mon-Fri 9:00 until two hours before each performance, Sat 9:00-12:00, closed Sun).

VIENNA

Standing-Room Tickets: Unless Placido Domingo is in town, it's easy to get one of 567 standing-room tickets (*Stehplätze*, €3 up top or €4 downstairs, can purchase one ticket/person). While the front doors open one hour before the show starts, a side door (middle of building, on the Operngasse side) opens 80 minutes before curtain time, giving those in the know an early grab at standing-room tickets. Just walk straight in, then head right until you see the ticket booth marked *Stehplätze*. If fewer than 567 people are in line, there's no need to line up early. If you're one of the first 160 in line, try for the €4 "Parterre" section and you'll end up dead-center at stage level, directly under the Emperor's Box. Otherwise, you can choose between the third floor *(Balkon)*, or the fourth floor *(Galerie)*, though regulars prefer these sections because each ticket holder gets a section of railing along with a digital screen to read the libretto. Dress is casual (but do your best) at the standing-room bar. Locals save their spot along the rail by tying a scarf to it. Once you've saved your spot with your scarf, you can leave to check your belongings.

Rick's Crude Tip: For me, three hours is a lot of opera. But just to see and hear Vienna's opera in action for a half-hour is a treat. And if you go, you'll get the added entertainment of seeing Vienna all dressed up. I'd buy a standing-room ticket and plan to just watch the first part of the show.

"Live Opera on the Square": Demonstrating its commitment to bringing opera to the masses, each spring and fall the Vienna State Opera projects several performances live on a huge screen on its building, puts out chairs for the public to enjoy...and it's all free. (These projected performances are noted as *Oper Live am Platz* in the official opera schedule—posted all around the opera building; they are also listed in the *Wien-Programm* brochure and at www.wiener-staatsoper.at—select "News," then "Staatsoper outdoors.")

Vienna Volksoper

For less-serious operettas and musicals, try Vienna's other opera house, located along the Gürtel, west of the city center (see *Wien-Programm* brochure or ask at TI for schedule, Währinger Strasse 78, tel. 01/5144-43670, www.volksoper.at).

Theater an der Wien

Considered the oldest theater in Vienna, this venue was designed in 1801 for Mozart operas—intimate, with just a thousand seats. It treats Vienna's music lovers to a different opera every month—generally Mozart with a contemporary setting and modern interpretation. Although Vienna now supports three opera companies, this is the only company playing through the summer (facing the Naschmarkt at Linke Wienzeile 6, tel. 01/58885, www.theater-wien.at).

Touristy Mozart and Strauss Concerts

Powdered-wig orchestra performances are given almost nightly in grand traditional settings (€30-60). You'll get second-rate chamber orchestras, clad in historic costumes, performing the greatest hits of Mozart and Strauss. These are casual, easygoing concerts with lots of tour groups attending. While there's not a Viennese person in the audience, the tourists generally enjoy the evening.

To sort through your options, check with the ticket office in the TI (same price as on the street, but with all venues to choose from). Savvy locals suggest getting the cheapest tickets, as no one seems to care if cheapskates move up to fill unsold pricier seats.

Mozarthaus Concert Venue

Of the many fine venues in Vienna, the **Sala Terrena at Mozarthaus** might be my favorite. Intimate chamber-music concerts take place in a small room richly decorated in Venetian Renaissance style (€49-59, Thu-Fri and Sun at 19:30, Sat at 18:00, near St. Stephen's Cathedral at Singerstrasse 7, tel. 01/911-9077, www.concert-in-vienna.com). Don't confuse this with the Mozarthaus Vienna Museum on Domgasse, which also holds concerts.

Strauss and Mozart Concerts in the Kursalon

For years, Strauss and Mozart concerts have been held in the Kursalon, the hall where the "Waltz King" himself directed wildly popular concerts 100 years ago (€42-65, concerts generally nightly at 20:15, Johannesgasse 33 at corner of Parkring, tram #2: Weihburggasse or U: Stadtpark, tel. 01/512-5790 to check on availability—generally no problem to reserve—or buy online at www.soundofvienna.at). Shows last two hours and are a mix of ballet, waltzes, and a 15-piece or-

chestra. It's touristy—tour guides holding up banners with group numbers wait out front after the show. Even so, the performance is playful, visually fun, fine quality for most, and with a tried-and-tested, crowd-pleasing format.

NIGHTLIFE

Vienna is a great place to just be out and about on a balmy evening. While tourists are attracted to the historic central district and its charming, floodlit corners, locals go else-where. Depending on your mood and taste, you can join them. Survey and then enjoy lively scenes with bars, cafés, trendy restaurants, and theaters in these areas: **Donaukanal** (the Danube Canal, especially popular in the summer for its imported beaches); **Naschmarkt** (after the produce stalls close up, the bars and eateries bring new life to the place through the evening; see page 897); **MuseumsQuartier** (surrounded by far-out museums, a young scene of bars with local students filling the courtyard; see page 894); and **City Hall** (on the parklike Rathausplatz, where in summer free concerts and a food circus of eateries attract huge local crowds—described next).

Open-Air Music-Film Series and Food Circus

A convivial, free-to-everyone people scene erupts each evening in summer (July-Aug) on Rathausplatz, the welcom-ing park in front of City Hall (right on the Ringstrasse). Thousands of people keep a food circus of simple stalls busy. There's not a plastic cup anywhere, just real plates and glasses—Vienna wants the quality of eating to be as high as the music that's about to begin. And most stalls are outposts of local restaurants—including some of Vienna's most esteemed—making this a fun and easy way to sample some of the city's most interesting options. About 2,000 spots on comfy benches face a 60-foot-wide screen up against the City Hall's Neo-Gothic facade. When darkness falls, an announcer explains the program, and then the music starts. The program is different every night—mostly films of opera and classical concerts, but with some jazz and R&B too. Ask at the TI or check www.filmfestival-rathausplatz.at for the schedule (programs generally last about 2 hours, starting when it's dark—between 21:30 in July and 20:30 in Aug).

Balls and Waltzing

Renowned for its ball scene, Vienna boasts hundreds of balls each year, where the classic dance is the waltz. The height of ball sea-son falls generally between December and February, when Vien-nese and visitors of all ages dress up and swirl to music ranging from waltzes to jazz to contemporary beats. Balls are put on by the Vienna Philharmonic, Vienna Boys' Choir, Vienna State Opera, and others (search for events at www.events.wien.info). The glam-orous **Hofburg Silvesterball** takes place on New Year's Eve at the Hofburg Palace, featuring big-name orchestras, bands, and opera singers, a sumptuous dinner, and champagne toast (www.hofburgsilvesterball.com).

English Cinema

Several great theaters offer three or four screens of English movies nightly (€6-9). **Burg Kino,** a block from the opera house, facing the Ring (see below), tapes its weekly schedule to the door—box office opens 30 minutes before each showing. **English Cinema Haydn** is near my recommended hotels on Mariahilfer Strasse (Mariahilfer Strasse 57, tel. 01/587-2262, www.haydnkino.at), and **Artis International Cinema** is right in the town center a few minutes from the cathedral (Schultergasse 5, tel. 01/535-6570).

The Third Man at Burg Kino

This movie is set in 1949 Vienna—when it was divided, like Berlin, between the four victorious Allies. Reliving the cinematic tale of a divided city about to fall under Soviet rule and rife with smuggling is an enjoyable two-hour experience while in Vienna (€7-9, in English; about 3 showings weekly—usually Sun afternoon, Fri evening, and Tue early evening; Opernring 19, tel. 01/587-8406, www.burgkino.at).

Third Man fans will love the quirky **Third Man Museum** (Dritte Mann Museum,) a lovingly curated collection of artifacts about the film, its popularity around the world, and postwar Vienna (€9, ask about Rick Steves discount, Sat only 14:00-18:00, also some guided tours on summer Wed at 14:00—confirm on website; U: Kettenbrückengasse, a long block south of the Naschmarkt at Pressgasse 25, tel. 01/586-4872, www.3mpc.net).

Sleeping in Vienna

Accommodations in Vienna are plentiful and relatively cheap—a €100 double here might go for €150 in Munich and €200 in Milan. Within the Ring, you'll need to shell out over €100 for a double room with bath. But around Mariahilfer Strasse, two people can stay comfortably for €75. Expect rates to spike for conventions (most frequent Sept-Oct) and to drop in November and from January to March.

Viennese elevators and stairwells can be confusing: In most of Europe, 0 is the ground floor, and 1 is the first floor up (our "second floor"). But in Vienna, thanks to a Habsburg-legacy quirk, older buildings have at least one extra "mezzanine" floor (labeled on elevators as P, H, M, and/or A) between the ground floor and the "first" floor, so floor 1 can actually be what we'd call the second, third, or even fourth floor.

Sleep Code

Hotels are classified based on the average price of a standard double room with breakfast in high season.

$$$$	**Splurge:** Most rooms over €170
$$$	**Pricier:** €130-170
$$	**Moderate:** €90-130
$	**Budget:** €50-90
¢	**Backpacker:** Under €50
RS%	**Rick Steves discount**

Unless otherwise noted, credit cards are accepted, hotel staff speak basic English, and free Wi-Fi is available. Comparison-shop by checking prices at several hotels (on each hotel's own website, on a booking site, or by email). For the best deal, *book directly with the hotel.* Ask for a discount if paying in cash; if the listing includes **RS%**, request a Rick Steves discount.

For more tips on accommodations, see the "Sleeping" section in the Practicalities chapter.

WITHIN THE RING, IN THE OLD CITY CENTER

You'll pay extra to sleep in the atmospheric old center, but if you can afford it, staying here gives you the classiest Vienna experience and enables you to walk to most sights.

$$$$ Hotel am Stephansplatz is a four-star business hotel with 56 rooms. It's plush but not over-the-top, and reasonably priced for its sleek comfort and incredible location facing the cathedral. Every detail is modern and quality, and breakfast is superb, with a view of the city waking up around the cathedral (air-con, elevator, gym and sauna, Stephansplatz 9, U: Stephansplatz, tel. 01/534-050, www.hotelamstephansplatz.at, office@hotelamstephansplatz.at).

$$$ Pension Aviano is a peaceful, family-run place and is the best value among my pricier listings. It has 17 rooms, all comfortable and some beautiful, with flowery carpets and other Baroque frills. It's high above the old-center action on the third and fourth floors of a typical city-center building (completely nonsmoking, fans, elevator, between Neuer Markt and Kärntner Strasse at Marco d'Avianogasse 1, tel. 01/512-8330, www.secrethomes.at, aviano@secrethomes.at, Frau Kavka).

$$$ Hotel Pertschy, circling an old courtyard, is big and hotelesque. Its 56 huge rooms are elegantly creaky, with chandeliers and Baroque touches. Those on the courtyard are quietest (non-smoking rooms, elevator, Habsburgergasse 5, U: Stephansplatz, tel. 01/534-490, www.pertschy.com, info@pertschy.com).

$$$ Hotel zur Wiener Staatsoper is quiet, with a more

Hotels in Central Vienna

1. Hotel am Stephansplatz
2. Pension Aviano
3. Hotel Pertschy
4. Hotel zur Wiener Staatsoper
5. Pension Nossek
6. Motel One Staatsoper
7. Pension A und A
8. Pension Suzanne
9. Schweizer Pension
10. Pension Neuer Markt
11. Pension Dr. Geissler

traditional elegance than many of my other listings. Its 22 tidy rooms come with high ceilings, chandeliers, and fancy carpets on parquet floors (fans on request, elevator, a block from the opera house at Krugerstrasse 11; U: Karlsplatz; tel. 01/513-1274, www. zurwienerstaatsoper.at, office@zurwienerstaatsoper.at, manager Claudia).

$$$ Pension Nossek offers 32 rooms right on the wonderful Graben...but an elevator takes you above any street noise into a calm realm tastefully decorated with lace and flowers, and with a small guest sitting room (air-con, elevator, Graben 17, U: Stephansplatz, tel. 01/5337-0410, www.pension-nossek.at, reservation@pension-nossek.at, Susanne).

$$$ Motel One Staatsoper, part of a German chain of "budget design hotels," features sleek, smallish, modern rooms outfitted with quality materials but no frills, a 24-hour reception but minimal service, fantastic lounge spaces, and refreshingly straightforward pricing. This location—right between the opera house and Karlsplatz—has 400 rooms, including some larger options, in a smartly renovated building that's kept its Old World charm (no triples but you can slip in a child under 13 for free, breakfast extra, air-con, elevator, Elisabethstrasse 5, U: Karlsplatz, tel. 01/585-0505, www.motel-one.com, wien-staatsoper@motel-one.com).

$$ Pension A und A, a friendly nine-room B&B run by Andreas and Andrea, offers an elegant, modern break from crusty old Vienna. This place, conveniently located just off the Graben, has a nice entryway and period elevator—but open the door and you'll find white minimalist hallways and contemporary style in the rooms (air-con, Habsburgergasse 3, U: Stephansplatz, tel. 01/890-5128, www.aunda.at, office@aunda.at).

$$ Pension Suzanne, as Baroque and doily as you'll find in this price range, is wonderfully located a few yards from the opera house. It's small, but run with the class of a bigger hotel. The 26 rooms are packed with properly Viennese antique furnishings and paintings (spacious apartment for up to 6 also available, fans on request, elevator, Walfischgasse 4; U: Karlsplatz and follow signs for Opera exit; tel. 01/513-2507, www.pension-suzanne.at, info@pension-suzanne.at, delightfully run by manager Michael).

$$ Schweizer Pension has been family-owned for four generations (and welcomed me on one of my first visits to Vienna). Anita and her son Gerald offer lots of tourist info and 11 homey rooms with parquet floors and a great price (four of the rooms have shared facilities). It does feel kind of Swiss—tidy and well-run (cash only, completely nonsmoking, elevator, full-service laundry-€18/load, Heinrichsgasse 2, U: Schottenring, tel. 01/533-8156, www.schweizerpension.com, office@schweizerpension.com). They also rent a quad with bath (too small for 4 adults but great for a family of 2 adults/2 kids under age 15).

$$ Pension Neuer Markt is family-run and perfectly central, with 37 comfy but faded rooms, and hallways with a cruise-ship ambience (in hot weather request a quiet courtyard-side room when you reserve, fans, elevator, Seilergasse 9, U: Stephansplatz, tel. 01/512-2316, www.hotelpension.at, neuermarkt@hotelpension.at, Wolfgang).

$ Pension Dr. Geissler, a respectable budget option, has 23 plain-but-comfortable rooms on the eighth floor of a modern, nondescript apartment building just off Schwedenplatz, about 10 blocks northeast of St. Stephen's, near the Bratislava ferry terminal (elevator, Wi-Fi in most rooms, Postgasse 14, U: Schwedenplatz— Postgasse is to the left as you face Hotel Capricorno, tel. 01/533-2803, www.hotelpension.at, dr.geissler@hotelpension.at).

ON OR NEAR MARIAHILFER STRASSE

Lively, pedestrianized Mariahilfer Strasse connects the Westbahn-hof and the city center. The U-3 subway line runs underneath the street on its way between the Westbahnhof and St. Stephen's Cathedral, and most of these listings are within a five-minute walk of a U-Bahn stop. This vibrant, inexpensive area is filled with stores, cafés, and even a small shopping mall. Its smaller hotels and pensions are generally immigrant-run, often by well-established Hungarian families. As you'd expect, the far end of Mariahilfer Strasse (around and past the Westbahnhof) is rougher around the edges, while the section near downtown is more gentrified.

Closer to Downtown

$$$ NH Atterseehaus Suites, part of a Spanish chain, is a stern, stylish-but-passionless business hotel on Mariahilfer Strasse. It rents 73 rooms, including a few "suites" that are ideal for families (breakfast is a lot extra, nonsmoking rooms, air-con, elevator, pay parking, Mariahilfer Strasse 78, U: Zieglergasse, tel. 01/524-5600, www.nh-hotels.com, nhatterseehaus@nh-hotels.com).

$$ Hotel Pension Corvinus is bright, modern, and proudly and warmly run by a Hungarian family: parents Miklós and Judit and sons Anthony and Zoltán. Its 15 comfortable rooms are spacious, and some are downright sumptuous, with nice extra touches (2 percent discount if you pay cash, ask about family rooms and apartments with kitchens, air-con, elevator, parking-€18/day, on the third floor at Mariahilfer Strasse 57, U: Neubaugasse, tel. 01/587-7239, www.corvinus.at, hotel@corvinus.at).

$$ Hotel Kugel is run with pride and attitude by the gentlemanly, hands-on owner, Johannes Roller. Its 25 fine rooms have Old World charm and are a good value, especially for families (free minibar, completely nonsmoking, some tram noise, Siebenstern-gasse 43, at corner with Neubaugasse, U: Neubaugasse, tel. 01/523-3355, www.hotelkugel.at, office@hotelkugel.at).

$$ Haydn Hotel is a formal-feeling business hotel one floor below Hotel Corvinus, with 21 bland, spacious, modern rooms (RS%, suites and family apartments, completely nonsmoking, air-con, elevator, pay parking, Mariahilfer Strasse 57, U: Neubaugasse, tel. 01/5874-4140, www.haydn-hotel.at, info@haydn-hotel.at, Nouri).

$ Hotel Pension Mariahilf's 12 rooms are clean, well-priced, and good-sized (if a bit outmoded), with high ceilings. Just steps from the U-Bahn, it's especially convenient (breakfast served in supermarket across the street Mon-Sat and in lobby Sun, elevator, pay parking, Mariahilfer Strasse 49, U: Neubaugasse, tel. 01/586-1781, www.mariahilf-hotel.at, info@mariahilf-hotel.at, Babak).

VIENNA

$ K&T Boardinghouse rents five modern, spacious rooms on the first floor of a quiet building a block off Mariahilfer Strasse (cash only but reserve with credit card, 2-night minimum, no breakfast, air-con–€8/day, coffee in rooms, Chwallagasse 2, U: Neubaugasse, tel. 01/523-2989, mobile 0676-553-6063, www.ktboardinghouse.at, kt2@chello.at, run by Tina, who also guides day trips to Hungary and Slovakia). From Mariahilfer Strasse, turn left at Café Ritter and walk down Schadekgasse one short block; tiny Chwallagasse is the first right.

$ Pension Kraml is a charming, 17-room place tucked away on a small street between Mariahilfer Strasse and the Naschmarkt. It's family-run and feels classic, with breakfast served in the per-fectly preserved family restaurant (no longer in operation) that the owner's grandmother ran in the 1950s. The rooms, which surround a pleasantly leafy courtyard, are big and quiet, with a homey, Old World ambience (family apartment available, no elevator, Brauer-gasse 5, midway between U: Zieglergasse and Pilgramgasse, tel. 01/587-8588, www.pensionkraml.at, pension.kraml@chello.at, Stephan Kraml).

$ Pension Hargita rents 24 bright and attractive rooms (most-ly twins) with woody Hungarian-village decor. While the pension is directly on bustling Mariahilfer Strasse, its windows block noise well. Don't let the dark entryway put you off—this spick-and-span, well-located place is a great value (cash preferred, breakfast extra, completely nonsmoking, lots of stairs and no elevator, air-con in common areas, bike parking, corner of Mariahilfer Strasse at Andreasgasse 1, right at U: Zieglergasse, tel. 01/526-1928, www.hargita.at, pension@hargita.at, Erika and Tibor).

Near the Westbahnhof

$$ Motel One Westbahnhof, a more affordable outpost of the

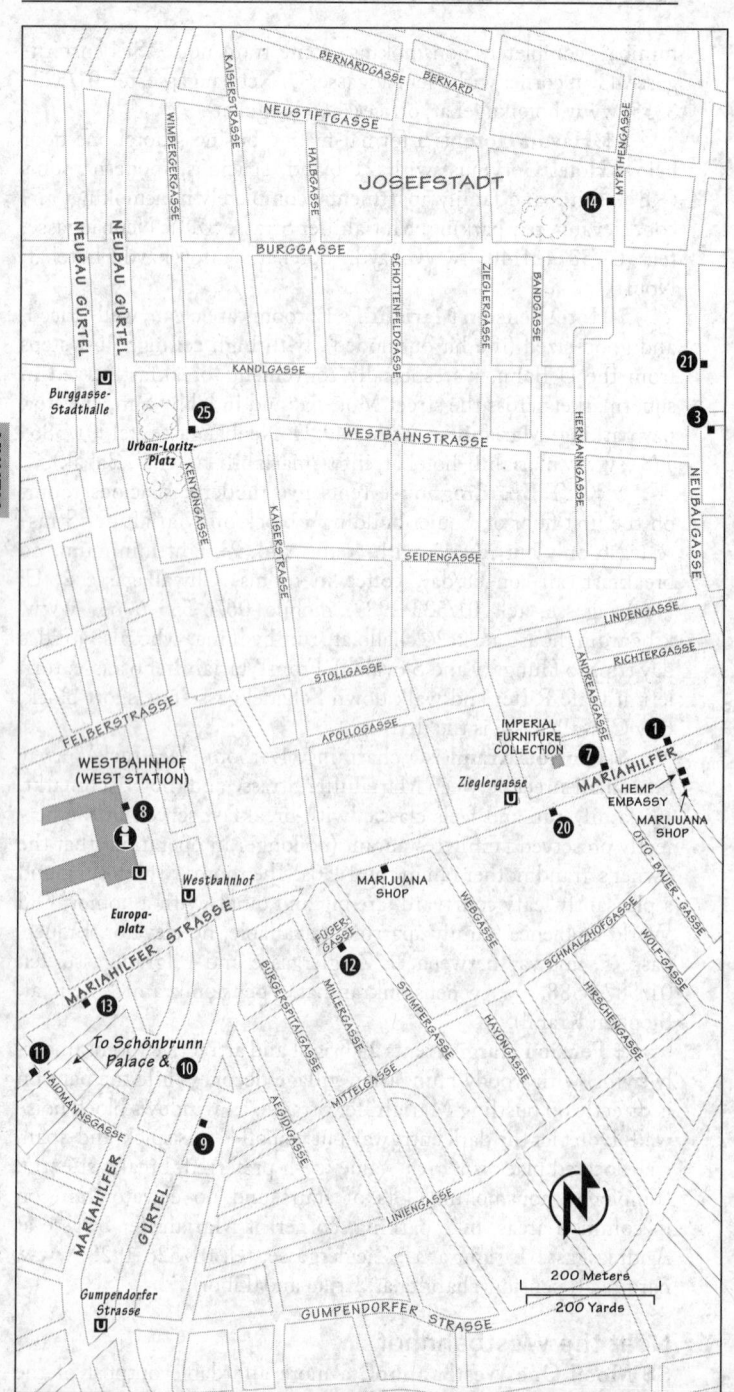

Hotels & Restaurants near Mariahilfer Strasse

VIENNA

Accommodations

❶ NH Atterseehaus Suites
❷ Hotel Pension Corvinus, Haydn Hotel & Cinema
❸ Hotel Kugel
❹ Hotel Pension Mariahilf
❺ K&T Boardinghouse
❻ Pension Kraml
❼ Pension Hargita
❽ Motel One Westbahnhof
❾ Hotel Ibis Wien Mariahilf
❿ To Pension Fünfhaus
⓫ Hostel Ruthensteiner
⓬ Westend City Hostel
⓭ Wombat's City Hostels (2)
⓮ Hostel Wien

Eateries & Other

⓯ Amerlingbeisl
⓰ Zu Ebener Erde und Erster Stock
⓱ Witwe Bolte
⓲ Plutzer Bräu
⓳ Glacis Beisl
⓴ Trześniewski
㉑ Schnitzelwirt
㉒ Akakiko Sushi & Merkur Supermarket
㉓ Naschmarkt
㉔ Café Sperl
㉕ Launderette

chain described on page 915, has 441 rooms (no triples but you can slip in a child under 13 for free, breakfast extra, air-con, pay parking, attached to the Westbahnhof at Europaplatz 3, tel. 01/359-350, www.motel-one.com, wein-westbahnhof@motel-one.com). They also have locations near the Hauptbahnhof (Gerhard-Bronner-Strasse 11, tel. 01/602-0000, wien-hauptbahnhof@motel-one.com) and near the Prater (Ausstellungsstrasse 40, tel. 01/729-7800, wien-prater@motel-one.com); prices at both are generally higher than the Westbahnhof location but lower than the Staatsoper location.

$ **Hotel Ibis Wien Mariahilf,** a modern high-rise hotel with American charm, is ideal for anyone tired of quaint old Europe. Its 341 cookie-cutter rooms are bright, comfortable, and modern, with all the conveniences (breakfast extra, air-con, elevator, pay parking; exit Westbahnhof to the right and walk 400 yards, Mariahilfer Gürtel 22, U: Westbahnhof; tel. 01/59998, www.ibishotel.com, h0796@accor.com).

$ **Pension Fünfhaus** is plain, clean, and bare-bones—almost institutional—with tile floors and 47 rooms. The neighborhood is, well...improving (you might see a few ladies loitering late at night), but really not that bad, and this "pension" does the job if you want rock-bottom prices and few services—but try Hargita or Kraml first (cash only, includes very basic breakfast, Wi-Fi in breakfast room, closed mid-Nov-Feb, Sperrgasse 12, U: Westbahnhof, tel. 01/892-3545, www.pension5haus.at, vienna@pension5haus.at, Frau Susi Tersch). Half the rooms are in the main building and half are in the annex at Grandgasse 8, which has good rooms, but its location near the train tracks is a bit sketchy at night. From the station, walk five minutes on Mariahilfer Strasse to #160, then turn right on Sperrgasse.

DORMS AND HOSTELS

These budget-minded options cluster near Mariahilfer Strasse and the Westbahnhof.

¢ **Hostel Ruthensteiner** is your smallest and coziest option, with 100 beds in 4- to 8-bed dorms and lots of little touches (private rooms available with towels included, towel rental in dorms-€1, breakfast extra, nonsmoking, laundry-€6/load, comfy common areas with piano and guitars, bike rental; Robert-Hamerling-Gasse 24; tel. 01/893-4202, www.hostelruthensteiner.com, info@hostelruthensteiner.com). From the Westbahnhof, follow Mariahilfer Strasse away from the center to #149, and turn left on Haidmannsgasse. Go one block, then turn right.

¢ **Westend City Hostel,** just a block from the Westbahnhof and Mariahilfer Strasse, is well-run and well-located in a residential neighborhood, so it's quiet after 20:00. It has a small lounge, high-ceilinged rooms, a tiny back courtyard, and 180 beds in 4- to 12-bed dorms, each with its own bath (cash only, private rooms available, towel purchase-€4.50, breakfast included when you book directly with the hostel, elevator, laundry-€7/load, Fügergasse 3, tel. 01/597-6729, www.westendhostel.at, info@westendhostel.at).

¢ **Wombat's City Hostel** has two well-run locations—both with about 250 beds and 4 to 6 beds per room (private rooms available, bar, generous public spaces; close to the Westbahnhof at Mariahilfer Strasse 137 and near the Naschmarkt at Rechte Wienzeile 35; tel. 01/897-2336, www.wombats-hostels.com, bookvienna@wombats.eu).

¢ **Hostel Wien** is your classic, huge, and well-run official youth hostel, with 260 beds (private rooms available, nonsmoking, towel purchase-€3, nonmembers pay €3.50 extra, Wi-Fi in lobby, always open, no curfew, coin-op laundry, Myrthengasse 7, take bus #48A from Westbahnhof, tel. 01/523-6316, www.1070vienna.at, hostel@chello.at).

Eating in Vienna

The Viennese appreciate the fine points of life, and right up there with waltzing is eating. The city has many atmospheric restaurants. As you ponder the Hungarian and Bohemian influence on many menus, remember that Vienna's diverse empire may be no more, but its flavors linger. In addition to restaurants, this section covers two uniquely Viennese institutions: the city's café culture and its *Heuriger* wine pubs. For a fun foodie guide to Vienna, see www.viennawuerstelstand.com.

EATING TIPS

Austrian Specialties: Traditional Austrian dishes tend to be meat-heavy (although fish is very popular and generally good in this landlocked country). The classic Austrian dish—and a stand-by on menus—is Wiener schnitzel (a veal cutlet that's been pounded flat, breaded, and fried). Pork schnitzel, which is cheaper, is also common. Austrian *Gulasch*, a meat stew, is a favorite comfort food.

Best of the Wurst: Sausage *(Wurst)* is a staple here. Most restaurants offer it (often as the cheapest thing on the menu), but it's more commonly eaten at a takeout stand *(Würstelstand)*.

Sausages can be boiled or grilled. The generic term *Bratwurst* simply means "grilled sausage." *Brühwurst* is boiled. Generally, the darker the weenie, the spicier it is.

At sausage stands, wurst usually comes in or with a roll *(Semmel*—not your typical hot-dog bun). You might be given the choice of a slice of bread *(Brot)*, a pretzel *(Breze)*, or in restaurants, potato salad. Sauces and sides include *Senf* (mustard; ask for *süss*—sweet,

---

Restaurant Price Code

I've assigned each eatery a price category, based on the average cost of a typical main course. Drinks, desserts, and splurge items (steak and seafood) can raise the price considerably.

$$$$	**Splurge:** Most main courses over €20
$$$	**Pricier:** €15-20
$$	**Moderate:** €10-15
$	**Budget:** Under €10

In Austria, a *wurst* stand or other takeout spot is **$**; a beer hall, *Biergarten,* or basic sit-down eatery is **$$**; a casual but more upscale restaurant is **$$$**; and a swanky splurge is **$$$$**.

---

or *scharf*—spicy), ketchup or curry-ketchup (*Currysauce*—curry-infused ketchup), *Kraut* (sauerkraut), and sometimes horseradish (called *Kren* in Austria and southern Germany).

Smoking in Restaurants: Austria instituted a ban on smoking in public places in 2009, but restaurants and cafés are largely exempt. Recent legislation has again mandated a complete smoking ban in restaurants and bars by 2018. In the meantime, some restaurants have nonsmoking sections, but expect secondhand smoke wherever you sit.

Cafés, Coffee, and Pastries: Vienna is known for its classic cafés—perfect places to sip some coffee and read a newspaper. A café is also a great place to try one of its famous desserts, as Vienna is the birthplace of the Sacher torte and a bevy of other cakes and pastry treats. See "Vienna's Café Culture," later in this section.

Heurigen: Make sure to check out a wine-garden restaurant (or *Heuriger;* the plural is *Heurigen*), nestled in the foothills of the Vienna Woods. At most *Heurigen,* you'll try the latest vintage wine, pick from an assortment of prepared foods, and listen to live music. For more on these, and a list of recommended places, see "*Wein* in Wien: Vienna's Wine Gardens," later in this section.

FINE DINING IN THE CENTER

The heart of the city offers plenty of options for a relaxing and expensive dining experience; here are some of my favorites. Reservations are always wise in the evening.

$$$ Lugeck serves the classics with a modern flair to a local "business casual" crowd with professional service but no pretense. Their slogan: "Genuine classics are always in fashion." Choose between a big, fresh, Art Deco interior and tables on a fine little square under a towering statue of Gutenberg. It's just a block from the recommended Zanoni & Zanoni gelato place—handy if you want a different scene for your dessert course (daily 11:30-23:00, Lugeck 4, tel. 01/512-5060, www.lugeck.com).

$$$ Artner Restaurant am Franziskanerplatz is a classy place with a smartly turned-out crowd (it's a favorite of Austrian politicians). Diners enjoy the cozy interior as well as the outside seating on a quaint square. They offer a meaty and inviting menu with nicely presented dishes, including gourmet hamburgers and great steaks (lunch specials, Mon-Sat 12:00-24:00, closed Sun, Franziskanerplatz 5, tel. 01/503-5034, www.artner.co.at).

Zum Schwarzen Kameel ("The Black Camel") is both a posh, pricey **$$$$** restaurant and a more casual (and affordable) **$$** wine bar. The elegant restaurant is a dark-wood, 12-table, Art Nouveau option serving fine gourmet Viennese cuisine (expensive wine, daily 12:00-24:00, Bognergasse 5, tel. 01/533-8125).

The wine bar, filled with a professional local crowd enjoying small plates from the fancy restaurant kitchen, is *the* place for horseradish and thin-sliced ham (*Beinschinken mit Kren; Achtung*—the horseradish is *hot*). Stand, grab a stool, find a table on the street, or sit anywhere you can—it's customary to share tables in the wine-bar section (no reservations). Fine Austrian wines are sold by the *Achtel* (eighth-liter glass) and listed on the board. They also have a buffet of tiny open-face finger sandwiches. Prices are the same inside or at their streetside outdoor tables.

$$$ Café Restaurant Palmenhaus overlooks the Palace Garden (Burggarten—see page 880). Tucked away in a green and peaceful corner two blocks behind the opera house in the Hofburg's backyard, this is a world apart. If you want to eat modern Austrian cuisine surrounded by palm trees rather than tourists, this is the place. And, since it's at the edge of a huge park, it's great for families. They specialize in fresh fish with generous vegetables—options are listed on the chalkboard (daily 10:00-24:00, Jan-Feb closed Mon-Tue; extensive fine-wine list, indoors in greenhouse or outdoors, Burggarten 1, tel. 01/533-1033).

CASUAL EATERIES AND TRADITIONAL STANDBYS
Near St. Stephen's Cathedral

Each of these eateries is within about a five-minute walk of the cathedral (U: Stephansplatz).

$ Gigerl Stadtheuriger offers a fun, near-*Heuriger* wine cellar experience without leaving the city center. It's self-service for food—just point to what looks good. As in other *Heurigen*, food is sold by the piece or weight; 100 grams *(10 dag)* is about a quarter-pound (cheese and cold meats cost about €5 per 100 grams, salads are about €2 per 100 grams; price sheet posted on wall to right of buffet line). The *Karree* pork with herbs is particularly tasty and tender. They also have entrées, spinach strudel, quiche, *Apfelstrudel*, and, of course, casks of new and local wines sold by the *Achtel*—

VIENNA

1. Lugeck
2. Artner Restaurant am Franziskanerplatz
3. Zum Schwarzen Kameel Rest. & Wine Bar
4. Café Rest. Palmenhaus
5. Gigerl Stadtheuriger
6. Zu den Drei Hacken
7. Trześniewski
8. Reinthaler's Beisl & Café Hawelka
9. Cantinetta La Norma
10. Akakiko Sushi (3)
11. Motto am Fluss Café & Restaurant
12. Aïda Café Konditorei
13. Zanoni & Zanoni Gelateria
14. Restaurant Ofenloch
15. Brezel-Gwölb
16. Biobar von Antun
17. Esterhazykeller

VIENNA

Restaurants in Central Vienna

18 Hopferl Bierhof

19 Julius Meinl am Graben Deli

20 Plachuttas Gasthaus zur Oper

21 Soho Kantine

22 Kurkonditorei Oberlaa, Le Bol Patisserie Bistro & Billa Corso

23 Danieli Ristorante

24 City Hall Food Circus

25 Café Central

26 Café Bräunerhof

27 Café Pruckel

28 Café Tirolerhof

29 Café Landtmann

30 Café Sacher

31 Demel

32 Billa Supermarket

about 4 oz (daily 15:00-24:00, indoor/outdoor seating; behind cathedral, a block off Kärntner Strasse, a few cobbles off Rauhensteingasse on Blumenstock, tel. 01/513-4431).

$$ Zu den Drei Hacken, a fun and typical *Weinstube* (wine pub), is famous for its local specialties (Mon-Sat 11:00-23:00, closed Sun, indoor/outdoor seating, Singerstrasse 28, tel. 01/512-5895).

$$ Trześniewski is an institution—justly famous for its elegant open-face finger sandwiches and small beers. Three different sandwiches and a *kleines Bier (Pfiff)* make a fun, light lunch. Point to whichever delights look tasty (or grab the English translation sheet and take time to study your 22 sandwich options). The classic favorites are *Geflügelleber* (chicken liver), *Matjes mit Zwiebel* (herring with onions), and *Speck mit Ei* (bacon and eggs). Pay for your sandwiches and a drink. Take your drink tokens to the lady on the right. Sit on the bench and scoot over to a tiny table when a spot opens up. You can grab an early, quick dinner here, but the selection can get paltry by the end of the day (Mon-Fri 8:30-19:30, Sat 9:00-17:00, closed Sun; 50 yards off the Graben, nearly across from Café Hawelka; Dorotheergasse 2, tel. 01/512-3291).

They have another branch at Mariahilfer Strasse 95 (near many recommended hotels—see map on page 919, Mon-Fri 8:30-19:00, Sat 9:00-18:00, closed Sun, U: Zieglergasse).

$$ Reinthaler's Beisl is a time warp that serves simple, traditional fare all day. It's handy for its location (a block off the Graben, across the street from Trześniewski) and because it's a rare restaurant in the center that's open on Sunday. Its fun, classic interior winds way back, and it also has a few tables on the quiet street outside (use the handwritten daily menu rather than the printed English one, daily 11:00-22:30, Dorotheergasse 4, tel. 01/513-1249).

$$$ Cantinetta La Norma, a short walk from the cathedral, serves tasty Italian dishes amid a cozy yet energetic ambience. Even on weeknights the small dining area is abuzz with friendly chatter among its multinational, loyal regulars (weekday lunch specials, daily 11:00-24:00, outdoor seating, Franziskaner Platz 3, tel. 01/512-8665, run by friendly Paco and Hany).

$$ Akakiko Sushi is a local chain of pan-Asian restaurants with a Japanese emphasis. Along with sushi, they serve noodle soups, rice dishes, and more, including decent-value bento box meals. With several convenient (and well-signed) locations, they're easy to find: Singerstrasse 4 (a block off Kärntner Strasse near the cathedral), Rotenturmstrasse 6 (also near the cathedral), Heidenschuss 3 (near other recommended eateries just off Am Hof, U: Herrengasse), and Mariahilfer Strasse 42 (fifth floor of Kaufhaus Gerngross, near many recommended hotels, U: Neubaugasse).

Though they lack charm, they're all fast, modern, air-conditioned, and reasonable (daily 10:30-23:30).

Motto am Fluss Café and Restaurant, on the upper floors of the Bratislava riverboat terminal, is good for a bite or drink over-looking the Danube Canal. The classy **$$** café, on the top floor, has indoor and outdoor tables (daily 8:00-24:00, tel. 01/252-5511); the pricier and elegant **$$$** restaurant is one floor down and serves modern cuisine (indoor seating only but with great canal-perch tables, extensive wine-by-the-glass list, three-course lunch specials, daily 11:30-14:30 & 18:00-24:00, tel. 01/252-5510).

$$ Aïda Café Konditorei, while not at all like the famed classic Vienna cafés, is a local fixture. You'll see branches all over town; the flagship is next to the cathedral with a view of the Graben. Locals appreciate the retro pink aprons and reliably good coffee, ice cream, and cakes (flagship café daily 8:00-22:00, 1010 Singer-strasse, tel. 01/890-8988).

Ice Cream: *Gelateria* **Zanoni & Zanoni,** run by an Italian family, is mobbed by happy Viennese hungry for their €2 two-scoop cones. Just two blocks from the cathedral, with a big terrace of tables, it's a classic scene for licking and people-watching (daily until 24:00, Lugeck 7, tel. 01/512-7979).

Near Am Hof Square

The streets around the square called Am Hof (U: Herrengasse) hide atmospheric medieval lanes with both indoor and outdoor eating action. The following eateries are all within a block or two of the square.

$$$ Restaurant Ofenloch serves good, traditional Viennese cuisine with formal service, both indoors and out. This delightfully intimate 300-year-old eatery has a refined yet relaxed ambience (Mon-Sat 11:00-23:00, closed Sun, Kurrentgasse 8, tel. 01/533-8844).

$$ Brezel-Gwölb, a Tolkienesque nook with tight indoor tables and outdoor dining on a quiet little square, serves Viennese classics in an unforgettable atmosphere. With its dark and candlelit interior and secretive-feeling outdoor seating, it's ideal for a roman-tic late-night glass of wine (three-course weekday lunch specials, daily 11:30-24:00; leave Am Hof on Drahtgasse, then take first left to Ledererhof 9; tel. 01/533-8811).

$$ Biobar von Antun is an earthy little place with a calm hippie interior and nice tables on a quiet square. They serve three-course vegan meals (soup, salad, and main course), hearty salads, and fancy juices (Tue-Sun 11:30-14:30 & 17:30-22:30, closed Mon, on Judenplatz at Drahtgasse 3, tel. 01/968-9351, Antun Petrovic).

$$ Esterhazykeller, both ancient and popular, has traditional fare in two serving areas. For a cheap and sloppy buffet, descend to the subbasement, a wine cellar that dates back to 1683. While the food is self-serve from the deli counter (a meal-sized plate costs around €10), you'll order drinks at your table (daily 16:00-23:00, closed July-mid-Sept). For table service from an only slightly pricier menu on a pleasant square, sit upstairs or outside (daily 11:00-23:00, just below Am Hof at Haarhof 1, tel. 01/533-3482).

$$$ Hopferl Bierhof, with lots of tables on the same square, might be a better option if it's hot and you're in the mood for a beer. It has a large, meaty menu and nice ambience, with Ottakringer beer on tap (daily 11:30-24:00, Naglergasse 13, tel. 01/533-4428).

Gourmet Supermarket: Located right on the Graben, **Julius Meinl am Graben,** with two floors of temptations, has been famous since 1862 as a top-end delicatessen with all the gourmet fancies. Assemble a meal from the picnic fixings on the shelves. There's also a café, with light meals and great outdoor seating; a stuffy and pricey restaurant upstairs; and a takeout counter with good benches for people-watching while you munch (shop open Mon-Fri 8:00-19:30, Sat 9:00-18:00, closed Sun; restaurant open Mon-Sat until 24:00, closed Sun; Am Graben 19, tel. 01/532-3334).

Near the Opera

These eateries are within easy walking distance of the opera house (U: Karlsplatz).

$$$ Plachuttas Gasthaus zur Oper, a proudly Austrian place a block from the opera, has a contemporary, classy interior and inviting seating on the street. It specializes in the local classics like *Tafelspitz* (boiled beef, Franz Josef's favorite dish) and Wiener schnitzel—they actually hand out a little souvenir recipe titled "the art of the perfect Wiener Schnitzel" (daily 11:00-24:00, Walfischgasse 5, tel. 01/512-2251).

$ Soho Kantine is a cave-like, government-subsidized cantina, serving the National Library staff but open to all, and offering unexciting, institutional sit-down lunches in the Hofburg. Pay for your meal—your choice of bland meat or bland vegetarian—and a drink at the bar, take your token to the kitchen, and then sit down and eat with the locals. Wednesday is schnitzel day and Friday is fish day (Mon-Fri 11:30-15:00, closed Sat-Sun and mid-July-Aug, hard to find—just past the butterfly house in a forlorn little square, look for *Soho* sign in entry corridor, Burggarten, mobile 0676-309-5161, Reni).

$$ Kurkonditorei Oberlaa may not have the royal and plush fame of Demel (see page 863), but this is where Viennese connoisseurs serious about the quality of their pastries go to get fat. With outdoor seating on Neuer Markt, it's particularly nice on a hot summer day. Upstairs has more temptations and good seating (three-course weekday lunch specials, great selection of cakes, daily 8:00-20:00, Neuer Markt 16, tel. 01/5132-9360).

$$ Le Bol Patisserie Bistro (next to Oberlaa) satisfies your need for something French. The staff speaks to you in French, serving fine salads, baguette sandwiches, and fresh croissants (Mon-Sat 8:00-22:00, Sun 10:00-20:00, Neuer Markt 14, mobile 0699-1030-1899).

$$$ Danieli Ristorante is your best classy Italian bet in the old town. White-tablecloth dressy, but not stuffy, it has reasonable prices. Dine in their elegant back room or on the street (daily 11:30-24:00, 30 yards off Kärntner Strasse opposite Neuer Markt at Himmelpfortgasse 3, tel. 01/513-7913).

Supermarkets: A top-end version of the Billa supermarket chain, **Billa Corso** has three floors of food and sells hot, gourmet, ready-made meals (by weight). You're welcome to sit and enjoy whatever you've purchased in either eating area: inside (air-conditioned) or out on the square. They also have a great deli selection of salads, soups, and picnic items (warm food—€2/100 grams, WC on ground floor, Mon-Fri 8:00-20:00, Sat until 19:00, closed Sun, Neuer Markt 17, on the corner where Seilergasse hits Neuer Markt, tel. 01/961-2133). A nongourmet **Billa** is on a side street around the corner from St. Stephen's Church (Mon-Sat 7:15-19:30, closed Sun, Singerstrasse 6).

Spittelberg

This charming cobbled grid of traffic-free lanes is a favorite dining neighborhood for the Viennese. It's handy, set between the MuseumsQuartier and Mariahilfer Strasse (U: Volkstheater/Museumsplatz). Tables tumble down sidewalks and into breezy courtyards; the charming buildings here date mostly from the early 1800s, before the Mariahilfer Strasse neighborhood was built. It's only worth a special trip on a balmy summer evening, as it's dead in bad weather. Stroll Spittelberggasse, Schrankgasse, and Gutenberggasse, then pick your favorite. Don't miss the vine-strewn wine garden at Schrankgasse 1. To locate these restaurants, see the map on page 919.

$ Amerlingbeisl, with a charming, casual atmosphere both on the cobbled street and in its vine-covered courtyard, is a great value, serving a mix of traditional Austrian and international dishes (check the board with daily specials—some vegetarian, daily 9:00-24:00, Stiftgasse 8, tel. 01/526-1660).

$$$ Zu Ebener Erde und Erster Stock (loosely translated as "Downstairs, Upstairs") is a charming little restaurant with a mostly traditional Austrian menu. Filling a cute 1750 building, it's true to its name, with two dining rooms: casual and woody downstairs (traditionally for the poor); and a fancy Biedermeier-style dining room with red-velvet chairs and violet tablecloths upstairs (where the wealthy convened). There are also a few al fresco tables along the quiet side street. Reservations are smart (seasonal specials, Mon-Fri 12:00-22:00, last seating at 20:00, closed Sat-Sun, Burggasse 13, tel. 01/523-6254, www.zu-ebener-erde-und-erster-stock.at).

$$$ Witwe Bolte is classy. The interior is tight, but its tiny square has a wonderful leafy ambience (daily 11:45-23:00, in July-Aug opens at 17:30 Mon-Fri, Gutenberggasse 13, tel. 01/523-1450).

$$ Plutzer Bräu, next door to Amerlingbeisl, feels a bit more commercial. It's a big, sprawling, impersonal brewpub serving stick-to-your-ribs pub grub: ribs, burgers, traditional dishes, Tirolean beer from the keg—and they also brew their own (daily 11:00-24:00, Schrankgasse 4, tel. 01/526-1215).

$$ Glacis Beisl, at the top edge of the MuseumsQuartier just before Spittelberg, is popular with locals. A gravelly wine garden tucked next to a city fortification, its outdoor tables and breezy ambience are particularly appealing on a balmy evening (weekday lunch specials, daily 11:00-24:00, Breitegasse 4, tel. 01/526-5660).

Mariahilfer Strasse and the Naschmarkt

Mariahilfer Strasse (see map on page 919) is filled with reasonable cafés serving all types of cuisine. For a quick yet traditional bite, consider the venerable **$$ Trześniewski** sandwich bar's branch at Mariahilfer Strasse 95 (see page 926), or its imitators (one is at #91).

$ Schnitzelwirt is an old classic with a 1950s patina and a mixed local and tourist clientele. In this smoky, working-class place, no one finishes their schnitzel (notice the self-serve butcher paper and plastic bags for leftovers). Walk to the nonsmoking section in the back, passing the kitchen piled high with breaded cutlets waiting for the deep fryer. The schnitzels are served with a starch or salad; if you order the smallest portion, you may want to add a side dish. They also serve Austrian standards including *Szegediner Gulasch*. You'll find no tourists, just cheap schnitzel meals (Mon-Sat 11:00-21:30, closed Sun, Neubaugasse 52, U: Neubaugasse, tel. 01/523-3771).

Supermarket: Merkur, in the basement of the Gerngross shopping mall at Mariahilfer Strasse 42, is big and open fairly late during the week (until 20:00, Sat until 18:00, closed Sun, U: Neubaugasse).

Naschmarkt: For a picnic or a trendy dinner, try the Naschmarkt, Vienna's sprawling produce market. This thriving Old World scene comes with plenty of fresh produce, cheap local-style eateries, cafés, kebab and sausage stands, and the best-value sushi in town (Mon-Fri 6:00-18:30, Sat until 17:00, closed Sun, closes earlier in winter; U: Karlsplatz, follow *Karlsplatz* signs out of the station). Picnickers can buy supplies at the market and eat on nearby Karlsplatz (plenty of chairs facing the Karlskirche) or pop into the Burggarten behind the famous Mozart statue.

In recent years, the Naschmarkt has become fashionable for dinner (or cocktails), with an amazing variety of local and ethnic eateries to choose from. Prices are great, the produce is certainly fresh, and the dinners are as local as can be. The best plan: Stroll through the entire market to survey the options, and then pick the place that appeals. For more on the Naschmarkt, see page 897.

VIENNA'S CAFÉ CULTURE

In Vienna, the living room is down the street at the neighborhood coffeehouse. This tradition is just another example of the Viennese expertise in good living. Each of Vienna's many long-established (and sometimes even legendary) coffeehouses has its individual character (and characters). These classic cafés can be a bit tired, with a shabby patina and famously grumpy waiters who treat you like an uninvited guest invading their living room. Yet these spaces somehow also feel welcoming, offering newspapers, pastries, sofas, quick and light workers' lunches, elegant ambience, and "take all the time you want" charm for the price of a cup of coffee. Rather than buy the *International New York Times* ahead of time, spend the money on a cup of coffee and read the paper for free, Vienna-style, in a café.

Café Tips: Once you claim a table or sofa in a café, make a trip to the glass display case to see the pastries of the day. The menu has all the standard offerings, but won't list the specials.

It's standard practice for your coffee to be served on a little silver tray, with a glass of tap water and perhaps a piece of chocolate on the side.

Coffee-Ordering Lingo: As in Italy and France, coffee drinks in Austria are espresso-based. *Kaffee* means coffee and *Milch* is milk; *Obers* is cream, while *Schlagobers* is whipped cream. Here are some Austrian coffee terms: Use them elsewhere, and you'll probably get a funny look (some are unique just to Vienna).

Schwarzer or *Mokka:* Straight, black espresso; order it *kleiner* (small) or *grosser* (big)

Verlängeter ("lengthened"): Espresso with water, like an Americano

Brauner: With a little milk

Schale Gold ("golden cup"): With a little cream (Vienna)

Melange: Like a cappuccino

Franziskaner: A *Melange* with whipped cream rather than foamed milk, often topped with chocolate flakes

Kapuziner: Strong coffee with a dollop of sweetened cream

Verkehrt ("incorrect") or *Milchkaffee:* Two-thirds milk and one-third coffee (Vienna)

Einspänner ("buggy"): With lots and lots of whipped cream, served in a glass with a handle. (It was the drink of horse-and-buggy drivers, who only had one hand free.)

Fiaker ("horse-and-buggy driver"): Black, with kirsch liqueur or rum, served with a *sliwowitz* (plum schnapps) or rum (Vienna)

(Wiener) Eiskaffee: Coffee with ice cream

Maria Theresia: Coffee with orange liqueur

Cafés in the Old Center

These are some of my favorite Viennese cafés located inside the Ring (see map on page 925).

VIENNA

$$ Café Central, while a bit touristy, remains a classic place, lavish under Neo-Gothic columns and celebrated by 19th-century Austrian writers. They serve fancy coffees, breakfasts, two-course weekday lunch specials, and traditional main dishes, and they entertain guests with live piano—schmaltzy tunes on a fine, Vienna-made Bösendorfer each evening from 17:00 to 22:00 (daily 7:30-22:00, Sun from 10:00, corner of Herrengasse and Strauchgasse, U: Herrengasse, tel. 01/533-3764).

$ Café Bräunerhof, between the Hofburg and the Graben, offers classic ambience with few tourists and live music on weekends (light classics, Sat-Sun 15:00-18:00), along with cheap lunches on weekdays (Mon-Fri 8:00-19:30, Sat 8:00-18:00, Sun 10:00-18:00, no hot food after 15:00, Stallburggasse 2, U: Stephansplatz, tel. 01/512-3893).

$ Café Hawelka has a dark, "brooding Trotsky" atmosphere, paintings by struggling artists who couldn't pay for coffee, a saloon-wood flavor, chalkboard menu, smoked velvet couches, an international selection of newspapers, and a phone that rings for regulars. Frau Hawelka died just a couple weeks after Pope John Paul II did. Locals suspect the pontiff wanted her much-loved *Buchteln* (marmalade-filled doughnuts) in heaven. The café, which doesn't serve hot food, remains family-run (daily 8:00-24:00, just off the Graben at Dorotheergasse 6, U: Stephansplatz, tel. 01/512-8230).

Other Classics in the Old Center: All of these places are open long hours daily: **$ Café Pruckel** (at Dr.-Karl-Lueger-Platz, across from Stadtpark at Stubenring 24); **$ Café Tirolerhof** (2 blocks from the opera house, behind the TI on Tegetthoffstrasse, at Führichgasse 8); and **$ Café Landtmann** (directly across from the City Hall on the Ringstrasse at Universitätsring 4). The Landtmann is unique, as it's the only grand café built along the Ring with all the other grand buildings.

Café Sacher (see page 858) and **Demel** (see page 863) are famous for their cakes, but they also serve good coffee drinks.

Near the Naschmarkt
$$ Café Sperl dates from 1880 and is still furnished identically to the day it opened—from the coat tree to the chairs (Mon-Sat 7:00-23:00, Sun 11:00-20:00 except closed in July-Aug, just off the Naschmarkt at Gumpendorfer Strasse 11, U: MuseumsQuartier, tel. 01/586-4158; see map on page 919).

WEIN IN WIEN: VIENNA'S WINE GARDENS
The *Heuriger* (HOY-rih-gur) is unique to Vienna, dating back to the 1780s, when Emperor Josef II decreed that vintners needed no special license to serve their own wines and juices to the public in their own homes. Many families grabbed this opportunity and opened *Heurigen* (HOY-rih-gehn)—wine-garden restaurants.

A tradition was born. Today, *Heurigen* are licensed, but do their best to maintain the old-village atmosphere, serving each fall's vintage until November 11 of the following year, when a new vintage year begins. To go with your wine, a *Heuriger* serves a variety of prepared foods that you choose from a deli counter. This is the most intimidating part of the *Heuriger* experience for tourists, but it's easily conquered—see the sidebar for tips. Some *Heurigen* compromise by offering a regular menu that you can order from. At many establishments, strolling musicians entertain—and ask for tips.

Hours: Most *Heurigen* open up in the afternoon (generally between 14:00 and 16:00) and close late (about 24:00), though some may stop serving food earlier (around 21:00). On Sundays, many places open up a few hours earlier. Some *Heurigen* may close in winter, during the grape-picking season, or just for vacation, so call or check websites if you have a specific place in mind.

Getting There: I've listed two good *Heuriger* neighborhoods, both on the northern outskirts of town. To get here from downtown Vienna, it's best to use public transit (cheap, 30 minutes, runs late in the evening, find specific directions under each section). You can also take a 15-minute taxi ride to any of these neighborhoods (about €20 from the Ring).

Choosing a Place: With more than 1,700 acres of vineyards within Vienna's city limits, there are countless *Heuriger* taverns. Each neighborhood I've described is a square or hub with two or three recommended spots and many other wine gardens worth considering. Wander around, then choose the *Heuriger* with the best atmosphere. Or ask a local—every Viennese will be only too glad to tell you about their favorite. (And for a near-*Heuriger* experience without leaving downtown Vienna, drop by Gigerl

The *Heuriger* Experience

To understand how a traditional *Heuriger* works, think of a full-service deli counter at an American supermarket, with a seating section nearby. Choose from the array of prepared items and hot dishes, pay at the buffet counter, and find a table—the staff will bring your food, nicely arranged on a plate. Then order (and pay for) your wine or other drinks from the waiter who will appear at your table. (That said, many of the *Heurigen* I've listed have regular menus and table service as well.)

A quarter-liter (*Viertel,* FEER-tehl, 8 oz) glass of new wine costs about €2-3. *Most* (mohst) is lightly alcoholic grape juice—wine in its earliest stages, and usually available only in autumn. Once it gets a little more oomph, it's called *Sturm* (shtoorm), also strictly a fall drink—sometimes only during the narrow "*Sturmzeit*" window (late Sept-mid-Oct). Teetotalers can order *Traubenmost* (TROW-behn-mohst), grape juice.

Food is generally sold by weight, often in "*10 dag*" units (that's 100 grams, or about a quarter-pound). The buffet has several sections: The core of your meal is a warm dish, generally meat (such as ham, roast beef, roast chicken, roulade, or meatloaf) carved off a big hunk. There are also warm sides *(Beilagen),* such as casseroles and sauerkraut, and a wide variety of cold salads and spreads. Rounding out the menu are bread and cheese (they'll slice it off for you).

Many *Heuriger* staff speak English, and pointing also works. Here's a menu decoder of items to look for...or to avoid:

Backhühner: Roasted chicken
Blutwurst or **Blunzn:** Blood sausage

Stadtheuriger—see page 923—which has the same deli-counter system as a *Heuriger,* but not the semirural atmosphere.)

Neustift am Walde

This district is farthest from the city but is still easy to reach by public transit. It feels a little less touristy than other places, and is the only area I list where you'll actually see the vineyards.

Getting There: Either take tram #D to Liechtenwerder Platz, or the U-6 subway to Nussdorfer Strasse, then ride bus #35A to the Neustift am Walde stop (leaves from stop across the street from north side of the U-Bahn station). To find the #35A bus stop from the Liechtenwerder Platz tram stop, walk a few steps up Augasse

Bohnen: Big white beans
Bratlfett: Gelatinous jelly made from fat drippings
Erdapfel: Potato
Fleckerl: Noodles
Fleischlaberln: Fried ground-meat patties
Kernöl: Vegetable oil
Knoblauch: Garlic
Knödl: Dumpling
Kornspitz: Whole-meal bread roll
Krapfen: Doughnut
Kren: Horseradish
Kummelbrate: Crispy roast pork with caraway
Lauch: Leek
Leberkäse: Finely ground corned beef, pork, bacon, and onions that's baked as a loaf
Liptauer: Spicy cheese spread
Presskopf: Jellied brains and innards
Roastbeef: Roast beef
Schinken: Ham
Schinkenfleckerln: Ham and noodle casserole
Schmalz: Spread made from rendered pig or goose fat
Spanferkel: Suckling pig
Speck: Fatty bacon
Specklinsen: Lentils with bacon
Stelze: Grilled knuckle of pork
Sulz: Gelatinous brick of meaty goo
Waldbauernflade: Rustic bread
Zwiebel: Onion

in the direction of the tram (away from the city), and around the corner to the right onto Liechtenwerder Platz.

$$ Fuhrgassl Huber, which brags it's the biggest *Heuriger* in Vienna, can accommodate 1,000 people inside and just as many outside. You can lose yourself in its sprawling backyard, with vineyards streaking up the hill from terraced tables. Musicians stroll most nights after 19:00 (opens at 14:00, a few steps past Das Schreiberhaus at Neustift am Walde 68, tel. 01/440-1405, family Huber).

$$ Das Schreiberhaus Heurigen-Restaurant is a popular, family-owned place right at the bus stop. Its creaky, old-time dining rooms are papered with celebrity photos. There are 600 spaces inside and another 600 outside, music nightly after 19:00 unless it's slow, and a cobbled backyard that climbs in steps up to the vineyards. Alone among my listings, this place offers a cheap all-you-can-eat lunch buffet on weekdays until 15:00 (opens at 11:00, Rathstrasse 54, tel. 01/440-3844).

$$ Weinhof Zimmermann, a 10-minute uphill walk from the bus stop, is my favorite. It's a sprawling farmhouse where the green tables on patios echo the terraced fields all around. While dining, you'll feel like you're actually right in the vineyard. The idyllic setting comes with rabbits in petting cages, great food, no city views but fine hillside vistas, and wonderful peace (opens at 15:00, closed Mon, tel. 01/440-1207). Get off bus #35A at the Agnesgasse stop (at the corner of Rathstrasse and Agnesgasse—one stop before the Neustift am Walde stop), then hike a block uphill on Agnesgasse and turn left on Mitterwurzergasse to #20.

Nussdorf

An untouristy district, characteristic and popular with the Viennese, Nussdorf has plenty of *Heuriger* ambience. This area feels very real, with a working-class vibe, streets lined with local shops, and characteristic *Heurigen* that feel a little bit rougher around the edges.

Getting There: Take tram #D from the Ringstrasse (stops include the Opera, Hofburg/Kunsthistorisches Museum, and City Hall); just after the Liechtenwerder Platz stop, keep your eyes peeled on the right for the colorful, fantastical Hundertwasser structure (actually a waste-incineration plant) hiding behind a complex of boring buildings. Ride tram #D to its endpoint, the Beethovengang stop (despite what it says on the front of the tram, the Nussdorf stop isn't the end—stay on for one more stop). Exit the tram, cross the tracks, go uphill 40 yards, and look for Schübel-Auer and Kierlinger on your left.

$ Schübel-Auer Heuriger is my favorite here—the back entrance is right at the tram stop, and it offers a big and user-friendly buffet (most dishes are labeled and the patient staff speaks English). Its rustic ambience can be enjoyed indoors or out (opens at 16:00, closed Sun-Mon and mid-Dec-mid-Feb, Kahlenberger Strasse 22, tel. 01/370-2222).

$ Heuriger Kierlinger, next door, is also good, with a particularly rollicking, woody room around its buffet (opens at 15:30, closed most of August and periodically in off-season, Kahlenberger Strasse 20, tel. 01/370-2264).

$$ Bamkraxler ("Tree-Climber") is not a *Heuriger,* but rather a *Biergarten* with a regular menu and table service—which some prefer to the *Heuriger* cafeteria line. It's a fun-loving, family-oriented place with fine keg beer (tapped daily at 17:00) and a big kids' playground (opens at 16:00, closed Mon, open all year, Kahlen-berger Strasse 17, tel. 01/318-8800). To get here from the tram, walk all the way through either of the other listings, pop out on Kahlenberger Strasse, and walk 20 yards uphill.

Vienna Connections

BY TRAIN

Vienna recently finished building an impressive new Hauptbahn-hof (main train station), and is consolidating most—but not all—train departures there. Be sure to confirm which station your train uses. From Vienna's two biggest stations, the handiest connection to the center is the U-Bahn (subway). For some stations, there's also a handy tram connection (see "Vienna's Public Transportation" map on page 848).

For schedules, check Germany's excellent all-Europe time-table at www.bahn.com. The Austrian federal railway's timetable at www.oebb.at includes prices, but it's not as user-friendly as the German site—and it doesn't always remind you about discounts or special passes. For general train information in Austria, call 051-717 (to get an operator, dial 2, then 2).

Wien Hauptbahnhof

Vienna's huge central station (just a few U-Bahn stops south of downtown) has 12 pass-through tracks, shopping, and all the ser-vices you may need—including baggage lockers, a TI desk (daily 9:00-19:00), food court (some outlets open very late), restaurants (including outposts of the recommended Oberlaa pastry shop and Akakiko Sushi), ATMs, grocery stores (some open daily until late), drugstores, bookstores, mobile-phone shops, a car-rental desk (Europcar), and a post office. Most shops are open Mon-Fri until 21:00, Sat until 18:00, and (unlike in the city center) many are open on Sunday.

Getting Between the Station and Vienna: To reach the city center, including all my recommended hotels in the center, ride the U-1 for two to four stops (direction: Leopoldau) to Karlsplatz, Stephansplatz, or Schwedenplatz—from the main hall follow the red *U1* signs; ticket machines are near the escalators. You can also take tram #D (which runs along the Ring) from outside the main entrance. To reach Mariahilfer Strasse, ride U-1 three stops to Stephansplatz, then change to U-3 (direction: Ottaring), or hop on bus #13A. Tram #O runs from the station to Landstrasse and the Wien-Mitte station (for airport trains).

When timing any train trip out of Vienna, keep in mind that the U-Bahn stop is a bit of a walk from the main train platforms—allow at least 10 minutes to get from the U-Bahn stop to your train.

Westbahnhof

This station (at the west end of Mariahilfer Strasse, on the U-3 and U-6 lines) has a modern, user-friendly mall of services, shops, and eateries (including the recommended Trześniewski—near track 9—with cheap-and-elegant finger sandwiches). You'll find travel agencies, grocery stores, ATMs, change offices, a post office, and baggage lockers (on the ground floor by the WC).

Getting Between the Station and Vienna: For the city center, follow orange signs to the U-3 (direction: Simmering). If your hotel is along Mariahilfer Strasse, your stop is on this line, but it may be simpler to walk.

Franz-Josefs-Bahnhof

This small station in the northern part of the city serves **Krems** and other points on the **north bank of the Danube.** Connections from Český Krumlov in the Czech Republic sometimes arrive here, too.

Getting Between the Station and Vienna: Although the station doesn't have an U-Bahn stop, convenient tram #D connects it to the city center. Also note that trains coming into town from this direction stop at the Spittelau station (on the U-4 and U-6 lines), one stop before they end at the Franz-Josefs-Bahnhof; consider hopping off your train at Spittelau for a handy connection to other points in Vienna. (Similarly, if you're headed out of town and you're not near the tram #D route, take the U-Bahn to Spittelau and catch your train there.)

Wien-Mitte Bahnhof

This smaller station, just west of the Ring, is the terminus for S-Bahn and CAT trains to the airport. Be aware that its U-Bahn station is called "Landstrasse." From here, take the U-3 to hotels near Stephansplatz or Mariahilfer Strasse, and the U-4 to hotels that are closer to the airport. It's also connected directly to the Hauptbahnhof by tram #O.

Train Connections

Before leaving your hotel, confirm which station your train leaves from.

From Vienna by Train to: Bratislava (2/hour, 1 hour, alternating between Bratislava's main station and Petržalka station, or try going by bus or boat; described on page 971), **Salzburg** (3/hour, 3 hours), **Hallstatt** (at least hourly, 4 hours, last connection leaves around 15:00, change in Attnang-Puchheim), **Budapest** (every 2 hours direct on express Railjet, 2.5 hours; more with changes; may be cheaper by Orange Ways bus: 4/day, 3 hours, www.orangeways. com), **Prague** (6/day direct, 4 hours; more with 1 change, 4.5 hours; 1 night train leaves Hauptbahnhof around 22:50, 7 hours), **Český**

Krumlov (5/day with 2 changes, 5 hours), **Munich** (6/day direct, 4 hours; otherwise about hourly, 4.5 hours, change in Salzburg or Plattling), **Zürich** (4/day direct, 8.5 hours; nearly hourly with 1-2 changes, 9 hours; night train), **Ljubljana** (1 convenient early-morning train, 6 hours; otherwise 3/day with change in Villach or Maribor, 6.5 hours), **Zagreb** (4/day, 7-9 hours, 1 direct, others with 1-3 changes), **Kraków** (2/day, 7 hours, change in Katowice; plus 1 night train, 9 hours), **Warsaw** (2/day direct, 7 hours; plus 1 night train, 10 hours), **Rome** (4/day, 12.5 hours, 2-3 changes; plus 1 night train, 14 hours), **Venice** (1 direct early-morning train, 8 hours; otherwise 5/day, 8-10 hours with changes—some involve bus connection; plus 1 direct night train, 12 hours), **Frankfurt** (5/day direct, 7 hours; plus 1 direct night train, 8 hours), **Paris** (10/day, 11-13 hours, 1-4 changes).

BY PLANE
Vienna International Airport
The airport, 12 miles from the center, is easy to reach from downtown (airport code: VIE, airport tel. 01/700-722-233, www.viennaairport.com). The arrivals hall has an array of services: TI, shops, ATMs, eateries, and a handy supermarket. Ramps lead down to the lower-level train station.

Getting Between the Airport and Central Vienna
By Train: Trains connect the airport with the Wien-Mitte Bahnhof, on the east side of the Ring (described earlier). Choose between two ways of getting to Wien-Mitte: the regular S-7 S-Bahn train (€4.40, 24 minutes), and the express CAT train (€12, 16 minutes). Both run twice an hour on the same tracks. The airport tries to steer tourists into taking the CAT train, but it's hard to justify spending almost €8 to save eight minutes of time. I'd take the S-7, unless the CAT is departing first and you're in a big hurry. Trains from downtown start running about 5:00, while the last train from the airport leaves about 23:30.

The **S-Bahn** works just fine and is plenty fast. From the arrivals hall, go down either of the big ramps, follow the red ÖBB signs, then buy a regular two-zone public transport ticket from the multilingual red "Fahrkarten" machines. The €4.40 price includes any transfers to other trams, city buses, S- and U-Bahn lines (see www.wienerlinien.at). Trains to downtown are marked "Floridsdorf." If you'll be using public transportation in Vienna a lot, consider buying a transit pass from the machines instead of a single ticket (see "Getting Around Vienna," page 847). As these passes are only valid in Vienna's central zone, you'll need to also buy a €2.10 single ticket to cover the stretch between the airport and the limits of the inner zone.

VIENNA

To take the fast **CAT** (which stands for City Airport Train), follow the green signage down the ramp to your right as you come out into the arrivals hall and buy a ticket from the green machines (one-way-€12, or €14 to also cover the connecting link from Wien-Mitte to your final destination by public transit; round-trip ticket valid 30 days-€19, 4 tickets-€38; usually departs both airport and downtown at :06 and :36 past the hour, www.cityairporttrain.com).

By Bus: Convenient express airport buses go to various points in Vienna: Morzinplatz/Schwedenplatz U-Bahn station (for city-center hotels, 20 minutes), Westbahnhof (for Mariahilfer Strasse hotels, 45 minutes), and Wien-Meidling Bahnhof (30 minutes). Double check your destination as you board (€8, round-trip-€13, 2/hour, buy ticket from driver, tel. 0810-222-333 for timetable info, www.viennaairportlines.at or www.postbus.at).

By Taxi: The 30-minute ride into town costs a fixed €36 from the several companies with desks in the arrivals hall. You can also take a taxi from the taxi rank outside; you'll pay the metered rate (plus a trivial baggage surcharge), which should come out about the same. Save by riding the cheap train/bus downtown, then taking a taxi to your destination.

Connecting the Airport and Other Cities

Direct buses serve **Bratislava** and its airport (roughly 1/hour, 1 hour, buses leave from platforms 7, 8, and 9; two companies: **Blaguss,** www.blaguss.sk, and **Slovak Lines/Postbus,** www.slovaklines.sk); **Budapest** (4/day, 3 hours, www.orangeways.com); **Prague** (4/day, 7 hours, www.studentagency.eu, also stops in **Brno**).

Bratislava Airport

The airport in nearby Bratislava, Slovakia—a hub for some low-cost flights—is an hour away from Vienna (see page 972 in the Bratislava chapter).

BY BOAT

High-speed boats connect Vienna to the nearby capitals of Bratislava (Slovakia) and Budapest (Hungary). While it's generally cheaper and faster to take the train—and the boat is less scenic and romantic than you might imagine—some travelers enjoy the Danube riverboat experience.

To Bratislava: The **Twin City Liner** runs 3-5 times daily from the terminal at Vienna's Schwedenplatz, where Vienna's town center hits the canal (€30-35 one-way, 75-minute trip downstream; U: Schwedenplatz, mid-April-Oct only, can fill up—reservations smart, Austrian tel. 01/58880, www.twincityliner.com). Their main competitor, **LOD,** is a bit cheaper, but runs only twice a day at most and is less convenient—since it uses Vienna's Reichsbrücke dock on the main river, farther from the city center (€25 one-way, €38 round-trip, 1.5-hour trip downstream; Handelskai 265, U: Vorgartenstrasse, tel. from Austria 00-421-2-5293-2226, www. lod.sk).

To Budapest: In the summer, the Budapest-based Mahart line runs daily high-speed hydrofoils down the Danube to Budapest (€109 one-way, €125 round-trip, runs Wed, Fri, and Sun, mid-May-Sept only). The boat leaves Vienna at 9:00 and arrives in Budapest at 14:30 (Budapest to Vienna: 9:00-15:30). In Vienna, you board at the DDSG Blue Danube dock at the Reichsbrücke (Handelskai 265, U: Vorgartenstrasse). To confirm times and prices, and to buy tickets, contact DDSG Blue Danube in Vienna (Austrian tel. 01/58880, www.ddsg-blue-danube.at) or Mahart in Budapest (Hungarian tel. 1/484-4013 or 1/484-4010, www. mahartpassnave.hu).

VIENNA

German Survival Phrases for Austria

When using the phonetics, pronounce ī sounds like the long i in "light."
Bolded syllables are stressed.

English	German	Pronunciation
Good day.	Grüss Gott.	**grews** gote
Do you speak English?	Sprechen Sie Englisch?	**shprehkh**-ehn zee **ehgn**-lish
Yes. / No.	Ja. / Nein.	yah / nīn
I (don't) understand.	Ich verstehe (nicht).	ikh fehr-**shtay**-heh (nikht)
Please.	Bitte.	**bit**-teh
Thank you.	Danke.	**dahng**-keh
I'm sorry.	Es tut mir leid.	ehs toot meer līt
Excuse me.	Entschuldigung.	ehnt-**shool**-dig-oong
(No) problem.	(Kein) Problem.	(kīn) proh-**blaym**
(Very) good.	(Sehr) gut.	(zehr) goot
Goodbye.	Auf Wiedersehen.	owf **vee**-der-zayn
one / two	eins / zwei	īns / tsvī
three / four	drei / vier	drī / feer
five / six	fünf / sechs	fewnf / zehkhs
seven / eight	sieben / acht	**zee**-behn / ahkht
nine / ten	neun / zehn	noyn / tsayn
How much is it?	Wieviel kostet das?	**vee**-feel **kohs**-teht dahs
Write it?	Schreiben?	**shrī**-behn
Is it free?	Ist es umsonst?	ist ehs oom-**zohnst**
Included?	Inklusive?	in-kloo-**zee**-veh
Where can I buy / find...?	Wo kann ich kaufen / finden...?	voh kahn ikh **kow**-fehn / **fin**-dehn
I'd like / We'd like...	Ich hätte gern / Wir hätten gern...	ikh **heh**-teh gehrn / veer **heh**-tehn gehrn
...a room.	...ein Zimmer.	īn **tsim**-mer
...a ticket to ___.	...eine Fahrkarte nach ___.	ī-neh **far**-kar-teh nahkh
Is it possible?	Ist es möglich?	ist ehs **mur**-glikh
Where is...?	Wo ist...?	voh ist
...the train station	...der Bahnhof	dehr **bahn**-hohf
...the bus station	...der Busbahnhof	dehr **boos**-bahn-hohf
...the tourist information office	...das Touristen-informations-büro	dahs too-**ris**-tehn-in-for-maht-see-**ohns**-**bew**-roh
...the toilet	...die Toilette	dee toh-**leh**-teh
men	Herren	**hehr**-rehn
women	Damen	**dah**-mehn
left / right	links / rechts	links / **rehkhts**
straight	geradeaus	geh-**rah**-deh-**ows**
What time does this open / close?	Um wieviel Uhr wird hier geöffnet / geschlossen?	oom **vee**-feel oor veerd heer geh-**urf**-neht / geh-**shloh**-sehn
At what time?	Um wieviel Uhr?	oom **vee**-feel oor
Just a moment.	Moment.	moh-**mehnt**
now / soon / later	jetzt / bald / später	yehtst / bahld / **shpay**-ter
today / tomorrow	heute / morgen	**hoy**-teh / **mor**-gehn

In a German/Austrian Restaurant

English	German	Pronunciation
I'd like / We'd like...	Ich hätte gern / Wir hätten gern...	ikh **heh**-teh gehrn / veer **heh**-tehn gehrn
...a reservation for...	...eine Reservierung für...	ī-neh reh-zer-**feer**-oong fewr
...a table for one / two.	...einen Tisch für eine Person / zwei Personen.	ī-nehn tish fewr ī-neh pehr- zohn / tsvī pehr-zohnehn
Non-smoking.	Nichtraucher.	**nikht**-rowkh-er
Is this seat free?	Ist hier frei?	ist heer frī
Menu (in English), please.	Speisekarte (auf Englisch), bitte.	**shpī**-zeh-kar-teh (owf **ehng**-lish) **bit**-teh
service (not) included	Trinkgeld (nicht) inklusive	**trink**-gehlt (nikht) in-kloo-**zee**-veh
cover charge	Eintritt	**īn**-trit
to go	zum Mitnehmen	tsoom **mit**-nay-mehn
with / without	mit / ohne	mit / **oh**-neh
and / or	und / oder	oont / **oh**-der
menu (of the day)	(Tages-) Karte	(**tah**-gehs-) **kar**-teh
set meal for tourists	Touristenmenü	too-**ris**-tehn-meh-**new**
specialty of the house	Spezialität des Hauses	**shpayt**-see-ah-lee-**tayt** dehs **how**-zehs
appetizers	Vorspeise	**for**-shpī-zeh
bread / cheese	Brot / Käse	broht / **kay**-zeh
sandwich	Sandwich	**zahnd**-vich
soup	Suppe	**zup**-peh
salad	Salat	zah-**laht**
meat	Fleisch	flīsh
poultry	Geflügel	geh-**flew**-gehl
fish	Fisch	fish
seafood	Meeresfrüchte	**meh**-rehs-**frewkh**-teh
fruit	Obst	ohpst
vegetables	Gemüse	geh-**mew**-zeh
dessert	Nachspeise	**nahkh**-shpī-zeh
mineral water	Mineralwasser	min-eh-**rahl**-vah-ser
tap water	Leitungswasser	**lī**-toongs-vah-ser
milk	Milch	milkh
(orange) juice	(Orangen-) Saft	(oh-**rahn**-zhehn-) zahft
coffee / tea	Kaffee / Tee	kah-**fay** / tay
wine	Wein	vīn
red / white	rot / weiß	roht / vīs
glass / bottle	Glas / Flasche	glahs / **flah**-sheh
beer	Bier	beer
Cheers!	Prost!	prohst
More. / Another.	Mehr. / Noch eins.	mehr / nohkh īns
The same.	Das gleiche.	dahs **glīkh**-eh
Bill, please.	Rechnung, bitte.	**rehkh**-noong **bit**-teh
tip	Trinkgeld	**trink**-gehlt
Delicious!	Lecker!	**lehk**-er

For more user-friendly German phrases, check out *Rick Steves' German Phrase Book and Dictionary* or *Rick Steves' French, Italian & German Phrase Book*.

SLOVAKIA

Slovensko

BRATISLAVA

The Slovak capital, Bratislava, long a drab lesson in the failings of the communist system, has become downright charming. Its old town bursts with colorfully restored facades, lively outdoor cafés, swanky boutiques, and in-love-with-life locals.

The rejuvenation doesn't end in the old town. The ramshackle quarter to the east is gradually being redeveloped into a new forest of skyscrapers. The hilltop castle gleams from a recent facelift. And even the glum commie suburb of Petržalka (PET-ur-ZHAL-kuh) is undergoing a Technicolor makeover. Bratislava and Vienna have forged a new twin-city alliance for trade and commerce, bridging Eastern and Western Europe.

It's easy to get the feeling that workaday Bratislavans—who strike some visitors as gruff—are being pulled to the cutting edge of the 21st century kicking and screaming. But many Slovaks embrace the changes and fancy themselves as the yang to Vienna's yin: If Vienna is a staid, elderly aristocrat sipping coffee, then Bratislava is a vivacious young professional jet-setting around Europe. Bratislava at night is a lively place; thanks in part to tens of thousands of university students, its very youthful center thrives.

Bratislava's priceless location—on the Danube (and the tourist circuit) smack-dab between Budapest and Vienna—makes it a very worthwhile "on the way" destination. I admit that Bratislava used to leave me cold. But all the recent changes have transformed it into a delightful destination.

PLANNING YOUR TIME

A few hours are plenty to get the gist of Bratislava. Head straight to the old town and follow my self-guided walk, finishing with a stroll along the Danube riverbank to the thriving, modern Eurovea development. With more time, take advantage of one or more of the city's fine viewpoints: Ascend to the "UFO" observation deck atop the funky bridge, ride the elevator up to the Sky Bar for a peek (and maybe a drink), or hike up to the castle for the views (but skip the ho-hum museum inside). If you spend the evening in Bratislava, you'll find it lively with students, busy cafés, and nightlife.

Note that all museums and galleries are closed on Monday.

Day-Tripping Tip: Bratislava can be done as a long side-trip from Budapest (or a short one from Vienna), but it's most convenient as a stopover to break up the journey between Budapest and Vienna. But pay careful attention to train schedules, as the Vienna connection alternates between Bratislava's two train stations (Hlavná Stanica and Petržalka). If checking your bag at the station, be sure that your return or onward connection will depart from there.

Orientation to Bratislava

Bratislava, with 430,000 residents, is Slovakia's capital and biggest city. It has a small, colorful old town *(staré mesto)*, with the castle on the hill above. This small area is surrounded by a vast construction zone of new buildings, rotting residential districts desperately in need of beautification, and some colorized communist suburbs (including Petržalka, across the river).

TOURIST INFORMATION

The helpful TI is at Klobučnícka 2, on Primate's Square behind the Old Town Hall (daily May-Oct 9:00-19:00, Nov-April 9:00-18:00, tel. 02/16186, www.visitbratislava.com). They also have a branch at the airport.

Discount Card: The TI sells the €12 Bratislava City Card, which includes free transit and sightseeing discounts for a full day—but it's worthwhile only if you're doing the old town walking tour (€14 without the card—see "Tours in Bratislava," later).

ARRIVAL IN BRATISLAVA

For information on Bratislava's trains, buses, riverboats, and airport, see "Bratislava Connections," at the end of this chapter.

HELPFUL HINTS

Wi-Fi: You'll find free Wi-Fi at the three major old-town squares (Hlavné Námestie—the main square, Primate's Square, and

BRATISLAVA

Slovakia Almanac

Official Name: Slovenská Republika, though locals call it Sloven-sko. The nation is the eastern half of the former Czechoslovakia (split peaceably in 1993).

Population: 5.5 million people. The majority are native Slovaks who are Roman Catholic and speak Slovak. But one in ten has Hungarian roots ("stranded" here when Hungary lost this land after WWI), and many—likely between 2 and 8 percent—are Roma (Gypsy). Slovakia has struggled to incorporate both of these large and often-mistreated minority groups.

Latitude and Longitude: 48°N and 19°E (similar latitude to Paris or Vancouver, BC).

Area: 19,000 square miles (the size of Massachusetts and New Hampshire put together).

Geography: The northeastern half of Slovakia features the beautiful rolling hills and spiky, jagged peaks of the Carpathian Mountains. The southwestern half is quite flat—a continuation of the Great Hungarian Plain. The climate is generally cool and cloudy.

Biggest Cities: Only two cities have more than 100,000 inhabitants: Bratislava in the west (the capital, 400,000) and Košice in the east (240,000).

Economy: The Gross Domestic Product is about $86 billion, and the GDP per capita is about $29,700.

Currency: Slovakia uses the euro (€1=about $1.10). You'll find ATMs at the train stations and airport.

Government: Slovakia's mostly figurehead president, Andrej Kiska, heads a government that isn't dominated by any single political party. Slovakia also has a 150-seat National Council (like a parliament), the leader of which is the prime minister, Robert Fico.

Flag: Horizontal bands of white, blue, and red with a shield bearing a "patriarchal cross" (with two crossbars instead of one) atop

Hviezdoslav Square), as well as along the entire Danube embankment.

Local Guidebook: For in-depth suggestions on Bratislava sightseeing, dining, and more, look for the excellent and eye-pleasing Bratislava Active guidebook by Martin Sloboda (see "Tours in Bratislava," next; around €10, sold at every postcard rack).

Toll Sticker: Slovakia requires cars on its expressways to display a toll sticker (vignette, €10/10 days, www.dialnicnenalepky.sk). If your car doesn't have one, buy one at a gas station when you cross the border. You don't need one if you'll be dipping into the country on minor roads—only for major highways.

three humps. The three humps represent three historic mountain ranges of Slovakia: Mátra (now in northern Hungary, near Eger),

Fatra, and Tatra. The double-barred cross represents St. Stephen (István) of Hungary, commemorating the many centuries that Slovakia was part of Hungary.

Cuisine: Today's Slovak cooking shows some Hungarian and Austrian influences, but it's closer to Czech—lots of starches and gravy, and plenty of pork, cabbage, potatoes, and dumplings. Keep an eye out for Slovakia's national dish, *bryndzové halušky* (small potato dumplings with sheep's cheese and bits of bacon).

Language: The official language is Slovak, which is closely related to Czech and Polish—although many Bratislavans also speak English. The local word used informally for both "hi" and "bye" is easy to remember: *ahoj* (pronounced "AH-hoy," like a pirate). "Please" is *prosím* (PROH-seem), "thank you" is *ďakujem* (DYAH-koo-yehm), "good" is *dobrý* (DOH-bree), and "Cheers!" is *Na zdravie!* (nah ZDRAH-vyeh).

Slovaks You May Recognize: Andy Warhol (American Pop artist who gained more than his 15 minutes of fame, born to Slovak immigrants), Martina Hingis (Swiss tennis player born in Slovakia), film director Ivan Reitman (*Ghostbusters, Stripes;* born in Slovakia to Jewish Holocaust survivors), actor Paul Newman (whose mother was born in Slovakia), Tomáš Garrigue Masaryk (founder of Czechoslovakia, whose father was Slovak), Alexander Dubček (leader of the 1968 Prague Spring uprising), and Štefan Banič (emigrated to America and invented the parachute).

BRATISLAVA

Tours in Bratislava

Walking Tours

The TI offers a one-hour old town walking tour in English every day in summer at 14:00 (free with €12 Bratislava City Card; for €14 you can arrange a tour on the hour at other times of day, book and pay at least two hours in advance). Travelers arriving by riverboat are accosted by guides selling their own 1.5-hour tours (half on foot and half in a little tourist train, €10, in German and English).

Local Guide

MS Agency, run by Martin Sloboda (a can-do entrepreneur and tireless Bratislava booster, and author of the great local guidebook

Welcome to Slovakia

In many ways, Slovakia is the West Virginia of Europe—relatively poor and undeveloped, but serenely beautiful in its own rustic way. Sitting quietly in the very center of Central Europe, wedged between bigger and stronger nations (Hungary, Austria, the Czech Republic, and Poland), Slovakia was brutally disfigured by the communists, then overshadowed by the Czechs. But in recent years, this fledgling republic has found its wings.

Recent economic reforms have caused two very different Slovakias to emerge: the modern, industrialized, flat, affluent west, centered on the capital of Bratislava; and the remote, poorer, mountainous, "backward" east, with high unemployment and traditional lifestyles. Slovakia has spent most of its history as someone else's backyard. For centuries, Slovakia was ruled from Budapest and known as "Upper Hungary." At other times, it was an important chunk of the Habsburg Empire, ruled from neighboring Vienna. But most outsiders think first of another era: the 75 years that Slovakia was joined with the Czech Republic as the country of "Czechoslovakia." From its start in the aftermath of World War I, this union of the Czechs and Slovaks was troubled; some Slovaks chafed at being ruled from Prague, while many Czechs resented the financial burden of their poorer neighbors to the east.

After they gained their freedom from the communists during 1989's peaceful Velvet Revolution, the Czechs and Slovaks began to think of the future. The Slovaks wanted to rename the country Czecho-Slovakia, and to redistribute power to give themselves more autonomy within the union. The Czechs balked, relations gradually deteriorated, and the Slovak nationalist candidate Vladimír Mečiar fared surprisingly well in the 1992 elections. Taking it as a sign that the two peoples wanted to part ways, politicians

described earlier, can set you up with a good guide (€130/3 hours, €160/4 hours); he can also help you track down your Slovak roots. Martin, who helped me put this chapter together, is part of the generation that came of age as communism fell and whose energy and leadership are reshaping the city (mobile 0905-627-265, www.msagency.sk, sloboda@msagency.sk).

pushed through (in just three months) the peaceful separation of the now-independent Czech and Slovak Republics. (The people in both countries never actually voted on the change, and most opposed it.) The "Velvet Divorce" became official on January 1, 1993.

At first the Slovaks struggled. Communist rule had been particularly unkind to them, and their economy was in a shambles. Visionary leaders set forth bold solutions, including the 2003 implementation of a flat tax (19 percent), followed by EU membership in 2004. Before long, major international corporations began to notice the same thing the communists had: This is a great place to build stuff, thanks to a strategic location (300 million consumers live within a day's truck drive), low labor costs, and a well-trained workforce. Not surprisingly, multiple foreign automakers have plants here. Today Slovakia produces one million cars a year, making the country the world's biggest car producer (per capita) and leading the *New York Times* to dub Slovakia "the European Detroit."

The flat tax and other aggressively pro-business policies have not been without their critics—especially in the very impoverished eastern half of the country, where poor people feel they're becoming even poorer. With the rollback of social services, some seem to have been left behind by Slovakia's bold new economy.

Even so, particularly if you zoom in on its success story around Bratislava, the evidence is impressive. Bratislava has only 5 percent unemployment, and 90 percent of its residents are satisfied living here (beating out Rome, Madrid, and even Paris). In 2009, Slovakia adopted the euro currency. While most of Europe is struggling through difficult economic times, much of Slovakia seems poised for its brightest future yet.

Bratislava Old Town Walk

This self-guided orientation walk passes through the heart of delightfully traffic-free old Bratislava and then down to its riverside commercial zone (figure 1.5 hours, not including stops). If you're coming from the station, make your way toward the green steeple of St. Michael's Gate (explained in "Bratislava Connections" at the end of this chapter). Before going through the passage into the old town, peek over the railing on your left to the pleasant garden below—once part of the city moat.

Bratislava

1. Hotel Marrol's
2. Hotel Michalská Brána
3. Penzión Virgo
4. Downtown Backpackers Hostel
5. 1. Slovak Pub
6. Bratislavský Meštiansky Pivovar
7. Lemon Tree/Sky Bar/Rum Club
8. Štúr
9. Coffee & Bagel Story;
   Café Roland; Kaffee Mayer
10. Billa Supermarket

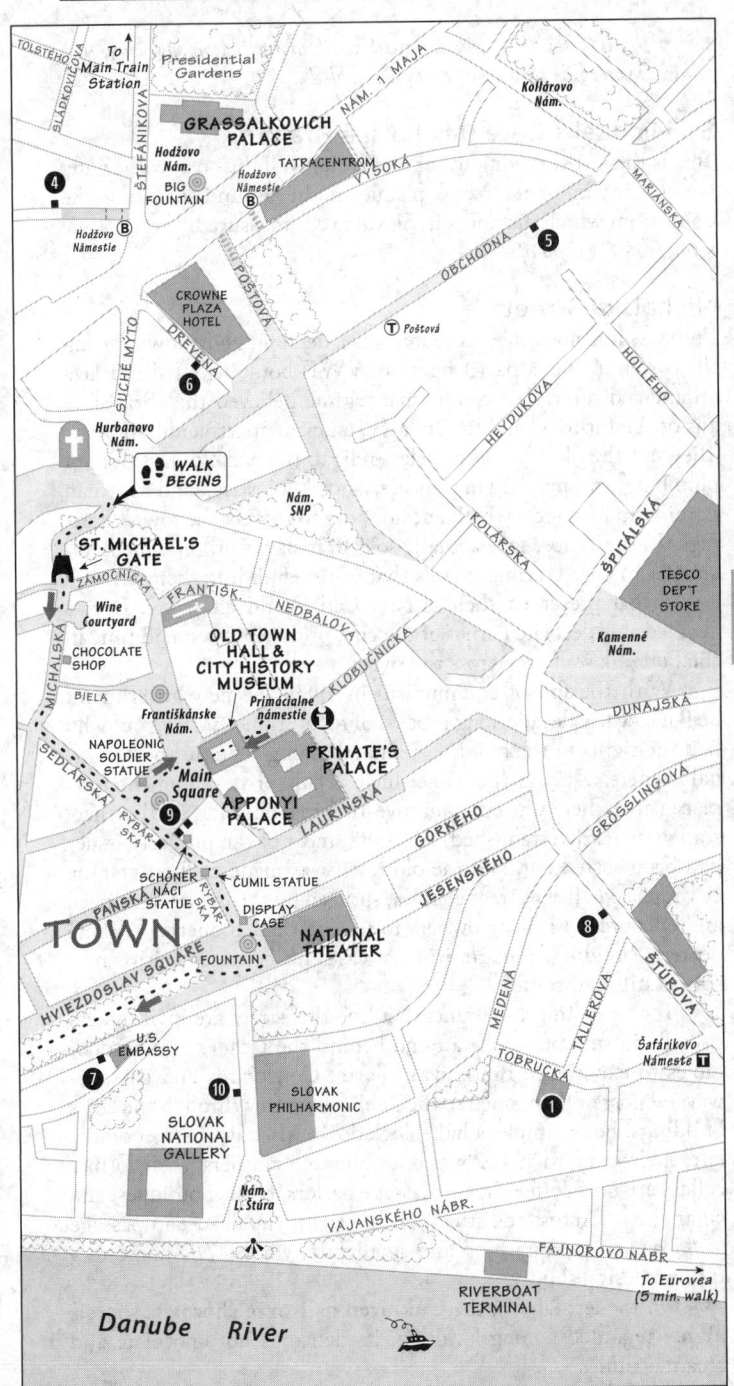

• *Step through the first, smaller gate, walk along the passageway, and pause as you come through the green-steepled…*

St. Michael's Gate (Michalská Brána)

This is the last surviving tower of the city wall. Just below the gate, notice the "kilometer zero" plaque in the ground, marking the point from which distances in Slovakia are measured.

• *You're at the head of…*

Michalská Street

Pretty as it is now, the old center was a decrepit ghost town during the communist era, partly because WWII bombing left Bratislava a damaged husk. The communist regime believed that Bratislavans of the future would live in large, efficient apartment buildings. They saw the old town as a useless relic of the bad old days of poor plumbing, cramped living spaces, social injustice, and German domination—a view which left no room to respect the town's heritage. In the 1950s, they actually sold Bratislava's original medieval cobbles to cute German towns that were rebuilding themselves in a way that preserved their elegant Old World character. Locals avoided this desolate corner of the city, preferring to spend time in the Petržalka suburb across the river.

With the fall of communism in 1989, the new government began a nearly decade-long process of restitution—sorting out who had the rights to the buildings, and returning them to their original owners. During this time, little repair or development took place (since there was no point investing in a building until ownership was clearly established). By 1998, most of the property issues had been sorted out, and the old town was made traffic-free. The city replaced all the street cobbles, spruced up the public buildings, and encouraged private owners to restore their property. (Where decrepit buildings remain, in most cases it's because their ownership is still in dispute.)

The cafés and restaurants that line this street are inviting, especially in summer. Poke around behind the facades and outdoor tables to experience Bratislava's charm. Courtyards and passageways—most of them open to the public—burrow through the city's buildings. For example, a half-block down Michalská street on the left, the courtyard at #12 was once home to vintners; their former cellars are now coffee shops, massage parlors, crafts boutiques, and cigar shops. Across the street, on the right, the dead-end passage at #5 has an antique shop and small café, while #7 is home to a fashion design shop.

On the left (at #6), the **Cukráreň na Korze** chocolate shop is highly regarded among locals for its delicious hot chocolate and creamy truffles.

Above the shop's entrance, the **cannonball** embedded in the wall recalls Napoleon's two sieges of Bratislava (the 1809 siege was 42 days long, which caused massive suffering—even worse than during World War II. It's one of several cannonballs around town. Keep an eye out for more of these reminders of one of Bratislava's darkest times.

• *Two blocks down from St. Michael's Gate, where the street jogs slightly right (and its name changes to Ventúrska), detour left along Sedlárska street and head to the...*

Main Square (Hlavné Námestie)

This modest square, the centerpiece of Bratislava's old town, feels too petite for a national capital. Its style is a mishmash—every

building around it seems to date from a different architectural period. Consider pausing at one of the cafés that line the square to sip a drink with Slovakia's best urban view.

Do a quick clockwise spin tour, starting at the top of the square with the impressive **Old Town Hall** (Stará Radnica), with its bold yellow tower that is both Gothic (at the base) and Baroque (at the top). Near the bottom of the tower, to the left of the window, notice a Napoleonic cannonball embedded in the facade.

Down the street to the right of the Old Town Hall are the historic apartments and wine museum at the **Apponyi House** (described under "Sights in Bratislava").

Turn farther right and note the venerable cafés at the far corner of the square. The classic choice is **Kaffee Mayer,** with red awnings and outdoor seating facing the fountain. This venerable café has been selling coffee and cakes to a genteel clientele since 1873. You can enjoy your pick-me-up in the swanky old interior or out

on the square. Just across the street, the Art Nouveau **Café Roland** is known for its 1904 Klimt-style mosaics and historic photos of the days when the city was known as Pressburg (Austrian times) or Pozsony (Hungarian times). The building, now home to an insurance company, was once a bank. These days the barista stands where a different kind of bean counter once did, guarding a vault that now holds coffee.

Keep spinning. Facing the fountain opposite Kaffee Mayer, a cartoonish statue of a **Napoleonic officer** peers over one of the benches (notice the French flag marking the embassy in the Rococo building right behind him). With bare feet and a hat pulled over his eyes, it's hardly a flattering portrait—you could call it the locals' revenge for Napoleon's sieges. Across the square, another soldier from that period stands at attention.

Finally, in the corner to the left of the Old Town Hall, you may see a jumble of cute **minikiosks**—sporting old-time cityscape engravings on their roofs—selling local handicrafts and knickknacks. In December, similar stalls fill the square, transforming this space into the city's popular and atmospheric **Christmas market.**

Now that you've spun back to the Old Town Hall, step through the passageway into the building's gorgeously restored **courtyard,** with its Renaissance arcades. (The **City History Museum**'s entrance is here—described later.)

To see another fine old square, continue through the other end of the courtyard into **Primate's Square** (Primaciálne Námestie). The pink mansion on the right is the **Primate's Palace,** with a fine interior decorated with six English tapestries (described later, but worth visiting now). At the far end of this square is the **TI.**

• *Backtrack to the main square. With your back to the Old Town Hall, go to the end of the square and take a left at the corner with Kaffee Mayer onto the street called Rybárska Brána. Just at the beginning of the street, as you exit the square, you'll pass a pair of...*

Whimsical Statues

Playful statues (such as the Napoleonic officer we met earlier) dot Bratislava's old town. Most date from the late 1990s, when city leaders wanted to entice locals back into the newly prettied-up center.

The jovial chap doffing his top hat is a statue of **Schöner Náci,** who lived in Bratislava until the 1960s. This eccentric old man, a poor carpet cleaner, would dress up in his one black suit and top hat, and go strolling through the city, offering gifts to the women he fancied. (He'd often whisper *"schön"*—German for "pretty," which is how he got his nickname.) Schöner Náci now gets to spend eternity greeting visitors outside his favorite café, Kaffee Mayer. Once he temporarily lost an arm when a bunch of drunks broke it off. (As Prague has grown more expensive, Bratislava has become an especially popular destination for weekend "stag parties," lured here by cheap flights and cheap beer.)

• *Continue down Rybárska.*

At the end of this block, at the intersection with Panská, watch out on the right for **Čumil** ("the Peeper"), grinning at passersby from a manhole. This was the first—and is still the favorite—of Bratislava's statues. There's no story behind this one—the artist simply wanted to create a fun icon and let the townspeople make up their own tales. Čumil has survived being driven over by a truck—twice—and he's still grinning.

• *Keep along Rybárska to reach the long, skinny square called...*

Hviezdoslav Square (Hviezdoslavovo Námestie)

At the near end is the impressive, silver-topped Slovak National Theater (Slovenské Národné Divadlo). Beyond that, the opulent yellow Neo-Baroque building is the Slovak Philharmonic (Slovenská Filharmónia). When the theater opened in the 1880s, half the shows were in German and half in Hungarian. Today, it's a proud Slovak institution—typical of the ethnic changes that have marked this city's life.

Right in front of the theater (by the McDonald's), look down into the glass display case to see the foundation of the one-time Fishermen's Gate into the city. Water surrounds the base of the gate: This entire square was once a tributary of the Danube, and the Carlton Hotel across the way was once a series of inns on different islands. The buildings along the old-town side of the square mark where the city wall once stood. Now the square is a lively zone on balmy evenings, with several fine restaurants (including some splurgy steakhouses) offering al fresco tables jammed with visiting businesspeople looking for good-quality, expense-account meals.

Stroll down the long square. After passing a statue of the square's namesake (Pavol Országh Hviezdoslav, a beloved Slovak poet), look for an ugly fence and barriers on the left, which mark the fortified US Embassy. Just past the embassy is the low-profile entrance to the recommended **Sky Bar,** an affordable rooftop restaurant with excellent views (ride elevator to seventh floor). The glass pavilion just outside is a popular venue for summer concerts. Behind it, across the square, is **Luculus,** where locals are likely lined up outside for some of the city's best ice cream. A few years

City of Three Cultures:
Pressburg, Pozsony, Bratislava

Historically more of an Austrian and Hungarian city than a Slovak one, Bratislava has always been a Central European melting pot. Over the years, a slew of notable visitors, from Hans Christian Andersen to Casanova, has sung the praises of this bustling burg on the Danube.

For most of its history, Bratislava was part of the Austrian Empire and known as Pressburg, with a primarily German-speaking population. (Only the surrounding rural areas were Slovak.) The Hungarians used Pozsony (as they called it) as their capital during the century and a half that Buda and Pest were occupied by Ottoman invaders.

By its turn-of-the-20th-century glory days, the city was a rich intersection of cultures—about 40 percent German, 40 percent Hungarian, and 20 percent Slovak. Shop clerks greeted customers in all three languages. It was said that the mornings belonged to the Slovaks (farmers who came into the city to sell their wares at market), the afternoons to the Hungarians (diplomats and office workers filling the cafés), and the evenings to the Austrians (wine producers who ran convivial neighborhood wine pubs where all three groups would gather). In those wine pubs, the vintner would listen to which language his customers used, then bring them a glass with the serving size expected in their home country: 0.3 liters for Hungarians, 0.25 liters for Austrians, and 0.2 liters for Slovaks (a distinction that still exists today). Jews (one-tenth of the population), and Roma (Gypsies) rounded out the city's ethnic brew.

When the new nation of Czechoslovakia was formed from the rubble of World War I, the city shed its German and Hungarian names, and took the newly-created Slavic name of Bratislava. The Slovak population was on the rise, but the city remained tricultural.

World War II changed all of that. With the dissolution of Czechoslovakia, Slovakia became an "independent" country under the thumb of the Nazis—who all but wiped out the Jewish population. Then, at the end of the war, a Czechoslovakia reunited under Soviet Russia rudely expelled the city's ethnic Germans and

ago the owner set the national record for number of scoops balanced on a single cone (150), but for me just a scoop or two is the perfect pick-me-up on this walk. On the right near the end of the park, a statue of Hans Christian Andersen is a reminder that the Danish storyteller enjoyed his visit to Bratislava, too.

• *Reaching the end of the square, you run into the barrier for a busy highway. Turn right and walk one block to find the big, black marble slab facing a modern monument.*

Hungarians in retribution for the misdeeds of Hitler and Horthy (Hungary's wartime leader).

Bratislava's urban heritage suffered terribly under the communists. The historic city's multilayered charm and delicate cultural fabric were ripped apart, then shrouded in gray. The communists were prouder of their ultramodern SNP Bridge than of the city's historic Jewish quarter—which they razed to make way for the bridge. Now the bridge and its highway slice through the center of the old town, and heavy traffic rattles the stained-glass windows of St. Martin's Cathedral. The city's Germanic heritage was also deliberately obscured.

But Bratislava's most recent chapter is one of great success. Since the fall of communism, the city has gone from gloomy victim to thriving economic center and social hub. With a healthy market economy, it now has the chance to re-create itself as Slovakia's national capital. Its population of about 430,000 includes some 60,000 students (at the city's six universities), creating an atmosphere of youthful energy and optimism. Its remarkable position on the Danube, a short commute from Vienna, is prompting its redevelopment as one of Europe's up-and-coming cities.

Bratislava and Vienna have realized that it's mutually beneficial to work together to bring the Slovak capital up to snuff. They're cooperating in a new "twin city" commerce super-zone. In the coming years, foreign investors talk of erecting a Bratislavan skyline of 600-foot-tall skyscrapers and a clutch of glittering megamalls. Bratislavans also have high hopes for revitalizing the city's transport infrastructure: The highway that barrels between the old town and the castle will be diverted underground (through a tunnel beneath the Danube); a bullet train will swoosh to a stop at a slick train station; a six-station subway line will lace the city together; and the entire riverfront will be transformed into a people-friendly park.

As the city pulls funding together, expect lots of construction during your visit. You'd never have guessed it a few years ago, but today calling Bratislava "the next Berlin on a smaller scale" is only a bit of a stretch.

BRATISLAVA

Holocaust Memorial

This was the site of Bratislava's original synagogue. You can see an etching of the building in the big slab.

At the base of the memorial sculpture, look for the word "Remember" carved into the base in Hebrew and Slovak, commemorating the 90,000 Slovak Jews who were deported to Nazi death camps. Nearly all were killed. The fact that the town's main synagogue and main church (to the right) were located side by side illustrates the tolerance that characterized Bratislava before Hitler.

Ponder the modern statue: The two pages of an open book, faces, hands in the sky, and bullets—all under the Star of David—evoke the fate of 90 percent of the Slovak Jews.

• *Now head toward the adjacent church, up the stairs.*

St. Martin's Cathedral (Dóm Sv. Martina)

If the highway thundering a few feet in front of this historic church's door were any closer, the off-ramp would go through the nave. Sad as it is now, the cathedral has been witness to some pretty important history. While Buda and Pest were occupied by Ottomans from 1543 to 1689, Bratislava was the capital of Hungary. Nineteen Hungarian kings and queens were crowned in this church—more than have been crowned anywhere in Hungary. In fact, the last Hungarian coronation (not counting the Austrian Franz Josef) was not in Budapest, but in Bratislava. A replica of the Hungarian crown still tops the steeple.

It's worth walking up to the cathedral's entrance to observe some fragments of times past (circle around the building, along the busy road, to the opposite, uphill side). Directly across from the church door is a broken bit of the 15th-century town wall. The church was actually built into the wall, which explains its unusual north-side entry. In fact, notice the fortified watchtower (with a WC drop on its left) built into the corner of the church just above you.

There's relatively little to see inside the cathedral—but if it's open, duck in (free to enter, €2.50 for treasury and choir). In the fairly gloomy interior you'll find some fine carved-wood altarpieces (a Slovak specialty), a dank crypt, and a treasury in the back with a whimsical wood carving of Jesus blessing Habsburg Emperor Franz Josef.

Outside, head back around the church for a good view (looking toward the river) of the huge bridge called **Most SNP**, the communists' pride and joy (the "SNP" stands for the Slovak National Uprising of 1944 against the Nazis, a common focus of communist remembrance). As with most Soviet-era landmarks in former communist countries, locals aren't crazy about this structure—not only for the questionable Starship Enterprise design, but also because of the oppressive regime it represented. However, the restaurant and observation deck up top have been renovated into a posh eatery called (appropriately enough) "UFO." You can visit it for the views, a drink, or a full meal.

• *You could end the walk here. Two sights (both described later, under "Sights in Bratislava") are nearby. To hike up to the **castle**, take the underpass beneath the highway, go up the stairs on the right marked by the Hrad/Castle sign, then turn left up the stepped lane marked Zámocké Schody. Or hike over the SNP Bridge (pedestrian walkway on lower level) to ride the elevator up the **UFO** viewing platform.*

*But to really round out your Bratislava visit, head for the river and stroll downstream (left) to a place where you get a dose of modern development in Bratislava—**Eurovea**. To reach it, walk about 10 minutes downstream, past the old town and boat terminals until you come to a big, slick complex with a grassy park leading down to the riverbank.*

Eurovea

Just downstream from the old town is the futuristic Eurovea, with four vibrant layers, each a quarter-mile long: a riverside park, luxury condos, a thriving modern shopping mall, and an office park. Walking out onto the view piers jutting into the Danube and surveying the scene, it looks like a computer-generated urban dreamscape come true. Exploring the old town gives you a taste of where this country has been. But wandering this riverside park, enjoying a drink in one of its chic outdoor lounges, and then browsing through the thriving mall, you'll enjoy a glimpse of where Slovakia is heading.

• *Our walk is finished.*

Sights in Bratislava

If Europe had a prize for "capital city with the most underwhelming museums," I'd cast my vote for Bratislava. You can easily have a great day here without setting foot in a museum. Focus instead on Bratislava's street life and the grand views from the castle and UFO restaurant. If it's rainy or you're in a museum-going mood, the Primate's Palace (with its cheap admission and fine tapestries) ranks slightly above the rest.

ON OR NEAR THE OLD TOWN'S MAIN SQUARE

These museums are all within a few minutes' walk of one another, on or very near the main square.

▲Primate's Palace (Primaciálny Palác)

Bratislava's most interesting museum, this tastefully restored French-Neoclassical mansion (formerly the residence of the archbishop, or "primate") dates from 1781. The religious counterpart of the castle, it filled in for Esztergom—the Hungarian religious capital—after that city was taken by the Ottomans in 1543. Even after the Ottoman defeat in the 1680s, this remained the winter residence of Hungary's archbishops.

Cost and Hours: €3, Tue-Sun 10:00-16:45, closed Mon, Primaciálne Námestie 1, tel. 02/5935-6394, www.bratislava.sk.

Visiting the Museum: The palace, which now serves as a government building, features one fine floor of exhibits. Follow signs for Expozícia up the grand staircase to the ticket counter. There are three main attractions: the Mirror Hall, the tapestries, and the archbishop's chapel.

The **Mirror Hall,** used for concerts, city council meetings, and other important events, is to the left as you enter and worth a glance (if it's not closed for an event).

A series of large public rooms, originally designed to impress, are now an art gallery. Distributed through several of these rooms is the museum's pride, and for many its highlight: a series of six English **tapestries,** illustrating the ancient Greek myth of the tragic love between Hero and Leander.

The tapestries were woven in England by Flemish weavers for the court of King Charles I (in the 1630s). They were kept in London's Hampton Court Palace until Charles was deposed and beheaded in 1649. Cromwell sold them to France to help fund his civil war, but after 1650, they disappeared...for centuries. But in 1903, restorers broke through a false wall in this mansion and discovered the six tapestries, neatly folded and perfectly preserved. Nobody knows how they got there (perhaps they were squirreled away during the Napoleonic invasion, and whoever hid them didn't survive). The archbishop—who had just sold the palace to the city, but emptied it of furniture before he left—cried foul and tried to get the tapestries back...but the city said, "A deal's a deal."

After traipsing through the grand rooms, find the hallway that leads through the smaller rooms of the archbishop's private quarters, now decorated with minor Dutch, Flemish, German, and Italian paintings. At the end of this hall, a bay window looks down into the archbishop's own private **chapel.** When the archbishop became too ill to walk down to Mass, this window was built for him to take part in the service.

On your way back to the entry, pause at the head of the larger corridor to study a 1900 view of the then-much-smaller town by Gustáv Keleti. The museum's entry hall also has grand portraits of Habsburg Empress Maria Theresa and her son Emperor Josef II.

City History Museum (Mestské Múzeum)

Delving into the bric-a-brac of Bratislava's past, this museum includes ecclesiastical art on the ground floor and a sprawling, chronological look at local history upstairs. The displays occupy rooms once used by the town council—courthouse, council hall, chapel, and so on. Everything is described in English, and the included audioguide tries hard, but nothing quite succeeds in bringing meaning to the place. On your way upstairs, you'll have a chance to climb up into the Old Town Hall's tower, offering so-so views over the square, cathedral, and castle.

Cost and Hours: €5, includes audioguide, €6 combo-ticket with Apponyi House, Tue-Fri 10:00-17:00, Sat-Sun 11:00-18:00, closed Mon, in the Old Town Hall—enter through courtyard, tel. 02/259-100-811, www.muzeum.bratislava.sk.

Apponyi House (Apponyiho Palác)

This nicely restored mansion of a Hungarian aristocrat is meaningless without the included audioguide (dull but informative). The museum has two parts. The cellar and ground floor feature an interesting exhibit on the vineyards of the nearby "Little Carpathian" hills, with historic presses and barrels, and a replica of an old-time wine-pub table. Upstairs are two floors of urban apartments from old Bratislava, called the Period Rooms Museum. The first floor up shows off the 18th-century Rococo-style rooms of the nobility— fine but not ostentatious, with ceramic stoves. The second floor up (with lower ceilings and simpler wall decorations) illustrates 19th-century bourgeois/middle-class lifestyles, including period clothing and some Empire-style furniture.

Cost and Hours: €4, includes audioguide, €6 combo-ticket with City History Museum, Tue-Fri 10:00-17:00, Sat-Sun 11:00-18:00, closed Mon, Radničná 1, tel. 02/5920-5135, www.muzeum.bratislava.sk.

BEYOND THE OLD TOWN
Bratislava Castle and Museum
(Bratislavský Hrad a Múzeum)

This imposing fortress, nicknamed the "upside-down table," is the city's most prominent landmark. The oldest surviving chunk is the

13th-century Romanesque watch-tower (the one slightly taller than the other three). When Habsburg Empress Maria Theresa took a liking to Bratislava in the 18th century, she transformed the castle from a military fortress to a royal residence suitable for holding court. She added a summer riding school (the U-shaped complex next to the castle), an enclosed winter riding school out back, and lots more. Maria Theresa's favorite daughter, Maria Christina, lived here with her husband, Albert, when they were newlyweds. Locals nicknamed the place "little Schönbrunn," in reference to the Habsburgs' summer palace on the outskirts of Vienna.

Turned into a fortress-garrison during the Napoleonic Wars, the castle burned to the ground in an 1811 fire started by careless soldiers, and was left as a ruin for 150 years before being reconstructed in 1953. Unfortunately, the uninviting communist rebuild left the inner courtyard feeling like a prison exercise yard.

The museum exhibits inside aren't really worth the cost of admission. The best visit is to simply hike up, enjoy the views over town, and take a close-up look at the stately old building. For the best walking route to the castle, see page 960.

Cost and Hours: Castle grounds—free, Castle museum—€7; Tue-Sun 10:00-18:00, closed Mon; ticket office to right of main river-facing entrance—enter exhibits from passage into central courtyard, tel. 02/2048-3110, www.snm.sk.

Visiting the Castle Museum: If you enter the palace, skip the misnamed Treasure Room (a sparse collection of ancient items found at the castle site) and the Knights Hall (offering a brief history lesson in the castle's construction and reconstruction). A blinding-white staircase with gold trim leads to the Music Hall, with a prized 18th-century Assumption altarpiece by Anton Schmidt (first floor); a collection of historical prints depicting Bratislava and its castle (second floor); and temporary exhibits (third/top floor). From the top floor, a series of very steep, modern staircases take you up to the Crown Tower (the castle's oldest and tallest) for views over town—though the vista from the terrace in front of the castle is much easier to reach and nearly as good.

▲▲SNP Bridge and UFO

Bratislava's bizarre, flying-saucer-capped bridge, completed in 1972 in heavy-handed communist style, has been reclaimed by

capitalists. The flying saucer-shaped structure called the UFO (at the Petržalka end of the bridge) is now a spruced-up, overpriced café/restaurant and observation deck, allowing sweeping 360-degree views of Bratislava from about 300 feet above the Danube. Think of it as the Slovak Space Needle.

Cost and Hours: €7.50, daily 10:00-23:00, elevator free if you have a meal reservation or order food at the pricey restaurant, restaurant opens at 12:00, tel. 02/6252-0300, www.redmonkeygroup.com.

Getting There: Walk across the bridge from the old town (walkways cross the bridge on a level below the road; the elevator entrance is a few steps down from the downstream-side walkway).

Visiting the UFO: The "elevator" that takes you up is actually a funicular—you may notice you're moving at an angle. At the top, walk up the stairs to the observation deck, passing photos of the bridge's construction.

Begin by viewing the **castle** and **old town.** The area to the right of the old town, between and beyond the skyscrapers, is a massive construction zone.

A time-lapse camera set up here over the next few years will catch skyscrapers popping up like dandelions. International investors are throwing lots of money at Bratislava. (Imagine having so much prime, undeveloped real

estate available downtown in the capital of an emerging European economic power...and just an hour down the road from Vienna, no less.) Most of the development is taking place along the banks of the Danube. In a decade, this will be a commercial center.

The huge TV tower caps a forested hill beyond the old town. Below and to the left of it, the pointy monument is **Slavín,** where more than 6,800 Soviet soldiers who fought to liberate Bratislava from the Nazis are buried. Under communist rule, a nearby church was forced to take down its steeple so as not to draw attention away from the huge Soviet soldier on top of the monument.

Now turn 180 degrees and cross the platform to face **Petržalka,** a planned communist suburb that sprouted here in the 1970s. The site was once occupied by a village, and the various districts of modern Petržalka still carry their original names (which now seem ironic): "Meadows" *(Háje),* "Woods" *(Lúky),* and "Courtyards" *(Dvory).* The ambitious communist planners envisioned a city laced with Venetian-style canals to help drain the marshy land, but the plans were abandoned after the harsh crackdown on the 1968 Prague Spring uprising. Without the incentives of private ownership, all they succeeded in creating was a grim and decaying sea of miserable concrete apartment *paneláky* ("panel buildings," so-called because they're made of huge prefab panels).

Today, one in four Bratislavans lives in Petržalka, and things are looking better. Like Dorothy opening the door to Oz, the formerly drab buildings have been splashed with bright new colors. Far from being a slum, Petržalka is a popular neighborhood for Bratislavan yuppies who can't yet afford to build their dream houses. Locals read the Czech-language home-improvement magazine *Panel Plus* for ideas on how to give their *panelák* apartments some style (browse it yourself at www.panelplus.cz).

Petržalka is also a big suburban-style shopping zone (note the supermall down below). But there's still some history here. The **park** called Sad Janka Kráľa (originally, in German, Aupark)—just downriver from the bridge—was technically the first public park in Europe in the 1770s and is still a popular place for locals to relax and court.

Scanning the **horizon** beyond Petržalka, two things stick out: on the left, the old communist oil refinery (which has been fully updated and is now state-of-the-art); and on the right, a forest of modern windmills. These are just over the border, in Austria...and

---

Sleep Code

Hotels are classified based on the average price of a standard double room with breakfast in high season.

$$$$	**Splurge:** Most rooms over €170
$$$	**Pricier:** €130-170
$$	**Moderate:** €90-130
$	**Budget:** €50-90
¢	**Backpacker:** Under €50
RS%	**Rick Steves discount**

Unless otherwise noted, credit cards are accepted, hotel staff speak basic English, and free Wi-Fi is available. Comparison-shop by checking prices at several hotels (on each hotel's own website, on a booking site, or by email). For the best deal, *book directly with the hotel.* Ask for a discount if paying in cash; if the listing includes **RS%,** request a Rick Steves discount.

Bratislava is sure to grow in that direction quickly. Austria is about three miles that way, and Hungary is about six miles farther to the left.

Before you leave, consider a drink at the café. If nothing else, be sure to use the memorable WCs (guys can enjoy a classic urinal photo).

Sleeping in Bratislava

I'd rather sleep in Budapest—particularly since good-value options in central Bratislava are slim, and service tends to be surly. Business-oriented places charge more on weekdays than on weekends. Expect prices to drop slightly in winter and in the hottest summer months. Hotel Michalská Brána is right in the heart of the old town, while the others are just outside it—but still within a 5-10-minute walk.

$$$$ Hotel Marrol's, on a quiet street, is the town's most enticing splurge. Although the immediate neighborhood isn't interesting, it's a five-minute walk from the old town, and its 53 rooms are luxurious and tastefully-appointed Old World country-style. While pricey, rates drop on weekends (elevator, air-con, loaner laptops, free minibar, gorgeous lounge, Tobrucká 4, tel. 02/5778-4600, www.hotelmarrols.sk, rec@hotelmarrols.sk). From the main train station, tram #1 takes you straight here—hop off at the fifth stop, Šafárikovo Námestie.

$ Hotel Michalská Brána is a charming boutique hotel just inside St. Michael's Gate in the old town. The 14 rooms are sleek, mod, and classy, and the location is ideal—right in the heart of town, but on a relatively sleepy lane just away from the hubbub (air-

BRATISLAVA

con, elevator, Baštová 4, tel. 02/5930-7200, www.michalskabrana.
com, reception@michalskabrana.com).

$ Penzión Virgo sits on a quiet residential street, an eight-
minute walk from the old town. The 12 boutiqueish rooms are
stylish and well-appointed (breakfast extra, reserve ahead for inexpensive parking, Panenská 14, mobile 0948-350-878, www.penzi-
onvirgo.sk, reception@penzionvirgo.sk).

¢ Downtown Backpackers Hostel is a funky but well-run
place located in an old-fashioned townhouse. Rooms are named for
famous artists and decorated with reinterpretations of their paintings (private rooms available, breakfast extra, bike rental, Panenská
31—across busy boulevard from Grassalkovich Palace, 10 minutes
on foot from main station or take bus #93, mobile 0905/259-714 or
0911/118-123, www.backpackers.sk, info@backpackers.sk).

Eating in Bratislava

For a fun drink and snack that locals love, try a Vinea grape soda
and a sweet *Pressburger* bagel in any bar or café.

Like the Czechs, the Slovaks produce excellent beer (*pivo*, PEE-voh). One of the top
brands is Zlatý Bažant ("Golden Pheasant").
Bratislava's beer halls are good places to sample
Slovak and Czech beers, and to get a hearty,
affordable meal of stick-to-your-ribs pub grub.
Long a wine-producing area, the Bratislava region makes the same wines that Vienna is famous for. But, as nearly all is consumed locally,
most outsiders don't think of Slovakia as wine
country.

The best plan may be to stroll the old town
and keep your eyes open for the setting and
cuisine that appeals to you most. Or consider
one of these options.

$ 1. Slovak Pub ("1." as in "the first") attracts a student crowd.
Enter from Obchodná, the bustling shopping street just above the
old town, and climb the stairs into a vast warren of rustic, old coun-
tryside-style pub rooms with uneven floors. Enjoy the lively, loud,
almost chaotic ambience while dining on affordable and truly authentic Slovak fare, made with products from the pub's own farm.
This is a good place to try the Slovak specialty, *bryndzové halušky*
(Mon 10:00-23:00, Tue-Sat until 24:00, Sun 12:00-23:00, Obchodná 62, tel. 02/5292-6367, www.slovakpub.sk).

$$ Bratislavský Meštiansky Pivovar ("Bratislava Town
Brewpub"), just above the old town behind the big Crowne Plaza
hotel, brews its own beer and also sells a variety of others. Seating

---

Restaurant Price Code

I've assigned each eatery a price category, based on the average cost of a typical main course. Drinks, desserts, and splurge items (steak and seafood) can raise the price considerably.

$$$$	**Splurge:** Most main courses over €20
$$$	**Pricier:** €15-20
$$	**Moderate:** €10-15
$	**Budget:** Under €10

In Slovakia, a takeout spot is **$**; a beer hall or basic sit-down eatery is **$$**; a casual but more upscale restaurant is **$$$**; and a swanky splurge is **$$$$**.

---

stretches over several levels in the new-meets-old interior (Mon-Sat 11:00-24:00, Sun until 23:00, Drevená 8, mobile 0944-512-265, www.mestianskypivovar.sk).

$$$ Lemon Tree/Sky Bar/Rum Club, a three-in-one place just past the fenced-in US Embassy on the trendy Hviezdoslavovo Námestie, features the same Thai-meets-Mediterranean menu throughout. But the real reason to come here is for the seventh-floor Sky Bar, with fantastic views of the old town and the SNP Bridge. It's smart to reserve a view table in advance if you want to dine here—or just drop by for a pricey vodka cocktail on the small terrace. You've got the best seat in town, and though prices are expensive for Bratislava, they're no more than what you'd pay for a meal in Vienna (daily 11:00-late, Sun from 12:00, Hviezdoslavovo Námestie 7, mobile 0948-109-400, www.spicy.sk).

At **$$$ Eurovea** (the recommended end to my walking tour, 10 minutes downstream from the old town), huge outdoor terraces rollicking with happy eaters line the swanky riverfront residential and shopping-mall complex. You'll pay high prices for the great atmosphere and views at international eateries—French, Italian, Brazilian—and a branch of the Czech beer-hall chain Kolkovna. Or you can head to the **$ food court** in the shopping mall, where you'll eat well for cheap.

$ Štúr is a hip, rustic-chic café (named for a revered 19th-century champion of Slovak culture, Ľudovít Štúr) with coffee drinks, sandwiches, and quiches (takeaway or table service, open long hours daily, just east of the old town, near Eurovea, at Štúrova 8).

$ Coffee & Bagel Story (a chain) sells...coffee and takeout bagel sandwiches. The handiest location is on the main square at Hlavné Námestie 8, with picnic tables right out front.

Supermarket: Try **Billa,** across from the Philharmonic, on Mostová street (Mon-Fri 7:00-21:00, Sat from 8:00, closed Sun).

Bratislava Connections

BY TRAIN

Bratislava has two major train stations: the main station, walkable to some accommodations and the old town (Hlavná Stanica, abbreviated "Bratislava hl. st." on schedules) and Petržalka station (sometimes called ŽST Petržalka), in a suburb across the river and linked to town by bus. When checking schedules, pay attention to which station your train uses. Frequent bus #93 connects the two stations (5-12/hour, 10 minutes; after 23:00 take bus #N93). For public transit info and maps, see http://imhd.zoznam.sk.

Hlavná Stanica (Main Train Station): This decrepit station is about a half-mile north of the old town. A left-luggage desk is to your right as you exit the tracks (*úschovňa batožín;* confirm open hours for pick-up). There are also a few lockers along track 1.

It's a 15-minute **walk** to the town center. Walk out the station's front door and follow the covered walkway next to the bus loop; it leads to a double pedestrian overpass. Cross on the nearer pedestrian overpass and head downhill on the busy main drag, Štefánikova, lined with Habsburg-era facades. You'll pass the presidential gardens, then Grassalkovich Palace, Slovakia's "White House" (with soldiers at guard out front). The old town—marked by the green steeple of St. Michael's Gate (the start of my self-guided walk)—is a long block ahead of you.

To shave a few minutes off the trip, ride from the station to Grassalkovich Palace on **bus** #93 (after 23:00, use bus #N93). Walk out the station's front door to the bus stops on the right. Buy a €0.70/15-minute *základný lístok/basic* ticket from the machine, and be sure to stamp it, either in the machine at the bus stop or on board.

Trams *(električky)* leave from an underground area outside the train station (same tickets as buses).

Petržalka Train Station (ŽST Petržalka): Half of the trains from Vienna arrive at this clean, quiet, modern little train station, across the river in the modern suburb of Petržalka (PET-ur-ZHAL-kuh). Luggage lockers are available here.

From this station, ride bus #93 (direction: Hlavná Stanica) or #94 (direction: STU) four stops to Zochova (the first stop after the bridge, near St. Michael's Gate); after 23:00, use bus #N93. Buy a €0.70/15-minute *základný lístok/basic* ticket from the machine, and be sure to stamp it.

From Bratislava by Train to: Budapest (every 1-2 hours to Keleti Station, 3 hours, more with transfers; also doable—and possibly cheaper—by Orange Ways bus, 1-4/day, 2.5 hours, www.orangeways.com), **Vienna** (2/hour, 1 hour; buy the €16 round-trip EU Regio day pass, which is cheaper than a one-way fare; departures alternate between the two stations—half from main station, half from Petržalka), **Sopron** (nearly hourly direct, 2.5 hours on RegionalExpress/REX; more with transfers at stations in downtown and/or suburban Vienna), **Prague** (5/day direct, 4.25 hours). To reach other Hungarian destinations (including **Eger** and **Pécs**), it's generally easiest to change in Budapest.

BY BUS

Two different companies run handy buses that connect Bratislava, Vienna, and the airports in each city: **Blaguss** (tel. 02/4363-7257, www.blaguss.sk) and **Slovak Lines/Postbus** (tel. 0810-222-3336, www.slovaklines.sk). You can book ahead online, or (if arriving at the airport) just take whichever connection is leaving first. The bus schedules are handily posted at www.bts.aero/en (find the "Transport" tab).

The buses run about hourly from Bratislava's airport to Bratislava (15 minutes, stop either at the main bus station east of the old town or at the Most SNP stop underneath the SNP Bridge), continue on to Vienna's airport (1 hour), and end in Vienna (1.25 hours, U: Erdberg). They then turn around and make the reverse journey (€5-7.50).

BY BOAT

Riverboats connect Bratislava to Vienna. Conveniently, these boats dock right along the Danube in front of Bratislava's old town. While they are more expensive, less frequent, and slower than the train, some travelers enjoy getting out on the Danube. It's prudent to bring your passport if crossing over for the day (though it's unlikely anyone will ask for it).

The **Twin City Liner** offers three to five daily boat trips between a dock at the edge of Bratislava's old town, along Fajnorovo nábrežie, and Vienna's Schwedenplatz (where Vienna's town center hits the canal; €30-35 each way, 75-minute trip, mid-April-Oct only; can fill up—reservations smart, Austrian tel. 01/58880, www.twincityliner.com).

The competing Slovak **LOD** line connects the cities a little more cheaply, but just twice a day. These boats are slower, as they use Vienna's less-convenient Reichsbrücke dock on the main river, farther from the city center (€25 one-way, €38 round-trip, 1.5-hour trip, tel. 02/5293-2226, www.lod.sk).

BY PLANE

You have two options for reaching Bratislava: You can fly into its own airport, or into the very nearby Vienna Airport.

Bratislava Airport (Letisko Bratislava)

This airport (airport code: BTS, www.bts.aero) is six miles northeast of downtown Bratislava. Budget airline Ryanair has many flights here. Some airlines market it as "Vienna-Bratislava," thanks to its proximity to both capitals. It's compact and manageable, with all the usual amenities.

From the Airport to Downtown Bratislava: The airport has easy **public bus** connections to Bratislava's main train station (Hlavná Stanica, €1.30, bus #61, 3-4/hour, 30 minutes). To reach the bus stop, exit straight out of the arrivals hall, cross the street, buy a ticket at the kiosk, and look for the bus stop on your right. For directions from the train station into the old town, see earlier. A taxi from the airport into central Bratislava should cost less than €20.

To Budapest: Take the bus or **taxi** to Bratislava's main train station (described above), then hop a train to Budapest.

To Vienna: Take either the Slovak Lines/Postbus bus, which runs to Vienna's Hauptbahnhof (€5, 1-2/hour, 1.5 hours, www.slovaklines.sk) or the Blaguss bus to the Erdberg stop on Vienna's U-3 subway line, on which it's a straight shot to Stephansplatz or Mariahilfer Strasse (€7.50, runs every 1-2 hours, 1 hour, www.blaguss.sk). Schedules for these buses are posted on the airport's website (www.bts.aero/en, under the "Transport" tab). A taxi from Bratislava Airport directly to Vienna costs €60-90 (depending on whether you use a cheaper Slovak or more expensive Austrian cab).

Vienna International Airport

This airport, 12 miles from downtown Vienna and 30 miles from downtown Bratislava, is well-connected both to both capitals (airport code: VIE, airport tel. 01/700-722-233, www.viennaairport.com). For a full description of this airport, see page 939.

To reach **Bratislava** from the airport, the easiest option is to take the Blaguss or Slovak Lines/Postbus bus described earlier (under "By Bus"). Check schedules on the airport website (under "Arrival & Parking") or ask the TI which bus is leaving first, then head straight out the door and hop on. After about 45 minutes, the bus stops in downtown Bratislava, then heads to the Bratislava airport. I'd skip the train connection, which takes longer and involves complicated changes (airport train to Wien-Mitte Bahnhof in downtown Vienna, S-Bahn/subway to Südbahnhof, train to Bratislava, figure 1.75 hours total).

MORE EASTERN EUROPE

MORE EASTERN EUROPE

The preceding chapters cover what I consider to be, for most travelers, the core of Eastern Europe. But in a sense, "Eastern Europe" is like the Louisiana Purchase...you can delve in as far as you like. That's where this section comes in.

The next five chapters offer a brief, practical overview for countries that lie just beyond the core of this book. Because this is designed to get you started—with candid advice about where to go, and what you'd do in each place—I've included only the most basic advice for logistics such as transportation, accommodations, and restaurants. These chapters are intended only as a first step—not the final word. In each one, I offer a quick overview, a rundown of practical country facts, some itinerary-planning advice, a few tips on the local cuisine and language, and a concise rundown of the best destinations (focusing on calling out the other attractions that are most worth your valuable time).

In the following pages, you'll find details on these destinations:

Croatia: Eastern Europe's Riviera is a natural add-on for travelers going to Slovenia—it's just down the road. For a quick taste of Croatia, you can dip into the northern Istrian Peninsula (which borders Slovenia) and enjoy one of Croatia's top seaside towns, Rovinj. Those taking the train between Budapest and Ljubljana will pass through Croatia's underrated capital, Zagreb, which is worth at least a few hours' exploration (or even a night or two). And if you have plenty of time, you can head south through the waterfall wonderland of Plitvice Lakes National Park to the Dalmatian Coast: Dubrovnik, Split, and the islands of Hvar and Korčula.

Bosnia-Herzegovina: Croatia wraps around this inviting country, with a dramatic landscape and a vibrant culture. I've focused on two top destinations: The small city of Mostar is an easy

More Eastern Europe at a Glance

Croatia Gorgeous coastline, islands, natural wonders (Plitvice Lakes), and great cities (Zagreb and Split).

Bosnia-Herzegovina A gregarious and gorgeous land with complex history, a rich Muslim tradition, and fascinating cities small (Mostar) and large (Sarajevo).

Montenegro Ruggedly beautiful landscape—from beaches to peaks—just south of Croatia.

Bulgaria Culturally-rich land with ancient artifacts, scintillating cities (Plovdiv, Sofia), charming towns (Veliko Tarnovo), great food, and kind people.

Romania Big and complex country with a thriving capital (Bucharest), Transylvanian castles and towns, vibrant folk culture (in Maramureş), and vividly painted monasteries (in Bucovina).

side-trip from Croatia's Dalmatian Coast, and offers an accessible and intriguing first look at Bosnia. With more time, it's rewarding to venture farther to the even more engaging capital, Sarajevo.

Montenegro: Just south of Croatia, Montenegro's glorious Bay of Kotor—with stunning scenery and characteristic seaside towns—is an easy side-trip for those based in Dubrovnik. With more time, you could head up into the hills to see the historic capital, Cetinje.

Bulgaria: A cultural detour that's well worth taking, Bulgaria involves a long overland journey (through the rugged Balkan Peninsula) or a quick flight from the core Eastern European countries. From the mellow and user-friendly capital, Sofia, you can head for the fun and fascinating second city, Plovdiv; the dramatically set historic capital, Veliko Tarnovo; and a variety of countryside sights: remote and majestic Rila Monastery, the ancient artifacts and fragrant rose fields of the Thracian Plain, and mountain-capping monuments including the bizarre communist-era conference hall called Buzludzha.

Romania: Romania is a big, crazy, fascinating, time-consuming destination—but for many, it's worth the effort. Romania borders Hungary, and parts are accessible on a long train ride or drive from Budapest. But given the long distances, it may be easier to fly into Bucharest (the capital) and continue from there. Bucharest deserves a quick look, but the main concentration of famous sights are a few hours north—in Transylvania. Choose a home-base town or two (the best options are Brașov—near castles; Sighișoara—near fortified churches; and Sibiu—best all-around town)...and then explore. If you're captivated by traditional folk life, you could take the long drive even farther north, to the rustic corner called Maramureș. And with even more time, consider swinging through the northeastern region of Bucovina, famous for its vividly painted monasteries.

Additional Information: In some cases—Croatia, Bosnia-Herzegovina, and Montenegro—you can find my complete coverage in a separate book: *Rick Steves Croatia & Slovenia*. In other cases—Bulgaria and Romania—I haven't produced a full-length book, but plenty of other guidebooks and online sources are available to fill in the gaps and advance your planning. (Also, in Bulgaria and Romania, local guides are particularly affordable and worth hiring to make your trip-planning easier—I've recommended my favorites in each country.)

CROATIA

Hrvatska

Sunny beaches, succulent seafood, and a taste of *la dolce vita*...in Eastern Europe?

With thousands of miles of inviting seafront, Croatia's coastline is Eastern Europe's Riviera. Holiday-makers love its pebbly beaches, predictably balmy summer weather, and dramatic mountains. Croatia is also historic. From ruined Roman arenas and Byzantine mosaics to Venetian bell towers, Habsburg villas, and even communist concrete, past rulers have left their mark. And for thoughtful travelers, a trip to Croatia comes with an opportunity to better understand Europe's most violent conflict since World War II: the breakup of Yugoslavia (see page 1101). All in all, Croatia offers something to everyone—there's good reason that it's one of Europe's hottest emerging destinations.

Where to Go: Croatia has more than 3,600 miles of coastline and more than a thousand islands. To be selective, zoom in on these three areas:

The **Dalmatian Coast,** a dramatic limestone coastline, features a bustling big city with the best ancient ruins in the country (Split); several alluring islands (most notably Korčula and Hvar); and Croatia's showcase city: romantic, walled Dubrovnik.

Istria, a wedge-shaped peninsula in northern Croatia, has rolling hills, wineries, truffles, charming hill towns, ancient ruins (in Pula), and the finest coastal town between Venice and Dubrovnik: Rovinj.

The **Croatian interior** boasts the country's surprisingly ap-

CROATIA

pealing capital, Zagreb, which lies near Hungary and Austria. And two hours south, deep in the countryside, is one of Europe's top natural wonders, Plitvice Lakes National Park.

For a quick visit of just a few days, focus either on the Dalmatian Coast (and possibly add in some Bosnia and Montenegro—covered in the next two chapters) or on the sights in the north (Istria and the interior). With more time—a week or more—you can hit the highlights of all three regions.

Seasonality: Croatia is the most seasonal destination in this book. July and August are the peak of peak—everything is jammed up with European vacationers, and prices are high. Late May, June, September, and early October are the best times to visit...it's cooler (but still warm) and less crowded. But off-season (after about mid-October, or before early May), while big cities like Dubrovnik and Split remain open for business, smaller towns close up tight.

Accommodations: Especially in the coastal towns, hotels tend to be big, overpriced resorts. Instead, carefully consider private accommodations: a *sobe* (room) or *apartman* (apartment). These offer double the cultural intimacy for a fraction the price of a big

Croatia Practicalities

Money: Croatia uses the kuna: $1 = about 7 kuna (kn, or HRK). One kuna is broken down into 100 lipa.

Geography and People: The country is 22,000 square miles, similar to West Virginia. Of the 4.5 million people, 90 percent are ethnic Croats (Catholic) and 4.5 percent are Serbs (Orthodox). Its biggest cities are the capital, Zagreb (pop. 790,000) and Split (pop. 178,000). The country's GDP is $80 billion ($18,000 GDP per capita).

Snapshot History: After losing their independence to Hungary in 1102, the Croats watched as most of their coastline became Venetian and their interior was conquered by Ottomans. Croatia was "rescued" by the Habsburgs, but after World War I it became part of Yugoslavia—a decision many Croats regretted until they finally gained independence in 1991 through a bitter war with their Serb neighbors. Today, Croatia is proudly independent.

Famous Croatians: Roman Emperor Diocletian, explorer Marco Polo, Nikoka Tesla (a Croatia-born Serb), and several Croatian-Americans, including Roger Maris, John Malkovich, John Kasich, and Dennis Kucinich.

Emergencies: Dial 92 for police; dial 112 for medical or other emergencies.

Consular Services in Zagreb: The US Embassy is at Ulica Thomasa Jeffersona 2 (tel. 01/661-2300, after-hours tel. 01/661-2400, http://zagreb.usembassy.gov). The Canadian Embassy is at Prilaz Đure Deželića 4 (tel. 01/488-1200, www. croatia.gc.ca). Call ahead for passport services.

Telephone Country Code: +385, then drop the initial 0 of the phone number.

Tourist Information: www.us.croatia.hr

CROATIA

hotel—and many are quite comfortable and hotelesque, with modern amenities and all of the independence you like. For the best prices, book directly (I've listed websites for my favorites).

Getting Around: Croatia's trains are of limited usefulness, but their bus network is strong (for schedules, see www.autobusni-kolodvor.com). Coastal destinations (including the islands) are well-connected by bus and by ferry—either big, lumbering car ferries (mostly operated by Jadrolinija, www.jadrolinija.hr) or speedy catamarans (handy ones on the Dalmatian Coast include www. jadrolinija.hr, www.krilo.hr, and www.gv-line.hr). Croatia is also easy for drivers, with excellent roads including a slick network of expressways (with tolls).

Croatian Cuisine: Like Italian fare, Croatian cooking includes lots of pasta, pizza, seafood, and *pršut* (prosciutto). Fill the tank at a pizzeria, but every so often splurge on a seafood feast. Try octopus salad or "black risotto" (a rice dish with cuttlefish simmered in its own ink). Ice-cream stands are abundant. In the interior, meat is popular (especially prepared with a *peka*—simmered under a metal baking lid covered in hot coals). While the cuisine scene in most of the famous coastal destinations is uninspired, Istria—with its proximity to Italy and abundant truffles—is a step above. Croatia also produces excellent wines (*bijelo* is white, *crno* is red).

Croatian Language: Most Croatians speak excellent English, so the language barrier is minimal. But just in case, here are a few helpful Croatian phrases: "Hello" is *Dobar dan* (formal) or *Bok* (informal); "please" is *molim;* "thank you" is *hvala;* and "Goodbye" is *Do viđenija.*

Top Croatian Destinations

The following sections are designed to get you started planning a trip to Croatia. For in-depth coverage—including self-guided walks and museum tours, detailed hotel and restaurant listings, and lots of practical advice—consider my *Rick Steves Croatia & Slovenia* guidebook.

THE DALMATIAN COAST
Of Croatia's long coastline, the southern third—stretching 200 miles from Zadar to Dubrovnik—contains many of the country's most popular destinations.

▲▲▲Dubrovnik
Dubrovnik is a living fairy tale that shouldn't be missed. It feels like a small town today, but 500 years ago, Dubrovnik was an independent city-state and major maritime power, with the third-biggest navy in the Mediterranean. Still jutting confidently into the sea and ringed by thick medieval walls, Dubrovnik deserves its nickname: the Pearl of the Adriatic. Within the ramparts, the traffic-free Old Town is a fun jumble of steep alleys, low-impact museums, al fresco cafés, and kid-

friendly squares. For tourist information, see www.tzdubrovnik.hr.

Visiting Dubrovnik: Though it's a sprawling city of 50,000 people, most visitors focus on its compact Old Town. Simply strolling the ▲▲▲ **Stradun** (main drag) is a highlight. Several churches, museums, and other attractions hide within the City Walls. All of them are skippable, but it's worth dipping into the fine ▲ **Cathedral** (with its quirky treasury collection); the restful cloisters of the ▲ **Franciscan and Dominican monasteries** (each with a modest museum); and the ▲ **Rector's Palace** (the historical residence of the rulers of this independent city-state). The Old Town also has a historical synagogue, a finely decorated Eastern Orthodox Church and icon collection, good ethnographic and maritime museums, an aquarium, and a poignant exhibition of wartime photography.

Dubrovnik's single-best attraction is strolling the scenic mile-and-a-quarter around the top of the remarkably well-preserved ▲▲▲ **City Walls.** As you meander along this lofty perch—with a sea of orange roofs on one side and the azure sea on the other—you'll get your bearings, peer into secluded gardens, and snap pictures like mad of the ever-changing views. Walk the walls early or late—the ticket line gets long with cruise-ship passengers midday.

For an even higher viewpoint, ride the ▲▲▲ **cable car** from just above the City Walls up to the summit of Mount Srđ. There you'll enjoy sweeping views down over the red rooftops of Dubrovnik, and out to offshore islands that recede into the sunset (www. dubrovnikcablecar.com).

The city can get very crowded midday, so it can be nice to escape to a nearby **beach** (several scenic spots line the road outside the Ploče Gate, southeast of the Old Town). Or head to the **Old Port**—at the mouth of the Old Town—where local captains offer sightseeing cruises. Popular destinations include little Lokrum Island (just offshore, great hiking and uncrowded beaches) and the Elaphite Islands (a trio of larger islands, each with small villages and beaches).

Sleeping in Dubrovnik: $$ Dubrovnik Gardens, an excellent value, is located in a private little garden inside the Old Town (Roberto and Marija, www.dubrovnikgardens.com). For private rooms on a sleepy, skinny, stepped lane inside the Old Town, try **$$ Villa Ragusa** (run by Pero, www.villaragusadubrovnik. com) or **$$ Apartments Paviša** (run by a different Pero, www. apartmentspavisa.com); if they're full, their neighbors often have rooms. Other good rooms around town include the simple but cheery **$ Plaza Apartments** (Lidija, www.apartmaniplaza.com), the classy **$$ Apartments Amoret** (Branka, www.dubrovnik-amoret.com), and the upscale and trendy **$$$$ Fresh Sheets Kathedral B&B** (Jon and Sanja, www.freshsheetskathedral.com).

Eating in Dubrovnik: Avoid the overpriced tourist traps on the main drag and on the glitzy "restaurant row," Prijeko street. One exception is **Nishta,** a well-run vegetarian eatery with an eclectic international menu (on Prijeko street, www.nishtarestaurant.com). For traditional Dalmatian food done well, try classy **Dalmatino** (Miha Pracata 6, www.dalmatino-dubrovnik.com) or **Kopun,** on a gravelly square facing a church (Poljana Ruđera Boškovića 7, www.restaurantkopun.com). To sample local wines (paired with light local dishes), don't miss **D'Vino Wine Bar** (Palmotićeva 4a, www.dvino.net). And for the most scenic setting in town, get a drink at one of two bars called **Cold Drinks "Buža"**—that means "hole in the wall"—which is literally what you'll have to climb through to reach these delightful perches, clinging like barnacles to the seaward side of the City Walls (ask locals for help to find the entrances).

Private Drivers: Many travelers splurge on hiring their own private driver for side-trips to destinations described in the next two chapters: Bosnia's Mostar and Montenegro's Bay of Kotor (figure around €250 for a full-day trip). Good options include **Pepo Klaić** (www.dubrovnikshoretrip.com) and **Petar Vlašić** (www.dubrovnikrivieratours.com).

▲▲Split

Split (pronounced as it's spelled) is Croatia's second city, bustling with 178,000 people. If you've been hopping along the coast, landing in urban Split feels like a return to civilization. While most Dalmatian coastal towns seem made for tourists, Split is real and vibrant—a shipbuilding city with ugly sprawl surrounding an atmospheric Old Town, which teems with Croatians living life to the fullest. As this is a transportation hub for the coast, you'll likely pass

through at some point. It's well worth spending a night (or more) to fully experience this underrated city. For tourist information, see www.visitsplit.com.

Though Split throbs to a modern, youthful beat, its history goes way back—all the way to the Roman Empire. And today, Split has some of the best Roman ruins this side of Italy. In the fourth century A.D., the Roman Emperor Diocletian (245-313) wanted to retire in his native Dalmatia, so he built a huge palace here. Eventually, the palace was abandoned. Then locals, fleeing seventh-century Slavic invaders, moved in and made themselves at home, and a medieval town sprouted from the rubble of the old palace.

This—combined with Venetian influence starting in the 15th century—has left Split a fascinating study in the layers of history.

Visiting Split: The city's top experience is exploring the ruins of ▲▲▲ **Diocletian's Palace,** which are integrated into the townscape of the Old Town. The Old Town's streets were literally the hallways of the palaces; you can see where later settlers grafted windows and doors onto the original structure. And those windows and doors are still in use today.

Begin by exploring **Diocletian's Cellars,** the cavelike foundation that Roman engineers built to support the massive palace.

Then head up to the **Peristyle**—once the palace's grand entryway, it's now the Old Town's main square. Café cushions line the steps (buy a drink if you want to rest on one), and up the stairs is a majestic entry vestibule where a cappella singers perform traditional Dalmatian *klapa* music.

Towering over the Peristyle is the **Cathedral of St. Domnius,** which began life as Diocletian's mausoleum. Inside, you can see what was supposed to be the final resting place of the emperor, who was notorious for torturing Christians. In a bit of poetic justice, today his mausoleum is a cathedral honoring those martyrs...and Diocletian is nowhere to be found.

Another wonderful experience is sauntering along Split's main pedestrian promenade, called **the Riva.** Filling the area between the Old Town (Diocletian's Palace) and the busy modern port, it's the perfect place to people-watch, lick an ice-cream cone, or nurse a coffee. Best around sunset—when it seems the whole town is out strolling—this mellow scene also sprawls up Marmontova street from the harbor.

Most of Split's museums (covering city history, archaeology, ethnography, and an old synagogue) are skippable. But one is a must: the ▲▲ **Meštrović Gallery,** displaying the works of local sculptor Ivan Meštrović (1883-1962). After a successful career in interwar Yugoslavia, Meštrović built a mansion and studio overlooking the Adriatic Sea on the outskirts of Split. Today that mansion—an easy bus or taxi ride from the Old Town—displays his expressive sculptures, which were greatly admired by his contemporary, Auguste Rodin. Meštrović's works still grace parks and squares all over Croatia (and in Chicago, where the artist fled after World War II).

Split is also a great city for relaxing. It has several distinctive and inviting squares; a green park peninsula, called **Marjan,** with hiking trails and beaches; and a lively, user-friendly nightlife scene.

Sleeping in Split: Just outside of the Old Town are some small, well-run guesthouses, including **$$ Villa Ana** (www.villaana-split. hr) and **$$ Villa Matejuška** (www.villamatejuska.hr). Within the Old Town—which can be noisy at night, especially on weekends— you can splurge at **$$$$ Marmont Hotel** (www.marmonthotel. com) or the cozy luxury B&B called **$$$$ Palača Judita** (www. juditapalace.com), or sleep more affordably at **$$ Kaleta Apart- ments** (www.kaletaapartments.com) or **$ Sobe "Base"** (www.base-rooms.com).

Eating in Split: You'll eat well inside the Old Town at the classic, fish-oriented **Trattoria Bajamont** (Bajamontijeva 3). Even better options are just a short walk west of the Old Town, in the Varoš neighborhood: cozy **Konoba Matejuška** (Tomića Stine 3), bustling **Šperun Restaurant** (Šperun 3), or the upscale **Paradigma** (Bana Jelačića ulica 3, www.jre.eu/paradigma).

▲▲Dalmatian Islands: Korčula and Hvar

Croatia is famous for its islands, and some of the most popular are in Dalmatia. Many travelers argue that *their* favorite island is the very best island, but I'll let you in on a little secret: They're all equally good. While each has its claim to fame, the Croatian is- lands are essentially variations on a theme: a warm stone Old Town with a Venetian bell tower, a tidy boat-speckled harbor, ample seafood restaurants, a few refurbished resort hotels on the edge of town, and *sobe* and *apartman* signs by every other doorbell. My two favorites are relatively well-connected to each other and to the mainland: ritzy Hvar and mellow, dramatically situated Korčula.

Hvar: Hvar's hip cachet, upscale-ritzy "Croatian Riviera" buzz, and easy proximity to Split (one hour by express catama- ran) have quickly turned this tidy Dalmatian fishing village into one of the most popular destinations in Croatia (www.tzhvar.hr). With a charming old town, a ruined fortress overhead, luxury yachts bobbing the harbor, and arguably the best night- life in Croatia, Hvar is an enjoyable place to be on vacation. You can tour its churches, or visit the Benedictine convent where nuns make delicate lace from natural plant fibers.

Or, to get out of town, enjoy one of the island's beaches, go for a hike, or take a boat ride to the offshore Pakleni Islands.

Good rooms in and near Hvar town include **$ Ivana and Paško Ukić** (in the steep lanes above the town center, www.hvar-apartments-center.com) and **$ Apartments Mare** (Marica and Gianni, a 10-minute walk west of the Old Town, www.apartments-mare-hvar.com). For a centrally-located splurge hotel, try **$$$$ Villa Nora** (http://villanora.incroatia.info) or **$$$$ Hotel Park** (www.hotelparkhvar.com).

For meals, consider **Konoba Menego,** serving Croatian classics tapas-style (in the steep lanes above the main square, www.menego.hr); **Alviž,** with simple but delicious meals near the bus station (Hanibala Lucića 1); or, for a splurge, **Gariful Restaurant,** with seafood along the harbor embankment (www.hvar-gariful.hr).

Korčula: The island town of Korčula (KOHR-choo-lah)—a bit closer to Dubrovnik, with workable connections—boasts an atmospheric Old Town, a smattering of little museums, and a dramatic, fjord-like mountain backdrop. Humbler and sleepier than its glitzy big sister Hvar, Korčula has an appealing backwater charm (www.visitkorcula.eu). The peninsular Old Town pokes out into the Adriatic, with fish-skeleton street plan, a variety of museums (including the supposed former home of Marco Polo, whom Korčulans claim was born here), and a variety of pizza, pasta, and seafood restaurants. Twice weekly in summer, Lazy Korčula snaps to life when locals perform a medieval folk dance called the *Moreška*.

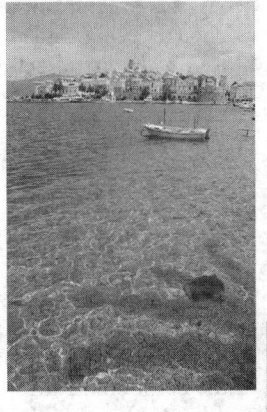

My favorite private rooms are **$$ Apartments Lenni** (Lenni and Pero, perisa.modrinic@du.t-com.hr), **$ Old Town Apartments** (Branko and Ulrike, www.juristic.de/korcula), and **$ Royal Apartments** (Zvonko and Marija, www.korcularoyalapartments.com). The best hotel option is **$$$$ Hotel Korsal** (www.hotelkorsal.com).

Several great restaurants—including **Aterina** and **Nonno**—are on the square called Trg Korčulanskih Klesara i Kipara. For a scenic setting, browse the eateries along the seawall, from the basic **Pizzeria Tedeschi** to the splurgy **Filippi.**

ISTRIA

Idyllic Istria, the wedge-shaped peninsula at Croatia's northwest corner, reveals itself to you gradually and seductively: Pungent truffles, Roman ruins, striking hill towns, quaint coastal villages, carefully cultivated food and wine, and breezy Italian culture all compete for your attention. The highlight is the gorgeous seaside town of Rovinj, but with more time (and a car), Istria has much to offer. Everything mentioned here is within a one-hour drive of Rovinj.

▲▲▲Rovinj

Among Croatian coastal towns, Rovinj (roh-VEEN) is particularly romantic (www.tzgrovinj.hr). Its streets are delightfully twisty, its ancient houses are characteristically crumbling, and its harbor—lively with real-life fishermen—is as salty as they come. Like a little Venice on a hill, Rovinj is the atmospheric setting of your Croatian seaside dreams.

Visiting Rovinj: Rovinj's main attraction is simply its gorgeous ▲▲▲ **Old Town**—rising dramatically from the Adriatic as though being pulled up to heaven by its grand bell tower. Enjoy stunning views from the town parking lot, then walk into town, pausing at the lively open-air market. Once inside the Old Town, you're swallowed up by a creaky and colorful townscape.

Narrow, stepped lanes climb up the hill to the ▲ **Church of St. Euphemia,** where you can learn about the local saint and climb rickety stairs up to the top of the bell tower. Rovinj has a few low-impact museums, including the ▲ **House of the Batana Boat,** celebrating a unique local fishing boat and the culture that goes along with it (www.batana. org). Rovinj has some rocky beaches, with sandy ones a short bike or boat ride away.

Sleeping in Rovinj: This town is a delightful home base for exploring Istria. The Old Town holds several appealing private rooms and guesthouses, including **$$$ Villa Markiz** (Andrej and Ivana, stylish apartments, www.markizrovinj.com), **$$ Casa Garzotto** (with rustic rooms and apartments scattered around the Old Town, www.casa-garzotto.com), and **$$ Villa Cissa** (tasteful apartments rented by engaging Veljko, www.villacissa.com).

Eating in Rovinj: Restaurants line up along Rovinj's "restaurant row" facing the harbor; good options include classy **Scuba,**

rustic **Veli Jože,** romantic **Santa Croce,** and—at the end of the strip—the scenic splurge **La Puntuleina.**

Rovinj also has delightful nightlife. Istrian wines are excellent, and Rovinj has two handy wine bars where you can learn more: **Bacchus Wine Bar,** just outside the Old Town gate at Carera 5 (Paolo), and **Piassa Granda,** on a charming little square right in the heart of the Old Town (Veli trg 1). For a memorable setting, keep an eye on the water as you stroll "restaurant row" to find **Valentino Cocktail Bar,** where you can nurse an overpriced drink "on the rocks"—literally—as the sun sets and fish come to investigate the underwater lights.

▲▲Istrian Hill Towns

Istria's interior is dotted with sleepy, picturesque hill towns, speckled with wineries and olive-oil farms, embedded with precious truffles, and grooved by meandering rural roads. Spend a half-day (or more) joyriding from town to town, stopping at some countryside wineries and making time for a truffle feast.

Visiting the Istrian Hill Towns: The most appealing hill town is **Motovun,** overlooking vineyards and truffle-filled oak forests. Hike up its shop-lined main street to the cute little square with a pretty church, a big hotel (the recommended Hotel Kaštel, www.hotel-kastel-motovun. hr), and views over the countryside. Motovun is also a foodie destination, with a pair of excellent restaurants

for an Istrian meal: the trendy but unpretentious **Mondo Konoba** (just below the Old Town's lower gate), and the more traditional **Konoba pod Voltom** (inside the Old Town's upper gate).

Other fine hill towns include **Grožnjan** (a time warp on a bluff—flatter and easier to drive to than Motovun), **Buje** (more workaday), and **Završje** (almost deserted and very atmospheric). Most towns have a restaurant specializing in truffle dishes, but Istria's gastronomic epicenter is **Livade,** in the valley below Motovun. This is home to the local Zigante truffle company, with a big shop and upscale restaurant.

Wine lovers enjoy stopping for tastings at countryside wineries, which are scattered across the region. Near Momjan (northwest of Motovun), good choices are the traditional **Kabola** (www.kabola.hr) and the sophisticated **Kozlović** (www.kozlovic.hr).

▲Pula

At Istria's southern tip, Pula is a big, industrial port city. But its urban core holds priceless ancient Roman ruins that rival Split's.

Park near the remarkably well-preserved amphitheater, which is worth touring. Then walk into the town center. On the main square (formerly the ancient forum) is a largely-intact ancient temple; a Roman floor mosaic hides behind some nearby shops.

THE CROATIAN INTERIOR

Most travelers to Croatia focus exclusively on the coast. That's a shame, because they miss the country's interior—with two of its best destinations: the capital city and a stunning natural wonder.

▲▲Zagreb

You can't get a complete picture of modern Croatia without a visit here—away from the touristy resorts, in the lively and livable city that is home to one out of every six

Croatians (pop. 790,000). In Zagreb, you'll find historic neighborhoods, a thriving café culture, my favorite urban people-watching in Croatia, a nearly Prague-like Old World streetscape, and virtually no tourists. The city is also the country's best destination for museum-going, and has Croatia's best foodie scene—both of which are in short supply along the coast.

Visiting Zagreb: Zagreb's main square, **Jelačić Square** (Trg bana Jelačića) is a hive of activity. Shoppers, commuters, and trams zip in and out of the square. The surrounding downtown zone is a delight to explore, with galleries, boutiques, and gourmet coffee shops.

Near Jelačić Square, a short funicular climbs up to Zagreb's old town, called Gradec. Its centerpiece is St. Mark's Square, where governmental buildings (including the parliament and president's residence) face the colorfully tiled roof of the Church of St. Mark.

Two of Croatia's top museums are within a block of St. Mark's Square. The small but riveting **▲▲▲ Croatian Museum of Naive Art** displays lovingly detailed works by self-taught peasant artists—dating from the early 20th century, when art-world insiders sought to prove that artistic ability was an inborn talent (www.hmnu.org).

And nearby, the innovative ▲▲ **Museum of Broken Relationships** collects true stories of failed couples from around the world, tells their story in their own words, and displays the tale alongside an actual item that embodies the relationship (https://brokenships.com). The Gradec area also has a fine city history museum and an atelier and collection of works of the great Croatian sculptor, Ivan Meštrović.

The adjacent, formerly walled district of Kaptol is home to Zagreb's ▲▲ **Cathedral**—containing various monuments celebrating the city's tumultuous history and Croatia's proud Catholic heritage.

Between Gradec and Kaptol is Zagreb's colorful (and largely untouristy) indoor-outdoor public **market,** a fun place to browse for a picnic. Nearby is the trendy café street called **Tkalčićeva,** with lots of lively al fresco eateries and the best people-watching in town.

Sleeping in Zagreb: Good, central choices include the cozy-yet-modern **$$ Jägerhorn Hotel** (www.hotel-jagerhorn.hr) or the big, well-located **$$$ Hotel Dubrovnik** (www.hotel-dubrovnik. hr). Smaller B&B-type options include **$ Sobe Zagreb 17** (www. sobezagreb17.com) or **$ 4 City Windows** (www.4citywindows. com).

Eating in Zagreb: It's fun to browse the restaurants along the bustling, traffic-free Tkalčićeva street, including the big, sloppy **Pivnica Mali Medo** (a Czech-style beer hall, at #36) or **La Štruk,** specializing in the local ravioli, *štrukli* (Skalinska 5). In Gradec, **Trilogija** feels upscale but still affordable and unpretentious (Kamenita 5, www.trilogija.com). And for foodie places in the downtown zone around Jelačić Square, check out **Lari & Penati** (Petrinjska 42A), **Bistro Fotić** (Ljudevita Gaja 25, www.bistrofotic.com), **Mundoaka** (international street food, Petrinjska 2), and **Nishta** (international vegetarian dishes, Masarykova 11).

▲▲▲Plitvice Lakes National Park

Plitvice (PLEET-veet-seh) is one of Europe's most spectacular natural wonders. Imagine Niagara Falls diced and sprinkled over a heavily forested Grand Canyon. There's nothing like this lush valley of 16 terraced lakes, separated by natural travertine dams and laced together by waterfalls, boat rides, and miles of pleasant plank walks (www.np-plitvicka-jezera.hr).

Visiting Plitvice: Deep in the countryside about two hours south of Zagreb (roughly on the way to Split), Plitvice is worth a little extra effort to reach. It's easiest for drivers, but many public buses from Zagreb or Split also stop here (bus stop along main road—ask locals or the driver to be clear on where to get off or on, best connections are provided by the summer-only Prijevoz Knežević express bus).

Once at the park, you can see the highlights in just a few hours' walk. It's easy (on well-tended paths and boardwalks), but can get crowded—in busy times, get an early start. (It works well to arrive in the evening, sleep near the park, hit the trails first thing the next morning, then move on to your next destination after lunch.) The lakes are divided into two sections, upper and lower. I prefer to buy my park ticket at Entrance 1 and do the Lower Lakes first. You'll hike

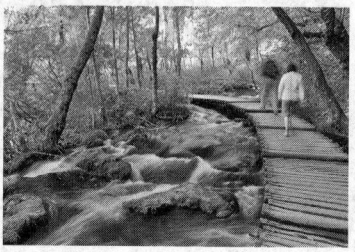

steeply down to the trail, then walk gradually uphill—past glorious cascades and pools of strangely colorful water—to the largest lake. From there, an electric boat shuttles you silently across to the Upper Lakes, which is yet another wonderland of boardwalks, waterfalls, and tranquil ponds. From the far end, you can ride a shuttle bus back to your starting point.

Sleeping and Eating at Plitvice: Most visitors stay at the national park lodges, which are functional but comfortable, and come with industrial-strength dining rooms. The best choices are **$$ Hotel Plitvice** and the slightly pricier **$$ Hotel Jezero** (book either through www.np-plitvicka-jezera.hr). For a more personal experience, drivers should stay at a family-run inn outside the park. My favorite, just a couple of minutes south of Plitvice, is the friendly **$$ Plitvice Mirić Inn** (www.plitvice-croatia.com). Others cluster near the road about 10 minutes' drive north of Plitvice, including the homey, picturesque **$ Villa Plitvička Sedra** (www.restoran-sedra.hr) and the big, roadside **$$ Hotel Degenija** (www.hotel-degenija.com). Each of these also has its own restaurant—ideal for dinner. For lunch near the trails, a few humble eateries—ranging from basic groceries selling sandwiches to sit-down places—cluster near the national park entrances and near the boat dock at the top of the Lower Lakes. But the food at these official national park eateries is nothing special; consider packing a picnic instead.

BOSNIA-HERZEGOVINA

Bosna i Hercegovina

The 1990s weren't kind to Bosnia-Herzegovina: War. Destruction. Genocide. But apart from the tragic way it separated from Yugoslavia, the country has long been—and remains—a remarkable place, with ruggedly beautiful terrain, a unique mix of cultures and faiths, kind and welcoming people who pride themselves on their hospitality, and some of the most captivating sightseeing in southeastern Europe. A visit here offers a fascinating opportunity to sample the cultures of three major faiths within a relatively small area: In the same day, you can inhale incense in a mystical-feeling Serbian Orthodox church, hear the subtle clicking of rosary beads in a Roman Catholic cathedral, and listen to the Muslim call to prayer echo across a skyline of prickly minarets.

Where to Go: The highlights of Bosnia are just a short drive from Croatia's Dalmatian Coast. Many side-trip from Dubrovnik or Split to **Mostar,** which is the country's most accessible and tourist-friendly town. But for a more authentic and complete Bosnian experience, it's worth going a few hours farther to reach **Sarajevo**—the gorgeously-set capital, with its fascinating history (both old and recent) and lively contemporary life. Three or four days is enough time to visit both great cities, with quick stops in some other towns and attractions in between, giving you an insightful first look at Bosnia.

Getting Around: Trains are slow and old; locals prefer to go by bus. Most buses are operated by the Bosniak-run companies

Bosnia-Herzegovina

CROATIA

SERBIA

Novi Grad

Bihać

Banja Luka

Doboj

Brčko

Bijelina

Bosna R.

Zvornik

BOSNIA-HERZEGOVINA

Zavidovići

Drvar

Jajce

Vrbas R.

Travnik

Zenica

Srebrenica

DINARIC ALPS

Bugojno

Visoko

Sarajevo

Višegrad

Ivan Planina

Goražde

Drina R.

Livno

Jablanica

Konjic

Foča

Neretva R.

Široki Brijeg

Mostar
Blagaj

Medugorje

Počitelj

Bileća

Trebinje

MONTE-NEGRO

100 Kilometers

100 Miles

Adriatic Sea

Dubrovnik

Podgorica

(www.autoprevoz-bus.ba and www.centrotrans.com), while other connections are Croat-operated (www.globtour.com)—check the options before you book. Bosnia is also a fine country for driving: The roads are surprisingly good (though there are few freeways), and traffic is light. Be aware that Google Maps navigation is not available in Bosnia. Given the mountainous terrain, affordable flights can save time; for example, Croatia Airlines often flies from Sarajevo to Zagreb for around $100 (www.croatiaairlines.com).

Bosnian Cuisine: The local food resembles what you may think of as "Greek" or "Turkish" food—with lots of tomatoes, peppers, soft cheeses, and grilled meats. The top street food is *burek*—a savory phyllo-dough pastry filled with meat, cheese, or spinach. Another Bosnian classic is *ćevapčići* (or *ćevapi*), a mix of minced meat (usually lamb and beef) formed into a sausage-link shape, then grilled. It's served with other grilled meats, chopped raw

Bosnia Practicalities

Money: Bosnia uses the Convertible Mark (Konvertibilna Marka, abbreviated KM locally, BAM internationally). The official exchange rate is $1 = about 1.80 KM. Euros and Croatian kunas are widely accepted in Mostar, but less so in Sarajevo.

People: The official population is about 3.9 million. A citizen of Bosnia-Herzegovina, regardless of ethnicity, is called a "Bosnian." But the population is divided into three major ethnic groups: Muslims, called "Bosniaks" (about half of the population); Eastern Orthodox Christians, called "Serbs" (about a third); and Roman Catholics, called "Croats" (about 15 percent).

Geography: Bosnia and Herzegovina are two distinct regions that share the same mountainous country. Bosnia constitutes the majority of the country (in the north, with the capital, Sarajevo—pop. 310,000), while Herzegovina is the southern tip (Mostar is its biggest city and de facto capital, with 130,000 people). It's fine to call the entire country "Bosnia" for short. The Dayton Peace Accords that ended the conflict here in 1995 gerrymandered the nation into two major, semi-autonomous zones: the Federation of Bosnia and Herzegovina (shared by Bosniaks and Croats, roughly in the western and central parts of the country) and the Republika Srpska (dominated by Serbs, generally to the north and east). For the most part, each of the three native ethnic groups stay in "their" part of this divided country, but tourists can move freely among them. While the Dayton Accords brought peace, the nation is still politically splintered and economically struggling—the per capita GDP is just $9,800.

Snapshot History: Bosnia's history was dominated first by the Illyrians, then by the Romans, and eventually by the Slavs. But in the late 15th century, it became part of the Ottoman Empire for 400 years (during which many Bosnians adopted Islam—their descendants remain Muslims today). Bosnia was briefly part of the Austro-Hungarian Empire beginning in 1878, then Yugoslavia after World War I, until it declared independence in the spring of 1992. The bloody three-way war that ensued came to an end in 1995. (For details, see "Understanding Yugoslavia" on page 1101.)

Emergencies: Dial 112.

Consular Services in Sarajevo: The US Embassy is at Ulica Robert C. Frasure 1 (tel. 033/704-000, sarajevo.usembassy. gov). The nearest Canadian Embassy is in Budapest, Hungary (see page 1109).

Telephone Country Code: +387, then drop the initial 0 of the phone number.

Tourist Information: www.bhtourism.ba

onions, a soft and spreadable cheese called *kajmak,* the pita-like *lepinje* bread, and the powerful red pepper and eggplant spread called *ajvar.* Bosnian desserts are gooey with honey: baklava or the shredded-wheat-style *kadaif.* And Bosnian coffee *(bosanska kafa)*— a hearty unfiltered brew simmered in a copper kettle and served in a little ceramic cup—is as much a slow-down-and-smell-the-tulips social ritual as it is a drink.

Bosnian Language: English is widely spoken, especially in tourist areas. Bosnian is very close to Croatian (in fact, until a generation ago they were considered one language); key phrases include these pleasantries: "Hello" is *Dobar dan* (formal) or *Zdravo* (informal); "please" is *molim;* "thank you" is *hvala;* and "goodbye" is *Do viđenija.* Bosniaks and Croats use basically the same Roman alphabet we do, while Serbs use the Cyrillic alphabet. You'll see both alphabets on currency, official documents, and road signs, but the Roman alphabet predominates in the destinations covered here.

Top Bosnian Destinations

The following sections are designed to get you started planning a trip to Bosnia. For in-depth coverage—including self-guided walks and museum tours, detailed hotel and restaurant listings, and lots of practical advice—pick up my *Rick Steves Croatia & Slovenia* guidebook.

▲▲▲Sarajevo

Though once torn by the wars of the 1990s, the Bosnian capital of Sarajevo—spectacularly situated in a mountain valley blanketed with cute Monopoly houses—is a comfortable and safe place to visit (www.sarajevo-tourism.com). It's a city of powerful experiences: Step into historic houses of worship from each of this region's four major faiths—Muslim, Catholic, Orthodox Christian, and Jewish— and notice the similarities. Visit the street corner where World War I

began. Climb up into the hills to the Olympic stadium that commanded the world's attention in 1984, or ascend even higher for sweeping views over the capital. Make friends with a gregarious Sarajevan—it's easy to do—and ask him the best way to prepare and drink Bosnian coffee. Ponder the scars of war, hunch over to squeeze through the tunnel that was the besieged Sarajevans' one lifeline to the world, and listen to a local relate personal stories from the harrowing time of the siege. Shop your way through the copper-laden canyons of the Turkish-style bazaar, bartering down the price of a hand-hammered Bosnian coffee set. Relax in a hidden caravansery, take a slow drag on a *šiša* (water pipe spewing sweet plumes of fruity smoke), and sample some honey-dripping pastry treats. Go ahead—it's OK to enjoy Sarajevo.

Visiting Sarajevo: Sarajevo is brought to life with the help of a good local guide; **Amir Telibečirović** is excellent and affordable (teleamir@gmail.com).

Begin in the Ottoman-flavored Old Town, called the **Baščaršija**—with cobbles, bazaars, minarets, and hardworking coppersmiths. In this area, ogle Sarajevo's iconic fountain (called Sebilj), do some window-shopping, and consider dropping into the good ▲ **City History Museum,** filling a former covered market. After hours, don't miss the atmospheric courtyard (behind the TI) called Trgovke—filled with gregarious locals, thumping Balkan music, and the sweet smoke of water pipes.

A few blocks to the west begins a totally different-feeling part of town, with Habsburg-style architecture from the late 19th and

early 20th centuries (the short-lived period when Bosnia was part of Austria-Hungary). The main drag, **Ferhadija,** feels worlds—rather than steps—away from the Baščaršija. During this Habsburg era, Sarajevo was the site of one of the most famous and important events in modern history: the assassination of the Habsburg heir, Franz Ferdinand, in 1914. You can see the riverside corner where the archduke and his wife were shot, visit the adjacent museum, or walk five minutes along the river to see the finest piece of architecture from this period, the Neo-Moorish City Hall, which Franz Ferdinand visited on that fateful day.

In this central zone of Sarajevo, various historic houses of worship sit a few steps apart. Stop in at Sarajevo's big, showpiece ▲▲ **Gazi Husrev-Bey Mosque** and associated buildings; the atmospheric ▲ **Old Serbian Orthodox Church,** with a museum of icons; the Neo-Gothic **Catholic Cathedral;** and the city's ▲▲ **Old Synagogue and Bosnian Jewish Museum.** (For more Jewish heritage, the sometimes-closed

National Museum displays the priceless Jewish prayer book called the Sarajevo Haggadah.)

Sarajevo offers many powerful lessons in the grotesque genocide of the Yugoslav Wars. In the early 1990s, this multiethnic city—surrounded by the snipers of Bosnian Serb leaders Radovan Karadžić and Ratko Mladić—withstood the longest siege in modern military history (more than 1,300 days). Many locals are willing to share their harrowing stories from that time—being relentlessly shelled and shot at, day in and day out, for three and a half years. All around the city, watch for blast craters in the pavement that have been filled with red resin; these memorials—called "Sarajevo roses"—have been preserved to commemorate that difficult time.

For sites relating to the siege, visit the still-busy **Markale Market,** the site of a notorious bombing that killed dozens of innocent shoppers. The emotion-

ally wrenching **Memorial to the Children of Sarajevo** pays respects to the more than 1,600 children who were among the estimated 10,000 Sarajevans killed during the siege. A few blocks away, you can freely walk through the skyscraper zone called Marijin Dvor, which was then known as **"Sniper Alley"**—where gunmen on the hillsides above would rain bullets down on civilians trying to live their lives in peace. Nearby, the ▲ **Historical Museum of Bosnia-Herzegovina** collects everyday items and "Sarajevo inventions" that allowed the Sarajevans to survive the siege. And in the town center, the ▲▲ **Srebrenica Exhibition** collects photography and video testimony about the brutal ethnic cleansing campaign that systematically murdered at least 8,000 residents of a small Bosnian town.

Perhaps the most powerful sight relating to the Siege of Sarajevo is the ▲▲ **Sarajevo War Tunnel Museum.** Here you can actually walk a few steps through the claustrophobic supply tunnel that ran a half-mile underneath the airport runway during the siege. This was the only safe way for besieged Sarajevans to escape to the outside world and bring home supplies to their loved ones (a taxi ride from downtown, www.tunelspasa.ba).

Sleeping in Sarajevo: Friendly, well-run guesthouses in or near the Old Town include **$ Ada Hotel** (www.adahotel.ba), **$ Hotel Old Town** (www.hoteloldtown.ba), and **$ Halvat Guest House** (www.halvat.com.ba).

Eating in Sarajevo: There are plenty of options for traditional Bosnian fare in the Old Town. My favorite *bureks* (savory phyllo pastry) are at **Buregdžinica Sač** (just off the main square, in the alley called Bravadžiluk Mali). Good choices for *ćevapčići* are **Mrkva** (Bravadžiluk 15) and **Petica** (Oprkanj 2). For a satisfying sit-down meal, try **Apetit** (tiny and with no printed menu—the server explains your options, Josipa Štadlera 6, www.apetit. ba) or **To Be ~~Or Not~~ To Be** (a classic buried in the Old Town, Čizmedžiluk 5). And for a scenic meal—with sweeping views over Sarajevo's valley—head up into the hills to the pricier (but still affordable) **Kibe Mahala** (Vrbanjuša 164, easiest to reach by taxi, www.kibemahala.ba).

▲▲Mostar

For those side-tripping into Bosnia from the Dalmatian Coast, Mostar is ideal: It's a convenient and very accessible microcosm

of the country. Mostar straddles the banks of the gorgeous Neretva River, with tributaries and waterfalls that carve their way through the rocky landscape. The sightseeing—mosques, old Turkish-style houses, and the city's spine-tingling Old Bridge—is engaging. And for those interested in recent history, the locals—who saw their

city torn apart by the Yugoslav Wars of the 1990s, and have worked hard to rebuild—are often eager to share their stories. If you're curious about Bosnia and only have a day to spend here, Mostar is the place.

Visiting Mostar: Almost everything of interest is within about a 15-minute walk in the town center. A local guide helps bring both the history and the powerful recent stories to life. I recommend **Alma Elezović** (aelezovic@gmail.com); her husband, Ermin, can be hired to drive you around Bosnia, or even to pick you up in Croatia.

The city's centerpiece and icon is its **Old Bridge,** commissioned in 1557 by the Ottoman Sultan Süleyman the Magnificent.

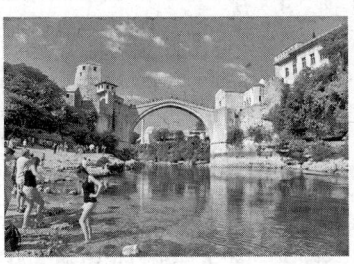

Dramatically arched and flanked by two boxy towers, the bridge is stirring. In 1993, as the various factions of the city fought amongst themselves, Serb artillery on the mountaintop above fired on the Bosniak-held bridge. It was destroyed and fell into the river. In 2004, the bridge was rebuilt and remains a symbol of reconciliation. And today, as they have for generations, local young men hustle for tips from tourists before they swan-dive from the bridge 75 feet down into the icy-cold Neretva below.

The area around the bridge has a few small historical and photo exhibitions about the war, and a cobbled bazaar (called Coppersmiths' Street) where locals sell trinkets to tourists.

While it continues to repair itself, Mostar also has several poignant reminders of the war. You'll still see a few bombed-out husks of buildings, tucked between rebuilt ones. And scattered around Mostar are poignant "new" cemeteries—former parks now filled with turban-shaped headstones, each one marked 1993 or 1994. When the Serb forces laid siege to the Muslims in Mostar's Old Town, bodies had to be buried in small parks in the city center, in the dark of night, for fear of snipers. Today, the city of Mostar remains effectively divided, between the Muslim community (around the Old Bridge, where most tourists go) and the Croat community (the modern sprawl to the west).

For those interested in Islam, Mostar offers the opportunity to visit various mosques. ▲ **Koski Mehmet-Pasha Mosque,** overlooking the Old Bridge, is the most representative and welcomes tourists. And you can step into a historical ▲ **Ottoman-style house,** to see how Mostarians lived under the rule of the sultans and pashas (the Bišćević House or the Muslibegović House—both just above the river not far from the bridge—are equally good). Across the river is the towering concrete steeple of the **Church of Sts. Peter and Paul**—built after the war by local Croats, seemingly to one-up the minarets all over town.

Sleeping in Mostar: Guesthouses here are a great value. I like the **$$ Muslibegović House** (a historical monument that also welcomes guests into its traditional rooms with modern comforts, www.muslibegovichouse.com), **$ Shangri La Mansion** (on the hill above the Old Bridge, www.shangrila.com.ba), **$ Villa Anri** (modern comfort near the Old Bridge, villa.anri@gmail.com), and **$ Hotel Kriva Ćuprija** (with lots of rooms tucked deep in the river valley near the Old Bridge—plus more in a modern annex, www. motel-mostar.ba).

Eating in Mostar: It seems all Mostar restaurants have the same tourist-oriented menu of Bosnian classics: grilled-meat *ćevapčići*, flaky *burek* pastries, and so on. Most visitors prioritize the view over the food, settling in at one of the places clinging to the lush cliffs overlooking the river, with stunning views of the Old

Bridge. For slightly better food (but less exciting views), **Restoran Hindin Han** has somewhat more refined food and a nice setting on a smaller canyon (Jusovina 10), and **Irma-Tima,** on the main drag near the Old Bridge, has great grilled meats (Onešćukova).

▲Sights near Mostar

Drivers exploring the area near Mostar can choose from several tempting stopovers.

Just outside of Mostar, the historical capital of **Blagaj** has an old dervish monastery *(tekija)* that sits at the bottom of a dramatic cliff face, where the Buna River bubbles up from underground.

On the main road between Mostar and the Dalmatian Coast, it's hard to resist stopping at **Počitelj**—dramatically set on chalky mountains, with a ruined castle and a proud mosque and minaret.

Also between Mostar and the coast—on a less-traveled route—is a powerful site of pilgrimage for Catholics: **Međugorje,** where six local teens claimed to have seen miraculous visions of the Virgin Mary in 1981. While there's little to see beyond a modern church, believers (and the curious) find something spiritually powerful here.

MONTENEGRO

Crna Gora

Small and rugged, Montenegro gets overlooked. It's tucked in a rocky and complicated part of the world between Croatia, Serbia, and Albania. And yet, it sits just a temptingly short drive away from the region's top destination, Dubrovnik. Today's Montenegro is a strange mix of big-money international investment (Russian-owned luxury resort hotels, the exclusive Porto Montenegro yacht harbor) and challenging local poverty (which is evident as you pass through ragtag cities and humble towns). But nothing can mar

Montenegro's natural beauty: Devote a day (or more) to making this easy side-trip, and you'll discover a land of stunning mountains, bays, and forests.

Where to Go: Most people see Montenegro as a quick side-trip from Dubrovnik—which, for those on a tight timeframe, is a smart plan. The main highlight (and the focus of this chapter) is the **Bay of Kotor,** with scenery that only improves on Croatia's Dalmatian Coast, some fine seaside towns (including tiny Perast and atmospheric Kotor), and the chance to ride out to a church-topped island in the middle of the bay, wrapped in 360 degrees of stunning scenery. With more time, beach bums can head for the **Budva Riviera;** celebrity-seekers can daydream about past glories at the striking hotel-peninsula of **Sveti Stefan;** and romantics can corkscrew up into the mountains to sample the Balkans' best smoked ham at **Njeguši** and visit the country's remote original capital at **Cetinje.**

Getting Around: Most visitors simply drive in for the day from Dubrovnik—using their own rental car, hiring a Dubrovnik-based private driver (listed in the "Dubrovnik" section on page 982), or joining a package tour. Be aware that Google Maps navigation is not available in Montenegro. Montenegro is also relatively well-served by buses (for connections to and from Kotor, see www.autobuskastanicakotor.me). It's also a popular and easy cruise port—ships put in right across the street from Kotor's Old Town.

Montenegrin Cuisine: Along the Bay of Kotor, the cuisine is similar to Croatia's—that means seafood, pasta, and pizza. *Njeguški pršut* is the rich, salty, smoky prosciutto from the village of Njeguši (described later) that goes well with the local cow's cheese—smoked, of course. Montenegro also produces some surprisingly good wines (Plantaže Podgorica is the biggest company): A good red is the dry, medium-bodied *vranac* (related to zinfandel), and for white, you'll see the dry, fruity *krstač* (similar to Riesling).

Montenegrin Language: Montenegrin is closely related to both Croatian and Bosnian. "Hello" is *Dobar dan* (formal) or *Zdravo* (informal); "please" is *molim;* "thank you" is *hvala;* and "Good-

Montenegro Practicalities

Money: Though it's not a member of the European Union, Montenegro officially uses the euro as its currency: €1 = about $1.10.

Geography and People: Montenegro (5,415 square miles, slightly smaller than Connecticut) is home to about 650,000 people. Of these, the vast majority are Eastern Orthodox Christians (45 percent Montenegrins, 29 percent Serbs), with minority groups of Muslims (including Bosniaks and Albanians, about 11 percent total) and Catholics (1 percent). The country is characterized by a rocky terrain that rises straight up from the Adriatic and almost immediately becomes a steep mountain range. Montenegro has 182 miles of coastline, about a third of which constitutes the Bay of Kotor. The only real city is the capital, Podgorica (190,000 people). Montenegro is a relatively poor country (per capita GDP is $15,000) that relies heavily on international investment.

Snapshot History: Named "Black Mountain" for the thickly forested hills that sailors saw when approaching this land, Montenegro was first inhabited by the ancient Illyrians (the mysterious distant ancestors of today's Albanians), who were later conquered by the Romans. Slavic migrants established a sovereign state here in the 10th century, and in the 14th century, the area flourished under the powerful Serbian emperor Dušan the Mighty. But soon, with the rising threat of the Ottomans, the Montenegrin coastline became part of the Republic of Venice for about 450 years (15th-19th centuries). In the 20th century, Montenegro joined Yugoslavia (and was often overshadowed by its "big brother," Serbia)—until it declared independence from Serbia, peacefully, in a landmark vote on June 3, 2006.

Emergencies: Dial 112.

Consular Services in Podgorica: The US Embassy is at Žona Džeksona 2 (tel. 020/410-500, http://podgorica.usembassy. gov); Canadians use the embassy in Belgrade, Serbia (tel. +381-11-306-3000).

Telephone Country Code: +382, then drop the initial 0 of the phone number.

Tourist Information: www.visit-montenegro.com or www. montenegro.travel bye" is *Do viđenija*. You'll see both "our" Roman alphabet and the Cyrillic alphabet used, more or less equally; for a crash course in Cyrillic, see page 1011.

Top Montenegrin Destinations

The following sections are designed to get you started planning a trip to Montenegro. For in-depth coverage—including a self-guided driving tour, detailed hotel and restaurant listings, and lots of practical advice—pick up my *Rick Steves Croatia & Slovenia* guidebook.

▲▲Bay of Kotor Driving Loop

For a look at the untamed Adriatic, take a spin on the winding road around Montenegro's steep and secluded Bay of Kotor. The

area's main town, also called Kotor, has been protected from centuries of would-be invaders by its position at the deepest point of the fjord—and by its imposing town wall, which scrambles in a zigzag line up the mountain behind it. Wander the enjoyably seedy streets of Kotor, drop into some Orthodox churches, and sip a coffee at an al fresco café.

Visiting the Bay of Kotor: Most people do a loop around the Bay of Kotor in one day from Dubrovnik. Here's the basic plan:

From Dubrovnik, head south on the main coastal road (signs to *Ćilipi*), past Cavtat and the airport; in about 40 minutes, you'll reach the **border** at Debeli Brijeg (where you'll need to show your passport and your rental car's proof-of-insurance "green card"). To avoid lines at the border, get an early start—on busy summer weekends, consider leaving Dubrovnik by 7:30 to beat the tour buses. (There's also a less crowded alternate border crossing called Konfin—ask locals for directions.)

Once across the border, you'll head through the big, dreary city of **Herceg Novi,** then curve around the headland at the **Verige Strait**—the quarter-mile-wide entrance to the huge, fjord-like bay (underlining Kotor's strategic importance). From here, you'll curl along the bay's waters—through crescendoing scenery and tiny towns—until you reach the village of ▲ **Perast.** Park, stretch your legs, and explore this tiny, well-preserved town (with a big waterfront main square and a half-built cathedral).

From Perast, pay a few euros per person to be shuttled out across the bay for a closer look at a pair of islands: **St. George** (Sv. Đorđe) and ▲▲ **Our Lady of the Rocks** (Gospa od Škrpjela). It's said that two local fishermen saw a light emanating from a reef deep below the surface near the isle of St. George. Discovering an icon of Mary, they were inspired to build a second island on that holy spot. So, for two centuries, locals dropped rocks and even sunk old ships there—eventually creating the island of Our Lady of the Rocks. You can stroll the island and dip into the church, filled with votives honoring the miraculous icon that was found here.

Back in Perast, get back on the road and carry on around the bay about another 30 minutes until you reach the town of **Kotor;** with more time, you can continue farther to the **Budva Riviera,** or head up into the mountains and **Cetinje** (all described later).

To return to Dubrovnik, just head back the way you came. Or, for a shortcut (and to see different scenery), you can continue around the bay past Kotor, then continue all the way around to Lepetani, where a frequent and easy ferry *(trajekt)* travels a few minutes across the bay to Kamenari—near Herceg Novi and a short drive from the Croatian border.

▲▲Kotor

Butted up against a steep cliff, cradled by a calm sea, naturally sheltered by its deep-in-the-fjord position, and watched over by an imposing network of fortifications, the town of Kotor is as impressive as it is well-protected. Though it's enjoyed a long and illustrious history, today's Kotor is a time-capsule retreat for travelers seeking an unspoiled Adriatic town (www.tokotor.me). For a good local guide, contact **Stefan Đukanović** (www.miroandsons.com, djukan@t-com.me).

Visiting Kotor: You can see the entire compact Old Town in a short stroll. Pass through the Main Town Gate (with a TI kiosk) and into the **Square of Arms,** fronted by a grand old palace and the town's bell tower. From here, get lost in the twisty lanes.

Make your way to the ▲ **Cathedral of St. Tryphon,** with its mismatched towers, fine interior, and quirky treasury collection (featuring an icon that, like Montenegro itself, seems to merge Eastern and Western Christian traditions). Just off the cathedral square, you can dip into the **Maritime Museum of Montenegro,** with modest exhibits on the bay's history and seafaring traditions (www.museummaritimum.com).

A few lanes over, ▲ **St. Luke's**

Square has two Eastern Orthodox Churches—one big, one little. Either offers a fascinating look at the Eastern Orthodox faith (see page 1017).

Kotor's main attraction—for those who are fit enough to tackle it—is climbing the ▲▲ **city walls** that climb up the sheer cliff face

behind town in a dizzying zigzag line. (If there's a more elaborate city wall in Europe, I haven't seen it.) This involves climbing 1,355 steps (an elevation gain of more than 700 feet)—don't overestimate your endurance or underestimate the heat. Find the ticket desk and trailhead at the back-left corner of the Old Town (near St. Mary's Church, through the alley with the two arches over it). Then get climbing, following a clockwise route that ascends to the Church of Our Lady of Health (the halfway mark), then all the way up to the Fortress of St. John. Allow at least an hour and a half round-trip, wear good shoes (uneven and rocky footing), and bring plenty of water and sun protection.

Sleeping in Kotor: I'd rather bunk in Dubrovnik—Kotor is pricey and can be noisy after dark. But if you need a bed, consider the stony-chic **$$$ Hotel Villa Duomo** (www.villaduomo. com), the businesslike and super-central **$$$ Hotel Vardar** (www. hotelvardar.com), or the affordable **$ D&Sons Apartments** (www. dandsons.com).

Eating in Kotor: City Restaurant has solid, basic food and outdoor tables next to the cathedral. **Cesarica** offers unpretentious seafood in a casual, stony interior buried deep in the Old Town (Stari Grad 375). And for a wine tasting or to browse bottles to take home, drop by **The Old Winery** (Stara Vinarija, at Stari Grad 483).

Budva Riviera

A 15-mile stretch of coarse-sand and fine-pebble beaches run along the coastline about 30 minutes south of Kotor. This "Budva Riviera" is unappealingly built up with a mix of cheap and luxury resort hotels. But the seafront is inviting, and the main town, **Budva,** has a charming Old Town crammed with souvenir shops and holiday-making Serbs and Russians. Two churches (Catholic and Orthodox) face each other near the town's imposing (but empty) citadel.

The main draw along the Budva Riviera is the famous hotel island of ▲ **Sveti Stefan**—which hovers like a mirage just offshore, about a 20-minute drive south of Budva. Once an actual, living town (connected to the mainland only by a narrow, natural causeway), Sveti Stefan was converted into a luxury hotel in the 1950s. Its promise of privacy attracted celebrities, rock stars, royalty, and dignitaries—from Sophia Loren to Kirk Douglas to Sly Stallone. More recently, it was again renovated into a super-exclusive, €1,000-plus-a-night Aman Resort

(www.aman.com). Only paying guests (no exceptions) can actually enter the island, but anyone is free to gaze over it from the road above, or to rent a pricey chair on the beaches that flank its causeway (there are a few free beach areas—ask the guard for pointers).

Montenegrin Interior

While the coastline gets all the buzz, the true heart of Montenegro beats behind the sheer wall of mountains rising up from that seafront. From near Kotor, an almost comically twisty road spirals up, up, up to the village of **Njeguši**—famous among Montenegrins for two reasons: as the hometown of the House of Petrović-Njegoš, the dynasty that ruled Montenegro for much of its history (1696-1918); and as the birthplace of Montenegrins' favorite food, the smoke-cured ham called *Njeguški pršut* (sold by various restaurants in town).

From here, the road winds across a startlingly desolate landscape to **Cetinje**—the now-humble historic capital of Montenegro. Stuck in an economic rut, Cetinje tickles romantic historians but has few tangible sights. On its main square are a collection of small museums, and nearby—marking the birthplace of the town—is the local monastery, dedicated to a charismatic local priest who famously carried a cross in one hand and a sword in the other, es-

tablished the first set of laws among Montenegrins, and inspired his people to defend Christian Montenegro against the Muslim Ottomans.

Even higher up from Cetinje, a winding road heads up to the mountaintop monument called **Lovćen,** which is capped by an elaborate mausoleum—designed by the great 20th-century Croatian sculptor Ivan Meštrović, and devoted to King Petar II Petrović-Njegoš. From here, you can ogle the grandiose statues of a long-forgotten dynasty and, in the turn of a head, see a significant percentage of Montenegro.

BULGARIA

България / Bălgariya

Endearing, surprising Bulgaria is a rewarding and all-too-often-overlooked destination. With a prime location at the intersection of cultures—going all the way back to antiquity—it has an unusually rich cultural heritage. Despite (or perhaps because of) the country's tumultuous history, the Bulgarian people are sweet and soulful—eager to share their homeland's many underappreciated gems. Travelers who venture here enjoy thriving cities, remarkable ancient sites, a flavorful cuisine, a ruggedly beautiful landscape, and powerful memories. If more travelers realized how impressive (and how affordable) Bulgaria is, it'd be jammed. But they don't...so it isn't. You'll feel like you're in on Eastern Europe's best-kept secret.

Where to Go: I've arranged this chapter's destinations in a counterclockwise loop that focuses on the highlights. On a short visit, the culturally rich "second city" of **Plovdiv** is the single most rewarding choice. With more time, the church-and-museum-packed modern capital of **Sofia** and the historic capital of **Veliko Tarnovo**—with its dramatic setting and chatty craftspeople—each deserve a day. With even more time, make a pilgrimage to the stunningly set **Rila Monastery** (worth the effort) and linger a bit at the **Thracian Plain** (ancient tombs) and **Shipka Pass** (modern monuments)—both between Plovdiv and Veliko Tarnovo. And if you have time to spare and want to hit the beach, consider adding the **Black Sea Coast.**

Getting Around: Trains (www.bdz.bg/en) and **buses** (www.bgrazpisanie.com) connect the country well—if slowly—and make sense for those linking up the cities. But if you want to explore the countryside, **driving** is (outside of congested Sofia) relatively easy in Bulgaria. Major roads are in good repair (though back roads can be somewhat deteriorated), traffic is fairly light, and drivers are generally courteous. To use expressways, you'll need a toll sticker (€8/week, €15/month)—cars rented in Bulgaria typically have one already.

Bulgarian Cuisine: Bulgaria boasts one of the tastiest and most interesting cuisines of Eastern Europe. Similar to Greek or Turkish food, Bulgarian cooking includes plenty of red peppers and tomatoes, hearty grilled meats, crumbly cheeses, and lots and lots of herbs and spices. (The pungent, powdered savory spice mix called *chubritsa*—used in just about everything—is a great culinary souvenir. The bright-red, tomatoes-peppers-and-eggplant condiment

lyutenitsa also packs a punch.) When in Bulgaria, I begin each meal with a shopska salad: chopped tomatoes, cucumbers, onions, parsley, and sometimes red peppers, all with a generous topping of feta-like cheese called *sirene*. Yogurt *(kiselo mlyako)* is big in Bulgaria. One of the tastiest ways to try it is in the refreshing cucumber-and-yogurt cold soup *tarator*—sprinkled with nuts, dill, and olive oil. For the main dish, you'll see lots of grilled meats; staples include *kyufte* (meatballs) and *kebapche* (kebabs). Another beloved dish is *sarmia*—stuffed grape or cabbage leaves. And the main Bulgarian

Bulgaria Practicalities

Money: The currency is the Bulgarian lev/лев (plural leva/лева), which is divided into 100 stotinki/стотинки. $1 = about 1.75 leva.

Geography and People: Bulgaria is 43,000 square miles, roughly the size of Tennessee, with just over 7 million people. About 85 percent are ethnic Bulgarians, with large minorities of Muslims (9 percent, mostly of Turkish ancestry) and Roma (an estimated 5 percent). It's fairly mountainous and bounded by the Danube to the north and the Black Sea to the east, but most of the population lives in cities in its central plain (including the capital, Sofia, pop. 1.2 million; Plovdiv, pop. 340,000; and Varna, pop. 335,000). Bulgaria is one of the European Union's poorest countries, with a per capita GDP of $19,100.

Snapshot History: At the intersection of the Greek, Turkish, and Slavic worlds, Bulgaria has more than its share of history. The Thracians had a rich and robust culture here during antiquity. After the fall of Rome, the Slavs (sixth century) and the Bulgars (seventh century) created the First Bulgarian Kingdom (9th-10th centuries)—which reached its peak during the reign of Simeon the Great (r. 893-927). After a period of decline, the Asen dynasty oversaw a medieval Golden Age (12th-14th centuries), when the Second Bulgarian Kingdom stretched from the Black Sea to the Adriatic. But then the Ottomans invaded, absorbing Bulgaria into their empire for 482 years. In 1877-1878, a Bulgarian-Russian army secured independence, giving rise to modern Bulgaria...and a series of devastating Balkan Wars with neighbors, which led directly into defeat in World War I. Since then, Bulgaria has taken a more peaceful tack, becoming part of the Soviet Bloc from 1945 to 1989, and now a fully modern, capitalistic, and democratic member of the European Union.

Famous Bulgarians: Spartacus (leader of a slave revolt) was born in ancient Thrace, and Cyril and Methodius—the missionary brothers who invented the Cyrillic alphabet and introduced Christianity to the Slavs in the ninth century—were born in Thessaloniki (then part of Bulgaria). In modern times, famous Bulgarians include opera singer Boris Christoff, "monument-wrapping" artist Christo, and actress Nina Dobrev.

Emergencies: Dial 112. You can also dial 150 for an ambulance, 160 for fire, or 166 for police.

Consular Services in Sofia: The US Embassy is at ulitsa Kozyak 16 (tel. 02-937-5100, bulgaria.usembassy.gov). Canadians use the embassy in Bucharest, Romania (see page 1031).

Telephone Country Code: +359, then drop the initial 0 of the phone number.

Tourist Information: www.bulgariatravel.org

street food is *banitsa*—a savory, cheesy phyllo-dough pastry (like a *burek* or a Greek *kopeta*) that's also popular at breakfast. And for dessert, Bulgarian sweets resemble Turkish ones: phyllo- and honey-based (baklava, *kadaif*) and halva (with sesame or sunflower-seed tahini). Bulgaria produces some decent wines that are worth trying...but not writing home about.

Bulgarian Language: Bulgarian is a Slavic language, closely related to Russian, Croatian, Bosnian, and Serbian. Bulgaria officially uses the Cyrillic alphabet—intimidating at first, but easy to sound out, once you've done a little studying (see sidebar). Many Bulgarians—particularly those in the tourist trade—speak some English. In this chapter, I've listed both the Cyrillic and "our" Roman spellings for key place names. Some key phrases: "Hello" is *Zdravejte/Здравейте* (formal) or just *Zdravei/Здравей* (informal); "Please" is *Molya te/Моля те*; "Thank you" is *Blagodarya/Благодаря*; and "Goodbye" is *Dovizhdane/Довиждане*.

Local Guide: In Bulgaria, hiring your own guide is a great investment. Stefan Bozadzhiev and the gang at **Lyuba Tours** offer everything from architectural walks of Sofia to fully guided, in-depth private tours around Bulgaria (www.lyubatours.com). Thanks to Stefan and Lyuba Tours for their help with the information in this chapter.

Top Bulgarian Destinations

The following sections are designed to get you started planning a trip to Bulgaria.

▲▲Sofia (София)

Bulgaria's capital, Sofia (locals say SOH-fee-yuh, not soh-FEE-ya) is delightfully livable. Its 1.2 million inhabitants enjoy an airy street plan, fine architecture, lush parks, snow-capped mountains on the horizon, and a relaxed pace of life (www.visitsofia.bg).

Visiting Sofia: Most of the sights mentioned here are in the easily walkable town center; a slick two-line Metro system and extensive tram network make longer jumps easy.

Sofia's ▲▲▲ **Alexander Nevsky Cathedral** is one of the largest Orthodox churches in Christendom—and the only national church I can think of that's named for an important saint of a different country: Russia. (The Bulgarians feel a Slavic kinship with Russia, who helped liberate them from nearly five centuries of Ottoman rule. The church is dedicated to Russian soldiers lost in that fight.)

Learning the Cyrillic Alphabet

If you're going to Bulgaria—even if just on a short visit—you'll have a much richer, smoother experience if you take the time to learn the Cyrillic alphabet. Once you know the basics, you can (slowly) sound out signs, and some of those very long, confusing words will become familiar.

The table shows the Cyrillic alphabet (both capital and lowercase), and in the second column, the Roman equivalent. Notice that the letters fall—very roughly—into four categories: Some letters are basically the same sound as in English, such as А, Е, К, М, О, and Т. Others are easy if you know the Greek alphabet: Г—gamma (g), Д—delta (d), П—pi (p), and Ф—phi (f). Some are unique to Cyrillic; most of these are "fricative" sounds, like ts, sh, ch, sht, or kh (Ж, З, Ц, Ч, Ш, Щ, Х). And the fourth category seem designed to trip you up: "false friends" that have a different sound than the Roman letter they resemble, such as В, С, Н, Р, Х, and У. It can be helpful to remember that the "backward" Roman consonants are actually vowels (И, Й, Я).

Cyrillic	Roman		Cyrillic	Roman
Аа	a		Пп	p
Бб	b		Рр	r
Вв	v		Сс	s
Гг	g		Тт	t
Дд	d		Уу	u
Ее	e		Фф	f
Жж	zh		Хх	kh
Зз	z		Цц	ts
Ии	i		Чч	ch
Йй	y		Шш	sh
Кк	k		Щщ	sht
Лл	l		Ъъ	uh
Мм	m		ьь	y
Нн	n		Юю	yu
Оо	o		Яя	ya

Built at about the same time as the Eiffel Tower, it's newer than it looks—with a steel frame clad in limestone veneer, and invisible buttresses that hold up its cascading gold and copper domes. The church is a pan-national creation: designed by Russian architects and decorated with Venetian mosaics, Slovenian oak doors, and Bohemian crystal chandeliers.

Inside, you're immersed in a rich aroma of incense and beeswax candle smoke. Shoulder-level candelabras represent prayers for the living; knee-level ones are for the deceased (buy candles in the entryway). Every available surface is slathered with gold-mosaic icons—depicting 247 saints and 25 scenes from the life of

Jesus. In front of the marble iconostasis are two marble thrones: One for the czar, and the other for the patriarch (head of the Bulgarian Orthodox Church). Per tradition, the czar's throne is bigger—demonstrating the Orthodox belief that a divinely ordained monarch has supremacy over the head of the church (the opposite of Catholic tradition). And yet, the czar's throne faces the pulpit, where an eagle (symbol of the Church) hovers in judgment over a lion (symbol of the czar)—a none-too-subtle reminder that the czar may call the shots on earth, but the final reckoning comes later. On the smaller iconostasis to the left of the main altar, a cheeky Czech artist infused his saints with personality rare in Orthodox church art. Mary looks like a real mom, tenderly kissing the arm of her Baby Jesus—who's not a serene cherub, but a fidgety toddler.

Across the street is Sofia's most historic church, and its namesake: the ▲ **Church of Sveta Sofia** ("Holy Wisdom"), with an austere brick basilica floor plan. The core of the church was built by the Byzantine Emperor Justinian in the sixth century. Underfoot sprawl lovingly excavated mosaic floors (now a museum). Outside, the **Tomb of the Unknown Soldier** is guarded by a stone lion—the national symbol—who looks not proud or fierce, but sad...suggesting the Bulgarians' generally pacifistic attitude after a grueling 20th century.

From this area, enjoy the parks, squares, and streets of Sofia's mellow downtown. Sofia even has an actual **yellow brick road.** When Austria's Emperor Franz Josef visited Sofia in 1907, he had to trudge through muddy streets. When he was invited back, he donated these bricks—made from a vivid-yellow limestone—to pave Sofia's streets.

A few blocks to the west (just follow the yellow brick road), you'll run into **Independence Square** (Ploshtad Nezavisimost)—ringed by an ensemble of severe communist-style governmental buildings called the Largo. The former Communist Party House—with its bold spire—faces a 65-foot-tall pillar that was once occupied by Vladimir Lenin. Today that pillar is topped by a statue of **Sveta Sofia** (Holy Wisdom). Near the pillar, head down

into the Metro underpass to see Roman ruins dating back two millennia. Archaeologists are constantly finding, excavating, and thoughtfully displaying fragments of the Roman town of "Serdica"—a reminder that an ancient world sprawls beneath the feet of modern commuters.

Just to the right of the former communist HQ is a little square fronted by the president's residence (featuring an extremely modest changing of the guard out front) and—housed in a huge former mosque—the ▲ **National Archaeological Museum,** with an exquisite collection of golden jewelry from ancient Thrace (www.naim.bg).

One block north of the Sveta Sofia monument is the **central market hall,** a great place to pick up a snack or some picnic fix-

ings. Tucked just behind the market, Europe's third-largest **synagogue**—designed by an Austrian architect in the early 20th century (www.sofiasynagogue.com)—feels like a celebration. Bulgaria was one of the only countries in Nazi territory that refused to turn its Jewish population over to Hitler. All 49,000 Bulgarian Jews survived the Holocaust.

Across the busy street from the market is the elegant, early-20th-century **Central Mineral Baths** complex, now renovated and gleaming (and home to the city history museum). Sofia prides itself on its natural springs, which attracted the first settlers here in ancient times. Poke through the park on the left (near the tram stop) to find a bunch of perpetually-flowing public taps, where locals fill up big jugs of warm, mineral-tasting, supposedly very healthy spring water.

From this area, the pedestrianized, shop-and-restaurant-lined **Vitosha Boulevard** runs to the south. This lively people zone is

where the people of Sofia promenade, nurse a coffee, and catch up with their friends. It leads to the communist-era **National Palace of Culture** and a surrounding park—with Sofians enjoying their city while ignoring the boldly socialist-style architecture. At the northern

end of the park, notice the partly dismantled monument. All over Bulgaria, controversy swirls around rusting communist monuments like this one—how long should they stand before being torn down?

Those interested in the communist period can track down some other intriguing artifacts. Just to the northeast, in Knyazheska Park, stands the **Monument of the Soviet Army,** honoring the Soviets who helped liberate Bulgaria in World War II. One panel on the side of the main plinth is regularly (and creatively) defaced with pointed political graffiti.

To see more statues that once intimidated the cityscape, head about three miles southeast of the center to the ▲ **Museum of Socialist Art.** You'll see—preaching their message to each other in an empty field—the Lenin that once topped the pillar in the center of town; Georgi Dimitrov, the "Bulgarian Lenin"; the red star that capped the Communist Party HQ; and several stoic soldiers and workers.

Two more important sights are in the Boyana district, in the foothills of the Mount Vitosha, about five miles southwest of the center. The humble brick ▲▲ **Boyana Church** contains a treasure trove of stunning 13th-century frescoes, combining a strong Orthodox faith with very early Renaissance Western European styles (think Giotto). The Boyana frescoes are unique in their early use of basic perspective, fluid motion, natural rather than stiff poses, subjects with real human emotions and personalities, and the skillful use of bold colors to suggest three dimensions—you can practically see bodies moving around under the subjects' clothes (www.boyanachurch.org). Nearby, housed in a particularly boxy old communist-era palace, is the ▲ **National Historical Museum,** with a fine collection of fragments from the full span of Bulgarian history (www.historymuseum.org).

Sleeping in Sofia: Two good options in the walkable town center are the professional, upscale **$$$ Crystal Palace Boutique Hotel** (www.crystalpalace-sofia.com), and the simpler **$$ Arte Hotel** (www.artehotelbg.com).

Eating in Sofia: It's easy to simply stroll Vitosha Boulevard, which is lined with tempting options. Along here I've eaten well at **Shtastliveca** (Щастливеца, long menu of traditional Bulgarian dishes in a kitschy mod-traditional setting, at #27, www.shtastliveca.com). A pocket of fun, trendier eateries is just west of Vistosha near Karnigradska and Solunska streets. And for a youthful, fast-changing foodie scene, explore the streets just east of the City Garden (behind the National Theatre). In this area, **Raketa Rakia Bar** is a trendy, communist-kitsch-themed nightspot with Bulgarian cuisine and more than 100 types of rakia (Balkan firewater; at Yanko Sakazov 17). Nearby, the **Club of the Architects** is the spot for a genteel dinner of international fare in a big yellow mansion, or (better yet) in its serene garden (Krakra 11).

▲▲▲Rila Monastery (Rilski Manastir/Рилски Манастир)

Bulgaria's spiritual heart and soul reside about 80 miles south of the capital, deep in the Rila (REE-lah) Mountains. Here you'll find Rila Monastery—a fortress on the outside, spiritual sanctuary inside. The monastery was founded in the 930s by Bulgaria's patron saint, St. John of Rila (or Ivan Rilski, as Bulgarians call him), who came here seeking a hermetic way of life. During the Dark Ages, monks at Rila kept the faint embers of Bulgarian Orthodox thought glowing. Later, during a period of Ottoman occupation—when conversion to Islam was strongly encouraged—remote monasteries like Rila became lifeboats for the Bulgarian faith, language, literature, and cultural artifacts. Today, Rila is a place of pilgrimage for Bulgarians, who consider it their faith's single most important site. And tourists are amazed by its pristine setting (tucked between mountains and forests), the reverent spirituality that fills its stony courtyard, and the vivid art that decorates its church.

Visiting Rila Monastery: The monastery is best for drivers, who can reach it in about two hours from Sofia (mostly on the slick A-3 expressway). It's also possible to reach by public bus, or—better—on a dedicated shuttle bus (also stops at Boyana Church—described earlier, reserve ahead, www.rilamonasterybus.com).

Stepping from the parking lot through the hulking outer wall, you emerge into a serene courtyard facing a red-and-white-striped church and a mountain backdrop. The stout **Hrelyo Tower** is the oldest part of the complex, from the 1330s; this was the place of last refuge in case of attack.

The complex's centerpiece church was built in the 1830s, after a fire. The walls and ceilings of its **porch** are slathered with

sumptuous, colorful frescoes—all crammed with details and symbolism. You'll see biblical stories, angels, devils, saints, and sinners. One elaborate scene shows the 40 days of trials your soul goes through after death, as a guardian angel accompanies the soul—represented by a small child—through a gauntlet of temptations.

The **church interior** is gloomy and atmospheric—air heavy with candle soot and incense. Next to each important icon hangs a small towel, used to wipe off smeared lipstick from reverent kisses. The right transept holds the heart of Czar Boris III, who capably led his country through World War II. Boris preserved Bulgarian sovereignty by politically allying with Nazi Germany. And yet, the czar defied orders to send Bulgaria's Jewish population to concentration camps, and refused to formally declare war on Bulgaria's biggest historic ally, the Soviet Union. Because Hitler needed easy access to Bulgaria's Black Sea ports—and lacked the resources to invade—he put up with it...until the summer of 1943, when Boris died mysteriously after a private audience with Hitler in Berlin. Many suspect a slow-acting poison, and Boris remains revered by the Bulgarian people.

Behind the church, find the **museum** holding treasures that devoted Bulgarians have donated or created to honor their most hallowed site. The highlight is the Rafail Cross, with 23 panels (each smaller than a deck of cards) depicting 36 Bible scenes populated by 650 toothpick-sized figures, all on a cross about the size of a hubcap. The monk who carved it over the course of 12 years literally went blind in the process—yet another remarkable act of devotion in this place that specializes in it.

Sleeping and Eating at Rila Monastery: While Rila is an active monastery (with resident monks), some of the **$ cells** have been converted into rustic accommodations for pilgrims and tourists (www.rilamonastery.pmg-blg.com). Just outside the north entrance to the monastery (opposite the parking lot) is a popular window selling fresh doughnuts and a good sit-down restaurant. Additional hotels and restaurants line the road between the monastery and the expressway.

▲▲▲Plovdiv (Пловдив)

If you visit only one city in Bulgaria, make it Plovdiv (PLOHV-div). The country's "second city" (with about 340,000 people), Plovdiv has it all: excellent sightseeing, a charming Old Town, and a bustling New Town (www.visitplovdiv.com). It's fascinating to explore and easy to enjoy. And people have enjoyed it for a very long time: Plovdiv claims to be one of the oldest continually inhabited cities in the world. The ancient Greeks dubbed it Philippopolis (for the father of Alexander the Great), and the Romans called it Trimontium (for the "three hills" it was built upon). Today you'll see a ruined acropolis, a well-preserved ancient theater, gorgeous 19th-century homes filled with the art of local painters, Bulgaria's most thriving pedestrian boulevard, and a hipster zone with creative restaurants and even more creative graffiti.

Visiting Plovdiv: Plovdiv has two parallel worlds, just steps apart and equally worth exploring: The Old Town (draped over a hill) and the New Town (filling the flat valley below). The city is compact—you can easily see everything on foot.

The **Old Town** blankets the slopes of some of the many

The Eastern Orthodox Church

Bulgaria is one of many Eastern European countries that is predominantly Eastern Orthodox Christian. (Others include entire nations—Russia, Serbia, and Greece—or a significant percentage of the population, as in Bosnia, Montenegro, and Slovenia.)

As you explore an Orthodox church, keep in mind that these churches carry on the earliest traditions of the Christian faith. Orthodox and Catholic Christianity came from the same roots, so the oldest surviving early-Christian churches (such as the stave churches of Norway) have many of the same features as today's Orthodox churches.

Notice that there are no pews. Worshippers stand through the service, as a sign of respect (though some older parishioners sit on the seats along the walls). Women stand on the left side, men on the right (equal distance from the altar—to represent that all are equal before God). The Orthodox Church uses essentially the same Bible as Catholics, but it's written in the Cyrillic alphabet, which you'll see displayed around any Orthodox church. Following Old Testament Judeo-Christian tradition, the Bible is kept on the altar behind the iconostasis, the big screen in the middle of the room covered with curtains and icons (golden paintings of saints), which separates the material world from the spiritual one. At certain times during the service, the curtains or doors are opened so the congregation can see the Holy Book.

Unlike the decorations in many Catholic churches, Orthodox icons are not intended to be lifelike. Packed with intricate symbolism, and cast against a shimmering golden background, they're meant to remind viewers of the metaphysical nature of Jesus and the saints rather than of their physical form, which is considered irrelevant. You'll almost never see a statue, which is thought to overemphasize the physical world...and, to Orthodox people, feels a little too close to violating the commandment, "Thou shalt not worship graven images." Orthodox services generally involve chanting (a dialogue that goes back and forth between the priest and the congregation), and the church is filled with the evocative aroma of incense.

The incense, chanting, icons, and standing up are all intended to heighten the experience of worship. While many Catholic and Protestant services tend to be more of a theoretical and rote consideration of religious issues (come on—don't tell me you've never dozed through the sermon), Orthodox services are about creating a religious experience. Each of these elements does its part to help the worshipper transcend the physical world and join in communion with the spiritual one.

hills that make up Plovdiv. Its rustic streets—with ankle-wrecking river-stone cobbles—are lined with dozens of homes in the eye-pleasing **Bulgarian National Revival style.** In the mid-19th century, when the ruling Ottoman Empire was in decline, the Bulgarians sought to celebrate their culture with this unique style: wooden-beam construction with upper floors that bulge outward, tastefully painted in vivid colors.

Today, many of these buildings house museums, including the ▲ **Hindliyan House**—dating from 1840 and decorated to the taste of its merchant owner. It still feels lived-in, with opulent sitting rooms, a starburst-painted ceiling, a Turkish-style hamam, a rose water fountain, and "souvenir" wall paintings showing off some of the merchant's far-flung business travels, from Stockholm to Venice.

Another house contains an art gallery celebrating a little-known but supremely talented Bulgarian painter. ▲▲▲ **Zlatyu Boyadzhiev** (1903-1976) was already a well-established artist when his health took a terrible turn. In 1951, he suffered a stroke that rendered his right hand useless. Boldly embarking on a second act, Boyadzhiev's left hand began painting scenes that looked nothing like the ones his right hand had produced. Over the next 25 years,

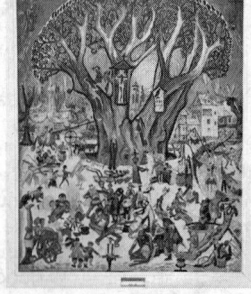

he reveled in bright colors with a childlike exuberance, slapping thick, Van Gogh-like brushstrokes onto the canvas. Boyadzhiev's best works feature timeless slices of peasant life: People praying not in temples, but under trees. Locals sitting around a public fountain sipping glasses of wine. Peasant women clustered around a fire, knitting as they eke out warmth. A fattened pig being slaughtered for Christmas; above the victim, each weathered face could tell a story.

Boyadzhiev also had a subversive streak. In *Public Prayer,* scrawny villagers come together to pray for good fortune; everyone is skinny...except the fat priest. In *The Orphanage,* a motley collection of disabled beggars (and their disabled pets) huddle behind their larger-than-life chieftain. Boyadzhiev was also captivated by the Karakachani, a nomadic tribe that herded their wooly sheep throughout the Balkans until the communists ended their way of life in the 1950s. Boyadzhiev worked under the communist regime, but managed to buck the predominant Socialist Realism style. Because he glorified peasant life, without threatening any of the communists' sacred cows, Boyadzhiev was allowed to carry on. This makes Boyadzhiev the rare artist who thrived under communism...and also had real talent.

The Old Town hillside also has some ancient sites. Up at the very top of town, the scant remains of the **acropolis** offer grand views over the modern skyline. And partway down the hill is a remarkably intact ▲▲ **ancient theater.** This 5,000-seat theater—built by Emperor Trajan—wasn't discovered until the 1960s. Now excavated, the theater's wall is mostly intact, the stony seats are still etched with their original numbers, and the acoustics remain perfect. Plays are performed here regularly.

Just below the theater, an underpass below the busy main thoroughfare leads to the **New Town.** The twisty streets straight ahead constitute the district called **Kapana** ("The Mousetrap"). Not long ago, this was a dreary, deserted, and dangerous quarter. But a recent initiative to pedestrianize and cobble the streets has turned the area into a hipster paradise. The streets are lined with bars, cafés,

and creative galleries (look for PLOVEdiv, with prints that put a whimsical pop-culture spin on old communist icons). This zone also has more than its share of creative, government-subsidized graffiti. Local authorities figure that street artists will tag buildings anyway—so they might as well focus all that creativity, and pay them to do it.

A couple of blocks south, you'll pop out at the ▲ **Dzhumaya Mosque.** Dating from the 1360s, this mosque is one of the few that remain of the dozens that filled the streets of Plovdiv during Ottoman times. Renovated in 2006, today the evocative mosque is an active house of worship serving Plovdiv's substantial Muslim population. Outside of prayer times, visitors are invited to step inside.

Directly in front of the mosque, they've excavated the seats at

the end of a long and skinny ▲▲ **stadium** built in the first century A.D. You can walk down to see the seats, or just enjoy a drink at the café. On some evenings, outdoor movies and other events fill this space.

From here, the ancient racecourse runs (unseen) beneath Plovidv's **main walking street** (officially named Knyaz Alexander I Street). Lined with cafés and busy shoppers, this drag is a delightful place to simply stroll. Partway down the street, at the grand staircase, look for the big blocky footprint in the middle of the street—marking what was the far end of the stadium. Those stairs lead up behind the burgundy-colored National Theatre; along its back wall is more city-sponsored graffiti (facing a rocky cliff with graffiti of Bulgarian VIPs).

Back on the main drag, continue heading south, past the American fast-food chain Макдоналдс. Soon after, the street opens up into an inviting fountain square. Just beyond is the giant, blocky, communist-era post office, anchoring the vast Central Square (Ploshtad Tsentralen)—which still has intimidating echoes of communist times, from the elite communist-era Hotel Trimontium (now a more run-of-the-mill Ramada) to the conceptual sculpture-fountain. Sprawling on your right is the gorgeous Tsar Simeon Garden, a well-used public park with footpaths, fountains, playgrounds, and the people of Plovdiv enjoying their city.

Sleeping in Plovdiv: In the Old Town, **$$ Hebros Hotel** fills a cozy old Bulgarian National Revival mansion with characteristic rooms and a great restaurant (www.hebros-hotel.com). The smaller **$$ Hotel Renaissance,** between the Old and New Towns, is also a good choice (www.renaissance-bg.com). At the other end of town, **$$$ Hotel Trimontium**—once the top-of-the-top communist-era hotel—is now a comfortable Ramada with easy access to the New Town's main drag (www.wyndhamhotels.com).

Eating in Plovdiv: The Kapana ("Mousetrap") district has several trendy bars and cafes, and the excellent **Pavaj** (Паваж) restaurant, which updates Bulgarian classics and international dishes with a hipster/foodie aesthetic (Zlatarska 7). The recommended **Hotel Hebros** restaurant has an upscale (but still affordable) vibe, with well-executed upscale Bulgarian dishes in a classy dining room or a leafy patio (www.hebros-hotel.com). On or near the New Town's main walking drag, consider the **Vino Culture** wine bar (Otets Paisiy 5); the tacky but popular **Happy** chain (basically the Applebees of Bulgaria, Vasil Levski 2, www.happy.bg); the more upscale-feeling **Hemingway** (Gurko 10, www.hemingway.bg); or the kitschy-touristy-traditional **Dayana** (Даяна, three branches— most central at Knyaz Al. Dondu- kov-Korsakov 4, www.dayanabg. com).

Nearby: About a half-hour south of Plovdiv, in the Rhodope Mountain foothills, is **Bachkovo Monastery** (Бачковски манастир).

It plays second fiddle to Rila—with a less romantic location and less dramatic frescoes—but for those based in Plovdiv, it's far easier to reach. Come here for an accessible look at a soulful Bulgarian Orthodox monastery. The two-story ossuary has some particularly fine frescoes from the 11th through 14th centuries.

▲Thracian Plain (Тракийска Низина)

Defined by Bulgaria's two major mountain ranges, the Thracian Plain was a busy funnel of trade throughout ancient times. This was the home of the Thracians (explained in the sidebar), who left behind tombs filled with ancient treasure.

Kazanlak (Казанлък, KAH-zahn-luk), with around 50,000 people, is the main town of the Thracian Plain. The workaday town—with a broad main square and a low-rise, communist-concrete aesthetic—is mainly of interest for sights relating to the Thracian Tombs (www.muzei-kazanlak.org).

In the town of Kazanlak itself, the **Kazanlak replica tomb** demonstrates how even in the afterlife, the deceased would be surrounded by colorful slices of Thracian life. You'll squeeze through a narrow passage, then crouch under a dome painted with vivid scenes: The eternal banquet of the Thracian who's buried here, flanked by servants, musicians, and horses.

Three more interesting tombs are within about a 10-minute drive of Kazanlak. At **Shushmanets** (Шушманец, SHOOSH-mah-nets), you can see how a single, stout column supported a heavy load. You'll also see a block with a well-worn hole, illustrating how the double stone doors could swing open and closed on a pivot. Nearby, **Ostrusha** (Оструша, OS-troo-sha) began as a temple. The entire block-like structure was carved out of one gigantic chunk of rock. That's 60 tons—triple the size of the blocks used for the Egyptian pyramids—transported here from the mountains 12 miles away. And then they had to carve it without cracking it. On the ceiling inside survives a fresco of a ghostly, enigmatic face—showing how Thracians were usually depicted as redheads. And **Kosmatka** (Косматка, kos-MAT-kah)—the tomb of Seuthes III—lets you peek into a multichambered tomb like the Kazanlak replica.

For a look at some of the breathtaking items found inside those tombs, back in Kazanlak, visit the ▲ **Iskra-Kazanlak Historical Museum**. The museum includes a room of Thracian artifacts: an intimidating helmet, with an attachable wreath of gilded leaves;

The Thracians and Their Tombs

Four centuries before Christ—when Socrates and Plato were doing their thing in Athens (about 300 miles to the south)—today's Bulgaria was known as Thrace, with a sophisticated civilization all its own. Famous Thracian figures include Spartacus (the charismatic leader of a Roman slave rebellion), Orpheus (a mythical musician and poet, likely based on an actual Thracian prince), and several emperors (including Justinian the Great). Thracians traded with other civilizations near and far. They had a reputation as redheads and fearsome fighters. And they had a remarkable skill for crafting jewelry as exquisite as anything you'll see today.

Thracians buried their royalty in distinctive, igloo-shaped tombs that were covered in earth. Dozens of these tombs (called *tumuli*) are scattered across the Thracian Plain, along with hundreds of decoy mounds designed to fool grave robbers. Buried deep under those piles of earth, the tombs were impressive feats of fourth-century-B.c. engineering. The dead were buried with troves of golden treasure, now displayed in museums throughout Bulgaria (including the museum in Kazanlak and Sofia's National Archaeological Museum and National Historical Museum).

Fans of ancient sites enjoy visiting a few of the tombs near Kazanlak, the region's main town (described in this chapter). True aficionados make a pilgrimage to the even bigger and more impressively decorated tomb at Sveshtari, in northeastern Bulgaria (about 4 hours from Kazanlak, or 2.5 hours from Veliko Tarnovo). Either way, you'll be impressed by the sophisticated engineering and delicate artistry of people who lived two and a half millennia ago.

a double-handled golden wine cup, or kylix; a solid-gold clamshell case; and some finely-detailed jewelry. Red-and-black Greek vases were likely obtained in exchange for Thracian copper ore and gold.

Kazanlak is also the capital of Bulgaria's **rose-oil** industry. (This area is known as the "Valley of the Roses.") Each May and June, hard-working laborers rise early to pick the delicate roses that have bloomed overnight, then take them to a distillery where they can be converted to fragrant oil. (It looks—and smells—like they're making very rosy moonshine.) Shops around town—and all over Bulgaria—sell the final product. It all culminates in Kazanlak's Rose Festival, usually in early June.

Sleeping in Kazanlak: The accommodations here are nothing special; **$ Hotel Palas** is central, just a short walk from the main square (www.hotel-palas.com).

▲▲Balkan Mountains and Shipka Pass

Between the Thracian Plain and Veliko Tarnovo run the Balkan Mountains (which gave their name to this entire peninsula). Crossing over this range, you'll pass several worthwhile sights. For a visual orientation, scan the mountainous horizon from the valley near Kazanlak and try to pick out three big landmarks: the flying-saucer shaped Buzludzha monument; the blocky Shipka Pass monument; and—down below that—the glimmering golden domes of Shipka Church.

▲▲ **Buzludzha** (Бузлуджа, BOOZ-lood-zhah)—an abandoned monument to the Bulgarian Communist Party—is easily worth ▲▲▲ for those captivated by Bulgaria's communist heritage.

This gigantic conference hall was built in the 1980s, in the waning days of communist rule. With the end of the Cold War and the arrival of capitalism, Buzludzha was abandoned. Today, you can drive up, up, up into the mountains and stand before this decaying souvenir of a failed system. The lyrics of the international communist anthem are literally falling off the walls. And the Coke-aping "Enjoy Communism" graffiti makes it clear who won the Cold War. You can try to find a way inside the structure (while officially closed, some intrepid visitors shimmy through gaps to get inside; this is—I cannot stress enough—at your own risk). The interior is an eerie, crumbling world of vandalized propaganda, muddy asbestos, a roof that's barely held up by its hammer and sickle, and disintegrating mosaics—once so proud, and now just a humble artifact. The monument is a twisty, 20-minute (each way) drive from the valley. To find the road up, look for the turnoff along the main road between Kazanlak and Shipka (marked by the stoic communist-era statue standing by a pillar).

The sumptuous ▲▲ **Shipka Church** sits on a hillside above the simple town of Shipka. The church—completed in 1902 by some of the leading Russian architects of the day—is exuberant "Muscovite-style"...over-the-top Baroque-meets-Byzantine. It's dedicated to the Russian and Bulgarian troops (now buried in the crypt) who fought fiercely to defeat the Ottomans in 1877 (see next). Stepping inside, you enter a world of glittering icons, a rich haze of incense, and hundreds of tall, skinny candles. The 175-foot-tall steeple, flanked by bulbous golden onion domes that shimmer in the sunshine, holds a giant bell cast from discarded artillery cartridges after the battle.

Higher up on the road to Veliko Tarnovo, you'll pass a turnoff for **Shipka Pass** (Shipchenski Prohod/Шипченски Проход). It's worth a quick detour to the monument marking the summit. A long staircase leads up to the boxy tower that honors the pivotal 1877 battle—fought right here—in which elite Russian forces came to help homegrown Bulgarian troops put an end to the nearly five centuries of Ottoman rule. This was a key turning point in Bulgarian history, and led directly to the creation of a modern, fully independent Bulgarian state. It also gave Bulgarians a soft spot for their big ally, Russia (unlike in most of Eastern Europe, where Russia is seen as an unwanted bully). This is partly why, a century later, Bulgaria was the most docile of the Soviet satellite states.

Descending from Shipka Pass on the north (Veliko Tarnovo) slope, you'll coast into the town of Palauzovo. Here you can turn off for a 30-minute drive to ▲ **Tryavna** (Трявна, tree-AHV-nah), a touristy village with an abundance of traditional Bulgarian National Revival-style homes. Stout stone bases support whitewashed walls and heavy slate roofs, and each door seems to lead to a souvenir shop. While you can also see a version of this style in Plovdiv and in Veliko Tarnovo, Tryavna is a pleasant stretch-your-legs small-town option. From here, you can simply continue north (via Tsareva Livada) to rejoin the main Veliko Tarnovo road.

If you skip the Tryavna turnoff, you'll pass through the big, gritty city of **Gabrovo** (Габрово). Filling an isolated valley with heavy industry, Gabrovo is the butt of many jokes for its people's thrifty ways. But these days, Gabrovo has the last laugh as the home of a museum called the House of Humor and Satire (you'll pass right by it on the main road, www.humorhouse.bg).

▲▲Veliko Tarnovo (Велико Търново)

One of Europe's most dramatically set cities, Veliko Tarnovo (VEH-lee-koh TAR-noh-voh) bunny-hops through a misty gorge at a sharp bend of the Yantra River. The town's hillsides are blanketed with both traditional homes and dreary concrete housing blocks. In this town that's more vertical than horizontal, going for a walk around the block feels like climbing a ladder. Tarnovo was the capital of the Second Bulgarian Kingdom, which was the medieval high-water mark of Bulgarian civilization. Today—with 70,000 inhabitants, and a prestigious university with around 18,000 students—it's called *Veliko* (Great) Tarnovo to honor its illustrious past. Aside from its stunning setting and rich history, Veliko Tarnovo offers the chance to meet some craftspeople, scramble around a ruined castle, and side-trip to some worthwhile sights (www. velikoturnovo.info).

Visiting Veliko Tarnovo: Perched on the rim of a gorge, Veliko Tarnovo is shaped like a natural amphitheater. And center stage—dominating a little peninsula defined by the tight river bend—is a giant sword thrusting skyward, ringed by fearsome horseback warriors. This monument commemorates the **Asen clan,** who ruled over the Second Bulgarian Kingdom (13th-14th centuries). According to legend, these brothers planted their sword on this spot and said, "Here shall be Bulgaria." While Bulgarian history can be obscure to outsiders, the Second Bulgarian Kingdom really was a big deal—an era when the Asen dynasty dominated the Balkan Peninsula from Ukraine to Greece. Their decline ushered in the Ottoman rule that would dominate Bulgarian history for nearly five centuries. You can circle all the way around town to find the bridge that goes out to the monument (and the art gallery just behind it); the best views from afar are along the charming, cobbled Gurko Street (near Hotel Gurko).

Veliko Tarnovo's town center lines up along **Stambolov Street,** which follows the curve of the river a few very steep blocks uphill. Branching off from this main drag is the town's most appealing lane, Rakovski Street—which I think of as ▲▲ **"Craftspeople Street."** Along this cobbled street are several talented artisans who enjoy inviting visitors to watch them create traditional crafts. Do some window-shopping, and drop in on any shop that grabs your attention: Silversmith Todor Kushlev creates intricate filigree jewelry by hand—or, in the case of his blowtorch—by mouth. Nina and her son create pottery with patterns dating back centuries. Miglena operates an old-fashioned loom. Rumi carves wooden items. Rashko painstakingly paints icons. And Greti carefully pours a thin stream of dough on a spinning griddle to create delicate shredded wheat-like strands for the honey-soaked treat, *kadaif.* (She doesn't sell the *kadaif,* mind you—just the strands. B.Y.O. honey.)

Farther south, Stambolov Street passes above what many consider to be the first parliament of Bulgaria—today the **Revival and Assembly Museum.** With the 1877-1878 expulsion of the Ottoman Empire (with Russian help), Bulgaria was free to create a modern nation. The National Assembly convened right here for the first time in 1879 and ratified a constitution. Today you can see the original assembly hall, and peruse a fine museum with vivid photographs documenting the Bulgarian National Revival movement and the creation of the modern Bulgarian state (www.museumvt.com). The building itself was designed by Kolyu Ficheto (1800-1881)—Bulgaria's leading 19th-century architect—who is honored by a statue out front. On a little crest just above, the striking, green-domed **Cathedral of the Nativity of the Virgin** (Rozhdestvo Bogorodichno, also designed by Ficheto) has a terrace with a great view over the gorge and castle.

Just over the ridge, the ruins of ▲ **Tsarevets Fortress** mark the site of the heavily-fortified Asen headquarters. While little survives, tourists enjoy aiming imaginary arrows from the bastions, taking in the views, and tiptoeing up to the so-called "Execution Rock"—where no ax or gallows were needed...just a firm shove into a deep gorge. The (reconstructed) church at the summit has unusual modern decorations. These were commissioned by Lyudmila Zhivkova (1942-1981)—the communist-era President of Art and Culture (and daughter of the Bulgarian dictator)—who, after surviving a car wreck and getting into yoga, used her influence to try to merge communist ideology with counterculture art and New Age philosophy. (She was being groomed as her father's heir apparent, and it would have been fascinating to see what direction she'd have steered the country...if she hadn't died—mysteriously, some say—of a brain tumor at age 38.) An elevator zips sightseers up to the steeple's crenelated top for the best high-altitude views in town.

Sleeping and Eating in Veliko Tarnovo: Friendly **$$ Hotel Gurko** enjoys an atmospheric Old Town setting (www.hotel-gurko.com). They also have a decent restaurant, but I prefer to hike (essentially straight uphill) to **Shtastliveca** (Щастливеца); ask for (or reserve) a table on the little cliff-hanging terrace with breathtaking canyon views (Stambolov 79, www.shtastliveca.com).

▲Arbanasi (Арбанаси)

The village of Arbanasi (ahr-bah-NAH-see), which overlooks Veliko Tarnovo from an adjacent ridge (about a 15-minute drive away), is a handy side-trip. The main attraction here is the ▲▲ **Church of the Nativity,** with magnificent frescoes in a dark, claustrophobic, wonderfully historic-feeling space. Typical of modest 16th- and 17th-century Orthodox church architecture (under Ottoman rule), it feels like a hay barn inside. The L-shaped gallery curves into the nave—and all of it is covered in still-vivid frescoes. Nearby, the **Konstantsalieva House** re-creates life here during Ottoman times. Also in Arbanasi, perched overlooking Veliko Tarnovo is the **Arbanasi Palace Hotel**—the former residence of communist dictator Todor Zhivkov, who ruled Bulgaria for 35 years (the longest of any socialist dictator in Europe). While definitely faded, the hotel still enjoys the same grand views over Veliko Tarnovo that lured Zhivkov here—and you can sleep in his presidential suite.

Black Sea Coast (Chernomorie/Черноморие)

With more time, consider venturing to the eastern edge of Bulgaria: the Black Sea Coast, a popular budget beach destination for in-the-know Brits and Europeans. While I'm more drawn to Bulgaria's cultural treasures (and beaches are better in Croatia or Greece), the Black Sea Coast has its fans, and helps round out your Bulgaria experience.

The main coastal city is **Varna** (Варна, VAR-nah, pop. 335,000). Varna has a skyscraper core; long, sandy resort-lined beaches; the lush and sprawling Primorski ("Seaside") Park; ancient ruins, including a second-century Roman bathhouse; beautiful churches; and the excellent Varna Archaeological Museum, displaying the oldest jewelry in the world (from the fifth millennium B.C.), discovered in a local necropolis (visit.varna.bg).

The small-town alternative is **Nesebar** (Несебър, neh-SAY-bar, pop. 15,000), connected to the rest of Bulgaria by a narrow isthmus watched over by an iconic windmill (www.visitnessebar.org). This little town has an unusually rich cultural heritage, with artifacts from ancient Greek, Roman, Byzantine, Ottoman, and Bulgarian National Revival times. Nesebar is known for its many fine, partly ruined, striped-brick, Byzantine-style churches. It's also an enjoyable place to simply let your pulse slow, hit the beach, go for a boat ride, and get to know some real, working fishermen. And, for a little more activity, Nesebar adjoins the hard-partying, aptly-named **Sunny Beach** (Slanchev Bryag/Слънчев бряг) resort—as popular now as when it was purpose-built in communist times.

ROMANIA

România

Still haunted by legends of Vlad the Impaler and Nicolae Ceauşescu, Romania is complex—with an epic history, a multifaceted ethnic mix, and an unusually rich cultural heritage. It may not be the easiest place to travel, but for adventurous souls, it's exceptionally rewarding. It's a land that layers gritty cities, charming cobbled towns, glorious castles, ragtag countryside, cut-glass peaks, playing chicken with horse carts, and connecting with kindhearted people living in a crazy world...sometimes all in the same day. Love it or hate it (and often both at once), Romania presents a powerful and memorable travel experience.

Where to Go: Romania is a vast and varied country. To focus your visit, break it into four chunks: Wallachia (Bucharest); Transylvania (cute towns and castles); Maramureş (traditional folk life); and Bucovina (painted monasteries).

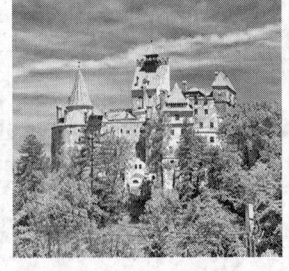

Wallachia consists of Romania's flatlands, wrapped around the Carpathian Mountains and stretching from Transylvania to the Danube (and Bulgaria). From a traveler's perspective, the only place here worth visiting is **Bucharest.** The exquisite **Peleş Castle** is also (just barely) in Wallachia, but feels closer to Transylvania.

Transylvania is Romania's heartland and where most visitors focus their time. You could spend many days here, sampling great cities, evocative castles and fortified churches, and a mountainous landscape. For home-base towns, big but charming **Braşov** works well for venturing into the mountains and touring castles (including **Bran, Râşnov,** and **Peleş**). Little, well-preserved **Sighişoara** is the most charming town and handy for touring fortified churches (such as the ones in **Biertan** and **Viscri**). **Sibiu** is Romania's most livable city, with a thriving historical core; it's relatively close to the dramatic **Corvin Castle.** And sprawling **Cluj-Napoca,** Transylvania's biggest city and de facto capital, has bustling squares, inviting parks, and busy nightlife.

Maramureș—in the far-north of the country, squeezed just inside the Ukrainian border—is time-consuming to reach. But it's definitely worth the effort for those interested in **traditional lifestyles** (and the gorgeous **Merry Cemetery**). Make a home base in the countryside near **Sighetu Marmației** and explore.

Bucovina, another traditional region to the east of Transylvania, is famous for its glorious **painted monasteries** (mostly near the town of Gura Humorului).

When planning your itinerary, don't underestimate the long distances (or the slow traffic—see next). To avoid spending all of your time on the road, be selective. With just a few days, focus on Transylvania, dividing your time between two home-base towns (Brașov and Sighișoara are handiest). With more time, add Maramureș and/or Bucharest. Bucovina's painted monasteries are beautiful, but the region has little else to see, and it's a time-consuming detour—include Bucovina only if you have ample time. For an even longer visit, the Dobrogea region (with the lush Danube Delta and the city of Constanța)—not covered in this book—is the most logical add-on.

Getting Around: Bucharest and other big cities are relatively well-connected by the slow **train** network (www.cfrcalatori.ro) or by **bus** (www.autogari.ro). But visitors wanting to scour the countryside—which is Romania's most appealing draw—are better off

driving. Roads are in decent condition, but progress is slow; there are virtually no expressways, country roads are generally two-lane, and city bypasses are rare—you'll usually have to drive right through the town center. On the other hand, drivers get a front-row seat for Romania's weird and wonderful ways—it's a fascinating place to just watch life unfold.

Romanian Cuisine: Romanian cooking is heavy peasant fare. Meals begin with a wooden platter of rustic mountain cheeses, greasy pork (including *jumări*—little strips of pork fat), and raw onions. Next is a simple but tasty soup *(supă);* a variety of "sour soups" called *ciorbă* are available (and typically delicious). Then comes the main course: pork, chicken, or fish. One popular protein is *mici* (MEE-chee)—minced-meat grilled sausages (like *ćevapčići* in the former Yugoslavia). Polenta *(mămăligă)*—often drizzled with sour cream—is the standard side, and *sarmale* (cabbage roll) is the national dish. A filling dessert is *papanași*—a baseball-sized fried doughnut smothered in jam and sour cream. Romanian wines and beers are nothing special, but try the fruity, 100-proof Romanian moonshine, *palinka* (a.k.a. *țuică*)...carefully. They say that when you drink *palinka*, "Your brain is OK, but your body is not OK."

Romanian Language: Romanian is a Romance language. If you speak French, Spanish, or Italian, you'll find that you may understand Romanian...a little. For example, "Good evening" is *Bună seara*. The character *ș* sounds like "sh," and *ț* is "ts." Some key survival phrases: "Hello" is *Bună ziua* (formal) or *Alo* (informal); "Please" is *Vă rog;* "Thank you" is *Mulțumesc* (or simply *Mersi*); and "Goodbye" is *La revedere*.

Local Guides: Hiring your own guide here is an exceptional investment. Prices are affordable, the guides I've recommended are top-notch, and Romania is much easier to take with a little local help. I've personally worked with each of the following guides, and highly recommend their services. While I've listed each one's area of specialty, most of them work throughout the country—consider hiring one to be with you for several stops (or even your entire trip): **Daniel Gheorghiță** at Covinnus Travel (throughout Romania, www.covinnus.com, office@covinnus.com), **Dan Nica** (Bucharest and beyond, www.tourguidesromania.com, dsnica@gmail.com), **Ana Adamoae** (Bucharest and Transylvania, www.guidedtoursbucharest.wordpress.com, aadamoae@gmail.com), **Ciprian "Chip" Slemco** at Hello Bucovina (Bucovina and throughout Romania—and beyond, www.hellobucovina.com, contact@hellobucovina.com), and **Teo Ivanciuc** (just Maramureș, www.maramurestour.com, teofilivanciuc@yahoo.com).

Romania Practicalities

Money: Romanians use the leu ("lion," plural *lei*): $1 = about 4 lei. One leu is broken down into 100 bani.

Geography and People: Romania is 92,000 square miles, about the size of Michigan or the United Kingdom. Of its 22 million people, the majority consider themselves ethnic Romanians (85 percent), with large minorities of Hungarians (just over 6 percent) and Roma (an estimated 3-4 percent); many Romanians are a mix of these, along with strong German and Russian/Ukrainian influences. The Carpathian Mountains take a big bite out of the middle of Romania, defining its biggest and most famous region, Transylvania (and several cultural fault lines). The capital and biggest city is Bucharest, with around 2 million people; other large cities, each with around 300,000 people, are Cluj-Napoca, Iaşi, Timişoara, and Braşov. Although a member of the EU since 2007, Romania still struggles economically (per capita GDP is $12,800).

Snapshot History: Romania's pagan Dacian tribes were taken over by soldiers of the Roman Empire, most of whom later returned to Rome—but left behind their DNA and their language (which evolved into today's Romanian). In the late ninth century came the Hungarians, who would rule the core of the region (Transylvania) for nearly a millennium. In the 12th century, seeking help to settle and defend the land, the ruling Hungarian dukes invited German (or "Saxon") merchants to establish towns, villages, and trade here. Meanwhile, powerful eastern neighbors—Russia and the Ottoman Empire—frequently invaded and occupied other parts of the Romanian lands. In the late 19th century, Romania finally threw off its foreign rulers and imported royalty from Germany (King Carol I) to help lead them into the modern age. But after World War II, Romania became part of the communist bloc, and had arguably one of the worst communist periods in Europe (under megalomaniacal strongman Nicolae Ceauşescu—see page 1034). In 1989, Ceauşescu was executed, and Romania began a new chapter: capitalistic, democratic, and fully independent.

Famous Romanians: Gymnast Nadia Comăneci (and coaches Béla and Márta Károlyi, of Hungarian ancestry), author Elie Wiesel (born to a Jewish family in Maramureş), composer George Enescu, and public radio commentator Andrei Codrescu.

Emergencies: Dial 112.

Consular Services in Bucharest: The US Embassy is at Bulevardul Dr. Liviu Librescu 4 (tel. 021-200-3300); the Canadian Embassy is at StradaTuberozelor 1 (tel. 021-307-5000).

Telephone Country Code: +40, then drop the initial 0 of the phone number.

Tourist Information: www.romaniatourism.com

Top Romanian Destinations

WALLACHIA
▲Bucharest (Bucureşti)

Romania's capital, Bucharest—with about two million people—is a muscular and gritty tangle of buildings. It can be hard to like at first glance, but with a thoughtful look, it reveals its charms. Between the dreary apartment blocks hides an impressive architectural heritage. Once called the "Little Paris of the East," Bucharest flourished in the late 19th century, when independent Romania was born. Later it was brutally disfigured by the communist dictator Ceauşescu,

who left behind a starkly Socialist-style residential zone and the city's main landmark (the Palace of the Parliament). But today's Bucharest is working hard to move forward. In recent years, they've rejuvenated the once-derelict Old Town—transforming it into one of the liveliest nightlife zones in Eastern Europe. Taken together, Bucharest is a fascinating place to grapple with for a day or two.

Visiting Bucharest: For a glimpse at Bucharest's genteel past, go for a stroll along ▲▲ **Victory Avenue** (Calea Victoriei)—with

grand belle époque architecture that has recently been scrubbed of its communist-era grime. Pause by the horseback statue of King Carol I (1839-1914), across the street from the Royal Palace. In the 1860s, Romania became a modern state for the first time. With no royal family to call their own, the Romanians went shopping for a king who could connect their country to the European mainstream. They found one in Germany, where a prince looking for a throne agreed to become King Carol I of Romania. King Carol embraced his new homeland: He learned the language and adopted the culture while bringing Western reforms and securing true independence for Romania. Under King Carol, Bucharest blossomed. He imported French architects to give Bucharest the romantic allure visitors still enjoy along Victory Avenue. Just up the street is the **Athenaeum** concert hall, one of the finest examples of Bucharest's Golden Age of architecture.

Nearby, **Revolution Square** (Piaţa Revoluţiei) is marked by a stark monument honoring the more than one thousand Romanians who died to bring freedom to their country in 1989. It stands in front of the former Communist Party Headquarters, where dictator Nicolae Ceaușescu would deliver speeches from the little balcony. On December 21, 1989—as revolution swept Romania—Ceaușescu had to abandon his podium midspeech when the crowd turned on him. (For the rest of the story, see the sidebar.)

Just a few blocks south sits Bucharest's ▲▲ **Old Town.** From communist times through the early 2000s, this area was deserted, dilapidated, and dangerous. But now it's being systematically rejuvenated. Grand, glittering belle époque buildings (including several bank headquarters) have been scrubbed and polished. Formerly abandoned shopping galleries are newly inviting. Historical monuments—like the delightful Hanul Manuc, an early 19th-century caravansery—have been painstakingly restored. And an al fresco dining and drinking scene enlivens the traffic-free streets. The lanes of the Old Town are a revelation after dark (especially on weekends), when the entire neighborhood feels like one big, sprawling cocktail party.

Also scattered around the Old Town are a few modest but colorfully decorated Romanian Orthodox churches. Observing

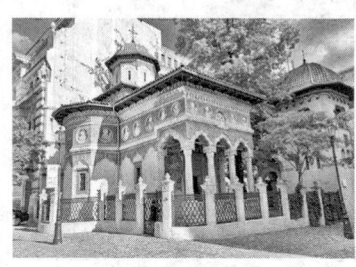

passersby in front of any church, you'll notice that—while religion was discouraged in communist times—these days, faith is an increasingly important part of everyday life. One of the best examples is the tiny ▲ **Biserica Stavropoleos convent,** unassumingly tucked between trendy restaurants and ritzy offices. Still tended by cloaked nuns, it feels like a transplanted time warp. A colorful *Last Judgment* painting fills the entranceway, and the little garden courtyard offers visitors a peaceful respite from the busy city.

Thriving as it is today, Bucharest's Old Town was lucky to survive the communist period. In the early 1980s, after an inspiring visit to North Korea, Nicolae Ceaușescu ripped out 80 percent of the historical center—30,000 houses, schools, and churches—to create the **Civic Center** (Centrul Civic) district, with wide boulevards, stone-faced apartment blocks, gurgling fountains, and a Pyongyang aesthetic. (Urban planners managed to save a few churches by secretly relocating them inside city blocks, where you can still find them today.) This area, just across the neglected little river from the Old Town, is worth a stroll to better understand the scale of Ceaușescu's ambition...and his ego.

In the core of the Civic Center, rows of fountains lead from

Nicolae Ceaușescu (1918-1989)

From uneducated peasant roots, Nicolae Ceaușescu (chow-SHESS-koo) rose through the communist ranks to take power in 1965. During his 24 years in power, Ceaușescu's brittle mental health and ballooning ego made him arguably Europe's most damaging communist dictator since Joseph Stalin. Early on, his aggressive deals with foreign leaders mortgaged Romania's future. (He turned his back on the Warsaw Pact and favored partnering with nonaligned countries in Asia and Africa—which made him paranoid about the likelihood of a Soviet invasion.) And later, Ceaușescu grew obsessed with paying off the country's debt just as he was becoming addicted to grandiose projects without budgets.

In the 1970s and 1980s, Ceaușescu erected massive factories and refineries, dammed the Danube, rerouted rivers for irrigation, and built an impossibly twisty road over the country's steepest mountains (see page 1037). And in his capital, Ceaușescu razed more than three-quarters of the historical quarter to build a new "Civic Center" district, capped by a palace fit for a megalomaniac.

Meanwhile, Ceaușescu exported vital resources even as his own people were starving. Expired frozen fish was all you could buy in grocery stores, and many Romanians resorted to subsistence farming and raised their own pigs to survive the harsh winters. As a cost-saving measure, power was routinely cut off at night, and hot and cold water were intermittent. To stem a dwindling population, Ceaușescu outlawed abortion and divorce, and extended elite status to mothers of multiple children. (Tens of thousands of unwanted children were later abandoned, creating a surge in US adoptions of Romanian orphans during the 1990s.) Ceaușescu also employed ruthless Stalinesque tactics to keep dissent at a minimum—through his huge, ruthless, KGB-style secret police force, the Securitate.

All of this created a powerful anti-Ceaușescu sentiment. And in the late fall of 1989, with winds of change sweeping across the Eastern Bloc, revolution reached Romania. As Ceaușescu delivered a speech, furious protesters filled the square. Ceaușescu ordered the police to open fire, while he fled to a dramatic rooftop helicopter rescue. But Ceaușescu and his wife were soon arrested, and a few days later were given a brief televised trial and shot, on Christmas Day 1989. To reassure the Romanians that their hated ruler was gone for good, the Ceaușescus' bodies were shown on national television. In all of Eastern Europe, Romania was the only country where the transition from communism to democracy came with a violent revolution—and the only one that ended in an execution.

Even now, decades later, Romanians are scarred from the Ceaușescu years. His legacy—economical, psychological, and physical—looms large. Looking back on Ceaușescu's excesses, Romanians say, "We can't even paint everything Ceaușescu built."

Unity Square (Piața Unirii) to the massive ▲▲▲ **Palace of Parliament**—the largest building in Europe (four million square feet, with more than a thousand rooms). Ceaușescu built this monstrosity as a symbol of his power. Today it houses the Romanian parliament, three skippable museums, and an international conference center—and is still about 70 percent vacant space.

Guided tours lead gawking visitors around its cavernous, empty, and dimly lit halls (if they turned on all the lights, the palace would consume as much electricity as a small city). On the one-hour tour (bring your passport, www.cic.cdep.ro/en), visitors see the grand entry hall; the theater, with its gargantuan five-ton crystal chandelier; and the ballroom, big enough to host a football match and with a glass ceiling that, it's rumored, could slide open to allow a helicopter to land. You'll also step out onto the balcony that Ceaușescu designed specifically for delivering speeches, while looking down a boulevard grand enough to echo his self-importance. (To be sure it met his expectations, builders erected full-scale cardboard models of facades along the entire street for his personal sign-off.)

Throughout the tour, ogle the details: The wall-to-wall carpets had to be delivered in pieces and sewn together on-site. The curtains are stitched with silver-and-gold threads. Garage-sized "pocket doors" slide up into marble frames. Huge as the building is above ground, it's built into the top of a hill—so there's even more of it below ground. Most of the structure is steel and concrete, wrapped in a marble veneer—more than 10 million square feet of it. The building sinks a quarter-inch each year under its sheer weight. They say underground tunnels go all the way to the airport—an emergency escape route for the paranoid Ceaușescu.

The dictator threw resources at his pet project like a crazed pharaoh. For six years, 700 architects and 20,000 laborers worked on it 24/7. Hundreds of workers died. Total cost: around three billion dollars. And even then, a third of the interior was never completed. Ceaușescu was executed halfway through its construction, and overnight, the "Presidential Palace" became the "Palace of the

People"—and those people were stuck with it. Nobody could possibly afford to buy the building, and finishing it was cheaper than tearing it down. When it finally opened in 1994, the Romanian people—whose food had been rationed for years to help pay for the palace—were both wonderstruck and repulsed when they wandered its opulent halls.

Next door, others are carrying on Ceauşescu's legacy of outsize projects. Just to the southwest, work crews are erecting the world's largest Orthodox church: The **Romanian People's Salvation Cathedral,** with a capacity of 6,000 worshippers, is scheduled to be consecrated in late 2018.

While Bucharest has plenty of fine museums, on a short visit I find it more interesting to simply explore the zones described above and tour the parliament. But to dig deeper into the story of Romania, consider the **National Museum of Romanian History** (right in the Old Town, www.mnir.ro) and the **National Museum of the Romanian Peasant** (folk-life artifacts on Victory Square/ Piaţa Victoriei, www.muzeultaranuluiroman.ro; this is redundant if you're heading to Maramureş).

Sleeping in Bucharest: The small, welcoming **$$ Rembrandt Hotel** is well-located, at the edge of the bustling Old Town dining and nightlife zone (www.rembrandt.ro). Also central is the more upscale, suite-oriented **$$$ Hotel Cişmigiu** (www.hotelcismigiu. ro).

Eating in Bucharest: The Old Town has ample dining options; for a memorable meal of Romanian classics, consider the classic upmarket-beer-hall vibe of **Caru' cu Bere** (www.carucubere. ro); the atmospheric caravansery setting of **Hanul' lui Manuc** (www.hanulluimanuc.ro); or the touristy and traditional **Crama Domnească** (www.cramadomneasca.net).

▲▲▲Peleş Castle

Peleş (PEH-lesh) Castle, on a wooded hillside above the lovely mountain resort town of Sinaia, is Romania's answer to Bavaria's Neuschwanstein: a fanciful, over-the-top, Romantic interpretation of a Gothic hunting palace, prickly with spires but far too pretty to repel an actual siege. Designed to impress, Peleş ranks among Europe's best Romantic Age palaces.

Background: Peleş was built in the 1880s by King Carol I, who had moved here from Germany. Carol was desperate to keep up with his rivals back home (such as "Mad" King Ludwig of Bavaria). And so, in a mountainous and forested landscape that reminded him of Germany, Carol imported German architects to create the ultimate palace. Here at Peleş, King Carol and Queen Elizabeth felt free from the stifling climate of German royalty: They slept together in the same bed, dressed in Romanian peasant costume, and decorated the place with Transylvanian folk themes. But Carol didn't abandon his German efficiency. Audiences took place standing at his upright desk and lasted about five minutes. His queen, Elizabeth (look for her portrait in traditional Romanian costume), used her Germanic know-how to both celebrate and elevate her adopted culture. Inspired by Transylvanian fairy tales, Elizabeth even wrote some of her own. It's no wonder that many contemporary Romanians still have great affection for their onetime-imported royalty.

Visiting Peleş Castle: You can get inside only with a guided tour (www.peles.ro). The interior is a rich world of sumptuous detail: cozy wood-paneled elegance, glittering Bohemian crystal chandeliers, whimsical paintings, colorful stoves, gilded stucco, Meissen porcelain, secret passages, and elaborate knickknacks (watch for the teak elephant table—a gift from the maharajah of India). Tours begin in the Hall of Honor—with its red carpets, grand staircase, venerable portraits, and inlaid-wood pictures of German castles (suggesting the king's sense of one-upsmanship). One particularly grandiose apartment—built for Emperor Franz Josef, who never actually slept here—has leather-tooled walls and a cozy breakfast room in the turret. In the Music Room, Queen Elizabeth hosted concerts and literary gatherings—and had scenes from her fairy tales painted on the walls. Meanwhile, the king's impressive armory collection (Europe's largest at the time) was designed both to intimidate and to stoke conversation. The private music halls and theaters were the site of many exclusive performances. And the library shows off the royal couple's passion for education. But remember: This was a Romantic Age, faux-medieval castle, built in the 1880s, so it also had all the modern conveniences: bathrooms with running water, forced-air heating, elevators, a central vacuum cleaner system, and even its own power plant.

If one castle isn't enough, you can also visit a second palace nearby, built by the next king (Carol's nephew)—a half-timbered mini-Peleş called **Pelişor Castle.**

▲▲Transfăgărăşan Road

The most challenging road connecting Bucharest to Transylvania—and, quite possibly, between any two points in Europe—is the Transfăgărăşan (trans-fah-gah-rah-SHAHN) Road. It twists and turns and bends back on itself several times as it crosses the cut-glass peaks of the Făgăraş Mountains, summiting at 6,670 feet.

This improbable road is another artifact of Nicolae Ceauşescu's rule. Following the 1968 Soviet invasion of Czechoslovakia to put down the Prague Spring uprising, a paranoid Ceaușescu wanted an escape route from Romania's flat capital to its easier-to-defend mountains. According to the story, Ceaușescu simply put his finger on a map and said, "Build it here." And they did. After incalculable costs and 40 workers' lives lost, Ceaușescu's dream was complete.

Today, the 56-mile-long Transfăgărășan Road has little practical value, but it's a popular scenic drive for tourists...as long as you're very comfortable with mountain driving. (Note that the road is only open when all snow has melted—typically late June through late October.) Consider the Transfăgărășan as a time-consuming but super-scenic alternate route for connecting Transylvania (it's off E-68, between Brașov and Sibiu) to Bucharest (via Pitești, where you can hop on the freeway).

At the southern (Bucharest) end of the pass, you'll pass **Poenari Castle.** Unlike the "Dracula Castle" at Bran (described later), Poenari has a real connection to Vlad Țepeș, who actually spent time here. (It's quite different than Bran, with a less striking interior; unless you have time and calories to burn, it's not worth the 1,400 stairs to reach the entrance.)

TRANSYLVANIA
▲Brașov

Brașov (BRAH-shohv, pop. 295,000), about a three-hour drive north of Bucharest, is scenically tucked against Carpathian foothills. Brașov was one of the original seven towns founded by Saxon settlers (see sidebar). It thrived then. It thrived during the Ceaușescu years, when it was aggressively developed into an industrial powerhouse. And it thrives today, with a rejuvenated old town center that's a popular springboard for the mountains: hiking in the summer, skiing in the winter, and castle-hopping anytime. Enjoyable but low-impact on its own, Brașov is an ideal home base for a Transylvanian "castle day"—with a car and an early start, you can easily side-trip to Peleș, Bran, and Râșnov in a single day.

Visiting Brașov: While Brașov's main appeal is its convenient location, its gorgeous main square and pe-

Transylvanian History

Transylvania's castle-capped hills and fortress-like churches are a testament to a hard-fought past. With a stout tower standing guard over every village, it's clear this region has frequently been a crossroads of history.

From the late ninth century until the end of World War I, Transylvania was part of Hungary. The Hungarian dukes who ruled this remote region called it Erdély (which, like "transsylvania," means "beyond the forest"). Seeking help to settle the rugged land, and to defend it against potential invasions from Tatars and Ottomans, the Hungarians invited merchants from today's Luxembourg, Belgium, and northwestern Germany to establish towns and trade here. Those settlers—called "Saxons"—founded seven fortified towns, including Brașov, Sighișoara, and Sibiu. (The German name for Transylvania is Siebenbürgen—"Seven Towns.") Meanwhile, German settlers in the countryside, who were outside of town walls and vulnerable to attack, beefed up their churches.

And so, for much of its history, Transylvania was divided along these societal strata: Hungarian rulers, German merchants, and Romanian peasants. But in modern times, things began to change. During a late-19th-century wave of emigration, many Saxons relocated to Germany. Then Hungary came up on the losing side of World War I, making Transylvania part of Romania. In the waning days of World War II, many Saxons fled the advancing Soviet Army, and under communism, the Romanian government literally sold its few remaining Saxons back to Germany.

And then there are the Roma (whom Romanians—eager to avoid any "Roma" vs. "Romanian" confusion—usually call Gypsies; see page 203). Today, Romania has one of Europe's largest Roma populations: officially 620,000 people, but—considering the difficulty of conducting a census of people who live off the grid—likely far more. The classic Roma stereotype is of desperately poor people living in shacks on the edge of town. You'll see plenty of that in Romania, but that's only part of the story. Most Roma live side-by-side with their Romanian neighbors, more or less integrated into mainstream society.

In today's Transylvania, the German minority is less than 1 percent. The Hungarian minority (about 6 percent of the population)—called Székelys—are scattered around Romania, but are concentrated in Hungarian-speaking enclaves in the central part of the country (east of Târgu Mureș). Travelers who can recognize each language are aware they're in a Balkan melting pot. Today, most Transylvanian towns are home to a mix of Romanians, Roma, Hungarians, and sometimes a few Germans—fitting for a region with such a rich and complex history.

destrianized core are a big bonus. The town is a fine mix of tourism and real, contemporary Romanian life. Its main square, **Piața Sfatului**—and the lively walking streets that flow away from it—are a delightful people zone.

Brașov's centerpiece is the **Black Church** (Biserica Neagră). The biggest Gothic church between Vienna and Istanbul, it got its nickname when it was charred by a 1689 fire. Inside, each bank of pews is lovingly decorated with the seal of the guild that financed it—suggesting the importance of trades and crafts in medieval Transylvania. The goldsmiths and other wealthy guilds sat near the front; poorer guilds, like the tailors and weavers, had the cheap seats in back. The mid-nave pews have backs that can be flipped to better see the grand pipe organ. And the most extensive Turkish carpet collection outside of Turkey fills the nave. These were donated by European traders, pilgrims, and crusaders who passed through this crossroads town on their way home from the Holy Land.

For a low-impact hike, head north across the little river and walk a few minutes up into the hills, where you can visit the **Black Tower** and the **White Tower**—part of the stout network of fortifications that protected the city in its medieval heyday. From the White Tower, you enjoy sweeping views over the tidy town center, the cable car that trundles to the adjacent mountaintop, and the big, white, Hollywood-like letters that spell out B-R-A-Ș-O-V.

Beyond the delightful urban core, Brașov features row after row of uniform concrete apartment blocks. But, revealing the city's relative affluence, many are now re-furbished and colorfully repainted. The sprawl is for good reason: Soon after the Iron Curtain slammed shut, Brașov was rechristened Orașul Stalin—"Stalintown." Ceaușescu built an extensive network of auto and armaments factories here, imported and retrained peasants from the wilds of Moldavia to staff them, and erected forests of concrete apartment blocks to house them. (For a time, Brașov was Romania's second-biggest city.) Trees with white bark were strategically planted on the hillside above to spell out the name S-T-A-L-I-N. And newlyweds felt compelled to have their picture taken with a big statue of "Father" Stalin in the park.

Sleeping in Brașov: Several cozy guesthouses are in the town center, including **$$ Hotel Bella Muzica** (www.bellamuzica.ro) and the simpler **$ Casa Albert** (www.casa-albert.ro). For a glitzy option near the train station (in the modern sprawl—a long walk or short drive from the Old Town), **$$$ Hotel Kronwell** is a big, slick design hotel with all the comforts (www.kronwell.com).

Eating in Brașov: You'll find plenty of options in the pedestrianized town center. **La Ceaun** ("The Cauldron") is good for traditional Romanian fare (www.laceaun.com), while the Italian-oriented **Prato** feels dressier but is still affordable (www.prato.ro). Both have appealing outdoor tables.

▲▲Castles near Brașov

You can link up all three of these castles in one busy day from Brașov. Or consider stopping off at Peleș on your way between Bucharest and Brașov, letting you linger and enjoy some time in Brașov itself.

The single best castle in the area (technically in Wallachia, just over the hills from Brașov) is **▲▲▲ Peleș Castle,** described earlier.

The mega-touristy **▲▲ Bran Castle** perches evocatively on a bluff overlooking a busy valley road (www.bran-castle.com). Despite the tacky vampire-themed kitsch that clutters the pathway up, Bran has virtually no real connection to Dracula or to Vlad the Impaler... but it sure is striking. Despite the fanciful legends, Bran actually is a good example of an authentic medieval fortress, dating from the 14th century. In the 1920s, Romania's royal family converted Bran into a rustic country retreat. And that, rather than vampires, is what you'll learn about in the whitewashed interior. As you follow the one-way route through the castle, exhibits introduce you to Romania's King Ferdinand I (the nephew of King Carol I) and his wife, Princess Marie (the granddaughter of Britain's Queen Victoria). Bran is also simply a fun kid-in-the-castle experience: Exploring the MC Escher floor plan, you'll discover a humble armory, a secret passage, and a fairy-tale courtyard.

▲ **Râşnov Castle** (RUZH-nohv) is your ruined-fortress-on-a-mountaintop experience. From the humble village of Râşnov (with its own Hollywood-like sign on the hills), you'll curl around the back of the hill, park, buy your ticket, then hike or ride a shuttle bus to the castle on top. Once inside the stout walls, a few houses and turrets still stand, which—along with

Dracula: Behind the Cape

Transylvania's tourist industry loves to milk its connection to Dracula. In reality, Dracula was the invention of a British novelist who never set foot in Transylvania, but was inspired, in part, by a real historical figure called Vlad the Impaler. Confused? To help you sort out fact from legend, here are the basics:

Vlad III (1431–1477) was a 15th-century prince of Wallachia who was taken captive by his Ottoman rivals. Some say he rotted in a prison, while others believe he apprenticed at the sultan's court in Constantinople. Either way, after six years the authorities believed him "rehabilitated" and returned him to his homeland—with the expectation that he would serve as their obedient puppet ruler of Wallachia.

Instead, Vlad quickly turned on his former captors, and joined the Hungarian fight to push back the Ottoman advance into Europe. According to later (and likely exaggerated) accounts, Vlad's methods for dealing with his enemies were brutal: Slowly and sadistically, he'd drive stakes into the bodies of his victims as they screamed in agony. Then he'd display their mutilated corpses along busy roads as a warning to would-be foes. Vlad dispatched tens of thousands of victims this way, earning him a vivid nickname: Vlad Țepeș—"the Impaler." He was also known by another name: Dracula, stemming from his father's membership in the chivalric "Order of the Dragon" (*Dracul* in Romanian).

While feared by the Transylvanian nobles, Vlad the Impaler was beloved by the peasants, who cheered his heroic defense of their homeland. And after his death, his legend only grew in a Europe terrified of the ever-looming threat of Ottoman invasion.

By the late 1800s, the English novelist Bram Stoker (1847-1912)—like many before and after him—found his imagination captivated by the sadism of Vlad the Impaler. Stoker was also inspired by completely separate Transylvanian folk tales of the undead. Stoker merged the two storylines and, in 1897, published the Victorian Gothic novel *Dracula*. Stoker never traveled to Romania to research his book; the vampire called Dracula, and his evocative Transylvanian settings, all came purely from Stoker's imagination.

All of this means that—from a sightseer's perspective—there are no actual sights in Romania relating to "Dracula," and only tenuous ties to Vlad the Impaler. Vlad may have lived for a brief time in Sighișoara. But it's likely that he never even set foot in the most famous "Dracula" sight, Bran Castle (at most, he spent a night or two there). Of course, the locals will never set you straight...all that Dracula lore is just too lucrative.

the foundations of others—give you a sense of the safety these castles provided during difficult times. Râșnov also enjoys grand views down over the valley.

▲▲Sighișoara

Sighișoara (sih-gih-SHO-rah, pop. 28,000) is Romania's showpiece jewel-box town—the Transylvanian version of Rothenburg

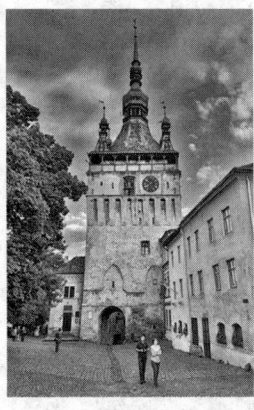

ob der Tauber or Český Krumlov. Sighișoara is the best-preserved of the original seven Saxon towns—it feels like a time warp. Sleep here if cuddly cobbles are your goal. Sighișoara is also a good home base for seeing the fortified churches, or as a stopover between Brașov and Maramureș.

Visiting Sighișoara: The entire fortified hilltop of Sighișoara—perched on a little plateau halfway up a wooded hill—forms the town's mighty **Citadel.** (Many tourists who come to Sighișoara ask, "So where's the castle?" They don't realize they're already in it.) This walled area was both a home to craftsmen and a place of last refuge in case

of invasions or raids—which were frequent. Nine of Sighișoara's 15 pointy-topped watchtowers still survive—each one named for the guild that defended it.

Sighișoara's icon is its **Clock Tower**—marked with symbols that proudly trumpet its special privileges. Inside, visitors spiral up and up on creaky wooden stairs, and peek out over the shoulders of the figures that change with the day of the week. At each landing are modest exhibits: a model of the town at its peak, and a display of the products of each of the main guilds that put this place on the map.

If you need a Dracula photo op, you'll find a statue of **Vlad Țepeș** (who may have lived here briefly) on the square called Piața Muzeului, just above the Monastery Church; nearby, a garden terrace features views over the rooftops of Sighișoara's workaday modern town.

From Sighișoara's town center, a covered staircase—called the **"Stairs of the Students"**—leads 175 steps up to the hilltop. After every sixth step is a landing—a reminder to rest on the seventh day.

At the top, a school, a church, and a cemetery honor those original Saxon pioneers. German names fill the graveyard. And inside the **church** is a collection of artifacts from smaller German churches around the region—most now all but abandoned. You can see how, when Lutheranism reached Transylvania, frugal village churches kept their old Catholic altars, but removed the showiest statues. Dowry chests were found squirrelled away in the attic of a village church, untouched for centuries. The tomb of a furrier recalls a time when it was cheaper to wear heavy cloaks on Sunday morning than to heat this huge space.

Sleeping in Sighișoara: Several quaint hotels and pensions line the cobbled streets of the Citadel. The biggest outfit is **$$ Hotel Sighișoara** and its annex, the upscale **$$$ Fronius Residence** (for both: www.sighisoarahotels.ro). Or try the simpler **$ Pension am Schneiderturm** (www.schneiderturm.ro).

Eating in Sighișoara: In this touristy town, don't go looking for a memorable meal—just pick the setting you enjoy best. I've eaten well at **Casa cu Cerb** (www.casacucerb.ro) and at recommended **Hotel Sighișoara.**

▲▲Fortified Saxon Churches

Some of Romania's best castles aren't castles at all—they're churches. While big towns like Sighișoara and Brașov were well protected, smaller Saxon settlements were vulnerable—especially after a devastating Tatar invasion in the 13th century. So what did the industrious settlers do? They fortified their churches.

Dozens of fortified German churches—mostly built in the 13th and 14th centuries—are scattered across Transylvania. From the outside, they look like medieval fortresses: beefy bastions, stout lookout towers, narrow slits for raining arrows on enemies, distinctly Transylvanian trapezoidal turrets (to shed the heavy snowfall), and wrap-around defensive galleries. While most Germans have long since left Romania, their heritage lives on here: The signs, the services, and the hymnals in the pews are all still in German. And periodically, some of these churches hold Lutheran services.

Visiting Fortified Churches: As you explore Transylvania—especially the area between Brașov and Sighișoara—you'll drive past several of these fortified churches (a particularly fine example is in Saschiz). But a few are worth going a bit out of your way to see.

Close to Brașov, **Prejmer** (PREHZH-mehr) has a particularly well-preserved, half-timbered-and-whitewashed courtyard, showing how townspeople could flock into the protection of the church in times of crisis. Each cell was reserved for one family—notice that each rustic door is labeled. You can even see the little one-room "schoolhouse" tucked into the wall. (Nearby, **Hărman** has another well-preserved example.)

Between Sighișoara and Sibiu, **Biertan** (BEER-tahn) has

one of the newest fortified churches (early 16th century)—illustrating the architecture style at its most evolved. Looking out from the top, you can see the surviving three concentric walls (of the original five) that protect the church. But stepping inside, you could be in any village church in medieval Germany. The original 16th-century stone pulpit still stands. And, like the Black Church in Braşov, each bank of pews is marked with the seal of a local guild. On the door to the left of the altar, the locksmiths' guild showed off

with an elaborate locking mechanism. In the church courtyard is a "divorce chamber," where a quarrelling couple would be forced to share one bed, one pot, and one plate—for however long it took to resolve their differences. (From 1500 to 1800, only one divorce was recorded.)

The whitewashed and ramshackle church of **Viscri** (VEE-scree, from the German Weiss Kirch—white church), hidden deep in the hills between Braşov

and Sighişoara, is one of the oldest (c. 1100). Most of the pews don't have backs. That's because of the starched dresses and long headdresses of traditional village women, who wanted to avoid creases. The pews with backs were for the only families who were from elsewhere: the minister and the teacher. The very humble dirt-street town of Viscri—where locals selling colorful woolens to tourists seems to be the only economy—is fun to explore. One of the houses belongs to (believe it or not) Prince Charles, who loves the anonymity this off-the-grid corner of Europe provides. Locals claim that Prince Charles and Prince Harry retreated here to hide from the press in the days following the 2011 royal wedding of William and Kate.

▲▲Sibiu

Charming Sibiu (SEE-bee-yoo) may be Romania's most livable city. Sibiu began life as Hermannstadt, the biggest and most important of the original seven Saxon towns. And today, while only about one in a hundred residents has German ancestry, Sibiu's tidy townscape still feels very Germanic. (In 2000, Sibiu elected Klaus Iohannis to be the first German mayor in Romania since World

War II; beloved and hugely successful locally, he went on to be elected Romania's president in 2014.) While not quite as practical a home base as Brașov or Sighișoara (it's farther from Transylvania's main sights), Sibiu is more appealing in its own right. It's just the right size to be interesting yet still manageable (pop. 150,000), and the creaky, cobbled, atmospheric, and mostly traffic-free city center is a delightful place to simply hang out.

Visiting Sibiu: The atmospheric Upper Town core consists of three interlocking squares, each with a different personality: The aptly named **Grand Square** (Piața Mare) dominates an inviting and wide-open expanse fronted by stately municipal buildings (climb the Council Tower for sweeping views over town). **Small Square** (Piață Mică) is quaint, lined with al fresco cafés and a double-decker street plan that offers fine views from the "Liar's Bridge." And

Huet Square (Piața Huet) is dominated by the gigantic German Protestant church—a reminder of Sibiu's strong Saxon pedigree.

From Grand Square, a pedestrian street called **Strada Nicolae Bălcescu** bursts with life as it proceeds several blocks south through the city center. Where the traffic-free zone ends, turn left and follow Strada Cetății along a tranquil park that delineates the former moat—passing three stout fortified brick **towers** that stand as bold reminders of Sibiu's militaristic past.

Beyond simply strolling its tidy core, Sibiu has some low-impact sightseeing options. Its giant, Neo-Byzantine-style ▲ **Holy Trinity Cathedral** is one of the country's most impressive Romanian Orthodox churches. The ▲ **Brukenthal Museum** collects a wealth of both Romanian and European artwork (www.brukenthalmuseum.ro). And ASTRA, a Romanian literature and culture society, operates several museums of its own, including one of the country's best ▲ **open-air folk museums** on the outskirts of town (www.muzeulastra.ro).

Sleeping in Sibiu: There are plenty of guesthouses to choose from. I slept well at **$$ Huet Residence** (www.huet-residence.ro).

▲▲Corvin Castle (Castelul Corvinilor; a.k.a. Hunyadi/Hunedoara Castle)

Corvin Castle may be the most visually striking reminder that Transylvania was part of Hungary for most of its history. This is the home castle of János Hunyadi, the hero of the 15th-century fight against the Ottomans; and his son, Mátyás Corvinus, who became the only Hungarian king in more than 600 years of foreign rule (see page 609). With a certain "Hogwarts Gothic" quality, Corvin is also one of the most picturesque castles in a country where picturesque castles are a forté. When Budapest was building a faux-"Transylvanian" castle in their City Park in 1896, they modeled it after this one (see page 600). The evocative but mostly-empty castle sits unceremoniously along a gritty road on the outskirts of Hunedoara—about an hour and a half drive west of Sibiu (www.castelulcorvinilor.ro). While striking, it's worth the long detour only if you're a connoisseur of Transylvanian castles, Hungarian history, or both (or if you're driving from central Transylvania to Timișoara or Hungary).

Nearby: The area around Hunedoara has one of Romania's highest concentrations of **"Gypsy palaces":** over-the-top-osten-tatious mansions built just outside city limits by powerful members of the Roma community. Striking and controversial (and rumored to be funded through illegal activity), these are worth a fascinating drive-by to appreciate one more facet of the Romanian Roma experi-

ence. Be discreet about stopping or taking photos—the people living here often don't appreciate unwanted attention. Several "Gypsy palaces" line up along road 687, at the south end of Hunedoara, on the way to Călan (beginning just east of Corvin Castle).

Cluj-Napoca

Cluj-Napoca—or simply Cluj (kloozh) for short—is Transylvania's de facto capital (pop. 324,000) and a major center of culture,

universities, and business. While the compact historical core has its charm, the busy sprawl of Cluj feels like an urban jungle—making it challenging to appreciate on a quick visit. For that reason, Cluj ranks lower on my list of "must-visit" Transylvanian cities. But if you go, you'll find a congested historic core that's worth a stroll.

Visiting Cluj: The city's landmarks reflect its multiethnic heritage—like Transylvania itself, it's a mix of Romanian, Hungarian, and German. Towering high above Unity Square (Piața Unirii) is the Gothic steeple of ▲ **St. Michael's Church,** built by Hungarian Catholics in the 15th century. Nearby stands a bulky statue of the Hungarian king **Mátyás Corvinus**—honoring Cluj's substantial Hungarian-speaking minority (about 15 percent of the population). But just a couple of blocks to the east—as if to one-up the Hungarians—stands the skinny, slotted dome of the ▲ **Dormition of the Theotokos Romanian Orthodox Cathedral,** and out front, a statue of Avram Iancu, a proud Romanian who fought *against* Hungarian influence in Transylvania. Just to the northwest, between the Old Town and the river, is Cluj's lively and inviting **Central Park,** with beautifully-restored pavilions and the city's cutting-edge soccer stadium. After hours, youthful Cluj is busy with nightlife. The university zone to the west—called Haşdeu—is edgy. Mellower and more inviting is the **Museum Square** (Piaţa Muzeului) pedestrian zone, tucked in the heart of the Old Town.

MARAMUREŞ

Maramureş (mah-rah-MOO-rehsh) is Europe's most traditional corner. Here you'll find time-warp locals farming fields, getting around by horse cart, and living agrarian—almost biblical—lifestyles, seemingly oblivious to the modern world just over the hills. This is the place in Romania to enjoy being off the beaten track: Slow down, go for a lazy drive, pull over at anything that catches your eye, and marvel at the simplicity of it all. While it takes some effort to reach, Maramureş is well worth the effort for those who want to see a real, living open-air folk museum.

Orientation: To the north of sprawling Transylvania, the tourist's Maramureş is small: a skinny sliver of land between the Gutâi Mountains and the Ukrainian border. From Transylvania, it's a long drive up to the main city of Maramureş—dreary Baia Mare, with Europe's third-tallest smokestack looming overhead—and even then, you're still more than an hour away, over a twisty mountain pass. The best corner of Maramureş clusters around the town of Sighetu Marmaţiei.

Local Guide: Particularly here in Maramureş, a good local guide is an essential investment to get the most of out of your time (and to make it worth the long drive here). Knowledgeable **Teo Ivanciuc** excels at putting you in touch with traditional lifestyles, and giving them meaning (www.maramurestour.com, teofilivanciuc@yahoo.com).

Sleeping in Maramureş: Expect rustic but cozy accommodations. While Sighetu Marmaţiei has some big hotels, for the full Maramureş experience, stay in the countryside. Local guide **$ Teo**

Ivanciuc, listed above, rents rooms (www.amizadil.com)—or can refer you to other locals who do. For a bigger but still-traditional option, try **Hotel Grădina Morii,** on the outskirts of Sighetu Marmației (www.hotelgradinamorii.ro).

Sighetu Marmației

With close to 40,000 inhabitants, "Sighet" (SEE-geht, as locals call it) is the area's main town. Actually, many locals don't even call it Sighet—they just call it "the town." With a scruffy main square (which hosts a daily farmers market) and dreary apartment blocks, Sighet is not particularly attractive—but you can't avoid passing through several times on your visit to Maramureș.

Sighet was the birthplace of the Holocaust survivor, author, and Nobel Peace Prize laureate **Elie Wiesel** (whose novel *Night* is a definitive work of Holocaust literature). His birthplace—near a synagogue that the Nazis burned down in 1944 (now rebuilt)—is now a modest museum, with informational signs and a few artifacts. Wiesel lived in Sighet until he was taken away to Auschwitz at age 16.

Thanks to its remote location—closer to Budapest than to Bucharest—communist-era Sighet became a sort of "Siberia of Romania." It was the site of the Securitate's main prison, where dissenters, intellectuals, clergy, journalists, and political opponents of the regime were sent to rot, far from mainstream society. Many died. Today, the prison houses the ▲▲ **Memorial for the Victims of Communism,** with a modern, powerful, well-presented exhibit detailing the communist period in Romania (www.memorialsighet. ro).

Sighet also has a good **Village Museum** (with wooden houses) and an **Ethnographic Museum,** but you don't really need them—Maramureș itself is the best sight.

▲▲▲Maramureș Joyriding

Maramureș is a rolling, pastoral landscape speckled with haystacks. Go for an aimless drive and just take it all in. Thanks to its

rugged landscape and its great distance from Bucharest, Maramureș avoided communist farm collectivization—so people still tend their small family plots by hand. Horse carts outnumber cows. Men in overalls and funny little straw hats pile hay onto their wooden wagons. Women wear big, puffy skirts just above the knee, babushkas on their heads, and baskets laden with heavy goods on their backs. While not ignorant of the modern world, Maramureș feels like Europe's Amish Country, where centuries-old ways endure. It's not for the benefit of tourists—it's just their lifestyle.

Locals are very open and welcoming to curious travelers. This is an ideal place to be an amateur anthropologist...simply observe the way people live. (While you can do this on your own, it's easier and more rewarding with a local guide.)

Wander through any village and peek into family compounds. Each one is marked with a huge, ceremonial wooden gateway—

just big enough for a hay-loaded horse cart to trot through. (These gateways show off the Romanian knack for flaunting whatever wealth you have...even if it's not much. Another status symbol is hanging colorful pots from tree branches.) The gates are carved with a whole iconography of local symbols: starburst (pagan sun worship), wolf teeth (protection), bull horns (masculinity), leaves (nature), and—most importantly—the "rope of life" motif, a helix-like design suggesting the continuity of life from generation to generation. Inside each courtyard, you'll usually see—in addition to the main house—a humble barn with a paddock, a garden patch, and an old-fashioned, hand-pulled well.

You'll be surprised how often you'll be invited inside. Many Maramureş residents are eager to show curious visitors their humble homes. Every house has a "show room," where people collect their nicest belongings: colorful piles of blankets, pillows, and so on (often from the dowry of the woman of the house). This room is reserved exclusively for guests, while the family spends most of their time in much humbler surroundings.

It's fine to simply wander around the area and see what you may stumble upon, but here are some areas you could focus on:

The little **Cosău River Valley**—especially the stretch between Călineşti and Budeşti (each with a wooden church)—is a picturesque throwback. The rushing river powers all manner of medieval industry. You'll see carpet laundries, where wooden canals channel water into a naturally-powered spin cycle. People use the flowing water to operate brandy stills, making their own plum firewater *(horinca)*. Grist mills grind grains into both polenta and animal feed. And tucked deep inside family compounds, people spin wool into yarn and use creaky old looms to weave it into a loose fabric. That fabric is then taken to a fulling mill, where water-powered wooden hammers pound and pound and pound, mashing it into a dense, heavy material that's used in the traditional winter costume. (Gheorghe Opris, in the village of Sârbi, operates a mill that

ROMANIA

does all these things; you can try dropping by, but as he speaks no English, it's better to visit with a local guide.)

For a scenic drive, take the **high road** between Călineşti and Văleni, offering high-altitude views over the rolling farm fields of Maramureş—and, if you're lucky, hardworking farmers making haystacks.

From Văleni, you can coast down into **Bârsana,** which has the busy wood workshop of Toader Bârsan. Out in the courtyard, young lumberjacks artfully carve new wooden gates that look old. Toader himself sits on the stoop, hand-carving trinkets and wearing his distinctive little Maramureş straw hat. He loves to explain how he once met Hillary Clinton. (The wooden Bârsana monastery complex—described later—is at the edge of this town.)

Horse Market: Ocna Şugatag, a larger, functional town sitting on a plateau, is fairly dull—except on Thursday mornings, when the weekly livestock market makes it feel like a 17th-century car show. The people-watching is marvelous.

▲▲▲Merry Cemetery (Cimitirul Vesel)

A 30-minute drive west of Sighet is one of Romania's top cultural treasures: the Merry Cemetery. In 1935, woodcarver Stan Ioan Pătraş—inspired by a long-forgotten local tradition for colorful grave markers—began filling the Săpânţa village cemetery with a forest of vivid memorials. Today there are more than 1,300—each one with a pointy roof to protect from the rain, a painting of the

departed doing something they loved (or in the moment of death), and a whimsical poem. It's all painted a cheery blue to match the

heavens where the souls are headed. The Merry Cemetery is a poignant celebration of each individual's life, a chronicle of village history, and an irreverent raspberry in the face of death.

Although the cemetery is dubbed "merry," many of the poems are downright morose. Tales of young lives cut short by tragic accidents, warriors mowed down in the prime of life, or people who simply never found happiness are a reminder that death, and life, are sometimes nothing to be cheerful about.

Even if you can't read the poems, the images speak volumes: Weaver. Loved bikes. Television repairman. Soldier. Hit by a car. Struck by lightning. Nagging mother-in-law.

Tucked behind the church, you can find the grave of the artist who started it all, Stan Ioan Pătraş, who died in 1977. His apprentices carry on the work today.

Nearby: Across the highway (and a half-mile back toward Sighet), **Săpânţa Peri Monastery Church** towers 250 feet tall. Completed in 2003, the church demonstrates that in Maramureş, wood remains as popular as it ever was. Inside, the technical mastery of Maramureş woodworkers is on display: chunky but precisely-cut dovetailing keeps massive walls firmly in place, and the artistic shinglework cascades tidily from peak to eaves.

▲▲Wooden Churches

In Maramureş, surrounded by thickly forested mountains, wood is king. And some of the finest wooden churches in Europe are right here. These centuries-old structures resemble Norwegian stave churches, but with less flair. They are graceful wooden pagodas with eye-pleasing lines angling up to the heavens. Inside, faded "wood frescoes" look like silly-puttied Sunday comics pages, stretched out and plastered against the wall—illustrating a medieval interpretation of Christianity. Dozens of these churches are scattered around the region, but most are generally closed to the public (local guides can usually get the key). Some of the churches are modern, including the **Săpânţa Peri** monastery church (near the Merry Cemetery, described previously) and a striking ensemble

of wooden ecclesiastical buildings at the **Bârsana** monastery complex (about a 30-minute drive southeast of Sighet).

BUCOVINA

Within the large, eastern Romanian region of Moldavia sits the smaller sub-region called Bucovina (BOO-koh-vee-nah)—known

for its traditional folk life, its rolling Carpathian foothills, and, most of all, its glorious painted monasteries. Unfortunately, Bucovina presents a time-consuming detour for travelers connecting the core of Transylvania with the folk-culture treasures of Maramureș. And if you're very tight on time, Bucovina is skippable—since there's relatively little to see in this region beyond the monasteries. But if you can make the time, the monasteries are worth the trip.

Local Tours: If you make a special trip to Bucovina, invest in a tour to connect the painted monasteries (and other cultural sights) and bring them to life. **Hello Bucovina,** well-run by Ciprian "Chip" Slemco, offers a range of well-designed tours, from a quick spin to the monasteries to multiday routes connecting Bucovina, the rest of Moldavia, and neighboring countries (www.hellobucovina.com).

▲▲▲Painted Monasteries of Bucovina

Remote and feisty Bucovina sits on the cusp of cultures. It's just outside the Carpathian Mountains, squeezed between two would-

be oppressors: The Hungarians of Transylvania to the west, and the Ottomans to the east. So maybe it's no surprise that this stubbornly traditional region chose to cling fast to its faith in the rough-and-tumble 15th and 16th centuries, erecting dozens of fortified and vividly decorated monasteries. And today, many of the churches still survive—their outside walls slathered in colorful Byzantine-style fresco murals of saints and bible stories.

Background: The tradition of painted monasteries began during the reign of Prince Stephen the Great of Moldavia (1433-1504)—a contemporary of Vlad the Impaler of Wallachia, King Mátyás Corvinus of Hungary, and Sultan Mehmet the Conqueror of the Ottoman Empire. It was a frightening time, as big egos struggled for control of the Romanian lands—but Stephen the Great stubbornly asserted his Romanian Orthodox faith. According to legend, to celebrate his many military victories, Stephen would climb a mountain, shoot arrows into the rolling hills, and build a monastery where each arrow fell. Stephen's son, Petru Rareș (1487-1546), was inspired by Renaissance frescoes on a visit to Florence, and decided to decorate the monasteries with a similar technique. Their Moldavian subjects were very poor, very religious, and eager to do God's work for low wages. And most people were illiterate, making the vivid illustrations a powerful educational tool. Of the dozens of monasteries built by Stephen the Great, nine still survive.

While each church has its own unique flourishes, all of them are wrapped in glorious, exceptionally well-preserved frescoes.

You'll see row after row of saintly icons, local religious figures, ancient philosophers, Bible stories, lush visions of heaven, terrifying depictions of hell, and epic historical scenes. Each church has its own distinctive coloring (for example, "Voroneț blue").

Each church has a giant *Last Judgment* **mural** on its western wall. These are packed with symbolism that's worth disentangling. (While this works best at Voroneț, the basic composition is standard across churches.) Striping the mural are five horizontal tiers (top to bottom):

1. At the top sits God, flanked by 12 signs of the zodiac—merging Christian and pagan beliefs, driving home the eternal nature of God, and evoking the 12 Apostles.

2. Floating in a celestial bubble is Jesus—in his "furious vengeance" mode. He's flanked by Mary, John the Baptist, and pews with 12 seated Apostles (with other saintly figures in the cheap seats behind them). From Jesus flows a river of flames that spreads out toward the lower-right corner...and the open mouth of a hideous, multiheaded Beelzebub.

3. A dove (the Holy Spirit) sits on the Throne of Judgment, flanked by Adam and Eve—who committed the original sin, and are now eyewitnesses to how it all turns out. To the right—cut off from the holiness by Jesus' river of flames—are condemned pagans (depicted as the Moldavians' historical enemies: Jews, Ottomans, Tatars, and Armenians). At the front of this pack, Moses gestures passionately with the Ten Commandments, hoping for some last-minute conversions. Meanwhile, to the left of the river of flames stand smug clumps of righteous believers: prophets, bishops, theologians, and so on.

4. Below the Holy Spirit, the hand of God holds the scales of judgment. Drama ensues, as angels and devils pile good and bad deeds on the scale in a struggle for the man's soul. On the right, hideous beasts prowl a barren landscape where souls emerge from tombs—hoping to be rescued by the angels. Below them, a female figure lovingly cradles a ship—representing salvation even for those lost at sea. Meanwhile, on the left end of this tier is a saintly legion, halos aglow.

5. Finally, along the bottom level, we see (from left to right) the saved, kicking back in the garden of paradise (look for Mary, the archangels Gabriel and Michael, Abraham, Isaac, Jacob, the face of Moses' burning bush, and the cross-toting thief who repented as he was crucified next to Jesus); the righteous waiting to enter heaven, led by St. Peter—about to use his key to open that golden

door; and King David playing a traditional Moldavian instrument (one of many subtle references to local culture) in a mountainous terrain, flanked by the deaths of a righteous man (saved by angels) and a sinner (skewered by devils).

Elsewhere on the church, you'll typically see a *Tree of Jesse,* tracing Jesus' family tree from Mary all the way back to Jesse and

King David. Another standard Orthodox theme is the *Deesis,* with Christ Pantocrator ("Ruler of All") enthroned in heaven and surrounded by saints. And many churches illustrate the Christian defense of Constantinople (today's Istanbul) during the Persian siege of 626. The "Persians" are dressed in Turkish clothes...a not-so-subtle reminder that these monasteries were built as bastions of Christendom against the rising tide of Islam.

You'll also see lots of unofficial decoration. Bucovina's painted monasteries were a popular destination in the Romantic Age of the late 19th century, when Bucovina was part of the Habsburg Empire. Mostly German-speaking tourists scratched their own initials into the colorful plaster—century-old-graffiti that's still readable.

Assuming there are no services going on, you can enter the church itself. People enter at the porch—traditionally, the unbaptized could go no farther. Inside, each church is divided into three sections, representing the holy trinity. First comes the pronous (pro-nave—sometimes outside on smaller churches), where regular people worshipped. Then comes the nous (nave), with benches for VIPs and a fresco of the donor who built the church. Finally there's the altar area, with the iconostasis. Each section is richly decorated with golden icons and colorful frescoes.

You may see a priest or nun walking around the courtyard, knocking on a piece of wood with a mallet. This means it's time for worship—and for tourists to leave the church interior.

Visiting the Painted Monasteries: The best painted monasteries are near the town of Gura Humorului (pop. 12,000). On a quick, targeted visit, you can simply visit Voroneț (the best one overall) and Humor—each about a 10-minute drive from Gura Humorului (in opposite directions). With more time, do a loop through the hills north of Gura Humorului to also see Moldovița and Sucevița. I've listed these in the order of an all-day loop.

Voroneț Monastery (voh-roh-NETS, from 1487) is the most striking and most famous—sometimes called the "Sistine Chapel of the East." Its vivid frescoes— with their distinctive "Voroneț blue" hue—are sumptuous and richly detailed. Voroneț also has the finest *Last Judgment* fresco. You could stare at it for hours, picking out details (for starters, see "Background," earlier). If you see only one painted monastery, make it this one.

Moldovița Monastery (MOHL-doh-veet-sah, from 1532) is less crowded, filling a serene courtyard, and has art nearly as impressive as Voroneț's. Moldovița has a particularly evocative fresco showing the siege of Constantinople; a fine *Tree of Jesse* mural; and the most evident examples of "graffiti" scratched into the plaster by 19th-century tourists (especially under the porch).

Between Moldovița and Sucevița, you'll twist up and over a dramatic mountain pass with great views.

Sucevița Monastery (SOO-cheh-veet-sah) was the final painted monastery built (1581), with the best-preserved fortifications and the biggest, richest interior. Even more than the others, from the outside it feels more like a fortress than a monastery. The frescoes include a particularly exquisite *Ladder to Paradise* (or *Jacob's Ladder*): The angled ladder (where each rung represents a holy virtue required to reach heaven) slices the composition in half, with a heavenly host of angels at the top and, below, grotesque beasts torturing sinners who missed a rung. If you're in shape, hike up the steep hill behind for a fine view down over the monastery, the valley, and the wooded hills.

Just west of Sucevița, and on the way to Humor, you'll pass through the workaday town of Marginea—famous for its many black pottery workshops.

Humor Monastery (a.k.a. Humorului, hoo-moo-ROO-lee, from 1530) is sleepier and lower-impact, with a lone fortified tower that stands taller than the church itself. Its *Last Judgment* fresco curls up under the roofline of the porch, protected from the elements.

Sleeping near the Painted Monasteries: The handiest home base is the functional crossroads town of Gura Humorului, which has several big hotels and smaller guesthouses. To sleep in the countryside, try **$ Casa Bunicilor,** a rustic but comfortable retreat a few minutes' drive out of town, near the Humor Monastery (www.casabunicilor.com).

Nearby: Suceava (soo-cheh-AH-vah, pop. 90,000), Bucovina's largest city, is about 25 miles to the east. It's workable as a home base, but its sparse sights (an empty-feeling old fortress and a mediocre open-air folk museum) and its distance from the monasteries make it less appealing than Gura Humorului.

PRACTICALITIES

This chapter covers the practical skills of European travel: how to get tourist information, pay for things, sightsee efficiently, find good-value accommodations, eat affordably but well, use technology wisely, and get between destinations smoothly. To study ahead and round out your knowledge and skills, check out "Resources from Rick Steves." If you're visiting Slovenia, Croatia, Bosnia-Herzegovina, or Montenegro, the "Understanding Yugoslavia" section gives you a good picture of how Yugoslavia was formed, and why it broke apart.

Tourist Information

BEFORE YOUR TRIP

National tourist offices are a wealth of information. Before your trip, get the free general information packet and request any specifics you may want (such as regional and city maps and festival schedules).

Czech Tourist Office: www.czechtourism.com

Polish Tourist Office: www.poland.travel
Hungarian Tourist Office: www.gotohungary.com
Slovenian Tourist Office: www.slovenia.info
Austrian Tourist Office: www.austria.info
Slovakian Tourist Office: www.slovakia.travel

IN EASTERN EUROPE

Your best first stop in every town is generally the tourist information office (abbreviated **TI** in this book). You'll find local TIs are usually well-organized and always have an English-speaking staff. While many TIs in Eastern Europe are still primarily government-run—and therefore have the sole priority of helping you have a better trip—others are in cahoots with local, private tour operators, which tends to color their advice. I find TIs a great place to flip through brochures, pick up a free map, and ask basic questions. But I supplement what I learn there with advice from my hotel, other local contacts, and online sources. TIs also offer information on public transit (including bus and train schedules), walking tours, special events, and nightlife. Some TIs have information on the entire country or at least the region, so try to pick up maps and printed information for destinations you'll be visiting later in your trip.

Travel Tips

Emergency and Medical Help: In all of the countries in this book, dial 112 for medical or other emergencies. Or ask at your hotel for help—they'll know the nearest medical and emergency services.

Theft or Loss: To replace a passport, you'll need to go in person to the appropriate embassy or consulate (see page 1109). If your credit and debit cards disappear, cancel and replace them (see "Damage Control for Lost Cards" on page 1065). File a police report, either on the spot or within a day or two; you'll need it to submit an insurance claim for lost or stolen rail passes or travel gear, and it can help with replacing your passport or credit and debit cards. For more information, see www.ricksteves.com/help.

Borders: All of the core countries in this book have officially joined the open-borders Schengen Agreement. That means that there are no border checks between any of these countries, or between them and Western European countries such as Germany, Austria, and Italy. You'll simply zip through the border without stopping.

Non-Schengen countries (including Bosnia-Herzegovina, Montenegro, Bulgaria, Romania, and Croatia) still have traditional border checkpoints—you'll still have to stop upon entering or exiting these countries. But whether traveling by car, train, or bus, you'll find that border crossings are generally a nonevent: Flash your passport, maybe wait a few minutes, and move on. Drivers may be asked to show proof of car insurance ("green card"), so be sure you have it when you pick up your rental car.

Even as border checkpoints fade, when you cross any international border, you must still change phone cards, postage stamps, currencies (in most cases), and underpants.

Time Zones: Most of the countries listed in this book are generally six/nine hours ahead of the East/West Coasts of the US. (Bulgaria and Romania are one hour ahead of the rest of these countries—that's seven/ten hours ahead of the East/West Coasts.) The exceptions are the beginning and end of Daylight Saving Time: Europe "springs forward" the last Sunday in March (two weeks after most of North America), and "falls back" the last Sunday in October (one week before North America). For a handy online time converter, see www.timeanddate.com/worldclock.

Weekends: Saturdays are virtually weekdays, with earlier closing hours and no rush hour (though transportation connections can be less frequent than on weekdays). Sundays have the same pros and cons as they do for travelers in the US (special events, limited hours, banks and many shops generally closed, limited public-transportation options, no rush hour). Rowdy evenings are rare on Sundays.

Watt's Up? Europe's electrical system is 220 volts, instead of North America's 110 volts. Most newer electronics (such as laptops, battery chargers, and hair dryers) convert automatically, so you won't need a converter, but you will need an adapter plug with two round prongs, sold inexpensively at travel stores in the US. Avoid bringing older appliances that don't automatically convert voltage; instead, buy a cheap replacement in Europe.

Discounts: Discounts for sights are generally not listed in this book. However, seniors (age 60 and over), youths under 18, and students and teachers with proper identification cards (www.isic.org) can get discounts at many sights. Always ask, though some discounts are available only for local residents or citizens of the European Union (EU).

Smoking: While the specifics vary by country, in almost all of the destinations in this book, smoking is generally banned indoors (though people still smoke like chimneys on terraces and other outdoor areas). The two exceptions are the Czech Republic and Austria. Czech businesses may decide whether to be smoking, nonsmoking, or have a designated nonsmoking section. Austrian restaurants and cafés currently are required to set aside at least half their space for nonsmokers; smaller establishments that physically can't accommodate two viable zones can go for smoking anywhere or entirely nonsmoking. However, new legislation has required a complete smoking ban in Austrian restaurants and bars by 2018. In all of these countries—as throughout Europe—there are more smokers than back home, so you'll still get a whiff of the nicotine-stained Old World. If you require a completely nonsmoking eating section or hotel room, be very specific in your request, and understand that it may not be granted.

Online Translation Tip: Google's Chrome browser instantly translates websites. You can also paste text or the URL of a foreign website into the translation window at translate.google.com. The Google Translate app converts spoken English into most European languages (and vice versa) and can also translate text it "reads" with your mobile device's camera.

Money

This section offers advice on how to pay for purchases on your trip (including getting cash from ATMs and paying with plastic), dealing with lost or stolen cards, VAT (sales tax) refunds, and tipping.

EXCHANGE RATES

Most of the countries in this book still use their traditional currencies. So far, only Slovenia, Austria, and Slovakia officially use the euro currency—and the others are unlikely to adopt it anytime soon. But even in countries that don't officially use the euro, many businesses (especially hotels) quote prices in euros anyway. (Even if they do, they typically prefer payment in the local currency.)

Here are the rough exchange rates for each country. I've also suggested a strategy for roughly converting prices into US dollars. Note that in some cases, I've favored easier-to-remember equations even if they offer less-precise conversions. For a more precise conversion, use the online tool at www.oanda.com/currency/converter.

1 euro (€) = about \$1.10 (used in Slovenia, Austria, and Slovakia). To convert prices in euros to dollars, add about 10 percent: €20 = about \$22, €50 = about \$55, and so on. Just like the dollar, one euro (€) is broken down into 100 cents. Coins range from €0.01 to €2, and bills from €5 to €200 (bills over €50 are rarely used; €500 bills are being phased out).

25 Czech crowns (*koruna*, Kč) = about \$1. To estimate prices in dollars, drop the last digit, multiply by 4, then drop the last digit again: 160 Kč = about \$6.

4 Polish złoty (zł, or PLN) = about \$1. To calculate prices in dollars, divide by four: 80 zł = about \$20.

275 Hungarian forints (Ft, or HUF) = about \$1. To very roughly figure dollars, divide by three and drop the last two digits: 1,000 Ft = about \$3 (actually \$3.60).

So, that 20-zł Polish woodcarving is about \$5, the 5,000-Ft

Hungarian dinner is about $17, and the 2,000-Kč taxi ride through Prague is...uh-oh.

WHAT TO BRING

Bring both a credit card and a debit card. You'll use the debit card at cash machines (ATMs) to withdraw local cash for most purchases, and the credit card to pay for larger items. Some travelers carry a third card, in case one gets demagnetized or eaten by a temperamental machine.

For an emergency stash, bring $100-200 in hard US cash. Although banks in some countries don't exchange dollars, in a pinch you can always find exchange desks at major train stations or airports—convenient but with crummy rates.

Cash

Although credit cards are widely accepted in Europe, day-to-day spending is generally more cash-based. I find local cash is the easiest—and sometimes only—way to pay for cheap food, bus fare, taxis, and local guides. Some vendors will charge you extra for using a credit card, some won't accept foreign credit cards, and some won't take any credit cards at all. Having cash on hand can help you avoid a stressful predicament if you find yourself in a place that won't accept your card.

Throughout Europe, ATMs are the easiest and smartest way for travelers to get cash. They work just like they do at home. To

withdraw money from an ATM (known as *Bankomat* in all of these countries), you'll need a debit card (ideally with a Visa or MasterCard logo), plus a PIN code (numeric and four digits). For increased security, shield the keypad when entering your PIN code, and don't use an ATM if anything on the front of the machine looks loose or damaged (a sign that someone may have attached a "skimming" device to capture account information). Try to withdraw large sums of money to reduce the number of per-transaction bank fees you'll pay.

When possible, use ATMs located outside banks—a thief is less likely to target a cash machine near surveillance cameras, and if your card is munched by a machine during banking hours, you can go inside for help. Stay away from "independent" ATMs such as Travelex, Euronet, YourCash, Cardpoint, and Cashzone, which charge huge commissions, have terrible exchange rates, and may try to trick users with "dynamic currency conversion" (described later). Although you can use a credit card to withdraw cash at an

ATM, this comes with high bank fees and only makes sense in an emergency.

While traveling, if you want to access your accounts online, be sure to use a secure connection (see page 1085).

Pickpockets target tourists. To safeguard your cash, wear a money belt—a pouch with a strap that you buckle around your waist like a belt and tuck under your clothes. Keep your cash, credit cards, and passport secure in your money belt, and carry only a day's spending money in your front pocket or wallet.

Credit and Debit Cards

For purchases, Visa and MasterCard are more commonly accepted than American Express. Just like at home, credit or debit cards work easily at larger hotels, restaurants, and shops. I typically use my debit card to withdraw cash to pay for most daily purchases. I use my credit card sparingly: to book and pay for hotel rooms, to buy advance tickets for events or sights, to cover major expenses (such as car rentals or plane tickets), and to pay for things online or near the end of my trip (to avoid another visit to the ATM). While you could instead use a debit card for these purchases, using a credit card offers a greater degree of fraud protection (because debit cards draw funds directly from your account).

Ask Your Credit- or Debit-Card Company: Before your trip, contact the company that issued your debit or credit cards.

Confirm that your **card will work overseas,** and alert them that you'll be using it in Europe; otherwise, they may deny transactions if they perceive unusual spending patterns.

Ask for the specifics on transaction **fees.** When you use your credit or debit card—either for purchases or ATM withdrawals—you'll typically be charged additional "international transaction" fees of up to 3 percent (1 percent is normal). If your card's fees seem high, consider getting a different card just for your trip: Capital One (www.capitalone.com) and most credit unions have low-to-no international fees.

Verify your daily ATM **withdrawal limit,** and if necessary, ask your bank to adjust it. I prefer a high limit that allows me to take out more cash at each ATM stop and save on bank fees; some travelers prefer to set a lower limit in case their card is stolen. Note that foreign banks also set maximum withdrawal amounts for their ATMs.

Get your bank's emergency **phone number** in the US (but not its 800 number, which isn't accessible from overseas) to call collect if you have a problem.

Ask for your credit card's **PIN** in case you need to make an emergency cash withdrawal or encounter payment machines using

EU Enlargement and the "New Europe"

The European Union (EU) began as a political and economic alliance of mostly Western European nations, with Germany, France, and Italy at the helm. But over the last decade and a half, the geographical and political center of Europe has shifted from Brussels to Prague. Since 2004, 11 formerly communist "Eastern European" countries—including most of the ones in this book—have joined the EU. And this enlargement has been a fitful process, both for the existing members and for the new ones.

Many Eastern Europeans, concerned that EU bureaucracy could threaten their prized traditions, have a "Euroskeptic" take on things. One Polish farmer grumbled that he has to get "passports" for each of his cows. EU hygiene standards are incompatible with slow-simmering national specialties. (My Czech friend complained, "The EU has made many of our best dishes illegal.") And many are simply exhausted after generations of outside meddling. A wise Czech grandmother pointed out that in her lifetime, her country had been ruled from Vienna (Habsburgs), Berlin (Nazis), and Moscow (communists). She said, "Now that we're finally ruled from Prague, why would we want to turn our power over to Brussels?"

Longstanding EU members have had their own doubts. Wealthy nations had already spent vast fortunes to improve the floundering economies of poorer member countries (such as Portugal, Greece, and Ireland), and were reluctant to take on more "charity cases." Some Westerners fretted about the influx of cheap labor from the East (see "The Polish Plumber Syndrome" on page 1070). Others felt threatened that their political clout would be diluted. And in the fall of 2015, a flood of refugees fleeing war in Syria used Eastern Europe as a route to reach better lives in more prosperous Western European countries. Each of these countries—pressured by their big EU allies—had to weigh their open-borders commitments against their own interests.

On the other hand, the advantages of the EU are evident everywhere. New expressways, train stations, public spaces, and museums throughout Eastern Europe were paid for, at least partly, by EU funds. Countries that have adopted the euro currency (including Slovenia and Slovakia) find they match up pretty well, economically, with their Western European counterparts. And, just as intended, Western companies are finding that easier access to the affordable resources and labor of Eastern Europe—thanks partly to all of those new highways—is a boon all around.

As the "New Europe" takes shape, players on both sides will continue to define their roles and seek compromise. But so far, despite the challenges, the general consensus in the East is that joining the EU was the right move.

the chip-and-PIN system; the bank won't tell you your PIN over the phone, so allow time for it to be mailed to you.

Chip and PIN: While much of Europe, including the Czech Republic and Austria, is shifting to a "chip-and-PIN" security system for credit cards, many Eastern European countries still use the old magnetic-swipe technology. (European chip-and-PIN cards are embedded with an electronic security chip, and require a four-digit PIN to make a purchase.) If you happen to encounter chip and PIN, it will probably be at payment machines, such as those at toll roads or unattended gas pumps. On the outside chance that a machine won't take your card, find a cashier who can make your card work (they can print a receipt for you to sign), or find a machine that takes cash. Most American travelers don't run into problems. Still, it pays to carry the local currency; remember, you can always use an ATM to withdraw cash with your magnetic-stripe debit card.

If you're concerned, ask if your bank offers a chip-and-PIN card. Andrews Federal Credit Union (www.andrewsfcu.org) and the State Department Federal Credit Union (www.sdfcu.org) offer these cards and are open to all US residents.

Dynamic Currency Conversion: If merchants or hoteliers offer to convert your purchase price into dollars (called dynamic currency conversion, or DCC), refuse this "service." You'll pay extra for the expensive convenience of seeing your charge in dollars.

Some ATMs and retailers try to confuse customers by presenting DCC in misleading terms. If an ATM offers to "lock in" or "guarantee" your conversion rate, choose "proceed without conversion." Other prompts might state, "You can be charged in dollars: Press YES for dollars, NO for euros." Always choose the local currency.

Damage Control for Lost Cards

If you lose your credit or debit card, you can stop people from using your card by reporting the loss immediately to the respective global customer-assistance centers. Call these 24-hour US numbers collect: Visa (tel. 303/967-1096), MasterCard (tel. 636/722-7111), and American Express (tel. 336/393-1111).

To make a collect call from any phone, use these numbers: Austria tel. 800-200-288; Czech Republic tel. 00-800-222-55288; Hungary tel. 06-800-011-11; Poland tel. 00-800-111-1111; Slovakia tel. 0800-000-101; Slovenia tel. 1180. Press zero or stay on the line for an English-speaking operator. European toll-free numbers (listed by country) can also be found at the websites for Visa and MasterCard.

If you are the secondary cardholder, you'll need to provide

VAT Rates

To be eligible to get a VAT refund, you usually need to spend the listed minimum at a single store.

Country of Purchase	VAT Standard Rate*	Minimum in Local Currency	Approx. Minimum in US $
Austria	20%	€75.01	$82
Czech Republic	21%	2,001 Kč	$100
Hungary	27%	52,001 Ft	$231
Poland	23%	200 zł	$67
Slovakia	20%	€175.01	$192
Slovenia	22%	€50.01	$55

*VAT rates fluctuate based on many factors, including what kind of item you are buying. Your refund will likely be less than the rate listed above, especially if it's subject to processing fees.

the primary cardholder's identification-verification details (such as birth date, mother's maiden name, or Social Security number). You can generally receive a temporary card within two or three business days in Europe (see www.ricksteves.com/help for more).

If you report your loss within two days, you typically won't be responsible for any unauthorized transactions on your account, although many banks charge a liability fee of $50.

TIPPING

Tipping in Europe isn't as automatic or as generous as in the US. While some waiters and taxi drivers in touristy cities have learned to expect Yankee-sized tips when they spot an American, you should feel free to "go local" and tip like the natives do. The proper amount depends on your resources, tipping philosophy, and the circumstances, but some general guidelines apply.

Restaurants: At sit-down eateries, tip a small amount by rounding up the bill 5-10 percent. For details on tipping in restaurants, see page 1080.

Taxis: For a typical ride, round up your fare a bit (for instance, if the fare is €42, pay €45). If the cabbie hauls your bags and zips you to the airport to help you catch your flight, you might want to toss in a little more. But if you feel like you're being driven in circles or otherwise ripped off, skip the tip.

Services: In general, if someone in the service industry does a super job for you, a small tip (the equivalent of a euro or two) is appropriate...but not required. If you're not sure whether (or how much) to tip for a service, ask your hotelier or the TI.

When in doubt, ask: If you're not sure whether (or how much) to tip, ask a local for advice.

GETTING A VAT REFUND

Wrapped into the purchase price of your Eastern European souvenirs is a Value-Added Tax (VAT) that varies per country. You're entitled to get most of that tax back if you make a purchase of more than a set amount at a store that participates in the VAT refund scheme. Typically, you must ring up the minimum at a single retailer—you can't add up your purchases from various shops to reach the required amount.

Getting your refund is usually straightforward and, if you buy a substantial number of souvenirs, well worth the hassle. (Note that if the store ships the goods to your US home, VAT is not assessed on your purchase.) You'll need to:

Get the paperwork. Have the merchant completely fill out the necessary refund document. You'll have to present your passport. Get the paperwork done before you leave the store to ensure you'll have everything you need (including your original sales receipt).

Get your stamp at the border or airport. Process your VAT document at your last stop in the country in which you made your purchase (or, if you bought it in the European Union, at your last stop in the EU). Arrive an additional hour before you need to check in for your flight to allow time to find the local customs office—and to stand in line. It's best to keep your purchases in your carry-on. If they're too large or dangerous to carry on (such as knives), pack them in your checked bags and alert the check-in agent. You'll be sent (with your tagged bag) to a customs desk outside security; someone will examine your bag, stamp your paperwork, and put your bag on the belt. You're not supposed to use your purchased goods before you leave. If you show up at customs wearing your chic Czech shirt, officials might look the other way—or deny you a refund.

Collect your refund. You'll need to return your stamped document to the retailer or its representative. Many merchants work with services, such as Global Blue or Premier Tax Free, that have offices at major airports, ports, or border crossings (either before or after security, probably strategically located near a duty-free shop). These services, which extract a 4 percent fee, can refund your money immediately in cash or credit your card (within two billing cycles). Other refund services may require you to mail the documents from home, or more quickly, from your point of departure (using an envelope you've prepared in advance or one that's been provided by the merchant). You'll then have to wait—it can take months.

CUSTOMS FOR AMERICAN SHOPPERS

You are allowed to take home $800 worth of items per person duty-free, once every 31 days. You can take home many processed and packaged foods: vacuum-packed cheeses, dried herbs, jams, baked goods, candy, chocolate, oil, vinegar, mustard, and honey. Fresh fruits and vegetables and most meats are not allowed, with exceptions for some canned items. As for alcohol, you can bring in one liter duty-free (it can be packed securely in your checked luggage, along with any other liquid-containing items).

To bring alcohol (or liquid-packed foods) in your carry-on bag on your flight home, buy it at a duty-free shop at the airport. You'll increase your odds of getting it onto a connecting flight if it's packaged in a "STEB"—a secure, tamper-evident bag. But stay away from liquids in opaque, ceramic, or metallic containers, which usually cannot be successfully screened (STEB or no STEB).

For details on allowable goods, customs rules, and duty rates, visit http://help.cbp.gov.

Sightseeing

Eastern Europe's best attractions are modern museums that chronicle the communist regime and celebrate its demise (such as Budapest's House of Terror and Memento Park, and Gdańsk's European Solidarity Center). But many museums here are dusty, old-fashioned collections of art or historical artifacts. While these don't quite rank with the Louvre or the Prado, many are surprisingly engaging if you take the time to learn more. With the right attitude, it's an exciting opportunity to be introduced to talented artists and important historical figures who are relatively unknown outside of their home countries. Generally, you'll follow a confusing, one-way tour route through a maze of rooms with squeaky parquet floors, monitored by grumpy grannies who listlessly point you in the right direction. While some museums label exhibits in English, most don't post full explanations; you'll have to buy a book or borrow laminated translations. In some cases, neither option is available.

Sightseeing can be hard work. Use these tips to make your visits to Eastern Europe's finest sights meaningful, fun, efficient, and painless.

MAPS AND NAVIGATION TOOLS

A good map is essential for efficient navigation while sightseeing. The maps in this book are concise and simple, designed to help you locate recommended destinations, sights, and local TIs, where you can pick up more in-depth maps. Maps with even more detail are sold at newsstands and bookstores.

You can also use a mapping app on your mobile device. Be aware that pulling up maps or looking up turn-by-turn walking directions on the fly requires an Internet connection: To use this feature, it's smart to get an international data plan (see page 1084) or only connect using Wi-Fi. With Google Maps or Apple Maps, it's possible to download a map while online, then go offline and navigate without incurring data-roaming charges, though you can't search for an address or get real-time walking directions. A handful of other apps—including City Maps 2Go, OffMaps, and Nav-free—also allow you to use maps offline.

PLAN AHEAD

Set up an itinerary that allows you to fit in all your must-see sights. For a one-stop look at opening hours, see the "At a Glance" sidebars for each major city (Prague, Kraków, Warsaw, Budapest, Ljubljana, and Vienna). Most sights keep stable hours, but in some destinations, hours tend to fluctuate from season to season. If you have your heart set on visiting particular sights, it's always smart to confirm the latest hours by checking their websites or asking at the local TI.

Don't put off visiting a must-see sight—you never know when a place will close unexpectedly for a holiday, strike, or restoration. Many museums are closed or have reduced hours at least a few days a year, especially on holidays such as Christmas, New Year's, and Labor Day (May 1). A list of holidays is on page 1110; check museums' websites for possible closures during your trip. In summer, some sights may stay open late; in the off-season, hours may be shorter.

Going at the right time helps avoid crowds. This book offers tips on the best times to see specific sights. Try visiting popular sights very early, at lunch, or very late. Evening visits are usually peaceful, with fewer crowds.

Study up. To get the most out of the sight descriptions in this book, read them before you visit. Note: To avoid redundancy, many cultural or historical details are explained for one sight in this book and not repeated for another; to get the full picture, read the entire chapter for each destination you'll visit.

AT SIGHTS

Here's what you can typically expect:

Entering: Be warned that you may not be allowed to enter if you arrive less than 30 to 60 minutes before closing time. And

The Polish Plumber Syndrome

You'll likely enjoy a taste of Eastern European culture on your next trip...to London or Dublin. When eight Eastern European countries joined the European Union in 2004, Great Britain and Ireland had to welcome their new comrades to work without a visa. This sparked a wave of immigration into the British Isles. Many Poles, Czechs, and Estonians ended up in the hospitality industry.

The transplants enjoyed more money and an irreplaceable cross-cultural experience. But Eastern Europe went through a somewhat alarming "brain drain," as many of its youngest and most westward-thinking residents rushed away. In Britain and Ireland, tourists began to encounter desk clerks who didn't quite speak fluent English. More recently, the global financial crisis has tightened up the job market—making immigration less appealing both to the expat workers, and to the native job-seekers in the countries that are hosting them. Quite a few of these transplants have lost their jobs and returned home to the East. And a general sentiment against immigrants (focused both on Eastern Europeans and those from farther away) partly propelled the "Brexit" vote in the summer of 2016. Britain's planned departure from the European Union poses serious questions about the status (societally, if not legally) of the Eastern Europeans who have put down roots and started families in the UK.

The EU has compelled other Western European countries to also open their borders—and rarely without controversy. One popular symbol—invented by a right-wing French politician—was an invading "Polish plumber" who'd put French plumbers out of a job. The Polish tourist board countered by putting up clever ads in France featuring an alluring Polish hunk stroking a pipe wrench, saying, "I'm staying in Poland...come visit me!"

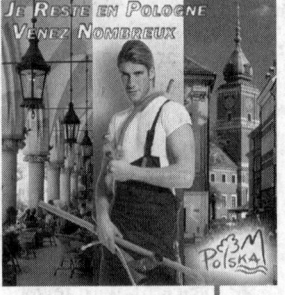

This is just one more step in the Europe-wide process of integration. European Gen Xers have been dubbed the "Erasmus Generation"—after the Erasmus Student Network, an EU organization that fosters study-abroad opportunities within Europe. As European thirtysomethings have grown up accustomed to attending universities in other countries, it seems natural for them to identify as "Europeans" rather than as Spaniards, Slovenes, or Swedes. Multilingualism, international résumés, and cross-cultural marriages are the norm. As the Brexit vote spurs conversation about how much European togetherness is *too much* togetherness, it will be interesting to see whether the idealistic vision of "European first" survives.

guards start ushering people out well before the actual closing time, so don't save the best for last.

Many important sights have a security check, where you must open your bag or send it through a metal detector. Allow extra time for these lines in your planning. Some sights require you to check daypacks and coats. (If you'd rather not check your daypack, try carrying it tucked under your arm like a purse as you enter.)

Photography: If the museum's photo policy isn't clearly posted, ask a guard. Generally, taking photos without a flash or tripod is allowed. Some sights ban photos altogether; others ban selfie sticks.

Temporary Exhibits: Museums may show special exhibits in addition to their permanent collection. Some exhibits are included in the entry price, while others come at an extra cost (which you may have to pay even if you don't want to see the exhibit).

Expect Changes: Artwork can be on tour, on loan, out sick, or shifted at the whim of the curator. Pick up a floor plan as you enter, and ask museum staff if you can't find a particular item.

Audioguides and Apps: Some sights rent audioguides, which generally offer recorded descriptions in English, though they're usually dull and rarely worth the cost (about $6-8). But if you like audioguide tours, bring your own earbuds—you can enjoy better sound and avoid holding the device to your ear. To save money, bring a Y-jack and share one audioguide with your travel partner. Museums and sights often offer free apps that you can download to your mobile device (check their websites). And, I've produced free, downloadable audio tours for my Prague City Walk, Vienna City Walk, Vienna's St. Stephen's Cathedral, and Vienna's Ringstrasse Tram Tour; look for the ∩ in this book. For more on my audio tours, see page 14.

Services: Important sights may have a reasonably-priced on-site café or cafeteria (handy places to rejuvenate during a long visit). The WCs at sights are free and generally clean.

Before Leaving: At the gift shop, scan the postcard rack or thumb through a guidebook to be sure that you haven't overlooked something that you'd like to see.

Every sight or museum offers more than what is covered in this book. Use the information in this book as an introduction—not the final word.

Sleeping

I favor hotels and restaurants that are handy to your sightseeing activities. Rather than list hotels scattered throughout a city, I choose hotels in my favorite neighborhoods. My recommendations run the gamut, from dorm beds to fancy doubles with all the comforts.

Extensive and opinionated listings of good-value rooms are a major feature of this book's "Sleeping" sections. I like places that are clean, central, relatively quiet at night, reasonably priced, friendly, English-speaking, professional-feeling but small enough to have a hands-on owner or manager and stable staff, and run with a respect for local traditions. I'm more impressed by a convenient location and a fun-loving philosophy than flat-screen TVs and a fancy gym. My favorites are small, family-run hotels and friendly local people who rent hotelesque private rooms without a reception desk. I've also thrown in a few hostels and other cheap options for budget travelers. Most places I recommend fall short of perfection. But if I can find a place with most of these features, it's a keeper.

Book your accommodations well in advance, especially if you want to stay at one of my top listings or if you'll be traveling during busy times. See page 1110 for a list of major holidays and festivals in Eastern Europe; for tips on making reservations, see page 1076.

Some people make reservations as they travel, calling hotels a few days to a week before their arrival. If you anticipate crowds (weekends are worst) on the day you want to check in, call hotels at about 9:00 or 10:00, when the receptionist knows who'll be checking out and which rooms will be available. Some apps—such as HotelTonight.com—specialize in last-minute rooms, often at business-class hotels in big cities. If you encounter a language barrier, ask the fluent receptionist at your current hotel to call for you.

RATES AND DEALS

Accommodations in Eastern Europe cost about as much as comparable beds in the West. While most accommodations listed in this book cluster at about $80-120 per double, they range from $15 bunks to $500-plus splurges (maximum plumbing and more).

I've described my recommended accommodations using a Sleep Code (see the sidebar). Prices listed are for one-night stays in peak season, and assume you're booking directly with the hotel (not through an online hotel-booking engine or TI). Booking services extract a commission from the hotel, which logically closes the door on special deals. Book directly.

My recommended hotels each have a website (often with a built-in booking form) and an email address; you can expect a response in English within a day (and often sooner).

Some accommodations quote their rates in euros, while others use the local currency. Occasionally I've converted a few prices to make it easier for you to compare hotel rates—so you might notice a little variation between the rates listed here and those quoted by hotels.

If you're on a budget, it's smart to email several hotels to ask for their best price. Comparison-shop and make your choice. This

Sleep Code

Hotels are classified based on the average price of a standard double room with breakfast in high season. Because relative values vary from country to country, I've assigned price ranges per country (rather than using the same for the entire book). These are noted in each chapter.

$$$$	**Splurge**
$$$	**Expensive**
$$	**Moderate**
$	**Budget**
¢	**Backpacker**
RS%	**Rick Steves discount**

Unless otherwise noted, credit cards are accepted, hotel staff speak basic English, and free Wi-Fi is available. Comparison-shop by checking prices at several hotels (on each hotel's own website, on a booking site, or by email). For the best deal, *book directly with the hotel.* Ask for a discount if paying in cash; if the listing includes **RS%,** request a Rick Steves discount.

is especially helpful when dealing with the larger hotels that use "dynamic pricing," a computer-generated system that predicts the demand for particular days and sets prices accordingly: High-demand days will often be more than double the price of low-demand days. This makes it impossible for a guidebook to list anything more accurate than a wide range of prices. I regret this trend. While you can assume that hotels listed in this book are good, it's very difficult to say which ones are the better value unless you email to confirm the price.

As you look over the listings, you'll notice that a few accommodations promise special prices to Rick Steves readers. To get these rates, you must book directly (that is, not through a booking site like TripAdvisor or Booking.com), mention this book when you reserve, and then show the book upon arrival. Rick Steves discounts apply to readers with ebooks as well as printed books. Because we trust hotels to honor this, please let me know if you don't receive a listed discount. Note, though, that discounts understandably may not be applied to promotional rates.

In general, prices can soften if you do any of the following: offer to pay cash, stay at least three nights, or mention this book. You can also try asking for a cheaper room or a discount, or offer to skip breakfast.

TYPES OF ACCOMMODATIONS
Hotels

In Eastern Europe, you can choose from a delightful variety of stylish and charming hotels and guesthouses. Hotel prices are roughly on par with midrange Western European countries: You can find a central, basic, comfortable double for $100 just about anywhere. Plan on spending $90-130 per double in big cities, and $60-90 in smaller towns. You can uncover some bar-gains, but I think it's worth pay-ing a little more for comfort and a

good location. Most hotels also offer single rooms, and some offer larger rooms for four or more people (I call these "family rooms" in the listings). Some hotels can add an extra bed (for a small charge) to turn a double into a triple. In general, a triple room is cheaper than the cost of a double and a single. Traveling alone can be ex-pensive: A single room can be close to the cost of a double.

When you check in, the receptionist will normally ask for your passport and keep it for a couple of hours. Don't worry. Ho-tels are legally required to register each guest with the local police. Americans are notorious for making this chore more difficult than it needs to be.

Breakfast, almost always served buffet-style, usually includes rolls, cold cuts, cheese, cereal, yogurt, fruit, coffee, milk, and juice; some places also provide eggs.

Hotel elevators, while becoming more common, are often very small—pack light. You may need to send your bags up one at a time. Most hotel rooms have a TV and telephone, and these days, most hotels offer free Wi-Fi. Pricier hotels also have air-condition-ing and minibars.

If you're arriving in the morning, your room probably won't be ready. Check your bag safely at the hotel and dive right into sightseeing.

Hoteliers can be a good source of advice. Most know their city well, and can assist you with everything from public transit and airport connections to finding a good restaurant, the nearest launderette, or a late-night pharmacy.

Some hotels occupy one floor of a building with a finicky vin-tage elevator or slightly dingy entryway. The hotelier doesn't con-trol the common areas of the building, so try not to let the entry-way atmosphere color your opinion of the hotel. Even at the best places, mechanical breakdowns occur: Sinks leak, hot water turns cold, toilets may gurgle or smell, the Wi-Fi goes out, or the air-conditioning dies when you need it most. Report your concerns clearly and calmly at the front desk. For more complicated prob-lems, don't expect instant results.

If you find that night noise is a problem (if, for instance, your room is over a nightclub), ask for a quieter room in the back or on an upper floor. To guard against theft in your room, keep valuables out of sight. Some rooms come with a safe, and other hotels have safes at the front desk. I've never bothered using one.

While it's customary to pay for your room upon departure, it can be a good idea to settle your bill the day before, when you're not in a hurry and while the manager's in. That way you'll have time to discuss and address any points of contention.

Above all, keep a positive attitude. Remember, you're on vacation. If your hotel is a disappointment, spend more time out enjoying the place you came to see.

Rooms in Private Homes

Private accommodations offer travelers a characteristic and money-saving alternative for a fraction of the price of a hotel. Rooms in private homes are called *sobe* in Slovenia and Croatia; the German word *Zimmer* works there, too, and throughout Eastern Europe. These places are inexpensive, at least as comfortable as a cheap hotel, and a good way to get some local insight. The boss changes the sheets, so people staying several nights are most desirable—and those who stay less than three nights are often charged a lot more (typically 20-50 percent; this surcharge is often waived outside of peak season). Renting a room in someone's home is a good option for those traveling alone, as you're more likely to find true single rooms—with just one single bed, and a price to match. While you can't expect your host to also be your tour guide, some may be interested in getting to know the travelers who come through their home.

Short-Term Rentals

A short-term rental—whether an apartment, house, or room in a local's home—is an increasingly popular alternative to a guest-house or hotel, especially if you plan to settle in one location for several nights. For stays longer than a few days, you can usually find a rental that's comparable to—or even cheaper than—a hotel room with similar amenities. Plus, you'll get a behind-the-scenes peek into how locals live.

The rental route isn't for everyone. Many places require a minimum-night stay, and compared to hotels, rentals usually have less-flexible cancellation policies. Also you're generally on your own: There's no hotel reception desk, breakfast, or daily cleaning service.

Finding Accommodations: Websites such as www.airbnb.com, www.roomorama.com, and www.vrbo.com let you browse properties and correspond directly with European property owners or managers. Or, for more guidance, consider using a rental agency such as www.interhomeusa.com or www.rentavilla.com. Agency-

Making Hotel Reservations

Given the erratic accommodations values in Eastern Europe (and the quality of the places I've found for this book), I recommend that you reserve your rooms several weeks or even months in advance—or as soon as you've pinned down your travel dates. Note that some national holidays merit your making reservations far in advance (see page 1110).

Requesting a Reservation: It's usually easiest to book your room through the hotel's website. (For the best rates, use the hotel's official site and not a booking agency's site.) If there's no reservation form, or for complicated requests, send an email. Most recommended hotels take reservations in English.

The hotelier wants to know:

- the size of your party and type of rooms you need
- your arrival and departure dates, written European-style—day followed by month and year (for example, 18/06/18 or 18 June 2018); include the total number of nights
- special requests (such as en suite bathroom vs. down the hall, cheapest room, twin beds vs. double bed, quiet room)
- applicable discounts (such as a Rick Steves reader discount, cash discount, or promotional rate)

Confirming a Reservation: Most places will request a credit-card number to hold your room. If they don't have a secure online reservation form—look for the **https**—you can email it (I do), but it's safer to share that confidential info via a phone call or fax.

Canceling a Reservation: If you must cancel, it's courteous—and smart—to do so with as much advance notice as possible,

represented apartments may cost more, but this route often offers more help and safeguards than booking directly.

Before you commit to a rental, be clear on the details, location, and amenities. I like to virtually "explore" the neighborhood using the Street View feature on Google Maps. Also consider the proximity to public transportation, and how well-connected it is with the rest of the city. Ask about amenities that are important to you (elevator, laundry, coffee maker, Wi-Fi, parking, etc.). Reading reviews from previous guests can help identify trouble spots that are glossed over in the official description.

Apartments: If you're staying somewhere for four nights or longer, it's worth considering an apartment or rental house (anything less than that isn't worth the extra effort involved, such as arranging key pickup, buying groceries, etc.). Apartment or house rentals can be especially cost-effective for groups and families. European apartments, like hotel rooms, tend to be small by US standards. But they often come with laundry machines and small,

From: rick@ricksteves.com
Sent: Today
To: info@hotelcentral.com
Subject: Reservation request for 19-22 July

Dear Hotel Central,

I would like to stay at your hotel. Please let me know if you have a room available and the price for:
• 2 people
• Double bed and en suite bathroom in a quiet room
• Arriving 19 July, departing 22 July (3 nights)

Thank you!
Rick Steves

PRACTICALITIES

especially for smaller family-run places. Cancellation policies can be strict; read the fine print or ask about these before you book. Many discount deals require prepayment, with no cancellation refunds.

Reconfirming a Reservation: Always call to reconfirm your room reservation a few days in advance. For B&Bs or very small hotels, I call again on my day of arrival to tell my host what time I expect to get there (especially important if arriving late—after 17:00).

Phoning: For tips on how to call hotels overseas, see page 1086.

equipped kitchens, making it easier and cheaper to dine in. If you make good use of the kitchen (and Europe's great produce markets), you'll save on your meal budget.

Other Options: Swapping homes with a local works for people with an appealing place to offer, and who can live with the idea of having strangers in their home (don't assume where you live is not interesting to Europeans). A good place to start is HomeExchange (www.homeexchange.com).

To sleep for free, Couchsurfing.com is a vagabond's alternative to Airbnb. It lists millions of outgoing members who host fellow "surfers" in their homes.

Hostels

A hostel provides cheap beds in dorms where you sleep alongside strangers for about $20-30 per night. Travelers of any age are welcome if they don't mind dorm-style accommodations and meeting other travelers. Most hostels offer kitchen facilities, guest comput-

PRACTICALITIES

The Good and Bad of Online Reviews

User-generated review sites and apps such as Yelp, Booking. com, and TripAdvisor are changing the travel industry. These sites can give you a consensus of opinions about everything from hotels and restaurants to sights and nightlife. If you scan reviews of a hotel and see several complaints about noise or a rotten location, it tells you something important that you'd never learn from the hotel's own website.

Review sites are only as good as the judgment of their reviewers. While these sites work to weed out bogus users, my hunch is that a significant percentage of user reviews are posted by friends or enemies of the business being reviewed. Ignore low and high grades. Focus on the median.

As a guidebook writer, my sense is that there is a big difference between this uncurated information and a guidebook. A user-generated review is based on the experience of one person, who likely stayed at one hotel and ate at a few restaurants, and doesn't have much of a basis for comparison. A guidebook is the work of a trained researcher who visited many alternatives to assess their relative value. I recently checked out some top-rated user-reviewed hotel and restaurant listings in various towns; when stacked up against their competitors, some were gems, while just as many were duds.

Both types of information have their place, and in many ways, they're complementary. If something is well-reviewed in a guidebook, and also gets good ratings on one of these sites, it's likely a winner.

ers, Wi-Fi, and a self-service laundry. Hostels almost always provide bedding, but the towel's up to you (though you can usually rent one for a small fee). Family and private rooms are often available.

Independent hostels tend to be easygoing, colorful, and informal (no membership required; www.hostelworld.com). You may pay slightly less by booking directly with the hostel.

Official hostels are part of Hostelling International (HI) and share an online booking site (www.hihostels.com). HI hostels typically require that you be a member or pay extra per night.

Eating

Eastern Europe offers good food for relatively little money—especially if you steer clear of the easy-to-avoid tourist-trap restaurants. This is affordable sightseeing for your palate.

Slavic cuisine has a reputation for being heavy and hearty, with lots of pork, potatoes, and cabbage. And, to be fair, some of that reputation is well-earned. But the food here is also delicious, and there's a lot more diversity from country to country than you might expect. For example, Hungarian cuisine is rich and spicy (think paprika), while Slovenia has a knack for Mediterranean cooking (seafood, pastas), and Polish food is more "northern" (with lots of dill, berries, and cream—like Russian cuisine). Tune in to the regional and national specialties and customs (see each country's introduction in this book for details).

For a change of pace, seek out vegetarian, Italian, Indian, Chinese, and similar places, which are especially good in big cities such as Prague, Budapest, or Kraków (I've listed a few tasty options).

When restaurant-hunting, choose a spot filled with locals, not the place with the big neon signs boasting, "We Speak English and Accept Credit Cards." Venturing even a block or two off the main drag leads to higher-quality food for less than half the price of the tourist-oriented places. Locals eat better at lower-rent locales. Most restaurants tack a menu on to their door for browsers and have an English menu inside. If the place isn't full, you can usually just seat yourself (get a waiter's attention to be sure your preferred table is OK)—the American-style "hostess," with a carefully managed waiting list, isn't common here. Once seated, feel free to take your time. In fact, it might be difficult to dine in a hurry. Only a rude waiter will rush you. Good service is relaxed (slow to an American).

When you're in the mood for something halfway between a restaurant and a picnic meal, look for take-out food stands, bakeries (with sandwiches and savory pastries to go), shops selling pizza by the slice, or simple little eateries offering fast and easy sit-down restaurant food. In Poland, don't miss the deliriously cheap "milk bar" cafeterias (see page 228). Many grocery stores sell sandwiches, and others might be willing to make one for you from what's in the deli case.

The Czech Republic is beer country, with Europe's best and cheapest brew. Poland also has fine beer, but the national drink is *wódka*. Hungary and Slovenia are known for their wines. Each country has its own distinctive liqueur, most of them a variation on *slivovice* (SLEE-voh-veet-seh)—a plum brandy so highly valued that it's the de facto currency of the Carpathian Mountains (often used for bartering with farmers and other mountain folk). Menus list drink size by the tenth of a liter, or deciliter (dl). Nondrinkers will find all the standard types of Coke and Pepsi, along with some fun-to-sample local alternatives (such as Slovenia's Cockta, described on page 709).

PRACTICALITIES

Restaurant Price Code

I've assigned each eatery a price category, based on the average cost of a typical main course. Drinks, desserts, and splurge items (steak and seafood) can raise the price considerably.

$$$$	**Splurge**
$$$	**Pricier**
$$	**Moderate**
$	**Budget**

Because relative values vary from country to country, I've assigned price ranges per country (rather than using the same for the entire book). These are noted in each chapter. In Eastern Europe, a milk bar or takeout spot is **$**; a basic sit-down eatery is **$$**; a casual but more upscale restaurant is **$$$**; and a swanky splurge is **$$$$**.

TIPPING

Tip only at restaurants that have table service. If you order your food at a counter, don't tip.

At restaurants that have a waitstaff, round up the bill 5-10 percent after a good meal. My rule of thumb is to estimate about 10 percent, then round slightly to reach a convenient total (for a 370-Kč meal, I pay 400 Kč—an 8-percent tip). I'm a little more generous in Budapest, where a minimum 10 percent tip is expected (I'll hand over 4,000 Ft for a 3,600-Ft bill—that's 11 percent).

Anywhere in Eastern Europe, a 15 percent tip is overly generous, verging on extravagant. At some tourist-oriented restaurants, a 10-15 percent "service charge" may be added to your bill, in which case an additional tip is not necessary. (More commonly, menus or bills remind you that the tip is *not* included.) If you're not sure whether your bill includes the tip, just ask.

RESTAURANT PRICING

I've categorized my recommended eateries based on price, indicated with a dollar-sign rating (see sidebar). The price ranges suggest the average price of a typical main course—but not necessarily a complete meal. Obviously, expensive items (like steak and seafood), fine wine, appetizers, and dessert can significantly increase your final bill.

The dollar-sign categories also indicate the overall personality and "feel" of a place:

$ Budget eateries include street food, takeaway, order-at-the-counter shops, basic cafeterias, and bakeries selling sandwiches.

$$ Moderate eateries are typically nice (but not fancy) sit-down restaurants, ideal for a straightforward, fill-the-tank meal.

Most of my listings fall in this category—great for getting a good taste of the local cuisine on a budget.

$$$ Pricier eateries are a notch up, with more attention paid to the setting, presentation, and cuisine. These are ideal for a memorable meal that's relatively casual and doesn't break the bank. This category often includes affordable "destination" or "foodie" restaurants.

$$$$ Splurge eateries are dress-up-for-a-special-occasion-swanky—Michelin star-type restaurants, typically with an elegant setting, polished service, pricey and intricate cuisine, and an expansive (and expensive) wine list.

I haven't categorized places where you might assemble a picnic, snack, or graze: supermarkets, delis, ice cream-stands, cafés or bars specializing in drinks, chocolate shops, and so on.

Staying Connected

One of the most common questions I hear from travelers is, "How can I stay connected in Europe?" The short answer is: more easily and cheaply than you might think.

The simplest solution is to bring your own device—mobile phone, tablet, or laptop—and use it just as you would at home (following the tips below, such as connecting to free Wi-Fi whenever possible). Another option is to buy a European SIM card for your mobile phone—either your US phone or one you buy in Europe. Or you can travel without a mobile device and use European landlines and computers to connect. Each of these options is described below; more details are at www.ricksteves.com/phoning. For a very practical one-hour lecture covering tech issues for travelers, see www.ricksteves.com/travel-talks.

USING YOUR OWN MOBILE DEVICE IN EUROPE

Without an international plan, typical rates from major service providers (AT&T, Verizon, etc.) for using your device abroad are about $1.70/minute for voice calls, 50 cents to send text messages, 5 cents to receive them, and $10 to download one megabyte of data. At these rates, costs can add up quickly. Here are some budget tips and options.

Use free Wi-Fi whenever possible. Unless you have an unlimited-data plan, you're best off saving most of your online tasks for Wi-Fi. You can access the Internet, send texts, and make voice calls over Wi-Fi.

Many cafés (including Starbucks and McDonald's) have free hotspots for customers; look for signs offering it and ask for the Wi-Fi password when you buy something. You'll also often find

Hurdling the Language Barrier

Many visitors are pleasantly surprised to learn that the language barrier in Eastern Europe is no bigger than in Western Europe. In fact, I find it much easier to communicate in Hungary or Slovenia than in Italy or Spain. Why is that? Because the Eastern European countries are small and not politically powerful, their residents realize that it's unreasonable to expect visitors to learn Hungarian (with only 12 million speakers worldwide) or Slovene (2 million). It's essential to find a common language with the rest of the world—so they learn English early and well. (I've had surprisingly eloquent conversations with Slovenian grade-schoolers.)

Of course, not everyone speaks English. In these situations, it's relatively easy to get your point across. I've often bought a train ticket simply by writing out the name of my destination (preferably with the local spelling—for example, "Praha" instead of "Prague"); the time I want to travel (using the 24-hour clock); and, if I'm not traveling on the same day I'm buying the ticket, I include the date I want to leave (day first, then the month as a Roman numeral, then the year). Here's an example of what I'd show a ticket-seller at a train station: "Warszawa, 17:30, 15.VII.18."

Eastern Europeans, realizing that their language intimidates Americans, often invent easier nicknames for themselves—so Šárka goes by "Sara," András becomes "Andrew," and Jaroslav tells you, "Call me Jerry."

The people in most of this book's destinations (except Hungary, Austria, and Romania) speak Slavic languages. These languages are closely related to one another and to Russian, and are, to varying degrees, mutually intelligible (though many spellings change—for example, Czech hrad, or "castle," becomes Slovene grad). Slavic languages have simple vocabularies but are highly inflected—that is, the meaning of a sentence depends on complicated endings that are tacked onto the ends of the words (as in Latin).

Slavic words are notorious for their seemingly unpronounceable, long strings of consonants. Slavic pronunciation can be tricky. In fact, when the Christian missionaries Cyril and Methodius came to Eastern Europe a millennium ago, they invented a whole new alphabet to represent these strange Slavic sounds. A modified version of that alphabet—called Cyrillic—is still used today in the eastern Slavic countries (such as Serbia and Russia).

Fortunately, nearly all of the destinations covered in this book use the same Roman alphabet we do, but they add lots of different diacritics—little markings below and above some letters—to represent a wide range of sounds (for example, č, ą, ó, đ, ł). I explain each of these diacritics in this book's various country introductions. (The Cyrillic alphabet is used throughout Bulgaria, and in parts of Bosnia and Montenegro—but even in these places, many signs are still in Roman. For a primer on the Cyrillic alphabet, see page 1011.)

Hungarian is another story altogether—it's completely unrelated to Slavic languages, German, or English. For more on the Magyar tongue, see page 535.

It's easy to throw up your arms in defeat and assume you'll never pronounce these words. But unlike English, Eastern European languages are entirely phonetic—you can always sound words out with confidence, once you learn a few basic rules. My advice: Take the time to wrestle with each language, and you'll be amazed how quickly you get comfortable.

German is spoken in Vienna. As part of the same language family as English, German sounds more familiar to American ears than the Slavic languages. Throughout Eastern Europe, speaking German can come in handy, especially if you're interacting with somebody over age 50 (while few people under communism learned English, German ranked right up there with Russian as a popular second language). A few words of Italian can come in handy in Slovenia and Croatia.

There are certain universal English words all Eastern Europeans know: hello, please, thank you, super, pardon, stop, menu, problem, and no problem. Another handy word that people throughout the region will understand is Servus (SEHR-voos)—the old-fashioned greeting from the days of the Austro-Hungarian Empire. If you draw a blank on how to say hello in the local language, just offer a cheery *"Servus!"*

Get an ear for the local language (see the language section in each of this book's country introductions), learn the key phrases (find survival phrases for each language in the country chapters), and travel with a phrase book. Consider Lonely Planet's good *Eastern Europe Phrasebook,* which covers all the languages spoken in the destinations in this book (except German).

Don't be afraid to interact with locals. Eastern Europeans can initially seem shy or even brusque—a holdover from the closed communist society—but often a simple smile is the only icebreaker you need to make a new friend. You'll find that doors open a little more quickly when you know a few words of the language. Give it your best shot, and the natives will appreciate your efforts.

PRACTICALITIES

Wi-Fi at TIs, city squares, major museums, public-transit hubs, airports, and aboard trains and buses.

Sign up for an international plan. Most providers offer a global calling plan that cuts the per-minute cost of phone calls and texts, and a flat-fee data plan. Your normal plan may already include international coverage (T-Mobile's does).

Before your trip, call your provider or check online to confirm that your phone will work in Europe, and research your provider's international rates. Activate the plan a day or two before you leave, then remember to cancel it when your trip's over.

Minimize the use of your cellular network. When you can't find Wi-Fi, you can use your cellular network to connect to the Internet, text, or make voice calls. When you're done, avoid further charges by manually switching off "data roaming" or "cellular data" (in your device's Settings menu; for help, ask your service provider or Google it). Another way to make sure you're not accidentally using data roaming is to put your device in "airplane" or "flight" mode (which also disables phone calls and texts), and then turn on Wi-Fi as needed.

Don't use your cellular network for bandwidth-gobbling tasks, such as Skyping, downloading apps, and streaming video: Save these for when you're on Wi-Fi. Using a navigation app such as Google Maps over a cellular network can take lots of data, so do this sparingly or use it offline.

Limit automatic updates. By default, your device constantly checks for a data connection and updates apps. It's smart to disable these features so your apps will only update when you're on Wi-Fi, and to change your device's email settings from "auto-retrieve" to "manual" (or from "push" to "fetch").

It's also a good idea to keep track of your data usage. On your device's menu, look for "cellular data usage" or "mobile data" and reset the counter at the start of your trip.

Use Skype or other calling/messaging apps for cheaper calls and texts. Certain apps let you make voice or video calls or send texts over the Internet for free or cheap. If you're bringing a tablet or laptop, you can also use them for voice calls and texts. All you have to do is log on to a Wi-Fi network, then contact any of your friends or family members who are also online and signed into the same service.

You can make voice and video calls using Skype, Viber, FaceTime, and Google+ Hangouts. If the connection is bad, try making an audio-only call. WhatsApp only offers voice calls. You can also make voice calls from your device to telephones worldwide for just a few cents per minute using Skype, Viber, or Hangouts if you buy credit first.

To text for free over Wi-Fi, try apps like Google+ Hangouts,

Tips on Internet Security

Using the Internet while traveling brings added security risks, whether you're getting online with your own device or at a public terminal using a shared network. Here are some tips for securing your data:

First, make sure that your device is running the latest version of its operating system and security software, and that your apps are up to date. Next, ensure that your device is password- or passcode-protected so thieves can't access it if your device is stolen. For extra security, set passwords on apps that access key info (such as email or Facebook).

On the road, use only legitimate Wi-Fi hotspots. Ask the hotel or café staff for the specific name of their Wi-Fi network, and make sure you log on to that exact one. Hackers sometimes create a bogus hotspot with a similar or vague name (such as "Hotel Europa Free Wi-Fi"). The best Wi-Fi networks require a password. If you're not actively using a hotspot, turn off your device's Wi-Fi connection so it's not visible to others.

Be especially cautious when accessing financial information online. Experts say it's best to use a banking app rather than sign in to your bank's website via a browser (the app is less likely to get hacked). Refrain from logging in to any personal finance sites on a public computer. Even if you're using your own mobile device at a password-protected hotspot, there's a remote chance that a hacker who's logged on to the same network could see what you're doing.

Never share your credit-card number (or any other sensitive information) online unless you know that the site is secure. A secure site displays a little padlock icon, and the URL begins with *https* (instead of the usual *http*).

WhatsApp, Viber, Facebook Messenger, and iMessage. Make sure you're on Wi-Fi to avoid data charges.

USING A EUROPEAN SIM CARD IN A MOBILE PHONE

This option works well for those who want to make a lot of voice calls at cheap local rates, and those who need faster connection speeds than their US carrier provides. With a European SIM card, you get a European phone number—and European rates.

You can buy a basic cell phone in Europe (as little as $20 from mobile-phone shops anywhere, including a SIM card). Or you can bring an "unlocked" US phone (check with your carrier about unlocking it) and swap out the original SIM card for one you buy in Europe. SIM cards are sold at mobile-phone shops, department-store electronics counters, newsstands, and vending machines. Costing about $5-10, they usually include about that much pre-paid calling credit, with no contract and no commitment. A SIM

How to Dial

International Calls

Whether phoning from a US landline or mobile phone, or from a number in another European country, here's how to make an international call. I've used one of my recommended Dubrovnik hotels as an example (tel. 385-20/453-834).

Initial Zero: Drop the initial zero from international phone numbers—except when calling Italy.

Mobile Tip: If using a mobile phone, the "+" sign can replace the international access code (for a "+" sign, press and hold "0").

US/Canada to Europe

Dial 011 (US/Canada international access code), country code (385 for Croatia), and phone number.

▶ To call the Dubrovnik hotel from home, dial 011-385-20/453-834.

Country to Country Within Europe

Dial 00 (Europe international access code), country code, and phone number.

▶ To call the Dubrovnik hotel from Slovakia, dial 00-385-20/453-834.

Europe to the US/Canada

Dial 00, country code (1 for US/Canada), and phone number.

▶ To call from Europe to my office in Edmonds, Washington, dial 00-1-425-771-8303.

Domestic Calls

In Eastern Europe, to call within the same country, except Hungary (such as from one Croatian landline or mobile phone to another), simply dial the phone number, including the initial 0 if there is one.

▶ To call a recommended Dubrovnik hotel from within Dubrovnik, dial 20/453-834.

Calls within Hungary

Calling in Hungary works slightly differently than elsewhere in Europe.

Landline Within the Same Hungarian City: Dial direct, with no area code.

▶ To call the Eger hotel from within Eger, dial 411-711.

Landline Long-Distance Call Within Hungary: Add the prefix 06, followed by the area code (36 for Eger).

▶ To call the Eger hotel from Budapest, dial 06-36/411-711.

card that also includes data (including roaming) will cost $20-40 more for one month of data within the country in which it was purchased. This can be faster than data roaming through your home provider. To get the best rates, buy a new SIM card whenever you arrive in a new country.

I like to buy SIM cards at a mobile-phone shop where there's

Hungarian Mobile Phones: Hungarian mobile phone numbers begin with +3620, +3630, +3631, or +3670. Use this prefix when calling from a mobile phone to another mobile phone. If you call these numbers from a landline within Hungary (such as from your hotel room phone), you'll need to replace the +36 with 06.

▶ To call a local guide with the number +3620-926-0557, dial exactly that from your US phone or Hungarian mobile phone—but from a Hungarian land line, dial 06-20-926-0557.

More Dialing Tips

Toll-Free Calls: International rates apply to US toll-free numbers dialed from any country in Eastern Europe—they're not free.

More Phoning Help: See www.howtocallabroad.com.

European Country Codes			
Austria	43	Ireland & N. Ireland	353 / 44
Belgium	32	Italy	39
Bosnia-Herzegovina	387	Latvia	371
Croatia	385	Montenegro	382
Czech Republic	420	Morocco	212
Denmark	45	Netherlands	31
Estonia	372	Norway	47
Finland	358	Poland	48
France	33	Portugal	351
Germany	49	Russia	7
Gibraltar	350	Slovakia	421
Great Britain	44	Slovenia	386
Greece	30	Spain	34
Hungary	36	Sweden	46
Iceland	354	Switzerland	41
		Turkey	90

PRACTICALITIES

a clerk to help explain the options and brands. Certain brands—including Lebara and Lycamobile, both of which are available in multiple European countries—are reliable and especially economical. Ask the clerk to help you insert your SIM card, set it up, and show you how to use it. In some countries—including Hungary—you'll be required to register the SIM card with your passport as an antiterrorism measure (which may mean you can't use the phone for the first hour or two).

Find out how to check your credit balance. When you run out of credit, you can top it up at newsstands, tobacco shops, mobile-phone stores, or many other businesses (look for your SIM card's logo in the window), or online.

UNTETHERED TRAVEL: PUBLIC PHONES AND COMPUTERS

It's possible to travel in Europe without a mobile device. You can check email or browse websites using public computers and Internet cafés, and make calls from your hotel room and/or public phones.

Phones in your **hotel room** generally have a fee for placing local and "toll-free" calls, as well as long-distance or international calls—ask for the rates before you dial. Since you're never charged for receiving calls, it's better to have someone from the US call you in your room.

If these fees are low, hotel phones can be used inexpensively for calls made with cheap international phone cards (sold at many newsstands, street kiosks, tobacco shops, and train stations). You'll either get a prepaid card with a toll-free number and a scratch-to-reveal PIN code, or a code printed on a receipt.

You'll see **public pay phones** in a few post offices and train stations. The phones generally come with multilingual instructions, and some work with insertable phone cards (sold at post offices, newsstands, etc.). With the exception of Great Britain, each European country has its own insertable phone card—so your Austrian card won't work in a Hungarian phone.

Public computers are easy to find. Many hotels have one in their lobby for guests to use; otherwise you can find them at Internet cafés and public libraries (ask your hotelier or the TI for the nearest location). If typing on a European keyboard, use the "Alt Gr" key to the right of the space bar to insert the extra symbol that appears on some keys. If you can't locate a special character (such as @), simply copy it from a Web page and paste it into your email message.

MAIL

You can mail one package per day to yourself worth up to $200 duty-free from Europe to the US (mark it "personal purchases"). If you're sending a gift to someone, mark it "unsolicited gift." For details, visit www.cbp.gov, select "Travel," and search for "Know Before You Go."

Eastern European postal services work fine, but for quick transatlantic delivery (in either direction), consider services such as DHL (www.dhl.com).

Transportation

In Eastern Europe, I travel mostly by public transportation. For long distances between big cities (such as Prague to Kraków, Warsaw to Budapest, or Vienna to Ljubljana), I prefer to take a cheap flight or a night train. For shorter distances (like Gdańsk to Warsaw or Budapest to Bratislava), I take a daytime train or bus. In areas with lots of exciting day-trip possibilities, such as the Czech countryside (castles) or Slovenia's Julian Alps (mountain scenery), I rent a car for a day or two. Or you can hire a local driver to take you around—freeing you up to enjoy the scenery...and the company (in this book, I recommend several drivers and tour guides with cars).

When deciding how to get between destinations in Europe, consider these factors: Cars are best for three or more traveling together (especially families with small kids), those packing heavy, and those delving into the countryside. Trains, buses, and boats are best for solo travelers, blitz tourists, city-to-city travelers, and those who don't want to drive in Europe. Intra-European flights are an increasingly inexpensive option. While a car gives you more freedom, trains, buses, and boats zip you effortlessly and scenically from city to city, usually dropping you in the center, often near a TI. Cars are great in the countryside, but an expensive headache in places like Prague, Budapest, and Vienna.

Throughout this book, I suggest whether trains, buses, or boats are better for a particular destination (in the "Connections" section at the end of each chapter).

TRAINS

Trains are punctual and cover cities well, but frustrating schedules make a few out-of-the-way recommendations difficult—or impossible—to reach (usually the bus will get you there instead; see "Buses," later).

Schedules: Pick up train schedules from stations as you go, or print them out from an online source. To study ahead on the Web, check www.bahn.com, Germany's excellent all-Europe timetable. Individual countries also have their own train timetable websites:

- **Czech Republic:** www.idos.cz
- **Poland:** www.rozklad-pkp.pl
- **Hungary:** www.elvira.hu
- **Slovenia:** www.slo-zeleznice.si
- **Austria:** www.oebb.at
- **Slovakia:** www.cp.sk

Tickets: Buy tickets at the train station (or on board, if the station is unstaffed). In many big-city train stations, it can be tricky to find the correct line (you'll see separate ticket windows for domestic trips, international journeys, immediate departures, and other

PRACTICALITIES

Public Transportation in Eastern Europe

Bus Route ┈┈┈┈

Ferry Route ┈┈┈┈

Railway

Border Station

concerns). Before getting in line, confirm with fellow travelers that you've chosen the right one. Many ticket-sellers speak limited English—be prepared to write out your destination and time. Bigger cities have train-ticket offices, either downtown (such as in Budapest) or in the station (such as in Warsaw and Ljubljana), where you can take a number to wait for an English-speaking clerk to sort through your options; I've listed these in this book. Especially if you have a complicated request (such as reserving a night-train berth a few days ahead), these offices can save you some frustration, and—in some cases—a needless trip to the station. While most short-haul journeys do not require a reservation, you are required to reserve on some high-speed trains (such as the Warsaw-Kraków express). It's also smart to reserve a sleeping berth if you're taking a night train.

Night Trains: To cover the long distances between the major destinations in this book, consider using night trains. Each night on the train saves a day for sightseeing. However, Eastern European night trains aren't as new, plush, or comfy as those in Western Europe (such as Austria's slick Nightjet). Expect a bumpy, noisy ride and gross WCs. In general, if a higher degree of comfort is important to you, look for an affordable flight (see "Flights," later), hire a driver to take you door-to-door (perhaps with some sightseeing stops en route), or take a day train. Thefts on night trains do occur, so lock the door and secure your belongings (to make it difficult—or at least noisy—for thieves to rip you off). When sleeping on a night train, I wear my money belt.

Rail Passes: Rail passes are rarely the best option for travel in Eastern Europe for two reasons: Point-to-point tickets are cheap and simple here, and most rail passes don't conveniently combine these countries. One handy option may be the European East Pass, covering the Czech Republic, Hungary, Slovakia, and Austria. Another option is the Global Pass, which covers all the countries in this book but is usually too expensive to be a good value. Each country except Slovakia and Bosnia has its own individual rail pass, valid for trips only within that country. Various preselected two- and three-country options are also available. Again, none of these passes is likely to save you much money, but if a pass matches your itinerary, give it a look and crunch the numbers.

For more detailed advice on figuring out the smartest rail pass options for your train trip, visit the Trains & Rail Passes section of my website at www.ricksteves.com/rail.

BUSES

While the train can get you most places faster than a bus can, this book covers a few areas where buses are worth considering. For example, Ljubljana and Lake Bled are connected by both train and bus—but the bus station is right in the town center of Bled, while the train station is a few miles away. And a few destinations are accessible only by bus. When in doubt, ask at the local TI for advice.

RENTING A CAR

If you're renting a car in Eastern Europe, bring your US driver's license. In Austria, Bosnia-Herzegovina, Hungary, Poland, and Slovenia you're also technically required to have an International Driving Permit (sold at your local AAA office for $20 plus the cost of two passport-type photos; see www.aaa.com). While that's the letter of the law, I generally rent cars without having this permit. How this is enforced varies from country to country: Get advice from your car-rental company.

Rental companies require you to be at least 21 years old and to have held your license for one year. Drivers under the age of 25 may incur a young-driver surcharge, and some rental companies do not rent to anyone 75 or older. If you're considered too young or old, look into leasing (covered later), which has less-stringent age restrictions.

Research car rentals before you go. It's cheaper to arrange most car rentals from the US. Consider several companies to compare rates.

Most of the major US rental agencies (including Avis, Budget, Enterprise, Hertz, and Thrifty) have offices throughout Eastern Europe. Also consider the two major Europe-based agencies, Europcar and Sixt. It can be cheaper to use a consolidator, such as Auto Europe/Kemwel (www.autoeurope.com—or the often-cheaper www.autoeurope.eu) or Europe by Car (www.europebycar.com), which compares rates at several companies to get you the best deal—but because you're working with a middleman, it's especially important to ask in advance about add-on fees and restrictions.

Always read the fine print carefully for add-on charges—such as one-way drop-off fees, airport surcharges, or mandatory insurance policies—that aren't included in the "total price." You may need to query rental agents pointedly to find out your actual cost.

For the best deal, rent by the week with unlimited mileage. To save money on fuel, you can request a diesel car. I normally rent the smallest, least-expensive model with a stick shift (generally cheaper than an automatic). Almost all rentals are manual by default, so if you need an automatic, request one in advance; be aware that these cars are usually larger models (not as maneuverable on narrow, winding roads).

Figure on paying roughly $230 for a one-week rental. Allow extra for supplemental insurance, fuel, tolls, and parking. For trips of three weeks or more, leasing can save you money on insurance and taxes. Be warned that one-way international trips, while ef-

Driving in Eastern Europe

PRACTICALITIES

Note: Your times may vary based on traffic, construction, and road conditions.

m = miles
h = hours
--- = car ferry

ficient, can be very expensive if the rental company assesses a drop-off fee for crossing a border (for details, see "International Drop-Off Fees," later).

As a rule, always tell your car-rental company up front exactly which countries you'll be entering. Some companies levy extra insurance fees for trips taken in certain countries with certain types of cars (such as BMWs, Mercedes, and convertibles). Double-check with your rental agent that you have all the documentation you need before you drive off (especially if you're crossing borders into non-Schengen countries, such as Bosnia-Herzegovina, where you might need to present proof of insurance).

Picking Up Your Car: Big companies have offices in most cities; ask whether they can pick you up at your hotel. Small local rental companies can be cheaper but aren't as flexible.

Compare pickup costs (downtown can be less expensive than the airport), and explore drop-off options. Always check the hours of the location you choose: Many rental offices close from midday Saturday until Monday morning and, in smaller towns, at lunchtime.

When selecting a location, don't trust the agency's description of "downtown" or "city center." In some cases, a "downtown" branch can be on the outskirts of the city—a long, costly taxi ride from the center. Before choosing, plug the addresses into a mapping website. You may find that the "train station" location is handier. But returning a car at a big-city train station or downtown agency can be tricky; get precise details on the car drop-off location and hours, and allow ample time to find it.

When you pick up the rental car, check it thoroughly and make sure any damage is noted on your rental agreement. Rental agencies in Europe are very strict when it comes to charging for even minor damage, so be sure to mark everything. Before driving off, find out how your car's gearshift, lights, turn signals, wipers, radio, and fuel cap function, and know what kind of fuel the car takes (diesel vs. unleaded). When you return the car, make sure the agent verifies its condition with you. Some drivers take pictures of the returned vehicle as proof of its condition.

International Drop-Off Fees

If you're planning a multicountry itinerary by car, be aware of often-astronomical international drop-off fees. There's typically no extra charge for picking up and dropping off a car in different towns within the same country, but you'll pay through the nose to drop off across the border. (For example, you can generally pick up a car in Zagreb, drive it nine hours to Dubrovnik, and turn it in there for no charge—but if you drive the same car from Zagreb just two hours to Ljubljana and drop it off, it can cost you hundreds of extra dollars.)

For some itineraries, you may just have to live with the extra expense. But in most cases, you can plan your itinerary smartly to avoid it. Some people plan a circular itinerary (for example, Prague-Kraków-Budapest-Bratislava-Vienna-Prague) to ensure they can drop the car off where they picked it up. Others connect the longer distances on their itinerary with trains or flights, then rent a car strategically for a day or two in places where it's warranted (such as the Czech or Slovenian countrysides). This is a particularly smart plan when you remember that in most big cities, a car is an expensive and worthless burden (i.e., fighting urban traffic and paying for pricey secure parking).

Car Insurance Options

When you rent a car, you are liable for a very high deductible, sometimes equal to the entire value of the car. Limit your financial risk with one of these options: Buy Collision Damage Waiver (CDW) coverage with a low or zero deductible from the car-rental company, get coverage through your credit card (free if your card automatically includes zero-deductible coverage), or get collision insurance as part of a larger travel-insurance policy.

Basic **CDW** includes a very high deductible (typically $1,000-1,500) costs $10-30 a day (figure roughly 30 percent extra), and reduces your liability, but does not eliminate it. When you reserve or pick up the car, you'll be offered the chance to "buy down" the basic deductible to zero (for an additional $10-30/day; this is sometimes called "super CDW" or "zero-deductible coverage").

If you opt for **credit-card coverage,** you'll technically have to decline all coverage offered by the car-rental company, which means they can place a hold on your card (which can be up to the full value of the car). In case of damage, it can be time-consuming to resolve the charges with your credit-card company. Before you decide on this option, quiz your credit-card company about how it works.

If you're already purchasing a **travel-insurance policy** for your trip, adding collision coverage can be an economical option. For example, Travel Guard (www.travelguard.com) sells affordable renter's collision insurance as an add-on to its other policies; it's valid everywhere in Europe except the Republic of Ireland, and some Italian car-rental companies refuse to honor it, as it doesn't cover you in case of theft.

For more on car-rental insurance, see www.ricksteves.com/cdw.

Leasing

For trips of three weeks or more, consider leasing (which automatically includes zero-deductible collision and theft insurance). By technically buying and then selling back the car, you save lots of money on tax and insurance. Leasing provides you a brand-new car with unlimited mileage and a 24-hour emergency assistance program. However, leases aren't generally available in Eastern Europe—you'll have to pick up and drop off the car elsewhere in Europe (such as Germany or Italy). You can lease for as little as 21 days to as long as five and a half months. Car leases must be arranged from the US. One of many companies offering affordable lease packages is Europe by Car.

Navigation Options

If you'll be navigating using your phone or a GPS unit from home, remember to bring a car charger and device mount.

Your Mobile Device: The mapping app on your mobile phone works fine for navigation in Europe, but for real-time turn-by-turn directions and traffic updates, you'll generally need access to a cellular network. A helpful exception is Google Maps, which provides turn-by-turn driving directions and recalibrates even when it's offline.

To use Google Maps offline, you must have a Google account and download your map while you have a data connection. Later—even when offline—you can call up that map, enter your destination, and get directions. View maps in standard view (not satellite view) to limit data demands.

GPS Devices: If you prefer the convenience of a dedicated GPS unit, consider renting one with your car ($10-30/day). These units offer real-time turn-by-turn directions and traffic without the data requirements of an app. Note that the unit may only come loaded with maps for its home country; if you need additional maps, ask. Also make sure your device's language is set to English before you drive off.

A less-expensive option is to bring a GPS device from home. Be aware that you'll need to buy and download European maps before your trip.

Maps and Atlases: Even when navigating primarily with a mobile app or GPS, I always make it a point to have a paper map. The free maps you get from your car-rental company usually don't have enough detail. It's smart to buy a better map before you go, or pick one up at a European gas station, bookshop, newsstand, or tourist shop.

DRIVING

Road Rules: Be aware of typical European road rules; for example, many countries—including most of the ones in this book—require headlights to be turned on at all times, and nearly all forbid talking on a mobile phone without a hands-free headset. In Europe, you're not allowed to turn right on a red light, unless there is a sign or signal specifically authorizing it, and on expressways it's illegal to pass drivers on the right. Ask your car-rental company about these rules, or check the US State Department website (travel.state.gov, search

for your country in the "Learn about your destination" box, then click on "Travel and Transportation").

Fuel: Gas is expensive—often about $6-8 per gallon. Diesel cars are more common in Europe than back home, so be sure you know what type of fuel your car takes before you fill up. Fuel pumps are color-coded for unleaded (green) or diesel (black).

Road Conditions: Eastern Europe is nearing the end of an impressive binge of superhighway construction. It's not unusual to discover that a much faster road has been built between major destinations since your five-year-old map was published. (This is another good reason to travel with the most up-to-date maps available and study them before each drive.) Over the last several years,

superhighways have opened between Dresden and Prague (A-17) and between Warsaw and Berlin (A-2). As soon as a long-enough section is completed, the roads are opened to the public.

Occasionally backcountry roads are the only option (especially in Poland). These can be bumpy and slow, but they're almost always paved (or, at least, they once were). In Poland, where the network of new expressways is far from complete, locals travel long distances on two-lane country roads. Since each lane is about a lane and a half wide, passing is commonplace. Slower drivers should keep to the far-right of their lane, and not be surprised when faster cars zip past them. Especially in Croatia and Slovenia, keep a close eye out for bikers—you'll see scads of them on mountain roads, struggling to earn a thrilling downhill run.

Tolls: In many countries, driving on highways requires a toll sticker (generally available at the border, post offices, gas stations, and sometimes car-rental agencies). You'll need a sticker in the **Czech Republic** (*dálniční známka*, 310 Kč/10 days, 440 Kč/1 month, www.sfdi.cz); **Slovakia** (*úhrada*, €10/10 days, €14/month, www.dialnicnenalepky.sk); **Hungary** (*autópálya matrica*, 2,975 Ft/week, 4,780 Ft/month, www.motorway.hu); **Slovenia** (*vinjeta*, €15/week, €30/month, www.dars.si); and **Austria** (*Vignette*, €8.90/10 days, €25.90/2 months, www.asfinag.at). Fines for not having a toll sticker can be stiff. Your rental car may already come with the necessary sticker—ask. In **Poland,** you'll take a toll ticket as you enter the expressway, then pay when you get off, based on how far you've traveled.

Parking: Parking is a costly headache in big cities. You'll pay about $10-25 a day to park safely. Rental-car theft can be a problem in cities (especially Prague), so ask at your hotel for advice.

FLIGHTS

The best comparison search engine for both international and intra-European flights is www.kayak.com. For inexpensive flights within Europe, try www.skyscanner.com.

Flying to Europe: Start looking for international flights at least four to six months before your trip, especially for peak-season travel. Off-season tickets can usually be purchased a month or so in advance. Depending on your itinerary, it can be efficient to fly into one city and out of another. If your flight requires a connection in Europe, see my hints on navigating Europe's top hub airports at www.ricksteves.com/hub-airports.

Flying Within Europe: If you're considering a train ride that's more than five hours long, a flight may save you both time and money. When comparing your options, factor in the time it takes to get to the airport and how early you'll need to arrive to check in.

Low-cost airlines allow you to cheaply connect many of the destinations in this book. Two well-established budget airlines are based in Eastern Europe: **Wizz Air** (www.wizzair.com, with hubs in Budapest, Prague, Warsaw, Gdańsk, and Katowice, near Kraków) and **Smart Wings** (www.smartwings.net, based in Prague). Well-

known cheapo airlines that
fly to Eastern European
destinations include **EasyJet**
(www.easyjet.com), **Ryanair**
(www.ryanair.com), **Air
Berlin** (www.airberlin.com),
and **Norwegian Air** (www.
norwegian.no).

Now that the estab-
lished airlines in Eastern Europe face more competition, they've
been forced to adapt. Many national carriers charge reasonable
fares for short-distance trips. For example, check out Poland's LOT
Airlines (www.lot.com). On recent trips, I've flown affordably on
LOT between Kraków and Ljubljana, and between Kraków and
Budapest, avoiding lengthy overland journeys.

But be aware of the potential drawbacks of flying with a discount airline: nonrefundable and nonchangeable tickets, minimal
or nonexistent customer service, stingy baggage allowances with
steep overage fees, and pricey and time-consuming treks to secondary airports (for example, some of Wizz Air's flights from
"Kraków" actually depart from Katowice, 50 miles away). If you're
traveling with lots of luggage, a cheap flight can quickly become a
bad deal. To avoid unpleasant surprises, read the small print before
you book. These days you can also fly within Europe on major airlines affordably—and without all the aggressive restrictions—for
around $100 a flight.

Flying to the US and Canada: Because security is extra tight
for flights to the US, be sure to give yourself plenty of time at the
airport. It's also important to charge your electronic devices before
you board because security checks may require you to turn them on
(see www.tsa.gov for the latest rules).

Resources from Rick Steves

Begin your trip at www.ricksteves.com: My mobile-friendly **website** is *the* place to explore Europe. You'll find thousands of fun articles, videos, photos, and radio interviews organized by country; a
wealth of money-saving tips for planning your dream trip; monthly
travel news dispatches; a collection of over 30 hours of practical
travel talks; my travel blog; my latest guidebook updates (www.
ricksteves.com/update); and my free Rick Steves Audio Europe
app. You can also follow me on Facebook and Twitter.

Our **Travel Forum** is an immense yet well-groomed collection of message boards where our travel-savvy community an-
swers questions and shares their personal travel experiences—and

our well-traveled staff chimes in when they can be helpful (www.ricksteves.com/forums).

Our **online Travel Store** offers travel bags and accessories that I've designed specifically to help you travel smarter and lighter. These include my popular carry-on bags (which I live out of four months a year), money belts, totes, toiletries kits, adapters, other accessories, and a wide selection of guidebooks and planning maps (www.ricksteves.com/shop).

Choosing the right **rail pass** for your trip—amid hundreds of options—can drive you nutty. Our website will help you find the perfect fit for your itinerary and your budget: We offer easy, one-stop shopping for rail passes, seat reservations, and point-to-point tickets.

Tours: Want to travel with greater efficiency and less stress? We organize **tours** with more than three dozen itineraries and more than 900 departures reaching the best destinations in this book...and beyond. Our 14-day Eastern Europe tour visits the Czech Republic, Poland, Hungary, Croatia, and Slovenia; our 14-day Adriatic tour focuses on Slovenia, Croatia, and a bit of Bosnia-Herzegovina. We also offer an 8-day tour of Prague and Budapest, a 12-day tour of Berlin, Prague, and Vienna, and a 12-day Best of Bulgaria tour. You'll enjoy great guides, a fun bunch of travel partners (with small groups of 24 to 28 travelers), and plenty of room to spread out in a big, comfy bus when touring between towns. You'll find European adventures to fit every vacation length. For all the details, and to get our Tour Catalog, visit www.ricksteves.com or call us at 425/608-4217.

Books: *Rick Steves Eastern Europe* is one of many books in my series on European travel, which includes country guidebooks (such as *Croatia & Slovenia*), city and region-al guidebooks (including *Budapest; Prague & the Czech Republic;* and *Vienna, Salzburg & Tirol*), Snapshot guidebooks (excerpted chapters from my country guides), Pocket guidebooks (full-color little books on big cities, including Vienna), "Best Of" guide-books (condensed country guides in a full-color, easy-to-scan format), and my budget-travel skills handbook, *Rick Steves Europe Through the Back Door*. Most of my titles are available as ebooks.

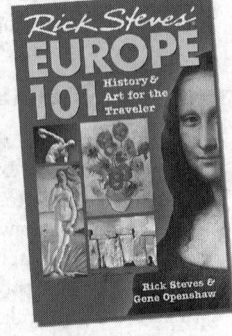

My phrase books—for German, French, Italian, Spanish, and Portuguese—are practical and budget-oriented. My other books include *Europe 101* (a crash course on art and history designed for travelers); *Mediterranean Cruise Ports* and *Northern European Cruise Ports* (how to make the most of your time in port); and *Travel as a Political Act* (a travelogue sprinkled with tips for bringing home a global perspective). A more complete list of my titles appears near the end of this book.

TV Shows: My public television series, *Rick Steves' Europe*, covers Europe from top to bottom with over 100 half-hour episodes. To watch full episodes online for free, see www.ricksteves.com/tv.

Travel Talks on Video: You can raise your travel I.Q. with video versions of our popular classes (including talks on travel skills, packing smart, cruising, tech for travelers, European art for travelers, travel as a political act, and individual talks covering most European countries). See www.ricksteves.com/travel-talks.

Audio: My weekly public radio show, *Travel with Rick Steves*, features interviews with travel experts from around the world. A complete archive of 10 years of programs (over 400 in all) is available at www.ricksteves.com/radio. I've also produced free, self-guided audio tours of some top sights and city walks in Vienna and Prague. Most of this audio content is available for free through my **Rick Steves Audio Europe app,** an extensive online library organized by destination. For more on my app, see page 14.

Understanding Yugoslavia

If you're struggling to understand the complicated breakup of Yugoslavia, read this admittedly oversimplified, as-impartial-as-possible history to get you started. (For a more complete version, see www.ricksteves.com/yugo.)

The Balkan Peninsula—between the Adriatic and the Black Sea, basically running from Hungary to Greece—has always been a crossroads of cultures, divided by a series of cultural, ethnic, and religious fault lines. The most important religious influences were **Western Christianity** (i.e., Roman Catholicism, introduced by Charlemagne and later championed by the Austrian Habsburgs), **Eastern Orthodox Christianity** (from the Byzantine Empire), and **Islam** (from the Ottomans).

Two major historical factors made the Balkans what they are today: The first was the **split of the Roman Empire** in the fourth century A.D., dividing the Balkans down the middle into Roman Catholic (west) and Byzantine Orthodox (east)—roughly along today's Bosnian-Serbian border. The second was the **invasion of the Ottomans** (from today's Turkey) in the 14th century, which kicked off five centuries of Islamic influence in Bosnia-Herzegovina and Serbia, further dividing the Balkans into Christian (north) and Muslim (south).

Yugoslav Succession

AUSTRIA
HUNGARY
ITALY
Ljubljana
SLOVENE
SLOVENIA
Zagreb
CROATIA
HUNGARIAN
VOJVODINA
Novi Sad
ROMANIA
BOSNIA-
HERZEGOVINA
Banja Luka
Belgrade
SERBIA
SERBO-CROATIAN
Adriatic Sea
Knin
Sarajevo
ITALY
MONTE-
NEGRO
Podgorica
Priština
KOSOVO
BULGARIA
ALBANIAN
Skopje
MACEDONIA

Former Yugoslavia Border
Current Borders
Province within Serbia
SLOVENE Language
"Serbian Krajina"
(Serb-Controlled Croatia
1991-1995)
Republika Srpska (Serb
territory in Bosnia-Herz.)

ALBANIA
GREECE
100 Kilometers
100 Miles

PRACTICALITIES

Because of these and other events, several distinct ethnic identities emerged. The major ethnicities of Yugoslavia are all considered "South Slavs." They're all descended from the same ancestors and speak closely-related languages, but are distinguished by their religious practices. Roman Catholic **Croats** and **Slovenes** are found mostly west of the Dinaric Mountains (Croats along the Adriatic coast and Slovenes farther north, in the Alps); Orthodox Christian **Serbs** live mostly east of the Dinaric range; and Muslim **Bosniaks** (whose ancestors converted to Islam under the Ottomans) live mostly in the Dinaric Mountains. The region also has several smaller ethnic groups: the Slavic **Montenegrins** and **Macedonians,** plus **Hungarians** (concentrated in the north) and **Albanians** (concentrated in Kosovo and the south). The groups overlapped a lot—which is exactly why the breakup of Yugoslavia was so contentious.

The lands of Yugoslavia were shuttled between various kingdoms and empires for much of their history, but by the late 19th century, most of the area was part of the Austro-Hungarian Empire. When that empire split apart at the end of World War I, the various mostly-Slavic groups in the region formed a new country: Yugoslavia ("Land of the South Slavs"). The union was almost immediately contentious, as various groups—especially Serbs and Croats—struggled to take control. By the dawn of World War II, it was already clear that Yugoslavia was a troubled proposition.

The seeds of the 1990s interethnic conflict were planted in World War II. Yugoslavia was invaded by Nazi Germany, then chopped up into puppet states for the Axis Powers. Some groups took advantage of changing circumstances in wartime Yugoslavia to exact revenge on their former compatriots. In occupied Croatia, the puppet Ustaše party imprisoned and executed large numbers of Serbs. In the eastern mountains, a Serbian royalist paramilitary group called the Četniks were every bit as brutal against Croats and Bosniaks. A third group—the homegrown Partisan Army—fought against Nazis, Ustaše, and Četniks to secure freedom for Yugoslavia. Unlike the other "Eastern European" countries, Yugoslavia was not liberated by the Soviet Union. This unique status allowed it to determine its own path after the war.

After the short but rocky Yugoslav union between the World Wars, it seemed that no one could hold the southern Slavs together in a single nation. But one man could, and did: Partisan war hero Josip Broz, who is better known by his code name, Tito. With a Slovene for a mother, a Croat for a father, a Serb for a wife, and a home in Belgrade, Tito was a true Yugoslav. Tito had a compelling vision that this fractured union of the South Slavs could function (see the sidebar).

Tito's new incarnation of Yugoslavia aimed for a more equitable division of powers. It was made up of six republics, each dominated by one ethnic group: **Croatia, Slovenia, Serbia, Bosnia-Herzegovina, Montenegro,** and **Macedonia.** Within Serbia, Tito set up two autonomous provinces, each one an enclave for an ethnicity that was a minority in greater Yugoslavia: Albanians in **Kosovo** (to the south) and Hungarians in **Vojvodina** (to the north). By allowing these two provinces some degree of independence, Tito hoped they would balance the political clout of Serbia, preventing a single republic from dominating the union.

While each republic had a measure of self-rule, the union was carefully overseen by President-for-Life Tito. Tito respected—and even celebrated—the diversity of his union, but he placed Yugoslav unity above all. He said that the borders between the republics should be "like white lines in a marble column."

Tito's Yugoslavia was communist, but it wasn't Soviet communism. He refused to formally join either the Warsaw Pact or NATO, and ingeniously played the East and the West against each other. Economically, Tito's vision was for a "third way," somewhere

Tito (1892-1980)

The Republic of Yugoslavia was the vision of a single man, who made it reality. Josip Broz—better known as Marshal Tito—presided over the most peaceful and prosperous era in this region's long and troubled history. Three decades after his death, Tito is beloved by many of his former subjects...and yet, he was a communist dictator who dealt brutally with his political enemies. This love-him-and-hate-him autocrat is one of the most complex figures in the history of this very complicated land.

Josip Broz was born in 1892 to a Slovenian mother and a Croatian father in the northern part of today's Croatia (then part of the Austro-Hungarian Empire). After growing up in the rural countryside, he was trained as a metalworker. He was drafted into the Austro-Hungarian army, went to fight on the Eastern Front during World War I, and was captured and sent to Russia as a prisoner of war. Freed by Bolsheviks, Broz fell in with the Communist Revolution...and never looked back.

At war's end, Broz returned home to the newly independent Yugoslavia, where he worked alongside the Soviets to build a national Communist Party. As a clandestine communist operative, he adopted the code name he kept for the rest of his life: Tito. Some believe this was a Spanish name he picked up while participating in that country's civil war, while others half-joke that the name came from Tito's authoritarian style: *"Ti, to!"* means "You, do this!" But one thing's clear: In this land where a person's name instantly identifies his ethnicity, "Tito" is ethnically neutral.

When the Nazis occupied Yugoslavia, Tito raised and commanded a homegrown, communist Partisan Army. Through guerilla tactics, Tito's clever maneuvering, and sheer determination, the Partisans liberated their country. And because they did so mostly without support from the USSR, Yugoslavia was able to set its own postwar course.

The war hero Tito quickly became the "president for life" of postwar Yugoslavia. But even as he introduced communism to his country, he retained some elements of a free-market economy—firmly declining to become a satellite of Moscow. He also pioneered the worldwide Non-Aligned Movement, joining with nations in Africa, the Middle East, Asia, and Latin America in refusing to ally with the US or USSR. Stubborn but suitably cautious, Tito expertly walked a tightrope between East and West.

There was a dark side to Tito. In the early years of his regime, Tito resorted to brutal, Stalin-esque tactics to assert his control. Immediately following World War II, the Partisan Army massacred tens of thousands of soldiers who had supported the Nazis. Then Tito systematically arrested, tried, tortured, or executed those who did not accept his new regime. Survivors whose lives were ruined during this reign of terror will never forgive Tito for what he did.

But once he gained full control, Tito moved away from strong-arm tactics and into a warm-and-fuzzy era of Yugoslav brotherhood. Tito believed that the disparate peoples of Yugoslavia could live in harmony. For example, every Yugoslav male had to serve in the People's Army, and Tito made sure that each unit was a microcosm of the complete Yugoslavia—with equal representation from each ethnic group. Yugoslavs from diverse backgrounds were required to work together and socialize—as a result, they became friends. He also worked toward economic diversification: Yugoslav tanks, some of the best in the world, were made of parts assembled in five different republics.

Tito's reign is a case study in the power of the cult of personality. Rocks on hillsides throughout Yugoslavia were rearranged to spell "TITO," and his portrait hung over every family's dinner table. Each of the six republics renamed one of its cities for their dictator. The main street and square in virtually every town were renamed for Tito. Each year, young people would embark on a months-long, Olympics-style relay, from each corner of Yugoslavia, to present a ceremonial baton to Tito on his official birthday (May 25). Tito also had vacation villas in all of Yugoslavia's most beautiful areas, including Lake Bled, the Brijuni Islands, and the Montenegrin coast. People sang patriotic anthems to their Druža (Comrade) Tito: "Comrade Tito, we pledge an oath to you."

Tito died in 1980 in a Slovenian hospital. His body went on a grand tour of the Yugoslav capitals: Ljubljana, Zagreb, Sarajevo, and Belgrade, where he was buried before hundreds of thousands of mourners, including more heads of state than at any other funeral in history. At his request, his tomb was placed in the greenhouse where he enjoyed spending time.

The genuine outpouring of grief at Tito's death might seem unusual for a man who was, on paper, an authoritarian communist dictator. But even today, many former Yugoslavs—especially Slovenes and Bosniaks—believe that his iron-fisted government was a necessary evil that kept the country strong and united. The eventual balance Tito struck between communism and capitalism, and between the competing interests of his ethnically diverse nation, led to this region's most stable and prosperous era. In a recent poll in Slovenia, Tito had a higher approval rating than any present-day politician, and 80 percent of Slovenes said they had a positive impression of him.

And yet, the Yugoslavs' respect for their former leader was not enough to keep them together. Tito's death began a long, slow chain reaction that led to the end of Yugoslavia. As the decades pass, the old joke seems more and more appropriate: Yugoslavia had eight distinct peoples in six republics, with five languages, three religions (Orthodox Christian, Catholic, and Muslim), and two alphabets (Roman and Cyrillic), but only one Yugoslav—Tito.

between communism and capitalism. While large industries were collectivized, small businesses were also permitted. Though Yugoslavs could not become really rich, through hard work it was possible to attain modest wealth to buy a snazzy car, a vacation home, Western imports, and other niceties. Yugoslavia was also the most free and open of the communist states. Tourists (from both East and West) flocked here for vacation, and Yugoslavs could travel to far more places abroad than could residents of the Eastern Bloc.

Tito died in 1980, and before long, the fragile union he had held together started to unravel. The breakup began in the late 1980s in the autonomous province of Kosovo, with squabbles between the Serb minority and the ethnic-Albanian majority. Serbian politician Slobodan Milošević traveled to Kosovo to rouse his Serb comrades, which alarmed some of the other republics. When Milošević-led Serbia annexed Kosovo soon after, and negotiations among the Yugoslav republics broke down, Croatia and Slovenia decided it was time to declare independence (both on June 25, 1991). Small, relatively homogenous Slovenia weathered a brief 10-day skirmish (see page 705), while Croatia—which had a large Serb minority—was pulled into a gruesome war lasting several years. Bosnia-Herzegovina declared its independence a few months later. But, because that republic was by far Yugoslavia's most ethnically diverse (with large populations of Muslim Bosniaks, Serbs, and Croats), its separation was hotly contested—plunging Bosnia into a horrifying four years of guerrilla warfare, medieval-style sieges, systematic rape, and ethnic cleansing.

Peace accords in 1995 brought an end to most of the hostilities throughout Yugoslavia, establishing the borders of Croatia and Bosnia that still exist today. Over the next several years, Slobodan Milošević and others accused of war crimes were arrested and tried by an international tribunal at The Hague, Netherlands (though Milošević died behind bars before a verdict was handed down). Later, additional parts of the former Yugoslavia split off, leaving behind seven independent nations where once was one: Croatia, Slovenia, Bosnia-Herzegovina, Montenegro, Serbia, Macedonia, and Kosovo.

Peace has reigned in these countries for more than two decades. The physical scars of war have mostly been repaired. And, considering that hospitality has been a forte of this region since long before the age of Yugoslavia, outside visitors feel welcome and safe—and are impressed at the candor of the people they meet, who are often willing to share their own wartime experiences. But, understandably, the psychological scars will take the longest to heal. Tensions still persist between formerly warring groups.

Thoughtful visitors to the former Yugoslavia grapple with

trying to understand what happened here just a generation ago. Many find it hard to get an impartial take on the current situation, or even on historical "facts." A very wise Bosniak once told me, "Listen to all three sides—Muslim, Serb, and Croat. Then decide for yourself what you think." A Serb told me a similar local saying: "You have to look at the apple from all sides."

APPENDIX

Useful Contacts

Emergency Needs

In all of the countries in this book, dial 112 for medical or other emergencies. For police, dial 112 in Slovakia, Hungary, Poland, or Austria; dial 158 in the Czech Republic; and dial 113 in Slovenia.

US Embassies and Consulates

Austria: Boltzmanngasse 16, tel. 01/313-390; consular services at Parkring 12a, Vienna, passport services available Mon-Fri 8:00-11:30, tel. 01/313-397-535, http://at.usembassy.gov.

Czech Republic: Tržiště 15, Prague, emergency passport services available Mon-Fri 8:00-11:30, tel. 257-022-000, http://cz.usembassy.gov.

Hungary: Szabadság tér 12, Budapest, passport services available Mon-Fri 8:00-17:00, tel. 1/475-4400, after-hours emergency tel. 1/475-4703 or 1/475-4924, http://hungary.usembassy.gov.

Poland: Ulica Piękna 12, Warsaw, appointments required for routine services, tel. 022-504-2784, after-hours emergency tel. 022-504-2000, http://pl.usembassy.gov; also a US Consulate in

Kraków at ulica Stolarska 9, appointments required for routine services, tel. 012-424-5100, https://pl.usembassy.gov/embassy-consulate/krakow.

Slovakia: Hviezdoslavovo námestie 4, Bratislava, passport services available Mon-Fri 8:00-11:45 & 14:00-15:15, tel. 02/5443-0861, http://slovakia.usembassy.gov.

Slovenia: Prešernova 31, Ljubljana, passport services available Mon-Fri 9:00-11:30 & 13:00-15:00, tel. 01/200-5595, after business hours tel. 01/200-5500, http://slovenia.usembassy.gov.

Canadian Embassies and Consulates

For after-hours emergencies, Canadian citizens can call collect to the Foreign Services Office in Ottawa at 613/996-8885.

Austria: Laurenzerberg 2, Vienna, passport services available Mon-Fri 8:30-12:30 & 13:30-15:30, tel. 01/531-383-000, www.austria.gc.ca.

Czech Republic: Ve Struhách 95/2, Prague, passport services Mon-Thu 9:00-12:00, Fri and afternoons by appointment, tel. 272-101-800, www.czechrepublic.gc.ca; also provides services for Slovakia.

Hungary: Ganz utca 12-14, Budapest, passport services available Mon-Thu 8:30-12:30 & 13:00-16:30, Fri 8:00-13:30, tel. 1/392-3360, www.hungary.gc.ca; also provides services for Bosnia-Herzegovina and Slovenia.

Poland: Ulica Jana Matejki 1-5, Warsaw, passport services available Mon-Fri 8:30-16:30, tel. 022-584-3100, www.poland.gc.ca.

Slovakia: Mostová 2, Bratislava, passport services available Mon-Fri 8:30-12:30 & 13:30-16:30, tel. 02/5920-4031; some services provided through Canadian Embassy in Prague, Czech Republic (listed above).

Slovenia (consulate office): Linhartova cesta 49a, Ljubljana; passport services available Mon, Wed, and Fri 8:00-12:00; tel. 01/252-4444, some services provided through Canadian Embassy in Budapest, Hungary (listed above).

Directory Assistance

Dial 1188 in the Czech Republic, 913 in Poland, 198 in Hungary, 988 in Slovenia, 1181 in Slovakia, and 118 in Austria.

Holidays and Festivals

This list includes selected festivals in this region, plus national holidays observed throughout Eastern Europe. Many sights and banks close on national holidays—keep this in mind when planning your itinerary. Catholic holidays are celebrated in Poland, Slovakia, and Slovenia (and to a lesser extent in Hungary and the Czech Republic). Before planning a trip around a festival, verify its dates by checking the festival's website or TI sites.

Jan 1	New Year's Day
Jan 6	Epiphany, Catholic countries
Jan 19	Anniversary of Jan Palach's Death, Prague (flowers in Wenceslas Square)
Feb 8	National Day of Culture, Slovenia (celebrates Slovenian culture and national poet France Prešeren)
Early March	One World International Human Rights Film Festival, Prague (www.oneworld.cz)
March 15	National Day, Hungary (celebrates 1848 Revolution)
Late March	Ski Jumping World Cup Finals, Planica, Slovenia (www.planica.info)
March/April	Easter weekend (Good Friday-Easter Monday): April 14-17, 2017; March 30-April 2, 2018
April	Budapest Spring Festival (2 weeks; opera, ballet, classical music; www.btf.hu)
April 27	National Resistance Day, Slovenia
April 30	Witches' Night, Czech Republic (similar to Halloween, with bonfires)
May	Ascension: May 25, 2017; May 10, 2018 (Catholic countries)
May 1	Labor Day
May 3	Constitution Day, Poland (celebrates Europe's first constitution)
May 8	Liberation Day, Czech Republic and Slovakia
May/June	Pentecost and Whitmonday: June 4-5, 2017; May 20-21, 2018 (Catholic countries)
May-June	Ramadan: May 26-June 25, 2017; May 15-June 14, 2018 (Muslim holy month)
May-June	Vienna Festival of Arts and Music (www.festwochen.at)
Early to mid-May	Prague International Marathon (www.pim.cz)
Mid- to late May	"Prague Spring" Music Festival (www.festival.cz)
Late May/early June	Corpus Christi: June 15, 2017; May 31, 2018 (Catholic countries)
June-July	Prague Proms, Prague (music festival, www.pragueproms.cz)

Mid-June	Celebration of the Rose, Český Krumlov, Czech Republic (medieval festival, music, theater, dance, knights' tournament)
June 25	National Day, Slovenia
Late June	Wianki Midsummer Festival, Kraków, Poland (wreaths on rafts in Vistula River, fireworks, music)
Late June	Jewish Culture Festival, Kraków, Poland (www.jewishfestival.pl)
Late June	Midsummer Eve celebrations, Austria
July 5	Sts. Cyril and Methodius Day, Czech Republic and Slovakia
July 6	Jan Hus Day, Czech Republic
July-mid-Sept	Ljubljana Summer Festival, Slovenia (www.ljubljanafestival.si)
Mid-July-mid-Aug	International Music Festival, Český Krumlov, Czech Republic (www.festivalkrumlov.cz)
Late July	Formula 1 races, Budapest (www.hungaroinfo.com/formel1)
Late July-mid-Aug	St. Dominic's Fair, Gdańsk, Poland (3 weeks of market stalls, music, and general revelry)
Early Aug	Sziget Festival, Budapest (rock and pop music, www.sziget.hu)
Aug 15	Assumption of Mary, Catholic countries
Aug 20	Constitution Day and St. Stephen's Day, Hungary (fireworks, celebrations)
Aug 29	National Uprising Day, Slovakia (commemorates uprising against Nazis)
Late Aug-early Sept	Jewish Summer Festival, Budapest (www.zsidonyarifesztival.hu)
Sept	Dvořák's Prague Music Festival, Prague (www.dvorakovapraha.cz)
Sept	Jewish High Holy Days (Rosh Hashanah: Sept 20-22, 2017, Sept 9-11, 2018; Yom Kippur: Sept 29-30, 2017, Sept 18-19, 2018; Jewish sites may close)
Sept 1	Constitution Day, Slovakia
Sept 28	St. Wenceslas Day, Czech Republic (celebrates national patron saint and Czech statehood)
Oct	International Jazz Festival, Prague (www.agharta.cz)
Mid-Oct	Café Budapest Festival (contemporary arts, www.cafebudapestfest.hu)

Oct 23	Republic Day, Hungary (remembrances of 1956 Uprising)
Oct 26	National Day, Austria
Oct 28	Independence Day, Czech Republic
Oct 31	Reformation Day, Slovenia
Nov 1	All Saints' Day/Remembrance Day, Catholic countries (religious festival, some closures)
Nov 11	Independence Day, Poland; St. Martin's Day (official first day of wine season), Slovenia
Nov 17	Velvet Revolution Anniversary, Czech Republic and Slovakia
Dec 5	St. Nicholas Eve, Prague (St. Nick gives gifts to children in town square)
Dec 24-25	Christmas Eve and Christmas Day
Dec 26	Boxing Day/St. Stephen's Day; Independence and Unity Day, Slovenia
Dec 31	St. Sylvester's Day, Prague and Vienna (fireworks)

Recommended Books and Films

To learn about Eastern Europe past and present, check out a few of these books and films.

NONFICTION

Lonnie Johnson's *Central Europe: Enemies, Neighbors, Friends* is the best historical overview of the countries in this book. Timothy Garton Ash has written several good "eyewitness account" books analyzing the fall of communism in Eastern Europe, including *History of the Present* and *The Magic Lantern*. Michael Meyer's *The Year that Changed the World* intimately chronicles the exciting events of 1989, culminating in the fall of the Berlin Wall. Anne Applebaum's *Iron Curtain: The Crushing of Eastern Europe 1944-1956* is a readable account of how the Soviets exerted their influence on the nations they had just liberated from the Nazis; her *Gulag: A History* delves into one particularly odious mechanism they used to intimidate their subjects. Tina Rosenberg's dense but thought-provoking *The Haunted Land* asks how those who actively supported communism in Eastern Europe should be treated in the postcommunist age. And Benjamin Curtis' *The Habsburgs: The History of a Dynasty* is an illuminating portrait of the Austrian imperial family that shaped so much of Eastern European history.

Patrick Leigh Fermor's *Between the Woods and the Water* is the vivid memoir of a young man who traveled by foot and on horseback across the Balkan Peninsula (including Hungary) in 1933. Rebecca West's classic, bricklike *Black Lamb and Grey Falcon* is the definitive travelogue of the Yugoslav lands (written during a journey between the two World Wars). For a more recent take, Croatian journalist Slavenka Drakulić has written a quartet of insightful essay collections from a woman's perspective: *Café Europa: Life After Communism; The Balkan Express; How We Survived Communism and Even Laughed;* and *A Guided Tour Through the Museum of Communism.*

Drakulić's *They Would Never Hurt a Fly* profiles Yugoslav war criminals. Dominika Dery's memoir, *The Twelve Little Cakes*, traces her experience growing up in communist Czechoslovakia in the 1970s. For a thorough explanation of how and why Yugoslavia broke apart, read *Yugoslavia: Death of a Nation* (by Laura Silber and Allan Little).

For information on Eastern European Roma (Gypsies), consider the textbook-style *We Are the Romani People* by Ian Hancock, and the more literary *Bury Me Standing* by Isabel Fonseca.

FICTION

The most prominent works of Eastern European fiction have come from the Czechs. These include *I Served the King of England* (Bohumil Hrabal), *The Unbearable Lightness of Being* (Milan Kundera), and *The Good Soldier Švejk* (Jaroslav Hašek). Czech existentialist writer Franz Kafka wrote many well-known novels, including *The Trial* and *The Metamorphosis*. Bruce Chatwin's *Utz* is set in communist Prague.

James Michener's *Poland* is a hefty look into the history of the Poles. *Zlateh the Goat* (Isaac Bashevis Singer) includes seven folktales of Jewish Eastern Europe. Joseph Roth's *The Radetzky March* details the decline of an aristocratic Slovenian family in the Austro-Hungarian Empire.

Imre Kertész, a Hungarian-Jewish Auschwitz survivor who won the Nobel Prize for Literature in 2002, is best known for his semiautobiographical novel *Fatelessness (Sorstalanság)*, which chronicles the experience of a young concentration-camp prisoner. Márai Sándor's reflective *Embers* paints a rich picture of cobblestoned, gaslit Vienna just before the empire's glory began to fade.

Arthur Phillips' confusingly-titled 2002 novel *Prague* tells the story of American expats negotiating young-adult life in postcommunist Budapest, where they often feel one-upped by their compatriots doing the same in the Czech capital (hence the title).

FILMS

Each of these countries has produced fine films. Below are a few highlights.

Czech Republic

The Czech film industry is one of the strongest in Eastern Europe; even under communism its films were seen and honored worldwide. Before he directed *One Flew Over the Cuckoo's Nest* and *Amadeus*, Miloš Forman directed *Loves of a Blonde* (1965), about the relationship between a rural Czech woman and a jazz pianist from Prague; and *The Firemen's Ball* (1967), a satirical look at small-town Czechoslovakia under communism. Another Czech New Wave film, *Intimate Lighting* (1965), finds two musicians reuniting in the 1960s.

In *Alice* (1988), Czech artist Jan Švankmajer adapts Lewis Carroll's *Alice's Adventures in Wonderland* in stop-motion animation combined with live action. The comedy *Czech Dream* (2004) features two film students who document the opening of a fake hypermarket in a hilarious, disturbing commentary on consumerism.

Two films directed by Jiří Menzel cover everyday life during World War II. The Oscar-winning *Closely Watched Trains* (1966) follows a young Czech man working at a German-occupied train station. *I Served the King of England* (2006), an adaptation of Bohumil Hrabal's novel, finds a man reminiscing about his past as an ambitious waiter who suffers the consequences of World War II.

Other great Czech films about World War II include *Divided We Fall* (2000), where a Czech couple hides a Jewish friend during Nazi occupation; *Protektor* (2009), whose main character must reconcile his job at a Nazi-propaganda radio station and his relationship with his Jewish wife; and *All My Loved Ones* (1999), the story of a Jewish family whose son is sent to England in the "Kindertransports" organized by Nicholas Winton (the British humanitarian who saved almost 700 Czech Jewish children).

Recent Czech films also cover life under communism and the Velvet Revolution. *The Elementary School* (1991), set in the late 1940s, looks at a rowdy classroom in suburban Prague that faces reform under the strict guidance of a war-hero teacher. The mystery *In the Shadow* (2012) tracks a burglary in 1950s Czechoslovakia that sets off a political investigation of Jewish immigrants. *Larks on a String* (1990) covers bourgeois Czechs who are forced into communist labor camps and struggle to maintain their humanity. The TV miniseries *Burning Bush* (2013) details the communist occupation of Czechoslovakia and the Prague Spring, focusing on Jan Palach, the Czech student who set himself on fire and died in protest against the Soviet occupation. In the Oscar-winning *Kolya* (1996), a concert-cellist in Soviet-controlled Czechoslovakia must care for an abandoned Russian boy just before the Velvet Revolution breaks out.

The Czechs also have a wonderful animation tradition that successfully competes with Walt Disney in Eastern Europe and

APPENDIX

China. The most popular character is Krtek (or Krteček, "Little Mole"), who gets in and out of trouble. You'll see plush black-and-white Krtek figures everywhere. Křemílek and Vochomůrka are brothers who live in the woods, Maxipes Fík is a clever dog, and the duo Pat and Mat are builders who can't seem to get anything right.

Poland

Several Polish films have won Oscars and major awards at Cannes. In *Katyń* (2007), acclaimed, Oscar-winning director Andrzej Wajda re-creates the Soviet Army's massacre of around 22,000 Polish officers, enlisted men, and civilians during World War II. Some of Wajda's earlier works include *Ashes and Diamonds* (1958), *The Promised Land* (1979), and the two-part series *Man of Marble* (1977) and *Man of Iron* (1981).

Polish filmmaker Krzysztof Kieslowski made several masterpieces, including *The Decalogue* (1989), consisting of 10 short films inspired by the Ten Commandments. Kieslowski also filmed the multilingual Three Colors Trilogy: *Red* (1994), *White* (1994), and *Blue* (1993).

Among other recent films, one Polish favorite is *Karol: A Man Who Became Pope* (2005), a Polish-Italian biopic made in English about the humble beginnings of St. John Paul II. Another fascinating religious tale is *Ida* (2014), the story of a young novitiate nun in 1960s Poland, who—just before taking her vows—discovers a terrible family secret.

Hungary

The surreal dark comedy *Kontroll* (2003) is about ticket inspectors on the Budapest Metró whose lives are turned upside down by a serial killer lurking in the shadows. *Fateless,* the 2005 adaptation of Imre Kertész's Nobel Prize-winning novel about a young man in a concentration camp, was scripted by Kertész himself. *The Witness* (a.k.a. *Without a Trace*, 1969), a cult classic about a simple man who mysteriously wins the favor of communist bigwigs, is a biting satire of the darkest days of Soviet rule. *Time Stands Still* (1981), a hit at the 1982 Cannes Film Festival, tells the story of young Hungarians in the 1960s. *Children of Glory* (2006) dramatizes the true story of the Hungarian water polo team that defiantly trounced the Soviets at the Olympics just after the 1956 Uprising.

Slovenia (and other Former Yugoslav Countries)

To grasp the wars that shook this region in the early 1990s, there's no better film than the Slovene-produced *No Man's Land*, which won the 2002 Oscar for Best Foreign Film. Angelina Jolie wrote and directed (but did not appear in) 2011's wrenching, difficult-to-watch *In the Land of Blood and Honey,* a love story set against the grotesque backdrop of the war in Bosnia.

On a lighter note, a classic from Tito-era Yugoslavia, *The Battle of Neretva* (1969), imported Hollywood talent in the form of Yul Brynner and Orson Welles to tell the story of a pivotal and inspiring battle in the fight against the Nazis. More recent Croatian films worth watching include *Border Post* (2006), about various Yugoslav soldiers working together just before the war broke out; and *When Father Was Away on Business* (1985), about a prisoner on the Tito-era gulag island of Goli Otok, near Rab. Other local movies include *Armin* (2007), *How the War Started on My Island* (1996), *Underground* (1995), and *Tito and Me* (1992).

Documentaries

Documentaries about this region are also worth looking for. The BBC produced a remarkable six-hour documentary series called *The Death of Yugoslavia,* featuring interviews with all of the key players (it's difficult to find on DVD, but try searching for "Death of Yugoslavia" on YouTube; the book *Yugoslavia: Death of a Nation,* noted earlier, was a companion piece to this film). The BBC also produced a harrowing documentary about the infamous Bosnian massacre, *Srebrenica: A Cry from the Grave* (also available on YouTube). The 1998 Oscar-winning documentary *The Last Days* recounts the fate of Jews when the Nazis took over Hungary in 1944.

Hollywood Meets Eastern Europe

Several award-winning films have covered key moments in Eastern European history. *Schindler's List* (1993), Steven Spielberg's Best Picture-winner, tells the story of a compassionate German businessman in Kraków who saved his Jewish workers during the Holocaust. Roman Polanski's *The Pianist* (2002) is a biopic about the struggle for survival of Władysław Szpilman (played by Adrien Brody, in an Oscar-winning role), a Jewish concert pianist in Holocaust-era Warsaw. *The Unbearable Lightness of Being* (1988), starring a young Daniel Day-Lewis, adapts the Milan Kundera novel about a love triangle set against the backdrop of the Prague Spring uprising. And *Sunshine* (1999, starring Ralph Fiennes, directed by István Szabó) somewhat melodramatically traces three generations of an aristocratic Jewish family in Budapest, from the Golden Age, through the Holocaust, to the Cold War.

Two acclaimed German movies offer excellent insight into the surreal and paranoid days of the Soviet Bloc. The Oscar-winning *Lives of Others* (2006) chronicles the constant surveillance that the communist regime employed to keep potential dissidents in line. For a funny and nostalgic look at postcommunist Europe's fitful transition to capitalism, *Good Bye Lenin!* (2003) can't be beat.

Eastern European filmmakers have always been very active in Hollywood. "Crossover" directors—who started out making films in their own countries and then turned out English-language Oscar winners—include Michael Curtiz (from Hungary; *Casablanca, White Christmas*), Miloš Forman (from Czechoslovakia; *One Flew Over the Cuckoo's Nest, Amadeus*) and Roman Polanski (from Poland; *Chinatown, The Pianist*).

You may recognize Eastern Europe backdrops in many blockbuster Hollywood movies—particularly Prague, whose low costs and well-trained filmmaking workforce appeal to studios. In many cases, Prague stands in for another European city. Films shot at least partly in Prague include everything from *Amadeus* to *Mission: Impossible;* from *The Chronicles of Narnia* to *Wanted;* from *The Bourne Identity* to the *Hostel* films; and from *Hannibal* to *Shanghai Knights.* Elsewhere in the Czech Republic, they've filmed the James Bond reboot *Casino Royale* and *The Illusionist.* Many American studios have taken advantage of Hungary's low prices to film would-be blockbusters in Budapest, including *Spy, A Good Day to Die Hard,* and *Mission: Impossible—Ghost Protocol.* More often, Budapest stands in for other cities—for example, as Buenos Aires in the 1996 film *Evita,* and as various European locales in Stephen Spielberg's 2005 film *Munich.*

Conversions and Climate

NUMBERS AND STUMBLERS

- Europeans write a few of their numbers differently than we do. 1 = 1, 4 = 4, 7 = 7.
- In Europe, dates appear as day/month/year, so Christmas is 25/12/18. In Hungary, dates are written as year/month/day, so Christmas 2018 is 2018/12/25 (or dots can be used instead: 2018.12.25).
- Commas are decimal points and decimals are commas. A dollar and a half is $1,50, one thousand is 1.000, and there are 5.280 feet in a mile.
- Hungarians usually list their surname first (for example, Bartók Béla instead of Béla Bartók).
- When counting with fingers, start with your thumb. If you hold up your first finger to request one item, you'll probably get two.
- What Americans call the second floor of a building is the first floor in Europe.
- On escalators and moving sidewalks, Europeans keep the left "lane" open for passing. Keep to the right.

METRIC CONVERSIONS

A kilogram is 2.2 pounds, and 1 liter is about a quart, or almost four to a gallon. A kilometer is six-tenths of a mile. I figure kilometers to miles by cutting them in half and adding back 10 percent of the original (120 km: 60 + 12=72 miles, 300 km: 150 + 30=180 miles).

1 foot = 0.3 meter	1 square yard = 0.8 square meter
1 yard = 0.9 meter	1 square mile = 2.6 square kilometers
1 mile = 1.6 kilometers	1 ounce = 28 grams
1 centimeter = 0.4 inch	1 quart = 0.95 liter
1 meter = 39.4 inches	
1 kilometer = 0.62 mile	32°F = 0°C

CLOTHING SIZES

When shopping for clothing, use these US-to-European comparisons as general guidelines (but note that no conversion is perfect).

Women: For clothing or shoe sizes, add 30 (US shirt size 10 = European size 40; US shoe size 8 = European size 38-39).

Men: For shirts, multiply by 2 and add about 8 (US size 15 = European size 38). For jackets and suits, add 10. For shoes, add 32-34.

Children: For clothing, subtract 1-2 sizes for small children and subtract 4 for juniors. For shoes up to size 13, add 16-18, and for sizes 1 and up, add 30-32.

EASTERN EUROPE'S CLIMATE

First line is the average daily high; second line, average daily low; third line, average number of rainy days. For more detailed weather statistics for destinations in this book (as well as the rest of the world), check www.wunderground.com.

J	F	M	A	M	J	J	A	S	O	N	D

AUSTRIA • Vienna

J	F	M	A	M	J	J	A	S	O	N	D
34°	38°	47°	58°	67°	73°	76°	75°	68°	56°	45°	37°
25°	28°	30°	42°	50°	56°	60°	59°	53°	44°	37°	30°
15	14	13	13	13	14	13	13	10	13	14	15

CZECH REPUBLIC • Prague

J	F	M	A	M	J	J	A	S	O	N	D
31°	34°	44°	54°	64°	70°	73°	72°	65°	53°	42°	34°
23°	24°	30°	38°	46°	52°	55°	55°	49°	41°	33°	27°
13	11	10	11	13	12	13	12	10	13	12	13

HUNGARY • Budapest

J	F	M	A	M	J	J	A	S	O	N	D
34°	39°	50°	62°	71°	78°	82°	81°	74°	61°	47°	39°
25°	28°	35°	44°	52°	58°	62°	60°	53°	44°	38°	30°
13	12	11	11	13	13	10	9	7	10	14	13

	J	F	M	A	M	J	J	A	S	O	N	D

POLAND • Kraków

32°	34°	45°	55°	67°	72°	76°	73°	66°	56°	44°	37°
22°	22°	30°	38°	48°	54°	58°	56°	49°	42°	33°	28°
16	15	12	15	12	15	16	15	12	14	15	16

SLOVENIA • Ljubljana

36°	41°	50°	60°	68°	75°	80°	78°	71°	59°	47°	39°
25°	25°	32°	40°	48°	54°	57°	57°	51°	43°	36°	30°
13	11	11	13	16	16	12	12	10	14	15	15

Fahrenheit and Celsius Conversion

Europe takes its temperature using the Celsius scale, while we opt for Fahrenheit. For a rough conversion from Celsius to Fahrenheit, double the number and add 30. For weather, remember that 28°C is 82°F— perfect. For health, 37°C is just right. At a launderette, 30°C is cold, 40°C is warm (usually the default setting), 60°C is hot, and 95°C is boiling. Your air-conditioner should be set at about 20°C.

APPENDIX

Packing Checklist

Whether you're traveling for five days or five weeks, you won't need more than this. Pack light to enjoy the sweet freedom of true mobility.

Clothing

- ❑ 5 shirts: long- & short-sleeve
- ❑ 2 pairs pants (or skirts/capris)
- ❑ 1 pair shorts
- ❑ 5 pairs underwear & socks
- ❑ 1 pair walking shoes
- ❑ Sweater or warm layer
- ❑ Rainproof jacket with hood
- ❑ Tie, scarf, belt, and/or hat
- ❑ Swimsuit
- ❑ Sleepwear/loungewear

Money

- ❑ Debit card(s)
- ❑ Credit card(s)
- ❑ Hard cash ($100-200 in US dollars)
- ❑ Money belt

Documents

- ❑ Passport
- ❑ Tickets & confirmations: flights, hotels, trains, rail pass, car rental, sight entries
- ❑ Driver's license
- ❑ Student ID, hostel card, etc.
- ❑ Photocopies of important documents
- ❑ Insurance details
- ❑ Guidebooks & maps
- ❑ Notepad & pen
- ❑ Journal

Toiletries Kit

- ❑ Basics: soap, shampoo, toothbrush, toothpaste, floss, deodorant, sunscreen, brush/comb, etc.
- ❑ Medicines & vitamins
- ❑ First-aid kit
- ❑ Glasses/contacts/sunglasses

- ❑ Sewing kit
- ❑ Packet of tissues (for WC)
- ❑ Earplugs

Electronics

- ❑ Mobile phone
- ❑ Camera & related gear
- ❑ Tablet/ebook reader/media player
- ❑ Laptop & flash drive
- ❑ Headphones
- ❑ Chargers & batteries
- ❑ Smartphone car charger & mount (or GPS device)
- ❑ Plug adapters

Miscellaneous

- ❑ Daypack
- ❑ Sealable plastic baggies
- ❑ Laundry supplies: soap, laundry bag, clothesline, spot remover
- ❑ Small umbrella
- ❑ Travel alarm/watch

Optional Extras

- ❑ Second pair of shoes (flip-flops, sandals, tennis shoes, boots)
- ❑ Travel hairdryer
- ❑ Picnic supplies
- ❑ Water bottle
- ❑ Fold-up tote bag
- ❑ Small flashlight
- ❑ Mini binoculars
- ❑ Small towel or washcloth
- ❑ Inflatable pillow/neck rest
- ❑ Tiny lock
- ❑ Address list (to mail postcards)
- ❑ Extra passport photos

Pronouncing Eastern European Place Names

Remember that in all of these languages, j is pronounced as "y," and c is pronounced "ts." Diacritical markings over most consonants (such as č, š, ś, or ž) have the same effect as putting an h after it in English; for example, č is "ch," š or ś is "sh," ž is "zh."

Name	Pronounced
Auschwitz (Concentration Camp, Poland)	OWSH-vits
Birkenau (Concentration Camp, Poland)	BEER-keh-now
Bled (Slovenia)	bled (as it's spelled); locals say "blayd"
Bohinj (Slovenia)	BOH-heen
Bovec (Slovenia)	BOH-vets
Bratislava (Slovakia)	brah-tee-SLAH-vah
Budapest (Hungary)	BOO-dah-pest in English, BOO-daw-pesht in Hungarian
Český Krumlov (Czech Republic)	CHESS-key KROOM-loff
Eger (Hungary)	EH-gehr
Egerszalók (Hungary)	EH-gehr-sah-lohk
Esztergom (Hungary)	EHS-tehr-gohm
Füzesabony (Hungary)	FOO-zesh-ah-boyn
Gdańsk (Poland)	guh-DAYNSK
Gdynia (Poland)	guh-DIN-yah
Gödöllő (Palace, Hungary)	GER-der-ler
Kazimierz (Poland)	kah-ZHEE-mezh
Kobarid (Slovenia)	KOH-bah-reed
Konopiště (Castle, Czech Republic)	KOH-noh-peesh-tyeh
Kraków (Poland)	KRACK-cow in English, KROCK-oof in Polish
Kutná Hora (Czech Republic)	KOOT-nah HO-rah
Ljubljana (Slovenia)	lyoob-lyee-AH-nah
Malbork (Castle, Poland)	MAHL-bork
Mostar (Bosnia-Herzegovina)	MOH-star
Nowa Huta (Poland)	NOH-vah HOO-tah
Oświęcim (Poland)	ohsh-VEENCH-im
Pécs (Hungary)	paych
Praha (Czech name for Prague, Czech Republic)	PRAH-hah
Radovljica (Slovenia)	rah-DOH-vleet-suh
Soča (River Valley, Slovenia)	SOH-chah
Sopot (Poland)	SOH-poht
Sopron (Hungary)	SHOH-prohn
Szentendre (Hungary)	SEHN-tehn-dreh

Name	Pronounced
Terezín (Concentration Camp, Czech Republic)	TEH-reh-zeen
Toruń (Poland)	TOH-roon
Vintgar (Gorge, Slovenia)	VEENT-gar
Visegrád (Hungary)	VEE-sheh-grahd
Vršič (Pass, Slovenia)	vur-SHEECH
Warszawa (Polish name for Warsaw, Poland)	vah-SHAH-vah
Wieliczka (Salt Mine, Poland)	veel-EECH-kah
Wien (German name for Vienna, Austria)	veen

INDEX

INDEX

MAP INDEX

Explore Europe

At ricksteves.com you can browse through thousands of articles, videos, photos and radio interviews, plus find a wealth of money-saving travel tips for planning your dream trip. And with our mobile-friendly website, you can easily access all this great travel information anywhere you go.

TV Shows

Preview the places you'll visit by watching entire half-hour episodes of Rick Steves' Europe (choose from all 100 shows) on-demand, for free.

ricksteves.com

your travel dreams into affordable reality

Radio Interviews

Enjoy ready access to Rick's vast library of radio interviews covering travel

tips and cultural insights that relate specifically to your Europe travel plans.

Travel Forums

Learn, ask, share! Our online community of savvy travelers is a great resource for first-time travelers to Europe, as well as seasoned pros. You'll find forums on each country, plus travel tips and restaurant/hotel reviews. You can even ask one of our well-traveled staff to chime in with an opinion.

Travel News

Subscribe to our free Travel News e-newsletter, and get monthly updates from Rick on what's happening in Europe.

Audio Europe™

Experience maximum Europe

Save time and energy

This guidebook is your independent-travel toolkit. But for all it delivers, it's still up to you to devote the time and energy it takes to manage the preparation and logistics that are essential for a happy trip. If that's a hassle, there's a solution.

Rick Steves Tours

A Rick Steves tour takes you to Europe's most interesting places with great

with minimum stress

guides and small groups of 28 or less. We follow Rick's favorite itineraries, ride in comfy buses, stay in family-run hotels, and bring you intimately close to the Europe you've traveled so far to see. Most importantly, we take away the logistical headaches so you can focus on the fun.

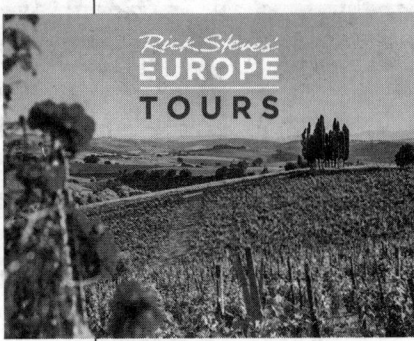

travelers—nearly half of them repeat customers— along with us on four dozen different itineraries, from Ireland to Italy to Istanbul. Is a Rick Steves tour the right fit for your travel dreams? Find out at ricksteves.com, where you can also request Rick's latest tour catalog. Europe is best

Join the fun

This year we'll take thousands of free-spirited experienced with happy travel partners. We hope you can join us.

See our itineraries at ricksteves.com

Rick Steves

   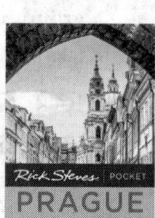

Maximize your travel skills with a good guidebook.

Loire Valley
Madrid & Toledo
Milan & the Italian Lakes District
Naples & the Amalfi Coast
Northern Ireland
Norway
Sevilla, Granada & Southern Spain
St. Petersburg, Helsinki & Tallinn
Stockholm

POCKET GUIDES

Amsterdam
Athens
Barcelona
Florence
Italy's Cinque Terre
London
Munich & Salzburg
Paris
Prague
Rome
Venice
Vienna

TRAVEL CULTURE

Europe 101
European Christmas
European Easter
Postcards from Europe
Travel as a Political Act

RICK STEVES' EUROPE DVDs

12 New Shows 2015–2016
Austria & the Alps
The Complete Collection 2000–2016

Eastern Europe
England & Wales
European Christmas
European Travel Skills & Specials
France
Germany, BeNeLux & More
Greece, Turkey & Portugal
The Holy Land: Israelis & Palestinians Today
Iran
Ireland & Scotland
Italy's Cities
Italy's Countryside
Scandinavia
Spain
Travel Extras

PHRASE BOOKS & DICTIONARIES

French
French, Italian & German
German
Italian
Portuguese
Spanish

PLANNING MAPS

Britain, Ireland & London
Europe
France & Paris
Germany, Austria & Switzerland
Ireland
Italy
Spain & Portugal

Credits

RESEARCHER
Gretchen Strauch

Before Gretchen became the online-content editor for Rick Steves' Europe, she lived in Konstanz, Germany, for three years, where she taught English and diligently researched the *Eiscafés* of southern Germany. She still does not like sauerkraut.

CONTRIBUTORS
Honza Vihan

Honza, who co-authors *Rick Steves Prague & the Czech Republic*, grew up roaming the Czech countryside in search of the Wild West. Once the borders opened, he set off for South Dakota. His journey took him to China, Honduras, India, and Iran, where he contributed to several travel guides. Honza lives in Prague with his family, teaches Chinese, and leads Rick Steves tours through Eastern Europe.

Gene Openshaw

Gene has co-authored a dozen *Rick Steves* books, specializing in writing walks and tours of Europe's cities, museums, and cultural sights. He also contributes to Rick's public television series, produces tours for Rick Steves Audio Europe, and is a regular guest on Rick's public radio show. Outside of the travel world, Gene has co-authored *The Seattle Joke Book*. As a composer, Gene has written a full-length opera called *Matter* (soundtrack available on Amazon), a violin sonata, and dozens of songs. He lives near Seattle with his daughter, enjoys giving presentations on art and history, and roots for the Mariners in good times and bad.

ACKNOWLEDGMENTS

The authors would like to acknowledge our friends and colleagues for their invaluable insights. Thanks to Ian Watson, Dave Hoerlein, Rick Garman, Trevor Holmes, and Ben Curtis; *Děkuji* to Honza Vihan (Czech Republic); *Dziękuję* to Katarzyna Derlicka and Agnieszka Syroka (Poland); *Köszönjük szépen* to Péter Pölczman, Andrea Makkay, Elemér Boreczky, George Farkas, Etelka Parine Berecz, István Koteczki, and Eszter Bokros (Hungary); *Hvala lepa* to Marijan Krišković, Tina Hiti, Sašo Golub, Amir Telibečirović, Bojan Kočar, Barbara Jakopić, and Gorazd Hiti (Slovenia, Croatia, and Bosnia); *D'akujeme* to Susana Minich (Slovakia); Благодаря ти много to Lyuba Boyanin and Stefan Bozadzhiev (Bulgaria); and *Mulţumim mult* to Daniel Gheorghiţă, Dan Nica, Ana Adamoae, Ciprian Slemco, and Teo Ivanciuc (Romania).

Avalon Travel
An imprint of Perseus Books
A Hachette Book Group company
1700 Fourth Street
Berkeley, CA 94710

For the latest on Rick's talks, guidebooks, Europe tours, public radio show, free audio tours, and public television series, contact Rick Steves' Europe, 130 Fourth Avenue North, Edmonds, WA 98020, 425/771-8303, www.ricksteves.com, rick@ricksteves.com.

ISBN 978-1-63121-613-8
9th edition

Rick Steves' Europe
Managing Editor: Jennifer Madison Davis
Special Publications Manager: Risa Laib
Editors: Glenn Eriksen, Tom Griffin, Katherine Gustafson, Suzanne Kotz, Cathy Lu, Carrie Shepherd
Editorial & Production Assistant: Jessica Shaw
Editorial Intern: Meesha Sundarum
Researcher: Gretchen Strauch
Graphic Content Director: Sandra Hundacker
Maps & Graphics: David C. Hoerlein, Lauren Mills, Mary Rostad

Avalon Travel
Senior Editor & Series Manager: Madhu Prasher
Editor: Jamie Andrade
Associate Editor: Sierra Machado
Copy Editor: Maggie Ryan
Proofreader: Kelly Lydick
Indexer: Stephen Callahan
Production & Typesetting: Rue Flaherty
Cover Design: Kimberly Glyder Design
Maps & Graphics: Kat Bennett, Mike Morgenfeld

Photo Credits
Front Cover: © Rudi1976/Dreamstime.com
Title Page: Prague Street Musicians © Dominic Arizona Bonuccelli
Front Matter Color: p. iv, Ulica Długa, Gdańsk, Poland © Cameron Hewitt
Full-page photos: p. 19 Charles Bridge, Prague; p. 213, Old Town Square, Warsaw; p. 513, Parliament, Budapest; p. 699, Julian Alps; p. 837, St. Peter's Church, Vienna; p. 945, St. Michael's Gate, Bratislava; p. 973, Shipka Church, Bulgaria.
Additional Photography: Dominic Arizona Bonuccelli, Barb Geisler, Cameron Hewitt, David C. Hoerlein, Sandra Hundacker, Debi Jo Michael, Gene Openshaw, Rhonda Pelikan, Rick Steves, Gretchen Strauch, Honza Vihan, Wikimedia Commons (PD-Art/PD-US)(photos are used by permission and are the property of the original copyright owners).

Want More Eastern Europe?
Maximize the experience with Rick Steves as your guide

Guidebooks
Prague, Budapest, and Croatia guides make side-trips smooth and affordable

Planning Maps
Use the map that's in sync with your guidebook

Rick's TV Shows
Preview where you're going with 7 shows on Eastern Europe

Free! Rick's Audio Europe™ App
Hear Eastern Europe travel tips from Rick's radio shows

Small Group Tours
Rick offers several great itineraries through Eastern Europe

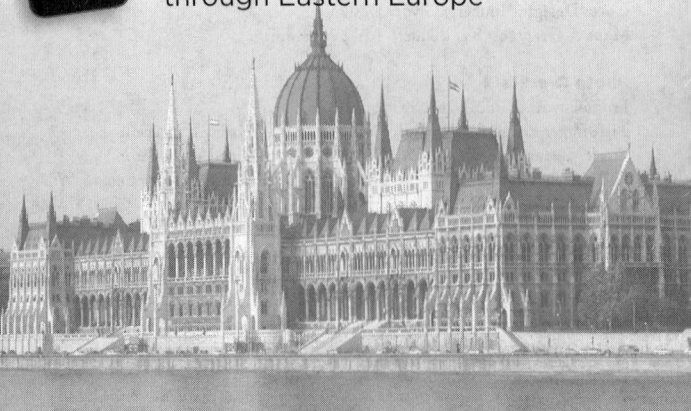

For all the details, visit ricksteves.com